T0180697

Lecture Notes in Computer Science 14084

Founding Editors

Gerhard Goos
Juris Hartmanis

Editorial Board Members

The series Lecture Notes in Computer Science (LNCS), including its subseries Lecture Notes in Artificial Intelligence (LNAI) and Lecture Notes in Bioinformatics (LNBI), has established itself as a medium for the publication of new developments in computer science and information technology research, teaching, and education.

LNCS enjoys close cooperation with the computer science R & D community, the series counts many renowned academics among its volume editors and paper authors, and collaborates with prestigious societies. Its mission is to serve this international community by providing an invaluable service, mainly focused on the publication of conference and workshop proceedings and postproceedings. LNCS commenced publication in 1973.

Helena Handschuh · Anna Lysyanskaya
Editors

Advances in Cryptology – CRYPTO 2023

43rd Annual International Cryptology Conference, CRYPTO 2023
Santa Barbara, CA, USA, August 20–24, 2023
Proceedings, Part IV

Springer

Editors
Helena Handschuh
Rambus Inc.
San Jose, CA, USA

Anna Lysyanskaya
Brown University
Providence, RI, USA

ISSN 0302-9743   ISSN 1611-3349 (electronic)
Lecture Notes in Computer Science
ISBN 978-3-031-38550-6   ISBN 978-3-031-38551-3 (eBook)
https://doi.org/10.1007/978-3-031-38551-3

This Springer imprint is published by the registered company Springer Nature Switzerland AG
The registered company address is: Gewerbestrasse 11, 6330 Cham, Switzerland

Preface

The 43rd International Cryptology Conference (CRYPTO 2023) was held at the University of California, Santa Barbara, California, USA, from August 20th to August 24th, 2023. It is an annual conference organized by the International Association for Cryptologic Research (IACR).

A record 479 papers were submitted for presentation at the conference, and 124 were selected, including two pairs of soft merges, for a total of 122 speaking slots. As a result of this record high, CRYPTO 2023 had three tracks for the first time in its history.

For the first time in its history as well, CRYPTO benefited from the great advice and tremendous help from six area chairs, covering the main areas of focus for the conference. These were Lejla Batina for Efficient and Secure Implementations, Dan Boneh for Public Key Primitives with Advanced Functionalities, Orr Dunkelman for Symmetric Cryptology, Leo Reyzin for Information-Theoretic and Complexity-Theoretic Cryptography, Douglas Stebila for Public-Key Cryptography and Muthuramakrishnan Venkitasubramaniam for Multi-Party Computation. Each of them helped lead discussions and decide which ones of the approximately 80 submissions in their area should be accepted. Their help was invaluable and we could not have succeeded without them.

To evaluate the submissions, we selected a program committee that consisted of 102 top cryptography researchers from all over the world. This was the largest program committee that CRYPTO has ever had, as well. Each paper was assigned to three program committee members who reviewed it either by themselves or with the help of a trusted sub-referee. As a result, we benefited from the expertise of almost 500 sub-referees. Together, they generated a staggering 1500 reviews. We thank our program committee members and the external sub-referees for the hard work of peer review which is the bedrock of scientific progress.

The review process was double-blind and confidential. In accordance with the IACR conflict-of-interest policy, the reviewing software we used (HotCRP) kept track of which reviewers had a conflict of interest with which authors (for example, by virtue of being a close collaborator or an advisor) and ensured that no paper was assigned a conflicted reviewer.

In order to be considered, submissions had to be anonymous and their length was limited to 30 pages excluding the bibliography and supplementary materials. After the first six or so weeks of evaluation, the committee chose to continue considering 330 papers; the remaining 149 papers were rejected, including five desk rejects. The majority of these received three reviews, none of which favored acceptance, although in limited cases the decision was made based on only two reviews that were in agreement. The papers that remained under consideration were invited to submit a response (rebuttal) to clarifications requested from their reviewers. Two papers were withdrawn during this second phase. Each of the 328 remaining papers received at least three reviews. After around five weeks of additional discussions, the committee made the final selection of the 124 papers that appear in these proceedings.

We would like to thank all the authors who submitted their papers to CRYPTO 2023. The vast majority of the submissions, including those that were ultimately not selected, were of very high quality, and we are very honored that CRYPTO was the venue that the authors chose for their work. We are additionally grateful to the authors of the accepted papers for the extra work of incorporating the reviewers' feedback and presenting their papers at the conference.

This year the Best Paper Award was awarded to Keegan Ryan and Nadia Heninger for their paper "Fast Practical Lattice Reduction Through Iterated Compression." The Best Early Career Paper Award went to Elizabeth Crites, Chelsea Komlo and Mary Maller for their paper "Fully Adaptive Schnorr Threshold Signatures." The runner up Best Early Career Paper was by Ward Beullens on "Graph-Theoretic Algorithms for the Alternating Trilinear Form Equivalence Problem." These three papers were subsequently invited to be submitted to the IACR Journal of Cryptology.

In addition to the presentations of contributed papers included in these proceedings, the conference also featured two plenary talks: Hugo Krawczyk delivered the IACR Distinguished Lecture, and Scott Aaronson gave an invited talk titled "Neurocryptography." The traditional rump session, chaired by Allison Bishop, took place on Tuesday, August 22nd, and featured numerous short talks.

Co-located cryptography workshops were held in the preceding weekend; they included the following seven events, "Crypto meets Artificial Intelligence—The Glowing Hot Topics in Cryptography," "MathCrypt—The Workshop on Mathematical Cryptology," "CFAIL—The Conference for Failed Approaches and Insightful Losses in Cryptography," "PPML—The Privacy-Preserving Machine Learning Workshop," "WAC6—The Workshop on Attacks in Cryptography 6," "ACAI—Applied Cryptology and Artificial Intelligence," and "RISE—Research Insights and Stories for Enlightenment." We gladly thank Alessandra Scafuro for serving as the Affiliated Events Chair and putting together such an enticing program.

All of this was possible thanks to Kevin McCurley and Kay McKelly without whom all of our review software would be crashing non-stop, and all of the Crypto presentations would be nothing but static. They are the true pillars of all of our IACR Crypto events and conferences. Last but not least we thank Britta Hale for serving as our General Chair and making sure the conference went smoothly and attendees had a great experience. Thank you to our industry sponsors, including early sponsors a16z, AWS, Casper, Google, JPMorgan, Meta, PQShield, and TII for their generous contributions, as well as to the NSF Award 2330160 for supporting Ph.D. student participants.

August 2023
                                                                Helena Handschuh
                                                                Anna Lysyanskaya

Organization

General Chair

Britta Hale   Naval Postgraduate School, USA

Program Co-chairs

Helena Handschuh   Rambus Inc., USA
Anna Lysyanskaya   Brown University, USA

Area Chairs

Lejla Batina *(for Efficient and*   Radboud University, the Netherlands
  Secure Implementations)
Dan Boneh *(for Public Key*   Stanford University, USA
  Primitives with Advanced
  Functionalities)
Orr Dunkelman *(for Symmetric*   University of Haifa, Israel
  Cryptology)
Leo Reyzin *(for*   Boston University, USA
  Information-Theoretic and
  Complexity-Theoretic
  Cryptography)
Douglas Stebila *(for Public-Key*   University of Waterloo, Canada
  Cryptography)
Muthu Venkitasubramaniam *(for*   Georgetown University, USA
  Multi-Party Computation)

Program Committee

Shweta Agrawal   IIT Madras, India
Ghada Almashaqbeh   University of Connecticut, USA
Benny Applebaum   Tel-Aviv University, Israel
Marshall Ball   New York University, USA
Fabrice Benhamouda   Algorand Foundation, USA

Nina Bindel	SandboxAQ, USA
Allison Bishop	Proof Trading and City University of New York, USA
Joppe W. Bos	NXP Semiconductors, Belgium
Raphael Bost	Direction Générale de l'Armement, France
Chris Brzuska	Aalto University, Finland
Benedikt Bünz	Stanford and Espresso Systems, USA
David Cash	University of Chicago, USA
Gaëtan Cassiers	TU Graz and Lamarr Security Research, Austria
Yilei Chen	Tsinghua University, China
Chitchanok Chuengsatiansup	The University of Melbourne, Australia
Kai-Min Chung	Academia Sinica, Taiwan
Carlos Cid	Simula UiB, Norway, and Okinawa Institute of Science and Technology, Japan
Sandro Coretti	IOHK, Switzerland
Geoffroy Couteau	CNRS, IRIF, Université Paris-Cité, France
Luca De Feo	IBM Research Europe, Switzerland
Gabrielle De Micheli	University of California, San Diego, USA
Jean Paul Degabriele	Technology Innovation Institute, UAE
Siemen Dhooghe	imec-COSIC, KU Leuven, Belgium
Itai Dinur	Ben-Gurion University, Israel
Christoph Dobraunig	Intel Labs, Intel Corporation, USA
Thomas Eisenbarth	University of Lübeck, Germany
Sebastian Faust	TU Darmstadt, Germany
Ben Fisch	Yale University, USA
Pierre-Alain Fouque	IRISA and University of Rennes, France
Georg Fuchsbauer	TU Wien, Austria
Chaya Ganesh	Indian Institute of Science, India
Rosario Gennaro	City University of New York, USA
Henri Gilbert	ANSSI, France
Niv Gilboa	Ben-Gurion University, Israel
Mike Hamburg	Rambus Inc., the Netherlands
David Heath	University of Illinois Urbana-Champaign, USA
Naofumi Homma	Tohoku University, Japan
Abhishek Jain	Johns Hopkins University, USA
Bhavana Kanukurthi	Indian Institute of Science, India
Shuichi Katsumata	PQShield, UK, and AIST, Japan
Jonathan Katz	University of Maryland and Dfns, USA
Nathan Keller	Bar-Ilan University, Israel
Lisa Kohl	CWI, the Netherlands
Ilan Komargodski	Hebrew University, Israel and NTT Research, USA

Anja Lehmann	Hasso-Plattner-Institute, University of Potsdam, Germany
Tancrède Lepoint	Amazon, USA
Benjamin Lipp	Max Planck Institute for Security and Privacy, Germany
Feng-Hao Liu	Florida Atlantic University, USA
Tianren Liu	Peking University, China
Patrick Longa	Microsoft Research, USA
Julian Loss	CISPA Helmholtz Center for Information Security, Germany
Fermi Ma	Simons Institute and UC Berkeley, USA
Mary Maller	Ethereum Foundation and PQShield, UK
Chloe Martindale	University of Bristol, UK
Alexander May	Ruhr-University Bochum, Germany
Florian Mendel	Infineon Technologies, Germany
Bart Mennink	Radboud University, the Netherlands
Brice Minaud	Inria and ENS, France
Kazuhiko Minematsu	NEC and Yokohama National University, Japan
Pratyush Mishra	Aleo Systems, USA
Tarik Moataz	MongoDB, USA
Jesper Buus Nielsen	Aarhus University, Denmark
Kaisa Nyberg	Aalto University, Finland
Miyako Ohkubo	NICT, Japan
Eran Omri	Ariel University, Israel
David Oswald	University of Birmingham, UK
Omkant Pandey	Stony Brook University, USA
Omer Paneth	Tel-Aviv University, Israel
Alain Passelègue	Inria and ENS Lyon, France
Arpita Patra	IISc Bangalore and Google Research, India
Léo Perrin	Inria, France
Thomas Peters	UCLouvain and FNRS, Belgium
Thomas Peyrin	Nanyang Technological University, Singapore
Stjepan Picek	Radboud University, the Netherlands
David Pointcheval	École Normale Supérieure, France
Antigoni Polychroniadou	J.P. Morgan AI Research, USA
Bart Preneel	University of Leuven, Belgium
Mariana Raykova	Google, USA
Christian Rechberger	TU Graz, Austria
Oscar Reparaz	Block, Inc., USA
Matthieu Rivain	CryptoExperts, France
Mélissa Rossi	ANSSI, France
Guy Rothblum	Apple, USA

Alexander Russell	University of Connecticut, USA
Paul Rösler	FAU Erlangen-Nürnberg, Germany
Kazue Sako	Waseda University, Japan
Alessandra Scafuro	North Carolina State University, USA
Patrick Schaumont	Worcester Polytechnic Institute, USA
Thomas Schneider	TU Darmstadt, Germany
André Schrottenloher	Inria, Univ. Rennes, CNRS, IRISA, France
Dominique Schröder	FAU Erlangen-Nürnberg, Germany
Benjamin Smith	Inria and École Polytechnique, France
Ling Song	Jinan University, China
Mehdi Tibouchi	NTT Social Informatics Laboratories, Japan
Yosuke Todo	NTT Social Informatics Laboratories, Japan
Alin Tomescu	Aptos Labs, USA
Dominique Unruh	University of Tartu, Estonia
Gilles Van Assche	STMicroelectronics, Belgium
Damien Vergnaud	Sorbonne Université, France
Jiayu Xu	Oregon State University, USA
Arkady Yerukhimovich	George Washington University, USA
Yu Yu	Shanghai Jiao Tong University, China

Additional Reviewers

Kasra Abbaszadeh	Christian Badertscher
Behzad Abdolmaleki	Shi Bai
Masayuki Abe	David Balbás
Ittai Abraham	Paulo Barreto
Hamza Abusalah	James Bartusek
Amit Agarwal	Andrea Basso
Akshima	Jules Baudrin
Gorjan Alagic	Balthazar Bauer
Martin Albrecht	Carsten Baum
Bar Alon	Josh Beal
Miguel Ambrona	Hugo Beguinet
Prabhanjan Ananth	Amos Beimel
Megumi Ando	Sana Belguith
Yoshinori Aono	Thiago Bergamaschi
Paula Arnold	Olivier Bernard
Gal Arnon	Sebastian Berndt
Arasu Arun	Ward Beullens
Gilad Asharov	Tim Beyne
Renas Bacho	Rishiraj Bhattacharyya
Matilda Backendal	Ritam Bhaumik

Mengda Bi
Alexander Bienstock
Bruno Blanchet
Olivier Blazy
Maxime Bombar
Xavier Bonnetain
Jonathan Bootle
Samuel Bouaziz-Ermann
Katharina Boudgoust
Alexandre Bouez
Charles Bouillaguet
Christina Boura
Clémence Bouvier
Ross Bowden
Pedro Branco
Anne Broadbent
Olivier Bronchain
Andreas Brüggemann
Anirudh Chandramouli
Eleonora Cagli
Matteo Campanelli
Pedro Capitão
Eliana Carozza
Kévin Carrier
Wouter Castryck
Pyrros Chaidos
Andre Chailloux
Suvradip Chakraborty
Gowri Chandran
Rohit Chatterjee
Albert Cheu
Céline Chevalier
Nai-Hui Chia
Arka Rai Choudhuri
Hien Chu
Hao Chung
Michele Ciampi
Valerio Cini
James Clements
Christine Cloostermans
Benoît Cogliati
Andrea Coladangelo
Jean-Sébastien Coron
Henry Corrigan-Gibbs
Craig Costello

Elizabeth Crites
Eric Crockett
Jan-Pieter D'Anvers
Antoine Dallon
Poulami Das
Gareth Davies
Hannah Davis
Dennis Dayanikli
Leo de Castro
Paola De Perthuis
Rafael del Pino
Cyprien Delpech de Saint Guilhem
Jeroen Delvaux
Patrick Derbez
Zach DeStefano
Lalita Devadas
Julien Devevey
Henri Devillez
Jean-François Dhem
Adam Ding
Yevgeniy Dodis
Xiaoyang Dong
Nico Döttling
Benjamin Dowling
Leo Ducas
Clément Ducros
Céline Duguey
Jesko Dujmovic
Christoph Egger
Maria Eichlseder
Reo Eriguchi
Andreas Erwig
Daniel Escudero
Thomas Espitau
Andre Esser
Simona Etinski
Thibauld Feneuil
Pouria Fallahpour
Maya Farber Brodsky
Pooya Farshim
Joël Felderhoff
Rex Fernando
Matthias Fitzi
Antonio Flórez-Gutiérrez
Cody Freitag

Sapir Freizeit
Benjamin Fuller
Phillip Gajland
Tarek Galal
Nicolas Gama
John Gaspoz
Pierrick Gaudry
Romain Gay
Peter Gaži
Yuval Gelles
Marilyn George
François Gérard
Paul Gerhart
Alexandru Gheorghiu
Ashrujit Ghoshal
Shane Gibbons
Benedikt Gierlichs
Barbara Gigerl
Noemi Glaeser
Aarushi Goel
Eli Goldin
Junqing Gong
Dov Gordon
Lénaïck Gouriou
Marc Gourjon
Jerome Govinden
Juan Grados
Lorenzo Grassi
Sandra Guasch
Aurore Guillevic
Sam Gunn
Aldo Gunsing
Daniel Günther
Chun Guo
Siyao Guo
Yue Guo
Shreyas Gupta
Hosein Hadipour
Mohammad Hajiabadi
Shai Halevi
Lucjan Hanzlik
Aditya Hegde
Rachelle Heim
Lena Heimberger
Paul Hermouet

Julia Hesse
Minki Hhan
Taiga Hiroka
Justin Holmgren
Alex Hoover
Akinori Hosoyamada
Kristina Hostakova
Kai Hu
Yu-Hsuan Huang
Mi-Ying Miryam Huang
Pavel Hubáček
Andreas Hülsing
Akiko Inoue
Takanori Isobe
Akira Ito
Ryoma Ito
Tetsu Iwata
Jennifer Jackson
Joseph Jaeger
Zahra Jafargholi
Jonas Janneck
Stanislaw Jarecki
Zhengzhong Jin
David Joseph
Daniel Jost
Nathan Ju
Seny Kamara
Chetan Kamath
Simon Holmgaard Kamp
Gabriel Kaptchuk
Vukašin Karadžić
Ioanna Karantaidou
Harish Karthikeyan
Mustafa Khairallah
Mojtaba Khalili
Nora Khayata
Hamidreza Khoshakhlagh
Eda Kirimli
Elena Kirshanova
Ágnes Kiss
Fuyuki Kitagawa
Susumu Kiyoshima
Alexander Koch
Dmitry Kogan
Konrad Kohbrok

Sreehari Kollath
Yashvanth Kondi
Venkata Koppula
Marina Krcek
Maximilian Kroschewski
Daniël Kuijsters
Péter Kutas
Qiqi Lai
Yi-Fu Lai
Philip Lazos
Jason LeGrow
Gregor Leander
Ulysse Léchine
Yi Lee
Charlotte Lefevre
Jonas Lehmann
Antonin Leroux
Baiyu Li
Chaoyun Li
Hanjun Li
Wenjie Li
Xin Li
Xingjian Li
Zhe Li
Mingyu Liang
Xiao Liang
Damien Ligier
Wei-Kai Lin
Helger Lipmaa
Guozhen Liu
Jiahui Liu
Linsheng Liu
Meicheng Liu
Qipeng Liu
Zeyu Liu
Chen-Da Liu-Zhang
Alex Lombardi
Johanna Loyer
Ji Luo
Vadim Lyubashevsky
Yiping Ma
Varun Madathil
Bernardo Magri
Luciano Maino
Monosij Maitra

Christian Majenz
Jasleen Malvai
Marian Margraf
Mario Marhuenda Beltrán
Erik Mårtensson
Ange Martinelli
Daniel Masny
Loïc Masure
Takahiro Matsuda
Kotaro Matsuoka
Christian Matt
Krystian Matusiewicz
Noam Mazor
Matthias Meijers
Fredrik Meisingseth
Pierre Meyer
Daniele Micciancio
Elena Micheli
Marine Minier
Helen Möllering
Charles Momin
Atsuki Momose
Hart Montgomery
Tal Moran
Tomoyuki Morimae
Kirill Morozov
Fabrice Mouhartem
Koksal Mus
Saachi Mutreja
Michael Naehrig
Marcel Nageler
Rishub Nagpal
Yusuke Naito
Anand Kumar Narayanan
Shoei Nashimoto
Ky Nguyen
Georgio Nicolas
Raine Nieminen
Valeria Nikolaenko
Oded Nir
Ryo Nishimaki
Olga Nissenbaum
Anca Nitulescu
Julian Nowakowski
Adam O'Neill

Sai Lakshmi Bhavana Obbattu
Maciej Obremski
Arne Tobias Ødegaard
Morten Øygarden
Cavit Özbay
Erdinc Ozturk
Jiaxin Pan
Dimitrios Papachristoudis
Aditi Partap
Anat Paskin-Cherniavsky
Rafael Pass
Sikhar Patranabis
Stanislav Peceny
Chris Peikert
Angelos Pelecanos
Alice Pellet-Mary
Octavio Perez-Kempner
Guilherme Perin
Trevor Perrin
Giuseppe Persiano
Pessl Peter
Spencer Peters
Duong Hieu Phan
Benny Pinkas
Bertram Poettering
Guru Vamsi Policharla
Jason Pollack
Giacomo Pope
Alexander Poremba
Eamonn Postlethwaite
Thomas Prest
Robert Primas
Luowen Qian
Willy Quach
Håvard Raddum
Shahram Rasoolzadeh
Divya Ravi
Michael Reichle
Jean-René Reinhard
Omar Renawi
Joost Renes
Nicolas Resch
Mahshid Riahinia
Silas Richelson
Jan Richter-Brockmann

Doreen Riepel
Peter Rindal
Bhaskar Roberts
Wrenna Robson
Sondre Rønjom
Mike Rosulek
Yann Rotella
Lior Rotem
Ron Rothblum
Adeline Roux-Langlois
Joe Rowell
Lawrence Roy
Keegan Ryan
Mark Ryan
Sherman S. M. Chow
Eric Sageloli
Antonio Sanso
Practik Sarkar
Yu Sasaki
Robert Schaedlich
Jan Schlegel
Martin Schläffer
Markus Schofnegger
Peter Scholl
Jan Schoone
Phillipp Schoppmann
Jacob Schuldt
Mark Schultz
Marek Sefranek
Nicolas Sendrier
Jae Hong Seo
Karn Seth
Srinath Setty
Yannick Seurin
Dana Shamir
Devika Sharma
Yaobin Shen
Yixin Shen
Danping Shi
Sina Shiehian
Omri Shmueli
Ferdinand Sibleyras
Janno Siim
Mark Simkin
Jaspal Singh

Amit Singh Bhati
Sujoy Sinha Roy
Naomi Sirkin
Daniel Slamanig
Christopher Smith
Tomer Solomon
Fang Song
Yifan Song
Pratik Soni
Jesse Spielman
Srivatsan Sridhar
Damien Stehlé
Marc Stevens
Christoph Striecks
Patrick Struck
Adam Suhl
Chao Sun
Siwei Sun
Berk Sunar
Ajith Suresh
Moeto Suzuki
Erkan Tairi
Akira Takahashi
Katsuyuki Takashima
Abdul Rahman Taleb
Quan Quan Tan
Er-Cheng Tang
Qiang Tang
Stefano Tessaro
Justin Thaler
Yan Bo Ti
Tyge Tiessen
Junichi Tomida
Dilara Toprakhisar
Andreas Trügler
Daniel Tschudi
Yiannis Tselekounis
Ida Tucker
Balazs Udvarhelyi
Rei Ueno
Florian Unterstein
Annapurna Valiveti
Gijs Van Laer
Wessel van Woerden
Akhil Vanukuri
Karolin Varner

Javier Verbel
Tanner Verber
Frederik Vercauteren
Corentin Verhamme
Psi Vesely
Fernando Virdia
Quoc-Huy Vu
Benedikt Wagner
Roman Walch
Hendrik Waldner
Han Wang
Libo Wang
William Wang
Yunhao Wang
Zhedong Wang
Hoeteck Wee
Mor Weiss
Weiqiang Wen
Chenkai Weng
Luca Wilke
Mathias Wolf
David Wu
Lichao Wu
Zejun Xiang
Tiancheng Xie
Alex Xiong
Anshu Yadav
Sophia Yakoubov
Hossein Yalame
Shota Yamada
Avishay Yanai
Kang Yang
Qianqian Yang
Tianqi Yang
Yibin Yang
Kan Yasuda
Eylon Yogev
Yang Yu
Arantxa Zapico
Hadas Zeilberger
Bin Zhang
Jiang Zhang
Ruizhe Zhang
Zhenda Zhang
Chenzhi Zhu
Jens Zumbraegel

Contents – Part IV

Faster Fully Homomorphic Encryption

Fast Blind Rotation for Bootstrapping FHEs 3
  Binwu Xiang, Jiang Zhang, Yi Deng, Yiran Dai, and Dengguo Feng

HERMES: Efficient Ring Packing Using MLWE Ciphertexts
and Application to Transciphering 37
  Youngjin Bae, Jung Hee Cheon, Jaehyung Kim, Jai Hyun Park,
  and Damien Stehlé

Accelerating HE Operations from Key Decomposition Technique 70
  Miran Kim, Dongwon Lee, Jinyeong Seo, and Yongsoo Song

Oblivious RAM

MacORAMa: Optimal Oblivious RAM with Integrity 95
  Surya Mathialagan and Neekon Vafa

Tri-State Circuits: A Circuit Model that Captures RAM 128
  David Heath, Vladimir Kolesnikov, and Rafail Ostrovsky

Limits of Breach-Resistant and Snapshot-Oblivious RAMs 161
  Giuseppe Persiano and Kevin Yeo

Cuckoo Hashing in Cryptography: Optimal Parameters, Robustness
and Applications 197
  Kevin Yeo

Obfuscation

The Pseudorandom Oracle Model and Ideal Obfuscation 233
  Aayush Jain, Huijia Lin, Ji Luo, and Daniel Wichs

Computational Wiretap Coding from Indistinguishability Obfuscation 263
  Yuval Ishai, Aayush Jain, Paul Lou, Amit Sahai, and Mark Zhandry

Secure Messaging

On Optimal Tightness for Key Exchange with Full Forward Secrecy
via Key Confirmation 297
   Kai Gellert, Kristian Gjøsteen, Håkon Jacobsen, and Tibor Jager

Security Analysis of the WhatsApp End-to-End Encrypted Backup Protocol ... 330
   *Gareth T. Davies, Sebastian Faller, Kai Gellert, Tobias Handirk,
Julia Hesse, Máté Horváth, and Tibor Jager*

On Active Attack Detection in Messaging with Immediate Decryption 362
   *Khashayar Barooti, Daniel Collins, Simone Colombo,
Loïs Huguenin-Dumittan, and Serge Vaudenay*

Fork-Resilient Continuous Group Key Agreement 396
   Joël Alwen, Marta Mularczyk, and Yiannis Tselekounis

Functional Encryption

Streaming Functional Encryption 433
   Jiaxin Guan, Alexis Korb, and Amit Sahai

Attribute-Based Multi-input FE (and More) for Attribute-Weighted Sums 464
   Shweta Agrawal, Junichi Tomida, and Anshu Yadav

How to Use (Plain) Witness Encryption: Registered ABE, Flexible
Broadcast, and More 498
   Cody Freitag, Brent Waters, and David J. Wu

Constant Input Attribute Based (and Predicate) Encryption from Evasive
and Tensor LWE 532
   Shweta Agrawal, Mélissa Rossi, Anshu Yadav, and Shota Yamada

Correlated Pseudorandomness

Correlated Pseudorandomness from the Hardness of Quasi-Abelian
Decoding 567
   Maxime Bombar, Geoffroy Couteau, Alain Couvreur, and Clément Ducros

Expand-Convolute Codes for Pseudorandom Correlation Generators
from LPN 602
   Srinivasan Raghuraman, Peter Rindal, and Titouan Tanguy

Proof Systems in the Discrete-Logarithm Setting

Correlation Intractability and SNARGs from Sub-exponential DDH 635
Arka Rai Choudhuri, Sanjam Garg, Abhishek Jain, Zhengzhong Jin,
and Jiaheng Zhang

Algebraic Reductions of Knowledge 669
Abhiram Kothapalli and Bryan Parno

On the Impossibility of Algebraic NIZK in Pairing-Free Groups 702
Emanuele Giunta

A Note on Non-interactive Zero-Knowledge from CDH 731
Geoffroy Couteau, Abhishek Jain, Zhengzhong Jin, and Willy Quach

Author Index 765

Faster Fully Homomorphic Encryption

Fast Blind Rotation for Bootstrapping FHEs

Binwu Xiang[1,2,3], Jiang Zhang[2]([✉]), Yi Deng[1,3], Yiran Dai[1,2,3], and Dengguo Feng[2]

[1] State Key Laboratory of Information Security, Institute of Information Engineering, Chinese Academy of Sciences, Beijing, China
{xiangbinwu,deng,daiyiran}@iie.ac.cn
[2] State Key Laboratory of Cryptology, P.O. Box 5159, Beijing 100878, China
zhangj@sklc.org, fengdg@263.net
[3] School of Cyber Security, University of Chinese Academy of Sciences, Beijing, China

Abstract. Blind rotation is one of the key techniques to construct fully homomorphic encryptions with the best known bootstrapping algorithms running in less than one second. Currently, the two main approaches, namely, AP and GINX, for realizing blind rotation are first introduced by Alperin-Sheriff and Peikert (CRYPTO 2014) and Gama, Izabachene, Nguyen and Xie (EUROCRYPT 2016), respectively.

In this paper, we propose a new blind rotation algorithm based on a GSW-like encryption from the NTRU assumption. Our algorithm has performance asymptotically independent from the key distributions, and outperforms AP and GINX in both the evaluation key size and the computational efficiency (especially for large key distributions). By using our blind rotation algorithm as a building block, we present new bootstrapping algorithms for both LWE and RLWE ciphertexts.

We implement our bootstrapping algorithm for LWE ciphertexts, and compare the actual performance with two bootstrapping algorithms, namely, FHEW/AP by Ducas and Micciancio (EUROCRYPT 2015) and TFHE/GINX by Chillotti, Gama, Georgieva and Izabachène (Journal of Cryptology 2020), that were implemented in the OpenFHE library. For parameters with ternary key distribution at 128-bit security, our bootstrapping only needs to store evaluation key of size 18.65 MB for blind rotation, which is about 89.8 times smaller than FHEW/AP and 2.9 times smaller than TFHE/GINX. Moreover, our bootstrapping can be done in 112 ms on a laptop, which is about 3.2 times faster than FHEW/AP and 2.1 times faster than TFHE/GINX. More improvements are available for large key distributions such as Gaussian distributions.

Keywords: Lattices · Fully Homomorphic Encryption · Bootstrapping · Blind Rotations

B. Xiang—This work was done while I was a visiting student in the group of Dr. Jiang Zhang during 2021–2023 at State Key Laboratory of Cryptology, Beijing, China.

H. Handschuh and A. Lysyanskaya (Eds.): CRYPTO 2023, LNCS 14084, pp. 3–36, 2023.
https://doi.org/10.1007/978-3-031-38551-3_1

1 Introduction

Fully homomorphic encryption (FHE) allows to perform computations on encrypted data without decryption and is one of the main cryptographic tools for privacy computation. Currently, almost all known FHE constructions follow the same paradigm introduced by Gentry [28]: 1) construct a somewhat homomorphic encryption (SHE) using noise-based encryptions (e.g., Regev encryption [42]) which typically can only support a limited number of homomorphic operations due to the increase of noise size; 2) design a bootstrapping algorithm that essentially homomorphically computes the decryption of SHE to reduce the noise size of ciphertexts. The initial attempts [9–11, 20, 21, 25, 43, 45] mainly focus on the construction of SHEs supporting the evaluation of their own (augmented) decryption circuits, and then use the bootstrapping theorem [28] to convert SHEs into FHEs. As bootstrapping is the central component for almost all existing FHEs and is much more complex than other elementary operations, it has become the main efficiency bottleneck in practical implementations.

Essentially, the decryption algorithm for most existing FHEs is to compute a function $g(\langle \mathbf{c}, \mathbf{s} \rangle \mod q) = g(\sum_i c_i s_i \mod q)$, where $\mathbf{c} = (c_0, \ldots, c_{n-1}) \in \mathbb{Z}_q^n$ is the ciphertext, $\mathbf{s} = (s_0, \ldots, s_{n-1}) \in \mathbb{Z}_q^n$ is the secret key, and g is a simple decoding algorithm that may vary depending on specific schemes. The most costly operation for bootstrapping is to homomorphically compute the modular function $f(\mathbf{c}, \mathbf{s}) = \sum_i c_i s_i \mod q$ for some integer modulus q. There are mainly three approaches to do this in practical implementations. The first approach focuses on BGV ciphertext [10] with decryption function $g(\langle \mathbf{c}, \mathbf{s} \rangle \mod q) = (\sum_i c_i s_i \mod q) \mod p$ for some integer p (e.g., $p = 2$). The central idea of this approach is to convert $f(\mathbf{c}, \mathbf{s}) = \sum_i c_i s_i \mod q$ with a general q to $f'(\mathbf{c}, \mathbf{s}) = \sum_i c_i s_i \mod q'$ with a special modulus $q' = p^r$ so that $g(\langle \mathbf{c}, \mathbf{s} \rangle \mod q)$ can be computed by extracting the bit decompositions of $\langle \mathbf{c}, \mathbf{s} \rangle$ in base p [9, 10, 12, 14, 25, 29, 32]. The second approach targets CKKS ciphertext [16] with decryption function $g(\langle \mathbf{c}, \mathbf{s} \rangle \mod q) = \sum_i c_i s_i \mod q$ for approximate numbers. The idea behind this approach is to use another math function, e.g., $\frac{q}{2\pi} \sin\left(\frac{2\pi}{q} \langle \mathbf{c}, \mathbf{s} \rangle\right)$, to approximate the modular function $\langle \mathbf{c}, \mathbf{s} \rangle \mod q$. Since this approach will inherently introduce extra noises to the resulting ciphertext, the choice of the approximate math functions significantly influences the computation performance and the quality of the result ciphertext [8, 13, 15, 16, 31, 36]. To perform the bootstrapping, both approaches above require to homomorphcially compute a polynomial (of the secret key $\mathbf{s}$) with relatively large degree, which not only need hundreds of megabytes to several gigabytes to store the bootstrapping keys, but also require tens/hundreds of seconds to bootstrap a single ciphertext.

The third approach is called blind rotation [5, 22], which allows to fast bootstrap a single ciphertext in less than one second. Basically, this approach uses two layers of encryptions: the first layer is a simple Regev-like encryption [42] which has very limited homomorphic capacity, and the second layer is a ring-based GSW-like encryption [30] which is specially designed to homomorphically compute the first-layer decryption algorithm. In more detail, let $R = \mathbb{Z}[X]/(X^N + 1)$

Table 1. Asymptotic comparison of different blind rotations in the number $\#R_Q$ of R_Q elements in the evaluation key and the number $\#$mul of multiplications in R_Q for computation (where B is an integer in bit-decomposing the first-layer ciphertexts for AP, and U is a public set in bit-decomposing the first-layer secret keys for GINX).

Method	$\#R_Q$	$\#$mul
AP [5,22,41]	$4d\lceil \log_B q \rceil (B-1)n$	$4d\lceil \log_B q \rceil n$
GINX [19,26]	$4d\lvert U \rvert n$	$4d\lvert U \rvert n^{\dagger}$
Lee et al. [37]	$2d(2n+q+1)$	$2d(3n+2)$
Ours	$d(n+q)$	$d(2n+1)$

† Recently, Bonte et al. [7] reduced the computational cost of GINX for the special case of ternary keys (i.e., $\lvert U \rvert = 2$) by a half, but still keep the evaluation key size unchanged. See Sect. 1.3 for more discussions.

with $q = 2N$ be the cyclotomic ring used in the second layer, then the modular function $f(\mathbf{c}, \mathbf{s}) = \sum_i c_i s_i \mod q$ in the first-layer decryption can be easily done in the exponent of the ring element $X \in R$ because the order of X is exactly q in R and $X^{f(\mathbf{c}, \mathbf{s})} = X^{\sum_i c_i s_i \mod q} = X^{\sum_i c_i s_i}$. By multiplying a rotation polynomial $r(X) = \sum_{i=0}^{q-1} i X^{-i}$, one can easily decode $\sum_i c_i s_i \mod q$ from the exponent of $X^{\sum_i c_i s_i}$ to the constant term of the polynomial $r(X) \cdot X^{\sum_i c_i s_i}$. The blind rotation actually refers to the procedure of computing $r(X) \cdot X^{\sum_i c_i s_i}$ from a given ciphertext vector $\mathbf{c} = (c_0, \ldots, c_{n-1})$ and some encryptions of the secret key $\mathbf{s} = (s_0, \ldots, s_{n-1})$. There are mainly two ways for realizing blind rotation, namely, AP [5,22,41] and GINX [19,26]. The first one [5,22,41] has performance asymptotically independent from the first-layer key distributions, but it has to store very large evaluation keys (e.g., more than 1.6GB at 128-bit security [39]). The second one [18,19,26] has performance linear in the bit-decomposition size of the first-layer secret key, which only needs to store very small evaluation keys for small key distributions (e.g., 54MB at 128-bit security for ternary key distribution [39]), but its evaluation keys will quickly increase to hundreds of megabytes when the secret key $\mathbf{s}$ is chosen from a distribution with large bit-decomposition size (e.g., Gaussian distributions as recommended in [1]). Recently, Lee et al. [37] presented a new blind rotation algorithm which has performance asymptotically independent from the first-layer key distributions as AP and outperforms GINX for large first-layer key distributions.

1.1 Our Results

In this work, we follow the two-layer framework to construct FHEs with fast bootstrapping algorithms. First, we present a second-layer GSW-like encryption based on the NTRU assumption, which supports very fast key-switching for ring automorphisms. Then, we propose a new blind rotation algorithm by crucially using ring automorphisms and its associated key-switchings. Our algorithm has performance asymptotically independent from the first-layer key distribution and

Table 2. Experimental comparison of different blind rotations using parameters at 128-bit security (where the column "Key distrib." denotes the key distributions used for the first-layer encryption; the column "EVK" denotes the evaluation key size for blind rotation; the last column "Timing" denotes the timing for running the whole bootstrapping algorithm).

Algorithms	Parameters	Key	EVK	Timing
	$(n, q, d, N, \log_2 Q, B, |U|)$	distrib.	(MB)	(ms)
FHEW/AP [6,22]	STD128 [39]	Ternary	1674	359
	(512,1024,4,1024,27,32,-)			
TFHE/GINX [6,19]	STD128 [39]	Ternary	54	234
	(512,1024,4,1024,27,-,2)			
Ours	P128T	Ternary	18.65	112
	(512,1024,5,1024,19.9,-,-)			
	P128G	Gaussian	17.90	100
	(465,1024,5,1024,19.9,-,-)			

outperforms AP and GINX in both the evaluation key size and the computation efficiency. By using our blind rotation algorithm as a building block, we construct new bootstrapping algorithms for both LWE-based and RLWE-based first-layer ciphertexts. Finally, we implement our bootstrapping algorithm for LWE-based first-layer ciphertexts, and the experiment shows that it can be efficiently done in 112 ms on a laptop for parameters at 128-bit security.[1]

In Table 1, we give a theoretical comparison of different blind rotations, where n, q are the dimension and modulus for the first-layer encryption; N, Q are the dimension and modulus of the ring $R_Q = \mathbb{Z}_Q[X]/(X^N + 1)$ for the second-layer GSW-like encryption; d is the bit-decomposition dimension for multiplying a second-layer GSW-like ciphertext; $|U|$ is the number of bits needed to represent the full range of secret key samples, e.g., $|U| = 2$ for ternary secrets. Since q is usually less than $2n$ for typically choices of parameters [39], one can see from Table 1 that our blind rotation has asymptotically the best performance in both evaluation key size and computational efficiency. We note that Lee et al.'s blind rotation [37] also has similar asymptotically performance as ours, but unlike us, they rely on an RLWE-based second-layer GSW-like encryption. Our NTRU-based GSW-like encryption allows us to obtain improvements over Lee et al. [37] by a factor about 2.7 times in the evaluation key size, and about 3 times in the computational efficiency.

In Table 2, we give an experimental comparison of different blind rotations. All the figures are obtained by running the corresponding algorithms on the same

---

[1] We note that the timing of 13 ms for a single GINX-like bootstrapping reported in [19] is obtained using implementation with binary secret keys (i.e., $|U| = 1$) and AVX2 instructions. The timing of their implementation using portable C language on our laptop is actually 227 ms for 128-bit security parameter, which is roughly 2 times slower than our algorithm, close to our theoretical estimation in Table 1.

laptop using parameters providing at least 128-bit security.[2] The parameter STD128 for FHEW/AP [22] and TFHE/GINX [19] is the default parameter provided in the OpenFHE 0.9.1 library [6] and recommended in [39]. For comparison, we choose two sets of parameters P128T and P128G: P128T is set to have the same parameters (n, q) and ternary key distribution with STD128 for the first-layer LWE encryption; while P128G is set to use a Gaussian key distribution with variance $4/3$. From Table 2, one can see that we only have to store an evaluation key of size 18.65 MB for blind rotation using parameter P128T, which is about 89.8 times smaller than FHEW/AP and 2.9 times smaller than TFHE/GINX. Moreover, our bootstrapping algorithm can be done in 112 ms, which is about 3.2 times faster than FHEW/AP and 2.1 times faster than TFHE/GINX. When using P128G with Gaussian key distribution, we can obtain an extra 10% improvements over P128T (while the performance of TFHE/GINX will become worse by roughly a factor of 1.5 when using our Gaussian key distribution).

1.2   Our Techniques

We now explain the techniques behind our results. Without loss of generality, a first-layer ciphertext is assumed to have a form of $(\mathbf{a}, b = \sum_{i=0}^{n-1} a_i s_i - \mathsf{noised}(m))$, where $\mathbf{a} = (a_0, \ldots, a_{n-1}), \mathbf{s} = (s_0, \ldots, s_{n-1}) \in \mathbb{Z}_q^n$ are respectively the randomness and the secret key used to encrypt some plaintext $m \in \mathbb{Z}_q$. Our goal is to homomorphically compute $\mathsf{noised}(m) = \sum_{i=0}^{n-1} a_i s_i - b \mod q$. At a high level, we want to remove the modulo q operation by choosing a ring $R_Q = \mathbb{Z}_Q[X]/(X^N+1)$ with N being a power of 2 and $q = 2N$ such that the order of X in R_Q is exactly q and the modulo q operation can be done for free in the exponent of X:

$$X^{\mathsf{noised}(m)} = X^{\sum_{i=0}^{n-1} a_i s_i - b \mod q} = X^{-b} X^{\sum_{i=0}^{n-1} a_i s_i}.$$

Then, by multiplying a rotation polynomial $r(X) = \sum_{i=0}^{q-1} iX^{-i} \in R_Q$ we can extract the value $\mathsf{noised}(m)$ from $X^{\mathsf{noised}(m)}$ to the constant term of the polynomial $r(X) \cdot X^{-b} X^{\sum_{i=0}^{n-1} a_i s_i}$, which is equal to

$$r(X) \cdot X^{\mathsf{noised}(m)} = \mathsf{noised}(m) + \sum_{i \neq \mathsf{noised}(m)} iX^{\mathsf{noised}(m)-i}.$$

The above procedure is called blind rotation [5,19,22,26,41], which can be extended to any (q, N) with $q|2N$ by multiplying a constant $2N/q$ in the exponent:

$$r(X^{\frac{2N}{q}}) \cdot X^{\frac{2N}{q}\mathsf{noised}(m)} = \mathsf{noised}(m) + \sum_{i \neq \mathsf{noised}(m)} iX^{\frac{2N}{q}(\mathsf{noised}(m)-i)}.$$

Note that $\mathbf{s} = (s_0, \ldots, s_{n-1})$ is the secret key, we can only compute

$$r(X^{\frac{2N}{q}}) \cdot X^{\frac{2N}{q}\mathsf{noised}(m)} = r(X^{\frac{2N}{q}}) \cdot X^{-\frac{2N}{q}b} X^{\frac{2N}{q}\sum_{i=0}^{n-1} a_i s_i}$$

---

[2] Table 2 does not include the bootstrapping algorithms in [7,37] because the code for [37] is not publicly available, and [7] did not use the recommended parameters (See Sect. 1.3 for more discussions).

by using ciphertexts that encrypt $\mathbf{s}$. Previously, this is done by either using the AP method [5,22,41] which relies on the decompositions of $a_i = \sum_j a_{i,j} B^j$ in some base B and encrypts all possible values of $a_{i,j} s_i \in \mathbb{Z}_q$ in the evaluation key, or using the GINX method [19,26] which relies on the bit decompositions of $s_i = \sum_{u \in U} s_{i,u} u$ for some public set U and encrypts all $s_{i,u} \in \{0,1\}$ in the evaluation key. Unlike AP and GINX, we use the idea of Lee et al. [37] to perform blind rotation by using ring automorphisms in R_Q. Basically, given a ciphertext $c(X) \in R_Q = \mathbb{Z}[X]$ that encrypts X^{s_i} using secret key $f(X)$, we can easily obtain a ciphertext $c(X^{a_i})$ that encrypts $X^{a_i s_i}$ by applying the automorphism $X \to X^{a_i}$ to $c(X)$ if $a_i \in \mathbb{Z}_q$ is coprime to $2N$. One problem is that $c(X^{a_i})$ is not a ciphertext under the original secret key $f(X)$ but a related secret key $f(X^{a_i})$. We need to perform a key-switching to convert $c(X^{a_i})$ back to a ciphertext that encrypts $X^{a_i s_i}$ under the secret key $f(X)$ to allow further homomorphic computations (recall that we have to homomorphically compute $r(X^{\frac{2N}{q}}) \cdot X^{-\frac{2N}{q} b} X^{\frac{2N}{q}(\sum_{i=0}^{n-1} a_i s_i)}$). The other problem is that each $a_i \in \mathbb{Z}_q$ in a given ciphertext $(\mathbf{a}, b)$ can be an even integer (with probability $1/2$) and thus is not coprime to $2N$. This means that $c(X^{a_i})$ may become an invalid ciphertext if we directly replace X with X^{a_i} in $c(X)$ for an even integer a_i. Fortunately, for most parameters used in practice [39] the requirement $q|N$ is satisfied, we can instead compute $X^{\frac{2N}{q} a_i s_i} = X^{(\frac{2N}{q} a_i + 1) s_i - s_i} = X^{w_i s_i} X^{-s_i}$, where $w_i = \frac{2N}{q} a_i + 1 < 2N$ is always an odd integer and thus is coprime to $2N$ for all $a_i \in \mathbb{Z}_q$ (recall that N is a power of 2). Thus, we can compute

$$r(X^{\frac{2N}{q}}) \cdot X^{-\frac{2N}{q} b} X^{\frac{2N}{q}(\sum_{i=0}^{n-1} a_i s_i)} = r(X^{\frac{2N}{q}}) \cdot X^{-\frac{2N}{q} b} X^{\sum_{i=0}^{n-1} w_i s_i} X^{-\sum_{i=0}^{n-1} s_i}$$

by using ring automorphisms almost without introducing extra restrictions on the choice of N. In the following, we first give an NTRU-based GSW-like encryption for the second layer such that the key-switching for ring automorphisms can be done as efficient as a single GSW-like homomorphic multiplication.

NTRU-Based GSW-Like Encryption. Let $f, f' \in R_Q$ be two polynomials with small coefficients that are invertible in R_Q. Let (τ, Δ) be two integer parameters depending on the encoding of m in $\mathsf{noised}(m)$ of the first-layer encryption. We define a scalar NTRU ciphertext that "encrypts" plaintext $u \in R_Q$ under secret key f as follows:

$$\mathrm{NTRU}_{Q,f,\tau,\Delta}(u) = \tau \cdot g/f + \Delta \cdot u/f \in R_Q,$$

where $g \in R_Q$ is a noise polynomial with small coefficients. Noted that both the noise term and the message are divided by f. This essentially requires by a circular-secure/KDM-secure assumption on NTRU, which is also used in [7,35]. Let B be an integer and $d = \lceil \log_B Q \rceil$, we also define a vector NTRU ciphertext that "encrypts" plaintext $v \in R_Q$ under secret key f' as follows:

$$\mathrm{NTRU}'_{Q,f',\tau}(v) := (\tau \cdot g_0/f' + v, \tau \cdot g_1/f' + B \cdot v, \cdots, \tau \cdot g_{d-1}/f' + B^{d-1} \cdot v) \in R_Q^d,$$

where $\{g_i\}_{0 \le i \le d-1}$ are also noise polynomials with small coefficients. Given a polynomial $c \in R_Q$, let $\mathrm{BitDecom}_B(c)$ be the deterministic function that converts

$c = \sum_{i=0}^{d-1} c_i \cdot B^i$ into a d-dimensional vector $(c_0, c_1, \ldots, c_{d-1}) \in R_B^d$. Now, we define the external product $\odot$ between a polynomial $c \in R_Q$ and a vector NTRU ciphertext $\mathbf{c}' = \mathrm{NTRU}'_{Q,f',\tau}(v)$ as follows:

$$c \odot \mathbf{c}' = \sum_{i=0}^{d-1} c_i c_i' = \tau \cdot \left(\sum_{i=0}^{d-1} g_i c_i \right) / f' + cv,$$

where $(c_0, \ldots, c_{d-1}) = \mathrm{BitDecom}_B(c) \in R_B^d$ and $\mathbf{c}' = (c_0', \ldots, c_{d-1}') \in R_Q^d$.

Note that if $c = \mathrm{NTRU}_{Q,f,\tau,\Delta}(u)$ is a scalar NTRU ciphertext with $f' = f$ and $v \in R_Q$ has small coefficients, we have that $c \odot \mathbf{c}' = \sum_{i=0}^{d-1} c_i c_i' = \tau \cdot g'/f + \Delta \cdot uv/f$ is a valid ciphertext $\mathrm{NTRU}_{Q,f,\tau,\Delta}(uv)$ that encrypts $uv \in R_Q$ with $g' = \sum_{i=0}^{d-1} g_i c_i + gv$. Moreover, in order to convert $c = \mathrm{NTRU}_{Q,f,\tau,\Delta}(u)$ into a ciphertext $\hat{c} = \mathrm{NTRU}_{Q,f',\tau,\Delta}(u)$ that encrypts the same plaintext u under another secret key f', it is sufficient to set $v = f/f'$ and $\hat{c} = c \odot \mathbf{c}' = \sum_{i=0}^{d-1} c_i c_i' = \tau \cdot \hat{g}/f' + \Delta \cdot u/f'$, where $\hat{g} = \sum_{i=0}^{d-1} g_i c_i + g$. This means that both homomorphic multiplication and key-switching can be efficiently done by using a single external product, which in turn only needs d multiplications in R_Q.

Fast Blind Rotation with Small Key Size. Recall that the goal of blind rotation is to homomorphically compute

$$r(X^{\frac{2N}{q}}) \cdot X^{-\frac{2N}{q}b} X^{\frac{2N}{q}(\sum_{i=0}^{n-1} a_i s_i)} = r(X^{\frac{2N}{q}}) \cdot X^{-\frac{2N}{q}b} X^{\sum_{i=0}^{n-1} w_i s_i} X^{-\sum_{i=0}^{n-1} s_i},$$

where both $r(X^{\frac{2N}{q}}) \cdot X^{-\frac{2N}{q}b} \in R_Q$ and $w_i = \frac{2N}{q} a_i + 1 < 2N$ can be publicly computed from the ciphertext $(\mathbf{a}, b = \sum_{i=0}^{n-1} a_i s_i - \mathsf{noised}(m))$ that needs to be bootstrapped. A key feature required for previous blind rotations [5,7,19,22,26, 41] is that $r(X^{\frac{2N}{q}}) \cdot X^{-\frac{2N}{q}b} \in R_Q$ can be naturally treated as a scalar "ciphertext" (with zero noise), so that one can directly multiply it with a vector ciphertext that encrypts $X^{\frac{2N}{q}(\sum_{i=0}^{n-1} a_i s_i)}$ by a single external product to obtain a (scalar) ciphertext that encrypts $r(X^{\frac{2N}{q}}) \cdot X^{-\frac{2N}{q}b} X^{\frac{2N}{q}(\sum_{i=0}^{n-1} a_i s_i)}$. However, this feature is not satisfied for our NTRU-based GSW-like encryption, because a scalar NTRU ciphertext that encrypts $r(X^{\frac{2N}{q}}) \cdot X^{-\frac{2N}{q}b}$ in our above scheme has the form of $\tau \cdot g/f + \Delta \cdot (r(X^{\frac{2N}{q}}) \cdot X^{-\frac{2N}{q}b})/f \in R_Q$, which cannot be publicly created even using zero noise $g = 0$.

Fortunately, we can solve this problem almost for free by carefully designing the evaluation key. Specifically, we create a set of ciphertexts that encrypts $\mathbf{s} = (s_0, \ldots, s_{n-1})$ as follows:

$$\mathbf{evk}_0 = \mathrm{NTRU}'_{Q,f,\tau}(X^{s_0}/f), \qquad \mathbf{evk}_i = \mathrm{NTRU}'_{Q,f,\tau}(X^{s_i}) \text{ for } 1 \le i < n,$$
$$\mathbf{evk}_n = \mathrm{NTRU}'_{Q,f,\tau}(X^{-\sum_{i=0}^{n-1} s_i}).$$

We also create a set of ciphertexts for the key-switchings associated with all the needed ring automorphisms as follows:

$$\mathbf{ksk}_j = \mathrm{NTRU}'_{Q,f,\tau}\left(f(X^j)/f(X)\right) \text{ for all } j \in S = \left\{ \frac{2N}{q} i + 1 : 1 \le i \le q - 1 \right\}.$$

The evaluation key is defined as $\mathbf{EVK}_{\tau,\Delta} = (\mathbf{evk}_0, \ldots, \mathbf{evk}_n, \{\mathbf{ksk}_j\}_{j \in S})$. Since each element in $\mathbf{EVK}_{\tau,\Delta}$ has d elements in R_Q, we only need to store $d(n+q)$ R_Q elements in total for the evaluation key.

Given $\mathbf{EVK}_{\tau,\Delta}$ and a ciphertext $(\mathbf{a}, b = \sum_{i=0}^{n-1} a_i s_i - \text{noised}(m))$, we now describe our new blind rotation algorithm. First, for each a_i in $\mathbf{a} = (a_0, \ldots, a_{n-1})$ and $w_i = \frac{2N}{q}a_i + 1$, we compute $w_i' = w_i^{-1} \mod 2N$. We also set $w_n' = 1$ for ease of presentation. Then, we compute $c_0(X) = \left(\Delta \cdot r(X^{\frac{2N}{q}w_0'}) \cdot X^{-\frac{2N}{q}bw_0'}\right) \odot \mathbf{evk}_0$. Since $\mathbf{evk}_0 = \text{NTRU}'_{Q,f,\tau}(X^{s_0}/f)$, one can easily check that

$$c_0(X) = \text{NTRU}_{Q,f,\tau,\Delta}(r(X^{\frac{2N}{q}w_0'}) \cdot X^{-\frac{2N}{q}bw_0'}X^{s_0}).$$

By applying the automorphism $X \to X^{w_0 w_1'}$ to $c_0(X)$ (note that $w_0 w_1'$ is always coprime to $2N$), we can obtain a ciphertext

$$c_0'(X) = c_0(X^{w_0 w_1'}) = \text{NTRU}_{Q,f(X^{w_0 w_1'}),\tau,\Delta}(r(X^{\frac{2N}{q}w_1'}) \cdot X^{-\frac{2N}{q}bw_1'}X^{w_0 w_1' s_0})$$

under secret key $f(X^{w_0 w_1'})$. For our goal, we want to switch it back to a ciphertext that encrypts the same plaintext $r(X^{\frac{2N}{q}w_1'}) \cdot X^{-\frac{2N}{q}bw_1'}X^{w_0 w_1' s_0}$ under secret key $f(X)$, which can be done by computing

$$\hat{c}_0(X) = \begin{cases} c_0'(X), & \text{if } w_0 w_1' = 1; \\ c_0'(X) \odot \mathbf{ksk}_{w_0 w_1'}, & \text{otherwise.} \end{cases}$$

Note that $2N/q$ is a factor of $2N$ and $w_0, w_1 \in S \cup \{1\}$. This means that we always have that $w_0 w_1' \in S \cup \{1\}$, and that $\mathbf{ksk}_{w_0 w_1'} = \text{NTRU}'_{Q,f,\tau}\left(f(X^{w_0 w_1'})/f(X)\right)$ is included in the evaluation key $\mathbf{EVK}_{\tau,\Delta}$. By the definition of external product we have that $\hat{c}_0(X) = \text{NTRU}_{Q,f,\tau,\Delta}(r(X^{\frac{2N}{q}w_1'}) \cdot X^{-\frac{2N}{q}bw_1'}X^{w_0 w_1' s_0})$.

Similarly, we can iteratively absorb X^{s_i} for $1 \le i \le n-1$ as follows. First, we compute $c_i(X) = \hat{c}_{i-1}(X) \odot \mathbf{evk}_i = \hat{c}_{i-1}(X) \odot \text{NTRU}'_{Q,f,\tau}(X^{s_i})$ to obtain $c_i(X) = \text{NTRU}_{Q,f,\tau,\Delta}(r(X^{\frac{2N}{q}w_i'}) \cdot X^{-\frac{2N}{q}bw_i'}X^{(\sum_{j=0}^{i-1} w_j s_j)w_i' + s_i})$. Then, apply the automorphism $X \to X^{w_i w_{i+1}'}$ to $c_i(X)$ and obtain

$$c_i'(X) = \text{NTRU}_{Q,f(X^{w_i w_{i+1}'}),\tau,\Delta}(r(X^{\frac{2N}{q}w_{i+1}'}) \cdot X^{-\frac{2N}{q}bw_{i+1}'}X^{(\sum_{j=0}^{i} w_j s_j)w_{i+1}'}).$$

Next, compute

$$\hat{c}_i(X) = \begin{cases} c_i'(X), & \text{if } w_i w_{i+1}' = 1 \\ c_i'(X) \odot \mathbf{ksk}_{w_i w_{i+1}'}, & \text{otherwise,} \end{cases}$$

to obtain $\hat{c}_i(X) = \text{NTRU}_{Q,f,\tau,\Delta}(r(X^{\frac{2N}{q}w_{i+1}'}) \cdot X^{-\frac{2N}{q}bw_{i+1}'}X^{(\sum_{j=0}^{i} w_j s_j)w_{i+1}'})$.

After the above iterative procedure, we compute and output $\hat{c}_{n-1}(X) \odot \mathbf{evk}_n$. Since $\mathbf{evk}_n = \text{NTRU}'_{Q,f,\tau}(X^{-\sum_{i=0}^{n-1} s_i})$ and $w_n' = 1$, we finally have that

$$\hat{c}_{n-1}(X) \odot \mathbf{evk}_n = \text{NTRU}_{Q,f,\tau,\Delta}\left(r(X^{\frac{2N}{q}}) \cdot X^{-\frac{2N}{q}b}X^{\sum_{j=0}^{n-1} w_j s_j}X^{-\sum_{j=0}^{n-1} s_j}\right),$$

which is the desired result for blind rotation. In all, our blind rotation only needs at most n automorphisms and $2n + 1$ external products (i.e., $n + 1$ for homomorphic multiplications and n for key switchings), which in turn only requires at most $d(2n + 1)$ multiplications in R_Q (note that the automorphisms in R_Q can be done cheaply by permuting the coefficients of R_Q elements with signs).

Bootstrapping LWE-Based First-Layer Ciphertexts. For ease of presentation, we only consider the case that the plaintext $m \in \mathbb{Z}_t$ is encoded in the higher bits of $\mathsf{noised}(m) = e + m \cdot \lfloor \frac{q}{t} \rceil$ for some noise e (but we note that our approach also applies to other kinds of encodings). Specifically, the first-layer ciphertext (in the secret-key setting) has a form of $(\mathbf{a}, b = \sum_{i=0}^{n-1} a_i s_i - (e + m \cdot \lfloor \frac{q}{t} \rceil)) \in \mathbb{Z}_q^n \times \mathbb{Z}_q$, where $\mathbf{a} = (a_0, \ldots, a_{n-1})$ and $\mathbf{s} = (s_0, \ldots, s_{n-1})$. Given an evaluation key $\mathbf{EVK}_{\tau,\Delta}$ with $(\tau, \Delta) = (1, \lfloor \frac{Q}{t} \rceil)$ as defined before, we can use the above blind rotation algorithm to obtain a ciphertext $c = \mathrm{NTRU}_{Q,f,\tau,\Delta}(u) = g/f + \Delta \cdot u/f$, where $u = r(X^{\frac{2N}{q}}) \cdot X^{-\frac{2N}{q}b} X^{\sum_{j=0}^{n-1} w_j s_j} X^{-\sum_{i=0}^{n-1} s_i} = \mathsf{noised}(m) + \sum_{i \neq \mathsf{noised}(m)} i X^{\frac{2N}{q}(\mathsf{noised}(m)-i)}$. We can actually further remove the noise e in $\mathsf{noised}(m)$ almost for free by setting $r(X) = \sum_{i=0}^{q-1} (\lfloor i/\lfloor q/t \rceil \rceil \mod t) X^{-i}$. Since $m = \lfloor \mathsf{noised}(m)/\lfloor q/t \rceil \rceil \mod t$ by the correctness of the first-layer encryption, we have

$$u = m + \sum_{i \neq \mathsf{noised}(m)} (\lfloor i/\lfloor q/t \rceil \rceil \mod t) X^{\frac{2N}{q}(\mathsf{noised}(m)-i)}.$$

Now, it suffices to show how to convert $c = \mathrm{NTRU}_{Q,f,\tau,\Delta}(u) = g/f + \Delta \cdot u/f$ into an LWE-based ciphertext that encrypts m under the original secret key $\mathbf{s}$. Let $\mathbf{c} = (c_0, \ldots, c_{N-1})$, $\mathbf{f} = (f_0, \ldots, f_{N-1})$, $\mathbf{g} = (g_0, \ldots, g_{N-1}) \in \mathbb{Z}_Q^N$ be the corresponding coefficient vectors of the polynomials $c, f, g \in R_Q$. We have that the constant term of the polynomial $fc \in R_Q$ is equal to $g_0 + \Delta \cdot m \in \mathbb{Z}_Q$, which in turn is equal to $f_0 c_0 - \sum_{i=1}^{N-1} c_i f_{N-i} \mod Q$. By setting $\hat{\mathbf{c}} = (c_0, -c_{N-1}, \ldots, -c_1) \in \mathbb{Z}_Q^N$, we have that $0 = \langle \hat{\mathbf{c}}, \mathbf{f} \rangle - (g_0 + \Delta \cdot m) \in \mathbb{Z}_Q$. This means that $(\hat{\mathbf{c}}, 0) \in \mathbb{Z}_Q^N \times \mathbb{Z}_Q$ can actually be seen as an LWE-based ciphertext that encrypts m under the secret key $\mathbf{f} \in \mathbb{Z}_Q^N$ and noise g_0. Thus, we can finally obtain a ciphertext in $\mathbb{Z}_q$ that encrypts m under the original secret key $\mathbf{s}$ by first making a key-switching from $\mathbf{f}$ to $\mathbf{s}$ and then a modulus switching from Q to q.

In summary, to bootstrap the ciphertext $(\mathbf{a}, b = \sum_{i=0}^{n-1} a_i s_i - (e + m \cdot \lfloor \frac{q}{t} \rceil)) \in \mathbb{Z}_q^n \times \mathbb{Z}_q$, we only need to set the parameters such that $g_0/Q \ll e/q$ and create a key-switching key from $\mathbf{f}$ to $\mathbf{s}$, which is essentially a set of ciphertexts that encrypts $\mathbf{f} \in \mathbb{Z}^N$ under the secret key $\mathbf{s} \in \mathbb{Z}^n$.

Bootstrapping RLWE-Based First-Layer Ciphertexts. Let $\hat{R}_q = \mathbb{Z}_q[X]/(X^n + 1)$ be the ring for the first-layer encryption. Given an RLWE ciphertext $(a, b = a \cdot s - \mathsf{noised}(m)) \in \hat{R}_q \times \hat{R}_q$, where $s \in \hat{R}_q$ is the secret key. Let $\mathbf{a} = (a_0, \ldots, a_{n-1}), \mathbf{s} = (s_0, \ldots, s_{n-1}), \mathbf{m} = (m_0, \ldots, m_{n-1}) \in \mathbb{Z}_q^n$ be the corresponding coefficient vectors of the polynomials $a, s, m \in \hat{R}_q$. By the fact that

$$a \cdot s = \sum_{i=0}^{n-1} \left(\sum_{j=0}^{i} s_j \cdot a_{i-j} - \sum_{j=i+1}^{n-1} s_j \cdot a_{i-j+n} \right) X^i \in \hat{R}_q,$$

we can actually get n LWE ciphertexts $(\mathbf{a}_i, b_i)$ that encrypts m_i under the secret key $\mathbf{s}$ for all $0 \le i \le n-1$, where $\mathbf{a}_i = (a_i, \ldots, a_0, -a_{n-1}, \ldots, -a_{i+1})$.

Then, for each LWE ciphertext $(\mathbf{a}_i, b_i)$, we run our blind rotation algorithm to get an NTRU ciphertext $c_i = \mathrm{NTRU}_{Q,f,\tau,\Delta}(u_i) \in R_Q$ such that the constant coefficient of $u_i \in R_Q$ is exactly m_i. Let $\mathbf{c}_i = (c_{i,0}, c_{i,1}, \ldots, c_{i,N-1}) \in \mathbb{Z}_Q^N$ be the coefficient vector of $c_i \in R_Q$. Let $\hat{\mathbf{c}}_i = (c_{i,0}, -c_{i,N-1}, \ldots, -c_{i,1}) \in \mathbb{Z}_Q^N$, then $(\hat{\mathbf{c}}_i, 0) \in \mathbb{Z}_Q^N \times \mathbb{Z}_Q$ is actually an LWE-based ciphertext that encrypts m_i under the secret key $\mathbf{f} = (f_0, f_1, \ldots, f_{N-1}) \in \mathbb{Z}_Q^N$. Finally, we can directly use the technique in [40] to pack the resulting LWE-based ciphertexts into a single RLWE-based ciphertext.

1.3   Other Related Work and Discussions

Bonte et al. [7] and Kluczniak [35] adapted the GINX-like blind rotation to the NTRU setting with better efficiency, also based on new second-layer GSW-like encryptions from the NTRU assumption, which are different from ours. In particular, our GSW ciphertext is designed to have the form of $(g + m)/f$ to support fast key-switching for ring automorphisms, while the ciphertext in [7] is $g/f + m$, and the ciphertext in [35] is $e_1 \cdot g/f + e_2 + m$. It seems that the NTRU-based GSW encryptions in both [7,35] do not support fast key-switching for ring automorphisms, which is very critical for our improvement.

In terms of concrete efficiency, for binary key distribution the blind rotation algorithms in [7,35] perform better than ours in terms of evaluation key size and computational efficiency. For ternary key distribution, Bonte et al. [7] presented a special CMux gate which results in a reduction of the computational efficiency of GINX-like blind rotation by half, while maintaining the evaluation key size unchanged. This makes the computational performance of their blind rotation asymptotically two times faster than ours in the setting of ternary key distribution. For other key distributions such as Gaussian distribution, they [7,35] have to use the general GINX approach to obtain blind rotations that have performance linear in the bit-decomposition size of the secret keys, and thus is asymptotically worse than ours (offering asymptotic overhead with factor $|U|$ in runtime and evaluation key size). For example, for uniform key distribution over $[-2, 2]$ (that is slightly larger than ternary distribution), the computational efficiency of our blind rotation is already asymptotically 1.5 times faster than that in [7,35]. We note that many existing FHE libraries, e.g., Helib, use small binary or ternary secrets for performance consideration. However, the literature has reported several attacks on existing libraries using small secret keys [2,3,24,44]. In fact, there are three types key distributions recommended in [1], namely, uniform, Gaussian, and ternary distribution, which do not include the binary secrets for security concerns [1]. Thus, it is of great theoretical and practical interest to improve the bootstrapping performance for large secret keys.

More recently, Lee et al. [37] proposed the first blind rotation algorithm that uses ring automorphisms. A key difference between [37] and ours is that their construction is based on an existing RLWE-based GSW encryption, while we have to carefully design a new GSW-like encryption from the NTRU assumption. As discussed in Sect. 1.2 and above, the adaption from the RLWE setting to the NTRU setting is non-trivial. In particular, unlike other known GSW encryptions including the one in [37], our NTRU-based GSW ciphertexts designed for fast key-switching cannot be publicly generated even for known plaintexts, which requires a careful design to the generation of evaluation keys.

1.4   Organization

After giving some background in Sect. 2, we give an NTRU-based GSW-like encryption in Sect. 3. In Sect. 4, we present our new blind rotation. We show how to bootstrap LWE-based and RLWE-based first-layer ciphertexts in Sect. 5 and Sect. 6, respectively. Finally, we report our implementation for bootstrapping LWE-based first layer ciphertexts in Sect. 7.

2   Preliminaries

2.1   Notation

The set of real numbers (integers) is denoted by $\mathbb{R}$ ($\mathbb{Z}$, resp.). We use $\leftarrow$ to denote randomly choosing an element from some distribution (or the uniform distribution over some finite set). Vectors are denoted by bold lower-case letters (e.g., $\mathbf{a}$). By $\|\cdot\|_2$ and $\|\cdot\|_\infty$, we denote the ℓ_2 and ℓ_∞ norms. By $\lceil\cdot\rceil$, $\lfloor\cdot\rfloor$ and $\lfloor\cdot\rceil$ we denote the ceiling, floor and round functions, respectively.

Let n, N, q, Q be positive integers with n, N being powers of 2. By R (resp., $\hat{R}$) and R_Q we denote the $2N$-th (resp., $2n$-th) cyclotomic ring $R = \mathbb{Z}[X]/(X^N + 1)$ (resp., $\hat{R}$) and its quotient ring $R_Q = R/QR$ (resp., $\hat{R}/q\hat{R}$). The norm of a ring element $a(X) \in R$ (or $\hat{R}$) is defined as the norm of its coefficient vector. There are N (resp., n) automorphisms ψ_t over R (resp., $\hat{R}$) given by $\psi_t : a(X) \to a(X^t)$ for all t that is coprime to $2N$ (resp., $2n$). Since $\psi_t(a(X))$ is essentially equivalent to a permutation with signs on the coefficient vector of $a(X)$, the norm of a polynomial is invariant under those N (resp., n) automorphisms.

2.2   Hard Problems and Ciphertexts

In this subsection, we first recall some backgrounds on hard problems.

Definition 1 (Decisional LWE Problem [42]). *For positive integers q and n, let χ be a noise distribution over $\mathbb{Z}$, the decisional LWE problem is to distinguish between $(\mathbf{a}, b = \langle\mathbf{a}, \mathbf{s}\rangle - e) \in \mathbb{Z}_q^n \times \mathbb{Z}_q$ and a pair uniformly chosen at random from $\mathbb{Z}_q^n \times \mathbb{Z}_q$, where $\mathbf{a}$ is drawn uniformly at random from $\mathbb{Z}_q^n$, $\mathbf{s}$ is drawn from some key distribution over $\mathbb{Z}^n$, and e is drawn from χ.*

Definition 2 (Decisional RLWE Problem [38]). *For positive integers N and Q, let $R = \mathbb{Z}[X]/(X^N + 1)$ and $R_Q = \mathbb{Z}_Q[X]/(X^N + 1)$. Let χ be a noise distribution over R. The decisional RLWE problem is to distinguish between $(a, b = a \cdot s - e) \in R_Q \times R_Q$ from a pair uniformly chosen at random from $R_Q \times R_Q$, where a is drawn uniformly at random from R_Q, s is drawn from some key distribution over R_Q, and e is drawn according to χ.*

Definition 3 (Decisional NTRU Problem [34]). *For positive integers N and Q, let $R = \mathbb{Z}[X]/(X^N + 1)$ and $R_Q = \mathbb{Z}_Q[X]/(X^N + 1)$. Let χ be a noise distribution over R. Let $f, g \leftarrow \chi$ and f has an inverse in R_Q, the decisional NTRU problem is to distinguish between $g/f \in R_Q$ and a uniform polynomial drawn uniformly at random from R_Q.*

We also need a variant of the NTRU assumption, which we call Decisional Vectorized-NTRU Problem.

Definition 4 (Decisional Vectorized-NTRU Problem). *For positive integers N and Q, let $R = \mathbb{Z}[X]/(X^N + 1)$ and $R_Q = \mathbb{Z}_Q[X]/(X^N + 1)$. Let χ be a noise distribution over R. For a positive integer d, let $f, g_0, \cdots, g_{d-1} \leftarrow \chi$ and f has an inverse in R_Q, the decisional Vectorized-NTRU problem is to distinguish between $(g_0/f, \cdots, g_{d-1}/f) \in R_Q^d$ and a d-dimensional uniform polynomial vector drawn uniformly at random from R_Q^d.*

As commented in [27, Section 1.2], the above problem is merely a syntactic extension of the standard NTRU problem and facilitates the encryption of longer messages, without an essential change in the security assumption.

Definition 5 (LWE Ciphertexts). *For positive integers q and n, an LWE-based encryption of $m \in \mathbb{Z}$ under secret key $\mathbf{s} \in \mathbb{Z}^n$ is defined as*

$$\mathrm{LWE}_{q,\mathbf{s}}(m) := (\mathbf{a}, b) = (\mathbf{a}, \langle \mathbf{a}, \mathbf{s} \rangle - \mathsf{noised}(m)) \in \mathbb{Z}_q^n \times \mathbb{Z}_q,$$

where $\mathbf{a} \leftarrow \mathbb{Z}_q^n$ is the randomness, and $\mathsf{noised}(m) \in \mathbb{Z}_q$ is an noised encoding of $m \in \mathbb{Z}$ using some noise $e \in \mathbb{Z}$ chosen from some distribution χ over $\mathbb{Z}$.

Definition 6 (RLWE ciphertexts). *For positive integers Q and N, an RLWE-based encryption of $m \in R$ under secret key $s \in R$ is defined as*

$$\mathrm{RLWE}_{Q,s}(m) := (a, a \cdot s - \mathsf{noised}(m)) \in R_Q \times R_Q,$$

where $a \leftarrow R_Q$ is the randomness, and $\mathsf{noised}(m) \in R_Q$ is an noised encoding of $m \in R$ using some noise $e \in R$ chosen from some distribution χ over R.

3 NTRU-Based GSW-Like Encryption

In this section, we give an NTRU-based GSW-like encryption that supports fast key switching for ring automorphisms on (scalar) ciphertexts.

Definition 7 (scalar NTRU ciphertexts). *Let τ, Δ be two integer parameters that will be determined later. Our scalar NTRU encryption of $u \in R_Q$ under a secret key $f \in R_Q$ (that is invertible in R_Q) is defined as*

$$\text{NTRU}_{Q,f,\tau,\Delta}(u) := \tau \cdot g/f + \Delta \cdot u/f \in R_Q,$$

where both $f, g \in R_Q$ are polynomials with small coefficients, which are usually taken from a ternary distribution in practice.

Looking ahead, we will set the two integer parameters (τ, Δ) depending on the encodings (namely, Regev-like [42], BGV-like [10], and CKKS-like [16]) of $m \in \mathbb{Z}_t$ in $\text{noised}(m)$ of the first-layer encryption over $\mathbb{Z}_q$ as follows:

$$(\tau, \Delta) = \begin{cases} \left(1, \left\lfloor \frac{Q}{t} \right\rfloor\right), & \text{if } \text{noised}(m) = e + \left\lfloor \frac{q}{t} \right\rfloor \cdot m; \\ (t, 1), & \text{if } \text{noised}(m) = t \cdot e + m; \\ (1, 1), & \text{if } \text{noised}(m) = e + m. \end{cases}$$

Definition 8 (vector NTRU ciphertexts). *Let B be an integer parameter, our vector NTRU encryption of $v \in R_Q$ under a secret key $f \in R$ (that is invertible in R_Q) is defined as*

$$\text{NTRU}'_{Q,f,\tau}(v) := (\tau \cdot g_0/f + B^0 \cdot v, \cdots, \tau \cdot g_{d-1}/f + B^{d-1} \cdot v) \in R_Q^d,$$

where $f, g_0, \cdots, g_{d-1} \in R_Q$ have small coefficients, and $d = \lceil \log_B Q \rceil$.

For any $a \in R_Q$, by $\text{BitDecom}_B(a) \in R_B^d$ we denote the decomposition vector $(a_0, \ldots, a_{d-1}) \in \mathbb{Z}_B^d$ of a in base B such that $a = \sum_{i=0}^{d-1} a_i \cdot B^i$. Now, we define the external product "$\odot$" between a polynomial $c \in R_Q$ and a vector NTRU ciphertext $\mathbf{c}' = \text{NTRU}'_{Q,f,\tau}(v) \in R_Q^d$ as the inner product between $\text{BitDecom}_B(c) = (c_0, \ldots, c_{d-1})$ and $\mathbf{c}' = (c'_0, \cdots, c'_{d-1})$:

$$c \odot \mathbf{c}' = \langle \text{BitDecom}_B(c), \mathbf{c}' \rangle = \sum_{i=0}^{d-1} c_i c'_i = \tau \cdot \sum_{i=0}^{d-1} c_i g_i/f + cv \in R_Q$$

Note that if $c \in \text{NTRU}_{Q,f,\tau,\Delta}(u)$ is a scalar NTRU ciphertext and v has small coefficients, then we have that the result of $c \odot \mathbf{c}'$ is a scalar NTRU ciphertext that encrypts uv, namely,

$$c \odot \mathbf{c}' = \text{NTRU}_{Q,f,\tau,\Delta}(u) \odot \text{NTRU}'_{Q,f,\tau}(v) = \text{NTRU}_{Q,f,\tau,\Delta}(uv).$$

Formally, we have the following lemma.

Lemma 1 (Homomorphic Multiplication). *Let $c = \text{NTRU}_{Q,f,\tau,\Delta}(u) \in R_Q$ be a scalar NTRU ciphertext using some noise distribution with variance $Var(g)$. Let $\mathbf{c}' = \text{NTRU}'_{Q,f,\tau}(v)$ be a vector NTRU ciphertext using some noise distribution with variance $Var(g')$. Then, we have that $\hat{c} = c \odot \mathbf{c}' = \tau \cdot \hat{g}/f + \Delta \cdot uv/f$ is a scalar NTRU ciphertext for uv, and the variance of $\hat{g}$ satisfies*

$$Var(g') \leqslant dN \frac{B^2}{12} Var(g') + \|v\|_2^2 \cdot Var(g).$$

In particular, if v is a monomial with binary coefficient, then we have

$$Var(g') \leqslant dN\frac{B^2}{12}Var(g') + Var(g).$$

Proof. By definition, we have $c = \tau \cdot g/f + \Delta \cdot u/f = \text{NTRU}_{Q,f,\tau,\Delta}(u)$, and $\mathbf{c}' = (c'_0, \ldots, c'_{d-1}) = \text{NTRU}'_{Q,f,\tau}(v)$ for some $c'_i = \tau \cdot g_i/f + B^i \cdot v$. Let $(c_0, \cdots, c_{d-1}) = \text{BitDecom}_B(c)$ be the decomposition of c in base B, i.e., $c = \sum_{i=0}^{d-1} = c_i \cdot B^i$. Then, we have

$$\hat{c} = c \odot \mathbf{c}' = \langle \text{BitDecom}_B(c), \mathbf{c}' \rangle = \sum_{i=0}^{d-1} c_i(\tau \cdot g_i/f + B^i \cdot v)$$

$$= \tau \cdot \sum_{i=0}^{d-1} c_i g_i/f + cv = \tau \cdot (\sum_{i=0}^{d-1} c_i g_i + gv)/f + \Delta \cdot uv/f$$

$$= \tau \cdot g'/f + \Delta \cdot uv/f \in R_Q$$

where $g' = \sum_{i=0}^{d-1} c_i g_i + gv$. Hence $\hat{c}$ is a scalar NTRU ciphertext for uv. Moreover, since $\|c_i\|_\infty < B$ for all $0 \leq i \leq d-1$, by assumption that g has variance $Var(g)$ and that all g_i's have the same variance $Var(g')$, we have that $Var(\hat{g}) \leqslant Var(\sum_{i=0}^{d-1} c_i g_i) + Var(gv) = dN\frac{B^2}{12}Var(g') + \|v\|_2^2 \cdot Var(g).$[3] This proves the first claim. The second claim directly follows from the fact that $\|v\|_2^2 \leq 1$ for any monomial v with binary coefficient. This completes the proof.

In the rest of this paper, we denote $\sigma_\odot^2 = dN\frac{B^2}{12}Var(g')$ as the variance of the increased noise (with respect to the input scalar NTRU ciphertext) for homomorphic multiplication.

3.1   Key Switching for Scalar NTRU Ciphertexts

In this subsection, we define a pair of algorithms (KSKGen, KS) for key switching scalar NTRU ciphertexts as follows:

- KSKGen(f_1, f_2): Given two secret keys $f_1, f_2 \in R_Q$ that are invertible in R_Q as inputs, the key-switching key from f_1 to f_2 is defined as

$$\mathbf{ksk}_{f_1,f_2} = (\tau \cdot g_0/f_2 + B^0 \cdot f_1/f_2, \cdots, \tau \cdot g_{d-1}/f_2 + B^{d-1} \cdot f_1/f_2).$$

Note that $\mathbf{ksk}_{f_1,f_2}$ is essentially a vector NTRU ciphertext $\text{NTRU}'_{Q,f_2,\tau}$ (f_1/f_2) that encrypts f_1/f_2 under the secret key f_2.
- KS$_{f_1 \to f_2}(c, \mathbf{ksk}_{f_1,f_2})$: Given a scalar ciphertext $\text{NTRU}_{Q,f_1,\tau,\Delta}(u)$ that encrypts u under the secret key f_1, and a key-switching key $\mathbf{ksk}_{f_1,f_2}$ as inputs, compute and output

$$\hat{c} = c \odot \mathbf{ksk}_{f_1,f_2}.$$

---

[3] This formula uses a simplification assumption that each coefficient of c_i is uniformly distributed over $[0, B-1]$.

Clearly, the above key-switching algorithm only needs a single external product, which is as efficient as a single homomorphic multiplication, and can be done by using d multiplications in R_Q. In the following lemma, we show that $\hat{c}$ is indeed a scalar NTRU ciphertexts that encrypts u under the secret key f_2.

Lemma 2 (Key Switching). *Let $c = \mathrm{NTRU}_{Q,f_1,\tau,\Delta}(u) \in R_Q$ be a scalar NTRU ciphertext that encrypts u using secret key f_1 and some noise distribution with variance $Var(g)$. Let $\mathbf{ksk}_{f_1,f_2} = \mathrm{KSKGen}(f_1, f_2) = \mathrm{NTRU}'_{Q,f_2,\tau}(f_1/f_2)$ be the key-switching key from f_1 to f_2 using some noise distribution with variance $Var(g')$. Then, we have that*

$$\hat{c} = \mathrm{KS}_{f_1 \to f_2}(c, \mathbf{ksk}_{f_1,f_2}) = c \odot \mathbf{ksk}_{f_1,f_2} = \tau \cdot \hat{g}/f_2 + \Delta \cdot u/f_2$$

is a scalar NTRU ciphertext that encrypts u under the secret key f_2, and the variance of $\hat{g}$ satisfies

$$Var(\hat{g}) \leqslant dN\frac{B^2}{12}Var(g') + Var(g).$$

Proof. By definition, we have $c = \tau \cdot g/f_1 + \Delta \cdot u/f_1 = \mathrm{NTRU}_{Q,f_1,\tau,\Delta}(u)$, and $\mathbf{ksk}_{f_1,f_2} = (c'_0, \dots, c'_{d-1}) = \mathrm{NTRU}'_{Q,f_2,\tau}(f_1/f_2)$ for some $c'_i = \tau \cdot g_i/f_2 + B^i \cdot f_1/f_2$. Let $(c_0, \cdots, c_{d-1}) = \mathrm{BitDecom}_B(c)$ be the decomposition of c in base B, i.e., $c = \sum_{i=0}^{d-1} = c_i \cdot B^i$. Then, we have

$$\hat{c} = \mathrm{NTRU}_{Q,f_1,\tau,\Delta}(u) \odot \mathbf{ksk}_{f_1,f_2} = \sum_{i=0}^{d-1} c_i(\tau \cdot g_i/f_2 + B^i \cdot f_1/f_2)$$

$$= \tau \cdot \sum_{i=0}^{d-1} c_i g_i/f_2 + cf_1/f_2 = \tau \cdot (\sum_{i=0}^{d-1} c_i g_i + g)/f_2 + \Delta \cdot u/f_2$$

$$= \tau \cdot g'/f_2 + \Delta \cdot u/f_2 \in R_Q$$

where $g' = \sum_{i=0}^{d-1} c_i g_i + g$. Hence $\hat{c}$ is a scalar NTRU ciphertext that encrypts u under secret key f_2. Moreover, since $\|c_i\|_\infty < B$ for all $0 \leq i \leq d-1$, by assumption that g has variance $Var(g)$ and that all g_i's have the same variance $Var(g')$, we have that $Var(g') \leqslant dN\frac{B^2}{12}Var(g') + Var(g)$.[4]

By $\sigma_{KS}^2 = dN\frac{B^2}{12}Var(g') = \sigma_\odot^2$ we denote the variance of the increased noise (with respect to the input scalar NTRU ciphertext) for key switching.

3.2 Automorphisms on Scalar NTRU Ciphertexts

Let N be a power of 2, and $R = \mathbb{Z}[X]/(X^N + 1)$. Recall that there are N automorphisms $\psi_t : R \to R$ given by $a(X) \to a(X^t)$ for all odd integers in $\mathbb{Z}_{2N}$. In this subsection, we show how to apply automorphism ψ_t on a plaintext

---

[4] Again, this formula uses a simplification assumption that each coefficient of c_i is uniformly distributed over $[0, B-1]$.

$u \in R_Q$ that is encrypted in a scalar NTRU ciphertext $c = \mathrm{NTRU}_{Q,f,\tau,\Delta}(u)$ to get a new ciphertext $\hat{c} = \mathrm{NTRU}_{Q,f,\tau,\Delta}(\psi_t(u)) = \mathrm{NTRU}_{Q,f,\tau,\Delta}(u(X^t))$ that encrypts $\psi(u)$ under the same secret key f. Looking ahead, we will achieve this by first applying ψ_t on c, and then making a key switching from $\psi_t(f) = f(X^t)$ to $f(X)$ on the resulting ciphertexts $\psi_t(c) = c(X^t)$. Formally, we define a pair of algorithms (AutoKGen, EvalAuto) for automorphisms as follows:

- AutoKGen(t, f) : Given an odd integer $t \in \mathbb{Z}_{2N}$ and a secret key $f \in R_Q$, compute $\mathbf{ksk}_t = \mathsf{KSKGen}(\psi_t(f), f) = \mathsf{KSKGen}(f(X^t), f(X))$.
- EvalAuto$_t(c, \mathbf{ksk}_t)$: Given a scalar NTRU ciphertext $c = \mathrm{NTRU}_{Q,f,\tau,\Delta}(u)$ that encrypts $u \in R_Q$ under the secret key $f \in R_Q$, and an automorphism key $\mathbf{ksk}_t$, compute $\psi_t(c) = c(X^t)$ and return

$$\hat{c} = \mathsf{KS}_{f(X^t) \to f(X)}(c(X^t), \mathbf{ksk}_t) = c(X^t) \odot \mathbf{ksk}_t.$$

Since the automorphism on $\psi_t : X \to X^t$ on the ciphertext c can be achieved by simply permuting the coefficient vector of $c \in R_Q$ with signs, the cost of the above automorphism algorithm is dominated by the single external product for key switching. We now show that $\hat{c}$ is a desired ciphertext that encrypts $\psi_t(u) = u(X^t)$ under the secret key f in the following lemma.

Lemma 3 (Automorphisms on Scalar NTRU Ciphertexts). *Let N be a power of 2, and let t be an odd integer. Let $c = \mathrm{NTRU}_{Q,f,\tau,\Delta}(u) \in R_Q$ be a scalar NTRU ciphertext that encrypts u using secret key f and some noise with variance $Var(g)$. Let $\mathbf{ksk}_t = \mathsf{AutoKGen}(t, f) = \mathsf{KSKGen}(f(X^t), f(X))$ be the key-switching key from $f(X^t)$ to $f(X)$ using some noise distribution with variance $Var(g')$. Then, we have that*

$$\hat{c} = \mathsf{EvalAuto}_t(c, \mathbf{ksk}_t) = \mathsf{KS}_{f(X^t) \to f(X)}(c(X^t), \mathbf{ksk}_t) = \tau \cdot \hat{g}/f + \Delta \cdot u(X^t)/f$$

is a scalar NTRU ciphertext that encrypts $u(X^t)$ under the secret key f, and the variance of $\hat{g}$ satisfies

$$Var(\hat{g}) \leqslant dN\frac{B^2}{12}Var(g') + Var(g).$$

Proof. By the definition of AutoKGen(t, f), we have that $\mathbf{ksk}_t$ is essentially a key-switching key from $f(X^t)$ to $f(X)$. Thus, by Lemma 2, it suffices to show that $\psi_t(c) = c(X^t)$ is a ciphertext that encrypts $u(X^t)$ under the secret key $f(X^t)$ with the same noise variance $Var(g)$ as c. Note that $c = \mathrm{NTRU}_{Q,f,\tau,\Delta}(u) = \tau \cdot g/f + \Delta \cdot u/f$. By the property of the automorphism ψ_t, we have that $\psi_t(c) = c(X^t) = \tau \cdot g(X^t)/f(X^t) + \Delta \cdot u(X^t)/f(X^t)$. Clearly, $c(X^t)$ is a ciphertext that encrypts $u(X^t)$ under secret key $\psi_t(f) = f(X^t)$ and noise $g(X^t)$. Since the coefficient vector of $g(X^t)$ is essentially a permutation of the coefficient vector of $g(X)$ with signs, we have $Var(g(X^t)) = Var(g(X))$. This completes the proof.

4 Fast Blind Rotation in the NTRU Setting

Given an LWE-based first-layer ciphertext $\mathrm{LWE}_{q,\mathbf{s}}(m) = (\mathbf{a}, b) \in \mathbb{Z}_q^n \times \mathbb{Z}_q$ that encrypts some plaintext $m \in \mathbb{Z}_q$ under the secret key $\mathbf{s} \in \mathbb{Z}_q^n$, a rotation polynomial $r(X) \in R_Q = \mathbb{Z}_Q[X]/(X^N + 1)$, the goal of blind rotation is to create a second-layer (scalar) NTRU ciphertext that encrypts $r(Y) \cdot Y^{-b+\langle \mathbf{a},\mathbf{s}\rangle} \in R_Q$ for some monomial $Y \in R_Q$ of order exactly q.

In this paper, we will set the parameter N such that N is a power of 2 and $q|N$. In this setting, the monomial $Y = X^{\frac{2N}{q}}$ has an order of exactly q. Before giving our construction of blind rotation, we first define a set $S = \left\{ \frac{2N}{q} i + 1 : 1 \leq i \leq q-1 \right\} \subset \mathbb{Z}_{2N}$ of size $q-1$ that will be used later. Since $q|N$, it is easy to check that all the numbers in S are odd integers, and thus have inverses in $\mathbb{Z}_{2N}$. Moreover, we have that $S \cup \{1\}$ is actually a multiplicative subgroup of $\mathbb{Z}_{2N}$. In fact, given any two numbers $w, \hat{w} \in S \cup \{1\}$, we have that their inverses $w^{-1}, \hat{w}^{-1} \in \mathbb{Z}_{2N}$ and their multiplication $w\hat{w} \in \mathbb{Z}_{2N}$ are also in the set $S \cup \{1\}$. This is because we always have $w^{-1} = \hat{w}^{-1} = w\hat{w} = 1 \mod \frac{2N}{q}$. Now, we are ready to give our blind rotation construction.

4.1 The Construction

Let τ, Δ be two integers depending on the encoding of m in the first-layer ciphertext. We define two algorithms (BRKGen, BREval) for blind rotation as follows:

- BRKGen$(\mathbf{s}, f)$: Given a secret key $\mathbf{s} = (s_0, \ldots, s_{n-1}) \in \mathbb{Z}_q^n$ for the first-layer encryption, and a secret key $f \in R_Q$ for the second-layer NTRU-based GSW-like encryption, the algorithm first computes a set of ciphertexts:

$$\mathbf{evk}_0 = \mathrm{NTRU}'_{Q,f,\tau}(X^{s_0}/f), \qquad \mathbf{evk}_i = \mathrm{NTRU}'_{Q,f,\tau}(X^{s_i}) \text{ for } 1 \leq i < n,$$
$$\mathbf{evk}_n = \mathrm{NTRU}'_{Q,f,\tau}(X^{-\sum_{i=0}^{n-1} s_i}).$$

Then, it computes a set of ciphertexts for automorphisms as follows:

$$\mathbf{ksk}_j = \mathsf{AutoKGen}(j, f) = \mathrm{NTRU}'_{Q,f,\tau}\left(f(X^j)/f(X)\right) \text{ for all } j \in S.$$

Finally, the algorithm outputs $\mathbf{EVK}_{\tau,\Delta} = (\mathbf{evk}_0, \ldots, \mathbf{evk}_n, \{\mathbf{ksk}_j\}_{j \in S})$ as the evaluation key for blind rotation.

- BREval$((\mathbf{a}, b), r, \mathbf{EVK}_{\tau,\Delta})$: Given an LWE-based ciphertext $\mathrm{LWE}_{q,\mathbf{s}}(m) = (\mathbf{a}, b) \in \mathbb{Z}_q^n \times \mathbb{Z}_q$, a rotation polynomial $r(X) \in R_Q$ and an evaluation key $\mathbf{EVK}_{\tau,\Delta}$ at inputs, computes and returns ACC as described in algorithm 1.

In Theorem 1, we show that the output ACC of the blind rotation is indeed a scalar NTRU ciphertext that encrypts $r(X^{\frac{2N}{q}}) \cdot X^{\frac{2N}{q}(-b+\sum_{i=0}^{n-1} a_i s_i)}$.

Theorem 1 (Correctness of Blind Rotation). *Let* $\mathrm{LWE}_{q,\mathbf{s}}(m) = (\mathbf{a}, b) \in \mathbb{Z}_q^n \times \mathbb{Z}_q$ *be an LWE-based ciphertext under secret key* $\mathbf{s} = (s_1, \ldots, s_{n-1}) \in \mathbb{Z}_q^n$, *where* $\mathbf{a} = (a_0, \ldots, a_{n-1}) \in \mathbb{Z}_q^n$. *Let* N *be a power of 2 and* $q|N$. *Let* $r(X) \in$

Algorithm 1. $\mathsf{BREval}((\mathbf{a}, b), r, \mathbf{EVK}_{\tau, \Delta})$

Input:

An LWE ciphertext $\mathsf{LWE}_{\mathbf{s},q}(m) = (\mathbf{a} = (a_0, \ldots, a_{n-1}), b) \in \mathbb{Z}_q^{n+1}$;

A rotation polynomial $r(X) \in R_Q$;

An evaluation key $\mathbf{EVK}_{\tau, \Delta} = (\mathbf{evk}_0, \ldots, \mathbf{evk}_n, \{\mathbf{ksk}_j\}_{j \in S}) \in R_Q^{d(n+q)}$.

Output:

An NTRU ciphertext $\mathsf{NTRU}_{Q,f,\tau,\Delta}\left(r(X^{\frac{2N}{q}}) \cdot X^{\frac{2N}{q}(-b+\sum_{i=0}^{n-1} a_i s_i)}\right)$.

1: **for** $i = 0; i < n; i = i + 1$ **do**
2:    $w_i = \frac{2N}{q} a_i + 1$
3:    $w_i' = w_i^{-1} \mod 2N$
4: **end for**
5: $w_n' = 1$
6: $\mathsf{ACC} \leftarrow \Delta \cdot r(X^{\frac{2N}{q} w_0'}) \cdot X^{-\frac{2N}{q} b w_0'}$
7: **for** $i = 0; i < n; i = i + 1$ **do**
8:    $\mathsf{ACC} \leftarrow \mathsf{ACC} \odot \mathbf{evk}_i$
9:    If $w_i w_{i+1}' \neq 1$
10:      $\mathsf{ACC} \leftarrow \mathsf{EvalAuto}_{w_i w_{i+1}'}(\mathsf{ACC}, \mathbf{ksk}_{w_i w_{i+1}'})$
11: **end for**
12: $\mathsf{ACC} \leftarrow \mathsf{ACC} \odot \mathbf{evk}_n$
13: **return** ACC

$R_Q = \mathbb{Z}_Q[X]/(X^N + 1)$ *be any rotation polynomial. Let* $f \in R_Q$ *be a polynomial that is invertible in* R_Q. *Then, for any* $\mathbf{EVK}_{\tau, \Delta} = \mathsf{BRKGen}(\mathbf{s}, f)$, *and* $\mathsf{ACC} = \mathsf{BREval}((\mathbf{a}, b), r, \mathbf{EVK}_{\tau, \Delta})$, *we have that* ACC *is a scalar NTRU ciphertext* $\mathsf{NTRU}_{Q,f,\tau,\Delta}(r(X^{\frac{2N}{q}}) \cdot X^{\frac{2N}{q}(-b+\sum_{i=0}^{n-1} a_i s_i)})$.

We can prove Theorem 1 following the sketch idea from Sect. 1.2 and we defer the proof to Appendix A.

4.2   Analysis and Comparisons

In this subsection, we analyze the performance of our blind rotation, and give a comparison with AP [5,22,41], GINX [19,26], and Lee et al.'s blind rotation [37].

Note that the evaluation key $\mathbf{EVK}_{\tau, \Delta}$ for our blind rotation consists of $n+1$ vector NTRU ciphertexts for encrypting $\mathbf{s}$ and $q-1$ vector NTRU ciphertexts for automorphisms. This leads to a total $n + q$ vector NTRU ciphertexts, and thus $d(n + q)$ R_Q elements in the evaluation key. Moreover, it is easy to check that starting from the initial value $\mathsf{ACC} = \Delta \cdot r(X^{\frac{2N}{q} w_0'}) \cdot X^{-\frac{2N}{q} b w_0'}$ in Algorithm 1, we need $n + 1$ homomorphic multiplications and at most n automorphisms for the whole blind rotation. Since each automorphism consists of a permutation on the coefficient vector of the input ciphertext (with signs) and an external product, we need at most $2n + 1$ external products, which leads to a total up to $d(2n + 1)$ multiplications in R_Q. Finally, let σ_e^2 be the noise variance for the second-layer GSW-like encryption. By Lemma 2 and Lemma 3, the variance of the increased noise introduced by a homomorphic multiplication is $\sigma_\odot^2 = dN \frac{B^2}{12} \sigma_e^2$ and by an automorphism is equal to $\sigma_{KS}^2 = \sigma_\odot^2 = dN\frac{B^2}{12}\sigma_e^2$. By the fact that the initial value ACC essentially has zero noise, we have that the final ciphertext of our blind rotation contains a noise with variance $\sigma_{BR}^2 = (2n+1)\sigma_\odot^2 = (2n+1)dN\frac{B^2}{12}\sigma_e^2$.

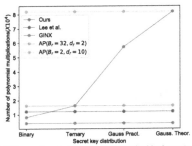
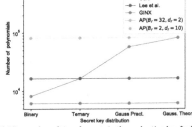

(a) The number of ring multiplications for blind rotation.

(b) The number of ring elements in the evaluation key for blind rotation.

Fig. 1. Comparison of blind rotations using different first-layer key distributions

In Table 1, we give a comparison of our blind rotation with AP/FHEW [5, 22,41], GINX/TFHE [19,26], and Lee et al.'s blind rotation [37] in terms of the number $\#R_Q$ of R_Q elements in the evaluation key and the number $\#mul$ of multiplications in R_Q for computation, where n, q are the dimension and modulus for the first-layer encryption; N, Q are the dimension and modulus of the ring $R_Q = \mathbb{Z}_Q[X]/(X^N + 1)$ for the second-layer GSW-like encryption; d is bit-decomposition dimension for multiplying a second-layer GSW-like ciphertext; B is a base parameter in bit-decomposing the first-layer ciphertexts for AP; and $|U|$ denote the size of the public set U in bit-decomposing the first-layer secret keys for GINX. Since q is usually less than $2n$ for typically choices of parameters [39], and $|U| \geq 1$ for all key distributions, one can see from Table 1 that our blind rotation has asymptotically the best performance in both evaluation key size and computational efficiency.

In Fig. 1, we give a comparison of different blind rotations using different first-layer key distributions. As in [37,39], we fix all other parameters, and only consider the use of different key distributions for the first-layer encryption. Specifically, we fix the parameters $(n, q, d) = (512, 1024, 4)$ for AP, GINX and Lee et al. that is recommended in STD128 [39] and $(n, q, d) = (512, 1024, 5)$ for our blind rotation using parameter P128T. We consider three types of key distributions, namely, binary distribution, ternary distribution, and Gaussian distribution. In Fig. 1, "Gauss Pract." and "Gauss. Theor." refer to Gaussian key distributions with standard deviation $\sigma = 3.19$ and $\sigma = \sqrt{n}$, respectively. We bound the size of an element chosen from Gaussian key distribution by using 12σ as in [39], which leads to a basis set U with size $|U| = 7$ and $|U| = 10$ corresponding to "Gauss Pract." and "Gauss. Theor." for GINX, respectively. As shown in Fig. 1, our bind rotation has performance asymptotically better than others for all key distributions.

Table 3. Estimation of noise variance for different blind rotations.

Methods	Noise variance	Ratio
AP [5,22,41]	$d_r dn N \frac{B^2}{6}\sigma_e^2$	$\frac{2d_r n}{2n+1} \approx d_r$
GINX [19,26]	$\lvert U \rvert dn N \frac{B^2}{3}\sigma_e^2$	$\frac{4\lvert U \rvert n}{2n+1} \approx 2\lvert U \rvert$
Lee et al. [37]	$(3n+2)dN\frac{B^2}{12}\sigma_e^2$	$\frac{3n+2}{2n+1} \approx 1.5$
Ours	$(2n+1)dN\frac{B^2}{12}\sigma_e^2$	\

In Table 3, we give a comparison of different blind rotations in terms of noise variance (i.e., the variance of the noise contained in the ciphertext output by the blind rotation). For AP, GINX and Lee et al.'s blind rotation, we use the formula given in [37]:

$$\sigma^2_{AP} = d_r dn N \frac{B^2}{6}\sigma_e^2, \sigma^2_{GINX} = 2\lvert U \rvert dn N \frac{B^2}{6}\sigma_e^2, \text{ and } \sigma^2_{Lee} = (3n+2)dN\frac{B^2}{12}\sigma_e^2.$$

Here $d_r = \lceil \log_{B_r} q \rceil$ for some integer parameter B_r in bit-decomposing the first-layer ciphertexts for AP. The column "Ratio" denotes the ratio between the considered blind rotation in that row and ours. As shown in Table 3, our blind rotation has the smallest noise variance, which makes it possible to use smaller parameters (e.g., N, Q) for the second-layer GSW-like encryption.

5   Bootstrapping LWE-Based First-Layer Ciphertexts

In this section, we describe how to apply our new blind rotation to bootstrap an LWE-based first-layer ciphertext. Our bootstrapping has a similar high-level structure as that in [5,19,22,26,37,41], which can be described as follows:

$$\text{LWE}_{q,s}(m) \xrightarrow[\text{Alg.1}]{\text{BREval}} \text{ACC} \xrightarrow[\text{[33]}]{\text{Ext}} \text{LWE}_{Q,\mathbf{f}}(m) \xrightarrow[\text{Lemma 4+Lemma 5}]{\text{ModSwitch+KeySwitch}} \text{LWE}_{q,\mathbf{s}}(m).$$

Given an LWE ciphertext $(\mathbf{a}, b) = (\mathbf{a}, \langle \mathbf{a}, \mathbf{s}\rangle - \text{noised}(m)) \in \mathbb{Z}_q^n \times \mathbb{Z}_q$, where $\text{noised}(m) = e + \lfloor \frac{q}{t}\rfloor m$ (here we take Regev-like ciphertexts [42] as an example, the same idea can be extended to BGV-like [10] and CKKS-like [16] ciphertexts by using different choice of (τ, Δ) and rotation polynomial $r(X) \in R_Q$). By first applying our blind rotation in Algorithm 1, we get a scalar NTRU ciphertext $c = \text{ACC}$ that encrypts $r(X^{\frac{2N}{q}}) \cdot X^{\frac{2N}{q}\text{noised}(m)}$ under secret key $f \in R_Q$. Let $r(X) = \sum_{i=0}^{q-1}(\lfloor i/\lfloor q/t\rfloor\rfloor \bmod t)X^{-i}$, one can easily check that the constant coefficient of $r(X^{\frac{2N}{q}}) \cdot X^{\frac{2N}{q}\text{noised}(m)}$ is m by the correctness of the first-layer encryption that $m = \lfloor \text{noised}(m)/\lfloor q/t\rfloor\rfloor$. Let $\mathbf{c} = (c_0,\ldots,c_{N-1})$, $\mathbf{f} = (f_0,\ldots,f_{N-1}) \in \mathbb{Z}_Q^N$ be the coefficient vectors of the polynomials $c, f \in R_Q$. Then, we can directly set $\hat{\mathbf{c}} = (c_0, -c_{N-1},\ldots, -c_1) \in \mathbb{Z}_Q^N$ the same as the LWE sample extraction algorithm Ext in [33] to get a ciphertext $\text{LWE}_{Q,\mathbf{f}}(m) = (\hat{\mathbf{c}} = (c_0, -c_{N-1},\ldots, -c_1), 0)$ that encrypts m under the secret key $\mathbf{f} \in \mathbb{Z}_Q^N$. Finally, we can use modulus-switching and key-switching to convert $\text{LWE}_{Q,\mathbf{f}}(m)$ to a desired $\text{LWE}_{q,\mathbf{s}}(m)$.

5.1   Modulus Switching for LWE-Based Ciphertexts

The modulus switching from Q to q can be easily achieved by multiplying the targeted ciphertext with q/Q, and rounding the results to the nearest integer.

Lemma 4 (Modulus switching for LWE, adapted from [22]). *Given a ciphertext* $\mathrm{LWE}_{Q,\mathbf{f}}(m) = (\mathbf{a}, b = \langle \mathbf{a}, \mathbf{f} \rangle - (e + \lfloor \frac{Q}{t} \rceil m)) \in \mathbb{Z}_Q^N \times \mathbb{Z}_Q$ *using some key distribution with variance* $Var(\mathbf{f})$ *and some noise distribution with variance* $Var(e)$ *and a targeted modulus* q, *define the modulus switching as*

$$(\mathbf{a}', b') = \mathsf{ModSwitch}(\mathrm{LWE}_{Q,\mathbf{f}}(m), q) = \left\lfloor \mathrm{LWE}_{Q,\mathbf{f}}(m) \cdot \frac{q}{Q} \right\rceil \quad \bmod q.$$

Then, $(\mathbf{a}', b')$ *is an LWE ciphertext that encrypts the same* m *under the same secret key* $\mathbf{f} \in \mathbb{Z}^N$. *Moreover, the noise variance of the resulting ciphertext* $(\mathbf{a}', b')$ *is bounded by* $\frac{q^2}{Q^2} Var(e) + \frac{1+NVar(\mathbf{f})}{12}$.

We denote $\sigma_{MS}^2 = \frac{1+NVar(\mathbf{f})}{12}$ as the variance of the increased noise (with respect to the input ciphertext) for modulus switching.

5.2   Key Switching for LWE-Based Ciphertexts

In this subsection, we define a pair of two algorithms $(\mathsf{LWE\_KSKG}, \mathsf{LWE\_KS})$ for key switching LWE ciphertexts as follows:

- $\mathsf{LWE\_KSKG}(\mathbf{f}, \mathbf{s}, q, B_{ks})$: Given two vectors $\mathbf{f} = (f_0, \ldots, f_{N-1}) \in \mathbb{Z}_q^N, \mathbf{s} \in (s_0, \ldots, s_{n-1}) \in \mathbb{Z}_q^n$ and two integers q, B_{ks} as inputs, the algorithm first computes $d_{ks} = \lceil \log_{B_{ks}} q \rceil$. Then, it creates a set of ciphertexts:

$$\mathbf{lksk}_{i,j,v} = (\mathbf{a}_{i,j,v}, b_{i,j,v} = \langle \mathbf{a}_{i,j,v}, \mathbf{s} \rangle - e_{i,j,v} - vB_{ks}^j f_i) \in \mathbb{Z}_q^n \times \mathbb{Z}_q$$

  for all $i \in \mathbb{Z}_N, j \in \mathbb{Z}_{d_{ks}}, 1 \leq v \leq B_{ks}$ by randomly choosing $\mathbf{a}_{i,j,v} \leftarrow \mathbb{Z}_q^n$ and noise $e_{i,j,v}$ from some noise distribution over $\mathbb{Z}$. Finally, it outputs $\mathbf{LKSK}_{\mathbf{f},\mathbf{s},q,B_{ks}} = \{\mathbf{lksk}_{i,j,v}\}_{i \in \mathbb{Z}_N, j \in \mathbb{Z}_{d_{ks}}, 1 \leq v \leq B_{ks}}$ as the key-switching key.

- $\mathsf{LWE\_KS}((\hat{\mathbf{a}}, \hat{b}), \mathbf{LKSK}_{\mathbf{f},\mathbf{s},q,B_{ks}})$: Given as inputs a ciphertext $\mathrm{LWE}_{q,\mathbf{f}}(m) = (\hat{\mathbf{a}}, \hat{b} = \langle \hat{\mathbf{a}}, \mathbf{f} \rangle - (\hat{e} + \lfloor \frac{q}{t} \rceil m)) \in \mathbb{Z}_q^N \times \mathbb{Z}_q$ for some $\hat{\mathbf{a}} = (\hat{a}_0, \ldots, \hat{a}_N) \in \mathbb{Z}_q^N$ and a key-switching key $\mathbf{LKSK}_{\mathbf{f},\mathbf{s},q,B_{ks}} = \{\mathbf{lksk}_{i,j,v}\}_{i \in \mathbb{Z}_N, j \in \mathbb{Z}_{d_{ks}}, 1 \leq v \leq B_{ks}}$ for some $\mathbf{lksk}_{i,j,v} = (\mathbf{a}_{i,j,v}, b_{i,j,v})$ as inputs, the algorithm first decomposes each $\hat{a}_i = \sum_{j=0}^{d_{ks}-1} v_{i,j} B_{ks}^j$ into a vector $(v_{i,0}, \ldots, v_{i,d_{ks}-1}) \in \mathbb{Z}_{B_{ks}}^{d_{ks}}$. Then, it computes

$$\hat{\mathbf{a}}' = \sum_{i=0}^{N-1} \sum_{j=0, v_{i,j} \neq 0}^{d_{ks}-1} \mathbf{a}_{i,j,v_{i,j}}, \quad \hat{b}' = \sum_{i=0}^{N-1} \sum_{j=0, v_{i,j} \neq 0}^{d_{ks}-1} b_{i,j,v_{i,j}} + \hat{b}.$$

Finally, it outputs $(\hat{\mathbf{a}}', \hat{b}') \in \mathbb{Z}_q^n \times \mathbb{Z}_q$.

Lemma 5. *[Key Switching for LWE Ciphertexts] Let $\mathbf{f} \in \mathbb{Z}_q^N, \mathbf{s} \in \mathbb{Z}_q^n$ be two vectors. Let $\mathrm{LWE}_{q,\mathbf{f}}(m) = (\hat{\mathbf{a}}, \hat{b}) \in \mathbb{Z}_q^N \times \mathbb{Z}_q$ be a ciphertext that encrypts $m \in \mathbb{Z}_q$ under the secret key $\mathbf{f} \in \mathbb{Z}_q^N$. Then, for any $\mathbf{LKSK}_{\mathbf{f},\mathbf{s},q,B_{ks}} = \mathsf{LWE\_KSKG}(\mathbf{f}, \mathbf{s}, q, B_{ks})$, we have that $(\hat{\mathbf{a}}', \hat{b}') = \mathsf{LWE\_KS}((\hat{\mathbf{a}}, \hat{b}), \mathbf{LKSK}_{\mathbf{f},\mathbf{s},q,B_{ks}}) \in \mathbb{Z}_q^n \times \mathbb{Z}_q$ is a ciphertext that encrypts $m \in \mathbb{Z}_q$ under the secret key $\mathbf{s} \in \mathbb{Z}_q^n$.*

Moreover, if the variance of the noise in $(\hat{\mathbf{a}}, \hat{b})$ is $Var(\hat{e})$, and the variance of the noise distribution used in generating $\mathbf{LKSK}_{\mathbf{f},\mathbf{s},q,B_{ks}}$ is $Var(e)$, we have that the variance $Var(\hat{e}')$ of the noise $\hat{e}'$ in $(\hat{\mathbf{a}}', \hat{b}')$ is upper bounded by $Nd_{ks}Var(e) + Var(\hat{e})$, where $d_{ks} = \lceil \log_{B_{ks}} q \rceil$.

We defer the proof of Lemma 5 to Appendix B, as it is also presented in [22]. Similarly, we use the symbol $\sigma_{LKS}^2 = Nd_{ks}Var(e)$ to denote the variance of the increased noise (with respect to the input ciphertext) for LWE key-switching.

5.3 The Bootstrapping Algorithm

In this section, we give the full description of our bootstrapping algorithm for LWE-based first-layer ciphertexts in Algorithm 2 (note that we use a modulus switching from Q to Q_{ks} for some $q < Q_{ks} < Q$ before key-switching to optimize the parameters for generating the LWE key-switching key).

Algorithm 2. Bootstrapping LWE-based First-layer Ciphertexts

Input:
    An LWE ciphertext $\mathrm{LWE}_{q,\mathbf{s}}(m) = (\mathbf{a} = (a_0, \ldots, a_{n-1}), b) \in \mathbb{Z}_q^{n+1}$;
    A rotation polynomial $r(X) \in R_Q$;
    Evaluation key $\mathbf{EVK}_{\tau,\Delta} = (\mathbf{evk}_0, \ldots, \mathbf{evk}_n, \{\mathbf{ksk}_j\}_{j \in S}) \in R_Q^{d(n+q)}$;
    LWE key-switching key $\mathbf{LKSK}_{\mathbf{f},\mathbf{s},Q_{ks},B_{ks}} = \{\mathbf{lksk}_{i,j,v}\}_{i \in \mathbb{Z}_N, j \in \mathbb{Z}_{d_{ks}}, 1 \le v \le B_{ks}}$;
Output:
    A refreshed LWE ciphertext $\mathrm{LWE}_{q,\mathbf{s}}(m) \in \mathbb{Z}_q^{n+1}$;
1: $\mathrm{ACC} \leftarrow \mathsf{BREval}((\mathbf{a}, b), r, \mathbf{EVK}_{\tau,\Delta})$
2: $\mathrm{LWE}_{Q,\mathbf{f}}(m) \leftarrow \mathsf{Ext}(\mathrm{ACC})$
3: $\mathrm{LWE}_{Q_{ks},\mathbf{f}}(m) \leftarrow \mathsf{ModSwitch}(\mathrm{LWE}_{Q,\mathbf{f}}(m), Q_{ks})$
4: $\mathrm{LWE}_{Q_{ks},\mathbf{s}}(m) \leftarrow \mathsf{LWE\_KS}(\mathrm{LWE}_{Q_{ks},\mathbf{f}}(m), \mathbf{LKSK}_{\mathbf{f},\mathbf{s},Q_{ks},B_{ks}})$
5: $\mathrm{LWE}_{q,\mathbf{s}}(m) \leftarrow \mathsf{ModSwitch}(\mathrm{LWE}_{Q_{ks},\mathbf{s}}(m), q)$

Theorem 2 (Bootstrapping LWE-based First-layer Ciphertexts). *Let $q < Q_{ks} < Q$ be positive integers. Given an LWE ciphertext $(\mathbf{a}, b = \langle \mathbf{a}, \mathbf{s} \rangle - \mathsf{noised}(m)) \in \mathbb{Z}_q^n \times \mathbb{Z}_q$ encrypting a plaintext $m \in \mathbb{Z}_t$ with $\mathsf{noised}(m) = \lfloor \frac{q}{t} \rceil m + e$, Algorithm 2 outputs a refreshed LWE ciphertext $(\mathbf{a}', b' = \mathbf{a}'\mathbf{s} - (\lfloor \frac{q}{t} \rceil m + e')) \in \mathbb{Z}_q^n \times \mathbb{Z}_q$ encrypting the same plaintext. And the noise e' of the refreshed ciphertext is bounded by a Gaussian with standard deviation*

$$\sqrt{\frac{q^2}{Q_{ks}^2}\left(\frac{Q_{ks}^2}{Q^2}\sigma_{BR}^2 + \sigma_{MS1}^2 + \sigma_{LKS}^2\right) + \sigma_{MS2}^2}$$

where $\sigma_{BR}^2 = (2n+1)dN\frac{B^2}{12}Var(g)$, $\sigma_{MS1}^2 = \frac{NVar(f)+1}{12}$, $\sigma_{LKS}^2 = Nd_{ks}Var(e)$, and $\sigma_{MS2}^2 = \frac{nVar(\mathbf{s})+1}{12}$ are the noise variances contributed respectively by the blind rotation, the first modulus switching, the key switching, and the second modulus switching in Algorithm 2, and $Var(g), Var(f), Var(e), Var(\mathbf{s})$ are respectively the noise variance and secret key variance of NTRU ciphertext and the noise variance and secret key variance of LWE ciphertext.

Proof. The correctness of Algorithm 2 directly follows from the correctness of the blind rotation in Theorem 1, the modulus switching in Lemma 4, and the LWE key switching in Lemma 5.

Next we analyze the noise of the resulting ciphertext. After the blind rotation in step 1, we get a scalar NTRU ciphertext with noise variance bounded by $\sigma_{BR}^2 = (2n+1)dN\frac{B^2}{12}Var(g)$ according to the analysis in Sect. 4.2. By a trivial Ext in step 2 we get an LWE ciphertext without increasing the noise variance. By Lemma 4, we have the noise variance after the first modulus switching from Q to Q_{ks} in step 3 is bounded by $\frac{Q_{ks}^2}{Q^2}\cdot\sigma_{BR}^2 + \sigma_{MS1}^2$ where $\sigma_{MS1}^2 = \frac{NVar(f)+1}{12}$. By Lemma 5, the noise variance after the key switching in step 4 is bounded by $\frac{Q_{ks}^2}{Q^2}\cdot\sigma_{BR}^2 + \sigma_{MS1}^2 + \sigma_{LKS}^2$, where $\sigma_{LKS}^2 = Nd_{ks}Var(e)$. Again, by Lemma 4, we have the noise variance after the second modulus switching in step 5 from Q_{ks} to q is bounded by $\frac{q^2}{Q_{ks}^2}\left(\frac{Q_{ks}^2}{Q^2}\sigma_{BR}^2 + \sigma_{MS1}^2 + \sigma_{LKS}^2\right) + \sigma_{MS2}^2$ where $\sigma_{MS2}^2 = \frac{nVar(\mathbf{s})+1}{12}$. This finally completes the proof.

6   Bootstrapping RLWE-Based First-Layer Ciphertexts

We now describe how to apply our blind rotation to bootstrap an RLWE-based first-layer ciphertext. Our bootstrapping has a high-level structure as follows:

$$\mathrm{RLWE}_{q,s}(m) \xrightarrow[\text{[33]}]{\text{Ext}} \{\mathrm{LWE}_{q,\mathbf{s}}(m_i)\} \xrightarrow[\text{Alg.}1+[33]]{\text{BREval+Ext}} \{\mathrm{LWE}_{Q,\mathbf{f}}(m_i)\} \xrightarrow[\text{Lemma 6}]{\text{Pack}} \mathrm{RLWE}_{Q,s}(m).$$

Given an RLWE ciphertext $\mathrm{RLWE}_{q,s}(m) = (a,b) \in \hat{R}_q \times \hat{R}_q$, and let $\mathbf{a} = (a_0, \ldots, a_{n-1})$, $\mathbf{s} = (s_0, \ldots, s_{n-1})$, $\mathbf{m} = (m_0, \ldots, m_{n-1}) \in \mathbb{Z}_q^n$ be the coefficients of $a, s, m \in \hat{R}_q$, one can easily extract n LWE ciphertexts $(\mathbf{a}_i, b_i)$ that encrypts m_i under secret $\mathbf{s}$ by the LWE sample extraction algorithm Ext in [33]. Then, for each LWE ciphertext $(\mathbf{a}_i, b_i)$, we apply our blind rotation algorithm BREval to obtain an NTRU ciphertext c_i that encrypts $r(X^{\frac{2N}{q}}) \cdot X^{\frac{2N}{q}\mathrm{noised}(m_i)}$ under the secret key f. Let $\mathbf{f} = (f_0, f_1, \ldots, f_{N-1}) \in \mathbb{Z}_Q^N$ and $\mathbf{c}_i = (c_{i,0}, c_{i,1}, \cdots, c_{i,N-1}) \in \mathbb{Z}_Q^N$ be the coefficient vectors of $f, c_i \in R_Q$. Let $\hat{\mathbf{c}}_i = (c_{i,0}, -c_{i,N-1}, \ldots, -c_{i,1}) \in \mathbb{Z}_Q^N$, then $(\hat{\mathbf{c}}_i, 0) \in \mathbb{Z}_Q^N \times \mathbb{Z}_Q$ is actually an LWE ciphertext that encrypts m_i under the secret key $\mathbf{f} = (f_0, f_1, \ldots, f_{N-1}) \in \mathbb{Z}_Q^N$. In particular, by setting appropriate rotation polynomial $r(X)$, we can always have that $\langle \hat{\mathbf{c}}_i, \mathbf{f} \rangle = \tau \cdot e_i + \Delta \cdot m_i$ for some noise e_i and integers (τ, Δ) depending on the encoding of m in $\mathrm{RLWE}_{q,s}(m)$. Finally, we can use the packing algorithm Pack in [40] pack the LWE ciphertexts into an RLWE ciphertext $\mathrm{RLWE}_{Q,s}(m) = (a', b') \in \hat{R}_Q \times \hat{R}_Q$. For completeness, we describe the packing algorithm in [40] in Sect. 6.1.

6.1 Packing LWE Ciphertexts to RLWE Ciphertexts

Let n, B, Q, τ, Δ be positive integers, and let $d = \lceil \log_B Q \rceil$. Without loss of generality, we assume that an LWE ciphertext $\mathrm{LWE}_{Q,\mathbf{f}}(m)$ has the form of $(\mathbf{a}, b = \langle \mathbf{a}, \mathbf{f} \rangle - (\tau \cdot e + \Delta \cdot m))$. Let $\hat{R}_Q = \mathbb{Z}[X]/(X^n + 1)$. We recall the algorithm for packing LWE ciphertexts into RLWE ciphertexts in [40]. Formally, we define two algorithms (PackKGen, Pack) as follows:

- PackKGen($\mathbf{f}, s$) : Given a vector $\mathbf{f} = (f_0, \cdots, f_{N-1}) \in \mathbb{Z}_Q^N$ and a ring element $s \in \hat{R}_Q$ as inputs, the algorithm first computes a set of ciphertexts

$$\mathbf{rpk}_{j,k} = (\hat{a}_{j,k}, \hat{b}_{j,k} = \hat{a}_{j,k}s - \tau \cdot \hat{e}_{j,k} - B^k f_j) \in \hat{R}_Q \times \hat{R}_Q$$

for all $j \in \mathbb{Z}_N, k \in \mathbb{Z}_d$ by randomly choosing $\hat{a}_{j,k} \leftarrow \hat{R}_Q$ and noise $\hat{e}_{j,k}$ from some distribution over $\hat{R}_Q$. Then, it outputs $\mathbf{RPK}_\tau = \{\mathbf{rpk}_{j,k}\}$.

- Pack($\{\mathrm{LWE}_{Q,\mathbf{f}}(m_i)\}, \mathbf{RPK}_\tau$): Given ciphertexts $\mathrm{LWE}_{Q,\mathbf{f}}(m_i) = (\mathbf{a}_i, b_i) \in \mathbb{Z}_Q^N \times \mathbb{Z}_Q$ for all $0 \leqslant i \leqslant n-1$ and $\mathbf{a}_i = (a_{i,0}, a_{i,1}, \cdots, a_{i,N-1}) \in \mathbb{Z}_Q^N$, and the packing key $\mathbf{RPK}_\tau = \{\mathbf{rpk}_{j,k}\}$ for some $\mathbf{rpk}_{j,k} = (\hat{a}_{j,k}, \hat{b}_{j,k})$ as inputs, the algorithm first computes $u_j = \sum_{i=0}^{n-1} a_{i,j} X^i$ for $0 \leq j \leq N - 1$, and $\mathrm{BitDecom}_B(u_j) = (u_{j,0}, \cdots, u_{j,d-1}) \in \hat{R}_B^d$ for some $u_j = \sum_{k=0}^{d-1} u_{j,k} B^k$. Then, it computes

$$u = \sum_{j=0}^{N-1} \sum_{k=0}^{d-1} u_{j,k} \hat{a}_{j,k}, \quad v = \sum_{j=0}^{N-1} \sum_{k=0}^{d-1} u_{j,k} \hat{b}_{j,k} + \sum_{i=0}^{n-1} b_i X^i.$$

Finally, it returns $(u, v) \in \hat{R}_Q \times \hat{R}_Q$ as the output.

Lemma 6 (Correctness of Packing). *Let $\mathbf{f} = (f_0, \cdots, f_{N-1}) \in \mathbb{Z}_Q^N$ be a vector, and let $s \in \hat{R}_Q$ be a ring element. For all $0 \leq i \leq n-1$, let $\mathrm{LWE}_{Q,\mathbf{f}}(m_i) = (\mathbf{a}_i, b_i = \langle \mathbf{a}_i, \mathbf{f} \rangle - (\tau \cdot e_i + \Delta \cdot m_i)) \in \mathbb{Z}_Q^N \times \mathbb{Z}_Q$ be an LWE ciphertext that encrypts m_i under secret key $\mathbf{f} = (f_0, \cdots, f_{N-1}) \in \mathbb{Z}_Q^N$. Then, for any $\mathbf{RPK}_\tau = \{\mathbf{rpk}_{j,k}\} = \mathrm{PackKGen}(\mathbf{f}, s)$, we have that $(u, v) = \mathrm{Pack}(\{\mathrm{LWE}_{Q,\mathbf{f}}(m_i)\}, \mathbf{RPK}_\tau) \in \hat{R}_Q \times \hat{R}_Q$ is a ciphertext that encrypts $m = \sum_{i=0}^{n-1} m_i X^i$ under the secret key $s \in \hat{R}_Q$.*

Moreover, if the variance of the noise in $\mathrm{LWE}_{Q,\mathbf{f}}(m_i)$ is $Var(e)$, and the variance of the noise distribution in generating $\mathbf{RPK}_\tau$ is $Var(\hat{e})$, then the variance $Var(e')$ of the noise in the resulting ciphertext (u, v) is upper bounded by $Var(e') \leqslant nNd\frac{B^2}{12} Var(\hat{e}) + Var(e)$.

We defer the proof of Lemma 6 to Appendix C, as it is also presented in [40].

6.2 The Bootstrapping Algorithm

In this subsection, we give the bootstrapping algorithm for RLWE-based first-layer ciphertexts in Algorithm 3, and prove the following theorem.

Algorithm 3. Bootstrapping RLWE-based First-layer Ciphertexts

---

Input:
  RLWE ciphertext $\text{RLWE}_{q,\mathbf{s}}(m) = (a, b) \in \hat{R}_q \times \hat{R}_q$;
  A rotation polynomial $r(X) \in R_Q$;
  Evaluation keys $\mathbf{EVK}_{\tau,\Delta} = (\mathbf{evk}_0, \ldots, \mathbf{evk}_n, \{\mathbf{ksk}_j\}_{j \in S}) \in R_Q^{d(n+q)}$;
  Packing keys $\mathbf{RPK}_\tau$;
Output:
  A refreshed RLWE ciphertext $(a', b') \in \hat{R}_Q \times \hat{R}_Q$;
1: **for** $i = 0, i < n, i = i + 1$ **do**
2:    $(\mathbf{a}_i, b_i) \leftarrow \text{Ext}(\text{RLWE}_{q,\mathbf{s}}(m))$
3:    $\text{ACC}_i \leftarrow \text{BREval}((\mathbf{a}_i, b_i), r, \mathbf{EVK}_{\tau,\Delta})$
4:    $\text{LWE}_{Q,\mathbf{f}}(m_i) \leftarrow \text{Ext}(\text{ACC}_i)$
5: **end for**
6: $\text{RLWE}_{Q,\mathbf{s}}(m) = (a', b') \leftarrow \text{Pack}(\{\text{LWE}_{Q,\mathbf{f}}(m_i)\}_{i \in [0,n-1]}, \mathbf{RPK}_\tau)$

Theorem 3 (Bootstrapping RLWE-based First-layer Ciphertexts).
Given an RLWE ciphertext $(a, b) = (a, as - \text{noised}(m)) \in \hat{R}_q \times \hat{R}_q$ encrypting a plaintext $m \in \hat{R}$, Algorithm 3 outputs a refreshed RLWE ciphertext $(a', b' = a's - (\tau \cdot e' + \Delta \cdot m)) \in \hat{R}_Q \times \hat{R}_Q$ encrypting the same plaintext. And the noise e' of the refreshed ciphertext is bounded by a Gaussian with standard deviation

$$\sqrt{nNd\frac{B^2}{12}Var(e) + Var(e) + (2n+1)dN\frac{B^2}{12}Var(g)}$$

where $Var(g), Var(e)$ represents the noise variance of NTRU ciphertext and the noise variance of RLWE ciphertext, respectively.

Proof. The correctness of Algorithm 3 directly follows from the correctness of the blind rotation in Theorem 1 and the LWE packing in Lemma 6.

Now, we analyze the noise of the resulting ciphertext. After each blind rotation in step 2, we get a scalar NTRU ciphertext with noise variance bounded by $Var(e) + \sigma_{BR}^2 = Var(e) + (2n+1)dN\frac{B^2}{12}Var(g)$. Then we extract the coefficients of NTRU ciphertext as LWE ciphertext, and use the packing algorithm to obtain a refreshed RLWE ciphertext in $\hat{R}_Q$ under large modulus Q. By Lemma 6, the refreshed noise is a Gaussian with standard deviation

$$\sqrt{nNd\frac{B^2}{12}Var(e) + Var(e) + (2n+1)dN\frac{B^2}{12}Var(g)}.$$

This completes the proof.

7   Security, Parameters and Implementation

In this section, we present the necessary security analysis and the experimental results of our bootstrapping algorithm for LWE-based first-layer ciphertexts, and compare its performance with that of FHEW/AP [22] and TFHE/GINX [19] running on the same laptop.

7.1   Security Analysis

The ciphertext of our first-layer encryption basically consists of (R)LWE samples, and thus it is indistinguishable from uniform based on the decisional (R)LWE assumptions. The ciphertext of our second-layer encryption contains scalar NTRU ciphertexts and vector NTRU ciphertexts. Our scalar NTRU encryption has form of $c = (\tau \cdot g + \Delta \cdot u)/f$. Since τ and Δ are publicly defined constants, this can be simplified as $c = (t \cdot g + u)/f$, where t is an integer. Because the standard NTRU encryption (in the symmetric key setting) has the form of $c = t \cdot g/f + m$, our ciphertext can be seen as a standard NTRU ciphertext that encrypts a key-dependent message $m = u/f$. Thus, the security of our second-layer encryption requires the circular-security/KDM-security assumption of the standard NTRU scheme, which is the same as that in [7,27,41]. Note that the construction of FHEs without such kind of assumptions is currently unknown. Moreover, the currently best algorithm solving $c = (t \cdot g + u)/f$, to the best of our knowledge, is to treat it as an RLWE instance (c, u) (as we can rewrite it as $u = cf - t \cdot g$), and the lattice used to solve this problem is very close to the standard NTRU lattice. Based on known algorithms solving (R)LWE and NTRU problems, we believe that this type of encryption $c = (t \cdot g + u)/f$ will not provide extra advantage to the adversary from the point of concrete attacks. Our vector NTRU ciphertext (for generating the evaluation keys $\mathbf{EVK}_{\tau,\Delta} = (\mathbf{evk}_0, \dots, \mathbf{evk}_n, \{\mathbf{ksk}_j\}_{j \in S})$) basically encrypts different messages using the same secret key as that in [7,41], whose security is essentially guaranteed by the decisional Vectorized-NTRU assumption.

    In all, the semantically (IND-CPA) security of our two-layer FHE scheme can be directly proved under the decisional (R)LWE problem, the decisional NTRU problem (with KDM security) and the decisional Vectorized-NTRU problem via a standard hybrid argument.

7.2   Parameters

In Table 4, we give all the parameters used in our experiment. The parameter STD128 (resp. STD192) is used for FHEW/AP [22] and TFHE/GINX [19], which is the default parameter for 128-bit (resp., 192-bit) security provided in the OpenFHE 0.9.1 library [6] and recommended in [39].

    For 128-bit security, we choose two types of parameters, namely, P128T and P128G, for our algorithms: P128T is set to have the same parameters (n, q) and ternary key distribution with STD128 for the first-layer LWE encryption; while P128G is set to use a Gaussian key distribution with variance $4/3$. We use the LWE estimator [4] to estimate the security of (R)LWE instances, and use the NTRU estimator offered by Ducas and van Woerden [23] to find the BKZ block size β needed by Dense Sublattice Discovery(DSD) attack. Then, we use the cost model $T(d, \beta) := 2^{0.292 \cdot \beta + 16.4 + \log_2(8 \cdot d)}$ (in the NTRU setting $d = 2N$) to estimate the concrete security. Both P128T and P128G are set to provide at least 128-bit security. Similar to [17,22,39], they are also set to satisfy the requirement that the decryption failure upper bound is less than 2^{-32}. We choose P192T and

Table 4. Parameters for bootstrapping LWE-based first-layer ciphertexts.

Parameters	Key distrib.	n	q	N	Q	B	Q_{ks}	B_{ks}
STD128 [39]	Ternary	512	1024	1024	2^{27}	2^7	2^{14}	2^7
P128T	Ternary	512	1024	1024	$995329 \approx 2^{19.9}$	2^4	2^{14}	2^7
P128G	Gaussian	465	1024	1024	$995329 \approx 2^{19.9}$	2^4	2^{14}	2^7
STD192 [39]	Ternary	1024	1024	2048	2^{37}	2^{13}	2^{19}	28
P192T	Ternary	1024	1024	2048	$44421121 \approx 2^{25.4}$	2^9	2^{19}	28
P192G	Gaussian	870	1024	2048	$44421121 \approx 2^{25.4}$	2^9	2^{17}	28

P192G to provide at least 192-bit security as STD192 using the same way as P128T and P128G.

For a NAND gate, we estimate the failure probability of decryption using the same formula $P = 1 - \text{erf}\left(\frac{q/8}{2\beta'}\right)$ (β' represents the standard deviation of the final noise) as that in [17, 22, 39]. The estimated decryption failure probabilities for our parameters are given by $P_{\text{P128T}} = 2^{-32}$, $P_{\text{P128G}} = 2^{-34}$, $P_{\text{P192T}} = 2^{-53}$ and $P_{\text{P192G}} = 2^{-42}$. Note that our parameters have modulus $Q < N^2$ (resp., $Q < N^{2.31}$) for both P128T and P128G (resp., P192T and P192G), which is smaller than the fatigue point $Q = N^{2.484}$ in [23] to avoid sublattice attacks on NTRU problems.

7.3 Experimental Results

We implement our bootstrapping algorithm for LWE-based first-layer ciphertexts in C++ on a laptop with an Intel(R) Core(TM) i5 CPU @ 2.30 GHz and 16 GB RAM, running Linux 4.4.0-19041-Microsoft. We compare the performance with FHEW/AP [22] and TFHE/GINX [19] that were implemented in the OpenFHE library [6]. All the experiments are running with a single thread at a single CPU core. In Table 5, we present the experimental results, where the timing figures are averaged over 1000 times running of the algorithms.

From Table 5, one can see that for parameters with ternary first-layer key distribution providing 128-bit security, we only need to store 18.65 MB for blind rotation, which is about 89.8 times smaller than FHEW/AP [6, 22] and 2.9 times smaller than TFHE/GINX [6, 19]. Moreover, our algorithm only needs 112 ms to evaluate a NAND gate followed by a bootstrapping, which is about 3.2 times faster than FHEW/AP and 2.1 times faster than TFHE/GINX. By using P128G with Gaussian key distribution, we can obtain an extra 10% improvement over P128T (we note that the performance of TFHE/GINX would become worse by roughly a factor of 1.5 when using the same Gaussian key distribution as ours). For parameters with ternary first-layer key distribution providing 192-bit security, the evaluation key size of our blind rotation is about 175 times smaller than FHEW/AP and 5.8 times smaller than TFHE/GINX; Our bootstrapping algorithm is about 3.7 times faster than FHEW/AP and 2.7 times faster than

Table 5. Timings and key sizes for bootstrapping (where the column "Timings" denotes the timing for performing a NAND gate followed by a bootstrapping, the column "EVK" denotes the evaluation key size for blind rotation; the column "KSK" denotes the key size for switching a second-layer ciphertext back to a first-layer one; the last column "Boots. key" denotes the whole bootstrapping key size.)

Algorithms	Parameters	Key distrib.	Timings (ms)	EVK (MB)	KSK (MB)	Boots. key (MB)
FHEW/AP [6,22]	STD128 [39]	Ternary	359	1674	224	1898
TFHE/GINX [6,19]	STD128 [39]	Ternary	234	54	224	278
Ours	P128T	Ternary	112	18.65	224	242.65
	P128G	Gaussian	100	17.90	203.44	221.34
FHEW/AP [6,22]	STD192 [39]	Ternary	1200	6682	532	7214
TFHE/GINX [6,19]	STD192 [39]	Ternary	859	222	532	754
Ours	P192T	Ternary	320	38.10	532	570.10
	P192G	Gaussian	273	34.30	404.41	438.71

TFHE/GINX. Again, by using P192G with Gaussian key distribution, we can obtain an extra 17% improvement over P192T.

Finally, we note that the whole bootstrapping key consists of the evaluation key for blind rotation and the key-switching key for converting a second-layer ciphertext (obtained from blind rotation) back to a first-layer ciphertext. Moreover, we also note that all the algorithms need a key-switching key of $nNB_{ks}d_{ks}\log_2 Q_{ks}$ bits. In Table 5, one can see that the size of the bootstrapping keys for TFHE/GINX and ours is mainly dominated by the key-switching key size. However, even if we use a key-switching key of the same size (namely, P128T and P192T) as TFHE/GINX, our blind rotation still provides a reduction in the total bootstrapping key size by about 12.7% for 128-bit security and 24.4% for 192-bit security. More improvements are available when using Gaussian key distributions.

Acknowledgements. We thank the anonymous reviewers of CRYPTO 2023 for their helpful comments and suggestions on earlier versions of our paper. Jiang Zhang, the corresponding author, is supported by the National Key Research and Development Program of China (Grant No. 2022YFB2702000), and by the National Natural Science Foundation of China (Grant Nos. 62022018, 61932019). Yi Deng is supported by the National Natural Science Foundation of China (Grant Nos. 61932019) and by Beijing Natural Science Foundation (Grant No. M22003).

A   Proof of Theorem 1

Proof. Note that by the definition of w_i and w_i', we have that $w_i w_{i+1}' \in S \cup \{1\}$ for all $0 \le i \le n-1$ and that $X^{\frac{2N}{q}(\sum_{i=0}^{n-1} a_i s_i)} = X^{\sum_{i=0}^{n-1} w_i s_i - \sum_{i=0}^{n-1} s_i}$. Let $\hat{c}_i$ for $0 \le i \le n-1$ be the value of ACC after evaluating the i-th loop in steps $7 \sim 10$ of Algorithm 1. Let $\hat{c}_n$ be the value of ACC in step 13 of Algorithm 1. For our purpose, it suffices to show that

$$\hat{c}_n = \text{NTRU}_{Q,f,\tau,\Delta}\left(r(X^{\frac{2N}{q}}) \cdot X^{-\frac{2N}{q}b} X^{\sum_{i=0}^{n-1} w_i s_i - \sum_{i=0}^{n-1} s_i}\right).$$

We first show that for all $0 \leq i \leq n-1$, we have

$$\hat{c}_i = \mathsf{NTRU}_{Q,f,\tau,\Delta}(r(X^{\frac{2N}{q}w'_{i+1}}) \cdot X^{-\frac{2N}{q}bw'_{i+1}} X^{(\sum_{j=0}^{i} w_j s_j)w'_{i+1}}).$$

Note that $\mathsf{ACC} = \Delta \cdot r(X^{\frac{2N}{q}w'_0}) \cdot X^{-\frac{2N}{q}bw'_0}$ before entering the loop in steps $7 \sim 10$, and that $\mathbf{evk}_0 = \mathsf{NTRU}'_{Q,f,\tau}(X^{s_0}/f) = (\tau \cdot g_0/f + B^0 X^{s_0}/f, \cdots, \tau \cdot g_{d-1}/f + B^{d-1}X^{s_0}/f)$. By the property of external product, one can easily check that

$$c_0(X) = \mathsf{ACC} \odot \mathbf{evk}_0 = \mathsf{NTRU}_{Q,f,\tau,\Delta}(r(X^{\frac{2N}{q}w'_0}) \cdot X^{-\frac{2N}{q}bw'_0} X^{s_0}).$$

If $w_0 w'_1 = 1 \mod 2N$, then we immediately have

$$\hat{c}_0(X) = c_0(X) = \mathsf{NTRU}_{Q,f,\tau,\Delta}(r(X^{\frac{2N}{q}w'_1}) \cdot X^{-\frac{2N}{q}bw'_1} X^{w_0 s_0 w'_1}).$$

Otherwise, the algorithm will compute $\hat{c}_0(X) = \mathsf{EvalAuto}_{w_0 w'_1}(c_0(X), \mathbf{ksk}_{w_0 w'_1})$. By Lemma 2, we still have that

$$\hat{c}_0(X) = \mathsf{NTRU}_{Q,f,\tau,\Delta}(r(X^{\frac{2N}{q}w'_1}) \cdot X^{-\frac{2N}{q}bw'_1} X^{w_0 s_0 w'_1}).$$

Now, it is enough to show that if

$$\hat{c}_k = \mathsf{NTRU}_{Q,f,\tau,\Delta}(r(X^{\frac{2N}{q}w'_{k+1}}) \cdot X^{-\frac{2N}{q}bw'_{k+1}} X^{(\sum_{j=0}^{k} w_j s_j)w'_{k+1}}),$$

for some $0 \leq k < n-1$, then $\hat{c}_{k+1}$ also has the same formula. Note that at the $(k+1)$-th loop, the algorithm will first compute $c_{k+1}(X) = \hat{c}_k \odot \mathbf{evk}_{k+1}$. Since $\mathbf{evk}_{k+1} = \mathsf{NTRU}'_{Q,f,\tau}(X^{s_{k+1}})$. By Lemma 1, we have that

$$c_{k+1} = \mathsf{NTRU}_{Q,f,\tau,\Delta}(r(X^{\frac{2N}{q}w'_{k+1}}) \cdot X^{-\frac{2N}{q}bw'_{k+1}} X^{(\sum_{j=0}^{k} w_j s_j)w'_{k+1}+s_{k+1}}).$$

Then, the algorithm will set $\hat{c}_{k+1} = c_{k+1}$ if $w_{k+1}w'_{k+2} = 1$, otherwise $\hat{c}_{k+1} = \mathsf{EvalAuto}_{w_{k+1}w'_{k+2}}(c_{k+1}(X), \mathbf{ksk}_{w_{k+1}w'_{k+2}})$. Again, by Lemma 2 we always have that

$$\hat{c}_{k+1} = \mathsf{NTRU}_{Q,f,\tau,\Delta}(r(X^{\frac{2N}{q}w'_{k+2}}) \cdot X^{-\frac{2N}{q}bw'_{k+2}} X^{(\sum_{j=0}^{k+1} w_j s_j)w'_{k+2}}).$$

After the loop, the algorithm will finally compute $\hat{c}_n = \hat{c}_{n-1} \odot \mathbf{ksk}_n$. Using the fact that $w'_n = 1$ and $\mathbf{evk}_n = \mathsf{NTRU}'_{Q,f,\tau}(X^{-\sum_{i=0}^{n-1} s_i})$, by Lemma 1 we have that

$$\hat{c}_n = \mathsf{NTRU}_{Q,f,\tau,\Delta}(r(X^{\frac{2N}{q}}) \cdot X^{-\frac{2N}{q}b} X^{\sum_{i=0}^{n-1} w_i s_i - \sum_{i=0}^{n-1} s_i}).$$

This finally completes the proof.

B Proof of Lemma 5

Proof. By definition, we have that $\mathsf{LWE}_{q,\mathbf{f}}(m) = (\hat{\mathbf{a}}, \hat{b} = \langle \hat{\mathbf{a}}, \mathbf{f} \rangle - (\hat{e} + \lfloor \frac{q}{t} \rceil m)) \in \mathbb{Z}_q^N \times \mathbb{Z}_q$ for some $\hat{\mathbf{a}} = (\hat{a}_0, \ldots, \hat{a}_N) \in \mathbb{Z}_q^N$, and that $\mathbf{LKSK}_{\mathbf{f},s,q,B_{ks}} = \{\mathsf{lksk}_{i,j,v}\}$

for some $\mathbf{lksk}_{i,j,v} = (\mathbf{a}_{i,j,v}, b_{i,j,v} = \langle \mathbf{a}_{i,j,v}, \mathbf{s} \rangle - e_{i,j,v} - vB_{ks}^{j}f_i)$. This lemma directly follows from the fact that $\hat{a}_i = \sum_{j=0}^{d_{ks}-1} v_{i,j}B_{ks}^{j}$ and that

$$
\begin{aligned}
\hat{b}' &= \sum_{i=0}^{N-1} \sum_{j=0,v_{i,j}\neq 0}^{d_{ks}-1} b_{i,j,v_{i,j}} + \hat{b} \\
&= \sum_{i=0}^{N-1} \sum_{j=0,v_{i,j}\neq 0}^{d_{ks}-1} (\langle \mathbf{a}_{i,j,v_{i,j}}, \mathbf{s} \rangle - e_{i,j,v_{i,j}} - v_{i,j}B_{ks}^{j}f_i) + \hat{b} \\
&= \langle \hat{\mathbf{a}}', \mathbf{s} \rangle - \sum_{i=0}^{N-1} \sum_{j=0,v_{i,j}\neq 0}^{d_{ks}-1} e_{i,j,v_{i,j}} - \sum_{i=0}^{N-1} \hat{a}_i f_i + \hat{b} \\
&= \langle \hat{\mathbf{a}}', \mathbf{s} \rangle - \sum_{i=0}^{N-1} \sum_{j=0,v_{i,j}\neq 0}^{d_{ks}-1} e_{i,j,v_{i,j}} - (\hat{e} + \lfloor \tfrac{q}{t} \rceil m)
\end{aligned}
$$

C   Proof of Lemma 6

Proof. By definition, we have that $\text{LWE}_{Q,\mathbf{f}}(m_i) = (\mathbf{a}_i, b_i = \langle \mathbf{a}_i, \mathbf{f} \rangle - \text{noised}(m_i))$ for some $\mathbf{a}_i = (a_{i,0}, \ldots, a_{i,N-1}) \in \mathbb{Z}_Q^N$ and $\text{noised}(m_i) = \tau \cdot e_i + \Delta \cdot m_i$ and that $\mathbf{RPK}_\tau = \{\mathbf{rpk}_{j,k}\}$ for some $\mathbf{rpk}_{j,k} = (\hat{a}_{j,k}, \hat{b}_{j,k})$ and $\hat{b}_{j,k} = \hat{a}_{j,k}s - \tau \cdot \hat{e}_{j,k} - B^k f_j$. By the fact that $u_j = \sum_{i=0}^{n-1} a_{i,j}X^i = \sum_{k=0}^{d-1} u_{j,k}B^k$, we have that

$$
\begin{aligned}
v &= \sum_{j=0}^{N-1}\sum_{k=0}^{d-1} u_{j,k}\hat{b}_{j,k} + \sum_{i=0}^{n-1} b_i X^i \\
&= \sum_{j=0}^{N-1}\sum_{k=0}^{d-1} u_{j,k}(\hat{a}_{j,k}s - (\tau \cdot \hat{e}_{j,k} + B^k f_j)) + \sum_{i=0}^{n-1} b_i X^i \\
&= us - \tau \cdot \sum_{j=0}^{N-1}\sum_{k=0}^{d-1} u_{j,k}\hat{e}_{j,k} - \sum_{j=0}^{N-1}\sum_{i=0}^{n-1} a_{i,j}f_j X^i + \sum_{i=0}^{n-1} b_i X^i \\
&= us - \tau \cdot \sum_{j=0}^{N-1}\sum_{k=0}^{d-1} u_{j,k}\hat{e}_{j,k} - \sum_{i=0}^{n-1} (\tau \cdot e_i + \Delta \cdot m_i)X^i \\
&= us - \tau \cdot e' - \Delta \cdot m
\end{aligned}
$$

where $e = \sum_{i=0}^{n-1} e_i X^i$, $m = \sum_{i=0}^{n-1} m_i X^i$ and $e' = \sum_{j,k} u_{j,k} \cdot \hat{e}_{j,k} + e$. This means that (u, v) is a ciphertext that encrypts m under the secret key $\mathbf{s} \in \hat{R}_Q$. Moreover, since $\|u_{j,k}\|_\infty < B$, we have that $Var(e') \leqslant nNd\frac{B^2}{12}Var(\hat{e}) + Var(e)$. This completes the proof.

References

1. Albrecht, M., et al.: Homomorphic encryption standard. In: Lauter, K., Dai, W., Laine, K. (eds.) Protecting Privacy through Homomorphic Encryption, pp. 31–62. Springer, Cham (2021). https://doi.org/10.1007/978-3-030-77287-1_2
2. Albrecht, M.R.: On dual lattice attacks against small-secret LWE and parameter choices in HElib and SEAL. In: Coron, J.-S., Nielsen, J.B. (eds.) EUROCRYPT 2017. LNCS, vol. 10211, pp. 103–129. Springer, Cham (2017). https://doi.org/10.1007/978-3-319-56614-6_4
3. Albrecht, M.R., Göpfert, F., Virdia, F., Wunderer, T.: Revisiting the expected cost of solving uSVP and applications to LWE. In: Takagi, T., Peyrin, T. (eds.) ASIACRYPT 2017. LNCS, vol. 10624, pp. 297–322. Springer, Cham (2017). https://doi.org/10.1007/978-3-319-70694-8_11
4. Albrecht, M.R., Player, R., Scott, S.: On the concrete hardness of learning with errors. J. Math. Cryptol. **9**(3), 169–203 (2015). https://doi.org/10.1515/jmc-2015-0016
5. Alperin-Sheriff, J., Peikert, C.: Faster bootstrapping with polynomial error. In: Garay, J.A., Gennaro, R. (eds.) CRYPTO 2014. LNCS, vol. 8616, pp. 297–314. Springer, Heidelberg (2014). https://doi.org/10.1007/978-3-662-44371-2_17
6. Badawi, A.A., et al.: OpenFHE: open-source fully homomorphic encryption library. Cryptology ePrint Archive, Paper 2022/915 (2022)
7. Bonte, C., Iliashenko, I., Park, J., Pereira, H.V., Smart, N.P.: Final: Faster fhe instantiated with NTRU and LWE. In: Agrawal, S., Lin, D. (eds.) ASIACRYPT 2022. LNCS, vol. 13792, pp. 188–215. Springer, Cham (2022). https://doi.org/10.1007/978-3-031-22966-4_7
8. Bossuat, J.-P., Mouchet, C., Troncoso-Pastoriza, J., Hubaux, J.-P.: Efficient bootstrapping for approximate homomorphic encryption with non-sparse keys. In: Canteaut, A., Standaert, F.-X. (eds.) EUROCRYPT 2021. LNCS, vol. 12696, pp. 587–617. Springer, Cham (2021). https://doi.org/10.1007/978-3-030-77870-5_21
9. Brakerski, Z.: Fully homomorphic encryption without modulus switching from classical GapSVP. In: Safavi-Naini, R., Canetti, R. (eds.) CRYPTO 2012. LNCS, vol. 7417, pp. 868–886. Springer, Heidelberg (2012). https://doi.org/10.1007/978-3-642-32009-5_50
10. Brakerski, Z., Gentry, C., Vaikuntanathan, V.: (leveled) fully homomorphic encryption without bootstrapping. In: ITCS 2012, pp. 309–325. ACM (2012). https://doi.org/10.1145/2090236.2090262
11. Brakerski, Z., Vaikuntanathan, V.: Fully homomorphic encryption from ring-LWE and security for key dependent messages. In: Rogaway, P. (ed.) CRYPTO 2011. LNCS, vol. 6841, pp. 505–524. Springer, Heidelberg (2011). https://doi.org/10.1007/978-3-642-22792-9_29
12. Brakerski, Z., Vaikuntanathan, V.: Efficient fully homomorphic encryption from (standard) LWE. SIAM J. Comput. **43**(2), 831–871 (2014). https://doi.org/10.1137/120868669
13. Chen, H., Chillotti, I., Song, Y.: Improved bootstrapping for approximate homomorphic encryption. In: Ishai, Y., Rijmen, V. (eds.) EUROCRYPT 2019. LNCS, vol. 11477, pp. 34–54. Springer, Cham (2019). https://doi.org/10.1007/978-3-030-17656-3_2
14. Chen, H., Han, K.: Homomorphic lower digits removal and improved FHE bootstrapping. In: Nielsen, J.B., Rijmen, V. (eds.) EUROCRYPT 2018. LNCS, vol. 10820, pp. 315–337. Springer, Cham (2018). https://doi.org/10.1007/978-3-319-78381-9_12

15. Cheon, J.H., Han, K., Kim, A., Kim, M., Song, Y.: Bootstrapping for approximate homomorphic encryption. In: Nielsen, J.B., Rijmen, V. (eds.) EUROCRYPT 2018. LNCS, vol. 10820, pp. 360–384. Springer, Cham (2018). https://doi.org/10.1007/978-3-319-78381-9_14

16. Cheon, J.H., Kim, A., Kim, M., Song, Y.: Homomorphic encryption for arithmetic of approximate numbers. In: Takagi, T., Peyrin, T. (eds.) ASIACRYPT 2017. LNCS, vol. 10624, pp. 409–437. Springer, Cham (2017). https://doi.org/10.1007/978-3-319-70694-8_15

17. Chillotti, I., Gama, N., Georgieva, M., Izabachène, M.: Faster fully homomorphic encryption: bootstrapping in less than 0.1 seconds. In: Cheon, J.H., Takagi, T. (eds.) ASIACRYPT 2016. LNCS, vol. 10031, pp. 3–33. Springer, Heidelberg (2016). https://doi.org/10.1007/978-3-662-53887-6_1

18. Chillotti, I., Gama, N., Georgieva, M., Izabachène, M.: Faster packed homomorphic operations and efficient circuit bootstrapping for TFHE. In: Takagi, T., Peyrin, T. (eds.) ASIACRYPT 2017. LNCS, vol. 10624, pp. 377–408. Springer, Cham (2017). https://doi.org/10.1007/978-3-319-70694-8_14

19. Chillotti, I., Gama, N., Georgieva, M., Izabachène, M.: TFHE: fast fully homomorphic encryption over the torus. J. Cryptol. **33**(1), 34–91 (2019). https://doi.org/10.1007/s00145-019-09319-x

20. Coron, J.-S., Mandal, A., Naccache, D., Tibouchi, M.: Fully homomorphic encryption over the integers with shorter public keys. In: Rogaway, P. (ed.) CRYPTO 2011. LNCS, vol. 6841, pp. 487–504. Springer, Heidelberg (2011). https://doi.org/10.1007/978-3-642-22792-9_28

21. van Dijk, M., Gentry, C., Halevi, S., Vaikuntanathan, V.: Fully homomorphic encryption over the integers. In: Gilbert, H. (ed.) EUROCRYPT 2010. LNCS, vol. 6110, pp. 24–43. Springer, Heidelberg (2010). https://doi.org/10.1007/978-3-642-13190-5_2

22. Ducas, L., Micciancio, D.: FHEW: bootstrapping homomorphic encryption in less than a second. In: Oswald, E., Fischlin, M. (eds.) EUROCRYPT 2015. LNCS, vol. 9056, pp. 617–640. Springer, Heidelberg (2015). https://doi.org/10.1007/978-3-662-46800-5_24

23. Ducas, L., van Woerden, W.: NTRU fatigue: how stretched is overstretched? In: Tibouchi, M., Wang, H. (eds.) ASIACRYPT 2021. LNCS, vol. 13093, pp. 3–32. Springer, Cham (2021). https://doi.org/10.1007/978-3-030-92068-5_1

24. Espitau, T., Joux, A., Kharchenko, N.: On a dual/hybrid approach to small secret LWE. In: Bhargavan, K., Oswald, E., Prabhakaran, M. (eds.) INDOCRYPT 2020. LNCS, vol. 12578, pp. 440–462. Springer, Cham (2020). https://doi.org/10.1007/978-3-030-65277-7_20

25. Fan, J., Vercauteren, F.: Somewhat practical fully homomorphic encryption. Cryptology ePrint Archive (2012)

26. Gama, N., Izabachène, M., Nguyen, P.Q., Xie, X.: Structural lattice reduction: generalized worst-case to average-case reductions and homomorphic cryptosystems. In: Fischlin, M., Coron, J.-S. (eds.) EUROCRYPT 2016. LNCS, vol. 9666, pp. 528–558. Springer, Heidelberg (2016). https://doi.org/10.1007/978-3-662-49896-5_19

27. Genise, N., Gentry, C., Halevi, S., Li, B., Micciancio, D.: Homomorphic encryption for finite automata. In: Galbraith, S.D., Moriai, S. (eds.) ASIACRYPT 2019. LNCS, vol. 11922, pp. 473–502. Springer, Cham (2019). https://doi.org/10.1007/978-3-030-34621-8_17

28. Gentry, C.: Fully homomorphic encryption using ideal lattices. In: STOC 2009, pp. 169–178 (2009). https://doi.org/10.1145/1536414.1536440

29. Gentry, C., Halevi, S., Smart, N.P.: Better bootstrapping in fully homomorphic encryption. In: Fischlin, M., Buchmann, J., Manulis, M. (eds.) PKC 2012. LNCS, vol. 7293, pp. 1–16. Springer, Heidelberg (2012). https://doi.org/10.1007/978-3-642-30057-8_1

30. Gentry, C., Sahai, A., Waters, B.: Homomorphic encryption from learning with errors: conceptually-simpler, asymptotically-faster, attribute-based. In: Canetti, R., Garay, J.A. (eds.) CRYPTO 2013. LNCS, vol. 8042, pp. 75–92. Springer, Heidelberg (2013). https://doi.org/10.1007/978-3-642-40041-4_5

31. Ha, J., Kim, S., Lee, B., Lee, J., Son, M.: Rubato: noisy ciphers for approximate homomorphic encryption. In: Dunkelman, O., Dziembowski, S. (eds.) EUROCRYPT 2022, LNCS, vol. 13275, pp. 581–610. Springer, Cham (2022). https://doi.org/10.1007/978-3-031-06944-4_20

32. Halevi, S., Shoup, V.: Bootstrapping for HElib. J. Cryptology **34**(1), 1–44 (2021). https://doi.org/10.1007/s00145-020-09368-7

33. Kim, A., et al.: General bootstrapping approach for RLWE-based homomorphic encryption. Cryptology ePrint Archive (2021)

34. Kirchner, P., Fouque, P.-A.: Revisiting lattice attacks on overstretched NTRU parameters. In: Coron, J.-S., Nielsen, J.B. (eds.) EUROCRYPT 2017. LNCS, vol. 10210, pp. 3–26. Springer, Cham (2017). https://doi.org/10.1007/978-3-319-56620-7_1

35. Kluczniak, K.: NTRU-ν-um: secure fully homomorphic encryption from NTRU with small modulus, pp. 1783–1797 (2022). https://doi.org/10.1145/3548606.3560700

36. Lee, J.-W., Lee, E., Lee, Y., Kim, Y.-S., No, J.-S.: High-precision bootstrapping of RNS-CKKS homomorphic encryption using optimal minimax polynomial approximation and inverse sine function. In: Canteaut, A., Standaert, F.-X. (eds.) EUROCRYPT 2021. LNCS, vol. 12696, pp. 618–647. Springer, Cham (2021). https://doi.org/10.1007/978-3-030-77870-5_22

37. Lee, Y., et al.: Efficient FHEW bootstrapping with small evaluation keys, and applications to threshold homomorphic encryption. In: Hazay, C., Stam, M. (eds.) EUROCRYPT 2023. LNCS, vol. 14006, pp. 227–256. Springer, Cham (2023). https://doi.org/10.1007/978-3-031-30620-4_8

38. Lyubashevsky, V., Peikert, C., Regev, O.: On ideal lattices and learning with errors over rings. In: Gilbert, H. (ed.) EUROCRYPT 2010. LNCS, vol. 6110, pp. 1–23. Springer, Heidelberg (2010). https://doi.org/10.1007/978-3-642-13190-5_1

39. Micciancio, D., Polyakov, Y.: Bootstrapping in FHEW-like cryptosystems. In: Proceedings of the 9th on Workshop on Encrypted Computing & Applied Homomorphic Cryptography, pp. 17–28 (2021). https://doi.org/10.1145/3474366.3486924

40. Micciancio, D., Sorrell, J.: Ring packing and amortized FHEW bootstrapping **107**, 100:1–100:14 (2018). https://doi.org/10.4230/LIPIcs.ICALP.2018.100

41. Pereira, H.V.L.: Bootstrapping fully homomorphic encryption over the integers in less than one second. In: Garay, J.A. (ed.) PKC 2021. LNCS, vol. 12710, pp. 331–359. Springer, Cham (2021). https://doi.org/10.1007/978-3-030-75245-3_13

42. Regev, O.: On lattices, learning with errors, random linear codes, and cryptography. J. ACM (JACM) **56**(6), 1–40 (2009). https://doi.org/10.1145/1568318.1568324

43. Smart, N.P., Vercauteren, F.: Fully homomorphic encryption with relatively small key and ciphertext sizes. In: Nguyen, P.Q., Pointcheval, D. (eds.) PKC 2010. LNCS, vol. 6056, pp. 420–443. Springer, Heidelberg (2010). https://doi.org/10.1007/978-3-642-13013-7_25

44. Son, Y., Cheon, J.H.: Revisiting the hybrid attack on sparse secret LWE and application to HE parameters. In: Proceedings of the 7th ACM Workshop on Encrypted Computing & Applied Homomorphic Cryptography, pp. 11–20 (2019). https://doi.org/10.1145/3338469.3358941

45. Stehlé, D., Steinfeld, R.: Faster fully homomorphic encryption. In: Abe, M. (ed.) ASIACRYPT 2010. LNCS, vol. 6477, pp. 377–394. Springer, Heidelberg (2010). https://doi.org/10.1007/978-3-642-17373-8_22

HERMES: Efficient Ring Packing Using MLWE Ciphertexts and Application to Transciphering

Youngjin Bae[1], Jung Hee Cheon[1,2], Jaehyung Kim[1], Jai Hyun Park[2(✉)], and Damien Stehlé[3]

[1] CryptoLab Inc., Seoul, Republic of Korea
{youngjin.bae,jaehyungkim}@cryptolab.co.kr
[2] Seoul National University, Seoul, Republic of Korea
{jhcheon,jhyunp}@snu.ac.kr
[3] CryptoLab Inc., Lyon, France
damien.stehle@cryptolab.co.kr

Abstract. Most of the current fully homomorphic encryption (FHE) schemes are based on either the learning-with-errors (LWE) problem or on its ring variant (RLWE) for storing plaintexts. During the homomorphic computation of FHE schemes, RLWE formats provide high throughput when considering several messages, and LWE formats provide a low latency when there are only a few messages. Efficient conversion can bridge the advantages of each format. However, converting LWE formats into RLWE format, which is called *ring packing*, has been a challenging problem.

We propose an efficient solution for ring packing for FHE. The main improvement of this work is twofold. First, we accelerate the existing ring packing methods by using bootstrapping and ring switching techniques, achieving practical runtimes. Second, we propose a new method for efficient ring packing, HERMES, by using ciphertexts in Module-LWE (MLWE) formats, to also reduce the memory. To this end, we generalize the tools of LWE and RLWE formats for MLWE formats.

On a single-thread implementation, HERMES consumes 10.2s for the ring packing of 2^{15} LWE-format ciphertexts into an RLWE-format ciphertext. This gives 41x higher throughput compared to the state-of-the-art ring packing for FHE, PEGASUS [S&P'21], which takes 51.7s for packing 2^{12} LWE ciphertexts with similar homomorphic capacity. We also illustrate the efficiency of HERMES by using it for transciphering from LWE symmetric encryption to CKKS fully homomorphic encryption, significantly outperforming the recent proposals HERA [Asiacrypt'21] and RUBATO [Eurocrypt'22].

1 Introduction

Fully Homomorphic Encryption (FHE) is a form of encryption that enables computations on encrypted data without decryption. Most of the known FHE

© International Association for Cryptologic Research 2023
H. Handschuh and A. Lysyanskaya (Eds.): CRYPTO 2023, LNCS 14084, pp. 37–69, 2023.
https://doi.org/10.1007/978-3-031-38551-3_2

schemes are based either on the learning-with-errors (LWE) problem [Reg09] or on the ring learning-with-errors (RLWE) problem [SSTX09,LPR10] for storing plaintexts. The main practical FHE schemes with plaintexts stored in LWE-format ciphertexts were proposed in [DM15] and [CGGI16]. Efficient FHE schemes with plaintexts stored in RLWE-format ciphertexts include BFV [Bra12, FV12], BGV [BGV14], and CKKS [CKKS17]. An RLWE ciphertext typically corresponds to a plaintext polynomial, whose degree is of the order of several thousands. Rather than placing the data in the coefficients of the polynomial, which is referred to coefficients-encoding, one often prefers slots-encoding: the data is placed in the frequency domain of a Fourier transform over a finite field (in the case of BGV/BFV) or over the complex numbers (in the case of CKKS). Each slot can be filled with a small modular integer, an element of a small finite field, or a real/complex number with moderate precision. By relying on slots, RLWE schemes can support Single Instruction Multiple Data (SIMD) additions and multiplications, which allow them to achieve amortized run-times. However, they are cumbersome for operations between data points stored in different slots or coefficients of the same ciphertext, and when there are only a few data points to be computed upon compared to the capacity of the ciphertext. On the other hand, LWE schemes are inefficient for handling many messages in parallel since they do not natively provide SIMD operations. Instead, they do not require a complex packing structure and provide low latency when only a few messages are considered.

Ring packing is the task of converting many LWE-format ciphertexts to an RLWE-format ciphertext. Below are several scenarios in which an efficient conversion can be particularly beneficial (some also require a reverse conversion, from RLWE-format to LWE-format, but this is typically easier to achieve).

- **Heterogeneous operation types**. Roughly speaking, RLWE schemes provide efficient addition and multiplication on small integers, complex numbers and finite field elements, while LWE schemes outperform them for table look-ups or computations on individual bits. Conversion applications to computations involving different types of operations are notably considered in [BGGJ20,LHH+21].

- **Heterogeneous computational widths**. A complex task may involve many data points at some stages, during which RLWE formats may be preferable, and much fewer at other stages, during which LWE formats may be considered. Notably, computations with plenty of inputs and a binary decision being taken at the end are considered in [BGGJ20].

- **Storing FHE ciphertexts**. The RLWE SIMD structure may be optimized depending on the specific computation to be performed. If the latter is not known in advance or diverse computations can be performed on the same data, it is interesting to store the data in LWE format, and convert it when a computation is launched. This is discussed, e.g., in [CGGI17].

- **Transciphering**. The large size of RLWE ciphertexts may be problematic when streaming data from small devices. It was suggested in [NLV11] to use a symmetric cipher for sending the data from a client to a server, and to let the server homomorphically decrypt it to obtain an FHE ciphertext. In [CDKS21], the authors use an LWE-based symmetric cipher, and homomorphic decryption reduces to ring packing.

Even though converting data stored in (many) LWE ciphertexts to a ciphertext in RLWE format is central to the above applications, the current approaches remain relatively inefficient. The algorithm from [LHH+21] takes $\approx 51.7\text{s}$ to pack 2^{12} LWE ciphertexts into a slots-encoded RLWE ciphertext of degree 2^{16} with a single-thread implementation (the run-time is obtained from [LHH+21, Table V] by adding the 'LT' and '$\mathcal{F}_{\text{mod}}$' timings). In [CDKS21, Table 2], the authors report that their algorithm allows pack 2^5 LWE ciphertexts into a coefficients-encoded RLWE ciphertext of degree 2^{14}, in 1.17s. The authors of [BGGJ20] mention a 7s timing to pack LWE ciphertexts into a slots-encoded RLWE ciphertext of degree 2^{12}. Note further that the experiments from [BGGJ20, CDKS21] are not satisfactory for packing the order of several hundreds or thousands LWE ciphertexts into an RLWE format that allows fully homomorphic computations and is hence bootstrappable (i.e., of degree $\geq 2^{15}$).

Contributions. Our main result is an efficient ring packing algorithm, for CKKS computations, based on ring packing for RLWE-format ciphertexts with small parameters. Its concrete efficiency is supported by experiments. Finally, we illustrate the usefulness of our efficient ring packing by focusing on the transciphering application.

Our ring packing algorithm is inspired from the one proposed in [CGGI17], itself based on the column method for matrix-vector multiplication described in [HS14]. We adapt it to fully homomorphic RLWE computations in a way that widely differs from [BGGJ20]. We leverage several techniques to optimize the efficiency: CKKS bootstrapping [CHK+18], ring switching [GHPS13], and intermediate Module-LWE computations [BGV14, LS15].

We implemented our algorithm in the HEaaN library [Cry]. One implementation allows to ring-pack 2^{15} LWE ciphertexts into a slots-encoded CKKS ciphertext of degree 2^{15} on which homomorphic computations can be directly performed, in 10.2s with a single thread. This is ≈ 41 times faster in terms of throughput than [LHH+21, Table V] mentioned above, for a similar task.

We use our ring packing algorithm for the transciphering application described in [CDKS21]. As illustrated in Table 1, compared to state of the art transciphering algorithms for the CKKS scheme [CHK+21, HKL+22], our approach achieves a significant reduction of server run-time while retaining a small bandwidth consumption. We refer to Sect. 5.4 for a more detailed comparison.

Table 1. Comparison between different transciphering schemes. Here N denotes the degree of the output RLWE ciphertext, and latency denotes the total transciphering time including online and offline phases of the client and server. The expansion ratio is the ratio between the ciphertext bit-size and the final plaintext precision multiplied by the number of slots. The first timings are borrowed from [CHK+21, HKL+22] and all timings are for single-thread implementations parametrized to encrypt 16 messages at once.

Scheme	N	Latency (s)	Expansion ratio
RtF-HERA [CHK+21]	2^{16}	142	1.24
RtF-Rubato [HKL+22]		71.1	1.31
This work		25.7	1.58

Although we focus on the CKKS scheme, we note that our techniques are also applicable to ring packing to RLWE formats that correspond to the BFV and BGV schemes and to RLWE formats that do not necessarily enable fully homomorphic encryption. Also, we chose to focus on the transciphering application, but note that the algorithmic improvements are also beneficial to the other applications mentioned above.

Technical Overview. Before delving into the technical ingredients of our ring packing algorithm, we take a step back and discuss the definition of ring packing.

Which Ring Packing? There have been several works on packing LWE ciphertexts into RLWE ciphertexts [CGGI17, MS18, BGGJ20, LHH+21, CDKS21]. Even though their high-level goals are similar, the ring packing task is underspecified and covers several application scenarios. It is not a priori obvious which RLWE degree N and modulus q should be targeted, and whether one should aim at slots-encoding or coefficients-encoding for the RLWE ciphertexts. Other parameters include the LWE dimension and modulus, as well as the number of ciphertexts to be ring-packed. This flexibility also makes it difficult to compare the various methods. For instance, the ring packing methods from [CGGI16, CDKS21, MS18] are for coefficients-encoding and small RLWE moduli. On the other hand, the ring packing methods from [BGGJ20, LHH+21] are designed for slots-encoding and large RLWE moduli.

A very important scenario for ring packing, encompassing all applications listed earlier, is to use the RLWE-formats for efficient homomorphic computations. Slot-encoding then seems a preferable choice as it enables SIMD operations. Very often, the aim is to be able to perform considerable computations on RLWE encryptions, which means the packed RLWE encryption should enjoy fully homomorphic computations. For example, consider the application of ring packing to bridging FHE computations on LWE-format ciphertexts and RLWE-format ciphertexts. Data stored in LWE-format ciphertexts can conveniently be manipulated in an atomic manner, and RLWE-format FHE schemes allow higher throughput thanks to the ring structure. With efficient ring packing methods, we can aggregate LWE ciphertexts into an RLWE ciphertext and utilize the efficient, structured computations of RLWE FHE schemes.

FHE Ring Packing. For the reasons mentioned above, the most desirable target for ring packing in the context of FHE computations is to obtain an RLWE-format ciphertext for parameters that support SIMD fully homomorphic computations with bootstrapping. The bootstrappability forces the RLWE degree to be sufficiently high. Also, such ring packing should enable computations immediately after the ring packing, without further processing. All known RLWE-format FHE schemes that support SIMD computations are leveled [BGV14]: ciphertexts are defined with respect to a modulus that belongs to a chain of moduli $Q_0 < Q_1 < \ldots$. A ciphertext is at the largest modulus $Q_{\texttt{comp}}$ right after bootstrapping and its modulus moves down while performing homomorphic computations. It eventually reaches the smallest modulus $Q_{\texttt{refresh}}$ that can be bootstrapped. In the context of FHE computations, the aim of ring packing should be to *output slots-encoded RLWE-format FHE ciphertexts in modulus $Q_{\texttt{comp}}$ and a bootstrappable degree.*

Existing Ring Packing Approaches. In ring packing, we are given several LWE-format ciphertexts $\mathbf{c}_i \in \mathbb{Z}_q^{K+1}$ for a common key $\mathbf{s}$: they satisfy $\mathbf{c}_i \cdot \mathbf{s} = m_i \bmod q$ for some message m_i. The goal is to obtain an RLWE-format ciphertext whose underlying plaintext polynomial contains the m_i's. Concretely, we aim at evaluating $\mathbf{C} \cdot \mathbf{s}$, where the matrix $\mathbf{C}$ whose rows are the $\mathbf{c}_i$'s is viewed as a plaintext, the LWE key $\mathbf{s}$ is given encrypted in RLWE format and the resulting vector should be encoded in RLWE format. In short, ring packing is an instance of (plaintext matrix)-(ciphertext vector) homomorphic multiplication.

Diverse approaches have been proposed for this task. In [CGGI17, MS18, BGGJ20], each entry in the key $\mathbf{s}$ is encrypted in RLWE format, each column $\mathbf{c}_j$ of $\mathbf{C}$ is interpreted as a polynomial, and one evaluates the weighted sum $\sum_j \mathbf{c}_j \cdot s_j$. This is an adaptation of the column method from [HS14] for matrix-vector multiplication. In the row method of [CDKS21], each column $\mathbf{c}_i$ of $\mathbf{C}$ is interpreted as a polynomial and the secret key $\mathbf{s}$ is stored in a single RLWE ciphertext; the ring automorphisms are used to remove the superfluous terms obtained when multiplying the polynomials corresponding to $\mathbf{c}_i$ and $\mathbf{s}$. In [LHH+21], the authors store the diagonals of $\mathbf{C}$ in polynomials and the secret key $\mathbf{s}$ is also stored in a single RLWE ciphertext; they use the SIMD property of RLWE encryption to compute $c_{ij} \cdot s_j$ for many j's in parallel. This is an extension of the diagonal method for matrix-vector multiplication described in [HS14] and attributed therein to Dan Bernstein.

Our Approach. Contrary to the most recent works on ring packing [CDKS21, LHH+21], our technique is based on the column method. We improve it to an extent that makes it outperform the strategies based on the row and diagonal methods.

Our first optimization stems from boostrapping itself. Indeed, bootstrapping includes steps that take a low-modulus coefficients-encoded ciphertext and convert it to a high-modulus slots-encoded one. The sequence of relevant components of bootstrapping is called HalfBoot in [CHK+21], where it was used in the context of converting outputs of BFV computations to CKKS ciphertexts. This strategy (which we rename HalfBTS for consistency with our notations) is motivated by the fact that bootstrapping is less costly than known ring packing methods to a high modulus such as Q_{comp}. We hence ring-pack to coefficients-encoded RLWE-ciphertexts at the smallest modulus that can be handled by HalfBTS (which is even lower than Q_{refresh}) and then HalfBTS to the target modulus. We stress that *FHE ring packing* is reduced to a *base ring packing* to a coefficients-encoded RLWE ciphertext with a small modulus. The rest of our improvements concern this base ring packing.

Secondly, by using the ring switching technique from [GHPS13], we decouple the ring packing dimension from the FHE dimension, and ring-pack from smaller LWE dimensions to smaller RLWE degrees: the only restriction is that the dimensions/degrees are high enough to provide security. As far as we are aware of, in the context of FHE computations, ours is the first work obtaining a significant practical gain by using the ring switching technique (see, e.g., the discussion in [HS21, Section 8]). These two techniques significantly improve the run-time of the column method.

The techniques above can also be used to improve the row and diagonal methods. We now explain why they benefit the column method the most. Thanks to HalfBTS, the aim is that the output of ring packing is coefficients-encoded at a small modulus. The modulus consumption during the (base) ring packing is therefore a key factor for efficiency, as computations must be performed at a higher modulus to end with the target small modulus. This is amplified by the fact that a higher modulus consumption requires a higher dimension, to maintain security. As the column method does not consume any modulus, it can fully be performed at the lowest modulus. On the other hand, the row method from [CDKS21] requires one rescaling, and the diagonal method from [LHH+21] requires many: the input modulus should be taken larger to anticipate the modulus loss. Finally, we note that the column method also benefits the most from the hoisting technique from [HS18, Section 5].

Reducing Memory Consumption. The column method still suffers from a significant drawback compared to the other approaches. Because each LWE secret key coefficient s_i is encrypted in an RLWE ciphertext, the whole key material requires a considerable amount of memory. To mitigate this, we propose *the block method*, which relies on ciphertexts in module-learning-with-errors (MLWE) format [BGV14,LS15].

We proceed as follows. Instead of decomposing the $N \times N$ matrix $\mathbf{C}$ into N columns and mapping each column to a degree N polynomial, we view it as a $\sqrt{N} \times \sqrt{N}$ matrix of blocks of dimensions $\sqrt{N} \times \sqrt{N}$. Each one of these blocks is associated with an MLWE ciphertext with dimension N. The key $(s_1, \ldots, s_N)$ is first decomposed into $\sqrt{N}$ segments of length $\sqrt{N}$, each segment of which can be stored in a single RLWE switching key of degree N. Each row of blocks from $\mathbf{C}$ is then packed into a single block by using module key switching, leading to an $N \times \sqrt{N}$ matrix that is encrypted under a temporary key. We then complete the process using the column method with $\sqrt{N}$ RLWE switching keys of degree N. Overall, the size of the key material has decreased from N RLWE ciphertexts of degree N to $2\sqrt{N}$ of them.

The method can be extended to multiple levels of recursion, leading to smaller key material sizes. The block method with t levels of recursion requires $tN^{1/t}$ RLWE switching keys of degree N. The column method is the case of $t = 1$, requiring N switching keys. The simplest block method, with $t = 2$, requires $2\sqrt{N}$ switching keys.

Transciphering. The existing FHE schemes suffer from high ciphertext expansion, with the notable exception of RLWE-based schemes at the smallest modulus, which encodes N messages into two degree N polynomials (the message precision is a little lower than the modulus, adding to the expansion factor). To further reduce this expansion factor, it is possible to implicitly represent the first polynomial as the output of an extendable output-format function (XOF) on a public seed. However, the granularity is very coarse, as a small expansion factor is achieved only if one starts with as many messages as the degree (e.g., set to 2^{15} or 2^{16} to enable bootstrapping in CKKS). The transciphering framework solves this problem using conversion between symmetric ciphers and homomorphic encryption schemes. In the context of CKKS, the state of the art transciphering approaches [HKL+22, CHK+21] rely on the Real-to-Finite-Field (RtF) transciphering framework from [CHK+21]. These works design stream ciphers for real numbers. The key stream is homomorphically evaluated with the BFV scheme (to perform finite field operations); the encrypted data is then added to the BFV encryption of the key stream to obtain a BFV encryption of the plaintext polynomial corresponding to the data; and then HalfBTS allows to obtain a slots-encoded CKKS ciphertext. This approach is quite heavy for the server, which has to run expensive BFV homomorphic computations. Further, the ciphers are specifically designed for this task, and their security is not well-established yet.

Instead of the RtF framework, we use the transciphering strategy described in [CDKS21], which consists in using an LWE-based symmetric cipher. Transciphering is then exactly ring packing. This approach was inefficient because so was ring packing, but our ring packing algorithm makes it outperform the proposals based on the RtF framework. The LWE ciphertexts are in a small dimension and with a small modulus. As all but one of the coordinates are implicitly represented using a seed, the expansion ratio is limited. Beyond efficiency, this approach achieves high granularity: each message is encrypted individually, as opposed to batches of 16 to 64 messages as in [HKL+22, CHK+21]. This granularity allows the client to send the data whenever it wishes, as it does not need to wait for completing it (alternatively, it could use a block of 16 to 64 messages with only one message, but this would damage the expansion ratio). Finally, the ring packing approach does not require to introduce any new assumption.

2   Preliminaries

For a power-of-2 integer $N \geq 2$, we define the polynomial ring $\mathcal{R}_N = \mathbb{Z}[X]/(X^N + 1)$. It is isomorphic to the ring of integers of the degree-N cyclotomic field. For $q \geq 2$, we define $\mathcal{R}_{q,N} = \mathbb{Z}_q[X]/(X^N + 1) = \mathcal{R}_N/q\mathcal{R}_N$. We will always choose q as a product of primes q_i such that $q_i = 1 \bmod 2N$ for all i. This enables fast multiplication over $\mathcal{R}_{q,N}$, based on the Chinese Remainder Theorem and the Number Theoretic Transform (NTT).

Let $K, q \geq 2$. An LWE_q^K ciphertext with modulus q and dimension K for a secret key $\mathbf{s} \in \mathbb{Z}^{K+1}$ and a plaintext $m \in \mathbb{Z}_q$ is an element $\mathbf{c} \in \mathbb{Z}_q^{K+1}$ such that $\langle \mathbf{c}, \mathbf{s} \rangle = m$. For N a power of 2, an $\mathsf{RLWE}_{q,N}$ ciphertext for a secret key $\mathbf{s} \in \mathcal{R}_N^2$ and a plaintext polynomial $m \in \mathcal{R}_{q,N}$ is an element $\mathbf{c} \in \mathcal{R}_{q,N}^2$ such that $\langle \mathbf{c}, \mathbf{s} \rangle = m$. We let $\mathsf{LWE}_q^K.\mathsf{Enc}(m)$ denote an LWE ciphertext decrypting to plaintext $m \in \mathbb{Z}_q$ and $\mathsf{RLWE}_{q,N}.\mathsf{Enc}(m)$ an RLWE ciphertext decrypting to plaintext $m \in \mathcal{R}_{q,N}$. We suppose the plaintexts in the notations contain small errors so that we can omit the contained error term e.

2.1   RLWE Key Switching

We describe RLWE key switching in terms of its substeps ModUp, ModDown and MultSwk. Key switching can be based on gadget decomposition and on the use of an intermediate integer. Typically, the de facto choice nowadays is a combination of these from [HK20]. For simplicity, we focus on explaining the case where the gadget decomposition number ($dnum$) is 1. The general case works similarly.

- ModUp : $\mathcal{R}_{q,N} \to \mathcal{R}_{qp,N}$ takes as input a polynomial in $\mathcal{R}_{q,N}$, embeds it into $\mathcal{R}_N$ by identifying $\mathbb{Z}_q$ with $[-q/2, q/2)$ and then reduces modulo qp.
- MultSwk : $\mathcal{R}_{qp,N} \times \mathcal{R}_{qp,N}^2 \to \mathcal{R}_{qp,N}^2$ takes as inputs a polynomial $\hat{a} \in \mathcal{R}_{qp,N}$ and a switching key $\mathsf{swk} \in \mathcal{R}_{qp,N}^2$, and simply computes $\hat{a} \cdot \mathsf{swk}$. It costs 2 Hadamard multiplications of degree N.
- ModDown : $\mathcal{R}_{qp,N}^2 \to \mathcal{R}_{q,N}^2$ takes as input a ciphertext $\mathsf{ct} \in \mathcal{R}_{qp,N}^2$ and computes an approximate division by p:

$$\mathsf{ct} = (\hat{b}, \hat{a}) \quad \mapsto \quad \left(\frac{\hat{b} - [\hat{b}]_p}{p}, \frac{\hat{a} - [\hat{a}]_p}{p} \right).$$

Given two secret keys s and s', the switching key from s to s' is defined as

$$\mathsf{swk} = (-\hat{a}s' + ps + \hat{e}, \hat{a}) \in \mathcal{R}_{qp,N}^2,$$

where $\hat{a}$ is a uniform polynomial in $\mathcal{R}_{qp,N}$ and $\hat{e} \in \mathcal{R}_N$ is random with small-magnitude coefficients. This switching key can be used to convert a ciphertext for s into a ciphertext for s' that encrypts the same plaintext (up to a small error). Let $\mathsf{ct} = (b, a) \in \mathcal{R}_{q,N}^2$ be a ciphertext for the secret key s so that $(b, a) \cdot (1, s) = b + as = m$ for the plaintext m. Key switching on ct with switching key swk is defined as follows:

$$\mathsf{KS}(\mathsf{ct}; \mathsf{swk}) = \mathsf{ModDown}\Big(\mathsf{MultSwk}(\mathsf{ModUp}(a), \mathsf{swk}) \Big) + (b, 0) \in \mathcal{R}_{q,N}^2.$$

Depending on the context, we sometimes use the notation $\mathsf{KS}_{s \to s'}(\mathsf{ct})$. When applying several automorphisms on a single ciphertext, $\mathsf{ModUp}(a)$ can be shared through key switching for automorphisms so computed only once. On the other hand, when summing up several key switching results, one can add everything before $\mathsf{ModDown}$ to avoid redundant $\mathsf{ModDown}$'s. Such techniques are referred to as hoisting in [HS18]. We introduce a notation for the second technique for later use. Suppose that $\mathsf{ct}_j = (b_j, a_j)$, $\hat{a}_j = \mathsf{ModUp}(a_j)$ for $0 \le j < \ell$ and $b = \sum_{0 \le j < \ell} b_j$. Then we write:

$$\mathsf{KS}\big((\mathsf{ct}_j)_{0 \le j < \ell}; (\mathsf{swk}_j)_{0 \le j < \ell}\big) = \mathsf{ModDown}\Big(\sum_{0 \le j < \ell} \mathsf{MultSwk}\big(\hat{a}_j, \mathsf{swk}_j\big) \Big) + (b, 0).$$

2.2 The Column Method for Ring Packing

We consider the task of packing N LWE ciphertexts in dimension N into a single RLWE ciphertext for degree N. By default, the column method is designed to handle as many input ciphertexts as the RLWE degree. We will see later that our algorithm offers more flexibility. By default, the column method output is a coefficients-encoded RLWE ciphertext.

Let $(b_0, \mathbf{a}_0), \ldots, (b_{N-1}, \mathbf{a}_{N-1}) \in \mathbb{Z}_q \times \mathbb{Z}_q^N$ be LWE ciphertexts such that

$$\forall i < N : \ b_i + \langle \mathbf{a}_i, \mathbf{s} \rangle = m_i$$

for some $m_0, \ldots, m_{N-1} \in \mathbb{Z}_q$ and where $\mathbf{s} \in \mathbb{Z}_q^N$ is an LWE secret key. We aim to get an RLWE ciphertext $(b, a) \in \mathcal{R}_{q,N}^2$ such that

$$(b, a) \cdot (1, s) = b(X) + a(X)s(X) = \sum_{i=0}^{N-1} m_i X^i,$$

where s is an RLWE secret key. Write $\mathbf{a}_i = (a_{i,0}, a_{i,1}, \ldots, a_{i,N-1})$ for $i < N$ and let $\alpha_j(X)$ be defined as

$$\alpha_j(X) = a_{0,j} + a_{1,j}X + \cdots + a_{N-1,j}X^{N-1},$$

for all $j < N$. Note that the coefficients of α_j correspond to the jth column obtained by stacking the $\mathbf{a}_i$'s on top of one another. This observation leads to the following equality, where we write $\mathbf{s} = (s_j)_{0 \le j < N}$:

$$\sum_{i=0}^{N-1} b_i X^{N-1} + \sum_{j=0}^{N-1} s_j \cdot \alpha_j(X) = \sum_{i=0}^{N-1} m_i X^i.$$

The column method [CGGI17] regards each s_j as a different secret key and performs a key switching from s_j to the RLWE key s for all $j < N$ and sums the results together. In more detail:

- (Switching key generation) For each j, compute

$$\mathsf{swk}_j = (-\hat{a}_j s + p s_j + \hat{e}_j, \hat{a}_j) \in \mathcal{R}_{qp,N}^2,$$

where $\hat{a}_j$ is a uniform polynomial in $\mathcal{R}_{qp,N}$ and $\hat{e}_j \in \mathcal{R}_N$ is random with small-magnitude coefficients.
- (Ring packing) Given the $\alpha_j(X)$'s for $j < N$ and $\sum_{i=0}^{N-1} b_i X^{N-1}$, we compute

$$\mathsf{modDown}\Big(\sum_{j=0}^{N-1} \mathsf{modup}(\alpha_j(X)) \cdot \mathsf{swk}_j \Big) + \Big(0, \sum_{i=0}^{N-1} b_i X^{N-1} \Big) \in \mathcal{R}_{q,N}^2,$$

which is an RLWE ciphertext that decrypts to $\approx \sum_{i=0}^{N-1} m_i X^i$.

2.3   The CKKS Scheme

We now provide a brief outline of the CKKS fully homomorphic encryption scheme [CKKS17, CHK+18].

Encoding and Decoding. In the CKKS scheme, messages are vectors in $\mathbb{C}^{N/2}$, while plaintexts are the elements of $\mathcal{R}_N$. There exists an approximate (scaled) isomorphism between these two spaces called encoding, whose inverse is referred to as decoding. In order to encrypt a message, one first converts the message into a plaintext via the inverse discrete Fourier transform (iDFT) and scales it up; this process is called encode and denoted as Ecd. The other direction maps a plaintext to a message and corresponds to evaluating the discrete Fourier transform (DFT) and scaling the result downwards; this process is called decode and is denoted as Dcd. To be more specific, $\mathsf{Ecd} : \mathbb{C}^{N/2} \to \mathcal{R}_N$ is defined as

$$z \quad \mapsto \quad \lfloor \Delta \cdot \mathsf{iDFT}(z) \rceil$$

where Δ is a scaling factor and $\lfloor \cdot \rceil$ denotes rounding. $\mathsf{Dcd} : \mathcal{R}_N \to \mathbb{C}^{N/2}$ is

$$m(x) \quad \mapsto \quad \frac{1}{\Delta} \cdot \mathsf{DFT}(m).$$

Slots and Coefficients. Let $\mathsf{ct} = (b, a) \in \mathcal{R}_{q,N}^2$ be a ciphertext encrypting a plaintext $m \in \mathcal{R}_N$. Since there is an approximately scaled isomorphism between the message and the plaintext polynomial, we can also view ct as encrypting the message $z = \mathsf{Dcd}(m)$. In this work, the *slots* of a ciphertext refer to the slots of z, and the *coefficients* of a ciphertext refer to coefficients of m.

Ciphertext Levels. Since encoding is a scaled homomorphism, we have an approximate identity

$$\mathsf{Ecd}(z_1) * \mathsf{Ecd}(z_2) \simeq \Delta \cdot \mathsf{Ecd}(z_1 \odot z_2)$$

where $*$ denotes the polynomial multiplication and $\odot$ denotes the componentwise multiplication. Hence, in order to maintain the scale, we should scale the result of every multiplication down by a factor Δ. This process is called rescale and reduces the ciphertext modulus q by a factor Δ: the new modulus is $\approx q/\Delta$. Since homomorphic operations including multiplication and addition can only be defined if two ciphertexts have the same ciphertext modulus, there is a notion of ciphertext level that is associated with its modulus. Concretely, the lowest modulus allowing meaningful decryption is designated as level 0 and we say that each rescale decreases the level by 1. We let Q_{Enc} denote the modulus of level 0 as it is the lowest modulus allowing meaningful encryption/decryption. We let Q_{KS} the modulus of level 1 as it is the lowest modulus at which we can perform key switching and obtain a ciphertext that still correctly decrypts.

CKKS Bootstrapping. Each multiplication/rescale consumes one level. When the level reaches to 0, we cannot proceed with further multiplications. Bootstrap is an operation that allows one to raise the modulus while keeping the underlying plaintext almost the same. CKKS bootstrapping consists of four steps:

- Slots-to-coeffs StC is a homomorphic evaluation of the DFT matrix. The coefficients of the resulting ciphertext become the slots of the input ciphertext.
- Modulus raises ModRaise raises the modulus via the canonical embedding, similarly to ModUp (the moduli are distinct, which justifies the different terminology). After mod-raising a ciphertext in $\mathcal{R}_{Q_{\mathsf{Enc}},N}$ with underlying m, one obtains a ciphertext in $\mathcal{R}_{Q_{\mathsf{top}},N}$ for a larger modulus Q_{top} with underlying plaintext equal to $m + Q_{\mathsf{Enc}}I$ for some small $I \in \mathcal{R}_N$.
- coefficients-to-slots CtS is a homomorphic evaluation of the iDFT matrix. The slots of the resulting ciphertext become the coefficients of the input ciphertext. In particular, this places the $Q_{\mathsf{Enc}}I$ terms in the slots.
- Modulo evaluation EvalMod removes the $Q_{\mathsf{Enc}}I$ part by homomorphically evaluating (an approximation of) the modular reduction function.

Since CtS and EvalMod consume modulus, the ciphertext modulus Q_{comp} after bootstrapping is smaller than the modulus Q_{top} of the output of ModRaise. Similarly, as StC consumes modulus, the ciphertext modulus Q_{refresh} before bootstrapping is larger than the modulus Q_{Enc} of the input of ModRaise. We provide basic information about a typical bootstrapping parameter set in Table 2.

Table 2. Data on the FGb parameter preset of the HEaaN library. Here $\log_2(QP)$ denotes the size of the largest ciphertext modulus that can be used with the parameters while maintaining the desired security. The bootstrapping time T_{BTS} is for a single thread and refers to the situation where all slots are used for data. The key size refers to the total size of the keys needed to bootstrap (the 'a' parts of the key components are represented with a seed, and an integer modulo q is represented on $\log_2 q$ bits).

N	$\log_2(QP)$	$\log_2(Q_{\mathsf{Enc}})$	$\log_2(Q_{\mathsf{refresh}})$	$\log_2(Q_{\mathsf{comp}})$	$\log_2(Q_{\mathsf{top}})$	T_{BTS}	Key size
2^{16}	1555	58	184	562	1258	27.4 s	667 MB

We note that when we start from a ciphertext whose data is packed into coefficients, we no longer need StC at the beginning. Following [CHK+21], we refer to bootstrapping without StC as HalfBTS.

Ring Degrees. There are several functionalities in the CKKS scheme. The simpler ones can be implemented with smaller ring degrees. We define N_{Enc} and N_{KS} as ring degrees that support RLWE encryption (with correct decryption) and RLWE key switching, respectively. We let N_{BTS} be a ring degree that supports CKKS bootstrapping. There are several possible choices for these degrees, but one typically would set $N_{\mathsf{Enc}} \leq N_{\mathsf{KS}} \leq N_{\mathsf{BTS}}$. For a message precision of 20 bits, we can set $N_{\mathsf{Enc}} = 2^{11}$ and $N_{\mathsf{KS}} = 2^{12}$. Among several options for N_{BTS}, we choose 2^{15} or 2^{16} throughout the paper.

3 Accelerating FHE Ring Packing

We present two techniques to accelerate FHE ring packing. The first one allows us to reduce FHE ring packing to a base ring packing towards coefficients-encoding RLWE ciphertexts with small modulus. The second one allows decreasing the RLWE ring degree.

3.1 Moduli Optimization

The cost of homomorphic computations highly depends on the working modulus. The modulus is much larger for high CKKS levels than for low levels, and so is the cost of computations. For instance, it is folklore to optimize homomorphic computations by scheduling the moduli of FHE ciphertexts. However, moduli optimization usually does not consider using bootstrapping since bootstrapping is much heavier than other homomorphic operations.

This convention is not justified when evaluating circuits as heavy as bootstrapping, or more. In that case, we argue that bootstrapping should be considered in the computing schedule. Indeed, for massive circuits, the improvement from lowering the moduli can overwhelm the cost of bootstrapping. In our ring packing scenario, this approach allows us to aggressively optimize the modulus.

Moduli-Optimized Ring Packing. Instead of performing ring packing in high-enough moduli to complete the computation at Q_{comp}, we perform ring packing in the lowest modulus Q_{Enc} and for coefficients-encoding, and then run HalfBTS to increase the modulus. As Q_{Enc} is much lower than Q_{comp}, the run-time saving on ring packing itself is very significant. Note that packing to coefficients rather than slots allows omitting StC during the bootstrapping, implying that HalfBTS suffices. In summary, we perform FHE ring packing as follows:

1. Ring-pack to a coefficients-encoding RLWE ciphertext with modulus Q_{Enc}. We call this step *base ring packing*.
2. Run HalfBTS.

Our moduli optimization strategy significantly improves the computational cost and key size of ring packing methods. These improvements come from the fact that ring packing is a more massive computation than bootstrapping. This aggressive moduli optimization is the most effective technique among those we introduce to decrease the runtime of ring packing.

We now explain why ring packing is a larger circuit than HalfBTS, which explains why performing it at a high level is so costly. All known ring packing methods are instances of (plaintext matrix)-(ciphertext vector) homomorphic multiplication. Further, the plaintext matrix is unstructured, making it difficult to optimize the matrix-vector product with special techniques such as decomposition to sparse matrices. HalfBTS also contains a (plaintext matrix)-(ciphertext vector) homomorphic multiplication, in its CtS step. But it can be efficiently evaluated, even if it occurs at a very high modulus, thanks to the algebraic structure of the plaintext matrix: it corresponds to an inverse DFT and can be decomposed as a product of sparse matrices. The rest of HalfBTS, namely ModRaise and EvalMod, can also be efficiently computed.

The aggressive moduli optimization is a general strategy that may be used to improve all ring packing methods (i.e., the column, row, and diagonal methods). The extent of the speed-up depends on how much the modulus can be lowered. This is why our aggressive moduli management benefits the column method the most, as shown in Table 9. The column method can be fully run at the lowest modulus, while the others should start at a little larger moduli since their level consumption is non-zero. This makes the column method competitive with the others. However, the large key size remains an issue, which we will mitigate in Sect. 4.

3.2   Ring Switching

Ring switching was introduced in [BGV14, Section 5.5] and further studied in [GHPS13]. It allows conversions between RLWE ciphertexts for rings of different degrees when the corresponding number fields are subfields of one another. In these works, the main focus is to lower the ring degree, but we will also switch to higher degree rings.

Ring Switching Revisited. We use ring switching for coefficients-encoded CKKS, while previous works mostly focus on slots-encoded BGV. This is because we utilize ring switching to optimize the base ring packing into coefficients-encoded CKKS.

Ring Switching via Modules. We first introduce a different view of ring switching via modules. When we have a ring extension, the large ring can be viewed as a module over the subring. Assume that we are given two powers of 2 integers, k and N, such that k divides N. Then we can view $\mathcal{R}_{q,N}$ as a rank-k $\mathcal{R}_{q,N/k}$-module. Let X_N and $X_{N/k}$ respectively denote the indeterminates corresponding to $\mathcal{R}_{q,N}$ and $\mathcal{R}_{q,N/k}$. By setting $\beta_i = X_N^i$ for all $i < k$, we obtain an $\mathcal{R}_{q,N/k}$-basis of $\mathcal{R}_{q,N}$: concretely, we have $\mathcal{R}_{q,N} \simeq \sum_{0 \le i < k} \mathcal{R}_{q,N/k} \cdot \beta_i$. We define the module decomposition map $\pi_{q,N}^k : \mathcal{R}_{q,N} \to (\mathcal{R}_{q,N/k})^k$ as $\pi_{q,N}^k(a) = (a_0, \cdots, a_{k-1})$, where $a = \sum_j a_j \beta_j$. Note that $\pi_{q,N}^k$ is an $\mathcal{R}_{q,N/k}$-linear. We also consider the ring embedding $\iota_{q,N}^k : \mathcal{R}_{q,N/k} \to \mathcal{R}_{q,N}$ defined by $\iota_{q,N}^k(X_{N/k}) = X_N^k$ and extended as an $\mathcal{R}_{q,N/k}$-homomorphism.

Consider a ciphertext $(b, a) \in \mathcal{R}_{q,N}^2$, with $b = -as + m$ and $s \in \mathcal{R}_{q,N/k}$. We have $s = \sum_j s_j \beta_j = s_0 \cdot 1$. We may then rewrite $b = -as + m$ as:

$$\sum_j b_j \beta_j = \sum_j (-a_j) s_0 \beta_j + \sum_j m_j \beta_j.$$

This is equivalent to

$$\forall j < k : \; b_j = -a_j s_0 + m_j.$$

To summarize, if a ciphertext is encrypted with a secret key that belongs to a subring of relative degree k, then the ciphertext can be split into k pieces, each encrypting a part of the plaintext. We call the conversion $(b_j, a_j)_j \mapsto (b, a)$ as Combine and $(b, a) \mapsto (b_j, a_j)_j$ as Split.

One can understand ring switching via Combine and Split. Ring switching to a higher degree is made of Combine to go from lower degree RLWE ciphertexts to a higher degree RLWE ciphertext with the same key, and of a switching key operation to obtain a higher degree key. Ring switching to a lower degree consists in switching the key of a large-degree RLWE ciphertext to a small-degree key (which belongs to the subring) and then applying Split.

In the case of coefficients-encoded CKKS, the bijection between $(b_j, a_j)_j$ and (b, a) is a direct sum, which means that it is just a rearrangement of coefficients, thus Split and Combine barely have any computation cost. This is the main improvement of our revisiting of ring switching for coefficients-encoded CKKS. Note that prior works on ring switching to slots-encoded BGV (such as [GHPS13]), in contrast, require multiplication by an appropriate (small) scalar during the ring switching.

Ring Switching in Ring Packing. Most of the existing works on ring packing do not consider parameters that would lead to bootstrappable RLWE ciphertexts. Indeed, their cost would be prohibitive, as this would require a sufficiently high ring packing degree (the ring degree of output RLWE ciphertexts), namely, it should then be no less that N_{BTS}. By using ring switching, we decouple the ring packing degree (which is much smaller) from the bootstrapping degree N_{BTS}.

The basic idea is to ring pack dimension-k LWE ciphertexts at a small modulus q into low-degree (n) RLWE ciphertexts and then combine them into a bootstrappable RLWE ciphertext of larger degree $N = N_{\mathsf{BTS}}$ by using ring switching. In particular, we first perform multiple base ring packings in the low parameters, yielding lower-degree RLWE ciphertexts. After that, we use ring switching to combine RLWE ciphertexts into a single RLWE ciphertext with a higher degree. We can then switch to slots-encoding at a high modulus Q by using HalfBTS, as explained above. The overall procedure can be summarized as follows.

1. Base-ring-pack from LWE ciphertexts to small-degree RLWE ciphertexts:

$$N \cdot \mathsf{LWE}_q^k \xrightarrow{\text{Base ring pack}} N/n \cdot \mathsf{RLWE}_{q,n}$$

2. Ring-switch, to combine the small-degree RLWE ciphertexts into one:

$$N/n \cdot \mathsf{RLWE}_{q,n} \xrightarrow{\text{Ring switch}} 1 \cdot \mathsf{RLWE}_{q,N}$$

3. HalfBTS to higher modulus:

$$1 \cdot \mathsf{RLWE}_{q,N} \xrightarrow{\text{HalfBTS}} 1 \cdot \mathsf{RLWE}_{Q,N}$$

By decoupling the base FHE ring packing dimension from N_{BTS}, our strategy substantially improves the computation and memory costs of FHE ring packing algorithms. Dividing the large ring packing into small ring packings does improve the speed and key size. Indeed, performing N/n ring packings to a small degree n is faster than a single ring packing to a large degree N, and the key size for a small ring packing is much smaller than it is for a large ring packing. The improvement is illustrated in Table 9.

We can lower the degree as long as RLWE remains secure under the current modulus. In particular, the only restriction is the security for the switching keys with respect to their moduli and lowered degrees. Thanks to the moduli optimization in Sect. 3.1, we perform base ring packing at the lowest modulus applicable, which means we can lower the base ring packing dimension meaningfully, even to N_{Enc}.

4   HERMES

The column method with the optimizations in Sect. 3 achieves a practical runtime. However, it still suffers from the requirement of a large key size. In this section, we propose a new ring packing algorithm, HERMES, which uses a substantially smaller key size but has a comparable running time with the optimized column method.

Intuitively, HERMES is a *block method*. Understanding ring packing as an instance of (plaintext matrix)-(ciphertext vector) multiplication, we classified the algorithms based on the way to store the plaintext matrix $\mathbf{C}$. Specifically, the column, row, and diagonal method stores each column, row, and diagonal of $\mathbf{C}$, respectively. For HERMES, we consider *subblocks* of $\mathbf{C}$. More concretely, we view $\mathbf{C}$ as a matrix of (rectangular) blocks consisting of N_{KS} entries each. The size of each subblock should be larger or equal to N_{KS} for the security, and less or equal to N_{KS} for the efficiency. We then introduce *module packing* to pack each row of blocks into a single block, resulting in reducing the width of $\mathbf{C}$. By recursively doing this, $\mathbf{C}$ finally would be reduced into a single column, which corresponds to a RLWE instance.

In order to store each block, we use ciphertexts in a module-LWE (MLWE) format, which is a generalization of LWE and RLWE. In the simplest case with only two levels of recursion, HERMES consists of two steps: (1) store the LWE instances in MLWE formats and *module pack* them into a smaller number of MLWE formats with a lower rank, and (2) *module pack* the MLWE formats into a single MLWE format of rank 1 which is an RLWE format. Since each step consists of module packing with $\sqrt{K}$ elementary switching keys, we significantly reduce the overall key size compared to the column method, from K to $2\sqrt{K}$ elementary switching keys. Here K is the dimension of input LWE ciphertexts.

As module packing is a generalization of ring packing, we aim to utilize the techniques of the column method. However, the ingredients (i.e., key switching and ring switching) of the column method cannot be used for MLWE formats directly. To this end, we propose MLWE key switching and MLWE ring switching in Sect. 4.2. By using the generalized ingredients, we finally describe ModPack, an algorithm for module packing, in Sect. 4.3, and its use for HERMES in Sects. 4.4 and 4.5.

For ease of discussion, in Sects. 4.2, 4.3 and 4.4, we mostly focus on the base ring packing problem, assuming the output modulus is Q_{Enc} and the output RLWE degree is the lowest possible, excluding the moduli optimization and the ring switching between RLWE formats introduced in Sect. 3. In Sect. 4.5, we put it all together to solve the FHE ring packing problem, introducing HERMES.

All throughout this section, we assume that ranks and degrees (N, k, ℓ, n, k' and k_i) are powers of 2, except for the input LWE dimension K which should be a multiple of a sufficiently large power of 2.

4.1   Module-LWE (MLWE)

We use bold font to indicate a vector and use square brackets to index ciphertext components. We also use subscripts for indexing an element of a vector, especially in the module context. We briefly review Module-LWE (MLWE) which was introduced in [BGV14,LS15]. Let $q \geq 2$ and k, n be powers of 2. An MLWE ciphertext with modulus q, rank k and degree n is denoted as $\mathsf{MLWE}_{q,n}^k$. It is an element $\mathbf{c} = (\mathbf{c}[0], \mathbf{c}[1], \cdots, \mathbf{c}[k]) \in (\mathcal{R}_{q,n})^{k+1}$. We also use the notation of $\mathbf{c} = (b, \mathbf{a})$ where $b = \mathbf{c}[0]$ and $\mathbf{a} = (\mathbf{c}[1], \cdots, \mathbf{c}[k])$. If $\langle \mathbf{c}, (1, \mathbf{s}) \rangle = b + \langle \mathbf{a}, \mathbf{s} \rangle = m$, then the ciphertext $\mathbf{c}$ is said to be an encryption of plaintext $m \in \mathcal{R}_{q,n}$ with secret key $\mathbf{s} = (s_1, \cdots, s_k) \in (\mathcal{R}_{q,n})^k$. To simplify the notations, we assume that the error is contained in m. We call $N = n \cdot k$ the dimension of the ciphertext. MLWE can be seen as a generalization of LWE and RLWE, as $\mathsf{MLWE}_{q,1}^k = \mathsf{LWE}_q^k$ and $\mathsf{MLWE}_{q,n}^1 = \mathsf{RLWE}_{q,n}$.

4.2   Building Blocks for ModPack

We describe two building blocks for ModPack: MLWE ring switching and MLWE key switching. Namely, we generalize Ring switching (Sect. 3.2) and key switching (Sect. 2.1) to MLWE.

MLWE Ring Switching. Suppose ℓ, k, n are powers of 2 and $(\mathbf{c}_j)_{0 \leq j < \ell}$ are MLWE ciphertexts of rank k and degree n, encrypted with the same secret key $\mathbf{s}$. Define $\mathbf{c}' = \mathsf{Combine}_{n,\ell}^k((\mathbf{c}_j)_{0 \leq j < \ell})$ as

$$\mathbf{c}'[t] = (\pi_{q,n\ell}^\ell)^{-1}((\mathbf{c}_j[t])_{0 \leq j < \ell})$$

for each $0 \leq t \leq k$. Then $\mathbf{c}'$ is an MLWE ciphertext of rank k and degree $n\ell$, encrypting the combined input data (i.e., its decryption contains the decryptions of the $\mathbf{c}_j$'s).

MLWE Key Switching. MLWE key switching is a technique to switch the key of an MLWE ciphertext using a RLWE switching as described in Sect. 2.1. It consists of the following three steps:

1. Embed the input MLWE ciphertext as part of an RLWE ciphertext of the same dimension but a higher degree;
2. Switch the key of the RLWE ciphertext;
3. Extract an MLWE ciphertext that encrypts valid data from the RLWE ciphertext.

These steps will be specified below. To describe them, we need to introduce some notations. We use the same notations as in Sect. 3.2. Additionally, we define $\epsilon_{q,N}^k : \mathcal{R}_{q,N} \to \mathcal{R}_{q,N/k}$ as $\epsilon_{q,N}^k(a) = a_0$: the $\epsilon_{q,N}^k$ map is extracting the first coefficient of an element of $\mathcal{R}_{q,N}$ viewed as an $\mathcal{R}_{q,N/k}$-module.

Example. *For $N = 8$ and $a = \sum_j a_j X_8^j \in \mathcal{R}_{q,8}$, we have*

$$\pi_{q,8}^2(a) = (a_0 + a_2 X_4 + a_4 X_4^2 + a_6 X_4^3, \; a_1 + a_3 X_4 + a_5 X_4^2 + a_7 X_4^3).$$

Further, we have $\epsilon_{q,8}^4(a) = a_0 + a_4 X_2$.

For $\mathbf{a} = (a_0, \cdots, a_{k-1}) \in (\mathcal{R}_{q,N/k})^k$, we define $\mathbf{a}^{tw}$, the twist of $\mathbf{a}$, as follows:

$$\mathbf{a}^{tw} := (a_0, a_{k-1} \cdot X_{N/k}^{-1}, a_{k-2} \cdot X_{N/k}^{-1}, \cdots, a_1 \cdot X_{N/k}^{-1}).$$

We define the inverse of the twist as

$$\mathbf{a}^{tw^{-1}} := (a_0, a_{k-1} \cdot X_{N/k}, a_{k-2} \cdot X_{N/k}, \cdots, a_1 \cdot X_{N/k}).$$

It may be checked that $\mathbf{a}^{tw^{-1} \circ tw} = (\mathbf{a}^{tw})^{tw^{-1}} = \mathbf{a}$.

Similarly, we can define the twist and its inverse for $a \in \mathcal{R}_{q,N}$ when a rank k is specified:

$$a^{tw,k} = (\pi_{q,N}^k)^{-1} \circ (\pi_{q,N}^k(a))^{tw}.$$

Then we observe the following.

Lemma 1. *For $a, s \in \mathcal{R}_{q,N}$, we have*

$$\epsilon_{q,N}^k\left(a^{tw,k} \cdot s\right) = \left\langle \pi_{q,N}^k(a), \pi_{q,N}^k(s) \right\rangle,$$

where $\langle \cdot, \cdot \rangle$ refers to the formal inner product over $(\mathcal{R}_{q,N/k})^k$.

Proof. Write $\pi_{q,N}^k(a) = (a_0, a_1, \cdots, a_{k-1})$ and $\pi_{q,N}^k(s) = (s_0, s_1, \cdots, s_{k-1})$ with $a_i, s_i \in \mathcal{R}_{q,N/k}$ for all i. Then we have

$$\epsilon_{q,N}^k\left(a^{tw,k} \cdot s\right) = \epsilon_{q,N}^k\left(a^{tw,k} \cdot \sum_{j=0}^{k-1} s_j X_N^j\right) = \sum_{j=0}^{k-1} \epsilon_{q,N}^k\left(a^{tw,k} \cdot s_j X_N^j\right).$$

As $a^{tw,k} = a_0 + \sum_{1 \leq j < k} a_{k-j} X_{N/k}^{-1} X_N^j$, we have $\epsilon_{q,N}^k\left(a^{tw,k} \cdot s_j X_N^j\right) = a_j s_j$ for each $0 \leq j < k$, which completes the proof. $\square$

We now explain how to view an MLWE ciphertext as an RLWE ciphertext (embedding) and the opposite (extraction). In general, we can view an MLWE ciphertext as an MLWE ciphertext with the same dimension but with a higher degree. In that case, as depicted in Fig. 1, the plaintext of the higher degree MLWE ciphertext includes the data of the lower degree one and the other plaintext slots are filled with random data. Also, we can extract a lower degree MLWE ciphertext from a higher degree MLWE ciphertext. The MLWE embedding map $\mathsf{Embed}_{q,N}^k : (\mathcal{R}_{q,N/k})^{k+1} \to (\mathcal{R}_{q,N})^2$ embeds an MLWE ciphertext of rank k and degree N/k into an RLWE ciphertext with dimension N. It is defined as

$$\mathsf{Embed}_{q,N}^k(b, \mathbf{a}) = \left(\iota_{q,N}^k(b), (\pi_{q,N}^k)^{-1}(\mathbf{a}^{tw})\right),$$

where $\iota_{q,N}^k : \mathcal{R}_{q,N/k} \to \mathcal{R}_{q,N}$ is the ring embedding and $\pi_{q,N}^k$ is the module decomposition map (as defined in Sect. 3.2). Then, by Lemma 1, we have

$$\mathsf{Embed}_{q,N}^k\left(\mathsf{MLWE}_{q,N/k}^k.\mathsf{Enc}_{\mathbf{s}}(m)\right) = \mathsf{RLWE}_{q,N}.\mathsf{Enc}_{(\pi_{q,N}^k)^{-1}(\mathbf{s})}(M). \qquad (1)$$

for some $M \in \mathcal{R}_{q,N}$ satisfying $\epsilon_{q,N}^k(M) = m$.

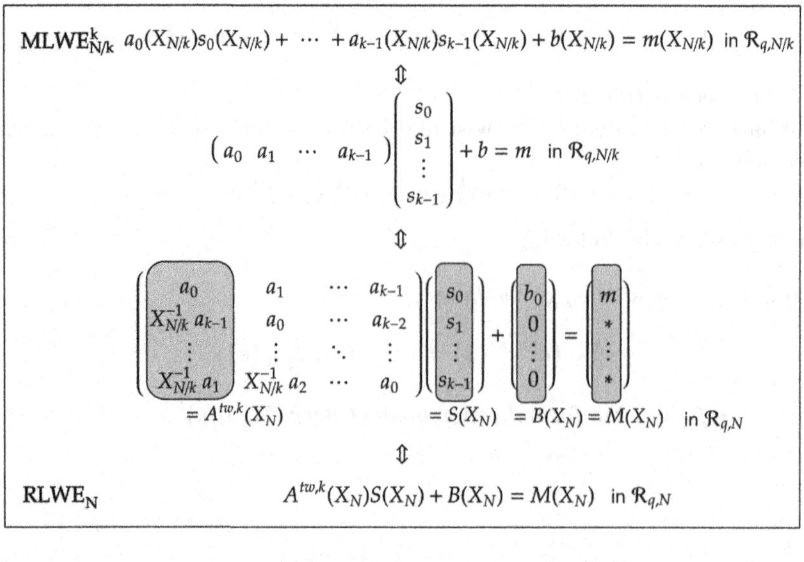

Fig. 1. MLWE embedding and extraction.

The MLWE extraction map $\text{Extract}_{q,N}^k : (\mathcal{R}_{q,N})^2 \to (\mathcal{R}_{q,N/k})^{k+1}$ extracts an MLWE ciphertext of rank k and degree N/k from an RLWE ciphertext of dimension N. It is defined as

$$\text{Extract}_{q,N}^k(\mathcal{B}, \mathcal{A}) = \left(\epsilon_{q,N}^k(\mathcal{B}), (\pi_{q,N}^k(\mathcal{A}))^{(tw,k)^{-1}}\right).$$

Then, by Lemma 1, we have

$$\text{Extract}_{q,N}^k\left(\text{RLWE}_{q,N}.\text{Enc}_s(m)\right) = \text{MLWE}_{q,N/k}^k.\text{Enc}_{\pi_{q,N}^k(s)}(\epsilon_{q,N}^k(m)). \qquad (2)$$

With Eqs. (1) and (2), we obtain the MLWE key switching procedure (Theorem 1). First, we view the input MLWE ciphertext as a part of an RLWE ciphertext. Then we switch the key of the RLWE ciphertext and extract an MLWE ciphertext as the result.

Theorem 1 (MLWE key switching). *Let $q \geq 2$, and k, N be powers of 2 such that $k \leq N$. Suppose that $\mathbf{c} = \text{MLWE}_{q,N/k}^k.\text{Enc}_\mathbf{s}(m)$ for some plaintext m. Let $\mathcal{S} = (\pi_{q,N}^k)^{-1}(\mathbf{s})$ and $\mathcal{S}' = (\pi_{q,N}^k)^{-1}(\mathbf{s}')$. Then the following holds:*

$$\text{Extract}_{q,N}^k \circ \text{KS}_{\mathcal{S} \to \mathcal{S}'} \circ \text{Embed}_{q,N}^k(\mathbf{c}) = \text{MLWE}_{q,N/k}^k.\text{Enc}_{\mathbf{s}'}(m).$$

Proof. Let $\mathbf{C} = \text{Embed}_{q,N}^k(\mathbf{c})$. With Eq. (1), we have $\mathbf{C} = \text{RLWE}_{q,N}.\text{Enc}_\mathcal{S}(M)$, where $M \in \mathcal{R}_{q,N}$ and $\epsilon_{q,N}^k(M) = m$. From Eq. (2), we obtain

$$\text{Extract}_{q,N}^k \circ \text{KS}_{\mathcal{S} \to \mathcal{S}'}(\mathbf{C}) = \text{Extract}_{q,N}^k(\text{RLWE}_{q,N}.\text{Enc}_{\mathcal{S}'}(M))$$
$$= \text{MLWE}_{q,N/k}^k.\text{Enc}_{\mathbf{s}'}(m).$$

This completes the proof.   □

4.3   ModPack: An Algorithm for Module Packing

In this section, we describe $\text{ModPack}_N^{K,k,k'}$, an algorithm for module packing, with the following signature:

$$k/k' \cdot \text{MLWE}_{q,N/k}^K \to \text{MLWE}_{q,N/k'}^{k'}. \qquad (3)$$

Here K refers to the rank of input MLWE ciphertexts. The degrees of input and output ciphertexts are N/k and N/k', respectively. For simplicity, we consider the case of an input data size that is the same as the output's. Since a degree d MLWE ciphertext has d plaintext slots, the number of input MLWE ciphertexts must be $(N/k')/(N/k) = k/k'$.

Let $\mathbf{s}$ be an $\text{MLWE}_{q,N/k}^K$ secret key and $\mathbf{s}'$ an $\text{MLWE}_{q,N/k'}^{k'}$ secret key. By viewing a K-dimensional vector as a concatenation of K/k' vectors of dimension k', we may write $\mathbf{s} = (\check{\mathbf{s}}_0, \check{\mathbf{s}}_1, \cdots, \check{\mathbf{s}}_{K/k'-1})$ with $\check{\mathbf{s}}_j \in \mathcal{R}_{q,N/k}^{k'}$ for each j. Let $\mathbf{s}_j = \iota_{q,N/k'}^{k/k'}(\check{\mathbf{s}}_j) \in \mathcal{R}_{q,N/k'}^{k'}$, $\mathcal{S}_j = (\pi_{q,N}^{k'})^{-1}(\mathbf{s}_j)$, $\mathcal{S}' = (\pi_{q,N}^{k'})^{-1}(\mathbf{s}')$ and $\text{swk}_j = \text{RLWE}_{qp,N}.\text{Enc}_{\mathcal{S}'}(p \cdot \mathcal{S}_j)$ for $0 \leq j < K/k'$. Given some $\text{MLWE}_{q,N/k}^K$ ciphertexts $(\mathbf{c}_j)_{0 \leq j < k/k'}$, where $\mathbf{c}_j$ decrypts to (m_j) under $\mathbf{s}$, $\text{ModPack}_N^{K,k,k'}$ (Algorithm 1) consists of the following steps:

1. $\mathbf{C} \leftarrow \mathsf{Combine}^K_{N/k,k,k'}((\mathbf{c}_j)_{0 \leq j < k/k'})$, then $\mathbf{C}$ is an $\mathsf{MLWE}^K_{N/k'}$ ciphertext encrypting

$$m' = (\pi^{k/k'}_{q,N/k'})^{-1}(m_0, \cdots, m_{k/k'-1}) \in \mathcal{R}_{q,N/k'}.$$

2. Write $\mathbf{C} = (\mathbf{C}[t])_{0 \leq t \leq K}$ and divide $\mathbf{C}$ into $(\mathbf{C}_j)_{0 \leq j < K/k'} \in (\mathcal{R}^{k'+1}_{q,N/k'})^{K/k'}$, where

$$\mathbf{C}_j = (0, \mathbf{C}[jk'+1], \mathbf{C}[jk'+2], \cdots, \mathbf{C}[jk'+k'])$$

for $j \neq 0$ and $\mathbf{C}_0 = (\mathbf{C}[0], \mathbf{C}[1], \cdots, \mathbf{C}[k'])$. Note that each $\mathbf{C}_j$ does not encrypt a valid data, while the decryption of their sum is m' if we assume that each $\mathbf{C}_j$ is encrypted with $\mathbf{s}_j$.

3. Use hoisted MLWE key switching to switch keys, i.e.,

$$\mathbf{C}' = \mathsf{Extract}^{k'}_{q,N} \circ \mathsf{KS}\left(\mathsf{Embed}^{k'}_{q,N}(\mathbf{C}_j)_{0 \leq j < K/k'}; (\mathsf{swk}_j)_{0 \leq j < K/k'}\right).$$

The output $\mathbf{C}'$ is an MLWE encryption of m' of rank k' and degree N/k', under secret key $\mathbf{s}'$. The algorithm is illustrated in Fig. 2.

Theorem 2 (ModPack). *Let* $\mathbf{s} = (\check{\mathbf{s}}_0, \check{\mathbf{s}}_1, \cdots, \check{\mathbf{s}}_{K/k'-1}) \in \mathcal{R}^K_{q,N/k}$ *with* $\check{\mathbf{s}}_j \in \mathcal{R}^{k'}_{q,N/k}$ *for each* j, *and* $\mathbf{s}' \in \mathcal{R}^{k'}_{q,N/k'}$. *Define* $\mathbf{s}_j = \iota^{k/k'}_{q,N/k'}(\check{\mathbf{s}}_j) \in \mathcal{R}^{k'}_{q,N/k'}$ *and* $\mathcal{S}_j = (\pi^{k'}_{q,N})^{-1}(\mathbf{s}_j)$ *for each* j, *and* $\mathcal{S}' = (\pi^{k'}_{q,N})^{-1}(\mathbf{s}')$. *Given as input* k/k' *MLWE ciphertexts* $\mathbf{c}_j = \mathsf{MLWE}^K_{q,N/k}.\mathsf{Enc}_{\mathbf{s}}(m_j)$ *for some* m_j *and* K/k' *switching keys* $\mathsf{swk}_j = \mathsf{RLWE}_{qp,N}.\mathsf{Enc}_{\mathcal{S}'}(p \cdot \mathcal{S}_j)$, *ModPack returns* $\mathbf{C}'$ *satisfying*

$$\mathbf{C}' = \mathsf{MLWE}^{k'}_{q,N/k'}.\mathsf{Enc}_{\mathbf{s}'}(m'),$$

where

$$m' = (\pi^{k/k'}_{q,N/k'})^{-1}(m_0, \cdots, m_{k/k'-1}) \in \mathcal{R}_{q,N/k'}.$$

Proof. Consider $\mathbf{C} = \mathsf{Combine}^K_{N/k,k,k'}((\mathbf{c}_j)_{0 \leq j < k/k'})$ and define $(\mathbf{C}_j)_{0 \leq j < K/k'} \in (\mathcal{R}^{k'+1}_{q,N/k'})^{K/k'}$ as in Equation (2.) for $j \neq 0$ and $\mathbf{C}_0 = (\mathbf{C}[0], \mathbf{C}[1], \cdots, \mathbf{C}[k'])$. Write $\mathbf{C} = (\mathbf{B}, \mathbf{A})$, $\mathbf{C}_j = (\mathbf{B}_j, \mathbf{A}_j)$, $\mathsf{Embed}^{k'}_{q,N}(\mathbf{C}_j) = (\mathcal{B}_j, \mathcal{A}_j)$, $\mathcal{B} = \sum_{0 \leq j < K/k'} \mathcal{B}_j$ and $\hat{\mathcal{A}}_j = \mathsf{ModUp}(\mathcal{A}_j)$ for each j. Then we have

$$\epsilon^{k'}_{q,N}\left(\sum_{0 \leq j < K/k'} \mathcal{A}_j \mathcal{S}_j + \mathcal{B}\right) = \sum_{0 \leq j < K/k'} \langle \mathbf{A}_j, \mathbf{s}_j \rangle + \mathbf{B} = \langle \mathbf{A}, \mathbf{s} \rangle + \mathbf{B} = m'. \quad (4)$$

Also, we have

$$\mathsf{KS}\left(\mathsf{Embed}^{k'}_{q,N}(\mathbf{C}_j)_{0 \leq j < K/k'}; (\mathsf{swk}_j)_{0 \leq j < K/k'}\right)$$

$$= \mathsf{ModDown}\left(\sum_{0 \leq j < K/k'} \mathsf{MultSwk}(\hat{\mathcal{A}}_j, \mathsf{swk}_j)\right) + (\mathcal{B}, 0)$$

$$= \mathsf{RLWE}_{q,N}.\mathsf{Enc}_{\mathcal{S}'}\left(\sum_{0 \leq j < K/k'} \mathcal{A}_j \mathcal{S}_j + \mathcal{B}\right).$$
$$(5)$$

From Equations (4), (5) and (2), we obtain

$$\mathbf{C}' = \mathsf{Extract}_{q,N}^{k'}\left(\mathsf{RLWE}_{q,N}.\mathsf{Enc}_{\mathcal{S}'}\left(\sum_{0 \leq j < K/k'} \mathcal{A}_j \mathcal{S}_j + \mathcal{B}\right)\right)$$

$$= \mathsf{MLWE}_{q,N/k'}^{k'}.\mathsf{Enc}_{\mathbf{s}'}(m'),$$

as desired. □

$\mathsf{ModPack}_N^{K,k,k'}$ consists of K/k' executions of ModUp, 1 execution of $\mathsf{ModDown}$ and $2K/k'$ Hadamard multiplications. The overall key consists of K/k' elementary switching keys. Each ModUp and $\mathsf{ModDown}$ involves $O(N \log N)$ integer operations since degree-N NTT dominates, and a Hadamard multiplication has $O(N)$ complexity. The size of a switching key is $2N \log(qp)$ since it is a degree-N RLWE ciphertext of modulus qp.

Algorithm 1: $\mathsf{ModPack}_N^{K,k,k'}$: $k/k' \cdot \mathsf{MLWE}_{q,N/k}^K \to \mathsf{MLWE}_{q,N/k'}^{k'}$

Input : $(\mathbf{c}_j)_{0 \leq j < k/k'}$
$\quad\quad\quad (\mathsf{swk}_j)_{0 \leq j < K/k'}$
Output: $\mathbf{C}'$
1 $\mathbf{C} \leftarrow \mathsf{Combine}_{N/k,k,k'}^K((\mathbf{c}_j)_{0 \leq j < k/k'})$
2 $\mathbf{C}_0 \leftarrow (\mathbf{C}[0], \mathbf{C}[1], \cdots, \mathbf{C}[k'])$
3 **for** $j = 1, \cdots, K/k'$ **do**
4 $\quad$ $\mathbf{C}_j \leftarrow (0, \mathbf{C}[jk'+1], \mathbf{C}[jk'+2], \cdots, \mathbf{C}[jk'+k'])$
5 **end for**
6 $\mathbf{C}' \leftarrow \mathsf{Extract}_{q,N}^{k'} \circ \mathsf{KS}(\mathsf{Embed}_{q,N}^{k'}(\mathbf{C}_j)_{0 \leq j < K/k'}; (\mathsf{swk}_j)_{0 \leq j < K/k'})$
7 **return** $\mathbf{C}'$

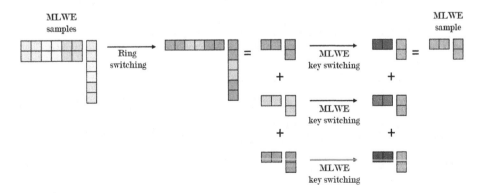

Fig. 2. Visualization of $\mathsf{ModPack}$, which packs multiple MLWE ciphertexts into a single MLWE ciphertext with the same dimension. The entries of each vector belong to quotient polynomial rings. A light color means a ring with a smaller degree while a dark color indicates a ring with a larger degree.

Note that $\mathsf{ModPack}_N^{N,N,1}$ is exactly the column method, and hence $\mathsf{ModPack}$ can be seen as a generalization of the column method.

4.4 BaseHERMES: A Base Ring Packing with MLWE Midpoints

Below, we describe how to reduce the switching key size by using $\mathsf{ModPack}$ (Algorithm 1), introducing $\mathsf{BaseHERMES}$, a composition of $\mathsf{ModPacks}$. To compose several $\mathsf{ModPacks}$ to form a base ring packing, we insert MLWE midpoints with intermediate degrees to split the ring packing procedure into several steps. Then, we apply $\mathsf{ModPack}$ at each step. We set the rank of the input LWE ciphertexts as $K \geq N_{\mathsf{Enc}}$ and set the number of input LWE ciphertexts as $N \geq N_{\mathsf{KS}}$. The dimension of switching key and the degree of the output RLWE ciphertexts are set to N. Base ring switching and hence $\mathsf{BaseHERMES}_N^{K,\kappa}$ have the following signature:

$$N \cdot \mathsf{LWE}_{Q_{\mathsf{Enc}}}^K \to 1 \cdot \mathsf{RLWE}_{Q_{\mathsf{Enc}},N} \tag{6}$$

Beyond the input LWE dimension K and output RLWE degree N, $\mathsf{BaseHERMES}$ is also parametrized by some $\kappa = \{k_1 > \cdots > k_t\}$. It refers to the set of ranks of the MLWE midpoints: t is the number of midpoints and k_j is the rank of jth midpoint for all j. We assume that $k_0 = N > k_j > 1 = k_{t+1}$ for all j. In case of $\kappa = \emptyset$, $\mathsf{BaseHERMES}_N^{K,\emptyset}$ is exactly $\mathsf{ModPack}_N^{K,k_0,k_1} = \mathsf{ModPack}_N^{K,N,1}$, which is the column method.

Single MLWE Midpoint. $\mathsf{BaseHERMES}_N^{K,\{k\}}$ consists in inserting an intermediate state "$k \cdot \mathsf{MLWE}_{Q_{\mathsf{Enc}},N/k}^k$" in (6), i.e., in splitting the base ring packing procedure into two steps:

$$N \cdot \mathsf{LWE}_{Q_{\mathsf{Enc}}}^K \xrightarrow{\text{Step 1}} k \cdot \mathsf{MLWE}_{Q_{\mathsf{Enc}},N/k}^k \xrightarrow{\text{Step 2}} 1 \cdot \mathsf{RLWE}_{Q_{\mathsf{Enc}},N}. \tag{7}$$

Step 1 is performed with k parallel executions of $\mathsf{ModPack}_N^{K,N,k}$, and Step 2 is itself implemented by calling $\mathsf{ModPack}_N^{k,k,1}$. More compactly, we may write:

$$\mathsf{BaseHERMES}_N^{K,\{k\}} = \mathsf{ModPack}_N^{k,k,1} \circ (k \cdot \mathsf{ModPack}_N^{K,N,k}).$$

The algorithm is illustrated in Fig. 3. Note that once the states are determined, there is a unique $\mathsf{ModPack}$ parametrization corresponding to it. The input of the first step consists of the N LWE ciphertexts of dimension K, which may be grouped and ordered arbitrarily, affecting the order of the plaintext slots of the output.

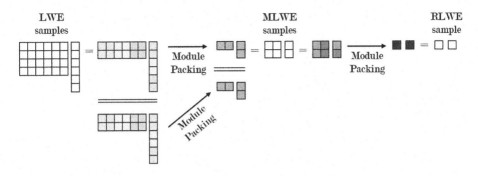

Fig. 3. Visualization of BaseHERMES with a single middle point.

Table 3 compares the costs and sizes of switching keys of the BaseHERMES$_N^{K,\emptyset}$ (the column method) and BaseHERMES$_N^{K,\{k\}}$ algorithms. It displays the number of executions of ModUp and ModDown (each of which has consumes $O(N \log N)$ arithmetic operations), the number of Hadamard multiplications and the number of elementary switching keys (an elementary switching key is a degree-N RLWE ciphertext of modulus Q_{KS} and thus has $N \log(Q_{KS})$ bit-size). For $K \geq \sqrt{N}$, which is the typical scenario, the value of k minimizing the number of switching keys is $\sqrt{K}$. It is therefore interesting to set k as the nearest power of two.

Table 3. Comparison between BaseHERMES$_N^{K,\emptyset}$ and BaseHERMES$_N^{K,\{k\}}$. Each cell provides the number of ModUp/ModDown/HadamardMult/SwitchingKey in each method. For time complexity, we mostly focus on ModUp and ModDown since they have higher cost $O(N \log N)$ than Hadamard multiplication's $O(N)$ cost.

Method		ModUp $O(N \log N)$	ModDown $O(N \log N)$	HadamardMult $O(N)$	SwitchingKey $O(N \log(Q_{KS}))$
BaseHERMES$_N^{K,\emptyset}$ (column method)		K	1	$2K$	K
BaseHERMES$_N^{K,\{k\}}$ (single midpoint)	Step 1	K	k	$2K$	K/k
	Step 2	k	1	$2k$	k
	Total	$K+k$	$k+1$	$2(K+k)$	$K/k+k$

To see the effectiveness of the new method, we consider the case of $K = N$ with $k = \sqrt{N}$ (see Table 4). In this case, the computational complexity difference is negligible compared to the main cost N executions of ModUp. However, the number of elementary switching keys significantly reduces from N for the column method to $2\sqrt{N}$ for the single midpoint method.

Table 4. Comparison between $\mathsf{BaseHERMES}_N^{N,\emptyset}$ and $\mathsf{BaseHERMES}_N^{N,\{\sqrt{N}\}}$.

Method		ModUp $O(N \log N)$	ModDown $O(N \log N)$	HadamardMult $O(N)$	SwitchingKey $O(N \log(Q_{\mathsf{KS}}))$
$\mathsf{BaseHERMES}_N^{N,\emptyset}$ (column method)		N	1	$2N$	N
$\mathsf{BaseHERMES}_N^{N,\{\sqrt{N}\}}$ (single midpoint)	Step 1	N	$\sqrt{N}$	$2N$	$\sqrt{N}$
	Step 2	$\sqrt{N}$	1	$2\sqrt{N}$	$\sqrt{N}$
	Total	$N + \sqrt{N}$	$\sqrt{N}+1$	$2(N+\sqrt{N})$	$2\sqrt{N}$

Generalization. By taking more MLWE midpoints, one can reduce the number of elementary switching keys for a limited slowdown in time performance. In general, we can insert t midpoints of rank k_j satisfying $N = k_0 > k_1 > \cdots > k_t > k_{t+1} = 1$ to build $\mathsf{BaseHERMES}_N^{K,\kappa}$ with $\kappa = \{k_1 > \cdots > k_t\}$. The state diagram of $\mathsf{BaseHERMES}_N^{K,\kappa}$ is as follows.

$$N \cdot \mathsf{LWE}_{Q_{\mathsf{Enc}}}^K \xrightarrow{\text{Step 1}} k_1 \cdot \mathsf{MLWE}_{Q_{\mathsf{Enc}}, N/k_1}^{k_1} \longrightarrow \cdots$$

$$\longrightarrow k_t \cdot \mathsf{MLWE}_{Q_{\mathsf{Enc}}, N/k_t}^{k_t} \xrightarrow{\text{Step } t+1} 1 \cdot \mathsf{RLWE}_{Q_{\mathsf{Enc}}, N}.$$

Step 1 is performed with k_1 parallel executions of $\mathsf{ModPack}_N^{K,k_0,k_1}$, whereas Step j for $j > 1$ consists in k_j parallel calls to $\mathsf{ModPack}_N^{k_{j-1},k_{j-1},k_j}$. To sum up, we have

$$\mathsf{BaseHERMES}_N^{K,\kappa} = (k_{t+1} \cdot \mathsf{ModPack}_N^{k_t,k_t,k_{t+1}}) \circ (k_t \cdot \mathsf{ModPack}_N^{k_{t-1},k_{t-1},k_t}) \circ \cdots$$
$$\circ (k_2 \cdot \mathsf{ModPack}_N^{k_1,k_1,k_2}) \circ (k_1 \cdot \mathsf{ModPack}_N^{K,k_0,k_1}).$$

Table 5 gives the costs and the number of elementary switching keys.

Table 5. Comparison between $\mathsf{BaseHERMES}_N^{K,\emptyset}$ and $\mathsf{BaseHERMES}_N^{K,\kappa}$.

Method		ModUp $O(N \log N)$	ModDown $O(N \log N)$	HadamardMult $O(N)$	SwitchingKey $O(N \log(Q_{\mathsf{KS}}))$
$\mathsf{BaseHERMES}_N^{K,\emptyset}$ (column method)		K	1	$2K$	K
$\mathsf{BaseHERMES}_N^{K,\kappa}$ (t midpoints)	Step 1	K	k_1	$2K$	K/k_1
	Step 2	k_1	k_2	$2k_1$	k_1/k_2
	$\cdots$	$-$	$-$	$-$	$-$
	Step $t+1$	k_t	1	$2k_t$	k_t
	Total	$K + \sum_{1 \leq j \leq t} k_j$	$\sum_{1 \leq j \leq t+1} k_j$	$2(K + \sum_{1 \leq j \leq t} k_j)$	$K/k_1 + \sum_{1 \leq j \leq t} k_j/k_{j+1}$

Increasing the number of mid-points t allows to significantly reduce key-size. For example, set $k_i = K^{1-i/(t+1)}$. Then the key consists of $(t+1) \cdot K^{1/(t+1)}$

elementary switching keys. The total number of ModUp's and ModDown's is $K + 2\sum_{i=1}^{t} K^{i/(t+1)} + 1$, which is no more than three times larger than that for BaseHERMES$_N^{K,\emptyset}$. Note that $K + 2\sum_{i=1}^{t} K^{i/(t+1)} + 1 = K + 2\frac{K - K^{1/(t+1)}}{K^{1/(t+1)} - 1} + 1 \leq 3K + 1$. Therefore, key size decreases fast with t, whereas the cost at most tripled.

In practice, as seen in Table 10, the single midpoint method already enjoys a very small key compared to the bootstrapping key, and reducing it further does not seem interesting in the FHE ring packing scenario.

4.5 HERMES

With ring switching, HalfBTS and BaseHERMES at hand, we can now describe HERMES. HERMES ring-packs N_{BTS} LWE$_{Q_{\mathsf{Enc}}, N_{\mathsf{Enc}}}^{K}$ ciphertexts into an RLWE$_{Q_{\mathsf{comp}}}$ ciphertext. It consists of three steps:

1. Group the given N_{BTS} LWE ciphertexts into $N_{\mathsf{BTS}}/N_{\mathsf{KS}}$ groups, each one with N_{KS} LWE ciphertexts; for each group, run BaseHERMES$_{N_{\mathsf{KS}}}^{K,\kappa}$, for some parameter κ, to obtain $N_{\mathsf{BTS}}/N_{\mathsf{KS}}$ RLWE$_{Q_{\mathsf{Enc}}, N_{\mathsf{KS}}}$ ciphertexts.
2. Ring switch the RLWE ciphertexts to form a single RLWE ciphertext.
3. Run HalfBTS on the RLWE ciphertext to raise the modulus to Q_{comp}.

The algorithm is illustrated in Fig. 4.

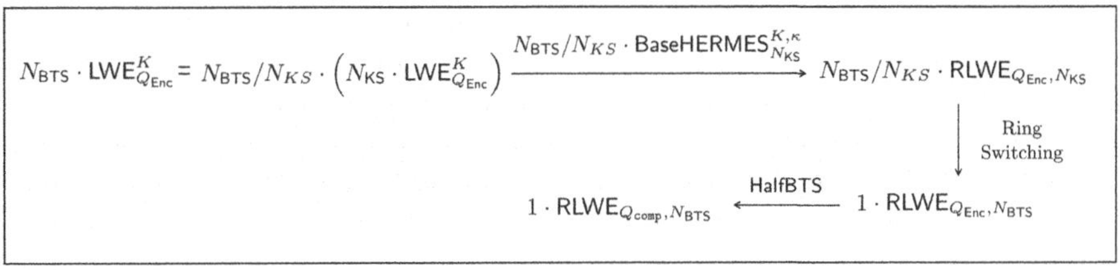

Fig. 4. Visualization of HERMES, which ring-packs N_{BTS} LWE$_{Q_{\mathsf{Enc}}}^{K}$ ciphertexts into an RLWE$_{Q_{\mathsf{comp}}, N_{\mathsf{BTS}}}$ ciphertext.

5 Implementation

We provide some proof-of-concept implementation results for our method. We used the C++ **HEaaN** library for the development. All experiments are measured on AMD® Ryzen 7 3700x 8-core processor with a single-threaded CPU.

In our (base) ring packing implementations, N denotes the degree of the output RLWE ciphertext, ℓ the number of input LWE ciphertexts, and K the dimension of the input LWE ciphertexts. The mean (resp. worst) precision is $-\log_2(\mathbb{E}(\|e\|_1/m))$ (resp. $-\log_2 \max \|e\|_\infty$), where $e \in \mathbb{R}^m$ denotes the overall (base) ring packing error; expectation and maximum are taken over 100 iterations for each implementation.

5.1   HERMES Implementation

We first describe our ring packing implementation and parameters. We start with 2^{16} LWE ciphertexts of dimension 2^{11} with scaling factor of $\Delta = 2^{42}$. Our method consists of the following procedures.

1. We either use the column method ($\mathsf{BaseHERMES}_{2^{12}}^{2^{11},\emptyset}$) or the single midpoint method ($\mathsf{BaseHERMES}_{2^{12}}^{2^{11},\{2^6\}}$) and obtain 2^4 RLWE ciphertexts of degree 2^{12}.
2. We use ring switching to combine 2^4 RLWE ciphertexts of degree 2^{12} into a single RLWE ciphertext of degree 2^{16}.
3. We perform HalfBTS, in order to bootstrap the ciphertext to modulus Q_{comp}.

We used the bootstrapping parameter set from Table 2. We let HERMES^0 denote the method based on the column method and HERMES^1 the method based on the single midpoint method. The latency of HERMES^0 and HERMES^1 are 29.1 s and 30.7 s, respectively, while their total key sizes including ring packing keys and BTS keys are 782 MB and 673 MB, respectively. We provide detailed information in Table 6.

5.2   Comparison to the State of the Art

The only previous work that provides implementation results for ring packing to RLWE slots at Q_{comp} is PEGASUS [LHH+21]. We provide a comparison between our method and [LHH+21] in Table 8. The value of $\log_2(Q_{\mathsf{comp}})$ in [LHH+21] is not given explicitly but we estimate from the data in [LHH+21, Section VI] that it is equal to $45 \cdot 6 = 270$. For fair comparison, we constructed a CKKS parameter with $\log_2(Q_{\mathsf{comp}}) = 270$, see Table 7. We use a smaller ring degree N than PEGASUS by using the technique of [BTPH22] and choosing appropriate Hamming weights. The PEGASUS figures in Table 8 are borrowed from [LHH+21, Table V].

Table 6. HERMES implementation results. The latency includes base ring packing and HalfBTS. The key size includes both ring packing keys and BTS keys. Let $\ell = 2^{16}$ be the number of input LWE ciphertexts.

	Latency (s)	Key size (MB)	Precision (mean-worst)
HERMES^0	29.1	782	$(23.8, 21.1)$
HERMES^1	30.7	673	$(24.9, 21.8)$

Table 7. Data on the parameter set constructed for comparison with PEGASUS. Here h and $\tilde{h}$ denote the Hamming weights of the dense and sparse secret keys, respectively, for the sparse-secret encapsulation technique from [BTPH22]. The column '$\log_2(QP)$' denotes the size of the largest ciphertext modulus that can be used with the parameters while maintaining the desired security. The key size refers to the total size of the keys needed to HalfBTS.

N	$(h, \tilde{h})$	$\log_2(QP)$	$\log_2(Q_{\mathsf{Enc}})$	$\log_2(Q_{\mathsf{comp}})$	$\log_2(Q_{\mathsf{top}})$	Key size
2^{15}	$(256, 32)$	820	45	270	765	542 MB

Table 8. Comparison between HERMES and PEGASUS. The key size includes both ring packing keys and BTS keys.

	N	$\log_2(Q_{\mathsf{comp}})$	ℓ	Latency (s)	Amortized time (ms/slot)	Key size (MB)
[LHH+21]	2^{16}	270	2^8	23.4	93.0	1870
			2^{10}	51.6	50.4	3540
			2^{12}	51.7	12.6	
HERMES[1]	2^{16}	562	2^8	19.4	75.8	1010
			2^{10}	20.4	19.9	1050
			2^{12}	21.9	5.35	927
			2^{16}	30.7	0.468	673
	2^{15}	270	2^8	6.15	24.0	812
			2^{10}	6.23	6.08	832
			2^{12}	6.68	1.63	718
			2^{15}	10.2	0.311	547

We compare HERMES[1] with $\log_2(Q_{\mathsf{comp}}) = 270$ and [LHH+21]. HERMES[1] is 3.8 to 7.7 times faster for the same value of ℓ. Our throughput may be optimized by choosing $\ell = 2^{15}$, which leads to a factor 41 improvement compared to [LHH+21] with $\ell = 2^{12}$. For $\ell < N$, we used the bootstrapping algorithm for sparsely packed ciphertexts from [CHK+18, Section 5.2].

All the other previous works including [CDKS21] and [CGGI17] should show similar or even slower latency than [LHH+21] because they homomorphically perform a linear transformation with moduli larger than Q_{comp}.

5.3   Impact of Our Ingredients

We introduced several optimizations including ring switching and modulus optimizations in Sect. 3. These optimizations are general ones that can be applied to all the base ring packing methods to improve performance. In Sect. 4, we proposed a method using multiple MLWE midpoints to reduce the key size of [CGGI17] while retaining a similar ring packing time. In this section, we provide some implementation results explaining how effective our ingredients are.

Optimizations. For comparison, we report in Table 9 experimental results for the improved versions of the row method [CDKS21] and the column method [CGGI17]. We first performed 2^4 many base ring packings for each method at dimension 2^{12}, gathered the ciphertexts into dimension 2^{16} via ring switching, and then performed HalfBTS. The improved row and column methods have a latency of 54.3s and 29.1s, respectively, which are fairly fast compared to the implementation of [LHH+21], meaning that our optimizations are indeed effective.

Table 9. Comparison between the improved row and column methods. Here T_{RP} denotes the total ring packing time including HalfBTS.

	N	K	T_{RP}	Base ring packing key size	BTS key size
The row method + ring switching + modulus optimization	2^{16}	2^{12}	54.3 s	670 KB	667 MB
The column method + ring switching + modulus optimization (HERMES⁰)		2^{11}	29.1 s	114 MB	

The improved row method gives a lower key size but is slower, and the column method is faster but has a significantly large key size. The key size of the row method is negligible compared to the BTS key size while it is not for the column method. Note that we used the BTS key reduction algorithm in [HS18], and BTS key size could be reduced even further with [KLK+22]. The trade-off between row and column methods gives a motivation for finding a hybrid method between the two.

MLWE Midpoints. In Table 10, we provide a comparison between different base ring packing methods, in terms of time and memory. Our single midpoint method is almost as fast as the improved column method but has a fairly small ring packing key size compared to the improved row method. The latency difference between the row method and the others comes from hoisting and the use of a smaller LWE dimension K. Since the row method with the same $\log_2 Q$ as the other methods gives significantly lower precision, we provide higher precision implementation results as well.

Table 10. Comparison of different base ring packing methods. Here T_{baseRP} denotes the base ring packing time. The bit size difference between output scaling factor and base modulus is set to 12 bits for fair comparison.

	N	K	$\log_2 Q$	T_{baseRP}	Key size	Precision (mean-worst)
Improved row method	2^{12}	2^{12}	54	1.78 s	664 KB	(22.5, 20.0)
			72	3.34 s	1.33 MB	(40.5, 37.9)
BaseHERMES$_N^{K,\emptyset}$ (improved column method)		2^{11}	54	231 ms	113 MB	(30.9, 28.4)
BaseHERMES$_N^{K,\{2^{\lceil \log_2 K/2 \rceil}\}}$ (single midpoint)			54	374 ms	5.31 MB	(32.8, 30.3)

5.4   Transciphering Using HERMES

The fundamental goal of the transciphering framework is to decrease the computational and communication costs for a client that sends FHE ciphertexts (e.g., CKKS ciphertexts) to a computing server. Beyond their size, another important drawback of CKKS ciphertexts in this context is their low granularity. They contain thousands of plaintext slots and the client has to wait and send a very large ciphertext if it wants to fully exploit the number of slots to decrease the expansion factor. To handle this, several works have focused on transciphering from a symmetric encryption scheme to CKKS. As CKKS encrypts approximations to real numbers with moderate precision rather than bits or finite field elements, some care is required to obtain efficient transciphering. For this purpose, HERA [HKL+22] and Rubato [CHK+21] rely on the so-called Real-to-Finite-field framework (RtF), using symmetric ciphers with plaintexts of bit-sizes slightly above the CKKS plaintext bit-sizes. The symmetric cipher is homomorphically decrypted with the discrete-plaintext BFV/BGV FHE schemes and the result is then mapped from BFV/BGV to CKKS.

HERMES provides a more direct solution. A client sends the encrypted data in LWE or small-degree MLWE format to achieve high granularity, and it uses an extendable output-format function (XOF) on a public seed to implicitly represent most of the ciphertext and achieve low ciphertext expansion. The server uses HERMES to construct FHE ciphertexts. Our approach directly encrypts approximations to real numbers in the LWE symmetric ciphers, hence allowing to bypass the costly BFV/BGV step in RtF framework. Thus, the efficiency of HERMES significantly reduces the server-side computational overhead even compared to the state-of-the-art transciphering approaches for CKKS [HKL+22,CHK+21]. Figure 5 (inspired from [CHK+21, Figure 2]) illustrates the offline and online phases of the client and server.

Using a XOF on a public seed makes much room for precomputation. Concretely, the $\boldsymbol{a}$ part in (M)LWE ciphertexts $((b = \langle \boldsymbol{a}, \boldsymbol{s} \rangle + m, \boldsymbol{a}))$ is computed as $\boldsymbol{a} = \mathrm{XOF}(\mathrm{seed})$ for a public seed. The client can precompute $\boldsymbol{a}$ and $\widehat{b} = \langle \boldsymbol{a}, \boldsymbol{s} \rangle$ using the secret key $\boldsymbol{s}$ and seed, and it computes $b = \widehat{b} + m$ in the online phase.

To reduce the communication cost due to b, the client can cut its least significant bits. Concretely, the client sends $\lfloor (2^{\hat{p}}/\Delta) \cdot b \rceil = \lfloor (2^{\hat{p}}/\Delta) \cdot (\hat{b} + m) \rceil \approx (2^{\hat{p}}/\Delta) \cdot \hat{b} + \lfloor (2^{\hat{p}}/\Delta) \cdot m \rceil$ instead of b, where $\hat{p}$ is the input precision. The server can scale up the received $\lfloor (2^{\hat{p}}/\Delta) \cdot b \rceil$ by a factor $\Delta/2^{\hat{p}}$, yielding an LWE encryption of m with sufficient precision $\approx \hat{p}$.

The server can precompute the $\boldsymbol{a}$ part of the (M)LWE ciphertexts using seed. It then pre-performs the base ring packing of HERMES for the ephemeral LWE ciphertexts $(0, \boldsymbol{a})$'s, and obtains a precomputed RLWE ciphertext $(\hat{B}(X), A(X))$. In the online phase, the server first appropriately rearranges the received b parts of input (M)LWE, yielding $\widetilde{B}(X)$. It then completes the ring packing by running HalfBTS on $(\hat{B}(X) + \widetilde{B}(X), A(X))$. Sending part of the HERMES computation to the offline phase works since through HERMES, the $A(X)$ part of the output RLWE ciphertext depends only on the $\boldsymbol{a}$ parts of input LWE ciphertexts.

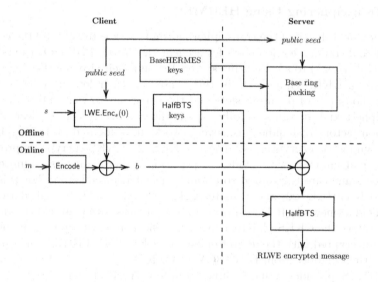

Fig. 5. Visualization of transciphering using HERMES.

Experimental Results. In Table 11, we compare HERMES transciphering with HERA [CHK+21, Table 5, Par-128a] and Rubato [HKL+22, Table 6], which are state-of-the-art for transciphering to CKKS. All parameter sets in the table achieve security of ≈ 128 bits.

As in [CHK+21] and [HKL+22], we compute the expansion ratio as the ratio between the ciphertext bit-size and the plaintext precision multiplied by the number of slots. It is equal to $(\log q)/(p+1)$, where $\log q$ is the bit size of the ciphertext modulus and p is the precision. Note that this excludes the seed used for $\boldsymbol{a} = \mathrm{XOF}(\mathrm{seed})$, though its bit size is negligible compared to the ciphertext bit size when amortized over many ciphertexts (by using a counter, only one seed needs to be sent). We have $\log_2(Q_0) = 58$, $\Delta = 2^{42}$ and $\hat{p} = 22$, implying that $\log_2(q) = 58 - 42 + 22 = 38$.

Our method allows some flexibility to choose n. For instance, we can choose $n = 1$ to achieve the highest granularity, i.e., to send ciphertexts corresponding to individual plaintexts. Rubato also considered several granularity levels, but for optimizing client throughput. For a consistent comparison, we started from MLWE ciphertexts of degrees n close to Rubato's block sizes. We use HERMES[1] with midpoint ring degree of $2^{\lceil \log_2(\sqrt{N_B n}) \rceil}$ for each n, where N_B is a ring dimension for BaseHERMES.

Our latency is 5.5 times smaller than HERA's, and at least 2.8 times smaller than Rubato's, while achieving similar precision and similar number of levels remaining after transciphering. Our expansion ratio is larger than those achieved by HERA and Rubato, but might be improved by using different parameter sets and/or the technique from [BCC+22] to increase the precision.

Table 11. Comparison between different transciphering schemes. Here n denotes the block size which corresponds to the MLWE degree in our method, and latency denotes the total transciphering time including online and offline phases of the client and server. Note that there is a difference in precision: it is due to the difference in bootstrapping algorithms used.

Scheme	N	n	Latency (s)	Expansion ratio	Mean precision
RtF-HERA [CHK+21]	2^{16}	16	142	1.24	19.1
RtF-Rubato [HKL+22]		64	106	1.26	18.9
		36	88.4	1.26	18.9
		16	71.1	1.31	18.8
Ours		64	25.8	1.58	23.0
		32	26.1	1.58	23.0
		16	25.7	1.58	23.0
		1	30.9	1.58	23.0

Acknowledgment. The research corresponding to this work was conducted while the fourth author was visiting CryptoLab Inc. as an intern student.

References

[BCC+22] Bae, Y., Cheon, J.H., Cho, W., Kim, J., Kim, T.: META-BTS: bootstrapping precision beyond the limit. In: CCS (2022)

[BGGJ20] Boura, C., Gama, N., Georgieva, M., Jetchev, D.: CHIMERA: combining ring-LWE-based fully homomorphic encryption schemes. J. Math. Cryptol. (2020)

[BGV14] Brakerski, Z., Gentry, C., Vaikuntanathan, V.: (Leveled) fully homomorphic encryption without bootstrapping. ACM Trans. Comput. Theory (2014)

[Bra12] Brakerski, Z.: Fully homomorphic encryption without modulus switching from classical GapSVP. In: Safavi-Naini, R., Canetti, R. (eds.) CRYPTO 2012. LNCS, vol. 7417, pp. 868–886. Springer, Heidelberg (2012). https://doi.org/10.1007/978-3-642-32009-5_50

[BTPH22] Bossuat, J.-P., Troncoso-Pastoriza, J., Hubaux, J.-P.: Bootstrapping for approximate homomorphic encryption with negligible failure-probability by using sparse-secret encapsulation. In: Ateniese, G., Venturi, D. (eds.) ACNS 2022. LNCS, vol. 13269, pp. 521–541. Springer, Cham (2022). https://doi.org/10.1007/978-3-031-09234-3_26

[CDKS21] Chen, H., Dai, W., Kim, M., Song, Y.: Efficient homomorphic conversion between (ring) LWE ciphertexts. In: Sako, K., Tippenhauer, N.O. (eds.) ACNS 2021. LNCS, vol. 12726, pp. 460–479. Springer, Cham (2021). https://doi.org/10.1007/978-3-030-78372-3_18

[CGGI16] Chillotti, I., Gama, N., Georgieva, M., Izabachène, M.: Faster fully homomorphic encryption: bootstrapping in less than 0.1 seconds. In: Cheon, J.H., Takagi, T. (eds.) ASIACRYPT 2016. LNCS, vol. 10031, pp. 3–33. Springer, Heidelberg (2016). https://doi.org/10.1007/978-3-662-53887-6_1

[CGGI17] Chillotti, I., Gama, N., Georgieva, M., Izabachène, M.: Faster packed homomorphic operations and efficient circuit bootstrapping for TFHE. In: Takagi, T., Peyrin, T. (eds.) ASIACRYPT 2017. LNCS, vol. 10624, pp. 377–408. Springer, Cham (2017). https://doi.org/10.1007/978-3-319-70694-8_14

[CHK+18] Cheon, J.H., Han, K., Kim, A., Kim, M., Song, Y.: Bootstrapping for approximate homomorphic encryption. In: Nielsen, J.B., Rijmen, V. (eds.) EUROCRYPT 2018. LNCS, vol. 10820, pp. 360–384. Springer, Cham (2018). https://doi.org/10.1007/978-3-319-78381-9_14

[CHK+21] Cho, J., et al.: Transciphering framework for approximate homomorphic encryption. In: Tibouchi, M., Wang, H. (eds.) ASIACRYPT 2021. LNCS, vol. 13092, pp. 640–669. Springer, Cham (2021). https://doi.org/10.1007/978-3-030-92078-4_22

[CKKS17] Cheon, J.H., Kim, A., Kim, M., Song, Y.: Homomorphic encryption for arithmetic of approximate numbers. In: Takagi, T., Peyrin, T. (eds.) ASIACRYPT 2017. LNCS, vol. 10624, pp. 409–437. Springer, Cham (2017). https://doi.org/10.1007/978-3-319-70694-8_15

[Cry] CryptoLab.inc. HEaaN private AI: Homomorphic encryption library

[DM15] Ducas, L., Micciancio, D.: FHEW: bootstrapping homomorphic encryption in less than a second. In: Oswald, E., Fischlin, M. (eds.) EUROCRYPT 2015. LNCS, vol. 9056, pp. 617–640. Springer, Heidelberg (2015). https://doi.org/10.1007/978-3-662-46800-5_24

[FV12] Fan, J., Vercauteren, F.: Somewhat practical fully homomorphic encryption (2012). http://eprint.iacr.org/2012/144

[GHPS13] Gentry, C., Halevi, S., Peikert, C., Smart, N.P.: Field switching in BGV-style homomorphic encryption. J. Comput. Secur. **21**, 663–684 (2013)

[HK20] Han, K., Ki, D.: Better bootstrapping for approximate homomorphic encryption. In: Jarecki, S. (ed.) CT-RSA 2020. Better bootstrapping for approximate homomorphic encryption., vol. 12006, pp. 364–390. Springer, Cham (2020). https://doi.org/10.1007/978-3-030-40186-3_16

[HKL+22] J. Ha, S. Kim, B. Lee, J. Lee, and M. Son. Rubato: Noisy ciphers for approximate homomorphic encryption. In: Dunkelman, O., Dziembowski, S. (eds.) EUROCRYPT 2022. LNCS, vol. 13275, pp. 581–610 (2022). https://doi.org/10.1007/978-3-031-06944-4_20

[HS14] Halevi, S., Shoup, V.: Algorithms in HElib. In: Garay, J.A., Gennaro, R. (eds.) CRYPTO 2014. LNCS, vol. 8616, pp. 554–571. Springer, Heidelberg (2014). https://doi.org/10.1007/978-3-662-44371-2_31

[HS18] Halevi, S., Shoup, V.: Faster homomorphic linear transformations in HElib. In: Shacham, H., Boldyreva, A. (eds.) CRYPTO 2018. LNCS, vol. 10991, pp. 93–120. Springer, Cham (2018). https://doi.org/10.1007/978-3-319-96884-1_4

[HS21] Halevi, S., Shoup, V.: Bootstrapping for HElib. J. Cryptol. **34**, 7 (2021)

[KLK+22] Kim, J., et al.: ARK: fully homomorphic encryption accelerator with runtime data generation and inter-operation key reuse. In: MICRO (2022)

[LHH+21] Lu, W.-J., Huang, Z., Hong, C., Ma, Y., Qu, H.: PEGASUS: bridging polynomial and non-polynomial evaluations in homomorphic encryption. In: S&P (2021)

[LPR10] Lyubashevsky, V., Peikert, C., Regev, O.: On ideal lattices and learning with errors over rings. In: Gilbert, H. (ed.) EUROCRYPT 2010. LNCS, vol. 6110, pp. 1–23. Springer, Heidelberg (2010). https://doi.org/10.1007/978-3-642-13190-5_1

[LS15] Langlois, A., Stehlé, D.: Worst-case to average-case reductions for module lattices. Des. Codes Crypt. **75**(3), 565–599 (2014). https://doi.org/10.1007/s10623-014-9938-4

[MS18] Micciancio, D., Sorrell, J.: Ring packing and amortized FHEW bootstrapping. In: ICALP 2018 (2018)

[NLV11] Naehrig, M., Lauter, K.E., Vaikuntanathan, V.: Can homomorphic encryption be practical? In: CCSW 2011 (2011)

[Reg09] Regev, O.: On lattices, learning with errors, random linear codes, and cryptography. J. ACM (2009)

[SSTX09] Stehlé, D., Steinfeld, R., Tanaka, K., Xagawa, K.: Efficient public key encryption based on ideal lattices. In: Matsui, M. (ed.) ASIACRYPT 2009. LNCS, vol. 5912, pp. 617–635. Springer, Heidelberg (2009). https://doi.org/10.1007/978-3-642-10366-7_36

Accelerating HE Operations from Key Decomposition Technique

Miran Kim[1], Dongwon Lee[2], Jinyeong Seo[2], and Yongsoo Song[2($\boxtimes$)]

[1] Department of Mathematics and Research Institute for Convergence
of Basic Science and Hanyang Institute of Bioscience and Biotechnology,
Hanyang University, Seoul, Republic of Korea
`miran@hanyang.ac.kr`
[2] Seoul National University, Seoul, Republic of Korea
`{dongwonlee95,jinyeong.seo,y.song}@snu.ac.kr`

Abstract. Lattice-based homomorphic encryption (HE) schemes are based on the noisy encryption technique, where plaintexts are masked with some random noise for security. Recent advanced HE schemes rely on a decomposition technique to manage the growth of noise, which involves a conversion of a ciphertext entry into a short vector followed by multiplication with an evaluation key. Prior to this work, the decomposition procedure turns out to be the most time-consuming part, as it requires discrete Fourier transforms (DFTs) over the base ring for efficient polynomial arithmetic. In this paper, an expensive decomposition operation over a large modulus is replaced with relatively cheap operations over a ring of integers with a small bound. Notably, the cost of DFTs is reduced from quadratic to linear with the level of a ciphertext without any extra noise growth. We demonstrate the implication of our approach by applying it to the key-switching procedure. Our experiments show that the new key-switching method achieves a speedup of 1.2–2.3 or 2.1–3.3 times over the previous method, when the dimension of a base ring is 2^{15} or 2^{16}, respectively.

Keywords: Homomorphic Encryption · Gadget Decomposition · External Product

1 Introduction

Homomorphic Encryption (HE) is a cryptosystem that allows us to compute on encrypted data without decrypting them. Since Gentry's pioneering work [17], a number of HE schemes have been proposed based on lattice cryptography. In particular, the current best-performing HE schemes rely on the hardness of the Learning with Errors (LWE) problem or its ring variant (RLWE) [28,29], which enables practically usable implementations using algebraic properties.

In (R)LWE-based HE schemes, a small noise is introduced when generating a public key or encrypting a plaintext to ensure security. This noise grows with homomorphic computation, so ciphertexts natively contain some errors which

© International Association for Cryptologic Research 2023
H. Handschuh and A. Lysyanskaya (Eds.): CRYPTO 2023, LNCS 14084, pp. 70–92, 2023.
https://doi.org/10.1007/978-3-031-38551-3_3

should be kept small enough for correct decryption. To reduce the noise growth
derived from nonlinear HE operations, recent advanced HE schemes such as
BGV [4], B/FV [3,16], GSW [19], FHEW/TFHE [12,14] and CKKS [9] commonly use a decomposition technique that transforms a ciphertext component
into a vector of small entries before multiplying it to a public (evaluation) key.
Such a combined operation of decomposition and multiplication (which will be
referred to as the *external product* in this paper) has been a core building block
of HE constructions.

Gentry et al. [18] proposed several optimization techniques, many of which
are still used extensively in HE implementations. For example, they introduced
polynomial representation methods based on a Residue Number System (RNS)
to support efficient polynomial arithmetic over a multi-precision modulus. Since
then, Bajard et al. [1] and the subsequent studies [8,20] presented "full RNS"
based constructions of B/FV and CKKS where all computations including gadget decomposition can be performed in an RNS representation. It enables a
significant enhancement in performance, and most state-of-the-art HE libraries
adopt RNS-friendly HE algorithms for efficiency.

More recently, much progress has been made towards improving the efficiency of bootstrapping technique [2,5,7,26,27] and investigating HE-compatible
approximations of non-polynomial functions [10,11]. But unfortunately, there
has been no remarkable theoretical advance in fundamental HE algorithms in
the past few years. Instead, recent studies and projects such as the Data Protection in Virtual Environments (DPRIVE) program [13] are aiming at optimizing implementations, for example, parallelization using GPU [23] and hardware
accelerator [25,30,31].

Our Contribution. Let $R = \mathbb{Z}[X]/(X^N + 1)$ be a ring of integers for a power-
of-two integer N and $R_Q = \mathbb{Z}_Q[X]/(X^N + 1)$ be its residue ring modulo an
integer Q. The external product is a dyadic operation that takes as its input a
polynomial $a \in R_Q$ and a vector $\mathbf{u} = (u_i)_{0 \le i < d} \in R_Q^d$.[1] More precisely, it first
transforms the input a into its *gadget decomposition*, say $(b_i)_{0 \le i < d}$, which is a
vector of small elements of R such that $a = \sum_i b_i \cdot g_i \pmod{Q}$ where $(g_i)_{0 \le i < d}$
is a fixed gadget basis over R_Q. And then, it returns the linear combination
$\sum_i b_i \cdot u_i \in R_Q$ of u_i's with coefficients b_i.

Our motivation stems from the observation that the previous external product method involves a pre-processing procedure before multiplications between
elements of R and R_Q. To be specific, the elements b_i's are first converted to
integers modulo Q (denoted $[b_i]_Q$), so that the products $b_i \cdot u_i = [b_i]_Q \cdot u_i$ can be
performed using modular multiplications over the modulus Q. As a result, the
performance of the external product mainly depends on the conversion process
$b_i \mapsto [b_i]_Q$, which is followed by discrete Fourier transforms (DFTs) over the ring
R_Q for efficient polynomial arithmetic. Note that these operations are performed
over the multi-precision modulus Q, so the complexity of the external product
is mainly dependent on the precision.

---

[1] Here we assume for simplicity that two inputs have the same modulus, but a more
general case will be discussed later.

In this paper, we present a new method to compute the external product more efficiently. A distinguishing feature of our approach is that $\mathbf{u} = (u_i)_{0 \leq i < d}$ is represented in a decomposed form, say $(v_{i,j})_{0 \leq i,j < d}$, when it is given as an input to our algorithm. That is, we have $u_i = \sum_j v_{i,j} \cdot \tilde{g}_j \pmod{Q}$ where $(\tilde{g}_j)_{0 \leq j < d}$ is another fixed gadget basis over R_Q. We observe that the external product between a and $\mathbf{u}$ can be expressed as a linear combination of the gadget basis:

$$\sum_{0 \leq j < d} \left(\sum_{0 \leq i < d} b_i \cdot v_{i,j} \right) \cdot \tilde{g}_j.$$

Hence, our algorithm mainly aims to compute $\sum_i b_i \cdot v_{i,j} \in R$ for all j, which only requires arithmetic operations between small elements of R without any modular reduction. We also point out that $\sum_i b_i \cdot v_{i,j}$ has an upper bound determined by the gadget decomposition and it is significantly smaller than the modulus Q. Therefore, this process can be implemented using DFTs on the element b_i over the polynomial ring with small coefficients rather than R_Q, and therefore the cost of DFTs is independent of the modulus Q. Notably, it is reduced from $O(\ell^2)$ to $O(\ell)$, where ℓ denotes the level of the input polynomial. As a result, the new external product method shows a significant speedup over the previous method.

Our algorithm has a wide range of applications since the external product is widely used in homomorphic operations such as the key-switching technique. For example, the external product between a ciphertext entry and an evaluation key (a gadget encryption of an old key under a new key) can be used to generate a new ciphertext that encrypts (approximately) the same plaintext under the new key. On the other hand, it is worth noting that the proposed method is to compute the same formula in a different way from the previous method, so it does not bring any extra noise growth during the computation. Furthermore, our method offers another advantage in flexibility such that it is compatible with commonly used HE techniques such as hoisting [21] and lazy key-switching [24].

Finally, we implement our external product algorithm and demonstrate its effectiveness through concrete performance. Our experimental results show that the key-switching method based on the new external product method achieves a speedup of 1.2–2.3 and 2.1–3.3 times over the previous method when the dimension of a base ring is 2^{15} and 2^{16}, respectively. For example, with the ring dimension $N = 2^{16}$, the previous key-switching and our key-switching take about 2.7 s and 0.8 s, respectively.

2   Preliminaries

Notations. Let N be a power of two and Q be an integer. We denote by $K = \mathbb{Q}[X]/(X^N + 1)$ the $(2N)$-th cyclotomic field, $R = \mathbb{Z}[X]/(X^N + 1)$ the ring of integers of K, and $R_Q = \mathbb{Z}_Q[X]/(X^N + 1)$ the residue ring of R modulo Q. We identify an element $a = \sum_{0 \leq i < N} a_i \cdot X^i \in R_Q$ with the vector of its coefficients $(a_0, \ldots, a_{N-1}) \in \mathbb{Z}_Q^N$. We use $\mathbb{Z} \cap (-Q/2, Q/2]$ as a representative of $\mathbb{Z}_Q$ for an integer q, and denote by $[a]_Q$ the reduction of an integer a modulo Q. For $a \in R$, we define $\|a\|_\infty$ as the ℓ_∞-norm of its coefficient vector.

For a real number r, $\lfloor r \rceil$ denotes the nearest integer to r, rounding upwards in case of a tie. For a finite set S, we use $x \leftarrow S$ to denote the sampling x according to the uniform distribution over S. For $\sigma > 0$, we denote by D_σ a distribution over R sampling N coefficients independently from the discrete Gaussian distribution of variance σ^2.

2.1 Ring Learning with Errors

Let χ be a distribution over R and $\sigma > 0$ a real. The ring learning with errors (RLWE) assumption with respect to the parameter (N, Q, χ, σ) is that given polynomially many samples of either (a, b) or $(a, as + e)$, where $a, b \leftarrow R_Q$, $s \leftarrow \chi$, $e \leftarrow D_\sigma$, it is computationally hard to distinguish which is the case. The lattice-based HE schemes such as B/FV [3,16] and CKKS [9] rely on the security on the RLWE assumption.

2.2 Gadget Decomposition and External Product

We give an overview of 'gadget toolkit' that is commonly used in lattice-based HE cryptosystems for noise reduction.

Definition 1 (Gadget Decomposition). *For a modulus Q, a function $h :$ $R_Q \rightarrow R^d$ is called a gadget decomposition if there exists a fixed vector $\mathbf{g} = (g_0, g_1, \ldots, g_{d-1}) \in R_Q^d$ and a real $B > 0$ such that the following holds for any $a \in R_Q$ and its decomposition $\mathbf{b} = (b_0, b_1, \ldots, b_{d-1}) \leftarrow h(a)$:*

$$\sum_{0 \leq i < d} b_i \cdot g_i = a \pmod{Q} \qquad and \qquad \|\mathbf{b}\|_\infty \leq B.$$

We call $\mathbf{g}$ a *gadget vector* and $B > 0$ a *bound* of h.

Definition 2 (External Product). *Let $\tilde{Q} = P \cdot Q$. The external product is a binary operation $\boxdot : R_Q \times R_{\tilde{Q}}^d \rightarrow R_Q$ defined as follows: for $a \in R_Q$ and $\mathbf{u} = (u_0, \ldots, u_{d-1}) \in R_{\tilde{Q}}^d$, compute $\mathbf{b} = (b_0, \ldots, b_{d-1}) \leftarrow h(a)$ and $\tilde{c} = \sum_{0 \leq i < d} b_i \cdot u_i$ $\pmod{\tilde{Q}}$, and return $c = \lfloor \frac{1}{P} \cdot \tilde{c} \rceil \pmod{Q}$.*

By a slight abuse of notation, we write $a \boxdot \mathbf{U} = (a \boxdot \mathbf{u}_0, a \boxdot \mathbf{u}_1) \in R_Q^2$ for any $a \in R_Q$ and $\mathbf{U} = [\mathbf{u}_0 | \mathbf{u}_1] \in R_{\tilde{Q}}^{d \times 2}$.

2.3 Homomorphic Encryption and Key-Switching

Homomorphic encryption is a cryptosystem that allows computation over encrypted data without decrypting them. We provide a description of the CKKS scheme [9] as an instantiation to explain how gadget decomposition and external product techniques are used in HE systems.

- $\texttt{CKKS.Setup}(1^\lambda)$: For given a security paramter λ, choose an RLWE dimension N, a ciphertext modulus Q, a special modulus P, a key distribution χ, and an error parameter $\sigma > 0$. Output the public parameter $\mathsf{pp} = (N, Q, P, \chi, \sigma)$. We write $\tilde{Q} = P \cdot Q$.
- $\texttt{CKKS.KeyGen}(\mathsf{pp})$: Given a public parameter pp, generate a secret key, a public key, a relinearization key, and an automorphism key as follows.
  - Sample $s \leftarrow \chi$ and return the secret key $\mathsf{sk} \leftarrow s$.
  - Sample $p_1 \leftarrow R_{\tilde{Q}}$ and $e_p \leftarrow D_\sigma$, and return the public key $\mathsf{pk} \leftarrow \mathbf{p} = (p_0, p_1) \in R_{\tilde{Q}}^2$ where $p_0 = -p_1 s + e_p \pmod{\tilde{Q}}$.
  - Sample $\mathbf{r}_1 \leftarrow R_{\tilde{Q}}^d$ and $\mathbf{e}_r \leftarrow D_\sigma^d$. Generate the relinearization key as $\mathsf{rlk} \leftarrow \mathbf{R} = [\mathbf{r}_0 | \mathbf{r}_1] \in R_{\tilde{Q}}^{d \times 2}$ where $\mathbf{r}_0 = -s \cdot \mathbf{r}_1 + P s^2 \cdot \mathbf{g} + \mathbf{e}_r \pmod{\tilde{Q}}$.
  - For an automorphism ϕ over K, sample $\mathbf{t}_1 \leftarrow R_{\tilde{Q}}^d$ and $\mathbf{e}_t \leftarrow D_\sigma^d$. Generate the automorphism key as $\mathsf{atk} \leftarrow \mathbf{T} = [\mathbf{t}_0 | \mathbf{t}_1] \in R_{\tilde{Q}}^{d \times 2}$ where $\mathbf{t}_0 = -s \cdot \mathbf{t}_1 + P \phi(s) \cdot \mathbf{g} + \mathbf{e}_t \pmod{\tilde{Q}}$.
- $\texttt{CKKS.Enc}(\mathsf{pk}; \mu)$: Given a public key $\mathsf{pk} = \mathbf{p}$ and a plaintext $\mu \in R^2$, output a ciphertext $\mathsf{ct} = \left\lfloor \frac{1}{P} \cdot (v \cdot \mathbf{p} + \mathbf{e}) \right\rceil + (\mu, 0) \pmod{Q}$ where $v \leftarrow \chi$ and $\mathbf{e} \leftarrow D_\sigma^2$.
- $\texttt{CKKS.Dec}(s; \mathsf{ct})$: Given a ciphertext $\mathsf{ct} = (c_0, c_1) \in R_Q^2$ and a secret key $s \in R$, output the plaintext $\mu = c_0 + s \cdot c_1 \pmod{Q}$.
- $\texttt{CKKS.Add}(\mathsf{ct}, \mathsf{ct}')$: Given two ciphertexts $\mathsf{ct}, \mathsf{ct}' \in R_Q^2$, output the ciphertext $\mathsf{ct}_{add} = \mathsf{ct} + \mathsf{ct}' \in R_Q^2$.
- $\texttt{CKKS.Mult}(\mathsf{rlk}; \mathsf{ct}, \mathsf{ct}')$: Given two ciphertexts $\mathsf{ct} = (c_0, c_1)$, $\mathsf{ct}' = (c_0', c_1') \in R_Q^2$ and a relinearization key $\mathsf{rlk} = \mathbf{R}$, let $d_0 = c_0 c_0' \pmod{Q}$, $d_1 = (c_0 c_1' + c_0' c_1) \pmod{Q}$, and $d_2 = c_1 c_1' \pmod{Q}$. Output a ciphertext $\mathsf{ct}_{mul} = (d_0, d_1) + d_2 \boxdot \mathbf{R} \in R_Q^2$.
- $\texttt{CKKS.Auto}(\mathsf{atk}, \phi; \mathsf{ct})$: Given a ciphertext $\mathsf{ct} = (c_0, c_1) \in R_Q^2$, an automorphism key $\mathsf{atk} = \mathbf{U}$, and an automorphism ϕ on R, output a ciphertext $\mathsf{ct}_{aut} = (\phi(c_0), 0) + \phi(c_1) \boxdot \mathbf{U} \in R_Q^2$.

A *gadget encryption* of a plaintext $\mu \in R$ under a secret key s is defined as $\mathbf{U} = [\mathbf{u}_0 | \mathbf{u}_1] \in R_{\tilde{Q}}^{d \times 2}$ where $\mathbf{u}_1 \leftarrow R_{\tilde{Q}}^d$, $\mathbf{e} \leftarrow D_\sigma^d$, and $\mathbf{u}_0 = -s \cdot \mathbf{u}_1 + P \mu \cdot \mathbf{g} + \mathbf{e} \pmod{\tilde{Q}}$. For example, the relinearization and automorphism keys are gadget encryptions of s^2 and $\phi(s)$. The external product can be used for multiplication of an arbitrary element in R_Q and a gadget encryption: for any $a \in R_Q$ and a gadget encryption $\mathbf{U} = [\mathbf{u}_0 | \mathbf{u}_1]$ of a plaintext $\mu \in R$ under a secret s, their external product $(c_0, c_1) \leftarrow a \boxdot \mathbf{U}$ satisfies that

$$c_0 + c_1 \cdot s \approx a \boxdot (\mathbf{u}_0 + s \cdot \mathbf{u}_1) \approx a \boxdot (P\mu \cdot \mathbf{g}) = a \cdot \mu \pmod{Q}.$$

---

[2] The original CKKS scheme enables to encode a vector of complex numbers to a plaintext in R. For the sake of brevity, we assume that an input of the encryption function is given as a plaintext polynomial.

The *key-switching* procedure is a major use-case of the external product. For given a ciphertext component a which is decryptable by a secret s', we can perform the external product with a gadget encryption $\mathbf{U}$ of s' under s (which is often referred as a key-switching key from s' to s) to transform it into an RLWE ciphertext under s while preserving the underlying plaintext. In other words, the resulting ciphertext $(c_0, c_1) \leftarrow a \boxdot \mathbf{U}$ satisfies that $c_0 + c_1 \cdot s \approx a \cdot s' \pmod{Q}$. For example, homomorphic multiplication and automorphism algorithms of CKKS involve the key-switching procedures from s^2 and $\phi(s)$ to s, respectively.

2.4 Polynomial Representations

The *Residue Number System* (RNS) enables representing a large integer as a tuple of small integers. Let $Q = q_0 \cdots q_{\ell-1}$ where q_k's are pairwise coprime integers. Then, we get an isomorphism $R_Q \rightarrow R_{q_0} \times \cdots \times R_{q_{\ell-1}}$, $a \mapsto ([a]_{q_0}, \ldots, [a]_{q_{\ell-1}})$ from the Chinese remainder theorem. The image $([a]_{q_0}, \ldots, [a]_{q_{\ell-1}})$ of an element $a \in R_Q$ is called the RNS representation of a. The main advantage of the RNS representation is that one can instantiate R_Q with smaller rings R_{q_k}'s. There have been several studies [1,8,20] to exploit the RNS representation for optimization of HE schemes by avoiding multi-precision arithmetic of a base ring.

We also define a discrete Fourier transformation over $\mathbb{Z}_{q_k}$, called *Number Theoretic Transform (NTT)*, for efficient polynomial arithmetic over R_{q_k}. Suppose that q_k is a prime integer such that $q_k = 1 \pmod{2N}$. Then, there exists a primitive $(2N)$-th root of unity ξ_k modulo q_k. It is easy to show that

$$a(X) \mapsto \big(a(\xi_k^i)\big)_{i \in \mathbb{Z}_{2N}^{\times}}$$

is an isomorphism from R_{q_k} to $\mathbb{Z}_{q_k}^N$. We call $\big(a(\xi_k^i)\big)_{i \in \mathbb{Z}_{2N}^{\times}}$ the NTT representation of $a \in R_{q_k}$. More generally, when Q is a product of distinct primes $q_0, \ldots, q_{\ell-1}$ such that $q_k = 1 \pmod{2N}$, we can combine NTTs over different moduli q_k to convert the RNS representation of $a \in R_Q$ between its coefficient and NTT forms. We will say that a ciphertext is in the coefficient (or NTT) form if its components are represented in the coefficient (or NTT, respectively) form.

3 A New External Product Method

Let $h : R_Q \rightarrow R^d$ be a gadget decomposition corresponding to a gadget vector $\mathbf{g} \in R_Q^d$. Recall that an external product of $a \in R_Q$ and $\mathbf{u} = (u_i)_{0 \le i < d} \in R_{\tilde{Q}}^d$ involves the computation of the gadget decomposition $\mathbf{b} = (b_i)_{0 \le i < d}$ of a, followed by the linear combination of $u_0, \ldots, u_{d-1} \in R_{\tilde{Q}}$ with coefficients $b_0, \ldots, b_{d-1} \in R$. Note that this operation is well-defined since $R_{\tilde{Q}}$ is an R-module.

In previous studies [8,20], the linear combination $\sum_i b_i \cdot u_i$ is obtained by converting $\mathbf{b} \in R^d$ into $[\mathbf{b}]_{\tilde{Q}} \in R_{\tilde{Q}}^d$ and computing the inner product between

$[\mathbf{b}]_{\tilde{Q}}$ and $\mathbf{u}$ over $R_{\tilde{Q}}$. The first step is particularly expensive since each conversion $b_i \mapsto [b_i]_{\tilde{Q}}$ involves NTT operations modulo the prime factors of $\tilde{Q}$.

In this section, we present a new approach to perform the external product operation more efficiently. In a nutshell, our approach employs gadget decomposition to represent the entries u_i as small elements in the ring of integers R. It enables us to express the external product using low-precision arithmetic over R. As a result, we can achieve performance improvements since the NTT operations over $R_{\tilde{Q}}$ are replaced with DFTs over R where the precision is determined by the (small) bounds of gadget decompositions rather than the (large) modulus $\tilde{Q}$.

3.1   Main Idea

Intuitively, the gadget decomposition can be understood as an operation to represent an arbitrary element of a residue ring as a linear combination of a fixed basis with small coefficients. Meanwhile, the external product involves a linear combination of arbitrary elements $u_i \in R_{\tilde{Q}}$ with small coefficients $b_i \in R$. The main observation is that, if u_i's are given as linear combinations with small coefficients, say $v_{i,j}$, then $\sum_i b_i \cdot u_i$ can be also expressed as a linear combination of the same basis where its coefficients can be obtained from $v_{i,j}$ and b_i.

Specifically, we introduce another gadget decomposition $\tilde{\mathbf{g}} = (\tilde{g}_0, \ldots, \tilde{g}_{\tilde{d}-1}) \in R_{\tilde{Q}}^{\tilde{d}}$ over $R_{\tilde{Q}}$ with a gadget vector $\tilde{h} : R_{\tilde{Q}} \to R^{\tilde{d}}$. For given $\mathbf{u} = (u_i)_{0 \le i < d} \in R_{\tilde{Q}}^d$, we decompose its entries via $\tilde{h}$ and get $\tilde{h}(u_i) = (v_{i,0}, \ldots, v_{i,\tilde{d}-1}) \in R^{\tilde{d}}$ for $0 \le i < d$. We write $\mathbf{V} := [v_{i,j}]_{0 \le i < d, 0 \le j < \tilde{d}}$ and denote its j-th column vector by $\mathbf{v}_j$ for $0 \le j < \tilde{d}$. Then, $\mathbf{V} = [\mathbf{v}_0 | \ldots | \mathbf{v}_{\tilde{d}-1}] \in R^{d \times \tilde{d}}$ can be viewed as gadget decomposition of $\mathbf{u}$ satisfying $\mathbf{u} = \sum_{0 \le j < \tilde{d}} \mathbf{v}_j \cdot \tilde{g}_j \pmod{\tilde{Q}}$. We note that $\mathbf{u}$ is usually a public material (such as a key-switching key generated by the key owner) in HE construction, so its gadget decomposition $\mathbf{V}$ can be pre-computed and reused during homomorphic evaluation.

Suppose that we are given $a \in R_Q$ and wish to compute the external product $a \boxdot \mathbf{u}$. Then, given the decomposition $\mathbf{b} = (b_i)_{0 \le i < d} \leftarrow h(a)$, the linear combination $\sum_i b_i \cdot u_i$ can be expressed using the gadget decomposition $\mathbf{V}$ of $\mathbf{u}$ as follows:

$$
\sum_{0 \le i < d} b_i \cdot u_i = \begin{bmatrix} b_0 \ldots b_{d-1} \end{bmatrix} \cdot \begin{bmatrix} u_0 \\ \vdots \\ u_{d-1} \end{bmatrix}
$$

$$
= \begin{bmatrix} b_0 \ldots b_{d-1} \end{bmatrix} \cdot \begin{bmatrix} v_{0,0} & \cdots & v_{0,\tilde{d}-1} \\ \vdots & \ddots & \vdots \\ v_{d-1,0} & \cdots & v_{d-1,\tilde{d}-1} \end{bmatrix} \begin{bmatrix} \tilde{g}_0 \\ \vdots \\ \tilde{g}_{\tilde{d}-1} \end{bmatrix}
$$

$$
= (\mathbf{b}^\top \cdot \mathbf{V}) \cdot \tilde{\mathbf{g}} = \sum_{0 \le j < \tilde{d}} \langle \mathbf{b}, \mathbf{v}_j \rangle \cdot \tilde{g}_j \pmod{\tilde{Q}}. \tag{1}
$$

Note that $\mathbf{b}$ and $\mathbf{v}_0, \ldots, \mathbf{v}_{\tilde{d}-1}$ are vectors in R^d, so the inner products $\langle \mathbf{b}, \mathbf{v}_j \rangle$ are defined over the ring R. As a result, $\sum_i b_i \cdot u_i$ is a linear combination of $\tilde{g}_0, \ldots, \tilde{g}_{\tilde{d}-1}$ with coefficients $\langle \mathbf{b}, \mathbf{v}_0 \rangle, \ldots, \langle \mathbf{b}, \mathbf{v}_{\tilde{d}-1} \rangle$.

Finally, we need to carry out multiplications between $\langle \mathbf{b}, \mathbf{v}_j \rangle$ and $\tilde{g}_j$ over $R_{\tilde{Q}}$ for $0 \leq j < \tilde{d}$ to complete the computation. Fortunately, this step can be very cheap when the gadget decomposition $\tilde{h}$ is chosen properly (which will be explained later in the next section). We also point out that the proposed method is purely an algorithmic optimization technique which outputs exactly the same result as before, thereby bringing no extra noise growth.

3.2 Representation and Arithmetic of Integral Polynomials

As discussed above, our external product method involves arithmetic operations over the ring R. Hence, it is necessary to estimate an upper bound of a given computational task to guarantee the correctness and efficiency of its implementation.

Let B and $\tilde{B}$ be upper bounds of two gadget decompositions h and $\tilde{h}$, respectively. In the new external product method, the inner products $\langle \mathbf{b}, \mathbf{v}_j \rangle$ are computed over the ring R, and these are bounded by

$$\|\langle \mathbf{b}, \mathbf{v}_j \rangle\|_\infty \leq dN \cdot \|\mathbf{b}\|_\infty \cdot \|\mathbf{v}_j\|_\infty \leq dN \cdot B\tilde{B}.$$

On the other hand, an element of R can be represented as the vector of its coefficients in $\mathbb{Z}^N$, but we use the DFT algorithm and its inverse over R to convert the coefficient vector into the DFT form and vice versa for efficient arithmetic operations. More specifically, we instantiate the polynomial ring R as $R_{B'}$ for some integer $B' > 2dN \cdot B\tilde{B}$ so that the reduction modulo B' does not occur during the computation of $\langle \mathbf{b}, \mathbf{v}_j \rangle \in R$ over $R_{B'}$. In our implementation, we set $B' = p_0 p_1 \ldots p_{r'-1}$ as a product of distinct word-size primes such that $p_j = 1 \pmod{2N}$ for a possibly minimal integer r', and use the isomorphism $R_{B'} \cong \prod_{0 \leq j < r'} R_{p_j}$ to represent the elements in $R_{B'}$ in the RNS form with moduli $p_0, \ldots, p_{r'-1}$. Then, the DFT over $R_{B'}$ can be efficiently implemented via small NTTs over $R_{p_0}, \ldots, R_{p_{r'-1}}$. Since $B' \approx 2dN \cdot B\tilde{B}$ is significantly smaller than $\tilde{Q}$, the unit complexity of the DFT algorithm over $R_{B'}$ in our external product method is much cheaper than that of the previous NTT operations over $R_{\tilde{Q}}$. A more detailed performance analysis will be provided in the next section.

4 Application to Key Switching

The external product operation is widely used in HE-based constructions such as the GSW scheme [19] and multi-key HE scheme [6]. In particular, as noted in Sect. 2.3, the key-switching operation in HE cryptosystems is a major application of the external product operation. More specifically, the key switching mechanism is extensively used in nonlinear homomorphic operations such as multiplication or automorphism; however, it is the main bottleneck affecting the performance of such homomorphic operations. For instance, the key-switching spends 86–93% of its time performing homomorphic multiplication (the detailed timing results will be provided later in Sect. 5.2). Therefore, improving the key-switching operation can lead to a substantial efficiency enhancement of HE schemes.

In the following, we will focus on the key-switching operation based on our new external product method. We first introduce a practical gadget decomposition that is compatible with the proposed key-switching method and explain how it can lead to performance improvements. We also provide a complexity analysis of the previous and our key-switching methods. We will count the number of unit NTT operations and unit Hadamard operations where NTT operation on R_q and Hadamard product on $\mathbb{Z}_q^N$ are set as unit NTT operation and unit Hadamard product for a word-sized prime integer q, respectively.

4.1 RNS-Based Gadget Decomposition

Since Gentry et al. [18] presented an RNS-based representation of polynomials, it has been extensively used in HE implementations to optimize arithmetic operations of a base polynomial ring. Moreover, recent studies [1,8,20,22] showed that it enables to construct HE schemes in a full-RNS manner where all computations are performed in RNS representation without any high-precision arithmetic. We provide a brief overview of RNS-friendly gadget decomposition methods presented in [22].

Throughout this section, let $Q = q_0 \cdots q_{\ell-1}$ for a set of distinct word-sized primes $\mathcal{B} = \{q_0, \ldots, q_{\ell-1}\}$. We partition this RNS base $\mathcal{B}$ into $\mathcal{B}_j = \{q_k : k \in I_j\}$ for $0 \leq j < d$ where $I_j \subseteq I = \{0, 1, \ldots, \ell - 1\}$ denotes the j-th index set. Note that the *digits* $D_j = \prod_{k \in I_j} q_k$ are pairwise coprime integers such that $Q = D_0 \ldots D_{d-1}$. We call $|I_j|$ the *length* of a digit D_j.

We define the RNS-based *digit decomposition* $h : R_Q \to R^d$ as $a \mapsto \mathbf{b} = (b_0, \ldots, b_{d-1})$ for $b_j = [a]_{D_j}$. We also write $\hat{D}_j = Q/D_j$ for $0 \leq j < d$ and let $\mathbf{g} = (g_0, \ldots, g_{d-1}) \in R_Q^d$ for $g_j = [\hat{D}_j^{-1}]_{D_j} \cdot \hat{D}_j$. Then, it is easy to show that h is a gadget decomposition corresponding to $\mathbf{g}$ with a bound $\|\mathbf{b}\|_\infty \leq B = \frac{1}{2} \max_{0 \leq j < d} \{D_j\}$ from the property that $g_j = 1 \pmod{D_j}$ and $g_j = 0 \pmod{D_{j'}}$ for $j' \neq j$.

The digit decomposition can be computed in an RNS representation using the *base conversion* algorithm [1,20], which can extend the RNS basis of a polynomial. Let $\hat{q}_k = D_j/q_k$ and $q_k^* = [\hat{q}_k^{-1}]_{\hat{q}_k}$ for $0 \leq j < d$ and $k \in I_j$. Suppose that we are given the RNS representation $(a_k = [a]_{q_k})_{0 \leq k < \ell}$ of an element $a \in R_Q$. Then, we get $a = \sum_{k \in I_j} [a_k \cdot q_k^*]_{q_k} \cdot \hat{q}_k \pmod{D_j}$ and obtain the following equations over R:

$$b_j = \sum_{k \in I_j} [a_k \cdot q_k^*]_{q_k} \cdot \hat{q}_k - D_j \cdot z_j, \tag{2}$$

where

$$z_j = \left\lfloor \frac{1}{D_j} \cdot \left(\sum_{k \in I_j} [a_k \cdot q_k^*]_{q_k} \cdot \hat{q}_k \right) \right\rceil = \left\lfloor \sum_{k \in I_j} \frac{[a_k \cdot q_k^*]_{q_k}}{q_k} \right\rceil. \tag{3}$$

Based on these formulae, we can represent the digit decomposition in a full-RNS manner as follows. Suppose that we are given $a_k = [a]_{q_k}$ for $k \in I_j$ and wish to compute $b_j = [a]_{D_j}$ modulo Q' for $0 \le j < d$. Then, for each prime factor q' of Q', we have

$$b_j = \left(\sum_{k \in I_j} [a_k \cdot q_k^*]_{q_k} \cdot [\hat{q}_k]_{q'} \right) - [D_j]_{q'} \cdot z_j \pmod{q'}, \tag{4}$$

where the constants such as $[\hat{q}_k]_{q'}$ and $[D_j]_{q'}$ are pre-computable independently from the input a. Hence, the RNS representation of b_j with respect to the modulus Q' is obtained by computing Eq. (4) for all prime factors q' of Q'.

4.2 Previous Key-Switching Method

We first review the concrete details of the previous key-switching method. We denote by $Q = q_0 \cdots q_{\ell-1}$ and $P = q_\ell \cdots q_{\tilde{\ell}-1}$ the ciphertext modulus and special modulus, respectively, for distinct word-sized primes $q_0, \ldots, q_{\tilde{\ell}-1}$, and let $\tilde{Q} = P \cdot Q = q_0 \cdots q_{\tilde{\ell}-1}$. We choose a partition of the RNS base $\mathcal{B} = \{q_0, \ldots, q_{\ell-1}\}$ and set digits D_j as in Sect. 4.1 so that the digit decomposition $h : R_Q \to R^d$ over R_Q is defined as $h : a \mapsto \mathbf{b} = (b_0, \ldots, b_{d-1})$ for $b_j = [a]_{D_j}$. We denote by $r_j = |I_j|$ the length of a digit D_j. We assume that all computations are performed in RNS representation even if not mentioned explicitly.

Previous key-switching operation

Input: A polynomial $a \in R_Q$ and a key-switching key $\mathbf{U} = [\mathbf{u}_0|\mathbf{u}_1] \in R_{\tilde{Q}}^{d \times 2}$.

Step 1 (Decomposition): Generate the RNS representation of $\mathbf{b} = (b_0, \ldots, b_{d-1}) \leftarrow h(a)$ modulo $\tilde{Q}$. Each $[b_j]_{\tilde{Q}}$ can be computed using Eq. (4) for all prime factors $q_0, \ldots, q_{\tilde{\ell}-1}$ of $\tilde{Q}$.

Step 2 (Inner product): Compute $\tilde{c}_0 = \langle \mathbf{b}, \mathbf{u}_0 \rangle \pmod{\tilde{Q}}$ and $\tilde{c}_1 = \langle \mathbf{b}, \mathbf{u}_1 \rangle \pmod{\tilde{Q}}$

Step 3 (Mod reduction): Compute $c_0' = \lfloor \frac{1}{P} \tilde{c}_0 \rceil \pmod{Q}$ and $c_1' = \lfloor \frac{1}{P} \tilde{c}_1 \rceil \pmod{Q}$.

Output: An RLWE ciphertext $(c_0', c_1') \in R_Q^2$.

The previous key-switching procedure consists of three steps – gadget decomposition, inner product, and modulus reduction. The first step aims to compute the gadget decomposition $h(a)$, but more precisely, its RNS representation over the modulus $\tilde{Q} = q_0 \cdots q_{\tilde{\ell}-1}$. Suppose that $a \in R_Q$ is given in the coefficient form. Then, we compute $b_j = [a]_{D_j}$ using Eqs. (3) and (4) for all prime factors $q' = q_0, q_1, \ldots, q_{\tilde{\ell}-1}$, and transform it into the NTT form over $R_{\tilde{Q}}$ for an efficient multiplication in the next step. In the second step, we perform two inner products $\tilde{c}_i = \langle \mathbf{b}, \mathbf{u}_i \rangle \pmod{\tilde{Q}}$ for $i = 0, 1$. We assume that the key-switching key $\mathbf{U} = [\mathbf{u}_0|\mathbf{u}_1] \in R_{\tilde{Q}}^{d \times 2}$ is given in the NTT form over $R_{\tilde{Q}}$ for efficiency. Then, each inner product between $\mathbf{b}$ and $\mathbf{u}_i$ is simply written as N inner products over $\mathbb{Z}_{\tilde{Q}}^d \cong \prod_{0 \le k < \tilde{\ell}} \mathbb{Z}_{q_k}^d$ since both are given in their NTT forms. At the end of this step, $\tilde{c}_0$ and $\tilde{c}_1$ are converted into the coefficient form for the next step. Finally, we perform the modulus reduction operation to scale the ciphertexts back down to Q, i.e., compute $c_i' = \lfloor \tilde{c}_i/P \rceil = (\tilde{c}_i - [\tilde{c}_i]_P)/P$ for $i = 0, 1$. This step involves a base conversion to obtain the RNS representation of $[\tilde{c}_i]_P$ modulo Q.

Complexity Analysis. For the sake of brevity, we assume that all the digit lengths r_j are the same and denoted by r, so we get $\ell = dr$. We first count the number of unit NTT operations in the previous key-switching operation. In the first step, we convert the decomposed element $[b_j]_{\tilde{Q}}$ to NTT representation for $0 \le j < d$. This procedure requires $d\tilde{\ell}$ unit NTT operations since the NTT operation over $R_{\tilde{Q}}$ requires $\tilde{\ell}$ unit NTT operations and we repeat this operation for each j. In the second step, it requires $2\tilde{\ell}$ unit NTT operations after performing inner products as the inverse NTT operation over $R_{\tilde{Q}}$ takes $\tilde{\ell}$ unit NTT operations and we repeat this operation for each $\tilde{c}_i$ to get its coefficient form. Therefore, the previous key-switching takes total $(d+2)\tilde{\ell}$ unit NTT operations.

We now count the number of unit Hadamard products. In the first step, the base conversion of $b_j = [a]_{D_j}$ to the modulus $\tilde{Q}$ requires $r_j(\tilde{\ell} - r_j) = r(\tilde{\ell} - r) \le r\tilde{\ell}$ unit Hadamard products, and we repeat this procedure for each $0 \le j < d$. Thus, the required number of unit Hadamard products in Step 1 is bounded by $dr\tilde{\ell} = \ell^2$. On the other hand, when $r = 1$, each D_j is a single prime number, and so the first step does not require any Hadamard products. In the second step, it takes $2d\tilde{\ell}$ unit Hadamard products since the Hadamard product over $R_{\tilde{Q}}$ requires $\tilde{\ell}$ unit Hadamard products and each inner product of $\tilde{c}_i = \langle \mathbf{b}, \mathbf{u}_i \rangle \pmod{\tilde{Q}}$ takes d Hadamard products over $R_{\tilde{Q}}$. To sum up, in the case of $r = 1$, the total number of unit Hadamard products required for the previous key-switching operation is $2d\tilde{\ell}$; otherwise, it is $\ell^2 + 2d\tilde{\ell}$.

We note that the gadget decomposition procedure is dominant in the cost of unit NTT operations. The computational cost of unit Hadamard products at the first step is roughly equivalent to the second step except for the case of $r = 1$. As a result, as noted in Sect. 3, the gadget decomposition step turns out to be the most time-consuming part of the previous key-switching operation.

4.3   Our Key-Switching Method

We now present our new approach based on the new external product operation. Our key-switching procedure is based on a digit decomposition over $R_{\tilde{Q}}$. For the RNS base $\tilde{\mathcal{B}} = \{q_0, \dots, q_{\tilde{\ell}-1}\}$ of the modulus $\tilde{Q}$, we choose a partition $\tilde{I}_0, \dots, \tilde{I}_{\tilde{d}-1}$ of $\{0, 1, \dots, \tilde{\ell}-1\}$ and digits $\tilde{D}_j = \prod_{k \in \tilde{I}_j} q_k$. Then, we can define an RNS-friendly gadget decomposition $\tilde{h} : R_{\tilde{Q}} \to R^{\tilde{d}}$ as $\tilde{h}(u) = (v_0, \dots, v_{\tilde{d}-1})$ for $v_j = [u]_{\tilde{D}_j}$, and its corresponding gadget vector is $\tilde{\mathbf{g}} = (\tilde{g}_0, \dots, \tilde{g}_{\tilde{\ell}-1}) \in R_{\tilde{Q}}^{\tilde{d}}$ such that $\tilde{g}_j = 1 \pmod{\tilde{D}_j}$ and $\tilde{g}_j = 0 \pmod{\tilde{D}_{j'}}$ for $j' \ne j$. We generate a key-switching key

$\mathbf{U} = [\mathbf{u}_0|\mathbf{u}_1] \in R_{\tilde{Q}}^{d \times 2}$ using the gadget encryption algorithm, and publish the decompositions of $\mathbf{u}_0$ and $\mathbf{u}_1$ with respect to $\tilde{h}$.

Similar to the previous method, our key-switching method consists of three steps. In the first step, the coefficient form of $a \in R_Q$ is given as an input. Then we compute the gadget decomposition $\mathbf{b} = h(a)$ and transform it into the DFT form over the ring R. As discussed in Sect. 3.2, since we instantiate R as $R_{B'}$ in our implementation, it suffices to transform the decomposition into the NTT form over $R_{B'}$. We remark that our method enjoys better performance than the previous approach since the decomposition is computed over $R_{B'}$ rather than $R_{\tilde{Q}}$. Therefore, the complexity of this step mainly depends on the upper bounds of the gadget decompositions h and $\tilde{h}$, which are significantly smaller than the modulus $\tilde{Q}$. In the second step, we compute $\tilde{c}_0 = \langle \mathbf{b}, \mathbf{u}_0 \rangle \pmod{\tilde{Q}}$ and $\tilde{c}_1 = \langle \mathbf{b}, \mathbf{u}_1 \rangle \pmod{\tilde{Q}}$ following the procedure below. First, we perform the inner products $\tilde{c}_{0,j} = \langle \mathbf{b}, \mathbf{v}_{0,j} \rangle$ and $\tilde{c}_{1,j} = \langle \mathbf{b}, \mathbf{v}_{1,j} \rangle$ for $0 \le j < \tilde{d}$, and convert them back to the coefficient form. Here, we can assume that $\mathbf{V}_0$ and $\mathbf{V}_1$ are given in the NTT form over $R_{B'}$, so these inner products can be computed efficiently over the NTT space of $R_{B'}$. Finally, it holds that

$$\tilde{c}_i = \langle \mathbf{b}, \mathbf{u}_i \rangle = \sum_{0 \le j < \tilde{d}} \langle \mathbf{b}, \mathbf{v}_{i,j} \rangle \cdot \tilde{g}_j = \sum_{0 \le j < \tilde{d}} \tilde{c}_{i,j} \cdot \tilde{g}_j \pmod{\tilde{Q}}$$

from Eq. (1), which implies that $\tilde{c}_i = \tilde{c}_{i,j} \pmod{\tilde{D}_j}$ for all $0 \le j < \tilde{d}$. Therefore, we have $\tilde{c}_i = \tilde{c}_{i,j} \pmod{q_k}$ for all $0 \le j < \tilde{d}$ and $k \in \tilde{I}_j$ from the property of digit decomposition, and the RNS representation of $\tilde{c}_i$ modulo $\tilde{Q}$ is obtained as $([\tilde{c}_{i,j}]_{q_k})_{0 \le j < \tilde{d}, k \in \tilde{I}_j} \in \prod_{0 \le k < \tilde{\ell}} R_{q_k}$. The last step of our key-switching is the modulus reduction process, which is identical to that of the previous method.

Our key-switching operation

Input: A polynomial $a \in R_Q$ and two decompositions $\mathbf{V}_i = [\mathbf{v}_{i,0}|\mathbf{v}_{i,1}|\dots|\mathbf{v}_{i,\tilde{d}-1}]$ of $\mathbf{u}_i$ for $i = 0, 1$, with respect to $\tilde{h}$ for a key-switching key $\mathbf{U} = [\mathbf{u}_0|\mathbf{u}_1] \in R_{\tilde{Q}}^{d \times 2}$.

Step 1 (Decomposition): Compute the gadget decomposition $\mathbf{b} = (b_0, \dots, b_{d-1}) \leftarrow h(a)$ over R using (2) and (3).

Step 2 (Inner product): Compute $\tilde{c}_{0,j} \leftarrow \langle \mathbf{b}, \mathbf{v}_{0,j} \rangle$ and $\tilde{c}_{1,j} \leftarrow \langle \mathbf{b}, \mathbf{v}_{1,j} \rangle$ over R for $0 \le j < \tilde{d}$. Compute the elements $\tilde{c}_0$ and $\tilde{c}_1$ of $R_{\tilde{Q}}$ such that $\tilde{c}_0 = \tilde{c}_{0,j} \pmod{D_j}$ and $\tilde{c}_1 = \tilde{c}_{1,j} \pmod{D_j}$ for $0 \le j < \tilde{d}$.

Step 3 (Mod reduction): Compute $c'_0 = \lfloor \frac{1}{P} \tilde{c}_0 \rceil \pmod{Q}$ and $c'_1 = \lfloor \frac{1}{P} \tilde{c}_1 \rceil \pmod{Q}$.

Output: An RLWE ciphertext $(c'_0, c'_1) \in R_Q^2$.

Complexity Analysis. We denote by $\tilde{r}_j = |\tilde{I}_j|$ the length of a digit $\tilde{D}_j$, and assume that all the digit lengths $\tilde{r}_j$ are the same and denoted by $\tilde{r}$, so we get

$\tilde{\ell} = \tilde{d}\tilde{r}$. We first count the number of unit NTT operations in our key-switching operation. As noted in Sect. 3.2, we assume that B' is a product of r' distinct word-sized primes. The NTT operation over $R_{B'}$ requires r' unit NTT operations and we repeat this operation for each entry of $\mathbf{b}$ to get its NTT representation, so this step requires dr' unit NTT operations. In the second step, it requires $2\tilde{d}r'$ unit NTT operations after performing inner products since we perform the inverse NTT operation over $R_{B'}$ on $\tilde{c}_{0,j}$ and $\tilde{c}_{1,j}$ to get their coefficient forms. Hence, the total number of unit NTT operations is $(d + 2\tilde{d})r'$.

We now count the number of unit Hadamard products. In the first step, the base conversion of $b_j = [a]_{D_j}$ to the modulus B' requires $r_j r' = rr'$ unit Hadamard products, and we repeat this procedure for each $0 \le j < d$. Thus, this step requires $drr' = \ell r'$ unit Hadamard products. On the other hand, when $r = 1$, it does not require any Hadamard products. In the second step, the Hadamard product over $R_{B'}$ requires r' unit Hadamard products and each inner product of $\tilde{c}_{i,j} = \langle \mathbf{b}, \mathbf{v}_{i,j} \rangle \pmod{B'}$ takes d Hadamard products over $R_{B'}$. We compute $\tilde{c}_{i,j}$ for $i = 0, 1$ and $0 \le j < \tilde{d}$, so it takes $2d\tilde{d}r'$ unit Hadamard products in total. At the end of the second step, the base conversion of $[\tilde{c}_{i,j}]_{B'}$ to the modulus q_k requires r' unit Hadamard products for each $0 \le i < 2$, $0 \le j < \tilde{d}$, $0 \le k \le \tilde{I}_j$. It follows from the assumption of digit lengths of $\tilde{I}_j$ that this procedure requires $2\tilde{d}\tilde{r}r' = 2\tilde{\ell}r'$ to get the RNS representation of $\tilde{c}_i$ modulo $\tilde{Q}$. To sum up, in the case of $r = 1$, the total number of unit Hadamard products is $(2d\tilde{d} + 2\tilde{\ell})r'$; otherwise, it is $(\ell + 2d\tilde{d} + 2\tilde{\ell})r'$.

We note that the computational cost of unit NTT operations at the first step is roughly equivalent to the second step. On the other hand, the second inner product step is dominant in the cost of unit Hadamard products since only this step is asymptotically quadratic in the level ℓ.

4.4   Complexity Comparison

We now provide an in-depth complexity comparison between previous and our key-switching methods. We analyze the computational complexity of two methods and then compare their space complexity.

Time Complexity. Table 1 summarizes the computational complexity of the previous and new key-switching methods in terms of number of unit operations.

As mentioned earlier, expensive NTT operations over $R_{\tilde{Q}}$ at the first decomposition step in the previous method are replaced by relatively cheaper NTT operations over $R_{B'}$ in our method (from $d\tilde{\ell}$ to dr' unit NTT operations). In other words, in the gadget decomposition step, a (large) value of $\tilde{\ell}$ in the previous method is reduced to a small value of r' in our method, and therefore the computational complexity of unit NTT operation in this step is reduced by a factor of $\tilde{\ell}/r'$. On the other hand, inverse NTT operations on the inner product results $\tilde{c}_i \in R_{\tilde{Q}}$ in the previous method are roughly equivalent to inverse NTT operations on the inner products $\tilde{c}_{i,j}$ in $R_{B'}$ in our method ($2\tilde{\ell} = 2\tilde{d}\tilde{r}$ vs. $2\tilde{d}r'$ unit NTT operations).

Table 1. Computational complexity comparison of the previous and our key-switching methods. Here, NTT and Hadamard Product indicate the corresponding unit operations. (d: the dimension of the gadget vector over R_Q, $\tilde{d}$: the dimension of the gadget vector over $R_{\tilde{Q}}$, ℓ: the level of the modulus Q, $\tilde{\ell}$: the number of distinct word-sized primes for the modulus $\tilde{Q} = PQ$, r': the number of distinct word-sized primes for the coefficient bound B')

Method	NTT	Hadamard Product	
		$r = 1$	$r > 1$
Previous	$d\tilde{\ell} + 2\tilde{\ell}$	$2d\tilde{\ell}$	$\ell^2 + 2d\tilde{\ell}$
Ours	$dr' + 2\tilde{d}r'$	$2(d\tilde{d} + \tilde{\ell})r'$	$\ell r' + 2(d\tilde{d} + \tilde{\ell})r'$

We now consider the cost of unit Hadamard products. The base conversion of an input to the large modulus $\tilde{Q}$ in the previous method requires about ℓ^2 unit Hadamard products, and this term increases significantly for a large level ℓ compared to those of the first and third steps in our method (ℓ^2 vs. $\ell r' + \tilde{\ell}r'$). In the second step, the computational cost of the previous method is roughly equivalent to the new key-switching method ($2d\tilde{\ell}$ vs. $2d\tilde{d}r'$). As a result, the number of unit Hadamard products in our method can be substantially reduced from the previous method as the value of ℓ increases.

To provide further intuition, we rephrase the complexity analysis in an asymptotic manner. By considering $r, \tilde{r}, r' \in O(1)$, we deduce $d, \tilde{d} \in O(\ell)$. Then, both unit NTT operations and Hadamard products in the previous key-switching have an asymptotic complexity of $O(\ell^2)$. Meanwhile, the asymptotic complexity of unit NTT operations in our algorithm is reduced to $O(\ell)$. Therefore, our algorithm reduces the number of NTT operations by a factor of $O(\ell)$ compared to the previous one, while the cost of Hadamard products keeps the same asymptotic computational complexity.

Consequently, our key-switching method provides a considerable speedup over the previous method for an evaluation of large-depth circuits. We note that it is a common practice in HE cryptosystems to use a sufficiently large value of ℓ, for example in the usage of bootstrapping. In particular, since NTT operations are relatively expensive than Hadamard products and the cost of NTT operations is reduced from quadratic to linear complexity in ℓ, it enables us to achieve a comparably better asymptotic complexity of the key-switching operation.

Space Complexity. In terms of space complexity, the key-switching key in the previous key-switching operation is viewed as a $(d \times 2)$ matrix over $R_{\tilde{Q}}$, so the bit-size of a key-switching key is $2d \cdot N \log \tilde{Q} \approx 2d\tilde{d} \cdot N \log \tilde{B}$. Meanwhile, the key-switching key in our new variant consists of two $d \times \tilde{d}$ matrices over R. As noted in Sect. 4.3, it can be given in the NTT form over $R_{B'}$ for efficient computation. Then the bit length of the key-switching key is $2d\tilde{d} \cdot N \log B'$, yielding an expansion factor of $\log B' / \log \tilde{B} \approx \log(2dN \cdot B\tilde{B}) / \log \tilde{B} = 1 + \log(2dNB) / \log \tilde{B}$. Alternatively, we can first generate a key-switching key as in the previous method. And then we decompose the key and convert it into an NTT representation before multiplying it by a ciphertext. As a result, we can speed up the key-switching operation while keeping the size of the switching key the same.

5 Implementation and Performance

We present the concrete parameters for the key-switching operation based on the new external product method. Then, we provide experimental results that demonstrate the effectiveness of our new key-switching method. Our source code is based on the CKKS scheme and the implementation is built on top of the Lattigo library [15] that supports the CKKS scheme in a full-RNS manner and with the RNS-based digit decomposition in [22]. The source code is available at https://github.com/SNUCP/fast-ksw. All experiments were performed with a single thread on a machine with Intel(R) Xeon(R) Platinum 8268 at 2.90GHz CPU and 192GB RAM running Ubuntu 20.04.3 LTS.

5.1 Parameter Setting

As noted in Sect. 3.2, the coefficient bound B' is a product of r' distinct ν-bit primes that satisfies the inequality $B' > 2dN \cdot B\tilde{B}$ where $B = \frac{1}{2}\max_{0 \le j < d}\{D_j\}$ and $\tilde{B} = \frac{1}{2}\max_{0 \le j < \tilde{d}}\{\tilde{D}_j\}$. Namely, it suffices to set r' as

$$r' \ge \left\lceil \frac{\log(2dN \cdot B\tilde{B})}{\nu} \right\rceil. \tag{5}$$

In our implementation, the key distribution χ samples each coefficient from $\{0, \pm 1\}$ with probability 0.25 for each of -1 and 1 and probability 0.5 for 0. The error distribution is the discrete Gaussian D_σ with $\sigma = 3.2$. We used two ring dimension parameters $N = 2^{15}$ and $N = 2^{16}$, which are commonly used for an evaluation of a circuit with a sufficiently large depth (e.g., bootstrapping operation). For each of these values of N, we derived an upper bound on the parameter $\tilde{Q}$ to achieve a 128-bit security level. For the modulus $\tilde{Q} = q_0 \cdots q_{\tilde{\ell}-1}$, we set all the primes q_i to be roughly the same size. We set the primes p_j to be $\nu \ge 59.9$ bits as an upper bound for these primes is set to 2^{60} in the Lattigo library. Table 2 summarizes upper bounds on the modulus $\tilde{Q}$ and the level $\tilde{\ell}$, along with approximate sizes for the primes q_i and p_j.

5.2 Experimental Results

We present experimental results of key-switching methods from our experiments. Tables 3 and 4 show the running time (in second) for the previous key-switching operation ("Prev") and the new key-switching operation ("Ours"). To be precise, we measured the time of the key switching operation taken to perform homomorphic multiplication of ciphertexts. We did this for various values of $\tilde{\ell}$ and r while using the parameters in Table 2. We processed the parameter r between 1 and 4 since the default digit length of the gadget decomposition is set as 3

Table 2. Parameters used in our experiments

N	$\log \tilde{Q}$	$\tilde{\ell}$	$\lceil \log q_i \rceil$	$\lceil \log p_j \rceil$
2^{15}	880	≤ 24	36	60
2^{16}	1761	≤ 48		

or 4 in the Lattigo library. In each table, the third column gives the level of an input ciphertext by $\ell = \tilde{\ell} - r$. Furthermore, as discussed in Sect. 4.3, our key-switching method relies on the parameters r, $\tilde{r}$, and r'. For each r and $\tilde{r}$, we chose the value of r' by Eq. (5). The last column gives a speedup of the fastest new key-switching operation among experiments with various parameters of $\tilde{r}$ and r' over the previous method.

We now consider the new key-switching method. Given fixed values of N, $\tilde{\ell}$, and r, if taking a large value of $\tilde{r}$, then a large value of r' is chosen by Eq. (5), whereas a small value of $\tilde{d}$ is taken by the fact of $\tilde{d} \approx \tilde{\ell}/\tilde{r}$. So, the first term dr' in the cost of unit NTT operations increases with the parameter $\tilde{r}$. However, because of the decreasing term $r'/\tilde{r}$ with $\tilde{r}$, the second term $2\tilde{d}r' (\approx 2\tilde{\ell}r'/\tilde{r})$ in the cost decreases as $\tilde{r}$ increases. Moreover, the dominant term in the cost of unit Hadamard products is $2d\tilde{d}r' \approx 2d\tilde{\ell}r'/\tilde{r}$, which also decreases with $\tilde{r}$. Therefore, we get an optimal computational complexity when all of these terms are balanced (e.g., $4 \leq \tilde{r} \leq 7$).

The previous key-switching operation is faster for a small value of $\tilde{\ell}$ and a large value of r (due to a small value of $d \approx \ell/r$), which closely aligns with theoretical complexity analysis in Table 1. In Fig. 1, the same tendency can be observed in our key-switching operation. Here, the running time is taken as the fastest result among experiments over various $\tilde{r}$ and r' for each $\tilde{\ell}$ and r. Compared to ours, given a fixed value of N, there is much variation in the running time of the previous key-switching operation as $\tilde{\ell}$ increases due to the quadratic and linear dependence of the number of NTTs on $\tilde{\ell}$ in the previous and our methods. Also, the running time of the previous method depends heavily on the value of r than ours.

Given fixed values of N and $\tilde{\ell}$, we get a further speedup of the new key-switching method over the previous method when a small value of r is used. This is because NTT operations are more costly than Hadamard products and the complexity of unit NTT operations for the gadget decomposition in our method is reduced by a factor of $\tilde{\ell}/r'$ compared to the previous method. As the optimal value of r' increases with r, the factor of $\tilde{\ell}/r'$ decreases with r. For example, we get a speedup of 3.3 if $\log N = 16, \tilde{\ell} = 48, r = 1$, and a speedup of 2.2 if $\log N = 16, \tilde{\ell} = 48, r = 4$. On the other hand, the factor of $\tilde{\ell}/r'$ increases with $\tilde{\ell}$. Consequently, our experiments indicate that the speedups for smaller r and larger $\tilde{\ell}$ are more significant and dramatic.

Table 3. Experimental results of the previous and our key-switching operations. The evaluation is examined on the full RNS variant of CKKS scheme with the ring dimension $N = 2^{15}$.

$\log N$	$\tilde{\ell}$	(ℓ, r)		Prev	Ours						Speedup
15	16	(15, 1)	$\tilde{r}$	−	1	2	3	4	5	6	
			r'	−	2	3	3	4	4	5	1.7
			Time	0.143	0.116	0.101	**0.084**	0.086	0.087	0.092	
		(14, 2)	$\tilde{r}$	−	2	3	4	5	6	7	
			r'	−	3	4	4	5	6	6	1.5
			Time	0.096	0.074	0.078	**0.062**	0.075	0.076	0.076	
		(13, 3)	$\tilde{r}$	−	2	3	4	5	6	7	
			r'	−	4	4	5	6	6	7	1.2
			Time	0.077	0.083	0.070	**0.066**	0.077	0.067	0.076	
	20	(19, 1)	$\tilde{r}$	−	1	2	3	4	5	6	
			r'	−	2	3	3	4	4	5	1.9
			Time	0.216	0.162	0.139	**0.112**	0.118	0.115	0.129	
		(18, 2)	$\tilde{r}$	−	2	3	4	5	6	7	
			r'	−	3	4	4	5	6	6	1.7
			Time	0.145	0.102	0.103	**0.085**	0.092	0.107	0.093	
		(17, 3)	$\tilde{r}$	−	2	3	4	5	6	7	
			r'	−	4	4	5	6	6	7	1.3
			Time	0.113	0.109	0.088	**0.087**	0.089	0.088	0.089	
	24	(23, 1)	$\tilde{r}$	−	1	2	3	4	5	6	
			r'	−	2	3	3	4	4	5	2.3
			Time	0.317	0.214	0.183	**0.140**	0.152	0.142	0.151	
		(22, 2)	$\tilde{r}$	−	2	3	4	5	6	7	
			r'	−	3	4	4	5	6	6	1.9
			Time	0.204	0.128	0.128	**0.110**	0.118	0.124	0.125	
		(21, 3)	$\tilde{r}$	−	2	3	4	5	6	7	
			r'	−	4	4	5	6	6	7	1.5
			Time	0.151	0.137	0.106	0.112	0.114	**0.101**	0.115	

Micro-benchmarks. To identify the improvements from the impact of the new key-switching method, we present micro-benchmarks for the individual procedures. Figure 2 shows the result with the parameters $N = 2^{16}$ and $\tilde{\ell} = 48$. We do this for various values of r defining the digit length of the gadget decomposition over R_Q. As discussed in Sect. 4.4, the gadget decomposition procedure including the base conversion and NTT operations is the most time-consuming part of the previous key-switching operation. In particular, the cost of NTT operations is dominant in the previous method; the key-switching spends 47–73% of its time performing NTT operations. In contrast, our key-switching proce-

Table 4. Experimental results of the previous and our key-switching operations. The evaluation is examined on the full RNS variant of CKKS scheme with the ring dimension $N = 2^{16}$.

$\log N$	$\tilde{\ell}$	(ℓ, r)		Prev	Ours						Speedup
16	32	$(31,1)$	$\tilde{r}$	–	1	2	3	4	5	6	
			r'	–	2	3	3	4	4	5	2.6
			Time	1.181	0.744	0.605	0.455	0.476	**0.451**	0.499	
		$(30,2)$	$\tilde{r}$	–	2	3	4	5	6	7	
			r'	–	3	4	4	5	6	6	2.4
			Time	0.854	0.414	0.427	**0.352**	0.399	0.408	0.388	
		$(29,3)$	$\tilde{r}$	–	2	3	4	5	6	7	
			r'	–	4	4	5	6	6	7	2.0
			Time	0.655	0.466	0.341	**0.335**	0.364	0.350	0.372	
		$(28,4)$	$\tilde{r}$	–	2	3	4	5	6	7	
			r'	–	4	5	6	6	7	7	1.6
			Time	0.486	0.403	0.357	0.343	0.319	0.318	**0.301**	
	40	$(39,1)$	$\tilde{r}$	–	1	2	3	4	5	6	
			r'	–	2	3	3	4	4	5	3.0
			Time	1.841	1.098	0.905	0.682	0.711	**0.604**	0.690	
		$(38,2)$	$\tilde{r}$	–	2	3	4	5	6	7	
			r'	–	3	4	4	5	6	6	2.7
			Time	1.378	0.621	0.623	**0.508**	0.531	0.574	0.532	
		$(37,3)$	$\tilde{r}$	–	2	3	4	5	6	7	
			r'	–	4	4	5	6	6	7	2.2
			Time	1.038	0.659	0.521	0.506	0.519	**0.479**	0.507	
		$(36,4)$	$\tilde{r}$	–	2	3	4	5	6	7	
			r'	–	4	5	6	6	7	7	2.1
			Time	0.929	0.581	0.554	0.514	0.456	0.481	**0.438**	
	48	$(47,1)$	$\tilde{r}$	–	1	2	3	4	5	6	
			r'	–	2	3	3	4	4	5	3.3
			Time	2.688	1.532	1.234	0.876	0.938	**0.818**	0.880	
		$(46,2)$	$\tilde{r}$	–	2	3	4	5	6	7	
			r'	–	3	4	4	5	6	6	3.0
			Time	1.980	0.823	0.791	**0.655**	0.702	0.727	0.670	
		$(45,3)$	$\tilde{r}$	–	2	3	4	5	6	7	
			r'	–	4	4	5	6	6	7	2.5
			Time	1.438	0.834	0.629	0.630	0.657	**0.585**	0.617	
		$(44,4)$	$\tilde{r}$	–	2	3	4	5	6	7	
			r'	–	4	5	6	6	7	7	2.2
			Time	1.191	0.738	0.670	0.650	0.589	0.592	**0.550**	

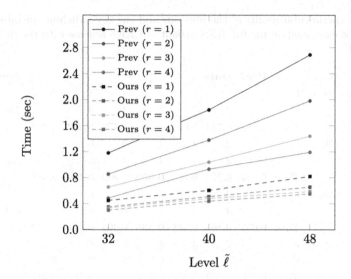

Fig. 1. Running time results of the key-switching methods with $N = 2^{16}$.

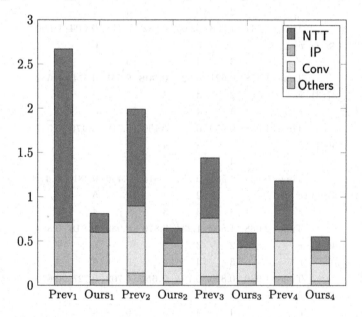

Fig. 2. The detailed proportion of each operation in the previous key-switching (Prev$_r$) and our key-switching (Ours$_r$) where $N = 2^{16}$ and $\tilde{\ell} = 48$. NTT stands for both NTT and its inverse, IP stands for inner product, and Conv stands for base conversion.

dure spends about 26–27% of its time performing NTT operations and the cost of inner products is dominant in the execution of the procedure. Notably, the NTT computation of our algorithm is around 4–9 times faster than that of the previous algorithm.

Application to Homomorphic Operations. As mentioned in Sect. 4, key-switching operation is a main bottleneck of homomorphic operations such as multiplication and automorphism. Table 5 shows the performance of multiplication and automorphism with the existing and our key-switching methods. We observe that the previous key-switching method accounts for about 86–93% and 90–95% of the execution times for multiplication and automorphism, respectively. By applying our new key-switching method, we get a speedup of up to 3 times for multiplication and automorphism.

Table 5. Experimental results of multiplication and automorphism with the previous and new key-switching operations when $\log N = 16$.

$\tilde{\ell}$	r	Previous			Ours		
		Key-switching	Mult	Auto	Key-switching	Mult	Auto
48	1	2.724 s	2.921 s	2.876 s	0.833 s	1.008 s	0.954 s
	2	1.909 s	2.103 s	2.057 s	0.660 s	0.835 s	0.781 s
	3	1.373 s	1.560 s	1.503 s	0.595 s	0.767 s	0.705 s
	4	1.143 s	1.324 s	1.261 s	0.562 s	0.729 s	0.681 s

6 Conclusion and Future Work

In this paper, we presented a new external product algorithm based on key decomposition technique. Prior to this work, a decomposed ciphertext is converted into the NTT form over a multi-precision modulus and then multiplied with a public evaluation key. We explore another way by refactoring the computation and exploiting the smallness of the gadget decomposition; therefore, we can significantly reduce the number of NTT operation. In our experiment, the key-switching operation based on the new external product method is up to 3 times faster than the previous key-switching operation over typical parameters.

One direction to explore is to take into account hardware implementation, for example, in a GPU environment. According to the recent study by Jung et al. [23], GPU can be used to accelerate the key-switching operation by optimizing the inner product procedure. A significant reduction in NTT operations in our method is a promising possibility that we believe will get a substantial performance improvement when combined with the existing GPU-based optimization techniques.

Acknowledgement. This work was supported by Samsung Research Funding & Incubation Center of Samsung Electronics under Project Number SRFC-TB2103-01.

References

1. Bajard, J.-C., Eynard, J., Hasan, M.A., Zucca, V.: A full RNS variant of FV like somewhat homomorphic encryption schemes. In: Avanzi, R., Heys, H. (eds.) SAC 2016. LNCS, vol. 10532, pp. 423–442. Springer, Cham (2017). https://doi.org/10. 1007/978-3-319-69453-5_23
2. Bossuat, J.-P., Mouchet, C., Troncoso-Pastoriza, J., Hubaux, J.-P.: Efficient boot-strapping for approximate homomorphic encryption with non-sparse keys. In: Canteaut, A., Standaert, F.-X. (eds.) Efficient bootstrapping for approximate homomorphic encryption with non-sparse keys. LNCS, vol. 12696, pp. 587–617. Springer, Cham (2021). https://doi.org/10.1007/978-3-030-77870-5_21
3. Brakerski, Z.: Fully homomorphic encryption without modulus switching from classical GapSVP. In: Safavi-Naini, R., Canetti, R. (eds.) CRYPTO 2012. LNCS, vol. 7417, pp. 868–886. Springer, Heidelberg (2012). https://doi.org/10.1007/978-3-642-32009-5_50
4. Brakerski, Z., Gentry, C., Vaikuntanathan, V.: (leveled) fully homomorphic encryption without bootstrapping. ACM Trans. Comput. Theory (TOCT) 6(3), 1–36 (2014)
5. Chen, H., Chillotti, I., Song, Y.: Improved bootstrapping for approximate homomorphic encryption. In: Ishai, Y., Rijmen, V. (eds.) EUROCRYPT 2019. LNCS, vol. 11477, pp. 34–54. Springer, Cham (2019). https://doi.org/10.1007/978-3-030-17656-3_2
6. Chen, H., Dai, W., Kim, M., Song, Y.: Efficient multi-key homomorphic encryption with packed ciphertexts with application to oblivious neural network inference. In: Proceedings of the 2019 ACM SIGSAC Conference on Computer and Communications Security, pp. 395–412 (2019)
7. Cheon, J.H., Han, K., Kim, A., Kim, M., Song, Y.: Bootstrapping for approximate homomorphic encryption. In: Nielsen, J.B., Rijmen, V. (eds.) EUROCRYPT 2018. LNCS, vol. 10820, pp. 360–384. Springer, Cham (2018). https://doi.org/10.1007/978-3-319-78381-9_14
8. Cheon, J.H., Han, K., Kim, A., Kim, M., Song, Y.: A full RNS variant of approximate homomorphic encryption. In: In: Cid, C., Jacobson Jr., M. (eds.) SAC 2018. LNCS, vol. 11349, pp. 347–368. Springer, Cham (2018). https://doi.org/10.1007/978-3-030-10970-7_16
9. Cheon, J.H., Kim, A., Kim, M., Song, Y.: Homomorphic encryption for arithmetic of approximate numbers. In: Takagi, T., Peyrin, T. (eds.) ASIACRYPT 2017. LNCS, vol. 10624, pp. 409–437. Springer, Cham (2017). https://doi.org/10. 1007/978-3-319-70694-8_15
10. Cheon, J.H., Kim, D., Kim, D.: Efficient homomorphic comparison methods with optimal complexity. In: Moriai, S., Wang, H. (eds.) ASIACRYPT 2020. LNCS, vol. 12492, pp. 221–256. Springer, Cham (2020). https://doi.org/10.1007/978-3-030-64834-3_8
11. Cheon, J.H., Kim, D., Kim, D., Lee, H.H., Lee, K.: Numerical method for comparison on homomorphically encrypted numbers. In: Galbraith, S.D., Moriai, S. (eds.) ASIACRYPT 2019. LNCS, vol. 11922, pp. 415–445. Springer, Cham (2019). https://doi.org/10.1007/978-3-030-34621-8_15
12. Chillotti, I., Gama, N., Georgieva, M., Izabachène, M.: TFHE: fast fully homomorphic encryption over the torus. J. Cryptol. 33(1), 34–91 (2020)
13. DARPA: Data protection in virtual environments (dprive). https://www.darpa.mil/program/data-protection-in-virtual-environments

14. Ducas, L., Micciancio, D.: FHEW: bootstrapping homomorphic encryption in less than a second. In: Oswald, E., Fischlin, M. (eds.) EUROCRYPT 2015. LNCS, vol. 9056, pp. 617–640. Springer, Heidelberg (2015). https://doi.org/10.1007/978-3-662-46800-5_24

15. EPFL-LDS: Lattigo v2.3.0. Online, October 2021. https://github.com/ldsec/lattigo

16. Fan, J., Vercauteren, F.: Somewhat practical fully homomorphic encryption. Cryptology ePrint Archive (2012)

17. Gentry, C.: Fully homomorphic encryption using ideal lattices. In: Proceedings of the 41st Annual ACM Symposium on Theory of Computing, pp. 169–178. ACM (2009)

18. Gentry, C., Halevi, S., Smart, N.P.: Homomorphic evaluation of the AES circuit. In: Safavi-Naini, R., Canetti, R. (eds.) CRYPTO 2012. LNCS, vol. 7417, pp. 850–867. Springer, Heidelberg (2012). https://doi.org/10.1007/978-3-642-32009-5_49

19. Gentry, C., Sahai, A., Waters, B.: Homomorphic encryption from learning with errors: conceptually-simpler, asymptotically-faster, attribute-based. In: Canetti, R., Garay, J.A. (eds.) CRYPTO 2013. LNCS, vol. 8042, pp. 75–92. Springer, Heidelberg (2013). https://doi.org/10.1007/978-3-642-40041-4_5

20. Halevi, S., Polyakov, Y., Shoup, V.: An improved RNS variant of the BFV homomorphic encryption scheme. In: Matsui, M. (ed.) CT-RSA 2019. LNCS, vol. 11405, pp. 83–105. Springer, Cham (2019). https://doi.org/10.1007/978-3-030-12612-4_5

21. Halevi, S., Shoup, V.: Faster homomorphic linear transformations in HElib. In: Shacham, H., Boldyreva, A. (eds.) CRYPTO 2018. LNCS, vol. 10991, pp. 93–120. Springer, Cham (2018). https://doi.org/10.1007/978-3-319-96884-1_4

22. Han, K., Ki, D.: Better bootstrapping for approximate homomorphic encryption. In: Jarecki, S. (ed.) CT-RSA 2020. LNCS, vol. 12006, pp. 364–390. Springer, Cham (2020). https://doi.org/10.1007/978-3-030-40186-3_16

23. Jung, W., Kim, S., Ahn, J.H., Cheon, J.H., Lee, Y.: Over 100x faster bootstrapping in fully homomorphic encryption through memory-centric optimization with GPUs. IACR Trans. Cryptographic Hardware Embedded Syst. 114–148 (2021)

24. Kim, M., Song, Y., Li, B., Micciancio, D.: Semi-parallel logistic regression for GWAS on encrypted data. BMC Med. Genomics **13**(7), 1–13 (2020)

25. Kim, S., Kim, J., Kim, M.J., Jung, W., Kim, J., Rhu, M., Ahn, J.H.: BTS: An accelerator for bootstrappable fully homomorphic encryption. In: Proceedings of the 49th Annual International Symposium on Computer Architecture, pp. 711–725 (2022)

26. Lee, J.-W., Lee, E., Lee, Y., Kim, Y.-S., No, J.-S.: High-precision bootstrapping of RNS-CKKS homomorphic encryption using optimal minimax polynomial approximation and inverse sine function. In: Canteaut, A., Standaert, F.-X. (eds.) EUROCRYPT 2021. LNCS, vol. 12696, pp. 618–647. Springer, Cham (2021). https://doi.org/10.1007/978-3-030-77870-5_22

27. Lee, Y., Lee, J.W., Kim, Y.S., Kim, Y., No, J.S., Kang, H.: High-precision bootstrapping for approximate homomorphic encryption by error variance minimization. In: Dunkelman, O., Dziembowski, S. (eds.) EUROCRYPT 2022. LNCS, vol. 13275, pp. 551–580. Springer, Cham (2022). https://doi.org/10.1007/978-3-031-06944-4_19

28. Lyubashevsky, V., Peikert, C., Regev, O.: On ideal lattices and learning with errors over rings. In: Gilbert, H. (ed.) EUROCRYPT 2010. LNCS, vol. 6110, pp. 1–23. Springer, Heidelberg (2010). https://doi.org/10.1007/978-3-642-13190-5_1

29. Regev, O.: On lattices, learning with errors, random linear codes, and cryptography. Journal of the ACM (JACM) **56**(6), 1–40 (2009)

30. Roy, S.S., Turan, F., Jarvinen, K., Vercauteren, F., Verbauwhede, I.: FPGA-based high-performance parallel architecture for homomorphic computing on encrypted data. In: 2019 IEEE International Symposium on High Performance Computer Architecture (HPCA), pp. 387–398. IEEE (2019)

31. Turan, F., Roy, S.S., Verbauwhede, I.: HEAWS: an accelerator for homomorphic encryption on the Amazon AWS FPGA. IEEE Trans. Comput. **69**(8), 1185–1196 (2020)

Oblivious RAM

MacORAMa: Optimal Oblivious RAM with Integrity

Surya Mathialagan$^{(\boxtimes)}$ and Neekon Vafa

MIT, Cambridge, MA 02139, USA
{smathi,nvafa}@mit.edu

Abstract. Oblivious RAM (ORAM), introduced by Goldreich and Ostrovsky (J. ACM '96), is a primitive that allows a client to perform RAM computations on an external database without revealing any information through the access pattern. For a database of size N, well-known lower bounds show that a multiplicative overhead of $\Omega(\log N)$ in the number of RAM queries is necessary assuming $O(1)$ client storage. A long sequence of works culminated in the asymptotically optimal construction of Asharov, Komargodski, Lin, and Shi (CRYPTO '21) with $O(\log N)$ worst-case overhead and $O(1)$ client storage. However, this optimal ORAM is known to be secure only in the *honest-but-curious* setting, where an adversary is allowed to observe the access patterns but not modify the contents of the database. In the *malicious* setting, where an adversary is additionally allowed to tamper with the database, this construction and many others in fact become insecure.

In this work, we construct the first maliciously secure ORAM with worst-case $O(\log N)$ overhead and $O(1)$ client storage assuming one-way functions, which are also necessary. By the $\Omega(\log N)$ lower bound, our construction is asymptotically optimal. To attain this overhead, we develop techniques to intricately interleave online and offline memory checking for malicious security. Furthermore, we complement our positive result by showing the impossibility of a *generic* overhead-preserving compiler from honest-but-curious to malicious security, barring a breakthrough in memory checking.

Keywords: Oblivious RAM · Memory checking · Malicious security

The first author was supported in part by the Siebel Scholars program. The second author is supported in part by NSF fellowship DGE-2141064. This research was supported in part by DARPA under Agreement No. HR00112020023, an NSF grant CNS-2154149, a grant from the MIT-IBM Watson AI, a grant from Analog Devices, a Microsoft Trustworthy AI grant, and a Thornton Family Faculty Research Innovation Fellowship from MIT. Any opinions, findings and conclusions or recommendations expressed in this material are those of the author(s) and do not necessarily reflect the views of the United States Government or DARPA.

© International Association for Cryptologic Research 2023
H. Handschuh and A. Lysyanskaya (Eds.): CRYPTO 2023, LNCS 14084, pp. 95–127, 2023.
https://doi.org/10.1007/978-3-031-38551-3_4

1   Introduction

Suppose a user would like to outsource their database to a server. While the user could encrypt the data to hide the contents within the database, it is possible that even the access pattern corresponding to the queries to the database could result in information leakage about the underlying data [12,33]. To solve this issue, Goldreich and Ostrovsky [28] propose the notion of *Oblivious RAM* (ORAM), a primitive that supports the same database queries but transforms the access pattern to remove any information leakage. As a general technique to ensure privacy of RAM computations, ORAM has many applications including cloud computing, multi-party protocols, secure processor design, and private contact discovery, the latter as implemented by the private messaging service Signal [9, 18,21,24,25,27,40,41,57,60,61].

To hide the access pattern, the ORAM client has to pay a communication cost. This cost is generally quantified in terms of *overhead*: the number of (physical) queries in the oblivious simulation per underlying (logical) database query. Note that ORAM is only interesting when we require both the overhead and the local storage of the client to be small. Otherwise, the client could simply conduct a linear scan of the whole database for every query or download the whole database and make queries locally.

Larsen and Nielsen [39] show that for a database of size N, $\Omega(\log N)$ overhead is necessary for $O(1)$ client space. After a long line of research [13–15, 20,28,29,38,50,53,57], the celebrated construction of OptORAMa by Asharov, Komargodski, Lin, Nayak, Peserico, and Shi [5] matches this lower bound with amortized $O(\log N)$ overhead and $O(1)$ client space. Asharov, Komargodski, Lin, and Shi [6] de-amortize this construction to fully match the lower bound with worst-case $O(\log N)$ overhead.

Tampering Adversaries. Many prior ORAM constructions, including OptORAMa [5] and its de-amortized counterpart [6], consider security against passive adversaries that can only observe access patterns. In reality, an adversary can potentially do a lot more. In many applications, the adversary can play an active role in learning information from access patterns by tampering with the memory [25,46,54]. A tampering adversary can clearly violate correctness by arbitrarily modifying the contents in the database. Critically, however, a tampering adversary can also breach *obliviousness*. In fact, we show in Sect. 2 that many ORAM constructions [5,6,14,15,53] are generally *not* oblivious when interacting with a tampering adversary.

As such, we view obliviousness against non-tampering adversaries as the *honest-but-curious* definition of obliviousness, whereas we consider security against tampering adversaries to be the natural *maliciously secure* notion of obliviousness. For a maliciously secure ORAM, we would like the following properties to hold (see Sect. 3.3 for a formal definition):

- The user's view should be indistinguishable from interacting with an honest RAM database (up until an abort).
- A malicious adversary should not be able to learn anything from tampering with the database except for the number of user RAM queries, even via the timing of a client abort.

Existing Constructions. The notion of maliciously secure ORAM (also called tamper-proof ORAM) was first proposed by Goldreich and Ostrovsky [28]. They argue that their ORAM constructions can be made maliciously secure with $O(1)$ blowup in overhead because it is possible to *time-stamp* all physical writes, i.e., to compute the number of times a given physical (not logical) address has been written to. Authenticating time-stamped messages prevents replay attacks, forcing the adversary to always respond honestly. However, their construction has overhead $O(\log^3 N)$.

Other works [54,58] use the tree-based paradigm to construct maliciously secure ORAMs. These works use hash functions to impose a Merkle tree [45] on the memory, with the root node stored locally by the client. Crucially, this does not add any asymptotic overhead since a Merkle tree can be naturally superimposed on the underlying tree. However, since these constructions follow the tree-based paradigm, they do not achieve the optimal $O(\log N)$ overhead for general word sizes.

Unfortunately, in Sect. 2, we argue that these techniques do not work for the existing optimal ORAM construction [6]. Indeed, there is no known $O(\log N)$ overhead ORAM that is maliciously secure. There are also no known lower bounds showing separations between the overhead needed for honest-but-curious ORAMs and maliciously secure ORAM. This motivates the following question:

Question 1. Does there exist a maliciously secure ORAM construction with $O(\log N)$ overhead and $O(1)$ client storage?

Generic Compilers for Malicious Security. One can ask more generally if there is a generic way to compile *any* honest-but-curious ORAM into one that is maliciously secure. In this setting, a *compiler* Π is a layer between any honest-but-curious ORAM $\mathcal{C}$ and the server, in the following sense: the compiler Π takes queries from $\mathcal{C}$ and interacts with the server to generate a response for $\mathcal{C}$, and we want the composition of Π and $\mathcal{C}$ to be a maliciously secure ORAM.

One solution to this would be *memory checking*, a notion first defined by Blum, Evans, Gemmell, Kannan, and Naor [11]. At a high level, a memory checker can be seen as a layer between the user and an unreliable memory which verifies the correctness of the memory's answers to the user's requests, using small, private, and reliable space. In fact, one can view both time-stamping and Merkle tree verification as special cases of memory checking.

Memory checking is clearly such a compiler, as the client can use a memory checker to make sure the adversary always answers honestly. If we had an $O(1)$-overhead memory checker, then we could compile the optimal honest-but-curious ORAM constructions into ones that are maliciously secure with $O(\log N)$ overhead. However, best known memory checker constructions have a bandwidth of $O(\log N)$ [11,23,30,31,48,52].[1] Therefore, applying such a memory checker to an optimal ORAM construction with $\Theta(\log N)$ overhead would result in a maliciously secure ORAM with $O(\log^2 N)$ overhead. Moreover, Dwork, Naor, Rothblum, and Vaikuntanathan [23] show that deterministic and non-adaptive memory checkers – capturing the known memory checking constructions – must have overhead $\Omega(\log N / \log \log N)$. Therefore, barring a major development in memory checking, this approach will not work.

But do compilers have to be memory checkers? Does a weaker compiler suffice? This leads us to the following question:

Question 2. Does an $O(1)$-overhead compiler from honest-but-curious to maliciously secure ORAM give an $O(1)$-overhead memory checker?

If so, this would present a memory checking barrier to generically compile any optimal honest-but-curious ORAM into an optimal maliciously secure ORAM.

1.1   Our Contributions

In this work, we resolve both questions. To answer Question 1, we construct MacORAMa, a maliciously secure oblivious RAM with worst-case $O(\log N)$ overhead. We compare MacORAMa to previous ORAM constructions in Table 1.

Theorem 1 (Informal version of Theorem 7). *Assuming the existence of one-way functions, for databases of size N and word size[2] $\omega(\log N)$, there is an ORAM construction with $O(\log N)$ worst-case overhead, $O(N)$ server storage, and $O(1)$ client storage that is secure against $\mathsf{poly}(N)$-time adversaries that can tamper with the database. Moreover, if the client (but not the adversary) is given access to a random oracle, our construction is unconditionally statistically secure, even against computationally unbounded adversaries.*

---

[1] *Bandwidth* refers to the ratio of the number of physical bits accessed to the number of bits being requested. While [52] achieves $O(\log N / \log \log N)$ overhead, its bandwidth is still $O(\log N)$ because the logical and physical word sizes differ by more than a constant factor. In our setting, the logical and physical word sizes will always differ by at most a constant factor, so overhead and bandwidth are asymptotically equivalent.

[2] See Sect. 2.4 for discussion about this choice of word size.

Table 1. This table outlines some of the known ORAM constructions secure against $\mathsf{poly}(N)$-time adversaries (i.e., for $\lambda = N$) for any word size $w = \omega(\log N)$ and $w \leq (\log N)^{1+\epsilon}$, for $0 < \epsilon < 1$. We justify this choice of word size in the malicious setting in Sect. 2.4. Client and server storage are measured in terms of the number of words. The assumption column refers to what assumptions the constructions use to prove security. "OWF" stands for the existence of one-way functions. Overheads with an asterisk (*) superscript denote amortized overheads.

Construction	Client Storage	Server Storage	Overhead	Assumption	Maliciously Secure
[28]	$\Theta(1)$	$\Theta(N \log N)$	$\Theta(\log^3 N)^*$	OWF	Yes
Path ORAM [58]	$\omega(\log N)$	$\Theta(N)$	$\Omega(\log^{2-\epsilon} N)$	None**	No
Path ORAM [58]	$\omega(\log N)$	$\Theta(N)$	$\Omega(\log^{2-\epsilon} N)$	OWF***	Yes
PanORAMa [53]	$\Theta(1)$	$\Theta(N)$	$\Theta(\log N \log\log N)^*$	OWF	No
OptORAMa [5]	$\Theta(1)$	$\Theta(N)$	$\Theta(\log N)^*$	OWF	No
[6]	$\Theta(1)$	$\Theta(N)$	$\Theta(\log N)$	OWF	No
Lower Bound [28,37,39]	$\Theta(1)$	$\Theta(N)$	$\Omega(\log N)$	–	–
MacORAMa (Our work)	$\Theta(1)$	$\Theta(N)$	$\Theta(\log N)$	OWF	Yes

**While the access-pattern is unconditionally statistically secure, one ultimately needs the existence of one-way functions to hide (i.e., encrypt) the underlying data.
***While the works of [54,58] use collision-resistant hash functions (CRHFs) to obtain malicious security, Ilan Komargodski and the authors independently observed that OWFs are sufficient for this transformation. For example, one can use universal one-way hash functions (UOWHFs) instead of CRHFs to instantiate the Merkle tree. Note that UOWHFs are implied by OWFs [35,55].

For word size $\omega(\log N)$, this not only matches the lower bound known for honest-but-curious ORAM [37,39], but also shows that malicious security is possible with *no additional asymptotic overhead*. Interestingly, even though maliciously secure ORAM is a stronger notion than memory checking, our construction matches the best known memory checker constructions (e.g., [11,23,30,31,48,52]) in terms of bandwidth. In other words, maliciously secure ORAM is a stronger primitive than both honest-but-curious ORAM and memory checking, and our construction achieves the best known bandwidth for both simultaneously.

Also, we observe that the existence of one-way functions is necessary for maliciously secure ORAM. One can easily show that the need for hiding the data itself (which is typically done via secret-key encryption) implies the existence of one-way functions. Furthermore, Naor and Rothblum [47] show that any memory checker, and hence maliciously secure ORAM, with local space s and overhead q (in bits) such that $s \cdot q = o(N)$ implies the existence of (almost) one-way functions. Therefore, our construction uses provably minimal assumptions.

To resolve Question 2, we show that any generic compiler from an honest-but-curious ORAM to a maliciously secure one needs to essentially be a memory checker.

Theorem 2 (Informal version of Theorem 3). *If there exists a generic honest-but-curious to maliciously secure ORAM compiler with $O(1)$ blowup, there exists a memory checker[3] with $O(1)$ overhead.*

Therefore, the existence of $O(1)$-overhead memory checkers exactly characterizes the existence of an $O(1)$-blowup compiler from honest-but-curious to maliciously secure ORAM. However, since the best memory checkers have bandwidth $O(\log N)$, this is a barrier to an overhead-preserving generic compiler. As a result, to construct our maliciously secure ORAM with $O(\log N)$ overhead, we use the existing optimal construction in a white-box way.

Our Techniques. To prove Theorem 1, we use more general notions of memory checking. Blum et al. [11] define an *online* memory checker as one which immediately verifies the correctness of every answer it gives the user and an *offline* memory checker as one that only needs to report that some error has occurred after a batch of requests. While all known online memory checkers incur an additional blowup of $\Omega(\log N)$, there exist offline memory checkers that achieve amortized $O(1)$ bandwidth [11,23]. Even though offline memory checking alone is insufficient to guarantee malicious security, we show how to intricately combine online and offline memory checking techniques to get $O(1)$ blowup and malicious security simultaneously. We describe these techniques in Sect. 2.3.

We believe that our techniques in combining online and offline memory checking are general enough to extend to future hierarchical ORAM constructions. Furthermore, as memory checking has other applications in cryptography and beyond [7,11,17,34,49,56], our techniques may be of independent interest.

1.2 Related Work

Server-Side Computation. The lower bounds of Goldreich and Ostrovsky [28], Larsen and Nielsen [39], and Komargodski and Lin [37] assume that the server is a "passive storage," i.e., supports only reads and writes. Crucially, they assume that the honest server does not do any additional work. While we only consider the passive storage model, we point out that prior work has in fact leveraged server-side computation to construct maliciously secure ORAMs with smaller client communication overhead [1,3,22,32]. For example, Devadas et al. [22] construct Onion ORAM, which is a maliciously secure ORAM with $O(1)$ communication overhead for word size $\tilde{\omega}(\log^6 N)$ (where $\tilde{\omega}$ hides $\log \log N$ factors) by relying on server-side computation. Hoang et al. [32] construct a *multi-server* maliciously secure ORAM with server-side computation achieving $O(1)$ communication overhead for word size $\omega(\log N)$. These constructions generally rely on poly-logarithmic server work.

---

[3] Technically, we consider a slightly different notion of memory checking that we show is both necessary and sufficient for compiling. See Sect. 5 for more details.

Multi-client Maliciously Secure ORAM. Several works have studied the problem of a multi-client ORAM [10,16,26,41–43,59]. In this setting, data owners can delegate access to their database to third party clients, while preserving the privacy of the clients. In particular, the access patterns must remain hidden not only from the server, but also from other clients. This problem has been studied in both the honest-but-curious and malicious setting. Blass et al. [10] consider the problem in the setting where only the server is malicious. Maffei et al. [42,43] further consider the model where both the server and the clients are malicious. However, most of these constructions at the core either rely on tree-based ORAM schemes interleaved with Merkle trees or apply a Merkle tree on top of a hierarchical scheme. Therefore, these do not achieve the desired efficiency for general word sizes and use assumptions (CRHFs) stronger than one-way functions.

Weaker Notions of Malicious Security. The work of Fletcher et al. [25] relies on the tree-based paradigm and recursively uses PRFs and authentication to cleverly compress the position map and to time-stamp in an alternate way. While the construction is extremely efficient in practice, they achieve a weaker notion of malicious security. Their construction promises obliviousness against honest-but-curious adversaries but guarantees only correctness against tampering adversaries. In particular, the timing of the client's abort in the presence of a tampering adversary can leak information about the user's access patterns.

1.3 Organization

In Sect. 2, we give a technical overview of our result. In Sect. 3, we motivate and give our definitions of malicious security. In Sect. 4, we define memory checking and give its connections to ORAM. In Sect. 5, we define a weaker notion of memory checking that we call *separated memory checkers*, and we show that a generic compiler is *equivalent* to this notion of memory checking. In Sect. 6, we define a notion of *write-deterministic* algorithms, and we argue that algorithms that are write-deterministic can be made maliciously secure with $O(1)$ blowup in overhead. In Sect. 7, we overview how the building blocks of the final ORAM construction can be made maliciously secure. In Sect. 8, we give a maliciously secure hash table construction that matches the efficiency of previous honest-but-curious constructions. Finally, in Sect. 9, we state our main theorem. We defer many technical definitions, theorems, and proofs to the full version [44].

2 Technical Overview

2.1 The Hierarchical ORAM Paradigm

The hierarchical ORAM framework was first introduced by Goldreich and Ostrovsky [28]. For a database D of size N, the corresponding hierarchical ORAM contains $L = \log_2 N$ *oblivious hash tables* $H_1, \ldots, H_L$, where H_i contains 2^i data items. Upon receiving a read or write to some address addr $\in D$:

- **Look-up phase:** Perform a hash table lookup for addr in each level $H_1, \ldots,$ H_L sequentially, until the key addr is found. If addr is found in level H_i, look up dummies in the subsequent layers $H_{i+1}, \ldots, H_L$. If the operation is a read, copy the data found in H_i to H_1 and return it. If it is a write, write the new value to H_1 that was provided as part of the access.
- **Rebuild phase:** Find the lowest level (i.e., smallest index) ℓ which is empty. If all levels are non-empty, set $\ell := L$. Merge all the elements in the first $\ell - 1$ layers $\bigcup_{1 \leq j \leq \ell - 1} H_i$ to layer ℓ, while only keeping the copy of any addr in the lowest possible level. Construct a new oblivious hash table at level ℓ with these contents. Now $H_1, \ldots, H_{\ell-1}$ are empty, and H_ℓ is non-empty.

For each access to D, we perform one hash table lookup in each H_i and one write to H_1. For these lookups to be efficient, we can use an *oblivious Cuckoo hashing* scheme [14,29,51] to achieve essentially $O(1)$ lookup time. Moreover, in the rebuild phase, the ith level is rebuilt every 2^i accesses. The work of Asharov et al. [5] achieves a linear rebuild time, giving an amortized overhead of $O(\log N) + \sum_{i=1}^{\log N} \frac{1}{2^i} \cdot O(2^i) = O(\log N)$. This complexity was then de-amortized in the work of Asharov et al. [6] to obtain $O(\log N)$ worst-case query complexity.

The main invariant maintained in the hierarchical construction is that any key corresponding to a real address will be looked up only once in the life span of an oblivious hash table H_i. To see this, note that once we find a key addr in level i, we search for dummies in subsequent layers. We then write back addr to H_1, and addr will always exist in a lower level than H_i until H_i is rebuilt. Therefore, the hash tables only need to guarantee obliviousness when this invariant is met.

2.2   Insufficiency of Standard Techniques

Authentication. For static databases (i.e., ones that do not support writes), one could use *message authentication codes* (MACs). MACs add tags to data (e.g., to ciphertexts) to make them difficult to modify or forge. However, when the database supports both reads and writes, MACs may not be sufficient because MACs do not protect against *replay attacks*, attacks where the server responds with old authenticated content. In particular, since ORAMs have to support dynamic updates, authentication alone is not sufficient. We show an explicit attack on hierarchical ORAMs including OptORAMa [5,6] and PanORAMa [53] even when MACs are added.

Replay Attack. First, suppose the user requests a read to address addr, and addr is found at hash table H_i. Consider a malicious database that effectively does not write the value of addr back to H_1. Now, suppose the user requests a write to address addr', and suppose that no rebuilding has happened between the two accesses (e.g., this happens when the number of total accesses so far is odd). If addr' = addr, since addr was not written back to H_1, the user looks up addr in all layers up to H_i, just as in the previous access. Therefore, the access pattern to tables $H_1, \cdots, H_i$ in both cases will look the same. On the other hand, if addr' $\neq$ addr, then the access pattern is very likely to be different. Hence, the adversary is able to distinguish between access patterns $A_1 = \{(\mathsf{read}, \mathsf{addr}), (\mathsf{write}, \mathsf{addr})\}$, and $A_2 = \{(\mathsf{read}, \mathsf{addr}), (\mathsf{write}, \mathsf{addr}')\}$, which breaks the obliviousness of the ORAM.

More generally, replay attacks can break the invariant that any key is looked up exactly once in the life span of an oblivious hash table. As a succinct summary, *obliviousness* of hash table lookups depends on the *correctness* of previous hash table lookups.

Time-Stamping. Goldreich and Ostrovsky [28] argue that their constructions are maliciously secure because it is possible to *time-stamp* all physical writes. Roughly speaking, time-stamping means that at any point in time, the client is able to locally compute the number of times any physical (not logical) address has been overwritten. If the client uses authenticated encryption to encrypt the data along with its time-stamp, any replay attack can be easily detected with essentially no blowup in overhead or local storage. In particular, since the hash tables in [28] are constructed using several AKS oblivious sorts [2], it is in fact time-stampable. Therefore, their construction gives a maliciously secure ORAM construction which achieves $O(\log^3 N)$ overhead. However, optimal ORAM schemes [5,6] do not seem to be time-stampable because they use techniques such as balls-in-bins hashing which do not have deterministic access patterns. Here is one example:

The Marking Problem. Consider the following arbitrary sequence of RAM operations, inspired by Lemma 3.3 of Dwork et al. [23].

– Initialize a database of size n and write 0 to all of the indices.
– Choose arbitrary $S \subseteq [n]$ of size $n/2$ and write 1 to all indices in S.

Claim 1. The Marking Problem as defined above cannot be time-stamped with $o(n)$ bits of memory.

Proof. A time-stamping function $T(i, t)$ outputs the number of times a given index i has been written to up to time t. Note that $T(i, 3n/2) = 2$ if and only if $i \in S$. Therefore, being able to compute $T(\cdot, \cdot)$ is sufficient to recover the set S. Since there are $2^{(1-o(1))n}$ possibilities for S, is clear that computing $T(\cdot, \cdot)$ must require $(1 - o(1)) \cdot n$ bits of space.

While this might seem like a contrived problem, this sequence of RAM operations shows up in OptORAMa and its de-amortized version [5,6] within the hash table implementation. In particular, whenever an address is visited in the hash table H_i at level i of the hierarchical ORAM, Asharov et al. [6] mark the visited elements and then remove these elements during the rebuild phase. Crucially, these hash table constructions [5,6] work off of Patel et al.'s [53] idea of reusing the residual randomness of *unvisited* elements to attain linear rebuild time. Therefore, it is important that all marked elements are memory checked and removed to achieve this guarantee. Since the sequence of logical addresses read could be arbitrary, by Claim 1, it is not possible to time-stamp this sequence in low space.

Merkle Trees. A common technique for checking consistency of data is Merkle trees [45], which are used in applications such as succinct argument systems for NP [36], trusted hardware [19], and blockchains. At a high level, a Merkle tree stores the database at the leaves of a binary tree, and each internal node contains hashes (e.g., using a collision resistant hash function) of its children nodes. One only has to locally store the root of the binary tree to be able to check consistency. While this would incur a $O(\log N)$ multiplicative overhead when applied to existing ORAM constructions in a black-box manner, Stefanov et al. [58] noticed that one can capitalize on the tree-based structure of path ORAM to superimpose a Merkle tree with $O(1)$ blowup. However, since the hierarchical ORAM constructions do not have a similar tree-based structure, it is not clear that a similar technique can be applied.

Memory Checking. More generally, one could use *memory checking* techniques [11] (defined in Sect. 4) to construct maliciously secure ORAMs. However, best known memory checkers are in fact tree-based, and they all have $O(\log N)$ bandwidth [11,23,52]. Therefore, generically applying existing memory checkers to optimal ORAM constructions will not give the desired overhead.

Generic Compilers. As posed in Question 2, one might ask if a more efficient generic compiler from honest-but-curious to maliciously secure ORAM exists. In Sect. 5, we show that such a compiler must also essentially be a memory checker. Intuitively, one could adversarially tamper with the database and embed an adversarially chosen access pattern into an honest-but-curious ORAM to force an incorrect response from the compiler. At this point, the (adversarially constructed) honest-but-curious ORAM can misbehave arbitrarily. We formalize this idea in Theorem 4 in Sect. 5.

More specifically, in Sect. 5, we define a variant of memory checking that only needs to be secure for user queries that are independent of the memory checker's server access pattern. In contrast, in the standard definition of memory checking, the user queries can adaptively depend on the memory checker's server access pattern. This variant of memory checking will allow us to separate out and embed adversarial user queries within an honest-but-curious ORAM. In fact, we show in Corollary 1 that this variant notion of memory checking is also *sufficient* for ORAM, crucially relying on the obliviousness of ORAM.

2.3   Our Techniques

As our starting point, we use the worst-case $O(\log N)$ overhead honest-but-curious ORAM construction of Asharov et al. [6]. Our main technique is carefully combining various forms of memory checking. Blum et al. [11] make the distinction between *online* and *offline* memory checkers. An *online memory checker* immediately verifies the correctness of every answer from the database. An *offline memory checker* is a batched version of online memory checking that only detects if *some* error has occurred after a long sequence of operations. We define these notions of memory checking formally in Sect. 4.

Online Memory Checking. Online memory checking is sufficient to guarantee malicious security, as any malicious response from the adversary can be immediately detected (as we prove in the full version [44]). Time-stamping is an online memory checking strategy that has $O(1)$ overhead. While most of the construction is time-stampable, as argued earlier, some parts of the algorithm have access patterns that are provably not time-stampable. Since the best known general online memory checkers have bandwidth $O(\log N)$, online memory checking alone does not seem sufficient to construct a maliciously secure ORAM with $O(\log N)$ overhead.

Offline Memory Checking. In offline memory checking, we require detection of an incorrect response only at the end of a given computation. It is possible with essentially only $O(1)$ amortized overhead [11,23]. However, offline memory checking does not necessarily prevent leakage. For example, the replay attack shows that if the outputs of the hash table lookups are tampered with, privacy leakage will occur before offline memory checking catches this error. To combat this issue, we characterize situations where offline memory checking is sufficient. We call an implementation *offline-safe* if directly applying offline memory checking results in a maliciously secure implementation.

Access-Deterministic Algorithms. Many sub-protocols of the construction have deterministic access patterns, i.e., access patterns that have no dependence on the input or any randomness. For example, in the AKS sorting network [2], the comparisons made by the algorithm are entirely determined by the edges of an expander graph, which is independent of the input array. In fact, many algorithms in OptORAMa, including tight compacting a bit array and interspersing two randomly shuffled arrays [5], have this flavor.

Since the access patterns of such algorithms are independent of the input in the honest-but-curious setting, it seems as though directly offline checking these algorithms is sufficient to make them maliciously secure. However, this is not always the case; the security of offline memory checking crucially depends on the implementation. We refer the reader to the full version [44] for a concrete example. To bypass these subtleties, we show (in Theorem 5) a generic way to convert access-deterministic algorithms into maliciously secure ones without worrying about implementation details. With this theorem, in Sect. 7, we compile many honest-but-curious building blocks from OptORAMa in an implementation-independent way into ones that are maliciously secure with $O(1)$ blowup.

One can view this as a strengthening of Goldreich and Ostrovsky's [28] notion of a time-stampable simulation, since an algorithm being access-deterministic, or more accurately, *write-deterministic* which we define in Sect. 6, is essentially equivalent to the existence of a (not necessarily efficiently computable) time-stamp function. However, Goldreich and Ostrovsky's algorithm [28] needs the time-stamp function to be efficiently computable in low space while ours just needs such a function to exist.

Access Patterns with Random Leakage. Some subprotocols in Asharov et al. [6] are in fact not access-deterministic. However, many such protocols only leak random values within intermediate stages. One such example is balls-in-bins hashing. Since the only values leaked in the process are the random values associated to each ball, this can be simulated and has no dependence on the input. Therefore, offline memory checking suffices in these cases as well. For a self-contained example, see the implementation of oblivious random permutation in the full version [44].

Conditionally Offline-Safe Access Patterns. Some subprotocols S in Asharov et al. [6] are neither time-stampable, access-deterministic, nor have only random leakage. However, the following is often true:

- These subprotocols S *are* offline-safe if we assume some other portion P of the memory is tamper-proof. We therefore call this protocol *conditionally offline-safe.*
- These portions of memory P are time-stampable, so we can use authentication to effectively assume that these portions cannot be tampered with.

Therefore, if we online memory check the time-stampable portions of memory, namely P, and simultaneously offline memory check the conditionally offline-safe portions, namely S, we can guarantee security against tampering adversaries. We give a concrete example (namely, the routing problem) of this technique in the full version [44]. We use this idea crucially in our hash table construction in Sect. 8 as well as in several of our building blocks in Sect. 7.

Post-Verifiable Offline Checking. Another issue is that as is, an adversary can tamper with the database after an offline check was conducted, making any reads to previously offline checked memory unreliable. To combat this, we modify the offline memory checking protocol of Blum et al. [11] to leave the memory in a *post-verifiable* state (using similar ideas as [4]). In particular, after an offline check of a batch of queries, the algorithm leaves the memory in a state that can be *online-checked* with query complexity $O(1)$ during future reads. This ensures that the contents of the memory cannot be tampered with after the offline check.

2.4   Word Size

Our results work for arbitrary word size w as long as $w = \omega(\log \lambda) = \omega(\log N)$ (for $N \leq \mathsf{poly}(\lambda)$, as it is in our setting) and $w \leq \mathsf{poly}(\lambda)$. Most prior work in the honest-but-curious regime focus on the setting where $w = \Theta(\log N)$. However, all existing techniques going from honest-but-curious to maliciously secure ORAM that preserve overhead require increasing the word size from $\Theta(\log N)$ to $\omega(\log N)$. For example, time-stamping requires separate MACs for each address, which each need to have length $\omega(\log \lambda)$. Also, collision-resistant hash functions (CRHFs), as used in Path ORAM [54,58], need to have output length $\omega(\log \lambda)$ to avoid birthday attacks.

In fact, we now give some barriers for going below word size $\omega(\log \lambda)$:

– The existing constructions of online memory checkers with $O(\log N)$ bandwidth need word size $\omega(\log \lambda)$ to guarantee $1 - \mathsf{negl}(\lambda)$ soundness [11,23,30, 31,48,52]. Since maliciously secure ORAM is a stronger primitive than online memory checking, this poses a barrier to constructing maliciously secure ORAM with $O(\log N)$ overhead and word size.

– Any online memory checker with $O(1)$ overhead and sublinear local space (i.e., in the computational soundness regime [47]) *must* have word size $\omega(\log \lambda)$, as otherwise, the adversary could simply return random values and break soundness with probability $1/\mathsf{poly}(\lambda)$ infinitely often. This captures the cases of time-stamping and CRHFs above.

– In the hierarchical paradigm, the replay attack shows that the correctness of each of the $\log N$ hash table lookups is necessary to guarantee obliviousness of the subsequent lookups. As a result, in the hierarchical paradigm, it seems that $O(1)$-overhead memory checking is necessary for each hash table lookup, and thus, making $\omega(\log \lambda)$ bits of communication necessary for each of the $\log N$ hash tables due to the previous argument.

3 Preliminaries

For a natural number $N \in \mathbb{N}$, we let $[N]$ denote the set $\{1, \ldots, N\}$. Throughout, we let λ denote the security parameter. We say a function $f : \mathbb{N} \to \mathbb{N}$ is *negligible* if for all constants $c \geq 0$, $\lim_{n \to \infty} f(n) \cdot n^c = 0$. We denote a negligible function in input λ by $\mathsf{negl}(\lambda)$. We say an algorithm is *PPT* if it runs in (non-uniform) probabilistic polynomial time.

For a (finite) set S, we use the notation $x \leftarrow S$ as shorthand for saying x is a random variable sampled uniformly from S. We abuse notation and write $x \leftarrow B()$ for saying that x is a sample from the output of a randomized algorithm B. For a stateful variable x, we often abuse notation and write $x \leftarrow y$ to denote the operation of updating the variable x to have value y. For $x, y \in \{0,1\}^n$, we use the notation $x \oplus y$ to denote bit-wise XOR of x and y, and for $x, y \in \{0,1\}^*$ we use the notation $x\|y$ and (x, y) to denote concatenation of x and y. We use the notation $\varnothing$ to denote an empty list or placeholder value, with the exact meaning being clear from context.

3.1 Random Access Memory

We work in the standard word RAM model throughout. Unless specified otherwise, the underlying RAM functionality we would like to make oblivious has N logical addresses and each memory cell indexed by $\mathsf{addr} \in [N]$ contains a word of size w, i.e., an element of $\{0,1\}^w$. (See Functionality 1 for more details.) For adversaries running in $\mathsf{poly}(\lambda)$ time to be able to store an N-word dictionary, we assume $w, N \leq \mathsf{poly}(\lambda)$.

To obliviously implement this RAM functionality (and other functionalities along the way), it will be convenient to work in a RAM model with a slightly larger word size $\overline{w}$ such that $\overline{w} = O(w)$. For clarity, we call w the *logical* or *plaintext* word size, and $\overline{w}$ the *physical* word size. Explicitly, we will set $\overline{w} = 10w$ such that $\overline{w} = \omega(\log \lambda)$ and $\overline{w} \leq \mathsf{poly}(\lambda)$, but we urge the reader to think of $\overline{w}$ as being an arbitrarily small function that is $\omega(\log \lambda)$. Since $\log(N) \leq O(\log \lambda) < \omega(\log \lambda) = \overline{w}$, physical words can contain a memory address, and we need $\overline{w} = \omega(\log \lambda)$ for security reasons so that ciphertexts and authentication tags can fit in a word and remain secure against $\mathsf{poly}(\lambda)$-time adversaries. (In particular, $2^{-\overline{w}} = \mathsf{negl}(\lambda)$.) See Sect. 2.4 for more details on this choice of word size.

As is standard in previous works, we assume that word-level addition and Boolean operations, and additionally pseudorandom function (PRF) evaluations, can be done in unit cost.

3.2 Cryptographic Primitives

In the full version [44], we formally define the cryptographic primitives we need, such as pseudorandom function families (PRFs), symmetric-key encryption, and message authentication codes (MACs).

3.3 Maliciously Secure Oblivious Simulation

Throughout this section, our definitions are inspired by Asharov et al. [5], but we crucially modify the definitions to describe security in the *malicious* setting. Recall that *honest-but-curious* security, as considered by Asharov et al. [5] and many prior works, only requires obliviousness of accesses with respect to a passive, non-tampering adversary, while *malicious* security requires obliviousness even if a tampering adversary can modify the database. Throughout the paper, we use the terms server, database, storage, and memory interchangeably, sometimes using adversary or $\mathcal{A}$ as a stand-in for the adversarial server.

Reactive Functionalities. Loosely speaking, a reactive functionality $\mathcal{F}$ is an interactive functionality that holds some internal state, and whenever it takes in a command cmd and input x, it gives some (possibly randomized) output $\mathcal{F}(\mathsf{cmd}, x)$, where the notational dependence on the internal hidden state is suppressed. One way to think of a reactive functionality is as a specification for a data structure problem (i.e., the desired behavior of a data structure), where the various types of queries are specified by cmd and the input to those queries are denoted by x.

Functionality 1. $\mathcal{F}_{\mathsf{RAM}}^{N,w}$: The RAM Functionality.

Syntax:
- cmd $\in \{\mathsf{read}, \mathsf{write}\}$;
- $x = (\mathsf{addr}, \mathsf{data}) \in [N] \times \{0,1\}^w$, where addr is an index into an N-entry RAM database, and data contains a word (to be used only if cmd = write).

Internal State: A memory array mem with N entries, each containing values in $\{0,1\}^w$, all initialized to 0^w.

Command $\mathcal{F}_{\mathsf{RAM}}^{N,w}(\mathsf{cmd}, x)$:
- If cmd = read, return mem[addr].
- If cmd = write, just update mem by mem[addr] $\leftarrow$ data and return nothing.

$\mathcal{F}_{\mathsf{RAM}}^{N,w}$ is an important example of a reactive functionality, and we describe it in Functionality 1. Another example of a reactive functionality that we will use is a hash table (see Functionality 4).

We formalize security for reactive functionalities by a simulation-based definition and require indistinguishability between a real-world and ideal-world experiment, as in Experiments 2 and 3. At a high level, for a fixed functionality $\mathcal{F}$, in the experiment, the (stateful) adversary $\mathcal{A}$ gets to adaptively choose (cmd, x) for the (stateful) client $\mathcal{C}$. In Experiments 2 and 3, the outer "while" loop corresponds to the adversary issuing multiple commands to the client, and the inner "while" loop corresponds to the client and adversary performing the RAM computation of the given command.

In the real world, the client $\mathcal{C}$, based on its knowledge of cmd and x, sends RAM queries $\mathsf{query} = (\mathsf{op}, \mathsf{addr}, \mathsf{data}) \in \{\mathsf{read}, \mathsf{write}\} \times [N] \times \{0,1\}^{\overline{w}}$ to the possibly malicious adversary $\mathcal{A}$. The adversary $\mathcal{A}$ can adaptively respond to each query with a possibly incorrect $\mathsf{data}^* \in \{0,1\}^{\overline{w}}$. At any point, $\mathcal{C}$ can abort (by setting flag = true, at which point the whole experiment ends), or it can claim it is finished and output out. This continues until either (a) $\mathcal{A}$ stops issuing commands or (b) $\mathcal{C}$ aborts at some point. In the ideal world, we require the existence of a simulator $\mathcal{S}$ that can simulate all the query and abort behavior of $\mathcal{C}$ without knowing x. We do not require the simulator to compute out, as this is in general impossible without knowing x. We instead (implicitly) set out $= \mathcal{F}(\mathsf{cmd}, x)$ and give this output to the adversary $\mathcal{A}$ in issuing its next command.

Our security definition is informally that no efficient $\mathcal{A}$ can distinguish between the two worlds. Since $\mathcal{A}$ jointly sees both the access pattern of $\mathcal{C}$ and the output of the computation, this indistinguishability asserts both obliviousness and correctness simultaneously. We present the formal definition in Definition 1.

Definition 1. *For a reactive functionality $\mathcal{F}$, we say a (stateful) RAM machine $\mathcal{C}_{\mathcal{F}}$ is a $(1 - \delta)$-maliciously secure oblivious implementation of a reactive functionality $\mathcal{F}$ if the following two conditions hold:*

1. **Obliviousness & Correctness**: *There is a (stateful) PPT simulator $\mathcal{S}$ such that for all (stateful) PPT $\mathcal{A}$, the adversary $\mathcal{A}$ distinguishes between* REAL($\mathcal{C}_{\mathcal{F}}, \mathcal{A}$) *(Experiment 2) and* IDEAL($\mathcal{F}, \mathcal{S}, \mathcal{A}$) *(Experiment 3) with advantage at most δ.*

2. **Completeness**: *For all (stateful) honest-but-curious $\mathcal{A}$, with probability $1-\delta$, the client $\mathcal{C}_{\mathcal{F}}$ never aborts, i.e., never sets* flag *to* true *throughout the whole execution of the real experiment.*

When δ is not specified, it is taken to mean an arbitrary negligible function in λ.

Experiment 2. REAL($\mathcal{C}, \mathcal{A}$).	Experiment 3. IDEAL($\mathcal{F}, \mathcal{S}, \mathcal{A}$).
$(\mathsf{cmd}, x) \leftarrow \mathcal{A}\left(1^{\lambda}\right)$	$(\mathsf{cmd}, x) \leftarrow \mathcal{A}\left(1^{\lambda}\right)$
while $\mathsf{cmd} \neq \perp$ **do**	**while** $\mathsf{cmd} \neq \perp$ **do**
$\quad$ out $\leftarrow \perp$	$\quad$ done $\leftarrow$ false
$\quad$ data$^{*} \leftarrow \perp$	$\quad$ data$^{*} \leftarrow \perp$
$\quad$ **while** out $= \perp$ **do**	$\quad$ **while** done $=$ false **do**
$\quad\quad$ (query, flag, out) $\leftarrow \mathcal{C}\left(1^{\lambda}, \mathsf{cmd}, x, \mathsf{data}^{*}\right)$	$\quad\quad$ (query, flag, done) $\leftarrow \mathcal{S}\left(1^{\lambda}, \mathsf{cmd}, \mathsf{data}^{*}\right)$
$\quad\quad$ **if** flag $=$ true **then return** $b \leftarrow \mathcal{A}\left(1^{\lambda}\right)$	$\quad\quad$ **if** flag $=$ true **then return** $b \leftarrow \mathcal{A}\left(1^{\lambda}\right)$
$\quad\quad$ data$^{*} \leftarrow \mathcal{A}\left(1^{\lambda}, \mathsf{query}\right)$	$\quad\quad$ data$^{*} \leftarrow \mathcal{A}\left(1^{\lambda}, \mathsf{query}\right)$
$\quad$ **end while**	$\quad$ **end while**
$\quad$ $(\mathsf{cmd}, x) \leftarrow \mathcal{A}\left(1^{\lambda}, \text{out}\right)$	$\quad$ $(\mathsf{cmd}, x) \leftarrow \mathcal{A}\left(1^{\lambda}, \mathcal{F}(\mathsf{cmd}, x)\right)$
end while	**end while**
return $b \leftarrow \mathcal{A}\left(1^{\lambda}\right)$	**return** $b \leftarrow \mathcal{A}\left(1^{\lambda}\right)$

We focus on three main complexity measures of implementations: *query complexity*, *local space complexity*, and *server space complexity*. The query complexity for a specific cmd refers to the number of RAM queries made by $\mathcal{C}$ needed to generate out for cmd. We use the terms *time*, *run-time*, and query complexity interchangeably. Local space complexity denotes the number of words an implementation $\mathcal{C}$ locally (and privately) stores, and server space complexity refers to the amount of space needed on the server by the implementation.

A special case of oblivious implementation is oblivious RAM (ORAM), where the reactive functionality being implemented is the RAM functionality itself:

Definition 2 (Oblivious RAM). *We say that $\mathcal{C}$ is a $(1 - \delta)$-maliciously secure oblivious RAM (ORAM) (or honest-but-curious $(1 - \delta)$-ORAM) for a database of size N with word size w if $\mathcal{C}$ is a $(1-\delta)$-maliciously secure oblivious (or honest-but-curious $(1 - \delta)$-oblivious, respectively) implementation of $\mathcal{F}_{\mathsf{RAM}}^{N,w}$. When δ is unspecified, we take it to mean an arbitrary function negligible in λ.*

We define the *overhead* of an ORAM $\mathcal{C}$ to be the maximum of the query complexities of the read and write commands for $\mathcal{C}$. In fact, our ORAM construction will also hide whether there the logical query is a read or write, making read or write part of the input, not the command. One can generically show that these definitions of ORAM are equivalent up to a multiplicative factor of two in the overhead, so we use them interchangeably.

4 Memory Checking

In this section, we define the main notions of memory checking that we will use, and we describe how memory checking can be used to construct maliciously secure oblivious implementations. Many details have been deferred to the full version [44].

4.1 Definitions

We recall the notion of memory checking from Blum et al. [11]. A memory checker M can be defined as a probablistic RAM program that interacts with a user $\mathcal{C}$ and server $\mathcal{A}$, where $\mathcal{C}$ is performing a RAM computation with memory held by $\mathcal{A}$. Specifically, without a memory checker, $\mathcal{C}$ sends $\mathsf{query}_{\mathcal{C}} = (\mathsf{cmd}, \mathsf{addr}, \mathsf{data}) \in \{\mathsf{read}, \mathsf{write}\} \times [N] \times (\{0,1\}^{\overline{w}} \cup \{\bot\})$ to $\mathcal{A}$, who may or may not correctly follow the RAM command, i.e., may send the wrong word back to $\mathcal{C}$ when $\mathsf{cmd} = \mathsf{read}$. With memory checker M, M now serves as an intermediary between $\mathcal{C}$ and $\mathcal{A}$ that takes in each $\mathsf{query}_{\mathcal{C}}$ from $\mathcal{C}$ and generates and sends (possibly multiple and adaptive) queries to $\mathcal{A}$. Whenever $\mathsf{cmd} = \mathsf{read}$, $\mathcal{C}$ once again generates and sends (possibly multiple and adaptive) queries to $\mathcal{A}$, and M is then required to either respond to $\mathcal{C}$ with some word or abort by sending $\bot$ to indicate a malicious $\mathcal{A}$. Once the memory checker aborts, the protocol is done. This continues in rounds until $\mathcal{C}$ is done sending queries, of which there are at most $\mathsf{poly}(\lambda)$.

Definition 3 (Online Memory Checker). *We say that M is an* online *memory checker for $\mathcal{C}$ if the following two properties hold:*

1. **Completeness**: *If $\mathcal{A}$ is honest (i.e., behaves according to $\mathcal{F}_{\mathsf{RAM}}$), then M never aborts and the responses that M sends to $\mathcal{C}$ are all correct with probability $1 - \mathsf{negl}(\lambda)$.*
2. **Soundness**: *For all PPT $\mathcal{A}$, the probability that M ever sends some incorrect response to $\mathcal{C}$ is $\mathsf{negl}(\lambda)$. That is, for each request from $\mathcal{C}$, if $\mathcal{A}$ sends an incorrect response to M, M can either independently recover the correct answer and send it to $\mathcal{C}$, or it can abort by sending $\bot$ to $\mathcal{C}$.*

We call this memory checker "online" because the memory checker must be able to catch incorrect responses from M as soon they are sent. On the other hand, one can define the notion of an "offline" memory checker:

Definition 4 (Offline Memory Checker). *We say that M is an* offline *memory checker for $\mathcal{C}$ if the following two properties hold:*

1. **Completeness**: *If $\mathcal{A}$ is honest (i.e., behaves according to $\mathcal{F}_{\mathsf{RAM}}$), then M never aborts, and the responses that M sends to $\mathcal{C}$ are all correct with probability $1 - \mathsf{negl}(\lambda)$.*
2. **Soundness**: *For all PPT $\mathcal{A}$, if M ever sends an incorrect response to $\mathcal{C}$, it must abort by the end of the last request made by $\mathcal{C}$ with probably at least $1 - \mathsf{negl}(\lambda)$.*[4]

---

[4] More formally, for the last request, the user $\mathcal{C}$ must send some "last request" symbol along with its query to indicate to M that it is the final request. We omit this technicality for simplicity.

That is, M may send many incorrect responses to $\mathcal{C}$, but if it does, by the end of the computation, M detects that there was an error at some point. We emphasize that M does not need to know where or when an error occurred.

Note that when we say M is an online or offline memory checker for an implementation $\mathcal{C}$, we mean this is true against adversaries that can both tamper with the server and adaptively feed commands and inputs into $\mathcal{C}$.

There are two main complexity measures we associate with (both online and offline) memory checkers: *(local) space complexity* and *query complexity* (or *overhead*). *Space complexity* is simply the amount of space (in words) used by the memory checker M, and worst-case (or amortized) *query complexity* is the worst-case (or amortized, respectively) number of requests made by M per request of $\mathcal{C}$ throughout the computation. We also sometimes explicitly consider the *server space complexity* of memory checkers, which refers to how many physical words are needed to be stored on the server. Unless specified otherwise, for a user $\mathcal{C}$ generating queries according to a RAM of size N, the server space complexity of memory checkers will be $O(N)$.

4.2   Memory Checking and ORAM

In the full version [44], we show the following.

- We show formally that online memory checking is sufficient to compile an honest-but-curious implementation into a maliciously secure one. As a corollary [28], time-stampable implementations can be made maliciously secure with no asymptotic overhead.
- As a corollary, we show that any implementation can be made maliciously secure with an $O(\log N)$ overhead using standard online memory checking techniques as proposed by Blum et al. [11].
- We define the notion of a post-verifiable offline checker and present a post-verifiable offline checker with amortized $O(1)$ query complexity during the offline-check and worst-case $O(1)$ query complexity for later reads.

5   Separated Memory Checkers

In this section, we define a variant of online memory checking that we show is both necessary and sufficient for generically compiling honest-but-curious ORAM clients into maliciously secure ones. At a high level, such an online memory checker M will be secure for arbitrary small-space RAM users $\mathcal{C}$ that do not interactively collude with the tampering server. As such, we call such memory checkers *separated memory checkers*. We give a formal definition below:

Definition 5 (Separated Memory Checker). *We say that M is a* separated memory checker for users with space c *(measured in words) if the following two properties hold:*

1. **Completeness**: *If $\mathcal{A}$ is honest (i.e., behaves according to $\mathcal{F}_{\mathsf{RAM}}$), then for all requests generated by a user $\mathcal{C}$ with space c, where $\mathcal{C}$ cannot see physical queries made by M, M never aborts with probability $1 - \mathsf{negl}(\lambda)$.*

2. **Soundness**: *For all PPT $\mathcal{A}$ and all c-space users $\mathcal{C}$, where $\mathcal{A}$ and $\mathcal{C}$ do not communicate throughout the entire protocol, the probability that M ever sends some incorrect response to $\mathcal{C}$ is $\mathsf{negl}(\lambda)$. That is, for each request from $\mathcal{C}$, if $\mathcal{A}$ sends an incorrect response to M, M can either independently recover the correct answer and send it to $\mathcal{C}$, or it can abort by sending $\perp$ to $\mathcal{C}$.*

The differences between this definition and the earlier memory checking definitions (Definitions 3 and 4) are as follows:

- While online memory checkers according to Definition 3 are defined in terms of specific users $\mathcal{C}$, as is convenient when describing time-stamping, in Definition 5, these memory checkers are defined for general low-space users $\mathcal{C}$.
- While offline memory checkers according to Definition 4 are phrased in terms of users $\mathcal{C}$ that are adaptively controlled by the server $\mathcal{A}$, here we explicitly separate $\mathcal{C}$ and $\mathcal{A}$ throughout the interactive protocol. However, since we quantify over all low-space $\mathcal{C}$ and PPT $\mathcal{A}$, the user and server can effectively collude beforehand to try to break the memory checker.
- We need completeness and soundness only against users with space c.

Remark 1. We note that the lower bound of Dwork et al. [23] can be adapted to show that that deterministic, non-adaptive separated memory checkers must also have $\Omega(\log N / \log \log N)$ overhead. Since we restrict the adversary to be separated, this definition is weaker than general purpose online memory checking, e.g., as in Blum et al. [11].

Throughout this section, for simplicity, we will consider ORAMs for a database of size N to have physical server space $O(N)$, as constructions with optimal overhead achieve this server space complexity. First, we show that a generic compiler must be a separated memory checker.

Theorem 3. *Suppose RAM program Π is such that that for all honest-but-curious ORAM $\mathcal{C}$ for a database of size N with local space at most c, the composition of Π and $\mathcal{C}$ is a maliciously secure ORAM size N. If Π has worst-case blowup in query complexity ℓ, then there is a separated memory checker for users with space $O(c)$ for a database of size N that has worst-case query complexity $O(\ell)$.*

In particular, if there does not exist a separated memory checker for users with space $O(1)$ (and a PRF key) with worst-case blowup in query complexity $O(1)$, then there is no worst-case $O(1)$-blowup Π such that composing an arbitrary honest-but-curious, $O(1)$ local space ORAM with Π will be maliciously secure.

Proof (sketch). We fix an honest-but-curious ORAM $\mathcal{C}$ with local space at most c and query complexity ℓ, and we construct a family of honest-but-curious ORAMs

$\{\mathcal{C}'_\mathcal{P}\}_\mathcal{P}$ by combining $\mathcal{C}$ with arbitrary RAM users $\mathcal{P}$ that use space c, so that each $\mathcal{C}'_\mathcal{P}$ has local space complexity $O(c)$ and query complexity $O(\ell)$. Furthermore, we augment $\mathcal{C}'_\mathcal{P}$ so that it detects any incorrect responses to queries from $\mathcal{P}$ with non-negligible probability, at which point it behaves arbitrarily (e.g., gives an incorrect response). We then construct a separated memory checker for $O(c)$ space users Π' by combining Π and $\mathcal{C}$. We argue that if there is some $\mathcal{P}$ for which Π' is not a memory checker, then composing Π with $\mathcal{C}'_\mathcal{P}$ is not maliciously secure, which is a contradiction.

We defer the proof of Theorem 3 to the full version [44]. Now, we show that such online memory checkers are sufficient to generically compile any honest-but-curious ORAM into a maliciously secure one.

Theorem 4. *Suppose that M is a separated memory checker for users with space $O(c)$. Then, for any honest-but-curious ORAM $\mathcal{C}$ with client space complexity c, M is an online memory checker for $\mathcal{C}$, in the sense of Definition 3.*

Proof (sketch). Since $\mathcal{C}$ has space complexity c, there exists a simulator $\mathcal{S}$ for $\mathcal{C}$ with space complexity $O(c)$. In particular, M is a good memory checker for $\mathcal{S}$ since $\mathcal{S}$ is *separated* from the ORAM user. Hence, $\mathcal{C}$ with arbitrary inputs is indistinguishable from a separated RAM user, namely $\mathcal{S}$. Therefore, we argue that if M doesn't satisfy either completeness or soundness for $\mathcal{C}$, one can use M to construct an *honest-but-curious* adversary $\mathcal{A}$ (i.e., one that does not send incorrect responses) that distinguishes $\text{REAL}(\mathcal{C}, \mathcal{A})$ and $\text{IDEAL}(\mathcal{F}_{\text{RAM}}, \mathcal{S}, \mathcal{A})$.

We defer the proof of Theorem 4 to the full version [44]. We now have the following immediate corollary.

Corollary 1. *Suppose that $\mathcal{C}$ is an honest-but-curious ORAM with client space complexity c, and suppose there is a separated memory checker M for users with space $O(c)$. Then, the composition of M and $\mathcal{C}$ is a maliciously secure ORAM.*

6   Write-Deterministic Implementations

In this section, we formalize how an *access-deterministic* honest-but-curious oblivious algorithm can be made oblivious against malicious servers with $O(1)$ blowup in overhead. In fact, we only need the *writes* to be deterministic, meaning that the reads can occur to arbitrary addresses. This motivates the following definition.

Definition 6. *We say a RAM program $\mathcal{C}$ is $(1 - \epsilon)$-write-deterministic if there exists a fixed set $S_\mathcal{C}$ of time and address pairs such that for all x, whenever $\mathcal{C}$ does not abort,*

$$\{(t, \mathsf{addr}) : \text{on input } x \text{ , } \mathcal{C} \text{ makes a write to } \mathsf{addr} \text{ at time } t\} = S_\mathcal{C}$$

when $\mathcal{C}$ is interacting with an honest RAM server, and for all x, $\mathcal{C}$ aborts with probability at most ϵ when interacting with an honest server. That is, for all x, *the timing and locations of writes that C makes are deterministic and completely independent of x. (This definition says nothing about the content of the writes or the contents or addresses of the reads, but it does implicitly fix the timing of the reads.) Whenever ϵ is unspecified, we take it to mean $\epsilon = 0$.*

Since the writes are deterministic, this definition can be seen as asserting the existence of a time-stamp function, or "time-labeling" in the sense of Goldreich and Ostrovsky [28], but without any requirement that such a function is computable in low space. We now show that this notion (without any efficiency requirements) is sufficient to get malicious security.

Theorem 5. *Suppose $C_{\mathcal{F}}$ is a $(1-\delta)$-honest-but-curious oblivious, $(1-\epsilon)$-write-deterministic implementation for a stateless functionality $\mathcal{F}$ with client space complexity c, server space s and query complexity q. Then, there exists a $(1 - O(\delta) - O(\epsilon) - \mathsf{negl}(\lambda))$-maliciously secure oblivious implementation $C'_{\mathcal{F}}$ for $\mathcal{F}$ with query complexity $O(q + s)$, server space complexity $O(q + s)$, and client space complexity $O(c)$ (and one PRF key).*

Proof (sketch). As mentioned in Sect. 2, offline memory checking a write-deterministic honest-but-curious oblivious algorithm directly may not be maliciously secure. We circumvent this by first running the honest-but-curious algorithm on some fixed dummy input (independent of the real input) to essentially build a time-stamp array. By offline-checking up until the array is built, we ensure correctness of the time-stamp array. Note that obliviousness is guaranteed throughout the offline check because nothing about the real input is used when building the array. After this check is finished, the algorithm now runs on the real input, using the post-verifiability of the time-stamp array to verify time-stamps in MACs in an online way. This allows one to catch any replay attacks by the adversarial server immediately.

We defer the algorithm and the full proof to full version [44].

In Sect. 7, we argue that many of our ORAM building blocks such as sorting, tight compaction and Cuckoo hashing are in fact access-deterministic and therefore write-deterministic. Therefore, these can be made maliciously secure with low overhead by directly applying Theorem 5.

7   Overview of Maliciously Secure Building Blocks

Our ORAM construction relies on several oblivious building blocks. We describe how we modify existing algorithms for these building blocks to be maliciously secure with small (usually $O(1)$) *blowup*, i.e., multiplicative increase in query complexity, relative to the honest-but-curious counterparts. For the explicit constructions and proofs, see the full version [44].

– **Maliciously Secure Oblivious RAM with $O(\log^4 n)$ overhead**: We modify the existing perfectly secure honest-but-curious ORAM with $O(\log^3 n)$

overhead due to Chan et al. [15] to obtain a maliciously secure ORAM with $O(\log^4 n)$ overhead with only a $\mathsf{negl}(\lambda)$ security loss independently of n, as long as $n \leq \mathsf{poly}(\lambda)$.

- **Oblivious Sorting Algorithms**: We argue that the sorting algorithm of Ajtai et al. [2] and the packed sorting algorithm of Asharov et al. [6,8] are access-deterministic, and thus can be made maliciously secure with $O(1)$ blowup in query complexity.
- **Oblivious Two-Key Dictionary**: Similarly to Asharov et al. [6], we give a maliciously secure implementation of a dictionary where each element has two keys such that one can pop elements with respect to either key. We do this by constructing a non-oblivious data structure and then composing it with the maliciously secure ORAM with $O(\log^4 n)$ overhead.
- **Oblivious Random Permutation**: We modify the random shuffling algorithm of Chan et al. [13] to be maliciously secure with $O(1)$ blowup using offline checking.
- **Oblivious Bin Placement**: A placement algorithm was proposed by Chan et al. [14] to obliviously route elements in an array. We argue that it is time-stampable and can be made maliciously secure with $O(1)$ blowup.
- **Oblivious Balls-into-Bins Sampling**: We adapt the algorithm of Asharov et al. [5] by applying online memory checking techniques to provide a maliciously secure algorithm for sampling balls-in-bins loads efficiently.
- **Tight Compaction, Intersperse, & Perfect Random Permutation**: Tight compaction takes as input an array where some elements are marked and outputs a permutation of the array so that all the marked elements appear before the unmarked elements. Intersperse is an algorithm which, given two randomly shuffled arrays, outputs a random shuffle of the concatenation of the two arrays. Asharov et al. [5] give an algorithm to randomly shuffle lists with $O(n \log n)$ queries with no failure probability. Since all of these algorithms are access-deterministic, we directly apply Theorem 5.
- **Oblivious Cuckoo Hashing**: Chan et al. [14] give an oblivious algorithm to compute Cuckoo hash tables with essentially $O(1)$ lookup time. We argue this algorithm can be made maliciously secure with $O(1)$ blowup because it is access-deterministic.
- **Deduplication**: Asharov et al. [6] give a linear-time oblivious algorithm to take a union of two randomly shuffled arrays while removing duplicates. We make this maliciously secure with $O(1)$ blowup using our maliciously secure hash table construction as given in Sect. 8.

8   Maliciously Secure Oblivious Hash Table

In this section, we construct an efficient maliciously secure oblivious implementation of the hash table functionality $\mathcal{F}_{\mathsf{HT}}$ (Functionality 4). Following previous works, in our ORAM construction, we use this hash table implementation to implement each layer of the hierarchical ORAM.

The works of Asharov et al. [5,6] provide an implementation CombHT of $\mathcal{F}_{\mathsf{HT}}$ with the following properties:

- The input array of size n satisfies $\log^{11} \lambda \leq n \leq \text{poly}(\lambda)$.
- Both CombHT.Build() and CombHT.Extract() run in $O(n)$ time.
- Each CombHT.Lookup() call takes $O(1)$ time ignoring linear scans over a $O(\log \lambda)$-sized stash, which in the final ORAM construction will end up being amortized over many lookups.

Functionality 4. $\mathcal{F}_{\mathsf{HT}}^n$: Hash Table Functionality for Non-Recurrent Lookups

Command $\mathcal{F}_{\mathsf{HT}}^n$.Build():
- **Input:** An array $\boldsymbol{I} = (a_1, \ldots, a_n)$ containing n elements, where each a_i is either dummy or a (key, value) pair denoted $(k_i, v_i) \in \{0,1\}^D \times \{0,1\}^D$ where $D := O(1) \cdot w$ where w is the plaintext word size.
- **Input assumptions:** The elements in the array are uniformly shuffled, and all real keys contained in $\{k_1, k_2, \ldots, k_n\}$ are distinct.
- **The procedure:** Initialize a list $\boldsymbol{P} \leftarrow \varnothing$. Initialize the internal state := $(\boldsymbol{I}, \boldsymbol{P})$.

Command $\mathcal{F}_{\mathsf{HT}}^n$.Lookup():
- **Input:** a key $k \in \{0,1\}^D \cup \{\bot\}$.
- **The procedure:** Parse the internal state as state = $(\boldsymbol{I}, \boldsymbol{P})$. If $k \in \boldsymbol{P}$, set $v^* = \bot$. If $k = \bot$ or $k \notin \boldsymbol{I}$, set $v^* = \bot$. Otherwise, set $v^* = v$ where v is the value that corresponds to the key k in $\boldsymbol{I}'$.
- **Output:** The element v^*.

Command $\mathcal{F}_{\mathsf{HT}}^n$.Extract():
- **The procedure:** Parse the internal state state = $(\boldsymbol{I}, \boldsymbol{P})$.Define an array $\boldsymbol{J} = \{a_1', a_2', \ldots, a_n'\}$ from $\boldsymbol{I}$ as follows: For $i \in [n]$, set $a_i' = a_i$ if $a_i \notin \boldsymbol{P}$, otherwise set $a_i' = \text{dummy}$. Shuffle $\boldsymbol{J}$ uniformly.
- **Output:** The array $\boldsymbol{J}$.

At a high level, this is achieved by hashing in two levels: the first level of hashing is a standard balls and bins hashing into $\frac{n}{\text{polylog}(\lambda)}$ bins (which they call BigHT), and each bin is then implemented as a $\text{polylog}(\lambda)$ size Cuckoo hash table (called SmallHT). In particular, they present CombHT in the SmallHT-hybrid model.

However, as presented, it is not clear how the CombHT construction in [5, 6] can be made obliviously secure with $O(1)$ multiplicative overhead. If each SmallHT instance is used in a black-box way, by a variant of the marking lower bound in Sect. 2, online memory checking which indices were accessed in each SmallHT instance (as needed to remove accessed elements when implementing SmallHT.Extract()) is not possible in low space.

Therefore, to make a maliciously secure version of CombHT with small local space, we combine the SmallHT instances in a non-black-box way. Specifically, in MalHT, we time-stamp a list of all accessed elements across SmallHT instances as the lookups occur, and then to support MalHT.Extract(), we do an offline memory check, as the access pattern will be conditionally write-deterministic on the time-stamped list of lookups.

Now, we present MalHT, a maliciously secure implementation of Functionality 4.

Algorithm 5. MalHT.Build(): Hash table for shuffled inputs.

Input: An array $I = (a_1, \ldots, a_n)$ containing n elements, where each a_i is either dummy or a (key, value) pair denoted (k_i, v_i) where both the key k and the value v are D-bit strings, where $D := O(1) \cdot w$.

Input assumptions: The elements in the array are uniformly shuffled, and all real keys contained in $\{k_1, k_2, \ldots, k_n\}$ are distinct.

Secret key: Sample a random PRF secret key sk. Use $\mathsf{PRF_{sk}}(\text{"Enc"}||\cdot)$ for all ciphertexts, and use $\mathsf{PRF_{sk}}(\text{"MAC"}||\cdot)$ for all MACs, where we now abuse notation and overload sk to denote the secret key for both.

Authenticated Encryption: Unless otherwise specified, for every write query (write, addr, data), data is replaced with $\mathsf{data}' := (\mathsf{ct} \leftarrow \mathsf{Enc_{sk}}(\mathsf{data}), \sigma \leftarrow \mathsf{MAC_{sk}}(\mathsf{ct}, \mathsf{addr}))$. Reads are passed through authenticated decryption, namely unpacking $\mathsf{data}' = (\mathsf{ct}^*, \sigma^*)$, checking $\mathsf{MACVer_{sk}}((\mathsf{ct}^*, \mathsf{addr}), \sigma^*) = 1$, aborting if verification fails, and otherwise returning $\mathsf{data}^* = \mathsf{Dec_{sk}}(\mathsf{ct}^*)$.

Memory checking: To make the algorithm maliciously obliviously secure, we combine both online and offline memory checking components. All portions that are post-verifiably offline memory checked are boxed out in gray (corresponding to the Read/Write phase), and all portions of memory that are not online-checkable via time-stamping will be indicated with superscript off. We time-stamp all other parts of this implementation.

The algorithm:

1. Let $\mu := \log^9 \lambda$, $\epsilon := \frac{1}{\log^2 \lambda}$, $\delta := e^{-\log \lambda \cdot \log \log \lambda}$, and $B := \lceil n/\mu \rceil$.
2. Initialize arrays $\mathsf{Bin}_1^{\mathsf{off}}, \mathsf{Bin}_2^{\mathsf{off}}, \ldots, \mathsf{Bin}_B^{\mathsf{off}}$ of size $\mu + 0.5 \cdot \epsilon\mu$ to $\varnothing$.
3. Initialize counters $c_1^{\mathsf{off}}, \ldots, c_B^{\mathsf{off}} := 0$.
4. *Balls in bins hashing to leave results in a post-verifiable state:*
   - For $i = 1, 2, \ldots, n$, throw real items $a_i = (k_i, v_i)$ into bin $\mathsf{Bin}_j^{\mathsf{off}}$ where $j = \mathsf{PRF_{sk}}(0||k_i) \pmod B$. If $a_i = $ dummy, throw it into a uniformly random bin. Concretely:
     - Every bin $\mathsf{Bin}_j^{\mathsf{off}}$ has an associated counter c_j^{off}.
     - Retrieve counter c_j^{off}. If $c_j^{\mathsf{off}} > |\mathsf{Bin}_j^{\mathsf{off}}|$, output $\perp$.
     - Place a_i in position $\mathsf{Bin}_j^{\mathsf{off}}[c_j^{\mathsf{off}}]$.
     - Increment c_j^{off}.
   - Initialize lists $\mathsf{Bin}_1, \ldots, \mathsf{Bin}_B$ to $\varnothing$.
   - For $i = 1, \ldots, B$, using the post-verifiability of the offline memory checker, copy over the contents of $\mathsf{Bin}_i^{\mathsf{off}}$ into Bin_i sequentially with appropriate timestamps.
5. *Sampling secret loads:*
   - Sample $(L_1, \ldots, L_B) \leftarrow \mathsf{SampleBinLoads}_{B,\delta}(n')$, where $n' = n \cdot (1 - \epsilon)$.
   - For any $i \in [B]$, if $||\mathsf{Bin}_i| - \mu| > 0.5\epsilon\mu$ or $\left|L_i - \frac{n'}{B}\right| > 0.5\epsilon\mu$, output $\perp$.
6. *Creating major bins:*
   - Initialize new bins $\mathsf{Bin}_1', \ldots, \mathsf{Bin}_B'$, each of size μ.

- For each $1 \leq i \leq B$, iterate in parallel over all of Bin_i and Bin'_i, and copy over the first L_i elements from Bin_i to Bin'_i, and fill the remaining $\mu - L_i$ slots of Bin'_i with dummy.

7. *Creating overflow pile.*
   - Iterate over all of Bin_i, and replace the first L_i positions with dummy, and rewrite the unmodified contents.
   - Concatenate $X = \mathsf{Bin}_1\|\mathsf{Bin}_2\|\ldots\|\mathsf{Bin}_B$.
   - Run $Y \leftarrow \mathsf{TightCompaction}(X)$ to move real elements to the front.
   - Truncate Y to length $2\epsilon \cdot n$.

8. *Prepare Cuckoo hash tables for efficient lookup:* For each $i = 1, 2, \ldots, B$:
   - Obtain the Cuckoo hashing initialized array $\boldsymbol{X}_i \leftarrow \mathsf{CuckooInit}(\mathsf{Bin}'_i)$ (note that this is not a hybrid call; we instead separate the pseudocode for readability). This subroutine intersperses dummies to pad the array to length $c_{\mathsf{cuckoo}} \cdot |\mathsf{Bin}_i| + \log \lambda$. See the full version [44] for the full description.
   - Iterate over indices j in $\boldsymbol{X}_i$ and create the metadata array $\mathbf{MD}_{\boldsymbol{X}_i}$ and do the following:
     • If $\boldsymbol{X}_i[j] = (k_j, v_j)$ is a real element, let $\mathbf{MD}_{\boldsymbol{X}_i}[j] := (\mathsf{choice}_{1,j}, \mathsf{choice}_{2,j})$ where $(\mathsf{choice}_{1,j}, \mathsf{choice}_{2,j}) \leftarrow \mathsf{PRF}_{\mathsf{sk}}(i\|k_j)$.
     • If $\boldsymbol{X}_i[j]$ is a dummy, let $\mathbf{MD}_{\boldsymbol{X}_i}[j] := (\bot, \bot)$.
   - Call the subroutine $\mathbf{Assign}_{\boldsymbol{X}_i} \leftarrow \mathsf{CuckooMD}(\mathbf{MD}_{\boldsymbol{X}_i})$ to obtain the Cuckoo hashing assignment, where we use the *packed* cuckooAssign algorithm that capitalizes on packed sorting. See the full version [44] for the details.
   - Initialize $\mathsf{CBin}_i^{\mathsf{off}}$ to be an empty array of size $\mu \cdot c_{\mathsf{cuckoo}}$, and initialize $\mathsf{S}_i^{\mathsf{off}}$ to be the stash of size $\log \lambda$ associated with $\mathsf{CBin}_i^{\mathsf{off}}$.
   - Route the elements of $\boldsymbol{X}_i$ according to $\mathbf{Assign}_{\boldsymbol{X}_i}$ to $\mathsf{CBin}_i^{\mathsf{off}} \cup \mathsf{S}_i^{\mathsf{off}}$ in the clear. More concretely, for $j = 1, 2, \ldots, |\boldsymbol{X}_i|$:
     • Let $(k, v) \leftarrow \boldsymbol{X}_i[j]$ (note that k may be a dummy).
     • Let $\mathsf{addr} \leftarrow \mathbf{Assign}_{\boldsymbol{X}_i}[j]$.
     • If $\mathsf{addr} \in \mathsf{CBin}_i^{\mathsf{off}}$, then write $\mathsf{CBin}_i^{\mathsf{off}}[\mathsf{addr}] := (k, v)$.
     • If $\mathsf{addr} \in \mathsf{S}_i^{\mathsf{off}}$, then write $\mathsf{S}_i^{\mathsf{off}}[\mathsf{addr}] := (k, v)$.
   - Initialize CBin_i to be an empty array of size $\mu \cdot c_{\mathsf{cuckoo}}$, and initialize S_i to be the stash of size $\log \lambda$ associated with CBin_i.
   - Using the post-verifiability of the offline memory checker, copy $\mathsf{CBin}_i^{\mathsf{off}} \cup \mathsf{S}_i^{\mathsf{off}}$ into $\mathsf{CBin}_i \cup \mathsf{S}_i$ sequentially with appropriate timestamps.

9. *Prepare Overflow Cuckoo hash table for efficient lookup:*
   - As described in the full version [44], run $\mathsf{cuckooAssign}(Y)$ (without packed sorting) with parameter δ and $\mathsf{PRF}_{\mathsf{sk}}(\text{``OF''}\|\cdot)$ to obtain the table and stash $(\mathsf{OF}, \mathsf{OF_S})$. Since $|Y| \leq 2\epsilon \cdot n = \frac{2n}{\log^2 \lambda}$, we have that the query and space complexity of this step is $O(|Y|\log|Y|) = O(n)$ since $n \leq \mathsf{poly}(\lambda)$.

10. *Prepare Stash Cuckoo hash table for efficient lookup:*
    - Let $\mathsf{S} = \bigcup_{i=1}^{B} \mathsf{S}_i$, i.e., the union of all stashes. Note that $|\mathsf{S}| \leq |B| \cdot \log \lambda \leq O\left(\frac{n}{\log^8 \lambda}\right)$.

- As described in the full version [44], run cuckooAssign(S) (without packed sorting) with parameter δ and $\mathsf{PRF}_{\mathsf{sk}}(\text{``SecS''}\|\cdot)$ to obtain the table and stash $(\mathsf{SecS}, \mathsf{SecS}_S)$. Since $|S| = O\left(\frac{n}{\log^8 \lambda}\right)$, we have that the query and space complexity of this step is $O(|S| \log |S|) = O(n)$.

Output: This command has no output.

State on Server:
- Bins
  - Main Cuckoo bins: $\mathsf{CBin}_1, \ldots, \mathsf{CBin}_B$.
  - Cuckoo hash tables for overflow pile and combined stash: $\mathsf{OF}, \mathsf{SecS}$.
- Two lists OF_S and SecS_S to lookup elements in the leftover stash.
- Array $\boldsymbol{P}$ of size n initialized $\varnothing$. This array will be used to track all lookups made to $\mathsf{CBin}_1, \ldots, \mathsf{CBin}_B, \mathsf{OF}, \mathsf{SecS}$.

Local State:
- Secret key: sk.
- Counter c initialized to 0. This counter will be used to track the number of lookups made.

Algorithm 6. MalHT.Lookup(k)

State on Server:
- Bins: $(\mathsf{CBin}_1, \ldots, \mathsf{CBin}_B, \mathsf{OF}, \mathsf{SecS}, \mathsf{OF}_S, \mathsf{SecS}_S)$.
- Array $\boldsymbol{P}$ of all lookups made.

Local State: Counter c and secret key sk.

Input: Key k to look for (which might be $\perp$ for dummy lookups).

Input Assumption: The key k has not been previously looked up, i.e., $k \notin \boldsymbol{P}$.

The algorithm:
1. Initialize $v := \perp$ and list $A_k \leftarrow \varnothing$.
2. If $k = \perp$:
   - Iterate linearly over OF_S, and write every element back unmodified.
   - Iterate linearly over SecS_S, and write every element back unmodified.
   - Lookup two random locations in OF, and add the locations to A_k.
   - Lookup two random locations in S, and add the locations to A_k.
   - Choose random bin $i \leftarrow [B]$, and lookup two random locations in CBin_i, and add the locations to A_k.
3. If $k \neq \perp$:
   - *Lookup in the stashes:*
     - Iterate linearly over OF_S. If $\mathsf{OF}_S[j]$ contains k, write $\perp$ back at $\mathsf{OF}_S[j]$, and store the value of v. Otherwise, perform a dummy write to $\mathsf{OF}_S[j]$.
     - Iterate linearly over SecS_S. If $\mathsf{SecS}_S[j]$ contains k, write $\perp$ back at $\mathsf{SecS}_S[j]$, and store the value of v. Otherwise, perform a dummy write to $\mathsf{SecS}_S[j]$.
     - Update the value of v.
   - *Lookup in overflow pile:*
     - If $v \neq \perp$ (i.e., v was found in the stashes), look up two random locations in OF.

- If $v = \bot$, let $\mathsf{choice}_{1,\mathsf{OF}}, \mathsf{choice}_{2,\mathsf{OF}} \leftarrow \mathsf{PRF}_{\mathsf{sk}}(\text{"OF"} \| k)$. Lookup $\mathsf{OF}[\mathsf{choice}_{1,\mathsf{OF}}]$ and $\mathsf{OF}[\mathsf{choice}_{2,\mathsf{OF}}]$. If key k lies in either of them, set v to be the corresponding value. Add both addresses to A_k.
- *Lookup in combined stash:*
  - If $v \neq \bot$, look up two random locations in SecS. Add the locations to A_k.
  - If $v = \bot$, compute $\mathsf{choice}_{1,\mathsf{SecS}}, \mathsf{choice}_{2,\mathsf{SecS}} \leftarrow \mathsf{PRF}_{\mathsf{sk}}(\text{"SecS"} \| k)$. Lookup $\mathsf{SecS}[\mathsf{choice}_{1,\mathsf{SecS}}]$ and $\mathsf{SecS}[\mathsf{choice}_{2,\mathsf{SecS}}]$. If key k lies in either of them, set v to be the corresponding value. Add both addresses to A_k.
- *Lookup in bins:*
  - If $v \neq \bot$, choose a random bin $i \leftarrow [B]$ and look up two random locations in CBin_i. Add both addresses to A_k.
  - If $v = \bot$,
    * Compute $i \leftarrow \mathsf{PRF}_{\mathsf{sk}}(0 \| k)$. Let $\mathsf{choice}_1, \mathsf{choice}_2 \leftarrow \mathsf{PRF}_{\mathsf{sk}}(i \| k)$.
    * Lookup $\mathsf{CBin}_i[\mathsf{choice}_1]$ and $\mathsf{CBin}_i[\mathsf{choice}_2]$. If key k lies in either, set v to be the corresponding value. Add both addresses to A_k.

Output: The value v.

Final State on Server:
- Bins: $(\mathsf{CBin}_1, \ldots, \mathsf{CBin}_B, \mathsf{OF}, \mathsf{SecS})$. Note that these remain *unchanged*.
- Two lists OF_S and SecS_S to look up elements in the leftover stash.
- Update $\boldsymbol{P}[c] \leftarrow (k, A_k)$. Here, A_k is a list of all 6 addresses (two addresses in OF, two addresses in SecS, and two addresses in CBin_i for some i) that were looked up in the table.

Final Local State: Increment $c \leftarrow c + 1$.

Algorithm 7. MalHT.Extract()

State on Server:
- Bins: $(\mathsf{CBin}_1, \ldots, \mathsf{CBin}_B, \mathsf{OF}, \mathsf{SecS}, \mathsf{OF}_\mathsf{S}, \mathsf{SecS}_\mathsf{S})$.
- Array $\boldsymbol{P}$ of all lookups made.

Local State: Counter c and secret key sk.

Input: This command has no input.

The algorithm:
1. Let $L = \mathsf{CBin}_1 \| \mathsf{CBin}_2 \| \ldots \| \mathsf{CBin}_B \| \mathsf{OF} \| \mathsf{SecS}$.
2. Initialize T^{off} to be an array of size $|L|$.
3. Copy the elements from L into T^{off}.
4. Iterate over $\boldsymbol{P}$, and sequentially do following:
   - If $\boldsymbol{P}[i] = (\bot, A_k)$, then access all addresses in A_k, and write back the contents without modifications.
   - If $\boldsymbol{P}[i] = (k, A_k)$ where $k \neq \bot$, access every $\mathsf{addr} \in A_k$:
     - If key k lies in $T^{\mathsf{off}}[\mathsf{addr}]$, rewrite the entry within T^{off} to $\bot$.
     - If key k does not lie in $T^{\mathsf{off}}[\mathsf{addr}]$, write back the contents within T^{off} without modifications.
5. Initialize an array T of size $|L|$ to $\varnothing$.

6. Using the post-verifiability of the offline memory checker, copy the contents of T^{off} into T sequentially with appropriate timestamps. Let $C\|\text{OF}'\|\text{SecS}' := T$, where C, OF' and SecS' correspond to the marked versions of $\text{CBin}_1, \cdots, \text{CBin}_B$, OF and SecS respectively.
7. Let $R \leftarrow \text{PerfectORP}(\text{OF}'\|\text{SecS}')$.
8. Let $T \leftarrow \text{Intersperse}(C\|R; |C|, |R|)$.
9. Let $T_\text{S} \leftarrow \text{PerfectORP}(\text{OF}_\text{S}\|\text{SecS}_\text{S})$.
10. Let $T' \leftarrow \text{Intersperse}(T\|T_\text{S}; |T|, |T_\text{S}|)$.
11. Let $T'' \leftarrow \text{TightCompaction}(T')$ considering all entries overwritten with $\perp$ as 0-balls (i.e., moved to end of array), and truncate the array to size n.
12. Let $X \leftarrow \text{IntersperseRD}_n(T'')$.

Output: The array X.

Final State on Server: Reset the state on the server to $\varnothing$.

Malicious Security. To make the algorithm maliciously obliviously secure, we combine both online and offline memory checking components. All portions that are offline memory checked are boxed out in gray, and all portions of memory that are not online-checkable via time-stamping will be indicated with superscript off. All such portions of memory are left in a post-verifiable state at the end of the offline checking portions. We then immediately copy the contents of this memory sequentially to fresh "online checkable" portions of memory with corresponding time-stamps. All other parts of this implementation can be time-stamped in the hybrid model. To see this, note that in both MalHT.Build() and MalHT.Extract(), all portions which are not offline-checked are linear scans over contiguous portions of memory. In MalHT.Lookup(), all of OF_S and SecS_S is updated every time, and hence can be time-stamped with just the knowledge of the number of lookups c. Moreover, only $\boldsymbol{P}[c]$ is modified in $\boldsymbol{P}$. Therefore, $\boldsymbol{P}$ can also be time-stamped.

Theorem 6. *Suppose* $\log^{11} \lambda \leq n \leq \text{poly}(\lambda)$. *MalHT is a maliciously secure implementation of $\mathcal{F}_{\text{HT}}$. Moreover, the run-time of the algorithm is $O(n)$ for Build, $O(\log \lambda)$ for Lookup and $O(n)$ for Extract.*

Proof (sketch). We highlight the main reasons why it is safe to offline-check various portions of the algorithm.

- Step 4. of MalHT.Build(), as discussed in Sect. 2, does not seem time-stampable. Nonetheless, offline checking is safe because the values leaked are either of the form $\text{PRF}_{\text{sk}}(0\|k_i)$ (with no duplicates) or uniformly random.
- In Step 8 of MalHT.Build(), we use the fact that $\textbf{Assign}_{X_i}$ is time-stamped and tamper-proof. Moreover, since the values of $\textbf{Assign}_{X_i}$ are safe to leak (because the input to MalHT.Build() is randomly shuffled), routing according to $\textbf{Assign}_{X_i}$ is *conditionally offline-safe*, as discussed in Sect. 2.3.

– Note that the array $\boldsymbol{P}$ was time-stamped as it was constructed during MalHT.Lookup() calls. Therefore, in Steps 3. and 4. of MalHT.Extract(), we use the fact that $\boldsymbol{P}$ is time-stamped and safe to leak (since $\boldsymbol{P}$ contains known addresses) to once again argue that it is conditionally offline-safe. Note that time-stamping $\boldsymbol{P}$ was not directly possible in the CombHT construction of Asharov et al. [5] since accesses to the small bins were abstracted out with SmallHT calls.

The proof has been deferred to the full version [44].

9   Maliciously Secure Optimal ORAM Construction

In this section, we state our main theorem.

Theorem 7 (Restatement of Theorem 1). *Let N be the capacity of the database, and let $\lambda \in \mathbb{N}$ be a security parameter such that $N \leq \mathsf{poly}(\lambda)$. Then, for word size $w = \omega(\log \lambda)$, there is a maliciously secure oblivious implementation of $\mathcal{F}_{\mathsf{RAM}}^{N,w}$, and each Access has worst-case query complexity $O(\log N + \log^5 \log \lambda)$. The local space complexity is $O(1)$ (and one PRF key), and the server space complexity is $O(N)$. Moreover, if the client (but not the adversary) has access to a random oracle, this implementation is statistically secure, even against computationally unbounded adversaries.*

We defer the construction and proof to the full version [44].

Acknowledgments. We are extremely grateful to Vinod Vaikuntanathan for suggesting this problem to us, engaging in many insightful discussions, and giving detailed feedback on our manuscript. We thank Ilan Komargodski for helpful discussions, especially about malicious security of Path ORAM. We thank Ran Canetti for helpful discussions about universal composability. We thank Moni Naor for helpful discussions about memory checking. We thank Alexandra Henzinger for giving valuable feedback on the manuscript. We also thank the anonymous reviewers for their many helpful comments.

References

1. Abraham, I., Fletcher, C.W., Nayak, K., Pinkas, B., Ren, L.: Asymptotically tight bounds for composing ORAM with PIR. In: Fehr, S. (ed.) PKC 2017, Part I. LNCS, vol. 10174, pp. 91–120. Springer, Heidelberg (2017). https://doi.org/10.1007/978-3-662-54365-8_5
2. Ajtai, M., Komlós, J., Szemerédi, E.: An $O(n \log n)$ sorting network. In: Proceedings of the Fifteenth Annual ACM Symposium on Theory of Computing, pp. 1–9 (1983)
3. Apon, D., Katz, J., Shi, E., Thiruvengadam, A.: Verifiable oblivious storage. In: Krawczyk, H. (ed.) PKC 2014. LNCS, vol. 8383, pp. 131–148. Springer, Heidelberg (2014). https://doi.org/10.1007/978-3-642-54631-0_8

4. Arasu, A., et al.: Concerto: a high concurrency key-value store with integrity. In: Proceedings of the 2017 ACM International Conference on Management of Data, pp. 251–266 (2017)
5. Asharov, G., Komargodski, I., Lin, W.K., Nayak, K., Peserico, E., Shi, E.: OptORAMa: optimal oblivious RAM. J. ACM **70**(1) (2022). https://doi.org/10.1145/3566049
6. Asharov, G., Komargodski, I., Lin, W.K., Shi, E.: Oblivious RAM with worst-case logarithmic overhead. J. Cryptol. **36**(2), 7 (2023). https://doi.org/10.1007/s00145-023-09447-5
7. Ateniese, G., et al.: Provable data possession at untrusted stores. In: Ning, P., De Capitani di Vimercati, S., Syverson, P.F. (eds.) ACM CCS 2007, pp. 598–609. ACM Press, October 2007. https://doi.org/10.1145/1315245.1315318
8. Batcher, K.E.: Sorting networks and their applications. In: Proceedings of the April 30–May 2, 1968, Spring Joint Computer Conference. AFIPS 1968 (Spring), New York, NY, USA, pp. 307–314. Association for Computing Machinery (1968). https://doi.org/10.1145/1468075.1468121
9. Bindschaedler, V., Naveed, M., Pan, X., Wang, X., Huang, Y.: Practicing oblivious access on cloud storage: the gap, the fallacy, and the new way forward. In: Ray, I., Li, N., Kruegel, C. (eds.) ACM CCS 2015, pp. 837–849. ACM Press, October 2015. https://doi.org/10.1145/2810103.2813649
10. Blass, E.-O., Mayberry, T., Noubir, G.: Multi-client oblivious RAM secure against malicious servers. In: Gollmann, D., Miyaji, A., Kikuchi, H. (eds.) ACNS 2017. LNCS, vol. 10355, pp. 686–707. Springer, Cham (2017). https://doi.org/10.1007/978-3-319-61204-1_34
11. Blum, M., Evans, W.S., Gemmell, P., Kannan, S., Naor, M.: Checking the correctness of memories. In: 32nd FOCS, pp. 90–99. IEEE Computer Society Press, October 1991. https://doi.org/10.1109/SFCS.1991.185352
12. Cash, D., Grubbs, P., Perry, J., Ristenpart, T.: Leakage-abuse attacks against searchable encryption. In: Ray, I., Li, N., Kruegel, C. (eds.) ACM CCS 2015, pp. 668–679. ACM Press, October 2015. https://doi.org/10.1145/2810103.2813700
13. Chan, T.-H.H., Chung, K.-M., Shi, E.: On the depth of oblivious parallel RAM. In: Takagi, T., Peyrin, T. (eds.) ASIACRYPT 2017. LNCS, vol. 10624, pp. 567–597. Springer, Cham (2017). https://doi.org/10.1007/978-3-319-70694-8_20
14. Chan, T.-H.H., Guo, Y., Lin, W.-K., Shi, E.: Oblivious hashing revisited, and applications to asymptotically efficient ORAM and OPRAM. In: Takagi, T., Peyrin, T. (eds.) ASIACRYPT 2017. LNCS, vol. 10624, pp. 660–690. Springer, Cham (2017). https://doi.org/10.1007/978-3-319-70694-8_23
15. Chan, T.-H.H., Nayak, K., Shi, E.: Perfectly secure oblivious parallel RAM. In: Beimel, A., Dziembowski, S. (eds.) TCC 2018. LNCS, vol. 11240, pp. 636–668. Springer, Cham (2018). https://doi.org/10.1007/978-3-030-03810-6_23
16. Chow, S.S.M., Fech, K., Lai, R.W.F., Malavolta, G.: Multi-client oblivious RAM with poly-logarithmic communication. In: Moriai, S., Wang, H. (eds.) ASIACRYPT 2020. LNCS, vol. 12492, pp. 160–190. Springer, Cham (2020). https://doi.org/10.1007/978-3-030-64834-3_6
17. Clarke, D.E., Suh, G.E., Gassend, B., Sudan, A., van Dijk, M., Devadas, S.: Towards constant bandwidth overhead integrity checking of untrusted data. In: 2005 IEEE Symposium on Security and Privacy, pp. 139–153. IEEE Computer Society Press, May 2005. https://doi.org/10.1109/SP.2005.24
18. Connell, G.: Technology deep dive: building a faster ORAM layer for enclaves (2022). https://signal.org/blog/building-faster-oram/

19. Costan, V., Devadas, S.: Intel SGX explained. Cryptology ePrint Archive, Report 2016/086 (2016). https://eprint.iacr.org/2016/086
20. Damgård, I., Meldgaard, S., Nielsen, J.B.: Perfectly secure oblivious RAM without random oracles. In: Ishai, Y. (ed.) TCC 2011. LNCS, vol. 6597, pp. 144–163. Springer, Heidelberg (2011). https://doi.org/10.1007/978-3-642-19571-6_10
21. Dauterman, E., Fang, V., Demertzis, I., Crooks, N., Popa, R.A.: Snoopy: Surpassing the scalability bottleneck of oblivious storage. In: Proceedings of the ACM SIGOPS 28th Symposium on Operating Systems Principles, pp. 655–671 (2021)
22. Devadas, S., van Dijk, M., Fletcher, C.W., Ren, L., Shi, E., Wichs, D.: Onion ORAM: a constant bandwidth blowup oblivious RAM. In: Kushilevitz, E., Malkin, T. (eds.) TCC 2016. LNCS, vol. 9563, pp. 145–174. Springer, Heidelberg (2016). https://doi.org/10.1007/978-3-662-49099-0_6
23. Dwork, C., Naor, M., Rothblum, G.N., Vaikuntanathan, V.: How efficient can memory checking be? In: Reingold, O. (ed.) TCC 2009. LNCS, vol. 5444, pp. 503–520. Springer, Heidelberg (2009). https://doi.org/10.1007/978-3-642-00457-5_30
24. Fletcher, C.W., Dijk, M.v., Devadas, S.: A secure processor architecture for encrypted computation on untrusted programs. In: Proceedings of the seventh ACM Workshop on Scalable Trusted Computing, pp. 3–8 (2012)
25. Fletcher, C.W., Ren, L., Kwon, A., van Dijk, M., Devadas, S.: Freecursive oram: [nearly] free recursion and integrity verification for position-based oblivious ram. In: Proceedings of the Twentieth International Conference on Architectural Support for Programming Languages and Operating Systems. ASPLOS 2015, New York, NY, USA, pp. 103–116. Association for Computing Machinery (2015). https://doi.org/10.1145/2694344.2694353, https://doi.org/10.1145/2694344.2694353
26. Franz, M., et al.: Oblivious outsourced storage with delegation. In: Danezis, G. (ed.) FC 2011. LNCS, vol. 7035, pp. 127–140. Springer, Heidelberg (2012). https://doi.org/10.1007/978-3-642-27576-0_11
27. Gentry, C., Halevi, S., Jutla, C., Raykova, M.: Private database access with HE-over-ORAM architecture. In: Malkin, T., Kolesnikov, V., Lewko, A.B., Polychronakis, M. (eds.) ACNS 2015. LNCS, vol. 9092, pp. 172–191. Springer, Cham (2015). https://doi.org/10.1007/978-3-319-28166-7_9
28. Goldreich, O., Ostrovsky, R.: Software protection and simulation on oblivious rams. J. ACM (JACM) 43(3), 431–473 (1996)
29. Goodrich, M.T., Mitzenmacher, M.: Privacy-preserving access of outsourced data via oblivious RAM simulation. In: Aceto, L., Henzinger, M., Sgall, J. (eds.) ICALP 2011. LNCS, vol. 6756, pp. 576–587. Springer, Heidelberg (2011). https://doi.org/10.1007/978-3-642-22012-8_46
30. Goodrich, M.T., Tamassia, R., Schwerin, A.: Implementation of an authenticated dictionary with skip lists and commutative hashing. In: Proceedings DARPA Information Survivability Conference and Exposition II. DISCEX 2001, vol. 2, pp. 68–82. IEEE (2001)
31. Hall, W.E., Jutla, C.S.: Parallelizable authentication trees. In: Preneel, B., Tavares, S. (eds.) SAC 2005. LNCS, vol. 3897, pp. 95–109. Springer, Heidelberg (2006). https://doi.org/10.1007/11693383_7
32. Hoang, T., Guajardo, J., Yavuz, A.A.: MACAO: a maliciously-secure and client-efficient active ORAM framework. In: NDSS 2020. The Internet Society, February 2020
33. Islam, M.S., Kuzu, M., Kantarcioglu, M.: Access pattern disclosure on searchable encryption: Ramification, attack and mitigation. In: NDSS 2012. The Internet Society, February 2020

34. Juels, A., Kaliski Jr., B.S.: PORS: proofs of retrievability for large files. In: Ning, P., De Capitani di Vimercati, S., Syverson, P.F. (eds.) ACM CCS 2007, pp. 584–597. ACM Press, October 2007. https://doi.org/10.1145/1315245.1315317
35. Katz, J., Koo, C.Y.: On constructing universal one-way hash functions from arbitrary one-way functions. Cryptology ePrint Archive, Report 2005/328 (2005). https://eprint.iacr.org/2005/328
36. Kilian, J.: A note on efficient zero-knowledge proofs and arguments (extended abstract). In: 24th ACM STOC, pp. 723–732. ACM Press, May 1992. https://doi.org/10.1145/129712.129782
37. Komargodski, I., Lin, W.-K.: A logarithmic lower bound for oblivious RAM (for All Parameters). In: Malkin, T., Peikert, C. (eds.) CRYPTO 2021. LNCS, vol. 12828, pp. 579–609. Springer, Cham (2021). https://doi.org/10.1007/978-3-030-84259-8_20
38. Kushilevitz, E., Lu, S., Ostrovsky, R.: On the (in)security of hash-based oblivious RAM and a new balancing scheme. In: Rabani, Y. (ed.) 23rd SODA, pp. 143–156. ACM-SIAM, January 2012
39. Larsen, K.G., Nielsen, J.B.: Yes, there is an oblivious RAM lower bound! In: Shacham, H., Boldyreva, A. (eds.) CRYPTO 2018. LNCS, vol. 10992, pp. 523–542. Springer, Cham (2018). https://doi.org/10.1007/978-3-319-96881-0_18
40. Liu, C., Wang, X.S., Nayak, K., Huang, Y., Shi, E.: ObliVM: a programming framework for secure computation. In: 2015 IEEE Symposium on Security and Privacy, pp. 359–376. IEEE Computer Society Press, May 2015. https://doi.org/10.1109/SP.2015.29
41. Lu, S., Ostrovsky, R.: Distributed oblivious RAM for secure two-party computation. In: Sahai, A. (ed.) TCC 2013. LNCS, vol. 7785, pp. 377–396. Springer, Heidelberg (2013). https://doi.org/10.1007/978-3-642-36594-2_22
42. Maffei, M., Malavolta, G., Reinert, M., Schröder, D.: Privacy and access control for outsourced personal records. In: 2015 IEEE Symposium on Security and Privacy, pp. 341–358. IEEE Computer Society Press, May 2015. https://doi.org/10.1109/SP.2015.28
43. Maffei, M., Malavolta, G., Reinert, M., Schröder, D.: Maliciously secure multi-client ORAM. In: Gollmann, D., Miyaji, A., Kikuchi, H. (eds.) ACNS 2017. LNCS, vol. 10355, pp. 645–664. Springer, Cham (2017). https://doi.org/10.1007/978-3-319-61204-1_32
44. Mathialagan, S., Vafa, N.: MacORAMa: Optimal Oblivious RAM with Integrity. Cryptology ePrint Archive, Paper 2023/083 (2023). https://eprint.iacr.org/2023/083
45. Merkle, R.C.: A certified digital signature. In: Brassard, G. (ed.) CRYPTO 1989. LNCS, vol. 435, pp. 218–238. Springer, New York (1990). https://doi.org/10.1007/0-387-34805-0_21
46. Mishra, P., Poddar, R., Chen, J., Chiesa, A., Popa, R.A.: Oblix: an efficient oblivious search index. In: 2018 IEEE Symposium on Security and Privacy, pp. 279–296. IEEE Computer Society Press, May 2018. https://doi.org/10.1109/SP.2018.00045
47. Naor, M., Rothblum, G.N.: The complexity of online memory checking. J. ACM (JACM) 56(1), 1–46 (2009)
48. Nissim, K., Naor, M.: Certificate revocation and certificate update. In: Rubin, A.D. (ed.) USENIX Security 98. USENIX Association, January 1998
49. Oprea, A., Reiter, M.K.: Integrity checking in cryptographic file systems with constant trusted storage. In: Provos, N. (ed.) USENIX Security 2007. USENIX Association, August 2007

50. Ostrovsky, R., Shoup, V.: Private information storage (extended abstract). In: 29th ACM STOC, pp. 294–303. ACM Press, May 1997. https://doi.org/10.1145/258533. 258606

51. Pagh, R., Rodler, F.F.: Cuckoo hashing. J. Algorithms $51(2)$, 122–144 (2004)

52. Papamanthou, C., Tamassia, R.: Optimal and parallel online memory checking. Cryptology ePrint Archive, Report 2011/102 (2011). https://eprint.iacr.org/2011/102

53. Patel, S., Persiano, G., Raykova, M., Yeo, K.: PanORAMa: oblivious RAM with logarithmic overhead. In: Thorup, M. (ed.) 59th FOCS, pp. 871–882. IEEE Computer Society Press, October 2018. https://doi.org/10.1109/FOCS.2018.00087

54. Ren, L., Fletcher, C.W., Yu, X., van Dijk, M., Devadas, S.: Integrity verification for path oblivious-ram. In: 2013 IEEE High Performance Extreme Computing Conference (HPEC), pp. 1–6 (2013). https://doi.org/10.1109/HPEC.2013.6670339

55. Rompel, J.: One-way functions are necessary and sufficient for secure signatures. In: 22nd ACM STOC, pp. 387–394. ACM Press, May 1990. https://doi.org/10.1145/100216.100269

56. Shacham, H., Waters, B.: Compact proofs of retrievability. J. Cryptol. $26(3)$, 442–483 (2012). https://doi.org/10.1007/s00145-012-9129-2

57. Shi, E., Chan, T.-H.H., Stefanov, E., Li, M.: Oblivious RAM with $O((\log N)^3)$ worst-case cost. In: Lee, D.H., Wang, X. (eds.) ASIACRYPT 2011. LNCS, vol. 7073, pp. 197–214. Springer, Heidelberg (2011). https://doi.org/10.1007/978-3-642-25385-0_11

58. Stefanov, E., et al.: Path ORAM: an extremely simple oblivious ram protocol. J. ACM $65(4)$ (2018). https://doi.org/10.1145/3177872

59. Stefanov, E., Shi, E.: Multi-cloud oblivious storage. In: Sadeghi, A.R., Gligor, V.D., Yung, M. (eds.) ACM CCS 2013, pp. 247–258. ACM Press, November 2013. https://doi.org/10.1145/2508859.2516673

60. Wang, X.S., Huang, Y., Chan, T.H.H., Shelat, A., Shi, E.: SCORAM: oblivious RAM for secure computation. In: Ahn, G.J., Yung, M., Li, N. (eds.) ACM CCS 2014, pp. 191–202. ACM Press, November 2014. https://doi.org/10.1145/2660267.2660365

61. Zahur, S., Wang, X.S., Raykova, M., Gascón, A., Doerner, J., Evans, D., Katz, J.: Revisiting square-root ORAM: Efficient random access in multi-party computation. In: 2016 IEEE Symposium on Security and Privacy, pp. 218–234. IEEE Computer Society Press, May 2016. https://doi.org/10.1109/SP.2016.21

Tri-State Circuits
A Circuit Model that Captures RAM

David Heath[1]($\boxtimes$), Vladimir Kolesnikov[2], and Rafail Ostrovsky[3]

[1] UIUC, Champaign, USA
daheath@illinois.edu
[2] Georgia Tech, Atlanta, Georgia
kolesnikov@gatech.edu
[3] UCLA, Los Angeles, USA
rafail@cs.ucla.edu

Abstract. We introduce *tri-state circuits* (TSCs). TSCs form a natural model of computation that, to our knowledge, has not been considered by theorists. The model captures a surprising combination of simplicity and power. TSCs are simple in that they allow only three wire values (0, 1, and undefined – $\mathcal{Z}$) and three types of fan-in two gates; they are powerful in that their statically placed gates fire (execute) eagerly as their inputs become defined, implying orders of execution that depend on input. This behavior is sufficient to efficiently evaluate RAM programs.

We construct a TSC that emulates T steps of any RAM program and that has only $O(T \cdot \log^3 T \cdot \log \log T)$ gates. Contrast this with the reduction from RAM to Boolean circuits, where the best approach scans all of memory on each access, incurring quadratic cost.

We connect TSCs with Garbled Circuits (GC). TSCs capture the power of garbling far better than Boolean Circuits, offering a more expressive model of computation that leaves per-gate cost essentially unchanged.

As an important application, we construct *authenticated Garbled* RAM (GRAM), enabling constant-round maliciously-secure 2PC of RAM programs. Let λ denote the security parameter. We extend authenticated garbling to TSCs; by simply plugging in our TSC-based RAM, we obtain authenticated GRAM running at cost $O(T \cdot \log^3 T \cdot \log \log T \cdot \lambda)$, outperforming all prior work, including prior semi-honest GRAM.

We also give semi-honest garbling of TSCs from a one-way function (OWF). This yields OWF-based GRAM at cost $O(T \cdot \log^3 T \cdot \log \log T \cdot \lambda)$, outperforming the best prior OWF-based GRAM by more than factor λ.

Keywords: Garbled RAM · MPC · Models of Computation · Malicious Security

1 Introduction

Boolean circuits form perhaps our simplest complete model of computation. The model allows only a small set of gate types, each of which computes a basic

H. Handschuh and A. Lysyanskaya (Eds.): CRYPTO 2023, LNCS 14084, pp. 128–160, 2023.
https://doi.org/10.1007/978-3-031-38551-3_5

function. Moreover, a circuit's structure is static and explicit. This simplicity is ideal for both theory and practice, making them popular in complexity theory and, in particular, in cryptography.

On the other hand, random access machine programs (RAM programs)[1] form our most ubiquitous practical model of computation. The random access capability approximates the power of real-world devices, so theoretical advances in RAM can more readily translate to real-world impact.

Unfortunately, it is difficult to connect Boolean circuits and RAM. Indeed, the two models seem inherently at odds. RAMs are inherently *dynamic*, allowing the program to quickly and arbitrarily access one element in an immense array; circuits are inherently *static*, requiring that the program fix the order in which it manipulates data before input is known.

It is therefore unsurprising that reductions from RAMs to Boolean gates are expensive. The straightforward reduction emulates each memory access by *linearly scanning the entire RAM memory*. This simple approach is also the *best known*. Since RAMs access memory at each step, this reduction yields a circuit that grows quadratically in the RAM runtime T.

Motivation for Introducing Tri-State Circuits: Constant Round 2PC. It is unfortunate that reductions from RAMs to circuits are so expensive. Many technologies are more compatible with circuits than with RAMs, and a concretely efficient reduction would automatically connect real-world RAM programs with circuit-based technologies.

As our crucial example, we consider Yao's Garbled Circuit (GC) [Yao86], a multiparty computation (MPC) technology that achieves symmetric-key-based constant-round protocols.

The GC literature is extensive, see [NPS99, ZRE15, HJO+16, GLNP18, RR21] and many more. Most GC works, including all listed above, garble Boolean gates only, suggesting a natural connection between garbling and circuits. On the other hand, the goal of GC is to enable secure computation of arbitrary programs, and many programs are best handled by RAMs, not by circuits.

It is possible – though challenging – to garble RAM programs. *Garbled RAM* (GRAM) [LO13] does so *without* reducing to circuits. GRAM also has a rich literature [GHL+14, GLO15, GLOS15, CH16, CCHR16, LO17, HKO22, PLS22]. The basic observation of GRAM is that it is possible to garble interconnected *collections* of circuits that execute in an order decided *at runtime*. This dynamic ordering breaks from the circuit model, where the order of execution is static.

Advancing GRAM was challenging. The problem was that reasoning about GRAM required reasoning simultaneously about multiple complex topics, including gate garbling techniques, the above dynamic circuit execution, and constructions of *Oblivious RAM* [GO96]. Worse still, the community lacked an effective vocabulary for discussing the dynamic mechanisms of GRAM; prior work

---

[1] The RAM model we consider is called the *word RAM model* [Hag98]; it is a RAM with a fixed word size that incurs unit cost per random access. We state the definition of the in Sect. 3. Throughout this work, by 'RAM' we mean 'word RAM'.

explained these mechanisms via a concept they called *dynamic language transla-tion*, see e.g. [GLO15, GLOS15, HKO22, PLS22]. Language translation is *deeply intertwined* with the specifics of circuit garbling, and thus understanding even the *basic* ideas of GRAM required intimate GC knowledge.

Matching the Power of Garbling to a Model of Computation. The mere existence of non-trivial GRAM, which leverages dynamic behavior, demonstrates that the circuit model poorly approximates the power of garbling. Clearly some additional expressive power is available, sufficient to efficiently execute RAM programs.

Thus, it is interesting to search for another model of computation – cheap to garble, simpler than RAM, and more expressive than Boolean circuits – that captures the dynamic power of garbling. Such a model would be useful, since it would decompose the GRAM problem into pieces, allowing us to think modularly about RAM constructions, untethered from garbling-specific concerns.

1.1   Our Contribution

We demonstrate that there exists a simple, circuit-like model of computation that closely approximates (within a polylogarithmic factor) the expressive power of RAM. Our *tri-state circuit* (TSC) model is strongly compatible with our target use-case of garbling, in the sense that it admits efficient and natural protocols.

Like a Boolean circuit, a TSC is composed from statically connected gates, each of which has one of only a small number (three) of possible gate types. Each gate computes a basic function of its two tri-value input wires. Despite their simplicity, TSCs are distinctly more powerful than Boolean circuits; they admit a primitive form of control flow where the order in which gates fire *depends on the input*. This basic control flow can *efficiently emulate RAM computation*. Thus, TSCs capture a surprising combination of conceptual simplicity and expressive power which, to our knowledge, has not been explored by theorists.[2,3]

We emphasize that while we feel the tri-state circuit model has intrinsic value, we are motivated by the concrete objective of improving symmetric-key-based constant-round secure computation (i.e., garbling).

Our contributions include:

---

[2] While tri-state circuits have not been theoretically explored, tri-state gates are used in practice. We chose our naming based on these real-world gates. A key gate in our model, which we call a *buffer*, exists as a digital logic element called a *tri-state buffer*. We show that RAM reduces to a relatively small number of such gates.

[3] Tri-state circuits are distinct from *ternary logic*. Ternary logic *has* been explored by theorists, even in the context of garbling [LY18, NPS99]. In ternary logic, wires can take three distinct values; however, the circuit executes in a standard topological order. In *tri-state circuits*, gates execute in a data-dependent order.

We formalize the tri-state circuit model.

We reduce RAM programs to (deterministic) tri-state circuits. Let T denote a runtime. We construct a tri-state circuit of size $O(T \cdot \log^4 T)$ that can emulate T steps of any RAM program.

We formalize randomized and *oblivious* tri-state circuits. In cryptography, data-independent orders of execution are useful for protecting privacy. *Basic* tri-state circuits discard input independence, losing cryptographic utility. *Oblivious* tri-state circuits reclaim this utility. A tri-state circuit is oblivious if its order of execution *appears* (to a distinguisher) independent of the input.

We reduce RAM programs to oblivious tri-state circuits. We construct an oblivious tri-state circuit of size $O(T \cdot \log^3 T \cdot \log \log T)$ that can simulate T steps of any RAM program. This oblivious reduction improves over our deterministic reduction by leveraging randomness.

We apply tri-state circuits to secure 2PC. Let λ denote the computational security parameter. We achieve two results:

– Our most exciting application is *authenticated GRAM*, a maliciously-secure constant-round 2PC RAM protocol. Our authenticated GRAM executes T RAM steps at cost $O(T \cdot \log^3 T \cdot \log \log T \cdot \lambda)$. Prior malicious GRAM relied on the expensive cut and choose technique, and was more than factor σ slower, for statistical security parameter σ.

– Our second application is improved semi-honest Garbled RAM from only one-way functions. Prior to our work, the best GRAMs were based on random-oracle-like assumptions [HKO22, PLS22]. The best GRAM avoiding such an assumption had quadratic scaling in λ [PLS22]. Our construction outperforms all prior RO-based GRAMs, and it relies only on one-way functions. It runs at cost $O(T \cdot \log^3 T \cdot \log \log T \cdot \lambda)$.

TSC garbling is lean. For example, Boolean circuits can be compiled to tri-state gates, and the communication cost of our resulting authenticated TSC protocol is less than $2\times$ that of state-of-the-art authenticated garbling of Boolean gates [DILO22], and with effort this overhead can likely be removed.

Impact on Garbled RAM. While [HKO22] and follow-on work [PLS22] substantially improved GRAM, these works left pressing and challenging open questions, including efficient malicious GRAM and standard-assumption-based GRAM.

We abstract garbled computation as tri-state circuits, not Boolean circuits, and the payoff is a modular approach to GRAM. This modularity allows us to make significant advances that would have been highly technically involved if expressed in the prior GRAM framework of language translation. We demonstrate that the above more challenging versions of GRAM can be constructed with overhead similar to basic GRAM. Going further, we discovered compatibility between a state-of-the-art Oblivious RAM construction [WCS15] and tri-state circuits, further improving GRAM's asymptotic cost.

Perhaps best of all, tri-state circuits markedly simplify GRAM fundamentals. Indeed, our new garbling procedures are extremely similar in complexity to their

Boolean-circuit-based counterparts. This reduced complexity will allow a broader cryptographic audience to understand, improve, and apply GRAM.

2   Background and Related Work

2.1   Garbled Circuits and Garbled RAM

Garbled Circuit (GC) [Yao86] is a fundamental MPC primitive that allows two parties – a garbler G and an evaluator E – to securely execute a program of their choice on their private inputs. GC is distinct from other secure computation primitives in that it allows for protocols that (1) run in a constant number of rounds and (2) rely almost entirely on fast symmetric key primitives.

Roughly speaking, GC splits program execution into two steps: garbling and evaluation. Garbling is independent of the input, and evaluation of the garbled program *appears* independent of the input. When these two steps are carried out by two different parties, we can arrange that each party's execution hides the input of the other, allowing privacy-preserving protocols.

While GC traditionally works in the Boolean circuit model, a number of works starting with [LO13] developed Garbled RAM (GRAM), an extension to the more expressive RAM model. [LO13] demonstrates that for a word-RAM program running in time T and for computational security parameter λ, we can garble the program at the following cost:

$$O(T \cdot \log^3 T \cdot \log^c \log T \cdot |\mathcal{C}_{prf}| \cdot \lambda) \qquad \text{[LO13]}$$

Here, c is an unspecified constant, and $|\mathcal{C}_{prf}|$ is the circuit size of a PRF with λ bits of output (asymptotic analysis by [PLS22]).

A sequence of works subsequently improved the Garbled RAM primitive, e.g. [GHL+14, GLOS15, GLO15, HKO22, PLS22]. The most recent garbled RAM constructions achieve the following costs:

$$O(T \cdot \log^4 T \cdot \lambda) \qquad \text{[HKO22]}$$
$$O(T \cdot \log^3 T \cdot (\log \log T)^2 \cdot \lambda) \qquad \text{[PLS22]}$$

[HKO22] and follow-on work [PLS22] far surpass prior GRAMs, bringing the technique's overhead in line with what is expected from more traditional Boolean-circuit-based GC.

Improving GRAM remains a crucial direction. In particular, it is interesting to (1) improve asymptotic cost, (2) extend GRAM to interesting and challenging settings, and (3) simplify the GRAM formalism, easing further exploration and application. Our work simultaneously achieves each of these goals.

Malicious GRAM. GC provides natural protection against *malicious* evaluator E, but protecting against *malicious* garbler G is more challenging. G can incorrectly garble the program, causing the program to, for instance, erroneously output bits of E's input. It is difficult to arrange that E can detect incorrectly garbled programs, because E's inability to reason about garbled programs is exactly the property that protects G's input.

Despite this challenge, prior work developed powerful techniques for efficient handling of malicious garbled *circuits* (see later discussion of authenticated garbling). Until this work, malicious garbled *RAM* was far less effective.

Prior work, e.g. [GGMP16, HY16, Mia20], demonstrated feasibility of malicious GRAM, but performance was poor, especially as compared to semi-honest GRAM. The best prior GRAM could be constructed by combining semi-honest GRAM [HKO22] (or the asymptotically more efficient [PLS22], framed as a garbling scheme [BHR12]) with the classic *cut and choose* technique, see e.g. [Lin13].

Cut and choose upgrades semi-honest garbling to the malicious setting. The idea is to have G garble many copies of the same program, then allow E to challenge a randomly selected subset of those programs. While this works, G must garble a number of copies that grows with the statistical security parameter σ, leading to highly undesirable factor σ slowdown as compared to the semi-honest execution. The best malicious GRAM had the following asymptotic cost:

$$O(T \cdot \log^3 T \cdot (\log \log T)^2 \cdot \lambda \cdot \sigma) \qquad \text{[PLS22] with Cut and Choose}$$

We avoid this factor σ slowdown by implementing tri-state circuits via the techniques of *authenticated garbling* (see next). Our maliciously secure GRAM dramatically improves over prior state of the art, achieving the following cost:

$$O(T \cdot \log^3 T \cdot \log \log T \cdot \lambda) \qquad \text{Our maliciously secure GRAM}$$

Authenticated Garbling. The breakthrough work [WRK17] introduced a far superior approach to malicious GC. Their *authenticated garbling* technique achieves performance that asymptotically matches semi-honest garbling, incurring only $O(n \cdot \lambda)$ cost for an n-gate circuit. The approach is also practically performant.

In classic GC, each wire value is represented by a length-λ *label*. These labels are used as keys to encrypt/decrypt subsequent labels in a way that achieves the program semantics. *Authenticated* GC extends each GC label with an additional σ bits, forming a MAC on the wire value. These MACs allow G to reveal particular wire values to E such that E is confident the value is indeed correct.

To securely evaluate each AND gate, the parties require an *authenticated multiplication triple*. Multiplication triples can be computed offline in a function-independent preprocessing phase. Improving the efficiency of authenticated garbling is the subject of a growing body of works [KRRW18, YWZ20, DILO22].

We demonstrate natural compatibility between authenticated garbling and tri-state circuits. Our construction achieves cost $O(n \cdot \lambda)$ for an n-gate *tri-state* circuit. While formal treatment of *any* non-trivial malicious technique is complex, authenticated garbling of tri-state circuits is – at least at an intuitive level – a straightforward extension of the core ideas given by the above prior works.

Standard-Assumption-Based GRAM. In the semi-honest setting, the fastest garbling techniques rely on a non-standard random-oracle-like assumption called a circular correlation robust hash (CCRH) function [CKKZ12]. This assumption stems from the classic "Free XOR" extension [KS08] whereby each GC wire has two labels related by a global correlation. The CCRH assumption is needed to achieve security in the presence of this correlation.

It is interesting to remove this assumption and to garble assuming only one-way functions (OWFs) [GLNP18].[4] Prior to our work, Garbled *RAM* from one-way functions was *far* inferior to GRAM based on Free XOR. Indeed, the best construction had the following cost (note the problematic scaling in λ):

$$O(T \cdot \log^3 T \cdot (\log \log T)^2 \cdot \lambda^2) \qquad \text{[PLS22]}$$

We demonstrate that classic OWF-based techniques from the literature can be almost directly applied to tri-state circuits. Indeed, our standard-assumption-based garbling scheme is relatively obvious, once the tri-state circuit model is understood. Applying this scheme in conjunction with our RAM constructions, we *as a corollary* achieve the best standard-assumption-based GRAM:

$$O(T \cdot \log^3 T \cdot \log \log T \cdot \lambda) \qquad \text{Our OWF-based semi-honest GRAM}$$

2.2   Oblivious RAM

Oblivious RAM (or ORAM, [GO96]) is a powerful technology that allows a weak client to outsource its database to a powerful untrusted server. The client can repeatedly query its sensitive database without the server learning what data is accessed, or even the pattern in which data elements are accessed. In ORAM, for each *logical* access, the client issues a sequence of queries to *physical* locations. These physical locations reveal nothing about the logical accesses, which can be formalized by showing that the server's view can be simulated.

ORAM is highly relevant to our notion of oblivious tri-state circuits. In particular, our reduction from RAM programs to oblivious tri-state circuits directly leverages the Circuit Oblivious RAM construction of [WCS15], implementing their ORAM algorithms via tri-state gates. Our reduction leverages this construction to hide memory access patterns, allowing for a circuit that executes RAM programs and whose gates execute in an order that can be simulated.

2.3   Other Models of Computation

The tri-state circuit model shows that, surprisingly, there exists a concrete set of gates that can efficiently (with polylog overhead) implement RAM. Said another

---

[4] Of course, full semi-honest GC protocols also use OT, which is not implied by OWFs. It is now traditional to view semi-honest GC as a *primitive*, independent of any particular protocol [BHR12]. This primitive, called a garbling scheme, can be meaningfully instantiated from OWFs alone.

way, tri-state circuits admit a small statically defined structure whose collection of use-once components jointly implement RAM. This capability distinguishes the model from other widely considered models.

Other models either *inefficiently* support RAM (e.g., Turing Machines, decision trees, Boolean circuits, arithmetic circuits, etc.), or have implicitly specified "static structure" that is either large or involves components that can be used repeatedly. For instance, while RAM can, of course, efficiently implement itself, it in some sense involves a very large static structure, where each RAM step is implicitly connected to each memory cell. Similarly *pointer machines* form a model of computation that proceeds by editing a directed graph, see e.g. [Sch80]; because of the large number of possible graphs that can emerge at runtime, pointer machines similarly have large implicit static structure.

Said yet another way, tri-state circuits require that we statically define a fixed "stage" that establishes explicit connections between computational elements and explicitly named memory cells. Runtime execution may only proceed within the connection constraints of this stage, and we measure cost in terms of the size of the stage, namely, the number of connections. Indeed, in GC, the garbler must account for each possible action and state of the evaluator. This accounting corresponds to generation of garbled tables – *garbling the stage*.

Despite these constraints, the model is expressive. It has sufficient freedom to (obliviously) implement RAM. This expressiveness in the presence of GC-compatible constraints is what makes tri-state circuits so useful in garbling.

While our focus is on secure computation and garbling, we envision that the tri-state circuit model may be interesting in other settings as well. For instance, it is intriguing that our tri-state circuit constructions can – at least in principle – be implemented via digital circuits, and the model may also have interesting connections to complexity theory.

3   Notation

Word RAM Model. In the word RAM model [Hag98], an abstract machine operates on length-w *words*. Basic operations, such as addition, comparisons, and, in particular, memory reads/writes are assumed to take constant time.

Let T denote RAM program runtime. We assume w is large enough to point into the program input (i.e., $w \geq \log_2 n$) and, for simplicity of analysis, we assume $w = \Theta(\log T)$. We assume that each non-memory-accessing instruction can be implemented by a Boolean circuit of size $O(w^2) = O(\log^2 T)$, sufficient to capture powerful operations such as multiplication. Throughout this work, we refer to word RAMs as RAMs.

Common Notation. $x \parallel y$ denotes the concatenation of strings x and y. We denote by $\langle x \rangle$ a Boolean encoding of the value x. E.g., if P is a RAM program, then $\langle P \rangle$ denotes a Boolean encoding of that RAM program. We leave the details of such encodings unspecified, as they are not interesting. σ denotes a statistical security parameter (e.g. 40 or 60). λ denotes a computational security parameter (e.g. 128). $X \overset{s}{=} Y$ denotes that distributions X and Y are *statistically close*.

$$
\begin{array}{c|ccc}
\oplus & 0 & 1 & \mathcal{Z} \\
\hline
0 & 0 & 1 & \mathcal{Z} \\
1 & 1 & 0 & \mathcal{Z} \\
\mathcal{Z} & \mathcal{Z} & \mathcal{Z} & \mathcal{Z}
\end{array}
$$

$$
\begin{array}{c|ccc}
/ & 0 & 1 & \mathcal{Z} \\
\hline
0 & \mathcal{Z} & 0 & \mathcal{Z} \\
1 & \mathcal{Z} & 1 & \mathcal{Z} \\
\mathcal{Z} & \mathcal{Z} & \mathcal{Z} & \mathcal{Z}
\end{array}
$$

$$
\begin{array}{c|ccc}
\bowtie & 0 & 1 & \mathcal{Z} \\
\hline
0 & 0 & \bot & 0 \\
1 & \bot & 1 & 1 \\
\mathcal{Z} & 0 & 1 & \mathcal{Z}
\end{array}
$$

1 **procedure** $notify(gate)$:
2    $(f, in_0, in_1, out) \leftarrow gate$
3    $x \leftarrow wires[in_0]$
4    $y \leftarrow wires[in_1]$
5    $z \leftarrow f(x, y)$
6   **if** $z \neq \mathcal{Z}$ and $wires[out] = \mathcal{Z}$:
7      $wires[out] \leftarrow z$
8   **for** $gate' \in subscribers(out)$:
9        $notify(gate')$

Fig. 1. The semantics of tri-state circuits. Tri-state circuits have three types of fan-in two gates: XORs ($\oplus$), buffers ($/$), and joins ($\bowtie$). We define the function of each gate type (left), and we define a recursive procedure $notify$ (right) which defines semantics. The array $wires$ is a global object that stores the value of each wire. Each wire can take on three different values: 0, 1, or $\mathcal{Z}$. $\mathcal{Z}$ indicates that a wire has not yet been assigned. At initialization, all non-input wires are set to $\mathcal{Z}$. The function $subscribers$ maps from wire ID w to the set of gates that take wire w as input. Circuit execution begins by calling $notify$ on each gate subscribed to an input wire. The symbol $\bot$ denotes an illegal state; if any join evaluates to $\bot$, we set all wires to $\bot$, execution terminates, and the circuit outputs $\bot$.

Tri-State Notation. Section 4 introduces the following; we catalog for reference.

Based on notation from digital circuits, $\mathcal{Z}$ denotes the distinguished tri-state *high impedance* value. $\mathcal{Z}$ can be pronounced "nil", and can be informally understood as the value of a wire that is not yet defined. A wire carrying 0 or 1 is **set**; a wire carrying $\mathcal{Z}$ is **not set**. We denote buffers by division[5] (written $/$or $\frac{x}{y}$), and joins by $\bowtie$. The second argument to each buffer is called its *control*. The symbol $\oplus$ denotes XOR. XOR is extended to tri-state values in a natural manner. Namely, if either XOR input is $\mathcal{Z}$, then the output is $\mathcal{Z}$ (see Fig. 1).

4 Tri-State Circuits

This section describes and formalizes the tri-state circuit model. Sections 5 and 6 later shows that tri-state circuits can efficiently implement RAM programs.

Tri-state circuits center on a non-Boolean gate that we call a *buffer*. A buffer takes two inputs, a *control wire* and a *data wire*:

---

[5] We chose division to denote buffers because buffer semantics produce the 'undefined' value $\mathcal{Z}$ when dividing by 0.

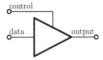

If the control is set to 1, then the output wire acquires the value of the data wire; if the control is set to 0, then the output wire *remains unassigned*, which we denote by stating the output wire has value $\mathcal{Z}$.[6] If the control is set to 1, we say that the buffer is **active** and that the output is **set**; else the buffer is **inactive** and the output is not set.

Because a buffer might not set its output, it is possible to implement interesting circuit arrangements, such as the following:

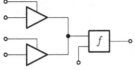

Here, we connect the outputs of two buffers, denoted by the black circle which we formalize as a gate that we refer to as a *join*. The join polls its two inputs, forwarding an input to its output as soon as some input is set. We connect the join's output to a subcircuit labelled f.

The crucial point is that the two buffers might be far apart in the circuit topology. Subcircuit f *eagerly fires* as soon as its inputs are set. Since the buffers fire at different times, the time at which f fires *depends on wire values*, not just the topology. This input-dependent order of execution is the key ingredient of tri-state circuits and is what distinguishes them from Boolean circuits.

Definition 1 (Tri-state Circuit). *A tri-state circuit is a circuit allowing cycles (i.e., its graph need not be acyclic) with three gate types: XORs, buffers, and joins. Each tri-state wire carries one of three values: 0, 1, or $\mathcal{Z}$. The semantics of each gate type and of circuit execution are formally specified in Fig. 1. Tri-state circuits may use two distinguished wires, named 0 and 1, which respectively carry the corresponding constants 0 and 1.*

Looking forward, we will consider constrained classes of tri-state circuits satisfying (combinations of) additional properties (see Definitions 4, 5 and 8).

The dynamic nature of tri-state circuits is formalized by *notify* (Fig. 1). When a wire is set to 0 or to 1 – i.e., when it is *not* $\mathcal{Z}$ – each gate **subscribed** to that wire (each gate taking the wire as input) is notified and fires.

At initialization, each non-input wire holds $\mathcal{Z}$. As gates fire, wire values change from $\mathcal{Z}$ to 0 or 1. Once set, a wire value cannot change again. Thus, the state of the wires converges to a final configuration, the **halt-time state**.

Definition 2 (Halt-time state). *The **halt-time state** of a tri-state circuit C is a wiring w (i.e., a map from circuit wires to wire values) such that there is no gate $g \in C$ where notify(g) changes w.*

---

[6] We use $\mathcal{Z}$, pronounced 'nil,' to denote 'no signal'. In digital circuits, the 'no signal' value is called *high impedance*, and is denoted 'hi-Z'. In GC, $\mathcal{Z}$ on a wire corresponds to E holding *no* key on that wire; see Sect. 7.

A gate only notifies its subscribers if it sets its output. This, combined with the fact that each gate has only two inputs, means that each gate is notified at most twice, tightly bounding the total runtime. I.e., it is a straightforward fact that a random access machine (e.g., a computer evaluating the TSC) can emulate a size-n tri-state circuit in time $O(n)$ by simply running *notify*.

The halt-time state of a tri-state circuit C is *unique*, even when we allow calls to *notify* to occur in an arbitrary order. Indeed, in Appendix A of the full version of this paper[7] we prove the following:

Lemma 1 (Halt-Time State Unique). *Let C be a TSC that, on input x and for some sequence of calls to* notify, *reaches a halt-time state w. Any sequence of calls to* notify *reaching a halt-time state will reach the same state w.*

Circuits with Cycles. Definition 1 explicitly allows circuit graphs with cycles. Indeed, cycles seem to be *essential* for implementing efficient RAM with TSCs.

Consider two executions of a RAM program. In the first execution, suppose we first access some index i, then we access some index j; in the second execution, suppose we first access index j, then index i. Ideally, we would save indexes i and j on particular collections of wires such that the two executions read the same two collections of wires, just in different orders. To achieve this, we *must* admit cycles in our circuits: there is a possible data path from the i wires to the j wires, and from the j wires to the i wires.

There is no inherent inconsistency in allowing circuits with cycles, so long as we are careful in our circuit designs. Namely, tri-state circuits are allowed to have cycles, but their runtime data paths *are not*. Consider the following example:

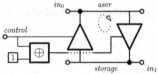

Here, we connect a wire named *user* to a wire named *storage*, allowing *user* to read from/write to *storage*. At first glance, the circuit appears to allow *user* to *write to itself*, a potentially problematic arrangement (especially when proving GC security). On closer inspection, it becomes clear that the wire *control* statically rules out this possibility: at most one buffer can activate, so there is no way for *user* to write to itself. This circuit has a cycle, but there is no possible cycle in the runtime data paths through the circuit.

We rule out runtime cycles by considering circuits that are *runtime acyclic*:

Definition 3 (Runtime Dependency). *A tri-state gate g is **runtime dependent** on another gate g' with respect to a circuit input x if:*

- *g is an XOR, join, or a buffer with control 1, and g is subscribed to the output wire of g'.*
- *g is a buffer with control 0 or $\mathcal{Z}$ (at halt-time), and g is subscribed to g' w.r.t. g's control wire (i.e., g' outputs the control of g).*

―――――
[7] https://eprint.iacr.org/2023/455.

We explicitly emphasize that a buffer with control 0 or $\mathcal{Z}$ (at halt-time) is not runtime dependent on the gate that outputs its data wire.

Definition 4 (Runtime Acyclic). *A tri-state circuit C is **runtime acyclic** if for all inputs x, there exists a winning strategy to a graph pebbling game with the following rules:*

- *The player is allowed to place a pebble on each circuit input.*
- *The player is allowed to place a pebble on a gate g iff there is a pebble on each of g's runtime dependencies with respect to x (Definition 3).*
- *The player wins if it successfully places a pebble on each gate.*

Roughly speaking, Definition 4 states that for any input, there is no data cycle; if there were, then it would be impossible to win the pebbling game, since pebbling a gate requires first pebbling each of that gate's runtime dependencies.[8] Note, the above example circuit *is* runtime acyclic. Indeed, if *control* = 0, then the left buffer is inactive, and we can pebble the cycle by first pebbling this left buffer; if instead *control* = 1, then we can first pebble the right buffer.

For the rest of this work, we only consider tri-state circuits that are runtime acyclic, and our formal security theorems (see Appendices C and D of the full version) require runtime acyclicity.

Subcircuit Sharing. Because tri-state gates run dynamically, we can arrange a trick that we call **subcircuit sharing**. Consider the following circuit:

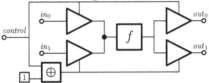

For sake of argument, suppose subcircuit f is composed from a large number of gates. Our example allows f to be called in two different ways: we can either set *control* = 1, running circuit f on **input port** in_0 and setting **output port** out_0, or we can symmetrically set *control* = 0, running f on input port in_1 and setting output port out_1. Since we can only set *control* to either 0 or 1, we can only activate *one* of the pairs of buffers, and so f is used only once. We again emphasize that the time at which f fires depends on *control*: in_0 and in_1 might each be set by the calling circuit at an arbitrary time.

Thus, f can be used in a *conditional manner*, solving a subproblem at one of two very different points in time. Crucially, our example is *efficient* in the sense that it contains only enough gates to implement f *once*; the gates in f are *shared* across the two call sites.

---

[8] One might wish to consider simpler definitions of runtime acyclicity, such as removing inactive buffers from the circuit, then requiring that the remaining graph is acyclic. Unfortunately, our attempts at such a definition admitted circuit designs for which we cannot prove GC security. Such designs feature cycles which set their own control wires. Our pebbling-game-based definition leads to a natural proof of GC security; it is inspired by pebbling-based techniques from adaptively secure GC [HJO+16].

RAM from Cyclic Circuits with Subcircuit Sharing. Subcircuit sharing is the **key idea** of our RAM reductions. In short – and as we later explain in detail – we arrange our RAM memory as a collection of small subcircuits, each of which stores RAM elements and is shared across many accesses. By sharing each such subcircuit, we allow each data-dependent access to consume only the subcircuit storing its desired element. Thus, the number of required gates is amortized across accesses; in total, we only need a number of gates that grows quasilinearly in the number of accesses. Each gate in our RAM can be used to satisfy a variety of different accesses because our RAM circuits feature *cycles*, allowing accessed memory elements to "flow backwards through the topology" to the particular RAM step where it is needed.

The complexity of our RAM constructions arises from arranging subcircuit sharing at a large scale. We ultimately share each of a large number of subcircuits across a large number of memory accesses. This is achieved by arranging subcircuits in a binary tree where each node is itself a shared subcircuit providing shared access to further subcircuits. Section 5 explains in detail.

Preventing Short Circuits. Definition 1 includes the possibility of *illegal states*, denoted $\perp$. One can erroneously join two wires where one wire holds 0 and the other holds 1. This causes a 'short circuit', and is ill defined. We must restrict ourselves to circuit designs that cannot enter an illegal state. For this reason, we focus on tri-state circuits that compute Boolean functions:

Definition 5 (Computing a Boolean function). *Let $f : \{0,1\}^n \to \{0,1\}^m$ denote a Boolean function and $\mathcal{C}$ denote a tri-state circuit. We say that $\mathcal{C}$ **computes** f if for all $x \in \{0,1\}^n$, $\mathcal{C}(x) = f(x)$.*

This definition rules out illegal states, because entering an illegal state causes the circuit to output $\perp$, which is not a possible output of a Boolean function.

Note, the property of computing a Boolean function (Definition 5) neither implies nor is implied by runtime acyclicity (Definition 4).

Completeness. Definition 1 does not include AND gates. Even without AND, tri-state circuits are as expressive as Boolean circuits. Indeed, for every Boolean circuit, there is a similarly-sized tri-state circuit computing the same function:

Theorem 1 (Emulating Boolean circuits; tri-state AND gates). *For any Boolean circuit $\mathcal{C}$, there exists a tri-state circuit $\mathcal{C}'$ such that:*

$$\mathcal{C}' \text{ computes } \mathcal{C} \quad \text{and} \quad |\mathcal{C}'| = O(|\mathcal{C}|)$$

Proof. By constructing Boolean gates from tri-state gates.

Indeed, it suffices to construct AND gates; XORs and constants are part of the tri-state circuit definition, and $\{\wedge, \oplus, 1\}$ is a complete Boolean basis. We use division to denote the buffer operation (Sect. 3). An AND gate can be constructed as follows:

$$AND(x, y) \triangleq \left(\frac{x}{y}\right) \bowtie \left(\frac{0}{y \oplus 1}\right)$$

The above definition can be read as follows: When the value of y is 1, the result is x; when the value of $y \oplus 1$ is 1, the result is 0. $\qquad\qquad\square$

4.1 Randomized and Oblivious Tri-State Circuits

In cryptographic settings, one of the principal advantages of non-tri-state circuits is their input independent order of execution. However, the entire point of the tri-state circuit model is its dependence on the input. This leads to a natural question: can we construct tri-state circuits where orders of execution – which depend on inputs – *appear* to be independent of the input?

Indeed, we can meaningfully define *oblivious* tri-state circuits. This definition is sufficient for cryptographic applications, as we demonstrate in Sect. 7. The definition of oblivious tri-state circuits is analogous to that of oblivious Turing Machines and of oblivious RAMs (ORAM, [GO96]).

In short, a tri-state circuit is *oblivious* if we can *simulate* all of its buffer control wires. I.e., there exists a poly-time simulator that outputs a distribution of control bits which – on every input – is close to the distribution of the *real* controls. This idea is reasonable because the order in which gates are executed can be deduced from the controls alone. Indeed, buffer control wires are the *only* mechanism in a tri-state circuit that can set a wire conditionally, and hence they determine the order of execution. Thus, if the controls can be simulated, then the order of gate execution hides the input.

Given our definitions so far, we cannot construct non-trivial oblivious circuits. So far, there is no mechanism for deviating from an order of execution that is deterministically prescribed by the input. Thus, the value on each control wire is a determined by the input, and we cannot simulate. Somehow we must *mask* each sensitive wire value before using it to control a buffer, e.g. by applying a one-time pad. Thus, we consider tri-state circuits with *randomized* inputs:

Definition 6 (Randomized Tri-State Circuit). *A **randomized tri-state circuit** is a pair consisting of a tri-state circuit C and a distribution of bit-strings $\mathcal{D}$. The execution of a randomized tri-state circuit on input x is defined by randomly sampling a string r from $\mathcal{D}$, then running C on x and r:*

$$(\mathcal{C}, \mathcal{D})(x) \triangleq \mathcal{C}(x; r) \qquad\qquad \textbf{where } r \in_\$ \mathcal{D}$$

A randomized tri-state circuit *obliviously* computes f if its *controls* (Definition 7) can be simulated:

Definition 7 (Controls). *Let C be a tri-state circuit with input $x \in \{0,1\}^n$. The **controls of C on** x, denoted $controls(C, x) \in \{0, 1, \mathcal{Z}\}^*$, is the set of all buffer control wire values (each labeled by its gate ID) at halt-time.*

Definition 8 (Obliviously computing a function). *Let $f : \{0,1\}^n \to \{0,1\}^m$ be a Boolean function. Let $\sigma \in \mathbb{N}$ be the statistical security parameter. Let $(\mathcal{C}, \mathcal{D})_{i \in [\mathbb{N}]}$ denote a family of randomized tri-state circuits. The family **obliviously computes** f if:*

1. *For all $x \in \{0,1\}^n$, $(\mathcal{C}, \mathcal{D})_\sigma$ outputs $f(x)$ with overwhelming probability:*

$$\Pr_{r \in_\$ \mathcal{D}} [\, \mathcal{C}(x; r) = f(x) \,] > 1 - \mathrm{negl}(\sigma)$$

2. *The distribution of controls of $(\mathcal{C}, \mathcal{D})_\sigma$ can be simulated. I.e., there exists a simulator $\mathcal{S}$ such that for all inputs $x \in \{0,1\}^n$ the following holds:*

$$\mathcal{S}(1^\sigma) \overset{s}{=} \{ \, controls(\mathcal{C}, (x; r)) \mid r \in_\$ \mathcal{D} \, \}$$

While only tri-state circuit *families* obliviously compute functions, we will sometimes slightly abuse notation and omit the explicit mention of families.

As a warm up, we show that for every Boolean circuit, there exists a similarly-sized randomized tri-state circuit obliviously computing the same function:

Theorem 2 (Obliviously Emulating Boolean Circuits). *For any Boolean circuit $\mathcal{C}$, there exists a randomized tri-state circuit $(\mathcal{C}', \mathcal{D})$ s.t.:*

$$(\mathcal{C}', \mathcal{D}) \text{ obliviously computes } \mathcal{C} \quad and \quad |\mathcal{C}'| = O(|\mathcal{C}|)$$

Proof. By reducing Boolean gates to tri-state gates with randomized input.

As in Theorem 1, we need only demonstrate how to build an oblivious AND gate, since XOR gates are part of the tri-state circuit definition.

To construct each AND gate, we use the classic idea of Beaver multiplication triples [Bea92]. For each AND gate, we define a distribution $\mathcal{D}$ as follows:

$$\mathcal{D} \triangleq \{ \, \alpha, \beta, \alpha \cdot \beta \mid \alpha, \beta \in_\$ \{0,1\} \, \}$$

Our oblivious AND gate uses the multiplication triple to mask its input bits before using them as buffer controls:

$$AND_{obv}(x, y; \alpha, \beta, \gamma = \alpha \cdot \beta) \triangleq$$
$$\left(\left(\frac{y}{x \oplus \alpha} \bowtie \frac{0}{(x \oplus \alpha) \oplus 1} \right) \oplus \left(\frac{\alpha}{y \oplus \beta} \bowtie \frac{0}{(y \oplus \beta) \oplus 1} \right) \right) \oplus \gamma$$

Both $x \oplus \alpha$ and $y \oplus \beta$ (and their complements) are controls, so to prove this gate is oblivious, we must simulate these values. This is straightforward: α and β act as one-time pads, masking x and y:

$$\mathcal{S}(1^\sigma) \triangleq \{ \, r_0, r_0 \oplus 1, r_1, r_1 \oplus 1 \mid r_0, r_1 \in_\$ \{0,1\} \, \}$$

Formally, the full circuit $(\mathcal{C}, \mathcal{D})$ consists of *many* such AND gates, each with its own triple, and we must jointly simulate *all* controls. This is trivial: multiplication triples are mutually independent and each is used only once.   □

Simple Distributions. The formal definition of randomized tri-state circuits allows *arbitrary* distributions $\mathcal{D}$. In practice, we cannot handle *any* distribution. For instance, some distributions are not computable. Moreover, in some settings – and in particular in the authenticated garbling setting – we wish to consider distributions that are as simple as possible, such that they are easy to sample.

Constructions presented in this work use simple distributions. In particular, our distributions can be described as the concatenation of independent copies of the following two sub-distributions: (1) a uniformly sampled bit $r \in_\$ \{0, 1\}$ and (2) a uniform multiplication triple $\{ \alpha, \beta, \alpha \cdot \beta \mid \alpha, \beta \in_\$ \{0, 1\} \}$. Uniform bits and multiplication triples suffice for our oblivious tri-state RAM.

Simple distributions are important because, as we will see, our approach to authenticated garbled tri-state circuits samples $\mathcal{D}$ via a (malicious) preprocessing functionality. Efficient protocols exist for our considered class of distributions [WRK17, KRRW18, YWZ20, DILO22].

5   Deterministic Tri-State RAM

In this section, we reduce RAM execution to deterministic tri-state circuits. We emphasize that this section constructs only RAM, not *oblivious* RAM.

Our focus is our later oblivious reduction (Sect. 6), which has utility in 2PC. We give a deterministic reduction here for two reasons. First, it explores the theoretical capabilities of TSCs. Second – and more importantly – our deterministic reduction is simpler than our oblivious reduction. Our deterministic RAM sets the stage for our more complex oblivious reduction, which mixes the same high-level ideas with the Oblivious RAM construction of [WCS15].

We set the stage by defining what it means for a TSC to emulate a RAM:

Definition 9 (T-Emulation). *Let $T \in \mathbb{N}$ denote a runtime. A tri-state circuit $\mathcal{C}$ T-emulates a RAM if $\mathcal{C}$ computes (Definition 5) the following function: Let P denote a word RAM program and $x \in \{0, 1\}^n$ denote a string. $\langle x \rangle$ denotes a Boolean encoding of value x.*

$$\mathcal{C}(\langle P \rangle, x) = \begin{cases} P(x) & \text{if } P \text{ halts on input } x \text{ within } T \text{ steps} \\ \langle \bot \rangle & \text{otherwise} \end{cases}$$

Theorem 3 (Deterministic Tri-State RAM). *For any runtime $T \in \mathbb{N}$, there is a tri-state circuit $\mathcal{C}$ s.t. $\mathcal{C}$ T-emulates a RAM and $|\mathcal{C}| = O(T \cdot \log^4 T)$.*

We describe our deterministic RAM. Our oblivious construction (Sect. 6) is more sophisticated, but builds on the ideas developed in this section.

The challenge of emulating a RAM is in accessing a large main memory. Other details – including operating on machine words and managing internal state – are straightforward, even without tri-state-specific capabilities. Thus we focus on repeatedly and arbitrarily accessing main memory.

Our approach is strongly inspired by the GRAM construction of [HKO22]; we show that their high level ideas are compatible with tri-state circuits, replacing their complex language translation mechanism by simple tri-state gates. We later asymptotically improve over [HKO22]'s construction.

Throughout the following discussion, we refer the reader to Fig. 2, which depicts our deterministic RAM construction.

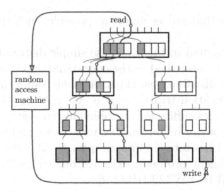

Fig. 2. Our deterministic tri-state RAM is arranged as a binary tree where memory elements are stored in the leaves. Each inner node has two stacks (concatenated rectangles) which allow the node to dynamically communicate with its two children. On each access, the RAM sets the desired leaf address on a top port of the RAM. This causes the circuit to dynamically traverse a path to the addressed leaf (example depicted in green). At each node, the RAM pops one stack and not the other, allowing the RAM to proceed either left or right. This establishes a path through which the requested element will flow back up to the root. Traversing the tree uses up parts of the circuit (previously used up components are in grey). Since the accessed memory element might be needed again later, the RAM writes an element back to a statically chosen and unused leaf. (Color figure online)

5.1   Deterministic Tri-State RAM Overview

Our main idea is to construct inside a tri-state circuit a binary tree of *nodes*, where each leaf holds one memory element, and where each internal node contains machinery needed to access its descendants.

On an access, the emulated RAM uses this machinery to dynamically traverse a path towards the particular leaf holding the target memory element. By leveraging **subcircuit sharing**, we ensure that while each traversal uses up some gates, it crucially does *not* use any gates off of its path. Thus, those gates can be used later. This basic idea leads to single circuit structure that is amortized across all RAM accesses.

Note that *Boolean* circuits cannot realize the above amortization since there is no mechanism by which to set aside a portion of the circuit for later use. In contrast, TSCs can, based on their dynamic order of execution and support for cyclic graphs. **This is the expressive advantage of TSCs.**

Communicating Nodes. Leveraging this ability to amortize gates, the next crucial insight of our deterministic RAM is to view each tree node as an *object* that can dynamically send messages to and receive messages from its two children, consuming only "on-the-path" TSC gates. (Boolean circuits do not have this ability, and each access to a child requires processing both children, ultimately resulting in a linear scan.) Messages are passed by *setting* particular collections of wires that we refer to as **ports**. By setting a child's **input port**, a parent can send a message to its child; by setting its own **output port**, the child can respond to its parent. The challenge is in allowing each parent to communicate with its children *dynamically*. Namely, we must arrange that a parent sends a message to its child if and only if that child is on a dynamically traversed path.

Circuit-Based Stacks. Like [HKO22], we arrange this dynamic communication via **circuit-based stacks** [ZE13]. Namely, there exists a Boolean-circuit-based analog of a stack data structure. These stacks are created with n elements and can support up to m *conditional pop* (cpop) operations. On each cpop, a stack takes as argument a single control bit p. If $p = 1$, then the stack indeed pops, returning and removing its top element; if $p = 0$, then the stack instead returns the all zeros string and its contents remain unchanged.

We can port stacks to tri-state gates by simply substituting ANDs by buffers and XORs by joins.[9] A stack with n w-bit elements supporting m cpop operations requires $O(w \cdot m \cdot \log n)$ tri-state gates. Thus, each of the m cpop operations requires only an amortized log number of gates. This straightforward substitution unlocks *substantial* utility. Leveraging tri-state semantics, we can use stacks as dynamic *communication channels* between nodes; see next.

Using Stacks. A parent node and its children communicate via a stack. The parent manages the stack's control bits and outputs. The child manages the stack's content: it appropriately connects the stack's content wires to its input/output ports. To communicate with its child, the parent pops the stack (the call to cpop with $p = 1$ is non-oblivious). This establishes a chain of buffers whose control wires are each set to 1, but whose data wires are not yet set. As soon as we set the data wire of the first buffer in the chain, the buffers will one-by-one fire, sending the data through the chain, from parent to child.

To enable two-way communication, we place two kinds of buffers in the stack. Some buffers are oriented from parent to child, allowing messages to flow from the parent into the input port of the child; other buffers are oriented from child to parent, allowing the child to set messages on its output port which will flow through the stack to its parent. (In Appendix B.1 of the full version, we formalize this notion by giving two variants of a stack, one that sends messages from inputs to outputs and the other that sends messages from outputs to inputs.) Thus, by calling cpop with $p = 1$, the parent dynamically connects itself to one input port and one output port of its child.

Now that ports are connected, the parent can send a message to its child by setting data wires on its side of the stack. These values automatically flow through the stack into the child's input port, causing gates in the child to fire, compute the relevant response, and load the response onto an output port, where it, again, automatically flows through the stack back to the parent.

---

[9] In addition to wires that store data elements, stacks include control logic that tracks element positions. Here, we do *not* simply replace ANDs by buffers (XORs by joins), but rather translate Boolean control logic into tri-state gates via Theorem 1.

Crucially, if the parent instead calls cpop with $p = 0$, no communication occurs. The parent does not connect to its child's port, and hence no gates inside the child fire, so all gates in the unused child remain ready for later use.

Inner Nodes. Let tree level 0 denote the root; level i has 2^i nodes. Let level ℓ denote the tree's largest level. Each node on level i has two stacks, each supporting $2^{\ell-i}$ calls to cpop, of which half can be called with $p = 1$. I.e., each stack allows the node to communicate with its respective child up to $2^{\ell-i-1}$ times.

Each node also consists of $2^{\ell-i}$ subcircuits, each of which performs the following task: (1) receive the address of some leaf from an input port, (2) use the first bit of this address as a stack control bit such that we pop only the stack corresponding to the subtree that stores the requested address, (3) save the remaining bits of the address on the output wires of each stack (sending the bits to the active child), (4) read the response from each child, (5) join the responses together, and (6) save the joined response on the output port. We note that as we inspect nodes closer and closer to the leaves, the nodes become progressively smaller, until the leaves are subcircuits capable of handling exactly one request.

Read Traversals. The RAM can read elements from memory by traversing full root-to-leaf paths through the tree. To do so, the RAM loads into the root the address of the target leaf. The root strips the most significant bit from this address and uses it to conditionally communicate with its two children, indeed popping (i.e. calling cpop with $p = 1$) the stack for the child on the target path, and not popping (i.e. calling cpop with $p = 0$) the other child's stack. The root can now forward a message to its child, so it forwards the address's remaining bits. The child then recursively computes this same procedure, and so on, until we reach the target leaf.

This leaf stores a single element, and it sets its single output port to this element. Based on the semantics of tri-state circuits, this automatically triggers a *cascade of events*. The element flows through the stack of its immediate parent, causing the parent to fire and set its own output port to this newly received element. This causes the element to flow through a stack in the next level of the tree, and so on until the element reaches the root. At this point, the RAM can read the element from the root, completing the memory read.

Direct Writes. Now that the RAM has read its desired element, it *must* write something back. Note, we require this even if the goal of the memory access is simply to read. The problem is that we have now used up the gates associated with the accessed leaf, so we cannot reach that same leaf again. Thus, we need to write back to a fresh leaf, allowing later reads to access the same element again.

It is straightforward to arrange that each step of the RAM is statically and directly connected to one leaf, allowing it to directly write back without a dynamic traversal. Note, these connections induce cycles in the circuit graph, but not at runtime (Definition 4).

Recursive Position Map. As just discussed, each time we read a memory element, we write it back to a fresh location. This introduces a problem: how does the RAM *remember* where it last placed a particular element? This problem is typical in Oblivious RAM constructions, e.g. [SvS+13, WCS15], and can be solved via recursion. Namely, we explicitly store the current position of each memory element in a smaller, recursively-instantiated *position map*.

We can ensure that each recursively instantiated memory holds half the number of elements as the last, so only $O(\log T)$ levels of memory are needed. To achieve this, we arrange that each position map element holds the positions of (at least) two elements in memory. To terminate the recursion, we instantiate the smallest, constant-sized memory via Boolean-logic-based linear scans.

In sum, the RAM construction is binary tree where each node on level i is capable of handling $2^{\ell - i}$ RAM read requests. We dynamically traverse the tree via tri-state-circuit-based stacks; each node holds two stacks, and on each access we pop only the stack on the path to the desired element.

5.2 Sources of Logarithmic Overhead

Our deterministic tri-state RAM has $O(T \cdot \log^4 T)$ gates. We characterize four distinct sources of cost, each of which adds a logarithmic factor:

1. **Word size.** The first source of scaling is unavoidable, as it stems simply from the size of RAM words. Words are assumed to have size $\Theta(\log T)$, and tri-state gates operate on only one bit at a time. Hence, each action on a word requires $O(\log T)$ gates. This factor highlights that the comparison between the word RAM model and the circuit model is "unfair". Word RAMs can manipulate entire words at unit cost; tri-state circuits cannot.
2. **Binary Tree.** On each access, our RAM traverses a path through a binary tree of size $O(T)$. Each traversal touches $O(\log T)$ nodes.
3. **Stacks.** During each traversal and at each tree node, our RAM calls cpop on a constant number of stacks, each of size $O(T)$. Circuit-based stacks of size n have $O(\log n)$ overhead per cpop, yielding an additional $O(\log T)$ factor. **Our oblivious construction** leverages randomness to reduce the size of stacks from $O(T)$ to only $O(\text{poly}(\log T))$, and hence reduces stack overhead from $O(\log T)$ to only $O(\log \log T)$. This is how our oblivious construction is able to improve over our deterministic RAM.
4. **Recursion.** To track positions of elements, we use $O(\log T)$ position maps.

It is difficult to foresee methods for achieving a tri-state RAM with fewer than $O(T \cdot \log^3 T \cdot \log \log T)$ gates. Indeed, each above source of scaling seems relatively inherent to our constructions, so further asymptotic improvement will likely require fundamentally new techniques.

5.3 Formal Construction

We present our formal reduction from RAM to deterministic tri-state circuits in Appendix B.2 of the full version of this paper. We emphasize that the circuit described there is simply a formalism of the key ideas explained in Sect. 5.1.

6   Oblivious Tri-State RAM

In this section, we reduce RAM programs to *oblivious* tri-state circuits. At the highest level, we demonstrate that techniques in Sect. 5 can be combined with the *Circuit Oblivious RAM construction* of [WCS15].

We note that as a proof of concept, one can achieve oblivious tri-state RAM by simply employing off-the-shelf ORAM. Namely, use our deterministic RAM construction to emulate an ORAM server, and use oblivious tri-state Boolean gates (Theorem 2) to emulate an ORAM client. This works, but introduces high overhead which we would like to avoid. Here, we give a direct construction that is far more efficient than this proof of concept.

We begin by formalizing our claim:

Definition 10 (Oblivious T-Emulation). *Let $T \in \mathbb{N}$ denote a runtime. A randomized tri-state circuit family $(\mathcal{C}, \mathcal{D})_{i \in [\mathbb{N}]}$ **obliviously T-emulates a RAM** if it obliviously computes the following function: Let P denote a word RAM program and $x \in \{0,1\}^n$ denote a string.*

$$\mathcal{C}(\langle P \rangle, x) = \begin{cases} P(x) & \text{if } P \text{ halts on input } x \text{ within } T \text{ steps} \\ \langle \bot \rangle & \text{otherwise} \end{cases}$$

Theorem 4 (RAM to Oblivious Tri-State Circuits). *For any runtime $T = \Theta(\text{poly}(\sigma))$, there is a randomized tri-state circuit family $(\mathcal{C}, \mathcal{D})_{i \in \mathbb{N}}$ such that $(\mathcal{C}, \mathcal{D})_\sigma$ obliviously T-emulates a RAM and $|\mathcal{C}| = O(T \cdot \log^3 T \cdot \log \log T)$*

6.1   Circuit ORAM [WCS15] Review

Our key idea is to implement inside a tri-state circuit the Circuit Oblivious RAM construction of [WCS15]. We thus review the relevant ideas of Circuit ORAM.

Circuit ORAM is a *statistically-secure* ORAM: it hides memory access patterns *without* computational assumptions. This property is achieved because the Circuit ORAM client does not use cryptographic primitives to choose its queries. The simplicity of the ORAM client is compatible with the tri-state circuit setting where implementing cryptographic primitives via gates is expensive.

Circuit ORAM arranges memory elements in a binary tree with $O(T)$ leaves. Each node holds up to a constant number (e.g., 3) of memory elements. The root is the only exception: it stores a larger *stash* with capacity $\Theta(\log T \cdot \log \log T)$.

When the ORAM client accesses an element, that element is retrieved from its node and moved to the stash. To prevent the stash from overflowing, Circuit ORAM consistently moves elements away from the root in a process called *eviction*. The key invariant – originally proposed by Path ORAM [SvS+13] – is that even as an element is evicted, it remains on the path to a *fixed leaf*.

To access an element, we scan only those nodes along that element's path. By the invariant, this scan is guaranteed to find the target element, and because each non-root node holds only a few elements, the scan is relatively cheap: the entire path – including the stash – holds only $O(\log T \cdot \log \log T)$ total elements.

Once the element is accessed, the ORAM places that element in the stash and reassigns the element to a fresh, uniformly chosen (with replacement) path.

Because each path is chosen randomly, it is easy to simulate Circuit ORAM's access pattern: the simulator handles each access by choosing a uniform path.

Remembering Paths. To access an element, the ORAM client must somehow *remember* that element's path. Recall that each element's path was chosen when it was last accessed, and there might be long gaps between accesses of a particular element. There are too many data elements for the client to remember paths locally, so the client remembers paths by recursively instantiating a smaller ORAM called the *position map*. See also our discussion of recursion in Sect. 5.

Eviction. After each access, the RAM deterministically chooses two paths and evicts elements along those paths. Each node on a chosen path evicts up to one RAM element to its child. To ensure that the RAM does not get 'stuck' with too many elements in the stash, the identity of evicted elements must be chosen carefully. The goal is to move elements towards the leaves – where there is more space – as quickly as possible. [WCS15]'s key contribution is an efficient procedure for deciding *which* element each node should evict.

Some details of this eviction strategy are *highly relevant* here, because we must implement the procedure with tri-state gates within our asymptotic budget.

[WCS15]*'s Eviction Strategy.* During eviction, [WCS15] first computes metadata, deciding for each path node which element to evict. This metadata computation scans the path twice, starting at the root, performing a (cheap) step of computation at each node towards the leaf, then performing a second scan starting from the leaf and returning to the root. Crucially, this metadata computation has *high locality*: each step only considers local information stored in the currently considered node, plus $O(\log T)$ bits from the previous step.

Jumping ahead to our construction, this locality is *absolutely essential*, because it bounds the amount of information that needs to be passed from a tree node to its parent/child, and hence bounds the amount of information that needs to pass through circuit-based stacks (see discussion in Sect. 5). Thus, our reduction can use stacks of small items, each of size $O(\log T)$ bits.

The remaining details of metadata computation are not crucial for understanding our construction, except that they ensure eviction prevents the stash from overflowing (except with negligible probability). For further detail, we refer the reader to [WCS15] (see their Algorithms 2 and 3 as well as their Fig. 2).

After metadata is computed, Circuit ORAM again performs a scan from root to leaf where each node evicts (up to) one element to its child. The identity of this child is chosen according to the metadata.

By evicting elements this way, Circuit ORAM maintains its crucial path invariant while ensuring that the root will never overflow.

6.2   Overview of Our Oblivious Tri-State RAM

In short, our oblivious tri-state RAM reuses almost every idea explained in Sect. 5. It similarly maintains a binary tree of nodes, each of which conditionally communicates with its two children via circuit-based stacks, and our RAM reads elements by traversing paths through the tree. Our oblivious construction improves over our deterministic RAM in two ways: it is *oblivious*, making it suitable for cryptographic use, and it is asymptotically smaller.

These properties are achieved by using tri-state circuits to directly implement the Circuit ORAM construction [WCS15]. We also leverage an insight described by [PLS22] that allows us to use smaller circuit-based stacks, reducing asymptotic cost. We describe our oblivious tri-state RAM by highlighting the differences as compared to our deterministic reduction (Sect. 5).

Storage in Every Node. In our deterministic RAM, only the leaves store memory elements. Our oblivious construction follows Circuit ORAM, where *each* node can hold $O(1)$ elements and where the root stores $O(\log T \cdot \log \log T)$ elements. When the RAM accesses an element, that element is written back to the root (and not written directly to a leaf). These elements subsequently move down the tree via Circuit ORAM's eviction strategy, implemented via tri-state gates.

Multi-purpose Node Subcircuits. In our deterministic construction, each node holds $O(T)$ subcircuits, each of which completes a basic task: conditionally pop both stacks, then join the resulting values and send them back to the parent. Our oblivious construction's subcircuits are more complex. They each conditionally perform various tasks, depending on the current need of the ORAM construction.

Each subcircuit conditionally performs one of three tasks: (1) **read**, including scanning the node's local content, (2) **evict**, including computing appropriate metadata and sending an element to a child, or (3) **do nothing** (the need for this option is explained when we discuss "smaller stacks"). While each subcircuit must include enough circuitry to complete *any* of these tasks, the subcircuit is small. This is achieved by reusing parts of the circuit across the different possible tasks. In particular, we need only two total calls to cpop per subcircuit.

Multiple Scans. In our deterministic RAM, each access scans a path twice, from root to leaf and then back to the root. Our *oblivious* tri-state RAM performs *three* scans. While only two scans are needed to read, three are needed to evict. When evicting, the RAM uses two scans to compute Circuit ORAM's relevant metadata, and it uses the third scan to evict elements from parent to child.

Our tri-state stacks are thus used multiple times per access: the parent sends a message to its child, receives a message back, and then sends a second message. We emphasize that there is no technical challenge in using a circuit-based stack to communicate more than once: just increase the size of stack elements and leverage tri-state semantics to send bits at the right time.

Even though our nodes use three scans, the total information flowing through stacks remains small. In total, each node sends/receives $O(\log T)$ bits of information. Keeping this amount of information small is crucial, because transmitted bits pass through stacks, and hence we must pay in additional gates for every bit of information transmitted between parent and child.

Smaller Stacks. In our deterministic RAM, each node communicates with each of its children via a circuit-based stack of size $O(T)$. Our oblivious construction improves on this by leveraging an elegant idea demonstrated by [PLS22], allowing much smaller stacks that hold only $O(\text{poly}(\log T))$ elements. The smaller stacks account for our oblivious construction's improved asymptotic size.

We explain [PLS22]'s observation – which is derived from an observation of [FNR+15] – in the context of Circuit ORAM. Recall that in Circuit ORAM, each memory access scans a uniformly chosen path.

Let $B = \Theta(\log^{1+\epsilon} \sigma)$ denote a parameter super-logarithmic in the security parameter for constant $\epsilon > 0$. We call B the *batch parameter*. Let level 0 denote the root of the RAM tree; each level i has 2^i nodes. Consider: how often will a particular node on level i be scanned over the course of $2^i \cdot B$ accesses?

[FNR+15]'s insight is that because elements are randomly assigned to leaves, accesses should be roughly evenly distributed amongst nodes on level i. Indeed, it is incredibly unlikely that a particular node will be scanned significantly more often than its peers. [FNR+15] proved that it is only negligibly likely that over $2^i \cdot B$ accesses any node on level i will be used more than $2 \cdot B$ times.

The upshot is that we need never instantiate a stack with more than $O(B)$ entries (e.g., 256 entries in practice), since it is unlikely that we will exhaust its entries over the course of $2^i \cdot B$ accesses. Instead, every $2^i \cdot B$ accesses, we insert a *reset* step, forcibly clearing all stacks on level i and instantiating fresh stacks. Since each cpop operation is made to a smaller stack, this strategy reduces stack overhead from factor $\log T$ to factor $\log \log T$.

Smaller stacks introduce nuance in implementing node subcircuits. Consider a particular node, consisting of many sequentially composed subcircuits. [PLS22]'s strategy partitions these subcircuits into *generations* of size $2 \cdot B$. After each generation, we insert a statically scheduled reset, preparing for the next generation. **For this to work**, we must ensure that over the course of $2^i \cdot B$ accesses, *every* subcircuit in the current generation is consumed. If not, the circuit is not well defined, since our reset will manipulate wires coming out of the generation's last subcircuit, and the wires of this last subcircuit are defined only if it and all of its predecessors have been used. Thus we must *ensure* that each subcircuit is ultimately used. Since subcircuits are used only if they are on a randomly chosen path, it is highly unlikely that *every* subcircuit will be used up naturally.

To account for this problem, we insert additional logic allowing a parent to burn through subcircuits in its children's current generations. This is the role of the **do nothing** subcircuit task. When a parent calls its child with a particular flag set, the child's subcircuit simply calls cpop on each of its respective stacks with $p = 0$, and no further action is taken. This burns the subcircuit.

Because we reset level i every $2^i \cdot B$ accesses, we reset level $i+1$ in synchrony with one out of every *two* resets of level i. On each second reset of level i, we add circuitry that causes each node on level i to call cpop on each of its stacks $2 \cdot B$ additional times, sending a message that instructs the corresponding child to burn a subcircuit (once all subcircuits are burned, the parent stops forwarding this message by instead calling cpop with $p = 0$). A statically known state, and we can correctly wire gates.

Oblivious Circuitry. To allow a simulator, our oblivious reduction uses oblivious Boolean gates (see Theorem 2). There is nuance here: circuit-based stacks continue to elide obliviousness, and the role each subcircuit ends up executing (read, evict, or do nothing) is leaked by the circuit. This leakage is fine, however, since this information is implied by the RAM's physical access pattern, and Circuit ORAM ensures that the physical access pattern hides the logical access pattern.

On the other hand, some oblivious gates *are* required. In particular, any circuitry that actually scans the content of a RAM node is oblivious. It is cheap to instantiate these components with oblivious ANDs (Theorem 2).

In sum, our oblivious reduction builds on the basic ideas of Sect. 5, and then layers in the key ideas of Circuit ORAM [WCS15] and of [PLS22]. Circuit ORAM's eviction procedure can be implemented by tri-state gates, allowing for a lean memory structure whose access pattern can be simulated. The resulting memory features an access pattern that touches nodes on each tree level uniformly, allowing us to use smaller stacks, reducing the size of circuitry required to support intra-node communication. Together, these ideas yield a circuit that obliviously simulates RAM and that has low poly-logarithmic overhead.

6.3 Formal Construction

We present our formal reduction from RAM to oblivious tri-state circuits in Appendix B.3 of the full version of this paper. We emphasize that the circuit described there is simply a formalism of the key ideas explained in Sect. 6.2.

7 Garbling Tri-State Circuits

In this section, we demonstrate how to garble tri-state circuits. We give two constructions. Our first construction garbles tri-state gates based only on one-way functions, achieving a *garbling scheme* [BHR12] suited to semi-honest protocols. Our second construction builds on *authenticated garbling* [WRK17] to achieve malicious security. Both constructions leverage similar high level ideas.

Intuition. In short, garbling of tri-state circuits is similar to classic garbling of Boolean circuits. Just as in classic garbling, the garbler G chooses two keys per wire. One key encodes logical zero, the other encodes one. To garble the circuit, G proceeds gate by gate. At each gate, G uses appropriate combinations of input keys to encrypt output keys according to the gate's function.

At runtime, the evaluator E obtains *at most* one key per wire. E walks the circuit, using keys to decrypt subsequent keys until obtaining output keys.

The crucial point is this: G *only* chooses keys that encode 0 and 1; the distinguished value $\mathcal{Z}$ is encoded by *the lack of a key*. If a particular wire holds

$\mathcal{Z}$ at halt-time, then E will *never* learn a key for that wire. The inability to decrypt certain wires differentiates tri-state garbling from classic garbling.

Throughout evaluation, E will keep track of which wires are set and which are not set. To arrange this, we *reveal to E the cleartext value of every buffer control wire.* (It is easy to arrange that E learns the cleartext values of particular wires.) Because E knows which wires hold $\mathcal{Z}$ and which do not, E can execute the circuit in a dynamic order, at each step handling those gates for which input keys are available. It is safe to reveal controls because the *obliviousness* (Definition 8) of the circuit ensures that these bits give E no information about the input.

Note the fit between garbling and the out-of-order nature of tri-state circuits: E can, of course, decrypt each GC gate *as soon as matching keys are obtained,* making it easy to execute gates in an order prescribed by *notify* (Fig. 1).

The following sections show how we garble tri-state gates. Our approaches build on known techniques for garbling from one-way functions (e.g., see [LP09]) and for authenticated garbling [WRK17].

7.1 Tri-State Garbling from One-Way Functions

Recall that tri-state circuits include XORs, buffers, and joins. We present our semi-honest garbling of each gate type from one-way functions.

Wire Keys; Point and Permute. For each wire w, G uniformly samples two length-λ keys K_w^0 and K_w^1. The first key encodes logical zero; the second encodes one.

We use the classic *point and permute* trick [NPS99]. In GC, each gate uses several ciphertexts, of which E should decrypt one. Point and permute allows E to decrypt the *correct* ciphertext without using awkward tricks like trying to decrypt a ciphertext and then checking if it decrypted correctly or not.

The trick requires that for each wire w, the least significant bits of K_w^0 and K_w^1 differ. G conditionally flips the least significant bit of K_w^1 to ensure it differs from that of K_w^0. G then *permutes* gate ciphertexts according to these keys.

In the following, we elide details of point and permute, opting for a simpler presentation. Appendix C of the full version presents a formal construction.

Gate Handling. With keys chosen, G garbles each gate one at a time. Consider a gate with input wires x and y and with output wire z. Let $Enc(\cdot, \cdot)$ denote CPA-secure encryption (which can be instantiated from one-way functions).

- **XOR.** For each XOR gate, G classically garbles the gate by encrypting each output key according to the appropriate combination of inputs keys:

$$Enc(K_x^0, Enc(K_y^0, K_z^0)) \qquad Enc(K_x^0, Enc(K_y^1, K_z^1))$$
$$Enc(K_x^1, Enc(K_y^0, K_z^1)) \qquad Enc(K_x^1, Enc(K_y^1, K_z^0))$$

These four ciphertexts are shuffled according to point and permute and sent to E. At runtime and when two input keys become available, E decrypts one ciphertext, obtaining the corresponding output key.

- **Buffer.** For each buffer, G ensures that E can obtain an output key iff E holds the one key for the control. Recall, E must *learn* the value of each control. To achieve this, G send to E the least significant bit of K_y^0; E can compare this to its own lsb and learn y. Altogether, G sends:

$$lsb(K_y^0) \qquad Enc(K_x^0, Enc(K_y^1, K_z^0)) \qquad Enc(K_x^1, Enc(K_y^1, K_z^1))$$

  The two encryptions are shuffled according to point and permute.

- **Join.** For each join, G ensures E obtains an output key if E holds *any* input key. G sends the following rows (shuffled wire-wise with point-and-permute):

$$Enc(K_x^0, K_z^0) \qquad Enc(K_x^1, K_z^1) \qquad Enc(K_y^0, K_z^0) \qquad Enc(K_y^1, K_z^1)$$

  As soon as E obtains *any* input key, E decrypts the appropriate ciphertext, obtaining a corresponding output key. Here it is *essential* that $(\mathcal{C}, \mathcal{D})$ computes a Boolean function, preventing the possibility of a short circuit (see discussion near Definition 5) which would allow E to learn *both* output keys.

Sampling $\mathcal{D}$. Recall that an oblivious tri-state circuit includes a distribution on bits $\mathcal{D}$. In the semi-honest setting, it is trivial to handle input randomness: G locally samples $r \in_\$ \mathcal{D}$, then sends to E wire keys corresponding to r.

In sum, our OWF-based garbling scheme is simple: we gate-by-gate garble the circuit, and each garbled gate has size $O(\lambda)$ bits. E evaluates the circuit as keys become available, implementing the dynamic behavior of the tri-state model.

Formal Construction. We present our OWF-based tri-state *garbling scheme* in Appendix C of the full version of this paper. We emphasize that the presentation there is just a formalization of the ideas presented above.

   In terms of security, our proof gives a simulator and a hybrid argument demonstrating that the garbled circuit hides the input. This proof is similar to classic proofs of GC security, e.g. [LP09], with *two key exceptions*: we use our oblivious tri-state circuit's simulator (Definition 8) to argue that the E's observed order of execution can be simulated, and we use runtime acyclicity (Definition 4) to guide our hybrid argument.

   By combining facts of Appendix C with Theorem 4, we obtain:

Corollary 1 (Garbled RAM from one-way functions). *Assuming one-way functions and in the OT-hybrid model, there exists a constant-round, semi-honest secure 2PC protocol for word-RAM programs such that for any program halting in T steps, communication cost is $O(T \cdot \log^3 T \cdot \log \log T \cdot \lambda)$ bits.*

7.2   Authenticated Garbling of Tri-State Circuits

In this section, we extend authenticated garbling [WRK17] to tri-state circuits. This extension implies an efficient constant-round maliciously-secure 2PC protocol for RAM programs.

   Our authenticated handling is similar to that of our standard-assumption -based garbling (Sect. 7.1). We highlight the key differences:

- **Doubly-authenticated labels.** In standard GC, we encode each wire by a pair of keys chosen by G. In authenticated GC, each key contains components chosen by *each* party. In particular, each key includes a MAC, allowing E to authenticate that certain values are well formed.
- **Preprocessing.** In Sect. 7.1, we allowed G to sample randomness $r \in_\$ \mathcal{D}$. In the authenticated setting, we instead require that G and E *jointly* sample r via a preprocessing functionality. This achieves two goals. First, it ensures that r is indeed sampled from $\mathcal{D}$, and not arbitrarily chosen by malicious G. Second it ensures that neither G nor E knows r. This (1) prevents E from learning wire values and (2) prevents G from performing *selective abort attacks*. Note, prior work on authenticated garbling also leverages preprocessed randomness in the form of *doubly authenticated multiplication triples*.
- **Correlations; Random Oracle Assumption.** In Sect. 7.1, we garbled tri-state gates using only one-way functions. Our authenticated approach uses a function H modeled as a random oracle. The use of RO stems from *correlations* in wire labels. It is typical to use RO for authenticated GC.

We next describe authenticated garbling in more detail.

Garblings. The crucial authenticated GC invariant [WRK17] is that on each wire, G and E hold XOR secret shares of two MACs, one that authenticates the cleartext value to G and one that authenticates the cleartext value to E.

These *garblings* are defined over two global secrets:

- $\Delta \in_\$ \{0,1\}^\lambda$ is a global key drawn by G and hidden from E. G uses Δ as a key with which to encrypt gates.
- $\mu \in_\$ \{0,1\}^\sigma$ is a global MAC drawn by E and hidden from G. E uses μ to check that values opened by G are honestly constructed.

For convenience of notation, we define a value $\Gamma \triangleq \Delta \parallel \mu \parallel 1$.

As the circuit executes, for each wire holding value x, G and E will hold XOR secret shares of the value $x \cdot \Gamma$. We refer to these shares as *garblings*:

Notation 1 (Distributed Pair). *We denote by $\langle\!\langle x, y \rangle\!\rangle$ a distributed pair of values, where G holds value x and E holds value y.*

Definition 11 (Garbling). *Let $x \in \{0, 1, \mathcal{Z}\}$ be a tri-state value. The **garbling** of x is a secret share held between G and E. G's share is a string $X \in \{0,1\}^{\lambda+\sigma+1}$. E's share is either (1) the symbol $\mathcal{Z}$ if $x = \mathcal{Z}$ or (2) the following:*

$$X \oplus (x \cdot \Delta \parallel x \cdot \mu \parallel x) = X \oplus x \cdot \Gamma$$

We denote a garbling of x by $[\![x]\!]$:

$$[\![x]\!] \triangleq \left\langle\!\!\left\langle X, \begin{cases} \mathcal{Z} & \text{if } x = \mathcal{Z} \\ X \oplus x \cdot \Gamma & \text{otherwise} \end{cases} \right\rangle\!\!\right\rangle$$

*For values $x \neq \mathcal{Z}$, we refer to the Δ component of a garbling as the **key part** of the garbling, to the μ component as the **MAC part**, and to the third component* *as the **value part**. We use key, mac, val to denote appropriate projections. I.e., when $x \neq Z$, we define the following projections:*

$$key([\![x]\!]) = \langle\!\langle X_0, X_0 \oplus x \cdot \Delta \rangle\!\rangle \qquad \textbf{where } X_0 \in \{0,1\}^\lambda$$
$$mac([\![x]\!]) = \langle\!\langle X_1, X_1 \oplus x \cdot \mu \rangle\!\rangle \qquad \textbf{where } X_1 \in \{0,1\}^\sigma$$
$$val([\![x]\!]) = \langle\!\langle X_2, X_2 \oplus x \rangle\!\rangle \qquad \textbf{where } X_2 \in \{0,1\}$$
$$\textbf{and } X_0 \mid\mid X_1 \mid\mid X_2 = X$$

Garbling XORs. Garblings are linearly homomorphic. Namely, if each party locally XORs the shares of two garbled bits, the result is itself a garbled bit. XOR gates are 'free' [KS08]:

Lemma 2 (Free XOR). $[\![x]\!] \oplus [\![y]\!] = [\![x \oplus y]\!]$

Revealing Values to E. Recall that in tri-state execution we reveal to E the cleartext value of each control bit. In the authenticated setting, we must be careful when revealing values. In particular, we must preserve two properties:

- **Privacy.** Revealed values should not leak G's input to E. Data privacy is preserved via tri-state *obliviousness* (Definition 8).
- **Authenticity.** Even a malicious G should not be able to reveal the wrong value. We prevent G from cheating via the MAC μ on the revealed wire.

It is relatively straightforward for G to reveal a circuit value $[\![x]\!]$ to E. The parties first compute:

$$\langle\!\langle X_1, X_1 \oplus x \cdot \mu \rangle\!\rangle \leftarrow mac([\![x]\!]) \qquad \langle\!\langle X_2, X_2 \oplus x \rangle\!\rangle \leftarrow val([\![x]\!])$$

If G is honest, G can reveal x by sending to E the strings X_1 and X_2. Of course, G might attempt to cheat, so it may be the case that G sends $X_1' \neq X_1$ and $X_2' \neq X_2$. Thus, E must check that the strings are well formed. Recall that E knows the MAC μ. E checks the following:

$$X_1' \oplus x' \cdot \mu \overset{?}{=} X_1 \oplus x \cdot \mu \qquad \text{where } x' = (X_2 \oplus x) \oplus X_2' \qquad (1)$$

If this passes, E is convinced that the wire indeed holds x'; otherwise, E aborts.

The above check passes whenever G indeed sends X_1 and X_2. Moreover, if G attempts to cheat, then the above check will only pass with probability negligible in σ. Indeed, to successfully reveal $x \oplus 1$, G must send $X_2' = X_2 \oplus 1$ and $X_1' = X_1 \oplus \mu$. However, G does not know μ, and so G's attempt to send $X_1 \oplus \mu$ requires guessing μ, which succeeds with probability at most $1/2^\sigma$.

Note that obliviousness ensures that each revealed value x can be simulated. This is important not only for protecting G's privacy, but also for protecting E's. In particular, G cannot employ a selective abort attack. Without obliviousness, G could cause E's check to fail iff x has a particular value; E's choice to abort/not abort reveals to G information about x. Indeed, G can still attempt such an "attack". However, the attempt is useless, since it only reveals information about a control wire which, by obliviousness, can be simulated anyway. Note that this argument crucially relies on the fact that G does not know the circuit randomness $r \in_\$ \mathcal{D}$, which is one reason r must be jointly computed in preprocessing.

Authenticated Buffers. Consider a buffer with data input $[\![x]\!]$ and control $[\![s]\!]$. Suppose $s \neq \mathcal{Z}$ and $x \neq \mathcal{Z}$. We show how the parties compute $[\![x \, / \, s]\!]$.

First, the parties reveal the control s to E, as described above. Now, let:

$$\langle\!\langle S, S \oplus s \cdot \Delta \rangle\!\rangle = key([\![s]\!]) \qquad \langle\!\langle X, X \oplus x \cdot \Gamma \rangle\!\rangle = [\![x]\!]$$

Honest G wishes to let E propagate $[\![x]\!]$ to the gate output iff $s = 1$. The parties publicly agree on gate-specific nonce ν, and G sets its output share as follows:

$$Y \triangleq H(S \oplus \Delta, \nu) \oplus X$$

At runtime, E checks if $s = 1$. Note that if $s = 1$, in an honest execution E holds $S \oplus \Delta$. In this case, E computes:

$$H(S \oplus \Delta, \nu) \oplus (X \oplus x \cdot \Gamma) = (Y \oplus X) \oplus (X \oplus x \cdot \Gamma) = Y \oplus x \cdot \Gamma$$

E places this value on the output wire, matching G's share Y. Thus, if $s = 1$, the output wire holds $[\![x]\!]$, as prescribed by buffer semantics. If instead $s = 0$ then the gate is indeed inactive: E cannot compute $H(S \oplus \Delta, \nu)$ without $S \oplus \Delta$.

Thus, a buffer is implemented by G revealing one value and having each party compute H at most once.

Authenticated Joins. Consider a join with inputs $[\![x]\!]$ and $[\![y]\!]$ and suppose that at runtime at least one input is set. We show how the parties compute $[\![x \bowtie y]\!]$.

Let the shares of $[\![x]\!]$, $[\![y]\!]$ be as follows:

$$[\![x]\!] = \langle\!\langle X, X_E \rangle\!\rangle = \langle\!\langle X, X \oplus x \cdot \Gamma \rangle\!\rangle \qquad [\![y]\!] = \langle\!\langle Y, Y_E \rangle\!\rangle = \langle\!\langle Y, Y \oplus y \cdot \Gamma \rangle\!\rangle$$

G sets its output share as X. Thus, if $x \neq \mathcal{Z}$ is set, then E simply copies its share $X \oplus x \cdot \Gamma$ onto the gate output wire. If instead $x = \mathcal{Z}$, then E must *translate* its share $Y \oplus y \cdot \Gamma$ to a format compatible with G's share. Hence, G includes in the GC the message $X \oplus Y$, which E can use to compute a matching share:

$$\left(\begin{cases} X_E & \text{if } y = \mathcal{Z} \\ Y_E \oplus X \oplus Y & \text{if } x = \mathcal{Z} \end{cases} \right) = \left(\begin{cases} X \oplus x \cdot \Gamma & \text{if } y = \mathcal{Z} \\ X \oplus y \cdot \Gamma & \text{if } x = \mathcal{Z} \end{cases} \right) = X \oplus (x \bowtie y) \cdot \Gamma$$

Thus, a join is implemented by having G send one correction value, which E conditionally XORs with its local value.

In sum, the authenticated garbling of tri-state gates is a relatively straightforward extension of existing techniques. Adding a MAC to each key prevents G from arbitrarily flipping wire values. Crucially, it remains possible for G to reveal values to E, allowing E to execute the dynamic behavior of the tri-state model.

Communication cost of our protocol is low. For example, plugging in Theorem 2, we evaluate an oblivious AND gate using an authenticated triple and $2\lambda + 4\sigma + 2$ additional communicated bits (two buffers, two joins). This is only slightly worse than the authenticated AND garbling of [KRRW18], which consumes an authenticated triple and $2\lambda + 1$ additional bits. For typical parameters $\lambda = 128$ and $\sigma = 40$, our approach is less than $2\times$ worse. Optimizations of [KRRW18] can likely be integrated with TSC handling, improving performance.

Formal Construction. We defer our full malicious protocol to Appendix D of the full version. Our protocol and its security proof are very similar to those of [WRK17], with the crucial difference that we use the above gate handling.

By combining facts proved in Appendix D with Theorem 4, we trivially obtain the following corollary:

Corollary 2 (Authenticated Garbled RAM). *In the random oracle/OT-hybrid model, there exists a constant-round, maliciously-secure 2PC protocol for word RAMs such that for any program halting in T steps, communication cost is $O(T \cdot \log^3 T \cdot \log \log T \cdot \lambda)$ bits.*

Acknowledgements. Distribution Statement "A": (Approved for Public Release, Distribution Unlimited). This research was developed with funding from the Defense Advanced Research Projects Agency (DARPA), supported in part by DARPA under Cooperative Agreement HR0011-20-2-0025, and DARPA Contract No. HR001120C0087, Algorand Centers of Excellence programme managed by Algorand Foundation, NSF grants CNS-2246353, CNS-2246354, CNS-2246355, CNS-2001096 and CCF-2220450, US-Israel BSF grant 2015782, Amazon Faculty Award, Cisco Research Award and Sunday Group. Any views, opinions, findings, conclusions or recommendations contained herein are those of the author(s) and should not be interpreted as necessarily representing the official policies, either expressed or implied, of DARPA, the Department of Defense, the Algorand Foundation, or the U.S. Government. The U.S. Government is authorized to reproduce and distribute reprints for governmental purposes not withstanding any copyright annotation therein.

References

[Bea92] Beaver, D.: Efficient multiparty protocols using circuit randomization. In: Feigenbaum, J. (ed.) CRYPTO 1991. LNCS, vol. 576, pp. 420–432. Springer, Heidelberg (1992). https://doi.org/10.1007/3-540-46766-1_34

[BHR12] Bellare, M., Hoang, V.T., Rogaway, P.: Foundations of garbled circuits. In: Yu, T., Danezis, G., Gligor, V.D. (eds.) ACM CCS 2012, pp. 784–796. ACM Press, October 2012

[CCHR16] Canetti, R., Chen, Y., Holmgren, J., Raykova, M.: Adaptive succinct garbled RAM or: how to delegate your database. In: Hirt, M., Smith, A. (eds.) TCC 2016. LNCS, vol. 9986, pp. 61–90. Springer, Heidelberg (2016). https://doi.org/10.1007/978-3-662-53644-5_3

[CH16]   Canetti, R., Holmgren, J.: Fully succinct garbled RAM. In: Sudan, M. (ed.) ITCS 2016, pp. 169–178. ACM, January 2016

[CKKZ12] Choi, S.G., Katz, J., Kumaresan, R., Zhou, H.-S.: On the security of the "Free-XOR" technique. In: Cramer, R. (ed.) TCC 2012. LNCS, vol. 7194, pp. 39–53. Springer, Heidelberg (2012). https://doi.org/10.1007/978-3-642-28914-9_3

[DILO22] Dittmer, S., Ishai, Y., Steve, L., Ostrovsky, R.: Authenticated garbling from simple correlations. In: Dodis, Y., Shrimpton, T. (eds.) CRYPTO 2022. LNCS, vol. 13510, pp. 57–87. Springer, Cham (2022). https://doi.org/10.1007/978-3-031-15985-5_3

[FNR+15] Fletcher, C., Naveed, M., Ren, L., Shi, E., Stefanov, E.: Bucket ORAM: single online roundtrip, constant bandwidth oblivious RAM. Cryptology ePrint Archive, Report 2015/1065 (2015). https://eprint.iacr.org/2015/1065

[GGMP16] Garg, S., Gupta, D., Miao, P., Pandey, O.: Secure multiparty RAM computation in constant rounds. In: Hirt, M., Smith, A. (eds.) TCC 2016. LNCS, vol. 9985, pp. 491–520. Springer, Heidelberg (2016). https://doi.org/10.1007/978-3-662-53641-4_19

[GHL+14] Gentry, C., Halevi, S., Lu, S., Ostrovsky, R., Raykova, M., Wichs, D.: Garbled RAM revisited. In: Nguyen, P.Q., Oswald, E. (eds.) EUROCRYPT 2014. LNCS, vol. 8441, pp. 405–422. Springer, Heidelberg (2014). https://doi.org/10.1007/978-3-642-55220-5_23

[GLNP18] Gueron, S., Lindell, Y., Nof, A., Pinkas, B.: Fast garbling of circuits under standard assumptions. J. Cryptol. 31(3), 798–844 (2018)

[GLO15] Garg, S., Lu, S., Ostrovsky, R.: Black-box garbled RAM. In: Guruswami, V. (ed.) 56th FOCS, pp. 210–229. IEEE Computer Society Press, October 2015

[GLOS15] Garg, S., Lu, S., Ostrovsky, R., Scafuro, A.: Garbled RAM from one-way functions. In: Servedio, R.A., Rubinfeld, R. (eds.) 47th ACM STOC, pp. 449–458. ACM Press, June 2015

[GO96] Goldreich, O., Ostrovsky, R.: Software protection and simulation on oblivious RAMs. J. ACM 43(3), 431–473 (1996)

[Hag98] Hagerup, T.: Sorting and searching on the word RAM. In: Morvan, M., Meinel, C., Krob, D. (eds.) STACS 1998. LNCS, vol. 1373, pp. 366–398. Springer, Heidelberg (1998). https://doi.org/10.1007/BFb0028575

[HJO+16] Hemenway, B., Jafargholi, Z., Ostrovsky, R., Scafuro, A., Wichs, D.: Adaptively secure garbled circuits from one-way functions. In: Robshaw, M., Katz, J. (eds.) CRYPTO 2016. LNCS, vol. 9816, pp. 149–178. Springer, Heidelberg (2016). https://doi.org/10.1007/978-3-662-53015-3_6

[HKO22] Heath, D., Kolesnikov, V., Ostrovsky, R.: EPIGRAM: practical garbled RAM. In: Dunkelman, O., Dziembowski, S. (eds.) EUROCRYPT 2022. LNCS, vol. 13275, pp. 3–33. Springer, Cham (2022). https://doi.org/10.1007/978-3-031-06944-4_1

[HY16] Hazay, C., Yanai, A.: Constant-round maliciously secure two-party computation in the RAM model. In: Hirt, M., Smith, A. (eds.) TCC 2016. LNCS, vol. 9985, pp. 521–553. Springer, Heidelberg (2016). https://doi.org/10.1007/978-3-662-53641-4_20

[KRRW18] Katz, J., Ranellucci, S., Rosulek, M., Wang, X.: Optimizing authenticated garbling for faster secure two-party computation. In: Shacham, H., Boldyreva, A. (eds.) CRYPTO 2018. LNCS, vol. 10993, pp. 365–391. Springer, Cham (2018). https://doi.org/10.1007/978-3-319-96878-0_13

[KS08] Kolesnikov, V., Schneider, T.: Improved garbled circuit: free XOR gates and applications. In: Aceto, L., Damgård, I., Goldberg, L.A., Halldórsson, M.M., Ingólfsdóttir, A., Walukiewicz, I. (eds.) ICALP 2008. LNCS, vol. 5126, pp. 486–498. Springer, Heidelberg (2008). https://doi.org/10.1007/978-3-540-70583-3_40

[Lin13] Lindell, Y.: Fast cut-and-choose based protocols for malicious and covert adversaries. In: Canetti, R., Garay, J.A. (eds.) CRYPTO 2013. LNCS, vol. 8043, pp. 1–17. Springer, Heidelberg (2013). https://doi.org/10.1007/978-3-642-40084-1_1

[LO13] Lu, S., Ostrovsky, R.: How to garble RAM programs? In: Johansson, T., Nguyen, P.Q. (eds.) EUROCRYPT 2013. LNCS, vol. 7881, pp. 719–734. Springer, Heidelberg (2013). https://doi.org/10.1007/978-3-642-38348-9_42

[LO17] Lu, S., Ostrovsky, R.: Black-box parallel garbled RAM. In: Katz, J., Shacham, H. (eds.) CRYPTO 2017. LNCS, vol. 10402, pp. 66–92. Springer, Cham (2017). https://doi.org/10.1007/978-3-319-63715-0_3

[LP09] Lindell, Y., Pinkas, B.: A proof of security of Yao's protocol for two-party computation. J. Cryptol. **22**(2), 161–188 (2009)

[LY18] Lindell, Y., Yanai, A.: Fast garbling of circuits over 3-valued logic. In: Abdalla, M., Dahab, R. (eds.) PKC 2018. LNCS, vol. 10769, pp. 620–643. Springer, Cham (2018). https://doi.org/10.1007/978-3-319-76578-5_21

[Mia20] Miao, P.: Cut-and-choose for garbled RAM. In: Jarecki, S. (ed.) CT-RSA 2020. LNCS, vol. 12006, pp. 610–637. Springer, Cham (2020). https://doi.org/10.1007/978-3-030-40186-3_26

[NPS99] Naor, M., Pinkas, B., Sumner, R.: Privacy preserving auctions and mechanism design. In: Proceedings of the 1st ACM Conference on Electronic Commerce, pp. 129–139. ACM (1999)

[PLS22] Park, A., Lin, W.-K., Shi, E.: NanoGRAM: garbled RAM with $\widetilde{O}(\log N)$ overhead. Cryptology ePrint Archive, Report 2022/191 (2022). https://eprint.iacr.org/2022/191

[RR21] Rosulek, M., Roy, L.: Three halves make a whole? Beating the half-gates lower bound for garbled circuits. In: Malkin, T., Peikert, C. (eds.) CRYPTO 2021. LNCS, vol. 12825, pp. 94–124. Springer, Cham (2021). https://doi.org/10.1007/978-3-030-84242-0_5

[Sch80] Schönhage, A.: Storage modification machines. SIAM J. Comput. **9**(3), 490–508 (1980)

[SvS+13] Stefanov, E., et al.: Path ORAM: an extremely simple oblivious RAM protocol. In: Sadeghi, A.-R., Gligor, V.D., Yung, M. (eds.) ACM CCS 2013, pp. 299–310. ACM Press, November 2013

[WCS15] Wang, X., Hubert Chan, T.-H., Shi, E.: Circuit ORAM: on tightness of the Goldreich-Ostrovsky lower bound. In: Ray, I., Li, N., Kruegel, C. (eds.) ACM CCS 2015, pp. 850–861. ACM Press, October 2015

[WRK17] Wang, X., Ranellucci, S., Katz, J.: Authenticated garbling and efficient maliciously secure two-party computation. In: Thuraisingham, B.M., Evans, D., Malkin, T., Xu, D. (eds.) ACM CCS 2017, pp. 21–37. ACM Press, October/November 2017

[Yao86] Yao, A.C.-C.: How to generate and exchange secrets (extended abstract). In: 27th FOCS, pp. 162–167. IEEE Computer Society Press, October 1986

[YWZ20] Yang, K., Wang, X., Zhang, J.: More efficient MPC from improved triple generation and authenticated garbling. In: Ligatti, J., Ou, X., Katz, J., Vigna, G. (eds.) ACM CCS 2020, pp. 1627–1646. ACM Press, November 2020

[ZE13] Zahur, S., Evans, D.: Circuit structures for improving efficiency of security and privacy tools. In: 2013 IEEE Symposium on Security and Privacy, pp. 493–507. IEEE Computer Society Press, May 2013

[ZRE15] Zahur, S., Rosulek, M., Evans, D.: Two halves make a whole - reducing data transfer in garbled circuits using half gates. In: Oswald, E., Fischlin, M. (eds.) EUROCRYPT 2015. LNCS, vol. 9057, pp. 220–250. Springer, Heidelberg (2015). https://doi.org/10.1007/978-3-662-46803-6_8

Limits of Breach-Resistant and Snapshot-Oblivious RAMs

Giuseppe Persiano[1,2] and Kevin Yeo[3(✉)]

[1] Università di Salerno, Salerno, Italy
[2] Google, New York, USA
[3] Google and Columbia University, New York, USA
kwlyeo@google.com

Abstract. Oblivious RAMs (ORAMs) are an important cryptographic primitive that enable outsourcing data to a potentially untrusted server while hiding patterns of access to the data. ORAMs provide strong guarantees even in the face of a *persistent adversary* that views the transcripts of all operations and resulting memory contents. Unfortunately, the strong guarantees against persistent adversaries comes at the cost of efficiency as ORAMs are known to require $\Omega(\log n)$ overhead.

In an attempt to obtain faster constructions, prior works considered security against *snapshot adversaries* that only have limited access to operational transcripts and memory. We consider (s, ℓ)-snapshot adversaries that perform s data breaches and views the transcripts of ℓ total queries. Promisingly, Du, Genkin and Grubbs [Crypto'22] presented an ORAM construction with $O(\log \ell)$ overhead protecting against $(1, \ell)$-snapshot adversaries with the transcript of ℓ consecutive operations from a single breach. For small values of ℓ, this outperforms standard ORAMs.

In this work, we tackle whether it is possible to further push this construction beyond a single breach. Unfortunately, we show that protecting against even slightly stronger snapshot adversaries becomes difficult. As our main result, we present a $\Omega(\log n)$ lower bound for any ORAM protecting against a $(3, 1)$-snapshot adversary that performs three breaches and sees the transcript of only one query. In other words, our lower bound holds even if an adversary observes only memory contents during two breaches while managing to view the transcript of only one query in the other breach. Therefore, we surprisingly show that protecting against a snapshot adversary with three data breaches is as difficult as protecting against a persistent adversary.

1 Introduction

In this work, we study the setting where a client wishes to outsource the storage of some data to a third-party service provider that we refer to as the server. For example, this is a natural problem that arises when users rely on cloud computing or cloud storage services. In terms of privacy, the client desires to keep all the data private even after outsourcing the data to the server. A straightforward attempt

The full version of this paper appears as ePrint paper 2023/811.

H. Handschuh and A. Lysyanskaya (Eds.): CRYPTO 2023, LNCS 14084, pp. 161–196, 2023.
https://doi.org/10.1007/978-3-031-38551-3_6

to secure the data is to require the client to encrypt all data before uploading to the server. This guarantees that the plaintext data may never be observed by anyone except the client. However, an adversary may still be able to observe patterns of access to the encrypted data. Prior works [IKK12, CGPR15, ZKP16, KKNO16, LMP18, GLMP19, BKM20, KPT21] have shown that access patterns may be utilized to reveal parts of the plaintext data in certain settings. Therefore, it is also important to also hide access patterns to the encrypted data.

Persistent Adversaries. Oblivious RAMs (ORAMs), introduced by Goldreich and Ostrovsky [GO96], are one cryptographic primitive that may be used to hide access patterns. At a high level, ORAMs guarantee that any adversary cannot distinguish between the access patterns to encrypted data incurred by any two equal-length operational sequences. These obliviousness guarantees hold even if the adversary has persistently compromised the server (for example, this may be the case if the adversary is the server operator). In this case, the *persistent adversary* observes server memory contents and all access to server memory (i.e., the operational transcript) during the entire execution of the ORAM.

A long line of work [GMOT12, KLO12, SvS+13, RFK+15, ZWR+16, PPRY18] has studied the best efficiency that is achievable by an ORAM leading to the best construction obtaining $O(\log n)$ overhead [AKL+20]. Recently, $\Omega(\log n)$ lower bounds [LN18] were proven showing the best ORAM constructions are optimal in the presence of persistent adversaries. Unfortunately, recent works have also shown that $\Omega(\log n)$ overhead is required to protect against persistent adversaries even with weaker privacy guarantees including differential privacy [PY19, PY23], searchable encryption leakage [PPY20], multiple non-colluding servers [LSY20] and hidden operational boundaries [HKKS19]. The same lower bounds have also been extended to other settings including small blocks [KL21].

Snapshot Adversaries. In an attempt to obtain faster constructions, prior works have considered weaker adversaries that model real-world scenarios. In most cases, users trust the service provider (server) to store data securely. However, attackers may try to breach these services to temporarily gain access to the system. During this time, adversaries may quickly download all data stored on the server or potentially even view transcripts of operations while being performed by the server. Eventually, the server operators will detect the system breach and remedy the situation to revoke access from the adversary. Recent reports [dbi] show that the above is a common theme in most real system attacks and remediation typically occurs within a couple of days after the attack starts.

To model the above, we introduce the notion of (s, ℓ)-snapshot adversaries where the adversary may breach the system at most s times. During each of these s breaches, the adversary receives a snapshot of the server memory and sees the transcript for a total of at most ℓ operations. When protecting against weaker snapshot adversaries (with small values of s and ℓ), we can hope to obtain sub-logarithmic efficiency for ORAMs. Prior works have studied constructions against such adversaries. Amjad, Kamara and Moataz [AKM19] considered breach-resistant data structures that were secure against $(s, 0)$-snapshot adversaries; these are adversary that only observed server memory contents and no operational transcripts. Unfortunately, their constructions still required $O(\log n)$ overhead in the worst case (see Sect. 5.2 for more details).

A recent work of Du, Genkin and Grubbs [DGG22] presented an ORAM construction secure against $(1, \ell)$-snapshot adversaries that required overhead of only $O(\log \ell)$. For small values of ℓ, this is significantly faster than the $O(\log n)$ overhead ORAMs that protect against persistent adversaries. It was also shown that $\Omega(\log \ell)$ overhead is necessary for ORAMs protecting against $(1, \ell)$-snapshot adversaries as such constructions can be used to construct ORAMs against persistent adversaries by setting ℓ to be an upper bound on the length of the operational sequence such as $\ell = n^{O(1)}$. However, this construction only protects against a single breach of the system ($s = 1$) leading to the following natural question that was also posed as an open problem in [DGG22]:

Is it possible to build sub-logarithmic overhead ORAMs that are secure against snapshot adversaries that may perform multiple breaches?

This is an important question as many real-world systems must run for long periods of time and may be compromised multiple times due to different attacks. For example, at least six large companies have been compromised by at least three data breaches in the past two decades (see [BRE]). In this paper, we tackle this open problem to answer whether it is possible to construct efficient ORAMs to protect against multiple data breaches.

1.1   Our Contributions

As our main result, we answer the open problem in the negative. In particular, we show that there is a $\Omega(\log n)$ lower bound for ORAMs protecting against $(3, 1)$-snapshot adversaries that perform only three breaches and view the transcript for one operation. Afterwards, we explore various settings where we can circumvent the lower bound and present sub-logarithmic constructions for some weaker primitives.

Lower Bounds for $(3, 1)$-Snapshot Oblivious RAMs. We begin by presenting our lower bound for ORAMs that protect against $(3, 1)$-snapshot adversaries. Recall that a $(3, 1)$-snapshot adversary is able to gain access to the system three times and view the transcripts for only a single query. That means, the $(3, 1)$-snapshot adversary only views the memory contents for two of the three breaches while observing the memory contents and the access patterns to server memory for only a single operation in the other breach. We present the following logarithmic lower bound for any oblivious RAMs that provide protection against $(3, 1)$-snapshot adversaries:

Theorem 1 (Informal). *Any $(3, 1)$-snapshot oblivious RAM for n b-bit entries with client storage c must have overhead $\Omega(\log(nb/c))$.*

Quite surprisingly, our main result proves that protecting against $(3, 1)$-snapshot adversaries with relatively weak access to the system is as challenging as protecting powerful persistent adversaries with unlimited access to the system. We note that our above lower bound asymptotically matches prior lower bounds for ORAMs with respect to persistent adversaries [LN18, PY19, HKKS19, KL21]. Our work shows that for any applications where protection of up to three breaches is required, one may use the logarithmic ORAM constructions [AKL+20] to obtain optimal overhead.

Our work is the first to prove a super-constant lower bound even when the adversary observes the transcript of only a constant number of operations. Previous lower bounds [LN18, PY19, HKKS19, LMWY20, PPY20, KL21, PY23] with persistent adversaries proved $\Omega(\log n)$ lower bounds, but required the adversary to observe the transcript of $\Theta(n)$ operations. Du, Genkin and Grubbs [DGG22] proved a $\Omega(\log \ell)$ lower bound for protecting against $(1, \ell)$-snapshot adversaries. However, the lower bound becomes trivial when the adversary views only $\ell = O(1)$ operational transcripts. Our lower bound shows that $\Omega(\log n)$ overhead is necessary even when $\ell = 1$ operational transcripts are observed. This is also the first lower bound that does not depend on the number of operational transcripts, ℓ, viewed by the adversary.

While our lower bound considers $(3, 1)$-snapshot adversaries, we note it also applies to any stronger adversaries. Formally, any ORAM requires logarithmic lower bound when consider security against a (s, ℓ)-snapshot adversary with $s \geq 3$ breaches and viewing the transcript of $\ell \geq 1$ operations. We note that our lower bound also applies to privacy guarantees that are weaker than obliviousness. Prior works have considered weaker notions including differential privacy [PY19], leakage functions commonly used in searchable encryption [PPY20] as well as read-only obliviousness. In our work, we show that our logarithmic lower bound may be extended to all three weaker privacy notions.

Sub-Logarithmic Constructions. Next, we explore various ways to circumvent the above logarithmic lower bound with respect to snapshot adversaries. In particular, we are trying to find constructions with sub-logarithmic lower bounds that still provide protections against $(3, 1)$-snapshot or stronger adversaries. As we know that this is impossible for RAMs (i.e., arrays), we explore functionalities that are weaker than RAMs that admit sub-logarithmic overhead.

- *No-Write Oblivious RAMs*[1]: Our lower bound for oblivious RAMs with respect to $(3, 1)$-snapshot adversaries critically leverages the ability to overwrite RAM entries. A natural question to study is a no-write ORAM that only enables reading entries. In Sect. 5.1, we show there exists a very simple construction for no-write ORAMs with $O(1)$ overhead that is secure against $(s, 1)$-snapshot adversaries for every $s \geq 1$. We note this is not surprising as no-write ORAMs never need to modify server memory to overwrite entries. However, no such separation is known for persistent adversaries as designing

---

[1] Prior works have also referred to this primitive as read-only ORAMs. However, similar names have also been used for read-only obliviousness where security is only provided against read operations, but write operations may not be private. To differentiate, we chose to rename this primitive as a no-write ORAM. Throughout our work, we will refer to read-only and write-only ORAMs as those that provide obliviousness for only read or write operations respectively.

a sub-logarithmic no-write ORAM remains an open problem. Furthermore, prior work showed significant barriers towards non-trivial lower bounds for no-write ORAMs even against persistent adversaries [WW18].

– *Oblivious Stacks and Queues*: We also consider stacks and queues that have weaker retrieval functionalities than a RAM data structure. We show that there exist simple constructions with $O(1)$ overhead secure against $(s, 1)$-snapshot adversaries for every $s \geq 1$. The constant overhead implementation of stacks and queues provides a separation with respect to snapshot adversaries. In contrast, it is known that oblivious RAMs and stacks/queues both require logarithmic overhead against persistent adversaries [JLN19].

1.2 Related Works

Lower Bounds and Barriers. The first lower bounds for oblivious RAMs were proven in the *balls-and-bins* model that makes a non-encoding assumption on each entry. Goldreich and Ostrovsky [GO96] proved the first logarithmic ORAM lower bounds in this model. Boyle and Naor [BN16] were the first to explicitly point out this non-encoding assumption and defined the balls-and-bins model. Further works prove lower bounds in this model such as for differentially private [PPY19], searchable encryption [BF19] and one-round ORAMs [CDH20]. PIR lower bounds were studied in models nearly identical to the balls-and-bins model including for public preprocessing [BIM04, PY22] and private preprocessing [CK20, CHK22, Yeo23]. To our knowledge, all balls-and-bins lower bounds were proven against persistent adversaries.

More general logarithmic lower bounds for ORAMs were proven by Larsen and Nielsen [LN18] in the cell probe model without any non-encoding assumptions. Follow-up works [JLN19] have considered lower bounds for other data structures and weaker security guarantees including differential privacy [PY19], searchable encryption leakage functions [PPY20] and multiple non-colluding servers [LSY20]. The highest lower bounds for oblivious data structures remains $\Omega(\log^2 n)$ for near-neighbor search [LMWY20]. Lower bounds were also proven for the setting of small block sizes in [KL21]. A recent work presented a framework for proving lower bounds for a wide range of data structures and security notions [PY23]. To our knowledge, all cell probe lower bounds were proven with respect to persistent adversaries.

Finally, several works have presented barriers for proving lower bounds. Boyle and Naor [BN16] showed that proving non-trivial lower bounds for *offline* ORAMs that receive all operations at once would imply unknown circuit lower bounds. A subsequent work by Weiss and Wichs [WW18] showed non-trivial lower bounds for no-write ORAMs would also imply unknown lower bounds for either circuits or locally decodable circuits (both of which are long-standing open problems).

Oblivious RAMs. Oblivious RAMs were first introduced by Goldreich and Ostrovsky [GO96] and have been studied extensively for decades thereafter. For examples, see [GO96, GMOT12, KLO12, SvS+13, RFK+15, ZWR+16,

PPRY18] and references therein. The best construction obtains logarithmic overhead [AKL+20]. ORAM constructions have been considered for various settings such as differential privacy [WCM18, PPY19], MPC [WHC+14, ZWR+16, Ds17], write-only obliviousness [LD13, BMNO14, RACM17] to list some examples. Of these results, write-only ORAMs are the closest to our notions. For completeness, we discuss their relation to the notion of snapshot security in Sect. 5.2.

Encrypted Search and Structured Encryption. Searching over encrypted data was first introduced by Song, Wagner and Perrig [SWP00]. Structured encryption was introduced by Chase and Kamara [CK10] to generalize the notion beyond encrypted indexes. In both primitives, the goal is to obtain efficient constructions while ensuring reasonable privacy upper bounded by a "sensible" leakage function. Follow-up works have considered adaptive adversaries [CGKO06], dynamic variants [KPR12, CJJ+14, HK14], forward and backward privacy [Bos16, BMO17], public-key settings [BDOP04, ACD+22], cache-efficiency [CT14, BBF+21, MR22], Boolean queries [CJJ+13, KM17, PPSY21], SQL queries [KM18], leakage suppression [KMO18, DPPS20, GKM21], and volume-hiding [KM19, PPYY19, APP+23]. Another line of work has studied the implications of various leakage profiles through abuse attacks [IKK12, CGPR15, ZKP16] [KKNO16, LMP18, GLMP19, BKM20, KPT21] and references therein.

2   Technical Overview

Reviewing Prior Lower Bounds. We start by reviewing the logarithmic lower bounds for ORAMs protecting against persistent adversaries, the first of which was proven by Larsen and Nielsen [LN18]. There are two main proof techniques, both originating from the data structure community: information transfer [PD06] and chronogram [FS89]. Prior works on lower bound for data structures guaranteeing different levels of privacy constructed similar persistent adversaries independent of the employed technique. These persistent adversaries consist of two main parts. First, the adversary observes the transcripts of a sequence of write ORAM operations where the transcript consists of all memory probes and whether the corresponding memory cell is overwritten. The adversary records a list of all memory cells that are updated and the operation responsible for the modification. Afterwards, the adversary views the transcript for one or more read ORAM operations and attempts to correlate probed memory cells and the operation that last modified the probed cell. At a high level, the adversary is attempting to estimate which ORAM write operation is responsible for the information returned by the ORAM read operation. As a result, this forces the ORAM to make additional memory probes to hide the real ORAM write operation responsible for the relevant information that needs to be returned.

The above adversary structure has been used by prior works regardless of whether they rely on the information transfer or chronogram technique. The main difference in the two techniques is the arrangement of counting disjoint memory probes that are forced by the adversary. The information transfer technique (used in [LN18, JLN19, HKKS19, PPY20, LSY20, KL21]) arranges a binary tree over a sequence of $\Theta(n)$ ORAM operations. Each ORAM operation is uniquely assigned to a leaf of a tree and every memory probe is uniquely assigned to a node in the tree by the adversary as follows. For any probe to a memory cell during operation i, the persistent adversary finds the last operation j responsible for modifying the contents of the memory cell. This probe is then assigned to the lowest common ancestor of leaf nodes associated to operations i and j. By a combination of correctness and privacy properties, it can be shown that, for sufficiently large m, each internal node with m leaf nodes must have $\Omega(m)$ assigned probes. In total, the entire tree has $\Omega(n \log n)$ assigned probes and, thus, an $\Omega(\log n)$ lower bound may be obtained.

The chronogram technique (used in [PY19,LMWY20,PY23]) takes a different approach by arranging $\Theta(n)$ ORAM write operations into partitions of geometrically decreasing size, for some constant factor $r > 1$. The leftmost partition contains $\Theta(n)$ operations, the second left most partition contains $\Theta(n/r)$ operations and so forth for a total of $p = \Theta(\log n)$ partitions. At last, a final ORAM read operation is performed after all $\Theta(n)$ ORAM write operations. If the last operation was chosen to read one random entry that was overwritten in the i-th partition, correctness implies that $\Omega(1)$ memory cells that were last overwritten by an operation during the i-th partition must be probed. On the other hand, privacy requires that this must be the case for all other p partitions thus obtaining an $\Omega(p) = \Omega(\log n)$ lower bound.

In either case, prior lower bounds heavily relied on the persistent nature of the adversary to view the transcripts for all operations. A weaker (s, ℓ)-snapshot adversary viewing transcripts for $\ell = O(1)$ operations will not be able to accumulate a log of all memory cell updates as done in the past.

New Techniques for Snapshot Adversaries. In our work, we develop new snapshot adversarial strategies for very weak compromise settings with only a constant $s = 3$ number of breaches and observing the transcript of just $\ell = 1$ operation. We first note that all prior persistent adversary strategies used the transcripts from all $\Theta(n)$ operations. In particular, they never utilized the contents of server memory that are also in the adversary's view. This is not surprising as a persistent adversary with transcripts from all operations can easily compute the exact contents of server memory at any point in time. However, one cannot compute the exact server memory when only observing the transcripts of a small subset of transcripts as is the case for snapshot adversaries with $\ell = 1$.

Instead, our new snapshot adversarial strategy will heavily utilize the contents of server memory that may be viewed during the $s = 3$ data breaches. Consider any pair of breaches where the adversary is able to view the contents of server memory. We observe that the adversary is able to compute the memory cells that have changed between the two snapshots of server memory. Therefore, a snapshot adversary is able to record memory cell updates between each of the s breaches that occur. The snapshot adversary is able to observe a list of all memory cell updates with coarser-grained update times where updates are only known to have occurred during operations between any pair of breaches. For $s = 3$, the snapshot adversary is able to categorize memory cell updates into three groups: cells updated before the first breach, cells updated between the first and second breach and cells updated between the second and third breach.

Next, we adapt the chronogram technique and show that it may still be used when a snapshot adversary is only able to sample and test a single adversarial event. Recall that the chronogram technique splits $\Theta(n)$ ORAM write operations into $p = \Theta(\log n)$ partitions. The goal is to prove that the final ORAM read operation must probe $\Omega(1)$ memory cells that were last overwritten from each of the p partitions. A persistent adversary is able to check whether all p events are satisfied (as done in prior works). In our proof, we instead show that it suffices for a snapshot adversary to randomly sample and test only one event. Suppose in fact that we have an ORAM construction that does not satisfy the conditions for one of the $p = \Theta(\log n)$ events with non-negligible probability q. Then, the snapshot adversary will sample this event and detect the violation with probability $q/p = \Omega(q/\log n)$ that is also non-negligible and thus privacy is violated. Therefore, a snapshot adversary only needs to test one random event. In our full proof, we extend this idea to constant adversarial advantage using randomization to hide the partitioning structure from the adversary.

Finally, we show that our seemingly weak snapshot adversarial strategy with $s = 3$ and $\ell = 1$ is sufficient to randomly sample and test one of the adversarial events. To do this, the snapshot adversary first samples one of the p partitions uniformly at random. Afterwards, the snapshot adversary chooses to perform breaches directly before and after all ORAM write operations of the sampled partition. In these two breaches, the snapshot adversary only sees server memory contents and no operational transcripts. Next, the adversary performs the third breach for the final ORAM read operation and views the transcript for this operation. Using the server memory from all three breaches, the adversary can determine the set of memory cells W that were updated by ORAM write operations during the sampled partition, but were not modified until the final ORAM read operation. As the last step, the adversary can check whether the intersection of the memory cells probed by the final ORAM read operation and W contains at least $\Omega(1)$ memory cells that is equivalent to testing the adversarial event corresponding to the sampled partition. Therefore, we show that an ORAM requires $\Omega(\log n)$ overhead against $(3, 1)$-snapshot adversaries.

As a side note, we chose to adapt the chronogram technique as it enables smaller values of $\ell = 1$. Our same techniques could be applied to the information transfer proof where the number of probes assigned to each internal node could be the adversarial event. Unfortunately, testing events associated to nodes with many leaf nodes would require the adversary to view the transcripts of $\ell = \Omega(n)$ operations. Thus the information tree methodology would use a stronger adversary and, thus, yield a weaker lower bound than what we obtain.

Sub-Logarithmic Constructions. We overview the simple constructions of our no-write ORAM secure against $(s, 1)$-snapshot adversaries for any $s \geq 1$. First, we note that security against an $(s, 0)$-snapshot attack is trivial for no-write ORAMs that never need to update server memory. For example, the server can store an encrypted array and perform reads by simply reading the i-th entry.

To protect against $(s, 1)$-snapshot attacks, we can simply have the server store a random permutation π of the encrypted array. For reads to entry i, the client simply downloads the $\pi(i)$-th entry of the encrypted array. This provides a separation for no-write and read-write ORAMs against $(3, 1)$-snapshot adversaries that is not known with respect to persistent adversaries.

Next, we show that we can obtain sub-logarithmic overhead for oblivious stacks and queues with weaker functionality than ORAMs. As stacks and queues may only push or pop entries to a fixed location, we can ensure that locations of memory updates only depend on the length of the operational sequence. This immediately obtains an $(s, 0)$-snapshot oblivious stack/queue for any $s \geq 1$. Using the same trick as done for no-write ORAMs, we can obtain $(s, 1)$-snapshot security using a random permutation. Therefore, we give a $O(1)$ overhead implementation of oblivious stacks/queues providing a separation from ORAMs. This separation is not possible for persistent adversaries where $\Omega(\log n)$ lower bounds are known for oblivious stacks/queues [JLN19].

3   Definitions

3.1   Snapshot Security

We start by defining (s, ℓ, ϵ)-*snapshot security* that guarantees that any PPT (s, ℓ)-snapshot adversary has advantage at most ϵ. Roughly speaking an (s, ℓ)-*snapshot* adversary is an adversary that perform a *snapshot attack* that consists of s *snapshot windows* for a total span of ℓ operations. When ϵ is clear from the context, we may drop ϵ and use (s, ℓ)-snapshot security.

More formally, we model an (s, ℓ)-snapshot adversary $\mathcal{A}$ as a two-part adversary $(\mathcal{A}_0, \mathcal{A}_1)$. Algorithm $\mathcal{A}_0(1^n)$ outputs two equal-length operational sequences, O_1 and O_2, as well as a sequence of *snapshot windows* denoted by

$$S = \big((t_1, \ell_1), (t_2, \ell_2), \ldots, (t_s, \ell_{|S|})\big)$$

describing the snapshot attack the adversary intends to mount. Specifically, a pair (t_i, ℓ_i) specifies a snapshot window of length ℓ_i starting with operation t_i. As a result of this snapshot window, the adversary will get the memory content before the operation with index t_i is executed and the server memory accesses for the following ℓ_i operations indexed $t_i, \ldots, t_i + \ell_i - 1$. Note that if $\ell_i = 0$ then the adversary only gets a snapshot of the memory content before operation t_i is performed and no memory access. Without loss of generality, we will also suppose that the snapshot windows are given in increasing order of the t_i and that they do not overlap.

Adversary $\mathcal{A}_1$ receives the leakage obtained from the snapshot attack specified by $\mathcal{A}_0$ when one of the two sequences of operations, O_1 and O_2, is executed. $\mathcal{A}_1$ outputs its guess as to which one has actually been used to produce the leakage. An adversary $\mathcal{A}$ is an (s, ℓ)-*snapshot adversary* if the following two conditions are satisfied: S contains at most s snapshot windows, that is $|S| \leq s$ and the total snapshot time $\ell_1 + \ldots + \ell_{|S|}$ is at most ℓ.

Read(x)	Write(x, y)	LRead(x)	LWrite(x, y)
1. Return $M[x]$.	1. Set $M[x] \leftarrow y$.	1. Set $\mathcal{L} \leftarrow \mathcal{L} \,\|\, (\text{read}, x)$.	1. Set $\mathcal{L} \leftarrow \mathcal{L} \,\|\, (\text{write}, x, y)$.
	2. Return $\bot$.	2. Return $M[x]$.	2. Set $M[x] \leftarrow y$.
			3. Return $\bot$.

Fig. 1. (Leaky) Memory Read and Write Oracles.

$\text{Expt}_{\text{DS}, \mathcal{A}}(n, \beta)$:

1. Execute $(O_0, O_1, S, \text{st}) \leftarrow \mathcal{A}_0(1^n)$.
2. Parse $S = \{(t_1, \ell_1), \ldots, (t_{|S|}, \ell_{|S|})\}$.
3. Set leakage $\mathcal{L} \leftarrow \emptyset$ and initialize DS with n blocks each consisting of randomly select blocks of b bits.
4. Set $i \leftarrow 1$.
5. While $i \leq |O_\beta|$:
   (a) If $i = t_j$ for some $j \in [|S|]$:
      i. Set $\mathcal{L} \leftarrow \mathcal{L} \,\|\, (\text{memory}, M)$.
      ii. For $k = 1, \ldots, \ell_j$:
         A. Execute $\text{DS}^{\text{LRead, LWrite}}(O_b[i])$.
         B. Set $i \leftarrow i + 1$.
   (b) Else:
      i. Execute $\text{DS}^{\text{Read, Write}}(O_b[i])$.
      ii. Set $i \leftarrow i + 1$.
6. Execute $\beta' \leftarrow \mathcal{A}_1(\text{st}, \mathcal{L})$.
7. Return β'.

Fig. 2. Experiment for (s, ℓ)-snapshot security.

We next define an experiment that is parameterized by the data structure DS and by a snapshot adversary $\mathcal{A}$ and a bit $\beta \in \{0, 1\}$. The experiment will execute the data structure DS on the sequence of operation O_β output by $\mathcal{A}_0$ and records the leakage of DS from the snapshot attacks specified by $\mathcal{A}_0$.

For any data structure DS, we will assume that DS has access to an underlying physical memory M that is indexed uniquely by integers from $[|M|]$. Access will be exclusively performed by means of two oracles: one for reading memory cells and one for writing to memory cells. In the experiment, DS will be equipped with standard oracles (Read and Write, see Fig. 1) except for the snapshot windows specified by the adversary during which the access to memory will be performed by means of leaky oracles (LRead and LWrite, see Fig. 1) that record the read/write operation performed for the adversary.

We present the formal definition of our experiment defining snapshot security in Fig. 2. Finally, we present the formal definition of (s, ℓ, ϵ)-snapshot security for data structures using the above defined experiment.

Definition 1 ((s, ℓ, ϵ)-Snapshot Security). *Let $s \geq 1$ and $\ell \geq 0$ be fixed integers and let $0 \leq \epsilon < 1$. A data structure DS is (s, ℓ, ϵ)-snapshot secure if for* *any PPT (s, ℓ)-snapshot adversary $\mathcal{A}$, the following holds:*

$$\left|\Pr[\mathsf{Expt}_{\mathsf{DS},\mathcal{A}}(n, 0) = 1] - \Pr[\mathsf{Expt}_{\mathsf{DS},\mathcal{A}}(n, 1) = 1]\right| \leq \epsilon,$$

for all sufficiently large n.

In our work, we will focus on RAM data structures that maintain an array of length n where the two supported operations are retrieving and update an entry. Throughout our work, we will denote a RAM data structure DS satisfying as (s, ℓ)-snapshot security as an (s, ℓ)-snapshot oblivious RAM or an oblivious RAM secure against (s, ℓ)-snapshot adversaries.

Discussion about Adaptive Adversary. In our above definition, we define the adversary to be non-adaptive. In particular, the adversary must pick the t snapshot windows at the beginning of the experiment. A stronger definition would be to enable the adversary to adaptively choose snapshot times and lengths that may depend on the leakage of previously seen snapshot leakage. As we are proving lower bounds, a weaker security definition implies a stronger lower bound. In other words, our lower bounds for non-adaptive adversaries would immediately apply to settings with more realistic adaptive adversaries.

Discussion about $\ell < s$. In our definition, we enable values of $\ell < s$. That is, the total snapshot time may be smaller than the number of snapshots. This is allowed because we allow snapshots of length 0 that is formally denoted by $\ell_i = 0$. In this case, note that the experiment only adds the current contents of memory cells M to the snapshot leakage $\mathcal{L}$ but not the memory access patterns for any operations performed by DS. This formalizes the setting where an adversary may perform a snapshot attack but no operations occur during the attack.

3.2   Cell Probe Model

In this work, we prove our lower bounds in the oblivious cell probe model introduced by Larsen and Nielsen [LN18] that adapts the cell probe model of Yao [Yao81]. In this model, there exists a client and a server with separate storage. The client has c bits of storage. The server's memory consists of memory cells that consist of $w \geq 1$ bits each. The only operation that is charged any cost is probing a cell in server memory to retrieve or update its contents. All other operations are free of cost including computation or accessing client storage. Additionally, we will assume there exists a long, but finite random string $\mathbf{R}$ that is accessible to both the client and the server without any cost. One can view $\mathbf{R}$ as a random oracle. As we consider a weak cost model, our lower bounds will apply for any reasonable model of computation.

4   Lower Bound

In this section, we prove a logarithmic lower bound for any RAM data structure DS that is $(3, 1)$-snapshot private. The adversary is able to employ three snapshot attacks at various time points. However, the three snapshot attacks are able to observe the memory access pattern of exactly one operation performed by the DS during one snapshot attack. In the other two snapshot attacks, the adversary may only view the current memory contents of DS. Even for such a weak snapshot adversary, we are able to prove the following lower bound:

Theorem 2. *For any* $0 \leq \epsilon \leq 1/16$, *let* DS *be a* $(3, 1, \epsilon)$-*snapshot private RAM data structure for* n *entries each of* $b \geq 1$ *bits implemented over* $w = \Omega(\log n)$ *bits using client storage of* $c \geq 1$ *bits in the cell probe model. If* DS *has amortized write time* t_w *and expected amortized read time* t_r *with failure probability at most* $1/3$, *then* $t_r + t_w = \Omega\left(b/w \cdot \log(nb/c)\right)$.

To do this, we actually prove the following lemma that assumes that the block size b is a sufficiently large constant ($b > 60$ is sufficient). Although, we show that this still implies the desired above theorem for all values of $b \geq 1$.

Lemma 1. *For any* $0 \leq \epsilon \leq 1/16$, *let* DS *be a* $(3, 1, \epsilon)$-*snapshot private RAM data structure for* n *entries each of* $b > 60$ *bits implemented over cells of size* $w = \Omega(\log n)$ *bits using client storage of* $c \geq 1$ *bits in the cell probe model. If* DS *has amortized write time* t_w *and expected amortized read time* t_r *with failure probability at most* $1/3$, *then* $t_r + t_w = \Omega\left(b/w \cdot \log(nb/c)\right)$.

We next show that the lemma above implies the main theorem.

Proof of Theorem 2. Assuming Lemma 1, we know that Theorem 2 holds for any $b > 60$. Towards a contradiction, suppose that Theorem 2 is false for some $1 \leq b \leq 60$. That is, there exists a DS with overhead that contradicts the lower bound $\Omega(b/w \cdot \log(nb/c)) = \Omega(\log(n/b)/w)$ as $b = \Theta(1)$. Note, we can construct DS$'$ for blocks of size 60 by simply keeping $60/b$ copies of DS. The resulting read and write overheads of DS$'$ are only a constant multiplicative factor higher than DS that would contradict Lemma 1. Therefore, Lemma 1 implies Theorem 2 for all values of $b \geq 1$. □

The remainder of this section is dedicated to proving Lemma 1. We prove the lower bound in the three following steps:

1. First, we will present a snapshot adversarial strategy that uses only three snapshots of which only one contains the memory access pattern of the operation. The adversarial algorithm will pick a hard sequence of operations as well as the locations and lengths of snapshots non-adaptively.
2. Next, we will analyze the adversarial method by relating the snapshot adversary's advantage to the efficiency of a one-way communication protocol that encapsulates the correctness guarantees of DS.
3. Finally, we show that we can derive our desired lower bounds using the analysis of the advantage of the snapshot adversarial strategy.

Discussion about Other Models. We note that prior works have considered lower bounds in other models including small blocks when w is small [KL21, PY23] and when operational boundaries are hidden from the adversary [HKKS19]. We believe that adapting prior techniques would enable extending our lower bound to these models, but we leave it as future work to not distract the readers from our main goal of studying snapshot security.

We do extend our lower bounds for weaker notions of snapshot security that may be easily adapted to our proof techniques. These weaker snapshot security notions include read-only obliviousness and differential private guarantees.

In our lower bound, if we restrict the adversary to only choose snapshots within a consecutive subset of Z operations, then our lower bound would be $\Omega(b/w \cdot \log(Zb/c))$ matching the construction in [DGG22].

4.1 Constructing a Snapshot Adversary

We start by presenting our $(3, 1)$-snapshot adversary that will be used to prove our lower bound. Recall that our snapshot adversary must submit two operational sequences O_0 and O_1 of equal length as well as a description of the times and lengths of the three snapshot attacks $S = \{(t_1, \ell_1), (t_2, \ell_2), (t_3, \ell_3)\}$ such that $\ell_1 + \ell_2 + \ell_3 = 1$ representing that only one snapshot can view the access patterns to memory for exactly one operation. Afterwards, the adversary receives the leakage from the s snapshot attacks and must output a bit b' that aims to distinguish whether O_0 or O_1 was executed.

Our adversary is inspired by the chronogram lower bound proof technique introduced by Fredman and Saks [FS89] and it outputs two sequences each consisting of m writes, for some $n/2 < m \le n$, followed by a single read, for a total of $m + 1$ operations. To describe the snapshot windows output by the adversary, we introduce the notion of a *partition* of the sequence of the m write operations The partitions are disjoint consecutive subsequences, whose sizes are geometrically increasing by some ratio $r > 1$ to be fixed. The write operations are naturally indexed $1, \ldots, m$ with 1 being the index of the first write to be executed and m the index of the last operations. Partitions are instead indexed in reverse order; that is, partition 0 is the rightmost partition and consists of the write operation of index m that is executed immediately before the read operation. The second partition consists of the r write operations that occur exactly before the last write operation; that is, it consists of the write operations indexed $m - r, \ldots, m - 1$. Generally, the i-th partition will consist of r^i consecutive write operations and there will be a total of $p = O(\log n / \log r)$ partitions. The $(p-1)$-th partition will be the leftmost and largest partition and the 0-th partition will be the rightmost and smallest partition. Finally, we will denote the index of the operation at the start of the i-th partition by p_i and we can see that $p_i + r^i - 1$ is the last operation of the i-th partition.

Now, we are ready to define the adversary's algorithm for generating the sequence of operations O_0, O_1 and the snapshot windows in S. The adversary $\mathcal{A}^{r,i} = (\mathcal{A}_0^{r,i}, \mathcal{A}_1^{r,i})$ is parameterized by rate $r > 1$ and an index i for a partition and proceeds as follows. $\mathcal{A}_0^{r,i}$ picks a random number m uniformly at random integer from the interval $[n/2 + 1, n]$. As already described above, O_0 and O_1 will consist of the same m write operations followed by a read operation that will differ between the two sequences. The first m operations will be write operations to indices $1, 2, \ldots, m$ of a uniformly random b-bit string. For O_0, the final operation will be a read to the index 1. For O_1, a read operation will be performed on a uniformly random index that was overwritten in the i-th partition. This can be done by picking an uniformly random index from the interval $[p_i, p_i + r^i - 1]$ to be used as input to the read. Finally, the snapshot windows outputs by the adversary are $(p_i, 0)$, $(p_i + r^i, 0)$ and $(m + 1, 1)$. In other words, the adversary elects to see the memory before partition i starts, just after it is completed, and before the read operation. In addition the adversary also sees the memory access performed by the read operation. A formal description of $\mathcal{A}_0^{r,i}$ is provided below:

$\mathcal{A}_0^{r,i}(1^n)$:

1. Pick integer m uniformly at random from interval $[n/2, n]$.
2. Generate m uniformly random b-bit strings $\mathbf{B}_1, \ldots, \mathbf{B}_m$.
3. Set $O_0 = (\text{write}(1, \mathbf{B}_1), \ldots, \text{write}(m, \mathbf{B}_m), \text{read}(1))$.
4. Pick a uniformly index $j \in [p_i, p_i + r^i - 1]$, where p_i is the index of the first operation in the i-th partition.
5. Construct $O_1 = (\text{write}(1, \mathbf{B}_1), \ldots, \text{write}(m, \mathbf{B}_m), \text{read}(j))$.
6. Set $S = ((p_i, 0), (p_i + r^i, 0), (m + 1, 1))$.
7. Return (O_0, O_1, S).

The leakage $\mathcal{L}$ associated with the snapshot attack output by $\mathcal{A}_0^{r,i}(1^n)$ consists of $((\text{memory}, M_{p_i}), (\text{memory}, M_{p_i+r^i}), (\text{memory}, M_m), \mathcal{T}_{m+1})$ where (memory, M_x) denotes the contents of all memory cells before the x-th operation in O_β and $\mathcal{T}_x \subseteq [|M|]$ is the access pattern to memory cells performed by the x-th operation.

The leakage $\mathcal{L}$ is passed as input to $\mathcal{A}_1^{r,i}$ that, roughly speaking, proceeds as follows. First it computes the set of memory locations that were last overwritten in the i-th partition and never overwritten until the final read operation. To do this, $\mathcal{A}_1^{r,i}$ computes the set of memory cell locations whose contents were changed in between the first and second snapshots, $U = \{j \in [|M|] \mid M_{p_i}[j] \neq M_{p_i+r^i}[j]\}$. Afterwards, the adversary computes a similar set of locations that changed between the second and third snapshot, $V = \{j \in [|M|] \mid M_{p_i+r^i}[j] \neq M_{m+1}[j]\}$. Lastly, the adversary computes the set difference $U \setminus V$ to obtain the desired set of memory cell locations that were last overwritten in the i-th partition. Finally, the adversary checks whether there exists any memory location in the intersection of $U \setminus V$ and $\mathcal{T}_{m+1}$. If the intersection is strictly less than $\rho \cdot b/w$ for some constant $\rho > 0$ that we will choose later, $\mathcal{A}_1^{r,i}$ outputs 0. Otherwise, $\mathcal{A}_1^{r,i}(\mathcal{L})$ returns 1 when the intersection is contains at least $\rho \cdot b/w$ locations. We formalize this adversarial algorithm below:

$\mathcal{A}_1^{r,i}(\mathcal{L})$:

1. Parse $\mathcal{L} = \{(\mathsf{memory}, M_{p_i}), (\mathsf{memory}, M_{p_i+r^i}), (\mathsf{memory}, M_{m+1}), \mathcal{T}_{m+1}\}$.
2. Compute $U_i = \{j \in [|M|] \mid M_{p_i}[j] \neq M_{p_i+r^i}[j]\}$.
3. Compute $V_i = \{j \in [|M|] \mid M_{p_i+r^i}[j] \neq M_{m+1}[j]\}$.
4. Compute $W_i = U_i \setminus V_i$.
5. If $|W_i \cap \mathcal{T}_{m+1}| < \rho \cdot b/w$, return 0.
6. Else if $|W_i \cap \mathcal{T}_{m+1}| \geq \rho \cdot b/w$, return 1.

Extension to Differential Privacy. We note that our adversary only submits two operational sequences that differ in exactly one operation (that is, the final read operation). Therefore, this adversary could also be applied to snapshot private data structures that are differentially private (following prior works such as [PY19]) where the adversarial advantage is a function of the number of differing operations in the two adversarially chosen sequences. As a result, our adversarial algorithm may be used to prove lower bounds snapshot private RAMs that are only differentially private.

Extension to Read-Only Obliviousness. Another property that is enjoyed by our adversarial algorithm is that the adversary only views memory access patterns for read operations. Therefore, we could also extend use the same adversary to extend our lower bound for snapshot private RAMs that only provide privacy for read operations while write operations may be completely public. Read-only obliviousness may be natural in certain settings where the underlying data is public while the sensitive information is the portion of the information that is of interest for the querier.

Extension to Structured Encryption Leakage. Most structured encryption schemes have some leakage functions known as key-equality revealing whether two operations are for the same index. Extending prior work [PPY20], we show that any ORAMs providing even slightly more security beyond key-equality also require $\Omega(\log n)$ overhead for snapshot security. See the full version for details.

Barriers for $(2, 1)$-Snapshot Security. Finally, we quickly discuss barriers towards extending our proof towards $(2, 1)$-snapshot security. In the above strategy, the adversary divides server memory updates into $p = \Theta(\log n)$ disjoint partitions. Afterwards, the adversary samples one partition and checks whether the final ORAM read operation accesses any memory in the sampled partition. To our knowledge, the most intelligent adversary requires three data breaches to perform this action: two data breaches for the beginning and end of the partition and one for the final ORAM read operation. Furthermore, all three data breaches seem necessary to perform this check.

4.2   Analyzing Adversarial Strategy

Next, we analyze the snapshot attack described in the previous section. In particular, we will use this specific snapshot adversary to prove certain properties about any RAM data structure that is $(3, 1)$-snapshot private. To do this, we will specifically analyze the set of operational sequences that the snapshot adversary will output as O_1. Recall that these are the sequences that picks a random index j to read from the set of r^i indices that are overwritten in the i-th partition. We show that for these sequences, the snapshot adversary is likely to output 1 with at least constant probability for many choices of partitions.

Formally, we define P to be the set of all partitions containing at least $\max(100c/b, 200 \log n/b)$ write operations. By our choice of $m = \Theta(n)$, we get

$$|P| = \log_r m - \max(\log_r(100c/b), \log_r(200 \log n/b)) = \Theta(\log(nb/c))$$

since $r \geq 2$ is a constant. First, we show that $(99/100)$-fraction of the partitions in P satisfy a certain property of distributions of memory accesses performed during the writes of the i-th partition. To do this, we define the following sets of memory cell accesses with respect to the i-th partition. Recall that we denote M_x to be the contents of memory before the x-th operation and T_x to be the set of memory locations that are accessed (either read or overwritten) during the x-th operation. Then, we define the following sets that are computed when executing the experiment $\mathsf{Expt}_{\mathsf{DS}, \mathcal{A}^{r,i}, 3, 1}(n, 1)$. Recall that is executing DS on the random operational sequence O_1 produced by the adversary $\mathcal{A}^{r,i}$.

- Denote U_i to be the set of memory locations that are overwritten by write operations in the i-th partition as defined in the description of $\mathcal{A}_1^{r,i}$. Formally,

$$U_i = \{j \in [|M|] \mid M_{p_i}[j] \neq M_{p_i + r^i}[j]\}.$$

- Denote Y_i to be the set of memory locations that are overwritten in the i-th partition and accessed by write operations after the i-th partition. Formally,

$$Y_i = U_i \cap (T_{p_i + r^i} \cup T_{p_i + r^i + 1} \cup \ldots \cup T_m).$$

Now, we show that for a large number of partitions $i \in P$, the size of Y_i cannot be too large assuming that the write overhead of the data structure DS beats the lower bound. We call these partitions the *critical* partitions.

Lemma 2. *Let* DS *be a* $(3, 1)$-*snapshot private RAM data structure for* n *b-bit entries run over a memory of* w-*bit cells using* c *bits of client storage and suppose that the amortized write time is* $t_w = o(b/w \cdot \log(nb/c))$. *For any* $r \geq 2$ *and sufficiently large* n, *there exists a set of* critical *partitions that contains at least* $(99/100)$-*fraction of the partitions* $i \in P$ *such that*

$$\mathbb{E}[|Y_i|] \leq r^{i-1} \cdot b/w.$$

Proof. We start by bounding the probability (taken over the choices of m) that a fix memory access belongs to Y_i, for a fixed partition i. We denote by β the index of the operation that performs the memory access and by $\alpha < \beta$ the index of the operation that last overwrote the cell before it is accessed by operation β. Observe that for the memory access to belong to Y_i it must be the case that operation α falls into partition i and that operation β falls into partition $j < i$. Let y denote the integer such that $z_{y-1} \leq \beta - \alpha < z_y$, where $z_y = 1 + r + \ldots + r^y$ is the number of operation in partitions 0 to y. Note that such a y is uniquely determined since z_y increases with y. Let us now distinguish two cases.

In the first case it holds that $i \leq y - 1$. Suppose that β is the last write operation (that is, it is executed just before the read operation). Since $\beta - \alpha \geq z_{y-1}$, operation α is executed before partition $y - 1$ is started and, since $i \leq y - 1$, before partition i is started. Therefore α cannot be one of the operation of partition i. If β is not the last operation then α will be executed even earlier and then will not be part of partition i for the same reason.

Let us now consider the case $i \geq y$. Observe that if β belongs to partition $j \leq i - 1$ then it must occur between the start of partition $i - 1$ and the last write operation. Therefore epoch $i - 1$ cannot start before operation $\beta - z_{i-1} + 1$. On the other hand, if α is in partition i then partition $i - 1$ cannot start after β for otherwise α and β are both in partition i. Therefore there at most z_{i-1} good choices for the start of epoch $i - 1$ each corresponding to a different choice of m. Moreover, epoch $i - 1$ must start between α and β and thus there are at most $\beta - \alpha < x_y$ good choices. As a result, the probe contributes to Y_i with probability at most $\min\{z_{i-1}, z_y\} \cdot 2/n$ for any $i \geq y$, as there are $n/2$ possible choices of m and each completely defines the partitioning.

By the two cases above, for every partition i, the contribution of a memory access to $|Y_i|/r^i$ is at most

$$\sum_{y \leq i} \frac{2}{r^i n} \cdot \min\{z_{i-1}, z_y\} \leq \sum_{y \leq i} \frac{4}{r^i n} \cdot \min\{r^{i-1}, r^y\} \leq \frac{4}{n}\left[\frac{1}{r} + \sum_{y \leq i-1} r^{y-i}\right] \leq \frac{12}{rn}.$$

since $z_{i-1} \leq 2r^{i-1}$ assuming $r \geq 2$. Each memory access can contribute to a single Y_i and thus, for a random partition i, the expected contribution of a memory access to $|Y_i|/r^i$ is at most $12/(rn|P|)$. Since there are at most $n \cdot t_w$ memory accesses, we can conclude that for a random partition i

$$\mathbb{E}[|Y_i|/r^i] \leq \frac{12}{r} \cdot \frac{t_w}{|P|} \leq \frac{1}{100 \cdot r} \cdot \frac{b}{w}$$

since, for some $\delta > 0$ and sufficiently large n, $|P| \geq \delta \log(nb/c)$ and $t_w \leq \delta/1200 \cdot b/w \cdot \log(nb/c)$. The lemma follows by Markov's inequality. $\square$

Using the above lemma, we can now derive properties about the advantage achieved by our snapshot adversary. We say that, for any partition i such that the above lemma applies, this partition i is *critical*. For any critical partition i, we show that $\mathcal{A}^{r,i}$ outputs 1 with constant probability when run for $\beta = 1$ (that is, it receives the leakage obtained from executing the sequence of operations O_1). The proof uses the correctness property of the data structure DS and shows that it is possible to derive a too-good-to-be-true, prefix-free compression scheme that will contradict Shannon's source coding theorem if the adversary does not output 1 with high enough probability. In other words, the DS provides an impossible method of storing and retrieving randomness without even requiring looking up the randomness in memory.

Lemma 3. *Let $b > 60$ and let DS be a $(3, 1)$-snapshot private RAM data structure for n b-bit entries run over a memory of w-bit cells using c bits of client storage. Suppose that the amortized write time of DS is $t_w = o(b/w \cdot \log(nb/c))$. For $r \geq 32$, $w = \Omega(\log n)$, and a sufficiently small but constant $\rho > 0$, the following holds for every critical partition $i \in P$,*

$$\Pr[\mathsf{Expt}_{\mathsf{DS}, \mathcal{A}^{r,i}}(n, 1) = 1] \geq 1/8.$$

Proof. Towards a contradiction, suppose that the above probability statement is false and let us unpack the implications of this assumption. Note, that $\mathcal{A}^{r,i}$ outputs 1 if and only if the final read operation accesses at least $\rho \cdot b/w$ memory locations whose contents were last changed by one of the r^i write operations in the i-th partition. The above assumption essentially means that the underlying DS will most likely only access a small number of memory locations that were changed by write operations in the i-th partition. Using this property, we will construct an impossibly efficient compression algorithm for random coin tosses. We show that we can use the i-th partition to compress random coin tosses in an efficient manner that will contradict Shannon's source coding theorem. At a high level, the idea is to execute DS where the encoding algorithm will embed the random coin tosses as blocks into the write operations of the i-th partition. Afterwards, the encoding algorithm will send enough information for the decoder to execute DS in an identical manner to retrieve the written random coin tosses.

Formally, both the encoder and the decoder will receive shared random public coins denoting the random blocks that will be inputs to write operations outside of the i-th partition. Only the encoding algorithm will receive the random blocks of write operations in the i-th partition. We denote $\mathbf{B}^{-i} = (\mathbf{B}_1, \ldots, \mathbf{B}_{p_i-1}, \mathbf{B}_{p_i+r^i}, \ldots, \mathbf{B}_m)$ as the set of blocks that in write operations outside of the i-th partition. Furthermore, let $\mathbf{B}^i = (\mathbf{B}_{p_i}, \mathbf{B}_{p_i+1}, \ldots, \mathbf{B}_{p_i+r^i-1})$ be the blocks in write operations inside the i-th partition. Finally, both algorithms will receive random coin tosses $\mathbf{R}$ that will be used as the internal randomness when executing DS. We will assume that $\mathbf{R}$ contains enough randomness to execute $m + 1$ operations on DS.

Encoding Algorithm: Receives $\mathbf{B}^{-i}, \mathbf{B}^i$ and $\mathbf{R}$ as input.

1. Set encoding $X = \emptyset$.
2. Execute the operations $\mathsf{write}(1, \mathbf{B}_1), \ldots, \mathsf{write}(p_i - 1, \mathbf{B}_{p_i-1})$ using DS and randomness $\mathbf{R}$. That is, execute all write operations occurring before the i-th partition.
3. Record the memory contents M_{p_i} before the first operation in the i-th partition.
4. Execute the operational sequence $\mathsf{write}(p_i, \mathbf{B}_{p_i}), \ldots, \mathsf{write}(p_i + r^i - 1, \mathbf{B}_{p_i+r^i-1})$ using DS and unused randomness from $\mathbf{R}$. That is, execute all write operations in the i-th partition.

5. Record the memory contents $M_{p_i+r^i}$ after the last operation in the i-th partition.
6. Append the c-bit content of client memory after the last operation in the i-th partition to encoding X.
7. Compute the set $U_i = \{j \in [|M|] \mid M_{p_i}[j] \neq M_{p_i+r^i}[j]\}$ that are the memory cells whose contents were changed during the i-th partition.
8. Execute the operations $\mathsf{write}(p_i+r^i, \mathbf{B}_{p_i+r^i}), \ldots, \mathsf{write}(m, \mathbf{B}_m)$ using DS and unused randomness from $\mathbf{R}$. That is, execute all write operations after the i-th partition. During the execution, record the transcripts $\mathcal{T}_{p_i+r^i}, \ldots, \mathcal{T}_m$ as the memory locations that are accessed during each of the write operations.
9. Record the memory contents M_{m+1} before the $(m+1)$-st and final read operation.
10. Compute the set $V_i = \{j \in [|M|] \mid M_{p_i+r^i}[j] \neq M_{m+1}[j]\}$ that are the memory cells whose contents were changed after the i-th partition.
11. Compute the set $W_i = U_i \setminus V_i$ that are the memory cells whose contents were last changed during the i-th partition and not by any operations after the i-th partition.
12. Compute $Y_i = U_i \cap (\mathcal{T}_{p_i+r^i} \cap \ldots \cap \mathcal{T}_m)$ that are the set of memory cells that were overwritten in the i-th partition and accessed by a write operation after the i-th partition. We will assume Y_i consists of both the memory cell locations and contents when they were accessed.
13. Append $|Y_i|$ and Y_i to encoding X.
14. Set $Q = \emptyset$,
15. For each $j = p_i, \ldots, p_i + r^i - 1$:
    (a) Execute $\mathsf{read}(j)$ using DS and unused randomness from $\mathbf{R}$ and keep track in $\mathcal{T}_{m+1}^j$ of the memory cells accessed during the read operation along with their content.
    (b) Compute $Q_i^j = \mathcal{T}_{m+1}^j \cap W_i$ consisting of the locations and contents of memory cells that were last overwritten in the i-th partition and accessed by $\mathsf{read}(j)$.
    (c) If $|Q_i^j| \leq \rho \cdot b/w$ and the output of operation $\mathsf{read}(j)$ is correct, append $(0, Q_i^j)$ to X and add j to Q. We pad Q_i^j with dummy values up to exactly $\rho \cdot b/w$ memory cells.
    (d) Otherwise when $|Q_i^j| > \rho \cdot b/w$ or the answer to $\mathsf{read}(j)$ is incorrect (that is, the read returns something different from $\mathbf{B}_j$), append $(1, \mathbf{B}_j)$ to X.
    (e) Rewind DS to its state before executing the $\mathsf{read}(j)$.
16. If $|Q| \geq r^i/4$, return $0 \parallel X$.
17. Otherwise when $|Q| < r^i/4$, return $1 \parallel \mathbf{B}^i$ where $\mathbf{B}^i = (\mathbf{B}_{p_i}, \ldots, \mathbf{B}_{p_i+r^i-1})$.

Decoding Algorithm: Receives $\mathbf{B}^{-i}, \mathbf{R}$ and the encoding X as input.

1. If the first bit of the encoding X is 1, then simply decode and return the next $r^i \cdot b$ bits as $\mathbf{B}^i = (\mathbf{B}_{p_i}, \ldots, \mathbf{B}_{p_i+r^i-1})$.
2. Otherwise, parse $X = 0 \parallel M^c \parallel |Y_i| \parallel Y_i \parallel (b_{p_i}, X_{p_i}) \parallel \cdots \parallel (b_{p_i+r^i-1}, X_{p_i+r^i-1})$.
3. Repeat Steps 15c–15d of the encoding algorithm using shared randomness $\mathbf{R}$ and inputs $\mathbf{B}^{-i}$.

4. Skip the operations in the i-th partition and update the client storage of DS to be M^c.
5. Execute the operational sequence $\mathsf{write}(p_i + r^i, \mathbf{B}_{p_i + r^i}), \ldots, \mathsf{write}(m, \mathbf{B}_m)$ using DS and randomness $\mathbf{R}$. That is, execute all write operations after the i-th partition. When executing operations, if any memory location encoded in Y_i is accessed, then use the contents of Y_i to continue execution. For all memory accesses outside of Y_i use the current memory contents of DS to continue execution.
6. For each $j = p_i, \ldots, p_i + r^i - 1$:
   (a) If $b_j = 1$, then parse $\mathbf{B}_j$ as X_j and continue to the next iteration of the loop.
   (b) If $b_j = 0$, then parse the next X_j as the locations and contents of $\rho \cdot b/w$ memory cells in Q_i^j.
   (c) Execute $\mathsf{read}(j)$ using DS and randomness $\mathbf{R}$. When executing the read operation, if any memory location encoded in Q_i^j is accessed, then use the encoded contents in Q_i^j. Otherwise, if any other memory location is accessed, use the current memory contents of DS.
   (d) Parse $\mathbf{B}_j$ as the answer of $\mathsf{read}(j)$.
   (e) Rewind DS to its state before executing the $\mathsf{read}(j)$.
7. Return $(\mathbf{B}_{p_i}, \ldots, \mathbf{B}_{p_i + r^i - 1})$.

Correctness. To show that encoding and decoding of $\mathbf{B}^i$ is successful, it suffices to show that both algorithms execute the operations for DS identically. Note, the execution of all write operations before the i-th partition are identical as both algorithms execute the same operations with the same randomness. Note that the encoder executes the write operations in the i-th partition while the decoder skips this subsequence of write operations. Both the encoder and decoder execute all operations after the i-th partition. We show that the decoder is able to execute identically to the encoder even though it is missing the write operations in the i-th partition. Consider the execution of any operation after the i-th partition by the decoder and any specific memory access. If the accessed memory location was not updated by any write operation in the i-th partition, then the decoder may simply use the current memory contents of DS to continue execution. If the memory location was modified during the i-th partition, we note that the contents are encoded by the encoder and used by the decoder. As a result, we can see that all operations after the i-th partition are executed identically by both the encoder and decoder. Therefore, we can see that the decoder always outputs the correct answer.

Length of Encoding. For the case that the encoding starts with a 1, we know that the encoding will always have bit length $1 + r^i \cdot b$. It remains us to upper bound the probability that the encoding starts with a 1 and the expected length of the encoding conditioned on it starting with a 0.

In this case, an encoding starts with c bits for client storage, $2 \log n$ bits for $|Y_i|$ and $2|Y_i| \cdot w$ bits for Y_i. Note that $|Y_i| \leq t_w \cdot n$ and thus at most $2 \log n$ are needed to represent $|Y_i|$. Moreover, since i is a critical partition,

$\mathbb{E}[|Y_i|] \leq r^{i-1} \cdot b/w$ meaning the encoding of Y_i has expected size $2 \cdot r^{i-1} \cdot b$ as each memory cell location and contents can be encoded using $2w$ bits.

The length of the part of the encoding produced at the for loop of Step 15, conditioned on the encoding starting with 0, is upper bounded by $r^i + (r^i \cdot 2\rho \cdot b) + \frac{3r^i \cdot b}{4}$. To see this, note that we use 1 bit to distinguish encoding output at Step 15c from those output at Step 15d. Moreover at most $(3/4)$-fraction of operations will encode the b-bit block and the remainder will encode $\rho \cdot (b/w)$ memory locations using $2w$ bits each. By choosing $\rho < 1/32$ and $b \geq 16$ we have

$$r^i + (r^i \cdot 2\rho \cdot b) + \frac{3r^i \cdot b}{4} \leq \frac{7r^i \cdot b}{8}.$$

Altogether, the expected length of encoding is upper bounded by

$$c + 2\log n + 2r^{i-1} \cdot b + \frac{7r^i \cdot b}{8} \leq \frac{19r^i \cdot b}{20}$$

by choosing $r \geq 32$ and noticing critical partition i belongs to P and therefore $r^i \geq \max(100c/b, 200\log n/b)$ meaning that $c \leq (1/100) \cdot r^i \cdot b$ and $2\log n \leq (1/100) \cdot r^i \cdot b$.

Finally, we lower bound the probability that the encoding starts with a 0. By our assumption towards a contradiction, we know that $\mathcal{A}^{r,i}$ outputs 1 with probability at most $1/8$ meaning that Q_i^j contains $\rho \cdot b/w$ locations with probability at least $7/8$. As the error probability of DS is at most $1/3$, both conditions are satisfied with probability at least $7/8 - 1/3 > 1/2$. By Markov's inequality, get that at least $1/4$ of these queries will encode $\rho \cdot b/w$ locations with probability at least $z \geq 1/3$. Using this bound, we get the expected encoding length is at most

$$1 + (1-z) \cdot r^i \cdot b + z \cdot \frac{19r^i \cdot b}{20} \leq 1 + \frac{59r^i \cdot b}{60} < r^i \cdot b$$

assuming $b > 60$.

Applying Shannon's Source Coding Theorem. Finally, we can use the expected length of the encoding to derive our contradiction. From the above, we already know that the expected length of the encoding for the i-th partition is strictly smaller than $r^i \cdot b$. Note that the protocol enables successful encoding and decoding of $\mathbf{B}^i$ that is independent of all other shared randomness. Therefore, $H(\mathbf{B}^i \mid \mathbf{B}^{-i}, \mathbf{R}) = H(\mathbf{B}^i) = r^i \cdot b$ as $\mathbf{B}^i$ consists of r^i uniformly random b-bit strings. This contradicts Shannon's source coding theorem stating that the expected length of any encoding scheme must be at least $r^i \cdot b$ completing the proof.   □

Comparison with Prior Works. We note that our compression protocol differs from prior lower bound works [LN18, PY19, PY23, PPY20, KL21, LSY20] to handle the weaker nature of a snapshot adversary. In our scheme, we have to handle the case that the snapshot adversary is unable to observe the majority of memory accesses. Instead, the snapshot adversary can only view the differences in memory contents between snapshot attacks and the memory accesses of the final read operation. To accommodate this restriction, our communication protocol only sends locations and contents of memory cells whose contents have changed. In contrast, prior works would send the locations and contents of memory cells that are accessed even if their contents were unchanged, which was wasteful.

4.3 Completing the Proof

To complete the proof, we will utilize Lemma 3 from the prior section that says that $\mathcal{A}^{r,i}$ is likely to output 1 with high probability when running experiment $\mathsf{Expt}_{\mathsf{DS},\mathcal{A}^{r,i}}(n,1)$ for at least $(99/100)$-fraction of partitions with at least $100c/b$ operations. By the snapshot privacy of DS, this immediately implies that $\mathcal{A}^{r,i}$ should also output 1 when running $\mathsf{Expt}_{\mathsf{DS},\mathcal{A}^{r,i}}(n,0)$. Note that for all partitions i, the operational sequence O_0 that is executed is identical. As a result, we show that this operational sequence is the hard distribution for which we can prove our desired lower bound. We formalize this argument to complete the proof of our lower bound below.

Proof of Lemma 1. To prove the condition of the theorem, we will first assume that $t_r = o(b/w \cdot \log(nb/c))$ and show that $t_w = \Omega(b/w \cdot \log(nb/c))$.

First, we utilize Lemma 3 that states that our adversary outputs 1 with high probability when running the experiment with bit $\beta = 1$, we know that

$$\Pr[\mathsf{Expt}_{\mathsf{DS},\mathcal{A}^{r,i},3,1}(n,1) = 1] \geq 1/8$$

for the critical partitions that constitute a $(99/100)$-fraction of the partitions from the set P of all partitions with at least $100c/b$ operations. For convenience, denote $I \subseteq P$ to be the set of critical partitions.

Next, we apply the fact that DS is $(3,1,\epsilon)$-snapshot private with $\epsilon \leq 1/16$. Note, this immediately implies that $\mathcal{A}^{r,i}$ must also output 1 when running the experiment with bit $\beta = 0$. Formally,

$$\Pr[\mathsf{Expt}_{\mathsf{DS},\mathcal{A}^{r,i}}(n,0) = 1] \geq 1/8 - \epsilon \geq 1/16 \tag{1}$$

for all critical partitions i.

Finally, we translate the above probabilities into the overhead of the final read operation. Note that $\mathsf{Expt}_{\mathsf{DS},\mathcal{A}^{r,i}}(n,0) = 1$ means that $\mathcal{A}^{r,i}$ output 1. This only occurs when the final read operation of O_0 accesses at least $\rho \cdot b/w$ memory locations that were last overwritten in the i-th partition. Furthermore, note that the randomized operational sequence O_0 produced by $\mathcal{A}^{r,i}$ is the same regardless of the choice of the partition i. Formally, recall that $\mathcal{A}^{r,i}$ defines the following:

- $U_i = \{j \in [|M|] \mid M_{p_i}[j] \neq M_{p_i+r^i}[j]\}$.
- $V_i = \{j \in [|M|] \mid M_{p_i+r^i}[j] \neq M_{m+1}[j]\}$.
- $W_i = U_i \setminus V_i$.

where W_i ends up being the set of memory locations that were last updated by write operations in the i-th partition. $\mathcal{A}^{r,i}$ only outputs 1 if the intersection of memory accesses by the final read operation $\mathcal{T}_m$ and W_i is at least $\rho \cdot b/w$. That is, $|\mathcal{T}_{m+1} \cap W_i| \geq \rho \cdot b/w$. Note that one way to compute the overhead of the final read operation is to lower bound the expected size of the set $\bigcup_{i \in P} (\mathcal{T}_{m+1} \cap W_i)$.

The main observation is that each of W_i are disjoints. Therefore, we can lower bound the number of memory accesses by the final read operation as

$$
\begin{aligned}
t_r &\geq \mathbb{E}\left[\left\lceil \left| \bigcup_{i \in P} (\mathcal{T}_{m+1} \cap W_i) \right| \right\rceil\right] \\
&\geq \sum_{i \in I} \mathbb{E}\left[|\mathcal{T}_{m+1} \cap W_i|\right] \\
&\geq \sum_{i \in I} \mathbb{E}\left[|\mathcal{T}_{m+1} \cap W_i| \mid \mathsf{Expt}_{\mathsf{DS}, \mathcal{A}^{r,i}}(n, 0) = 1\right] \\
&\geq \frac{99}{100} \cdot |P| \cdot \Pr[\mathsf{Expt}_{\mathsf{DS}, \mathcal{A}^{r,i}}(n, 0) = 1] \cdot \rho \cdot b/w \\
&= \Omega(b/w \cdot \log(nb/c))
\end{aligned}
$$

as we know that $|I| \geq (99/100) \cdot |P|$, $|P| = \Theta(\log(nb/c))$ and $\rho = \Theta(1)$. □

5   Snapshot Oblivious RAMs

In this section, we study no-write snapshot ORAMs that only enable clients to read entries. We present a very simple $O(1)$ construction secure against $(s, 1)$-snapshot adversaries for any $s \geq 1$ providing a separation with our lower bound for read-write ORAMs. Such a separation is not known between no-write and read-write ORAMs with respect to persistent adversaries. We also survey prior works with slightly different security notions and show that they also provide security against $(s, 0)$-snapshot adversaries.

5.1   No-Write Snapshot ORAMs

In a no-write ORAM, the client can only access the data but cannot overwrite any entries. Constructing a no-write ORAM secure against $(s, 0)$-snapshot attacks for every $s \geq 1$ is straightforward. The client uploads all n entries in encrypted form to the server with an encryption key stored by the client. To query for the i-th entry, the client simply downloads the i-th encrypted entry and decrypts to retrieve the i-th entry. Since no block is overwritten, the snapshot adversary receives the same server memory for any sequence of operations. This construction can be upgraded to security against $(s, 1)$-snapshot adversary, for every $s \geq 1$. To do this, the client simply samples a random key for a pseudorandom permutation (PRP) and uploads the encrypted n entries in a permuted manner. Retrieving the i-th entry becomes retrieving the i-th entry according to the PRP.

Even though the adversary observes the transcript of a single ORAM read operation, we note that the transcript simply contains a memory read to a random entry.

Theorem 3. *Assuming the existence of one-way functions, there exists a no-write ORAM with $O(1)$ overhead that is secure against $(s, 1)$-snapshot attacks for any $s \geq 1$.*

The theorem above must be contrasted with the our current understanding of the overhead needed for no-write ORAMs secure against persistent adversaries. Specifically, the current best construction for no-write ORAMs is the generic $O(\log n)$ overhead construction for ORAMs supporting both read and write operations. On the lower bound front, Weiss and Wichs [WW18] proved that showing lower bounds for no-write ORAMs even against persistent adversaries will give corresponding lower bounds on sorting circuit size or on the query complexity and size of locally decodable codes. Both are long-standing, important open problems in the area of computational complexity.

5.2   Snapshot ORAMs from Prior Works

Next, we show that prior works have studied slightly different privacy notions that may be reinterpreted as snapshot security.

Breach-Resistant Structured Encryption. Amjad et al. [AKM19] introduced the notion of a breach-resistant structured encryption. A structured encryption scheme (STE) encrypts a data structures so that it can be privately queried. Special cases of STE include graphs, dictionaries, multi-maps and RAMs that are the primary focus of this paper. They consider adversaries that only perform breaches to see the contents of server memory. Their goal is to design breach *breach-resistant* multi-maps where only the size of the underlying data is revealed to the adversary. If we restrict the multi-map to be an array, we can view their work as constructing ORAMs that are secure against $(s, 0)$-snapshot adversaries for some $s \geq 1$. However, the snapshot adversary considered in [AKM19] is stronger[2] than ours as it is allowed to adaptively decide on the next batch of operations after having seen the leakage from the previous batch. More precisely, the snapshot adversary considered in [AKM19] works in rounds. At the start of each round, the adversary receives a snapshot of the memory and decides for the next round of operations to be executed. The following result is implicit in [AKM19]:

Theorem 4 ([AKM19]). *If one-way functions exist, then there exists an ORAM with $O(\log n)$ overhead secure against $(s, 0)$-snapshot adversary for any s.*

---

[2] As the main goal of our paper was the lower bound, we only considered weaker non-adaptive snapshot adversaries since weaker adveraries imply stronger lower bounds. Although, we note that all the constructions presented in our paper can also be proven secure against adaptive snapshot adversaries.

Write-only ORAM. Write-only ORAMs [LD13, BMNO14, RACM17] are closely related to snapshot security. A write-only ORAM relaxes the security notion of an ORAM by requiring only the write operations to be oblivious with respect to a persistent adversary. In other words, the adversary receives the access pattern to server memory for all write operations. This is somewhat similar to security with respect to $(s, 0)$-snapshot adversary. In write-only ORAMs, the view of the adversary is filtered based upon the type of the logical ORAM operation type whereas in $(s, 0)$-snapshot attack the filtering occurs at the physical level (whether a server memory location is updated or not).

The work of Amjad et al. [AKM19] proved that breach-resistant arrays implied write-only obliviousness. In this work, we show that write-only obliviousness under certain restrictions also implies $(s, 0)$-snapshot security for any s. Specifically, we assume that ORAM read operations perform no physical writes to server memory. We view this as a mild assumption as the most efficient write-only ORAMs satisfy this property (see [RACM17]).

Theorem 5. *Any write-only ORAM that implements logical ORAM read operations with no physical writes to server memory during read operations is secure against $(s, 0)$-snapshot adversaries for any s.*

Proof. As any logical ORAM read operations do not modify server memory, the leakage viewed by a $(s, 0)$-snapshot adversary after ORAM read operations is trivial. Furthermore, by definition, write-only ORAMs are oblivious for any logical write operations. Therefore, any write-only ORAM with the condition that ORAM read operations perform no server memory overwrites is also $(s, 0)$-snapshot secure.   □

Using the above, we can see that prior write-only ORAM constructions are also secure against $(s, 0)$-snapshot adversaries. To our knowledge, the Det-WoORAM construction [RACM17] satisfies the conditions of the above theorem and is the most efficient write-only ORAM to date. Therefore, we get that:

Theorem 6 ([RACM17]). *If one-way functions exist then for any s there exists an ORAM with $O(\log n)$ overhead secure against $(s, 0)$-snapshot adversary.*

State-of-the-Art for $(s, 0)$-Snapshot Security. To our knowledge, the above constructions for breach-resistance and write-only ORAMs achieve the best concrete overhead for $(s, 0)$-snapshot ORAMs. One could also use standard ORAMs secure against persistent adversaries [AKL+20] to also obtain $O(\log n)$ overhead. As our lower bounds do not apply for $(s, 0)$-snapshot security, we leave it as an open to resolve the optimal overhead for $(s, 0)$-snapshot security. However, we present several barriers towards designing sub-logarithmic $(s, 0)$-snapshot secure ORAMs in Sect. 7. In fact, it is not hard to show that both above constructions are also $(s, 1)$-snapshot secure meaning that they must have $\Omega(\log n)$ overhead to not contradict our lower bound. In other words, an improved $(s, 0)$-snapshot secure ORAM would require a vastly different approach that the ones above.

6   Snapshot Oblivious Stacks and Queues

In this section, we show that we can also construct stacks and queues with constant overhead that is secure against $(s, 1)$-snapshot adversaries for any $s \geq 1$. This provides a separation between snapshot oblivious RAMs and stacks/queues. In contrast, oblivious RAMs and stacks/queues require $\Omega(\log n)$ overhead against persistent adversaries [LN18, JLN19]. Throughout, we will describe constructions only for stacks, but it is trivial to derive queue (or even deque) constructions.

First, we will show a simple construction that obtains $(s, 0)$-snapshot security for any $s \geq 1$. Afterwards, we show that a simple trick using permutations would enable $(s, 1)$-snapshot security. We chose to present our construction this way to showcase that it seems easy to upgrade $(s, 0)$-snapshot security to $(s, 1)$-snapshot security. This is a similar approach that was taken for no-write ORAMs in Sect. 5.1 as well. We present further discussion on this topic in Sect. 7.

6.1 $(s, 0)$-Snapshot Secure Oblivious Stack

We start by describing an implementation of the stack data structure that is secure with respect to an $(s, 0)$-snapshot adversary for any $s \geq 1$. That is, an adversary that receives an initial snapshot of the server memory and the snapshot of the memory after each operation. The server memory consists of n locations indexed $0, \ldots, n - 1$. All memory is initialized to contain the all 0-bit string. The client memory will consists of two components: an IND-CPA encryption key, cnt to track the number of operations and top to track the current server index of the top of the stack. Next, we formally describe the stack algorithms for initialization Init, pushing an item Push and popping an item Pop.

- Init(1^λ): Initialization sets the two variables cnt and top to 0 and -1 respectively and also randomly generates a λ-bit encryption key $K \leftarrow \{0, 1\}^\lambda$ for an IND-CPA encryption scheme. All three are stored in client memory.
- Push(v): To push the value v, the clients encrypts Enc($K, (v, \text{top})$) and uploads it to the location with index cnt. This pair consists of the value v and a pointer to the previous top of the stack. Finally, top is set equal to cnt and cnt is incremented.
- Pop(): To pop the top of the stack, the client downloads and decrypts the pair at the server location top to obtain (v, pTop) consisting of the value at the top of the stack and a pointer to the previous top of the stack. Next, a dummy pair is encrypted Enc($K, (\bot, \bot)$) and uploaded to server memory at location cnt. Finally, top is set equal to pTop and cnt is incremented. The value v is returned.

Theorem 7. *Assuming one-way functions exist there exists an oblivious stack with $O(1)$ overhead secure against $(s, 0)$-snapshot adversaries for any s.*

Proof. The above stack construction clearly has $O(1)$ overhead as it only downloads and updates $O(1)$ entries. To argue security, we simply need to focus on the server locations that are updated as the $(s, 0)$-snapshot adversary does not observe operational transcripts. For each operation (regardless of Push or Pop), the stack will always encrypt and upload a pair to the server memory location indexed by cnt. By IND-CPA security, we know that the encryption is indistinguishable from random. Recall that cnt is the number of operations that have been executed. Therefore, all operational sequences of the same length will result in the same view for a $(s, 0)$-snapshot adversary for any $s \geq 1$.

As a final remark, we observe that the Pop operation downloads the encrypted pair stored at index top whereas Push do not. However, the location is not rewritten and this different behavior between operations goes undetected to an $(s, 0)$-snapshot adversary that does not observe operational transcripts. □

6.2 Upgrading to $(s, 1)$-Snapshot Security

Next, we upgrade the construction from the previous section to $(s, 1)$-snapshot security that includes adversaries that also obtain the transcript of one operation of their choice. The previous construction is not $(s, 1)$-snapshot secure because the memory accesses in the Pop operation reveals the size of the real stack (and, thus, reveals the number of Push and Pop operations total).

To remedy this, we simply permute memory contents according to a pseudorandom permutation F generated using a randomly selected λ-bit seed K_π. We modify the stack so that it accesses locations $F(K_\pi, \text{top})$ and $F(K_\pi, \text{cnt})$ instead of top and cnt. Even if an adversary views the memory access of a Pop operation, the resulting read memory is essentially uniformly random enabling $(s, 1)$-snapshot security. More precisely, we have the following modifications:

- Init(1^λ) proceeds identically as before, but also randomly selects a λ-bit seed $K_\pi \leftarrow \{0, 1\}^\lambda$ for a PRP family of functions F. The key K_π is stored in client memory.
- Push(v) must be modified in two ways. First, the client must also read a memory location to be indistinguishable from Pop operations. To do this, the client will download the encrypted pair currently stored at $F(K_\pi, \text{top})$. The downloaded result is discarded immediately. Secondly, the encrypted Enc$(K, (v, \text{top})$ is stored at server location $F(K_\pi, \text{cnt})$ as opposed to cnt.
- Pop$()$ must be modified in two ways as well. First, the top of the stack is downloaded from server location $F(K_\pi, \text{top})$ as opposed to just top. Additionally, the encrypted dummy pair Enc$(K, (\bot, \bot))$ is stored at location $F(K_\pi, \text{cnt})$ as opposed to cnt.

Theorem 8. *Assuming one-way functions exist, there exists an oblivious stack with $O(1)$ overhead that is secure against $(s, 1)$-snapshot adversaries for any $s \geq 1$.*

Proof. The proof follows from Theorem 7 for $(s, 0)$-snapshot security. To see security against $(s, 1)$-snapshot security, we observe that the operational transcript for any Push or Pop operation involves reading a random location and updating a random location with a random entry due to the security of the underlying PRP and IND-CPA encryption schemes. □

Remark About $(2,2)$**-Snapshot Attacks.** We note that the construction above ceases to be snapshot-secure if the adversary is allowed to see the transcript of two operations. The attack relies on the fact that both Push and Pop download the current top of the stack. More precisely, consider sequences $O_1 = (\text{Push}, \text{Push}, \text{Pop}, \text{Push})$ and $O_2 = (\text{Push}, \text{Push}, \text{Push}, \text{Push})$. Note that in O_1, but not in O_2, the top of the stack is at the same location before the second operation and before the fourth operation. This is so because the third operation in O_1 is a Pop and "undoes" the previous push. The third operation in O_2 instead is a push and the top does not go back. In other words, even though for any single operation the accessed memory location is random, the memory locations accessed by two operations might not be independent.

7   Potential Obstacles to $(s, 0)$-Snapshot Security

In our constructions for both no-write ORAMs and oblivious stacks/queues that are secure against $(s, 1)$-snapshot adversaries, we took the approach of first constructing a simple $(s, 0)$-snapshot secure protocol. Afterwards, we applied a PRP on the server memory to obtain a $(s, 1)$-snapshot secure construction. In both cases, the transformation from $(s, 0)$-snapshot security to $(s, 1)$-snapshot security was the same transformation using a PRP.

This provides some evidence that it may be easy to transform most $(s, 0)$-snapshot secure oblivious data structures into ones that are also $(s, 1)$-snapshot secure. To our knowledge, we are unaware of a blackbox reduction. However, we have shown that many natural $(s, 0)$-snapshot secure constructions can be easily upgraded using our PRP transformation. As an application, we tried to apply the PRP transformation to the $(s, 0)$-snapshot secure ORAMs from breach-resistance and write-only ORAMs in Sect. 5.2. It turns out that both the constructions can be upgraded to $(s, 1)$-snapshot security in a straightforward manner. Therefore, it is not surprising (and, in fact, necessary) that these constructions have $O(\log n)$ overhead to not contradict our $\Omega(\log n)$ lower bound for ORAMs against $(3, 1)$-snapshot adversaries.

We note that this acts as an obstacle towards constructing sub-logarithmic $(s, 0)$-snapshot secure ORAMs. If one wishes to design sub-logarithmic $(s, 0)$-snapshot ORAMs, the construction must not enable the above PRP transformation to $(s, 1)$-snapshot security. In particular, for the case when $s \geq 3$, we know that $(s, 1)$-snapshot secure ORAMs requires $\Omega(\log n)$ overhead. Therefore, the above acts as a barrier and guiding principle if one wishes to try and construct efficient $(s, 0)$-snapshot ORAMs.

8   Extensions of Our Lower Bound

In this section, we strengthen our lower bound for differential privacy and for read-only obliviousness. The extension to Structured Encryption is discussed in the full version.

8.1   Differential Privacy

Definition 2 (Differentially Private $(s, \ell, \epsilon, \delta)$-Snapshot Security). *Let $s \geq 1$ and $\ell \geq 0$ be fixed integers and let $0 \leq \epsilon, \delta < 1$. A data structure* DS *is $(s, \ell, \epsilon, \delta)$-snapshot secure if for any PPT (s, ℓ)-snapshot adversary $\mathcal{A} = (\mathcal{A}_0, \mathcal{A}_1)$ such that $\mathcal{A}_0$ outputs two challenge sequences that differ in only one operation, the following holds for all $b \in \{0, 1\}$:*

$$\Pr[\mathsf{Expt}_{\mathsf{DS},\mathcal{A}}(n, b) = 1] \leq e^\epsilon \Pr[\mathsf{Expt}_{\mathsf{DS},\mathcal{A}}(n, 1 - b) = 1] + \delta,$$

for all sufficiently large n.

The above is a weaker notion of the snapshot security that was defined in Definition 1. For example, if we set $\epsilon = 0$ and $\delta = \mathsf{negl}(n)$, then we obtain a notion that is equivalent to standard snapshot security with negligible adversarial advantage. We show that ORAMs satisfying this definition still requires logarithmic overhead. The only modification needed is in lower bounding the advantage of the adversary in Eq. 1 for which we use the following series of inequalities:

$$e^\epsilon \cdot \Pr[\mathsf{Expt}_{\mathsf{DS},\mathcal{A}^{r,i}}(n, 0) = 1] + \delta \geq \Pr[\mathsf{Expt}_{\mathsf{DS},\mathcal{A}^{r,i}}(n, 1) = 1]$$
$$\Pr[\mathsf{Expt}_{\mathsf{DS},\mathcal{A}^{r,i}}(n, 0) = 1] \geq (1/8 - \delta)/e^\epsilon$$
$$\Pr[\mathsf{Expt}_{\mathsf{DS},\mathcal{A}^{r,i}}(n, 0) = 1] \geq 1/(16e).$$

Theorem 9. *For any $0 \leq \epsilon \leq 1$ and any $0 \leq \delta \leq 1/16$, let* DS *be a differentially private $(3, 1, \epsilon, \delta)$-snapshot secure RAM data structure for n entries each of b bits implemented over $w = \Omega(\log n)$ bits using client storage of c bits in the cell probe model. If* DS *has amortized write time t_w and expected amortized read time t_r with failure probability at most $1/3$, then $t_r + t_w = \Omega\left(b/w \cdot \log(nb/c)\right)$.*

8.2   Read-Only Obliviousness

Next, we consider a weaker privacy notion where obliviousness is only to be provided for ORAM read operations. This notion is relevant when write operations are public information, but read operations are sensitive (e.g., a medical research database). We consider the security experiment ROExpt in which leakage to memory is returned only write operations.

Definition 3 (Read-Only (s, ℓ, ϵ)-Snapshot Security). *Let $s \geq 1$ and $\ell \geq 0$ be fixed integers and let $0 \leq \epsilon < 1$. A data structure* DS *is (s, ℓ, ϵ)-snapshot private if for any PPT (s, ℓ)-snapshot adversary $\mathcal{A} = (\mathcal{A}_0, \mathcal{A}_1)$ such that $\mathcal{A}_0$ outputs two challenge sequences with the same number of read operations and the following holds:*

$$\left|\Pr[\mathsf{ROExpt}_{\mathsf{DS},\mathcal{A}}(n, 0) = 1] - \Pr[\mathsf{ROExpt}_{\mathsf{DS},\mathcal{A}}(n, 1) = 1]\right| \leq \epsilon,$$

for all sufficiently large n.

Our snapshot adversary from Sect. 4.1 outputs two operational sequences with exactly one ORAM read operation. Furthermore, the transcript viewed by the snapshot adversary is always the single ORAM read operation. Therefore, our snapshot adversary from Sect. 4.1 is also a read-only snapshot adversary and the lower bound holds without modification.

Theorem 10. *For any $0 \leq \epsilon \leq 1/16$, let* DS *be a read-only $(3,1,\epsilon)$-snapshot secure RAM data structure for n entries each of b bits implemented over $w = \Omega(\log n)$ bits using client storage of c bits in the cell probe model. If* DS *has amortized write time t_w and expected amortized read time t_r with failure probability at most $1/3$, then $t_r + t_w = \Omega\left(b/w \cdot \log(nb/c)\right)$.*

9   Conclusions and Open Problems

In this work, we present a negative answer to the open problem posed in [DGG22] of whether it is possible to build sub-logarithmic ORAM constructions secure against multiple breaches. We present a $\Omega(\log n)$ lower bound for ORAMs secure against $(3,1)$-snapshot adversaries. In other words, we show that protecting against three breaches is as challenging as protecting against a persistent adversary. Furthermore, we prove some separations by presenting $O(1)$ overhead constructions for no-write ORAMs and oblivious stacks/queues secure against $(s,1)$-snapshot adversaries for any $s \geq 1$. We leave the following open problems:

- Our work rules out sub-logarithmic overhead against $(3,1)$-snapshot adversaries with three data breaches. However, it remains open to resolve the correct overhead for snapshot adversaries with two data breaches. Is it possible to construct a $o(\log n)$ overhead ORAM construction to protect against $(2,\ell)$-snapshot adversaries for any $\ell \geq 1$?
- The lower bound presented in our work shows that snapshot adversaries are as powerful as persistent adversaries if they can see the transcript of one operation. It is also natural to consider adversaries that never see the transcript of any operation. Unfortunately, current constructions from prior works [RACM17,AKM19] still require $O(\log n)$ overhead to protect against $(s,0)$-snapshot adversaries. Is it possible to construct a $o(\log n)$ ORAM that is secure against $(s,0)$-snapshot adversaries for any $s \geq 2$? We provide some evidence towards barriers for sub-logarithmic constructions in Sect. 7.
- Are there any other meaningful weakenings of security for ORAMs that admit sub-logarithmic constructions while still enabling wide applicability in practical applications?

Acknowledgements. The authors would like to thank Yang Du and Paul Grubbs for posing the question of multiple data breaches and Wei-Kai Lin and Daniel Wichs for initial discussions about the problem.

References

[ACD+22] Aronesty, E., et al.: Encapsulated search index: public-key, sub-linear, distributed, and delegatable. In: Hanaoka, G., Shikata, J., Watanabe, Y. (eds.) PKC 2022, Part II. LNCS, vol. 13178, pp. 256–285. Springer, Cham (2022). https://doi.org/10.1007/978-3-030-97131-1_9

[AKL+20] Asharov, G., Komargodski, I., Lin, W.-K., Nayak, K., Peserico, E., Shi, E.: OptORAMa: optimal oblivious RAM. In: Canteaut, A., Ishai, Y. (eds.) EUROCRYPT 2020, Part II. LNCS, vol. 12106, pp. 403–432. Springer, Cham (2020). https://doi.org/10.1007/978-3-030-45724-2_14

[AKL+22] Asharov, G., Komargodski, I., Lin, W.-K., Peserico, E., Shi, E.: Optimal oblivious parallel ram. In: Proceedings of the 2022 Annual ACM-SIAM Symposium on Discrete Algorithms (SODA), pp. 2459–2521. SIAM (2022)

[AKLS21] Asharov, G., Komargodski, I., Lin, W.-K., Shi, E.: Oblivious RAM with *Worst-Case* logarithmic overhead. In: Malkin, T., Peikert, C. (eds.) CRYPTO 2021, Part IV. LNCS, vol. 12828, pp. 610–640. Springer, Cham (2021). https://doi.org/10.1007/978-3-030-84259-8_21

[AKM19] Amjad, G., Kamara, S., Moataz, T.: Breach-resistant structured encryption. PoPETs **2019**(1), 245–265 (2019)

[APP+23] Amjad, G., Patel, S., Persiano, G., Yeo, K., Yung, M.: Dynamic volume-hiding encrypted multi-maps with applications to searchable encryption. PoPETs (2023, to appear)

[BBF+21] Bossuat, A., Bost, R., Fouque, P.-A., Minaud, B., Reichle, M.: SSE and SSD: page-efficient searchable symmetric encryption. In: Malkin, T., Peikert, C. (eds.) CRYPTO 2021, Part III. LNCS, vol. 12827, pp. 157–184. Springer, Cham (2021). https://doi.org/10.1007/978-3-030-84252-9_6

[BCP16] Boyle, E., Chung, K.-M., Pass, R.: Oblivious parallel RAM and applications. In: Kushilevitz, E., Malkin, T. (eds.) TCC 2016, Part II. LNCS, vol. 9563, pp. 175–204. Springer, Heidelberg (2016). https://doi.org/10.1007/978-3-662-49099-0_7

[BDOP04] Boneh, D., Di Crescenzo, G., Ostrovsky, R., Persiano, G.: Public key encryption with keyword search. In: Cachin, C., Camenisch, J.L. (eds.) EUROCRYPT 2004. LNCS, vol. 3027, pp. 506–522. Springer, Heidelberg (2004). https://doi.org/10.1007/978-3-540-24676-3_30

[BF19] Bost, R., Fouque, P.-A.: Security-efficiency tradeoffs in searchable encryption. PoPETs **2019**(4), 132–151 (2019)

[BIM04] Beimel, A., Ishai, Y., Malkin, T.: Reducing the servers' computation in private information retrieval: PIR with preprocessing. J. Cryptol. **17**(2), 125–151 (2004)

[BKM20] Blackstone, L., Kamara, S., Moataz, T.: Revisiting leakage abuse attacks. In: NDSS 2020. The Internet Society, February 2020

[BMNO14] Blass, E.-O., Mayberry, T., Noubir, G., Onarlioglu, K.: Toward robust hidden volumes using write-only oblivious RAM. In: Ahn, G.-J., Yung, M., Li, N. (eds.) ACM CCS 2014, pp. 203–214. ACM Press, November 2014

[BMO17] Bost, R., Minaud, B., Ohrimenko, O.: Forward and backward private searchable encryption from constrained cryptographic primitives. In: Thuraisingham, B.M., Evans, D., Malkin, T., Xu, D. (eds.) ACM CCS 2017, pp. 1465–1482. ACM Press, October/November 2017

[BN16] Boyle E., Naor, M.: Is there an oblivious RAM lower bound? In: Sudan, M. (ed.) ITCS 2016, pp. 357–368. ACM, January 2016

[Bos16] Bost, R.: Σοφος: forward secure searchable encryption. In: Weippl, E.R., Katzenbeisser, S., Kruegel, C., Myers, A.C., Halevi, S. (eds.) ACM CCS 2016, pp. 1143–1154. ACM Press, October 2016

[BRE] List of data breaches. https://en.wikipedia.org/wiki/List_of_data_breaches

[CDH20] Cash, D., Drucker, A., Hoover, A.: A lower bound for one-round oblivious RAM. In: Pass, R., Pietrzak, K. (eds.) TCC 2020, Part I. LNCS, vol. 12550, pp. 457–485. Springer, Cham (2020). https://doi.org/10.1007/978-3-030-64375-1_16

[CGKO06] Curtmola, R., Garay, J.A., Kamara, S., Ostrovsky, R.: Searchable symmetric encryption: improved definitions and efficient constructions. In: Juels, A., Wright, R.N., De Capitani di Vimercati, S. (eds.) ACM CCS 2006, pp. 79–88. ACM Press, October/November 2006

[CGPR15] Cash, D., Grubbs, P., Perry, J., Ristenpart, T.: Leakage-abuse attacks against searchable encryption. In: Ray, I., Li, N., Kruegel, C. (eds.) ACM CCS 2015, pp. 668–679. ACM Press, October 2015

[CHK22] Corrigan-Gibbs, H., Henzinger, A., Kogan, D.: Single-server private information retrieval with sublinear amortized time. In: Dunkelman, O., Dziembowski, S. (eds.) EUROCRYPT 2022, Part II. LNCS, vol. 13276, pp. 3–33. Springer, Heidelberg (2022). https://doi.org/10.1007/978-3-031-07085-3_1

[CJJ+13] Cash, D., Jarecki, S., Jutla, C., Krawczyk, H., Roşu, M.-C., Steiner, M.: Highly-scalable searchable symmetric encryption with support for Boolean queries. In: Canetti, R., Garay, J.A. (eds.) CRYPTO 2013, Part I. LNCS, vol. 8042, pp. 353–373. Springer, Heidelberg (2013). https://doi.org/10.1007/978-3-642-40041-4_20

[CJJ+14] Cash, D., et al.: Dynamic searchable encryption in very-large databases: data structures and implementation. In: NDSS 2014. The Internet Society, February 2014

[CK10] Chase, M., Kamara, S.: Structured encryption and controlled disclosure. In: Abe, M. (ed.) ASIACRYPT 2010. LNCS, vol. 6477, pp. 577–594. Springer, Heidelberg (2010). https://doi.org/10.1007/978-3-642-17373-8_33

[CK20] Corrigan-Gibbs, H., Kogan, D.: Private information retrieval with sublinear online time. In: Canteaut, A., Ishai, Y. (eds.) EUROCRYPT 2020, Part I. LNCS, vol. 12105, pp. 44–75. Springer, Cham (2020). https://doi.org/10.1007/978-3-030-45721-1_3

[CLT16] Chen, B., Lin, H., Tessaro, S.: Oblivious Parallel RAM: Improved Efficiency and Generic Constructions. In: Kushilevitz, E., Malkin, T. (eds.) TCC 2016, Part II. LNCS, vol. 9563, pp. 205–234. Springer, Heidelberg (2016). https://doi.org/10.1007/978-3-662-49099-0_8

[CT14] Cash, D., Tessaro, S.: The locality of searchable symmetric encryption. In: Nguyen, P.Q., Oswald, E. (eds.) EUROCRYPT 2014. LNCS, vol. 8441, pp. 351–368. Springer, Heidelberg (2014). https://doi.org/10.1007/978-3-642-55220-5_20

[dbi] DBIR: Data Breach Investigations Report. https://www.verizon. com/business/resources/T61c/reports/dbir/2022-data-breach-investigations-report-dbir.pdf

[DGG22] Yang, D., Genkin, D., Grubbs, P.: Snapshot-oblivious RAMs: sub-logarithmic efficiency for short transcripts. In: Dodis, Y., Shrimpton, T. (eds.) CRYPTO 2022, Part IV. LNCS, vol. 13510, pp. 152–181. Springer, Heidelberg (2022). https://doi.org/10.1007/978-3-031-15985-5_6

[DPPS20] Demertzis, I., Papadopoulos, D., Papamanthou, C., Shintre, S.: SEAL: attack mitigation for encrypted databases via adjustable leakage. In: Capkun, S., Roesner, F. (eds.) USENIX Security 2020, pp. 2433–2450. USENIX Association, August 2020

[Ds17] Doerner, J., Shelat, A.: Scaling ORAM for secure computation. In: Thuraisingham, B.M., Evans, D., Malkin, T., Xu, D. (eds.) ACM CCS 2017, pp. 523–535. ACM Press, October/November 2017

[FS89] Fredman, M.L., Saks, M.E.: The cell probe complexity of dynamic data structures. In: 21st ACM STOC, pp. 345–354. ACM Press, May 1989

[GKM21] George, M., Kamara, S., Moataz, T.: Structured encryption and dynamic leakage suppression. In: Canteaut, A., Standaert, F.-X. (eds.) EUROCRYPT 2021, Part III. LNCS, vol. 12698, pp. 370–396. Springer, Cham (2021). https://doi.org/10.1007/978-3-030-77883-5_13

[GLMP19] Grubbs, P., Lacharité, M.-S., Minaud, B., Paterson, K.G.: Learning to reconstruct: Statistical learning theory and encrypted database attacks. In: 2019 IEEE Symposium on Security and Privacy, pp. 1067–1083. IEEE Computer Society Press, May 2019

[GMOT12] Goodrich, M.T., Mitzenmacher, M., Ohrimenko, O., Tamassia, R.: Privacy-preserving group data access via stateless oblivious RAM simulation. In: Rabani, Y. (ed.) 23rd SODA, pp. 157–167. ACM-SIAM, January 2012

[GO96] Goldreich, O., Ostrovsky, R.: Software protection and simulation on oblivious rams. J. ACM (JACM) (1996)

[HK14] Hahn, F., Kerschbaum, F.: Searchable encryption with secure and efficient updates. In: Ahn, G.-J., Yung, M., Li, N. (eds.) ACM CCS 2014, pp. 310–320. ACM Press, November 2014

[HKKS19] Hubáček, P., Koucký, M., Král, K., Slívová, V.: Stronger lower bounds for online ORAM. In: Hofheinz, D., Rosen, A. (eds.) TCC 2019, Part II. LNCS, vol. 11892, pp. 264–284. Springer, Cham (2019). https://doi.org/10.1007/978-3-030-36033-7_10

[IKK12] Islam, M.S., Kuzu, M., Kantarcioglu, M.: Access pattern disclosure on searchable encryption: ramification, attack and mitigation. In: NDSS 2012. The Internet Society, February 2012

[JLN19] Jacob, R., Larsen, K.G., Nielsen, J.B.: Lower bounds for oblivious data structures. In: Chan, T.M. (ed.) 30th SODA, pp. 2439–2447. ACM-SIAM, January 2019

[KKNO16] Kellaris, G., Kollios, G., Nissim, K., O'Neill, A.: Generic attacks on secure outsourced databases. In: Weippl, E.R., Katzenbeisser, S., Kruegel, C., Myers, A.C., Halevi, S. (eds.) ACM CCS 2016, pp. 1329–1340. ACM Press, October 2016

[KL21] Komargodski, I., Lin, W.-K.: A logarithmic lower bound for oblivious RAM (for all parameters). In: Malkin, T., Peikert, C. (eds.) CRYPTO 2021, Part IV. LNCS, vol. 12828, pp. 579–609. Springer, Cham (2021). https://doi.org/10.1007/978-3-030-84259-8_20

[KLO12] Kushilevitz, E., Lu, S., Ostrovsky, R.: On the (in)security of hash-based oblivious RAM and a new balancing scheme. In: Rabani, Y. (ed.) 23rd SODA, pp. 143–156. ACM-SIAM, January 2012

[KM17] Kamara, S., Moataz, T.: Boolean searchable symmetric encryption with worst-case sub-linear complexity. In: Coron, J.-S., Nielsen, J.B. (eds.) EUROCRYPT 2017. LNCS, vol. 10212, pp. 94–124. Springer, Cham (2017). https://doi.org/10.1007/978-3-319-56617-7_4

[KM18] Kamara, S., Moataz, T.: SQL on structurally-encrypted databases. In: Peyrin, T., Galbraith, S. (eds.) ASIACRYPT 2018, Part I. LNCS, vol. 11272, pp. 149–180. Springer, Cham (2018). https://doi.org/10.1007/978-3-030-03326-2_6

[KM19] Kamara, S., Moataz, T.: Computationally volume-hiding structured encryption. In: Ishai, Y., Rijmen, V. (eds.) EUROCRYPT 2019, Part II. LNCS, vol. 11477, pp. 183–213. Springer, Cham (2019). https://doi.org/10.1007/978-3-030-17656-3_7

[KMO18] Kamara, S., Moataz, T., Ohrimenko, O.: Structured encryption and leakage suppression. In: Shacham, H., Boldyreva, A. (eds.) CRYPTO 2018, Part I. LNCS, vol. 10991, pp. 339–370. Springer, Cham (2018). https://doi.org/10.1007/978-3-319-96884-1_12

[KPR12] Kamara, S., Papamanthou, C., Roeder, T.: Dynamic searchable symmetric encryption. In: Yu, T., Danezis, G., Gligor, V.D. (eds.) ACM CCS 2012, pp. 965–976. ACM Press, October 2012

[KPT21] Kornaropoulos, E.M., Papamanthou, C., Tamassia, R.: Response-hiding encrypted ranges: revisiting security via parametrized leakage-abuse attacks. In: 2021 IEEE Symposium on Security and Privacy, pp. 1502–1519. IEEE Computer Society Press, May 2021

[LD13] Li, L., Datta, A.: Write-only oblivious RAM based privacy-preserved access of outsourced data. Cryptology ePrint Archive, Report 2013/694 (2013). https://eprint.iacr.org/2013/694

[LMP18] Lacharité, M.-S., Minaud, B., Paterson, K.G.: Improved reconstruction attacks on encrypted data using range query leakage. In: 2018 IEEE Symposium on Security and Privacy, pp. 297–314. IEEE Computer Society Press, May 2018

[LMWY20] Larsen, K.G., Malkin, T., Weinstein, O., Yeo, K.: Lower bounds for oblivious near-neighbor search. In: Chawla, S., (ed.) 31st SODA, pp. 1116–1134. ACM-SIAM, January 2020

[LN18] Larsen, K.G., Nielsen, J.B.: Yes, there is an oblivious RAM lower bound! In: Shacham, H., Boldyreva, A. (eds.) CRYPTO 2018, Part II. LNCS, vol. 10992, pp. 523–542. Springer, Cham (2018). https://doi.org/10.1007/978-3-319-96881-0_18

[LSY20] Larsen, K.G., Simkin, M., Yeo, K.: Lower bounds for multi-server oblivious RAMs. In: Pass, R., Pietrzak, K. (eds.) TCC 2020, Part I. LNCS, vol. 12550, pp. 486–503. Springer, Cham (2020). https://doi.org/10.1007/978-3-030-64375-1_17

[MR22]   Minaud, B., Reichle, M.: Dynamic local searchable symmetric encryption. In: Dodis, Y., Shrimpton, T. (eds.) CRYPTO 2022, Part IV. LNCS, vol. 13510, pp. 91–120. Springer, Heidelberg (2022). https://doi.org/10.1007/978-3-031-15985-5_4

[PD06]   Patrascu, M., Demaine, E.D.: Logarithmic lower bounds in the cell-probe model. SIAM J. Comput. (2006)

[PPRY18]   Patel, S., Persiano, G., Raykova, M., Yeo, K.: PanORAMa: oblivious RAM with logarithmic overhead. In: Thorup, M. (ed.) 59th FOCS, pp. 871–882. IEEE Computer Society Press, October 2018

[PPSY21]   Patel, S., Persiano, G., Seo, J.Y., Yeo, K.: Efficient Boolean search over encrypted data with reduced leakage. In: Tibouchi, M., Wang, H. (eds.) ASIACRYPT 2021. LNCS, vol. 13092, pp. 577–607. Springer, Cham (2021). https://doi.org/10.1007/978-3-030-92078-4_20

[PPY19]   Patel, S., Persiano, G., Yeo, K.: What storage access privacy is achievable with small overhead? In: ACM PODS (2019)

[PPY20]   Patel, S., Persiano, G., Yeo, K.: Lower bounds for encrypted multi-maps and searchable encryption in the leakage cell probe model. In: Micciancio, D., Ristenpart, T. (eds.) CRYPTO 2020. LNCS, vol. 12170, pp. 433–463. Springer, Cham (2020). https://doi.org/10.1007/978-3-030-56784-2_15

[PPYY19]   Patel, S., Persiano, G., Yeo, K., Yung, M.: Mitigating leakage in secure cloud-hosted data structures: Volume-hiding for multi-maps via hashing. In: Cavallaro, V., Kinder, J., Wang, X.F., Katz, J. (eds.) ACM CCS 2019, pp. 79–93. ACM Press, November 2019

[PY19]   Persiano, G., Yeo, K.: Lower bounds for differentially private RAMs. In: Ishai, Y., Rijmen, V. (eds.) EUROCRYPT 2019, Part I. LNCS, vol. 11476, pp. 404–434. Springer, Cham (2019). https://doi.org/10.1007/978-3-030-17653-2_14

[PY22]   Persiano, G., Yeo, K.: Limits of preprocessing for single-server PIR. In: Annual ACM-SIAM Symposium on Discrete Algorithms (2022)

[PY23]   Persiano, G., Yeo, K.: Lower bound framework for differentially private and oblivious data structures. In: Hazay, C., Stam, M. (eds.), EUROCRYPT 2023, Part I, vol. 14004, LNCS, pp. 487–517. Springer, Cham (2023). https://doi.org/10.1007/978-3-031-30545-0_17

[RACM17]   Roche, D.S., Aviv, A.J., Choi, S.G., Mayberry, T.: Deterministic, stash-free write-only ORAM. In: Thuraisingham, B.M., Evans, D., Malkin, T., Xu, D. (eds.) ACM CCS 2017, pp. 507–521. ACM Press, October/November 2017

[RFK+15]   Ren, L., et al.: Constants count: practical improvements to oblivious RAM. In: Jung, J., Holz, T. (eds.) USENIX Security 2015, pp. 415–430. USENIX Association, August 2015

[SvS+13]   Stefanov, E., et al.: Path ORAM: an extremely simple oblivious RAM protocol. In: Sadeghi, A.-R., Gligor, V.D., Yung, M. (eds.) ACM CCS 2013, pp. 299–310. ACM Press, November 2013

[SWP00]   Song, D.X., Wagner, D., Perrig, A.: Practical techniques for searches on encrypted data. In: 2000 IEEE Symposium on Security and Privacy, pp. 44–55. IEEE Computer Society Press, May 2000

[WCM18]   Wagh, S., Cuff, P., Mittal, P.: Differentially private oblivious ram. In: Proceedings on Privacy Enhancing Technologies (2018)

[WHC+14] Wang, X.S., Huang, Y., Hubert Chan, T.-H., Shelat, A., Shi, E.: SCO-RAM: oblivious RAM for secure computation. In: Ahn, G.-J., Yung, M., Li, N. (eds.) ACM CCS 2014, pp. 191–202. ACM Press, November 2014

[WW18] Weiss, M., Wichs, D.: Is there an oblivious RAM lower bound for online reads? In: Beimel, A., Dziembowski, S. (eds.) TCC 2018, Part II. LNCS, vol. 11240, pp. 603–635. Springer, Cham (2018). https://doi.org/10.1007/978-3-030-03810-6_22

[Yao81] Yao, A.C.-C.: Should tables be sorted? J. ACM (JACM) (1981)

[Yeo23] Yeo, K.: Lower bounds for (batch) PIR with private preprocessing. In: Hazay, C., Stam, M. (eds.) EUROCRYPT 2023, Part I. LNCS, vol. 14004, pp. 518–550. Springer, Cham (2023). https://doi.org/10.1007/978-3-031-30545-0_18

[ZKP16] Zhang, Y., Katz, J., Papamanthou, C.: All your queries are belong to us: The power of file-injection attacks on searchable encryption. In: Holz, T., Savage, S. (eds.), USENIX Security 2016, pp. 707–720. USENIX Association, August 2016

[ZWR+16] Zahur, S., et al.: Revisiting square-root ORAM: efficient random access in multi-party computation. In: 2016 IEEE Symposium on Security and Privacy, pp. 218–234. IEEE Computer Society Press, May 2016

Cuckoo Hashing in Cryptography: Optimal Parameters, Robustness and Applications

Kevin Yeo[1,2(✉)]

[1] Google, New York City, USA
[2] Columbia University, New York City, USA
kwlyeo@cs.columbia.edu

Abstract. Cuckoo hashing is a powerful primitive that enables storing items using small space with efficient querying. At a high level, cuckoo hashing maps n items into b entries storing at most ℓ items such that each item is placed into one of k randomly chosen entries. Additionally, there is an overflow stash that can store at most s items. Many cryptographic primitives rely upon cuckoo hashing to privately embed and query data where it is integral to ensure small failure probability when constructing cuckoo hashing tables as it directly relates to the privacy guarantees.

As our main result, we present a more query-efficient cuckoo hashing construction using more hash functions. For construction failure probability ϵ, the query overhead of our scheme is $O(1 + \sqrt{\log(1/\epsilon)/\log n})$. Our scheme has quadratically smaller query overhead than prior works for any target failure probability ϵ. We also prove lower bounds matching our construction. Our improvements come from a new understanding of the locality of cuckoo hashing failures for small sets of items.

We also initiate the study of robust cuckoo hashing where the input set may be chosen with knowledge of the hash functions. We present a cuckoo hashing scheme using more hash functions with query overhead $\tilde{O}(\log \lambda)$ that is robust against $\mathsf{poly}(\lambda)$ adversaries. Furthermore, we present lower bounds showing that this construction is tight and that extending previous approaches of large stashes or entries cannot obtain robustness except with $\Omega(n)$ query overhead.

As applications of our results, we obtain improved constructions for batch codes and PIR. In particular, we present the most efficient explicit batch code and blackbox reduction from single-query PIR to batch PIR.

1 Introduction

Cuckoo hashing, introduced by Pagh and Rodler [52], is a powerful tool that enables embedding data from a very large universe into memory whose size is linear in the total size of the data while enabling very efficient retrieval. In more detail, the original cuckoo hashing scheme enables taking a set of n items from a universe U and stores them into approximately $2n$ entries such that querying any item x requires searching only two entries. A huge advantage of cuckoo

---

The full version of this paper may be found at [66].

© International Association for Cryptologic Research 2023
H. Handschuh and A. Lysyanskaya (Eds.): CRYPTO 2023, LNCS 14084, pp. 197–230, 2023.
https://doi.org/10.1007/978-3-031-38551-3_7

hashing is that the storage overhead is optimal up to a small constant factor and independent of the universe size $|U|$ while query overhead (the number of possible locations for any item) is $O(1)$. Due to the power of cuckoo hashing, it has found usage in a wide range of applications such as high-performance hash tables [13,68], databases [61], caching [25] and cuckoo filters [26]. Furthermore, many follow-up works have studied further properties and variants of cuckoo hashing including [4,7,21,23,28–30,41,43,45].

Cuckoo Hashing in Cryptography. One important area where cuckoo hashing has found wide usage is cryptography. Cuckoo hashing is a core component of many cryptographic primitives such as private information retrieval (PIR) [1,2,20], private set intersection (PSI) [14,15,57–59], symmetric searchable encryption (SSE) [11,55] and oblivious RAM (ORAM) [5,33,37,53,56].

A common method used in cryptographic primitives is to leverage cuckoo hashing to *privately* embed data while enabling efficient queries when necessary. For example, suppose one party has a database of identifier-value pairs $\{(\mathsf{id}_1, v_1), \ldots, (\mathsf{id}_n, v_n)\}$ that it wishes to outsource to another potentially untrusted third party for storage. As the third party is untrusted, the data must be outsourced in a private manner such that the third party cannot see the data in plaintext. For utility, the data owner should still be able to query and retrieve certain values efficiently. To do this, many works leverage cuckoo hashing with two modifications. First, the underlying random hash functions are replaced with cryptographic hash functions (typically, pseudorandom functions). Secondly, the contents of the resulting cuckoo hash tables are encrypted in some manner such as standard IND-CPA encryption. The keys for the cryptographic hash function and encryption are typically kept by the data owner to ensure privacy. To query, the data owner executes the cuckoo hashing query algorithm using the private keys when necessary to retrieve all possible locations for a queried item. The above does not comprehensively cover all usages of cuckoo hashing in cryptography, but was elaborated to provide readers with intuition on an example usage of cuckoo hashing to privately embed and query data.

To our knowledge, all cryptographic applications use cuckoo hashing where all n items are provided ahead of time to construct a hash table that is not modified in the future. However, this does not preclude the usage of cuckoo hashing for cryptographic primitives where data may be updated frequently (such as oblivious RAM). Throughout our work, we will focus on the setting of constructing a static cuckoo hash table and ignore features that enable inserting items. See Sect. 4.1 for more discussion on our choice of abstraction.

Failure Probability and Adversarial Advantage. Requirements of cuckoo hashing for usage in cryptography differs significantly from other applications. In cuckoo hashing, there is a non-zero probability that it is impossible to allocate a set of n items using the sampled random hash functions. We will refer to this as the *construction failure probability*. For standard cuckoo hashing, it was shown that the failure probability is $1/\mathsf{poly}(n)$. Without privacy concerns, one can simply sample new random hash functions and repeat the construction algorithm to handle the failure. As the failure probability is $1/\mathsf{poly}(n)$, this would increase the expected running time of construction by a minimal amount.

For cryptography, the failure probability has much larger implications with respect to privacy and adversarial advantage. Suppose we consider a cuckoo hashing instantiation with failure construction probability ϵ over the randomly sampled hash function $\mathcal{H}$. This means that, if we choose a uniformly random set of n items, the set of n items cannot be allocated correctly according to $\mathcal{H}$ with probability ϵ. In other words, an ϵ-fraction of inputs will behave differently from the remaining inputs. At a high level, an adversary can leverage this property to compromise privacy of the inputs when ϵ is too large. Suppose the adversary picks two input sets S_1 and S_2. An ideal cryptographic protocol would pick $\eta \in \{0, 1\}$ at random and execute with S_η as input. Given the transcript of the protocol, the adversary should not be able to guess η with probability better than $1/2 + \mathsf{negl}(\lambda)$ probability. If the adversary picks S_1 and S_2 at random, it is not hard to see that exactly one of S_1 or S_2 will fail to be allocated by cuckoo hashing with probability approximately $O(\epsilon)$. As the transcripts will be different when cuckoo hashing fails to construct the hash table, the adversary has advantage approximately $1/2 + \epsilon$ of guessing η. So, it is essential that the construction failure probability ϵ is negligible to ensure privacy of the embedded data. In fact, prior works have shown insecurity of protocols when $\epsilon = 1/\mathsf{poly}(n)$ such as [42]. Therefore, standard cuckoo hashing with $1/\mathsf{poly}(n)$ failure cannot be used in most cryptographic applications. Instead, we must come up with new cuckoo hashing schemes with negligible failure for usage in cryptography.

Cuckoo Hashing with Negligible Failure. To systematically study cuckoo hashing, we will consider several tunable parameters: number of hash functions k, number of entries b, size of each entry ℓ and size of the overflow stash s. The main table will consist of b entries that can each store up to ℓ items. Each item is randomly assigned to k different entries using the hash functions where the item may be allocated. Additionally, there is an overflow stash of size s to store any items that cannot fit in the main table. We denote the *query overhead* as the total number of possible locations that need to be checked when querying an item. With these parameters, the query overhead is exactly $k\ell + s$ that checks all ℓ locations in each of the k entries as well as the stash. To our knowledge, the above encapsulates all variants of cuckoo hashing used in cryptography.

Obtaining negligible (or even zero) failure in cuckoo hashing is trivial. For example, if we set the stash size to be $s = n$, no failures will ever occur. The real challenge is obtaining negligible failure while keeping small query overhead that directly relates to the efficiency of the cryptographic application. While the above example obtains zero failure, the resulting query overhead is $k\ell + s = O(n)$.

It is an important question to study the query overhead of cuckoo hashing with negligible failure due to its heavy usage in cryptographic primitives. To date, there are two constructions that obtain the smallest query overhead. The first is cuckoo hashing with a large stash introduced by Kirsch, Mitzenmacher and Wieder [41]. By picking stash size $s = O(1 + \log(1/\epsilon)/\log n)$, it can be proven that cuckoo hashing will fail only with ϵ probability [7]. Another approach considers entries that can store a large number of items ℓ. For $\ell = O(1 + \log(1/\epsilon)/\log n)$, it has been shown that failure probability ϵ may be achieved by Minaud and

	Hash Functions k	Entry Size ℓ	Entries b	Stash Size s	Failure ϵ	Query Overhead
Cuckoo Hashing [52]	2	1	$O(n)$	0	$1/n^{O(1)}$	$O(1)$
Large-Sized Entries [23]	2	$O(1)$	$(1+\alpha)n/\ell$	0	$1/n^{O(1)}$	$O(1)$
Large-Sized Entries [45]	2	$O(1+\log(1/\epsilon)/\log n)$	$O(n/\ell)$	0	ϵ	$O(1+\log(1/\epsilon)/\log n)$
Constant-Sized Stash [41]	2	1	$O(n)$	$O(1)$	$1/n^{O(1)}$	$O(1)$
Large-Sized Stash [7]	2	1	$O(n)$	$O(1+\log(1/\epsilon)/\log n)$	ϵ	$O(1+\log(1/\epsilon)/\log n)$
More Hash Functions [28]	$O(1+\log(1/\epsilon)/\log n)$	1	$O(n)$	0	ϵ	$O(1+\log(1/\epsilon)/\log n)$
Our Work	$O(1+\sqrt{\log(1/\epsilon)/\log n})$	1	$O(n)$	0	ϵ	$O(1+\sqrt{\log(1/\epsilon)/\log n})$

Fig. 1. Comparison table of known cuckoo hashing instantiations. The query overhead $k\ell + s$ is the number of locations to search when retrieving an item.

Papamanthou [45]. A final approach considers standard cuckoo hashing that utilizes large-scale experiments to estimate the failure probability [2,15] without providing any provable failure bounds. The above approaches all obtain negligible failure probabilities in different ways. It is unclear that the above approaches are most efficient way to obtain negligible failure leading us to the following question:

> *What is the smallest query overhead achievable with provably negligible failure probability for cuckoo hashing?*

As our major result, we present an approach with provable failure bounds that is quadratically smaller query overhead than previous constructions. We also prove lower bounds matching our construction.

Adversarial Robustness. In the prior discussions, we overlooked a subtle, but important, assumption used in cuckoo hashing. The failure probabilities assumed that the chosen inputs were independent of the sampled random hash functions. Instead, if we assume that an adversary is given the hash functions to choose the input set for cuckoo hashing, the previous construction failure bounds no longer apply. In many settings, it is natural that the adversary has knowledge of the random hash functions. Two such examples include if the adversary may view or control the randomness in the system or if the hash functions need to be published publicly for use by multiple parties.

We initiate the study of *robust cuckoo hashing* that provide negligible construction failure probabilities for inputs chosen adversarially with knowledge of the hash functions. This leads to the following natural question:

> *What is the smallest query overhead achievable for robust cuckoo hashing?*

In our work, we present constructions for robust cuckoo hashing with optimal query overhead that match our lower bounds.

1.1   Our Contributions

Improved Query and Failure Trade-offs. As our major result, we present a new cuckoo hashing construction that achieves better trade-offs between query overhead and failure probabilities. To obtain failure probability ϵ, we prove it suffices to use $k = O(1 + \sqrt{\log(1/\epsilon)/\log n})$ hash functions with $b = O(n)$ entries of size $\ell = 1$ and no stash, $s = 0$. Therefore, the resulting query overhead is $O(1 + \sqrt{\log(1/\epsilon)/\log n})$. If we restrict to the case when $\epsilon \leq 1/n$, we get that $\log(1/\epsilon) \geq \log n$. Then, we can drop the case when ϵ is too large and simply state

	Hash Functions k	Entry Size ℓ	Entries b	Stash Size s	Robustness	Query Overhead
Our Work	$O(f(\lambda)\log\lambda), f(\lambda)=\omega(1)$	1	$O(n)$	0	$(\lambda, \mathsf{negl}(\lambda))$	$O(f(\lambda)\log\lambda)$
Our Work	$\omega(\log\lambda)$	$o(n)$	$O(n/\ell)$	$o(n)$	$(\lambda, 1/2)$	$\omega(\log\lambda)$
Our Work	$O(\log\lambda)$	$\Omega(n)$	$O(n/\ell)$	$o(n)$	$(\lambda, 1/2)$	$\Omega(n)$
Our Work	$O(\log\lambda)$	$o(n)$	$O(n/\ell)$	$\Omega(n)$	$(\lambda, 1/2)$	$\Omega(n)$

Fig. 2. A table of bounds for cuckoo hashing parameters where (λ, ϵ)-robustness means that any adversary running in probabilistic $\mathsf{poly}(\lambda)$ time cannot cause a construction failure with probability greater than ϵ.

that the number of hash functions and query overhead is $O(\sqrt{\log(1/\epsilon)/\log n})$. We will assume $\epsilon \leq 1/n$ through the rest of the section for convenience.

For any target failure probability $\epsilon \leq 1/n$, our construction requires quadratically smaller query overhead than any prior known scheme. To date, the best query overhead achievable was $O(\log(1/\epsilon)/\log n)$ of cuckoo hashing schemes instantiated with large stashes [7] or larger entries [45]. We also prove matching lower bounds showing that our construction is optimal and provides the smallest query overhead across all possible instantiations using the four considered parameters. Our results and comparisons to prior work can be found in Fig. 1.

Robust Cuckoo Hashing. We also study the best query overhead achievable for robust cuckoo hashing. We say cuckoo hashing is (λ, ϵ)-robust if any adversary running in $\mathsf{poly}(\lambda)$ time cannot find an input set that will incur a construction failure with probability greater than ϵ. We present a $(\lambda, \mathsf{negl}(\lambda))$-robust construction with $k = O(f(\lambda)\log\lambda)$ hash functions, for any super-constant function $f(\lambda) = \omega(1)$, with $b = O(n)$ entries of size $\ell = 1$ and no stash, $s = 0$. Therefore, our construction has query overhead $O(f(\lambda)\log\lambda)$. For polynomial time adversaries with $\lambda = n$, the resulting query overhead is essentially $\tilde{O}(\log n)$.

We also prove matching lower bounds showing our construction is optimal. If we restrict ourselves to sub-linear query overhead constructions with sub-linear sized entries and stash, $s = o(n)$ and $\ell = o(n)$, we show that the number of hash functions must be $\omega(\log\lambda)$. The above also shows that the only way to obtain sub-linear query overhead is using a large number of hash functions. For example, any instantiation with $k = O(\log\lambda)$ requires that $s+\ell = \Omega(n)$ meaning that query overhead is linear. All our results are summarized in Fig. 2.

Applications. Using our new cuckoo hashing constructions with large number of hash functions, we present improved constructions for several primitives:

- *Probabilistic Batch Codes (PBC).* PBCs are a primitive that aim to encode a database D of n entries into m buckets such that any subset of q entries may be retrieved efficiently by accessing at most t codewords from each bucket. The total number of codewords is denoted by N and the goal is to maximize the rate n/N and to keep the buckets m as close to q as possible. Utilizing our efficient cuckoo hashing scheme, we obtain a PBC with rate $O(\sqrt{\lambda/\log\log n})$, $m = O(q)$ and $t = 1$ with error probability $2^{-\lambda}$. Our construction has quadratically better rate than prior provable PBCs.
- *Robust PBCs.* We also initiate the study of *robust PBCs* where the subset of q entries may be chosen by an adversary with knowledge of the system's randomness. By leveraging our robust cuckoo hashing constructions, we obtain

robust PBCs with rate $O(\log \lambda)$ while ensuring that a PPT adversary cannot find an erring input except with probability $\mathsf{negl}(\lambda)$. To our knowledge, this is the most efficient explicit robust PBC to date. All prior perfect PBCs with zero error are either less efficient or are non-explicit.

- *Single-Query to Batch PIR.* Private information retrieval (PIR) considers the setting where a client wishes to privately retrieve an entry from an array stored on a server. Batch PIR is the extension where the client wishes to retrieve a subset of q entries at once. A standard way to build batch PIR is to compose a single-query PIR with a (probabilistic) batch code (see [2, 39]). To our knowledge, these compositions are the most concretely efficient ways to build batch PIRs to date. Using our new PBCs, we obtain a more asymptotically efficient blackbox reduction from single-query PIR to batch PIR.

- *Re-usable Batch PIR.* We also consider re-usable batch PIR where the server must efficiently handle multiple sequential queries. The standard reduction from single-query to batch PIR requires the server to encode a database using a PBC where the construction failure probability becomes the error probability. In the case of multiple queries (i.e. re-usable protocols), the hash functions must be made public to all parties. As a result, adversarially chosen queries can be made to fail with very high probability. To solve this problem, we utilize robust PBCs to construct a re-usable batch PIR that guarantees a PPT adversary will be unable to find erring query subsets.

- *Other Applications.* We also show that our new cuckoo hashing schemes may also be applied to improve other primitives including private set intersection, encrypted search, vector oblivious linear evaluation and batch PIR with private preprocessing.

1.2   Related Works

Cuckoo Hashing Variants. Following the seminal work of Pagh and Rodler [52], there have been many follow-up works studying cuckoo hashing. We will focus on the variants that enable negligible failure probability. Cuckoo hashing where entries can store $\ell > 1$ items was studied in [23, 41, 45]. A variant of cuckoo hashing with an overflow stash that may store $s \geq 1$ items was studied in [7, 41, 45]. Finally, cuckoo hashing with $k > 2$ hash functions was studied in [22, 28].

Cuckoo Hashing in Cryptography. Many prior works have relied heavily upon cuckoo hashing to build many primitives including private information retrieval (PIR) [1, 2, 20], private set intersection (PSI) [14, 15, 24, 47, 57–59], symmetric searchable encryption (SSE) [11, 55], oblivious RAMs [5, 33, 37, 53], history-independent data structures [49] and hardness-preserving reductions [10]. We also point readers to references therein for more prior works.

Adversarial Robustness. Similar notions of adversarial robustness has been studied in prior works outside of cuckoo hashing where it is assumed the adversary has knowledge of the system's randomness. Some examples of prior works include sketching [36, 46], streaming [9], probabilitic data structures [18, 50] and property-preserving hash functions [12, 27, 38].

Other Hashing Schemes. We note that there are other schemes beyond cuckoo hashing to obtain efficient allocations. For example, the "power-of-two" choice paradigm inserts items into the least loaded of two bins [8,64]. A variant with a stash to obtain negligible failure was presented in [54]. Examples of other schemes include simple tabulation [62] and multi-dimensional balanced allocations [6].

2   Technical Overview

In this section, we present a technical overview for our improved cuckoo hashing constructions. To start, we consider a failed modification that provides insights into cuckoo hashing failures. Equipped with these insights, we derive both our improved constructions and matching lower bounds.

Insights from a Failed Construction. A standard instantiation of cuckoo hashing used in cryptography including oblivious RAM [5,53] and encrypted search [55] uses a stash of size $s = O(1 + \log(1/\epsilon)/\log n)$, $k = 2$ hash functions and $b = O(n)$ entries of size $\ell = 1$ to obtain ϵ failure probability. A straightforward modification may be to try and recursively apply cuckoo hashing on the overflow items in the stash of logarithmic size. In particular, we can try to build a second cuckoo hashing table with $b = O(n)$ entries of size $\ell = 1$ and $k = 2$ hash functions for all items in the stash. This seems like a simpler task as there are only a logarithmic number of items to place in a table with $O(n)$ entries. If the resulting stash becomes zero, we would make the query overhead to be $O(1)$ as only $2k$ locations need to be checked. Even if the resulting stash was smaller, we could apply this technique recursively to obtain smaller query overhead. Unfortunately, this approach is unsuccessful as the second table also requires the stash size to be $s = O(1 + \log(1/\epsilon)/\log n)$ if we re-do the failure analysis in [7].

However, we develop the following insights from the failed construction. The failure of cuckoo hashing seems to be fairly localized and only depend on a small sets of items. We observe that handling the $O(1 + \log(1/\epsilon)/\log n)$ overflow items in the second table required preparing for a similar number of overflows as the first table with n items. On the positive side, once a cuckoo hashing construction can handle overflows for a small set of items, it seems that this will scale to a large set of items easily. In other words, if one designs a cuckoo hashing scheme that can handle small sets of items, that scheme should also be able to handle larger sets of items. We see this as the first table requires the same asymptotic stash size for n items as the second table for a logarithmic number of items. We rely on these insights for our constructions and lower bounds.

Our Improved Construction. To obtain our improved construction, we will heavily utilize our observation that cuckoo hashing failures are very local to sets of small sizes. We need to find a way to ensure that small sets of items will not cause significant overflows requiring large entries or stashes. One way to do this is to split the table of b entries into k disjoint sub-table of b/k entries. Each of the k hash functions will be used to pick a random entry from each of the k sub-tables. Using the approach, we deterministically guarantee that any set of

$k\ell$ items will never cause an overflow. In the worst case, all $k\ell$ items will hash to the same k entries. However, there are $k\ell$ locations to allocate all $k\ell$ items.

By considering larger values of k and/or ℓ, we could increase the size of the sets that are handled deterministically by disjoint sub-tables. To figure out which is the better choice, we consider one more item that needs to be allocated even if the prior k items were allocated to the same k entries. This item would cause an overflow only if it was also allocated to the same k entries that occurs with probability at most $(1/(b/k))^k = (k/b)^k$ that decreases exponentially for larger values of k. Therefore, a promising approach seems to be use k disjoint sub-tables along with a larger number of hash functions k.

To analyze the failure probability of our new construction, we utilize prior connections (used in [7,28] for example) between the cuckoo hashing and matchings in biparite graphs. At a high level, we construct a bipartite graph with n left nodes representing the n inserted items and $b\ell + s$ right nodes representing table locations in the b entries of size ℓ and the stash. There is an edge if and only if an item may be allocated to the potential location as denoted by the k hash functions. We note that each left node has degree exactly $k\ell + s$ corresponding to the k assigned entries by the k hash functions and the overflow stash. Finally, we note that there exists an allocation of the n items as long as there exist a perfect left matching in the bipartite graph. To analyze the existence of a perfect left matching, we utilize Hall's Theorem that states such a perfect left matching exists if and only if every the neighborhood of every subset of left nodes contains at least as many right nodes. Using this analysis, we are able to show that $k = O(1 + \sqrt{\log(1/\epsilon)/\log n})$ hash functions, $b = O(n)$ entries of size $\ell = 1$ and no stash $s = 0$ is sufficient to obtain ϵ failure probability. As a result, this construction has quadratically smaller query overhead than prior instantiations.

We also note that prior work by Fotakis *et al.* [28] had studied cuckoo hashing with many hash functions. However, they considered a single shared table where each of the k hash functions picks any of the b entries at random. Their analysis showed that $k = O(1 + \log(1/\epsilon)/\log n)$ hash functions were required that we will later show is necessary for a single shared table.

Deriving a Lower Bound. Next, we attempt to derive a lower bound using the observation that it seems equally challenging to handle a small number of items as it is to handle a large number of items. By looking at a small number of items, we can prove a very simple lower bound. Consider any instantiation with $k \geq 1$ hash functions, $\ell \geq 1$ entry sizes, $b = O(n)$ entries and a overflow stash of $s \geq 0$ items. First, we consider the case where we consider k disjoint sub-tables as done in our construction. We analyze the probability that $k\ell + s + 1$ items are allocated to the same k entries. This would mean that $s + 1$ items are assigned to the stash that would incur a construction failure. After doing exercises in probability, one can obtain the following lower bound of $k^2\ell + ks = \Omega(\log(1/\epsilon)/\log n)$. Immediately, we see that our above construction with $k = O(\sqrt{\log(1/\epsilon)/\log n})$ hash functions and $\ell = 1$ and $s = 0$ is optimal.

Finally, we can also see that it is critical to utilize disjoint sub-tables to systematically handle smaller sets of items. By re-doing the above analysis for a single shared table where the k hash functions pick any of the b entries at random, we can immediately obtain the lower bound $k = \Omega(\log(1/\epsilon)/\log n)$ when $b = O(n)$ and $s = \ell = O(1)$. In other words, the analysis in [28] for the same setting of a single, shared table is optimal.

Extending to Robustness. Lastly, we extend our results to the case of robust cuckoo hashing where an adversary may have knowledge of the underlying randomness and hash functions used in the cuckoo hashing scheme. In particular, we want cuckoo hashing instantiations with small failure even if the adversary chooses bad input sets using the hash functions.

For our construction, we use the same insights to use a large number of hash functions k along with k disjoint sub-tables. We modify the analysis for robustness. We start with an adversary that is limited to at most Q evaluations of the underlying hash functions. Without loss of generality, we also assume the n submitted items by the adversary were also evaluated meaning at most $Q+n$ hash evaluations are performed. Afterwards, we consider the same bipartite graph where the left nodes consists of the at most $Q + n$ items for which the adversary knows the hash evaluations. Using a similar analysis, we analyze the probability that any subset of left nodes would violate the requirements of Hall's theorem. We get that $k = O(\log(Q/\epsilon))$ hash functions is sufficient to obtain ϵ failure probability when $b = O(n)$, $\ell = 1$ and $s = 0$. For poly(λ) time adversaries, we extend this to show that $k = O(f(\lambda) \log \lambda + \log(1/\epsilon))$, for any $f(n) = \omega(1)$, suffices to obtain ϵ failure probability. In other words, there exists a robust cuckoo hashing instantiation with roughly logarithmic query overhead.

One may notice that the above analysis may seem too pessimistic. It computes the probability whether there exists a subset amongst the $Q+n$ items that would violate Hall's theorem. However, finding such a violating set is non-trivial and may not be efficiently computable by an adversary. Nevertheless, we show that this construction is optimal by presenting a matching query overhead lower bound $k = \omega(\log \lambda)$ for robust cuckoo hashing against poly(λ) adversaries. To do this, we show it suffices to consider an adversary that simply attempts to find a set of n items that all allocate into the first half of each of the k disjoint sub-tables. Restricting to sub-linear query overhead with sub-linear sized entries and stashes, $\ell = o(n)$ and $s = o(n)$, we show that $k = \omega(\log \lambda)$ hash functions is necessary. In other words, if the number of hash functions is even slightly smaller at $k = O(\log n)$, then it must be that $\ell + s = \Omega(n)$ meaning that query overhead must be linear. Therefore, the only way to obtain efficient query overhead for robust cuckoo hashing is a large number of hash functions.

3   Definitions

3.1   Random Hash Functions

We start by presenting definitions of the various random hash functions that may be utilized by our cuckoo hashing instantiations.

Definition 1 (t-Wise Independent Hash Functions). *Let $\mathcal{H}$ be a family of hash functions where $H : \mathcal{D} \to \mathcal{R}$ for every hash function $H \in \mathcal{H}$. $\mathcal{H}$ is a t-wise independent hash family if, for any distinct $x_1, \ldots, x_t \in \mathcal{D}$ and any $y_1, \ldots, y_t \in \mathcal{R}$, the following is true:*

$$\Pr[H(x_1) = y_1, \ldots, H(x_t) = y_t] = |\mathcal{R}|^{-t}.$$

Next, we define a variant of hash families that behave like a t-wise independent hash family on every set of t inputs except with probability ϵ. In other words, we can treat such hash families as t-wise independence except with probability ϵ over the choice of the hash function (not the input set).

Definition 2 ((t, ϵ)-Wise Independent Hash Functions). *Let $\mathcal{H}$ be a family of hash functions where $H : \mathcal{D} \to \mathcal{R}$ for every hash function $H \in \mathcal{H}$. $\mathcal{H}$ is a (t, ϵ)-wise independent hash family if, for any distinct $S = \{x_1, \ldots, x_t\} \in \mathcal{D}$ and any $y_1, \ldots, y_t \in \mathcal{R}$, the following is true:*

– *There exists an event E_S such that $\Pr[\overline{E_S}] \leq \epsilon$.*
– *$\Pr[H(x_1) = y_1, \ldots, H(x_t) = y_t : E_S] = |\mathcal{R}|^{-t}$.*

These weaker variants of hash functions have been studied in the past (such as [7,51]). It has been shown they can be constructed using lower independence hash functions and faster evaluation. Regardless for both t-wise and (t, ϵ)-wise, for usable regimes of ϵ, independent hash functions require $\Omega(t)$ storage to represent a random hash function from the hash family.

The cost of storage for explicit random hash functions is large. Instead, we can resort to cryptographic assumptions to obtain random functions. The above definition of (t, ϵ)-wise independent hash functions considers the failure event E_S from a statistical viewpoint. Instead, we could also consider computational assumptions where we can use pseudorandom functions (PRFs) that are indistinguishable from random functions and may be represented succinctly.

Definition 3 (Pseudorandom Functions). *For a security parameter λ, a deterministic function $F : \{0,1\}^s \times \{0,1\}^n \to \{0,1\}^m$ is a λ-PRF if:*

– *Given any $k \in \{0,1\}^s$ and $x \in \{0,1\}^n$, there exists a polynomial time algorithm A to compute $F(k,x)$.*
– *For any PPT adversary A, $\left|\Pr\left[A^{F(k,\cdot)}(1^\lambda) = 1\right] - \Pr\left[A^{R(\cdot)}(1^\lambda) = 1\right]\right| \leq \mathsf{negl}(\lambda)$ where k is drawn randomly from $\{0,1\}^s$ and R is a random function from $\{0,1\}^n \to \{0,1\}^m$.*

We note that PRFs can be viewed as $(\mathsf{poly}(\lambda), \mathsf{negl}(\lambda))$-wise independent hash functions against all PPT adversaries. For $t = \mathsf{poly}(\lambda)$, a λ-PRF is a $(t, \mathsf{negl}(\lambda))$-wise independent hash function in the view of a PPT adversary. This is stronger as it applies to any $t = \mathsf{poly}(\lambda)$ as opposed to a fixed t.

Finally, we can also consider the ideal random oracle model (ROM) where there is an oracle $\mathcal{O}$ that always output random values $\mathcal{O}(x)$ for each input x. For any repeated inputs, $\mathcal{O}$ returns the same consistent output.

Definition 4 (Random Oracle Model). *In the random oracle model (ROM), there exists an oracle $\mathcal{O}$ such that for new input x, $\mathcal{O}(x)$ is uniformly random. For any repeated input, the same output $\mathcal{O}(x)$ is returned.*

Choosing the Hash Function. Throughout our work, we will assume that the hash function outputs are random. To do this, we can choose to instantiate our hash functions using any of the above options. The main differences are that t-wise and (t, ϵ)-wise independence require larger storage while PRFs and ROM require stronger underlying assumptions. In any of our results, we can switch between the above choices using different assumptions and storage costs.

3.2   Hashing Schemes

We start by defining the notion of hashing schemes. At a high level, the goal of a hashing scheme is to take n identifier-value pairs $\{(\mathsf{id}_1, v_1), \ldots, (\mathsf{id}_n, v_n)\}$ with n distinct identifiers from a potentially large identifier universe U^{id} and allocate them into a hash table T whose size depends only on n and not the universe size $|U^{\mathsf{id}}|$. Throughout the rest of our work, we will refer to an identifier-value pair (id, v) as an *item*. Furthermore, the hash table T should enable efficient queries for any identifier $\mathsf{id} \in U^{\mathsf{id}}$. We will focus on the setting of constructing hash tables from an input data set as this closely corresponds to the usage of cuckoo hashing in cryptography.

Definition 5 (Hashing Schemes). *A hashing scheme for size n, identifier universe U^{id} and value universe U^V consists of the following efficient algorithms:*

- *$\mathcal{H} \leftarrow \mathsf{Sample}(1^\lambda)$: A sampling algorithm that is given a security parameter λ as input and returns a set of one or more hash functions H.*
- *$T \leftarrow \mathsf{Construct}(H, X)$: A construct algorithm that is given the set of hash functions $\mathcal{H}$ and a set $X = \{(\mathsf{id}_1, v_1), \ldots, (\mathsf{id}_n, v_n)\} \subseteq U^{\mathsf{id}} \times U^V$ of items such that $\mathsf{id}_i \neq \mathsf{id}_j$ for all $i \neq j \in [n]$ and returns a hash table T allocating X or $\perp$ otherwise.*
- *$v \leftarrow \mathsf{Query}(H, T, \mathsf{id})$: A query algorithm that is given the set of hash functions $\mathcal{H}$, the hash table T and an identifier id and returns a value v if $(\mathsf{id}, v) \in X$ or $\perp$ otherwise.*

As mentioned earlier, we consider $\mathsf{Construct}$ that enables a hashing scheme to get all items X that need to be allocated at once. We choose to focus on this setting as it more closely aligns to the usage of cuckoo hashing in cryptographic applications where one party encodes their entire input using cuckoo hashing.

Next, we move onto the definition of error probabilities for hashing schemes. We will focus on the notion of *construction error probabilities* that measures the probability that a set X of identifier-value pairs cannot be constructed into a hash table according to the public parameters and the sampled set of hash functions over the randomness of the sampling and construct algorithms. We emphasize that this definition assumes that the input set X is chosen independent of the sampled hash functions (see Sect. 3.3 for stronger definitions).

Definition 6 (Construction Error Probability). *A hashing scheme for size n, identifier universe U^{id} and value universe U^V has construction error probability ϵ if, for any set of items $X = \{(id_1, v_1), \ldots, (id_n, v_n)\} \subseteq U^{id} \times U^V$ such that $id_i \neq id_j$ for all $i \neq j \in [n]$, the following holds:*

$$\Pr[\mathsf{Construct}(H, X) = \bot : H \leftarrow \mathsf{Sample}(1^\lambda)] \leq \epsilon.$$

In cryptography, the typical requirement for ϵ would be to be negligible in the input size n. However, in many constructions, cuckoo hashing is used as a sub-system on a smaller subset of the input size (for example, subsets of $\log n$ size). For these settings, ϵ is still required to be negligible in n even though the cuckoo hashing scheme considers significantly less than n items. Therefore, the above definition considers generic error probability ϵ as there are various settings where the error probability may need to be much smaller than negligible.

Throughout our paper, we will consider *perfect construction algorithms*. A perfect construction algorithm will always be able to find a successful allocation for the input set X if at least one such allocation exists. The main benefit of perfect construction algorithms is that construction failures only occur if the set of sampled hash functions $\mathcal{H}$ does not emit a proper allocation for the input set X. Even with this restriction, we obtain asymptotically optimal query overhead that match our lower bounds. We formally define these algorithms below:

Definition 7 (Perfect Construction Algorithms). *A hashing scheme for size n, identifier universe U^{id} and value universe U^V has a perfect construction algorithm $\mathsf{Construct}$ if, for any set of items $X = \{(id_1, v_1), \ldots, (id_n, v_n)\} \subseteq U^{id} \times U^V$ such that $id_i \neq id_j$ for all $i \neq j \in [n]$, the following holds:*

$$\Pr\left[\mathsf{Construct}(\mathcal{H}, X) \neq \bot : \begin{array}{l} \mathcal{H} \leftarrow \mathsf{Sample}(1^\lambda) \\ \exists T \text{ a successful allocation of } X \text{ according to } \mathcal{H} \end{array}\right] = 1.$$

Next, we also consider query error probability. Throughout our work, we will only consider hashing schemes with zero query error probability. In other words, if the construction algorithm succeeds, every query will always be correct.

Definition 8 (Query Error Probability). *A hashing scheme for size n, identifier universe U^{id} and value universe U^V has query error probability ϵ_q if, for any set of items $X = \{(id_1, v_1), \ldots, (id_n, v_n)\} \subseteq U^{id} \times U^V$ such that $id_i \neq id_j$ for all $i \neq j \in [n]$ and for any query $id \in U^{id}$,*

$$\Pr\left[\mathsf{Query}(\mathcal{H}, T, id) \neq v_{id} : \begin{array}{l} \mathcal{H} \leftarrow \mathsf{Sample}(1^\lambda) \\ T \leftarrow \mathsf{Construct}(\mathcal{H}, X), T \neq \bot \end{array}\right] \leq \epsilon_q$$

where $v_{id} = v_q$ if $id = id_q$ or $v_{id} = \bot$ otherwise.

3.3 Robust Hashing Schemes

In the prior section, we defined the construction error probability with respect to input sets X of identifier-value pairs that are chosen independently of the sampled hash functions. We define the notion of adversarially robust hashing schemes where an adversary is given the sampled hash functions $\mathcal{H}$ and aims to produce a set X of identifier-value pairs that will fail to allocate.

Definition 9 (((Q, ϵ)-Robust Hashing Schemes). *A hashing scheme for size* n, *security parameter* λ, *identifier universe* U^{id} *and value universe* U^V *is* (Q, ϵ)-*robust if, for any adversary* $\mathcal{A}$ *with running time* $O(Q)$, *the following holds:*

$$
\Pr\left[\mathsf{Construct}(\mathcal{H}, X) = \bot : \begin{array}{c} \mathcal{H} \leftarrow \mathsf{Sample}(1^\lambda) \\ X = \{(\mathsf{id}_1, v_1), \ldots, (\mathsf{id}_n, v_n)\} \leftarrow \mathcal{A}(\mathcal{H}) \\ \mathsf{id}_i \neq \mathsf{id}_j, \forall i \neq j \in [n] \end{array} \right] \leq \epsilon.
$$

Once again, we define robustness in a more fine-grained manner for adversaries running in expected time in $O(Q)$ and arbitrary probabilities ϵ. Typically, we would use $Q = \mathsf{poly}(n)$ to consider efficient adversaries and ϵ to be negligible in n. As mentioned earlier, cuckoo hashing may be used as a sub-system for smaller inputs where we have to consider adversaries with running time larger than polynomial in the cuckoo hashing size and probabilities smaller than negligible in the cuckoo hashing size.

Finally, we define strongly robust to consider all polynomial time adversaries.

Definition 10 (Strongly Robust Hashing Schemes). *A hashing scheme is* (λ, ϵ)-*strongly robust if, for any polynomial* $t(n, \lambda)$, *it is* (t, ϵ)-*robust.*

4   Cuckoo Hashing

In this section, we re-visit cuckoo hashing. We will consider a generic version of cuckoo hashing that considers arbitrary numbers of hash functions k, number of entries b, entry sizes ℓ and overflow stash sizes s. We will exclusively consider the variant of cuckoo hashing with k disjoint sub-tables of size b/k such that each item is assigned to one entry in each sub-table according to the k hash functions.

4.1   Description

Cuckoo hashing aims to allocate a set X of n identifier-value pairs into $k \geq 2$ disjoint sub-tables $T_1, \ldots, T_k$ with b/k entries in each table. For convenience, we will assume that k divides b evenly. Each entry is able to store at most $\ell \geq 1$ items. The hash table may also consist of an overflow stash that may be able to store at most $s \geq 0$ items that were not allocated into any of the k tables.

Each identifier-value pair is mapped to a random entry in each of the k tables using k random hash functions, $(H_1, \ldots, H_k)$ such that $H_i : \{0, 1\}^* \to [b/k]$. For convenience, we can use a single hash function H that can simulate k hash functions by setting $H_i(\cdot) = H(i \,\|\, \cdot)$. Therefore, the Sample algorithm for cuckoo hashing simply samples a hash function H. See Sect. 3.1 for various choices of these random hash functions. Any identifier-value pair (id, v) is mapped to the $H_1(\mathsf{id})$-th entry of T_1, the $H_2(\mathsf{id})$-th entry of T_2 and so forth. The pair (id, v) is guaranteed to be stored in any of the k entries specified by $H_1, \ldots, H_k$ or the overflow stash. The Query algorithm checks all possible locations for the queried item including the k entries specified by $H_1, \ldots, H_k$ as well as the overflow stash. So, the query overhead is exactly $k\ell + s$. Furthermore, assuming the construction is successful, the query algorithm will never fail to provide the correct answer (i.e., the query error will always be 0). For the Construct algorithm, there are several options that we will outline later in Sect. 4.3 once we have defined the necessary graph terminology.

We also define the storage overhead describing the size of the resulting table. For our parameters, the storage overhead is $b\ell + s$ for the b entries and the stash.

Definition 11. *The cuckoo hashing scheme* CH(k, b, ℓ, s) *refers to the algorithm using k hash functions, b entries across k disjoint tables storing at most ℓ items and an overflow stash storing at most s items with* Sample *and* Query *as described above and any perfect construction algorithm* Construct *from Sect. 4.3. The query overhead is $k\ell + s$ and the storage overhead is $b\ell + s$.*

Discussion about Static Tables. Dynamic variants of cuckoo hashing enable inserting items into a table. We chose to study the static variant as insertions are not used in cryptographic applications. This is due to the fact that insertions are highly dependent on whether certain entries are populated or empty that is detrimental for privacy (see full version for further discussion).

Discussion about Non-Adaptive Querying. In our abstraction, we define the query overhead to be $k\ell + s$ that is total number of possible locations for any item. This is due to the fact that we assume non-adaptive querying where all possible locations for the queried item in one round. Instead, one could consider an adaptive approach where locations that are more likely to contain the queried item are retrieved first (such as non-stash locations). If the item is not found, the query algorithm can proceed with the remaining locations (such as stash locations). This approach has two downsides. First, the querier and cuckoo table storage provider are different parties. Therefore, the above adaptive query would require multiple roundtrips. Secondly, the querying algorithm reveals whether certain entries are populated or empty that is detrimental for privacy (similar to insertions). For these reasons, to our knowledge, all usages of cuckoo hashing in cryptography rely on non-adaptive querying with overhead $k\ell + s$. See the full version for more details about the problems with adaptive queries.

4.2 Cuckoo Bipartite Graphs

To be able to analyze cuckoo hashing, we define the notion of cuckoo bipartite graphs to accurately model the behavior of cuckoo hashing. The left vertex set will consist of the n items that should be allocated. The right vertex set represents all potential slots that an item can be stored. If a cuckoo hashing scheme has b entries each storing at most ℓ items and an stash storing at most s items, there will be $b\ell + s$ total right vertices. An edge between an item vertex v and an entry vertex v' means that the item may be allocated to the corresponding entry. As each item can be stored in at most k entries or one of the s slots in the stash, each left vertex will have degree exactly $k\ell + s$. Each of the k hash functions will be a random function, so the above description can be modelled as drawing randomly from a distribution of bipartite graphs that we define as follows.

Definition 12. *Let $\mathcal{G}(n, k, b, \ell, s)$ denote the distribution of random bipartite cuckoo graph generated in the following way:*

- *The left vertex set contains n vertices representing the n items to be allocated.*
- *The right vertex set contains $b\ell + s$ vertices that are partitioned into $b + 1$ sub-groups in the following way. The first b sub-groups contain ℓ vertices while the last sub-group S contains s vertices corresponding to b entries and the stash respectively. We further group together the first b sub-groups (i.e., b entries) as follows. The group B_1 consists of the first b/k sub-groups, the group B_2 consists of the second b/k sub-groups and so forth to obtain k groups $B_1, \ldots, B_k$ that each correspond to a disjoint table of b/k entries each.*
- *Each left vertex is connected to $k\ell + s$ vertices by choosing a uniformly random sub-group from each group $B_1, \ldots, B_k$ and adding an edge to all ℓ vertices in each of the k chosen sub-groups corresponding to picking a random entry of size ℓ from each of the k tables. Finally, each vertex is assigned to all s vertices in S corresponding to the stash.*

The major benefit of modelling cuckoo hashing in this manner is that we can directly map item allocations to matchings in the bipartite graph. In particular, we can choose an edge between an item and entry slot if and only if that item was allocated into that entry's slot. Therefore, we can see that any successful allocation directly corresponds to a *left perfect matching* meaning that there exists a set of edges where each left vertex is adjacent to exactly one edge and each right vertex is adjacent to at most one edge. Throughout our paper, our proofs will consist of analyzing the probability of the existence of left perfect matchings for various parameter settings for random graphs drawn from the distribution $\mathcal{G}(n, k, b, \ell, s)$.

As a note, the entire bipartite graph may be quite large but does not need to be represented explicitly. In particular, the graph can be fully re-created using only the parameters (n, k, b, ℓ, s), the hash functions $H_1, \ldots, H_k$ and the set of items to be allocated. Additionally, we note that any allocation of n items can be stored using $O(n)$ storage of the corresponding edges.

4.3   Perfect Construction Algorithms

Finally, we present perfect construction algorithms. We note that one can rephrase a construction algorithm as finding a perfect left matching. This amounts to finding an alternating path from each node to a free right vertex (i.e., empty entry). To do this, we could perform breadth first search (BFS) starting from each of the n left vertices that guarantees a perfect construction algorithm. One can also use the more popular random walk algorithm. However, random walks are not guaranteed to terminate. To make it a perfect construction algorithm, one can bound the random walk to $O(n)$ length before running BFS. Finally, one can also use the local search allocation algorithm of [40] that runs in $O(nk)$ time with high probability. In the full version [66], we describe the construction algorithms in detail and analyze the running times. As most prior works consider constant k, we modify their proofs to obtain bounds for super-constant values of k.

5   Cuckoo Hashing with Negligible Failure

We will systematically study cuckoo hashing across all four parameters of the number of hash functions k, the number of entries b, entry size ℓ and stash size s. As our major contribution, we show that using large k with k disjoint sub-tables obtains the smallest query overhead for any failure probability ϵ. We present our construction with large k below:

Theorem 1. *If H is a (nk)-wise independent hash function, then the cuckoo hashing scheme* $\mathsf{CH}(k, b, \ell, s)$ *has construction failure probability at most ϵ when $k = O(1 + \sqrt{\log(1/\epsilon)/\log n})$, $\ell = 1$, $s = 0$ and $b = O(n)$. The query overhead is $O(1 + \sqrt{\log(1/\epsilon)/\log n})$ and storage overhead is $O(n)$.*

We can compare with the best query overhead achievable by prior schemes. Cuckoo hashing with a stash requires $s = O(\log(1/\epsilon)/\log n)$ [7] and cuckoo hashing with larger entries requires $\ell = O(\log(1/\epsilon/\log n)$ [45]. The resulting query overheads of these instantiations is $O(\log(1/\epsilon)/\log n)$ that is quadratically larger than the our construction for any $\epsilon \leq 1/n$. This includes negligible failure probability $\epsilon = \mathsf{negl}(n)$ that is typically required in cryptography. For convenience, we will consider $\epsilon \leq 1/n$ for the remainder of this section so that we can write $k = O(1 + \sqrt{\log(1/\epsilon)/\log n}) = O(\sqrt{\log(1/\epsilon)/\log n})$.

We will also show that all these parameter dependencies are asymptotically optimal by proving a matching lower bound in Sect. 5.3. In other words, we show that the gap in efficiency is inherent and cuckoo hashing with more hash functions and disjoint sub-tables is the most efficient approach.

Different Parameter Sets. In our construction, we considered extreme parameter regime of large k. One could also consider parameters that aim to balance between various parameter choices using our techniques. However, it turns out that the best choice remains using large values of k. We refer to Sect. 5.3 for further discussions using the lower bound.

Different Values for b. Throughout our work, we considered fixed values of $b = O(n/\ell)$. We did this to ensure that we restricted to constructions with $O(n)$ storage overhead. For completeness, we present tight bounds for parameters with large b in the full version [66]. We show one must have $b = \Omega(1/\epsilon)$ when considering parameters with small number of hash functions k, entry sizes ℓ and stashes s. For small $\epsilon < 1/n$, this would result in super-linear storage overhead.

Choice of Random Hash Function. In our above results, we assumed that H is a (nk)-wise independent hash function. One could, instead, plug in a (nk, ϵ_H)-wise independent hash function and obtain similar results with construction failure probability increased by an additive ϵ_H factor. One could also use PRFs or random oracles for H requiring stronger assumptions.

5.1 Technical Lemmas

We start with a technical lemma that relates the existence of an allocation of n items to perfect left matchings in bipartite graphs. From there, we can utilize Hall's Theorem [35] to get a very simple characterization of when an allocation for any n items via cuckoo hashing exists. We abstract out these lemmas as we will re-use them when constructing robust cuckoo hashing in Sect. 6.1. We note similar analytical tools were used in the past (such as [7,28]).

For any subset of left nodes X, we denote the neighborhood $N(X)$ as the subset of all right nodes that are directly connected a left node in the set X. Using neighborhoods, we get the following characterization:

Lemma 1. *Consider any cuckoo hashing scheme* $\mathsf{CH}(k,b,\ell,s)$ *with a perfect insertion algorithm where H is a (qk)-wise independent hash function. Then, for any set S of q items, the construction failure probability is equal to the probability that there exists a subset of left vertices X such that $|N(X)| < |X|$ for a random graph drawn from the distribution $\mathcal{G}(q,k,b,\ell,s)$.*

Proof. As we consider cuckoo hashing schemes with perfect insertion algorithms, we know that if there exists a proper allocation that successfully allocates all q items, then the construction will be successful. Therefore, the cuckoo hashing scheme fails to insert if and only if no allocation fitting all the q items exists.

We can directly map a successful allocation of the q items to a perfect left matching in the corresponding cuckoo graph. Consider any cuckoo hashing scheme given q items to construct after fixing the hash function. Then, there exists a corresponding bipartite graph G in the support of the distribution $\mathcal{G}(q,k,b,\ell,s)$. There exists a correct allocation if and only if each of the q items is assigned uniquely to a bin or stash location. In other words, a correct allocation exists if and only if there exists a left perfect matching in G where the allocation of an item to a bin corresponds to an edge in the matching. By Hall's Theorem [35], no left perfect matching exists in a bipartite graph if and only if there exists some subset X of left vertices such that its neighbor vertex set is strictly smaller than X, that is, $|N(X)| < |X|$. □

Lemma 2. *Let $q,k,b,\ell \geq 1$ and $s \geq 0$ and consider the distribution of random bipartite cuckoo graphs $\mathcal{G}(q,k,b,\ell,s)$. The probability that there exists a subset X of left vertices of size t such that it has less than t neighbors, $|N(X)| < t$, for any $k\ell + s + 1 \leq t \leq \min\{q, b/2\}$ is at most*

$$\Pr[\exists X : |X| = t, |N(X)| < t] \leq \binom{q}{t} \cdot \binom{b}{\lfloor (t-s-1)/\ell \rfloor} \cdot \left(\frac{2(t-s-1)}{b\ell}\right)^{k \cdot t}.$$

For $t \leq k\ell + s$, the above probability is 0.

Proof. Fix any vertex set X of size t. For the case of $t \leq k\ell + s$, it is impossible to find a subset X since every left vertex has degree $k\ell + s$. Consider $t > k\ell + s$. We know that X immediately has s neighbors in the stash vertices. Therefore, X must have at most $t - s - 1$ neighbors outside of the stash vertices. So, X must connect to at most $\lfloor (t - s - 1)/\ell \rfloor$ bins that consist of ℓ vertices each. Suppose that these bins are chosen such that a_1 come from the first table, a_2 come from the second table and so forth such that $a_1 + \ldots + a_k \leq \lfloor (t - s - 1)/\ell \rfloor$. We note that the total number of ways to choose these bins is at most $\binom{b}{\lfloor (t-s-1)/\ell \rfloor}$. For any vertex $x \in X$, the probability that the k random hash functions pick edges in these bins is at most $(a_1 k/b) \cdots (a_k k/b)$ as there are b/k bins in each of the tables. Therefore, we get the probability upper bound of

$$\Pr[|N(X)| < t] \leq \binom{b}{a_1 + \ldots + a_k} \cdot \left(\prod_{i=1}^{k} \frac{a_i k}{b} \right)^t \leq \binom{b}{\lfloor (t - s - 1)/\ell \rfloor} \cdot \left(\prod_{i=1}^{k} \frac{a_i k}{b} \right)^t$$

since $t \leq b/2$. The right side of the equation is maximized when the product $a_1 \cdots a_k$ is maximized. Therefore, we get an upper bound by setting each $a_i = \lceil (t - s - 1)/(\ell k) \rceil \leq 2(t - s - 1)/(\ell k)$. Plugging this in as well as taking a final Union Bound over all $\binom{q}{t}$ choices of X we get the following upper bound

$$\Pr[\exists X : |X| = t, |N(X)| < t] \leq \binom{q}{t} \cdot \binom{b}{\lfloor (t - s - 1)/\ell \rfloor} \cdot \left(\frac{2(t - s - 1)}{b\ell} \right)^{k \cdot t}$$

to complete the proof.   □

5.2   Our Construction

Next, we prove that our cuckoo hashing construction with more hash functions (i.e., larger k) results in quadratically smaller query overhead. Recall our construction from Theorem 1 uses $k = O(\sqrt{\log(1/\epsilon)/\log n})$ hash functions, $b = O(n)$ entries of size $\ell = 1$ and no stash, $s = 0$.

Proof of Theorem 1. To prove this, we will leverage Lemma 1 that provides a tight characterization between a successful insertion in cuckoo hashing and left perfect matchings in random bipartite graphs. We start from the probability upper bound from Lemma 2 and plug in our values of k, ℓ, b and s to get the following for values of $k + 1 \leq t \leq n$ assuming $b \geq 2n$:

$$\Pr[\exists X : |X| = t, |N(X)| < |X|] \leq \binom{n}{t} \cdot \binom{b}{t - 1} \cdot \left(\frac{2(t - 1)}{b} \right)^{k \cdot t}$$

$$\leq \left(\frac{en}{t} \right)^t \cdot \left(\frac{eb}{t - 1} \right)^{t - 1} \cdot \left(\frac{2(t - 1)}{b} \right)^{k \cdot t}$$

$$\leq \left(\frac{eb}{t - 1} \right)^{2(t - 1)} \cdot \left(\frac{eb}{t - 1} \right)^{t - 1} \cdot \left(\frac{2(t - 1)}{b} \right)^{k \cdot t}$$

$$\leq (2e)^{kt} \cdot \left(\frac{t - 1}{b} \right)^{(k - 3)t}.$$

Note that we used Stirling's approximation that $\binom{x}{y} \leq (ex/y)^y$ in the second inequality. For the second and third inequality, we use that $n \leq b$ and $t \geq k \geq 3$. Note, if we set $b \geq (2e)^5 \cdot n$ appropriately and assume that $k \geq 4$, we get the following inequality:

$$\Pr[\exists X : |X| = t, |N(X)| < |X|] \leq \left(\frac{t-1}{2n}\right)^{(k-3)(t-1)}.$$

We break the analysis into two parts depending on the value of t. We start with the case that for the smaller range $k + 1 \leq t \leq n^{0.75}$. As a result, we can upper bound the probability by $(1/n^{0.25})^{(k-3)(k-1)}$. For the other case, assume that $n^{0.75} < t \leq n$. Therefore, we can upper bound the probability by $(1/2)^{(k-3)\cdot(n^{0.75})} \leq (1/n)^{(k-3)(n^{0.75}/\log n)}$. Finally, we know that

$$\max\{(1/n^{0.25})^{(k-3)(k-1)}, (1/n)^{(k-3)(n^{0.75}/\log n)}\} \leq (1/n^{0.25})^{(k-3)(k-1)}$$

for sufficiently large n. Applying a Union Bound for all values of $k + 1 \leq t \leq n$, we get that

$$\Pr[\exists X : |N(X)| < |X|] \leq (n - k) \cdot (1/n^{0.25})^{(k-3)(k-1)} = (1/n)^{\Theta(k^2)}.$$

We solve the following inequality to get a lower bound on k based on ϵ

$$(1/n)^{\Theta(k^2)} \leq \epsilon \implies k = O(\sqrt{\log(1/\epsilon)/\log n}).$$

As k must be at least 4, we get that $k = O(1 + \sqrt{\log(1/\epsilon)/\log n})$.   □

Necessity of k Disjoint Tables. Prior work [28] aimed to analyze the failure probabilities for cuckoo hashing with arbitrary k hash functions when $b = O(n)$, $\ell = 1$ and $s = 0$. Rephrasing their results, the prior result required $k = O(\log(1/\epsilon)/\log n)$ that is quadratically higher than our result. The core difference between the two results is that our work analyzes the setting where there are k disjoint sub-tables while the prior result [28] considered a single shared table. With k disjoint sub-tables, we guarantee that any set of at most k left vertices will have k distinct neighbors. Therefore, our analysis only needs to consider left vertex sets of larger size. For the setting where each of the k hash functions may choose any of the b entries in a single shared table, we note a result similar to ours is impossible. Consider the setting of left vertex sets of size 2, $|X| = 2$. The probability that all $2k$ hash function evaluations resulting in the same entry is already $(1/b)^{2k}$. If $b = \Theta(n)$, this immediately implies that $k = \Omega(\log(1/\epsilon)/\log n)$ for failure probability ϵ. By avoiding this case using disjoint tables, we are able to obtain the same failure probability with a quadratically smaller number of hash functions.

5.3   Lower Bounds

Next, we prove lower bounds on the best possible parameters obtainable in cuckoo hashing. In particular, we will show that the chosen parameters in Theorem 1 are asymptotically optimal for failure probabilities ϵ.

Our lower bounds do not make any assumptions on the construction algorithm used. In other words, the results apply regardless of the construction algorithm (such as whether they are perfect or whether they are efficient). Additionally, we only make the assumption that the underlying hash function H is a $(k\ell + s + 1)$-wise independent hash function to mimic standard cuckoo hashing constructions.

At a high level, we will present a simple attack relying on the insight that cuckoo hashing failure is hard for small sets. By the structure of our cuckoo hashing scheme using k disjoint sub-tables and a stash, we know that any set of $k\ell + s$ will be allocated correctly. Our goal is to simply pick a random set of $k\ell + s + 1$ items and lower bound the probability that all these items will hash into the exact same k entries. In this case, the construction algorithm would fail.

Theorem 2. *Let $k \geq 1$, $\ell \geq 1$, $1 \leq b \leq n^{O(1)}$, $s \geq 0$ such that $k\ell + s + 1 \leq n$. The failure probability of $\mathsf{CH}(k, b, \ell, s)$ cuckoo hashing scheme where H is a $(k\ell + s + 1)$-wise independent hash function satisfies the following:*

$$k^2\ell + ks = \Omega(\log(1/\epsilon)/\log(n)). \tag{1}$$

Proof. We know that the first item will be successfully inserted. Consider the k distinct locations that were chosen for the first item denoted by S. Suppose that another $k\ell + s$ different items were also assigned to the same k locations or a subset of the k locations. In this case, there are $k\ell + s + 1$ items that must be assigned to $k\ell + s$ locations in the k entries and the stash that is impossible and will result in an insertion failure regardless of the choice of the insertion algorithm. To obtain our lower bound, we simply lower bound this probability. Consider the other $k\ell + s$ to be inserted. Each of these $k\ell + s$ items will pick k locations uniformly at random from each of the k disjoint tables. Therefore, the probability that the k choices will be a subset of S is $(k/b)^k$. As all choices are independent, the probability that this is true for all $k\ell$ items is $(k/b)^{k(k\ell+s)}$. Therefore, the probability of an insertion failure is at least $\epsilon \geq (k/b)^{k^2\ell+ks}$. Applying logs to both sides gets that $k^2\ell + ks \geq \log(1/\epsilon)/\log(b/k)$. Using the fact that $b \leq n^{O(1)}$ and $k \geq 1$, we get that $\log(b/k) = O(\log n)$. Therefore, we get the inequality $k^2\ell + ks = \Omega(\log(1/\epsilon)/\log n)$ completing the proof.   □

Theorem 3. *Let $1 \leq k \leq n^{2/5}$ and $1 \leq \ell \leq n^{2/5}$. Suppose that the cuckoo hashing scheme $\mathsf{CH}(k, b, \ell, s)$ where H is a $(k\ell + s + 1)$-wise independent hash function. Then, the following are true:*

- *If $\ell = O(1), b = n^{O(1)}$ and $s = O(1)$, then $k = \Omega(\sqrt{\log(1/\epsilon)/\log n})$.*
- *If $k = O(1), b = n^{O(1)}$ and $s = O(1)$, then $\ell = \Omega(\log(1/\epsilon)/\log n)$.*
- *If $k = O(1), b = n^{O(1)}$ and $\ell = O(1)$, then $s = \Omega(\log(1/\epsilon)/\log n)$.*

Proof. Plug in the values for each parameter regime into Theorem 2.   □

We note that the above corollary shows that our construction in Theorem 1 is asymptotically optimal. Furthermore, we also show that the constructions of large stashes [7] and large entries [45] are also tight.

Balancing Parameters. For our constructions, we only consider the extreme regime of large k while the other parameters s and ℓ remain very small. Instead, we could consider trying to balance the parameters to obtain more efficient constructions. Using Theorem 2, we can see why the choice of large k is the most efficient approach. Recall that the query overhead is $O(k\ell + s)$. However, it must be that $k^2\ell + ks = \Omega(\log(1/\epsilon)/\log n)$. In other words, we want to minimize $k\ell + s$ while satisfying the above condition. It is not hard to see that the optimal approach is to set $k = O(\sqrt{\log(1/\epsilon)/\log n})$ as we do in our constructions.

Implications to Other Primitives. As our lower bounds do not make any assumptions on the construction algorithm, our results can apply to other hashing schemes other than cuckoo hashing. For example, we can consider multiple-choice allocation schemes [8,64] where items are allocated to multiple entries and placed into the entry with the current smallest load. In general, one can apply our lower bounds to any scheme that limits the candidate entries for any item to at most k locations and can set an upper limit on the number of items per entry to ℓ.

Our lower bounds apply to other primitives that heavily rely on cuckoo hashing techniques such as cuckoo filters [26] and oblivious key-value stores [31] that encode data using cuckoo hashing (see the full version [66] for more details).

Assumptions in Our Lower Bounds. In the above theorem, we made the assumptions that $k \leq n^{2/5}$ and $\ell \leq n^{2/5}$. We do not believe these limit the applicability of our lower bounds as, otherwise, the query overhead of cuckoo hashing will be too large. As query overhead is $O(k\ell + s)$, either condition being false immediately implies $\Omega(n^{2/5})$ query overhead that is impractical.

One or Two Hash Functions. These lower bounds match constructions for cuckoo hashing with large stashes [7] and entries [45] with $k = 2$. Our lower bound does not preclude obtaining the same results with $k = 1$. However, it turns out that $k \geq 2$ is necessary as one can use analysis from "balls-into-bins" analysis to show that $k = 1$ is impossible. For completeness, we include impossibility results for $k = 1$ in the full version of this paper [66].

Comparison with Prior Lower Bounds. We note that prior work [45] also proved lower bounds for constant values of s and ℓ and fixed $k = 2$. In particular, for $k = 2$, constant entry size $\ell \geq 1$, constant stash size $s \geq 0$, and $b = O(n/\ell)$, they proved that $\epsilon = \Omega(n^{-s-\ell})$. Our lower bounds improve upon this as we can consider arbitrary s and ℓ.

6 Robust Cuckoo Hashing

In this section, we study robust cuckoo hashing where the input set can be chosen by an adversary that is also given input to the hash function H. To model this, we consider the adversary having access to an oracle $\mathcal{O}$ for hash evaluations. We will present variants of cuckoo hashing that can still guarantee smaller construction failures even when the input set is chosen adversarially by efficient adversaries with knowledge of the randomness (that is, the hash function H). In particular, we study (λ, ϵ)-strong robustness where $\mathsf{poly}(\lambda)$ adversaries cannot find a failing input set except with probability ϵ.

6.1   Robustness Constructions

Recall that in the prior section, we required that $k = O(\sqrt{\log(1/\epsilon)/\log n})$ to obtain ϵ construction failure probabilities. We show that increasing the number of hash functions by a small amount suffices to obtain robustness. To analyze robust cuckoo hashing, we will consider a hash oracle $\mathcal{O}$ that may be queried by the adversary. We consider an adversary with running time Q that may query at most Q hash evaluations. Afterwards, we analyze the probability there exists a subset of n items amongst the Q queried items that would incur a failure under the hash functions. We will also show our choice of k is optimal in Sect. 6.2.

Lemma 3. *For any $0 < \epsilon < 1$, let $k = O(\log(Q/\epsilon))$, $s = 0$, $\ell = 1$, $b = \alpha n$ for some constant $\alpha \geq 1$. If H is a random hash function and for any $Q \geq n$, the cuckoo hashing scheme $\mathsf{CH}(k, b, \ell, s)$ is (Q, ϵ)-robust.*

Proof. We will consider hash oracle $\mathcal{O}$ that returns $\mathcal{O}(x) = (H_1(x), \ldots, H_k(x))$ on input x. That is, a single oracle query will return the outputs of all k hash functions. Without loss of generality, we will assume that if the adversary returns a set S of n items, then the adversary has computed $H_1(s), \ldots, H_k(s)$ for all $s \in S$. This only increases the number of queries of the adversary by at most $n \leq Q$ for a total of at most $2Q$ hash queries. Let U be the set of all items that the adversary has queried to the hash functions. That is, if $u \in U$, then the adversary knows the values $\mathcal{O}(u) = (H_1(u), \ldots, H_k(u))$. We know that $|U| \leq 2Q$.

To show that the scheme is robust, we will show that a random graph drawn from the distribution $\mathcal{G}(|U|, k, b, \ell, s)$ does not contain any set of left vertices X such that $|X| \leq n$ and $|N(X)| < |X|$. By proving no such set of left vertices X exists, it will be impossible for the adversary to identify any input set that would cause the cuckoo hashing scheme $\mathsf{CH}(k, b, \ell, s)$ to fail.

By applying Lemma 2 with our parameters of $s = 0$, $\ell = 1$ and $b = \Theta(n)$, we get the following for probability upper bounds for the values of $k + 1 \leq t \leq n$:

$$\Pr[\exists X : |X| = t, |N(X)| < |X|] \leq \binom{|U|}{t} \cdot \binom{b}{t-1} \cdot \left(\frac{2(t-1)}{b}\right)^{k \cdot t}$$

$$\leq \left(\frac{2eQ}{t}\right)^t \cdot \left(\frac{eb}{t-1}\right)^{t-1} \cdot \left(\frac{2(t-1)}{b}\right)^{k \cdot t}$$

$$\leq (2Q)^t \cdot (2e)^{k} \cdot \left(\frac{t-1}{b}\right)^{(k-3)t}$$

$$\leq (2Q)^t \cdot \left(\frac{t-1}{2n}\right)^{(k-3)t}$$

$$\leq \left(\frac{t^{k-3} \cdot (2Q)}{(2n)^{k-3}}\right)^t.$$

Since $k + 1 \leq t \leq n$, we can upper bound the above probability by

$$\Pr[\exists X : |X| = t, |N(X)| < |X|] \leq \left(\frac{2Q}{2^{k-3}}\right)^{k+1}.$$

As this needs to be at most ϵ, we can derive the following inequalities

$$\left(\frac{2Q}{2^{k-3}}\right)^{k+1} \leq \epsilon \implies (k+1)(k-3-\log(2Q)) \geq \log(1/\epsilon).$$

If we set $k = O(\log(Q/\epsilon))$, we get the desired bound that completes the proof.

□

Next, we show that this may be extended to the notion of strongly robust that applies to any polynomial time adversaries.

Theorem 4. *For security parameter λ and error $0 < \epsilon < 1$, let $k = O(f(\lambda) + \log(1/\epsilon))$ for some function $f(\lambda) = \omega(\log \lambda)$, $s = 0$, $\ell = 1$ and $b = \alpha n$ for some constant $\alpha \geq 1$. If H is a random hash function, then the cuckoo hashing scheme $\mathsf{CH}(k, b, \ell, s)$ is (λ, ϵ)-strongly robust.*

Proof. The adversary runs in polynomial time and, more importantly, makes at most $\mathsf{poly}(\lambda)$ queries to the hash oracle. We fix $Q = 2^{\omega(\log \lambda)} = \lambda^{\omega(1)}$ to be any function super-polynomial in λ and, thus, Q is larger than the running time of any $\mathsf{poly}(\lambda)$ time algorithm. By applying Lemma 3 with $Q = 2^{\omega(\log \lambda)}$ to obtain robustness except with probability ϵ, we get that $k = O(\log(Q/\epsilon)) = \omega(\log \lambda) + O(\log(1/\epsilon))$ suffices to complete the proof.   □

Finally, we can apply our above theorem for standard values of $\lambda = n$ and $\epsilon = n^{f(n)}$ for any $f(n) = \omega(1)$ that is negligible in n to get the following corollary.

Corollary 1. *Let $\epsilon = n^{f(n)}$ for any function $f(n) = \omega(1)$. Let $k = O(f(n) \log n)$, $s = 0$, $\ell = 1$ and $b = \alpha n$ for some constant $\alpha \geq 1$. Then, the cuckoo hashing scheme $\mathsf{CH}(k, b, \ell, s)$ is $(n, \mathsf{negl}(n))$-strongly robust.*

Instantiation of Hash Function. In this section, we made the assumption that the hash function H is indistinguishable from random and that H may also be queried by the adversary. We leave it as an open problem to consider hash functions from other assumptions.

6.2   Lower Bounds for Robustness

In this section, we prove lower bounds for the required parameters to ensure that cuckoo hashing is robust. We will show that our construction in Theorem 4 is asymptotically optimal in the regime of sub-linear stash and entry sizes. First, we will assume that the stash and entry size are sub-linear, $s = o(n)$ and $\ell = o(n)$, and that the number of entries is $b = O(n/\ell)$. We prove our lower bound with respect to $(\lambda, 1/2)$-robustness. As we are proving lower bounds, our result also applies to smaller, more reasonable, failure probabilities such as negligible failure.

At a high level, our lower bound consists of a simple adversary. The goal of the adversary is to find a set of n items that are allocated into the first half of each of the k disjoint sub-tables. By analyzing the probability of finding such an input set, we obtain a matching lower bound.

Theorem 5. *Suppose that $k, \ell \geq 1$ and $s \geq 0$ such that $\ell = o(n)$, $s = o(n)$ and $b = O(n/\ell)$. If H is a random hash function and the cuckoo hashing scheme $\mathsf{CH}(k, b, \ell, s)$ is $(\lambda, 1/2)$-robust for $\lambda \geq n$, then it must be that $k = \omega(\log \lambda)$.*

Proof. To prove this, we assume a contradiction that $k = O(\log \lambda)$ and we will show that there exists a $\mathsf{poly}(\lambda)$ time adversary that outputs a set S of n items to insert such that all n items hash to the same $n/(2\ell)$ bins except with at most $1/2$ probability. In this case, we note that the $n/(2\ell)$ bins and the stash can store at most $n/(2\ell) \cdot \ell + s = n/2 + o(n) \leq 3n/4$ that cannot store all n items in the set S that would complete the proof.

To construct our adversary, we will leverage that $k = O(\log \lambda)$. Assuming that H is a random hash function, we know that for any input x,

$$\Pr[H_1(x) \leq n/(2\ell k) \wedge \ldots \wedge H_k(x) \leq n/(2\ell k)] = \left(\frac{n/(2\ell k)}{b/k}\right)^k = \left(\frac{n}{2\ell b}\right)^k.$$

As $b = O(n/\ell)$, there exists some constant $\alpha > 0$ such that $b \leq \alpha n/(2\ell)$ meaning that $(n/(2\ell b))^k \leq (1/\alpha)^k$. Suppose that $k \leq c \log_\alpha n$ for some constant $c > 0$ since $k = O(\log n)$ and α is a positive constant, then we know that $\Pr[H_1(x) \leq n/(2\ell k) \wedge \ldots \wedge H_k(x) \leq n/(2\ell k)] \leq (1/\alpha)^k \leq 1/\lambda^c$. Next, we construct the following adversary using the above probability that aims to find a set S of n items such that all items satisfy the above property in the following way:

Adversary $\mathcal{A}(H_1, \ldots, H_k)$:

1. Let $S \leftarrow \emptyset$.
2. Let $\mathsf{cnt} \leftarrow 0$.
3. While $|S| < n$ and $\mathsf{cnt} \leq \lambda^{c+2}$:
   (a) If $H_1(\mathsf{cnt}) \leq n/(2\ell k) \wedge \ldots \wedge H_k(\mathsf{cnt}) \leq n/(2\ell k)$, set $S \leftarrow S \cup \{\mathsf{cnt}\}$.
   (b) Set $\mathsf{cnt} \leftarrow \mathsf{cnt} + 1$.
4. If $|S| < n$, return $\bot$.
5. Return S as the n items to insert.

We analyze a slight modification of the adversary that executes all λ^{c+2} iterations before returning. Let $X_i = 1$ if and only if the i-th iteration (when $\mathsf{cnt} = i$) succeeds in being placed into S. Let $X = X_1 + \ldots + X_{n^{c+2}}$. We know that the adversary outputs $\bot$ if and only if $X < n$. Note that $\Pr[X_i = 1] = 1/\lambda^c$, so $\mu = \mathbb{E}[X] = \lambda^{c+2}/\lambda^c = \lambda^2$. As each X_i is independent due to the random hash functions and $\lambda \geq n$, we can apply Chernoff's Bound to get that $\Pr[X < n] \leq \Pr[X < \lambda^2/2] = \Pr[X < \mu/2] \leq 2^{-\Theta(\lambda^2)}$. In other words, the adversary outputs the desired set S with probability at least $1 - 2^{-\Theta(\lambda^2)} > 1/2$ as required. Note the adversary is polynomial time as each of the λ^{c+2} iteration requires $O(k) = O(\log \lambda)$ time by assumption. Therefore, the adversary's running time is $O(\lambda^{c+2} \log \lambda)$ that is polynomial in λ as c is a positive constant. $\square$

The above shows that if we consider sub-linear s and t, then it must be that $k = \omega(\log \lambda)$. We can consider the contrapositive of the above theorem. Suppose that $k = O(\log \lambda)$ that is slightly smaller than the lower bound above.

PBC	Size (N)	Buckets (b)	Explicit?	Error
Subset [39]	$O(n)$	$q^{O(1)}$	✓	0
Expander Graphs [39]	$O(n \log n)$	$O(q)$	×	0
Balbuena Graphs [63]	$O(n)$	$O(q^3)$	✓	0
Pung [3]	$4.5n$	$9q$	✓	$2^{-20}*$
3-way Cuckoo Hashing [2]	$3n$	$1.5q$	✓	$2^{-40}*$
Our Work	$O(n \cdot \sqrt{\lambda / \log \log n})$	$O(q)$	✓	$2^{-\lambda}$

Fig. 3. A comparison table of prior PBC constructions with $t = 1$. Constructions with only experimental evaluations are marked with asterisks(*).

Assuming that $b = O(n/\ell)$ to ensure storage of the hash table remains linear, this immediately implies that either $s = \Omega(n)$ or $\ell = \Omega(n)$. In other words, either the stash or entry must be able to store almost all n inserted items and the resulting query overhead is $O(n)$. These parameter sets are essentially trivial as it is equivalent to retrieving the entire cuckoo hash table.

Theorem 6. *Suppose that $k, \ell \geq 1$ and $s \geq 0$ such that $k = O(\log \lambda)$ and $b = O(n/\ell)$. If the cuckoo hashing scheme $\mathsf{CH}(k, b, \ell, s)$ is $(\lambda, 1/2)$-robust for $\lambda \geq n$, then it must be that $s + \ell = \Omega(n)$ with query overhead $\Omega(n)$.*

7 Batch Codes

7.1 Probabilistic Batch Codes

The notion of batch codes was introduced by Ishai, Kushilevitz, Ostrovsky and Sahai [39]. At a high level, the goal of a batch code is to distribute a database of n entries into m buckets such that any subset of q entries may be retrieved by querying at most t codewords from each of the m buckets. The size parameter N denotes the total codewords across all m buckets and we denote the rate of the batch code by n/N. When constructing batch codes, the goal is to maximize the rate n/N while keeping the number of buckets m as close to q as possible, ideally $m = O(q)$, and minimizing t, ideally $t = 1$.

Leveraging our results in cuckoo hashing, we will present improved constructions for batch codes. In particular, we will present a probabilistic batch code (PBC) with quadratically smaller rate compared to prior works (see Fig. 3).

Probabilistic batch codes (PBCs) were introduced by Angel, Chen, Laine and Setty [2]. Unlike batch codes, PBCs are able to err on a subset of potential queries with the goal of obtaining more efficient parameters. To date, state-of-the-art PBCs are built from either directly adapting batch codes with zero error or constructions whose error probabilities have only been experimentally evaluated. By adapting our analysis of cuckoo hashing, we are able to construct a PBC with provable error probabilities that have better parameters than all prior works. To our knowledge, our batch code either has quadratically better rate or cubically smaller number of buckets than the best prior construction (including non-explicit ones). We point readers to Fig. 3 for more details.

Before we present our constructions, we formally define the notion of PBCs. Note, we will construct *systematic* or *replication* batch codes where each codeword must be one of the n entries in the database.

Definition 13 (Probabilistic Batch Codes). *A (n, N, q, m, t)-systematic PBC consists of the following four efficient algorithms:*

- prms ← Init(1^λ): *The initialization algorithm takes the security parameter and outputs parameters.*
- $(C_1, \ldots, C_m)$ ← Encode(prms, DB): *The encode algorithm takes a database DB of n entries as input and outputs m buckets such that the total number of codewords is at most N. Furthermore, each $(C_i)_j$ must be one of the n database entries in the set $\{DB_i\}_{i \in [n]}$.*
- $(S_1, \ldots, S_m)$ ← Schedule(prms, Q): *The schedule algorithm takes as input a query Q of q distinct elements and outputs a schedule of the indices of each bucket to read such that each $|S_i| \leq t$.*
- A ← Decode(prms, Q, $(C_1)_{i \in S_1}, \ldots, (C_m)_{i \in S_m}$): *The decode algorithm takes as input a query Q of q distinct elements in $[n]$ and the scheduled indices of each code and outputs the queried database entries.*

Furthermore, the PBC has error at most ϵ if, for all database DB and queries Q of q distinct elements, the following holds:

$$
\Pr\left[R \neq (DB_i)_{i \in Q} : \begin{array}{l} \text{prms} \leftarrow \text{Init}(1^\lambda) \\ (C_1, \ldots, C_m) \leftarrow \text{Encode}(\text{prms}, \text{DB}) \\ (S_1, \ldots, S_m) \leftarrow \text{Schedule}(\text{prms}, Q) \\ R \leftarrow \text{Decode}(\text{prms}, Q, (C_1)_{i \in S_1}, \ldots, (C_m)_{i \in S_m}) \end{array} \right] \leq \epsilon.
$$

As a note, we only consider PBCs whose queries do not contain duplicate entries (i.e., each query is to a unique entry). In most practical applications, the querier can handle duplicate entries in the scheduling algorithm by removing duplicates and then duplicating them in the decode algorithm. This assumption is not limiting in most practical applications such as PIR (see Sect. 8.1).

Next, we show that a cuckoo hashing scheme may be used to construct PBCs with similar parameters. We note that a similar reduction was informally shown in [2] previously. We present the proof in the full version [66].

Lemma 4. *If there exists a cuckoo hashing $CH(k, b, \ell, s)$ for q items that has failure probability at most ϵ, then there exists a $(n, (k + \lceil s/\ell \rceil)n, q, b + \lceil s/\ell \rceil, \ell)$-systematic PBC for a universe U of size n with error at most ϵ.*

As an immediate consequence of this lemma, one can immediately construct a PBC with negligible error using prior cuckoo hashing with large stash results [7, 41,45]. For example, one can obtain a $(n, O(n\lambda), q, O(q), 1)$-PBC with error $2^{-\lambda}$. We omit the proof as it was already known to exist in folklore.

Using the above reduction, we can construct an efficient PBC with rate $1/O(\sqrt{\lambda/\log\log n})$ from Theorem 1 with quadratically better rate than prior constructions with $b = O(q)$. We point to Fig. 3 for further comparisons. The proof may be found in the full version [66].

PBC	Size (N)	Buckets (b)	Explicit?
Subset [39]	$O(n)$	$q^{O(1)}$	✓
Expander Graphs [39]	$O(n \log n)$	$O(q)$	✗
Balbuena Graphs [63]	$O(n)$	$O(q^3)$	✓
Our Work	$O(n \cdot (f(n) + \lambda)), f(n) = \omega(\log n)$	$O(q)$	✓

Fig. 4. A comparison table of $(2^{-\lambda})$-robust PBC constructions with $t = 1$.

Theorem 7. *For all $1 \leq q \leq n$, there exists a (n, N, q, b, ℓ)-systematic PBC with at most $2^{-\lambda}$ error where $b = O(q)$, $\ell = 1$ and $N = O(n \cdot \sqrt{\lambda / \log \log n})$.*

7.2   Robust Probabilistic Batch Codes

We introduce the notion of adversarially robust PBCs that lies in between batch codes with zero error and PBCs with negligible error. Robust PBCs guarantee that even, if there does exist an input that would err, no PPT adversary will be able to find the erring input with non-negligible probability. In other words, robust PBCs provide stronger guarantees compared to normal PBCs. However, we note that batch codes with zero error are robust PBCs as no erring input exists. We show this relaxation enables more efficient explicit constructions. We will also show later in Sect. 8.2 that robust PBCs may be useful for batch PIR schemes where hash functions must be made public.

We present robust PBC constructions from robust cuckoo hashing. Our robust PBC is the best explicit construction with $O(q)$ buckets. To our knowledge, all other robust PBCs come directly from zero-error batch codes. Furthermore, the most efficient zero-error schemes from expander graphs are non-explicit. See Fig. 4 for more comparison. At a high level, the PPT adversary is given the parameters of the scheme (including the hash functions) and the database. The goal of the adversary is to produce a subset Q that cannot be correctly decoded by the scheme.

For our construction, we will simply use a robust cuckoo hashing scheme and follow the exact same approach as Lemma 4. The additional work needed is to show that one can build robust PBCs using robust cuckoo hashing. The proof of the following may be found in the full version.

Theorem 8. *For all $1 \leq q \leq n$ and any function $f(n) = \omega(\log n)$, there exists a (n, N, q, b, ℓ)-systematic PBC that is $(2^{-\lambda})$-robust where $b = O(q)$, $\ell = 1$ and $N = O(n \cdot (f(n) + \lambda))$.*

8   Private Information Retrieval

Private information retrieval (PIR) [16,17] is a powerful cryptographic primitive that considers the setting where a client wishes to retrieve the i-th entry from a server hold an n-entry database. For privacy, the server should not learn the index i that is queried by the client. In this section, we present improved constructions of PIR utilizing our new cuckoo hashing instantiations.

Explicit Batch PIR	Computational Time	Queries	Error
Subset [39]	$O(n)$	$q^{O(1)}$	0
Balbuena Graphs [63]	$O(n)$	$O(q^3)$	0
Pung [3]	$4.5n$	$9q$	2^{-20*}
3-way Cuckoo Hashing [2]	$3n$	$1.5q$	2^{-40*}
Our Work	$O(n \cdot \sqrt{\lambda/\log\log n})$	$O(q)$	$2^{-\lambda}$

Fig. 5. A comparison table of explicit blackbox single to batch PIR transformations. The error probability considers queries chosen independently of the hash functions. Asterisks (*) denote experimental error probabilities.

8.1 Single-Query to Batch PIR Reductions

Batch PIR is an extension of standard PIR where the client wishes to perform *batch queries*. The client holds a set $Q \subseteq [n]$ of q queries and wishes to return the i-th entry for all $i \in Q$. We present a formal definition in the full version.

We consider the problem of taking a PIR construction for a single-query and efficiently transform it to a batch-query PIR. The standard way to do this is to utilize a (probabilistic) batch code to encode the database to reduce the problem of a batch PIR query of size q to executing q single-query PIR schemes (for example, see [2,39]). To our knowledge, these approaches result in the most efficient blackbox transformations that do not make any other assumptions about the single query PIR scheme.

We present an improved transformation that leverages our explicit batch codes in Theorem 7. Using our cuckoo hashing based PBC with more hash functions, we obtain a transformation with quadratically smaller computational overhead compared to prior works. The proof can be found in the full version [66]. We point readers to Fig. 5 for a comparison.

Theorem 9. *Suppose there exists a single-query PIR scheme Π with communication $c(n)$ and computation $O(n)$. Then, there exists a batch-query PIR scheme for q queries with communication $q \cdot c(O(n\sqrt{\lambda/\log\log n}/q + \lambda))$ and computation $O(n \cdot \sqrt{\lambda/\log\log n})$ with error probability $2^{-\lambda}$.*

Note, if we plug in any of the asymptotically optimal single-query PIR schemes with $\tilde{O}(\log n)$ communication and $O(n)$ communication, the resulting batch PIR for q queries has communication $\tilde{O}(q\log(n\lambda))$ and computation $O(n\sqrt{\lambda/\log\log n})$ that is nearly optimal except for the $\tilde{O}(\sqrt{\lambda/\log\log n})$ multiplicative factor in computation.

We note that optimal batch PIR constructions were shown by Groth, Kiayias and Lipmaa [34] by utilizing the properties of a specific single-query PIR scheme of Gentry and Ramzan [32] that is not a blackbox transformation. While asymptotically optimal, more recent PIR schemes based on lattice-based assumptions are more practically efficient (such as [1,44,48]). The most practical batch PIR schemes do make use of the above transformation using PBCs and state-of-the-art lattice-based PIR constructions (for example, see [2]).

Explicit Batch PIR	Computational Time	Queries	Adversarial Error
Subset [39]	$O(n)$	$q^{O(1)}$	0
Balbuena Graphs [63]	$O(n)$	$O(q^3)$	0
Pung [3]	$4.5n$	$9q$	$\geq 1/2$
3-way Cuckoo Hashing [2]	$3n$	$1.5q$	$\geq 1/2$
Our Work	$O(n \cdot (f(n) + \lambda)), f(n) = \omega(\log n)$	$O(q)$	$2^{-\lambda}$

Fig. 6. A comparison table of explicit re-usable batch PIR schemes.

8.2   Adversarial Error for Re-usable Batch PIR

In the above batch PIR constructions and prior works [2,3] that utilize PBCs instantiated through cuckoo hashing, the error probabilities are considered for batch queries chosen independent of the hash functions. In practice, this means that the fresh random hash functions are chosen for each batch query issued by the client to ensure that query indices are independent. Unfortunately, this requires the server to constantly generate new databases for each set of hash functions and, thus, each query perform by a client.

In an ideal setting, we would like for the server to generate a single database that could be re-used for multiple batch PIR queries. Ideally, a set of public hash functions are sampled once and made available to all clients that may issue batch PIR queries. The server would only need to encode the database according the hash functions a single time. Unfortunately, this means that an adversary during the challenge phase may be able to use the hash functions to pick two batch PIR queries such that only one of the two batch PIR queries would fail to allocate. For example, the PPT adversary could choose to employ any of the attacks that we outline in Theorem 5 using knowledge of the hash functions. If the adversary's view is different for queries that would fail to allocate correctly, the resulting batch PIR scheme would be insecure.

To our knowledge, we are unaware of any batch PIR scheme that enable re-usability. Prior works [2,3] build batch PIR from PBCs with non-robust cuckoo hashing where adversaries could employ the attack above. To solve this problem, we introduce the notion of *adversarial error* where the PPT adversary can aim to choose inputs that will cause query errors and/or failure to encode databases. By using our robust PBC schemes, we can guarantee that error remain low even with databases and batch queries chosen by a PPT adversary. In other words, we can construct *re-usable batch PIR* schemes with low error rates even with adversarially chosen inputs. We point readers to Fig. 6 for comparisons with prior works. See the formal definition in the full version.

We follow the same approach of building batch PIR using a PBC and a single query PIR. The main difference is that we utilize a robust PBC. Given a robust PBC, if there exists a PPT adversary that can find erring queries, the same adversary can also find subsets of items that cannot be decoded by the robust PBC. Our approach results in the most efficient explicit construction with negligible adversarial error for the regime of $O(q)$ queries. The next theorem follows in a similar way as Theorem 9 using our robust PBC from Theorem 8.

Theorem 10. *Suppose there exists a single-query PIR scheme Π with communication $c(n)$ and computation $O(n)$. Fix any $k = \omega(\log n) + \lambda$. Then, there exists a batch-query PIR scheme for q queries with communication $q \cdot c(O(nk/q + \lambda))$ and computation $O(nk)$ with adversarial error $2^{-\lambda}$.*

9 Other Applications

Private Set Intersection. PSI considers the problem where two parties have input sets X and Y and wish to compute the intersection $X \cap Y$. PSI rely on cuckoo hashing to enable the two parties to co-ordinate similar data into buckets. Prior works [14, 19, 58, 60] utilized experimental evaluation to pick parameters for a cuckoo hashing and chose $k \in \{2, 3\}$ hash functions with $b = O(n)$ entries of size $\ell = 1$ and no stash, $s = 0$. Plugging in our constructions, one can obtain provable failure at the cost of larger asymptotic overhead.

Encrypted Search. Recent work [55] employed cuckoo hashing for volume-hiding multi-maps where the goal is to hide the size of value tuples. Using our scheme with $k = O(1 + \sqrt{\log(1/\epsilon)/\log n})$, $b = O(n)$, $\ell = 1$ and $s = 0$, we can reduce the query overhead quadratically (see the full version for more details).

Vector Oblivious Linear Evaluation (VOLE). Cuckoo hashing is also used in a recent VOLE protocol [65]. At a very high level, the construction utilizes batch codes in a similar way as batch PIR. As a result, the improvements to batch codes in Sect. 7 can be plugged into their construction to obtain improvements.

Batch PIR with Private Preprocessing. A recent work [67] presented a blackbox construction for batch PIR with private preprocessing using a standard single-query PIR with private preprocessing and any batch code. Using our batch codes from Sect. 7, we immediately obtain improved blackbox reductions.

10 Conclusions

In this paper, we present new cuckoo hashing constructions that obtain better trade-offs between query overhead and failure probabilities. For any fixed failure probability, the query complexity of our new schemes are quadratically smaller than prior constructions. Furthermore, we define the notion of robust cuckoo hashing where the adversary has knowledge of the underlying hash functions. We show that we can extend our schemes with a large number of hash functions to obtain robustness while prior approaches cannot be extended except with linear query overhead. We also present matching lower bounds for all parameters. Finally, we obtain state-of-the-art constructions for probabilistic batch codes and blackbox reductions from single-query to batch PIR.

Acknowledgements. The author would like to thank Mo (Helen) Zhou for feedback on earlier manuscripts and Daniel Noble for pointing out an error and fix in a proof. This research was supported in part by the Algorand Centres of Excellence programme managed by Algorand Foundation. Any opinions, findings, and conclusions or recommendations expressed in this material are solely those of the authors.

References

1. Ali, A., et al.: Communication-computation trade-offs in PIR. In: 30th USENIX Security (2021)
2. Angel, S., Chen, H., Laine, K., Setty, S.: PIR with compressed queries and amortized query processing. In: 2018 IEEE S&P (2018)
3. Angel, S., Setty, S.: Unobservable communication over fully untrusted infrastructure. In: 12th USENIX OSDI (2016)
4. Arbitman, Y., Naor, M., Segev, G.: De-amortized cuckoo hashing: provable worst-case performance and experimental results. In: ICALP (2009)
5. Asharov, G., Komargodski, I., Lin, W.-K., Nayak, K., Peserico, E., Shi, E.: OptORAMa: optimal oblivious RAM. In: Canteaut, A., Ishai, Y. (eds.) EUROCRYPT 2020. LNCS, vol. 12106, pp. 403–432. Springer, Cham (2020). https://doi.org/10.1007/978-3-030-45724-2_14
6. Asharov, G., Naor, M., Segev, G., Shahaf, I.: Searchable symmetric encryption: optimal locality in linear space via two-dimensional balanced allocations. In: ACM STOC (2016)
7. Aumüller, M., Dietzfelbinger, M., Woelfel, P.: Explicit and efficient hash families suffice for cuckoo hashing with a stash. Algorithmica $70(3)$, 428–456 (2014)
8. Azar, Y., Broder, A.Z., Karlin, A.R., Upfal, E.: Balanced allocations. In: ACM Symposium on Theory of Computing (1994)
9. Ben-Eliezer, O., Jayaram, R., Woodruff, D.P., Yogev, E.: A framework for adversarially robust streaming algorithms. In: ACM PODS (2020)
10. Berman, I., Haitner, I., Komargodski, I., Naor, M.: Hardness-preserving reductions via cuckoo hashing. J. Cryptol. $32(2)$, 361–392 (2019)
11. Bossuat, A., Bost, R., Fouque, P.-A., Minaud, B., Reichle, M.: SSE and SSD: page-efficient searchable symmetric encryption. In: Malkin, T., Peikert, C. (eds.) CRYPTO 2021. LNCS, vol. 12827, pp. 157–184. Springer, Cham (2021). https://doi.org/10.1007/978-3-030-84252-9_6
12. Boyle, E., LaVigne, R., Vaikuntanathan, V.: Adversarially robust property-preserving hash functions. In: 10th Innovations in Theoretical Computer Science (2019)
13. Breslow, A.D., Zhang, D.P., Greathouse, J.L., Jayasena, N., Tullsen, D.M.: Horton tables: fast hash tables for in-memory data-intensive computing. In: 2016 USENIX Annual Technical Conference (2016)
14. Chen, H., Huang, Z., Laine, K., Rindal, P.: Labeled PSI from fully homomorphic encryption with malicious security. In: ACM CCS (2018)
15. Chen, H., Laine, K., Rindal, P.: Fast private set intersection from homomorphic encryption. In: ACM CCS (2017)
16. Chor, B., Gilboa, N.: Computationally private information retrieval. In: ACM Symposium on Theory of Computing (1997)
17. Chor, B., Kushilevitz, E., Goldreich, O., Sudan, M.: Private information retrieval. J. ACM 53, 68–73 (1998)
18. Clayton, D., Patton, C., Shrimpton, T.: Probabilistic data structures in adversarial environments. In: ACM CCS (2019)
19. Cong, K., et al.: Labeled psi from homomorphic encryption with reduced computation and communication. In: Proceedings of the 2021 ACM SIGSAC Conference on Computer and Communications Security, pp. 1135–1150 (2021)
20. Demmler, D., Rindal, P., Rosulek, M., Trieu, N.: PIR-PSI: scaling private contact discovery. Proc. Priv. Enh. Technol. $2018(4)$, 159–178 (2018)

21. Devroye, L., Morin, P.: Cuckoo hashing: further analysis. Inf. Process. Lett. **86**(4), 215–219 (2003)
22. Dietzfelbinger, M., Goerdt, A., Mitzenmacher, M., Montanari, A., Pagh, R., Rink, M.: Tight thresholds for cuckoo hashing via XORSAT. In: Abramsky, S., Gavoille, C., Kirchner, C., Meyer auf der Heide, F., Spirakis, P.G. (eds.) ICALP 2010. LNCS, vol. 6198, pp. 213–225. Springer, Heidelberg (2010). https://doi.org/10.1007/978-3-642-14165-2_19
23. Dietzfelbinger, M., Weidling, C.: Balanced allocation and dictionaries with tightly packed constant size bins. Theoret. Comput. Sci. **380**, 47–68 (2007)
24. Duong, T., Phan, D.H., Trieu, N.: Catalic: delegated PSI cardinality with applications to contact tracing. In: Moriai, S., Wang, H. (eds.) ASIACRYPT 2020. LNCS, vol. 12493, pp. 870–899. Springer, Cham (2020). https://doi.org/10.1007/978-3-030-64840-4_29
25. Fan, B., Andersen, D.G., Kaminsky, M.: MemC3: compact and concurrent Mem-Cache with dumber caching and smarter hashing. In: USENIX NSDI (2013)
26. Fan, B., Andersen, D.G., Kaminsky, M., Mitzenmacher, M.D.: Cuckoo filter: practically better than bloom. In: Proceedings of the 10th ACM International on Conference on emerging Networking Experiments and Technologies (2014)
27. Fleischhacker, N., Larsen, K.G., Simkin, M.: Property-preserving hash functions for hamming distance from standard assumptions. In: Dunkelman, O., Dziembowski, S. (eds.) EUROCRYPT 2022. LNCS, vol. 13276, pp. 764–781. Springer, Cham (2022). https://doi.org/10.1007/978-3-031-07085-3_26
28. Fotakis, D., Pagh, R., Sanders, P., Spirakis, P.: Space efficient hash tables with worst case constant access time. Theory Comput. Syst. **38**, 229–248 (2005)
29. Fountoulakis, N., Panagiotou, K., Steger, A.: On the insertion time of cuckoo hashing. SIAM J. Comput. **42**(6), 2156–2181 (2013)
30. Frieze, A., Melsted, P., Mitzenmacher, M.: An analysis of random-walk cuckoo hashing. In: Dinur, I., Jansen, K., Naor, J., Rolim, J. (eds.) APPROX/RANDOM -2009. LNCS, vol. 5687, pp. 490–503. Springer, Heidelberg (2009). https://doi.org/10.1007/978-3-642-03685-9_37
31. Garimella, G., Pinkas, B., Rosulek, M., Trieu, N., Yanai, A.: Oblivious key-value stores and amplification for private set intersection. In: Malkin, T., Peikert, C. (eds.) CRYPTO 2021, Part II. LNCS, vol. 12826, pp. 395–425. Springer, Cham (2021). https://doi.org/10.1007/978-3-030-84245-1_14
32. Gentry, C., Ramzan, Z.: Single-database private information retrieval with constant communication rate. In: Caires, L., Italiano, G.F., Monteiro, L., Palamidessi, C., Yung, M. (eds.) ICALP 2005. LNCS, vol. 3580, pp. 803–815. Springer, Heidelberg (2005). https://doi.org/10.1007/11523468_65
33. Goodrich, M.T., Mitzenmacher, M.: Privacy-preserving access of outsourced data via oblivious RAM simulation. In: Aceto, L., Henzinger, M., Sgall, J. (eds.) ICALP 2011. LNCS, vol. 6756, pp. 576–587. Springer, Heidelberg (2011). https://doi.org/10.1007/978-3-642-22012-8_46
34. Groth, J., Kiayias, A., Lipmaa, H.: Multi-query computationally-private information retrieval with constant communication rate. In: Nguyen, P.Q., Pointcheval, D. (eds.) PKC 2010. LNCS, vol. 6056, pp. 107–123. Springer, Heidelberg (2010). https://doi.org/10.1007/978-3-642-13013-7_7
35. Hall, P.: On representatives of subsets. In: Classic Papers in Combinatorics (1987)
36. Hardt, M., Woodruff, D.P.: How robust are linear sketches to adaptive inputs? In: ACM Symposium on Theory of Computing (2013)

37. Hemenway Falk, B., Noble, D., Ostrovsky, R.: Alibi: a flaw in cuckoo-hashing based hierarchical ORAM schemes and a solution. In: Canteaut, A., Standaert, F.-X. (eds.) EUROCRYPT 2021. LNCS, vol. 12698, pp. 338–369. Springer, Cham (2021). https://doi.org/10.1007/978-3-030-77883-5_12
38. Holmgren, J., Liu, M., Tyner, L., Wichs, D.: Nearly optimal property preserving hashing. Cryptology ePrint Archive (2022)
39. Ishai, Y., Kushilevitz, E., Ostrovsky, R., Sahai, A.: Batch codes and their applications. In: ACM Symposium on Theory of Computing (2004)
40. Khosla, M.: Balls into bins made faster. In: Bodlaender, H.L., Italiano, G.F. (eds.) ESA 2013. LNCS, vol. 8125, pp. 601–612. Springer, Heidelberg (2013). https://doi.org/10.1007/978-3-642-40450-4_51
41. Kirsch, A., Mitzenmacher, M., Wieder, U.: More robust hashing: Cuckoo hashing with a stash. SIAM J. Comput. $39(4)$, 1543–1561 (2010)
42. Kushilevitz, E., Lu, S., Ostrovsky, R.: On the (in) security of hash-based oblivious ram and a new balancing scheme. In: Proceedings of the Twenty-Third Annual ACM-SIAM Symposium on Discrete Algorithms (2012)
43. Kutzelnigg, R.: Bipartite random graphs and cuckoo hashing. Discrete Math. Theor. Comput. Sci. (2006)
44. Menon, S.J., Wu, D.J.: Spiral: fast, high-rate single-server PIR via FHE composition. Cryptology ePrint Archive (2022)
45. Minaud, B., Papamanthou, C.: Note on generalized cuckoo hashing with a stash. arXiv preprint arXiv:2010.01890 (2020)
46. Mironov, I., Naor, M., Segev, G.: Sketching in adversarial environments. SIAM J. Comput. $40(6)$, 1845–1870 (2011)
47. Mohassel, P., Rindal, P., Rosulek, M.: Fast database joins and PSI for secret shared data. In: ACM CCS (2020)
48. Mughees, M.H., Chen, H., Ren, L.: OnionPIR: response efficient single-server PIR. In: ACM CCS (2021)
49. Naor, M., Segev, G., Wieder, U.: History-independent cuckoo hashing. In: Aceto, L., Damgård, I., Goldberg, L.A., Halldórsson, M.M., Ingólfsdóttir, A., Walukiewicz, I. (eds.) ICALP 2008. LNCS, vol. 5126, pp. 631–642. Springer, Heidelberg (2008). https://doi.org/10.1007/978-3-540-70583-3_51
50. Naor, M., Yogev, E.: Bloom filters in adversarial environments. In: Gennaro, R., Robshaw, M. (eds.) CRYPTO 2015. LNCS, vol. 9216, pp. 565–584. Springer, Heidelberg (2015). https://doi.org/10.1007/978-3-662-48000-7_28
51. Pagh, A., Pagh, R.: Uniform hashing in constant time and optimal space. SIAM J. Comput. $38(1)$, 85–96 (2008)
52. Pagh, R., Rodler, F.F.: Cuckoo hashing. J. Algorithms 51, 122–144 (2004)
53. Patel, S., Persiano, G., Raykova, M., Yeo, K.: PanORAMa: oblivious RAM with logarithmic overhead. In: IEEE FOCS (2018)
54. Patel, S., Persiano, G., Yeo, K.: What storage access privacy is achievable with small overhead? In: ACM PODS (2019)
55. Patel, S., Persiano, G., Yeo, K., Yung, M.: Mitigating leakage in secure cloud-hosted data structures: Volume-hiding for multi-maps via hashing. In: CCS (2019)
56. Pinkas, B., Reinman, T.: Oblivious RAM revisited. In: Rabin, T. (ed.) CRYPTO 2010. LNCS, vol. 6223, pp. 502–519. Springer, Heidelberg (2010). https://doi.org/10.1007/978-3-642-14623-7_27
57. Pinkas, B., Rosulek, M., Trieu, N., Yanai, A.: PSI from PaXoS: fast, malicious private set intersection. In: Canteaut, A., Ishai, Y. (eds.) EUROCRYPT 2020. LNCS, vol. 12106, pp. 739–767. Springer, Cham (2020). https://doi.org/10.1007/978-3-030-45724-2_25

58. Pinkas, B., Schneider, T., Segev, G., Zohner, M.: Phasing: private set intersection using permutation-based hashing. In: USENIX Security Symposium (2015)
59. Pinkas, B., Schneider, T., Weinert, C., Wieder, U.: Efficient circuit-based PSI via cuckoo hashing. In: Nielsen, J.B., Rijmen, V. (eds.) EUROCRYPT 2018. LNCS, vol. 10822, pp. 125–157. Springer, Cham (2018). https://doi.org/10.1007/978-3-319-78372-7_5
60. Pinkas, B., Schneider, T., Zohner, M.: Scalable private set intersection based on OT extension. ACM Trans. Priv. Secur. (TOPS) 21(2), 1–35 (2018)
61. Polychroniou, O., Raghavan, A., Ross, K.A.: Rethinking SIMD vectorization for in-memory databases. In: ACM SIGMOD (2015)
62. Pătraşcu, M., Thorup, M.: The power of simple tabulation hashing. J. ACM (JACM) 59, 1–50 (2012)
63. Rawat, A.S., Song, Z., Dimakis, A.G., Gál, A.: Batch codes through dense graphs without short cycles. IEEE Trans. Inf. Theory 62, 1592–1604 (2016)
64. Richa, A.W., Mitzenmacher, M., Sitaraman, R.: The power of two random choices: a survey of techniques and results. Combinatorial Optimization (2001)
65. Schoppmann, P., Gascón, A., Reichert, L., Raykova, M.: Distributed Vector-OLE: improved constructions and implementation. In: Proceedings of the 2019 ACM SIGSAC Conference on Computer and Communications Security, pp. 1055–1072 (2019)
66. Yeo, K.: Cuckoo hashing in cryptography: optimal parameters, robustness and applications. Cryptology ePrint Archive, Paper 2022/1455 (2022). https://eprint.iacr.org/2022/1455
67. Yeo, K.: Lower bounds for (batch) PIR with private preprocessing. In: Hazay, C., Stam, M. (eds.) EUROCRYPT 2023, Part I. LNCS, vol. 14004, pp. 518–550. Springer, Cham (2023). https://doi.org/10.1007/978-3-031-30545-0_18
68. Zhang, K., Wang, K., Yuan, Y., Guo, L., Lee, R., Zhang, X.: Mega-KV: a case for GPUs to maximize the throughput of in-memory key-value stores. VLDB 8, 1226–1237 (2015)

Obfuscation

Obfuscation

The Pseudorandom Oracle Model and Ideal Obfuscation

Aayush Jain[1($\boxtimes$)], Huijia Lin[2($\boxtimes$)], Ji Luo[2($\boxtimes$)] (ID), and Daniel Wichs[3,4($\boxtimes$)]

[1] Carnegie Mellon University, Pittsburgh, USA
aayushja@andrew.cmu.edu
[2] University of Washington, Seattle, USA
{rachel,luoji}@cs.washington.edu
[3] Northeastern University, Boston, USA
wichs@ccs.neu.edu
[4] NTT Research, Sunnyvale, USA

Abstract. We introduce a new idealized model of hash functions, which we refer to as the *pseudorandom oracle* (Pr$\mathcal{O}$) model. Intuitively, it allows us to model cryptosystems that use the code of an ideal hash function in a non-black-box way. Formally, we model hash functions via a combination of a pseudorandom function (PRF) family and an ideal oracle. A user can initialize the hash function by choosing a PRF key k and mapping it to a public handle h using the oracle. Given the handle h and some input x, the oracle can also be called to evaluate the PRF at x with the corresponding key k. A user who chooses the PRF key k therefore has a complete description of the hash function and can use its code in non-black-box constructions, while an adversary, who just gets the handle h, only has black-box access to the hash function via the oracle.

As our main result, we show how to construct ideal obfuscation in the Pr$\mathcal{O}$ model, starting from functional encryption (FE), which in turn can be based on well-studied polynomial hardness assumptions. In contrast, we know that ideal obfuscation cannot be instantiated in the basic random oracle model under any assumptions. We believe our result provides heuristic justification for the following: (1) most natural security goals implied by ideal obfuscation can be achieved in the real world; (2) obfuscation can be constructed from FE at polynomial security loss.

We also discuss how to interpret our result in the Pr$\mathcal{O}$ model as a construction of ideal obfuscation using simple hardware tokens or as a way to bootstrap ideal obfuscation for PRFs to that for all functions.

1 Introduction

Hash Functions and Random Oracles. Hash functions are one of the most important cryptographic primitives and are ubiquitous in both theoretical and practical cryptosystem designs. The basic security property of a hash function is collision resistance, which is already sufficient for many applications. However, there is a widespread belief that good hash functions can satisfy a much wider range of security properties beyond collision resistance. This belief is captured in

© International Association for Cryptologic Research 2023
H. Handschuh and A. Lysyanskaya (Eds.): CRYPTO 2023, LNCS 14084, pp. 233–262, 2023.
https://doi.org/10.1007/978-3-031-38551-3_8

the *random oracle model* (ROM) [12], where we model a hash function as a truly random public function and give the honest users as well as the adversary oracle access to this function. The random oracle is an ideal functionality relative to which we can construct cryptosystems and formally prove their security. We then take a heuristic leap of faith that such cryptosystems remain secure even when we replace the random oracle by a real, well-designed hash function (like SHA-3). While the second step is heuristic and has no formal justification, it captures the intuition that an adversary cannot do anything meaningful with a well-designed hash function other than treating it as a random oracle. The random oracle heuristic is immensely popular and successful. Almost all cryptosystems used in practice, from TLS to Bitcoin, rely on it to justify their security. On the theory side, there are contrived examples where the random oracle heuristic fails — specially designed cryptosystems that are provably secure in the random oracle model, but are insecure when instantiated with any real hash function [9, 27]. Nevertheless, outside of such specially crafted counterexamples, the random oracle heuristic gives extremely strong evidence of security in real life, and there is no known example of it ever leading to a security flaw in a natural real-world cryptosystem.

Indistinguishability or Ideal Obfuscation. A scenario analogous to the one above also plays out in the upper reaches of cryptography when it comes to obfuscation [11]. We have a standard-model definition of obfuscation security called *indistinguishability obfuscation* ($i\mathcal{O}$) [11], and as of recently, we even have instantiations under well-studied assumptions [35, 36]. While $i\mathcal{O}$ suffices for some applications, it does not suffice for many others, or results in exceedingly complex and cumbersome constructions. Similarly to hash functions, we believe obfuscators are capable of satisfying a much wider range of security properties beyond $i\mathcal{O}$. Similarly to the random oracle model for hash functions, we can define an *ideal obfuscation model*, where we model obfuscation as an ideal functionality that only gives the adversary black-box access to the obfuscated programs.[1] Analogously to the ROM, we can design cryptosystems and prove their security in the ideal obfuscation model, which is extraordinarily powerful and allows for very simple constructions. We can then make a heuristic leap of faith that such cryptosystems remain secure when we replace the ideal obfuscator by $i\mathcal{O}$. Also analogously to the random oracle model, one can come up with contrived counterexamples (e.g., [11]) where this heuristic fails, but the intuition is that it should be secure in almost all natural use cases that come up in real life.

---

[1] Ideal obfuscation is similar to virtual black-box (VBB) obfuscation [11], except that we consider it to be an idealized model rather than a security definition. In contrast, VBB was originally intended as a security definition, with some artificial choices (restricting adversaries to only 1-bit output) to rule out obvious counterexamples. Nevertheless, the main result of [11] shows that even with these restrictions, VBB security is unachievable in its full generality in the plain model.

Our Work: Ideal Obfuscation from Ideal Hash Functions. Summarizing the above discussion, we have the analogy that collision-resistant hash functions are to random oracles as $i\mathcal{O}$ is to ideal obfuscation. Modeling hash functions as random oracles is well-established, yet there was little study on the idealization of obfuscators. We wonder:

> *Can we justify the ideal obfuscation model, e.g.,*
> *by constructing ideal obfuscation from ideal hash functions?*

As a starting point, we might try constructing ideal obfuscation in the random oracle model under appropriate additional standard-model assumptions. Such a result would formalize that the ideal obfuscation heuristic is just a special case of the ROM heuristic. Unfortunately, the work of [19] rules out the above attempt by showing that it is impossible to construct ideal obfuscation in the ROM.

Nevertheless, in this work, we re-examine the question of constructing ideal obfuscation from ideal hash functions, and show that it is indeed possible! To get around the previous negative result, we need to tweak our modeling of ideal hash functions. Instead of the random oracle model, we introduce a new and more flexible idealized model of hash functions that we call the *pseudorandom oracle* (Pr$\mathcal{O}$) *model*. We argue that the Pr$\mathcal{O}$ model captures the same intuition as the usual ROM, but provides more technical flexibility. As our main result, we show how to construct ideal obfuscation in the Pr$\mathcal{O}$ model. Our construction assumes (single-key, sublinearly succinct) functional encryption (FE), a strong yet standard-model primitive. We believe that this result formalizes the following intuition:

> *Heuristically assuming that we have ideal obfuscation*
> *is not worse or "crazier" than*
> *heuristically assuming that we have ideal hash functions.*

As such, confidence in the latter supports confidence in the former. Furthermore, our construction of ideal obfuscation from FE in the Pr$\mathcal{O}$ model only incurs a polynomial security loss. Combined with the fact that FE can be based on well-studied polynomial assumptions [35,36], we obtain a heuristic obfuscator based on polynomial hardness. In contrast, constructions of $i\mathcal{O}$ from FE in the standard model incur an exponential security loss.

Organization. We explain the basics of the pseudorandom oracle (Pr$\mathcal{O}$) model in Sect. 1.1, provide the interpretations of our result in Sect. 1.2, further justify the Pr$\mathcal{O}$ model in Sect. 1.3, and discuss related works in Sect. 1.4. We overview our techniques of constructing ideal obfuscation in Sect. 2. After providing preliminaries in Sect. 3, we define the Pr$\mathcal{O}$ model in Sect. 4 and ideal obfuscation in Sect. 5. We present our construction of ideal obfuscation in Sect. 6 and its simulator in Sect. 7. Due to space constraints, we refer the readers to the full version [34] for the proofs.

1.1   Basics of the Pseudorandom Oracle (Pr$\mathcal{O}$) Model

Just like the ROM, the Pr$\mathcal{O}$ model is defined in terms of a formally specified ideal functionality that all parties (honest users as well as the adversary) have access to. The ideal functionality for Pr$\mathcal{O}$ is specified relative to some (standard-model) pseudorandom function (PRF) family H_k and has two interfaces. The first interface *initializes* a hash function when provided with a PRF key k as input — the ideal functionality maps the PRF key k to a random *handle* h and outputs it. The second interface *evaluates* the hash function when provided with a handle h and an input x — the ideal functionality finds the PRF key k corresponding to h and outputs $H_k(x)$.

A Pr$\mathcal{O}$ can be used as a basic RO. Consider an honest user who chooses a random PRF key k, uses the Pr$\mathcal{O}$ to get the corresponding handle h, and then discards k and publishes h. In that case, the adversary essentially just gets oracle access to the hash function H_k by querying the oracle with the handle h. By the pseudorandomness of H_k, this is indistinguishable from a truly random oracle.

The Pr$\mathcal{O}$ model also provides additional flexibility in allowing the honest user who chose k to use the code of the hash function H_k in a non-black-box way (e.g., inside fully homomorphic encryption, functional encryption, or garbled circuits). In other words, the Pr$\mathcal{O}$ allows different users of the cryptosystem to use different descriptions of the same hash function. The first description is given via the key k, which specifies the full code of the hash function H_k and allows for evaluating it in a non-black-box way without making any oracle calls. The second description is given via the handle h, which only provides black-box access to the hash function H_k via oracle queries. The first description is useful for functionality, but provides no security guarantee — since we only assume PRF security for H_k, if the adversary ever sees the PRF key k, all security is lost. The second description is useful for security, but provides no functionality advantage over the basic ROM. The power of the Pr$\mathcal{O}$ comes from the fact that it simultaneously gives us both descriptions for the same hash function and allows us to model different levels of access to the same hash function for different users.

However, the Pr$\mathcal{O}$ model is very conservative about what kind of security guarantees it provides, and proving security in the Pr$\mathcal{O}$ is generally very subtle and requires extreme care. In particular, if the adversary ever receives any information about k via the non-black-box use of H_k, then all security guarantees are lost! Our analysis can only make use of Pr$\mathcal{O}$ security in hybrid games where all information about the key k is removed from the view of the adversary. This implies that although our overall cryptosystem may rely on non-black-box use of the hash function, for the Pr$\mathcal{O}$ model to be helpful in security proofs, such use must be indistinguishable from black-box use in the eyes of the adversary.

Using the Pr$\mathcal{O}$. Looking ahead, it is illustrative to examine the role of the Pr$\mathcal{O}$ in our construction of ideal obfuscation. For obfuscation, we have two users with different roles — the *obfuscator* who creates the obfuscated program, and the *evaluator* who gets the obfuscated program and evaluates it on various inputs. The obfuscator will choose several PRF keys k_i and the obfuscated program will encrypt the keys k_i into some functional encryption (FE) ciphertext. The evaluator will get the FE ciphertext as well as the corresponding handles h_i, which will be sufficient for evaluating the obfuscated program on any input. In the security analysis, the adversary plays the role of the evaluator. Although it does not get keys k_i directly, it gets an FE ciphertext containing them. To argue security, we will need a careful sequence of hybrids in each of which we replace the $\text{Pr}\mathcal{O}$ outputs for some handle h_i by random values after removing the corresponding PRF key k_i from the FE ciphertext.

1.2   Interpreting Our Result of Ideal Obfuscation

Ideal obfuscation cannot be realized by any standard-model obfuscation scheme, similar to the fact that a random oracle cannot be realized by any standard-model hash function. However, also similar to random oracles, ideal obfuscation provides a formal model in which we can design and analyze cryptosystems. We can instantiate them using a real-world obfuscator based on the intuition that a good obfuscator is sufficient to achieve the security required by the cryptosystem from ideal obfuscation in most reasonable scenarios. This heuristic is powerful.

1. It allows us to reach security goals outside the current scope of standard-model proofs. The literature already contains an impressive list of such examples: doubly efficient PIR [18], FHE for RAM [30], virtual gray-box obfuscation [13], input-hiding obfuscation for evasive functions [10], public-coin differing-input obfuscation, obfuscation for input-unbounded Turing machines [32], extractable witness encryption, attribute-based encryption for RAM [28], OT over binary erasure channels [1], wiretap-channel coding [31], refuting the dream XOR lemma [8], etc. This list is sure to grow.[2]
2. It enables (conceptually) simple constructions. Consider for instance the task of building FE. Using ideal obfuscation, we can simply set the secret key for a function f to be an obfuscated program that decrypts ciphertexts of a (CCA-secure) public-key encryption and then computes the function f on the decryption result. In contrast, $i\mathcal{O}$ applications typically involve more sophisticated techniques (such as puncturing [48]) to overcome the weak security of $i\mathcal{O}$, producing cumbersome constructions with complex proofs of security. The ideal obfuscation heuristic gives strong evidence that such complication is actually unnecessary.
3. For many real-life security goals such as protecting software patches, creating crippleware with parts of the functionality redacted, obfuscating machine learning models, etc., $i\mathcal{O}$ security is insufficient. In these specific natural contexts, virtual black-box security is plausible (the impossibility of [11] does not apply) and can be heuristically instantiated.

When it comes to which concrete obfuscator to use when instantiating the ideal obfuscation heuristic, in the literature, the standard-model $i\mathcal{O}$ construction is

---

[2] We note that after the initial pre-print and prior to the publication of this work, DE-PIR, FHE for RAM [42], and ABE for TM/RAM [3,33] are achieved in the standard model.

typically used. Our construction of ideal obfuscation in the Pr$\mathcal{O}$ model, when instantiated with a well-designed hash function, provides another option. An advantage of our obfuscator is that it can be based on polynomial hardness assumptions, as opposed to requiring subexponential hardness.

Comparison with Best-Possible Obfuscation. Goldwasser and Rothblum showed that $i\mathcal{O}$ is a "best-possible obfuscator" [29], in the sense that if some obfuscator is capable of hiding some information of the program, then so does $i\mathcal{O}$. Intuitively, it says that *if* a program can be obfuscated with stronger security, then $i\mathcal{O}$ is a good candidate achieving the stronger security. However, it does not address the question when the premise is true. Our result that ideal obfuscation is feasible in the Pr$\mathcal{O}$ model gives supporting evidence that *natural* programs can be obfuscated with stronger security, under the heuristic that Pr$\mathcal{O}$ can be instantiated using real-world hash functions in *natural* scenarios. It suggests that obfuscation with stronger security is possible in most natural applications.

Alternative Interpretations: Hardware Tokens and Bootstrapping. Our result can also be interpreted as constructing ideal obfuscation using hardware tokens. The obfuscator chooses the PRF key k and releases a hardware token that implements the PRF H_k (acting as the handle in the Pr$\mathcal{O}$ model to provide black-box access to H_k) and the obfuscated program containing encrypted k. There are several prior works showing how to construct obfuscation using hardware tokens [15,23,45]. However, in all cases, the hardware token is significantly more complex than just implementing a PRF. Therefore, our work also provides an interesting new take on how to construct obfuscation using extremely simple hardware tokens.

Alternatively, we can interpret our result as showing that ideal obfuscation for PRFs implies ideal obfuscation for general functions. Indeed, the Pr$\mathcal{O}$ model can be thought of as exactly an ideal obfuscation for a PRF family H_k. The handle h is an ideal obfuscated program computing H_k.[3] In the literature, there are several bootstrapping theorems [7,20,25] transforming obfuscation for weak classes of functions to that for general functions. In these works, the weak classes are typically weaker from a complexity-theoretic perspective, e.g., belonging to NC^1 or TC^0, but are expressive enough to hardcode an arbitrary circuit in the function description (e.g., verifying that a ciphertext is obtained by homomorphically evaluating a circuit on some input ciphertexts, and if so, decrypting that ciphertext). In comparison, our bootstrapping theorem starts with obfuscation of a single PRF family H_k, apparently without the ability to embed the logic related to arbitrary computation.

---

[3] This is yet another reason why the Pr$\mathcal{O}$ model and the ROM are morally equivalent. The ROM essentially says that good hash functions are "self-obfuscated PRFs" since having the full description of a hash function is no better than just having oracle access to a random function, which is also what the Pr$\mathcal{O}$ model stipulates.

1.3   Further Discussion on the Pr$\mathcal{O}$ Model

The motivation behind the usual ROM is providing a rigorous and well-defined model capturing the intuition that outputs of a good hash function "appear random", and enabling formal security analysis based on this intuition. To be well-defined, the ROM completely removes non-black-box access to the hash function. Intuitively, the Pr$\mathcal{O}$ model is a new well-defined ideal functionality capturing the same intuition (as discussed earlier, it subsumes the random oracle model), and additionally allowing us to formally reason about cryptosystems that make non-black-box use of the hash function.

Formalizing *Ad Hoc* Non-Black-Box Uses of Hash Functions. The ROM was motivated and guided by heuristic uses of hash functions that preceded it (e.g., the Fiat–Shamir transformation [24]). However, the benefits of having an explicit ideal model go beyond providing partial justification to these usages. It greatly facilitates future design, as witnessed in the explosion of cryptosystems designed in the ROM since its introduction [12]. In recent years, we saw heuristic *non-black-box* uses of hash functions, for instance, in recursive composition of SNARKs [14], in simulation-secure FE [22], and in CCA-secure FHE [21]. It is well-motivated to formalize a variant of the ROM capable of capturing some non-black-box uses of hash functions. However, such efforts quickly meets the contradiction that one cannot simultaneously model hash functions as random functions and assume efficient code representation. As a result, previous heuristic non-black-box uses of hash functions have been deemed less satisfactory than heuristics justified in the ROM.

The Pr$\mathcal{O}$ model side-steps the contradiction — the oracle evaluates pseudorandom functions $H_k(\cdot)$ with efficient code representation. However, as discussed earlier, security proofs in the Pr$\mathcal{O}$ model are subtle since we do not assume any security of $H_k(\cdot)$ when the key k is around. In effect, this means that the Pr$\mathcal{O}$ model only allows us to rely on RO-style modeling of $H_k(\cdot)$ in hybrid games where all non-black-box use of k is removed.

We believe that the Pr$\mathcal{O}$ model is a natural and more flexible variant of the ROM that enables us to formally reason about cryptosystems making non-black-box use of hash functions, while being "morally analogous" to the ROM.

(Non-)Contradiction of *Non-Black-Box Ideal* Hash Functions. At first sight, the idea of an ideal model capturing non-black-box use of hash functions may seem unnatural — if the cryptosystem makes non-back box use of the hash function, why can't the adversary? The Pr$\mathcal{O}$ model gives a satisfactory answer to this from two perspectives. In the formal security proof, we can only invoke Pr$\mathcal{O}$ security in hybrids where all non-black-box use of the hash function has been removed, in which case it is reasonable to assume that the adversary also only has black-box access. Conceptually, this means that the Pr$\mathcal{O}$ model is only useful for a cryptosystem if its non-black-box use of hash functions is indistinguishable to black-box use of them, so it is again reasonable to assume only black-box access from the adversary.

Putting a Real-World Cryptosystem into the $\text{Pr}\mathcal{O}$ Model. Suppose a real-world cryptosystem uses some hash function, say SHA-3 with a *public salt k*. Parts of the cryptosystem will only make black-box calls to $\text{SHA3}(k\|\cdot)$, but do not rely on the code otherwise, while other parts of the cryptosystem may use the code of $\text{SHA3}(k\|\cdot)$ in a non-black-box way. In the usual ROM, we model the former usage by replacing all calls to $\text{SHA3}(k\|\cdot)$ by oracle calls to a truly random public oracle, but do not have any way of capturing the latter usage. In the $\text{Pr}\mathcal{O}$ model, we can set $H_k(\cdot) = \text{SHA3}(k\|\cdot)^4$ and replace all black-box calls to $\text{SHA3}(k\|x)$ by oracle evaluation calls on (h, x), where h is the handle to k. Additionally, if the original cryptosystem also uses $\text{SHA3}(k\|\cdot)$ in a non-black-box way, the $\text{Pr}\mathcal{O}$ model allows parties knowing k to make non-black-box use of H_k and ensures that the black-box use via oracle evaluation calls is consistent with it.

The $\text{Pr}\mathcal{O}$ Paradigm. Like the ROM, the $\text{Pr}\mathcal{O}$ model articulates an explicit design paradigm. For a cryptographic notion Π, to design a good scheme or protocol P for Π:

1. Find a formal definition of Π in the model of computation where all parties (including the adversary) share the pseudorandom oracle $\text{Pr}\mathcal{O}^H$ for some PRF family H_k.
2. Devise an efficient scheme P for Π in this $\text{Pr}\mathcal{O}$ model.
3. Prove that P satisfies the definition of Π in the $\text{Pr}\mathcal{O}$ model.
4. Instantiate $\text{Pr}\mathcal{O}^H$ for some real hash function H.

In the above $\text{Pr}\mathcal{O}$ paradigm, as well as the traditional RO paradigm, the proof of security (Step 3) is in an ideal model and the instantiation (Step 4) is heuristic in nature. There are known schemes/protocols secure in the ROM, but never secure when instantiated with real hash functions, e.g., [9, 27]. These counterexamples extend to the $\text{Pr}\mathcal{O}$ model. In addition, our construction of ideal obfuscation is an example separating the $\text{Pr}\mathcal{O}$ model and the ROM. Despite these counterexamples, for the same reasons that apply to the RO paradigm, having a security proof in the $\text{Pr}\mathcal{O}$ model maintains significant benefits. First, schemes secure in the $\text{Pr}\mathcal{O}$ model are secure against generic attacks that make only black-box calls to the hash functions. Second, under the *uber heuristic* that in *natural use cases*, no adversary can effectively make use of the code of well-designed hash functions beyond making black-box calls, we obtain heuristically secure schemes in the standard model. The uber heuristic is the same as the heuristic backing the RO paradigm.

Instantiating the $\text{Pr}\mathcal{O}$ Model. Suppose some hash function H is suitable for instantiating the ROM, we argue that the salted version of H is good for the $\text{Pr}\mathcal{O}$ model. For example, to instantiate the $\text{Pr}\mathcal{O}$ model with SHA-3, we

- set $H_k(x) = \text{SHA3}(k\|x)$,
- replace the handle h by k itself (!), and
- replace every evaluation call on (h, x) by $\text{SHA3}(h\|x)$.

---

[4] We assume that $\text{SHA3}(k\|\cdot)$ is a PRF with k being the *(secret) key*, which is a very mild assumption for real-world hash functions.

Note the glaring difference between practice and formalism. The $\text{Pr}\mathcal{O}$ model defines the handle as a random string,[5] yet the suggested instantiation simply sets $h = k$.

Our rationale is based on the random oracle heuristics — since SHA-3 is suitable for the ROM, an adversary, given the public salt $h = k$, cannot do anything meaningful about k other than evaluating it at various inputs with prefix k. This is exactly what the $\text{Pr}\mathcal{O}$ model demands from the hash function! Also, when regarding the $\text{Pr}\mathcal{O}$ model as ideal obfuscation of PRF, the handle h is the obfuscated PRF and the key k is hidden inside h, but we can redefine the PRF as $H'_h(x) = h(x) = H_k(x)$ so h becomes *the* key, i.e., it is sensible to set $h = k$. This matches the idea that hash functions suitable for the ROM are "self-obfuscated PRFs". Lastly, yet another reason to go with this simple instantiation is that the choice of making h a random string is merely a formalism, a modeling method to enable invocation of PRF security when k is absent. The means should not be taken as the ends.

1.4   Related Works

Several prior works have attempted to rely on the random oracle heuristics of a hash function while making non-black-box use of the hash function at the same time. For example, the work of Valiant [50] constructs incrementally verifiable proofs of knowledge and the work of [22] constructs simulation-secure FE using this type of approach. However, these works do not define a fully specified formal model in which one can state the given results, making it difficult to even write down a meaningful theorem. This is in contrast to our $\text{Pr}\mathcal{O}$ model, which gives a formally specified idealized model in which we can state and prove propositions. On the other hand, the $\text{Pr}\mathcal{O}$ model only allows very careful non-black-box use of the hash function, where we can only make use of $\text{Pr}\mathcal{O}$ security in hybrids where all non-black-box use of the hash function is removed. It does not appear that the constructions of [22,50] could be directly translated into results in the $\text{Pr}\mathcal{O}$ model.

2   Technical Overview

Now we describe the main ideas behind our construction. Our starting point is the insights of [4,17] and the follow-ups [16,38,39,41], which establish that $i\mathcal{O}$ can implemented generically from subexponentially secure single-key functional encryption (FE) scheme, a seemingly weaker primitive. These works additionally require the FE scheme to satisfy certain encryption efficiency guarantees. In the

---

[5] This is similar to Shoup's generic group model [49]. Alternatively, we can define the handle as a special symbol that cannot be operated on, like in Maurer's GGM [43]. The two models are studied in the recent work of [51]. We choose Shoup's flavor for its potential flexibility, although our construction is compatible with Maurer's. However, in either flavor, per definition, h is independent of k, and the difference between practice and formalism still prevails.

overview below, we assume that the FE scheme satisfies adaptive indistinguishability security and has linear-time encryption.[6]

FE-to-$i\mathcal{O}$ Transformation. In order to obfuscate circuit $C : \{0,1\}^D \to \{0,1\}$, we give out an FE ciphertext ct_ε encrypting C. We think of this ciphertext as being associated with the root of a perfect binary tree of depth D. We also give out FE secret keys for each of the D levels in the tree, for functions that themselves compute FE encryptions. By defining such functions carefully, we can expand any ciphertext ct_χ for some prefix $\chi \in \{0,1\}^{<D}$ associated with some internal node in the tree into two ciphertexts $\mathsf{ct}_{\chi\|0}, \mathsf{ct}_{\chi\|1}$ for its children, with each such child ciphertext again carrying information about C. Lastly, for leaf ciphertexts ct_x with $x \in \{0,1\}^D$, we give out an FE secret key that allows one to recover the output $C(x)$. This allows an evaluator to compute $C(x)$ starting from ct_ε by going down the appropriate path in the tree.

In more detail, the obfuscator does the following:

- For $0 \le d \le D$, sample fresh FE key pairs $(\mathsf{mpk}_d, \mathsf{msk}_d)$.
- Compute $\mathsf{ct}_\varepsilon \overset{\$}{\leftarrow} \mathsf{Enc}(\mathsf{mpk}_0, \mathsf{info}_\varepsilon)$, where $\mathsf{info}_\varepsilon = (C, \varepsilon, \star)$ with $\star$ being a slot for miscellaneous information to be specified later as needed.
- For $0 \le d \le D$, generate $\mathsf{sk}_d \overset{\$}{\leftarrow} \mathsf{KeyGen}(\mathsf{msk}_d, f_d)$. Under normal functioning, f_d for $i < D$ takes $\mathsf{info}_\chi = (C, \chi, \star)$ as input and outputs two ciphertexts $(\mathsf{ct}_{\chi\|0}, \mathsf{ct}_{\chi\|1})$ encrypting $\mathsf{info}_{\chi\|b} = (C, \chi\|b, \star)$ for $b \in \{0,1\}$ under mpk_{d+1}, and f_D takes $\mathsf{info}_x = (C, x \in \{0,1\}^D, \star)$ as input and outputs $C(x)$.

The obfuscated circuit is $\widehat{C} = (\mathsf{ct}_\varepsilon, \{\mathsf{sk}_d\}_{0 \le d \le D})$. To evaluate $\widehat{C}$ on $x \in \{0,1\}^D$, one computes ct_x at level D, then decrypts it using sk_D to recover $C(x)$. The process of computing ct_x is inductive and proceeds like a binary tree traversal. Let $x_{\le d}$ be the prefix of x of length d. We start by decrypting $\mathsf{ct}_{x_{\le 0}} = \mathsf{ct}_\varepsilon$ using sk_0 to obtain $(\mathsf{ct}_0, \mathsf{ct}_1)$. For $1 \le d < D$, we inductively decrypt $\mathsf{ct}_{x_{\le d}}$ using sk_d to derive $(\mathsf{ct}_{x_{\le d}\|0}, \mathsf{ct}_{x_{\le d}\|1})$, then use $\mathsf{ct}_{x_{\le d+1}}$ to further traverse down the tree.

The scheme satisfies *polynomial slowdown*. At every level, ct_χ encrypts info_χ and the running time of f_d is $\mathsf{poly}(\lambda, |\mathsf{info}_\chi|)$, so each f_d is polynomial-sized. Some care is needed to ensure that the $\star$ slots used by the ciphertexts do not blow up as the levels increase — the proof is designed in a way that this happens.

The security proof is slightly tricky. Given the obfuscation, there are around 2^D FE ciphertexts, ct_χ for $\chi \in \{0,1\}^{\le D}$, encrypting $\mathsf{info}_\chi = (C, \chi, \star)$, containing the circuit C being obfuscated. For two equivalent circuits C_0, C_1, we want to show $\widehat{C}_0 \approx \widehat{C}_1$. Since the adversary is given ct_ε and $\mathsf{sk}_0, \dots, \mathsf{sk}_D$, it can compute ct_χ for any $\chi \in \{0,1\}^{\le D}$ of its choice, and can do so internally without the reduction knowing the χ's "of the adversary's interest". Therefore, the proof resorts to switching ct_χ from containing C_0 to C_1 for *every* $\chi \in \{0,1\}^{\le D}$, taking around 2^D steps (hybrids) and creating a security loss of $\Omega(2^D)$.

---

[6] The encryption time is $|z| \mathsf{poly}(\lambda)$, where z is the plaintext. This is independent of the functions for which secret keys are issued.

Why the Scheme Fails to Be an Ideal Obfuscation. In ideal obfuscation, we require that $\widehat{C}$ can be simulated by a *polynomial-time* simulator having only oracle access to C. This implies that the simulator must come up with a short ciphertext ct_ε (ignoring the [short] keys for now) capable of evaluating C at every $x \in \{0,1\}^D$ from just black-box access to C. Assuming that hard-to-learn functions exist, this is impossible as the simulator can only query C at a polynomial number of points. Indeed, this simple argument shows that ideal obfuscation cannot exist, which is also implied by the the work of [11] showing that even a more restricted notion, VBB obfuscation, cannot exist. In this work, one of our primary goals is to identify a reasonable model capturing real-world adversaries in which ideal obfuscation is possible. We take inspiration from the random oracle model [12] — there are several applications that are known to be impossible in the standard model but can be constructed in the ROM.

Simplified Idea Using Random Oracles. From the observation discussed earlier, one of the obstacles to proving ideal security of the scheme above is that once the reduction or the simulator produces some ciphertext ct_ε, it has implicitly specified *all* the ciphertexts in the tree and all the outputs of the circuit. There is no place to "program" any information. The random oracle could be useful in solving this issue. Imagine a world where ct_ε makes the first decryption yield $H(\varepsilon) \oplus (\mathsf{ct}_0 \| \mathsf{ct}_1)$ so that adversary has to query $H(\varepsilon)$ to unmask the next layer ciphertexts. Similarly, assume that the result of decrypting ct_χ for $\chi \in \{0,1\}^{\leq D-1}$ is $H(\chi) \oplus (\mathsf{ct}_{\chi\|0} \| \mathsf{ct}_{\chi\|1})$.

If the above were possible, we would be able to come up with a simulation strategy. The random oracle offers two powerful capabilities, *observability* and *programmability*, that enable such simulation. As the evaluator queries H at various χ, the simulator can keep track of the paths the adversary is taking to evaluate the circuit. By programming, one can enter a hybrid where ct_χ decrypts to a random value v_χ and (simultaneously) the random oracle responds to $H(\chi)$ by answering $v_\chi \oplus (\mathsf{ct}_{\chi\|0} \| \mathsf{ct}_{\chi\|1})$.

Once this is done, any ct_χ can only be accessed by querying the oracle. The issue of programming space would be resolved as the random oracle provides an exponentially large one. In addition, since the adversary only makes polynomially many queries, the proof only has to switch a polynomial number of ciphertexts, reducing the security loss to polynomial. In particular, the proof would replace ct_χ for $\chi \in \{0,1\}^{\leq D-1}$ by dummy ciphertexts independent of C, and ct_x for $x \in \{0,1\}^D$ by simulated ciphertexts containing $C(x)$, *only* for χ's and x's at which H is queried.

Unfortunately, so far this is just wishful thinking! There is a fundamental flaw with the above idea that must be addressed before we can materialize this approach.

Using the Pr$\mathcal{O}$ Model. The flaw with the aforementioned idea is the premise itself. We assume that decrypting ct_χ yields $H(\chi) \oplus (\cdots)$, but this requires the FE scheme to evaluate the hash function H. This makes sense only if the FE key functions f_d contain the code of H, meaning that H must be a real hash function and not a random oracle! We now have seemingly conflicting requirements — we need the code of the hash function to define the scheme syntactically, but we also need to idealize the hash function as a public random function to take advantage of observability and programmability.

This is where our model comes in. We precisely show that the above approach can be done in the PrO model. Let us briefly recall the model. There are two oracle algorithms hGen and hEval with syntax

$$\mathcal{O}(\mathsf{hGen}, k) \mapsto h, \quad \mathcal{O}(\mathsf{hEval}, h, x) \mapsto H(k, x),$$

where $\mathcal{O}(\mathsf{hGen}, \cdot)$ maps a key k into a handle h and $\mathcal{O}(\mathsf{hEval}, h, x)$ maps the handle h back into its key k and outputs $H(k, x)$ for some fixed function H. The handle map is a random permutation and can be efficiently implemented using lazy sampling. Furthermore, we require that H is a pseudorandom function — this implies that given a handle h for a random k, when k is *absent* from the view of the adversary, $\mathcal{O}(\mathsf{hEval}, h, \cdot) = H(k, \cdot)$ is indistinguishable from a random function.

The PrO model provides the right abstraction needed to solve our problem. A random key k can be used *inside* the FE ciphertext, together with the code of H in the FE keys, to compute $H(k, \chi) \oplus (\mathsf{ct}_{\chi\|0}\|\mathsf{ct}_{\chi\|1})$, and the corresponding handle h can be used *outside* the FE scheme when evaluating the obfuscated circuit. At the same time, if k is absent from the adversary's view, we can still program $\mathcal{O}(\mathsf{hEval}, h, \cdot)$. Of course, the difficulty is that the key k is part of the adversary's view whenever it is (encrypted) inside the FE ciphertext. Therefore, we must come up with a careful proof strategy involving a sequence of hybrids to first remove k then program the oracle. We explain how to do so below.

First Attempt. Let $G : \{0,1\}^\lambda \rightarrow \{0,1\}^{4\lambda}$ be a PRG for deriving the encryption randomness of the intermediate FE ciphertexts. Here, we assume that both PrO hash keys and encryption randomness are of length λ. To obfuscate C, one computes ct_ε encrypting $(C, \varepsilon, k, s_\varepsilon)$, where k is a fresh hash key (with h being its handle) and s_ε is a fresh PRG seed. The function f_0 on input $(C, \varepsilon, k, s_\varepsilon)$ outputs $H(k, \varepsilon) \oplus (\mathsf{ct}_0\|\mathsf{ct}_1)$, and $f_1, \ldots, f_D$ are defined analogously. The obfuscator outputs $\hat{C} = (h, \mathsf{ct}_\varepsilon, \{\mathsf{sk}_d\}_{0 \leq d \leq D})$. We give an outline in Fig. 1.

Evaluating such an obfuscated circuit is straightforward. Given $x \in \{0,1\}^D$, for each prefix χ of x starting from ε, decrypting ct_χ yields the child ciphertexts masked by $H(k, \chi)$, which the evaluator can unmask by querying $(\mathsf{hEval}, h, \chi)$ before proceeding to the next level. Lastly, decrypting ct_x yields $C(x)$.

As envisioned, the simulator programs $\mathcal{O}(\mathsf{hEval}, h, \cdot)$ and changes the ciphertexts into some simulation mode. A natural idea to prove security is to replace the (intermediate) ciphertexts layer by layer in a sequence of hybrids, starting from the root ct_ε. This approach faces an immediate obstacle. In the PrO model, $\mathcal{O}(\mathsf{hEval}, h, \cdot)$ can only be programmed if the key k is not given to the adversary, but in the scheme, k appears inside all the intermediate ciphertexts. Therefore, it is not clear how to switch even just ct_ε into simulation, as k appears in the deeper ciphertexts in both hybrids. We would have to first remove k from all the

---

Input. C, the circuit being obfuscated.

Steps.
1. Sample $k \xleftarrow{\$} \{0,1\}^\lambda$ and obtain its handle h from PrO.
2. Sample $s_\varepsilon \xleftarrow{\$} \{0,1\}^\lambda$.
3. For $0 \leq d \leq D$, sample fresh FE key pair $(\mathsf{mpk}_d, \mathsf{msk}_d)$ and run $\mathsf{sk}_d \xleftarrow{\$} \mathsf{KeyGen}(\mathsf{msk}_d, f_d)$ for f_d defined below.
4. Run $\mathsf{ct}_\varepsilon \xleftarrow{\$} \mathsf{Enc}(\mathsf{mpk}_0, \mathsf{info}_\varepsilon)$ with $\mathsf{info}_\varepsilon = (\mathsf{normal}, \varepsilon, k, s_\varepsilon)$. Here, normal is a flag indicating the mode of the ciphertext.
5. Output $\widehat{C} = (h, \mathsf{ct}_\varepsilon, \{\mathsf{sk}_d\}_{0 \leq d \leq D})$.

Functions. (normal mode)
- For $0 \leq d < D$, the function $f_d(\mathsf{normal}, \chi, k, s_\chi)$
  1. computes $s_{\chi\|0}\|r_{\chi\|0}\|s_{\chi\|0}\|r_{\chi\|0} \leftarrow G(s_\chi)$;
  2. for $b \in \{0,1\}$, runs $\mathsf{ct}_{\chi\|b} \leftarrow \mathsf{Enc}(\mathsf{mpk}_{d+1}, \mathsf{info}_{\chi\|b}; r_{\chi\|b})$, where $\mathsf{info}_{\chi\|b} = (\mathsf{normal}, C, \chi\|b, k, s_{\chi\|b})$;
  3. outputs $H(k, \chi) \oplus (\mathsf{ct}_{\chi\|0}\|\mathsf{ct}_{\chi\|1})$.
- For $d = D$, the function $f_D(\mathsf{normal}, C, x, k, s_x)$ outputs $C(x)$.

Fig. 1. First Attempt of Ideal Obfuscator.

intermediate ciphertexts to appeal to the programmability of $\mathcal{O}(\mathsf{hEval}, h, \cdot)$. This appears rather difficult without first simulating the ciphertexts by programming, i.e., there is a circularity issue.

Second Attempt. To circumvent the issue, we use different key/handle pairs (h_i, k_i) for each layer as opposed to the same pair. Now, a ciphertext ct_χ for $\chi \in \{0,1\}^d$ at level d will only contain $\{(h_i, k_i)\}_{d \leq i < D}$. Note that each ciphertext is independent of the keys for the previous layers, thus breaking the circularity. The scheme is described in Fig. 2.

The simulator now programs $\mathcal{O}(\mathsf{hEval}, h_d, \cdot)$'s accordingly. Our proof strategy is again hybridizing over the layers. Suppose the ciphertexts ct_χ for $\chi \in \{0,1\}^{<\delta}$ are already simulated so that they contain no information about $C, k_0, \ldots, k_{\delta-1}$, and we want to simulate ct_χ's for $\chi \in \{0,1\}^\delta$. Now that k_δ only appears in ct_χ's for $\chi \in \{0,1\}^\delta$ and nowhere else, it is easier to completely remove k_δ, at which point we can observe and program $\mathcal{O}(\mathsf{hEval}, h_\delta, \cdot)$ and replace ct_χ's by dummy ciphertexts.

Take $\delta = 0$ as an example, for which our goal is to change ct_ε from encrypting $(\mathsf{normal}, C, \varepsilon, \{k_i\}_{0 \leq i < D}, s_\varepsilon)$ to being simulated and to program $\mathcal{O}(\mathsf{hEval}, h_0, \cdot)$. This can be done in three steps:

1. Change ct_ε to encrypting $(\mathsf{sim}, H(k_0, \varepsilon) \oplus (\mathsf{ct}_0\|\mathsf{ct}_1))$. Seeing the sim flag, the function f_0 simply outputs the second component, the *hardwired* output. This change is indistinguishable to the security of FE.
2. Replace the appearance of $H(k_0, \varepsilon)$ in ct_ε and the response to $\mathcal{O}(\mathsf{hEval}, h_0, \varepsilon)$ by a random string otp_ε. This change is indistinguishable by the PRF security of H.

Input. C, the circuit being obfuscated.

Steps.
1. For $0 \leq i < D$, sample $k_i \xleftarrow{\$} \{0,1\}^\lambda$ and obtain its handle h_i from PrO.
2. Sample $s_\varepsilon \xleftarrow{\$} \{0,1\}^\lambda$.
3. For $0 \leq d \leq D$, sample fresh FE key pair $(\mathsf{mpk}_d, \mathsf{msk}_d)$ and run $\mathsf{sk}_d \xleftarrow{\$} \mathsf{KeyGen}(\mathsf{msk}_d, f_d)$ for f_d defined below.
4. Run $\mathsf{ct}_\varepsilon \xleftarrow{\$} \mathsf{Enc}(\mathsf{mpk}_0, \mathsf{info}_\varepsilon)$ with $\mathsf{info}_\varepsilon = (\mathsf{normal}, \varepsilon, \{k_i\}_{0 \leq i < D}, s_\varepsilon)$.
5. Output $\widehat{C} = (\{h_i\}_{0 \leq i < D}, \mathsf{ct}_\varepsilon, \{\mathsf{sk}_d\}_{0 \leq d \leq D})$.

Functions. (normal mode)
- For $0 \leq d < D$, the function $f_d(\mathsf{normal}, \chi, \{k_i\}_{d \leq i < D}, s_\chi)$
   1. computes $s_{\chi\|0}\|r_{\chi\|0}\|s_{\chi\|0}\|r_{\chi\|0} \leftarrow G(s_\chi)$;
   2. for $b \in \{0,1\}$, runs $\mathsf{ct}_{\chi\|b} \leftarrow \mathsf{Enc}(\mathsf{mpk}_{d+1}, \mathsf{info}_{\chi\|b}; r_{\chi\|b})$, where $\mathsf{info}_{\chi\|b} = (\mathsf{normal}, C, \chi\|b, \{k_i\}_{d+1 \leq i < D}, s_{\chi\|b})$;
   3. outputs $H(k_d, \chi) \oplus (\mathsf{ct}_{\chi\|0}\|\mathsf{ct}_{\chi\|1})$.
- For $d = D$, the function $f_D(\mathsf{normal}, C, x, s_x)$ outputs $C(x)$.
   (There are no k's in the leaf ciphertexts.)

Fig. 2. Second Attempt of Ideal Obfuscator.

3. Change ct_ε to encrypting $(\mathsf{sim}, v_\varepsilon)$ and replace the response to $\mathcal{O}(\mathsf{hEval}, h_0, \varepsilon)$ by $v_\varepsilon \oplus (\mathsf{ct}_0\|\mathsf{ct}_1)$, where v_ε is a random string. This is identical to the previous hybrid.

(After these steps, we are ready to work with $\mathsf{ct}_0, \mathsf{ct}_1$.) This strategy generalizes to every layer of the tree, except that each leaf ct_x will hardwire $C(x)$ instead of a random v_x during simulation. Moreover, the simulator only creates $\mathsf{ct}_{\chi\|0}, \mathsf{ct}_{\chi\|1}$ when the adversary queries $\mathcal{O}(\mathsf{hEval}, h_{|\chi|}, \chi)$, and only queries $C(x)$ if it has to create ct_x. This implies that the simulator is polynomial-time and the security loss of the proof is polynomial.

While the intuition is simple, there is still an important issue that we overlooked. The problem is that the *plaintext* inside ct_χ is of length $|\mathsf{ct}_{\chi\|0}\|\mathsf{ct}_{\chi\|1}|$, *twice* as long as a (one-layer-deeper) *ciphertext*. As such, $|\mathsf{ct}_\varepsilon|$ grows at least exponentially as D increases. To resolve this issue, we revisit the simulation strategy at the very first layer and then apply the idea to the all layers.

Fixing Simulation Efficiency. To fix the simulator itself, instead of a long, truly random v_ε, we encrypt a short PRG seed in ct_ε and let f_0 output the PRG expansion during simulation. We must also not hardwire the complete decryption result into ct_ε in Step 1 above. The solution is to work on the decryption result block by block. The scheme is outlined in Fig. 3.

To demonstrate that, let $|\mathsf{ct}|$ be (an upper bound of) FE ciphertext length. We define two parameters B, the number of blocks, and L, the length of each block, which we set so that $LB \geq 2|\mathsf{ct}|$. Now, instead of one key/handle pair

(h_0, k_0) for the first layer, we use B pairs $\{(h_{0,j}, k_{0,j})\}_{1 \leq j \leq B}$. We also assume $H(k, \cdot)$ is of length L. To switch ct_ε from real to simulation, consider the following series of hybrids for $1 \leq \beta \leq B$:

1. Remove $k_{0,\beta}$ from ct_ε and hardwire $H(k_{0,\beta}, \varepsilon) \oplus [\mathsf{ct}_0 \| \mathsf{ct}_1]_\beta$, the βth block of the output, into ct_ε. Here, $[\cdot]_\beta$ is the βth block of a string.
2. Replace the hardwired block in ct_ε by random and program $\mathcal{O}(\mathsf{hEval}, h_{0,\beta}, \varepsilon)$ for consistency. This is allowed since $k_{0,\beta}$ has been removed from the view of the adversary.
3. Replace the hardwired block in ct_ε by PRG expansion (while reprogramming $\mathcal{O}(\mathsf{hEval}, h_{0,\beta}, \varepsilon)$ for consistency). This change is indistinguishable due to the security of PRG.
4. Undo hardwiring by putting the PRG seed into ct_ε.

This idea can be generalized to every node in every layer, except that the last layer is handled using $C(x)$. The hybrid argument will proceed layer by layer, and inside each layer, block by block. For each block, all the (queried) ciphertexts are switched together.

To see that the lengths are under control, note that the plaintext contains (at most) the circuit, an input prefix, DB hash keys, one L-bit block, and B PRG seeds. Recall that we assume linear-time encryption in this overview, so $|\mathsf{ct}| = O(|C| + D + DB\lambda + L + B\lambda)$. The constraint $LB \geq 2|\mathsf{ct}|$ can be easily satisfied by setting $L = B = \Theta(|C|D\lambda)$.

Input. C, the circuit being obfuscated.

Steps.
1. For $0 \leq i < D, 1 \leq j \leq B$, sample $k_{i,j} \xleftarrow{\$} \{0,1\}^\lambda$ and obtain its handle $h_{i,j}$ from $\mathrm{Pr}\mathcal{O}$.
2. Sample $s_\varepsilon \xleftarrow{\$} \{0,1\}^\lambda$.
3. For $0 \leq d \leq D$, sample fresh FE key pair $(\mathsf{mpk}_d, \mathsf{msk}_d)$ and run $\mathsf{sk}_d \xleftarrow{\$} \mathsf{KeyGen}(\mathsf{msk}_d, f_d)$ for f_d defined below.
4. Run $\mathsf{ct}_\varepsilon \xleftarrow{\$} \mathsf{Enc}(\mathsf{mpk}_0, \mathsf{info}_\varepsilon)$ with $\mathsf{info}_\varepsilon = (\mathsf{normal}, \varepsilon, \{k_{i,j}\}_{\substack{0 \leq i < D \\ 1 \leq j \leq B}}, s_\varepsilon)$.
5. Output $\widehat{C} = (\{h_{i,j}\}_{\substack{0 \leq i < D \\ 1 \leq j \leq B}}, \mathsf{ct}_\varepsilon, \{\mathsf{sk}_d\}_{0 \leq d \leq D})$.

Functions. (normal mode)
- For $0 \leq d < D$, the function $f_d(\mathsf{normal}, \chi, \{k_{i,j}\}_{\substack{d \leq i < D \\ 1 \leq j \leq B}}, s_\chi)$
    1. computes $s_{\chi\|0} \| r_{\chi\|0} \| s_{\chi\|0} \| r_{\chi\|0} \leftarrow G(s_\chi)$;
    2. for $b \in \{0,1\}$, runs $\mathsf{ct}_{\chi\|b} \leftarrow \mathsf{Enc}(\mathsf{mpk}_{d+1}, \mathsf{info}_{\chi\|b}; r_{\chi\|b})$, where $\mathsf{info}_{\chi\|b} = (\mathsf{normal}, C, \chi\|b, \{k_{i,j}\}_{\substack{d+1 \leq i < D \\ 1 \leq j \leq B}}, s_{\chi\|b})$;
    3. outputs $(H(k_{d,1}, \chi) \| \cdots \| H(k_{d,B}, \chi)) \oplus (\mathsf{ct}_{\chi\|0} \| \mathsf{ct}_{\chi\|1})$.
- For $d = D$, the function $f_D(\mathsf{normal}, C, x, s_x)$ outputs $C(x)$. (There are no k's in the leaf ciphertexts.)

Fig. 3. Final Construction of Ideal Obfuscator.

3   Preliminaries

We denote by λ the security parameter, and use the standard notions $\approx, \approx_s, \equiv$ for computational indistinguishability, statistical indistinguishability, and identity. The order of tuples of ordered objects is lexicographical, so $(a, b) \leq (c, d)$ means either $a = c$ and $b \leq d$ or $a < c$, for integers a, b, c, d. For two strings x, y, we write $x \| y$ for their concatenation. The empty string is denoted by ε. Given a string x and a length $0 \leq i \leq |x|$, we let $x_{\leq i}$ be the length-i prefix of x. In the context where strings are canonically split into blocks, $[x]_j$ denotes the jth block of x for $j \geq 1$. For a circuit C, we write $C[w]$ for C with w hardwired into its leading portion of input.

Pseudorandom Generators and Pseudorandom Functions. We assume that the PRG seed length is always λ, that its output length ℓ_{out} can be freely specified, and that its running time is $\ell_{\text{out}} \operatorname{poly}(\lambda)$. Similarly, we assume that the PRF key is uniformly random over $\{0, 1\}^\lambda$, that its input/output lengths $\ell_{\text{in}}, \ell_{\text{out}}$ can be freely specified, and that its running time is $\ell_{\text{in}} \ell_{\text{out}} \operatorname{poly}(\lambda)$.[7]

Functional Encryption. We base our obfuscation scheme on 1-key functional encryption, which is weaker than the standard notion:[8]

Definition 1 (1-key FE [17]). *A (public-key) 1-key functional encryption scheme (for circuits) consists of 3 efficient algorithms:*

- $\mathsf{Gen}(1^\lambda, f)$ *takes a circuit* $f : \{0, 1\}^n \to \{0, 1\}^*$ *as input. It outputs a pair* $(\mathsf{pk}, \mathsf{sk}_f)$ *of public (encryption) key and secret (decryption) key for* f.
- $\mathsf{Enc}(\mathsf{pk}, z)$ *takes as input the public key and some plaintext* $z \in \{0, 1\}^n$. *It outputs a ciphertext* ct.
- $\mathsf{Dec}(\mathsf{sk}_f, \mathsf{ct})$ *takes as input the secret key and a ciphertext. It is supposed to compute* $f(z)$.

The scheme must be correct, *i.e., for all* $\lambda \in \mathbb{N}$, *circuit* $f : \{0, 1\}^n \to \{0, 1\}^*$, *input* $z \in \{0, 1\}^n$, *it holds that*

$$\Pr\left[\begin{array}{c} (\mathsf{pk}, \mathsf{sk}_f) \xleftarrow{\$} \mathsf{Gen}(1^\lambda, f) \\ \mathsf{ct} \xleftarrow{\$} \mathsf{Enc}(\mathsf{pk}, z) \end{array} : \mathsf{Dec}(\mathsf{sk}_f, \mathsf{ct}) = f(z)\right] = 1.$$

We require the encryption algorithm to run in time subquadratic in $|z|$ and sublinear in $|f|$:

Definition 2 (efficiency). *A 1-key FE scheme* $(\mathsf{Gen}, \mathsf{Enc}, \mathsf{Dec})$ *(Definition 1) has* subquadratic-sublinear efficiency *(or* sufficiently efficient *for the purpose of this work) if* Enc *runs in time*

$$(n^{2-2\varepsilon} + m^{1-\varepsilon}) \operatorname{poly}(\lambda) \qquad \text{for some constant } \varepsilon > 0,$$

where $n = |z|$ *is the input length of* f *and* $m = |f|$ *is the circuit size of* f.

---

[7] The required properties can be achieved by standard PRG extension techniques and indifferentiable domain extension of random oracles.

[8] In retrospect, this notion is an interpolation between functional encryption and unary function-revealing encryption [37].

By a standard result [47] in circuit complexity, a circuit of Enc of subquadratic-sublinear size can be efficiently computed. Hereafter, we will use such a bound for uniform circuit complexity of Enc.

We need the 1-key FE scheme to be *adaptively* secure:

Definition 3 (adaptive security). *A 1-key FE scheme* (Gen, Enc, Dec) *(Definition 1) is adaptively secure if* $\mathsf{Exp}^0_{\text{1-key}} \approx \mathsf{Exp}^1_{\text{1-key}}$, *where* $\mathsf{Exp}^b_{\text{1-key}}(1^\lambda)$ *with adversary* $\mathcal{A}$ *proceeds as follows:*

- **Setup.** *Launch* $\mathcal{A}(1^\lambda)$, *receive a circuit* $f : \{0,1\}^n \to \{0,1\}^*$ *from* $\mathcal{A}$, *run*

$$(\mathsf{pk}, \mathsf{sk}_f) \xleftarrow{\$} \mathsf{Gen}(1^\lambda, f),$$

  and send $(\mathsf{pk}, \mathsf{sk}_f)$ *to* $\mathcal{A}$.
- **Challenge.** $\mathcal{A}$ *chooses two inputs* $z_0, z_1 \in \{0,1\}^n$. *Run* $\mathsf{ct} \xleftarrow{\$} \mathsf{Enc}(\mathsf{pk}, z_b)$ *and send* ct *to* $\mathcal{A}$.
- **Guess.** $\mathcal{A}$ *outputs a bit* $b' \in \{0,1\}$. *The outcome of the experiment is* b' *if* $f(z_0) = f(z_1)$. *Otherwise, the outcome is set to* 0.

There is a long series of works [2,5,6,17,26,33,39,40] studying the transformations among functional encryption schemes with various security and efficiency guarantees. It is known [33,46] that standard public-key FE with encryption time $m^{1-\varepsilon} \operatorname{poly}(\lambda, n)$ and weak selective security against one key query implies standard public-key FE with encryption time $n \operatorname{poly}(\lambda)$ and full adaptive security against unbounded collusion.[9] The latter can be used as a sufficiently efficient and adaptively secure 1-key FE.

We can assume, without loss of generality (neither efficiency nor security), that Enc uses a uniformly random λ-bit string as its randomness, by using a PRG with efficiency stated earlier in this section.

Idealized Model. We will define ideal obfuscation with respect to an idealized model, and construct such a scheme in a particular idealized model.

Definition 4 (idealized model). *In an idealized model with oracle* $\mathcal{O}$, *all algorithms, including adversaries, are given access to* $\mathcal{O}$. *The oracle is programmable, i.e., security reductions as well as simulators in simulation-based security notions can provide an alternative implementation of* $\mathcal{O}$.

As an example, the standard model is an idealized model with $\mathcal{O}() = \perp$.

---

[9] In a standard public-key FE, the scheme is set up for a master public/secret key pair not tied to f, and a key for f can be derived separately from the master secret key. Weak selective security means that the adversary chooses f, z_0, z_1 independent of the master public key. Full adaptive security against unbounded collusion means that the adversary can choose z_0, z_1 and arbitrarily many f_q's after seeing the master public key and in an arbitrary interleaving manner.

Oracle Circuits. In an idealized model, we may consider circuits containing gates calling into an oracle, referred to as *oracle circuits*. Like a usual circuit, the description $C^\bullet$ of an oracle circuit consists of its gates and wires, with the convention that oracle gates are just placeholders, i.e., $C^\bullet$ does not specify the behavior of the oracle. The circuit can be evaluated given an input x and an oracle $\mathcal{O}$ (with appropriate input/output lengths), which is denoted by $C^{\mathcal{O}}(x)$.

4   The Pseudorandom Oracle (Pr$\mathcal{O}$) Model

We now formally define the pseudorandom oracle model.

Definition 5 (Pr$\mathcal{O}$M). *Let H be a pseudorandom function. The* pseudorandom oracle model *for H is the idealized model with the oracle $\mathcal{O}$ that internally uses a random permutation*

$$\mathsf{hMap} : \{0,1\}^\lambda \to \{0,1\}^\lambda$$

and that responds to the following 2 types of queries:

$$\mathcal{O}(\mathsf{hGen}, k) = \mathsf{hMap}(k), \quad \mathcal{O}(\mathsf{hEval}, h, t) = H(\mathsf{hMap}^{-1}(h), t).$$

5   Ideal Obfuscation

We still define ideal obfuscators as algorithms and security properties in idealized models, instead of an idealized model itself. The reason is elaborated after the security definition.

Definition 6 ((circuit) obfuscation). *A (circuit) obfuscation scheme in an idealized model with oracle $\mathcal{O}$ is an efficient algorithm $\mathsf{Obf}^{\mathcal{O}}(1^\lambda, C)$ that, given a circuit C as input, outputs an oracle circuit $\widehat{C}^\bullet$. The scheme must be correct, i.e., for all $\lambda \in \mathbb{N}$, circuit $C : \{0,1\}^D \to \{0,1\}^*$, input $x \in \{0,1\}^D$, it holds that*

$$\Pr\left[\widehat{C}^\bullet \xleftarrow{\$} \mathsf{Obf}^{\mathcal{O}}(1^\lambda, C) : \widehat{C}^{\mathcal{O}}(x) = C(x)\right] = 1.$$

We remark that the scheme can only obfuscate *vanilla* circuits, which do not use the idealized model oracle $\mathcal{O}$, yet the oracle $\mathcal{O}$ can be used during evaluation. This gap is necessary to avoid the impossibility results [11].

Our definition of ideal obfuscation in an idealized model is inspired by the indifferentiability framework [44]:

Definition 7 (ideal obfuscation). *An obfuscation scheme $\mathsf{Obf}^{\mathcal{O}}$ (Definition 6) is an* ideal obfuscation (with universal simulation) *if there exists an efficient simulator $\mathcal{S} = (\mathcal{S}_1, \mathcal{S}_2, \mathcal{S}_3)$ (with shared state) such that for all efficient adversary $\mathcal{A} = (\mathcal{A}_1, \mathcal{A}_2)$ (with shared state), its advantage is negligible:*

$$\Pr\left[\begin{array}{l} C \xleftarrow{\$} \mathcal{A}_1^{\mathcal{O}}(1^\lambda) \\ \widehat{C}^\bullet \xleftarrow{\$} \mathsf{Obf}^{\mathcal{O}}(1^\lambda, C) \end{array} : \mathcal{A}_2^{\mathcal{O}}(\widehat{C}^\bullet) = 1 \right]$$

$$-\Pr\left[\begin{array}{l} C \xleftarrow{\$} \mathcal{A}_1^{\mathcal{S}_1}(1^\lambda) \\ \widetilde{C}^\bullet \xleftarrow{\$} \mathcal{S}_2^C(1^\lambda, 1^D, 1^S) \end{array} : \mathcal{A}_2^{\mathcal{S}_3^C}(\widetilde{C}^\bullet) = 1 \right].$$

Here, $D = |x|$ is the input length of C, and $S = |C|$ is the circuit size of C.

Although Definition 7 does not guarantee security when multiple circuits are obfuscated, the simulator for our construction readily extends to handle multiple circuits.

We add a remark about our security definition and the ideal obfuscation model alluded to in the introduction. The idealized model IdealObf is as follows:

- IdealObf(hGen, C) takes a circuit $C : \{0,1\}^n \to \{0,1\}$ as input and outputs a handle h.
- IdealObf(hEval, h, x) takes as input a handle h and some $x \in \{0,1\}^n$, and outputs $C(x)$, where C is the circuit corresponding to h.

The usual way of defining that Obf is a construction of IdealObf in (or from) $\mathcal{O}$ via indifferentiability [44] is to require

$$(\mathsf{Obf}^{\mathcal{O}}, \mathcal{O}) \approx (\mathsf{IdealObf}, \mathcal{S}^{\mathsf{IdealObf}})$$

for some (potentially distinguisher-dependent) simulator $\mathcal{S}$, where $\mathcal{S}$ does not get to observe or respond to IdealObf queries. In contrast, Definition 7 allows the simulator to partially observe (namely, the input length and the circuit size of) and create the response to an obfuscation query, for two reasons:

1. Unlike hash functions (often considered for indifferentiability), whose output is supposedly a random string, an obfuscated circuit is a structured object, whose format depends on the obfuscator and cannot be uniformly specified *a priori*.
2. The simulator in our construction can only respond indistinguishably from, but not identically to, the real obfuscation algorithm.

Due to the first reason and the fact that security is defined differently from indifferentiability, we choose to not formally define the ideal obfuscation model. Nevertheless, we consider Definition 7 essentially indifferentiability with some "interface gluing".

6 Construction of Ideal Obfuscation in the Pr$\mathcal{O}$ Model

Similar to many prior works [4,17] building obfuscation from FE, our construction involves a binary tree of FE ciphertexts, yet its structure is slightly different to take advantage of the Pr$\mathcal{O}$ model. The binary tree structure is instructive for understanding the correctness, as well as the security proof in Sect. 7, of our construction.

The obfuscation of a circuit C with D-bit input involves a perfect binary tree of $(D + 1)$ levels, as depicted in Fig. 4. Each node is identified by its root-to-node path, each leaf an input x to C, and each internal node a proper prefix of x. For each $\chi \in \{0,1\}^{\leq D}$, node χ is associated with ct_χ encrypting C, χ plus some other information. The behavior of decrypting ct_χ is as follows:

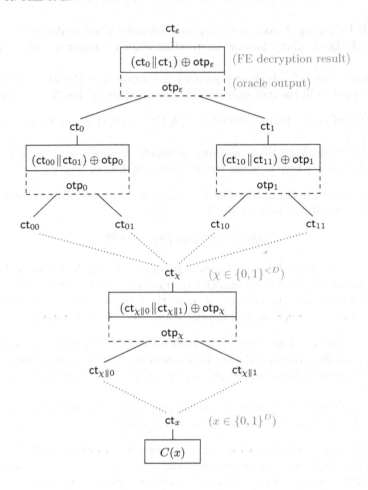

Fig. 4. The binary tree of ciphertexts in Construction 1 (normal behavior).

- For an internal node, $\chi \in \{0,1\}^{<D}$ is a proper fix of the input, and decrypting ct_χ yields its children $\mathsf{ct}_{\chi\|0}$ and $\mathsf{ct}_{\chi\|1}$ *padded* by the one-time pad otp_χ associated with χ, which is the PrOM oracle output.
- For a leaf, $\chi = x \in \{0,1\}^D$ is the input, and decrypting ct_x yields $C(x)$.

The obfuscated circuit $\widehat{C}^\bullet$ contains the root ciphertext ct_ε, FE secret keys, and handles of PrOM. To evaluate $C(x)$, starting from the root ciphertext ct_ε, for each proper prefix χ of x, we decrypt ct_χ, *unpad* the result using otp_χ, and keep either $\chi_{\chi\|0}$ or $\mathsf{ct}_{\chi\|1}$ (depending on the next bit of x), until we reach ct_x, which we decrypt one last time for $C(x)$.

Ingredients of Construction 1. Let

- D be the input length of the circuit C to be obfuscated;
- S the circuit size of C;

- L the block length, a parameter to be determined later;
- B the number of blocks, a parameter to be determined later;
- $H : \{0,1\}^\lambda \times \{0,1\}^D \to \{0,1\}^L$ the PRF of $\mathrm{Pr}\mathcal{O}\mathrm{M}$;
- $G_{sr} : \{0,1\}^\lambda \to \{0,1\}^{4\lambda}$ the PRG for encryption randomness;
- $G_v : \{0,1\}^\lambda \to \{0,1\}^L$ the PRG for decryption result simulation;
- $(\mathsf{Gen}, \mathsf{Enc}, \mathsf{Dec})$ an FE scheme whose Enc uses λ-bit uniform randomness.

We construct an obfuscation scheme in the $\mathrm{Pr}\mathcal{O}$ model for H:

Construction 1 (obfuscation). $\mathsf{Obf}^\mathcal{O}(1^\lambda, C)$ does the following.

1. It sets up $(D+1)$ FE instances:

$$(\mathsf{pk}_D, \mathsf{sk}_D) \xleftarrow{\$} \mathsf{Gen}(1^\lambda, \mathsf{Eval}),$$

$$(\mathsf{pk}_d, \mathsf{sk}_d) \xleftarrow{\$} \mathsf{Gen}(1^\lambda, \mathsf{Expand}_d[\mathsf{pk}_{d+1}]) \quad \text{for } d = D-1, \ldots, 0,$$

   where Expand_d and Eval are defined in Figs. 5 and 7.
2. It samples keys of H and obtains their handles:

$$k_{i,j} \xleftarrow{\$} \{0,1\}^\lambda, \quad h_{i,j} \leftarrow \mathcal{O}(\mathsf{hGen}, k_{i,j}) \qquad \text{for } 0 \le i < D, 1 \le j \le B.$$

3. It samples the seed and the encryption randomness for the root ciphertext, sets its flag and information, and computes ct_ε:

$$s_\varepsilon \xleftarrow{\$} \{0,1\}^\lambda, \qquad r_\varepsilon \xleftarrow{\$} \{0,1\}^\lambda,$$

$$\mathsf{flag}_\varepsilon \leftarrow \mathsf{normal}, \qquad \mathsf{info}_\varepsilon \leftarrow (C, \{k_{i,j}\}_{0 \le i < D, 1 \le j \le B}, s_\chi),$$

$$\mathsf{ct}_\varepsilon \leftarrow \mathsf{Enc}(\mathsf{pk}_0, \mathsf{flag}_\varepsilon, \varepsilon, \mathsf{info}_\varepsilon; r_\varepsilon).$$

4. It outputs $\widehat{C}^\bullet[\mathsf{ct}_\varepsilon, \{\mathsf{sk}_d\}_{0 \le d \le D}, \{h_{i,j}\}_{0 \le i < D, 1 \le j \le B}]$, defined in Fig. 6, as an obfuscation of C.

Correctness. $\widehat{C}^\mathcal{O}$ in Fig. 6 follows the tree structure in Fig. 4. Correctness readily follows by inspecting the branches of Expand_d and Eval in Fig. 5 and noting

$$H(k_{d,1}, \chi_d \| 0^{D-d}) \| \cdots \| H(k_{d,B}, \chi_d \| 0^{D-d})$$

$$= \mathcal{O}(\mathsf{hEval}, h_{d,1}, \chi_d \| 0^{D-d}) \| \cdots \| \mathcal{O}(\mathsf{hEval}, h_{d,B}, \chi_d \| 0^{D-d}).$$

Remarks. In our construction, the domain/codomain of the hash function are dependent on (the size and the input length of) the circuit being obfuscated. Formally, our obfuscator works in different $\mathrm{Pr}\mathcal{O}$ models (relative to different PRFs) for circuits of different sizes and input lengths. However, it is simple to tweak the construction as well as the security proof so that the obfuscator works in a single $\mathrm{Pr}\mathcal{O}$ model for $H : \{0,1\}^\lambda \times \{0,1\}^* \to \{0,1\}$ for all circuits. This is similar to how $\{0,1\}^* \to \{0,1\}$ implements the ROM for every domain/codomain by domain separation.

$\text{Expand}_d[\text{pk}_{d+1}](\text{flag}_\chi, \chi, \text{info}_\chi)$ — **Function for Level** $0 \leq d < D$

Hardwired. pk_{d+1}, public key for level $(d+1)$.

Input. $\text{flag}_\chi \in \{\text{normal}, \text{hyb}, \text{sim}\}$, flag associated with χ;
$\chi \in \{0,1\}^d$, proper prefix of circuit input;
info_χ, information associated with χ, format varying by flag_χ.

Output.
$$\begin{cases} \text{Expand}_{d,\text{normal}}[\text{pk}_{d+1}](\chi, \text{info}_\chi), & \text{if } \text{flag}_\chi = \text{normal}; \\ \text{Expand}_{d,\text{hyb}}[\text{pk}_{d+1}](\chi, \text{info}_\chi), & \text{if } \text{flag}_\chi = \text{hyb}; \\ \text{Expand}_{d,\text{sim}}(\chi, \text{info}_\chi), & \text{if } \text{flag}_\chi = \text{sim}. \end{cases}\right\} \text{Fig. 7}$$

$\text{Eval}(\text{flag}_\chi, \chi, \text{info}_\chi)$ — **Function for Level** D

Input. $\text{flag}_\chi \in \{\text{normal}, \text{sim}\}$, flag associated with χ;
$\chi \in \{0,1\}^D$, circuit input;
info_χ, information associated with χ, format varying by flag_χ.

Output.
$$\begin{cases} \text{Eval}_{\text{normal}}(\chi, \text{info}_\chi), & \text{if } \text{flag}_\chi = \text{normal}; \\ \text{Eval}_{\text{sim}}(\chi, \text{info}_\chi), & \text{if } \text{flag}_\chi = \text{sim}. \quad (\text{Fig. 7}) \end{cases}$$

$\text{Expand}_{d,\text{normal}}[\text{pk}_{d+1}](\chi, \text{info}_\chi)$

Hardwired. pk_{d+1}, public key for level $(d+1)$.

Input. $\chi \in \{0,1\}^d$, proper prefix of circuit input;
$\text{info}_\chi = (C, \{k_{i,j}\}_{d \leq i < D, 1 \leq j \leq B}, s_\chi)$:
C, circuit being obfuscated;
$k_{i,j}$, keys of H for level $d, \ldots, D-1$;
s_χ, seed of G_{sr} associated with χ.

Output. Computed as follows.

$s_{\chi\|0} \| r_{\chi\|0} \| s_{\chi\|1} \| r_{\chi\|1} \leftarrow G_{sr}(s_\chi)$

for $\eta = 0, 1$:

    $\text{flag}_{\chi\|\eta} \leftarrow \text{normal}$

    $\text{info}_{\chi\|\eta} \leftarrow (C, \{k_{i,j}\}_{d+1 \leq i < D, 1 \leq j \leq B}, s_{\chi\|\eta})$

    $\text{ct}_{\chi\|\eta} \leftarrow \text{Enc}(\text{pk}_{d+1}, \text{flag}_{\chi\|\eta}, \chi\|\eta, \text{info}_{\chi\|\eta})$

    $\text{otp}_\chi \leftarrow H(k_{d,1}, \chi\|0^{D-d}) \| \cdots \| H(k_{d,B}, \chi\|0^{D-d})$

    output $v_\chi \leftarrow (\text{ct}_{\chi\|0} \| \text{ct}_{\chi\|1}) \oplus \text{otp}_\chi$

$\text{Eval}_{\text{normal}}(\chi, \text{info}_\chi)$

Input. $\chi \in \{0,1\}^D$, circuit input;
$\text{info}_\chi = (C, s_\chi)$:
C, circuit being obfuscated;
s_χ, unused.

Output. $C(\chi)$, computed by evaluating a universal circuit at (C, χ).

Fig. 5. The circuits Expand_d and Eval in Construction 1 (branches for correctness).

$$\widehat{C}^{\mathcal{O}}[\mathsf{ct}_\varepsilon, \{\mathsf{sk}_d\}_{0 \le d \le D}, \{h_{i,j}\}_{0 \le i < D, 1 \le j \le B}](x)$$

Hardwired. ct_ε, root ciphertext;
 sk_d, secret keys;
 $h_{i,j}$, handles of Pr$\mathcal{O}$M.

Input. $x \in \{0,1\}^D$, circuit input.

Output. Computed as follows.

    for $d = 0, \ldots, D-1$:

$$\chi_d \leftarrow x_{\le d}$$
$$v_{\chi_d} \leftarrow \mathsf{Dec}(\mathsf{sk}_d, \mathsf{ct}_{\chi_d})$$
$$\mathsf{otp}_{\chi_d} \leftarrow \mathcal{O}(\mathsf{hEval}, h_{d,1}, \chi_d \| 0^{D-d}) \| \cdots \| \mathcal{O}(\mathsf{hEval}, h_{d,B}, \chi_d \| 0^{D-d})$$
$$\mathsf{ct}_{\chi_d \| 0} \| \mathsf{ct}_{\chi_d \| 1} \leftarrow v_{\chi_d} \oplus \mathsf{otp}_{\chi_d}$$

    output $\mathsf{Dec}(\mathsf{sk}_D, \mathsf{ct}_x)$

Fig. 6. The circuit $\widehat{C}^\bullet$ in Construction 1.

7 Security Proof of Ideal Obfuscation in the Pr$\mathcal{O}$ Model

Theorem 1. *Assuming PRF security of H, PRG security of G_{sr}, G_v, adaptive security (Definition 3) of $(\mathsf{Gen}, \mathsf{Enc}, \mathsf{Dec})$, and appropriate choice of L, B [34], then Construction 1 is an ideal obfuscation (Definition 7) in the Pr$\mathcal{O}$ model (Definition 5) for H.*

We specify the simulator in Sect. 7.1. The proof of Theorem 1 can be found in the full version [34].

Branches for Proof and Hybrid Template. The simulator for Construction 1 and the proof of Theorem 1 use the branches of Expand_d and Eval defined in Fig. 7.

The hybrids as well as the simulator follow a common template shown in Fig. 8, and we define a hybrid by specifying the placeholders in the hybrid. The three phases of the interaction are as follows:

- $\mathcal{S}_1$ (pre-obfuscation Pr$\mathcal{O}$M). In this phase, $\mathcal{S}_1$ efficiently implements the Pr$\mathcal{O}$M using lazy sampling.
- $\mathcal{S}_2$ (creating the obfuscation). In this phase, $\mathcal{S}_2$ generates FE keys, samples ("special") Pr$\mathcal{O}$M handles and keys used in the obfuscation, generates the root ciphertext ct_ε, and outputs the obfuscation. The handles are distinct, but the keys are not necessarily distinct (to facilitate application of PRF security), and not all handles correspond to a key. The placeholders specify which handles have a corresponding key and how ct_ε is generated.
- $\mathcal{S}_3$ (post-obfuscation Pr$\mathcal{O}$M). There are multiple cases, depending on whether the query is related to the "special" handles and keys:

$$\text{Expand}_{d,\text{hyb}}[\text{pk}_{d+1}](\chi, \text{info}_\chi)$$

Hardwired. pk_{d+1}, public key for level $(d+1)$.

Input. $\chi \in \{0,1\}^d$, proper prefix of circuit input;
$\quad \text{info}_\chi = (C, \{k_{i,j}\}_{d<i<D, 1\le j\le B}, s_\chi, \beta,$
$\qquad\qquad \{\sigma_{\chi,j}\}_{1\le j<\beta}, w_\chi, \{k_{d,j}\}_{\beta<j\le B})$:
$\qquad C$, circuit being obfuscated;
$\qquad k_{i,j}$, keys of H for level $d+1,\dots,D-1$;
$\qquad s_\chi$, seed of G_{sr} associated with χ;
$\qquad \beta$, hybrid index;
$\qquad \sigma_{\chi,j}$, seeds of G_v associated with χ (gradually introduced);
$\qquad w_\chi$, hardwired block of decryption result;
$\qquad k_{d,j}$, keys of H for level d (gradually removed).

Output. Computed as follows ($\boxed{\text{difference}}$ from $\text{Expand}_{d,\text{normal}}$).

$\quad s_{\chi\|0}\|r_{\chi\|0}\|s_{\chi\|1}\|r_{\chi\|1} \leftarrow G_{sr}(s_\chi)$
$\quad$ **for** $\eta = 0, 1$:
$\qquad \text{flag}_{\chi\|\eta} \leftarrow \text{normal}$
$\qquad \text{info}_{\chi\|\eta} \leftarrow (C, \{k_{i,j}\}_{d+1\le i<D, 1\le j\le B}, s_{\chi\|\eta})$
$\qquad \text{ct}_{\chi\|\eta} \leftarrow \text{Enc}(\text{pk}_{d+1}, \text{flag}_{\chi\|\eta}, \chi\|\eta, \text{info}_{\chi\|\eta})$
$\qquad$ **output** $v_\chi \leftarrow \boxed{G_v(\sigma_{\chi,1})\|\cdots\|G_v(\sigma_{\chi,\beta-1})\|w_\chi}$
$\qquad\qquad \| \big([\text{ct}_{\chi\|0}\|\text{ct}_{\chi\|1}]_{\beta+1} \oplus H(k_{d,\beta+1}, \chi\|0^{D-d})\big)\|\cdots$
$\qquad\qquad \| \big([\text{ct}_{\chi\|0}\|\text{ct}_{\chi\|1}]_{B} \oplus H(k_{d,B}, \chi\|0^{D-d})\big)$

$$\text{Expand}_{d,\text{sim}}(\chi, \text{info}_\chi)$$

Input. $\chi \in \{0,1\}^d$, proper prefix of circuit input;
$\quad \text{info}_\chi = \{\sigma_{\chi,j}\}_{1\le j\le B}$, seeds of G_v associated with χ.

Output. $v_\chi \leftarrow G_v(\sigma_{\chi,1})\|\cdots\|G_v(\sigma_{\chi,B})$.

$$\text{Eval}_{\text{sim}}(\chi, \text{info}_\chi)$$

Input. $\chi \in \{0,1\}^D$, circuit input;
$\quad \text{info}_\chi = y_\chi$, hardwired circuit output at χ.

Output. y_χ.

Fig. 7. The circuits Expand_d and Eval in Construction 1 (branches for security proof).

Hybrid Template with $\boxed{\text{Placeholders}}$

Shared State:

$\mathcal{T}_{\text{other}}$, set of (k, h) pairs for hMap, initially $\varnothing$, with

$$\mathsf{Keys}(\mathcal{T}_{\text{other}}) \overset{\text{def}}{=\joinrel=} \{\, k \mid \exists h \text{ such that } (k, h) \in \mathcal{T}_{\text{other}} \,\},$$

$$\mathsf{Handles}(\mathcal{T}_{\text{other}}) \overset{\text{def}}{=\joinrel=} \{\, h \mid \exists k \text{ such that } (k, h) \in \mathcal{T}_{\text{other}} \,\};$$

C, circuit being obfuscated, available in $\mathcal{S}_2$ and $\mathcal{S}_3$;

$\{h_{i,j}\}_{0 \leq i < D, 1 \leq j \leq B}$, handles of PrOM in obfuscation, initially $\bot$;

$\{\mathsf{pk}_d, \mathsf{sk}_d\}_{0 \leq d \leq D}$, public and secret keys, initially $\bot$;

$\boxed{\{k_{i,j}\}}$, keys of H in obfuscation, initially $\bot$;

$\boxed{\{F_{i,j}\}, F_\sigma, F_r, F_s}$, random functions (lazily sampled) for

non-programmed portion of $\mathcal{O}(\mathsf{hEval}, h_{i,j}, \star)$, and $\sigma_{\chi,j}, r_\chi, s_\chi$;

$\boxed{\mathsf{flag}_\chi, \mathsf{info}_\chi, r_\chi}$, components of

$\mathsf{ct}_\chi = \mathsf{Enc}(\mathsf{pk}_{|\chi|}, \mathsf{flag}_\chi, \chi, \mathsf{info}_\chi; r_\chi)$, available in $\mathcal{S}_2$ and $\mathcal{S}_3$.

$\mathcal{S}_1(\mathsf{hGen}, k)$:

    if $\nexists h$ such that $(k, h) \in \mathcal{T}_{\text{other}}$:

        $h \overset{\$}{\leftarrow} \{0, 1\}^\lambda \setminus \big(\mathsf{Handles}(\mathcal{T}_{\text{other}}) \cup \{h_{i,j}\}\big)$

        $\mathcal{T}_{\text{other}} \leftarrow \mathcal{T}_{\text{other}} \cup \{(k, h)\}$

    output the unique h such that $(k, h) \in \mathcal{T}_{\text{other}}$

$\mathcal{S}_1(\mathsf{hEval}, h, t)$:

    if $\nexists k$ such that $(k, h) \in \mathcal{T}_{\text{other}}$:

        $k \overset{\$}{\leftarrow} \{0, 1\}^\lambda \setminus \mathsf{Keys}(\mathcal{T}_{\text{other}})$

        $\mathcal{T}_{\text{other}} \leftarrow \mathcal{T}_{\text{other}} \cup \{(k, h)\}$

    output $H(k, t)$ for the unique k such that $(k, h) \in \mathcal{T}_{\text{other}}$

$\mathcal{S}_2$:

    generate $\{\mathsf{pk}_d, \mathsf{sk}_d\}_{0 \leq d \leq D}$ as specified in Construction 1

    sample uniformly random distinct $h_{i,j}$ from $\{0, 1\}^\lambda \setminus \mathsf{Handles}(\mathcal{T}_{\text{other}})$

    $\{k_{i,j}\} \overset{\$}{\leftarrow} \{0, 1\}^\lambda$

    output $\widehat{C}^\bullet[\mathsf{ct}_\varepsilon, \{\mathsf{sk}_d\}_{0 \leq d \leq D}, \{h_{i,j}\}_{0 \leq i < D, 1 \leq j \leq B}]$

$\mathcal{S}_3(\mathsf{hGen}, k)$:

    if $k = k_{i,j}$ for $\boxed{\text{``}k \overset{?}{=} k_{i,j}\text{''}, \text{ range of } (i, j) \text{ being tested}}$:

        output $h_{i,j}$ for the smallest such (i, j)

    else: same as $\mathcal{S}_1(\mathsf{hGen}, k)$

$\mathcal{S}_3(\mathsf{hEval}, h, t)$:

    if $h = h_{i,j}$:

        if $t = \chi \| 0^{D-i}$ for $\chi \in \{0, 1\}^i$:

            $\boxed{\text{``}h_{i,j} : \chi\text{''}, \text{ response to } \mathcal{S}_3(\mathsf{hEval}, h_{i,j}, t = \chi \| 0^{D-i})}$

        else:

            $\boxed{\text{``}h_{i,j} : t\text{''}, \text{ response to } \mathcal{S}_3(\mathsf{hEval}, h_{i,j}, t \neq \chi \| 0^{D-i})}$

    else: same as $\mathcal{S}_1(\mathsf{hEval}, h, t)$

Fig. 8. The hybrid template for the security proof of Construction 1.

- For $(\mathsf{hGen}, k_{i,j})$, the output is $h_{i,j}$, as it should be. Not all $k_{i,j}$'s are considered in all hybrids (specified by the placeholders). Intuitively, this case can happen only with negligible probability, yet this very fact is proved using the hybrids and the branch is gradually removed as the proof proceeds.
- For $(\mathsf{hEval}, h_{i,j}, \chi \| 0^{D-i})$, its output is supposed to unmask $\mathsf{Dec}(\mathsf{sk}_{|\chi|}, \mathsf{ct}_\chi)$ and specified by the placeholders.
- For $(\mathsf{hEval}, h_{i,j}, \cdot)$, the output is unrelated to obfuscation and specified by the placeholders.
- For the other queries (excluded from $(\mathsf{hGen}, k_{i,j})$ or unrelated to "special" handles and keys), it is the same as $\mathcal{S}_1$.

7.1   Simulator

The simulator is specified in Table 1:

- ct_χ is in *simulation* mode and uses *truly random* r_χ for Enc;
- *no* $h_{i,j}$ has a corresponding PRF key; and
- ct_χ for $\chi \neq \varepsilon$ is *not computed* by $\mathsf{Expand}_{|\chi|-1}$, but *programmed* into the $\mathsf{Pr}\mathcal{OM}$ responses to $h_{|\chi|-1,j}$'s.

Although the template in Fig. 8 has C (the circuit being obfuscated) as part of its share state, the template itself does not use C. The simulator only uses evaluations of C in $\mathcal{S}_3$ (to generate ct_χ for $|\chi| = D$ on demand), hence adheres to the required syntax of a simulator in Definition 7.

Table 1. Specification of the simulator (see Fig. 8).

$\{k_{i,j}\}$	non-existent
$\{F_{i,j}\}$	$\{0,1\}^D \to \{0,1\}^L$ for $0 \leq i < D,\, 1 \leq j \leq B$
F_σ	$\{0,1\}^{<D} \times \{1,\dots,B\} \to \{0,1\}^\lambda$
F_r	$\{0,1\}^{\leq D} \to \{0,1\}^\lambda$
F_s	non-existent
flag_χ	sim
info_χ	$\begin{cases} \{F_\sigma(\chi, j)\}_{1 \leq j \leq B}, & \text{if } |\chi| < D; \\ C(\chi), & \text{if } |\chi| = D. \end{cases}$
r_χ	$F_r(\chi)$
state $\uparrow$ $\mathcal{S}_3 \downarrow$	in simulator
$k \overset{?}{=} k_{i,j}$	non-existent
$h_{i,j} : \chi$	$G_v(F_\sigma(\chi, j)) \oplus [\mathsf{ct}_{\chi\|0} \| \mathsf{ct}_{\chi\|1}]_j$
$h_{i,j} : t$	$F_{i,j}(t)$

Acknowledgments. Aayush Jain was supported by gifts from CyLab of CMU and Google. Huijia Lin and Ji Luo were supported by NSF CNS-1936825 (CAREER), CNS-2026774, a JP Morgan AI Research Award, a Cisco Research Award, and a Simons Collaboration on the Theory of Algorithmic Fairness. Daniel Wichs was supported by NSF CNS-1750795, CNS-2055510, and the JP Morgan Faculty Research Award. The authors thank the anonymous reviewers for their valuable feedback.

References

1. Agrawal, S., et al.: Secure computation from one-way noisy communication, or: anti-correlation via anti-concentration. In: Malkin, T., Peikert, C. (eds.) CRYPTO 2021. LNCS, vol. 12826, pp. 124–154. Springer, Cham (2021). https://doi.org/10.1007/978-3-030-84245-1_5

2. Ananth, P., Brakerski, Z., Segev, G., Vaikuntanathan, V.: From selective to adaptive security in functional encryption. In: Gennaro, R., Robshaw, M. (eds.) CRYPTO 2015. LNCS, vol. 9216, pp. 657–677. Springer, Heidelberg (2015). https://doi.org/10.1007/978-3-662-48000-7_32

3. Ananth, P., Chung, K.M., Fan, X., Qian, L.: Collusion-resistant functional encryption for RAMs. In: Agrawal, S., Lin, D. (eds.) Advances in Cryptology – ASIACRYPT 2022. ASIACRYPT 2022. Lecture Notes in Computer Science, vol. 13791, pp. 160–194. Springer, Cham (2022). https://doi.org/10.1007/978-3-031-22963-3_6

4. Ananth, P., Jain, A.: Indistinguishability obfuscation from compact functional encryption. In: Gennaro, R., Robshaw, M. (eds.) CRYPTO 2015. LNCS, vol. 9215, pp. 308–326. Springer, Heidelberg (2015). https://doi.org/10.1007/978-3-662-47989-6_15

5. Ananth, P., Jain, A., Sahai, A.: Indistinguishability obfuscation from functional encryption for simple functions. Cryptology ePrint Archive, Report 2015/730 (2015). https://eprint.iacr.org/2015/730

6. Ananth, P., Sahai, A.: Functional encryption for turing machines. In: Kushilevitz, E., Malkin, T. (eds.) TCC 2016. LNCS, vol. 9562, pp. 125–153. Springer, Heidelberg (2016). https://doi.org/10.1007/978-3-662-49096-9_6

7. Applebaum, B.: Bootstrapping obfuscators via fast pseudorandom functions. In: Sarkar, P., Iwata, T. (eds.) ASIACRYPT 2014. LNCS, vol. 8874, pp. 162–172. Springer, Heidelberg (2014). https://doi.org/10.1007/978-3-662-45608-8_9

8. Badrinarayanan, S., Ishai, Y., Khurana, D., Sahai, A., Wichs, D.: Refuting the dream XOR lemma via ideal obfuscation and resettable MPC. In: Dachman-Soled, D. (ed.) ITC 2023. LIPIcs, vol. 230, pp. 1–21. Schloss Dagstuhl (2022). https://doi.org/10.4230/LIPIcs.ITC.2022.10

9. Barak, B.: How to go beyond the black-box simulation barrier. In: 42nd FOCS, pp. 106–115. IEEE Computer Society Press, October 2001. https://doi.org/10.1109/SFCS.2001.959885

10. Barak, B., Bitansky, N., Canetti, R., Kalai, Y.T., Paneth, O., Sahai, A.: Obfuscation for evasive functions. In: Lindell, Y. (ed.) TCC 2014. LNCS, vol. 8349, pp. 26–51. Springer, Heidelberg (2014). https://doi.org/10.1007/978-3-642-54242-8_2

11. Barak, B., et al.: On the (Im)possibility of obfuscating programs. In: Kilian, J. (ed.) CRYPTO 2001. LNCS, vol. 2139, pp. 1–18. Springer, Heidelberg (2001). https://doi.org/10.1007/3-540-44647-8_1

12. Bellare, M., Rogaway, P.: Random oracles are practical: a paradigm for designing efficient protocols. In: Denning, D.E., Pyle, R., Ganesan, R., Sandhu, R.S., Ashby, V. (eds.) ACM CCS 93, pp. 62–73. ACM Press, November 1993. https://doi.org/10.1145/168588.168596

13. Bitansky, N., Canetti, R.: On strong simulation and composable point obfuscation. In: Rabin, T. (ed.) CRYPTO 2010. LNCS, vol. 6223, pp. 520–537. Springer, Heidelberg (2010). https://doi.org/10.1007/978-3-642-14623-7_28

14. Bitansky, N., Canetti, R., Chiesa, A., Tromer, E.: Recursive composition and bootstrapping for SNARKS and proof-carrying data. In: Boneh, D., Roughgarden, T., Feigenbaum, J. (eds.) 45th ACM STOC, pp. 111–120. ACM Press, June 2013. https://doi.org/10.1145/2488608.2488623

15. Bitansky, N., Canetti, R., Goldwasser, S., Halevi, S., Kalai, Y.T., Rothblum, G.N.: Program obfuscation with leaky hardware. In: Lee, D.H., Wang, X. (eds.) ASIACRYPT 2011. LNCS, vol. 7073, pp. 722–739. Springer, Heidelberg (2011). https://doi.org/10.1007/978-3-642-25385-0_39

16. Bitansky, N., Nishimaki, R., Passelègue, A., Wichs, D.: From cryptomania to obfustopia through secret-key functional encryption. In: Hirt, M., Smith, A. (eds.) TCC 2016. LNCS, vol. 9986, pp. 391–418. Springer, Heidelberg (2016). https://doi.org/10.1007/978-3-662-53644-5_15

17. Bitansky, N., Vaikuntanathan, V.: Indistinguishability obfuscation from functional encryption. In: Guruswami, V. (ed.) 56th FOCS, pp. 171–190. IEEE Computer Society Press, October 2015. https://doi.org/10.1109/FOCS.2015.20

18. Boyle, E., Ishai, Y., Pass, R., Wootters, M.: Can we access a database both locally and privately? In: Kalai, Y., Reyzin, L. (eds.) TCC 2017. LNCS, vol. 10678, pp. 662–693. Springer, Cham (2017). https://doi.org/10.1007/978-3-319-70503-3_22

19. Canetti, R., Kalai, Y.T., Paneth, O.: On obfuscation with random oracles. In: Dodis, Y., Nielsen, J.B. (eds.) TCC 2015. LNCS, vol. 9015, pp. 456–467. Springer, Heidelberg (2015). https://doi.org/10.1007/978-3-662-46497-7_18

20. Canetti, R., Lin, H., Tessaro, S., Vaikuntanathan, V.: Obfuscation of probabilistic circuits and applications. In: Dodis, Y., Nielsen, J.B. (eds.) TCC 2015. LNCS, vol. 9015, pp. 468–497. Springer, Heidelberg (2015). https://doi.org/10.1007/978-3-662-46497-7_19

21. Canetti, R., Raghuraman, S., Richelson, S., Vaikuntanathan, V.: Chosen-ciphertext secure fully homomorphic encryption. In: Fehr, S. (ed.) PKC 2017. LNCS, vol. 10175, pp. 213–240. Springer, Heidelberg (2017). https://doi.org/10.1007/978-3-662-54388-7_8

22. De Caro, A., Iovino, V., Jain, A., O'Neill, A., Paneth, O., Persiano, G.: On the achievability of simulation-based security for functional encryption. In: Canetti, R., Garay, J.A. (eds.) CRYPTO 2013. LNCS, vol. 8043, pp. 519–535. Springer, Heidelberg (2013). https://doi.org/10.1007/978-3-642-40084-1_29

23. Döttling, N., Mie, T., Müller-Quade, J., Nilges, T.: Basing obfuscation on simple tamper-proof hardware assumptions. Cryptology ePrint Archive, Report 2011/675 (2011). https://eprint.iacr.org/2011/675

24. Fiat, A., Shamir, A.: How to prove yourself: practical solutions to identification and signature problems. In: Odlyzko, A.M. (ed.) CRYPTO 1986. LNCS, vol. 263, pp. 186–194. Springer, Heidelberg (1987). https://doi.org/10.1007/3-540-47721-7_12

25. Garg, S., Gentry, C., Halevi, S., Raykova, M., Sahai, A., Waters, B.: Candidate indistinguishability obfuscation and functional encryption for all circuits. In: 54th FOCS, pp. 40–49. IEEE Computer Society Press, October 2013. https://doi.org/10.1109/FOCS.2013.13

26. Garg, S., Srinivasan, A.: Single-key to multi-key functional encryption with polynomial loss. In: Hirt, M., Smith, A. (eds.) TCC 2016. LNCS, vol. 9986, pp. 419–442. Springer, Heidelberg (2016). https://doi.org/10.1007/978-3-662-53644-5_16
27. Goldwasser, S., Kalai, Y.T.: On the (in)security of the Fiat-Shamir paradigm. In: 44th FOCS, pp. 102–115. IEEE Computer Society Press, October 2003. https://doi.org/10.1109/SFCS.2003.1238185
28. Goldwasser, S., Kalai, Y.T., Popa, R.A., Vaikuntanathan, V., Zeldovich, N.: How to run Turing machines on encrypted data. In: Canetti, R., Garay, J.A. (eds.) CRYPTO 2013. LNCS, vol. 8043, pp. 536–553. Springer, Heidelberg (2013). https://doi.org/10.1007/978-3-642-40084-1_30
29. Goldwasser, S., Rothblum, G.N.: On best-possible obfuscation. In: Vadhan, S.P. (ed.) TCC 2007. LNCS, vol. 4392, pp. 194–213. Springer, Heidelberg (2007). https://doi.org/10.1007/978-3-540-70936-7_11
30. Hamlin, A., Holmgren, J., Weiss, M., Wichs, D.: On the plausibility of fully homomorphic encryption for RAMs. In: Boldyreva, A., Micciancio, D. (eds.) CRYPTO 2019. LNCS, vol. 11692, pp. 589–619. Springer, Cham (2019). https://doi.org/10.1007/978-3-030-26948-7_21
31. Ishai, Y., Korb, A., Lou, P., Sahai, A.: Beyond the Csiszár-korner bound: best-possible wiretap coding via obfuscation. In: Dodis, Y., Shrimpton, T. (eds.) Advances in Cryptology – CRYPTO 2022. CRYPTO 2022. Lecture Notes in Computer Science, vol. 13508. Springer, Cham (2022). https://doi.org/10.1007/978-3-031-15979-4_20
32. Ishai, Y., Pandey, O., Sahai, A.: Public-coin differing-inputs obfuscation and its applications. In: Dodis, Y., Nielsen, J.B. (eds.) TCC 2015. LNCS, vol. 9015, pp. 668–697. Springer, Heidelberg (2015). https://doi.org/10.1007/978-3-662-46497-7_26
33. Jain, A., Lin, H., Luo, J.: On the optimal succinctness and efficiency of functional encryption and attribute-based encryption. In: Hazay, C., Stam, M. (eds.) Advances in Cryptology – EUROCRYPT 2023. EUROCRYPT 2023. Lecture Notes in Computer Science, vol. 14006, pp. 479–510. Springer, Cham (2023). https://doi.org/10.1007/978-3-031-30620-4_16
34. Jain, A., Lin, H., Luo, J., Wichs, D.: The pseudorandom oracle model and ideal obfuscation. Cryptology ePrint Archive, Report 2022/1204 (2022). https://eprint.iacr.org/2022/1204
35. Jain, A., Lin, H., Sahai, A.: Indistinguishability obfuscation from well-founded assumptions. In: Khuller, S., Williams, V.V. (eds.) 53rd ACM STOC, pp. 60–73. ACM Press, June 2021. https://doi.org/10.1145/3406325.3451093
36. Jain, A., Lin, H., Sahai, A.: Indistinguishability obfuscation from LPN over $\mathbb{F}_p$, DLIN, and PRGs in NC^0. In: Dunkelman, O., Dziembowski, S. (eds.) Advances in Cryptology –EUROCRYPT 2022. EUROCRYPT 2022. Lecture Notes in Computer Science, vol. 13275, pp. 670–699. Springer, Cham (2022). https://doi.org/10.1007/978-3-031-06944-4_23
37. Joye, M., Passelègue, A.: Function-revealing encryption. In: Catalano, D., De Prisco, R. (eds.) SCN 2018. LNCS, vol. 11035, pp. 527–543. Springer, Cham (2018). https://doi.org/10.1007/978-3-319-98113-0_28
38. Kitagawa, F., Nishimaki, R., Tanaka, K.: Obfustopia built on secret-key functional encryption. In: Nielsen, J.B., Rijmen, V. (eds.) EUROCRYPT 2018. LNCS, vol. 10821, pp. 603–648. Springer, Cham (2018). https://doi.org/10.1007/978-3-319-78375-8_20

39. Kitagawa, F., Nishimaki, R., Tanaka, K., Yamakawa, T.: Adaptively secure and succinct functional encryption: improving security and efficiency, simultaneously. In: Boldyreva, A., Micciancio, D. (eds.) CRYPTO 2019. LNCS, vol. 11694, pp. 521–551. Springer, Cham (2019). https://doi.org/10.1007/978-3-030-26954-8_17

40. Li, B., Micciancio, D.: Compactness vs collusion resistance in functional encryption. In: Hirt, M., Smith, A. (eds.) TCC 2016. LNCS, vol. 9986, pp. 443–468. Springer, Heidelberg (2016). https://doi.org/10.1007/978-3-662-53644-5_17

41. Lin, H., Pass, R., Seth, K., Telang, S.: Indistinguishability obfuscation with non-trivial efficiency. In: Cheng, C.-M., Chung, K.-M., Persiano, G., Yang, B.-Y. (eds.) PKC 2016. LNCS, vol. 9615, pp. 447–462. Springer, Heidelberg (2016). https://doi.org/10.1007/978-3-662-49387-8_17

42. Lin, W.K., Mook, E., Wichs, D.: Doubly efficient private information retrieval and fully homomorphic RAM computation from ring LWE. In: Saha, B., Servedio, R.A. (eds.) 55th ACM STOC, pp. 595–608. ACM Press (Jun 2023). https://doi.org/10.1145/3564246.3585175

43. Maurer, U.: Abstract models of computation in cryptography. In: Smart, N.P. (ed.) Cryptography and Coding 2005. LNCS, vol. 3796, pp. 1–12. Springer, Heidelberg (2005). https://doi.org/10.1007/11586821_1

44. Maurer, U., Renner, R., Holenstein, C.: Indifferentiability, impossibility results on reductions, and applications to the random oracle methodology. In: Naor, M. (ed.) TCC 2004. LNCS, vol. 2951, pp. 21–39. Springer, Heidelberg (2004). https://doi.org/10.1007/978-3-540-24638-1_2

45. Nayak, K., et al.: HOP: hardware makes obfuscation practical. In: NDSS 2017. The Internet Society (Feb/Mar 2017). https://doi.org/10.14722/ndss.2017.23349

46. Nishimaki, R.: Personal communication (2022)

47. Pippenger, N., Fischer, M.J.: Relations among complexity measures. J. ACM **26**(2), 361–381 (1979). https://doi.org/10.1145/322123.322138

48. Sahai, A., Waters, B.: How to use indistinguishability obfuscation: deniable encryption, and more. In: Shmoys, D.B. (ed.) 46th ACM STOC, pp. 475–484. ACM Press (May/Jun 2014). https://doi.org/10.1145/2591796.2591825

49. Shoup, V.: Lower bounds for discrete logarithms and related problems. In: Fumy, W. (ed.) EUROCRYPT 1997. LNCS, vol. 1233, pp. 256–266. Springer, Heidelberg (1997). https://doi.org/10.1007/3-540-69053-0_18

50. Valiant, P.: Incrementally verifiable computation or proofs of knowledge imply time/space efficiency. In: Canetti, R. (ed.) TCC 2008. LNCS, vol. 4948, pp. 1–18. Springer, Heidelberg (2008). https://doi.org/10.1007/978-3-540-78524-8_1

51. Zhandry, M.: To label, or not to label (in generic groups). In: Dodis, Y., Shrimpton, T. (eds.) Advances in Cryptology – CRYPTO 2022. CRYPTO 2022. Lecture Notes in Computer Science, vol. 13509, , pp. 66–96. Springer, Cham (2022). https://doi.org/10.1007/978-3-031-15982-4_3

Computational Wiretap Coding
from Indistinguishability Obfuscation

Yuval Ishai[1], Aayush Jain[2], Paul Lou[3], Amit Sahai[3], and Mark Zhandry[4(✉)]

[1] Technion, Haifa, Israel
`yuvali@cs.technion.ac.il`
[2] Carnegie Mellon University, Pittsburgh, USA
`aayushja@andrew.cmu.edu`
[3] UCLA, Los Angeles, USA
`{pslou,sahai}@cs.ucla.edu`
[4] NTT Research, Sunnyvale, USA
`mzhandry@gmail.com`

Abstract. A wiretap coding scheme for a pair of noisy channels (ChB, ChE) enables Alice to reliably communicate a message to Bob by sending its encoding over ChB, while hiding the message from an adversary Eve who obtains the same encoding over ChE.

A necessary condition for the feasibility of wiretap coding is that ChB is not a *degradation* of ChE, namely Eve cannot simulate Bob's view. While insufficient in the information-theoretic setting, a recent work of Ishai, Korb, Lou, and Sahai (Crypto 2022) showed that the non-degradation condition *is* sufficient in the computational setting, assuming idealized flavors of obfuscation. The question of basing a similar feasibility result on standard cryptographic assumptions was left open, even in simple special cases.

In this work, we settle the question for all discrete memoryless channels where the (common) input alphabet of ChB and ChE is *binary*, and with arbitrary finite output alphabet, under standard (sub-exponential) hardness assumptions: namely those assumptions that imply indistinguishability obfuscation (Jain-Lin-Sahai 2021, 2022), and injective PRGs. In particular, this establishes the feasibility of computational wiretap coding when ChB is a binary symmetric channel with crossover probability p and ChE is a binary erasure channel with erasure probability e, where $e > 2p$.

On the information-theoretic side, our result builds on a new polytope characterization of channel degradation for pairs of binary-input channels, which may be of independent interest.

1 Introduction

A primary focus of algorithmic coding theory is the construction of codes enabling efficient decoding of noisily perturbed codewords. Along the way, however, we often run into the hardness of recovering from different kinds of noise. For example, a random binary linear code of constant rate allows for efficient decoding of a codeword where each bit of the codeword is *erased* and replaced

H. Handschuh and A. Lysyanskaya (Eds.): CRYPTO 2023, LNCS 14084, pp. 263–293, 2023.
https://doi.org/10.1007/978-3-031-38551-3_9

with a special $\perp$ symbol with some constant probability. In contrast, despite decades of study, we have no efficient algorithms for decoding random binary linear codes when each bit of the codeword can be flipped with any constant probability. Indeed, the conjectured hardness of this task is formalized as the Learning Parity with Noise (LPN) assumption [5]. On the flip side, the contrast between efficient decoding from one kind of noise and hardness of decoding from another serves as a useful basis for a variety of cryptographic primitives, including public-key encryption [2] and much more.

In this work we ask: *How general is this phenomenon?*

For example, can we turn things around and construct a specially-designed code (not a random binary linear code) that allows for efficient decoding from a constant probability p of bit flipping, but where any constant probability $e > 2p$ of erasures makes decoding computationally intractable? Note that if $e \leq 2p$, then the task becomes impossible, since a probability e erasure can be transformed into a probability p bit-flip by simply replacing $\perp$ symbols with random bits. At the same time, to make the question meaningful, we need to choose the parameters so that the erasure decoding problem is still information-theoretically possible.

As far as we know, even this very natural and simple question did not have any affirmative answers until very recently – and before this paper, this question had no affirmative answer where the hardness we seek can be reduced to well-studied hardness conjectures.

Wiretap Coding. An information-theoretic study of the above question, where computational hardness is replaced by information loss, was pioneered in the seminal work of Wyner [20] on wiretap channels. Wiretap coding enables secure message transmission using only *unidirectional* communication over noisy channels. This should be contrasted with the use of public-key cryptography for exchanging secret keys, which inherently requires bidirectional communication. In a sense, wiretap coding trades reduced interaction for physical assumptions. Wyner's work has spawned a large body of work in the borderline of information theory and cryptography, and serves as the basis of a research area known as physical layer security. See, e.g., [16] for a survey.

More concretely, given a pair of noisy channels (ChB, ChE) (here we only consider discrete memoryless channels), a wiretap coding scheme enables Alice to reliably send a message m to an honest Bob by sending a (randomized) encoding of m over ChB. Given the noisy encoding, Bob should be able to decode m with negligible failure probability. On the other hand, an adversary Eve who obtains the same encoding through the channel ChE, should learn essentially nothing about m.

For which pairs of channels (ChB, ChE) is wiretap coding at all possible? A simple necessary condition is captured by the following notion of (stochastic) *degradation*: We say that ChB is a degradation of ChE if there is a probabilistic function S such that, for every input x, the output of ChB(x) is identically distributed to S(ChE(x)). In such a case, it is possible for Eve to use S to perfectly simulate Bob's view, and wiretap coding is clearly impossible.

Is wiretap coding possible whenever ChB is *not* a degradation of ChE? Somewhat unexpectedly, the answer is no. This is implied by a general characterization due to Csiszár and Korner [7]. In the special case where ChB is a binary symmetric channel BSC_p (flipping each bit with probability p) and ChE is a binary erasure channel BEC_e (erasing each bit with probability e), wiretap coding is possible if and only if $e > 4p(1 - p)$ [15], whereas ChB is not a degradation of ChE whenever $e > 2p$.

Computational Wiretap. The above gap naturally begs the following question: Is the non-degradation condition sufficient for *computational* wiretap coding, where all parties are computationally bounded? In particular, here security should only hold against a polynomial-time Eve. This question was studied in the recent work of Ishai, Korb, Lou, and Sahai [11], who showed that the non-degradation condition *is* sufficient in this setting, assuming *idealized flavors of obfuscation.* Concretely, rather than rely on the standard *indistinguishability obfuscation* ($i\mathcal{O}$) primitive, which can now be based on well-studied cryptographic assumptions [13,14], the construction required Alice to send an obfuscated program over a channel, but its analysis treated the program as an oracle, relying on an idealized notion of "virtual black-box" obfuscation [4]. The question of basing a similar feasibility result on standard cryptographic assumptions was left open in [11], even in simple special cases such as the $(\mathsf{BSC}_p, \mathsf{BEC}_e)$ case.

While we now have a sophisticated toolbox of techniques to replace ideal obfuscation by $i\mathcal{O}$ [8,17], these techniques apply in the context of obfuscating a cryptographic primitive, such as a pseudorandom function, building on the security properties of the primitive. In contrast, the constructions of [12] obfuscate non-cryptographic "evasive" functions [3], which pose a challenge to current techniques of leveraging $i\mathcal{O}$.

1.1 Our Contribution

Our main result settles the computational wiretap coding question, under the standard assumptions that $i\mathcal{O}$ and injective pseudorandom generators (PRGs) exist, for the case where the (common) input alphabet of ChB and ChE is binary. Here the output alphabets can be of any (finite) size.

Theorem 1.1. *Assuming the existence of $i\mathcal{O}$ and injective PRGs, there exists a computational wiretap coding scheme for any pair of binary-input channels* (ChB, ChE) *such that* ChB *is not a degradation of* ChE.

As a special case, under the same standard assumptions, there is computational wiretap coding for $(\mathsf{BSC}_p, \mathsf{BEC}_e)$ if (and only if) $e > 2p$. In fact, this settles the broad coding question posed in the beginning of the introduction, with respect to *probabilistic* encoding, for the case of *binary* error-correcting codes with arbitrary channel noise.

On the information-theoretic side, a technical tool we develop for proving Theorem 1.1 is a complete *polytope characterization* of stochastic channel degradation for pairs of binary-input channels. To state this characterization, we will need the following definition.

Definition 1.2 (Channel Polytope). *Let* $\mathbf{A}$ *be a real-valued matrix of non-negative entries. We associate to* $\mathbf{A}$ *the following polytope, denoted* $\mathcal{P}(\mathbf{A})$, *which can be defined in either of the following equivalent ways:*

- $\mathcal{P}(\mathbf{A})$ *is the convex hull of all subset-sums of columns of* $\mathbf{A}$.
- $\mathcal{P}(\mathbf{A}) = \{\mathbf{A} \cdot \mathbf{s} : \mathbf{0} \leq \mathbf{s} \leq \mathbf{1}\}$

Theorem 1.3. *Let* $\mathbf{B}, \mathbf{E}$ *be two non-negative matrices, representing* ChB *and* ChE *respectively, with two rows that satisfy* $\mathbf{B} \cdot \mathbf{1} = \mathbf{E} \cdot \mathbf{1}$. *Then* $\mathcal{P}(\mathbf{B}) \subseteq \mathcal{P}(\mathbf{E})$ *if and only if* ChB *is a degradation of* ChE.

We also show that this characterization does not extend to general input alphabets of size greater than two. That is, we show an explicit counterexample for the case of $\mathbf{B}, \mathbf{E}$ with three rows (ternary input alphabets) where $\mathcal{P}(\mathbf{B}) \subseteq \mathcal{P}(\mathbf{E})$ yet ChB is not a degradation of ChE.

Perspective: Average-Case Complexity with Side-Information. One can also view our main result from the lens of average-case complexity in the presence of side-information. One way to design a computational wiretap coding scheme is by constructing hard average-case planted problems (e.g. a planted random CSP or a planted graph problem) with sharp algorithmic thresholds with respect to side information about the planted assignment. We can model such a problem as an inversion problem where we denote $y = \mathsf{P}_{e,p}(x)$ (where the problem P is parameterized by the erasure and flip probabilities) as the instance and the planted assignment $x \leftarrow \{0,1\}^n$ is chosen at random. The properties we want are:

- If one is additionally given x' that is formed by erasing e bits of x at random, inverting x should appear hard.
- On the other hand, given x' that is formed by flipping p bits of x at random, inverting x becomes easy.

We desire these properties to hold even when e is barely greater than $2 \cdot p$, and thereby requiring a very sharp threshold. As an example, when $e = 0.22$ and $p = 0.1$, in this case x'_{flip} that is formed by flipping agrees with x on roughly 90% fraction number of bits where as x'_{erasure} erases out a 22% fraction. By randomly guessing on non-erased we can come up with a string r_{erasure} that agrees with x on 89% bits of x which is barely more than the number of agreements of x'_{flip} with x.

To our surprise, this seemingly very natural class of problems has not been very well studied. One notable example of such study is in the context of Goldreich's one-way functions, that have been shown to have a self-correction property. In particular, Goldreich's one-way functions satisfy [6] the property above when $e = 1$ and $p = \frac{1}{2} - \epsilon$ for any constant $\epsilon > 0$. In this work, we show that relying on well-studied hardness assumptions we can construct a problem with these exact properties for any choice of parameters satisfying $e > 2p$.

Open Questions. Our work gives rise to several natural open questions.

- Can Theorem 1.1 be extended to an arbitrary pair of channels satisfying the non-degradation condition, removing the binary-input requirement? The failure of Theorem 1.3 to extend to this general case is the most immediate roadblock.
- Are strong cryptographic assumptions such as $i\mathcal{O}$, or even "public-key" assumptions, necessary? For instance, does computational wiretap coding for $(\mathsf{BSC}_{0.1}, \mathsf{BEC}_{0.3})$ imply secret key exchange in the plain model?
- Theorem 1.1 implies *randomized* encoding schemes which support efficient decoding of 0.1-fraction of random errors but cannot be efficiently decoded from a 0.3-fraction of random erasures (though inefficient decoding is possible). Can such codes be constructed more directly? Can the encoding function be made deterministic? See Sect. 4.1 for discussion.
- Can our technique for replacing ideal obfuscation of a "non-cryptographic" program by $i\mathcal{O}$ be extended to apply to other applications, such as secure computation over unidirectional noisy channels [1]?

2   Technical Overview

We will represent a channel ChB by a row-stochastic matrix $\mathbf{B} \in [0,1]^{2\times n_B}$ and ChE is by a row-stochastic matrix $\mathbf{E} \in [0,1]^{2\times n_E}$ where the (i,j)-th entry of the matrix gives the probability that the ith input alphabet symbols maps to the jth output alphabet symbol when passed through the channel. We are given that ChB is not a degradation of ChE: This means that there does not exist ChS (represented by a row stochastic matrix $\mathbf{S} \in [0,1]^{n_E \times n_B}$) such that $\mathsf{ChB} = \mathsf{ChS} \circ \mathsf{ChE}$ (equivalently $\mathbf{B} = \mathbf{E} \cdot \mathbf{S}$). Throughout this technical overview, we will refer to channels and their row-stochastic matrix representations interchangeably.

2.1   A Construction for BSC_p and BEC_e channels

We begin with might seem like a warmup case: the setting in which Bob's channel $\mathbf{B}$ is a BSC_p channel (a sent bit b is received as $1 - b$ with probability p and received as b with probability $1 - p$) and Eve's channel $\mathbf{E}$ is a BEC_e channel (a sent bit b is erased with probability e and received as b with probability $1 - e$) for some channel parameters p and e. As we will see below, handling this case will be fundamental to handling the general case.

The Degradation Condition. In this setting, it is easy to see that ChB is *not* a degradation of ChE if and only if $e > 2p$. That is, Eve's best guessing strategy for each of her erasures to randomly guess a bit, so if $e > 2p$, then Eve cannot hope in expectation to produce a received string with a p error rate. And if $e \leq 2p$, Eve perfectly simulates receiving an output form ChB by randomly assigning a random bit for each of her received erasures (and depending on p, possibly introducing more intentional errors in her received non-erasures).

We now introduce some useful notation. Consider a randomly chosen string $x \in \{0,1\}^\lambda$ for a large (security) parameter λ passed through ChB and ChE. Let z^B denote the string that is received by Bob and z^E the string that is received by Eve. Denote by $\Delta_H(\star, \star)$ the Hamming distance function between two strings and by $\Delta_c(\star, \star)$ the function that outputs the number of indices on which the input strings agree. Since Bob's channel is BSC_p, we have that with high probability $\Delta_c(z^B, x) \approx (1 - p)\lambda$ where $\approx$ subsumes $o(\lambda^{0.51})$ additive error given by a standard Chernoff bound. On the other hand, when x is passed through Eve's channel BEC_e we will receive a string $z^E \in \{0, 1, \perp\}^\lambda$ where $\perp$ denote erasures. Let $S_\perp$ denote the indices where the erasures occur and $\overline{S_\perp}$ denote the remaining indices. For every index in $\overline{S_\perp}$, z^E will completely agree with x. On the other hand, we have no information about $x_{S_\perp}$ given z^E. Therefore the best we can do is produce a random string v which agrees with $x_{S_\perp}$ at roughly $\frac{|S_\perp|}{2}$ locations. This lets us come up with a string r^E for which $\Delta_c(x, r^E) \approx \frac{|S_\perp|}{2} + |\overline{S_\perp}|$. With high probability, this number is roughly $(1 - \frac{e}{2}) \cdot \lambda$.

When Bob's channel is not a degradation of Eve's channel we have $\frac{e}{2} > p$. As a consequence, Bob's received string z^B for which $\Delta_c(x, z^B) \approx (1 - p) \cdot \lambda$ agrees with x at approximately $(1 - p) \cdot \lambda - (1 - \frac{e}{2}) \cdot \lambda = (\frac{e}{2} - p) \cdot \lambda$ more locations than the best string r^E that Eve can construct for which $\Delta_c(x, r^E) \approx (1 - \frac{e}{2}) \cdot \lambda$. We want to make use of this fact to build our wiretap coding scheme.

Prior Work: Using Ideal Obfuscation. How do we use this observation to construct a computational wiretap coding scheme for this case? Prior work [12] leverages an ideal obfuscation scheme and exactly exploits the above idea. Recall that in the ideal obfuscation model, one can obfuscate any circuit C to produce a functionally equivalent obfuscated circuit $\tilde{C} = \mathcal{O}(C)$, and any efficient adversary that obtains $\tilde{C}$ can be computationally simulated by a polynomial time algorithm Sim that gets oracle access to C but doesn't get $\tilde{C}$ itself. To encode a bit $m \in \{0, 1\}$, the prior work suggested that we obfuscate, using an ideal obfuscation scheme, the circuit $C_{x,m}$ given below. In the encoding scheme, x is chosen at random from $\{0,1\}^\lambda$ and the circuit $C_{x,m}$ in Fig. 1 is constructed. The encoding algorithm sends out $\tilde{C}_{x,m}$ encoded using an appropriate error-correcting coding scheme for ChB, so that Bob can receive $\tilde{C}_{x,m}$ completely. Further, x is sent out through the channel ChB as is. At the end Bob receives $\tilde{C}_{x,m}$ and $\mathsf{ChB}(x) = z^B$. On the other hand, Eve will receive $\mathsf{ChE}(x) = z^E$, and for the security analysis, we assume that Eve is also able to recover $\tilde{C}_{x,m}$. Based on the previous insight, we now make the following observations:

- (Correctness for Bob): As described previously, with overwhelming probability, $\Delta_c(x, z^B) > (1 - p) \cdot \lambda - o(\lambda^{0.51})$. Therefore, the first check in the description of $C_{x,m}$ will pass if we evaluate it on z^B. Thus, Bob can recover m by computing $\tilde{C}_{x,m}(z^B)$.
- (Security against Eve): We start with the observation that the best string that Eve can construct agrees at about constant fraction $(\frac{e}{2} - p)$ fewer number of indices than the required threshold $(1 - p) \cdot \lambda - \lambda^{0.9}$. Furthermore, recall that Eve can be simulated by an efficient Sim that only has oracle access to $C_{x,m}$.

$C_{x,m}(z)$:

Input: $z \in \{0,1\}^{\lambda}$

Hardwired: $x \in \{0,1\}^{\lambda}$, $m \in \{0,1\}$

1. Check $\Delta_c(x,z) > (1-p) \cdot \lambda - \lambda^{0.9}$.
2. If the check passes, output m otherwise output $\perp$.

Fig. 1. Circuit C

Putting these two observations together, we observe that having oracle access to $C_{x,m}$ is worthless: all queries to query $C_{x,m}$ will produce an output of $\perp$. Thus, the message m is hidden from Eve.

In [12], the authors show that the same template described above can be extended to construct wiretap computational encoding scheme for arbitrary (multi-input/multi-output) channel pairs (ChB, ChE) satisfying the non-degradation condition.

Leveraging Indistinguishability Obfuscation. The above solution relies on ideal obfuscation, and uses it in a very interesting way. Our goal, however, is to try to solve the wiretap coding problem based on well-studied hardness conjectures, and unfortunately this type of ideal obfuscation is not known to exist under well-studied hardness conjectures. On the other hand, indistinguishability obfuscation $i\mathcal{O}$ has recently been achieved from well-studied hardness conjectures [13]. However, $i\mathcal{O}$ provides a fundamentally different kind of security guarantee compared to ideal obfuscation. $i\mathcal{O}$ guarantees that any two circuits C_0, C_1 of same size and identical input-output behavior must yield computationally indistinguishable obfuscations. What makes it hard to use $i\mathcal{O}$ is that in this case circuit $C_{x,m}$ in Fig. 1 is not functionally equivalent to the always-$\perp$ circuit. In fact, these circuits differ at any points for which $\Delta_c(x,z) > (1-p) \cdot \lambda - \lambda^{0.9}$, which could be an exponential number of points.

Using $i\mathcal{O}$ instead of ideal obfuscation will require some new tools. We now elaborate:

Gadget: PRG with Self-Correction. Consider the following variant of an injective pseudorandom generator denoted by SC-PRG. SC-PRG$_{\epsilon}$ is indexed with a parameter $\epsilon \in (0, \frac{1}{2}]$ which is some constant. This PRG satisfies the following properties:

- (Polynomial Stretch and Pseudorandomness) Just like a regular PRG, SC-PRG$_{\epsilon}$: $\{0,1\}^{\lambda} \to \{0,1\}^{p_{\epsilon}(\lambda)}$ maps λ bits to $p_{\epsilon}(\lambda)$ bits for some polynomial $p_{\epsilon}(\lambda) \gg 2 \cdot \lambda$ (that could depend on ϵ). Further, for a randomly chosen seed Seed $\in \{0,1\}^{\lambda}$, $y = $ SC-PRG$_{\epsilon}$(Seed) is computationally indistinguishable to a truly random string y'.
- (Self-Correction) There exists an efficient algorithm SC-PRG$_{\epsilon}$.Self-Correct(y, Seed$'$) with the property that for overwhelming choices of Seed $\in \{0,1\}^{\lambda}$ it holds that given $y = $ SC-PRG$_{\epsilon}$(Seed) along with

an arbitrary side-information string $\mathsf{Seed}' \in \{0,1\}^\lambda$ that agrees with Seed on at least $(\frac{1}{2}+\epsilon)$ fraction of bits — that is, such that $\Delta_c(\mathsf{Seed}, \mathsf{Seed}') > (\frac{1}{2}+\epsilon)\lambda$ — the algorithm will be able to successfully recover Seed itself.

In fact, the work of [6] showed that Goldreich PRGs (even with linear stretch $\Omega_\epsilon(\lambda)$) satisfy the self-correction property we are looking for. In our work (see below for more intuition), we show how to construct a PRG with self-correction from any injective PRG.

Using PRG with Self-Correction with iO. We now describe how this new gadget can help us leverage the power of $i\mathcal{O}$ in our security proof. To encode $m \in \{0,1\}$, we give out $\tilde{C}_{x,m} = i\mathcal{O}(C_{x,m})$ as an obfuscation of the circuit $C_{x,m}$, described in Fig. 1, which is encoded using an appropriate coding scheme for Bob's channel ChB so that Bob can reconstruct it. Further x is transported to Bob without any encoding via ChB. In this case, Eve's view consist of $\tilde{C}_{x,m}$ and $\mathsf{ChE}(x) = z^E$. We now describe how we can switch computationally un-detectably an obfuscation of $\tilde{C}_{x,m}$ (even given z^E) from an obfuscation of the circuit in Fig. 1 to an obfuscation of the always-$\bot$ circuit, from Eve's point of view.

Step 1: Hardwiring Part of Eve's View Into the Circuit. As a crucial first step, we observe that in the proof, we can have intermediate hybrids where the circuit to be obfuscated actually depends on Eve's received string z^E, where z^E is a string in $\{0, 1, \bot\}^\lambda$ and $\bot$ denotes an erasure. If $S_\bot$ is the set of erased locations and $\overline{S_\bot}$ is the set of non erased locations, then, we have that $z^E_{S_\bot} = \bot^{|S_\bot|}$ and $z^E_{\overline{S_\bot}} = x_{\overline{S_\bot}}$. In the first step, we replace $\tilde{C}_{x,m}$ to now be an $i\mathcal{O}$ obfuscation of the circuit $C^{(1)}_{x,m,S_\bot}$ described in Fig. 2. Notice that circuits $C^{(1)}_{x,m,S_\bot}$ and $C_{x,m}$ are functionally equivalent. This equivalence is because $\Delta_c(x, z) = \Delta_c(x_{S_\bot}, z_{S_\bot}) + \Delta_c(x_{\overline{S_\bot}}, z_{\overline{S_\bot}})$ since the set $S_\bot$ and $\overline{S_\bot}$ form a partition of $[\lambda]$. Therefore, due to $i\mathcal{O}$ security the change is computationally indistinguishable assuming we pad the circuits appropriately before computing the $i\mathcal{O}$ obfuscation.

$C^{(1)}_{x,m,S_\bot}(z)$:

Input: $z \in \{0,1\}^\lambda$

Hardwired: $x \in \{0,1\}^\lambda$, $m \in \{0,1\}$, set $S_\bot$ and $\overline{S_\bot}$

1. Check $\Delta_c(x_{S_\bot}, z_{S_\bot}) + \Delta_c(x_{\overline{S_\bot}}, z_{\overline{S_\bot}}) > (1-p) \cdot \lambda - \lambda^{0.9}$.
2. If the check passes, output m otherwise output $\bot$.

Fig. 2. Circuit $C^{(1)}_{x,m,S_\bot}(z)$

Step 2: Using the $\mathsf{SC\text{-}PRG}_\epsilon$ Scheme. So far, it may seem that we have not done anything interesting. The change was merely syntactical. But now, we observe that Eve has absolutely zero information about $x_{S_\bot}$, while Bob does! This fact enables us to leverage the self-correcting properties of the SC-PRG scheme. We compute $\mathsf{SC\text{-}PRG}_\epsilon(x_{S_\perp}) = y$ where we describe how we set the constant $\epsilon > 0$ shortly. In the new circuit $C^{(2)}_{x_{\overline{S_\perp}},m,S_\perp,\varepsilon,y}$ (Fig. 3), we no longer hardwire x completely. This time, we will only hardwire the non-erased portion $x_{\overline{S_\perp}}$ and instead of hardwiring $x_{S_\perp}$, we hardwire $\mathsf{SC\text{-}PRG}_\epsilon(x_{S_\perp}) = y$. To maintain functional equivalence, the circuit $C^{(2)}_{x_{\overline{S_\perp}},m,S_\perp,\varepsilon,y}$ will derive $x_{S_\perp}$ from y.

$C^{(2)}_{x_{\overline{S_\perp}},m,S_\perp,\varepsilon,y}(z)$:

Input: $z \in \{0,1\}^\lambda$

Hardwired: $x_{\overline{S_\perp}} \in \{0,1\}^{|\overline{S_\perp}|}$, $m \in \{0,1\}$, set $S_\perp$ and $\overline{S_\perp}$, $\epsilon = (\frac{1}{2} - \frac{p}{e}) \cdot \frac{1}{2} \in (0, \frac{1}{4}]$ and $y = \mathsf{SC\text{-}PRG}_\epsilon(x_{S_\perp})$,

1. Run $\mathsf{SC\text{-}PRG}_\epsilon.\mathsf{Self\text{-}Correct}(y, z_{S_\perp}) = s$ and check if $s = x_{S_\perp}$ by checking if $\mathsf{SC\text{-}PRG}_\epsilon(s) = y$. If the check fails output $\perp$. Else set $x_{S_\perp} = s$ and continue,
2. Check $\Delta_c(x_{S_\perp}, z_{S_\perp}) + \Delta_c(x_{\overline{S_\perp}}, z_{\overline{S_\perp}}) > (1 - p) \cdot \lambda - \lambda^{0.9}$.
3. If the check passes, output m otherwise output $\perp$.

Fig. 3. Circuit $C^{(2)}_{x_{\overline{S_\perp}},m,S_\perp,\varepsilon,y}$

The idea is that if the following check passes on any given input z:

$$\Delta_c(x_{S_\perp}, z_{S_\perp}) + \Delta_c(x_{\overline{S_\perp}}, z_{\overline{S_\perp}}) > (1 - p)\lambda - \lambda^{0.9}, \tag{1}$$

that means that:

$$\Delta_c(x_{S_\perp}, z_{S_\perp}) > (1 - p) \cdot \lambda - \lambda^{0.9} - \Delta_c(x_{\overline{S_\perp}}, z_{\overline{S_\perp}}).$$

The maximum value of $\Delta_c(x_{\overline{S_\perp}}, z_{\overline{S_\perp}}) = |\overline{S_\perp}|$. With overwhelming probability, $|S_\perp| \in [e \cdot \lambda - \lambda^{0.9}, e \cdot \lambda + \lambda^{0.9}]$ and therefore $|\overline{S_\perp}| \in [(1-e) \cdot \lambda - \lambda^{0.9}, (1-e) \cdot \lambda + \lambda^{0.9}]$. Therefore, we have that with overwhelming probability over the size of $S_\perp$, for any z satisfying the check in Eq. 1, we have:

$$\Delta_c(x_{S_\perp}, z_{S_\perp}) > (e - p) \cdot \lambda - 2 \cdot \lambda^{0.9}.$$

Since with overwhelming probability over erasures, $|S_\perp| \in [e \cdot \lambda - \lambda^{0.9}, e \cdot \lambda + \lambda^{0.9}]$, the above equation can be rephrased as:

$$\Delta_c(x_{S_\perp}, z_{S_\perp}) > \underbrace{(1 - \frac{p}{e})}_{\frac{1}{2} + \epsilon' \ (\epsilon' = \frac{1}{2} - \frac{p}{e})} \cdot |S_\perp| - O(\lambda^{0.9}).$$

Therefore, with overwhelming probability over the number of erasures, for any z satisfying Eq. 1 it must hold that $z_{S_\perp}$ agrees with $x_{S_\perp}$ at roughly $1 - \frac{p}{e} = \frac{1}{2} + \epsilon'$ fraction of indices (ignoring the $O(\lambda^{-0.9})$ term), where $\epsilon' = \frac{1}{2} - \frac{p}{e}$. Since $e > 2p$ because of the non-degradation condition, we have $\epsilon' > 0$. To be on the conservative side, we choose the self-correction threshold $\epsilon = \frac{\epsilon'}{2} > 0$.

Putting this all together, in the circuit $C^{(2)}_{x_{\overline{S_\perp}}, m, S_\perp, \varepsilon, y}$, we have $y = $ SC-PRG$_\epsilon(x_{S_\perp})$ hardwired. The circuit will takes input z, and uses it to "derive" $x_{S_\perp}$ by running SC-PRG$_\epsilon$.Self-Correct$(y, z_{S_\perp})$. Then it will perform all the checks as before. Due to self-correction property of SC-PRG, with overwhelming probability over the locations $S_\perp$, $\overline{S_\perp}$ and the choice of $x_{S_\perp}$ the circuits $C^{(2)}_{x_{\overline{S_\perp}}, m, S_\perp, \varepsilon, y}$ and $C^{(1)}_{x, m, S_\perp}(z)$ are functionally equivalent. For any input z that satisfies the check in $C^{(1)}_{x, m, S_\perp}(z)$ given by Eq. 1, we will also have that $z_{S_\perp}$ will agree with $x_{S_\perp}$ on at least $\frac{1}{2} + \epsilon$ fraction of indices as argued before. With high probability over $x_{S_\perp}$, it holds that SC-PRG$_\epsilon$.Self-Correct$(y, r) = x_{S_\perp}$ for every r that agrees with $x_{S_\perp}$ on at least $\frac{1}{2} + \epsilon$ fraction of indices. Therefore with overwhelming probability on the choice of $S_\perp$ and $x_{S_\perp}$, on input any such z that passes check in Eq. 1, we can recover $x_{S_\perp}$ uniquely. Therefore, the two circuits are functionally identical; if the check in Eq. 1 does not pass, both circuits output $\perp$ anyway. Because of this, we can appeal to $i\mathcal{O}$ security and argue computational indistinguishability for the change.

The Final Step: Exploiting Eve's Ignorance. Recall that given z^E and conditioned on erased indices $S_\perp$, the distribution $x_{S_\perp}$ is identically uniform. Therefore, we can switch the $i\mathcal{O}$ obfuscation of the circuit $C^{(2)}_{x_{\overline{S_\perp}}, m, S_\perp, \varepsilon, y}$ with an obfuscation of $C^{(3)}_{x_{\overline{S_\perp}}, m, S_\perp, \varepsilon, y}$ described in Fig. 4 where the only change is that now y is sampled as a uniformly random string in $\{0, 1\}^{p_\epsilon(|S_\perp|)}$ as opposed to being $y = $ SC-PRG$_\epsilon(x_{S_\perp})$. With overwhelming probability $|S_\perp| = \Omega(\lambda)$ and therefore, this change is indistinguishable due to the security of SC-PRG.

Finally observe that if SC-PRG is sufficiently expanding, with overwhelming probability for any y that is chosen at random, there will not exist any $x_{S_\perp}$ such that $y = $ SC-PRG$_\epsilon(x_{S_\perp})$. Therefore, with overwhelming probability over y, the circuit $C^{(3)}_{x_{\overline{S_\perp}}, m, S_\perp, \varepsilon, y}$ is functionally equivalent to the always-$\perp$ circuit. Thus using $i\mathcal{O}$ security, we can switch $\tilde{C}_{x,m}$ to be an obfuscation of the always-$\perp$ circuit. This finishes the overview of the proof of security of the wiretap scheme.

Constructing Self-Correcting PRGs from any Injective PRGs. One issue that we should address is that as far as we know the only currently known instantiations

$C^{(3)}_{x_{\overline{S_\perp}},m,S_\perp,\varepsilon,y}(z)$:

Input: $z \in \{0,1\}^\lambda$

Hardwired: $x_{\overline{S_\perp}} \in \{0,1\}^{\overline{S_\perp}}$, set $S_\perp$ and $\overline{S_\perp}$, $\epsilon = (\frac{1}{2} - \frac{p}{e}) \cdot \frac{1}{2} \in (0, \frac{1}{4}]$ and $y \leftarrow \{0,1\}^{p_\epsilon(|S_\perp|)}$,

1. Run SC-PRG$_\epsilon$.Self-Correct$(y, z_{S_\perp}) = s$ and check if $s = x_{S_\perp}$ by checking if SC-PRG$_\epsilon(s) = y$. If the check fails abort. Else set $x_{S_\perp} = s$ and continue,
2. Check $\Delta_e(x_{S_\perp}, z_{S_\perp}) + \Delta_e(x_{\overline{S_\perp}}, z_{\overline{S_\perp}}) > (1-p) \cdot \lambda - \lambda^{0.9}$.
3. If the check passes, output m otherwise output $\perp$.

Fig. 4. Circuit $C^{(3)}_{x_{\overline{S_\perp}},m,S_\perp,\varepsilon,y}$

of such self-correcting PRGs are Goldreich PRGs [6]. We in fact show that any injective PRG suffices for constructing a self-correcting PRG.

Suppose we have an injective PRG $G : \{0,1\}^\lambda \rightarrow \{0,1\}^\kappa$ mapping λ bits to κ bits for some polynomial $\kappa(\lambda)$ that we will work out below. Additionally, we use a powerful tool from coding theory: a polynomial rate list-decodable code $\mathcal{C}_{\epsilon'} = (\text{Enc}, \text{Dec})$. The code is parameterized with any constant $\epsilon' \in (0, \frac{1}{2})$ and satisfies the following properties:

- (Polynomial rate) The encoding algorithm Enc is a polynomial deterministic algorithm mapping Enc : $\{0,1\}^\lambda \rightarrow \{0,1\}^n$ for some polynomial $n(\lambda) > \lambda$.
- (List Decoding) The Dec algorithm is a polynomial time algorithm with the property that for any c such that $\Delta_H(c, \text{Enc}(\alpha)) < (\frac{1}{2} - \epsilon') \cdot n$, the algorithm outputs a list of size at most $\text{poly}(\lambda, \frac{1}{\epsilon'})$ of elements in $\{0,1\}^\lambda$ that contains α.

Such a coding scheme exists by [19] and many appropriate schemes have been well-explored [9,10,18]. Once we have both these ingredients, the function SC-PRG$_\epsilon$ can be described as follows. On input a string $x = (x_1 \in \{0,1\}^n, x_2 \in \{0,1\}^\lambda)$, to compute SC-PRG$_\epsilon(x) = y$ we evaluate $y_2 = G(x_2)$ and $r = \text{Enc}(x_2)$. We then set $y_1 = r \oplus x_1$ and output $y = (y_1, y_2)$. If n and ϵ' satisfy some mild parameteric requirements that we arrive at below, we claim that this construction satisfies the properties we need.

Observe that SC-PRG$_\epsilon$ is injective. Given SC-PRG$_\epsilon(x_1, x_2) = (y_1, y_2)$, y_2 binds x_2 uniquely as $y_2 = G(x_2)$ and G is injective. As a consequence $y_1 = x_1 \oplus \text{Enc}(x_2)$ binds x_1 once x_2 is determined. Similarly, SC-PRG$_\epsilon(x_1, x_2) = (y_1, y_2)$ also satisfies pseudorandomness. This is because $y_1 = x_1 \oplus \text{Enc}(x_2)$ and $y_2 = G(x_2)$. Since x_1 is random and independent of x_2, we have that y_1 hides x_2. As a consequence given y_1, it is the case that $y_2 = G(x_2)$ is pseudorandom due to the security of G. Therefore (y_1, y_2) is pseudorandom.

Most importantly, if the parameters are set appropriately, SC-PRG$_\epsilon$ also satisfies the self-correction property. Imagine we have $(y_1, y_2) = $ SC-PRG$_\epsilon(x_1, x_2)$ and z such that $\Delta_H(z, (x_1, x_2)) < (\frac{1}{2} - \epsilon)|x| = (\frac{1}{2} - \epsilon)(\lambda + n)$. We want to show that such a z lets us recover x.

Note that $\Delta_H(z, (x_1, x_2)) < (\frac{1}{2} - \epsilon)(\lambda + n)$ means that $\Delta_H(z_1, x_1) < (\frac{1}{2} - \epsilon)n + \lambda$ where $z_1 \in \{0, 1\}^n$ is the first n length sub-string of z. If $n \gg \lambda$, we have $\Delta_H(z_1, x_1) < (\frac{1}{2} - \epsilon')n$ for some constant ϵ' barely less than ϵ. If the list decodable coding scheme can correct from $(\frac{1}{2} - \epsilon')$ fractions of errors and G is injective, given such a z we can derive x using the following steps:

- We first compute $c = y_1 \oplus z_1$ and then compute a list $L = \text{Dec}(c)$ of polynomial size.
- Find $\alpha \in L$ such that $G(\alpha) = y_2$ (such an α must be equal to x_2).
- Finally, output x_1 computing $y_1 \oplus \text{Enc}(x_2)$.

The reason why this algorithm succeeds is that $y_1 = \text{Enc}(x_2) \oplus x_1$ and if z_1 is such that $\Delta_H(z_1, x_1) < (\frac{1}{2} - \epsilon')n$, we have that $y_1 \oplus z_1$ satisfies $\Delta_H(y_1 \oplus z_1, \text{Enc}(x_2)) < (\frac{1}{2} - \epsilon')n$. Therefore, due to the list decoding property of the code and the injectivity of G the second condition will produce $\alpha = x_2$. Since $y_1 = x_1 \oplus \text{Enc}(x_2)$, we can derive x_1 correctly in the third step.

2.2 Tackling General Channels with Binary Input Alphabets: An Overview

Above we saw our construction for a simple pair of binary input channels based on $i\mathcal{O}$ and an injective PRG. We now need to build a computational wiretap coding scheme for pairs of general binary input channels. Before we give detailed technical ideas, we first provide a guide to the remainder of this technical overview.

Step 1: Coding scheme for BAC-BAEC *pair.* In the first step, we will construct a coding scheme for a case that is just a little more general than the case considered above. In this case, Bob's channel matrix **B** is an arbitrary binary channel in $[0, 1]^{2 \times 2}$ (such channels are called binary asymmetric channels BAC, see Definition 3.4). Such BAC's are a generalization of a binary symmetric channel. While there is a single parameter p that determines a binary symmetric channel BSC_p (the probability of flipping a bit b to $1 - b$ is p independently of the bit b), there are two parameters p_0, p_1 for the binary asymmetric channel BAC_{p_0, p_1} that respectively define the probability of a 0 flipping and the probability of a 1 flipping, and these probabilities p_0 and p_1 may differ. Eve's channel is a generalization of the binary erasure channel, called a binary asymmetric erasure channel (BAEC, see Definition 3.5) whose row-stochastic matrix representation is in $[0, 1]^{2 \times 3}$. While a binary erasure channel BEC_e is parameterised by a single parameter e, where the probability of erasing any given bit $b \in \{0, 1\}$ is e independently of b, there are two parameters e_0, e_1 for the asymmetric channel BAEC_{e_0, e_1} where the probability of erasure for any given bit b is e_b and these two parameters may differ. We will show how to build a computational wiretap encoding scheme that works as long as Bob's channel BAC_{p_0, p_1} is not a degradation of Eve's channel BAEC_{e_0, e_1}.

Step 2: Bootstrapping Step 1 to the General Binary Input Case. Why should a computational wiretap coding scheme for the case when Bob's channel is of the form BAC_{p_0,p_1} and Eve's channel is of the form BAEC_{e_0,e_1} suffice for the general binary input case? In general, $\mathbf{B}$ and $\mathbf{E}$ can be completely arbitrary channels with arbitrary constant-sized input and output alphabets.

We show that as long as $\mathbf{B} \in [0,1]^{2 \times n_B}$ and $\mathbf{E} \in [0,1]^{2 \times n_E}$ are binary input channels (with potentially larger constant sized output alphabets), the above solution is fully general! To obtain this result, we show a series of implications:

- (Polytope characterization of non-degradation) For any channel $\mathbf{C} \in \mathbb{R}^{2 \times n_C}$, we define $\mathcal{P}(\mathbf{C})$ as the bounded convex set:

$$\mathcal{P}(\mathbf{C}) = \left\{ \mathbf{C} \cdot \mathbf{u} \mid \mathbf{u} \in [0,1]^{n_c \times 1} \right\}.$$

In simple words, this is a bounded convex-set in the two-dimensional plane $\mathbb{R}^2$ that is generated by the taking combinations of columns of $\mathbf{C}$ where the coefficients of each column in the combination are in $[0,1]$. Our main characterization theorem states that for any pair of binary-input channels (with potentially a different number of outputs) $\mathbf{B} \in \mathbb{R}^{2 \times n_B}$ and $\mathbf{E} \in \mathbb{R}^{2 \times n_E}$:

$$\mathbf{B} \text{ is a degradation of } \mathbf{E} \iff \mathcal{P}(\mathbf{B}) \subseteq \mathcal{P}(\mathbf{E}).$$

It turns out that this characterization does not extend to non-binary input alphabets. We give an explicit counter-example to the claim if the input alphabet is ternary.

- Using the simple characterization described above, for any binary input channel pair $(\mathbf{B}, \mathbf{E})$ where $\mathbf{B}$ is not a degradation of $\mathbf{E}$, we (efficiently) find two channels $\mathbf{B}' \in \mathbb{R}^{2 \times 2}$ and $\mathbf{E}' \in \mathbb{R}^{2 \times 3}$ such that the following properties hold:
  - $\mathbf{B}'$ is of the form BAC_{p_0,p_1} for some p_0, p_1 and $\mathbf{E}'$ is of the form BAEC_{e_0,e_1} for some e_0, e_1.
  - $\mathcal{P}(\mathbf{B}') \subseteq \mathcal{P}(\mathbf{B})$. In other words, using the characterization above, $\mathbf{B}'$ can be simulated by $\mathbf{B}$.
  - $\mathcal{P}(\mathbf{E}) \subseteq \mathcal{P}(\mathbf{E}')$. In other words, using the characterization above, $\mathbf{E}$ can be simulated by $\mathbf{E}'$.
  - Further, $\mathcal{P}(\mathbf{B}') \not\subseteq \mathcal{P}(\mathbf{E}')$. In other words, using the characterization above, $\mathbf{B}'$ is not a degradation of $\mathbf{E}'$.

- Using the observations above, we can use the computational wiretap coding scheme for the BAC-BAEC case to construct a computational wiretap coding scheme for the general binary input case where we use the base encoding scheme for the BAC-BAEC case effectively treating Bob's channel as $\mathbf{B}'$ and Eve's channel as $\mathbf{E}'$. In slightly more detail, while the physical channel to Bob is given by $\mathbf{B}$, Bob can simulate $\mathbf{B}'$ via a post-processing procedure allowing Bob to recover the message bit using the base encoding scheme. On the other hand, while the physical channel to Eve is given by $\mathbf{E}$, we show that an even more leaky BAEC channel $\mathbf{E}'$ which is enough to simulate $\mathbf{E}$ would not suffice to recover the message bit.

We describe the intuition behind both these steps next. In Sect. 2.3, we describe how we extend the above construction ideas to a computational wiretap coding scheme for the BAC-BAEC case. Finally, in Sect. 2.4, we discuss the polytope characterization for non-degradation of binary input channels and how use this polytope characterization to find channels $\mathbf{B}'$ and $\mathbf{E}'$ as described above to bootstrap our computational wiretap coding scheme for the BAC-BAEC case to a construction for *any* pair of non-degraded binary input channels.

2.3 Generalization to Asymmetric Erasures/Flips

To describe the ideas behind our base computational wiretap encoding scheme for the case when $\mathbf{B}$ is of the form BAC_{p_0,p_1} and $\mathbf{E}$ is of the form BAEC_{e_0,e_1}, let us understand for what parameter settings of p_0, p_1 and e_0, e_1, we have that BAC_{p_0,p_1} is not a degradation of BAEC_{e_0,e_1}. Without loss of generality, we can assume that p_0 is less than or equal to $\frac{1}{2}$. If this is not the case, we can post-process ChB with the channel given by the permutation matrix:

$$\mathbf{P} = \begin{bmatrix} 0 & 1 \\ 1 & 0 \end{bmatrix}$$

yielding Bob's channel to be $\mathsf{BAC}_{p_0'=1-p_0,p_1'=1-p_1}$ which satisfies our requirement $p_0' \leq \frac{1}{2}$. This transformation also does not change the polytope for Bob as this transformation just swaps the columns of Bob's matrix.

Relation Between Erasure/Flip Probabilities for Non-Degradation. If $\mathbf{B}$ is a matrix corresponding to a BAC_{p_0,p_1} then, it can be expressed as:

$$\mathbf{B} = \begin{bmatrix} 1 - p_0 & p_0 \\ p_1 & 1 - p_1 \end{bmatrix}.$$

Similarly, if $\mathbf{E}$ is a matrix corresponding to a BAEC_{e_0,e_1} then, it can be expressed as:

$$\mathbf{E} = \begin{bmatrix} 1 - e_0 & 0 & e_0 \\ 0 & 1 - e_1 & e_1 \end{bmatrix}.$$

Recall that as described above $\mathbf{B}$ is not a degradation of $\mathbf{E}$ if and only if $\mathcal{P}(\mathbf{B}) \not\subseteq \mathcal{P}(\mathbf{E})$.

One can draw these polytopes in $\mathbb{R}^2$, and a representative picture looks like the one we describe in Fig. 5. The red polytope depicts the polytope $\mathcal{P}(\mathbf{E})$ and the blue polytope represents $\mathcal{P}(\mathbf{B})$. In order to show non-degradation, by the polytope criterion, we only need to show that the point $(p_0, 1 - p_1)$ is not inside $\mathcal{P}(\mathbf{E})$. This translates to having the point $(p_0, 1 - p_1)$ to be on the opposite side of the line joining $(e_0, 1)$ with $(0, 1 - e_1)$ as the origin. When we compute this condition, we get the criterion:

$$e_0 \cdot e_1 > p_1 \cdot e_0 + p_0 \cdot e_1. \tag{2}$$

A formal proof can be found in the full version.

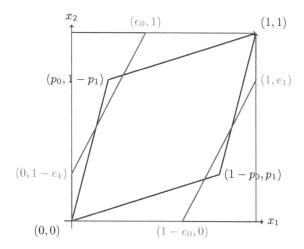

Fig. 5. An example of polytope non-containment for binary asymmetric channels and binary asymmetric erasure channels. Here, x_1 and x_2 are indeterminates. The blue polytope is $\mathcal{P}(\mathsf{BAC}_{p_0,p_1})$ for parameters $p_0 = 1/5, p_1 = 1/4$. The red polytope is $\mathcal{P}(\mathsf{BAEC}_{e_0,e_1})$ for parameters $e_0 = 2/5$, $e_1 = 3/4$. (Color figure online)

Extending the Construction to the Asymmetric Setting. We now describe how to extend our construction ideas to handle the general (asymmetric) case when Bob's channel is BAC_{p_0,p_1} and Eve's channel is BAEC_{e_0,e_1} where the parameters p_0, p_1, e_0, e_1 are potentially differing values (conditioned on ChB not being a degradation of ChE). Below, we recall the mathematical formulation of the non-degradation condition described in Eq. 2.

$$e_0 \cdot e_1 > p_1 \cdot e_0 + p_0 \cdot e_1.$$

Our construction in this case is largely similar to the construction for the $\mathsf{BSC}_p\text{-}\mathsf{BEC}_e$ case with some important modifications.

As before, to encode a message $m \in \{0,1\}$, as a first step we sample a string $x \in \{0,1\}^\lambda$. However, instead of sampling each bit of x uniformly at random from $\{0,1\}$, we sample each bit of x independently to be zero with probability $\eta = \frac{e_1}{e_0+e_1}$ and one with probability $1 - \eta = \frac{e_0}{e_0+e_1}$ (therefore the distribution $\mathsf{Ber}^\lambda_{1-\eta}$). The second modification is the threshold condition in the circuit we will obfuscate. Once we have such an x, we compute $\tilde{C}$ which is now an obfuscation of the circuit C in Fig. 6.

Notice that in the circuit C described in Fig. 6, the threshold for the number of agreeing bits has changed to a constant fraction $(1 - \frac{(p_0 e_1 + p_1 e_0)}{e_0 + e_1})$.

We now describe why these two changes yield a computational wiretap encoding scheme for this case. The rationale behind this is that x is chosen so that each bit of x is zero with probability $\eta = \frac{e_1}{e_0+e_1}$. Further, Bob's channel ChB is BAC_{p_0,p_1} and flips a bit b with probability p_b. As a consequence, Bob's received

---

$C(z)$:

Input: $z \in \{0,1\}^\lambda$

Hardwired: $x \in \{0,1\}^\lambda$

1. Check $\Delta_c(x,z) > (1 - \frac{(p_0 e_1 + p_1 e_0)}{e_0 + e_1})\lambda - \lambda^{0.9}$.
2. If the check passes, output m otherwise output $\perp$.

Fig. 6. Circuit C

string z^B will agree with x on an expected $(1 - p_0)\eta + (1 - p_1)(1 - \eta) = \left(1 - \frac{(p_0 e_1 + p_1 e_0)}{e_0 + e_1}\right)$ fraction of bits, which is more than the threshold we set.

What can Eve do? Eve will receive a string $z^E \in \{0,1\}^\lambda$ that contains erasures and is in $\{0,1,\perp\}^\lambda$. As before, by let $z^E_{S_\perp}$ denote the erased part and $z^E_{\overline{S_\perp}}$ denote the rest of the string which is also equal to $x_{\overline{S_\perp}}$. For this distribution, the size $|\overline{S_\perp}|$ in expectation can be computed to be $((1 - e_0)\eta + (1 - e_1)(1 - \eta))\lambda = \left(1 - \frac{2e_0 e_1}{e_0 + e_1}\right) \cdot \lambda$. What is also crucial for us and sheds a light on how η is chosen is that one can show using a simple probability analysis that conditioned on z^E (equivalently $x_{\overline{S_\perp}}$), the conditional distribution of the erased part $x_{S_\perp}$ is actually a uniform distribution. Therefore, to come up with a maximum number of agreeing bits, what Eve can essentially do is to use up every bit of z^E corresponding to the non-erased set $\overline{S_\perp}$ and make a random guess v corresponding to the set $S_\perp$. This lets Eve come up with a string r such that $r_{\overline{S_\perp}} = x_{\overline{S_\perp}}$ and $r_{S_\perp} = v$, which satisfies:

$$\Delta_c(r,x) \approx \frac{|S_\perp|}{2} + |\overline{S_\perp}|$$

In expectation, this value is a fraction $(1 - \frac{2e_0 e_1}{e_0 + e_1}) + \frac{e_0 e_1}{e_0 + e_1} = 1 - \frac{e_0 e_1}{e_0 + e_1}$.

This implies that Bob's string agrees with x at $\epsilon' = \left(1 - \frac{(p_0 e_1 + p_1 e_0)}{e_0 + e_1}\right) - \left(1 - \frac{e_0 e_1}{e_0 + e_1}\right) = \frac{e_0 e_1 - (p_0 e_1 + p_1 e_0)}{e_0 + e_1}$ more locations than Eve's best string r. The non-degradation condition that we work out in Eq. 2 posits that $e_0 e_1 > p_1 e_0 + p_0 e_1$ and this implies that $\epsilon' > 0$. For a successful Eve this means that it must come up with a string r such that $r_{S_\perp}$ agrees with $x_{S_\perp}$ on at least $(\frac{1}{2} + \gamma')|S_\perp|$ indices for some constant $\gamma' > 0$.

This rough intuition can be massaged into a proof. As before, we will make the following indistinguishable changes:

- As before, for the first change, we will program the string $z^E, S_\perp$ and $\overline{S_\perp}$ into the obfuscated circuit. We will replace the check $\Delta_c(x,z) > (1 - \frac{(p_0 e_1 + p_1 e_0)}{e_0 + e_1})\lambda - \lambda^{0.9}$ with a functionally equivalent check $\Delta_c(x_{S_\perp}, z_{S_\perp}) + \Delta_c(x_{\overline{S_\perp}}, z_{\overline{S_\perp}}) > \left(1 - \frac{(p_0 e_1 + p_1 e_0)}{e_0 + e_1}\right)\lambda - \lambda^{0.9}$.
- Then, just like in the symmetric case, instead of hardwiring $x_{S_\perp}$ in the circuit we will hardwire the value $y = \text{SC-PRG}_\gamma(x_{S_\perp})$ where we set γ to be a constant barely less than γ'. Then, instead of using $x_{S_\perp}$ which we no

longer have, the program will first derive $x_{S_\perp}$ using self-correction feature of SC-PRG$_\gamma$ relying on y and a z that successfully pass our check. This circuit is indistinguishable because with high probability, for any input z that satisfies $\Delta_c(x_{S_\perp}, z_{S_\perp}) + \Delta_c(x_{\overline{S_\perp}}, z_{\overline{S_\perp}}) > \left(1 - \frac{(p_0 e_1 + p_1 e_0)}{e_0 + e_1}\right)\lambda - \lambda^{0.9}$, it must also hold that $\Delta_c(x_{S_\perp}, z_{S_\perp}) > \left(\frac{1}{2} + \gamma\right)|S_\perp|$ as argued above.

- Next, we will replace y with a truly random string. This change is indistinguishable due to the security of SC-PRG$_\gamma$. Observe that because the conditional distribution $x_{S_\perp}$ given z^E is uniform and $|S_\perp| = \Omega(\lambda)$, $y = $ SC-PRG$_\gamma(x_{S_\perp})$ is pseudorandom.
- Once y is a random string, with high probability it will no longer have preimages with respect to SC-PRG. Therefore, with high probability, the circuit under consideration is functionally equivalent to an all reject circuit. We can now use $i\mathcal{O}$ security to replace this circuit with an all reject circuit.

2.4 Reducing the General Binary Input Case to the Asymmetric Setting

We now describe how we construct a computational wiretap coding scheme for pairs of general non-degraded binary-input channels. To this extent, a reader might wonder why the polytope characterization below is both natural and useful for this purpose.

Theorem 2.1. *(Informal) Let $\mathbf{B} \in \mathbb{R}^{2 \times n_B}$ and $\mathbf{E} \in \mathbb{R}^{2 \times n_E}$ be arbitrary row-stochastic matrices. Then, $\mathbf{B} \neq \mathbf{E} \cdot \mathbf{S}$ for every row stochastic matrix $\mathbf{S}$ if and only if $\mathcal{P}(\mathbf{B}) \not\subseteq \mathcal{P}(\mathbf{E})$.*

The usefulness of this theorem is found by considering the following natural approach to construct a computational wiretap encoding scheme for a general binary input channel pair $(\mathbf{B} \in \mathbb{R}^{2 \times n_B}, \mathbf{E} \in \mathbb{R}^{2 \times n_E})$ such that $\mathbf{B}$ is not a degradation of $\mathbf{E}$:

- **Output Reduction for Bob:** Find a stochastic matrix $\mathbf{S}_B \in \mathbb{R}^{n_B \times 2}$ such that $\mathbf{B}' = \mathbf{B} \cdot \mathbf{S}_B$ is not a degradation of $\mathbf{E}$. In particular, at the end of this step, this yields us with a BAC channel $\mathbf{B}'$ such that there does not exist a stochastic matrix $\mathbf{S}$ such that $\mathbf{B} \cdot \mathbf{S}_B = \mathbf{B}' = \mathbf{E} \cdot \mathbf{S}$.
- **Simulating Eve's channel by a BAEC:** In the next step, we want to find an erasure channel BAEC$_{e_0,e_1}$, $\mathbf{E}' \in \mathbb{R}^{2 \times 3}$ such that $\mathbf{E} = \mathbf{E}' \cdot \mathbf{S}_E$ for some stochastic matrix $\mathbf{S}_E$ (in other words Eve's channel is a degradation of $\mathbf{E}'$). Importantly, it must hold that $\mathbf{B}'$ must not be a degradation of $\mathbf{E}'$. That is, there should not exist any stochastic matrix $\mathbf{S}$ such that $\mathbf{B}' = \mathbf{E}' \cdot \mathbf{S}$.
- **Using a solution for BAC$_{p_0,p_1}$-BAEC$_{e_0,e_1}$:** Once we have $\mathbf{B}'$ and $\mathbf{E}'$ satisfying the criteria described above, we can leverage a computational wiretap scheme for the BAC$_{p_0,p_1}$-BAEC$_{e_0,e_1}$ case. We will treat Bob's channel to be $\mathbf{B}'$ (which can be simulated by Bob) and Eve's channel to be $\mathbf{E}'$ (which can simulate Eve).

The question is: can such matrices $\mathbf{B}'$ and $\mathbf{E}'$ be found? We show that for the above approach to materialize, for the binary input channels the polytope condition in Theorem 2.1 is both necessary and sufficient.

The necessity can be seen just from the first condition. We want that there must exist a stochastic $\mathbf{S}_B \in \mathbb{R}^{n_B \times 2}$ such that there does not exist any stochastic matrix $\mathbf{S} \in \mathbb{R}^{n_E \times 2}$ for which it holds that:

$$\mathbf{B} \cdot \mathbf{S}_B = \mathbf{E} \cdot \mathbf{S}$$

Notice that $\mathbf{B}' = \mathbf{B} \cdot \mathbf{S}_B$ is of a very special form. It is of the form $\mathbf{B}' = [\mathbf{v}|\mathbf{v}']$ where due to the properties of stochastic matrices, the first column is some vector $\mathbf{v} \in \mathcal{P}(\mathbf{B})$, whereas the second column is simply $\mathbf{v}' = \mathbf{1} - \mathbf{v}$ where $\mathbf{1}$ is the all ones column matrix. When we have that $[\mathbf{v}|\mathbf{v}'] \neq \mathbf{E} \cdot \mathbf{S}$, then this must mean that $\mathbf{v} \notin \mathcal{P}(\mathbf{E})$. If it was not the case, then $\mathbf{v} = \mathbf{E}\mathbf{w}$ for a column vector $\mathbf{w} \in [0,1]^{n_E}$. Then, we can set $\mathbf{S} = [\mathbf{w}|\mathbf{1} - \mathbf{w}]$ which will satisfy $[\mathbf{v}|\mathbf{v}'] = \mathbf{E} \cdot \mathbf{S}$ giving us a contradiction.

Constructing $\mathbf{B}'$ and $\mathbf{E}'$. Assuming that Theorem 2.1 holds, how do we find such a $\mathbf{B}'$ and $\mathbf{E}'$ in finite time (we assume that channel description is "constant-sized").

Finding $\mathbf{B}'$. To find such a matrix $\mathbf{B}'$ one can find a vector $\mathbf{v} \in \mathcal{P}(\mathbf{B}) \setminus \mathcal{P}(\mathbf{E})$. For such a vector, $\mathbf{v} = \mathbf{B} \cdot \mathbf{a}$ for some $\mathbf{a} \in [0,1]^{n_B \times 1}$. We can set $\mathbf{B}' = [\mathbf{v} \mid \mathbf{1} - \mathbf{v}] = \mathbf{B} \cdot \mathbf{S}_B$ for the stochastic matrix $\mathbf{S}_B$ where $\mathbf{S}_B = [\mathbf{a} \mid \mathbf{1} - \mathbf{a}]$. Observe that $\mathbf{v} \in \mathcal{P}(\mathbf{B}') \setminus \mathcal{P}(\mathbf{E})$, therefore $\mathbf{B}'$ is not a degradation of $\mathbf{E}$ as per Theorem 2.1.

How do we find $\mathbf{v}$? Note that both $\mathcal{P}(\mathbf{B})$ and $\mathcal{P}(\mathbf{E})$ are convex bodies with finitely many extreme points. Since $\mathcal{P}(\mathbf{B})$ is not contained inside $\mathcal{P}(\mathbf{E})$, there must be an extreme point of $\mathcal{P}(\mathbf{B})$ not contained inside $\mathcal{P}(\mathbf{E})$. Furthermore, the set of extreme points of $\mathcal{P}(\mathbf{B})$ are contained inside the set $\{\mathbf{B} \cdot \mathbf{b} \mid \mathbf{b} \in \{0,1\}^{n_B}\}$. For each of these points, the non-containment can also be checked efficiently using a linear program.

Finding $\mathbf{E}'$. Perhaps what might seem really surprising is that we can actually find a channel matrix $\mathbf{E}'$ that is highly structured (of the form BAEC_{e_0,e_1}) so that it is powerful enough to simulate $\mathbf{E}$, but not enough to simulate $\mathbf{B}'$, for any pair of channel matrices $\mathbf{B}' \in \mathbb{R}^{2 \times 2}$ and $\mathbf{E} \in \mathbb{R}^{2 \times n_E}$ satisfying the non-degradation condition.

The equivalent polytope condition actually gives rise to a very intuitive geometric approach to show this. The idea is that $\mathcal{P}(\mathbf{E})$ is a bounded convex body in $[0,1]^2$, and there is a point $\mathbf{v} \in \mathcal{P}(\mathbf{B}') \setminus \mathcal{P}(\mathbf{E})$ so there exists a separating hyperplane that strictly separates $\mathbf{v}$ from $\mathcal{P}(\mathbf{E})$. This separating hyperplane, a line in two-dimensions, will form a facet of a new channel polytope that defines a binary asymmetric erasure channel. Since $(0,0)$ and $(1,1)$ are in both $\mathcal{P}(\mathbf{B}')$ and $\mathcal{P}(\mathbf{E})$ the line should stay "above" the line joining $(0,0)$ and $(1,1)$. This line will intersect the line $x_1 = 0$ at a point $(0, 1 - e_1)$ for some $e_1 > 0$ and the line $x_2 = 1$ at $(e_0, 1)$ some $e_0 > 0$. By two-fold rotational symmetry, we can find another parallel line intersecting $x_2 = 0$ at $(1 - e_0, 0)$ and $x_1 = 1$ at $(1, e_1)$ that separates the point $\mathbf{1} - \mathbf{v}$ from $\mathcal{P}(\mathbf{E})$. The area formed that is between the two parallel lines inside $[0,1]^2$ can be represented by the channel matrix as required:

$$\mathbf{E}' = \begin{bmatrix} 1 - e_0 & 0 & e_0 \\ 0 & 1 - e_1 & e_1 \end{bmatrix}.$$

See Fig. 7 for a visual depiction.

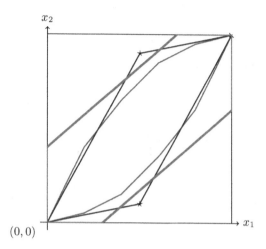

Fig. 7. The blue polytope (for ChB) is not contained in the red polytope (for ChE), so ChB is not a degradation of ChE. Using separating hyperplanes (olive-colored lines) we can strictly separate the blue extreme points from the red polytope. The olive polytope corresponds to a binary asymmetric erasure channel ChE' that contains the red polytope but does not contain the blue polytope, i.e. ChE is a degradation of ChE' and ChB is not a degradation of ChE'. (Color figure online)

Proving the Polytope Characterization. To show the polytope character-ization theorem (Theorem 2.1), we first observe that one direction is straight-forward. To show that if ChB is a degradation of ChE, then $\mathcal{P}(\mathbf{B}) \subseteq \mathcal{P}(\mathbf{E})$, we simply open up all the definitions. By definition of the polytope formulation, for any point $\mathbf{x} \in \mathcal{P}(\mathbf{B})$ there exists a vector $\mathbf{s}$ such that $\mathbf{x} = \mathbf{B} \cdot \mathbf{s}$ where $\mathbf{0} \leq \mathbf{s} \leq \mathbf{1}$. From the definition of stochastic degradation, there is a row-stochastic matrix $\mathbf{S}$ such that $\mathbf{B} = \mathbf{E} \cdot \mathbf{S}$. Then $\mathbf{x} = \mathbf{E} \cdot (\mathbf{S} \cdot \mathbf{s}) = \mathbf{E} \cdot \mathbf{s}'$ where $\mathbf{0} \leq \mathbf{s}' \leq \mathbf{1}$ since $\mathbf{S}$ is stochastic.

Showing the converse that $\mathcal{P}(\mathbf{B}) \subseteq \mathcal{P}(\mathbf{E})$ implies the existence of a row-stochastic matrix $\mathbf{S}$ such that $\mathbf{B} = \mathbf{E} \cdot \mathbf{S}$ is more involved. A natural approach is by induction on the number of columns of $\mathbf{B}$. For this induction approach, we will relax the row-stochastic condition on $\mathbf{B}$ and $\mathbf{S}$, which states that non-negative matrices $\mathbf{B}$ and $\mathbf{E}$ satisfy $\mathbf{B} \cdot \mathbf{1} = \mathbf{1} = \mathbf{E} \cdot \mathbf{1}$, and instead assume the more general condition $\mathbf{B} \cdot \mathbf{1} = \mathbf{E} \cdot \mathbf{1}$ for non-negative matrices $\mathbf{B}$ and $\mathbf{E}$.

1. In the base case, if $\mathbf{B}$ consists of one column, then $\mathbf{B} \cdot \mathbf{1} = \mathbf{B}$ so we can take the row-stochastic $\mathbf{S} = \mathbf{1}$ and observe that $\mathbf{E} \cdot \mathbf{1} = \mathbf{B} \cdot \mathbf{1} = \mathbf{B}$.

2. In the induction step, we consider a matrix $\mathbf{B}'$ which is constructed from $\mathbf{B}$ by removing a column of $\mathbf{B}$ so that $\mathbf{B} = \begin{bmatrix} \mathbf{v} | \mathbf{B}' \end{bmatrix}$. Observe that $\mathbf{B}' \cdot \mathbf{1} = \mathbf{B} \cdot \mathbf{1} - \mathbf{v}$. The induction hypothesis is that if $\mathcal{P}(\mathbf{B}') \subseteq \mathcal{P}(\mathbf{E}')$ for some matrix $\mathbf{B}'$ of fewer columns than $\mathbf{B}$, and some $\mathbf{E}'$ such that $\mathbf{B}' \cdot \mathbf{1} = \mathbf{E}' \cdot \mathbf{1}$, then there exists a row-stochastic matrix $\mathbf{S}'$ such that $\mathbf{B}' = \mathbf{E}' \cdot \mathbf{S}'$.

   To see how we might apply the induction hypothesis, observe that $\mathcal{P}(\mathbf{B}') = \mathcal{P}(\mathbf{B}) \cap (\mathcal{P}(\mathbf{B}) - \mathbf{v})$ where we define the set $\mathcal{P}(\mathbf{B}) - \mathbf{v} := \{\mathbf{u} - \mathbf{v} : \mathbf{u} \in \mathcal{P}(\mathbf{B})\}$. This immediately implies the following polytope containment relation

   $$\mathcal{P}(\mathbf{B}') = \mathcal{P}(\mathbf{B}) \cap (\mathcal{P}(\mathbf{B}) - \mathbf{v}) \subseteq \mathcal{P}(\mathbf{E}) \cap (\mathcal{P}(\mathbf{E}) - \mathbf{v})$$

   To apply the induction hypothesis, we need to find a matrix $\mathbf{E}'$ such that $\mathcal{P}(\mathbf{E}') = \mathcal{P}(\mathbf{E}) \cap (\mathcal{P}(\mathbf{E}) - \mathbf{v})$ such that $\mathbf{E}' \cdot \mathbf{1} = \mathbf{B}' \cdot \mathbf{1}$. To find this matrix $\mathbf{E}'$, we turn to the (two-dimensional) geometric view of the polytopes: $\mathcal{P}(\mathbf{E}) \cap (\mathcal{P}(\mathbf{E}) - \mathbf{v})$ is the intersection of a polytope and its translated polytope. This intersection, visually, is a polytope obtained by starting with the polytope $\mathcal{P}(\mathbf{E})$ and shrinking the length of its facets (lines) by some multiplicative factor in the interval $[0, 1]$. This geometric intuition is exactly captured by the existence of some diagonal matrix $\mathbf{D}$, whose entries are in the closed interval $[0, 1]$, such that $\mathcal{P}(\mathbf{E}) \cap (\mathcal{P}(\mathbf{E}) - \mathbf{v}) = \mathcal{P}(\mathbf{E} \cdot \mathbf{D})$. Thus, we set $\mathbf{E}' = \mathbf{E} \cdot \mathbf{D}$.

   It remains to show that $\mathbf{E} \cdot \mathbf{D} \cdot \mathbf{1} = \mathbf{B}' \cdot \mathbf{1}$. To see why this is true, observe that by non-negativity $\mathbf{E} \cdot \mathbf{1}$ is the maximal element (in the ℓ_1-norm) of $\mathcal{P}(\mathbf{E})$ so $\mathbf{E} \cdot \mathbf{1} - \mathbf{v}$ is the maximal element of $\mathcal{P}(\mathbf{E}) - \mathbf{v}$. Then, $\mathbf{E} \cdot \mathbf{1} - \mathbf{v} \in \mathcal{P}(\mathbf{E})$ by definition of the polytope formulation ($\mathbf{v} = \mathbf{E} \cdot \mathbf{u}'$ for some $\mathbf{0} \leq \mathbf{u}' \leq \mathbf{1}$). Therefore, $\mathbf{E} \cdot \mathbf{1} - \mathbf{v}$ is the maximal element of $\mathcal{P}(\mathbf{E}) \cap (\mathcal{P}(\mathbf{E}) - \mathbf{v}) = \mathcal{P}(\mathbf{E} \cdot \mathbf{D})$. This fact implies that $\mathbf{E} \cdot \mathbf{D} \cdot \mathbf{1} = \mathbf{E} \cdot \mathbf{1} - \mathbf{v} = \mathbf{B} \cdot \mathbf{1} - \mathbf{v} = \mathbf{B}' \cdot \mathbf{1}$.

   Applying the induction hypothesis, we now have a row-stochastic matrix $\mathbf{S}'$ such that $\mathbf{B}' = \mathbf{E} \cdot \mathbf{D} \cdot \mathbf{S}'$. To conclude the induction step, we set $\mathbf{S} = \begin{bmatrix} \mathbf{1} - \mathbf{D} \cdot \mathbf{1} | \mathbf{D} \cdot \mathbf{S}' \end{bmatrix}$ and observe that $\mathbf{E} \cdot \mathbf{S} = \mathbf{B}$ and $\mathbf{S} \cdot \mathbf{1} = \mathbf{1}$.

Counterexample for the Many Input-Case. At first glance, it may seem to be without loss of generality to consider binary input channels, since Alice is honest and can anyway choose to use only binary inputs. However, there can exist channels with non-binary inputs where Bob's channel is not a degradation of Eve's channel, and yet every projection of those channels to only two inputs always yields channels where Bob's channel is a degradation of Eve's channel. Such pairs of channels, however, are not common. Nevertheless, if future work is to tackle the case of non-binary input channels, this issue will present a challenge.

One might wonder if our polytope characterization holds for channels with larger number of inputs $k > 2$. Such a claim would indeed be useful to extend our approach to handle to an arbitrary case when $\mathbf{B} \in \mathbb{R}^{k \times n_B}$ and $\mathbf{E} \in \mathbb{R}^{k \times n_E}$. Unfortunately it turns out that such a claim is untrue whenever $k \geq 3$. Intriguingly, we can come up with an explicit choice for stochastic matrices $\mathbf{B} \in \mathbb{R}^{3 \times 3}$ and $\mathbf{E} \in \mathbb{R}^{3 \times 4}$ such that $\mathcal{P}(\mathbf{B}) \subseteq \mathcal{P}(\mathbf{E})$ and yet there does not exist any stochastic matrix such that $\mathbf{B} = \mathbf{E} \cdot \mathbf{S}$. See the full version for a counterexample.

3   Preliminaries

Throughout this paper, we will use the notation $[n] = \{1, 2, 3, \ldots, n\}$. Let $\mathbf{1}$ denote the all-ones column vector whose length can be clearly inferred in the various contexts. We will use the usual convention that rows are probability vectors. A row-stochastic matrix $\mathbf{M}$ is a matrix whose rows add up to 1; equivalently, $\mathbf{M}$ satisfies $\mathbf{M} \cdot \mathbf{1} = \mathbf{1}$.

3.1   Channels and Wiretap Coding

Definition 3.1 (Discrete Memoryless Channel). *A discrete memoryless channel (DMC)* $\mathsf{ChW} : \mathcal{X} \to \mathcal{Y}$ *is a randomized function from input alphabet* $\mathcal{X}$ *to output alphabet* $\mathcal{Y}$*. Let* $p_W(y \mid x)$ *denote the probability that we observe* $y \in \mathcal{Y}$ *after sending* $x \in \mathcal{X}$ *through* ChW*. For* $x \in \mathcal{X}$*, we use* $\mathsf{ChW}(x)$ *to denote a random variable over* $\mathcal{Y}$ *such that for* $y \in \mathcal{Y}$*,*

$$\Pr[\mathsf{ChW}(x) = y] = p_W(y \mid x).$$

We associate ChW *with its row-stochastic matrix* $\mathbf{W} = [p_W(y \mid x)]_{x \in \mathcal{X}, y \in \mathcal{Y}}$ *so that* $\mathbf{W} \cdot \mathbf{1} = \mathbf{1}$*. For* $n \in \mathbb{N}$ *and* $r = (r_1, \ldots, r_n) \in \mathcal{X}^n$*, we define*

$$\mathsf{ChW}(r) = \mathsf{ChW}(r_1) \ldots \mathsf{ChW}(r_n).$$

For two channels $\mathsf{ChW} : \mathcal{X} \to \mathcal{Y}$ *and* $\mathsf{ChV} : \mathcal{Y} \to \mathcal{Z}$*, we use* $\mathsf{ChV} \circ \mathsf{ChW}$ *to denote their concatenation* $\mathsf{ChV}(\mathsf{ChW}(\cdot))$*. Whenever we discuss channels in the context of efficient algorithms, we assume all channels have finite description size with constant alphabet size and rational probabilities.*

Definition 3.2 (Binary Symmetric Channel (BSC)). *A binary symmetric channel with crossover probability* p*, denoted as* BSC_p *is a DMC with binary input and binary output such that on input bit* b*, it outputs* $1 - b$ *with probability* p *and* b *otherwise.*

Definition 3.3 (Binary Erasure Channel (BEC)). *A binary erasure channel with erasure probability* e*, denoted as* BEC_e*, is a DMC with binary input and output* $\{0, 1, \perp\}$ *such that on input bit* b*, it outputs* $\perp$ *(i.e. erases the bit) with probability* e *and* b *otherwise.*

Definition 3.4 (Binary Asymmetric Channel (BAC)). *A binary asymmetric channel with crossover probabilities* (p_0, p_1)*, denoted as* BAC_{p_0, p_1}*, is a DMC with binary input and binary output such that on input bit* b*, the channel outputs* $1 - b$ *with probability* p_b *and* b *with probability* $1 - p_b$*. The associated row-stochastic matrix is given by*

$$\begin{bmatrix} 1 - p_0 & p_0 \\ p_1 & 1 - p_1 \end{bmatrix}.$$

Definition 3.5 (Binary Asymmetric Erasure Channel (BAEC)). *A binary asymmetric channel with erasure probabilities* (e_0, e_1), *denoted as* BAEC_{e_0, e_1}, *is a DMC with binary input and ternary output in* $\{0, 1, \bot\}$ *such that on input bit* b, *the channel outputs* $\bot$ *with probability* e_b *and* b *with probability* $1 - e_b$. *The associated row-stochastic matrix is given by*

$$\begin{bmatrix} 1 - e_0 & 0 & e_0 \\ 0 & 1 - e_1 & e_1 \end{bmatrix}.$$

Remark 3.6. In the symmetric case, we can assume that a channel BSC_p has $p \leq 1/2$ without loss of generality because the receiver can always flip its interpretation of the received bit. In the asymmetric setting, by the same reasoning we can assume without loss of generality that $p_0 \leq 1/2$ (but not both p_0 and p_1).

If one channel can be used to simulate another channel, we say that the latter is a degradation of the former. More formally, we recall the well-established notion of stochastic channel degradation.

Definition 3.7 (Stochastic Degradation). *We say that channel* ChB *is a degradation of channel* ChE *if there exists a channel* ChS *such that* $\mathsf{ChB} = \mathsf{ChS} \circ \mathsf{ChE}$. *Equivalently,* ChB *is a degradation of* ChE *if there exists a row-stochastic matrix* $\mathbf{S}$ *such that* $\mathbf{B} = \mathbf{E} \cdot \mathbf{S}$, *where* $\mathbf{B}$ *is the row-stochastic matrix of* ChB *and* $\mathbf{E}$ *is the row-stochastic matrix of* ChE.

Definition 3.8 (Wiretap Channel). *A wiretap channel is a pair of DMCs* $(\mathsf{ChB}, \mathsf{ChE})$ *where* $\mathsf{ChB} : \mathcal{X} \rightarrow \mathcal{Y}$ *and* $\mathsf{ChE} : \mathcal{X} \rightarrow \mathcal{Z}$ *share the same input alphabet* $\mathcal{X}$.

We now recall the definition of wiretap coding schemes in the setting of a computationally bounded adversary.

Definition 3.9 (Computational wiretap coding [11]). *A pair of* PPT *algorithms* $\Pi = (\mathsf{Enc}, \mathsf{Dec})$ *is a computational secure wiretap coding scheme for wiretap channel* $(\mathsf{ChB}, \mathsf{ChE})$ *and message space* $\mathcal{M} = \{0, 1\}$, *if there exists a negligible function* $\epsilon(\lambda)$ *such that*

- **Correctness:** *For every message* $m \in \{0, 1\}$,

$$\Pr[\mathsf{Dec}(1^\lambda, \mathsf{ChB}(\mathsf{Enc}(1^\lambda, m))) = m] \geq 1 - \epsilon(\lambda)$$

- **Security:** *For all polynomial-time non-uniform adversaries* $\mathcal{A}$,

$$\Pr[\mathcal{A}(1^\lambda, \mathsf{ChE}(\mathsf{Enc}(1^\lambda, b))) = b] \leq \frac{1}{2} + \epsilon(\lambda)$$

where b *is uniformly distributed over* $\{0, 1\}$.

3.2 Error-Correcting Codes

For any two binary strings x and y of the same length n, let $\Delta_H(x, y)$ denote their Hamming distance and let $\delta_H(x, y) = \frac{\Delta_H(x,y)}{n}$ denote their relative Hamming distance.

Definition 3.10. *A q-ary code of block length n and dimension k is given by a function $C : \mathcal{M} \to \subseteq [q]^n$ where $|\mathcal{M}| = q^k$ and $\mathcal{M}$ is the message space and $[q]$ is the alphabet of C. Such a code is also referred as a $(n, k)_q$ code.*

Definition 3.11. *An ensemble of codes $\{C_\lambda : \mathcal{M}_\lambda \to [q_\lambda]^{n_\lambda}\}$ is $(p(\cdot), L(\cdot))$-list decodable, where $p : \mathbb{N} \to (0, 1)$ and let $L : \mathbb{N} \to \mathbb{N}$ are functions in some parameter λ, if there is a polynomial-time algorithm ListDec such that for all $\lambda \in \mathbb{N}$, for all $y \in [q_\lambda]^{n_\lambda}$, ListDec$(\lambda, y)$ outputs a list S of size at most $L(\lambda)$ messages such that S contains all $m \in \mathcal{M}_\lambda$ such that $\delta_H(C_\lambda(m), y) \le p(\lambda)$.*

Lemma 3.12 (Implicit in [19], also Theorem 9 in [18]). *For every ε, k, if $n \ge \mathsf{poly}\left(k, \frac{1}{\varepsilon}\right)$, there exists an $(n, k)_2$ code with a polynomial time list-decoding algorithm for up to $\left(\frac{1}{2} - \varepsilon\right) \cdot n$ errors.*

4   The **BSC-BEC** Case

We first consider the simpler setting when Bob's channel is BSC_p and Eve's channel is BEC_e where Bob's channel is not a degradation of Eve's (which happens exactly when $e > 2p$). In this setting, we present a simple construction of a computational wiretap coding scheme based on the existence of $i\mathcal{O}$ and an injective one-way function. Our "code-offset" based construction for this setting also motivates our construction for the general binary input wiretap channels which can be found in the full version.

Theorem 4.1 (Computational wiretap for the BSC-BEC case). *Assuming the existence of $i\mathcal{O}$ and an injective one-way function, there exists a computational wiretap coding scheme for a wiretap channel of the form $(\mathsf{BSC}_p, \mathsf{BEC}_e)$ if and only if $e > 2p$.*

The "only if" direction follows from the fact that when $e \le 2p$, Bob's channel BSC_p is a degradation of Eve's channel BEC_e. In fact, this direction holds unconditionally. We thus focus on constructing a computational wiretap coding scheme when $e > 2p$ using $i\mathcal{O}$ and an injective one-way function. The construction is described in the following figure.

Coding Scheme 1 *(Computational Wiretap Coding for $(\mathsf{BSC}_p, \mathsf{BEC}_e)$)*
For the construction, we will use an $i\mathcal{O}$ scheme and any error-correcting coding scheme $\mathcal{C}_B = (\mathcal{C}_B.\mathsf{Enc}, \mathcal{C}_B.\mathsf{Dec})$ for the channel BSC_p $(p < 1/2)$ such that for all $x \in \{0, 1\}^*$,

$$\Pr[\mathcal{C}_B.\mathsf{Dec}(1^\lambda, \mathsf{BSC}_p(\mathcal{C}_B.\mathsf{Enc}(1^\lambda, x))) = x] \ge 1 - \varepsilon(\lambda)$$

for some negligible function ε. For example, even a simple repetition code of block length λ suffices. $\mathsf{Enc}(1^\lambda, b)$:

---

1. Let $\delta_{th} = \lambda^{-0.1}$.
2. Sample $r \leftarrow \{0,1\}^\lambda$ uniform randomly.
3. Construct a circuit (whose size is determined by λ) for the function f : $\{0,1\}^\lambda \to \{0,1,\bot\}$ defined as follows:

$f_\lambda(x)$:
Input: $x \in \{0,1\}^\lambda$.
Hardwired constants: r, b.
  1. If the Hamming distance $\Delta_H(x,r) < (p + \delta_{th}) \cdot \lambda$, then output b. Else, output $\bot$.

4. Output $(\mathcal{C}_B.\mathsf{Enc}(1^\lambda, i\mathcal{O}(f_\lambda)), r)$ where f_λ is padded to be the maximum circuit size of itself and $\{f_\lambda^{(i)}\}_{i \in [4]}$ which are described below.

$\mathsf{Dec}(1^\lambda, \hat{f}, z)$:

1. Let $f \leftarrow \mathcal{C}_B.\mathsf{Dec}(1^\lambda, \hat{f})$.
2. Output $f(z)$.

Having explained the intuition for the above coding scheme in the technical overview (Sect. 2), we proceed to the formal proofs.

Lemma 4.2 (Correctness of the Computational Wiretap Encoding Scheme). *There exists a negligible function $\varepsilon : \mathbb{N} \to [0,1]$ such that for every message bit $b \in \{0,1\}$,*

$$\Pr[\mathsf{Dec}(1^\lambda, \mathsf{ChB}(\mathsf{Enc}(1^\lambda, b))) = b] \geq 1 - \varepsilon(\lambda).$$

Proof. We will use (f, r) to denote random variables representing the output of $\mathsf{Enc}(1^\lambda, b)$ and we will use $(\tilde{f}, \tilde{r})$ to denote random variables representing the output of the channel $\mathsf{ChB}(f, r)$. Using the notation $\Delta_H(\cdot, \cdot)$ to denote Hamming distance (non-relative), we note that the expected value of the Hamming distance of $\tilde{r}$ from r is given as $\mathbb{E}_{\mathsf{ChB,Enc}}[\Delta_H(\tilde{r}, r)] = p \cdot \lambda$. Then the probability over the channel randomness and the coins used by the encoding algorithm $\mathsf{Enc}(\cdot, \cdot)$ that the received string $\tilde{r}$ fails the statistical check is given by an additive Chernoff bound:

$$\Pr_{\mathsf{ChB,Enc}}[\Delta_H(\tilde{r}, r) \geq (p + \delta_{th}) \cdot \lambda] \leq \exp\left(-2 \cdot \delta_{th}^2 \cdot \lambda\right) = \exp\left(-2 \cdot \lambda^{0.8}\right)$$

which is negligible in λ.

Lemma 4.3. *Let ChB be a BSC_p channel and let ChE be a BEC_e channel such that $e > 2p$. For all polynomial-time non-uniform algorithms $\mathcal{A}$, there exists a negligible function $\mu : \mathbb{N} \to [0,1]$ such that*

$$\Pr[\mathcal{A}(1^\lambda, \mathsf{ChE}(\mathsf{Enc}(1^\lambda, b))) = b] \leq \frac{1}{2} + \mu(\lambda)$$

where b is uniformly distributed over $\{0,1\}$.

Proof. We will proceed through the following series of hybrids (experiments) that model Eve's view. We will show that what Eve receives from this encoding process is computationally indistinguishable from Eve receiving a null circuit, thereby rendering Eve unable to recover the message bit b except with negligible advantage. In each of the following hybrids, each function (viewed as a circuit) is padded to be the maximum circuit size of the circuits in $\{f_\lambda\} \cup \left\{f_\lambda^{(i)}\right\}_{i \in [4]}$ where f_λ is defined in the construction and $f_\lambda^{(i)}$ are defined in each of the below hybrids.

1. $H_0(1^\lambda)$: In the real world, Alice sends $\text{Enc}(1^\lambda, b) = (\mathcal{C}.\text{Enc}(i\mathcal{O}(f)), r)$ through ChE and Eve receives the output of the channel, $\text{ChE}((\mathcal{C}.\text{Enc}(i\mathcal{O}(f))), r)$. We assume that Eve successfully recovers $i\mathcal{O}(f)$, since such an assumption only gives Eve more information. The output of the experiment is $(i\mathcal{O}(f), \text{ChE}(r))$.

2. $H_1(1^\lambda)$: In this hybrid, we consider a slight variation of the above experiment. Let $r \leftarrow \{0,1\}^\lambda$ be chosen as in $\text{Enc}(1^\lambda, b)$ where each bit r_i is independently identically sampled uniform randomly. Then let $\hat{r} := \text{ChE}(r) \in \{0,1,\bot\}^\lambda$. Let $S_\bot \subseteq [\lambda]$ be the set of indices for which $\hat{r}_i = \bot$ and let $\overline{S_\bot} := [\lambda] \setminus S_\bot$. Let $\kappa := |S_\bot|$. Define the finite subsequence (a string) $r_{S_\bot} := (r_{i_j})_{i_j \in S_\bot \text{ s.t. } i_j < i_{j+1}} \in \{0,1\}^\kappa$ consisting of the bits from the indices from $S_\bot$ and analogous finite subsequence $r_{\overline{S_\bot}} := (r_{i_j})_{i_j \in \overline{S_\bot} \text{ s.t. } i_j < i_{j+1}} \in \{0,1\}^{\lambda-\kappa}$ of the bits from the indices from $\overline{S_\bot}$.
We now give an alternate encoding method where instead of constructing the function f as in Coding Scheme 1, Alice instead uses the following function $f_\lambda^{(1)}$:

$f_\lambda^{(1)}(x)$:
Input: $x \in \{0,1\}^\lambda$
Hardwired constants: $r_{S_\bot}, r_{\overline{S_\bot}}, b, e_0, e_1, p_0, p_1, S_\bot$.
  1. If the Hamming distances satisfy $\Delta_H(x_{S_\bot}, r_{S_\bot}) + \Delta_H(x_{\overline{S_\bot}}, r_{\overline{S_\bot}}) \leq (p + \delta_{th}) \cdot \lambda$, then output b. Else, output $\bot$.

The output of the experiment is $(i\mathcal{O}(f_\lambda^{(1)}), \hat{r})$.

3. $H_2(1^\lambda)$: Let $r \leftarrow \{0,1\}^\lambda$ be chosen as in $\text{Enc}(1^\lambda, b)$ where each bit r_i is sampled uniform randomly. Then let $\hat{r} := \text{ChE}(r) \in \{0,1,\bot\}^\lambda$. Let $S_\bot \subseteq [\lambda]$ be the set of indices for which $\hat{r}_i = \bot$ and let $\overline{S_\bot} := [\lambda] \setminus S_\bot$. Let $\kappa := |S_\bot|$. Define the finite subsequence (a string) $r_{S_\bot} := (r_{i_j})_{i_j \in S_\bot \text{ s.t. } i_j < i_{j+1}} \in \{0,1\}^\kappa$ consisting of the bits from the indices from $S_\bot$ and analogous finite subsequence $r_{\overline{S_\bot}} := (r_{i_j})_{i_j \in \overline{S_\bot} \text{ s.t. } i_j < i_{j+1}} \in \{0,1\}^{\lambda-\kappa}$ of the bits from the indices from $\overline{S_\bot}$.
We now give an alternate encoding method where instead of constructing the function $f^{(1)}$ as in $H_1(1^\lambda)$, Alice will do the following in order to construct a different function $f^{(2)}$ which we will define shortly:

(a) Let $\varepsilon = \frac{1}{4} - \frac{p}{2e}$. Let $C_{LD,\kappa} : \{0,1\}^{\kappa^d} \to \{0,1\}^{\kappa}$ be a code from a $(1/2 - \varepsilon, q(\kappa, 1/\varepsilon))$-list decodable ensemble of binary codes for some constant $0 < d < 1$ and some polynomial $q(\kappa, 1/\varepsilon)$. We will use $C_{LD,\kappa}.\mathsf{ListDec}(\cdot)$ to denote an efficient list-decoding function for $C_{LD,\kappa}$.

(b) Sample $\alpha \in \{0,1\}^{\kappa^d}$ uniform randomly and set $c \leftarrow C_{LD,\kappa}(\alpha)$ so $c \in \{0,1\}^{\kappa}$.

(c) Let $z = c \oplus r_{S_\perp}$.

(d) Let $G : \{0,1\}^{\kappa^d} \to \{0,1\}^{3 \cdot \kappa^d}$ be a length-tripling injective PRG.

$f_\lambda^{(2)}(x)$:

Input: $x \in \{0,1\}^\lambda$

Hardwired constants: $r_{\overline{S_\perp}}, z, G(\alpha), b, e_0, e_1, p_0, p_1, S_\perp$.

1. Let $D \leftarrow C_{LD,\kappa}.\mathsf{ListDec}(z \oplus x_{S_\perp})$. D is a list of at most $q(\kappa, 1/\varepsilon)$ many elements in $\{0,1\}^{\kappa^d}$.
2. If $G(s) \neq G(\alpha)$ for all strings $s \in D$, output $\perp$. Otherwise, set α' to be the string s such that $G(s) = G(\alpha)$.
3. Set $r_{S_\perp} \leftarrow C_{LD,\kappa}(\alpha') \oplus z$.
4. If the Hamming distances satisfy $\Delta_H(x_{S_\perp}, r_{S_\perp}) + \Delta_H(x_{\overline{S_\perp}}, r_{\overline{S_\perp}}) \leq (p + \delta_{th}) \cdot \lambda$, then output b. Else, output $\perp$.

The output of the experiment is $(i\mathcal{O}(f_\lambda^{(2)}), \hat{r})$.

4. $H_3(1^\lambda)$: Let $r \leftarrow \{0,1\}^\lambda$ be chosen as in $\mathsf{Enc}(1^\lambda, b)$ where each bit r_i is independently identically sampled uniform randomly. Then let $\hat{r} := \mathsf{ChE}(r) \in \{0,1,\perp\}^\lambda$. Let $S_\perp \subseteq [\lambda]$ be the set of indices for which $\hat{r}_i = \perp$ and let $\overline{S_\perp} := [\lambda] \setminus S_\perp$. Let $\kappa := |S_\perp|$. Define the finite subsequence (a string) $r_{S_\perp} := (r_{i_j})_{i_j \in S_\perp \text{ s.t. } i_j < i_{j+1}} \in \{0,1\}^\kappa$ consisting of the bits from the indices from $S_\perp$ and analogous finite subsequence $r_{\overline{S_\perp}} := (r_{i_j})_{i_j \in \overline{S_\perp} \text{ s.t. } i_j < i_{j+1}} \in \{0,1\}^{\lambda-\kappa}$ of the bits from the indices from $\overline{S_\perp}$.

We now give an alternate encoding method where instead of constructing the function $f^{(1)}$ as in $H_1(1^\lambda)$, Alice will do the following in order to construct a different function $f^{(2)}$ which we will define shortly:

(a) Let $\varepsilon = \frac{1}{4} - \frac{p}{2e}$. Let $C_{LD,\kappa} : \{0,1\}^{\kappa^d} \to \{0,1\}^\kappa$ be a code from a $(1/2 - \varepsilon, q(\kappa, 1/\varepsilon))$-list decodable ensemble of binary codes for some constant $0 < d < 1$ and some polynomial $q(\kappa, 1/\varepsilon)$. We will use $C_{LD,\kappa}.\mathsf{ListDec}(\cdot)$ to denote an efficient list-decoding function for $C_{LD,\kappa}$.

(b) Sample $\alpha \in \{0,1\}^{\kappa^d}$ uniform randomly and set $c \leftarrow C_{LD,\kappa}(\alpha)$ so $c \in \{0,1\}^\kappa$.

(c) Let $z \leftarrow c \oplus r_{S_\perp}$.

(d) Let $G : \{0,1\}^{\kappa^d} \to \{0,1\}^{3 \cdot \kappa^d}$ be a length-tripling injective PRG.

(e) Let R be a string sampled uniform randomly from $\{0,1\}^{3 \cdot \kappa^d}$.

$f_\lambda^{(3)}(x)$:

Input: $x \in \{0,1\}^\lambda$

Hardwired constants: $r_{\overline{S_\perp}}, z, R, b, e_0, e_1, p_0, p_1, S_\perp$.

1. Let $D \leftarrow C_{LD,\kappa}.\mathsf{ListDec}(z \oplus x_{S_\perp})$. D is a list of at most $q(\kappa, 1/\varepsilon)$ many elements in $\{0,1\}^{\kappa^d}$.
2. If $G(s) \neq R$ for all strings $s \in D$, output $\perp$. Otherwise, set α' to be the string s such that $G(s) = G(\alpha)$.
3. Set $r_{S_\perp} \leftarrow C_{LD,\kappa}(\alpha') \oplus z$.
4. If the Hamming distances satisfy $\Delta_H(x_{S_\perp}, r_{S_\perp}) + \Delta_H(x_{\overline{S_\perp}}, r_{\overline{S_\perp}}) \leq (p + \delta_{th}) \cdot \lambda$, then output b. Else, output $\perp$.

The output of the experiment is $(i\mathcal{O}(f_\lambda^{(3)}), \hat{r})$.

5. $H_4(1^\lambda)$: We now consider when Eve simply gets the $i\mathcal{O}$ of a null circuit. Let $r \leftarrow \{0,1\}^\lambda$ be chosen as in $\mathsf{Enc}(1^\lambda, b)$ where each bit r_i is independently uniform randomly sampled. Then let $\hat{r} := \mathsf{ChE}(r) \in \{0,1,\perp\}^\lambda$.

$f_\lambda^{(4)}(x)$:
Input: $x \in \{0,1\}^\lambda$
1. Output $\perp$.

The output of the experiment is $(i\mathcal{O}(f_\lambda^{(4)}), \hat{r})$.

We now make the following claims:

1. $H_0(1^\lambda) \approx_c H_1(1^\lambda)$: First, $\hat{r}$ is sampled identically as $\mathsf{ChE}(r)$. Then, observe that for any subset $S_\perp \subseteq [\lambda]$, the function $f_\lambda^{(1)}(\cdot)$ is functionally equivalent to f_λ because for any string $x \in \{0,1\}^\lambda$, $\Delta_H(x_{S_\perp}, r_{S_\perp}) + \Delta_H(x_{\overline{S_\perp}}, r_{\overline{S_\perp}}) = \Delta_H(x, r)$. Therefore, the claim follows by the indistinguishability of the $i\mathcal{O}$ scheme.

2. $H_1(1^\lambda) \approx_c H_2(1^\lambda)$: We claim that $f_\lambda^{(2)}$ is functionally equivalent to $f_\lambda^{(1)}$ with overwhelming probability over the coins used in generation of $\hat{r} \in \{0,1,\perp\}^\lambda$. For the functional equivalence to hold we require that on inputs $x \in \{0,1\}^\lambda$, that if $\Delta_H(x_{S_\perp}, r_{S_\perp}) + \Delta_H(x_{\overline{S_\perp}}, r_{\overline{S_\perp}}) \leq (p + \delta_{th}) \cdot \lambda$, then the list decoding algorithm is able to recover α. The list decoding algorithm recovers α when $\Delta_H(x_{S_\perp}, r_{S_\perp}) \leq (\frac{1}{2} - \varepsilon) \cdot \kappa$. Now viewing κ as a random variable, a sufficient condition for this implication to occur is, therefore, that $(p + \delta_{th}) \cdot \lambda \leq (\frac{1}{2} - \varepsilon) \cdot \kappa$. A standard Chernoff argument shows that κ satisfies this inequality with overwhelming probability for our choice of parameters.

In detail, let κ_i be a $0/1$ indicator random variable for the event that $\hat{r}_i = \perp$, and let $\kappa := \sum_{i \in [\lambda]} \kappa_i$. Note that $\mathbb{E}[\kappa] = e \cdot \lambda$. By a standard additive Chernoff, we have $\Pr[\kappa < (e - \lambda^{-0.1}) \cdot \lambda] \leq \exp(-2 \cdot \lambda^{0.8})$. Recall that our objective is to show that $(\frac{1}{2} - \varepsilon) \cdot \kappa \geq (p + \delta_{th}) \cdot \lambda$ with high probability so that on inputs of small Hamming distance less that $(p + \delta_{th}) \cdot \lambda$, our new function $f_\lambda^{(2)}$ successfully recovers α via a list decoding procedure. For there to exist a setting of ε such that the following probability is overwhelming: $\Pr[(\frac{1}{2} - \varepsilon) \cdot \kappa \geq (p + \delta_{th}) \cdot \lambda]$ it suffices to choose a constant ε such that

$$\left(\frac{1}{2} - \varepsilon\right)^{-1} \cdot (p + \delta_{th}) \cdot \lambda \leq (e - \lambda^{-0.1}) \cdot \lambda.$$

To see why, observe that if this inequality holds, then the same Chernoff above implies that $\Pr\left[\kappa < \left(\frac{1}{2}-\varepsilon\right)^{-1}\cdot(p+\delta_{th})\cdot\lambda\right] \leq \exp(-2\cdot\lambda^{0.8})$. Rearranging the above inequality, we obtain an equivalent inequality: $\varepsilon \leq \frac{1}{2}-\frac{p\cdot\lambda^{0.1}+1}{e\cdot\lambda^{0.1}-1}$. Then observe that the degradation condition guarantees that $p < \frac{e}{2}$, so by choosing any constant $\varepsilon \in \left[0,\frac{1}{2}-\frac{p}{e}\right]$, the above inequality holds for sufficiently large $\lambda \in \mathbb{N}$. Therefore, we conclude that by choosing any constant $\varepsilon \in \left[0,\frac{1}{2}-\frac{p}{e}\right]$, for sufficiently large λ,

$$\Pr\left[\left(\frac{1}{2}-\varepsilon\right)\cdot\kappa > (p+\delta_{th})\cdot\lambda\right] \geq 1-\exp(-2\cdot\lambda^{0.8})$$

Conditioning on the event that $\kappa > \left(\frac{1}{2}-\varepsilon\right)^{-1}\cdot(p+\delta_{th})\cdot\lambda = \Omega(\lambda)$, we can analyze the behavior of $f_\lambda^{(2)}$:

(a) If the input x satisfies that $\Delta_H(x_{S_\perp}, r_{S_\perp}) \leq (p+\delta_{th})\cdot\lambda$, then the Hamming weight of $x_{S_\perp} \oplus r_{S_\perp}$ satisfies

$$\mathsf{wt}_H(x_{S_\perp} \oplus r_{S_\perp}) \leq (p+\delta_{th})\cdot\lambda \leq \left(\frac{1}{2}-\varepsilon\right)\cdot\kappa.$$

The $(1/2-\varepsilon, q(\kappa, 1/\varepsilon))$-list decodable property, implies that the preimage α of the randomly chosen codeword c will be recovered in the list D. By the injectivity of the PRG, there is a unique such preimage α and therefore, the function $f_\lambda^{(2)}$ can correctly compute $C_{LD,\kappa}(\alpha)$ and recover $r_{S_\perp}$. Finally, Step 3 is exactly computing $f_\lambda^{(1)}(r')$.

(b) If the input x instead satisfies the complement relation $\Delta_H(x_{S_\perp}, r_{S_\perp}) > p+\delta_{th}$, then observe that either $f_\lambda^{(2)}$ will output $\perp$ either due to Step 2, or due to Step 3. This is exactly the output behavior of $f_\lambda^{(1)}$.

Therefore, conditioning on the event that $\kappa > \left(\frac{1}{2}-\varepsilon\right)^{-1}\cdot(p+\delta_{th})\cdot\lambda = \Omega(\lambda)$, we have that $f_\lambda^{(2)}$ has the same input-output behavior as $f_\lambda^{(1)}$ on all inputs and we appeal to the indistinguishability of the $i\mathcal{O}$ scheme to show that $(i\mathcal{O}(f^{(1)}),\hat{r}) \approx_c (i\mathcal{O}(f^{(2)}),\hat{r})$. This event occurs with all but negligible probability, so the two hybrids are computationally indistinguishable.

3. $H_2(1^\lambda) \approx_c H_3(1^\lambda)$: We will use the computationally indistinguishability of the PRG G to show this statement. Again, we condition on the event that the number of observed erasures, κ, satisfies $\kappa > \left(\frac{1}{2}-\varepsilon\right)^{-1}\cdot(p+\delta_{th})\cdot\lambda = \Omega(\lambda)$. This event occurs with all but negligible probability in λ where the probability is over the coins used in the generation of $\hat{r}$.

If there is a polynomial-time non-uniform algorithm $\mathcal{A}$ that can distinguish between $(i\mathcal{O}(f^{(2)}),\hat{r})$ and $(i\mathcal{O}(f^{(3)}),\hat{r})$, then we can construct a polynomial-time non-uniform algorithm $\mathcal{B}$ that can distinguish between the output of G on a random string of length κ^d and a uniform random string of length $3\cdot\kappa^d$. Namely, $\mathcal{B}$ on input $R_{Challenge}$ follows the construction template of the experiment $H_2(1^\lambda)$ and uses $R_{Challenge}$ in-place of $G(\alpha)$ to obtain some output $(\hat{f},\hat{r})$. Crucially, observe that z is independently sampled from $G(\alpha)$ because $r_{S_\perp}$ is uniform randomly sampled and $r_{S_\perp}$ is not a hardcoded constant in the function. If $R_{Challenge}$ is sampled from the distribution $G(U_{p(\lambda)})$, where $U_{p(\lambda)}$ is the uniform distribution on $p(\lambda)$ bits, then $\mathcal{B}$ has exactly sampled $(\hat{f}, \hat{r})$ from the distribution of $H_3(1^\lambda)$'s output. Otherwise, $R_{Challenge}$ is sampled from the distribution $U_{3 \cdot p(\lambda)}$, where $U_{3 \cdot p(\lambda)}$ is the uniform distribution on $3 \cdot p(\lambda)$ bits, then $\mathcal{B}$ has exactly sampled $(\hat{f}, \hat{r})$ from the distribution of $H_4(1^\lambda)$'s output. Then $\mathcal{B}$ passes $(\hat{f}, \hat{r})$ as input, as well as the appropriate advice string, to $\mathcal{A}$ who distinguishes between the two with non-negligible probability in λ. Therefore, $\mathcal{B}$ breaks the security of the PRG with non-negligible probability in λ.

4. $H_3(1^\lambda) \approx_c H_4(1^\lambda)$: Again, we condition on the event that $\kappa > \left(\frac{1}{2} - \varepsilon\right)^{-1} \cdot (p + \delta_{th}) \cdot \lambda = \Omega(\lambda)$. Observe that in $H_3(1^\lambda)$, with all but negligible probability in λ, the uniform randomly chosen string R is not in the image of G. Then with all but negligible probability in λ, $f_\lambda^{(3)}$ always outputs $\bot$ so $f_\lambda^{(3)}$ is identical to the null circuit $f_\lambda^{(4)}$ that always outputs $\bot$. Then, by the indistinguishability property of the $i\mathcal{O}$ scheme, we have that $H_3(1^\lambda) \approx_c H_4(1^\lambda)$.

This series of hybrids show that Eve's view is computationally indistinguishable from receiving a null circuit. Therefore, there cannot exist any polynomial-time non-uniform algorithm that is able to recover b efficiently from the real output of the coding scheme with non-negligible advantage.

4.1 Application: Codes with Easy Error Correction and Hard Erasure Correction

In any error-correcting code, correcting t erasures is (by definition) no harder than correcting t errors. But suppose we allow the error bound t to be smaller than the erasure bound v, while still insisting that erasure-decoding is information-theoretically possible. Then we have a fundamental coding-theoretic complexity question, unexplored before [11] and our work: Can we design an (efficiently encodable, binary) error-correcting code for which t errors can be corrected in polynomial time whereas correcting v erasures requires super-polynomial time?

What makes the problem challenging is the fact that most useful classes of error-correcting codes that support efficient decoding are *linear*. For linear codes, if correcting v erasures is information-theoretically possible, then it can also be done in polynomial time by solving a system of linear equations. Thus, a solution to the above question must inherently rely on efficiently decodable *nonlinear* codes, for which fewer natural examples exist.

A simple corollary of Theorem 4.1 gives a solution to this problem where the encoding function is *probabilistic* and the noise pattern is *random* (for both errors and erasures). This is captured by the following theorem.

Corollary 4.4 (Easy-hard codes). *Suppose $i\mathcal{O}$ and injective one-way functions exist. Then, for every $p, e \in (0, 1)$ such that $2p < e < 4p(1 - p)$, there exists a PPT encoding algorithm $E : \{0, 1\}^k \to \{0, 1\}^{n(k)}$ such that the following holds:*

- **Easy p-error correction.** *There is a polynomial-time decoder D and a negligible ϵ such that for all $x \in \{0, 1\}^k$ we have $\Pr[D(\tilde{y}_p) \neq x] \leq \epsilon(k)$, where $\tilde{y}_p$*

is obtained by first computing $y \leftarrow E(x)$ and then flipping each bit of y with probability p.

- **Hard e-erasure correction.** For every non-uniform polynomial-time decoder D^* there is a negligible μ such that for a uniformly random $x \in \{0,1\}^k$, $\Pr[D^*(\tilde{y}_e) = x] \leq \mu(k)$ where $\tilde{y}_e$ is obtained by first computing $y \leftarrow E(x)$ and then erasing each bit of y with probability e.

- **Nontriviality.** There exists a computationally unbounded decoder D^∞ and a negligible ϵ such that for a random $x \in \{0,1\}^k$, where $\tilde{y}_e$ is obtained by first computing $y \leftarrow E(x)$ and then erasing each bit of y with probability e, we have $\Pr[D^\infty(\tilde{y}_e) = x] \geq 1 - \epsilon(k)$.

Proof (sketch). Both easy p-error correction and hard e-erasure correction essentially immediately follow from Theorem 4.1 and non-triviality follows from the impossibility of information-theoretic wiretap coding when $e < 4p(1 - p)$ and the amplification techniques in [7] (see also [11]). A more detailed proof is in the full version.

A natural question is whether it is possible to prove a variant of Corollary 4.4 in which the encoding function E is *deterministic*. Note that if we use a random oracle to determine the randomness for E based on the message, then the above proof still applies. This gives rise to a heuristic solution using a cryptographic hash function to replace the random oracle. We leave open the question of eliminating the random oracle by relying on cryptographic or derandomization assumptions.

Finally, an intriguing question is whether instances of similar "easy-hard codes" can be obtained (even heuristically) via a natural construction, without relying on the power of general-purpose obfuscation.

Acknowledgments. Y. Ishai was supported in part by ERC Project NTSC (742754), BSF grant 2018393, ISF grant 2774/20, and a Google Faculty Research Award. A. Jain is supported in part by the Google Research Scholar Award and through various gifts from CYLAB, CMU. A. Sahai was supported in part from a Simons Investigator Award, DARPA SIEVE award, NTT Research, BSF grant 2018393, a Xerox Faculty Research Award, a Google Faculty Research Award, and an Okawa Foundation Research Grant. This material is based upon work supported by the Defense Advanced Research Projects Agency through Award HR00112020024.

References

1. Agrawal, S., et al.: Secure computation from one-way noisy communication, or: anti-correlation via anti-concentration. In: Malkin, T., Peikert, C. (eds.) CRYPTO 2021. LNCS, vol. 12826, pp. 124–154. Springer, Cham (2021). https://doi.org/10.1007/978-3-030-84245-1_5
2. Alekhnovich, M.: More on average case vs approximation complexity. In: 44th Symposium on Foundations of Computer Science (FOCS 2003), 11–14 October 2003, Cambridge, MA, USA, Proceedings, pp. 298–307. IEEE Computer Society (2003). https://doi.org/10.1109/SFCS.2003.1238204

3. Barak, B., Bitansky, N., Canetti, R., Kalai, Y.T., Paneth, O., Sahai, A.: Obfuscation for evasive functions. In: Lindell, Y. (ed.) TCC 2014. LNCS, vol. 8349, pp. 26–51. Springer, Heidelberg (2014). https://doi.org/10.1007/978-3-642-54242-8_2
4. Barak, B., et al.: On the (Im)possibility of obfuscating programs. In: Kilian, J. (ed.) CRYPTO 2001. LNCS, vol. 2139, pp. 1–18. Springer, Heidelberg (2001). https://doi.org/10.1007/3-540-44647-8_1
5. Blum, A., Furst, M., Kearns, M., Lipton, R.J.: Cryptographic primitives based on hard learning problems. In: Stinson, D.R. (ed.) CRYPTO 1993. LNCS, vol. 773, pp. 278–291. Springer, Heidelberg (1994). https://doi.org/10.1007/3-540-48329-2_24
6. Bogdanov, A., Qiao, Y.: On the security of Goldreich's one-way function. Comput. Complex. **21**(1), 83–127 (2012)
7. Csiszár, I., Korner, J.: Broadcast channels with confidential messages. IEEE Trans. Inf. Theory **24**(3), 339–348 (1978)
8. Garg, S., Gentry, C., Halevi, S., Raykova, M., Sahai, A., Waters, B.: Candidate indistinguishability obfuscation and functional encryption for all circuits. SIAM J. Comput. **45**(3), 882–929 (2016). https://doi.org/10.1137/14095772X
9. Guruswami, V.: List decoding of binary codes–a brief survey of some recent results. In: Chee, Y.M., Li, C., Ling, S., Wang, H., Xing, C. (eds.) IWCC 2009. LNCS, vol. 5557, pp. 97–106. Springer, Heidelberg (2009). https://doi.org/10.1007/978-3-642-01877-0_10
10. Guruswami, V., Sudan, M.: List decoding algorithms for certain concatenated codes. In: 32nd ACM STOC, pp. 181–190. ACM Press, May 2000
11. Ishai, Y., Korb, A., Lou, P., Sahai, A.: Beyond the Csiszár-Körner bound: best-possible wiretap coding via obfuscation. In: Crypto 2022 (2022)
12. Ishai, Y., Korb, A., Lou, P., Sahai, A.: Beyond the csiszár-korner bound: Best-possible wiretap coding via obfuscation. In: Dodis, Y., Shrimpton, T. (eds.) Advances in Cryptology - CRYPTO 2022, Part II. LNCS, vol. 13508, pp. 573–602. Springer, Cham (2022). https://doi.org/10.1007/978-3-031-15979-4_20
13. Jain, A., Lin, H., Sahai, A.: Indistinguishability obfuscation from well-founded assumptions. In: Proceedings of the 53rd Annual ACM SIGACT Symposium on Theory of Computing, pp. 60–73 (2021)
14. Jain, A., Lin, H., Sahai, A.: Indistinguishability obfuscation from LPN over $\mathbb{F}\_p$, dlin, and prgs in nc^0. In: Dunkelman, O., Dziembowski, S. (eds.) Advances in Cryptology - EUROCRYPT 2022. Part I. LNCS, vol. 13275, pp. 670–699. Springer, Cham (2022). https://doi.org/10.1007/978-3-031-06944-4_23
15. Nair, C.: Capacity regions of two new classes of two-receiver broadcast channels. IEEE Trans. Inf. Theory **56**(9), 4207–4214 (2010)
16. Poor, H.V., Schaefer, R.F.: Wireless physical layer security. In: Proceedings of the National Academy of Sciences, vol. 114, no. 1, 19–26 (2017). https://www.pnas.org/content/114/1/19
17. Sahai, A., Waters, B.: How to use indistinguishability obfuscation: deniable encryption, and more. SIAM J. Comput. **50**(3), 857–908 (2021). https://doi.org/10.1137/15M1030108
18. Sudan, M.: List decoding: algorithms and applications. In: van Leeuwen, J., Watanabe, O., Hagiya, M., Mosses, P.D., Ito, T. (eds.) TCS 2000. LNCS, vol. 1872, pp. 25–41. Springer, Heidelberg (2000). https://doi.org/10.1007/3-540-44929-9_3
19. Sudan, M., Trevisan, L., Vadhan, S.P.: Pseudorandom generators without the XOR lemma (extended abstract). In: 31st ACM STOC, pp. 537–546. ACM Press, May 1999
20. Wyner, A.D.: The wire-tap channel. Bell Syst. Tech. J. **54**(8), 1355–1387 (1975)

Secure Messaging

On Optimal Tightness for Key Exchange with Full Forward Secrecy via Key Confirmation

Kai Gellert[1]([⊠]), Kristian Gjøsteen[2], Håkon Jacobsen[3,4], and Tibor Jager[1]

[1] University of Wuppertal, Wuppertal, Germany
{kai.gellert,jager}@uni-wuppertal.de
[2] Norwegian University of Science and Technology, Trondheim, Norway
kristian.gjosteen@ntnu.no
[3] Thales Norway, Oslo, Norway
[4] University of Oslo, Oslo, Norway
hakon.jacobsen@its.uio.no

Abstract. A standard paradigm for building key exchange protocols with *full* forward secrecy (and *explicit* authentication) is to add key confirmation messages to an underlying protocol having only *weak* forward secrecy (and *implicit* authentication). Somewhat surprisingly, we show through an impossibility result that this simple trick must nevertheless incur a linear tightness loss in the number of parties for many natural protocols. This includes Krawczyk's HMQV protocol (CRYPTO 2005) and the protocol of Cohn-Gordon et al. (CRYPTO 2019).

Cohn-Gordon et al. gave a very efficient underlying protocol with *weak* forward secrecy having a linear security loss, and showed that this is optimal for certain reductions. However, they also claimed that *full* forward secrecy could be achieved by adding key confirmation messages, and *without any additional loss*. Our impossibility result disproves this claim, showing that their approach, in fact, has an overall *quadratic* loss.

Motivated by this predicament we seek to restore the original linear loss claim of Cohn-Gordon et al. by using a different proof strategy. Specifically, we start by lowering the goal for the underlying protocol with weak forward secrecy, to a *selective* security notion where the adversary must commit to a long-term key it cannot reveal. This allows a *tight* reduction rather than a linear loss reduction. Next, we show that the protocol can be upgraded to full forward secrecy using key confirmation messages with a linear tightness loss, even when starting from the weaker selective security notion. Thus, our approach yields an *overall* tightness loss for the fully forward-secret protocol that is only linear, as originally claimed. Finally, we confirm that the underlying protocol of Cohn-Gordon et al. can indeed be proven selectively secure, tightly.

This work has been supported by the European Research Council (ERC) under the European Union's Horizon 2020 research and innovation programme, grant agreement 802823.

© International Association for Cryptologic Research 2023
H. Handschuh and A. Lysyanskaya (Eds.): CRYPTO 2023, LNCS 14084, pp. 297–329, 2023.
https://doi.org/10.1007/978-3-031-38551-3_10

1   Introduction

A security reduction is said to be *tight* if it preserves the security of the object being reduced to. The benefit of a tight reduction is that it allows to closely relate the security of a complex object to a simpler and, hopefully, more easy to analyze object. Moreover, a tight reduction allows cryptographic schemes to be instantiated with optimal parameters in a theoretically sound way. Unfortunately, for key exchange protocols the security reductions have historically been inordinately *non-tight*. But recent works have started to address these deficiencies either by doing more careful analyses of existing protocols, or by proposing new protocols more suitable for tighter reductions. Typically the approach has either been to use digital signatures with tight multi-user security [2,16,17,25], or signature-less protocols based on some variant of Diffie-Hellman [10,19]. While the latter tend to be more efficient than the signature-based approaches in practice, the comparison isn't completely fair since the signature-based protocols provide *full* forward secrecy and *explicit* authentication (AKE) while the protocols based on Diffie-Hellman ones only give *weak* forward secrecy and *implicit* authentication.

Forward Secrecy, Authentication and Key Confirmation. *Full* forward secrecy refers to the ability of a protocol to provide security of session keys even if the long-term secret key of a communicating party is leaked [7]. It is considered an essential standard security goal for modern key exchange protocols. *Weak* forward secrecy achieves this property under the assumption that the adversary does not actively interfere with the protocol messages in the sessions it attacks. The notions of weak and full forward secrecy are intimately connected to authentication [4,8,13].

Explicit authentication guarantees that the intended communication partner is indeed "online" and has actively participated in the protocol. Implicit authentication guarantees that only the intended peer will be able to derive the same session key. However, it does not guarantee that the peer actually has participated in the protocol. Typically, for key exchange protocols having only implicit authentication, an adversary can efficiently impersonate Alice towards Bob, in the sense that it sends messages on behalf of Alice and such that Bob derives a session key that he believes is suitable for communicating with Alice, but the adversary will still not be able to distinguish this session key from a random one. The question then becomes: how can we upgrade from weak forward secrecy and implicit authentication to full forward secrecy and explicit authentication, while still maintaining tightness and efficiency?

A very natural idea is to have the participants send *key confirmation* messages derived from the session key. This solution is simple, efficient, and has already been treated in multiple works [4,10,13,15,20,27]. Key confirmation ensures that a second protocol participant has indeed computed the same session key and thus turns an implicitly authenticated protocol into an explicitly authenticated protocol [13]. However, key confirmation also serves a dual role as a simple tool for upgrading weak forward secrecy to full forward secrecy. The HMQV-C [20] protocol is a notable example of this usage. In this paper we use key confirmation in both senses above.

Finally, while implicit (resp. explicit) authentication often corresponds to weak (resp. full) forward secrecy, we note that these are in fact separate notions. Protocols having explicit authentication but no forward secrecy are common (see for instance the AKEP1 protocol in [5, Fig. 2]). Examples of protocols achieving full forward security without explicit authentication are given in [8, Protocol 4] and [12, Fig. 3].

Does Key Confirmation Preserve Tightness? Suppose Π is an arbitrary key exchange protocol providing weak forward secrecy and implicit authentication. The protocol participants exchange a session key using Π and from this derive key confirmation messages as well as a new session key using a pseudorandom function (PRF). They then exchange and verify the confirmation messages before outputting the new session key. Call this extended protocol Π^+. Intuitively, protocol Π^+ should achieve explicit authentication via a *tight* reduction to the implicit authentication of protocol Π as well as the multi-user security of the PRF. Indeed, this is the claim of Theorem 6 in [10]. Unfortunately, this claim turns out to be wrong. In fact, as we will show, for certain natural protocols, such as the protocol from Cohn-Gordon et al. [10] and HMQV [20], adding key confirmation messages like this or in any other deterministic way must *necessarily* lose a factor of U, where U is the number parties in the protocol. Hence, it seems that the notions of weak forward secrecy and implicit authentication are too weak to be *tightly* upgraded to full forward secrecy and explicit authentication by simply adding key confirmation messages. Interestingly and surprisingly, we will however also argue that an even weaker *selective* security notion is sufficient to obtain security with the same linear loss, which provides a new approach to obtain full forward secrecy with optimal linear tightness loss.

The Flaw in Cohn-Gordon et al. [10] . The high-level idea of the security reduction from protocol Π^+ to protocol Π in [10] is as follows. The reduction uses Test or Reveal queries to get the session keys from Π and uses these to simulate the key confirmation messages of protocol Π^+. However, the reduction must decide which session keys it will reveal and which it will issue a Test query for. The trivial standard strategy would be to guess which session the adversary will test, but this cannot be deployed in [10] as it would immediately incur a linear security loss in the number of users *times* the number of sessions per user. Instead, the reduction proceeds as follows: once a session has reached an accepting state in the underlying AKE protocol Π, the reduction will base its decision on which query to use on the *current* freshness of the session. If the session is not fresh, it will issue a Reveal query. If the session is fresh, it will issue a Test query.

The problem with this strategy is that the freshness notion is with respect to protocol Π, which is only guaranteeing *weak* forward secrecy. Unfortunately this notion is too weak (i.e., too restrictive) to accommodate the reduction. More specifically, in a weak forward secrecy model the adversary is forbidden from both being active in a Test session and revealing the long-term secret of its peer. This is due to a classic attack described by [4] and [20] (see [8] and [12] for further discussions).

In this attack the adversary $\mathcal{A}$ impersonates Alice towards Bob by creating the DH share g^x on her behalf. Once Bob receives this message he creates its own DH share g^y and accepts in protocol Π. Since $\mathcal{A}$ has not (yet) revealed the long-term key of Alice, Bob is at this point still fresh in protocol Π according to weak forward secrecy. Consequently, the reduction will issue a Test query in order to simulate its key confirmation message. However, if $\mathcal{A}$ now reveals the long-term key of Alice, then Bob will no longer be fresh (in protocol Π). At this point the reduction is stuck. This means that the reduction in Theorem 6 of Cohn-Gordon et al. [10] does not work. This issue has been confirmed by the authors of [10].

1.1 Our Contributions

While the reduction of [10] does not work, can the result nevertheless be salvaged? On the one hand, we show that a tight reduction from full forward secrecy and explicit authentication to weak forward secrecy and implicit security is impossible for a large class of compilers and protocols of interest for practical applications. In particular, this includes the common key confirmation message compiler discussed above and the key exchange protocol of [10]. We prove this using a meta-reduction described in more detail below.

On the other hand, by considering what the actual *end goal* of [10] is, we can in fact recover the intended result by a rearranging of arguments. That is, the end goal is to create an as efficient as possible key exchange protocol having full forward secrecy and explicit authentication, with optimal tightness. Here, tightness is with respect to the lowest level building block of the protocol. In the case of [10] this is the strong Diffie-Hellman (stDH) assumption [1]. It was shown in [10] that a large class of DH-based implicitly authenticated key exchange protocols must lose a factor of U when reducing to stDH, where U is the number of parties. If the reduction from Π^+ to Π had been tight, as mistakenly claimed in [10], then the overall result would have been a protocol Π^+ with full forward secrecy and an optimal tightness loss of U to the stDH assumption. However, in light of our impossibility result, the best one can hope for using this approach is a loss of U^2, since there is a tightness loss of U going from Π^+ to Π and a tightness loss of U going from Π to stDH.

But this begs the question: if we know from the beginning that we at least have to lose a factor of U, is there some other way of structuring our arguments in order to avoid a quadratic loss? The solution is to first reduce the security of protocol Π^+ to an even *weaker* notion of implicit security for protocol Π, taking the "hit" of U here. Then, we show that this weaker notion for Π can be reduced further to stDH but now *tightly*. Thus, overall we obtain a modular reduction from Π^+ down to stDH losing only a factor of U.

What is this weaker notion for Π? It is a type of *selective security* game where the adversary needs to commit to a single party it will not reveal the long-term key of. This is related to the selective security notion from [21], but differs in two important ways. First, the requirement that one long-term key must stay *unrevealed*—rather than simply being involved in some event—makes the two notions technically incomparable (see Remark 1). Second, in [21] the adversary commits to *both* parties *and their sessions* involved in the event. This incurs a quadratic security loss, making it unsuitable for our purposes.

In summary, our main results are:

- We give a generic impossibility result showing that no security proof for adding key confirmation to a weakly forward-secret key exchange protocol can avoid a loss factor of U (Sect. 6).
- We provide an optimal security proof (i.e., with a linear loss in U) for adding key confirmation, which reduces to a weaker security notion for the underlying key exchange protocol (Sect. 4). This weaker notion allows us to avoid a tightness loss when proving the underlying protocol secure.
- Finally, we give a tight proof of the CCGJJ protocol [10] under the weaker notion, showing that the overall strategy achieves the end goal (Sect. 5).

One important consequence of our work is that future key exchange protocols having only weak forward secrecy can now be designed towards the goal of selective key secrecy, not full key secrecy. As shown by the analysis of CCGJJ [10], this may simplify proofs significantly.

Basic Idea of the Impossibility Result. Our impossibility result shows essentially that if one constructs a protocol Π^+ from an underlying implicitly authenticated protocol Π by extending Π with two additional key confirmation messages, and if the security analysis of Π^+ includes a reduction $\mathcal{R}$ to the security of Π, then $\mathcal{R}$ loses a factor which is at least linear in the number U of parties. The basic idea of the argument is as follows.

We first define a (hypothetical) adversary $\mathcal{A}$, which proceeds in four steps:

1. First $\mathcal{A}$ receives the public keys $\mathsf{pk}_1, \ldots, \mathsf{pk}_U$ of all parties.
2. Then it interacts with $\mathcal{R}$ to create a session $s_{i,j}$ of protocol Π^+ for every pair of parties i, j. In all of these sessions the protocol is executed until $\mathcal{R}$ outputs the first of the two key confirmation messages.
   Note that $\mathcal{R}$ may simulate messages of Π^+ that correspond to messages of the underlying protocol Π by relaying these messages to its own security experiment. However, $\mathcal{R}$ also has to simulate the first key confirmation messages, which depend on the session key k of protocol Π.
3. Finally, $\mathcal{A}$ reveals the long-term secret keys of all but one party, receiving sk_i for all $i \in \{1, \ldots, U\} \setminus \{i^*\}$, where i^* is chosen at random by $\mathcal{A}$. Then $\mathcal{A}$ uses these secret keys to verify all key confirmation messages received from $\mathcal{R}$ for all sessions $s_{i,j}$ with $i \neq i^*$. If at least one of these key confirmation messages is invalid, then $\mathcal{A}$ terminates.
4. If all key confirmation messages are correct, then $\mathcal{A}$ breaks the security of Π^+ in a target session $s_{i^*,j}$ for some j.

$\mathcal{A}$ is a valid adversary that breaks Π^+ in the security experiment with maximal advantage. The choice of i^* is perfectly hidden from the reduction until Step 3 of $\mathcal{A}$, as all queries in Step 2 are independent of i^*. Note in particular that we can trivially simulate $\mathcal{A}$, if $\mathcal{R}$ outputs at least one invalid key confirmation message for any session $s_{i,j}$, $i \neq i^*$. Furthermore, note that we can always simulate the first three steps of $\mathcal{A}$ efficiently.

We will essentially argue that the reduction $\mathcal{R}$ is only able to simulate all key confirmation messages of sessions $s_{i,j}$ of parties $i \neq i^*$ properly, if it asks its security experiment to reveal the corresponding session keys $k_{i,j}$. However, at the same time $\mathcal{R}$ must not ask its security experiment to reveal the session key $k_{i^*,j}$ of the target session $s_{i^*,j}$, as otherwise it cannot leverage $\mathcal{A}$ to break the security of this session. Hence, the reduction faces the challenge that it has to "predict" i^* already in Step 2 of the adversary, in order to make sure that the key confirmation messages are simulated correctly, but still $\mathcal{A}$ can be leveraged to break the security of Π. Since i^* is chosen uniformly from $\{1, \ldots, U\}$, this yields a linear loss in U.

We stress that this sketch of the impossibility result is simplified, the actual formal result is more involved and subtle. For instance, in (Sect. 6.1 we formulate precise conditions on which classes of reductions, protocols Π, and which constructions of Π^+ are covered by the impossibility result. These will cover the construction from [10] but also many other natural constructions.

The common way of arguing that a reduction $\mathcal{R}$ does not "need" $\mathcal{A}$ in certain cases is to perform a meta-reduction where $\mathcal{A}$ can efficiently be simulated in these cases. Normally, the standard approach of meta-reductions used in many prior works, such as [3, 18, 23], is to *rewind* $\mathcal{R}$ in order to be able to simulate $\mathcal{A}$ properly. Unfortunately, these results are usually only able to rule out reductions to *non-interactive* hardness assumptions. In contrast, the assumption that Π is secure is *interactive*. By rewinding $\mathcal{R}$ and running it multiple times with different queries from the "snapshot" state, we might cause $\mathcal{R}$ to make a sequence of queries that is not allowed in the key exchange security experiment of Π, such as revealing and then testing the same session s. Hence, we need to find another argument that avoids rewinding.

The main technical novelty of this result is that it consists of a combination of several different meta-reductions that enable us to argue that the reduction indeed "commits" itself to one particular choice of i^* after simulating the key confirmation messages in Step 2 of $\mathcal{A}$. The proof consists of several meta-reductions that do not perform rewinding and only simulate the first two or three steps of $\mathcal{A}$ (which can be done efficiently), in combination with a careful argument showing that this is indeed sufficient.

2 Definitions

The formalism and definitions we use to model key exchange protocols are adapted from de Saint Guilhelm et al. [13]. Unlike the traditional Bellare–Rogaway [4–6] and (e)CK models [9,22], security in this model is not formulated as a single all-in-one game that implicitly captures all the properties a protocol should have. Instead, security is split into many smaller definitions that each captures a single "atomic" security property. This leads to a slight increase in the number of definitions, as well as the number proofs one have to carry out in order to establish a protocol as "secure". On the other hand, the advantage of this approach is that each definition/property is much simpler and focused, and many of the proofs will similarly also be very simple.

2.1 Syntax

A *key exchange protocol* is a tuple of algorithms (KeyGen, Init, Run) where KeyGen is the long-term key generation algorithm; Init creates a *session state* at party i having intended peer j and role role, and returns this session's initial message (empty if a responder role); and Run takes as input a session state st and a message m and outputs an updated state st' and response message m'.

Session State. A *session state* st consists of the following variables.

- accept $\in \{$true, false, $\perp\}$ – indicates the status of the key exchange run; initialized to $\perp$ and indicates a running, non-completed, session.
- key $\in \{0,1\}^* \cup \{\perp\}$ – the local session key derived during the key exchange run; set once accept $=$ true.
- role $\in \{$init, resp$\}$ – the role of the session in the key exchange run.
- party – the party identity to which this session belongs.
- peer – the party identity of the intended peer for this key exchange run.
- sk – the secret long-term key of the party this session belongs to.
- pk – the public long-term key of the intended peer of the session.
- transcript – the (ordered) transcript of all messages sent and received by session s. We use transcript$^-$ to denote the transcript minus the last message.
- aux – auxiliary protocol specific state, such as internal randomness and ephemeral values.

Security Experiment. We shall use the generic formal experiment $\mathbf{Exp}_{\Pi,U}^{\mathsf{Pred}}(\mathcal{A})$ given in Fig. 1 to define the various security properties of a key exchange protocol (see Sect. 3). The experiment is parameterized on a *security predicate* Pred that captures the security property being modeled. The experiment uses a number of counters, variables and collections for bookkeeping purposes.

- query_ctr – incremented for each query made by the adversary. Used to order events in time; needed to define (full) forward secrecy.
- session_ctr – incremented for each new session created. Each session state is associated with a unique session number which functions as an administrative label for that session (state). The session number is also given to the adversary which can use it as an opaque handle to refer to a given session in its queries. We use the notation "$s.x$" to refer to the variable x of the session state identified by the administrative session number s. Note that the adversary cannot "dereference" a session number in order to obtain internal variables of the session state.
- Accepted, Tested, Revealed, RevealedLTK – associative arrays that records when a session accepted, was tested, or when its session or long-term key was revealed.

$\mathbf{Exp}_{\Pi,U}^{\mathsf{Pred}}(\mathcal{A})$

101: $i^* \leftarrow \mathcal{A}$
102: $b \xleftarrow{\$} \{0,1\}$
103: query_ctr $\leftarrow 0$
104: session_ctr $\leftarrow 0$
105: Accepted $\leftarrow$ Dict
106: Revealed $\leftarrow$ Dict
107: RevealedLTK $\leftarrow$ Dict
108: Tested $\leftarrow$ Dict
109: $\mathbf{sk}, \mathbf{pk} \leftarrow$ Dict
110: for $i \in [1 \ldots U]$:
111:      $(\mathbf{sk}[i], \mathbf{pk}[i]) \xleftarrow{\$} \Pi.\mathsf{KeyGen}$
112:      RevealedLTK$[i] \leftarrow 0$
113: $b' \leftarrow \mathcal{A}^{\mathsf{O}}(\mathbf{pk})$
114: return Pred

NewSession$(i \in [1, U], j \in [1, U], \mathsf{role})$

201: query_ctr++
202: session_ctr++
203: $s \leftarrow$ session_ctr
204: Accepted$[s] \leftarrow 0$
205: Revealed$[s] \leftarrow 0$
206: Tested$[s] \leftarrow 0$
207: $(m, st) \leftarrow \Pi.\mathsf{Init}(i, j, \mathsf{role}, \mathbf{pk}[j], \mathbf{sk}[i])$
208: $s.st \leftarrow st$
209: return (s, m)

Send(s, m)

401: query_ctr++
402: $(m', st') \leftarrow \Pi.\mathsf{Run}(s.st, m)$
403: $s.st \leftarrow st'$
404: if $s.\mathsf{accept} = \mathsf{true}$:
405:      Accepted$[s] \leftarrow$ query_ctr
406: return m'

Reveal(s)

501: query_ctr++
502: Revealed$[s] \leftarrow$ query_ctr
503: return $s.\mathsf{key}$

RevealLTK$(i \in [1, U])$

601: if RevealedLTK$[i] \neq 0$:
602:      return $\perp$
603: if $i = i^*$:
604:      return $\perp$
605: query_ctr++
606: RevealedLTK$[i] \leftarrow$ query_ctr
607: return $\mathbf{sk}[i]$

Test(s)

701: query_ctr++
702: if Tested$[s] \neq 0$:
703:      return $\perp$
704: if $s.\mathsf{accept} \neq \mathsf{true}$:
705:      return $\perp$
706: Tested$[s] \leftarrow$ query_ctr
707: $K_0 \leftarrow s.\mathsf{key}$
708: $K_1 \xleftarrow{\$} \mathcal{K}$
709: return K_b

Fig. 1. Generic experiment parameterized on winning predicate Pred, where $\mathcal{A}$ can make the queries in $\mathsf{O} = \{\mathsf{NewSession}, \mathsf{Send}, \mathsf{Reveal}, \mathsf{RevealLTK}, \mathsf{Test}\}$. Code in dashed boxes is only for the key secrecy game; code in filled boxes is only for the selective key secrecy game. The notation $s.st \leftarrow st'$ means to assign all the variables in st' to the corresponding variables associated with session s. Dict defines an associative array.

Common Predicates. It will be useful to introduce a number of predicates on the security experiment.

Definition 1 (Origin sessions). *A (possibly non-accepted) session s' is an origin-session for an accepted session s if predicate $\mathsf{Orig}(s, s')$ holds true, where*

$$\mathsf{Orig}(s, s') \iff s'.\mathsf{transcript} \in \{s.\mathsf{transcript}, s.\mathsf{transcript}^-\}. \tag{1}$$

Definition 2 (Partnering). *Two sessions s, s' are partners if they have matching conversations; that is, if the predicate $\mathsf{Partner}(s, s')$ holds true, where*

$$\mathsf{Partner}(s, s') \iff s.\mathsf{transcript} = s'.\mathsf{transcript}. \tag{2}$$

Like [13] we do not require partners to agree upon each other's identities. This is an authentication property which will be covered by other definitions in Sect. 3. Unlike [13] we use matching conversations instead of abstract session identifiers as our partnering mechanism. This is mainly done for the sake of concreteness and is not a fundamental difference, although certain well-known pitfalls need to be avoided when using matching conversations [24].

Definition 3 (SameKey). *The predicate $\mathsf{SameKey}(s, s')$ holds true if the sessions both have established a session key and they are equal, that is*

$$\mathsf{SameKey}(s, s') \iff [s.\mathsf{key} = s'.\mathsf{key} \neq \bot]. \tag{3}$$

Definition 4 (Authentication fresh). *A session is authentication fresh if the long-term key of its intended peer has not been revealed, that is:*

$$\mathsf{aFresh}(s) \iff \mathsf{RevealedLTK}[s.\mathsf{peer}] = 0. \tag{4}$$

Finally, we define freshness predicates used for the key secrecy games. These come in two flavors: *weak forward secrecy* and *full forward secrecy* [4]. Common to both is that the adversary cannot reveal the session key of a tested session or its partner. The difference is how long-term key leakage is handled. For weak forward secrecy the adversary is forbidden from revealing the long-term key of a session's peer if it was actively interfering in the protocol run of the session (indicated by the lack of an origin-session for the session in question). For full forward secrecy this restriction is lifted, provided the leak happened *after* the session in question accepted.

Definition 5 (Session key freshness). *Let $s.\mathsf{peer} = j$. The $\mathsf{kFreshWFS}(s)$ (resp. $\mathsf{kFreshFFS}(s)$ predicate hold if:*

$$\mathsf{Revealed}[s] = 0 \tag{5}$$

$$\forall s' :: \mathsf{Partner}(s, s') \implies \mathsf{Revealed}[s'] = 0 \wedge \mathsf{Tested}[s'] = 0 \tag{6}$$

$$(\text{wFS}) \quad \{s' \mid \mathsf{Orig}(s, s')\} = \emptyset \implies \mathsf{aFresh}(s) \tag{7}$$

$$(\text{fFS}) \quad \{s' \mid \mathsf{Orig}(s, s')\} = \emptyset \implies \mathsf{aFresh}(s) \vee (\mathsf{RevealedLTK}[j] > \mathsf{Accepted}[s]) \tag{8}$$

3   Protocol Security Properties

This section defines the security properties a secure key exchange protocol ought to have. The breakdown follows that of [13] and consists of: soundness properties (match and key-match soundness); various authentication properties (implicit/explicit key and entity authentication); and session key secrecy. An application will typically require all of these properties. Refer to [13] for further discussion and background.

3.1   Match Soundness

Match soundness is primarily a sanity check on the choice of partnering mechanism. Namely, partnered sessions should derive the same session key (9); and sessions will at most have one partner (10).

Definition 6 (Match soundness).   *The* Match *predicate evaluates to 1 iff* $\forall s, s', s''$:

$$\mathsf{Partner}(s, s') \implies \mathsf{SameKey}(s, s') \tag{9}$$

$$(\mathsf{Partner}(s, s') \land \mathsf{Partner}(s, s'')) \implies s' = s'' \tag{10}$$

The match soundness advantage *of an adversary* $\mathcal{A}$ *is*

$$\mathbf{Adv}_{\Pi,U}^{\mathsf{Match}}(\mathcal{A}) \overset{\text{def}}{=} \Pr[\mathbf{Exp}_{\Pi,U}^{\mathsf{Match}}(\mathcal{A}) \Rightarrow 1] \tag{11}$$

3.2   Key-Match Soundness

Key-match soundness (KMSound) is basically the converse of Match soundness. While Match soundness says (among other things) that partners should have equal session keys, KMSound says that sessions having equal session keys should be partners.

Definition 7 (Key-match soundness).   *The* KMSound *predicate evaluates to 1 if and only if*

$$\forall s :: (\mathsf{aFresh}(s) \land s.\mathsf{accept}) \implies \forall s' :: (\mathsf{SameKey}(s, s') \implies \mathsf{Partner}(s, s')) \tag{12}$$

The key-match soundness advantage *of an adversary* $\mathcal{A}$ *is*

$$\mathbf{Adv}_{\Pi,U}^{\mathsf{KMSound}}(\mathcal{A}) \overset{\text{def}}{=} \Pr[\mathbf{Exp}_{\Pi,U}^{\mathsf{KMSound}}(\mathcal{A}) \Rightarrow 1]. \tag{13}$$

3.3   Implicit Key Authentication

Implicit key authentication stipulates that two sessions that derive the same session key should agree upon *whom* they are sharing this key with.

Definition 8 (Implicit key authentication). *The* iKeyAuth *predicate evaluates to 1 if and only if*

$$\forall s :: s.\mathsf{accept} \implies \forall s' :: (\mathsf{SameKey}(s, s') \implies s.\mathsf{peer} = s'.\mathsf{party})$$

The implicit key authentication advantage *of an adversary* $\mathcal{A}$ *is*

$$\mathbf{Adv}_{\Pi,U}^{\mathsf{iKeyAuth}}(\mathcal{A}) \stackrel{\text{def}}{=} \Pr[\mathbf{Exp}_{\Pi,U}^{\mathsf{iKeyAuth}}(\mathcal{A}) \Rightarrow 1]. \tag{14}$$

3.4 Explicit Key Authentication

Explicit key authentication stipulates that any two sessions that derive the same session key should agree upon whom they are sharing this key with (as for implicit key authentication), and as long as the session is authentication fresh some other session deriving the same session key should exist.

Obviously, the session that sends the last message can never guarantee that this message arrives at its destination, which means that this session can only achieve the notion of *almost-full* key authentication, namely that an origin session should exist and any origin session that has derived a session key has derived the same key. A session that receives the last message, however, can guarantee that another session exists that has derived the same key, and thereby achieve *full* key authentication.

Let $\mathcal{L}_{\mathsf{rcv}}$ denote the collection of all sessions that *receives* the last message of the protocol, and let $\mathcal{L}_{\mathsf{send}}$ denote the collection of all sessions that *sends* the last message of the protocol.

Definition 9 (Explicit key authentication). *The* fexKeyAuth *predicate (resp.* afexKeyAuth *predicate) evaluates to 1 if and only if*

$$\forall s \in \mathcal{L}_{\mathsf{rcv}} \ (\text{resp. } \mathcal{L}_{\mathsf{send}}) :: s.\mathsf{accept} \implies \forall s' :: (\mathsf{SameKey}(s, s') \Rightarrow s.\mathsf{peer} = s'.\mathsf{party}) \tag{15}$$

$$\wedge$$

$$\text{(full)} \qquad\qquad\qquad \mathsf{aFresh}(s) \Rightarrow \exists s' :: \mathsf{SameKey}(s, s')$$

$$\text{(almost-full)} \qquad \mathsf{aFresh}(s) \Rightarrow \exists s' :: \Big(\mathsf{Orig}(s, s') \wedge [s'.\mathsf{key} \neq \bot \implies \mathsf{SameKey}(s, s')]\Big)$$

The full (resp. almost-full) explicit key authentication advantage *of* $\mathcal{A}$ *is*

$$\mathbf{Adv}_{\Pi,U}^{\mathsf{fexKeyAuth}}(\mathcal{A}) \stackrel{\text{def}}{=} \Pr[\mathbf{Exp}_{\Pi,U}^{\mathsf{fexKeyAuth}}(\mathcal{A}) \Rightarrow 1] \tag{16}$$

$$\mathbf{Adv}_{\Pi,U}^{\mathsf{afexKeyAuth}}(\mathcal{A}) \stackrel{\text{def}}{=} \Pr[\mathbf{Exp}_{\Pi,U}^{\mathsf{afexKeyAuth}}(\mathcal{A}) \Rightarrow 1] \tag{17}$$

3.5 Explicit Entity Authentication

Explicit *entity* authentication is almost identical to explicit *key* authentication, the only difference being that the former is based on the Partner predicate while the latter is based on the SameKey predicate. Basically, explicit key authentication says that if a session with an honest peer accepts then there *is* some other session holding the same session key, while explicit entity authentication says that if a session with an honest peer accepts then it *has* a partner session.

Explicit key authentication and explicit entity authentication are closely related, as shown in [13] and further expounded in the full version.

Definition 10 (Explicit entity authentication). *The* fexEntAuth *predicate (resp.* afexEntAuth *predicate) evaluates to 1 if and only if*

$$\forall s \in \mathcal{L}_{\mathsf{rcv}} \text{ (resp. } \mathcal{L}_{\mathsf{send}}) :: s.\mathsf{accept} \implies \forall s' :: (\mathsf{Partner}(s, s') \implies s.\mathsf{peer} = s'.\mathsf{party})$$

$$\wedge$$

$$\text{(full)} \qquad\qquad\qquad \mathsf{aFresh}(s) \implies \exists s' :: \mathsf{Partner}(s, s')$$

$$\text{(almost-full)} \quad \mathsf{aFresh}(s) \implies \exists s' :: \Big(\mathsf{Orig}(s,s') \wedge [s'.\mathsf{accept} \implies \mathsf{Partner}(s, s')]\Big)$$

The full (resp. almost-full) *explicit entity authentication advantage of* $\mathcal{A}$ *is*

$$\mathbf{Adv}_{\Pi,U}^{\mathsf{fexEntAuth}}(\mathcal{A}) \overset{\text{def}}{=} \Pr[\mathbf{Exp}_{\Pi,U}^{\mathsf{fexEntAuth}}(\mathcal{A}) \Rightarrow 1] \qquad (18)$$

$$\mathbf{Adv}_{\Pi,U}^{\mathsf{afexEntAuth}}(\mathcal{A}) \overset{\text{def}}{=} \Pr[\mathbf{Exp}_{\Pi,U}^{\mathsf{afexEntAuth}}(\mathcal{A}) \Rightarrow 1] \qquad (19)$$

3.6 Key Secrecy

Key secrecy is defined as usual with the adversary using a Test query to get the real session key or a random key of a session. Note that the adversary may make multiple test queries, and they all share the same challenge bit, so that either all Test queries return real session keys, or all Test queries return random (and independently) sampled keys. Our experiment does not prevent the adversary from making Test queries for sessions that are not key fresh, so we need to account for this in the definition of advantage (called the *penalty-style* in [26]).

Definition 11 (Key secrecy). *If* $\forall s \in$ Tested $:: \mathsf{kFreshWFS}(s) = $ true *(resp.* $\mathsf{kFreshFFS}(s) = $ true*), the* KeySecWFS *(resp.* KeySecFFS *) predicate returns 1 if and only if* $b' = b$. *Else it returns* b. *The* weak (resp. full) forward key secrecy *advantage of an adversary* $\mathcal{A}$ *is*

$$\mathbf{Adv}_{\Pi,U}^{\mathsf{KeySecWFS}}(\mathcal{A}) \overset{\text{def}}{=} 2 \cdot \Pr[\mathbf{Exp}_{\Pi,U}^{\mathsf{KeySecWFS}}(\mathcal{A}) \Rightarrow 1] - 1 \qquad (20)$$

$$\mathbf{Adv}_{\Pi,U}^{\mathsf{KeySecFFS}}(\mathcal{A}) \overset{\text{def}}{=} 2 \cdot \Pr[\mathbf{Exp}_{\Pi,U}^{\mathsf{KeySecFFS}}(\mathcal{A}) \Rightarrow 1] - 1 \qquad (21)$$

Selective Key Secrecy. The *selective* key secrecy experiment is defined over the experiment given in Fig. 1, where now the code inside the blue boxes is included. In the selective security experiment the adversary has to commit to one party it will not reveal the long-term key of throughout the game.

Definition 12 (Selective key secrecy). *If* $\forall s \in$ Tested :: kFreshWFS$(s) =$ true, *the* S-KeySecWFS *predicate returns 1 if and only if* $b' = b$. *Else it returns* b. *The* selective key secrecy advantage *of an adversary* $\mathcal{A}$ *is*

$$\mathbf{Adv}_{\Pi,U}^{\mathsf{S\text{-}KeySecWFS}}(\mathcal{A}) \stackrel{\text{def}}{=} 2 \cdot \Pr[\mathbf{Exp}_{\Pi,U}^{\mathsf{S\text{-}KeySecWFS}}(\mathcal{A}) \Rightarrow 1] - 1. \tag{22}$$

Remark 1. Ordinary key secrecy does not reduce trivially to selective key secrecy with a U tightness loss as one might expect. Specifically, for an adversary that starts by revealing *all* long-term keys a reduction to selective key secrecy will not be able to simulate the one key it committed to. This makes our selective security notion incomparable to the selective notion of [21].

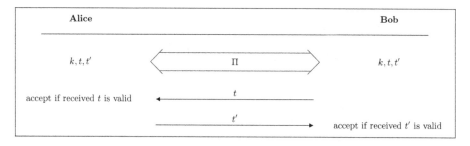

Fig. 2. Protocol Π^+ obtained by extending protocol Π with key confirmation tags. All session variables in Π^+ are inherited from Π, except for **accept** which is defined as shown. The session sending the last message in protocol Π sends tag t, and the session receiving the last message in protocol Π sends tag t'.

4   The Security of Adding Key Confirmation

Let Π denote an arbitrary key exchange protocol, and let Π^+ denote the protocol that extends Π by adding key confirmation messages from each side as illustrated in Fig. 2. Conventionally, the key confirmation messages are derived from the session key of Π using a PRF (and possibly a MAC) but in order to simplify the later analysis we assume that Π produces session keys of the form (k, t, t') directly. Protocol Π^+ is then derived from Π simply by defining its session key to be k, and the key confirmation tags to be t and t'. Using this trick we can relate the security of protocol Π^+ purely to the security of protocol Π without having to rely on PRFs or MACs.

Unfortunately, defining Π^+ in terms of the key triple output by Π introduces one technicality. We will often want to make an assertion of the form "if s and s' have equal keys in protocol Π^+ (meaning k), then they also have equal keys in protocol Π (meaning (k, t, t'))". While this assertion easily follows in practice—for instance if (k, t, t') is derived from the session transcript using a function for which getting a collision just in k is unlikely, such as an extendable-output function or a random oracle—in the generality we have presented Π and Π^+ above the assertion does not automatically follow. Thus, to cleanly state and prove our generic results we introduce the implication "equal k $\implies$ equal (k, t, t')" as an explicit security property.

To this end, let prefix : $\{0,1\}^* \to \{0,1\}^*$ be a function that returns a prefix of a particular length (left unspecified) from its argument and define

$$\mathsf{SamePrefix}(s, s') \iff [s.\mathsf{key}, s'.\mathsf{key} \neq \bot \wedge \mathsf{prefix}(s.\mathsf{key}) = \mathsf{prefix}(s'.\mathsf{key})]. \quad (23)$$

Definition 13 (Same prefix security). *The* $\mathsf{PreEqAllEq}$ *predicate evaluates to 1 if and only if*

$$\forall s \in \mathcal{L}_{\mathsf{rcv}} :: s.\mathsf{accept} \implies \forall s' :: (\mathsf{SamePrefix}(s, s') \implies \mathsf{SameKey}(s, s')). \quad (24)$$

The same prefix advantage *of* $\mathcal{A}$ *is*

$$\mathbf{Adv}_{\Pi,U}^{\mathsf{PreEqAllEq}}(\mathcal{A}) \overset{\text{def}}{=} \Pr[\mathbf{Exp}_{\Pi,U}^{\mathsf{PreEqAllEq}}(\mathcal{A}) \Rightarrow 1]. \quad (25)$$

We now state the first main theorem of the paper: a protocol with weak forward secrecy can be upgraded to full forward secrecy by adding key confirmation messages, and, moreover, this upgrade can be achieved with a linear security loss in the number of parties. The second main theorem of the paper is that this linear security loss is unavoidable for a larger class of compilers (see Sect. 6).

Theorem 1. *Let* $\mathcal{A}$ *be an adversary against key secrecy for* Π^+. *Then there exist adversaries* $\mathcal{B}_1, \mathcal{B}_2, \ldots, \mathcal{B}_6$, *all with about the same runtime as* $\mathcal{A}$, *such that*

$$\mathbf{Adv}_{\Pi^+,U}^{\mathsf{KeySecFFS}}(\mathcal{A}) \leq 4 \cdot U \cdot \mathbf{Adv}_{\Pi,U}^{\mathsf{S\text{-}KeySecWFS}}(\mathcal{B}_1) + 8 \cdot \mathbf{Adv}_{\Pi,U}^{\mathsf{iKeyAuth}}(\mathcal{B}_2) + \frac{4US}{2^{\mathsf{taglen}}}$$

$$+ 12 \cdot \mathbf{Adv}_{\Pi,U}^{\mathsf{Match}}(\mathcal{B}_3) + 4 \cdot \mathbf{Adv}_{\Pi,U}^{\mathsf{KMSound}}(\mathcal{B}_4) + 12 \cdot \mathbf{Adv}_{\Pi,U}^{\mathsf{PreEqAllEq}}(\mathcal{B}_5)$$

$$+ 4 \cdot \mathbf{Adv}_{\Pi,U}^{\mathsf{KeySecWFS}}(\mathcal{B}_6),$$

where taglen *is the length of the key confirmation tags used by* Π^+ *and* S *is the number of sessions.*

The proof of Theorem 1 is given in the full version. At a high level the proof consists of two parts: one where all accepting sessions with peers whose long-term keys are unrevealed have an origin session, and one where they don't. In the first case full forward key secrecy of protocol Π^+ reduces straightforwardly to the weak forward key secrecy of protocol Π. The main challenge is to deal with the second case, namely to prove that protocol Π^+ achieves explicit entity authentication. In fact, the main technical tool for this is to prove that Π^+ achieves explicit *key* authentication, which is where we use the *selective* key secrecy notion. The proof of explicit key authentication is the focus of Sect. 4.1.

4.1 Implicit to Explicit Key Authentication

In this section, we establish that explicit key authentication can be based on *selective* key secrecy, implicit key authentication, and same prefix security. This is a key technical result needed to restore the tight security of the explicitly authenticated protocol of [10]. The use of selective security may have further applications in constructing highly efficient explicitly authenticated key exchange protocols with full forward secrecy in the future.

Lemma 1. *Let $\mathcal{A}$ be an adversary against full explicit key authentication for Π^+. Then there exists an adversary $\mathcal{B}_2$ against selective key secrecy and an adversary $\mathcal{B}_1$ against implicit key authentication and same prefix security, both with the same runtime as $\mathcal{A}$, such that*

$$\mathbf{Adv}_{\Pi^+,U}^{\mathsf{fexKeyAuth}}(\mathcal{A}) \leq \mathbf{Adv}_{\Pi,U}^{\mathsf{iKeyAuth}}(\mathcal{B}_1) + \mathbf{Adv}_{\Pi,U}^{\mathsf{PreEqAllEq}}(\mathcal{B}_1) + U \cdot \mathbf{Adv}_{\Pi,U}^{\mathsf{S\text{-}KeySecWFS}}(\mathcal{B}_2) + \frac{US}{2^{\mathsf{taglen}}},$$

where taglen *is the length of the key confirmation tags used by Π^+ and S is the number of sessions.*

We need to deal with two cases. The first case considers attacks on explicit authentication that result from breaking implicit authentication of the underlying protocol Π. This case does not incur a tightness loss.

The second case considers attacks on explicit authentication that rely on breaking the weak forward secrecy of the underlying protocol Π. The important point is that in order to break explicit authentication, the partner long-term key must be unrevealed at the point in time where authentication is broken. This means that the session will be fresh at the time authentication is broken, which means that we can deduce the challenge bit at the point in time where authentication is broken. Any subsequent reveal of the partner long-term key can therefore be ignored.

Proof. The proof is structured as a sequence of games. Let Win_{G_i} denote the event that $\mathcal{A}$ wins in Game i. Winning in this case means that full explicit key authentication in (15) from Definition 9 does not hold.

Game 0. This is the original game for protocol Π^+. We have that

$$\mathbf{Adv}_{\Pi^+,U}^{\mathsf{fexKeyAuth}}(\mathcal{A}) = \Pr[\mathsf{Win}_{G_0}]. \tag{26}$$

Game 1. We modify the game so that if (15) does not hold for the Π part of a session of Π^+, then that session never accepts. Let Except_{G_1} be the event that this happens.

It is immediate that until Except_{G_1} happens, Game 1 proceeds exactly as Game 0, so

$$|\Pr[\mathsf{Win}_{G_1}] - \Pr[\mathsf{Win}_{G_0}]| \leq \Pr[\mathsf{Except}_{G_1}]. \tag{27}$$

We create an adversary $\mathcal{B}_1$ against implicit key authentication for Π that runs a copy of $\mathcal{A}$ and uses its experiment to run the Π part of Π^+. When a session of Π outputs a session key, $\mathcal{B}_1$ reveals the session key and uses that to simulate sending and receiving the key confirmation messages. Let $\mathsf{Win}_{\mathcal{B}_1}$ denote the probability that $\mathcal{B}_1$ wins.

It is immediate that $\mathcal{B}_1$ and its experiment together simulate the experiment in Game 0 perfectly with respect to the copy of $\mathcal{A}$ run by $\mathcal{B}_1$. Since SameKey for Π^+ implies SamePrefix for Π, if (15) does not hold for Π^+ in an execution, either it will not hold when we consider the game as an execution of Π, or PreEqAllEq will not hold when we consider the game as an execution of Π. In other words,

$$\Pr[\mathsf{Except}_{G_1}] \leq \Pr[\mathsf{Win}_{\mathcal{B}_1}^{\mathsf{iKeyAuth}}] + \Pr[\mathsf{Win}_{\mathcal{B}_1}^{\mathsf{PreEqAllEq}}]. \tag{28}$$

Game 2. We modify the game by sampling $j \in \{1, 2, \ldots, U\}$ at the start. Let Win'_{G_2} be the event that Win_{G_2} happens and one session for which authentication is broken has the jth key as its peer's public key. Clearly,

$$\Pr[\mathsf{Win}'_{G_2}] \geq \frac{1}{U} \Pr[\mathsf{Win}_{G_2}] = \frac{1}{U} \Pr[\mathsf{Win}_{G_1}]. \tag{29}$$

Game 3. We modify the game so that if (15) holds for a session of Π^+ that has the jth key as its peer public key but it has no origin session, then that session samples random tags to use for the Π^+ part of the protocol, instead of the tags output by Π.

It is immediate that

$$\Pr[\mathsf{Win}'_{G_3}] \leq \frac{S}{2^{\mathsf{taglen}}}. \tag{30}$$

We create an adversary $\mathcal{B}_2$ against selective key secrecy for Π that runs a copy of $\mathcal{A}$ and uses its experiment to run the Π part of Π^+, simulating the sending and receiving of key confirmation messages as modified in Game 2, further modified as follows:

- At the start, $\mathcal{B}_2$ selects an integer $j \in \{1, 2, \ldots, U\}$.
- When a session of Π, using the ith key as its peer key, outputs a session key, (15) holds for the session and it has no origin session, then:
  - If $i \neq j$, then $\mathcal{B}_2$ reveals the session key of the session and uses that key to simulate the Π^+ part of the session.
  - If $i = j$, then $\mathcal{B}_2$ tests the Π instance and uses that key to simulate the Π^+ part of the session.
- If $\mathcal{A}$ reveals the jth long-term key, $\mathcal{B}_2$ outputs 0 and stops.

If $\mathcal{A}$ breaks authentication for a session with the jth key as its peer key, $\mathcal{B}_2$ outputs 1, otherwise $\mathcal{B}_2$ outputs 0.

Let $\mathsf{Win}'_{\mathcal{B}_2, b}$ denote the event that $\mathcal{B}_2$ outputs 1, when its experiment has the secret bit b. We have that

$$\mathbf{Adv}_{\Pi, U}^{\mathsf{S\text{-}KeySecWFS}}(\mathcal{B}_2) = |\Pr[\mathsf{Win}_{\mathcal{B}_2, 0}] - \Pr[\mathsf{Win}_{\mathcal{B}_2, 1}]|. \tag{31}$$

If the experiment's secret bit $b = 0$, then $\mathcal{B}_2$ perfectly simulates Game 2 with respect to the Win'_{G_2} event, since the only observable difference is that

$\mathcal{B}_2$ terminates when Win'_{G_2} no longer can occur (when the jth long-term key is revealed), so

$$\Pr[\mathsf{Win}_{\mathcal{B}_2,0}] = \Pr[\mathsf{Win}'_{G_2}]. \tag{32}$$

If the experiment's secret bit $b = 1$, then $\mathcal{B}_2$ perfectly simulates Game 3 with respect to the Win'_{G_2} event, again because of termination, so

$$\Pr[\mathsf{Win}_{\mathcal{B}_2,1}] = \Pr[\mathsf{Win}'_{G_2}]. \tag{33}$$

The claim follows from (26)–(33). □

The same argument proves the similar statement:

Lemma 2. *Let $\mathcal{A}$ be an adversary against almost full explicit key authentication for Π^+. Then there exists an adversary $\mathcal{B}_2$ against selective key secrecy and an adversary $\mathcal{B}_1$ against implicit key authentication and same prefix security, both with the same runtime as $\mathcal{A}$, such that*

$$\mathbf{Adv}^{\mathsf{afexKeyAuth}}_{\Pi^+,U}(\mathcal{A}) \leq \mathbf{Adv}^{\mathsf{iKeyAuth}}_{\Pi,U}(\mathcal{B}_1) + \mathbf{Adv}^{\mathsf{PreEqAllEq}}_{\Pi,U}(\mathcal{B}_1) + U \cdot \mathbf{Adv}^{\mathsf{S\text{-}KeySecWFS}}_{\Pi,U}(\mathcal{B}_2) + \frac{US}{2^{\mathsf{taglen}}},$$

where taglen *is the length of the key confirmation tags used by* Π^+.

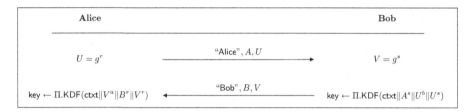

Fig. 3. The CCGJJ protocol from [10] for prime-ordered group G with generator g. Alice has secret key a, public key A; Bob has secret key b, public key B. Their context ctxt contains their names, their public keys and the two messages U and V. We include names and public keys in the messages; in practice they may be communicated in other ways.

4.2   Additional Security Reductions

Lemma 1 is *the* key result needed to show that protocol Π^+ achieves explicit authentication from the implicitly authenticated protocol Π in a manner that only incurs a tightness loss of U. From this result all the other security properties defined in Sect. 3 follow in a straightforward and modular way. That is, in the full version we show that Π^+ has all the security properties from Sect. 3 via reductions to the same properties of protocol Π, in addition to same prefix security. Moreover, none of these reductions loses more than a factor of U (in fact, most of the reductions are fully tight, and those that are not only accrue the U term as a result of invoking Lemma 1).

5   The CCGJJ Protocol

The CCGJJ protocol from Cohn-Gordon et al. [10] is a highly efficient implicitly authenticated key exchange protocol with optimal tightness. We use this protocol to illustrate our framework, which means that we need to prove various properties for the protocol (Fig. 3).

We begin by proving that the protocol has the basic properties we want, in particular match soundness, key match soundness and the same prefix property.

Proposition 1. *Let $\mathcal{A}$ be an adversary against the CCGJJ protocol. Then*

$$\mathbf{Adv}_{CCGJJ,U}^{\mathsf{Match}}(\mathcal{A}) \leq \frac{S^2}{2^{|\mathsf{key}|}}, \quad \mathbf{Adv}_{CCGJJ,U}^{\mathsf{KMSound}}(\mathcal{A}) \leq \frac{S^2}{|G|} \quad and \quad \mathbf{Adv}_{CCGJJ,U}^{\mathsf{iKeyAuth}}(\mathcal{A}) \leq \frac{S^2}{2^{|\mathsf{key}|}}.$$

Proposition 2. *Let $\mathcal{A}$ be an adversary against the CCGJJ protocol. Then*

$$\mathbf{Adv}_{CCGJJ,U}^{\mathsf{PreEqAllEq}}(\mathcal{A}) \leq \frac{S^2}{2^{|\mathsf{key}|-2\mathsf{taglen}}}.$$

Proposition 3. *Let $\mathcal{A}$ be an adversary against selective key secrecy for CCGJJ. Then there exists adversaries $\mathcal{B}_1$, $\mathcal{B}_2$ and $\mathcal{B}_3$ against strong Diffie-Hellman (in group G with generator g) with essentially the same runtime as $\mathcal{A}$ such that*

$$\mathbf{Adv}_{CCGJJ,U}^{\mathsf{S\text{-}KeySecWFS}}(\mathcal{A}) \leq \mathbf{Adv}_G^{\mathsf{stDH}}(\mathcal{B}_1) + \mathbf{Adv}_G^{\mathsf{stDH}}(\mathcal{B}_2) + \mathbf{Adv}_G^{\mathsf{stDH}}(\mathcal{B}_3) + \frac{US^2}{|G|}$$

The proof closely follows the structure of the proof in [10], modelling $\Pi.\mathsf{KDF}$ as a random oracle.

6   Impossibility of Tightly-Secure Explicit Authentication via Key Confirmation

In this section we show that a large, natural, and widely-used class of compilers for turning implicitly authenticated protocols into explicitly authenticated protocols, inevitably must incur a linear security loss in the number of parties. The class includes the generic compiler from [10] which was incorrectly claimed to achieve tight security but also the MAC-based approach to turn HMQV into HMQV-C [20] (which does not give explicit security bounds) and the compiler by Yang [27] (which has a linear loss in the number of parties times sessions per party).

6.1   Requirements on Π and Π^+

We want to consider *generic* approaches that turn *any* implicitly authenticated key exchange protocol Π into an explicitly authenticated protocol Π^+. To this end, we will in the sequel focus on underlying protocols Π and constructions Π^+ that satisfy certain requirements that we will define in this section.

Messages of Π are Independent of the Secret Key. We consider protocols Π where the messages sent by a party are *independent* of the long-term secret key of this party (and the long-term secret is only used during session key computation). More precisely, we consider n-message protocols $\Pi = (\text{KeyGen}, \text{Init}, \text{Run})$, with two associated session key computation algorithms $\Pi.\text{KDF}, \Pi.\text{KDF}'$. Recall that Run is a state-dependent algorithm, i.e., the state "prescribes" which protocol message needs to be generated next. The algorithms are executed as follows.

1. The initiator samples randomness r_I uniformly from some space (depending on the protocol) and uses this to compute the first protocol message and session state as

$$(m_1, st_1) \leftarrow \Pi.\text{Init}(I, R, \text{init}, \text{pk}_R, -).$$

   Here pk_R is the public key of the intended communication partner (the responder). Note that I's secret long-term key sk_I is not used to produce m_1, st_1.
2. Upon receiving message m_1 the responder samples uniform randomness r_R and initializes a session state as $st_2' \leftarrow \Pi.\text{Init}(R, I, \text{resp}, \text{pk}_I, -)$, then computes the second protocol message and an updated state as

$$(m_2, st_2) \leftarrow \Pi.\text{Run}(st_2', m_1).$$

   Again, note that R's secret long-term key sk_R is not used to produce m_2, st_2.
3. If $n > 2$, then the parties keep exchanging messages until the protocol is finished. Hence, whenever a party with state st_{i-1} receives a message m_i with $i < n$, then it computes a message m_{i+1} and an updated state st_{i+1} as

$$(m_{i+1}, st_{i+1}) \leftarrow \Pi.\text{Run}(st_{i-1}, m_i).$$

4. When a party receives the $(n-1)^{\text{th}}$ message m_{n-1}, then it computes the nth message and updated state st_n as above, and—using the updated state and secret long-term key sk—additionally outputs a session key as

$$k \leftarrow \Pi.\text{KDF}(st_n, \text{sk}).$$

5. Similarly, when a party receives the nth message m_n, it uses this, together with its current state st_{i-1} and secret long-term key sk, to derive

$$k \leftarrow \Pi.\text{KDF}'(st_{n-1}, \text{sk}, m_n).$$

The messages must be independent of the secret key because we will construct an efficient adversary which has to send messages on behalf of other parties without knowing their secret keys. This includes typical implicitly authenticated protocols, such as protocols where each party sends a group element g^x for random $x \leftarrow \mathbb{Z}_p$ and the long-term secret keys are only used during key derivation at the end of the protocol. Many typical implicitly authenticated high-efficiency protocols have messages that are independent of the secret key. This includes in particular the implicitly authenticated variant of the CCGJJ19 protocol [10] but also protocols such as HMQV [20].

One class of protocols which is *not* covered by this assumption are those based on digital signatures, such as the signed Diffie-Hellman protocol. Digitally signing messages is thus a way to circumvent our impossibility result. However, note that implicitly authenticated key exchange protocols, such as [10,20], typically avoid the use of digital signatures since they add a very significant overhead (w.r.t. computation and communication) to the protocol. This holds in particular when tightness is considered, where the most efficient signature schemes with fully tight multi-user security (in the random oracle model) [14] are significantly more expensive than corresponding schemes without tight security.

An extension to NAXOS-like protocols [22], where parties send a group element g^x where $x = H(sk, r)$ depends on the secret key of the sending party and some randomness r, as well as to reductions in the random oracle model, is discussed in Sect. 6.3.

Π^+ *Adds Key Confirmation Messages with Canonical Verification to* Π. In the sequel let Π be an (implicitly authenticated) n-message protocol as defined above. We consider $(n + 1)$-messages protocols Π^+ defined in terms of Π, and two associated functions Π^+.Conf and Π^+.KDF, where Π^+.Conf computes the *key confirmation messages* added to the protocol and Π^+.KDF may perform additional key derivation. The first three steps of an execution of protocol Π^+ are identical to Π as described above. The remaining steps proceed as follows (cf. Fig. 4).

4. When a party receives the $(n-1)^{\text{th}}$ message m_{n-1}, then it computes the nth message of Π and updated state st_n as above, and derives the session key of Π as an *intermediate* key $k \leftarrow \Pi$.KDF(st_n, sk)
Then it computes a *key confirmation* message $m_{n+1} \leftarrow \Pi^+$.Conf(k, T_n), depending on k and the transcript $T_n = (m_1, \ldots, m_n)$ of all protocol messages as sent and received by this party so far. The nth message of Π^+ now consists of the tuple (m_n, m_{n+1}), that is, the nth message of Π plus the key confirmation message.
5. When a party receives the nth message of Π^+ (m_n, m_{n+1}), then it derives an *intermediate* key as $k \leftarrow \Pi$.KDF$'(st_{n-1}, \text{sk}, m_n)$ using its current state st_{n-1}, long-term secret key sk, and message m_n.
Then it checks the first key confirmation message by computing $m'_{n+1} \leftarrow \Pi^+$.Conf$(k, T_n)$ and setting accept $\leftarrow$ true if and only if $m_{n+1} = m'_{n+1}$.
If accept = false, then it outputs $k' = \bot$. If accept = true, then it sends a second *key confirmation* message $m_{n+2} \leftarrow \Pi^+$.Conf(k, T_{n+1}) and outputs $k' \leftarrow \Pi^+$.KDF(k, T_{n+2}), where $T_{n+2} = (m_1, \ldots, m_{n+2})$.
6. Finally, when a party receives the $(n+1)^{\text{th}}$ message of Π^+, i.e., the second key confirmation message, then it computes $m'_{n+2} \leftarrow \Pi^+$.Conf$(k, T_{n+1})$ and sets accept = true if and only if $m_{n+2} = m'_{n+2}$. If accept = false, then it outputs $k' = \bot$. If accept = true, then it outputs $k' \leftarrow \Pi^+$.KDF(k, T_{n+2}).

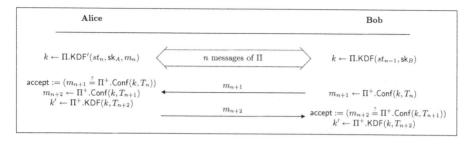

Fig. 4. Protocol Π^+ extending protocol Π with key-confirmation messages. In this concrete example Bob would have sent the last message m_n of Π.

Remark 2. We have defined Π^+ such that the first key confirmation message is sent along with the last message of Π, and then the second key confirmation message is sent as a reply. This adds *one* extra message to Π, that is, Π^+ is an $(n + 1)$-message protocol. Alternatively, we could have defined Π^+ so that the first key confirmation is sent as a *reply* to m_n. This would have added *two* messages to Π, making Π^+ an $(n + 2)$-message protocol. We consider the former approach more natural, and is the approach used in CCGJJ19 [10] and HMQV-C [20]. The latter approach is used by Yang [27]. Even though we only treat the former variant here, our results apply equally to both variants.

Definition 14. *Let Π^+.Conf be such that key confirmation messages are elements of $\{0,1\}^\beta$ We say that Π^+.Conf is δ-entropy-preserving, if for every $m \in \{0,1\}^\beta$ and every string T' holds that*

$$\Pr_{k \xleftarrow{\$} \mathcal{K}} \left[\Pi^+.\mathsf{Conf}(k, T') = m \right] \le \delta$$

Security of Π^+ from Π via a Valid Black-Box Reduction. We want to consider generic constructions of a fully forward secret (and explicitly authenticated) protocol Π^+ based on the assumption that the underlying Π is a weakly forward secret (and implicitly authenticated) protocol, plus possibly some additional assumptions, e.g., on the primitives used to create the key confirmation messages, and so on. This excludes artificial constructions of Π^+ which run Π as a redundant subroutine but where security is achieved in a completely different way, so that Π is actually superfluous.

The most natural way to establish security of Π^+ based on the security of Π is to have a security analysis of Π^+ which includes (possibly among other arguments and reductions) at least one reduction $\mathcal{R}$ to the KeySecWFS security of Π. We will argue that such a reduction cannot be tight. The full security analysis of Π^+ might include further arguments, such as reductions to the security of primitives used in the key confirmation messages.

More precisely, we assume that the security proof of Π^+ includes a black-box reduction $\mathcal{R}$, which treats the adversary $\mathcal{A}$ as a black box by submitting inputs and receiving outputs from $\mathcal{A}$ as specified in the explicitly authenticated security model, and which is able to leverage any successful $\mathcal{A}$ (independently of how $\mathcal{A}$ works internally) to break the KeySecWFS security of Π. Reduction $\mathcal{R}$ has access to the KeySecWFS security experiment of protocol Π, and to an adversary $\mathcal{A}$ on the KeySecFFS security of Π^+. We require that for every party i of the Π^+ experiment, there exists a unique corresponding party i' in the Π security experiment, and that $\mathcal{R}$ relays all messages of Π between the adversary and its security experiment. Hence, for every session $s_{i,j}$ of Π^+ there exists a unique session $s'_{i,j}$ of Π. The additional key confirmation messages of Π^+ are simulated by $\mathcal{R}$ (in any arbitrary way).

We also assume that the reduction is always "valid", i.e., it never makes any trivially invalid queries in its KeySecWFS security experiment. For example asking Reveal(s) and Test(s) against the same session s. We assume that a reduction rather aborts instead of making invalid queries. Obviously, any reduction $\mathcal{R}'$ that does not satisfy this can be generically transformed into a reduction $\mathcal{R}$ that does, with essentially the same running time and advantage, by simply putting a wrapper around $\mathcal{R}'$ that relays all queries and their replies but terminates $\mathcal{R}'$ when it asks the first trivially invalid query.

Π *has Unique and Efficiently Verifiable Secret Keys.* We assume that the public key pk of every party running protocol Π *uniquely* determines a matching secret key sk, and that one can efficiently and perfectly verify that a given sk matches a given pk. Note that this also holds for many typical implicitly authenticated high-efficiency protocols, in particular the CCGJJ19 protocol [10], but also HMQV [20], NAXOS [22], and many more, where a public key is a group element y of a group of order p and the matching secret key is the unique $x \in \mathbb{Z}_p$ such that $g^x = y$.

It is known that it is generally difficult to reduce the security of a protocol Π with unique secret keys tightly to the hardness of some non-interactive complexity assumption, due to the general impossibility results of Bader *et al.* [3]. However, note that our impossibility result is not about the tightness of security proofs for Π and reductions to non-interactive hardness assumptions, but rather about the tightness of reducing the security of a protocol Π^+ with key confirmation to the security of some underlying protocol Π (which then may or may not have a tight reduction to some hardness assumption). Hence, it is independent of the question of whether Π has a tight security proof under some (non-interactive) hardness assumption or not. Note also that in order to rule out tight generic constructions of explicit authentication via key confirmation, it is sufficient to rule out such constructions for protocols with unique secret keys, as a generic construction should work in particular for protocols with unique keys.

6.2   Impossibility Result

Theorem 2. *Let Π be an AKE protocol and let Π^+ be an AKE protocol constructed by extending Π with δ-entropy-preserving key confirmation. Let $\mathcal{R}$ be a reduction which converts any adversary $\mathcal{A}$ against the KeySecFFS security of Π^+*

into an adversary $\mathcal{R}(\mathcal{A})$ *against the implicitly authenticated* KeySecWFS*-security of* Π, *such that* Π, Π^+, *and* $\mathcal{R}$ *satisfy all requirements described in Sect. 6.1. Let* ϵ *denote an upper bound on the advantage* $\mathbf{Adv}_{\Pi,U}^{\mathsf{KeySecWFS}}(\mathcal{B})$ *of any efficient adversary* $\mathcal{B}$ *in the* KeySecWFS *security experiment for* Π *with* U *parties.*

There exists a hypothetical adversary $\mathcal{A}$ *with* $\mathbf{Adv}_{\Pi^+,U}^{\mathsf{KeySecFFS}}(\mathcal{A}) = 1 - 1/2^{|\mathsf{key}|}$ *such that for every reduction* $\mathcal{R} = \mathcal{R}(\mathcal{A})$ *holds that*

$$\mathbf{Adv}_{\Pi,U}^{\mathsf{KeySecWFS}}(\mathcal{R}(\mathcal{A})) \leq \frac{2}{U} + 5 \cdot \epsilon + \frac{1}{2^{|\mathsf{key}|-1}} + \delta$$

Interpretation of Theorem 2. If Π is secure (otherwise a reduction to the security of Π is meaningless anyway), then ϵ is negligible. Furthermore, we can assume that $\frac{1}{2^{|\mathsf{key}|-1}}$ and δ are negligibly small, too, as otherwise there are trivial attacks on Π^+. Hence, we obtain that the advantage of any reduction $\mathcal{R}$ must be negligibly close to $O(1/U)$. However, note that the adversary $\mathcal{A}$ against Π^+ in the above theorem has advantage ≈ 1. Hence, a reduction $\mathcal{R}$ cannot be tight, as it must have a linear loss in the number of parties U.

Theorem 2 is formulated in terms of key secrecy, as it considers reductions leveraging an adversary $\mathcal{A}$ breaking the full forward secrecy (KeySecFFS) of Π^+. However, the impossibility result could equally have been phrased in terms of entity authentication. To see this, note that while the proof of Theorem 2 describes a meta-reduction which simulates a hypothetical adversary $\mathcal{A}$ breaking key secrecy, in Step 4 of this hypothetical adversary $\mathcal{A}$ also breaks entity authentication. Therefore one can equally phrase the theorem in terms of entity authentication, the overall proof and arguments all remaining the same. Consequently, Theorem 6 of [10], which is technically a claim about entity authentication and not about key secrecy, cannot be correct by Theorem 2. This was confirmed by the authors of [10].

Proof. As common in proofs based on meta-reductions [3,18,23] we first describe an (inefficient) hypothetical adversary. Then we explain how this hypothetical adversary is leveraged to prove the result, by showing that one can efficiently simulate $\mathcal{A}$ for any reduction $\mathcal{R}$ that is "too tight", which yields a contradiction.

Description of the Hypothetical Adversary. Consider the following (hypothetical) adversary $\mathcal{A}$ for the explicitly authenticated security experiment.

1. $\mathcal{A}$ receives a dictionary **pk** containing all the public keys of all users. It picks $i^* \xleftarrow{\$} \{1, \ldots, U\}$ at random.
2. $\mathcal{A}$ initiates $U(U-1)$ protocol sessions as follows. For every party i it picks $U-1$ random values $r_{i,j}$ for all $j \neq i$, that is, one for every party different from party i. Then it uses the fact that protocol messages of Π are independent of the secret long-term key to execute a run of protocol Π^+ such that the experiment outputs the *first* key confirmation message on behalf of j. $\mathcal{A}$ does not respond with the second key confirmation message.

More precisely, if Π is an n-message protocol and n is even, then $\mathcal{A}$ impersonates every party i as an initiator by querying

$$s_{i,j} \leftarrow \mathsf{NewSession}(j, i, \mathsf{resp})$$

to create a session id $s_{i,j}$. Note that in our notation the session $s_{i,j}$ refers to a session where the adversary impersonates party i towards a session of party j with session id $s_{i,j}$ in the experiment. Then $\mathcal{A}$ uses $r_{i,j}$ to compute

$$(m_{i,j,1}, st_{i,j,1}) \leftarrow \Pi.\mathsf{Init}(i, j, \mathsf{init}, \mathsf{pk}_j, -)$$

and queries $\mathsf{Send}(s_{i,j}, m_{i,j,1})$ in order to send $m_{i,j,1}$ to the experiment on behalf of party i.

> If Π is a two-message protocol, then the experiment will respond with the second message of Π and the key confirmation message on behalf of j. If Π has more than two messages (i.e., $n \in \{4, 6, 8, \ldots\}$), then $\mathcal{A}$ continues to simulate all further messages of Π using $st_{i,j,1}$ on behalf of i by appropriate Send queries, until the experiment outputs the first key confirmation message.

> If Π is an n-message protocol for odd n, then $\mathcal{A}$ proceeds similarly, except that instead of sending the first protocol message, it queries $(m_{i,j,1}, s_{i,j}) \leftarrow \mathsf{NewSession}(j, i, \mathsf{init})$ in order to receive the first protocol message $m_{i,j,1}$ from j to i and a corresponding session id $s_{i,j}$.

Thus, in total $\mathcal{A}$ obtains $U(U-1)$ key confirmation messages from its security experiment. We will later consider reductions $\mathcal{R}$ simulating the experiment of Π^+ by relaying all messages of Π to the security experiment of Π. But since the key confirmation messages exist only in Π^+ and not in Π, $\mathcal{R}$ is forced to somehow simulate the key confirmation messages. However, we will argue that these key confirmation messages are difficult to simulate properly for any $\mathcal{R}$ without predicting the index i^* chosen by $\mathcal{A}$ in its next step.

3. So far all queries of $\mathcal{A}$ were independent of i^*. Now $\mathcal{A}$ reveals the long-term keys of all users except for i^*, by querying $\mathsf{RevealLTK}(i)$ for all $i \in \{1, \ldots, U\} \setminus \{i^*\}$. The adversary aborts if anything is wrong. More precisely:

   (a) It checks whether all secret keys returned by the experiment match the public keys and aborts if not. Here we use that Π has unique and efficiently verifiable secret keys.

   Intuitively, this forces a reduction $\mathcal{R}$ simulating the experiment to relay all $\mathsf{RevealLTK}$ queries to the security experiment of Π. Otherwise, we can leverage $\mathcal{R}$ to break Π due to the fact that it is able to output a valid, *non-revealed*, long-term secret key. We prove this below.

   (b) For all $i \in \{1, \ldots, U\} \setminus \{i^*\}$ and all $j \neq i$, $\mathcal{A}$ uses its randomness $r_{i,j}$ and sk_i to compute all *intermediate* session keys $k_{i,j}$ (i.e., the session key of protocol Π of the session between i and j). To this end, it computes

$$k_{i,j} \leftarrow \Pi.\mathsf{KDF}'(st_{i,j,n-1}, \mathsf{sk}_i, m_{i,j,n})$$

and then uses $k_{i,j}$ and the transcript $T_{i,j,n}$ of the first n protocol messages of the session between i and j to test whether the key confirmation message produced by the security experiment in this session indeed match the correct key confirmation message determined by $k_{i,j}$ and the protocol transcript $T_{i,j,n}$. This is done by computing

$$m'_{i,j,n+1} \leftarrow \Pi^+.\mathsf{Conf}(k_{i,j}, T_{i,j,n})$$

and checking whether $m_{i,j,n+1} = m'_{i,j,n+1}$. $\mathcal{A}$ aborts if any key confirmation message is incorrect.

Intuitively, this forces a reduction $\mathcal{R}$ simulating the security experiment to produce correct key confirmation messages for all sessions where $\mathcal{R}$ simulates party j. Below we'll argue that this is difficult for a reduction without predicting the index i^*, which incurs a linear security loss.

4. This last step is the "hypothetical" part of the adversary. $\mathcal{A}$ computes the unique value sk_{i^*} that corresponds to the secret key of party i^*. We intentionally do not specify precisely how this is done, as a black-box reduction should be able to leverage any adversary that somehow accomplishes this in some way. Then $\mathcal{A}$ finishes the key exchange protocol on behalf of i^* with *any* party j, for instance for $j = 1$.

To this end, it computes the *intermediate* key from Π as

$$k_{i^*,j} \leftarrow \Pi.\mathsf{KDF}'(st_{i^*,j,n-1}, \mathsf{sk}_{i^*}, m_{i^*,j,n})$$

and sets $\mathsf{accept} \leftarrow \mathsf{true}$ if and only if $m_{i^*,j,n+1} = \Pi^+.\mathsf{Conf}(k_{i^*,j}, T_{i^*,j,n+1})$, where $T_{i^*,j,n+1}$ is the transcript of all protocol messages of the session between i^* and j as observed by $\mathcal{A}$. If $\mathsf{accept} = \mathsf{false}$, then $\mathcal{A}$ aborts.

If $\mathsf{accept} = \mathsf{true}$, then $\mathcal{A}$ derives and sends the second key confirmation message of Π^+.[1] Since $s_{i^*,j}$ has not been revealed and no partner has been revealed, corrupted, or tested, it is eligible for a Test query.

Now $\mathcal{A}$ asks $\mathsf{Test}(s_{i^*,j})$ and receives back a key k', which is either the "real" session key or a random key. $\mathcal{A}$ then computes $k \leftarrow \Pi^+.\mathsf{KDF}(k, T_{i^*,j,n+2})$, where $T_{i^*,j,n+2}$ is the transcript of all protocol messages of the session between i^* and j as observed by $\mathcal{A}$. It outputs 1 if $k = k'$ and 0 otherwise.

Note that $\mathcal{A}$ is a correct (hypothetical) adversary against the explicitly authenticated KeySecFFS security of Π^+ with

$$\mathbf{Adv}^{\mathsf{KeySecFFS}}_{\Pi^+, U}(\mathcal{A}) = 1 - 1/2^{|\mathsf{key}|}$$

The term $1/2^{|\mathsf{key}|}$ is the probability that a random key k' equals the "real" session key k "by accident", which is the only case where $\mathcal{A}$ answers incorrectly. Note that this is the best possible advantage that an adversary that asks only a single

---

[1] This step already breaks entity authentication of Π^+ since the long-term key of $s_{i^*,j}$'s peer has not been revealed. However, since we focus on forward security here we let $\mathcal{A}$ continue.

Test query can achieve in the security experiment. Hence, any black-box reduction $\mathcal{R}$ that works for any correct adversary should work in particular for $\mathcal{A}$. As common in proofs based on meta-reductions, such as [3,11,18,23] our hypothetical adversary is not efficient but we will show how it can be efficiently *simulated* if the reduction $\mathcal{R}$ is tight. This yields that either the reduction must be non-tight, or the underlying hardness assumption (that Π is secure in an implicitly authenticated sense) must be wrong. Since we assume that Π is secure (as otherwise any reduction to the security of Π is meaningless and trivial, anyway), we conclude that $\mathcal{R}$ must be non-tight.

Analysis of $\mathcal{R}$. Consider the following sequence of games, where we denote with X_i the advantage of $\mathcal{R}(\mathcal{A})$ in the KeySecWFS security experiment of Π in Game i. Proofs for the lemmas can be found in the full version.

Game 0. As described in Sect. 6.1, we consider reductions $\mathcal{R}$ which have access to the KeySec security experiment of protocol Π, and to an adversary $\mathcal{A}$ on the *explicitly authenticated* KeySec security of Π^+. This game consists of an execution of any such reduction $\mathcal{R}$ with our hypothetical adversary. We have

$$X_0 = \mathbf{Adv}_{\Pi,U}^{\mathsf{KeySecWFS}}(\mathcal{R}(\mathcal{A}))$$

Recall from Sect. 6.1 that for every party i of the Π^+ experiment, there exists a unique corresponding party i' in the Π security experiment. Recall also that $\mathcal{R}$ relays all messages of Π between the adversary and its security experiment, such that for every session $s_{i,j}$ of Π^+ there exists a unique session $s'_{i,j}$ of Π, and that we assume that $\mathcal{R}$ does not make any invalid queries in its security experiment that make $\mathcal{R}$ trivially "lose" the KeySec security experiment.

Game 1. Recall that according to Definition 1 the origin predicate evaluates to $\mathsf{Orig}(s, s') = \mathsf{true}$ for two sessions s, s', if the transcript of s' is equal to or a prefix of the transcript of s. Recall also that session key freshness (Definition 5) allows to reveal the long-term key of s's peer if there exists s' with $\mathsf{Orig}(s, s') = \mathsf{true}$.

Note that $\mathcal{A}$ impersonates one communication partner of every session created with $\mathcal{R}$ using independent randomness, and that $\mathcal{R}$ relays all protocol messages of Π between its own experiment and $\mathcal{A}$. Hence, intuitively it should be unlikely that there exist any two sessions s, s' of Π such that $\mathsf{Orig}(s, s') = \mathsf{true}$, and thus long-term key reveals of peers should not be allowed (as this would enable a trivial attack, where $\mathcal{A}$ sends a message on behalf of a party *and* it knows the corresponding secret key, such that it can trivially compute the session key and break the KeySec security). However, it might happen by coincidence, e.g., if $\mathcal{A}$ and the security experiment of Π happen to choose the same randomness.

The security of Π implies that the probability of this to happen is negligibly small. In Game 1 we ensure that indeed there are no two sessions s, s' such that $\mathsf{Orig}(s, s') = \mathsf{true}$ holds "by accident". Note that all sessions of Π are created in Step 2 of $\mathcal{A}$, therefore it suffices to consider the experiment until the end of Step 2 of $\mathcal{A}$, that is, before $\mathcal{A}$ asks the first RevealLTK query in Step 3.

Game 1 is identical to Game 0, except that we raise event WrongOrigin and abort, if at the end of Step 2 of the adversary there exist any two sessions s, s' such that $\mathsf{Orig}(s, s') = \mathsf{true}$. We have

$$|X_1 - X_0| \le \Pr[\mathsf{WrongOrigin}]$$

Hence, after Game 1 we are guaranteed that there are no two sessions s, s' such that $\mathsf{Orig}(s, s') = \mathsf{true}$, and thus $\mathcal{R}$ is not allowed to reveal the long-term key of a test session's peer.

Lemma 3. *There exists an efficient adversary $\mathcal{B}_1$ against the key secrecy of Π with*

$$\mathbf{Adv}_{\Pi, U}^{\mathsf{KeySecWFS}}(\mathcal{B}_1) \ge \Pr[\mathsf{WrongOrigin}]$$

Game 2. This game is identical to Game 1, except that we abort if the event $\mathsf{NotAllRevLTK}(i)$ happens, where $\mathsf{NotAllRevLTK}(i)$ is the event that $\mathcal{R}$ has not asked $\mathsf{RevealLTK}(i)$ for all $i \ne i^*$ before $\mathcal{A}$ reaches Step 4. In other words, if $\mathsf{NotAllRevLTK}(i)$ happens, then when $\mathcal{A}$ reaches Step 4 there exists an index $i \ne i^*$ such that $\mathcal{R}$ has never queried $\mathsf{RevealLTK}(i)$. We have

$$|X_2 - X_1| \le \Pr[\mathsf{NotAllRevLTK}(i)]$$

Hence, from Game 2 on we are guaranteed that every reduction $\mathcal{R}$ must satisfy all the following properties simultaneously throughout its execution:

- Throughout its execution, $\mathcal{R}$ eventually asks $\mathsf{RevealLTK}(i)$ for all $i \ne i^*$, as otherwise event $\mathsf{NotAllRevLTK}(i)$ occurs.
- $\mathcal{R}$ does *not* query $\mathsf{RevealLTK}(i^*)$, because this would mean that $\mathcal{R}$ learns *all* parties' long-term keys, which would make the reduction trivially invalid, since it could not issue a Test query to any session started by our $\mathcal{A}$.
- $\mathcal{R}$ does *not* query $\mathsf{Test}(s_{i,j})$ for any session $s_{i,j}$ with $i \ne i^*$, as for none of the sessions $s_{i,j}$ there exists an origin session and therefore this would violate session key freshness (Definition 5), and so the reduction would be trivially invalid.

Lemma 4. *There exists an efficient adversary $\mathcal{B}_1$ against the key secrecy of Π with*

$$\mathbf{Adv}_{\Pi, U}^{\mathsf{KeySecWFS}}(\mathcal{B}_1) \ge \Pr[\mathsf{NotAllRevLTK}(i)] - 1/2^{|\mathsf{key}|}.$$

Game 3. This game is identical to Game 2, except that we abort if the event $\mathsf{IncorrectConf}$ happens, where $\mathsf{IncorrectConf}$ is the event that $\mathcal{R}$ outputs at least one key confirmation message such that $\mathcal{A}$ aborts in Step 3. Note that $\mathsf{IncorrectConf}$ occurs, if there exists any session $s_{i,j}$ with $i \ne i^*$ where $\mathcal{R}$ outputs a key confirmation message $m_{i,j,n+1}$ such that

$$m_{i,j,n+1} \ne \Pi^+.\mathsf{Conf}(k_{i,j}, T_{i,j,n})$$

where $k_{i,j} \leftarrow \Pi.\mathsf{KDF}'(st_{i,j,n-1}, \mathsf{sk}_i, m_{i,j,n})$ and $st_{i,j,n-1}$ is the session state determined by sk_i and transcript $T_{i,j,n}$. We have

$$|X_3 - X_2| \leq \Pr[\mathsf{IncorrectConf}]$$

Hence, from Game 3 on we are guarenteed that $\mathcal{R}$ outputs correct key confirmation messages for all $s_{i,j}$ with $i \neq i^*$.

Lemma 5. *There exists an efficient adversary $\mathcal{B}_3$ against the key secrecy of Π with*

$$\mathbf{Adv}_{\Pi,U}^{\mathsf{KeySecWFS}}(\mathcal{B}_3) \geq \Pr[\mathsf{IncorrectConf}]$$

Observe that the decision whether $\mathcal{A}$ aborts is already made at the end of Step 2 of the adversary, where all queries of $\mathcal{A}$ are independent of i^*, and in particular before $\mathcal{A}$ asks any $\mathsf{RevealLTK}$ query in Step 3. Intuitively, this forces $\mathcal{R}$ to output correct key confirmation messages for all sessions $s_{i,j}$ with $i \neq i^*$.

Game 4. This game is identical to Game 3, except that we abort if $\mathcal{R}$ queries $\mathsf{Test}(s_{i^*,j})$ for any session of party j with i^*, where i^* is the index chosen by $\mathcal{A}$, before Step 2 of $\mathcal{A}$ ends, that is, before $\mathcal{A}$ makes the first $\mathsf{RevealLTK}$ query.

Recall that we have already established in Game 2 that $\mathcal{R}$ cannot make a $\mathsf{Test}(s_{i,j})$ query for any session $s_{i,j}$ with $i \neq i^*$ throughout the game. Hence, if $\mathcal{R}$ makes a $\mathsf{Test}(s_{i^*,j})$ query already in Step 2 of $\mathcal{A}$, then it correctly predicts the random i^*. Since all queries of $\mathcal{A}$ are independent of i^* until the beginning of Step 3, we have

$$|X_4 - X_3| \leq \frac{1}{U}$$

Game 5. Now we additionally abort if $\mathcal{R}$ queries $\mathsf{Reveal}(s_{i^*,j})$ for *all* sessions with party i^*, where i^* is the index chosen by $\mathcal{A}$, before Step 2 of $\mathcal{A}$ ends, that is, before $\mathcal{A}$ makes the first $\mathsf{RevealLTK}$ query in its Step 3. We claim that

$$|X_4 - X_3| = 0.$$

Note that none of the sessions created by $\mathcal{R}$ with its security experiment has an origin-session due to the construction of $\mathcal{A}$ and since we have ruled out the event $\mathsf{WrongOrigin}$ in Game 1. Recall also that $\mathcal{R}$ must eventually ask $\mathsf{RevealLTK}(i)$ for all $i \neq i^*$, as established in Game 2. Hence, $\mathcal{R}$ must not ask a $\mathsf{Test}(s_{i,j})$ query for any session $s_{i,j}$ with $i \neq i^*$, as this would violate the $\mathsf{aFresh}(s_{i,j})$ predicate of the $\mathsf{kFreshWFS}(s_{i,j})$ definition. However, if $\mathcal{R}$ would now also query $\mathsf{Reveal}(s_{i^*,j})$ for *all* sessions of party i^*, then $\mathcal{R}$ would not be allowed to query $\mathsf{Test}(s_{i,j})$ for any session $s_{i,j}$ with $i = i^*$, as this would violate the $\mathsf{kFreshWFS}(s_{i,j})$ definition.

In this case, no fresh session would remain for which $\mathcal{R}$ could make a Test query. Hence, this would be an invalid sequence of queries, and since we assume that $\mathcal{R}$ does not make any such invalid queries this cannot happen.

Game 6. This game is identical to Game 5, except that we abort if the event AllConfCorrect happens, where AllConfCorrect occurs if $\mathcal{R}$ outputs *all* key confirmation messages correctly in Step 2. Specifically, AllConfCorrect occurs if

$$m_{i,j,n+1} = \Pi^+.\mathsf{Conf}(k_{i,j}, T_{i,j,n})$$

holds for *all* sessions $s_{i,j}$, and thus for all sessions $s_{i^*,j}$ for some j. We have

$$|X_6 - X_5| \leq \Pr\left[\mathsf{AllConfCorrect}\right]$$

Hence, from Game 6 on we are guarenteed that $\mathcal{R}$ outputs correct key confirmation messages for all $s_{i,j}$ with $i \neq i^*$ as otherwise we abort due to Game 5, but there must be at least one incorrect key confirmation message for a session $s_{i^*,j}$, as otherwise we abort due to Game 6.

Lemma 6. *There exists an efficient adversary* $\mathcal{B}_6$ *against the key secrecy of* Π *with*

$$\mathbf{Adv}_{\Pi,U}^{\mathsf{KeySecWFS}}(\mathcal{B}_6) \geq \frac{\Pr\left[\mathsf{AllConfCorrect}\right]}{2} - \frac{1}{2^{|\mathsf{key}|}} - \delta \qquad (34)$$

Analysis of Game 6. Finally, we claim that

$$X_6 \leq \frac{1}{U}.$$

In order to see this, consider the state of $\mathcal{R}$ in Game 6 immediately after it has output all key confirmation messages, that is, after Step 2 and *before* Step 3 of $\mathcal{A}$. We have established that $\mathcal{R}$ must output correct key confirmation messages for all sessions $s_{i,j}$ with $i \neq i^*$, as otherwise event IncorrectConf occurs. However, it also must output at least one incorrect key confirmation messages in Step 2 of $\mathcal{A}$, as otherwise event AllConfCorrect occurs. However, before Step 3, all queries made by $\mathcal{A}$ are independent of i^*, so essentially $\mathcal{R}$ has to "predict" the uniform choice of $i^* \xleftarrow{\$} \{1, \ldots, U\}$, which happens with probability at most $1/U$. $\qquad \square$

6.3 Discussion of Extensions and Generalizations

Extension to NAXOS-Like Protocols. One limitation of the impossibility result is that it requires that all protocol messages are independent of the long-term secret key. As already discussed, this holds for many implicitly-authenticated, in particular those aiming at maximal efficiency. However, one interesting class of protocols that are unfortunately excluded are NAXOS-like protocols [22], where parties send a group element g^x where $x = H(sk, r)$ depends on the secret key of the sending party and some randomness r.

We expect that Theorem 2 can also be generalized to such protocols, though. Recall that our hypothetical adversary $\mathcal{A}$ establishes protocol sessions between all parties in its Step 2. However, since it did not yet reveal any parties' long-term keys at this step, it cannot compute $x = H(sk, r)$ for the real secret key sk of a party. Observe, though that in such NAXOS-like protocols a party receiving g^x

is not able to verify that $x = H(sk, r)$, because the receiving party also doesn't know sk (and also not r). Even though a reduction $\mathcal{R}$ might somehow be able to check consistency of x (e.g., using the random oracle queries made by $\mathcal{A}$), it would still have to continue the key exchange protocol like the real security experiment. Hence, $\mathcal{A}$ could simply pick x at random and send g^x to $\mathcal{R}$, and $\mathcal{R}$ would have to continue the protocol and send a key confirmation message at the end, which leads to a similar security loss as in the proof of Theorem 2, with almost exactly the same argument that it essentially requires $\mathcal{R}$ to "predict" the index i^* chosen by $\mathcal{A}$ already in Step 2 of $\mathcal{A}$.

The reason why we did not consider this extension is because it seems that we would either have to consider specific protocols concretely, such as specifically NAXOS, which would reduce the generality of the result, or alternatively we would have had to define a general notion of "efficient simulatability" of secret-key-dependent protocol messages. We refrained from the former to obtain a general impossibility result which explains the core reason of the inherent security loss of standard ways to do key confirmation, and from the latter because the argument in the proof of Theorem 2 is already relatively complex due to the inherent complexity of key exchange security models, and we preferred an as-clean-as-possible and more rigorous argument over full generality.

Extension to Key Confirmation in the Random Oracle Model. Note that the argument in the proof of Theorem 2, specifically the construction of adversary $\mathcal{B}_6$ in Lemma 6, uses the key confirmation m_{n+1} as a "test value" to check whether a given challenge key k is real or random. This exploits that the message m_{n+1} produced by $\mathcal{R}$ in the tested session is computed deterministically as

$$m_{n+1} = \Pi^+.\mathsf{Conf}(k', T_n)$$

from the real session key k' and the public transcript T_n of protocol messages. Note that this accurately models the approach to do key confirmation used and incorrectly claimed to be tightly secure in [10]. It also covers the new approach described in the present paper, which additionally leverages selective security, since both are in the standard-model, that is, without random oracles.

Given that most highly-efficient implicitly authenticated protocols are proven secure in the random oracle model, one might ask whether it is possible to give a tightly-secure construction of Π^+ from Π in the random oracle model. For instance, one could consider computing the key confirmation message as

$$m_{n+1} = H(k', T_n)$$

If H is modeled as a random oracle, then this could enable a reduction to avoid the "commitment" implied by the key confirmation messages that it has to simulate properly, by just sending random strings m_{n+1} that then might later be "explained" as proper hash values by the $\mathcal{R}$, if necessary.

We expect that this approach also fails and once again we have an inherent tightness loss. The reason for this is because the reduction would also have to simulate the random oracle H consistently. But in order to achieve this, $\mathcal{R}$ would have to be able to distinguish a random oracle query $H(k', T_n)$ using the "real" key (in which case it would have to return m_{n+1}) from a query $H(k'', T_n)$ using an independent string k''. Since k' is the session key of Π, the reduction would thus have to be able to distinguish session keys of Π from random, which should give rise to another attacker $\mathcal{B}$ on Π that proceeds as follows:

1. $\mathcal{B}$ is again a meta-reduction, which runs $\mathcal{R}$ as a subroutine, relays all queries between $\mathcal{R}$ and its security experiment, and simulates our hypothetical adversary $\mathcal{A}$ until the end of Step 2.
2. Then $\mathcal{B}$ picks an arbitrary random session $s_{i,j}$ and queries $\mathsf{Test}(s_{i,j})$ to the security experiment of Π, receiving back a challenge key k.
3. Now $\mathcal{B}$ issues many random oracle queries of the form $H(k_i, T_n)$ to $\mathcal{R}$, where $k_1, ..., k_Q$ are chosen at random, but $k_\ell := k$ is defined as the challenge key k for some random index $\ell \xleftarrow{\$} \{1, ..., Q\}$.
4. Now either $\mathcal{R}$ is able to distinguish the query with a "real" key k from a "random" one. In this case, $\mathcal{B}$ can also distinguish the real key from a random one, by checking whether $m_{n+1} = H(k_\ell, T_n)$.
   Or $\mathcal{R}$ is not able to distinguish the query with a "real" key k from a "random" one. In this case, $\mathcal{R}$ will fail with probability $1 - 1/Q$, so that once again we can simulate $\mathcal{A}$ efficiently because it aborts if $\mathcal{R}$ fails.

The above proof idea is only a sketch, and we expect a rigorous proof to be significantly more complex and subtle. Therefore we chose to focus on the simpler and cleaner case of ruling out tight standard model constructions, as this is also what was claimed in [10] and is achieved in the present paper.

References

1. Abdalla, M., Bellare, M., Rogaway, P.: The oracle Diffie-Hellman assumptions and an analysis of DHIES. In: Naccache, D. (ed.) CT-RSA 2001. LNCS, vol. 2020, pp. 143–158. Springer, Heidelberg (2001). https://doi.org/10.1007/3-540-45353-9_12
2. Bader, C., Hofheinz, D., Jager, T., Kiltz, E., Li, Y.: Tightly-secure authenticated key exchange. In: Dodis, Y., Nielsen, J.B. (eds.) TCC 2015, Part I. LNCS, vol. 9014, pp. 629–658. Springer, Heidelberg (2015). https://doi.org/10.1007/978-3-662-46494-6_26
3. Bader, C., Jager, T., Li, Y., Schäge, S.: On the impossibility of tight cryptographic reductions. In: Fischlin, M., Coron, J.-S. (eds.) EUROCRYPT 2016, Part II. LNCS, vol. 9666, pp. 273–304. Springer, Heidelberg (2016). https://doi.org/10.1007/978-3-662-49896-5_10
4. Bellare, M., Pointcheval, D., Rogaway, P.: Authenticated key exchange secure against dictionary attacks. In: Preneel, B. (ed.) EUROCRYPT 2000. LNCS, vol. 1807, pp. 139–155. Springer, Heidelberg (2000). https://doi.org/10.1007/3-540-45539-6_11
5. Bellare, M., Rogaway, P.: Entity authentication and key distribution. In: Stinson, D.R. (ed.) CRYPTO 1993. LNCS, vol. 773, pp. 232–249. Springer, Heidelberg (1994). https://doi.org/10.1007/3-540-48329-2_21
6. Bellare, M., Rogaway, P.: Provably secure session key distribution: the three party case. In: 27th ACM STOC, pp. 57–66. ACM Press (1995). https://doi.org/10.1145/225058.225084

7. Boyd, C., Gellert, K.: A modern view on forward security. Comput. J. **64**(4), 639–652 (2020). https://doi.org/10.1093/comjnl/bxaa104

8. Boyd, C., Nieto, J.G.: On forward secrecy in one-round key exchange. In: Chen, L. (ed.) IMACC 2011. LNCS, vol. 7089, pp. 451–468. Springer, Heidelberg (2011). https://doi.org/10.1007/978-3-642-25516-8_27

9. Canetti, R., Krawczyk, H.: Analysis of key-exchange protocols and their use for building secure channels. In: Pfitzmann, B. (ed.) EUROCRYPT 2001. LNCS, vol. 2045, pp. 453–474. Springer, Heidelberg (2001). https://doi.org/10.1007/3-540-44987-6_28

10. Cohn-Gordon, K., Cremers, C., Gjøsteen, K., Jacobsen, H., Jager, T.: Highly efficient key exchange protocols with optimal tightness. In: Boldyreva, A., Micciancio, D. (eds.) CRYPTO 2019, Part III. LNCS, vol. 11694, pp. 767–797. Springer, Cham (2019). https://doi.org/10.1007/978-3-030-26954-8_25

11. Coron, J.-S.: Optimal security proofs for PSS and other signature schemes. In: Knudsen, L.R. (ed.) EUROCRYPT 2002. LNCS, vol. 2332, pp. 272–287. Springer, Heidelberg (2002). https://doi.org/10.1007/3-540-46035-7_18

12. Cremers, C., Feltz, M.: Beyond eCK: perfect forward secrecy under actor compromise and ephemeral-key reveal. Des. Codes Crypt. **74**(1), 183–218 (2013). https://doi.org/10.1007/s10623-013-9852-1

13. de Saint Guilhem, C., Fischlin, M., Warinschi, B.: Authentication in key-exchange: definitions, relations and composition. In: Jia, L., Küsters, R. (eds.) CSF 2020 Computer Security Foundations Symposium, pp. 288–303. IEEE Computer Society Press (2020). https://doi.org/10.1109/CSF49147.2020.00028

14. Diemert, D., Gellert, K., Jager, T., Lyu, L.: More efficient digital signatures with tight multi-user security. In: Garay, J.A. (ed.) PKC 2021, Part II. LNCS, vol. 12711, pp. 1–31. Springer, Cham (2021). https://doi.org/10.1007/978-3-030-75248-4_1

15. Fischlin, M., Günther, F., Schmidt, B., Warinschi, B.: Key confirmation in key exchange: a formal treatment and implications for TLS 1.3. In: 2016 IEEE Symposium on Security and Privacy, pp. 452–469. IEEE Computer Society Press (2016). https://doi.org/10.1109/SP.2016.34

16. Gjøsteen, K., Jager, T.: Practical and tightly-secure digital signatures and authenticated key exchange. In: Shacham, H., Boldyreva, A. (eds.) CRYPTO 2018, Part II. LNCS, vol. 10992, pp. 95–125. Springer, Cham (2018). https://doi.org/10.1007/978-3-319-96881-0_4

17. Han, S., et al.: Authenticated key exchange and signatures with tight security in the standard model. In: Malkin, T., Peikert, C. (eds.) CRYPTO 2021, Part IV. LNCS, vol. 12828, pp. 670–700. Springer, Cham (2021). https://doi.org/10.1007/978-3-030-84259-8_23

18. Hofheinz, D., Jager, T., Knapp, E.: Waters signatures with optimal security reduction. In: Fischlin, M., Buchmann, J., Manulis, M. (eds.) PKC 2012. LNCS, vol. 7293, pp. 66–83. Springer, Heidelberg (2012). https://doi.org/10.1007/978-3-642-30057-8_5

19. Jager, T., Kiltz, E., Riepel, D., Schäge, S.: Tightly-secure authenticated key exchange, revisited. In: Canteaut, A., Standaert, F.-X. (eds.) EUROCRYPT 2021, Part I. LNCS, vol. 12696, pp. 117–146. Springer, Cham (2021). https://doi.org/10.1007/978-3-030-77870-5_5

20. Krawczyk, H.: HMQV: a high-performance secure Diffie-Hellman protocol. In: Shoup, V. (ed.) CRYPTO 2005. LNCS, vol. 3621, pp. 546–566. Springer, Heidelberg (2005). https://doi.org/10.1007/11535218_33

21. Krawczyk, H., Paterson, K.G., Wee, H.: On the security of the TLS protocol: a systematic analysis. In: Canetti, R., Garay, J.A. (eds.) CRYPTO 2013, Part I. LNCS, vol. 8042, pp. 429–448. Springer, Heidelberg (2013). https://doi.org/10.1007/978-3-642-40041-4_24

22. LaMacchia, B., Lauter, K., Mityagin, A.: Stronger security of authenticated key exchange. In: Susilo, W., Liu, J.K., Mu, Y. (eds.) ProvSec 2007. LNCS, vol. 4784, pp. 1–16. Springer, Heidelberg (2007). https://doi.org/10.1007/978-3-540-75670-5_1

23. Lewko, A., Waters, B.: Why proving HIBE systems secure is difficult. In: Nguyen, P.Q., Oswald, E. (eds.) EUROCRYPT 2014. LNCS, vol. 8441, pp. 58–76. Springer, Heidelberg (2014). https://doi.org/10.1007/978-3-642-55220-5_4

24. Li, Y., Schäge, S.: No-match attacks and robust partnering definitions: defining trivial attacks for security protocols is not trivial. In: Thuraisingham, B.M., Evans, D., Malkin, T., Xu, D. (eds.) ACM CCS 2017, pp. 1343–1360. ACM Press (2017). https://doi.org/10.1145/3133956.3134006

25. Pan, J., Qian, C., Ringerud, M.: Signed Diffie-Hellman key exchange with tight security. In: Paterson, K.G. (ed.) CT-RSA 2021. LNCS, vol. 12704, pp. 201–226. Springer, Cham (2021). https://doi.org/10.1007/978-3-030-75539-3_9

26. Rogaway, P., Zhang, Y.: Simplifying game-based definitions. In: Shacham, H., Boldyreva, A. (eds.) CRYPTO 2018, Part II. LNCS, vol. 10992, pp. 3–32. Springer, Cham (2018). https://doi.org/10.1007/978-3-319-96881-0_1

27. Yang, Z.: Modelling simultaneous mutual authentication for authenticated key exchange. In: Danger, J.-L., Debbabi, M., Marion, J.-Y., Garcia-Alfaro, J., Zincir Heywood, N. (eds.) FPS -2013. LNCS, vol. 8352, pp. 46–62. Springer, Cham (2014). https://doi.org/10.1007/978-3-319-05302-8_4

Security Analysis of the WhatsApp
End-to-End Encrypted Backup Protocol

Gareth T. Davies[1], Sebastian Faller[2,3]($\boxtimes$), Kai Gellert[1], Tobias Handirk[1]($\boxtimes$),
Julia Hesse[2], Máté Horváth[1], and Tibor Jager[1]

[1] Bergische Universität Wuppertal, Wuppertal, Germany
davies@uni-wuppertal.de , tobias.handirk@uni-wuppertal.de
[2] IBM Research Europe – Zurich, Rüschlikon, Switzerland
[3] ETH Zurich, Zürich, Switzerland
sebastian.faller@ibm.com

Abstract. WhatsApp is an end-to-end encrypted (E2EE) messaging
service used by billions of people. In late 2021, WhatsApp rolled out
a new protocol for backing up chat histories. The E2EE WhatsApp
backup protocol (WBP) allows users to recover their chat history from
passwords, leaving WhatsApp oblivious of the actual encryption keys.
The WBP builds upon the OPAQUE framework for password-based key
exchange, which is currently undergoing standardization.

While considerable efforts have gone into the design and auditing of
the WBP, the complexity of the protocol's design and shortcomings in
the existing security analyses of its building blocks make it hard to understand the actual security guarantees that the WBP provides.

In this work, we provide the first formal security analysis of the WBP.
Our analysis in the universal composability (UC) framework confirms
that the WBP provides strong protection of users' chat history and passwords. It also shows that a corrupted server can under certain conditions
make more password guesses than what previous analysis suggests.

1 Introduction

WhatsApp is the most popular instant messaging app in the world with over 100
billion messages sent per day, containing personal and business communications.
WhatsApp provides *end-to-end encrypted* (E2EE) communications [32], where
no party but sender and receiver should be able to read (or modify) messages.
This specifically prevents the WhatsApp service provider from breaking security
guarantees such as confidentiality if the service gets compromised. E2EE is considered a default standard for modern secure messaging protocols, and several

Gareth T. Davies, Tobias Handirk, and Tibor Jager have been supported by the European Research Council (ERC) under the European Union's Horizon 2020 research and
innovation programme, grant agreement 802823. Julia Hesse was supported by the
Swiss National Science Foundation (SNSF) under the AMBIZIONE grant "Cryptographic Protocols for Human Authentication and the IoT". Máté Horváth has been
supported by the German Research Foundation (DFG), project JA2445/6-1.

H. Handschuh and A. Lysyanskaya (Eds.): CRYPTO 2023, LNCS 14084, pp. 330–361, 2023.
https://doi.org/10.1007/978-3-031-38551-3_11

formal analyses of the E2EE messaging protocol used by WhatsApp and other messaging apps such as Signal exist [2, 4, 5, 10, 13, 14, 24, 29, 30].

Bypassing E2EE via Backups. Protecting the *transmission* of confidential data is necessary to enable secure messaging, however, it is not sufficient. WhatsApp clients can back up the user's chat history so that they can recover it if the device is lost, for example by theft or switching to a new phone. Naturally, the backup mechanism must offer strong protection as well, so as not to undermine the security of the E2EE messaging protocol.

Before the end of 2021, whenever a user[1] initiated the procedure for backing up their messages (to be stored on iCloud or Google Drive), they would encrypt these messages using a key that was known to WhatsApp. While this simple approach allowed WhatsApp to return the backup encryption key to the user if the original device were to be lost, it allowed access to backed up messages beyond the control of the user. For example, by US law, federal governments could have forced WhatsApp to reveal the backup key (and the storage provider to reveal the encrypted contents) through a court order, and the previously well protected private communication suddenly becomes evidence in a lawsuit [27]. More generally, the fact that the E2EE security can be circumvented by accessing the backups harbors a great potential for abuse, for instance by malfeasant governments, malicious employees, or in case of a compromise of both the storage provider's servers and WhatsApp's servers.

WhatsApp E2EE Backups. In late 2021, WhatsApp rolled out an improved protocol for protecting backups [31], with the aim to extend the E2EE security guarantees in a user-friendly way that enables users to restore their backup keys from a password in case a device is lost. By early 2023, over 100 million WhatsApp users have already switched to this option [12]. The underlying protocol, which we call the *WhatsApp backup protocol* (WBP) in this work, makes use of hardware security modules (HSMs). Intuitively, an HSM can be programmed once with code and then "locked" in such a way that it is infeasible to change its code afterwards. This enables even the protection of a protocol against corruption of the party running the HSM (here, the WhatsApp servers). The challenge now lies in designing the code run by the HSM in such a way that (1) users can retrieve their backup keys from a password, but (2) WhatsApp servers not knowing the user password cannot retrieve the backup key.

The core idea of the WBP is to outsource all cryptographic computations to the client and the HSM, while the WhatsApp "main server" essentially only relays messages (with some minor modifications) between client and HSM. The protocol is designed such that during the initialization phase[2] both client and HSM enter a secret value (a password pw for the client, and a "per-client-secret"[3] for the HSM). Furthermore, the client chooses a symmetric backup key K and the HSM receives an encrypted version of the key, without either of them learning

---

[1] In this paper we will refer to the people using a device that runs the WhatsApp client software as *users*, to the device as a *client*, and to the servers that provide the WhatsApp chat and backup service as *servers*.

[2] Note that WhatsApp refer to this phase as *registration*.

[3] It is actually a "per-backup-secret", which is determined during initialization. If a client were to re-register, a new "per-backup-secret" would be chosen.

the secret input of the counterparty. The client uses the backup key K to encrypt the backup data. If a user loses their device, they can initiate a recovery protocol from a new client device. To this end, the new client and the WhatsApp "main server" (which, again, relays messages to the HSM) execute a protocol where the client recovers the backup key, with the password pw used during initialization and the HSM contributing the same per-client-secret as during initialization.

The password-based nature of the WBP introduces several technical challenges. Firstly, being password-based while aiming at keeping the stored key from a potentially compromised WhatsApp server implies that the protocol must not leak user passwords to the server. To this end, the WBP deploys OPAQUE [23], an asymmetric password-based key exchange protocol (aPAKE) [19] that allows a key exchange from a password without disclosing the password itself to the server. Another essential feature the WBP aims to provide is security against *password guessing attacks*, where a malicious client repeatedly executes the recovery protocol with password guesses pw'. If the password guess pw' equals the password pw used during initialization, an adversary would gain access to the secret backup key. Note that this attack is especially effective if the user password only has low entropy, which is often the case for human-memorable passwords in practice. The deployed protocol limits the number of admissible incorrect guesses to ten [18,31], after which the HSM destroys the encrypted version of the backup key (and thus makes the backup irrecoverable). This guarantee should even hold if the WhatsApp server were to be compromised.

Contributions. The WBP protocol is a widely-used real-world cryptographic protocol that addresses the fundamental problem of recovering data from encrypted backups based on human-memorizable secrets. It aims to provide strong security properties that match the E2EE-security of the messaging protocol, even against a corrupted service provider. This work presents the first rigorous security analysis of the WBP. Concretely, our results can be summarized as follows.

- We formalize the security properties expected from the WBP protocol in terms of a *password-protected key retrieval* (PPKR) scheme, where users store cryptographic keys on an untrusted server, retrievable with a password. This formalization serves as a foundation for our work, and may also support future analyses of alternative (potentially non-HSM-based) PPKR protocols and their comparison.
- We provide a *full description* of the cryptographic core of the WBP protocol. This description is based on a whitepaper published by WhatsApp [31], a public security assessment of the backup system conducted by the NCC Group [18], and personal correspondence with the WBP designers [1] to fill subtle but essential technical gaps left in the protocol descriptions of [18,31].
- We present the *first formal security analysis* of the WBP protocol. Our analysis is conducted in the universal composability (UC) framework [9], which is simulation-based and therefore facilitates the consideration of low-entropy passwords. We formally confirm several prior statements about the security guarantees of the WBP.

- We describe how a corrupted server could get more than ten password guesses per encrypted backup, even though prior security analysis [18] claimed that after ten incorrect tries the account is irremediably locked by the HSM software, and the backup data cannot be retrieved in plaintext. Concretely, we show that a corrupted server can get ten password guesses *per backup initialization*. For example, a corrupted server could suppress protocol messages to simulate a failed initialization, such that either the WhatsApp client app retries sending of initialization messages automatically, or the user re-initializes a backup manually, in order to increase the number of password guesses against the HSM.
- We give a formal analysis of the 2HashDH oblivious pseudorandom function [21] (that is used in OPAQUE) in the multi-key setting, where the domains of the two hash functions used as a building block are not assumed to be separated for different keys. For our work, this result is required since the WBP does not apply hash domain separation. Beyond that, our findings provide the basis for analyzing the *about-to-be-standardized* version of OPAQUE [6][4] and the 2HashDH protocol currently in last call at the IRTF [16] even under the usage of *multiple* OPRF keys.

Paper Organization. The remainder of this work is structured as follows. Section 2 contains technical preliminaries and Sect. 3 provides a full protocol description of the WBP. We then describe our model for PPKR in Sect. 4 and give our formal result in Sect. 5 (the full proof can be found in the full version [17]). Our work concludes with a discussion in Sect. 6.

Responsible Disclosure. The research conducted for this work did not impact the entire WhatsApp system or the privacy of WhatsApp users. In particular, there was no interaction with the WhatsApp servers, HSMs, or any WhatsApp users. The protocol description was written with the help of WhatsApp employees [1], and no reverse-engineering of any implemented code took place. The scenario in which a *corrupt* WhatsApp server can increase the number of password guesses against a user was never demonstrated in practice, but it was acknowledged by WhatsApp that this would indeed be possible. WhatsApp does not object to the publication of this paper.

1.1 Related Work

Password-protected secret sharing (PPSS) [3,21] allows a user to share a secret value among a number of servers and later retrieve it using a partial set of the servers (in the event that one or more servers become compromised or unavailable) if and only if the password used during retrieval is the same as the one

---

[4] The existing formal analysis of the OPAQUE protocol [23] assumes hash domain separation in 2HashDH and hence does not apply to the version of OPAQUE in the most recent Internet Draft [6].

used during the sharing step. This primitive has been analyzed in the UC framework [8,21], and several constructions based on oblivious pseudorandom functions (OPRF) exist (an overview can be found in [11]).

The WhatsApp approach can be viewed as a one-out-of-one version of PPSS, where WhatsApp's HSM is the only server. This makes comparisons with work on PPSS difficult: we need to model corruption of the WhatsApp communication server (but not the HSM) and assess security in this context, something that prior models that do not split the server's role cannot capture. Nonetheless, our formalization of PPKR in the UC model takes great inspiration from existing functionalities for PPSS [21].

Beyond PPSS, there are several works that aim at bootstrapping encryption keys (or symmetric encryptions directly) from user passwords with the assistance of a server. Updatable oblivious key management [22] relies on server assistance to let a user derive file-specific encryption keys from a password, while requiring strong user authentication. The distributed password-authenticated symmetric encryption scheme DPaSE [15] aims for the same, while relying on the assistance of several servers but not requiring user authentication. Like the WBP, all the above schemes rely on OPRFs to shield passwords from curious servers, but none of them aims to provide a restriction in the number of guessing attempts after the compromise of the server, which the WBP aims for.

Password-hardened encryption services [7,26] let users outsource the encryption to a fully trusted frontend server. The protocols do not require OPRFs and can hence provide better throughput, at the cost of revealing the user's password to the frontend server.

2 Preliminaries

Notation. We denote the security parameter as λ. For any $\lambda \in \mathbb{N}$ let 1^λ be the unary representation of λ and let $[\ell] = \{1, \ldots, \ell\}$. We write $x \xleftarrow{\$} S$ to indicate that we choose an element x uniformly at random from set S. For a probabilistic polynomial-time algorithm $\mathcal{A}$ we define $y \xleftarrow{\$} \mathcal{A}(x_1, \ldots, x_\ell)$ as the execution of $\mathcal{A}$ (with fresh random coins) on input $x_1, \ldots, x_\ell$ and assigning the output to y.

We use records of form $\langle x_1, x_2, x_3 \rangle$ for bookkeeping in our formal arguments. For convenience, we introduce a notation that combines retrieval and assignment of such records, i.e., when retrieving $\langle \mathsf{value}, *, * \rangle$, we retrieve a record that contains the value value in the first field and arbitrary values in the second and third field (denoted by a wildcard symbol $*$). Additionally, we use brackets to indicate variable assignment after retrieval, i.e., when retrieving $\langle \mathsf{value}, [x_2], [x_3] \rangle$, we retrieve the record holding the value value in its first entry and assign the second and third entry to the variables x_2 and x_3, respectively.

Cryptographic Building Blocks and Their Security. Due to the lack of space, we do not recap definitions of standard cryptographic building blocks and their security. We refer to the full version [17] for formal definitions.

3   E2EE Backups in WhatsApp

In this section, we give a detailed description of the WBP. Our presentation is based on a whitepaper published by WhatsApp [31], a public security assessment of the backup system conducted by NCC Group [18], and personal correspondence with WhatsApp (Meta) staff [1].

We will start with a simplified explanation of the overall protocol layout in Sect. 3.1 to give a high-level overview of its main idea. Then, to prepare the detailed protocol description, we will discuss the creation of a communication channel between clients and the backup server via the WhatsApp client registration protocol in Sect. 3.2. In Sect. 3.3, we elaborate on how WhatsApp uses HSMs; in Sect. 3.4, we outline how these HSMs outsource storage to servers that are considered untrusted. In Sect. 3.5, we then provide a detailed description of the actual WBP. We conclude with Sect. 3.6, where we describe how a malicious server can increase the admissible number of password guesses in certain settings.

3.1   High-Level Protocol Overview

There are four entities in the system: the user, a WhatsApp client running on the user's device, the WhatsApp server, and the HSM that only the WhatsApp server can communicate with. We will now focus on the latter three. In this high-level overview, we simplify by describing the WhatsApp server as merely relaying messages between the HSM and the client. In the actual WBP protocol it additionally authenticates clients and stores files encrypted by the HSM. As the encryption and outsourced storage of the data at a cloud provider is done using symmetric encryption, we focus on the initialization and recovery of the encryption key from a password.

Initialization. When activating WhatsApp's E2EE backups for the first time, the client chooses a backup key K to encrypt the chat history and the WBP key initialization phase is executed (see Fig. 1). To this end, the client first runs the OPAQUE protocol with the HSM, which takes a password pw from the client and a key K_{OPRF} from the HSM as inputs. It then outputs a key K^{export} to the client[5] and the "envelope" env to the HSM. This envelope is encrypted under the key K^{export} (which is derived using both pw and K_{OPRF}) and contains freshly chosen key material of the client that is used during recovery to perform, e.g., a Diffie–Hellman key exchange, among other things.

---

[5] The option to derive this additional key was originally not part of OPAQUE [23]. However, it exists in the OPAQUE Internet Draft version 03 [25], which is deployed by the WBP.

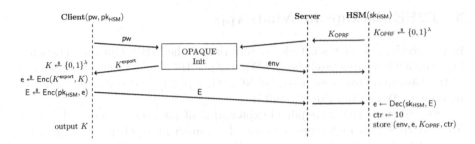

Fig. 1. The WBP key initialization, high-level layout. The value K_{OPRF} is freshly chosen by the HSM for each initialization request.

To conclude initialization, the client encrypts the backup key K first under the symmetric key K^{export} and then under the HSM's public encryption key pk_{HSM}, and sends the result E to the HSM. The HSM removes the outer encryption layer and stores the encrypted backup key e, the OPAQUE envelope env, the key K_{OPRF}, and a counter ctr initialized with 10 that tracks password guessing attempts.

Key Recovery. If the client has lost their client device (and thus lost their backup key K), they can re-authenticate their new client device with WhatsApp (via a challenge-response protocol that takes place after re-installing the WhatsApp application), and subsequently start the recovery part of the WBP depicted in Fig. 2.

The first step of the recovery phase is that client and HSM engage in the key exchange phase of the OPAQUE protocol. To this end, the client uses a value pw' as input and the HSM contributes the values K_{OPRF} and env as established during the initialization phase. If the password pw' entered by the client is equal to the password pw during initialization, the OPAQUE protocol guarantees that (1) the client recovers the former export key $\bar{K}^{export} = K^{export}$ and (2) both client and HSM derive the same value shk' = shk. However, if pw' ≠ pw, the client will have to abort instead.

The HSM decrements its counter for attempted password guesses each time a recovery procedure is initiated. If the client can convince the HSM that it has computed the same value shk' = shk (via a key confirmation), the HSM will learn that the entered password pw' was indeed correct and hence reset its counter to ten and send the stored ciphertext c to the client. Lastly, the client can use the derived $\bar{K}^{export}$ to decrypt the ciphertext c and recover their backup key K. This concludes the high-level overview of the cryptographic core of the WBP.

3.2 Client Registration

The WBP essentially relies on a communication channel between clients and the backup server, which is realized in an indirect way. Upon installing the

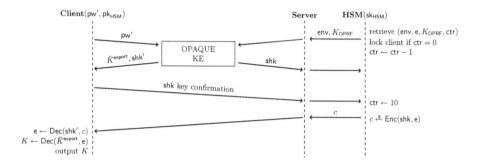

Fig. 2. The WBP key recovery, high-level layout.

WhatsApp application, the main WhatsApp server sets up a mutually authenticated channel with each new client. In the WhatsApp ecosystem this is done by a server called ChatD, which is physically distinct form the WhatsApp server handling the WBP. We decided to view all WhatsApp servers as a single WhatsApp server entity, since a distinction would make the already complex protocol description and security analysis unnecessarily more complex without providing additional insight.[6]

That is, at first, a secure channel is set up between the client and WhatsApp using the Noise framework [28]. Then WhatsApp uses SMS authentication to verify that the phone number it received via the freshly set up Noise channel belongs to the client. Upon conclusion, the client stores WhatsApp's public key pk_{WA}^{Noise} and WhatsApp stores the freshly generated client's public key $pk_{ID_C}^{Noise}$ together with a unique client identifier ID_C. Subsequently, the WhatsApp server handles all incoming client requests via the Noise channel and also mediates the WBP messages between the client and the backup service.

Client with phone number no	WhatsApp server
Noise Pipe Setup →	
no *via Noise Pipe* →	choose ID_C
← n_{SMS} *via SMS*	$n_{SMS} \stackrel{\$}{\leftarrow} \{0,1\}^\lambda$
n'_{SMS} *via Noise Pipe* →	if $n'_{SMS} \neq n_{SMS}$
	return FAIL
	else return $(pk_{ID_C}^{Noise}, ID_C)$
return pk_{WA}^{Noise}	

Fig. 3. The WhatsApp client registration that is independent from the WBP. Upon conclusion, the client can be identified via a unique identifier ID_C, and both client and server are mutually authenticated.

---

[6] For example, we want a corruption of the WhatsApp server to model a malicious WhatsApp service provider, and therefore we want to consider the entire service as corrupted in this case, without a need to distinguish between the ChatD and the backup server.

3.3   Hardware Security Modules

The WBP deploys HSMs as a core component of their PPKR protocol. Intuitively, an HSM is a hardware device that can be programmed once with code and then "locked" in such a way that it is infeasible to change its code afterwards. After the HSMs are set up they hence serve as an incorruptible entity in the backup ecosystem. In the WBP, the HSM performs most cryptographic relevant computations on the "WhatsApp side" (with minor computations performed by a different, non-HSM WhatsApp "main server") and is responsible for coordinating the secure storage of backup keys.

Trusted Setup Ceremony. For the HSM to serve as an incorruptible entity in the system, it must be ensured that (1) its secret key material is not leaked and that (2) its code cannot be modified after setup. This is usually ensured via a process called *trusted setup ceremony* or *key ceremony*. During such a ceremony, a ceremony leader essentially unpacks new modules, sets them up with program code, and generates fresh key material for the HSM (where public keys are copied and secret keys remain secret). After setup, the HSM's "programming key" is destroyed, ensuring that it cannot be modified after the ceremony has taken place. The public key material of the HSM is hard-coded into the WhatsApp application [18]. Naturally, this procedure can only be trusted if it was executed faithfully. For the remainder of this work we assume that the setup ceremony was conducted such that

- the following key material has been generated
  - a symmetric encryption key $K_{\mathsf{HSM}}^{\mathsf{Enc}} \xleftarrow{\$} \{0,1\}^{\lambda}$,
  - a signature key pair $(\mathsf{sk}_{\mathsf{HSM}}^{\mathsf{Sig}}, \mathsf{pk}_{\mathsf{HSM}}^{\mathsf{Sig}}) \xleftarrow{\$} \Sigma.\mathsf{KeyGen}(1^{\lambda})$,
  - a public-key encryption key pair $(\mathsf{sk}_{\mathsf{HSM}}^{\mathsf{Enc}}, \mathsf{pk}_{\mathsf{HSM}}^{\mathsf{Enc}}) \xleftarrow{\$} \mathsf{PKE}.\mathsf{KeyGen}(1^{\lambda})$,
  - a static Diffie–Hellman key pair $(\mathsf{sk}_{\mathsf{HSM}}^{\mathsf{DH}}, \mathsf{pk}_{\mathsf{HSM}}^{\mathsf{DH}}) \xleftarrow{\$} \mathsf{DH}.\mathsf{KeyGen}(1^{\lambda})$;
- the HSM uses the secret key material to execute the WBP's computations via predefined interfaces for each protocol step;
- the HSM can only be queried by a WhatsApp server, and only via the specified interfaces. In particular, the HSM does not leak any of its secret key material.

We remark that the HSM solution deployed by WhatsApp consists of multiple HSMs, which ensures that user cannot get locked out of their backup if an HSM breaks down. All HSMs are set up such that they coordinate their state changes via a consensus protocol, ensuring that each HSM behaves in the same manner towards a user [1]. Without loss of generality, we treat this set of HSMs as a single HSM entity. The analysis of the HSM consensus protocol is beyond the scope of this work.

3.4 Secure Outsourced Storage

One might be tempted to store sensitive data along with key material in an HSM. However, storing data in the internal memory of an HSM is very expensive and limited in capacity. Thus, the internal storage of an HSM is not viable to store large quantities of sensitive data for millions or billions of users. Therefore WhatsApp uses storage fully controlled by the WhatsApp server. The HSM uses a dedicated symmetric encryption key $K_{\mathsf{HSM}}^{\mathsf{Enc}} \xleftarrow{\$} \{0,1\}^{\lambda}$ which is used for authenticated encryption, and this essentially ensures confidentiality and integrity of stored records. Whenever the HSM requests a stored record, it decrypts the record and verifies its integrity before processing it. In addition, a Merkle tree based protocol is deployed to "tie" the encrypted records together and to prevent a replay of old state records that were previously deleted by the HSM. Whenever the WhatsApp server provides an encrypted record to the HSM, it also has to provide a proof (using the Merkle tree) that this ciphertext is consistent with the current state of the encrypted database. The HSM verifies this against a locally stored root of the Merkle tree. If this verification fails, the HSM rejects the record. A formal analysis of this mechanism is beyond the scope of our work. Therefore we model the interaction of the HSM with the outsourced storage mechanism via function calls, which are defined as follows.

- $\mathsf{sec\_store}(\mathsf{id}, \mathsf{data})$ takes as input a unique identifier id and to-be-stored data value data. It encrypts the data using the approach described above. The record can be identified via id.
- $\mathsf{sec\_retr}(\mathsf{id})$ takes as input an identifier id and retrieves the record associated with identifier id. The returned record is processed as described above.
- $\mathsf{sec\_delete}(\mathsf{id})$ takes as input an identifier id and "tombstones" the record associated with identifier id, in that its existing data is overwritten with the information that is has been deleted.
- For brevity, we define one additional function call that allows the HSM to change counter values. $\mathsf{sec\_set\_ctr}(\mathsf{id}, \mathsf{ctr})$ takes as input an identifier id and an integer ctr with $0 \leq \mathsf{ctr} \leq 10$. It takes the record associated with identifier id and sets the corresponding counter to the value ctr. Integrity and authenticity is ensured via the process described above.

Should any of the function calls fail (e.g., due to a non-existing record or a failed integrity check), the respective function call would return an error symbol $\perp$. We assume that this mechanism provides secure outsourced storage for the HSM, which is immutable for any entity but the HSM.

3.5   WhatsApp Backup Protocol (WBP) Description

The detailed descriptions of the WBP's key initialization and recovery phases are depicted in Fig. 4 and Fig. 5, respectively. As already discussed in Sect. 3.1, the WBP builds on the OPAQUE Internet Draft v3 [25], the steps of which are highlighted in the figures. For a comparison of these OPAQUE steps with [25], we refer to the full version [17]. Note that the figures include events like **return**(INTERFACE, value). These can bee seen as messages delivered to higher-level application processes, which, e.g., output a successfully established symmetric backup key to be used for backing up the actual data. We make these calls explicit since they will also appear in parts of our security model.

Participants. There are three participants in the protocol. Client refers to the WhatsApp client application of a user with unique identifier ID_C. The client is

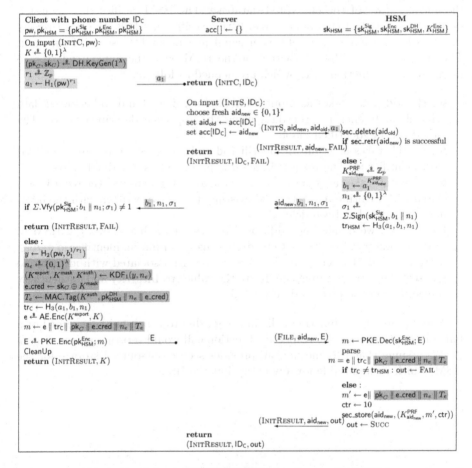

Fig. 4. The WBP initialization. Light blue boxes indicate 2HashDH instructions of OPAQUE; dark gray boxes denote other OPAQUE instructions; non-colored parts were added by WhatsApp. $\overset{a}{\longrightarrow}\bullet$ is the ID_C-authenticated transmission of a.

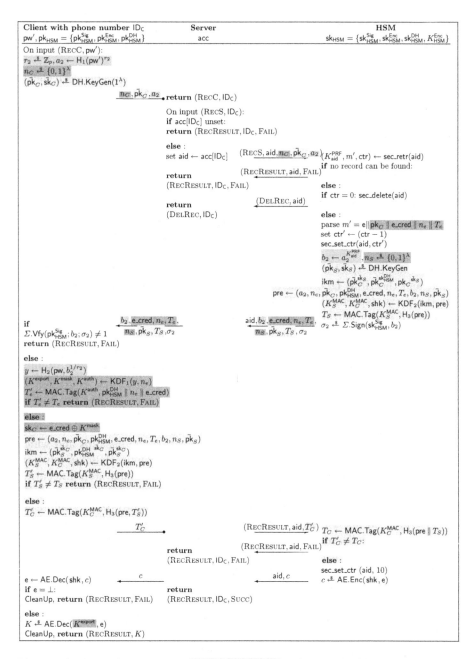

Fig. 5. The WBP key recovery. Light blue boxes indicate 2HashDH instructions of OPAQUE; light gray boxes mark 3DH of OPAQUE; dark gray boxes denote other OPAQUE instructions; non-colored parts were added by WhatsApp. $\xrightarrow{\ \ a\ \ }\bullet$ is the $\mathsf{ID_C}$-authenticated transmission of a.

in possession of the HSM's public key, which is composed of a public key for a signature scheme pk_{HSM}^{Sig}, an encryption public key pk_{HSM}^{Enc}, and a static Diffie–Hellman public key pk_{HSM}^{DH}. Those keys are hard-coded into the WhatsApp client and thus authenticated.

The server is run by WhatsApp and it mostly relays messages between clients and the HSM. For this it communicates with the client via the previously established ID_C-authenticated channel (see Fig. 3) and with the HSM directly through a TLS channel. The server also maintains an array $acc[\cdot]$ of identifier pairs (ID_C, aid), which "tie" a so-called *account identifier* aid (described below) to the client identifier ID_C. If some ID_C is not contained in acc, we let $acc[ID_C] = \bot$. As already described in Sect. 3.4, the server also acts as an external (untrusted) storage medium for the HSM.

Finally the HSM is (a trusted entity that is) in possession of the secret keys sk_{HSM}^{Sig}, sk_{HSM}^{Enc}, sk_{HSM}^{DH} corresponding to the respective public keys, as well as a key K_{HSM}^{Enc} that is used to encrypt records stored on the server (see Sect. 3.3).

Dealing with Unexpected Protocol Messages. We assume that the client, the server, and the HSM ignore messages that are sent out-of-order, i.e., messages that the party expects at a different point in the protocol execution. The first messages of an initialization (i.e., a_1) and recovery (i.e., $(n_C, \bar{pk}_C, a_2)$) can be sent anytime, leading to the parties deleting all temporary data of the non-finished initialization/recovery and starting with a new initialization/recovery. This implies that there is never more than one initialization/recovery running at a time.

Key Initialization. A user with password pw and ID_C initializes the backup as follows. On input of pw, the WhatsApp client app first chooses a uniformly random backup key K that can be used for encrypting the backups and which is going to be preserved via WBP. Next, it samples a Diffie–Hellman key-pair (pk_C, sk_C) that will be used later in the OPAQUE key exchange step. Executing the 2HashDH OPRF protocol [20] with the HSM, the client samples $r_1 \xleftarrow{\$} \mathbb{Z}_p$ uniformly at random. This is then used to blind the password pw by computing $a_1 \leftarrow H_1(pw)^{r_1}$ using a hash function $H_1 \colon \{0,1\}^* \to \mathbb{G}$. The client sends a_1 to the server over the ID_C-authenticated channel.

Upon receiving a_1 from ID_C, the server chooses a fresh $aid_{new} \in \{0,1\}^*$ that is called "account identifier" by WhatsApp[7] and checks if the client with ID_C has ever initiated the protocol and thus has already an aid in its array acc. If so, it sets $aid_{old} \leftarrow acc[ID_C]$ and $acc[ID_C] \leftarrow aid_{new}$, otherwise it sets $aid_{old} = \bot$. Finally, the server sends $aid_{new}, aid_{old}, a_1$ to the HSM. Observe that the HSM *never* receives any identifying information (e.g., ID_C) about the clients other than the value aid. That is, the HSM is *not* aware of the concept of a client ID_C.

---

[7] We remark that this terminology is slightly misleading, as aid does not identify a client's account but is rather a "backup identifier". If the same client initializes many backups, possibly with different passwords, then each backup will be assigned a new aid and only the most recent backup is kept.

Upon receiving the server's message, the HSM "tombstones" all information associated with $\mathsf{aid_{old}}$ from its outsourced storage (with the instruction $\mathsf{sec\_delete}(\mathsf{aid_{old}})$). Then it checks whether $\mathsf{aid_{new}}$ has ever been used before.[8] If it was, then the HSM aborts and outputs $\mathsf{aid_{new}}, \text{FAIL}$ to the server. If the HSM sees $\mathsf{aid_{new}}$ for the first time, it picks a random key $K^{\mathsf{PRF}}_{\mathsf{aid_{new}}} \xleftarrow{\$} \mathbb{Z}_p$ for that specific $\mathsf{aid_{new}}$ to be used in the 2HashDH OPRF. The HSM then uses the client's blinded password a_1 to compute $b_1 \leftarrow a_1^{K^{\mathsf{PRF}}_{\mathsf{aid_{new}}}}$. Furthermore, the HSM samples a nonce $n_1 \xleftarrow{\$} \{0,1\}^\lambda$ uniformly at random and signs $b_1 \parallel n_1$ under its secret key $\mathsf{sk}^{\mathsf{Sig}}_{\mathsf{HSM}}$. Finally, it computes a transcript hash $\mathsf{tr_{HSM}}$ of the values a_1, b_1, n_1 with a hash function $\mathsf{H_3} \colon \{0,1\}^* \to \{0,1\}^\lambda$, and sends back $\mathsf{aid_{new}}, b_1, n_1$ together with the resulting signature σ_1 to the server, which relays b_1, n_1, σ_1 to the client.

After receiving the HSM's message from the server, the client first verifies σ_1 using $\mathsf{pk}^{\mathsf{Sig}}_{\mathsf{HSM}}$ and aborts if the verification fails. Otherwise, it unblinds the server's response b_1 using the randomness r_1 and derives the OPRF output $y \leftarrow \mathsf{H_2}(\mathsf{pw}, b_1^{1/r_1})$ with hash function $\mathsf{H_2} \colon \{0,1\}^* \to \{0,1\}^\lambda$. Next, further keys $K^{\mathsf{export}}, K^{\mathsf{mask}}, K^{\mathsf{auth}}$ are derived from the OPRF output y with the help of a key derivation function $\mathsf{KDF_1}$. The obtained keys are used as follows. K^{mask} is used as an XOR mask to obtain $\mathsf{e\_cred}$, hiding the client's Diffie-Hellman secret $\mathsf{sk_C}$. K^{auth} is used to compute a MAC tag T_e over $\mathsf{pk}^{\mathsf{DH}}_{\mathsf{HSM}} \parallel n_e \parallel \mathsf{e\_cred}$, where n_e is a randomly sampled nonce of length λ. Finally, K^{export} is used to encrypt K to produce the envelope[9] $\mathsf{e} \leftarrow \mathsf{AE.Enc}(K^{\mathsf{export}}, K)$. Similarly to the HSM, the client also computes a transcript hash $\mathsf{tr_C} \leftarrow \mathsf{H_3}(a_1, b_1, n_1)$ and compose a message $m \leftarrow \mathsf{e} \parallel \mathsf{tr_C} \parallel \mathsf{pk_C} \parallel \mathsf{e\_cred} \parallel n_e \parallel T_e$, which is then encrypted under the HSM's public key ($E \leftarrow \mathsf{PKE.Enc}(\mathsf{pk}^{\mathsf{Enc}}_{\mathsf{HSM}}, m)$) to hide its content from the intermediary server. The encrypted envelope E is sent to the server over the $\mathsf{ID_C}$-authenticated channel. The client runs $\mathsf{CleanUp}$ to delete all assigned variables and received messages[10] (including $r_1, \mathsf{sk_C}$) and outputs the backup key K.

Upon receiving E from a client with $\mathsf{ID_C}$, the server looks up $\mathsf{acc}[\mathsf{ID_C}] \leftarrow \mathsf{aid_{new}}$ and forwards $\mathsf{aid_{new}}, E$ to the HSM. After receiving the message, the HSM decrypts E and checks whether the received transcript hash $\mathsf{tr_C}$ matches its own view of the transcript ($\mathsf{tr_{HSM}}$). If the transcripts do not match, it aborts sending $\mathsf{aid_{new}}, \text{FAIL}$ to the server that outputs $\mathsf{ID_C}, \text{FAIL}$. In case of matching transcripts, the HSM initializes a counter ctr that aims to track the unsuccessful key recovery attempts and stores in the secure storage the tuple ($\mathsf{aid_{new}}, K^{\mathsf{PRF}}_{\mathsf{aid_{new}}}, \mathsf{e} \parallel \mathsf{pk_C} \parallel \mathsf{e\_cred} \parallel n_e \parallel T_e, \mathsf{ctr}$). Finally, it informs the server about the successful completion of the initialization phase by sending $\mathsf{aid_{new}}, \text{SUCC}$ that outputs $\mathsf{ID_C}, \text{SUCC}$ concluding the key initialization.

---

[8] To this end, the HSM tries to retrieve a backup associated with $\mathsf{aid_{new}}$ from the secure storage. If $\mathsf{aid_{new}}$ is currently in use, this will succeed. If $\mathsf{aid_{new}}$ was previously used but corresponds to an already deleted backup, an empty "tombstoned" backup is returned to the HSM, showing that $\mathsf{aid_{new}}$ is not fresh.

[9] Note that the WBP's envelope is not equivalent to an OPAQUE envelope.

[10] We note that the abstract $\mathsf{CleanUp}$ instruction might be implemented without any explicit deletion, e.g., by keeping these ephemeral values only in volatile memory and never storing them persistently.

Key Recovery. The goal of the WBP recovery phase is to enable users, who do not have access anymore to their backup key K, to recover it using the password they entered during key initialization. On input of pw', the WhatsApp client app first prepares its input r_2, a_2 to the 2HashDH OPRF the same way as during initialization, samples an ephemeral Diffie–Hellman key-pair $(\bar{pk}_C, \bar{sk}_C)$ for the 3DH protocol, and also samples a uniformly random nonce n_C. Then $n_C, \bar{pk}_C, a_2$ are sent to the server over the ID_C-authenticated channel.

Upon receiving the client's message, the server checks the array acc and if it does not contain ID_C, then it aborts because no user with the identifier ID_C initialized any backup keys. Otherwise, it attaches the account identifier $aid \leftarrow acc[ID_C]$ to the client's message and sends these to the HSM.

When receiving the server's message, the HSM retrieves the record from the secure storage that is indexed by aid. If no such record is found, it returns failure to the server. Otherwise the HSM retrieves the record containing the per-client OPRF-key K_{aid}^{PRF}, the current counter value ctr, and m' that is parsed as $m' = e \parallel pk_C \parallel e\_cred \parallel n_e \parallel T_e$. If $ctr = 0$, then the HSM deletes the record indexed with aid from the storage and informs the server of this. If $ctr > 0$, then its value is decreased by one and the stored record for aid is updated with the new ctr value. Next, as in the key initialization phase, the HSM computes $b_2 \leftarrow a_2^{K_{aid}^{PRF}}$ as a step of 2HsahDH. After sampling a uniformly random nonce n_S, the execution of the 3DH protocol steps follows. The HSM samples an ephemeral Diffie–Hellman key pair $(\bar{pk}_S, \bar{sk}_S)$ and computes three shared Diffie–Hellman secrets: $\bar{pk}_C^{\bar{sk}_S}, \bar{pk}_C^{sk_{HSM}^{DH}}, pk_C^{\bar{sk}_S}$. Using these shared secrets and the preamble pre, which is essentially a concatenation of the full protocol transcript $(a_2, n_c, \bar{pk}_C, pk_{HSM}^{DH}, e\_cred, n_e, T_e, b_2, n_S, \bar{pk}_S)$, it derives the keys K_S^{MAC}, K_C^{MAC}, and shk from a key derivation function KDF_2. Finally, with K_S^{MAC} it computes a MAC tag T_S over the hashed preamble, signs b_2 with sk_{HSM}^{Sig} to get signature σ_2 and sends its response composed of $aid, b_2, e\_cred, n_e, T_e, n_S, \bar{pk}_S, T_S, \sigma_2$ to the server, who removes aid from the message and forwards the rest to the client.

After receiving the HSM's response from the server, the client first verifies the signature σ_2 and aborts if the verification fails. It then again derives the keys $K^{export}, K^{mask}, K^{auth}$ and verifies the MAC T_e that was created during the initialization. If the verification failed, it aborts. Otherwise it continues to reconstruct sk_C by unmasking e_cred with K^{mask} and then to derive the keys $K_S^{MAC}, K_C^{MAC}, shk$ from the three shared Diffie–Hellman secrets $\bar{pk}_S^{\bar{sk}_C}, sk_{HSM}^{DH \, sk_C}, \bar{pk}_S^{sk_C}$ and the preamble pre. Using K_S^{MAC} it verifies the MAC T_S and aborts if this is not successful. Otherwise the client computes MAC T_C' over a hash of $pre \parallel T_S$ with the key K_C^{MAC}, which it then sends to the server through the ID_C-authenticated channel.

After attaching aid to T_C', the server forwards these values to the HSM. Since the HSM knows all values for computing the MAC tag that it has just received, it can verify the MAC. Note that with the MAC verification it essentially checks whether $pw = pw'$. If the MAC verification fails, it aborts, otherwise it resets the counter ctr to 10. Finally, the HSM encrypts e using shk and sends the resulting ciphertext c and aid to the server who forwards c to the client.

As the final steps of the recovery phase, the client first decrypts c to obtain e (it aborts if the AE decryption fails) and then decrypts e using the key K^{export} to obtain the backup key K. As in case of the initialization, before returning any output, the client always deletes all assigned variables and received messages (including $\text{shk}, \text{sk}_C \bar{\text{sk}}_C, r_2$).

3.6   Extending the Number of Password Guesses

As we already noted in the protocol description in Sect. 3.5, the WBP only authenticates the client towards the server but not towards the HSM. The usage of the so-called "account identifier" aid aims to bridge this gap. The way it is used ensures that the HSM always associates every recovery request from the same ID_C with the same unique aid that was assigned for this ID_C during its last successful key initialization request. Furthermore, the HSM only keeps records of the last key initialization of a user under the aid that was assigned to the corresponding ID_C during this last initialization. Recall that in order to limit the number of password guesses against some account, each password guess has to be associated with the targeted account. It turns out that this cannot be guaranteed in case of the WBP when the server is malicious. The reason for this is that the server is in charge of assigning aids for ID_Cs, and neither the client nor the HSM can check this because the former never sees their assigned aid, and the latter never learns the ID_C of clients. This allows the server to increase the number of password guesses in certain cases.

We demonstrate the attack with an example. Let us assume that some client with identity ID_C has already initialized a key and the HSM stored the corresponding record under aid. Now if the same client runs key initialization again with the same password,[11] the server is assumed to instruct the HSM to delete the previous record by setting $\text{aid}_{\text{old}} \leftarrow \text{aid}$. However, the execution of this step completely depends on the server acting honestly. A malicious server might however proceed as if it has never seen ID_C before and make the HSM store q_I records for ID_C, if the client with ID_C runs the key initialisation q_I times. If the client used the same password pw all q_I times, the malicious server will have $10q_I$ password guessing opportunities, since it knows all the q_I aids that are associated with ID_C's records.

Mitigating the Attack. If the transcripts tr_{HSM} and tr_C contained information about the client identity ID_C, in a way that both the client and the HSM can verify this, then they would be able to notice if the server is dishonest about the client identity. However, note that this countermeasure is very difficult to deploy retroactively, since any changes in the programming of the HSM would require the setup ceremony to be performed again.

---

[11] WhatsApp is for mobile devices, connection loss may happen leading to a failure. After an unsuccessful attempt, the user would most probably re-run initialization, likely with the same password.

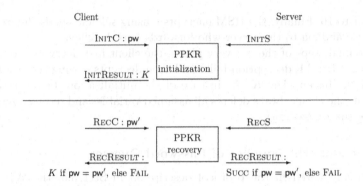

Fig. 6. Schematic overview of password-protected key retrieval with initialization on top and recovery at the bottom, already using the interface names of our functionality $\mathcal{F}_{\mathsf{PPKR}}$. In both phases, the server does not provide any particular input but still has to participate in the protocol for the client to successfully initialize and recover a key K, which is modeled in the ideal functionality by letting it provide the INITS and RECS messages.

4   Password-Protected Key Retrieval

In this section we give a formal definition of password-protected key retrieval (PPKR) in terms of an ideal functionality. For the unfamiliar reader, we provide a short introduction to the basic UC framework in the full version [17].

The Cryptographic Abstraction of the WBP. We introduce the concept of a *password-protected key retrieval* (PPKR) protocol, which is a 2-party protocol executed by a client and a server. (Note that in the WBP protocol, this client is the user's WhatsApp client and this server is the combination of the WhatsApp server and the HSM.) A PPKR protocol consists of two phases: (1) an initialization phase, where the client generates a symmetric encryption key and, using a password, securely stores it with a server, and (2) a recovery phase, where the client can recover their symmetric encryption key using a password.

The server may neither learn any information about the client's password, nor their key from these interactions, but only whether a recovery was successful. To provide a high-level intuition, we depict the input-output behavior of the PPKR functionality in Fig. 6. Besides this, we demand several properties from a PPKR scheme that seem relevant for such a primitive in practice. These include protection against online and offline dictionary attacks, and that it provides cryptographically strong encryption keys.

Remark 1. We note here that alternative modelings are possible. For example, one could case-tailor the definition to the WhatsApp setting and formulate a variant of PPKR with three parties: the client, the server, and the HSM. However, our notion with only two parties is more versatile: it can be used to analyze protocols where the server relies on an HSM, as well as protocols where the server acts on its own, or relies on arbitrarily many other entities, such as a cloud provider, offline storage, etc. The reason why this is possible is that usage of such "helpers" is well integrated into the UC framework [9] through the notion of so-called *hybrid functionalities*, which can be modularly "plugged" into protocol descriptions without "spilling" into the definition of the underlying primitive.

Expected Security Properties. We now describe which security properties we intuitively expect from a PPKR scheme, and thus want to formalize in an ideal PPKR functionality $\mathcal{F}_{\mathsf{PPKR}}$. The key K that is generated in a PPKR scheme should be usable without restrictions in any other application, thus we require that K is indistinguishable from random. Note that in particular this implies that neither the server nor the adversary can influence the generation of K in any way. Moreover, we expect K to remain secret from everyone but the client that computed it throughout the lifetime of the PPKR protocol. Hence, $\mathcal{F}_{\mathsf{PPKR}}$ should leak no information on the key, and any output given by $\mathcal{F}_{\mathsf{PPKR}}$ to the server or the adversary must be independent from K, unless the server gets corrupted and correctly guesses the client's password. In order to limit the ability to guess passwords via dictionary attacks, we expect $\mathcal{F}_{\mathsf{PPKR}}$ to (1) not leak any information about a password used by some client to any other party beyond whether a password used in a recovery is the same as in the most recent initialization by that client, and (2) allow only a small number of failed recovery attempts before K is deleted. We further expect that clients are authenticated towards the server[12] and cannot be impersonated by other clients or the adversary, to ensure that any client's key remains secret from all other clients even if they knew the correct password. However, note that a corrupt server might be able to skip client authentication[13] and execute the protocol on behalf of any client by itself, i.e., without interacting with any client. Further, we expect that the server is authenticated towards clients and cannot be impersonated by the adversary.

We summarize the list of expected security properties below.

- **Pseudorandomness of** K: Honest clients compute pseudorandom keys K, even if the server acts maliciously.
- **Secrecy of** K: Initialized and recovered keys of any honest client remain hidden from even a malicious server as long as the server does not correctly guess the honest client's password.
- **Uniqueness of** K: If the server is honest, initialization of a key K by user C buries any key that C previously initialized.

---

[12] We leave the concrete means of authentication to the application. In the case of the WBP, SMS-based authentication is used, creating a one-to-one correspondence between ID_C and phone numbers of WhatsApp users. Other authentication methods such as biometrics (where ID_C would correspond to, e.g., a fingerprint) or even device-bound strong authentication using signatures are possible as well.

[13] We opted for a general treatment here, i.e., allowing client impersonation by the server. In fact, we could strengthen this (see Sect. 4.2 for more details) but this depends on which mechanisms on the server side are corruptible.

- **Oblivious passwords**: The initialization phase does not leak any information about the password to even a malicious server.
- **No online dictionary attacks**: The recovery phase does not leak any information (1) about the password used by the client to even a malicious server, and (2) about the initialized password to even a malicious client, beyond whether the password used during recovery matches the one used to create the backup.
- **Limited number of recovery attempts with wrong passwords**: Let K denote the key initialized by honest client C, and assume that C later runs the recovery phase 10 times consecutively with a wrong password. Then the server erases all K-dependent information, i.e., K cannot be recovered anymore. This must hold even if the client becomes maliciously corrupted after initializing K.
- **Limited number of offline guesses**: The above guarantee extends to maliciously corrupted servers, i.e., after 10 wrong password guesses to recover any honestly initialized key K, K is buried and cannot be retrieved by anyone anymore.[14]
- **Client authentication**: Only the client who initialized K or a malicious server can attempt to recover K. This must hold even if the password used during initialization becomes publicly known.
- **Server authentication**: There is only one server in the system and it cannot be impersonated by the adversary, unless the server gets corrupted.

4.1   A PPKR Functionality

In Figs. 7 and 8 we describe the ideal functionality $\mathcal{F}_{PPKR}$ for password-protected key retrieval. On a high level, $\mathcal{F}_{PPKR}$ implements a password protected lookup table that contains clients' keys. When some client executes the initialization phase, an entry for that client is created in the lookup table or updated if an entry already existed. By executing the recovery phase, clients can access their entry in the table and recover their key, but only if they pass password authentication. If they fail password authentication 10 times in a row, $\mathcal{F}_{PPKR}$ "buries the key" by erasing the corresponding table entry of that user. Note that while $\mathcal{F}_{PPKR}$ maintains the table entries using client *identifiers*, $\mathcal{F}_{PPKR}$ does not enforce the initialization and recovery processes to run on the same physical client machine. In our model, we understand the client's party identifier as the identity under which the client device can authenticate. This way, if multiple devices can authenticate under the same identity (as is possible, e.g., for the SMS-based authentication in the WBP), INITC and RECC can be called from different machines.

---

[14] Note that the phrasing "any initialized" here reflects that the adversary can extend the number of admissible password guesses, as described in Sect. 3.6. This is necessary to model the security achieved by WhatsApp's protocol. We will discuss in Sect. 4.2 how the functionality can be strengthened.

Next we will explain the interfaces and record keeping of $\mathcal{F}_{\mathsf{PPKR}}$. In Figs. 7 and 8 we labeled all instructions for easy referencing. $\mathcal{F}_{\mathsf{PPKR}}$ interacts with arbitrary clients and a single server S, where S is encoded in the session identifier sid (**server authentication**). The functionality internally maintains different types of records to keep track of ongoing and finished initialization and recovery phases. If $\mathcal{F}_{\mathsf{PPKR}}$ ever tries to retrieve a record that does not exist, it ignores the query causing this.

Initialization Phase. Whenever a client $\mathsf{ID_C}$ starts a new initialization, it calls the INITC interface with the password pw the user has chosen. $\mathcal{F}_{\mathsf{PPKR}}$ then (IC.1) generates a fresh key $K \xleftarrow{\$} \{0,1\}^\lambda$ (ensuring **pseudorandomness** of K) for $\mathsf{ID_C}$ and records that $\mathsf{ID_C}$ has started a new initialization by creating a record $\langle$INITC, sid, $\mathsf{ID_C}$, pw, $K \rangle$ (IC.2). This newly created record overwrites any existing record of type INITC for $\mathsf{ID_C}$, which ensures that a client can only have one ongoing intialization session. Finally, the functionality informs the server S and the adversary $\mathcal{A}$ that the client $\mathsf{ID_C}$ has started a new initialization (IC.3).

If the server agrees to participate in the initialization with $\mathsf{ID_C}$, it calls the INITS interface, which takes as input two (not necessarily distinct) client identities $\mathsf{ID_C}$ and $\mathsf{ID_C}^*$. The additional identity $\mathsf{ID_C}^*$ is only effective if the server is corrupt, and reflects that a malicious server can simply ignore client authentication and claim a different identity has authenticated to him. $\mathcal{F}_{\mathsf{PPKR}}$ now retrieves the INITC record of $\mathsf{ID_C}$, which ensures that the query only proceeds if $\mathsf{ID_C}$ has started a new initialization (IS.1). Then it creates a FILE record containing the password pw and key K from the retrieved INITC record and, depending on whether the server is honest or corrupt, either the identity $\mathsf{ID_C}$ or $\mathsf{ID_C}^*$ (IS.2 and IS.3). Thus, a corrupt server can freely choose for which identity the FILE record is created, while FILE records created for an honest server always contain the same identity as the corresponding INITC record. A newly created record overwrites any existing record of the same identity to ensure that any key K' that may have been generated in a previous initialization by $\mathsf{ID_C}$ cannot be recovered anymore (**Uniqueness of the key**). However, since a malicious server can make $\mathcal{F}_{\mathsf{PPKR}}$ store files under different identities $\mathsf{ID_C}^*$, this guarantee holds only as long as the server is honest. Indeed, $\mathcal{F}_{\mathsf{PPKR}}$ allows a malicious server to make $\mathcal{F}_{\mathsf{PPKR}}$ store *all the password-protected key records* that any honest client ever initialized (see Sect. 4.2 for a discussion of this weakness).

After the server agreed to participate in the initialization with $\mathsf{ID_C}$, the adversary may let $\mathcal{F}_{\mathsf{PPKR}}$ compute the output of the initialization phase for the client with either the interface COMPLETEINITC or COMPLETEINITC-DOS and for the server with either COMPLETEINITS or COMPLETEINITS-DOS. The functionality does not enforce an order in which the parties receive their output and leaves this decision to the adversary $\mathcal{A}$. All these interfaces ensure that only one output can be generated towards client and server for every ongoing initialization session, by retrieving (CIC.1, CICD.1) and deleting (CIS.1, CISD.1) the corresponding session records (in the case of CIS.1, the record is not deleted but assigned a special marking - see below for details). The adversary's choices are as follows:

$\mathcal{F}_{\text{PPKR}}$ is parameterized with a security parameter λ. $\mathcal{F}_{\text{PPKR}}$ talks to a server S where S is encoded in sid. $\mathcal{F}_{\text{PPKR}}$ also talks to the adversary $\mathcal{A}$, and arbitrary clients ID_C. If the functionality tries to "retrieve a record" that does not exist, it ignores the incoming message. We write $\text{tx}_{\text{sid}}[\cdot]$ for a list of counters.

Offline attacks

On input $(\text{MALICIOUSINIT}, \text{sid}, \text{ID}_C, \text{pw}^*, K^*)$ from $\mathcal{A}$: // A corrupt server can impersonate an either honest or corrupt ID_C and initialize on his behalf.
    MI.1 If S is honest ignore this input.
    MI.2 Record $\langle \text{FILE}, \text{sid}, \text{ID}_C, \text{pw}^*, K^* \rangle$, overwriting any existing record $\langle \text{FILE}, \text{sid}, \text{ID}_C, *, * \rangle$. Set $\text{tx}_{\text{sid}}[\text{ID}_C] \leftarrow 10$

On input $(\text{MALICIOUSREC}, \text{sid}, \text{ID}_C, \text{pw}^*)$ from $\mathcal{A}$: // Attacking an honest client's stored key: bury the key after 10 subsequent wrong password guesses.
    MR.1 If S is honest ignore this input. // Server needs to be corrupt to mount an offline attack.
    MR.2 Retrieve record $\langle \text{FILE}, \text{sid}, \text{ID}_C, [\text{pw}], [K] \rangle$ marked STORED.
    MR.3 If $\text{tx}_{\text{sid}}[\text{ID}_C] = 0$, delete record $\langle \text{FILE}, \text{sid}, \text{ID}_C, \text{pw}, K \rangle$ and output $(\text{DELREC}, \text{sid}, \text{ID}_C)$ to $\mathcal{A}$ // The key is buried if zero guesses remain.
    MR.4 If $\text{pw}^* = \text{pw}$, set $\text{tx}_{\text{sid}}[\text{ID}_C] \leftarrow 10$ and output (sid, K) to $\mathcal{A}$. Otherwise, set $\text{tx}_{\text{sid}}[\text{ID}_C] \leftarrow \text{tx}_{\text{sid}}[\text{ID}_C] - 1$ an output $(\text{sid}, \text{FAIL})$ to $\mathcal{A}$

Initialization phase

On input $(\text{INITC}, \text{sid}, \text{ID}_C, \text{pw})$ from ID_C (or $\mathcal{A}$ if ID_C is corrupt): // Client always starts initialization
    IC.1 Choose $K \xleftarrow{\$} \{0,1\}^\lambda$
    IC.2 Record $\langle \text{INITC}, \text{sid}, \text{ID}_C, \text{pw}, K \rangle$, overwriting any existing record $\langle \text{INITC}, \text{sid}, \text{ID}_C, *, * \rangle$ // Storing ID_C's current init state; a client can only be in one initialization session
    IC.3 Send $(\text{INITC}, \text{sid}, \text{ID}_C)$ to $\mathcal{A}$ and to S

On input $(\text{INITS}, \text{sid}, \text{ID}_C, \boxed{\text{ID}_C^*})$ from S (or $\mathcal{A}$ if S is corrupt): // Server agrees to assist ID_C in initialization. If S is corrupt, $\mathcal{A}$ can reroute the initialization to a different ID_C^*. Note that ID_C^* does not have to be the identity of an existing client and can be an arbitrary identity
    IS.1 Retrieve $\langle \text{INITC}, \text{sid}, \text{ID}_C, [\text{pw}], [K] \rangle$ // Continue only if ID_C started initialization already
    IS.2 $\boxed{\text{If S is honest,}}$ record $\langle \text{FILE}, \text{sid}, \text{ID}_C, \text{pw}, K \rangle$, overwriting any existing record $\langle \text{FILE}, \text{sid}, \text{ID}_C, *, * \rangle$, and send $(\text{INITS}, \text{sid}, \text{ID}_C)$ to $\mathcal{A}$ // Storing S's current init state; the server can only be in one initialization session. Invariant: There is only one key stored
    IS.3 $\boxed{\text{Otherwise, record } \langle \text{FILE}, \text{sid}, \text{ID}_C^*, \text{pw}, K \rangle, \text{ overwriting any existing record}}$ $\boxed{\langle \text{FILE}, \text{sid}, \text{ID}_C^*, *, * \rangle.}$

On input $(\text{COMPLETEINITC}, \text{sid}, \text{ID}_C)$ from $\mathcal{A}$: // Client completes the protocol and outputs a key
    CIC.1 Retrieve record $\langle \text{INITC}, \text{sid}, \text{ID}_C, *, [K] \rangle$ and delete it
    CIC.2 Output $(\text{INITRESULT}, \text{sid}, K)$ to ID_C (or $\mathcal{A}$ if ID_C is corrupt)

On input $(\text{COMPLETEINITS}, \text{sid}, \text{ID}_C)$ from $\mathcal{A}$: // Server concludes initialization with file storage
    CIS.1 Retrieve record $\langle \text{FILE}, \text{sid}, \text{ID}_C, *, * \rangle$ not marked STORED and mark it STORED // Note: there is only one such record thanks to overwriting in INITS interface. This becomes the stored key now!
    CIS.2 Set $\text{tx}_{\text{sid}}[\text{ID}_C] \leftarrow 10$
    CIS.3 Send $(\text{INITRESULT}, \text{sid}, \text{ID}_C, \text{SUCC})$ to S (or $\mathcal{A}$ if S is corrupt)

Attacks on Initialization Phase

On input $(\text{COMPLETEINITC-DoS}, \text{sid}, \text{ID}_C)$ from $\mathcal{A}$: // DoS attack against ID_C, who concludes the initialization session with failure.
    CICD.1 Retrieve record $\langle \text{INITC}, \text{sid}, \text{ID}_C, *, * \rangle$ and delete it
    CICD.2 Output $(\text{INITRESULT}, \text{sid}, \text{FAIL})$ to ID_C (or $\mathcal{A}$ if ID_C is corrupt)

On input $(\text{COMPLETEINITS-DoS}, \text{sid}, \text{ID}_C)$ from $\mathcal{A}$: // DoS attack against the server, such that it cannot store a file
    CISD.1 Delete any record $\langle \text{FILE}, \text{sid}, \text{ID}_C, *, * \rangle$ // Server's state in current initialization session no longer needed
    CISD.2 Send $(\text{INITRESULT}, \text{sid}, \text{ID}_C, \text{FAIL})$ to S (or $\mathcal{A}$ if S is corrupt)

Fig. 7. Ideal functionality $\mathcal{F}_{\text{PPKR}}$ for password-protected key retrieval, offline attacks and initialization interfaces. For a stronger version of $\mathcal{F}_{\text{PPKR}}$, boxed code can be dropped (see Sect. 4.2).

Recovery Phase

On input $(\text{RecC}, \text{sid}, \text{ID}_C, \text{pw}')$ from ID_C (or $\mathcal{A}$ if ID_C is corrupt):

RC.1 Record $\langle\text{RecC}, \text{sid}, \text{ID}_C, \text{pw}'\rangle$, overwriting any existing record $\langle\text{RecC}, \text{sid}, \text{ID}_C, *\rangle$ // Storing ID_C's current init state; a client can only be in one recovery session.

RC.2 Send $(\text{RecC}, \text{sid}, \text{ID}_C)$ to $\mathcal{A}$ and S. // S learns which clients started recovery, with the guarantee that attempts by honest clients cannot be faked.

On input $(\text{RecS}, \text{sid}, \text{ID}_C, \text{ID}_C^*)$ from S (or $\mathcal{A}$ if S is corrupt): // Server agrees to assist ID_C in recovery. If S is corrupt, $\mathcal{A}$ can reroute the recovery to a different ID_C^*. Note that ID_C^* does not have to be the identity of an existing client and can be an arbitrary identity

RS.1 If S is honest, set $\text{ID}_C' \leftarrow \text{ID}_C$, $\boxed{\text{otherwise set } \text{ID}_C' \leftarrow \text{ID}_C^*}$

RS.2 Retrieve record $\langle\text{RecC}, \text{sid}, \text{ID}_C, [\text{pw}']\rangle$ // Continue only if ID_C started recovery already

RS.3 If there exists no record $\langle\text{File}, \text{ID}_C', \text{sid}, [\text{pw}], [K]\rangle$ marked STORED, send $(\text{RecResult}, \text{aid}, \text{Fail})$ to S (or $\mathcal{A}$ if S is corrupt). Else retrieve the record. // The currently stored K and pw (for ID_C') are used. If ID_C' re-inits afterwards, it has no effect on this recovery session.

RS.4 If $\text{tx}_{\text{sid}}[\text{ID}_C'] = 0$, delete record $\langle\text{File}, \text{sid}, \text{ID}_C', \text{pw}, K\rangle$ marked STORED and send $(\text{DelRec}, \text{sid}, \text{ID}_C')$ to S and $\mathcal{A}$ Else continue.

RS.5 Set $\text{tx}_{\text{sid}}[\text{ID}_C'] \leftarrow \text{tx}_{\text{sid}}[\text{ID}_C'] - 1$

RS.6 Append pw and K to record $\langle\text{RecC}, \text{sid}, \text{ID}_C, \text{pw}'\rangle$, overwriting any existing record $\langle\text{RecC}, \text{sid}, \text{ID}_C, *, *, *\rangle$ // The recovery session of ID_C is used

RS.7 Send $(\text{RecS}, \text{sid}, \text{ID}_C', \text{pw} \stackrel{?}{=} \text{pw}')$ to $\mathcal{A}$ // A ppKR protocol may not hide whether recovery was successful or not

On input $(\text{CompleteRecC}, \text{sid}, \text{ID}_C)$ from $\mathcal{A}$:

CRC.1 Retrieve record $\langle\text{RecC}, \text{sid}, \text{ID}_C, [\text{pw}'], [\text{pw}], [K]\rangle$. If record is marked RECOVERED, delete it. Otherwise, mark it RECOVERED. // Ensures that record can be retrieved twice before deletion.

CRC.2 Determine the output as follows:
   (1) If pw = pw' then set $K' \leftarrow K$ // Recovering the key!
   (2) In all other cases, set $K' \leftarrow \text{Fail}$

CRC.3 Send $(\text{RecResult}, \text{sid}, K')$ to ID_C (or $\mathcal{A}$ if ID_C is corrupt).

On input $(\text{CompleteRecS}, \text{sid}, \text{ID}_C)$ from $\mathcal{A}$ // Server finishes recovery session by learning whether the password was correct or not:

CRS.1 Retrieve record $\langle\text{RecC}, \text{sid}, \text{ID}_C, [\text{pw}], [\text{pw}'], [K]\rangle$. If record is marked RECOVERED, delete it. Otherwise, mark it RECOVERED. // Ensures that record can be retrieved twice before deletion.

CRS.2 If pw = pw', set $\text{tx}_{\text{sid}}[\text{ID}_C] \leftarrow 10$ and send $(\text{RecResult}, \text{sid}, \text{ID}_C, \text{Succ})$ to S.

CRS.3 If pw $\neq$ pw', then send $(\text{RecResult}, \text{sid}, \text{ID}_C, \text{Fail})$ to S (or $\mathcal{A}$ if S is corrupt).

Attacks on Recovery Phase

On input $(\text{CompleteRecC-DoS}, \text{sid}, \text{ID}_C)$ from $\mathcal{A}$ // Network attacker or malicious server can always make the client fail:

CRCD.1 Retrieve record $\langle\text{RecC}, \text{sid}, \text{ID}_C, *, *, *\rangle$ and delete it.

CRCD.2 Send $(\text{RecResult}, \text{sid}, \text{Fail})$ to ID_C (or $\mathcal{A}$ if ID_C is corrupt).

On input $(\text{CompleteRecS-DoS}, \text{sid}, \text{ID}_C)$ from $\mathcal{A}$: // Server finishes with failure. In particular, it never learns if the password was correct

CRSC.1 Retrieve record $\langle\text{RecC}, \text{sid}, \text{ID}_C, *, *, *\rangle$ and delete it.

CRSD.2 Output $(\text{RecResult}, \text{sid}, \text{ID}_C, \text{Fail})$ to S (or $\mathcal{A}$ if S is corrupt).

Fig. 8. Ideal functionality $\mathcal{F}_{\text{PPKR}}$, recovery interfaces.

- COMPLETEINITC outputs K from the session record to the client ($\boxed{\text{CIC.2}}$)
- COMPLETEINITC-DoS outputs FAIL to the client ($\boxed{\text{CICD.2}}$)
- COMPLETEINITS outputs SUCC to the server ($\boxed{\text{CIS.3}}$)
- COMPLETEINITS-DoS outputs FAIL to the server ($\boxed{\text{CISD.2}}$)

Additionally to these outputs, the COMPLETEINITS interface ensures that $\mathcal{F}_{\text{PPKR}}$ installs a password-protected backup key file for ID_C that contains K. This works as follows: instead of deleting it, $\mathcal{F}_{\text{PPKR}}$ marks the FILE record of ID_C

as STORED (CIS.1). Looking ahead, in the recovery phase clients can only recover keys from FILE records that are marked STORED. $\mathcal{F}_{\mathsf{PPKR}}$ then initializes a counter $\mathsf{tx}_{\mathsf{sid}}[\mathsf{ID_C}]$ to 10 (CIS.2), which indicates the remaining recovery attempts for the newly created FILE record, and sends the output (INITRESULT, sid, $\mathsf{ID_C}$, SUCC) to the server (CIS.3).

This concludes the description of $\mathcal{F}_{\mathsf{PPKR}}$'s initialization phase. The absence of any K- or pw-dependent information in the outputs towards the server (IC.3, CIS.3, CISD.2) and the adversary (IS.2) ensures **secrecy of** K **and password obliviousness** during initialization.

Recovery Phase. The general structure of record keeping and interfaces of the recovery phase are very similar to the initialization phase. First, a client starts a recovery session with the RECC interface, then the server has to agree in participating in the recovery with the RECS interface, and finally there are again for each party two interfaces to let $\mathcal{F}_{\mathsf{PPKR}}$ output either success or failure to the parties. For the RECC interface, $\mathsf{ID_C}$ provides as input the password pw' it chose for this recovery attempt. $\mathcal{F}_{\mathsf{PPKR}}$ then records this in a RECC record (RC.1), again overwriting any existing RECC record, and outputs to S and $\mathcal{A}$ that $\mathsf{ID_C}$ started a recovery session (RC.2).

If the server agrees to participate in the recovery session with $\mathsf{ID_C}$ it calls the RECS interface with two (not necessarily distinct) client identities $\mathsf{ID_C}$ and $\mathsf{ID_C}^*$, where again the second identity $\mathsf{ID_C}^*$ being given by the server allows a malicious server to ignore client authentication and claim a different identity is recovering. $\mathcal{F}_{\mathsf{PPKR}}$ now does three things:

- $\mathcal{F}_{\mathsf{PPKR}}$ checks whether $\mathsf{ID_C}$ has started recovery in the first place by looking for a corresponding client recovery session (RS.2) and drops the query otherwise.
- Then, $\mathcal{F}_{\mathsf{PPKR}}$ grabs password and key from the stored key record with identity $\mathsf{ID_C}'$ (RS.3), and writes them into the client's recovery session record. With this, $\mathcal{F}_{\mathsf{PPKR}}$ lets a *corrupt* server, who can let $\mathsf{ID_C}'$ be any $\mathsf{ID_C}^*$ (RS.1), re-route the recovery attempt of any honest client to the password-protected key record of *any other* honest client, which is again motivated by the fact that a malicious server can simply skip client authentication. Conversely, if the server is honest, $\mathcal{F}_{\mathsf{PPKR}}$ ensures $\mathsf{ID_C}' = \mathsf{ID_C}$ and hence gives access to some FILE record containing an identity $\mathsf{ID_C}$ only to a client with that identity (**Client authentication** during recovery).
- After finding a file for a recovery attempt in the previous step, $\mathcal{F}_{\mathsf{PPKR}}$ checks if the recovery attempt counter for $\mathsf{ID_C}'$ has reached zero (RS.4). In that case, it deletes the FILE record of $\mathsf{ID_C}'$ marked STORED to ensure that the key contained in that record cannot be recovered anymore (**limited number of recovery attempts with wrong passwords**) and outputs DELREC to S and $\mathcal{A}$. Otherwise, the recovery attempt counter for $\mathsf{ID_C}'$ is decremented (RS.5) and the password pw and key K obtained from the FILE record are appended to the RECC record (RS.6).

Extending the record again serves the purpose of recording that S agreed to participate in the recovery with ID_C. Note that this extended record is not deleted if ID_C starts a new recovery session with another call to the RECC interface. This reflects the fact that the server should still be able to finish a recovery session until it agrees to participate in another recovery session with ID_C. Finally, the functionality gives the output (RECS, sid, ID_C', pw $\stackrel{?}{=}$ pw$'$) to the adversary $\mathcal{A}$ (RS.7). We let $\mathcal{F}_{PPKR}$ leak the latter bit to the adversary because many protocols, including the WBP, leak via their communication pattern whether the client used the correct password or not. For example, a server might only send its last message to the client if it has previously learned that the client's password was correct.

To complete the recovery session, the adversary calls either COMPLETERECC or COMPLETERECC-DoS and either COMPLETERECS or COMPLETERECS-DoS, again with $\mathcal{F}_{PPKR}$ enforcing no order in which the interfaces are called. In COMPLETERECC the functionality retrieves the extended RECC record (CRC.1) and compares the two password pw and pw$'$ contained in it (CRC.2). If they are the same, it outputs the key K contained in the record to the client and otherwise outputs FAIL to the client. To ensure that both the client and the server can finish the recovery in any order, the RECC record is marked as RECOVERED or deleted if it already is marked as RECOVERED (CRC.1). Similarly, in the COMPLETERECS interface $\mathcal{F}_{PPKR}$ retrieves the extended RECC record (CRS.1) and outputs either SUCC or FAIL to the server depending on whether the passwords pw and pw$'$ in the RECC record match (CRS.2 and CRS.3). Additionally, if the passwords match, the recovery attempt counter $tx_{sid}[ID_C]$ is reset to 10 (CRS.2). To again enforce no order on which party receives its outputs first, the RECC record is marked as RECOVERED or deleted if it already is marked as RECOVERED. Using this mechanism both parties receive their output once, and the record is deleted after both parties received their output.

The two interfaces COMPLETERECC-DoS and COMPLETERECS-DoS behave exactly the same. The RECC record of ID_C is deleted (CRCD.1 and CRSD.1) and $\mathcal{F}_{PPKR}$ outputs FAIL to the corresponding party (CRCD.2 and CRSD.2). In these interface we do not use the mechanism of marking the record RECOVERED, since we assume that if either party produces the output FAIL the other party cannot successfully finish the recovery anymore.

It can be seen from the outputs towards the server (RC.2, CRS.2-3, CRSD.2) and the adversary (RS.7) that only one bit of information about the password used by an honest client during recovery (i.e., match or no match) is leaked, protecting the client from **online dictionary attacks**. Similarly, adversary and client learn only the match bit about the password contained in the file that the server uses during a recovery session (RS.7, CRC.3, CRCD.2).

Offline Attacks. The adversary has access to two interfaces MALICIOUSREC and MALICIOUSINIT to mount offline attacks. In both interfaces the adversary impersonates some client ID_C, however, as described in the discussion of the expected security properties, a client can only be impersonated if the server is corrupt. Therefore, both queries are ignored by $\mathcal{F}_{\mathsf{PPKR}}$ if S is honest (MR.1 and MI.1).

With the MALICIOUSINIT interface the adversary impersonates a client ID_C and executes a new initialization for ID_C. For this, $\mathcal{A}$ can choose a new password pw^* and a new key K^*, which are then stored in a new FILE record marked STORED that overwrites any existing FILE record for ID_C (MI.2). $\mathcal{F}_{\mathsf{PPKR}}$ resets the counter $\mathsf{tx_{sid}}$ to 10 since with any new initialization the client gets 10 new recovery attempts.

With the interface MALICIOUSREC the adversary impersonates a client and tries to recover a client's key from a guessed password. To this end, $\mathcal{A}$ inputs the client identity ID_C and a password guess pw^*. $\mathcal{F}_{\mathsf{PPKR}}$ retrieves the FILE record of ID_C marked STORED (MR.2) and checks if ID_C has any recovery attempts left by checking if $\mathsf{tx_{sid}}[\mathsf{ID}_C] = 0$. If ID_C has no recovery attempts left, it deletes the FILE record of ID_C (**limited number of offline guesses**) and outputs (DELREC, sid, ID_C) to $\mathcal{A}$ to notify $\mathcal{A}$ that the record was deleted (MR.3). Otherwise, the functionality proceeds to check whether the guessed password pw^* matches the password pw from the FILE record. If the passwords match, the adversary gets access to the key stored in the FILE record, and otherwise $\mathcal{F}_{\mathsf{PPKR}}$ returns FAIL to the adversary (MR.4).

Differences Between PPKR and 1-PPSS A password-protected secret sharing scheme [3] allows a user to retrieve a password-protected secret from a set of servers. The servers cannot derive or offline-attack the user's data unless a certain subset of them colludes. A PPKR scheme could be interpreted as a 1-PPSS scheme, i.e., where only one server is involved in storing and retrieving the password-protected secret. While both primitives are very similar considering only honest parties, it is actually the server corruption model that greatly differs for PPKR and 1-PPSS. Intuitively, the one server of a 1-PPSS scheme holds the only share of a secret (or key, in the terminology of PPKR), i.e., the full secret. If such a server is compromised, unlimited offline guesses on the shared user secret are unavoidable. PPKR is stronger: upon server compromise, only a *limited* number of password guesses are allowed on user secrets. Hence, PPKR never falls back to 1-PPSS, due to the stronger guarantees upon server compromise.

4.2   On Strengthening $\mathcal{F}_{\mathsf{PPKR}}$

We discuss a potential strengthening of $\mathcal{F}_{\mathsf{PPKR}}$ regarding the limitation of offline guesses by a malicious server. While $\mathcal{F}_{\mathsf{PPKR}}$ buries keys of honest users whenever a user re-initializes (e.g., when refreshing the key, or when changing the password) as long as the server is honest, it does not guarantee uniqueness of clients' backup keys if the server is corrupted. Consequently, the limitation of offline guessing attempts holds only *per initialized key* of a user, and not *per user*. The reason why we go with the weaker $\mathcal{F}_{\mathsf{PPKR}}$ is that the WBP cannot guarantee the stronger version, and thus we have to reflect this weakness for the security analysis of the actual protocol. However, for completeness, we state here the properties that we would ideally like to demand from $\mathcal{F}_{\mathsf{PPKR}}$, and the corresponding functionality can be read from Fig. 7 by dropping the $\boxed{\text{boxed code}}$. Figure 8 does not change. A bit more detailed, we could strengthen $\mathcal{F}_{\mathsf{PPKR}}$ by disallowing the adversary to reroute initializations of honest clients ID_C to new identities $\mathsf{ID}_C{}^*$, such that upon honest re-initialization, $\mathcal{F}_{\mathsf{PPKR}}$ always buries the former key of that client. The security guarantees are then strengthened as follows.

- **Uniqueness of** K: ~~If the server is honest,~~ initialization of a key K by user C buries any key that C previously initialized, *even if the server is malicious*.
- **Limited number of offline guesses**: The above guarantee extends to maliciously corrupted servers, i.e., after 10 wrong password guesses to recover ~~any honestly initialized~~ *the latest honestly initialized key K of any client*, K is buried and cannot be retrieved by anyone anymore.

5 Security Analysis

The Difficulty of a Security Analysis. One might hope that the security of the WBP directly follows from the security of its OPAQUE component. There are two main reasons why that does not hold true. First, OPAQUE is a *key exchange* protocol that results in two parties sharing a key, while the goal of the WBP is to *hide the key from the server*. Second, the WBP deploys version 03 of the OPAQUE Internet Draft [25] to which the security analysis of the OPAQUE framework [23] does not apply.

The main challenge when performing a security analysis of the WBP is to tame its complexity (cf. Figure 4 and Fig. 5). Since we want to focus on the actual cryptographic protocol, we do not to include the way in which the HSM outsources data storage in the security analysis. WhatsApp deploys a Merkle tree based outsourced storage routine that lets the HSM put encrypted data onto the WhatsApp server's storage, which should guarantee integrity of the data and the ability of the HSM to detect malicious erasures by the WhatsApp server. We leave the analysis of this scheme as a future task, and in this work simply make the exact same assumptions about it that are claimed in the WBP whitepaper [31]. To further tame the complexity of the proof of the WBP, we modularize the security proofs of the underlying OPRF and the authenticated key exchange (AKE) scheme 3DH. Since previous security analyses did not apply to the protocol versions deployed by the WBP, we first show their security separately, which may be of independent interest. Then we use the resulting simulators as subcomponents of the WBP simulator. This proof technique, which was already used for AKE in [23], avoids formulating the WBP in the AKE- and OPRF-hybrid model. The latter is not even possible, due to the non-black-box use that the WBP makes of these components. Altogether, our analysis (1) shows a lower bound on the security of the WBP, (2) shows the security of the multi-key 2HashDH OPRF and AKE building blocks as deployed by the OPAQUE internet draft version 3 [25], as well as malicious client security of that OPAQUE version.[15]

---

[15] Our proof considers the security of OPAQUE only against a malicious client, since the OPAQUE server is run on the incorruptible HSM.

Modeling the HSM. We model the HSM as a hybrid functionality $\mathcal{F}_{\mathsf{HSM}}$ that can be queried by the server as in Fig. 4 and Fig. 5. That is, $\mathcal{F}_{\mathsf{HSM}}$ contains exactly the code that the HSM contains in these figures. For completeness and clarity, $\mathcal{F}_{\mathsf{HSM}}$ is depicted in Fig. 9. In addition, $\mathcal{F}_{\mathsf{HSM}}$ provides an interface for clients to retrieve $\mathsf{pk}_{\mathsf{HSM}}$, which models the setup process that ensures that clients have the "right" WhatsApp public key hard-coded into their smartphones.[16]

In the UC framework, messages sent between some party and an ideal functionality are perfectly secure, meaning no network adversary can intercept them or tamper with them. So modeling the HSM key distribution as idealized communication expresses our assumptions

- that the user installs the correct WhatsApp client on her phone,
- that WhatsApp's setup ceremony of the HSM leads to honestly generated keys being distributed to the clients,
- and that only the HSM knows the secret key of the HSM.

However, analyzing the mechanisms to ensure the above assumptions is not in the scope of this work.

Treatment of Out-of-Order Messages. We assume that the protocol parties ignore messages that are received out-of-order. That means that during an initialization or a recovery, the parties do nothing upon receiving a message that is not formatted as expected. The only exception to this is the respective first message of an initialization or recovery, i.e., a_1 for initialization or $(n_C, \bar{\mathsf{pk}}_C, a_2)$ for recovery. If such a message is received, the currently running initialization (or recovery, resp.) is discarded and the new initialization (or recovery, resp.) is continued. This way, there is never more than one initialization (or recovery, resp.) running per user.

Corruption Model. All corruptions are malicious, meaning that the adversary can fully control not only the communication but also the behavior of a corrupted party. We consider adaptive corruptions of clients and the server. However, we add the restriction that clients cannot be corrupted during an ongoing initialization or recovery session. More precisely, the environment is not allowed to corrupt some client ID_C if, following the most recent ($\textsc{InitC}, *$) input from the environment to ID_C, ID_C did not produce a corresponding output ($\textsc{InitResult}, *$) yet. Analogously, if following the most recent ($\textsc{RecC}, *$) input from the environment to ID_C, ID_C did not produce a corresponding output ($\textsc{RecResult}, *$) yet, the environment is not allowed to corrupt ID_C as well. We deem this reasonable, since the time it takes to execute the initialization or recovery protocol is relatively short. Formally, this means that the effect of adaptive client corruptions

---

[16] One might be tempted to model this by giving the HSM's public key as input to the client instead. However, that would mean that the UC environment machine can give public keys to clients for which the environment knows the corresponding secret key. For WBP the clients have a hard-coded public key for which only the HSM knows the secret key, so this would not adequately model WBP and make the already complex security analysis unreasonably more complex.

Ideal functionality $\mathcal{F}_{\mathsf{HSM}}$

The functionality talks to a server S hardcoded in sid and to arbitrary other parties P.

Initially:

$K_{\mathsf{HSM}}^{\mathsf{Enc}} \xleftarrow{\$} \{0,1\}^\lambda$

$(\mathsf{sk}_{\mathsf{HSM}}^{\mathsf{Sig}}, \mathsf{pk}_{\mathsf{HSM}}^{\mathsf{Sig}}) \xleftarrow{\$} \Sigma.\mathsf{KeyGen}(1^\lambda)$

$(\mathsf{sk}_{\mathsf{HSM}}^{\mathsf{Enc}}, \mathsf{pk}_{\mathsf{HSM}}^{\mathsf{Enc}}) \xleftarrow{\$} \mathsf{PKE}.\mathsf{KeyGen}(1^\lambda)$

$(\mathsf{sk}_{\mathsf{HSM}}^{\mathsf{DH}}, \mathsf{pk}_{\mathsf{HSM}}^{\mathsf{DH}}) \xleftarrow{\$} \mathsf{DH}.\mathsf{KeyGen}(1^\lambda)$

$\mathsf{pk}_{\mathsf{HSM}} = \{\mathsf{pk}_{\mathsf{HSM}}^{\mathsf{Sig}}, \mathsf{pk}_{\mathsf{HSM}}^{\mathsf{Enc}}, \mathsf{pk}_{\mathsf{HSM}}^{\mathsf{DH}}\}$

$\mathsf{sk}_{\mathsf{HSM}} = \{\mathsf{sk}_{\mathsf{HSM}}^{\mathsf{Sig}}, \mathsf{sk}_{\mathsf{HSM}}^{\mathsf{Enc}}, \mathsf{sk}_{\mathsf{HSM}}^{\mathsf{DH}}, K_{\mathsf{HSM}}^{\mathsf{Enc}}\}$

On input (GETPK) from $\mathsf{P} \in \{\mathsf{ID}_C, \mathsf{S}, \mathcal{A}\}$

return $\mathsf{pk}_{\mathsf{HSM}}$ to P

On input (INITS, $\mathsf{aid}_{\mathsf{new}}$, $\mathsf{aid}_{\mathsf{old}}$, a_1) from S :

$\mathsf{sec\_delete}(\mathsf{aid}_{\mathsf{old}})$

if $\mathsf{sec\_retr}(\mathsf{aid}_{\mathsf{new}})$ is successful:

   return (INITRESULT, $\mathsf{aid}_{\mathsf{new}}$, FAIL)

else :

$K_{\mathsf{aid}_{\mathsf{new}}}^{\mathsf{PRF}} \xleftarrow{\$} \mathbb{Z}_p$

$b_1 \leftarrow a_1^{K_{\mathsf{aid}_{\mathsf{new}}}^{\mathsf{PRF}}}$

$n_1 \xleftarrow{\$} \{0,1\}^\lambda$

$\sigma_1 \xleftarrow{\$} \Sigma.\mathsf{Sign}(\mathsf{sk}_{\mathsf{HSM}}^{\mathsf{Sig}}; b_1 \| n_1)$

$\mathsf{tr}_{\mathsf{HSM}} \leftarrow \mathsf{H}_3(a_1, b_1, n_1)$

return $(\mathsf{aid}_{\mathsf{new}}, b_1, n_1, \sigma_1)$ to S

On input (FILE, $\mathsf{aid}_{\mathsf{new}}$, E) :

$m \leftarrow \mathsf{PKE}.\mathsf{Dec}(\mathsf{sk}_{\mathsf{HSM}}^{\mathsf{Enc}}; \mathsf{E})$

parse $m = (\mathsf{e} \| \mathsf{tr}_C \| \mathsf{pk}_C \| \mathsf{e\_cred} \| n_e \| T_e)$

if $\mathsf{tr}_C \neq \mathsf{tr}_{\mathsf{HSM}}$:

   return (INITRESULT, $\mathsf{aid}_{\mathsf{new}}$, FAIL) to S

else :

$\mathsf{sec\_store}(\mathsf{aid}_{\mathsf{new}}, (K_{\mathsf{aid}_{\mathsf{new}}}^{\mathsf{PRF}},$

   $\mathsf{e} \| \mathsf{pk}_C \| \mathsf{e\_cred} \| n_e \| T_e, \mathsf{ctr} \leftarrow 10))$

return (INITRESULT, $\mathsf{aid}_{\mathsf{new}}$, SUCC) to S

On input (RECS, $\mathsf{aid}, n_c, \bar{\mathsf{pk}}_C, a_2$) :

$(K_{\mathsf{aid}}^{\mathsf{PRF}}, m, \mathsf{ctr}) \leftarrow \mathsf{sec\_retr}(\mathsf{aid})$

if no record can be found:

   return (RECRESULT, aid, FAIL)

parse $m = \mathsf{e} \| \mathsf{pk}_C \| \mathsf{e\_cred} \| n_e \| T_e$

if $\mathsf{ctr} = 0$:

   return (DELREC, aid)

else :

   set $\mathsf{ctr}' \leftarrow \mathsf{ctr} - 1$

   $\mathsf{sec\_set\_ctr}(\mathsf{aid}, \mathsf{ctr}')$

   $b_2 \leftarrow a_2^{K_{\mathsf{aid}}^{\mathsf{PRF}}}$

   $n_S \xleftarrow{\$} \{0,1\}^\lambda$

   $(\bar{\mathsf{pk}}_S, \bar{\mathsf{sk}}_S) \xleftarrow{\$} \mathsf{DH}.\mathsf{KeyGen}$

   $\mathsf{pre} \leftarrow (a_2, n_c, \bar{\mathsf{pk}}_C, \mathsf{pk}_{\mathsf{HSM}}^{\mathsf{DH}}, \mathsf{e\_cred},$

      $n_e, T_e, b_2, n_S, \bar{\mathsf{pk}}_S)$

   $\mathsf{ikm} \leftarrow (\bar{\mathsf{pk}}_C^{\bar{\mathsf{sk}}_S}, \bar{\mathsf{pk}}_C^{\mathsf{sk}_{\mathsf{HSM}}^{\mathsf{DH}}}, \mathsf{pk}_C^{\bar{\mathsf{sk}}_S})$

   $(K_S^{\mathsf{MAC}}, K_C^{\mathsf{MAC}}, \mathsf{shk}) \leftarrow \mathsf{KDF}_2(\mathsf{ikm}, \mathsf{pre})$

   $T_S \leftarrow \mathsf{MAC}.\mathsf{Tag}(K_S^{\mathsf{MAC}}, \mathsf{H}_3(\mathsf{pre}))$

   $\sigma_2 \xleftarrow{\$} \Sigma.\mathsf{Sign}(\mathsf{sk}_{\mathsf{HSM}}^{\mathsf{Sig}}; b_2)$

   return $(\mathsf{aid}, b_2, \mathsf{e\_cred}, n_e, T_e, n_S, \bar{\mathsf{pk}}_S, T_S, \sigma_2)$

On input (RECRESULT, aid, T_C') :

$T_C \leftarrow \mathsf{MAC}.\mathsf{Tag}(K_C^{\mathsf{MAC}}, \mathsf{H}_3(\mathsf{pre} \| T_S))$

if $T_C' \neq T_C$:

   return (RECRESULT, aid, FAIL) to S

else :

   $c \xleftarrow{\$} \mathsf{AE}.\mathsf{Enc}(\mathsf{shk}; \mathsf{e})$

   $\mathsf{sec\_set\_ctr}(\mathsf{aid}, 10)$

   return (aid, c) to S

Fig. 9. The ideal functionality $\mathcal{F}_{\mathsf{HSM}}$.

is that the adversary (1) learns all values that the client stores after completion of an initialization or recovery phase, namely key K, and (2) controls the client behavior from that point on.

Let AE' be the AE scheme that is implicitly used in Figs. 4 and 5 to encrypt sk_C, that is:

- $\mathsf{KeyGen}'(1^\lambda) \to (K^{\mathsf{mask}}, K^{\mathsf{auth}})$, where $K^{\mathsf{mask}}, K^{\mathsf{auth}} \xleftarrow{\$} \{0,1\}^\lambda$
- $\mathsf{Enc}'((K^{\mathsf{mask}}, K^{\mathsf{auth}}), m) \to (m \oplus K^{\mathsf{mask}}, \mathsf{MAC}.\mathsf{Tag}(K^{\mathsf{auth}}, m \oplus K^{\mathsf{mask}}))$
- $\mathsf{Dec}'((K^{\mathsf{mask}}, K^{\mathsf{auth}}), (\mathsf{e\_cred}, T_e)) \to \begin{cases} \perp \text{ if } \mathsf{MAC}.\mathsf{Vfy}(K^{\mathsf{auth}}, m) = 0 \\ \mathsf{e\_cred} \oplus K^{\mathsf{mask}} \text{ else} \end{cases}$

Theorem 2. *Let* $\mathsf{H}_1, \mathsf{H}_2, \mathsf{KDF}_1, \mathsf{KDF}_2$ *be random oracles such that 2HashDH UC-realizes the "multi-key" functionality* $\mathcal{F}_{\mathsf{OPRF}}$ *and 3DH UC-realizes the* authenticated key exchange functionality $\mathcal{F}_{\mathsf{AKE\text{-}KCI}}$, which are formally defined in the full version [17]. Let $\Sigma = (\Sigma.\mathsf{KeyGen}, \Sigma.\mathsf{Sign}, \Sigma.\mathsf{Vfy})$ be an sEUF-CMA-secure signature scheme, $\mathsf{MAC} = (\mathsf{MAC.Tag}, \mathsf{MAC.Vfy})$ be an sEUF-CMA-secure MAC, $\mathsf{PKE} = (\mathsf{PKE.KeyGen}, \mathsf{PKE.Enc}, \mathsf{PKE.Dec})$ be an IND-CPA-secure public key encryption scheme, $\mathsf{AE} = (\mathsf{AE.KeyGen}, \mathsf{AE.Enc}, \mathsf{AE.Dec})$ be an authenticated encryption scheme, $\mathsf{AE}' = (\mathsf{KeyGen}', \mathsf{Enc}', \mathsf{Dec}')$ have random-key robustness, and $\mathsf{H}_3 : \{0,1\}^* \to \{0,1\}^\lambda$ be a collision resistant hash function.

Then the WBP as described in Fig. 4 and Fig. 5 UC-realizes the PPKR functionality of Fig. 7 and Fig. 8 in the $\mathcal{F}_{\mathsf{HSM}}$-hybrid model, assuming malicious adaptive corruption of clients as defined above, malicious adaptive corruption of the server, and a client-authenticated channel between clients and the server. Concretely, for any efficient adversary against WBP (interacting with $\mathcal{F}_{\mathsf{HSM}}$), there is an efficient simulator SIM that interacts with $\mathcal{F}_{\mathsf{PPKR}}$ and produces a view such that for every efficient environment $\mathcal{Z}$, it holds that

$$
\begin{aligned}
\mathbf{Dist}_{\mathcal{Z}}^{\mathsf{WBP}, \{\mathcal{F}_{\mathsf{PPKR}}, \mathrm{SIM}\}}(\lambda) \leq{} & \mathbf{Dist}_{\mathcal{Z}^*}^{\mathsf{2HashDH}, \{\mathcal{F}_{\mathsf{OPRF}}, \mathrm{SIM}_{\mathsf{OPRF}}\}}(\lambda) \\
& + \mathbf{Dist}_{\mathcal{Z}^*}^{\mathsf{3DH}, \{\mathcal{F}_{\mathsf{AKE\text{-}KCI}}, \mathrm{SIM}_{\mathsf{3DH}}\}}(\lambda) \\
& + \mathbf{Adv}_{\mathcal{B},\Sigma}^{\mathsf{sEUF\text{-}CMA}}(\lambda) + 2Q_{\mathrm{REC}} \mathbf{Adv}_{\mathcal{B},\mathsf{MAC}}^{\mathsf{sEUF\text{-}CMA}}(\lambda) \\
& + 2\mathbf{Adv}_{\mathcal{B},\mathsf{H}_3}^{\mathsf{CR}}(\lambda) + Q_{\mathrm{INIT}} \mathbf{Adv}_{\mathcal{B},\mathsf{PKE}}^{\mathsf{IND\text{-}CPA}}(\lambda) \\
& + Q_{\mathrm{REC}} \mathbf{Adv}_{\mathcal{B},\mathsf{AE}}^{\mathsf{IND\text{-}CPA}}(\lambda) + Q_{\mathrm{REC}} \mathbf{Adv}_{\mathcal{B},\mathsf{AE}}^{\mathsf{INT\text{-}CTXT}}(\lambda) \\
& + \binom{Q_{\mathrm{INIT}}}{2} 2^{-\lambda} + \binom{Q_{\mathrm{REC}}}{2} 2^{-\lambda+1} + \binom{Q_{\mathsf{KDF}_1}}{2} \mathbf{Adv}_{\mathcal{B},\mathsf{AE}'}^{\mathsf{RKR}}(\lambda),
\end{aligned}
$$

where $Q_{\mathrm{INIT}} \in \mathbb{N}$ is an upper bound on the number of initializations, $Q_{\mathrm{REC}} \in \mathbb{N}$ is an upper bound on the number of recoveries, Q_{KDF_1} is an upper bound on the number of KDF_1 queries, and $\mathcal{B}$, resp. $\mathcal{Z}^*$, is the adversary in the corresponding security experiments.

Proof. A proof sketch outlining the proof steps, the full proof, as well as a discussion of the proof can be found in the full version [17].

6 Conclusion and Future Work

We have presented the first formal security analysis of the widely-used WhatsApp backup protocol and confirmed that the WBP indeed provides strong security guarantees such as online protection of the password, and the strength and secrecy of the backup key. However, we also show how a compromised WhatsApp server can increase the number of admissible password guesses from only ctr on the most recent password of the user, to $q_{\mathsf{pw}} * \mathsf{ctr}$ on any password pw ever entered by the user, where q_{pw} is the number of initializations performed with pw by the WhatsApp client device. Our analysis and formal modeling further spans a multitude of interesting research questions, that we divide into three categories.

Widening the Scope of the Analysis. In this work we have only focused on the cryptographic core of the WBP. Potential avenues for future research include a formal analysis of the (Merkle tree based) protocol which the HSM uses to securely outsource storage to untrusted servers. Another interesting direction would be to extend the corruption model to *proactive corruptions*, which allows to investigate whether WBP participants can recover faithfully from corruptions, e.g., after having granted compelled access at border control.

Direct Improvements of the WBP. The increased number of password guesses is only possible because the HSM cannot authenticate the client but has to trust the WhatsApp server that it indeed only acts on demand of honest clients. This can, e.g., be achieved if the client directly authenticates towards the HSM. That way, the server cannot impersonate clients towards the HSM anymore. However, this approach also requires WhatsApp to modify its authentication infrastructure, which is currently independent of the WBP. An "easy" modification of WBP is to let the HSM sign *all* messages. This provides direct protection of replay attacks by the adversary, against which the WBP protects implicitly using message authentication codes (MACs). Such "full" signing would greatly simplify the analysis of the protocol. This raises also the interesting question whether other potentially more costly protection mechanisms of the integrity of messages could be dropped if signing ensures HSM-authenticated channels, ending up with a more efficient protocol overall. Lastly, regarding efficiency improvements, one could look into whether a "less secure" (and potentially more efficient) version of OPAQUE could be plugged into the WBP, where protection against server compromise is dropped. Server compromise seems not a realistic attack scenario in this particular application of OPAQUE, because the OPAQUE server part is run on an HSM, which needs to be trusted anyway.

We note here that the above discussed efficiency improvements might not be of immediate interest to WhatsApp, where the WBP is only seldomly executed per user. Improvements regarding the security must be carefully analyzed and justified, since updating the HSM code of WBP requires WhatsApp to replace all HSMs with new ones and to perform the setup ceremony again.

Constructing PPKR Differently. The WBP is built around the OPAQUE protocol, which in turn deploys an oblivious pseudorandom function (OPRF) and an authenticated key exchange (AKE) protocol. The authenticated key exchange part serves as a tool for convincing the HSM of correctness of the client's password, which is necessary to ensure that the guess attempt counter can be reset to 10 guesses. It is an interesting open question whether this could be achieved from simpler primitives, such as symmetric primitives, which are more efficient than the public-key-based AKE.

References

1. Direct correspondences with Kevin Lewi and other members of the WhatsApp engineering team, 2022–2023
2. Alwen, J., Coretti, S., Dodis, Y.: The double ratchet: security notions, proofs, and modularization for the signal protocol. In: Ishai, Y., Rijmen, V. (eds.) EURO-CRYPT 2019, Part I. LNCS, vol. 11476, pp. 129–158. Springer, Cham (2019). https://doi.org/10.1007/978-3-030-17653-2_5
3. Bagherzandi, A., Jarecki, S., Saxena, N., Lu, Y.: Password-protected secret sharing. In: ACM CCS 2011, pp. 433–444. ACM Press (2011)
4. Bellare, M., Singh, A.C., Jaeger, J., Nyayapati, M., Stepanovs, I.: Ratcheted encryption and key exchange: the security of messaging. In: Katz, J., Shacham, H. (eds.) CRYPTO 2017, Part III. LNCS, vol. 10403, pp. 619–650. Springer, Cham (2017). https://doi.org/10.1007/978-3-319-63697-9_21
5. Bienstock, A., Fairoze, J., Garg, S., Mukherjee, P., Raghuraman, S.: A more complete analysis of the signal double ratchet algorithm. In: Dodis, Y., Shrimpton, T. (eds.) CRYPTO 2022, Part I. LNCS, vol. 13507, pp. 784–813. Springer, Heidelberg (2022). https://doi.org/10.1007/978-3-031-15802-5_27
6. Bourdrez, D., Krawczyk, D.H., Lewi, K., Wood, C.A.: The OPAQUE Asymmetric PAKE Protocol. Internet-Draft draft-irtf-cfrg-opaque-09, Internet Engineering Task Force (2022). https://datatracker.ietf.org/doc/draft-irtf-cfrg-opaque/09/. Work in Progress
7. Brost, J., Egger, C., Lai, R.W.F., Schmid, F., Schröder, D., Zoppelt, M.: Threshold password-hardened encryption services. In: ACM CCS 2020, pp. 409–424. ACM Press (2020)
8. Camenisch, J., Lysyanskaya, A., Neven, G.: Practical yet universally composable two-server password-authenticated secret sharing. In: ACM CCS 2012, pp. 525–536. ACM Press (2012)
9. Canetti, R.: Universally composable security: A new paradigm for cryptographic protocols. In: 42nd FOCS, pp. 136–145. IEEE Computer Society Press (2001)
10. Canetti, R., Jain, P., Swanberg, M., Varia, M.: Universally composable end-to-end secure messaging. In: Dodis, Y., Shrimpton, T. (eds.) CRYPTO 2022, Part II. LNCS, vol. 13508, pp. 3–33. Springer, Heidelberg (2022). https://doi.org/10.1007/978-3-031-15979-4_1
11. Casacuberta, S., Hesse, J., Lehmann, A.: SoK: oblivious pseudorandom functions. In: IEEE EuroS&P 2022. IEEE (2022)
12. Cathcart, W.: (2022). https://twitter.com/wcathcart/status/1600603826477617152
13. Chase, M., Perrin, T., Zaverucha, G.: The signal private group system and anonymous credentials supporting efficient verifiable encryption. In: ACM CCS 2020, pp. 1445–1459. ACM Press (2020)
14. Cohn-Gordon, K., Cremers, C., Dowling, B., Garratt, L., Stebila, D.: A formal security analysis of the signal messaging protocol. In: EuroS&P, pp. 451–466. IEEE (2017)
15. Das, P., Hesse, J., Lehmann, A.: DPaSE: distributed password-authenticated symmetric-key encryption, or how to get many keys from one password. In: ASI-ACCS 2022, pp. 682–696. ACM Press (2022)
16. Davidson, A., Faz-Hernandez, A., Sullivan, N., Wood, C.A.: Oblivious Pseudorandom Functions (OPRFs) using Prime-Order Groups. Internet-Draft draft-irtf-cfrg-voprf-17, Internet Engineering Task Force (2023). https://datatracker.ietf.org/doc/draft-irtf-cfrg-voprf/17/. Work in Progress

17. Davies, G.T., et al.: Security analysis of the whatsapp end-to-end encrypted backup protocol. Cryptology ePrint Archive, Paper 2023/843 (2023). https://eprint.iacr. org/2023/843

18. Doussot, G., Lacharité, M.S., Schorn, E.: End-to-End Encrypted Backups Security Assessment (2021). https://research.nccgroup.com/wp-content/uploads/2021/10/ NCC_Group_WhatsApp_E001000M_Report_2021-10-27_v1.2.pdf

19. Gentry, C., MacKenzie, P., Ramzan, Z.: A method for making password-based key exchange resilient to server compromise. In: Dwork, C. (ed.) CRYPTO 2006. LNCS, vol. 4117, pp. 142–159. Springer, Heidelberg (2006). https://doi.org/10. 1007/11818175_9

20. Jarecki, S., Kiayias, A., Krawczyk, H.: Round-optimal password-protected secret sharing and T-PAKE in the password-only model. In: Sarkar, P., Iwata, T. (eds.) ASIACRYPT 2014. LNCS, vol. 8874, pp. 233–253. Springer, Heidelberg (2014). https://doi.org/10.1007/978-3-662-45608-8_13

21. Jarecki, S., Kiayias, A., Krawczyk, H., Xu, J.: Highly-efficient and composable password-protected secret sharing (or: how to protect your bitcoin wallet online). In: IEEE European Symposium on Security and Privacy, EuroS&P 2016, Saarbrücken, Germany, 21–24 March 2016, pp. 276–291. IEEE (2016)

22. Jarecki, S., Krawczyk, H., Resch, J.K.: Updatable oblivious key management for storage systems. In: ACM CCS 2019, pp. 379–393. ACM Press (2019)

23. Jarecki, S., Krawczyk, H., Xu, J.: OPAQUE: an asymmetric PAKE protocol secure against pre-computation attacks. In: Nielsen, J.B., Rijmen, V. (eds.) EURO-CRYPT 2018, Part III. LNCS, vol. 10822, pp. 456–486. Springer, Cham (2018). https://doi.org/10.1007/978-3-319-78372-7_15

24. Jost, D., Maurer, U., Mularczyk, M.: A unified and composable take on ratcheting. In: Hofheinz, D., Rosen, A. (eds.) TCC 2019, Part II. LNCS, vol. 11892, pp. 180–210. Springer, Cham (2019). https://doi.org/10.1007/978-3-030-36033-7_7

25. Krawczyk, D.H., Lewi, K., Wood, C.A.: The OPAQUE Asymmetric PAKE Protocol. Internet-Draft draft-irtf-cfrg-opaque-03, Internet Engineering Task Force (2021). https://datatracker.ietf.org/doc/draft-irtf-cfrg-opaque/03/. Work in Progress

26. Lai, R.W.F., Egger, C., Reinert, M., Chow, S.S.M., Maffei, M., Schröder, D.: Simple password-hardened encryption services. In: USENIX Security 2018, pp. 1405–1421. USENIX Association (2018)

27. Novak, M.: Paul Manafort Learns That Encrypting Messages Doesn't Matter If the Feds Have a Warrant to Search Your iCloud Account (2018). https://gizmodo. com/paul-manafort-learns-that-encrypting-messages-doesnt-ma-1826561511

28. Perrin, T.: The noise protocol framework. http://noiseprotocol.org/noise.html

29. Rösler, P., Mainka, C., Schwenk, J.: More is less: on the end-to-end security of group chats in signal, whatsapp, and threema. In: EuroS&P, pp. 415–429. IEEE (2018)

30. Vatandas, N., Gennaro, R., Ithurburn, B., Krawczyk, H.: On the cryptographic deniability of the signal protocol. In: Conti, M., Zhou, J., Casalicchio, E., Spognardi, A. (eds.) ACNS 2020, Part II. LNCS, vol. 12147, pp. 188–209. Springer, Cham (2020). https://doi.org/10.1007/978-3-030-57878-7_10

31. WhatsApp: Security of End-to-End Encrypted Backups (2021). https://www. whatsapp.com/security/WhatsApp_Security_Encrypted_Backups_Whitepaper.pdf

32. WhatsApp: WhatsApp Encryption Overview (2021). https://www.whatsapp.com/ security/WhatsApp-Security-Whitepaper.pdf

On Active Attack Detection in Messaging with Immediate Decryption

Khashayar Barooti, Daniel Collins$^{(\boxtimes)}$, Simone Colombo,
Loïs Huguenin-Dumittan, and Serge Vaudenay

EPFL, Lausanne, Switzerland
{khashayar.barooti,daniel.collins,simone.colombo,
lois.huguenin-dumittan,serge.vaudenay}@epfl.ch

Abstract. The widely used Signal protocol provides protection against
state exposure attacks through forward security (protecting past messages) and post-compromise security (for restoring security). It supports
immediate decryption, allowing messages to be re-ordered or dropped at
the protocol level without affecting correctness. In this work, we consider strong *active attack detection for secure messaging with immediate
decryption*, where parties are able to immediately detect active attacks
under certain conditions. We first consider in-band active attack detection, where participants who have been actively compromised but are
still able to send a single message to their partner can detect the compromise. We propose two complementary notions to capture security, and
present a compiler that provides security with respect to both notions.
Our notions generalise existing work (RECOVER security) which only
supported in-order messaging. We also study the related out-of-band
attack detection problem by considering communication over out-of-
band, authenticated channels and propose analogous security notions.
We prove that one of our two notions in each setting imposes a linear
communication overhead in the number of sent messages and security
parameter using an information-theoretic argument. This implies that
each message must information-theoretically contain all previous messages and that our construction, that essentially attaches the entire message history to every new message, is asymptotically optimal. We then
explore ways to bypass this lower bound and highlight the feasibility of
practical active attack detection compatible with immediate decryption.

1 Introduction

Since the Snowden revelations and given the unprecedented rise of mass surveil-
lance, several messaging solutions strengthened their security guarantees. The
susceptibility to state exposure attacks pushed both researchers and practi-
tioners to develop ratcheting-based schemes, which enables forward secrecy—
confidentiality of messages sent before a state exposure—and post-compromise
security—automatic healing of confidentiality upon compromise [15].

The full version of this paper is available at [6].

© International Association for Cryptologic Research 2023
H. Handschuh and A. Lysyanskaya (Eds.): CRYPTO 2023, LNCS 14084, pp. 362–395, 2023.
https://doi.org/10.1007/978-3-031-38551-3_12

The asynchronicity of messaging and the unreliability of some network protocols drove the design of ratcheting-based schemes with *immediate decryption* [1,16,31], i.e., the support of out-of-order delivery and message loss on the *protocol level*. This property ensures that legitimate messages can be immediately decrypted by the receiver upon arrival and placed correctly among other received messages. Furthermore, communication can continue even if some messages are permanently lost. The Signal protocol, the current de-facto messaging standard, supports immediate decryption. By contrast, many schemes in the literature fail if even a single message is lost (see [7,11,14,21,32] for a non-exhaustive list).

The aforementioned security notions do not guarantee message authentication when the adversary impersonates parties, e.g., through state compromise. The lack of authentication implies that parties cannot *detect* active attacks. A recent phishing attack against Signal's phone number verification service enabled attackers to re-register accounts to another device, demonstrating the practicality of impersonation attacks via secret state compromise [35]. Similar attacks that steal verification codes to hijack accounts affect a plethora of messaging applications. The proliferation of spyware such as Pegasus represents an additional—and worrying—threat for secret exfiltration [34].

The most widely used mechanisms for detecting active attacks use an *out-of-band* authenticated channel. All such mechanisms we are aware of, either deployed in practice [28] or proposed in the literature [17,19] assume such a channel. Solutions like Signal's safety numbers [28] enables parties to authenticate long-term keys by comparing QR codes in person. However, as observed by Dowling and Hale [18,19], Signal's approach—and all similar methods to our knowledge—fails to provide guarantees after a user's state is exposed, since safety numbers only authenticate initial keys (for Signal, the keys that the X3DH key agreement protocol generates).

To remedy this situation, Dowling and Hale [19] proposed to add an additional authentication key to each iteration of Signal's asymmetric ratchet for on-demand use in out-of-band authentication. Their construction allows parties to immediately—that is, without additional communication rounds—authenticate their entire *asymmetric ratchet* out of band. However messages forged under symmetric keys will never be detected. The only other construction in the literature to our knowledge, proposed by Dowling, Günter and Poirrier [17], requires *three rounds* of in-band communication before an out-of-band hash comparison can take place. Contrary to Dowling and Hale's solution, this approach authenticates all messages (albeit does not formally treat out-of-order messages), but imposes additional rounds, which is especially problematic in the presence of an active adversary. This raises our first research question:

1. Can we authenticate *all* messages in a *single round* of out-of-band communication to detect active attacks in the immediate decryption setting?

Out-of-band authentication is not always practical or even possible. A convenient alternative is to detect active attacks *in-band*, i.e., using the same channel as the messaging protocol. The adversary can, in the worst case, block all messages sent by honest parties, thereby forcing users to resort to out-of-band communication, but mounting such a persistent attack requires considerable resources. Durak and Vaudenay [21] introduce RECOVER security: if a party receives a forgery, then this party does not accept subsequent messages sent honestly by his counterpart. Caforio et al. [11] extend RECOVER security to enable a party to detect whether their *partner* was compromised, i.e., whether they received a forgery. By contrast to out-of-band authentication, no additional messages are required to support attack detection: in-band ciphertexts contain the authentication information. However, these notions and the corresponding constructions assume in-order message delivery and fail on message dropping. This raises a second question, first suggested by Alwen et al. [1]:

2. Can we achieve extended RECOVER security—immediate in-band active attack detection—while supporting immediate decryption?

To detect active attacks, parties need to authenticate their *entire* message history: each message may be a forgery, i.e., the result of an active attack. With immediate decryption, parties cannot be sure which messages their partner has received until they receive an honest reply from them. Intuitively, each message needs to "contain" the message history up until when it was sent. We prove this intuition, which motivates the exploration of performance/security trade-offs and optimisations. In this regard, existing protocols for both in-band and out-of-band active attack detection represent only a subset of the potential design space. Consequently we also ask:

3. What are the *communication costs* of in- and out-of-band active attack detection for messaging with immediate decryption, and what useful performance/security *trade-offs* can be made?

1.1   Our Contributions

In this paper, we explore the aforementioned questions. In more detail:

- We introduce (Sect. 3) a new primitive that we call *authenticated ratcheted communication*, which captures immediate decryption and models communication through both insecure in-band and authentic out-of-band channels.
- In Sect. 4, we formalise in-band active attack detection for immediate decryption, by extending RECOVER security [11,21], with two notions, namely r-RID and s-RID security, for detecting active attacks towards the receiver and on reception of messages from the sender after they were attacked; combined, these two notions comprise RID (recover with immediate decryption) security. We propose a scheme secure under these notions.
- We consider *out-of-band* active attack detection for immediate decryption messaging in Sect. 5. We introduce notions r-UNF and s-UNF (which combine to UNF for unforgeable), which are analogous to the notions for in-band detection. Demonstrating their similarity, we construct an UNF-secure scheme from a RID-secure scheme. We also construct an UNF-secure ARC scheme given a RC scheme.

- In Sect. 6, we prove with an information-theoretic argument that ciphertexts in a scheme satisfying either r-RID or r-UNF security must grow *linearly* in the number of messages sent. As our constructions demonstrate, s-RID and s-UNF security are comparatively cheaper and practical.
- In Sect. 7, we consider different ways to bypass the aforementioned lower bounds. First we discuss ways to optimize the s-RID-secure scheme. We show how one can drastically reduce the overhead as long as the communication between the two parties is balanced. The details of this optimization are given in the full version of this paper [6], which we believe is the most suitable scheme for use in practice that we propose. We also focus on optimizing the *authenticated* out-of-band channel variant, by exploring pruning-based optimizations, where parties securely prune messages as soon as they are authenticated. We finally discuss the performance advantages resulting from a three-move authentication procedure.

1.2 Paper Overview

We assume a network where parties communicate over two types of channels: insecure channels and out-of-band authenticated channels. The adversary has full control over insecure channels. In particular, she can read, deliver, modify and delay messages. In the authenticated channels, the integrity and authenticity of the messages are protected, that is, the adversary can read, deliver, duplicate and delay messages but not modify them. In the Signal application, the insecure channel is the usual network, whereas the out-of-band channel is that used for safety number verification [28], typically in-person.

(Authenticated) Ratcheted Communication. We introduce a syntax for ratcheted communication (RC) in which sent and received messages are associated with totally ordered *ordinals* (epoch/index pairs in Signal [1]). Ordinals enable our protocol to support *immediate decryption* [1], i.e., message loss and re-ordering on the network. We build on this syntax to define *authenticated ratcheted communication*, or ARC, which comprises two additional functions AuthSend and AuthReceive. A party can use AuthSend to send an authentication tag through the out-of-band channel that the counterpart processes with AuthReceive. AuthSend outputs an ordinal that is at least as large as the last *sent* ordinal for that party. AuthReceive, if successful, should authenticate all messages up to that ordinal; this is captured in UNF security. Our notion ORDINALS enforces these semantics even in presence of forgeries.

RID *security.* We revisit the definitions of RECOVER security [11,21] in the immediate decryption setting. We define two complementary security notions for RID security:

- r-RID ensures that the receiver of a forgery does not accept honest messages with ordinals *larger* than that of the forgery.
- s-RID security enables a party to detect if their counterpart has ever received a forgery (i.e., a forgery from the sender).

If a scheme is both r-RID- and s-RID-secure, then it is RID-secure. These notions are orthogonal to forward security and post-compromise security.

We propose a construction that transforms any ratcheted communication scheme into a provably RID-secure one. In the construction, both parties keep track of messages they have sent and received. Every time they send a message, they attach *all* messages (i.e., the ciphertexts from the underlying RC) they have sent and received so far to their ciphertext. When a party receives a message that "contradicts" what it has sent or received, it can deduce that an active attack took place.

To reduce bandwidth, parties send ordinals and hashes of messages, instead of complete ciphertexts. For r-RID security, a receiver $\overline{\mathcal{P}}$ compares the input message and the sender $\mathcal{P}$'s supposed set of sent messages with what $\overline{\mathcal{P}}$ has received previously. For s-RID, it suffices for a receiver $\overline{\mathcal{P}}$ (who knows exactly what it sent) to check whether the sender claims to have received anything that $\overline{\mathcal{P}}$ did not send. Here, $\mathcal{P}$ only needs to send a *single* hash alongside the set of received ordinals (which are generally smaller than hashes), since $\overline{\mathcal{P}}$ can recompute the hash locally. Since the channel is insecure, parties need to perform a series of checks on the ciphertexts to prevent the adversary from tampering with the sets of sent and received messages sent. Both r-UNF- and s-UNF-security build on the collision resistance of the hash function.

UNF *security.* We define notions analogous to r-RID and s-RID for *authenticated* ratcheted communication schemes. The r-UNF (receiver unforgeable) notion ensures that a party does not accept authentication tags after receiving a forgery, whereas s-UNF (sender unforgeable) ensures that a party does not accept authentication tags coming from a counterpart that received a forgery. We show that a RID-secure scheme can be turned into a UNF-secure scheme. The transformation highlights the similarity between RID and UNF security. In the former, parties authenticate all messages they have sent and received in band, whereas in the latter the messages are authenticated out of band. Concretely, the transformation uses the ciphertext of a RID-secure RC scheme as the authentication tag for an ARC scheme, by moving authentication material to the out-of-band channel.

Communication Costs. We prove a linear lower bound on the ciphertext size of any r-RID-secure RC: each ciphertext must capture all information contained in previously sent ones. In fact, the security notion requires that the receiving party is able to immediately detect if *any* subset of previous ciphertexts contains a forgery, since the sender does not know what has been received and ciphertexts can be arbitrarily re-ordered or dropped.

For the proof, we construct an (inefficient) encoder/decoder pair for a list of input messages $(m_1, \ldots, m_n)$ and randomness R, that uses the r-RID RC to compress the input. More precisely, the encoder uses the RC to send messages $(m_1, \ldots, m_n)$ with randomness R to get a list of ciphertexts $(\mathsf{ct}_1, \ldots, \mathsf{ct}_n)$, and outputs only (ct_n, R). Next, the decoder uses the RC to receive ciphertext ct_n, generates every possible ct_1 for all possible messages m_1 with randomness R and attempts to successfully receive one of them. If this succeeds, it means m_1 was the same message as the one input to the encoder (i.e., the "honest" one). Then, the decoder continues with m_2 and so on, eventually outputting $(m_1, \ldots, m_n, R)$. Finally, by setting the distributions of the messages and randomness as uniform, one can argue by Shannon's theorem that the ciphertext space must be exponentially large in $n \cdot |m_i|$. The formal proof is actually more complicated as the r-RID security does not need to be perfect and many ciphertexts might be successfully received when decoding.

Then, following a nearly identical proof, we prove a linear lower bound on the authentication tag size of any r-UNF-secure ARC. These proofs might be of independent interest. Following similar arguments we show that the state (i.e. secret key) of any public key puncturable encryption (PKPE) scheme must grow linearly with the number of punctures.

Practical Active Attack Detection. We explore how to overcome the linear communication complexity that r-RID and r-UNF impose. We first observe that ciphertexts can be much smaller to achieve s-RID or s-UNF security. As noted above, it suffices for $\mathcal{P}$ to send a single hash of all received messages with the corresponding ordinals, since partner $\overline{\mathcal{P}}$ can recompute the hash if it stores all messages it sends. Assuming each ordinal uses c space, ciphertexts reduce in size from $O(n(\lambda + c))$ to $O(\lambda + nc)$ given $\mathcal{P}$ has received n messages.

Motivating this comparison, we observe that parties achieve r-RID/r-UNF-like guarantees after one round of communication from s-RID/s-UNF security. If $\mathcal{P}$ detects that their partner $\overline{\mathcal{P}}$ has received a forgery, $\mathcal{P}$ can let $\overline{\mathcal{P}}$ know, and thus $\overline{\mathcal{P}}$ can learn that they have received a forgery (which is what r-RID/r-UNF guarantee). We formalise this by proposing a lightweight three-move protocol, and a corresponding security model, over the out-of-band channel which provides bidirectional message authentication. Participant $\mathcal{P}$ (resp. $\overline{\mathcal{P}}$) sends their set of received messages to their partner in the first and second moves. In the second and third moves, $\overline{\mathcal{P}}$ (resp. $\mathcal{P}$) sends a bit that indicates whether the set of received messages was consistent with what they actually sent.

In the aforementioned protocols, performance degrades *linearly* in the number of exchanged messages, even for s-RID/s-UNF security. We observe that for UNF security the authentication tags can be compressed over time by including acknowledgements in tags. Since the out-of-band channel is authentic, parties are sure that the authentication information—that is, the sets of sent and received messages—coming from the counterpart is correct. This enables parties to prune already authenticated messages. For r-RID security, pruning-based optimizations are more difficult to obtain, since parties do not know which messages are authentic, i.e., have really been sent or received by the counterpart.

1.3 Additional Related Work

A growing line of work considers the performance and security of messaging in both the two-party [5,7,11,21,25,33] and more general group settings [2–4] settings. Some of these works provide similar [25] and sometimes weaker [26] guarantees for in-band active attack detection assuming in-order communication.

To our knowledge, in-band active attack detection is not explicitly explored in group messaging, but schemes like MLS ensure that if the state of two parties is forked then their states become incompatible, in some protocol-specific sense.

Naor et al. [29] introduced the concept of immediate key delivery for key exchange: if one goes offline, the remaining ones should be able to complete it successfully by returning a shared secret. This property is orthogonal to immediate decryption as it focuses on keys instead of messages.

Apart from Durak and Vaudenay and Caforio et al. who introduced the RECOVER notions, Dowling et al. [20] provide r-RECOVER, but not s-RECOVER security via signatures, while providing anonymity guarantees even upon state exposure. Dowling et al. [17] frame their authentication guarantees as follows: if no long-term keys are compromised, then all messages exchanged are authentic. Otherwise, active attacks can be detected out-of-band. They achieve this by signing all messages with long-term keys. Our protocols and security notions can be adapted to achieve these guarantees. In distributed computing, the problem is formalised in terms of accountability, which enables parties to detect faulty (Byzantine) nodes [12,22]. In multi-party computation, a line of work has explored security with *identifiable abort* [23] which ensures that if parties fail to compute a given function, they can identify the party that caused the failure.

The encoder/decoder technique that we use to prove the lower bounds in Sect. 6 have been used before in cryptography [24,27]. While the basic idea is the same, the technical details of the proofs are not comparable as the primitives are different. Related work in group messaging achieves communication lower bounds in a symbolic model of execution [9] and in a black-box impossibility setting [8].

2 Notation

We consider two parties, A and B. Let $\mathcal{P}$ be one party (A resp. B) and $\overline{\mathcal{P}}$ be their partner (B resp. A). We use maps, or associative arrays, which associate keys with values: $m[\cdot] \leftarrow x$ defines a new map with values initially set to x and $m[k]$ returns the element indexed by key k. Keys are tuples of any length $n \geq 1$. We index maps with integers starting from 1; in this case, $m[a : b]$ returns the list of elements whose keys are between a and b. We access the element of a tuple using the dot notation. The function $\mathsf{length}(m)$ returns the number of keys in map m. The empty string is denoted by ε. Given a set S, S^* (respectively S^n) is the set of all strings of arbitrary length (resp. of length n) whose elements are in S. PPT abbreviates 'probabilistic polynomially bounded', which we use in the context of algorithms bounded in terms of the security parameter λ.

3 (Authenticated) Ratcheted Communication

In this section we introduce the *ratcheted communication* (RC) cryptographic primitive and an extension *authenticated ratcheted communication* (ARC) supporting out-of-band authentication. These primitives augment classic ratcheted secure messaging schemes [1,11,26] in two ways: (i) sent and received messages are associated with *ordinals*, and, for ARC, (ii) the syntax encompasses two additional stateful algorithms AuthSend and AuthReceive.

Ordinals associated with messages enable a party to (1) order incoming messages immediate decryption setting; (2) keep track of how many messages have passed through the communication channel; and (3) infer which messages have been authenticated using the out-of-band channel. Ordinals of the form num can be elements of any set on which a total order is defined. In Alwen et al.'s [1] and Bienstock et al.'s [10] modelling of the Signal protocol, an ordinal num is defined as a pair of integers (e, c) such that $(e, c) < (e', c')$ if $e < e'$ or both $e = e'$ and $c < c'$. We formally define an RC scheme below.

Definition 1 (Ratcheted communication (RC)). *A ratcheted communication (RC) scheme comprises the following PPT algorithms:*

- Setup(1^λ) → pp *takes the security parameter* $\lambda \in \mathbb{N}$, *expressed in unary, and outputs public parameters* pp.
- Init(pp) → (st_A, st_B, z) *takes public parameters* pp *and outputs a state* $st_\mathcal{P}$ *for* $\mathcal{P} \in \{A, B\}$, *and public information* z.
- Send($st_\mathcal{P}$, ad, pt) → $(st'_\mathcal{P}, num, ct)$ *takes a state* $st_\mathcal{P}$, *associated data* ad *and a plaintext* pt *and outputs a new state* $st'_\mathcal{P}$, *an ordinal* num *and ciphertext* ct.
- Receive($st_\mathcal{P}$, ad, ct) → $(acc, st'_\mathcal{P}, num, pt)$ *takes a state* $st_\mathcal{P}$, *associated data* ad *and ciphertext* ct *and outputs an acceptance bit* $acc \in \{true, false\}$, *state* $st'_\mathcal{P}$, *ordinal* num *and plaintext* pt.

The Receive *algorithm returns dummy* $st'_\mathcal{P}$, num, pt *which are ignored when* acc = false.

Remark 1. Signal can be viewed as an RC. In the work of Alwen et al. [1], a secure messaging scheme consists of an initialisation algorithm and party-specific Send and Receive algorithms with no associated data. The Receive algorithms, but not the Send algorithms, output an epoch/index pair $(e, i) \in \mathbb{N}^2$ which plays the role of an ordinal. Signal as defined by Alwen et al. [1] can thus be considered an RC by modifying its Send algorithm to output each (e, i) pair as an ordinal and enforcing that ad = $\bot$ is always input to Send and Receive.

In an ARC, parties rely on AuthSend and AuthReceive to authenticate the communication using a (possibly narrowband) out-of-band authenticated channel. AuthSend inputs state and outputs an updated state, an authentication tag and an ordinal, whereas AuthReceive takes a state and an authentication tag to output an authentication bit, an updated state and an ordinal. Intuitively, the authentication tag is sent via the out-of-band authenticated channel and it enables the receiver to detect active attacks using the AuthReceive algorithm. Participants can decide when to invoke the algorithms and thus use the authentication tag on-demand, e.g., when an out-of-band channel is available.

AuthSend and AuthReceive outputs ordinals with the same semantics as Send and Receive. Namely, the num that AuthSend outputs is greater or equal to the last num that Send outputs; besides ordering authentication tags with respect to messages the party has sent or received, the ordinal indicates which messages (all up until num) the authentication tag authenticates. Similarly, for AuthReceive, the ordinal num indicates that all messages with num$'$ $\leq$ num have been authenticated with the received tag.

Definition 2 (Authenticated ratcheted communication (ARC)). *An authenticated ratcheted communication (ARC) scheme comprises the following PPT algorithms:*

- Setup, Init, Send, Receive *defined as in RC (Definition 1).*
- AuthSend($st_\mathcal{P}$) $\rightarrow$ ($st'_\mathcal{P}$, num, at) *takes a state* $st_\mathcal{P}$ *and outputs a new state* $st'_\mathcal{P}$, *an ordinal* num *and an authentication tag* at.
- AuthReceive($st_\mathcal{P}$, at) $\rightarrow$ (auth, $st'_\mathcal{P}$, num) *takes a state* $st_\mathcal{P}$ *and authentication tag* at *and outputs an authentication bit* auth $\in$ {true, false}, *an updated state* $st'_\mathcal{P}$ *and an ordinal* num.

The AuthReceive *algorithm returns dummy* $st'_\mathcal{P}$, num *which the scheme ignores when* auth = false.

Remark 2. One could alternatively define AuthSend/AuthReceive to output sets of ordinals, rather than single ones, corresponding to which messages have been authenticated. Our security notions ensure that this information can be efficiently computed by parties using the ordinal that the algorithms output.

We define *correctness* for an RC and ARC scheme with the CORRECT game presented in Fig. 1. The game takes a security parameter and a schedule sched as inputs. We use a schedule to model the message flow between the participants, which can (1) send a message, (2) receive a message, and for ARC only, (3) send an authentication tag, or (4) receive a sent authentication tag. More precisely, sched is an ordered list of instructions either of the form $(\mathcal{P}, \text{``send''}, \text{ad}, \text{pt})$, $(\mathcal{P}, \text{``rec''}, j)$, and for ARC only, $(\mathcal{P}, \text{``authsend''})$, and $(\mathcal{P}, \text{``authrec''}, j)$, where $\mathcal{P} \in \{\mathsf{A}, \mathsf{B}\}$, ad denotes associated data, pt denotes a plaintext, and $j \in \mathbb{N}$ indicates either the (ad, ct) pair or the at to be received—that is, to be processed by Receive or AuthReceive respectively.

A correct (A)RC scheme must recover the correct plaintext from the corresponding associated data/ciphertext pair. Moreover, the scheme must satisfy the following properties.

- Subsequent calls to the Send algorithm outputs increasing ordinals (line 7 in Fig. 1).
- Ordinals are equal for corresponding calls to Send (resp. AuthSend for ARC) and Receive (resp. AuthReceive for ARC) (lines 12 and 22).
- For ARC, AuthSend outputs an ordinal greater or equal to the ordinal returned by the last call to Send.

We encode these properties in the CORRECT game for clarity. We require that these properties hold in the adversarial setting (in particular when forgeries are received) and enforce them in the ORDINALS game presented in Fig. 3. We formally define correctness for an (A)RC scheme in Definition 3.

Game CORRECT(1^λ, sched)
1:    pp $\leftarrow$ Setup(1^λ); $(\mathsf{st_A}, \mathsf{st_B}, z) \leftarrow$ Init(pp)
2:    $\mathsf{ad}_*[\cdot], \mathsf{pt}_*[\cdot], \mathsf{ct}_*[\cdot]_* [\cdot] \leftarrow \perp$; received$[\cdot]$, sent$[\cdot] \leftarrow$ false; sent-num $\leftarrow 0$
3:    for $i = 1$ to length(sched) do
4:      if sched$[i]$ parses as $(\mathcal{P}, \text{"send"}, \mathsf{ad}, \mathsf{pt})$ for ad, pt then
5:        $(\mathsf{st}_\mathcal{P}, \mathsf{num}, \mathsf{ct}) \leftarrow$ Send($\mathsf{st}_\mathcal{P}, \mathsf{ad}, \mathsf{pt}$)
6:        $(\mathsf{num}', \cdot) \leftarrow \mathsf{pt}_\mathcal{P}[i-1]$
7:        if $i > 1 \wedge \mathsf{num}' \geq \mathsf{num}$ then return 1
8:        sent$[i] \leftarrow$ true; $\mathsf{ad}_\mathcal{P}[i] \leftarrow \mathsf{ad}$; $\mathsf{pt}_\mathcal{P}[i] \leftarrow (\mathsf{num}, \mathsf{pt})$; $\mathsf{ct}_\mathcal{P}[i] \leftarrow \mathsf{ct}$; sent-num $\leftarrow$ num
9:      elseif sched$[i]$ parses as $(\mathcal{P}, \text{"rec"}, j)$ for $j \in \mathbb{N}$ then
10:        if $\neg$sent$[j] \vee$ received$[j] \vee_{\overline{\mathcal{P}}} [j] \neq \perp$ then continue
11:        $(\mathsf{acc}, \mathsf{st}'_\mathcal{P}, \mathsf{num}, \mathsf{pt}) \leftarrow$ Receive($\mathsf{st}_\mathcal{P}, \mathsf{ad}_{\overline{\mathcal{P}}}[j], \mathsf{ct}_{\overline{\mathcal{P}}}[j]$)
12:        if $\neg$acc $\vee ((\mathsf{num}, \mathsf{pt}) \neq \mathsf{pt}_{\overline{\mathcal{P}}}[j])$ then return 1
13:        received$[j] \leftarrow$ acc; $\mathsf{st}_\mathcal{P} \leftarrow \mathsf{st}'_\mathcal{P}$
14:      elseif sched$[i]$ parses as $(\mathcal{P}, \text{"authsend"})$ then
15:        $(\mathsf{st}_\mathcal{P}, \mathsf{num},) \leftarrow$ AuthSend($\mathsf{st}_\mathcal{P}$)
16:        if num $<$ sent-num then return 1
17:        sent$[i] \leftarrow$ true; $\mathcal{P}[i] \leftarrow (\mathsf{num},)$; sent-num $\leftarrow$ num
18:      elseif sched$[i]$ parses as $(\mathcal{P}, \text{"authrec"}, j)$ for $j \in \mathbb{N}$ then
19:        if $\neg$sent$[j] \vee$ received$[j] \vee_{\overline{\mathcal{P}}} [j] = \perp$ then continue
20:        $(\mathsf{num}_{\overline{\mathcal{P}}, \overline{\mathcal{P}}}) \leftarrow_{\overline{\mathcal{P}}} [j]$
21:        $(\mathsf{auth}, \mathsf{st}'_\mathcal{P}, \mathsf{num}) \leftarrow$ AuthReceive($\mathsf{st}_{\mathcal{P}, \overline{\mathcal{P}}}$)
22:        if $\neg$auth $\vee$ num $\neq \mathsf{num}_{\overline{\mathcal{P}}}$ then return 1
23:        received$[j] \leftarrow$ true; $\mathsf{st}_\mathcal{P} \leftarrow \mathsf{st}'_\mathcal{P}$
24:    return 0

Fig. 1. Correctness game for an RC/ARC scheme. Highlighted statements are only executed for when considering an ARC.

Definition 3 (CORRECT). *Consider the correctness game* CORRECT *presented in Fig. 1. An RC (resp. ARC) scheme is* correct *if, for all $\lambda \in \mathbb{N}$, and all sequences of the form* sched *with elements of the form* $(\mathcal{P}, \text{"send"}, \mathsf{ad}, \mathsf{pt})$, $(\mathcal{P}, \text{"rec"}, j)$, *(resp. also of the form* $(\mathcal{P}, \text{"authsend"})$, $(\mathcal{P}, \text{"authrec"}, j))$, *for* $\mathcal{P} \in \{\mathsf{A}, \mathsf{B}\}$, *we have* $\Pr[\mathsf{CORRECT}(1^\lambda, \mathsf{sched}) \Rightarrow 1] = 0$.

Remark 3. Correctness states that AuthSend must output an ordinal greater or equal to the ordinal that the last call to Send returned. If AuthSend does not increase the ordinal, then it is clear which messages are authenticated; if the ordinal increases in AuthSend, the application designer must keep track of the last num that Send returned to infer what the tag authenticates. Nonetheless, the latter case may be desirable to ensure that all ordinals output by Send and AuthSend are distinct.

Security notions for RC and ARC schemes build on a common set of oracles, introduced in Fig. 2. The SEND (resp. RECEIVE) oracle enables the adversary to send (resp. receive) a message on behalf of a party $\mathcal{P}$. In SEND, the caller can specify the randomness used by Send or let the challenger sample randomness uniformly. For ARC, AUTHSEND enables the adversary to send an authentication tag on behalf of a party $\mathcal{P}$, whereas AUTHRECEIVE handles AuthReceive. The oracles $\mathsf{EXP}_{pt}(j)$ and $\mathsf{EXP}_{st}(j)$ expose plaintexts and states, respectively.

Oracle SEND($\mathcal{P}$, ad, pt, r)

1 : $i \leftarrow i + 1$
2 : if $r = \varepsilon$ then $r \leftarrow_s \mathcal{R}$
3 : $(\mathsf{st}_\mathcal{P}, \mathsf{num}, \mathsf{ct}) \leftarrow \mathsf{Send}(\mathsf{st}_\mathcal{P}, \mathsf{ad}, \mathsf{pt}; r)$
4 : $\mathsf{state}[i] \leftarrow \mathsf{st}_\mathcal{P}$
5 : $\mathsf{plaintext}[i] \leftarrow \mathsf{pt}$
6 : $\mathsf{log}[i] \leftarrow (\text{"send"}, \mathcal{P}, \mathsf{num}, \mathsf{ad}, \mathsf{ct})$
7 : **return** $(\mathsf{num}, \mathsf{ct})$

Oracle RECEIVE($\mathcal{P}$, ad, ct)

1 : $(\mathsf{acc}, \mathsf{st}, \mathsf{num}, \mathsf{pt}) \leftarrow \mathsf{Receive}(\mathsf{st}_\mathcal{P}, \mathsf{ad}, \mathsf{ct})$
2 : if $\neg\mathsf{acc}$ then **return** $\bot$
3 : $i \leftarrow i + 1$
4 : $\mathsf{st}_\mathcal{P} \leftarrow \mathsf{st}$; $\mathsf{state}[i] \leftarrow \mathsf{st}_\mathcal{P}$
5 : $\mathsf{plaintext}[i] \leftarrow \mathsf{pt}$
6 : $\mathsf{log}[i] \leftarrow (\text{"rec"}, \mathcal{P}, \mathsf{num}, \mathsf{ad}, \mathsf{ct})$
7 : **return** num

Oracle AUTHSEND($\mathcal{P}$)

1 : $i \leftarrow i + 1$
2 : $(\mathsf{st}_\mathcal{P}, \mathsf{num},) \leftarrow \mathsf{AuthSend}(\mathsf{st}_\mathcal{P})$
3 : $\mathsf{auth}[(\mathcal{P}, i)] \leftarrow$
4 : $\mathsf{state}[i] \leftarrow \mathsf{st}_\mathcal{P}$
5 : $\mathsf{log}[i] \leftarrow (\text{"authsend"}, \mathcal{P}, \mathsf{num},)$
6 : **return** $(\mathsf{num},)$

Oracle $\mathsf{EXP}_{pt}(j)$

1 : $i \leftarrow i + 1$
2 : $\mathsf{log}[i] \leftarrow (\text{"ptexp"}, j)$
3 : **return** $\mathsf{plaintext}[j]$

Oracle AUTHRECEIVE($\mathcal{P}, j$)

1 : $\leftarrow \mathsf{auth}[(\overline{\mathcal{P}}, j)]$
2 : if $= \bot$ then **return** $\bot$
3 : $(\mathsf{auth}, \mathsf{st}, \mathsf{num}) \leftarrow \mathsf{AuthReceive}(\mathsf{st}_\mathcal{P},)$
4 : if $\neg\mathsf{auth}$ then **return** $\bot$
5 : $i \leftarrow i + 1$
6 : $\mathsf{st}_\mathcal{P} \leftarrow \mathsf{st}$; $\mathsf{state}[i] \leftarrow \mathsf{st}_\mathcal{P}$
7 : $\mathsf{log}[i] \leftarrow (\text{"authrec"}, \mathcal{P}, \mathsf{num},)$
8 : **return** num

Oracle $\mathsf{EXP}_{st}(j)$

1 : $i \leftarrow i + 1$
2 : $\mathsf{log}[i] \leftarrow (\text{"stexp"}, j)$
3 : **return** $\mathsf{state}[j]$

Fig. 2. Oracles which use variables state, plaintext, log, auth, st_* and i, all initialized in games where the oracles are used. AUTHSEND and AUTHRECEIVE are only used when considering ARC.

The oracles of Fig. 2 models a communication network composed of insecure inband and authentic out-of-band channels. The SEND and RECEIVE oracles enable the adversary to read, deliver, modify and delay messages, but AUTHSEND and AUTHRECEIVE do not allow the modification of authentication tags.

Remark 4. We assume an *always-authentic* out-of-band channel. To our knowledge, all deployed solution for out-of-band authentication and relevant literature [17,18] assume this. One can define a stronger model where the out-of-band channel is authentic only in some cases, e.g., the tampering rate is bounded, or multiple out-of-band channels exist but the adversary can compromise only a subset of them. As a not-always-authentic out-of-band channel is a stronger version of an insecure in-band channel, the discussions in Sect. 4 apply.

For RC and ARC schemes we require that even in the presence of an adversary that injects forgeries, the Send and Receive (as well as AuthSend and AuthReceive for ARC schemes) algorithms output correct ordinals. An RC or ARC scheme has *correct ordinals* if (1) the Send algorithm always outputs increasing ordinals with respect to all previously sent or received ordinals; (2) corresponding calls to Send and Receive (resp. to AuthSend and AuthReceive) output the same ordinal; and (3) for an ARC scheme, AuthSend outputs an ordinal greater or equal to the ordinal returned by the last call to Send. We consider these properties in CORRECT (Fig. 1), but they must hold also in presence of forgeries. We formalize this notion with the ORDINALS game in Fig. 3.

In this game the challenger verifies three predicates, which correspond to the conditions for correct ordinals presented above. In Definition 4 we formalize ORDINALS-security for (A)RC schemes.

Game ORDINALS$^{\mathcal{A}}(1^\lambda)$

1 : $\mathsf{pp} \leftarrow \mathsf{Setup}(1^\lambda); (\mathsf{st_A}, \mathsf{st_B}, z) \leftarrow \mathsf{Init}(\mathsf{pp})$

2 : $\mathsf{state}[\cdot], \mathsf{plaintext}[\cdot], \mathsf{log}[\cdot], \mathsf{auth}[\cdot], \mathsf{st_*} \leftarrow \bot$

3 : $i \leftarrow 0$

4 : $\mathcal{A}^{\mathsf{SEND},\mathsf{RECEIVE},\mathsf{EXP_{pt}},\mathsf{EXP_{st}},\mathsf{AUTHSEND},\mathsf{AUTHRECEIVE}}(z)$

5 : **if** $\exists \, \mathcal{P}, \mathsf{num}, \mathsf{num}', \mathsf{ad}, \mathsf{ct}, x, y :$

6 : $\mathsf{not\text{-}increasing}(\mathsf{log}, \mathcal{P}, \mathsf{num}, \mathsf{num}', x, y) \vee \mathsf{different}(\mathsf{log}, \mathcal{P}, \mathsf{num}, \mathsf{num}', \mathsf{ad}, \mathsf{ct},) \vee$

7 : $\mathsf{auth\text{-}monotonic}(\mathsf{log}, \mathcal{P}, \mathsf{num}, x)$ **then**

8 :   **return** 1

9 : **return** 0

$\mathsf{not\text{-}increasing}(\mathsf{log}, \mathcal{P}, \mathsf{num}, \mathsf{num}', x, y)$

1 : **return** $((\text{``send''}, \mathcal{P}, \mathsf{num}, \cdot, \cdot) = \mathsf{log}[x] \vee (\text{``rec''}, \mathcal{P}, \mathsf{num}, \cdot, \cdot) = \mathsf{log}[x]) \wedge$

2 : $(\text{``send''}, \mathcal{P}, \mathsf{num}', \cdot, \cdot) = \mathsf{log}[y] \wedge (0 < x < y) \wedge (\mathsf{num} \geq \mathsf{num}')$

$\mathsf{different}(\mathsf{log}, \mathcal{P}, \mathsf{num}, \mathsf{num}', \mathsf{ad}, \mathsf{ct},)$

1 : **return** $(((\text{``send''}, \mathcal{P}, \mathsf{num}, \mathsf{ad}, \mathsf{ct}) \in \mathsf{log} \wedge (\text{``rec''}, \overline{\mathcal{P}}, \mathsf{num}', \mathsf{ad}, \mathsf{ct}) \in \mathsf{log})) \vee$

2 : $((\text{``authsend''}, \mathcal{P}, \mathsf{num}, ) \in \mathsf{log} \wedge (\text{``authrec''}, \overline{\mathcal{P}}, \mathsf{num}',) \in \mathsf{log}))) \wedge (\mathsf{num} \neq \mathsf{num}')$

$\mathsf{auth\text{-}monotonic}(\mathsf{log}, \mathcal{P}, \mathsf{num}, x)$

1 : $\mathsf{num}' \leftarrow 0$

2 : **if** $(\text{``send''}, \mathcal{P}, \cdot, \cdot, \cdot) \in \mathsf{log}$ **then** $\mathsf{num}' \leftarrow \max\{\mathsf{num}'' : (\text{``send''}, \mathcal{P}, \mathsf{num}'', \cdot, \cdot) = \mathsf{log}[y] \wedge y < x\}$

3 : **return** $(\text{``authsend''}, \mathcal{P}, \mathsf{num}, \cdot, \cdot) = \mathsf{log}[x] \wedge (\mathsf{num} < \mathsf{num}')$

Fig. 3. ORDINALS game. Highlighted statements are only considered for an ARC.

Definition 4 (ORDINALS). *Consider the* ORDINALS *game in Fig. 3. We say that an (authenticated) ratcheted communication scheme is* ORDINALS *secure if, for all possibly unbounded adversaries* $\mathcal{A}$ *we have* $\Pr[\mathrm{ORDINALS}^{\mathcal{A}}(1^{\lambda}) \Rightarrow 1] = 0$.

Remark 5. The ORDINALS game in Fig. 3 is not suited to the case where ordinals can be arbitrary and in particular collide between parties. Thus, each party must be associated with disjoint ordinals: practical schemes like the Signal protocol do this by associating one party with even epochs and the counterpart with odd epochs.

4 In-band Active Attack Detection: RECOVER

In this section we consider *in-band* active attack detection in the immediate decryption setting.

Caforio et al. [11] define RECOVER security, which encompasses both r-RECOVER security and s-RECOVER security, by assuming that the channel ensures in-order message delivery. Intuitively, r-RECOVER security prevents a party from being able to deliver an honest message *after* delivering a forgery, and s-RECOVER security allows a party to detect and stop communication when their partner has delivered a forgery. We extend these notions to handle out-of-order message delivery by introducing r-RID and s-RID, which we present in Fig. 4 and illustrate in Fig. 5. Combined, these two properties ensure RID security. Note that these definitions are orthogonal to the usual forward and post-compromise security notions that the ratcheting literature considers [1,7].

The winning condition in RID consists of three predicates:

- forgery verifies whether a forgery was accepted by one of the participants by taking into account both injection and modification of messages. In the predicate, we denote the impersonated party as $\mathcal{P}$ and the recipient of the forgery as $\overline{\mathcal{P}}$.
- bad-$\overline{\mathsf{P}}$ checks whether the recipient of the forgery manages to detect the attack. This predicate corresponds to r-RID security.
- bad-P establishes whether $\mathcal{P}$, i.e., the participant that the adversary impersonates to send the forgery, fails to detect the attack. Since $\overline{\mathcal{P}}$ is the recipient of the forgery, the detection of the attack by $\mathcal{P}$ relies on a ciphertext sent by $\overline{\mathcal{P}}$ and honestly delivered. This predicate corresponds to s-RID security.

The game imposes that if forgery returns true, then at least one between bad-P and bad-$\overline{\mathsf{P}}$ must return true for the adversary to win the game.

Definition 5 (RID). *A RC is* (q, t, ϵ)*-r-RID (resp.* s-RID*) secure, if for all adversaries* $\mathcal{A}$ *which make at most* q *oracle queries and which run in time at most* t, *we have:* $\Pr[\text{r-RID}^{\mathcal{A}}(1^{\lambda}) \Rightarrow 1] \leq \epsilon$ *(resp.* $\Pr[\text{s-RID}^{\mathcal{A}}(1^{\lambda}) \Rightarrow 1] \leq \epsilon$), *where game* r-RID$^{\mathcal{A}}$ *(resp.* s-RID$^{\mathcal{A}}$*) is defined in Fig. 4.*

Although r-RID seems to be a stronger than s-RID at first glance, the two notions are not comparable. There exist schemes which provide r-RID and not s-RID security and vice versa, e.g., the scheme proposed in Fig. 6 if the checks for either r-RID or s-RID are removed from the checks subroutine.

However, we note the following link between both notions. Suppose we use a s-RID scheme. This means that $\mathcal{P}$ is able to know that $\overline{\mathcal{P}}$ received a forged message. Then, if $\mathcal{P}$ sends an "abort" message to $\overline{\mathcal{P}}$, $\overline{\mathcal{P}}$ would be able to detect the forgery after *one* honest round-trip of messages. In other words, s-RID RC schemes can be transformed (by adding an "abort" message) into RC schemes with a weak variant of r-RID security: r-RID after a honest round-trip.

Remark 6. Suppose A sends messages with num $\in \{1, \ldots, 5\}$, B receives a forgery with num $= 1000$, and then A sends messages with num $\in \{6, \ldots, 10\}$. If B never sends, i.e., A is the sender and B the receiver, RID-security only guarantees that the forgery might be detected when A sends the honest message with num' $= 1001$. (cf. the condition "num $<$ num'" in predicate bad-$\overline{\mathsf{P}}$ in Fig. 4.). Intuitively, B should be able to detect the forgery on receipt of honest message with num $= 6$ since this message is "independent" of the forgery with num $= 1000$. By the not-increasing predicate of the ORDINALS security, all messages that A sends after one round-trip will have num > 1000, so such an attack will nevertheless be eventually detected. Fine-grained security capturing these scenarios can be formalised by tracking state exposures and message delivery timing at the cost of greater definitional complexity; we leave it open to do so. Some forgeries will be defeated by our construction below but it is likely required to leverage the security of the underlying RC to build a secure scheme. Looking ahead, this remark also applies to UNF ARC schemes defined in Sect. 5.

Game r-RID$^{\mathcal{A}}(1^\lambda)$ | s-RID$^{\mathcal{A}}(1^\lambda)$

1 : $\mathsf{pp} \leftarrow \mathsf{Setup}(1^\lambda)$; $(\mathsf{st_A}, \mathsf{st_B}, z) \leftarrow \mathsf{Init}(\mathsf{pp})$
2 : $\mathsf{state}[\cdot], \mathsf{plaintext}[\cdot], \mathsf{log}[\cdot] \leftarrow \perp$
3 : $\mathsf{auth}[\cdot], \mathsf{st_*} \leftarrow \perp$
4 : $i \leftarrow 0$
5 : $\mathcal{A}^{\mathcal{O}}(z)$
6 : **if** $\exists \mathcal{P}, \mathsf{num}, \mathsf{num}', \mathsf{ad}, \mathsf{ct}, \mathsf{ad}', \mathsf{ct}', x, y :$
7 : $\mathsf{forgery}(\mathsf{log}, \mathcal{P}, \mathsf{num}, \mathsf{ad}, \mathsf{ct}, x) \wedge$
8 : $\mathsf{bad}\text{-}\overline{\mathsf{P}}(\mathsf{log}, \mathcal{P}, \mathsf{num}, \mathsf{num}', \mathsf{ad}', \mathsf{ct}')$ **then**
9 : $\mathsf{bad}\text{-}\mathsf{P}(\mathsf{log}, \mathcal{P}, \mathsf{num}', \mathsf{ad}', \mathsf{ct}', x, y)$ **then**
10 :   **return** 1
11 : **return** 0

Game RID$^{\mathcal{A}}(1^\lambda)$

1 : **return** r-RID$^{\mathcal{A}}(1^\lambda) \vee$ s-RID$^{\mathcal{A}}(1^\lambda)$

$\mathsf{forgery}(\mathsf{log}, \mathcal{P}, \mathsf{num}, \mathsf{ad}, \mathsf{ct}, x)$

1 : **return** ("send", $\mathcal{P}, \mathsf{num}, \mathsf{ad}, \mathsf{ct}) \notin \mathsf{log} \wedge$
2 :   ("rec", $\overline{\mathcal{P}}, \mathsf{num}, \mathsf{ad}, \mathsf{ct}) = \mathsf{log}[x]$

$\mathsf{bad}\text{-}\overline{\mathsf{P}}(\mathsf{log}, \mathcal{P}, \mathsf{num}, \mathsf{num}', \mathsf{ad}', \mathsf{ct}')$

1 : **return** ("rec", $\overline{\mathcal{P}}, \mathsf{num}', \mathsf{ad}', \mathsf{ct}') \in \mathsf{log} \wedge$
2 :   ("send", $\mathcal{P}, \mathsf{num}', \mathsf{ad}', \mathsf{ct}') \in \mathsf{log} \wedge$
3 : $(\mathsf{num} < \mathsf{num}')$

$\mathsf{bad}\text{-}\mathsf{P}(\mathsf{log}, \mathcal{P}, \mathsf{num}', \mathsf{ad}', \mathsf{ct}', x, y)$

1 : **return** $(y > x) \wedge$
2 :   ("send", $\overline{\mathcal{P}}, \mathsf{num}', \mathsf{ad}', \mathsf{ct}') = \mathsf{log}[y] \wedge$
3 :   ("rec", $\mathcal{P}, \mathsf{num}', \mathsf{ad}', \mathsf{ct}') \in \mathsf{log}$

Fig. 4. r-RID, s-RID and RID games for $\mathcal{O} = \{\mathsf{SEND}, \mathsf{RECEIVE}, \mathsf{EXP_{pt}}, \mathsf{EXP_{st}}\}$.

4.1   A RID-Secure RC

In this section we build a RID-secure RC scheme given a correct and ORDINALS-secure RC scheme and a collision-resistant hash function $\mathcal{H}$. We present our transformation in Fig. 6.

Scheme Description. Each party $\mathcal{P}$ keeps track of every message it has sent and received (in S and R, respectively). This information is communicated to $\overline{\mathcal{P}}$ every time $\mathcal{P}$ calls Send (via variables S and R′).

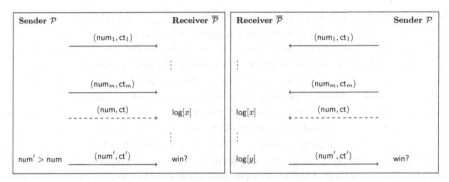

Fig. 5. Visualizing r-RID (left) and s-RID (right). Each figure showcases an adversary's winning condition in the respective game. The dashed arrows are forged messages. If $\overline{\mathcal{P}}$ accepts the message at time "win?" then the adversary wins.

The Send procedure prepares the set R′, which contains the ordinals and a hash of all received messages (line 3). This step can be optimized by using an incremental hash function as we discuss in Sect. 7.1. Next, the procedure calls RC.Send with input $((ad, S, R′), pt)$. The ciphertext ct is the concatenation of ct′ and both sets S and R′ (which are authenticated in ad′). Finally, the procedure adds the pair (num, h) to S (line 8), where the hash h is computed as $\mathcal{H}.Eval(st_{\mathcal{P}}.hk, (ad, ct))$, where $ct = (ct′, S, R′)$. Intuitively, (num, h) comprises a summary of $\mathcal{P}$'s state after calling RC.Send which can be checked by $\overline{\mathcal{P}}$ for inconsistency.

When $\overline{\mathcal{P}}$ invokes Receive, the procedure calls RC.Receive, which outputs num′ (which is such that num = num′ given $\mathcal{P}$ and $\overline{\mathcal{P}}$ are correct). Since ct contains $R^{\overline{\mathcal{P}}}$, $\overline{\mathcal{P}}$ checks that what $\mathcal{P}$ received so far was correct (line 3 in checks). In addition, using the S set contained in the ciphertext, $\overline{\mathcal{P}}$ can further check whether the ciphertexts it received so far have indeed been sent by $\mathcal{P}$. This is verified in line 5 of checks and from line 7 to 18. These latter checks detect tampering of ct by the adversary (e.g. ct.S should not contain ordinals larger than the one of the current ciphertext, or if ct was sent earlier than another ciphertext already received, ct.S should be consistent with messages already acknowledged, etc.). If everything verifies, Receive stores (num, h) in R and adds ct.S to the set of acknowledged messages (lines 9 and 10).

Remark 7. The sets S and R′ included in the ciphertext are also included in the authenticated data passed to the underlying RC: the tuple $(S, R′)$ is always authenticated in Fig. 6. This is actually not needed for RID security, but for authentication and confidentiality. Even if we do not define authentication and confidentiality for (A)RC, we use authenticated encryption for completeness.

Remark 8. In case of forgery detection the scheme outputs the generic error symbol $\perp$. In practice it could be necessary to distinguish between different kinds of errors. For instance, a RID forgery made by an adversary that exposed the state could be interpreted by the application as a failure of the underlying RC.Receive function. In that case, the application could decide to continue and accept subsequent ciphertexts, although this should not happen.

RRC.Setup(1^λ)

1 : $pp_0 \leftarrow$ RC.Setup(1^λ)

2 : $hk \leftarrow \mathcal{H}$.KGen($1^\lambda$)

3 : $hk' \leftarrow \mathcal{H}$.KGen($1^\lambda$)

4 : $pp \leftarrow (pp_0, hk, hk')$

5 : **return** pp

RRC.Send($st_\mathcal{P}, ad, pt$)

1 : $(st'_\mathcal{P}, hk, hk', S, R, \cdot, \cdot) \leftarrow st_\mathcal{P}$

2 : $nums' \leftarrow \{num' : (num', \cdot) \in R\}$

3 : $R' \leftarrow (nums', \mathcal{H}.\text{Eval}(hk', R))$

4 : $ad' \leftarrow (ad, S, R')$

5 : $(st_\mathcal{P}.st'_\mathcal{P}, num, ct') \leftarrow$ RC.Send($st'_\mathcal{P}, ad', pt$)

6 : $ct \leftarrow (ct', S, R')$

7 : $h \leftarrow \mathcal{H}.\text{Eval}(hk, (num, ad, ct))$

8 : $st_\mathcal{P}.S \leftarrow S \cup \{(num, h)\}$

9 : **return** ($st_\mathcal{P}, num, ct$)

RRC.Receive($st_\mathcal{P}, ad, ct$)

1 : $(ct', S^{\overline{\mathcal{P}}}, R^{\overline{\mathcal{P}}}) \leftarrow ct$

2 : $(st'_\mathcal{P}, hk, hk', \cdot, R, S_{ack}, max\text{-}num) \leftarrow st_\mathcal{P}$

3 : $ad' \leftarrow (ad, S^{\overline{\mathcal{P}}}, R^{\overline{\mathcal{P}}})$

4 : $(acc, st'_\mathcal{P}, num, pt) \leftarrow$ RC.Receive($st'_\mathcal{P}, ad', ct'$)

5 : **if** $\neg acc$ **then return** (false, $st_\mathcal{P}, \perp, \perp$)

6 : $h \leftarrow \mathcal{H}.\text{Eval}(hk, (num, ad, ct))$

7 : **if** checks($st_\mathcal{P}, ct, h, num$) **then**

8 :   **return** (false, $st_\mathcal{P}, \perp, \perp$)

9 : $st_\mathcal{P}.R \leftarrow R \cup \{(num, h)\}$

10 : $st_\mathcal{P}.S_{ack} \leftarrow S_{ack} \cup S^{\overline{\mathcal{P}}}$

11 : $st_\mathcal{P}.st'_\mathcal{P} \leftarrow st'_\mathcal{P}$

12 : **return** ($acc, st_\mathcal{P}, num, pt$)

RRC.Init(pp)

1 : $(pp_0, hk, hk') \leftarrow$ pp

2 : $(st'_A, st'_B, z') \leftarrow$ RC.Init(pp_0)

3 : $max\text{-}num \leftarrow 0$

4 : $S, R, S_{ack} \leftarrow \emptyset$

5 : $st_A \leftarrow (st'_A, hk, hk', S, R, S_{ack}, max\text{-}num)$

6 : $st_B \leftarrow (st'_B, hk, hk', S, R, S_{ack}, max\text{-}num)$

7 : $z \leftarrow (z', pp)$

8 : **return** (st_A, st_B, z)

checks($st_\mathcal{P}, ct, h, num$)

1 : $(nums', h') \leftarrow ct.R$

2 : $R^* \leftarrow \{(num', \cdot) \in st_\mathcal{P}.S : num' \in nums'\}$

3 : $s\text{-}bool \leftarrow (\mathcal{H}.\text{Eval}(st_\mathcal{P}.hk', R^*) \neq h')$

4 : $R' \leftarrow \{(num', \cdot) \in st_\mathcal{P}.R : num' \leq num\}$

5 : $r\text{-}bool \leftarrow (R' \not\subseteq ct.S)$

6 : $r\text{-}bool \leftarrow r\text{-}bool \lor$

7 : $(\exists(num^*, \cdot) \in ct.S : num^* \geq num)$

8 : **if** $num < st_\mathcal{P}.max\text{-}num$ **then**

9 : $r\text{-}bool \leftarrow r\text{-}bool \lor ((num, h) \notin st.S_{ack})$

10 : $r\text{-}bool \leftarrow r\text{-}bool \lor (ct.S \not\subseteq st.S_{ack})$

11 : $S_{ack}' \leftarrow \{(num', \cdot) \in st_\mathcal{P}.S_{ack} :$

12 : $num' < num\}$

13 : $r\text{-}bool \leftarrow r\text{-}bool \lor (S_{ack}' \not\subseteq ct.S)$

14 : **else**

15 : $st_\mathcal{P}.max\text{-}num \leftarrow num$

16 : $r\text{-}bool \leftarrow r\text{-}bool \lor$

17 : $(\exists(num', \cdot) \in st.S_{ack} \setminus ct.S :$

18 : $num' < st_\mathcal{P}.max\text{-}num)$

19 : **return** $r\text{-}bool \lor s\text{-}bool$

Fig. 6. RID-secure RC scheme RRC based on a RC scheme RC (Definition 1). RRC requires the following variables: max-num represents the largest received num. S is the set of (num, h) pairs; R is the set of received (num, h) pairs; S_{ack} is the set of (num, h) which are expected to be received (according to the received ciphertext ct). All sets are append-only.

Security Analysis. Correctness of the RRC scheme follows from the correctness of the underlying scheme RC and the fact that the checks always outputs false when only honest messages are received. Similarly, ORDINALS-security follows from the ORDINALS-security of RC, as RRC outputs the num that RC outputs. As the next theorems state, the construction of Fig. 6 is r-RID-secure (Theorem 1) and s-RID-secure (Theorem 2). The construction is therefore RID-secure.

Theorem 1. *Let $\mathcal{H}$ be a (t_{cr}, ϵ_{cr}) collision resistant hash function. Then RRC (defined in Fig. 6) is a (q, t, ϵ_{cr})-r-RID-secure RC where $t_{cr} \approx t$ and q is upper bounded by t.*

Theorem 2. *Let $\mathcal{H}$ be a (t_{cr}, ϵ_{cr}) collision resistant hash function. Then RRC (defined in Fig. 6) is a (q, t, ϵ_{cr})-s-RID-secure RC where $t_{cr} \approx t$ and q is upper bounded by t.*

Optimization. The s-RID notion imposes less average overhead than r-RID: the construction can be further optimized and still provide s-RID security. We give here an intuition about this optimization and refer the reader to the full version of this paper [6] for the details.

In the optimized version, parties keep track of epochs. Party A starts with epoch $= 0$ and B with epoch $= 1$. While sending each message parties attach the epoch alongside. If $\text{epoch}_A = t$, A does not accept any messages with epoch $> t+1$ and if A receives a message with epoch $= t + 1$ they update their epoch $\leftarrow t + 2$. The observation is that epoch values only increase when both parties have received a message. Using this fact, it can be shown that it suffices to convey information about the messages received in the last two epochs to provide s-RID security. If an honest message was sent from A to B after A received a forged message, either this forgery was received in the last 2 epochs, or there was another forgery and honest message pair after it, as otherwise the epoch values would be out of sync. Although this optimization does not change the worst-case complexity of Fig. 6, if the direction of the conversation changes frequently enough the overhead significantly decreases.

5   Out-of-Band Active Attack Detection: UNF

In-band active attack detection is not always possible, as an adversary may block all honest messages in the network. For example, modern messaging solutions use a possibly malicious third party server to relay messages between participants, thereby introducing a single point of failure for in-band communication. This brings us to consider out-of-band active attack detection.

An ARC scheme is *unforgeable* if, as soon as one of the two parties accepts a forgery, both parties can detect this out-of-band. We formalize this security notion through the UNF game (Fig. 7), which, similarly to RID, encompasses r-UNF and s-UNF. The winning condition in UNF consists of three predicates: forgery, bad-$\overline{\text{P}}$ (corresponds to r-UNF) and bad-P (corresponds to s-UNF) that are essentially the same as the predicates that we use to define RID security (Definition 5), except they rely on authentication tags instead of ciphertexts for forgery detection.

Definition 6 (UNF). *Consider the* r-UNF *(resp.* s-UNF*) game in Fig. 7. We say that an ARC scheme is* (q, t, ϵ)-r-UNF *(resp.* s-UNF*) secure if, for all adversaries* $\mathcal{A}$ *which make at most* q *oracle queries, and which run in time at most* t*, we have:* $\Pr[\text{r-UNF}^{\mathcal{A}}(1^{\lambda}) \Rightarrow 1] \le \epsilon$ *(resp.* $\Pr[\text{s-UNF}^{\mathcal{A}}(1^{\lambda}) \Rightarrow 1] \le \epsilon$*).*

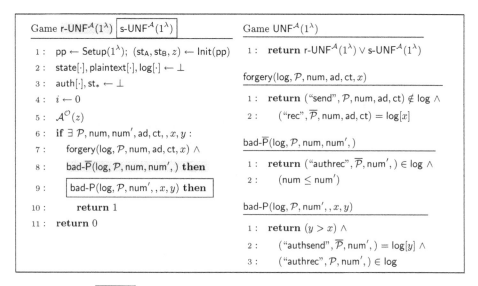

Fig. 7. r-UNF, s-UNF and UNF games for $\mathcal{O} = \{\text{SEND}, \text{RECEIVE}, \text{EXP}_{\text{pt}}, \text{EXP}_{\text{st}}, \text{AUTHSEND}, \text{AUTHRECEIVE}\}$.

Remark 9. As for RC schemes, we do not define message indistinguishability for ARC schemes. All the schemes include in the authentication tag only *public* material, i.e., messages that have already transited through the insecure channel. Since the adversary already has access to the entire transcript of the insecure channel, the authentication material does not give any additional advantage for distinguishing.

5.1 RID RC ⇒ UNF ARC

We show in this section that RID-secure RC schemes imply UNF-secure ARC ones. More precisely, one can easily build an UNF-secure ARC scheme from a RID-secure RC. The ARC scheme uses the Setup, Gen, Init, Send, Receive function of RC. To send an authentication tag with AuthSend, the ARC scheme calls the Send function on a dummy message to generate a ciphertext ct that acts as the authentication tag. The function AuthReceive is then implemented as a Receive call on the authentication tag/ciphertext. The construction is detailed in Fig. 8.

Then, we can show the following theorem, which also implies that the scheme of Fig. 8 is also r-UNF- and s-UNF-secure.

Theorem 3. *Let* RC *be a RC scheme and* RC-ARC *be the ARC scheme built out of* RC *as shown in Fig. 8. If* RC *is* RID, ORDINALS-*secure and correct, then* RC-ARC *is* UNF-, ORDINALS-*secure and correct.*

Proof. Correctness follows from the correctness of the underlying RRC and the use of domain separation for tags and ciphertexts.

RC-ARC.Setup(1^λ)
_____

1 : **return** RRC.Setup(1^λ)

RC-ARC.Init(pp)
_____

1 : **return** RRC.Init(pp)

RC-ARC.Send($\mathrm{st}_\mathcal{P}$, ad, pt)
_____

1 : $\mathrm{ct}' \leftarrow$ RRC.Send($\mathrm{st}_\mathcal{P}$, ad, pt)

2 : $\mathrm{ct} \leftarrow (0, \mathrm{ct}')$

3 : **return** ct

RC-ARC.Receive($\mathrm{st}_\mathcal{P}$, ad, ct)
_____

1 : $(b, \mathrm{ct}') \leftarrow \mathrm{ct}$

2 : **if** $b \neq 0$ **then return** (false, $\bot, \bot, \bot$)

3 : **return** RRC.Receive($\mathrm{st}_\mathcal{P}$, ad, ct')

RC-ARC.AuthSend($\mathrm{st}_\mathcal{P}$)
_____

1 : $(\mathrm{st}'_\mathcal{P}, \mathrm{num}, \mathrm{ct}) \leftarrow$ RRC.Send($\mathrm{st}_\mathcal{P}, 0, 0$)

2 : **return** $(\mathrm{st}'_\mathcal{P}, \mathrm{num}, (1, \mathrm{ct}))$

RC-ARC.AuthReceive($\mathrm{st}_\mathcal{P}$,)
_____

1 : $(b,') \leftarrow$

2 : **if** $b \neq 1$ **then return** (false, $\bot, \bot$)

3 : $(\mathrm{acc}, \mathrm{st}'_\mathcal{P}, \mathrm{num}, \mathrm{pt}) \leftarrow$ RC.Receive($\mathrm{st}_\mathcal{P}, 0,'$)

4 : **return** (acc, $\mathrm{st}'_\mathcal{P}$, num)

Fig. 8. UNF-secure ARC scheme based on a RID-secure RC scheme RRC.

Now, we sketch the proof that RID security of RC implies UNF security of RC-ARC. For any adversary $\mathcal{A}$ playing the UNF game with RC-ARC, we build a RID adversary $\mathcal{B}$ for RC. Each query made by $\mathcal{A}$ to the oracles SEND, RECEIVE, $\mathsf{EXP_{pt}}$, $\mathsf{EXP_{st}}$ are forwarded by $\mathcal{B}$ to its own corresponding oracles (and domain separation is correctly implemented where needed). Queries of the form AUTHSEND($\mathcal{P}$) are simulated by $\mathcal{B}$ querying $\mathsf{at'} \leftarrow \mathsf{SEND}(\mathcal{P}, 0, 0)$ and setting $\mathsf{at} \leftarrow (1, \mathsf{at'})$, which perfectly simulates the generation of a tag in ARC. Finally, AUTHRECEIVE queries are simulated using the RECEIVE oracle on the tag/ciphertext. $\mathcal{B}$ can perfectly simulate the UNF game for $\mathcal{A}$.

Now, let us assume that the UNF adversary $\mathcal{A}$ wins with the forgery and bad-P predicates evaluating to true. It means a forgery was received by a party $\mathcal{P}$, then, later, that party sent a tag (i.e. a ciphertext in the RID game played by $\mathcal{B}$) that is honestly and successfully delivered to a party $\overline{\mathcal{P}}$. That implies that in the RID game played by $\mathcal{B}$, a party received a forgery, then sent a message that was successfully delivered, which is a winning condition for $\mathcal{B}$.

The second case is when the UNF adversary $\mathcal{A}$ wins with the forgery and bad-$\overline{\mathsf{P}}$ predicates evaluating to true. This means that a forgery was received by a party $\mathcal{P}$ with ordinal num, then a tag with ordinal num' $\geq$ num was successfully received. Note that in our RC-ARC construction the tags are ciphertexts, thus the ordinals are strictly increasing, i.e., num' > num. Therefore, in the RID game played by $\mathcal{B}$, a forgery with ordinal num was received by $\mathcal{P}$, then later a honest ciphertext with ordinal num' > num was successfully delivered to $\mathcal{P}$, making the bad-$\overline{\mathsf{P}}$ predicate in the RID game true.

Hence, for any adversary $\mathcal{A}$ winning the UNF game, there exists a RID adversary $\mathcal{B}$ that wins with at least the same probability.

ORDINALS-security follows from the construction. $\qquad\square$

5.2 A UNF-Secure ARC Scheme

We present a non-optimized UNF-secure ARC scheme given a RC scheme (Definition 1), i.e. we define the two additional algorithms AuthSend and AuthReceive. We present our scheme in Fig. 9.

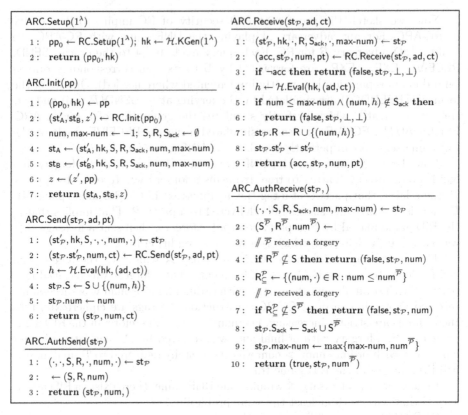

Fig. 9. UNF-secure ARC scheme based on a RC scheme RC (Definition 1). The scheme uses four additional variables compared to RC: S is the set of sent (num, h); R is the set of received (num, h); S_{ack} is the set of (num, h) which are expected to be received (according to the received authentication tag); max-num represents the largest num received in an . All sets are append-only. For simplicity of exposition, we omit the optimisation where R is sent as a single hash and n ordinals as done in Fig. 6 for RID security.

Scheme Description. The Send and Receive procedures call the respective procedures of the underlying RC scheme. The Send procedure stores the hash of (ad, ct) for the message being sent, together with the corresponding num that the underlying RC.Send algorithm returns. The tuple composed of num and the hash is stored in a set S, which is in turn stored in the internal state of the party. The Send algorithm also updates the ordinal num in the state. The Receive procedure verifies if the RC.Receive algorithm accepts the inputs and that the received message is not a forgery on a previously authenticated message, which is by construction contained in S_{ack}. If both checks pass, Receive stores the hash of (ad, ct) together with the ordinal num returned by RC.Receive in a set R.

AuthSend puts in the authentication tag at the hashes of the sent and received messages together with the last num returned by RC.Send. Intuitively, the num in the authentication tag at indicates which messages are authenticated in the S messages. Since the adversary can reorder messages both in the normal channel and in the out-of-band channel, the ordinal indicates to the recipient of the authentication tag which messages they should compare against at. AuthReceive parses the authentication tag and checks whether the messages received by the counterpart are in the local S set. Then it verifies whether the local set of received messages, without the messages not encompassed by at, is a subset of the messages sent by the counterpart. If one of these conditions is not satisfied, then a forgery is detected. The sent messages authenticated by the counterpart are stored in a set S_{ack}. Receive uses this set to avoid forgeries on already authenticated num's.

Remark 10. The size of the authentication tags and the state of each party in the scheme of Fig. 9 is linear in the number of sent and received messages as we show in Sect. 6. Messages can nevertheless be efficiently exchanged out-of-band in practice, e.g., using Bluetooth. Otherwise, parties can send authentication information over the insecure channel and authenticate it using the out-of-band channel by hashing and comparing digests [30]. If we assume that the underlying network channel is ordered (e.g., by using TCP), then the hashes of the last sent and received messages suffice to detect forgeries [11].

Security Analysis. We now analyze the security properties of the scheme in Fig. 9. Correctness of the scheme follows from the correctness of the underlying RC scheme. Similarly, ORDINALS security follows from the ORDINALS security of RC, as the scheme of Fig. 9 outputs the same num that RC outputs.

The UNF-security of the ARC scheme presented in Fig. 9, lies in the collision resistance of the hash function that the scheme uses. When one party $\mathcal{P}$ wants to authenticate the communication it produces an authentication tag containing the hashes of all the messages inboxed and outboxed by $\mathcal{P}$. These hashes can be compared with the counterpart $\overline{\mathcal{P}}$ to detect if any forgery has been received and accepted by one of the participants. In what follows we prove that the scheme of Fig. 9 is UNF-secure.

Theorem 4 (Unforgeability of ARC). *Let $\mathcal{H}$ be a (t_{cr}, ϵ_{cr})-collision resistant hash function. Then the ARC scheme, that we present in Fig. 9, is (q, t, ϵ_{cr})-UNF secure ARC scheme where $t \approx t_{cr}$.*

6   Communication Costs for Attack Detection

We study in this section the size of both ciphertexts and authentication tags of r-RID RC and r-UNF ARC schemes, respectively. In particular, all our constructions of such schemes imply a linear growth of ciphertexts (and tags) in the number of messages sent, in the worst case. We show here that one cannot hope for better by proving two lower bounds. More precisely, we show that the ciphertext space (resp. tag space) of a r-RID RC (resp. r-UNF ARC) grows exponentially in the number of messages sent. Note that we cannot prove a lower bound on the ciphertext size directly as it is always possible that *some* ciphertext is small. However, our bounds imply that at least n bits are required to represent any ciphertext or tag in their respective domain after the n-th message.

6.1   Communication Cost of r-RID RC

In what follows, we consider a RC that is perfectly correct: for all randomness r, valid states $\mathsf{st}_\mathcal{P}$ and associative data ad, the function $\mathsf{Send}(\mathsf{st}_\mathcal{P}, \mathsf{ad}, \cdot; \mathsf{r})$ mapping a plaintext to a ciphertext is injective.

The next theorem proves that ciphertext size in a r-RID RC grows linearly in the number of messages (times either the security parameter or message size).

Theorem 5. *Let Π be a perfectly correct RC, n_s and λ be fixed, and T_{λ,n_s} be the time complexity of the (efficient) adversary given on the left of Fig. 10. In addition, let $\gamma \in \mathbb{Z}$ be such that for all adversaries $\mathcal{A}$ running in at most time T_{λ,n_s} which send at most n_s messages, we have:* $\Pr[\text{r-RID}_\Pi^\mathcal{A}(1^\lambda) \Rightarrow 1] \leq \frac{1}{2^\gamma}$. *Let $\mathcal{M} = \{0,1\}^n$ and $\mathcal{C} = \{0,1\}^k$ be the plaintext and ciphertext space associated to Π, respectively. Then,*

$$k \geq n + (n_s - 1)(\gamma - 2), \ \text{if } \gamma \leq n$$
$$k \geq 2 + n_s(n - 2), \ \text{if } \gamma > n.$$

A third lower bounds gives

$$k \geq nn_s - \frac{1}{1 - \frac{2^n n_s}{2^\gamma}},$$

which is tighter for low values of n (e.g. $n = 1, 2$) and when $\gamma > n + \log(n_s)$.

Proof. We show that if k is smaller than the given bounds, one can build an encoder/decoder for a uniform source s.t. the expected bit-length of a codeword is strictly lower than the entropy (i.e. the log of the size of the sampling set), contradicting Shannon's source coding theorem.

More formally, we consider a source that samples uniformly at random from the set $\{0,1\}^{n \times n_s} \times \{0,1\}^r$, where r is the maximal number of bits (i.e. random coins) needed by the two procedures Setup and Init of Π and n_s invocations of Send. We present an encoder and decoder for such a source in Fig. 11 (the non-boxed instructions in the encoder, and the decoder shown on the left). First assume that the RC used in the encoder/decoder has perfect r-RID security. Then, the sender sends n_s honestly generated ciphertexts $\mathsf{ct}_1, \ldots, \mathsf{ct}_{n_s}$, and the receiver receives the last ciphertext ct_{n_s}. By perfect r-RID security, for any $i < n_s$, any ciphertext $\mathsf{ct}'_i \neq \mathsf{ct}_i$ should be rejected by the receiver. Thus, one can build an (inefficient) decoder that tests all ct'_i to find the correct one and recovers the corresponding message. In a sense, all ct_i must be encoded in the last ciphertext ct_{n_s}. The actual encoding is more complicated as if the r-RID security is not perfect, there will be a number of false positives (i.e. $\mathsf{ct}_i' \neq \mathsf{ct}_i$ but ct_i' is accepted by the receiver). Note that w.l.o.g., we omit the associated data throughout the proof (or assume $\mathsf{ad} = \bot$) as it plays no role.

Lemma 1. *Our encoder (Fig. 11) is perfectly correct, i.e.*

$$\Pr[\mathsf{Decode}(\mathsf{Encode}(m_1,\ldots,m_{n_s},R)) = (m_1,\ldots,m_{n_s},R)] = 1 \ .$$

Proof. The value R output by Decode is the same as the one input in Encode. Since the initial states depend only on R and Π is correct, ct_{n_s} will decrypt to m_{n_s}. The states st_A^i will be identical in both the encoding and decoding procedures as they are generated from st_A^{i-1}, the previously recovered message m_{i-1} and randomness R_i. This implies that the sets of accepting messages S_i will be the same as they depend only on st_B^1 and st_A^{i-1}. In addition, by the perfect correctness of Π, each message m_i will be in the corresponding set S_i. Hence, the decoder can recover each message m_i by reading S_i at the index given in the input.   □

Lemma 2. *Let C be the random variable corresponding to the codeword length output by Encode. In addition, let $F_i := S_i \setminus \{m_i\}$ be the set of false positives, where S_i and m_i are as in Encode. Then, $\mathbb{E}[C] \leq k+r+\sum_{i=1}^{n_s-1} 1+\log(\mathbb{E}[|F_i|]+1)$.*

Proof. By design, the encoder outputs a codeword of $k + r + \sum_{i=1}^{n_s-1} \lceil\log(|S_i|)\rceil$ bits. Therefore, we have

$$\mathbb{E}[C] = k+r+ \sum_{i=1}^{n_s-1} \mathbb{E}[\lceil\log(1 + |F_i|)\rceil] \leq k+r+ \sum_{i=1}^{n_s-1} 1 + \mathbb{E}[\log(1 + |F_i|)]$$

which is upper bounded by $k + r + \sum_{i=1}^{n_s-1} 1 + \log(\mathbb{E}[|F_i|] + 1)$, by the linearity of expectation and the definition of F_i, the fact that $\lceil x\rceil \leq 1 + x$, and Jensen's inequality, respectively.   □

Finally, we show the following key lemma.

Lemma 3. *Let F_i, $i \in [n_s - 1]$ be defined as above and n,γ as in the statement of the Theorem. Then, $\mathbb{E}[|F_i|] \leq 2^{n-\gamma}$.*

Proof. We proceed by contradiction. That is, we show that if $\mathbb{E}[|F_i|] > 2^{n-\gamma}$, then there exists an adversary $\mathcal{A}_i$ s.t. $\Pr[\mathsf{r\text{-}RID}_\Pi^{\mathcal{A}_i}(1^\lambda) \Rightarrow 1] > \frac{1}{2^\gamma}$.

We present such an adversary $\mathcal{A}_i$ on the left of Fig. 10. The adversary samples n_s messages $m_1,\ldots,m_{n_s}$ at random and makes A send these with randomness $R_1,\ldots,R_{n_s}$, respectively. Then, $\mathcal{A}_i$ makes B receive the last ciphertext ct_{n_s}. Next, $\mathcal{A}_i$ samples a random message m, sends it using state st_A^{i-1} and randomness R_i to get a ciphertext ct and makes B receive it. Now, as ct_{n_s} is sent after ct (ct_{n_s} is sent with $\mathsf{st}_A^{n_s-1}$ and ct with st_A^{i-1}), ct_{n_s} and ct will decrypt respectively to num_{n_s} and num_i s.t. $\mathsf{num}_{n_s} > \mathsf{num}_i$ by correctness. Then, if $m \neq m_i$, then ct is different from the i-th ciphertext ct_i (as we assume $\mathsf{Send}(\mathsf{st}_A^{i-1}, \cdot; R_i)$ is injective). Therefore, if ct is accepted and $m \neq m_i$, then ct and num_i satisfy the forgery

$\mathcal{A}_i$		$\mathcal{A}_i$	
1:	$m_1,\ldots,m_{n_s} \leftarrow\!\!\$\ \{0,1\}^{n\times n_s}$	1:	$m_1,\ldots,m_{n_s} \leftarrow\!\!\$\ \{0,1\}^{n\times n_s}$
2:	$R_{-1},R_0,\ldots,R_{n_s} \leftarrow\!\!\$\ \{0,1\}^r$	2:	$R_{-1},R_0,\ldots,R_{n_s} \leftarrow\!\!\$\ \{0,1\}^r$
3:	for $j \in \{1,\ldots,n_s\}$ do	3:	for $j \in \{1,\ldots,n_s\}$ do
4:	if $j = i$ then	4:	if $j = i$ then
5:	$\mathsf{st}_A^{i-1} \leftarrow \mathsf{EXP}_{\mathsf{st}}(A)$	5:	$\mathsf{st}_A^{i-1} \leftarrow \mathsf{EXP}_{\mathsf{st}}(A)$
6:	$(\mathsf{ct}_j,\mathsf{num}_j) \leftarrow \mathsf{SEND}(A,\emptyset,m_j,R_j)$	6:	$(\mathsf{ct}_j,\mathsf{num}_j) \leftarrow \mathsf{SEND}(A,\emptyset,m_j,R_j)$
7:	$\mathsf{RECEIVE}(B,\emptyset,\mathsf{ct}_{n_s})$	7:	$(\mathsf{num},) \leftarrow \mathsf{AUTHSEND}(A)$
8:	$m \leftarrow\!\!\$\ \{0,1\}^n$	8:	$i \leftarrow$ index of
9:	$\_,\_,\mathsf{ct} \leftarrow \mathsf{Send}(\mathsf{st}_A^{i-1},m;R_i)$	9:	$\mathsf{AUTHRECEIVE}(B,i)$
10:	$\mathsf{RECEIVE}(B,\emptyset,\mathsf{ct})$	10:	$m \leftarrow\!\!\$\ \{0,1\}^n$
11:	return B	11:	$\_,\_,\mathsf{ct} \leftarrow \mathsf{Send}(\mathsf{st}_A^{i-1},m;R_i)$
		12:	$\mathsf{RECEIVE}(B,\emptyset,\mathsf{ct})$
		13:	return B

Fig. 10. Adversary for the proof of Theorem 5 (resp. Theorem 6) on the left (resp. on the right).

predicate of the r-RID game in Fig. 4. In addition, as ct_{n_s} is sent and delivered honestly, the conditions on lines 7 and 8 of the r-RID game always hold for num_{n_s} and ct_{n_s}, and the adversary wins (i.e. the bad-$\overline{\mathsf{P}}$ predicate is satisfied). We call this event win.

We now compute the probability that win happens, which is the probability that $\mathsf{ct}_i \neq \mathsf{ct}$ and B accepts ct. Let $m_1,\ldots,m_{n_s}$ and the whole randomness R ($R = R_{-1},R_0,\ldots,R_{n_s}$) be fixed. As before, let S_i be the set of messages m s.t. $\mathsf{Receive}(\mathsf{st}_B^{i-1},\mathsf{ct})$ accepts, for $\mathsf{ct} = \mathsf{Send}(\mathsf{st}_A^{i-1},m;R_i)$. Note that since S_i depends only $(m_1,\ldots,m_{n_s},R)$ (which are now fixed), it is deterministic. Therefore, conditioned on $m_1,\ldots,m_{n_s},R$, we have

$$\Pr_m[\mathsf{win}] = \Pr_m[m \in S_i \wedge m \neq m_i] = \Pr_m[m \in F_i] = \frac{|F_i|}{2^n}$$

as m is sampled uniformly at random. Hence, overall

$$\Pr_{m,m_1,\ldots,m_{n_s},R}[\mathsf{win}] = \mathbb{E}_{m_1,\ldots,m_{n_s},R}[\Pr_m[m \in F_i]] = \frac{\mathbb{E}[|F_i|]}{2^n}.$$

Note that both the source and the adversary sample $m_1,\ldots,m_{n_s},R$ uniformly at random. Finally, if $\mathbb{E}[|F_i|] > 2^{n-\gamma}$, then $\Pr[\mathsf{win}] > \frac{2^{n-\gamma}}{2^n} = 2^{-\gamma}$, which leads to the contradiction. $\square$

By the previous lemma, we have $\log(\mathbb{E}[|F_i|]+1) \leq \log(2^{n-\gamma}+1) \leq \max(0,n-\gamma)+1$. Plugging this result into Lemma 2, we get $\mathbb{E}[C] \leq k+r+(n_s-1)(\max(0,n-\gamma)+2)$. In addition, as our encoder outputs a uniquely decodable code, we know that $n_s n + r \leq \mathbb{E}[C]$ by Shannon's source coding theorem. Hence, we get

$$k+r+(n_s-1)(n-\gamma+2) \geq n_s n + r \iff k \geq n + (n_s-1)(\gamma-2)$$

if $\gamma \leq n$ and otherwise

$$k + r + (n_s - 1)2 \geq n_s n + r \iff k \geq 2 + n_s(n - 2).$$

Now that the first two lower bounds have been shown, we prove the final bound in the following lemma.

Lemma 4. *Let k, n, n_s, γ as in the statement of the theorem. Then,*

$$k \geq nn_s - \frac{1}{1 - \frac{2^n n_s}{2^\gamma}} \ .$$

Proof. In order to prove this lemma, we build another encoder/decoder pair very similar to the previous one. They are shown in Fig. 11 (*with* the boxed instructions for the encoder and the boxed decoder on the right). The only difference in the encoder is that if *one* false positive is found, the encoder outputs a bit set to zero and the trivial encoding of the input. Let's call this event fail. If fail does not occur, a bit set to 1, the last ciphertext and the randomness are output.

In the decoder, either the first bit of the input is set to 0 and the input is returned straightaway, or $b = 1$ and the decoder proceeds as before. However, as there are no false positives, the m_i can be recovered without using the indices e_i (i.e. the correct message would be the only element of S_i). Overall, the expected codeword length is $\mathbb{E}[C] = 1 + \alpha nn_s + (1 - \alpha)k + r$, where $\alpha := \Pr[\mathsf{fail}]$, as if fail occurs a trivial encoding (on $1 + nn_s + r$ bits) is used, and otherwise the encoder outputs $1 + k + r$ bits. By Shannon source coding theorem, we obtain

$$1 + \alpha nn_s + (1 - \alpha)k + r \geq nn_s + r \iff k \geq nn_s - \frac{1}{1 - \alpha}$$

In addition, we have $\alpha := \Pr[\mathsf{fail}] = \Pr[\cup_{i=1}^{n_s - 1}\{|F_i| \geq 1\}] \leq \sum_{i=1}^{n_s - 1} \Pr[|F_i| \geq 1]$ as fail occurs if at least one of the sets of false positives F_i contains an element. Then, we have $\Pr[|F_i| \geq 1] \leq \mathbb{E}[|F_i|] \leq 2^{n-\gamma}$, where the first inequality follows from Markov's inequality and the second from Lemma 3. Overall, we get $\alpha \leq \frac{n_s 2^n}{2^\gamma}$. Hence,

$$k \geq nn_s - \frac{1}{1 - \alpha} \geq nn_s - \frac{1}{1 - \frac{2^n n_s}{2^\gamma}} \ .$$

Finally, some algebra shows that this bound is tighter than the second one when

$$2^\gamma \geq 2^n n_s \frac{2 - 2n_s}{3 - 2n_s} \ ,$$

that is, when γ is larger than $\approx n + \log(n_s)$. $\qquad\square$

Encode($m_1, \ldots, m_{n_s}, R$)

1:   parse $R_{-1}, R_0, \ldots, R_{n_s} \leftarrow R$; pp $\leftarrow$ Setup($1^\lambda; R_{-1}$); $st_A^0, st_B^0, z \leftarrow$ Init(pp; R_0)
2:   for $i \in \{1, \ldots, n_s\}$ do// send the n_s messages
3:      st_A^i, num, $ct_i \leftarrow$ Send($st_A^{i-1}, m_i; R_i$)
4:   acc, st_B^1, num, $m'_{n_s} \leftarrow$ Receive(st_B^0, ct_{n_s})// Receive ct_{n_s}: $m'_{n_s} = m_{n_s}$ by perfect corr.
5:   // Collecting false positives + correct messages:
6:   for $i \in \{1, \ldots, n_s - 1\}$ do
7:      $S_i \leftarrow \emptyset$
8:      for $m \in \{0,1\}^n$ do
9:         $\_, \_, ct' \leftarrow$ Send($st_A^{i-1}, m; R_i$)
10:        acc, $\_, \_, m' \leftarrow$ Receive(st_B^1, ct')
11:        if acc then
12:           $\boxed{\text{if } m \neq m_i \text{ then return } (0, m_1, \ldots, m_{n_s}, R)}$
13:           $S_i \leftarrow S_i \cup \{m\}$
14:     $L_i \leftarrow$ sort(S_i)
15:     $e_i \leftarrow$ index of m_i in L_i (in binary with $\lceil \log(|L_i|) \rceil$ bits)
16: encode ct_{n_s} with k bits
17: $\boxed{\text{return } (1, ct_{n_s}, R)}$
18: return ($ct_{n_s}, R, e_0 \| \ldots \| e_{n_s - 1}$)

Decode(ct_{n_s}, R, E)

1:   parse $R_{-1}, R_0, \ldots, R_{n_s} \leftarrow R$
2:   pp $\leftarrow$ Setup($1^\lambda; R_{-1}$)
3:   $st_A^0, st_B^0, z \leftarrow$ Init(pp; R_0)
4:   acc, st_B^1, num, $m_{n_s} \leftarrow$ Receive(st_B^0, ct_{n_s})
5:   // Collecting false positives:
6:   for $i \in \{1, \ldots, n_s - 1\}$ do
7:      $S_i \leftarrow \emptyset$
8:      for $m \in \{0,1\}^n$ do
9:         $\_, \_, ct' \leftarrow$ Send($st_A^{i-1}, m; R_i$)
10:        acc, $\_, \_, m' \leftarrow$ Receive(st_B^1, ct')
11:        if acc then $S_i \leftarrow S_i \cup \{m\}$
12:     $L_i \leftarrow$ sort(S_i)
13:     $e_i \leftarrow$ read next $\lceil \log(|L_i|) \rceil$ bits of E
14:     $m_i \leftarrow L_i[e_i]$
15:     $st_A^i, \_, \_ \leftarrow$ Send($st_A^{i-1}, m_i; R_i$)
16: return ($m_1, \ldots, m_{n_s}, R$)

Decode(b, data, R)

1:   if $b = 0$ then
2:      $(m_1, \ldots, m_{n_s}) \leftarrow$ data
3:      return ($m_1, \ldots, m_{n_s}, R$)
4:   else $ct_{n_s} \leftarrow$ data
5:   parse $R_{-1}, R_0, \ldots, R_{n_s} \leftarrow R$
6:   pp $\leftarrow$ Setup($1^\lambda; R_{-1}$); $st_A^0, st_B^0, z \leftarrow$ Init(pp; R_0)
7:   acc, st_B^1, num, $m_{n_s} \leftarrow$ Receive(st_B^0, ct_{n_s})
8:   // Collecting false positives:
9:   for $i \in \{1, \ldots, n_s - 1\}$ do
10:     $S_i \leftarrow \emptyset$
11:     for $m \in \{0,1\}^n$ do
12:        $\_, \_, ct' \leftarrow$ Send($st_A^{i-1}, m; R_i$)
13:        acc, $\_, \_, m' \leftarrow$ Receive(st_B^1, ct')
14:        if acc then $m_i \leftarrow m$
15:     $st_A^i, \_, \_ \leftarrow$ Send($st_A^{i-1}, m_i; R_i$)
16: return ($m_1, \ldots, m_{n_s}, R$)

Fig. 11. Encoder without (resp. with) $\boxed{\text{boxed}}$ instructions and decoder on the left (resp. right) for proving the first 2 (resp. third) lower bound(s) in Theorem 5.

On Non-Perfect Correctness. For simplicity in the proof, we only considered RC schemes which are perfectly correct. Note, however, that it should be possible to obtain a slightly worse bound for RC schemes that are *not* perfectly (computationally or statistically) correct. In more detail, perfect correctness is used twice in the proof of Theorem 5: 1. in the encoder to argue that the encoded messages will decrypt properly and 2. in the reduction to argue that $m \neq m_i \Rightarrow \text{ct} \neq \text{ct}_i$. Then, if the probability that a correctness error arises is at most δ, we can argue as follows. In case 1., we can simply use the trick of the 3rd bound (i.e. output the trivial encoding if the encoded message does not decrypt properly) to get the same bounds $-1/(1 - \delta \cdot n_s)$. Then, in case 2., we will have $\Pr[\text{win}] > 2^{-\lambda} - \delta$ as we need to take into account the probability that m triggers a correctness error. This might incur an additional $\approx -\log(\delta)$ loss in the bound. Overall the proof still holds with $\delta > 0$, and if it is small then the bounds remain nearly identical.

6.2 Communication Cost of r-UNF ARC

We consider a perfectly correct ARC (i.e. the function $\mathsf{Send}(\mathsf{st}_\mathcal{P}, \mathsf{ad}, \cdot; r)$ is injective for all randomness r, valid states $\mathsf{st}_\mathcal{P}$ and associative data ad). The following theorem states that the tag size of a secure ARC grows linearly in the number of messages (times either the security parameter or message size).

Theorem 6. *Let Π be a perfectly correct ARC, n_s and λ be fixed, and T_{λ,n_s} be the time complexity of the (efficient) adversary given on the right of Fig. 10. In addition, let $\gamma \in \mathbb{Z}$ be such that for all adversaries $\mathcal{A}$ running in at most time T_{λ,n_s} which send at most n_s messages, we have: $\Pr[\text{r-UNF}_\Pi^\mathcal{A}(1^\lambda) \Rightarrow 1] \leq \frac{1}{2^\gamma}$. Let $\mathcal{M} = \{0,1\}^n$ and $\mathcal{T} = \{0,1\}^k$ be the plaintext and tag space associated to Π, respectively. Then, $k \geq n_s(\gamma - 2)$, if $\gamma \leq n$, and $k \geq n_s(n-2)$, if $\gamma > n$. A third lower bounds gives*

$$k \geq nn_s - \frac{1}{1 - \frac{2^n(n_s+1)}{2^\gamma}},$$

which is tighter for low values of n (e.g. $n = 1, 2$) and when $\gamma > n + \log(n_s)$.

This theorem can be proven almost identically to Theorem 5; the minor changes to the proof are presented in the full version [6].

7 Performance and Security Trade-Offs

In Sect. 6 we showed that r-RID and r-UNF impose a linear communication complexity for RC and ARC schemes. In this section we explore ways to bypass these lower bounds and propose practical protocols for active attack detection. We first argue that s-RID/s-UNF security can be achieved at a much lower cost than the counterparts r-RID/r-UNF. Motivating this analysis, we propose a lightweight three-move protocol that authenticates communication in both direction over the out-of-band channels. Noting that ciphertexts size is unbounded in the schemes that we presented up to this point, we then propose an optimised scheme for UNF security that prunes unnecessary messages included in authentication tags.

Table 1. Overhead induced by the two RID security notions. We assume that n messages are received and c is the space needed to encode an ordinal. The variable n_{fresh} refers to the number of messages received in the last two epochs.

Notion	r-RID	s-RID
Overhead	$\mathcal{O}(n(\lambda + c))$	$\mathcal{O}(\lambda + nc)$
Optimized overhead (cf. full version [6])	N/A	$\mathcal{O}(\lambda + n_{fresh}c)$

7.1   On the Practicality of s-RID and s-UNF security

We focus here on s-RID security, but similar arguments hold for s-UNF security. The RRC scheme in Fig. 6 achieves s-RID security by sending to the counter part the list of received nums and an *hash* of the R set. Informally, this suffices for security because a party can immediately detect when their counterpart has received a forgery (by keeping in state their sent messages and recomputing the hash). Table 1 summarizes the overheads of the two notions together with the optimized variant of s-RID, where only information about messages received during the two last epochs is sent.

One can reduce ciphertext size further by optimising for the "good case" scenario where messages are delivered in-order; in this case, ordinals can be encoded in ranges. For epochs with no lost messages, it suffices to encode only the last index. In any case, as the size of a single message in today's secure messaging applications can be several kilobytes, the overhead that s-RID imposes seems reasonable. We leave a deeper and concrete analysis to determine the impact of RID/UNF security in practice to future work.

In Fig. 6, the entire set of received messages is hashed (using a regular hash function) every time a message is sent by $\mathcal{P}$. Consequently, when $\mathcal{P}$ receives a new message, the entire hash must be re-computed when $\mathcal{P}$ sends their next message. To avoid this, the scheme can use an *incremental hash function* such that, when a message is received, an efficient operation only depending on the new message and the previous digest can be executed to derive the new digest. Hash digests can be as small as a group element [13]. This enables parties to prune their set of sent/received messages in state. For example, if $\mathcal{P}$ receives a message m claiming that $\overline{\mathcal{P}}$ has received the first k messages from $\mathcal{P}$, and $\mathcal{P}$ has received messages for all possible ordinals that precede the ordinal of m, then $\mathcal{P}$ can safely store just the incrementally-hashed value corresponding to the first k messages, since $\overline{\mathcal{P}}$ can no longer claim to have only received a strict subset of the k messages.

7.2 Lightweight Bidirectional Authentication

We propose a three-move bidirectional authentication protocol. Figure 12 describes the protocol at a high level. Parties include in the authentication tag only the set of *received* messages. The receiver of the tag compares then the set of received messages from the counterpart with the set of sent messages.

We envision this approach to be used when participants meet in person or online and can both authenticate the respective views of the conversation at the same time. This is already required in Signal—with the verification of safety numbers [28]—and other messaging solutions. For readers interested in the formal investigation of the scheme, we refer them to the full version of this paper [6].

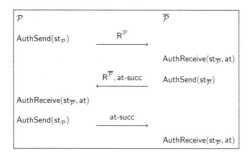

Fig. 12. Description of the three-move authentication procedure. The boolean at-succ indicates whether the counterpart's set of received messages is a subset of the local set of sent messages.

7.3 Reducing Bandwidth for UNF Security

In Fig. 13, we present a scheme that optimises bandwidth consumption for UNF security. A complete description and security proof are given in the full version [6]. Our scheme takes advantage of the fact that messages sent out-of-band cannot be forged. Suppose that $\mathcal{P}$ sends an authentication tag to $\overline{\mathcal{P}}$, then $\overline{\mathcal{P}}$ acknowledge the reception of the tag to $\mathcal{P}$. At this point, $\mathcal{P}$ no longer needs to send the information that $\overline{\mathcal{P}}$ has already obtained. As usual, our scheme supports out-of-order communication even on the authenticated channels. This approach is complicated by the fact that parties have to keep track of, e.g., which tags their partner has received to determine what is safe to prune from state (in $\mathsf{S_{at}}$-Seen), which incurs relatively small overhead in typical executions.

ARC-OP.Setup(1^λ)

1 : $pp_0 \leftarrow$ RC.Setup(1^λ); hk $\leftarrow \mathcal{H}$.KGen(1^λ)

2 : **return** (pp_0, hk)

ARC-OP.Init(pp)

1 : (pp_0, hk) $\leftarrow$ pp

2 : (st'_A, st'_B, z') $\leftarrow$ RC.Init(pp)

3 : num, max-num, cnt_{at}, max-cnt_{at}, $\leftarrow 0$

4 : S, R, S_{ack}, S_{at}, S_{at}-Seen $\leftarrow \emptyset$

5 : $st_A \leftarrow$ (st'_A, hk, S, R, S_{ack}, num, max-num,

6 : cnt_{at}, max-cnt_{at}, S_{at}, S_{at}-Seen)

7 : $st_B \leftarrow$ (st'_B, hk, S, R, S_{ack}, num, max-num,

8 : cnt_{at}, max-cnt_{at}, S_{at}, S_{at}-Seen)

9 : $z \leftarrow$ (z', pp)

10 : **return** (st_A, st_B, z)

ARC-OP.Send($st_\mathcal{P}$, ad, pt)

1 : ($st'_\mathcal{P}$, hk, S, ·, ·, num, ·) $\leftarrow st_\mathcal{P}$

2 : ($st_\mathcal{P}.st'_\mathcal{P}$, num, ct) $\leftarrow$ RC.Send($st'_\mathcal{P}$, ad, pt)

3 : $h \leftarrow \mathcal{H}$.Eval(hk, (ad, ct))

4 : $st_\mathcal{P}.S \leftarrow S \cup \{(num, h)\}$

5 : $st_\mathcal{P}.num \leftarrow$ num

6 : **return** ($st_\mathcal{P}$, num, ct)

ARC-OP.AuthSend($st_\mathcal{P}$)

1 : (·, ·, S, R, ·, num, ·,

2 : cnt_{at}, S_{at}, S_{at}-Seen) $\leftarrow st_\mathcal{P}$

3 : $st_\mathcal{P}.cnt_{at} \leftarrow st_\mathcal{P}.cnt_{at} + 1$

4 : $\leftarrow$ (S, R, num, cnt_{at}, S_{at}-Seen)

5 : $st_\mathcal{P}.S_{at}[st_\mathcal{P}.cnt_{at}] \leftarrow S$

6 : $st_\mathcal{P}.S_{at}$-Seen $\leftarrow \emptyset$

7 : **return** ($st_\mathcal{P}$, num,)

ARC-OP.Receive($st_\mathcal{P}$, ad, ct)

1 : ($st'_\mathcal{P}$, hk, ·, R, S_{ack}, ·, max-num) $\leftarrow st_\mathcal{P}$

2 : (acc, $st'_\mathcal{P}$, num, pt) $\leftarrow$ RC.Receive($st'_\mathcal{P}$, ad, ct)

3 : **if** ¬acc **then return** (false, $st_\mathcal{P}$, $\bot$, $\bot$)

4 : $h \leftarrow \mathcal{H}$.Eval(hk, (ad, ct))

5 : **if** num $\leq$ max-num $\wedge$ (num, h) $\notin S_{ack}$ **then**

6 :   **return** (false, $st_\mathcal{P}$, $\bot$, $\bot$)

7 : $st_\mathcal{P}.R \leftarrow R \cup \{(num, h)\}$

8 : $st_\mathcal{P}.st'_\mathcal{P} \leftarrow st'_\mathcal{P}$

9 : **return** (acc, $st_\mathcal{P}$, num, pt)

ARC-OP.AuthReceive($st_\mathcal{P}$,)

1 : (·, ·, S, R, S_{ack}, num, max-num,

2 : cnt_{at}, max-cnt_{at}, S_{at}, S_{at}-Seen) $\leftarrow st_\mathcal{P}$

3 : ($S^{\overline{\mathcal{P}}}$, $R^{\overline{\mathcal{P}}}$, $num^{\overline{\mathcal{P}}}$, $cnt_{at}^{\overline{\mathcal{P}}}$, S_{at}-Seen$^{\overline{\mathcal{P}}}$) $\leftarrow$

4 : **if** $cnt_{at}^{\overline{\mathcal{P}}} \leq$ max-cnt_{at} **then**

5 :   **return** (true, $st_\mathcal{P}$, $num^{\overline{\mathcal{P}}}$)

6 : // $\overline{\mathcal{P}}$ received a forgery

7 : **if** $R^{\overline{\mathcal{P}}} \not\subseteq S$ **then return** (false, $st_\mathcal{P}$, num)

8 : $R_{\subseteq}^{\mathcal{P}} \leftarrow \{(num, ·) \in R : num \leq num^{\overline{\mathcal{P}}}\}$

9 : // $\mathcal{P}$ received a forgery

10 : **if** $R_{\subseteq}^{\mathcal{P}} \not\subseteq S^{\overline{\mathcal{P}}}$ **then return** (false, $st_\mathcal{P}$, num)

11 : $st_\mathcal{P}.S_{ack} \leftarrow st_\mathcal{P}.S_{ack} \cup S^{\overline{\mathcal{P}}}$

12 : $st_\mathcal{P}.$max-num $\leftarrow \max\{$max-num, $num^{\overline{\mathcal{P}}}\}$

13 : $st_\mathcal{P}.$max-$cnt_{at} \leftarrow \max\{cnt_{at}^{\overline{\mathcal{P}}}, st_\mathcal{P}.$max-$cnt_{at}\}$

14 : // garbage collection

15 : $st_\mathcal{P}.S_{at}$-Seen $\leftarrow st_\mathcal{P}.S_{at}$-Seen $\cup \{cnt_{at}^{\overline{\mathcal{P}}}\}$

16 : $st_\mathcal{P}.R \leftarrow st_\mathcal{P}.R \setminus R_{\subseteq}^{\mathcal{P}}$

17 : **for** $i \in S_{at}$-Seen$^{\overline{\mathcal{P}}}$ **do**

18 : $st_\mathcal{P}.S \leftarrow st_\mathcal{P}.S \setminus st_\mathcal{P}.S_{at}[i]$; $st_\mathcal{P}.S_{at}[i] \leftarrow \emptyset$

19 : **return** (true, $st_\mathcal{P}$, $num^{\overline{\mathcal{P}}}$)

Fig. 13. Optimised UNF-secure ARC scheme ARC-OP based on a RC scheme RC (Definition 1). The sets S, R and S_{ack} are as in Fig. 6. The variable max-num represents the largest num received in an . The counters cnt_{at} and max-cnt_{at} keep track of how many have been sent and largest cnt_{at} received in an , respectively. S_{at}-Seen is the list of cnt_{at} of received since the last sent one; $S_{at}[i]$ contains the content of S sent in the ith . All sets are append-only.

8   Conclusion

This work considers active attack detection for secure messaging with immediate decryption, including its inherent performance limitations and how to overcome them. We conclude with some avenues for future work: 1) Analyze the *practical* overhead of in- and out-of-band authentication; and 2) Define RID and UNF notions and corresponding constructions in the group setting.

Acknowledgement. Khashayar Barooti and Loïs Huguenin-Dumittan are supported by a grant (project no. 192364) of the Swiss National Science Foundation (SNSF). We thank Olivier Becker and Nathan Duchesne for pointing out bugs in our constructions and proofs, and the anonymous reviewers of this paper for their feedback, notably the reviewer who proposed the epoch-based s-RID optimisation.

References

1. Alwen, J., Coretti, S., Dodis, Y.: The double ratchet: security notions, proofs, and modularization for the signal protocol. In: Ishai, Y., Rijmen, V. (eds.) EURO-CRYPT 2019. LNCS, vol. 11476, pp. 129–158. Springer, Cham (2019). https://doi.org/10.1007/978-3-030-17653-2_5
2. Alwen, J., Coretti, S., Dodis, Y., Tselekounis, Y.: Modular design of secure group messaging protocols and the security of MLS. In: CCS (2021)
3. Alwen, J., Coretti, S., Jost, D., Mularczyk, M.: Continuous group key agreement with active security. In: TCC (2020)
4. Alwen, J., Jost, D., Mularczyk, M.: On the insider security of MLS. In: Dodis, Y., Shrimpton, T. (eds.) CRYPTO 2022. LNCS, vol. 13508, pp. 34–68. Springer, Cham (2022). https://doi.org/10.1007/978-3-031-15979-4_2
5. Balli, F., Rösler, P., Vaudenay, S.: Determining the core primitive for optimally secure ratcheting. In: Moriai, S., Wang, H. (eds.) ASIACRYPT 2020. LNCS, vol. 12493, pp. 621–650. Springer, Cham (2020). https://doi.org/10.1007/978-3-030-64840-4_21
6. Barooti, K., Collins, D., Colombo, S., Huguenin-Dumittan, L., Vaudenay, S.: On Active Attack Detection in Messaging with Immediate Decryption. IACR Cryptology ePrint Archive (2023)
7. Bellare, M., Singh, A.C., Jaeger, J., Nyayapati, M., Stepanovs, I.: Ratcheted encryption and key exchange: the security of messaging. In: Katz, J., Shacham, H. (eds.) CRYPTO 2017. LNCS, vol. 10403, pp. 619–650. Springer, Cham (2017). https://doi.org/10.1007/978-3-319-63697-9_21
8. Bienstock, A., Dodis, Y., Garg, S., Grogan, G., Hajiabadi, M., Rösler, P.: On the Worst-Case Inefficiency of CGKA. In: Kiltz, E., Vaikuntanathan, V. (eds.) TCC 2022. LNCS, vol. 13748, pp. 213–243. Springer, Cham (2022). https://doi.org/10.1007/978-3-031-22365-5_8
9. Bienstock, A., Dodis, Y., Rösler, P.: On the price of concurrency in group ratcheting protocols. In: Pass, R., Pietrzak, K. (eds.) TCC 2020. LNCS, vol. 12551, pp. 198–228. Springer, Cham (2020). https://doi.org/10.1007/978-3-030-64378-2_8
10. Bienstock, A., Fairoze, J., Garg, S., Mukherjee, P., Raghuraman, S.: A More Complete Analysis of the Signal Double Ratchet Algorithm. In: Dodis, Y., Shrimpton, T. (eds.) CRYPTO 2022. LNCS, vol. 13507, pp. 784–813. Springer, Cham (2022)
11. Caforio, A., Durak, F.B., Vaudenay, S.: Beyond security and efficiency: on-demand ratcheting with security awareness. In: Garay, J.A. (ed.) PKC 2021. LNCS, vol. 12711, pp. 649–677. Springer, Cham (2021). https://doi.org/10.1007/978-3-030-75248-4_23
12. Civit, P., et al.: Crime and punishment in distributed byzantine decision tasks. Cryptology ePrint Archive (2022)

13. Clarke, D., Devadas, S., van Dijk, M., Gassend, B., Suh, G.E.: Incremental multiset hash functions and their application to memory integrity checking. In: Laih, C.-S. (ed.) ASIACRYPT 2003. LNCS, vol. 2894, pp. 188–207. Springer, Heidelberg (2003). https://doi.org/10.1007/978-3-540-40061-5_12

14. Cohn-Gordon, K., Cremers, C., Dowling, B., Garratt, L., Stebila, D.: A formal security analysis of the signal messaging protocol. In: EuroS&P (2017)

15. Cohn-Gordon, K., Cremers, C., Garratt, L.: On post-compromise security. In: CSF (2016)

16. Cremers, C., Zhao, M.: Provably post-quantum secure messaging with strong compromise resilience and immediate decryption. IACR Cryptology ePrint Archive (2022)

17. Dowling, B., Günther, F., Poirrier, A.: Continuous authentication in secure messaging. In: Atluri, V., Di Pietro, R., Jensen, C.D., Meng, W. (eds.) ESORICS 2022. LNCS, vol. 13555, pp. 361–381. Springer, Cham (2022). https://doi.org/10.1007/978-3-031-17146-8_18

18. Dowling, B., Hale, B.: There Can Be No Compromise: The Necessity of Ratcheted Authentication in Secure Messaging. IACR Cryptology ePrint Archive (2020)

19. Dowling, B., Hale, B.: Secure messaging authentication against active man-in-the-middle attacks. In: EuroS&P (2021)

20. Dowling, B., Hauck, E., Riepel, D., Rösler, P.: Strongly anonymous ratcheted key exchange. In: Agrawal, S., Lin, D. (eds.) ASIACRYPT 2022. LNCS, vol. 13793, pp. 119–150. Springer, Cham (2022)

21. Durak, F.B., Vaudenay, S.: Bidirectional asynchronous ratcheted key agreement with linear complexity. In: Attrapadung, N., Yagi, T. (eds.) IWSEC 2019. LNCS, vol. 11689, pp. 343–362. Springer, Cham (2019). https://doi.org/10.1007/978-3-030-26834-3_20

22. Haeberlen, A., Kouznetsov, P., Druschel, P.: PeerReview: practical accountability for distributed systems. SIGOPS 41(6), 175–188 (2007)

23. Ishai, Y., Ostrovsky, R., Zikas, V.: Secure multi-party computation with identifiable abort. In: Garay, J.A., Gennaro, R. (eds.) CRYPTO 2014. LNCS, vol. 8617, pp. 369–386. Springer, Heidelberg (2014). https://doi.org/10.1007/978-3-662-44381-1_21

24. Jacob, R., Larsen, K.G., Nielsen, J.B.: Lower bounds for oblivious data structures. In: SODA (2019)

25. Jaeger, J., Stepanovs, I.: Optimal channel security against fine-grained state compromise: the safety of messaging. In: Shacham, H., Boldyreva, A. (eds.) CRYPTO 2018. LNCS, vol. 10991, pp. 33–62. Springer, Cham (2018). https://doi.org/10.1007/978-3-319-96884-1_2

26. Jost, D., Maurer, U., Mularczyk, M.: Efficient ratcheting: almost-optimal guarantees for secure messaging. In: Ishai, Y., Rijmen, V. (eds.) EUROCRYPT 2019. LNCS, vol. 11476, pp. 159–188. Springer, Cham (2019). https://doi.org/10.1007/978-3-030-17653-2_6

27. Larsen, K.G., Nielsen, J.B.: Yes, there is an oblivious RAM lower bound! In: Shacham, H., Boldyreva, A. (eds.) CRYPTO 2018. LNCS, vol. 10992, pp. 523–542. Springer, Cham (2018). https://doi.org/10.1007/978-3-319-96881-0_18

28. Marlinspike, M.: Safety number updates (2017). https://signal.org/blog/verified-safety-number-updates/. Accessed 22 May 2022

29. Naor, M., Rotem, L., Segev, G.: Out-of-band authenticated group key exchange: from strong authentication to immediate key delivery. In: ITC (2020)

30. Pasini, S., Vaudenay, S.: An optimal non-interactive message authentication protocol. In: Pointcheval, D. (ed.) CT-RSA 2006. LNCS, vol. 3860, pp. 280–294. Springer, Heidelberg (2006). https://doi.org/10.1007/11605805_18
31. Pijnenburg, J., Poettering, B.: On Secure Ratcheting with Immediate Decryption. In: Agrawal, S., Lin, D. (eds.) ASIACRYPT 2022. LNCS, vol. 13793, pp. 89–118. Springer, Cham (2022). https://doi.org/10.1007/978-3-031-22969-5_4
32. Poettering, B., Rösler, P.: Asynchronous ratcheted key exchange. IACR Cryptology ePrint Archive (2018)
33. Poettering, B., Rösler, P.: Towards bidirectional ratcheted key exchange. In: Shacham, H., Boldyreva, A. (eds.) CRYPTO 2018. LNCS, vol. 10991, pp. 3–32. Springer, Cham (2018). https://doi.org/10.1007/978-3-319-96884-1_1
34. Scott-Railton, J., et al.: CatalanGate: Extensive Mercenary Spyware Operation against Catalans Using Pegasus and Candiru (2022). https://citizenlab.ca/2022/04/catalangate-extensive-mercenary-spyware-operation-against-catalans-using-pegasus-candiru/. Accessed 22 May 2022
35. Support, S.: Twilio Incident: What Signal Users Need to Know (2022). https://support.signal.org/hc/en-us/articles/4850133017242. Accessed 03 Oct 2022

Fork-Resilient Continuous Group Key Agreement

Joël Alwen[1]([⊠]), Marta Mularczyk[1], and Yiannis Tselekounis[2]

[1] AWS-Wickr, Seattle, USA
{jalwen,mulmarta}@amazon.com
[2] Carnegie Mellon University, Pittsburgh, USA
itseleko@cs.cmu.edu

Abstract. Continuous Group Key Agreement (CGKA) lets an evolving group of clients agree on a sequence of group keys. An important application of CGKA is scalable end-to-end (E2E) encrypted group messaging. A major problem preventing the use of CGKA over unreliable infrastructure are so-called forks. A *fork* occurs when group members have diverging views of the group's history (and thus its current state); e.g. due to network or server failures. Once communication channels are restored, members *resolve* a fork by agreeing on the state of the group again. Today's CGKA protocols make fork resolution challenging, as natural resolution strategies seem to conflict with the way the protocols enforce group state agreement and forward secrecy. Meanwhile, secure group messaging protocols which do support fork resolution do not scale nearly as well as CGKA does.

In this work, we pave the way to practical scalable E2E messaging over unreliable infrastructure. To that end, we generalize CGKA to *Fork Resilient*-CGKA which allows clients to process significantly more types of out-of-order network traffic. This is important for many natural fork resolution procedures as they are based, in part, on replaying missed traffic. Next, we give two FR-CGKA constructions: a practical one based on the CGKA underlying the MLS messaging standard and an optimally secure one (albeit with only theoretical efficiency). To further assist with fork resolution, we introduce a simple new abstraction to describe a client's local protocol state. The abstraction describes all and only the information relevant to natural fork resolution, making it easier for higher-level fork resolution procedures to work with and reason about. We define a black-box extension of an FR-CGKA which maintains such a description of a client's internal state. Finally, as a proof of concept, we give a basic fork resolution protocol.

1 Introduction

End-to-end (E2E) encrypted secure messaging is a widely used class of cryptographic applications allowing groups of clients to communicate securely with

Y. Tselekounis—Work done at CMU and partially supported by a Packard Fellowship, NSF awards #CNS-2128519, #CNS-2044679, ONR award #N000142212064, Algorand Foundation and JP Morgan Faculty Research Award.

H. Handschuh and A. Lysyanskaya (Eds.): CRYPTO 2023, LNCS 14084, pp. 396–429, 2023.
https://doi.org/10.1007/978-3-031-38551-3_13

each other over untrusted network and server infrastructure. Here, "secure" has come to denote (at least) message authenticity and a strong flavour of message confidentiality known as *Post Compromise Forward Secrecy* (PCFS) [5,22]. Intuitively, PCFS means that current messages remain semantically secure from an adversary that controls all network traffic and can leak all participants' local states both in the past (PCS) and future (FS) but not currently.

A new class of messaging applications are based on underlying Continuous Group Key Agreement (CGKA) protocols, including the IETF's upcoming *Messaging Layer Security* (MLS) standard [15]. Most of the functionality, security and efficiency properties of these protocols is inherited directly from their underlying CGKAs [6]. This has made CGKA a growing subject of cryptographic research in recent years. (See the related work section below for some highlights.)

Put simply, CGKA provides an E2E secure group state management for dynamic groups, i.e., groups whose properties (including its membership) evolve over time. Every change of the group's properties initiates a new *epoch*. The goal of CGKA is to equip the group members in each epoch with a symmetric *group key* known only to them. In line with the E2E security paradigm, clients can affect and authenticate changes to their group's state (including adding/removing members) on their own. That is, without relying on specially designated group members or trusted third parties (beyond some form of PKI). Finally, as sessions may last for years, at any point clients can perform a *PCS update*. This injects fresh entropy into all of the client's cryptographic secrets related to the CGKA session so as to hedge against the client's local state being leaked mid-session.

To be useful for messaging applications, CGKAs must provide all group members with a *consistent* view of the group's state. That is, group members that have a common view of a group state and subsequently see the same (or equivalent, as defined by the protocol) "packets" (aka. protocol messages) will end up with the same new group state. This state includes the group's membership and other data (e.g. the group's name).

The CGKA-based approach to group messaging comes with various improvements over previous generations of messaging protocols. Most notably, CGKAs are designed to scale to orders of magnitude larger group sizes n (e.g. $100x$ larger) opening up new use cases in the domain of IoT and large scale events while reducing the bandwidth requirements of today's use cases. To enable this scalability, they reduce the $O(n)$ communication (and computational) complexities of older messaging protocols' (e.g. when removing a group member or doing a PCS update) [25,33,38,48] down to $O(\log(n))$; albeit, under some relatively mild assumptions about clients online/offline behavior. This type of complexity is sometimes informally referred to as "fair-weather complexity" and it is a hallmark of CGKA protocols. Other improvements of CGKA over older protocols include mechanisms for exporting shared keys (for use by higher level applications), importing PSKs and other arbitrary external contexts, dynamically updating ciphersuites, client capabilities and even the protocol version mid-session and a mechanism for recovering from faults. They are also very extensible allowing applications to define custom group properties, business logic, and protocol functionality as needed.

Consistency For Reliable Infrastructure. One of the main tasks in designing a messaging system (and CGKA) is to ensure all participants maintain a *consistent* view of the group's state under minimal network assumptions. Indeed, the vast majority of messaging applications are designed for asynchronous communication. That is, they allow clients to participate in groups even when no other group member is currently online. Whenever a client does come online it quickly catches up to the current group state by processing any packets it missed while offline.

A common method of ensuring consistency is to implement a single source of truth determining the group state; e.g. via an server which buffers all packets for a group and forwards them *in the same order* to all group members as they come online. This implicitly establishes a fixed order of events in the group that all clients can agree on and based on which they can determine the new group state.[1] Alternatively, the server may maintain its own view of the group sate (possibly obliviously so [21]) which serves as a more direct single source of truth.

Consistency for Unreliable Infrastructure. Unfortunately, when infrastructure such as the network or server are *unreliable*, depending so critically on a central server can become problematic as it introduces a single point of failure (and a bottleneck) for the group. A client that cannot reach the server cannot participate in the group at all. Unfortunately (and unnecessarily as it turns out) that is even true when clients can still reach each other somehow over the network.

Yet many secure messaging use cases must contend with unreliable infrastructure. For example, in disaster relief scenarios, when communicating via ad-hoc mesh networks or when operating in contested environments. Even in a federated setting (where clients' packets are routed via host servers as with email) it can happen that host servers lose connectivity with each other for extended periods of time.[2] In such cases, we could ask that clients can still participate in groups with each other as long as their host servers remain in contact (or they are hosted on the same server).

Fortunately, as a consequence of enabling asynchronous messaging, most CGKA and secure messaging protocols already, in principle, allow arbitrary subsets of clients in a group to process each other's packets without any further

---

[1] We note such delivery servers are not trusted for confidentiality, authenticity or agreement of the CGKA / messaging application. Instead, we rely on them only for availability. The agreement property ensures that for two clients to be in the same epoch (a prerequisite for exchanging E2E encrypted messages in a CGKA-based messaging protocol) the clients must first have the same view of the group state.

[2] Federated messaging is used widely in practice, especially in the enterprise and public sectors. [25,28,33,34,42,44]. One reason is that by administering their own host servers, organizations can better manage their members' clients. For example, organizations can better control incoming/outgoing communication flows by determining to which external host servers their own server can connect.

interaction with the group members outside their subset [15,25,33,37]. Thus, one way to improve resilience of a messaging application is for clients to forward packets directly to each other whenever possible as permitted by the communication infrastructure.

But forgoing a central server also means living without the single source of truth it provided. So, to guarantee consistency a new method is needed that allows for "fork resolution". A *fork* occurs when clients in a group have diverging views of the group's event history, e.g. due to network links going down for some time. Once connectivity is restored, the fork resolution method must provide a way for clients to reconcile their divergent views in order to agree on a new group state from which to proceed.

For example, consider a group in a federated setting where some members are hosted on a host server S_A and the rest on host server S_B. Now suppose the link connecting the two servers goes down, partitioning the group into two subsets that can continue to communicate with each other via their shared host servers. Alice, who is hosted on server S_A adds Anthony to the group who joins from the perspective of all clients hosted on S_A. Meanwhile Bob, who is hosted on S_B, removes Alice from the group. Thus we now have a fork. Later, the link between the servers is restored. A fork resolution method must now provide a way for all clients in the group to resolve their fork to reach consensus on a common view of the group state (in particular, in this case, its membership).

Natural Fork Resolution. Fork resolution for CGKA and messaging have both been considered before. To the best of our knowledge, they all adhere to the following high-level outline we shall call *natural fork resolution*. First, clients determine which network packets each one is missing. Next, they obtain those packets (e.g. from each other via a gossip protocol). Finally, after processing the new packets they determine a new group state based on their, now updated, view of all events in the group. This final step is often implemented non-interactively by running an algorithm (sometimes called a "state resolution" algorithm [26]) which maps an initial group state and a set of causally dependent events in the group to a new group state.

The Matrix messaging application, the DCGKA protocol of [47] and the messaging protocol of [23] employ the natural fork resolution paradigm. Along with a state resolution algorithm, each also introduces a group messaging protocol that allows processing packets delivered in any causality respecting order.

An event E_1 is *causally dependent* on event E_0 if E_1 happened after E_0 from the point of view of the client that created event E_1 [46]. For example Alice must join the group (E_0) before she sends a message to the group (E_1). In a slight abuse of notation we use the same terminology for packets to denote that the sender of a packet P_1 already received packet P_0 when sending P_1. A sequence of events (or packets) is *causality respecting* if every event (or packet) appears in the sequence after all events (or packets) upon which it is causally dependent. Note that an otherwise unreliable network that does ensure packets from the same origin to the same destination are received in the order they are sent guarantees that packets in a session are delivered in an arbitrary but causality respecting order to all group members.[3]

However, neither Matrix nor the protocols from [23,47] are designed with the type of scalability that characterizes CGKA protocols. In particular, rather than fair-weather logarithmic complexity, removing a group member requires $O(n)$ download bandwidth for each client, as does a single PCS update.[4] Conversely, the (experimental) fair-weather dMLS messaging protocol (adapted from MLS by the Matrix team [39]) allows for processing packets in any causality respecting order. However it does so at the cost of seriously weakening forward secrecy for message confidentiality.

Nevertheless, their state resolution algorithms (or something similar) seem like useful building blocks for a fork resilient fair weather complexity messaging protocol. But before we can apply them we must first overcome a fundamental problem with today's CGKA protocols. Forks can result in sender and receiver of a packet receiving packets in different orders. Thus, the natural fork resolution paradigm requires that clients can process incoming packets in arbitrary causally respecting order while ending up with the same interpretation of events encoded in those packets.

In the example above, clients hosted by server S_A will see Alice's packet inviting Anthony before they see Bob's packet removing Alice while clients hosted by server S_B will see the packets in reverse. Yet, to date, no CGKA supports this level of flexibility. Instead, to ensure forward secrecy of old epoch keys, protocols mandate critical key material in an epoch state be deleted as soon as it is used to transition to a new epoch. The unfortunate side effect is that no other transitions (e.g. due to forks) can be made out of the old epoch. Thus, clients are effectively only able to process events in a single sequence, making consistency in the face of unreliable networks very challenging.

1.1 Our Contribution

In this work we pave the way towards scalable secure group messaging (and CGKA) over unreliable communication infrastructure. That is, we define and construct a new type of CGKA that supports processing packets in any causally respecting order. This removes the main roadblock preventing natural fork resolution for CGKA based messaging. We do so without compromising on the standard CGKA security properties. Furthermore, we provide a simple abstraction clients can use to reason and communicate about their local states, and to help determine what events (i.e. packets) they are missing and which missing ones they could still process.

---

[3] Most protocols make it easy to recognize any causal dependencies of packets using sequence or epoch numbers so local buffering of packets delivered prior to causal dependencies effectively implements a causality respecting network from one with eventual delivery from a clients point of view.

[4] We also note that, unlike almost all other protocols in this work, the Matrix protocol has little to no forward secrecy, though we believe this could be fixed relatively easily; albeit at the likely cost to availability in the case of failure and device loss [1].

Fork-Resilient CGKA. We begin with a fresh approach to CGKA, called *fork-resilient CGKA* (FR-CGKA). We observe that, up till now, a typical way of thinking about regular CGKA relies heavily on the concept of a client's *current epoch*. For example, this resulted in defining authenticity for CGKA to mean that a member only accepts packets from group members in a single, i.e. the receiver's "current", epoch [7–9]. Consequently, all CGKA protocols to date are incapable of processing packets with events pertaining to older epochs.

To address this, a key conceptual novelty of FR-CGKA is to replace the focus on a current epochs with a focus on a current *view of the group's history*. This history is represented as a directed tree of epochs called the *history graph* [6] where an edge from an epoch E_0 to E_1 represents an event modifying E_0's state, giving rise to the new epoch E_1. Each new FR-CGKA protocol packet corresponds to creating a new edge and epoch in the history graph. Clients can create a child epoch E_1 of any epoch E_0 in their view, i.e., they can send a packet *from epoch E_0* to convey to other group members some event changing E_0's state defining the new epoch E_1. Clients can also receive packets sent from any epoch E_0 in their view thus adding the new epoch node E_1 to their view and connecting it as a child of E_0. We adapt the standard CGKA security notions accordingly. For example, authenticity now requires that if a member accepts a packet as having been sent by some client C, then C is a member in E_0 and C did in fact create E_1. In particular, correctness of FR-CGKA ensures that packets can be processed in any causality respecting order.

Our model for defining FR-CGKA is based on server-aided CGKA [8] inheriting its advantages, e.g. a flexible definition parameterized by security predicates and enabling better efficiency, as members receive personalized, smaller packets.

The Pebbling Abstraction For Local States. To implement the natural fork resolution paradigm, clients that re-establish communication after a fork must determine which packets they have received (and which not) as well as which of the packets they didn't receive, yet which they are still able to process.

To help with this, we introduce a comparatively simple abstraction of a clients local state which captures precisely this (and no more) information about the client. In essence, it captures which epochs and their relations a client is aware of, for which of those epochs it can still send and receive and for which it still knows the epoch key. In a bit more detail, we call the abstraction the client's *pebbled history graph*. At any given moment, the local state of a client can be represented using this abstraction. There are three types of pebbles which can be placed on nodes (i.e. on epochs in the history graph): *move* pebbles, *visited* pebbles and *key* pebbles. A node can have at most one pebble of each type on it. A move pebble on epoch E denotes that the client can send and receive from E. A visited pebble on E denotes that the packet leading to E can *not* be processed any more. (Not being able to process previously received packets is crucial to ensure forward secrecy of messages in a CGKA-based messaging protocol.) Finally, a *key* pebble on epoch E indicates that the client still has the epoch key in their local state. Move and key pebbles can be deleted from old epochs at any time (as this simply corresponds to deleting cryptographic keys from the client's local state). A visited pebble E cannot be removed though as its presence implies that some critical cryptographic secret required to process the packet for the E's incoming edge has already been deleted. To summarize; to be able to process a packet sent from epoch E_0 to create child epoch E_1 the client must already have a move pebble on E_0 and, if E_1 is already in their view, then have no visited pebble on E_1. Processing the packet then (adds E_1 as a child of E_0 if not already there and) places a move, visited and key pebble on E_1. Thus, the pebbled history graph of a client fully determines which packets it has and still can process. We give a simple protocol in the FR-CGKA hybrid model for clients to obtain and manipulate their current pebbling state. This presents a minimal interface to the underlying FR-CGKA for use by a fork resolution procedure. In particular, it abstracts away all details about the underlying cryptographic state.

We note that FR-CGKA is a generalization of CGKA in the following sense. A CGKA can be built black-box from any FR-CGKA by keeping only the newly placed move pebble and removing all old ones whenever a new packet is processed.

Natural Fork Resolution Example for FR-CGKA. As a brief proof-of-concept demonstrating how FR-CGKA and the pebbling abstraction can be used for fork resolution we give an example natural fork resolution procedure (in Sect. 5). At a high level, when users discover that they are out of sync, they exchange their respective pebbled history graphs and missing packets and run a local state resolution algorithm to get a "current" group state consistent with their combined views. Then one of them chooses some epoch E and creates its child E_0 (or a chain of descendants ending with E_0) whose state matches the "current" one. (E should be chosen so that the cost of creating and/or transitioning to E_0 is minimized.) For state resolution, we can, for example, use the algorithm of [26], as the "event graphs" it uses are similar to history graphs.

Practical FR-CGKA. As our next contribution we give a practical protocol, FREEK, based on the SAIK protocol [8], which in turn builds on MLS [15].

It turns out that modifying MLS (or SAIK) without compromising on security is not entirely straightforward. For example, the distributed MLS (dMLS) protocol of [40], which modifies MLS to allow processing packets in any causally respecting order, ends up with far weaker forward secrecy (FS) than FS-CGKA (and MLS) guarantee. Concretely, to enable processing packets from old epochs, dMLS stores old secrets (thus, removing MLS's instructions to delete them). So for example, corrupting Alice while she has a move pebble on epoch E can reveal the epoch keys (and thus messages sent by clients in those epochs since dMLS is a CGKA-based messaging protocol) of many descendant epochs of E, *even those she has already deleted.* In contrast, FREEK ensures that these keys are secure.

The main idea of FREEK is as follows. SAIK (and MLS) derive the epoch key of an epoch E_1 by mixing secret entropy from the state of its parent epoch E_0 with fresh entropy sampled by the client creating E_1. Concretely, init_secret, which is part of E_0's cryptographic state, is hashed with a fresh commit_secret distributed in a packet to the group by the creator of E_1. Recall that CGKA must provide strong FS for epoch keys. Unfortunately, the decryption keys clients use to recover commit_secret from a packet may not be rotated out for many epochs into the future which means we get weaker than desired FS for commit_secret. So instead, SAIK (and MLS) improve the FS of E_1's epoch keys by immediately deleting the init_secret of E_0. Thus, a leaked client's state might reveal enough to allow recovering commit_secret but not init_secret which is also needed to recompute the epoch key.

However, this creates a problem for FR-CGKA, as the deleted init_secret is needed to transition to other child epochs of E_0. Therefore, if the packets for those epochs arrive later, the client can no longer process them.

Based on this observation, we take a more fine-grained approach to enforcing FS by being more selective about which information is deleted. In particular, in FREEK the init_secret of E_0 is now the key to a puncturable PRF (PPRF). Puncturable PRFs allow puncturing their key on any subset of inputs S such that the key reveals nothing about the output of the PRF on those inputs but can still be used to evaluate the PRF on all other inputs. The epoch key of E_1 is now derived by mixing a fresh commit_secret with the PPRF output produced using init_secret of E_0 as the PPRF key and a *challenge* distributed in the packet by the creator of E_1. So, instead of deleting init_secret, FREEK only punctures it on the challenge, providing FS for E_1's epoch key while maintaining the ability to process future packets with other commit_secret values.

It remains to choose the challenge, which turns out to be a bit tricky. For example, using commit_secret is a bad idea, because a punctured PPRF key may reveal the inputs it was punctured on (this is actually the case for the common GGM-based PPRF). Therefore, using such a construction would leak old commit secrets, making FS worse again. Using instead a random challenge (attached to the packet) is also a bad idea, because it opens the door to denial-of-service attacks (and it increases bandwidth). In such an attack, a malicious group member Malory creates a packet P_1 with the challenge copied from some honest packet P_2, and delivers P_1 to Bob before P_2. As a result, Malory blocks Bob from receiving P_1, since Bob already punctured his init_secret. As a result, FREEK constructs the challenge from a cryptographic commitment to the new epoch's public state and half of the commit secret (the other half becomes what was previously the commit secret). See Sect. 3 for details on challenge selection.

Optimally Secure FR-CGKA. Finally, we construct a second FR-CGKA protocol with optimal security predicates. That is, all epochs whose security does not contradict the protocol's correctness are secure. To achieve this, we expand the techniques of [7] which constructs standard CGKA with optimal security using hierarchical identity-based encryption (HIBE). To extend the CGKA of [7] to the FR-CGKA setting, parties would have to store old CGKA states, which destroys optimal security. We show how to fix this using HIBE with a binary identity space, which achieves both HIBE and puncturable PKE [30].

1.2   Related Work

Besides those already mentioned in the introduction, there various works about fork resolution and about CGKA. First, several (also non-cryptographic) decentralized systems in practice can be cast as using resolution algorithms to provide consistency, some more explicitly than others. For example some messaging applications [23,25,34,42], most blockchain protocols (e.g. [20,41]) and CRDT based systems like collaborative document editing applications [12,29] all use either implicit or even explicit [25] resolution algorithms. Further, [24] provides a way to deal with a different type of fork; namely ones caused by malicious insiders deviating from the honest protocol in the setting with a server trusted to deliver packets in order.

Another related line of work considers *concurrent CGKA* protocols [3,4,15, 16] which allow for concurrent PCS updates (e.g. due to a network partition). However for these protocols, concurrency is only supported within one epoch. That is, once a client decides to apply one or more concurrently generated PCS updates (or other modifications) to its state, it enters a new epoch at which point it can no longer process any other incoming events pertaining to the previous epoch. In particular, it has no way of processing delayed packets pertaining to the old group state. As such, these protocols provide a very limited type of fork resilience.

The most prominent CGKA protocol, the one underlying the MLS [15] messaging standard, received a lot of attention from academia. The works [9,18] provide cryptographic analysis of the whole protocol, while [19] analyzes its key schedule. Further, [45] gives a formally verified implementation of MLS with security proofs in F*. Apart from MLS, other CGKA protocols have been proposed, improving efficiency and/or security. In terms of security, RTreeKEM [5] improves PCFS while [32] provides better metadata privacy. The works of [13,35] consider CGKA with flexible authorization. Protocols with better efficiency (at least in certain scenarios) include TTKEM [10] and the protocol of [2]. The work [17] proposes a (potentially) more efficient but also more restricted variant of CGKA. Another way to improve efficiency is to consider *server-aided* CGKA [8,31,36], where parties download (smaller) personalized packets prepared by an untrusted mailboxing service (instead of communicating via broadcast as is typical for CGKA).

2   Fork-Resilient CGKA

In the current section we define the notion of Fork-Resilient Continuous Group Key Agreement (FR-CGKA). Our model is based on the model of [8], which in turn builds on [7], i.e., our definitions and protocols are in the server-aided CGKA setting. In Sect. 2.1 we first recall the core ideas behind CGKA in general, and then, in Sects. 2.2 and 2.3, we present our FR-CGKA definition.

2.1   (Server-Aided) CGKA

A CGKA protocol enables a dynamic group of parties to continuously agree on shared, symmetric secret keys, while ensuring the *confidentiality* and *authenticity* of those keys. The protocol is run over a network and parties may be online/offline at arbitrary times, while the communication between parties is assumed to be handled by an untrusted mailboxing service. A PKI is also assumed, that enables parties to exchange initial key material so that they can be added while offline.

Syntax. A CGKA protocol execution proceeds in *epochs*. Each epoch defines a fixed set of group properties, most importantly the member set and the shared group key. Any group member can modify the group properties, which means that they create a new epoch. In this work, we consider three types of operations they can do: (1) the *addition* of new members, (2) the *removal* of existing ones, and (3) the *update* of the group key. Each protocol operation is performed by creating a single message, which is uploaded to the untrusted mailboxing service. Afterwards, each group member can download a possibly personalized message, and, if they accept it, they transition to the new epoch. When adding a member, a CGKA protocol may contact a *key service* to fetch a so-called key package previously uploaded by the added member. This way the added member does not need to be online. A key package can only be used once and it must be group-agnostic—a member does not know to which groups they will be added.

Adversary. The adversary can fully control the mailboxing service and repeatedly expose secret states for parties. Note that this combination allows it to inject messages on behalf of parties whose states were exposed (they have no more secrets). Intuitively, this means that if Alice's state is exposed and her message is delivered first, then she can heal. However, if a message injected on her behalf is delivered first, then Alice is doomed—the only way for the group to heal is to remove the adversary impersonating Alice and add Alice again.

History Graphs. A useful tool when thinking of CGKA are *history graphs* introduced in [6]. Intuitively, a history graph is a symbolic representation of group evolution. Epochs are represented as nodes and group modifications are represented as directed edges. For instance, assume a group with a single member, Alice in epoch U. If Alice decides to add Bob, she creates an epoch V with an edge from U to V, and after Bob joins they are both in epoch V. If Alice then decides to update the group key, she creates an epoch W (every epoch has its own key). The history graph also stores information about parties' current epochs, adversary's actions, etc.

Ideally, the history graph of a CGKA protocol execution should be a chain, i.e., each epoch should have only a single child epoch in which the epoch creator transitions to it instantly, while other parties transition as soon as they go online (or they join the group) and process the creator's message. However, this is not true since forks can also be created: if two parties simultaneously create new epochs, an active adversary can deliver different messages to different parties, causing them to follow different branches, creating a fork. Furthermore, it can make parties join fake groups by injecting messages that invite them. Epochs in fake groups form what we call *detached trees*, where in presence of such trees the history graph becomes a *forest*.

Security. Using the language of history graphs, [8] identifies the following CGKA security properties. We also add correctness which is not considered in [8].

Agreement: Any two parties in the same epoch agree on the group state, i.e., the set of current members, the group key, the last group modification and the previous epoch. One consequence of the property is agreement on the transcript, that is, any two parties in a given epoch reached it by executing the same sequence of group modifications since the latter one joined.

Confidentiality: An epoch U is confidential if the adversary has no information about its group key. An active adversary may destroy confidentiality in certain epochs. CGKA security is parameterized by a *confidentiality predicate* which decides if an epoch U is confidential.

Authenticity: Authenticity for a party A in an epoch U is preserved if the following holds: If a party in U transitions to a child epoch V and identifies A as the sender creating V, then A indeed created V. Again, an active adversary may destroy authenticity for certain epochs and parties. CGKA security is parameterized by an *authenticity predicate* which decides if authenticity of a party A in epoch E is preserved.

Strong Correctness: An honestly-generated message transitioning from epoch U to V is accepted by a party in U. This holds even in the presence of corruptions, e.g. when U is created by the adversary (via injections).

2.2 FR-CGKA Protocols

The intuition from the previous subsection leads to CGKA protocols and definitions which make fork resolution very problematic. In such CGKAs, each party knows only about *one current* epoch. If two parties end up with current epochs in different branches, they will never be able to reach the same current epoch and, hence, communicate; see the example in Fig. 1. The reason is that agreement requires a common group history (including all ancestors of the current epoch), and reaching the same epoch from different branches clearly contradicts that.

FR-CGKA enables fork resolution without giving up agreement. At a high level, we replace the notion of a party's current epoch by *its current view of the history graph*. This means that a party is not in one epoch but in many epochs at once. In the FR-CGKA syntax, when a party creates a new epoch, it specifies a history-graph node which should be its parent. When a party receives a message, it simply learns about a new node (and its parent). We say that it traverses the edge in such case. Further, it can fetch the group keys from different nodes.

More precisely, a party's view is represented by a pebbling of the history graph. See the example in Figs. 2, 3 4. Each party has three types of pebbles: A party A has a *move pebble* on an epoch U if it has information required to transition to (non-visited) children of U. That is, A can create a child epoch of U and transition to a child of U created by another party. A's *key pebble* on U indicates that A can output the group key for epoch U. A key can only be fetched once for forward secrecy. Finally, forward secrecy requires that after traversing an edge from U to V, a party A removes the information needed to do that. A's *visited pebble* on V denotes that A already traversed the edge.

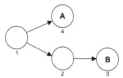

Fig. 1. A fork blocks CGKA : Alice (A) in epoch 4 will never be able to read messages sent by Bob (B) in epoch 3.

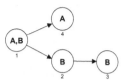

Fig. 2. Resolving a fork in FR-CGKA : A and B can process messages from epoch 1, i.e., each has a move pebble on 1. Also, B has move pebbles on 2 and 3, and A has a move pebble on 4. (Color figure online)

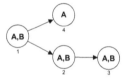

Fig. 3. Resolving a fork in FR-CGKA : Once Alice receives messages $(1, 2)$ and $(2, 3)$, she gets move pebbles on epochs 2 and 3 and she can talk to Bob (she needs *both* messages to get to epoch 3.) (Color figure online)

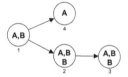

Fig. 4. FS of FR-CGKA : B's state doesn't contain information needed to transition to epochs he already visited, i.e., 2 and 3, marked by his visited pebbles. So, if B is corrupted in the situation above, the adversary learns the group key in epoch 4 but not in 2, 3.

In addition, the syntax of FR-CGKA allows for deleting move pebbles. It provides FS for old epochs from which a party no longer needs to move.

All security properties of CGKA also apply to FR-CGKA. The only difference is that agreement now mandates that for any epoch *in the view of* two parties, the parties agree on the group state in this epoch. Note that when the state of a party A is exposed, the adversary can traverse edges from all nodes on which A has a move pebble except those on the ends of which she has a visited pebble.

2.3 FR-CGKA Security Definition

We define security of FR-CGKA protocols in the UC framework, i.e., we consider a real-world experiment where an environment $\mathcal{A}$ interacts with an FR-CGKA protocol π, denoted by $\text{REAL}_\pi(\mathcal{A})$, and an ideal-world experiment where $\mathcal{A}$ interacts with an ideal FR-CGKA functionality $\mathcal{F}_{\text{FR-CGKA}}$ and a simulator $\mathcal{S}$, denoted

---

Functionality $\mathcal{F}_{\text{FR-CGKA}}$

Parameters: **conf**, **auth**, packet extraction function $\text{Ext}(C) \to c$, group creator $\text{id}_{\text{creator}}$

Initialization // Executed on first input.
  $\text{Eps}[*] \leftarrow \bot$
  Receive U_0 from the simulator
  $\text{Eps}[U_0] \leftarrow *\text{new} - \text{ep}(\text{sndr} = \text{id}_{\text{creator}}, \text{par} = \bot, \text{act}$
    $= \text{'create'}, \text{mem} = \{\text{id}_{\text{creator}}\}, \text{packet} = \text{'create'})$
  $\text{Move}^{\mathcal{A}}, \text{Key}^{\mathcal{A}}, \text{Visited}^{\mathcal{A}} \leftarrow \varnothing$
  $\text{Move}, \text{Key}, \text{Visited} \leftarrow \{(\text{id}_{\text{creator}}, U_0)\}$
  return U_0 to $\text{id}_{\text{creator}}$

Input (**Send**, U, $\text{act} \in \{\text{'up'}, \text{'add'}\text{-id}_t, \text{'rem'}\text{-id}_t\}$)
                              from id
  Send (**Send**, id, U, act) to sim., receive (V, C, ack)
  req $ack \wedge \text{Eps}[V] = \bot$
  // Compute the new epoch created by the action.
  $\text{Eps}[V] \leftarrow *\text{new} - \text{ep}(\text{sndr} = \text{id}, \text{par} = U, \text{act},$
            $\text{mem} = *\text{mem}(U, \text{act}), \text{packet} = C)$
  $\text{Move}, \text{Key}, \text{Visited} +\leftarrow (\text{id}, V)$
  $*\text{assert} - \text{agree} - \text{auth} - \text{preserved}$
  return (V, C)

Input (**Receive**, c) **from** id
  Send (**Receive**, id, c) to sim.
  if $\exists V : c = \text{Ext}(\text{Eps}[V].\text{packet})$ **then**
    req $*\text{step} - \text{correct}(\text{Move}, \text{Key}, \text{Visited}, \text{id}, V)$
  else
    Receive (ack, V) from the sim.; **req** ack
  if $\text{Eps}[V] \neq \bot$ **then**
    $(\text{sndr}, \text{act}, U) \leftarrow (\text{Eps}[V].\text{sndr},$
                $\text{Eps}[V].\text{act}, \text{Eps}[V].\text{par})$
  else
    Receive $(\text{sndr}, \text{act}, U)$ from sim.
    $\text{Eps}[V] \leftarrow *\text{new} - \text{ep}(\text{sndr}, \text{par} = U, \text{act},$
          $\text{mem} = *\text{mem}(U, \text{act}), \text{packet} = \text{'inj'})$
  if $\text{act} \neq \text{'rem'}\text{-id}$ **then**
    $\text{Move}, \text{Key}, \text{Visited} +\leftarrow (\text{id}, V)$
  $*\text{assert} - \text{agree} - \text{auth} - \text{preserved}$
  return $(U, V, \text{sndr}, \text{act})$

Input (**Join**, c) **from** id // Note : id may already
                    be in the group in another epoch
  Send (**Join**, id, c) to sim., receive (ack, U)
  req ack
  if $\text{Eps}[U] \neq \bot$ **then**
    $(\text{sndr}, \text{act}, \text{mem}) \leftarrow (\text{Eps}[U].\text{sndr},$
                  $\text{Eps}[U].\text{act}, \text{Eps}[U].\text{mem})$
  else
    Receive $(\text{sndr}, \text{act}, \text{mem})$ from sim.
    $\text{Eps}[U] \leftarrow *\text{new} - \text{ep}(\text{sndr}, \text{par} = \bot, \text{act},$
                    $\text{mem}, \text{packet} = \text{'inj'})$
  assert $\text{act} = \text{'add'}\text{-id}$
  $\text{Move}, \text{Key}, \text{Visited} +\leftarrow (\text{id}, U)$
  $*\text{assert} - \text{agree} - \text{auth} - \text{preserved}$
  return $(U, \text{sndr}, \text{mem})$

Input (**GetKey**, U) **from** id
  req $(\text{id}, U) \in \text{Key}$
  Send (**Key**, id, U) to the sim. and receive I.
  if $\text{Eps}[U].\text{key} = \bot$ **then**
    if $\text{conf}(U, \text{Eps}, \text{Move}^{\mathcal{A}}, \text{Key}^{\mathcal{A}}, \text{Visited}^{\mathcal{A}})$ **then**
      $\text{Eps}[U].\text{key} \xleftarrow{\$} \{0,1\}^{\kappa}$; $\text{Eps}[U].\text{chall} \leftarrow \text{true}$
    else
      $\text{Eps}[U].\text{key} \leftarrow I$
  $\text{Key} -\leftarrow (\text{id}, U)$
  return $\text{Eps}[U].\text{key}$

Input (**DeleteMovePebble**, U) **from** id
  Send (**DeleteMovePebble**, id, U) to sim.
  $\text{Move} -\leftarrow (\text{id}, U)$

Corruption (**Expose**, id)
  $\text{Key}^{\mathcal{A}} +\leftarrow \{U : (\text{id}, U) \in \text{Key}\}$
  for U s.t. $(\text{id}, U) \in \text{Move} \setminus \text{Move}^{\mathcal{A}}$ **do**
    $\text{Move}^{\mathcal{A}} +\leftarrow (\text{id}, U)$
    $\text{Visited}^{\mathcal{A}} +\leftarrow \{(\text{id}, V) :$
                  $U = \text{Eps}[V].\text{par} \wedge (\text{id}, V) \in \text{Visited}\}$
  $*\text{assert} - \text{agree} - \text{auth} - \text{preserved}$
  //
  Avoids commitment problem.
  only allowed if $\nexists U : \text{Eps}[U].\text{chall} \wedge$
              $\neg\text{conf}(U, \text{Eps}, \text{Move}^{\mathcal{A}}, \text{Key}^{\mathcal{A}}, \text{Visited}^{\mathcal{A}})$

Helper $*\text{new} - \text{ep}(\text{sndr}, \text{par}, \text{act}, \text{mem}, \text{packet})$
  return new epoch with given sndr, par,
  act, mem and packet, and with key $= \bot$,
  exp $= \varnothing$, chall $= \text{false}$.

Helper $*\text{mem}(U, \text{act})$
  $G \leftarrow \text{Eps}[U].\text{mem}$
  if $\text{act} = \text{'add'}\text{-id}_t$ **then** $G +\leftarrow \text{id}_t$
  else if $\text{act} = \text{'rem'}\text{-id}_t$ **then** $G -\leftarrow \text{id}_t$
  req $\text{act} = \text{'up'} \vee G \neq \text{Eps}[U].\text{mem}$
  return G

Helper $*\text{assert} - \text{agree} - \text{auth} - \text{preserved}$
  assert HG has no cycles
  for U s.t. $\text{Eps}[U] \neq \bot$ **do**
    assert $\{\text{id} : (\text{id}, U) \in \text{Visited}\} \subseteq \text{Eps}[U].\text{mem}$
    assert $\text{Eps}[U].\text{par} = \bot \vee \text{Eps}[U].\text{mem} =$
                    $*\text{mem}(\text{Eps}[U].\text{par}, \text{Eps}[U].\text{act})$
  assert $\nexists V : \text{Eps}[V].\text{packet} = \text{'inj'} \wedge \text{auth}(V,$
                $\text{Eps}, \text{Move}^{\mathcal{A}}, \text{Key}^{\mathcal{A}}, \text{Visited}^{\mathcal{A}})$

Helper $*\text{step} - \text{correct}(\text{Move}, \text{Visited}, \text{id}, V)$
  return $(\text{id}, \text{Eps}[V].\text{par}) \in \text{Move} \wedge (\text{id}, V) \notin \text{Visited}$

Fig. 5. The ideal CGKA functionality.

by IDEAL$_{\mathcal{F}_{\text{FR-CGKA}},\mathcal{S}}(\mathcal{A})$. In this setting, a protocol π is secure if for all $\mathcal{A}$ there exists an $\mathcal{S}$ such that the difference between the probability that $\mathcal{A}$ outputs 1 in REAL$_\pi(\mathcal{A})$ and the probability that $\mathcal{A}$ outputs 1 in IDEAL$_{\mathcal{F}_{\text{FR-CGKA}},\mathcal{S}}(\mathcal{A})$, is negligible. Due to space limitations, basic ideas behind the UC framework and the security model of [8] are deferred to the full version [11].

We now formally define our ideal functionality, $\mathcal{F}_{\text{FR-CGKA}}$, presented in Fig. 5. The functionality is parameterized by the confidentiality and authenticity predicates, **conf** and **auth**, respectively, the packet extraction function $\text{Ext}(C, \text{id}) \rightarrow c$ and the id of the group creator, denoted by $\text{id}_{\text{creator}}$. Note that our security definition is generic enough to capture arbitrary predicates **conf**, **auth**, admitting protocols with different levels of security. The (deterministic) Ext function is (only) used to express correctness. Ext is defined by the FR-CGKA protocol realizing $\mathcal{F}_{\text{FR-CGKA}}$ for the mailboxing service to extract from an uploaded packet C, a packet c downloaded by id.

Notation. We use the keyword **assert** followed by a condition **cond**, to restrict the simulator's actions as follows: if the condition **cond** is false, then the functionality permanently halts, making the real and ideal worlds easily distinguishable. We use **only allowed if** followed by a condition **cond** to restrict the environment. That is, our statements quantify only over environments who, when interacting with $\mathcal{F}_{\text{FR-CGKA}}$ and any simulator, never make **cond** false. We write *"Receive x from the simulator"* to denote that the functionality sends a dummy value to it, waits until it sends a value x back and asserts via **assert** that the received value is of the correct format.

History Graph. The functionality $\mathcal{F}_{\text{FR-CGKA}}$ maintains a history graph represented as an array Eps, where Eps[U] denotes the epoch identified by U. Each epoch, say E, has a number of attributes, listed below, and we use the standard object-oriented notation to access their values, e.g., E.mem returns the set of group members in E. Epoch identifiers U are arbitrary, i.e., chosen by the simulator, subject to some natural conditions such as that, when a group member creates a new epoch, its identifier must not already exist in the graph.

E.par	The parent epoch of E
E.sndr	The party who created E by performing a group operation
E.packet	If E was created honestly, the packet C creating it; else, a special value '*inj*'
E.act	The group modification performed when E was created
E.mem	The set of group members
E.key	The shared group key
E.chall	A flag indicating if a random group key has been outputted

Pebbling History Graph Nodes. Besides maintaining the history graph, the $\mathcal{F}_{\text{FR-CGKA}}$ functionality also pebbles and unpebbles the history graph nodes depending on the input operation. In particular, $\mathcal{F}_{\text{FR-CGKA}}$ stores sets Move, Key and Visited. We say that id has a move (resp., key or visited) pebble on U if $(\text{id}, U) \in$ Move (resp., $(\text{id}, U) \in$ Key or $(\text{id}, U) \in$ Visited).

Whenever a party id gets corrupted, the history graph is pebbled with *adversarial pebbles* that capture the knowledge gained by the adversary. In particular, all group keys that can be computed by id can also be computed by the adversary. $\mathcal{F}_{\text{FR-CGKA}}$ marks this by putting an adversarial key pebble on each U on which id has a key pebble. Formally, for all $(\text{id}, U) \in$ Key, it adds U to a set $\text{Key}^{\mathcal{A}}$. Second, for each epoch U on which id has a move pebble, the adversary gains the ability to transition to those children V of U for which id does not have a visited pebble on the edge from U to V. This means that the adversary can create children of U on behalf of id and transition to some (honestly created) children of U. $\mathcal{F}_{\text{FR-CGKA}}$ marks this by putting an adversarial move pebble on U and adversarial visited pebbles on some of its children. Formally, for each $(\text{id}, U) \in$ Move, $\mathcal{F}_{\text{FR-CGKA}}$ adds (id, U) to a set $\text{Move}^{\mathcal{A}}$ and for each child V of U such that $(\text{id}, V) \in$ Visited, it adds (id, V) to a set $\text{Visited}^{\mathcal{A}}$.

Inputs from Parties. **Initialization** is executed on the first input to $\mathcal{F}_{\text{FR-CGKA}}$. The functionality initializes an empty history graph ($\text{Eps}[*] \leftarrow \perp$) and creates the first epoch using the $*\text{new} - \text{ep}$ helper (see below), with epoch id U_0, chosen by the simulator. It also initializes the sets that store pebbles, described above.

On input **Send**, followed by an epoch id U and action act, $\mathcal{F}_{\text{FR-CGKA}}$ first sends all input values to the simulator and awaits for the acknowledgement flag *ack* (which indicates whether the send operation succeeds or fails with output $\perp$), message C and new epoch id V. In case of success the history graph is updated and a new epoch is created using the helper $*\text{new} - \text{ep}$. Furthermore, (id, V) is added to Move, Key, Visited, since immediately after sending the message from epoch U, id transitions to V, and is *allowed to move, compute the group key, and has already visited, V*. Finally, the helper $*\text{assert} - \text{agree} - \text{auth} - \text{preserved}$ is called to enforce agreement of the history graph and authenticity (see below).

On input (**Receive**, c), from id, $\mathcal{F}_{\text{FR-CGKA}}$ first forwards the input values to the simulator and via the first "if" statement checks if the message c corresponds to an existing target epoch id V. In the first case it enforces correctness of the transition to V (from the parent epoch $\text{Eps}[V].\text{par}$) via the helper $*\text{step} - \text{correct}$ (see below), while in the latter, the target epoch V is provided by the simulator. Subsequently, if V already exists, the sender, action and parent epoch are recovered, otherwise, a new epoch is created via $*\text{new} - \text{ep}$, with inputs provided by the simulator. If act is not for removal, the receiver transitions to the epoch V and Move, Key, Visited, are updated as in **Receive**. Agreement and authenticity are enforced via $*\text{assert} - \text{agree} - \text{auth} - \text{preserved}$. On **Join**, $\mathcal{F}_{\text{FR-CGKA}}$ acts similarly.

On input (**GetKey**, U) from id, $\mathcal{F}_{\text{FR-CGKA}}$ outputs the group key of the party with id id. The key is set to a uniformly random value if confidentiality for U holds (this is checked **conf**), otherwise is set to an arbitrary value chosen by the simulator. The operation requires (id, U) to be in the set of key pebbles, Key, and is removed afterwards, which enforces forward secrecy of CGKA protocols.

On input $(\texttt{DeleteMovePebble}, U)$ from id, (id, U) is removed from Move, indicating that id can no longer move from U to any other epoch.

When id gets corrupted, all pebbles related to id are added to the adversarial sets of pebbles. In particular, for all key pebbles $(\text{id}, U) \in$ Key, U is added to $\text{Key}^{\mathcal{A}}$; for all move pebbles (id, U) not in $\text{Move}^{\mathcal{A}}$, (id, U) is added to $\text{Move}^{\mathcal{A}}$ and similar for $\text{Visited}^{\mathcal{A}}$. The above are only allowed if the corruption is not violating confidentiality of a challenged epoch, while agreement and authenticity are enforced as in previous operations.

Helpers. The $\ast\texttt{new} - \texttt{ep}$ creates a new epoch with creator sndr, parent epoch par, action act, group members mem, and packet packet. $\ast\texttt{mem}$ receives epoch U and action act and updates the set of group members based on the type of action, while $\ast\texttt{assert} - \texttt{agree} - \texttt{auth} - \texttt{preserved}$ enforces agreement and authenticity via the following assertions: (1) all ids visited an epoch U they should belong to the set of group members for that epoch, (2) the history graph has no cycles, (3) $\ast\texttt{mem}$ should update group membership consistently w.r.t. parent epoch and action, and (4) there is no epoch that satisfies the authenticity predicate **auth**, that has been created via an injected packet. Finally, $\ast\texttt{step} - \texttt{correct}$ receives $(\text{Move}, \text{Visited}, \text{id}, V)$ and checks validity of id moving to V, as follows: there should be a move pebble for id w.r.t. the parent of V and id should have not visited V.

Security Properties. Intuitively, $\mathcal{F}_{\text{FR-CGKA}}$ captures the security properties of Sect. 2, as follows. Regarding *Agreement*, observe that for each epoch $\mathcal{F}_{\text{FR-CGKA}}$ stores and returns to the caller the same group key, parent epoch, last group modification (action), and group members (set at the time the epoch is created), and if this doesn't hold for the protocol, real and ideal would be easily distinguishable. Further, the 2nd and 3rd assertions inside the $\ast\texttt{assert} - \texttt{agree} - \texttt{auth} - \texttt{preserved}$ enforce consistency in the way that the set of group members is updated w.r.t. the actions issued by the callers, enforcing the same behaviour for the real world protocol. *Confidentiality* is captured by the fact that the adversary is allowed to make calls to the $\texttt{GetKey}$ operation, that, for epochs for which confidentiality has not been violated via corruptions (this is checked by the predicate **conf**), the operation returns a uniformly random key (instead of the actual protocol key). This implies that for confidential epochs the actual group key is indistinguishable from a uniformly random value. *Authenticity* is enforced via the last assertion in $\ast\texttt{assert} - \texttt{agree} - \texttt{auth} - \texttt{preserved}$, which requires that there should be no injected epoch that satisfies the authenticity predicate **auth**. If the assertion fails, the execution halts, making the real and ideal worlds easily distinguishable. *Strong correctness*, is enforced by the fact that for an honestly generated epoch V, $\mathcal{F}_{\text{FR-CGKA}}$ requires (via $\ast\texttt{step} - \texttt{correct}$) that the receiver has a move pebble on the parent of, and hasn't already visited, V, in which case it always returns the corresponding outputs. This means that for $\mathcal{F}_{\text{FR-CGKA}}$ the receiver should be able to process the incoming message, and if this is not the case for the real world protocol, then real and ideal are easily distinguishable.

2.4 (Sub-)Optimal Security Predicates

We now introduce generic security predicates for confidentiality and authenticity, depicted in Fig. 6, which are used by both our protocols (and potentially other FR-CGKAs). The predicates are parameterized by a protocol-specific predicate P. Intuitively, P identifies epochs which are insecure only due to the protocol's sub-optimal security. That is, P of an optimal FR-CGKA is always false.

First of all, both predicates are false for epochs in detached trees, i.e., not descendants of the root epoch created on Initialization. The reason is that, as in [8], we do not consider security in detached trees for simplicity. Note that detached epochs may become secure once attached. In the remainder of this section, we do not consider detached epochs.

In general, both predicates are defined as follows. We start with an initial configuration of adversary's pebbles, as recorded by $\mathcal{F}_{\text{FR-CGKA}}$ on corruptions. Then we add more adversary's pebbles, in any way that conforms with pebbling-step

---

Generic security predicates

$\text{conf}_P(U, \text{Eps}, \text{Move}_0^{\mathcal{A}}, \text{Key}_0^{\mathcal{A}}, \text{Visited}_0^{\mathcal{A}})$ is true if U is a descendant of the epoch created on Initialization and there is no sequence of P-valid pebbling steps from $(\text{Move}_0^{\mathcal{A}}, \text{Key}_0^{\mathcal{A}}, \text{Visited}_0^{\mathcal{A}})$ to $(\text{Move}^{\mathcal{A}}, \text{Key}^{\mathcal{A}}, \text{Visited}^{\mathcal{A}})$ such that $U \in \text{Key}^{\mathcal{A}}$.

$\text{auth}_P(V, \text{Eps}, \text{Move}_0^{\mathcal{A}}, \text{Key}_0^{\mathcal{A}}, \text{Visited}_0^{\mathcal{A}})$ is true iff V is a descendant of the epoch created on Initialization and there is no sequence of P-valid pebbling steps from $(\text{Move}_0^{\mathcal{A}}, \text{Key}_0^{\mathcal{A}}, \text{Visited}_0^{\mathcal{A}})$ to $(\text{Move}^{\mathcal{A}}, \text{Key}^{\mathcal{A}}, \text{Visited}^{\mathcal{A}})$ s.t. there is a move pebble for the creator $\text{id} = \text{Eps}[V].\text{sndr}$ of V on its parent $U = \text{Eps}[V].\text{par}$.

P-valid pebbling step

Let P be a predicate on a history graph Eps, a party id, an epoch V and a pebbling configuration $(\text{Move}^{\mathcal{A}}, \text{Key}^{\mathcal{A}}, \text{Visited}^{\mathcal{A}})$. A pair of adversarial pebbling configurations $(\text{Move}_0^{\mathcal{A}}, \text{Key}_0^{\mathcal{A}}, \text{Visited}_0^{\mathcal{A}})$ and $(\text{Move}_1^{\mathcal{A}}, \text{Key}_1^{\mathcal{A}}, \text{Visited}_1^{\mathcal{A}})$ on a history graph Eps is P-valid if all of the following conditions hold.

1. In addition, move pebbles for id cannot be put on V if id is the sender or is not a member:

$$(\text{id}, V) \in (\text{Move}_1^{\mathcal{A}} \setminus \text{Move}_0^{\mathcal{A}}) \wedge U \neq \bot \rightarrow \text{id} \in \text{Eps}[V].\text{mem} \wedge \text{id} \neq \text{Eps}[V].\text{sndr}$$

2. Move pebbles are only put a node V if A) the parent $U = \text{Eps}[V].\text{par}$ already has a move pebble for id and there is no visited pebble on V, or B) $\text{subopt} = P(\text{Eps}, \text{id}, V, \text{Move}_0^{\mathcal{A}}, \text{Key}_0^{\mathcal{A}}, \text{Visited}_0^{\mathcal{A}})$ is true.

$$(\text{id}, V) \in (\text{Move}_1^{\mathcal{A}} \setminus \text{Move}_0^{\mathcal{A}}) \wedge U \neq \bot \rightarrow \left((\text{id}, U) \in \text{Move}_0^{\mathcal{A}} \wedge (\text{id}, V) \notin \text{Visited}_0^{\mathcal{A}}\right) \vee \text{subopt}$$

3. Key pebbles are put on nodes V only if a move pebble for some id is put on it:

$$U \in (\text{Key}_1^{\mathcal{A}} \setminus \text{Key}_0^{\mathcal{A}}) \wedge U \neq \bot \rightarrow \exists \text{id}(\text{id}, U) \in \text{Move}_1^{\mathcal{A}} \setminus \text{Move}_0^{\mathcal{A}}$$

4. Visited pebbles for an id are removed from an edge (U, V) only if a move pebble is put on its parent U:

$$(\text{id}, V) \in (\text{Visited}_0^{\mathcal{A}} \setminus \text{Visited}_1^{\mathcal{A}}) \wedge U \neq \bot \rightarrow (\text{id}, U) \in \text{Move}_1^{\mathcal{A}} \setminus \text{Move}_0^{\mathcal{A}}$$

Fig. 6. Generic security predicates for both our protocols.

P-validity, defined in the bottom part of the figure. An epoch U is confidential, i.e., $\mathbf{conf}(U, \mathsf{Eps}, \mathsf{Move}_0^{\mathcal{A}}, \mathsf{Key}_0^{\mathcal{A}}, \mathsf{Visited}_0^{\mathcal{A}})$ is true, if there is no way we can get to a configuration where $U \in \mathsf{Key}^{\mathcal{A}}$, that is, if the adversary cannot *deduce* a configuration where it knows the key in U. Further, authenticity for V is guaranteed, i.e., $\mathbf{auth}(V, \mathsf{Eps}, \mathsf{Move}_0^{\mathcal{A}}, \mathsf{Key}_0^{\mathcal{A}}, \mathsf{Visited}_0^{\mathcal{A}})$ is true if the adversary cannot deduce a configuration with a move pebble for the creator of V on its parent.

Pebbling-Step Validity. A step from a configuration $(\mathsf{Eps}, \mathsf{Move}_0^{\mathcal{A}}, \mathsf{Key}_0^{\mathcal{A}}, \mathsf{Visited}_0^{\mathcal{A}})$ to $(\mathsf{Eps}, \mathsf{Move}_1^{\mathcal{A}}, \mathsf{Key}_1^{\mathcal{A}}, \mathsf{Visited}_1^{\mathcal{A}})$ is valid w.r.t. the predicate P (or *P-valid*), if rules 1), 2), 3), 4) on Fig. 6 hold. Rules 1), 2) define when the adversary can add a move pebble for id on V, i.e., transition to a configuration such that $(\mathsf{id}, V) \in \mathsf{Move}_1^{\mathcal{A}}$. Intuitively, being able to add a move pebble means that the adversary can deduce secrets known to id in V from the secrets it has given in the first configuration 0. For an optimal protocol, i.e., with $P(\cdot) = \mathtt{false}$, this is only possible if the adversary can transition to V by executing id's protocol. This is only possible if 1) id didn't create, and is a member of, V, 2) there is a move pebble on the parent of V for id and id doesn't have a visited pebble on V. Observe that this is the same as the $*\mathtt{step} - \mathtt{correct}$ predicate in $\mathcal{F}_{\text{FR-CGKA}}$. Intuitively, 1) captures PCS—the group heals from id's compromise when id sends a message or is no longer a group member, and 2) captures FS—corrupting id after it transitioned to V does not give the adversary the ability to transition.

The above cases cover what we consider as *optimal* security. Additional, *protocol specific*, weaknesses that enable the adversary to deduce *more* information about the parties' protocol states are captured by the "$\vee P(\cdot)$" part of the generic security predicate, which enables the adversary to deduce "more pebbles", by mounting protocol specific attacks that set $P(\cdot)$ to $\mathtt{true}$.

3 The **FREEK** Protocol

In this section we present the practical FR-CGKA called FREEK. It builds on the SAIK protocol of [8], which in turn builds on the MLS protocol of [14]. We note that all our techniques can be easily applied to MLS too.

Overview of SAIK. For this overview, we distinguish three components of SAIK: *key schedule*, the *TreeKEM protocol* and *message framing*. The key schedule generates for each epoch U a bunch of secrets: the *application, membership, init* and *epoch*, secrets (and a *joiner*, which is only relevant for adding new members, so we ignore it for now). A secret of U is a κ-bit value known only to the members in U. The *application secret* is the CGKA *group key*. The rest we explain soon.

When a party A creates an epoch V as a child of U, the key schedule generates secrets for V as follows. First, the *init secret* of U is hashed with the *commit secret* of V and the *group context* of V to compute the *epoch secret* of V. The commit secret is a fresh random value which A generates and communicates to all other group members using TreeKEM (TreeKEM guarantees PCS).[5] The context is a cryptographic commitment to all relevant information about V, e.g. the member set and the parent epoch. Finally, all other secrets of V are derived by hashing its epoch secret with different labels.

The main idea behind the FS and PCS security of SAIK is as follows. Regarding FS, observe that the secrets in V look random (in the RO model) if the adversary does not know the secrets of U, while for PCS, the secrets of V also look random even if the adversary knows the secrets of U, assuming that A generated the commit secret for V, honestly. SAIK also achieves agreement because agreement on the secrets implies agreement on the group context which commits to all information we want the group members to agree on. Finally, SAIK achieves authenticity using the message-framing component. This component equips each member with a signature key pair. When A creates V, her message is framed by signing it with her secret key and MACing with the *membership secret* in U. A's message also includes a new key pair for herself, which provides PCS.

Problems with Forks. In SAIK, when a party B transitions from epoch U to V, he immediately deletes the init secret of U. Indeed, this is essential for FS as in this way, if B gets corrupted, say, five epochs later, the secrets of V remain secure, since the adversary does not know the init secret of U. Note that, TreeKEM does not guarantee security of the commit secret of V after the corruption, as the adversary could learn the secret key that decrypts the ciphertext that carries it (this happens if B does not issue an update after epoch V and before getting corrupted). The above creates issues in the presence of forks. For concreteness, say there is a network partition and some party, A', not knowing about A creating V, creates another child of U, say V'. When the connectivity is restored and B learns about V', he would like to derive its secrets (this way he can e.g. read messages encrypted using the CGKA group key in the other partition). However, this is not possible since the same init secret in U protects the group keys in both V and V'. Therefore by deleting it in order to achieve FS of V, B lost the ability to derive the key in V'. A trivial solution to solve this issue would be to *store the old init secrets*, but clearly this completely destroys FS.

Our FR-CGKA Protocol. In a high level, our idea to solve the above problem is to modify the key schedule so that it can derive *many init secrets* of an epoch U, one for each child of U. We refer to those secrets as *child init secrets*. That is, the secrets of a child V of U are generated by hashing the *child init secret* (instead of the *init secret* hashed in the old key schedule) of V with its commit secret. After deriving the child init for V, the key schedule deletes all information about it.

---

[5] For the purpose of this overview, one can think of a simplified TreeKEM where each party has a PKE key pair. The sender encrypts a random commit secret to each party and generates a new PKE key pair for themselves.

The above key schedule can be easily constructed using puncturable PRF, PPRF (we recall the primitive in the full version [11]). In particular, each epoch U has a *parent init secret* which is a PPRF key. To derive the child init for V, the key schedule evaluates the PPRF on input a *challenge* for V (we discuss choosing the challenge soon) and punctures the parent init secret on the challenge.

To summarize, our FR-CGKA protocol works as follows. When B transitions to a child V of U, he generates the secrets of V and stores the entire SAIK state in U, except with the parent init secret punctured on the challenge for V. This means that B keeps one SAIK state for each epoch on which he has a move pebble. To delete a pebble, B simply deletes the state. In this way we get FS: corrupting B after he transitions to a child V does not allow the adversary to re-compute the secrets of V because the parent init of U has been punctured. Moreover, we get fork resilience – if some party A' creates another child V' of U, B can generate its secrets, because the parent init of U has not been punctured on the challenge for V' (and he kept the TreeKEM state).

Choosing the Challenge for V. The first idea may be to have the party creating V pick a random challenge and attach it to the packet. However, this increases bandwidth cost and opens the door to denial-of-service (DoS) attacks. For example, say A creates an epoch V as a child of U and picks a random challenge r. Before B sees her packet, a corrupted C creates a child V' of U and sets the challenge for V' to the same r. If B transitions to V' first, he cannot process the honest packet from A because he already punctured the parent init of U on r.

The second idea is to make the challenge be the context of V (recall, the context is a commitment to information about V produced by SAIK). Unfortunately, the context does not bind the commit secret of V which brings back the DoS attack. In particular, the corrupted C can still create V' with the exact same context as V (same group modification etc.) but with a different commit secret. Again, if B transitions to V', he can no longer transition to V. The third idea is to include both the commit secret and the context in the challenge. However, this is insecure, because a punctured PPRF key generally may reveal the point it was punctured on. Therefore, a corruption of B would reveal old commit secrets via the punctured parent init secrets, destroying FS.

One may try to fix this by setting the challenge to a hash of the commit secret and the context (which is fine if the hash is modeled as an RO). However, this still allows some DoS attacks. At a high level, the problem is that a *removed* member does not know the commit secret of the new epoch (clearly, since they are no longer in the group) and therefore cannot validate the challenge. Concretely, in our running example, say the corrupted C creates V' by *removing* B. After receiving the packet, B punctures his parent init secret on the identifier of V'. B has no way of computing or verifying the identifier, so he must trust C that it is correct. Therefore, C can again claim that the identifier is the same as that of the honest epoch V. After puncturing, B can no longer transition to V.

The final solution is to include in the challenge half of the commit secret and use the other half to generate the secrets of V. That is, let us call the commit secret produced by TreeKEM the path secret (commit is one of path secrets TreeKEM internally generates). The challenge is set to (a hash of) the context and the hash of the path secret with label '*conf*', called *commit confirmation*. The secrets of V are generated using the new commit secret which is the hash of the path secret with label '*comm*'. Removed members receive the commit confirmation from their removers. Moreover, we choose *epoch identifiers* equal to the challenges. This means that, intuitively, there is a 1-1 correspondence between identifiers and challenges. This prevents the above attack because B can now compute the epoch identifier the same way as other members. This means that injecting a message creating V' in a way that makes B puncture on an honest identifier V is equivalent to delivering the honest message creating V. The reason is that, as we identify epochs by challenges, the above implies $V = V'$. Further, B can check that the epoch removes him (using the context).

Authentication. We use a simplified version of SAIK's framing component. Roughly, each member A generates a signature key pair and updates it each time she sends a message. Further, a secret called the *membership key*, used as a MAC key, is generated by the key schedule for each epoch U. When A creates an epoch V as a child of U, she signs and MACs the identifier V.

Note on Correctness. Say a party A creates an epoch by sending C. In SAIK the adversary can, without corruptions, successfully deliver different packets c' not outputted by Ext, as long as they transition to the honest epoch created by the sender of C. (Trying to make c unique is too stringent, requiring inefficient solutions.) Therefore, it can happen that a party B receives c' first, punctures the parent init and then receives c outputted by Ext. Recall that correctness requires that B accepts c. Thus, when receiving a packet claiming to transition to a V (the identifier is included in the packet), B checks if V is already in his state, and returns its stored semantics (while throwing error would be more natural).

3.1   The FREEK Protocol

In the current section we formally define our FR-CGKA protocol, FREEK, based on SAIK [8], which, as most CGKA protocols, relies on a PKI infrastructure, called Authenticated Key Service (AKS) in [8]. In our protocol description, calls to AKS are made implicitly via calls to SAIK's operations.

Our protocol relies on the following primitives: (1) a multi-recipient multi-message PKE, mmPKE, (2) a puncturable PRF, PPRF, (3) a signature scheme, Sig, (4) a message authentication code, MAC, and (4) HKDF. Our protocol is depicted in Fig. 7, and includes FREEK's main algorithms (that make calls to SAIK's ones), the key schedule, and the message framing. Due to space limitations, SAIK's unmodified algorithms are deferred to the full version of this paper [11].

The FREEK protocol executed by a party id keeps track of epochs using an array St. For each epoch with identifier U on which id has a move pebble, $St[U]$ stores a modified SAIK state in that epoch. Further, the protocol keeps track of all outputs of Join and Receive operations in an array Semantics (cf. the "Note on correctness" paragraph in Sect. 3). Both arrays are initialized when id creates the group using Initialization or joins for the first time. Note that id may join multiple times to different epochs (which is only possible in *FR*-CGKA).

Send. The Send operation receives U and act, recovers SAIK's state for epoch U ($\gamma \leftarrow St[U]$) and uses it to generate a message C and a new state γ' via SAIK.Send(γ, act). Internally (not in Fig. 7) the latter algorithm runs TreeKEM to create and encrypt a value pathSec, which it then inputs to the $*\mathsf{derive} - \mathsf{keys}$ function of the key schedule to compute the secrets of γ'. To enable joining, SAIK also encrypts the joinerSec computed in $*\mathsf{derive} - \mathsf{keys}$ to all new members (they cannot run $*\mathsf{derive} - \mathsf{keys}$, since they should not know the init secret—this may allow them to compute group keys for other forks where they are not members).

We modify $*\mathsf{derive} - \mathsf{keys}$ as follows; this is one of the core changes made by FREEK. The function computes a distinct init secret for γ', denoted by initChildSec. This value is the output of PPRF.eval over the PPRF key, initSec, of γ, and the epoch id of γ', where the latter is the output of HKDF.Exp over the group context, grpCtxt(γ'), and the confirmation secret, comSecConf. The joiner's secret, joinerSec, is now computed w.r.t. the group context, grpCtxt(), initChildSec and the commit secret, commitSec, and from joinerSec, all other secretes are derived as in SAIK. Obverse that the PPRF key in γ is punctured over the id of γ', and this enables FS, i.e., if the user's PPRF key is leaked after processing the incoming message creating γ', the adversary can no longer evaluate the PPRF over its identifier and compute the initChildSec.

The rest of the Send operation fetches from γ' the epoch identifier U created by $*\mathsf{derive} - \mathsf{keys}$ and stores the state in St. Finally, it MACs and signs U (SAIK MACs and signs a different value which is not useful for us.)

FREEK: Algorithms

```
Initialization
    γ ← SAIK.Init
    St[*] ← ε; γ.eid ← 0; St[0] ← γ
    Semantics[*] ← ⊥
    return γ.eid

Input (Send, U, act ∈ { 'up', 'add'-id_t, 'rem'-id_t }) from id
    γ ← St[U]
    // Run SAIK to get new epoch's state and a packet
    (γ', C) ← SAIK.Send(γ, act)
    U' ← γ'.eid; St[U'] ← γ
    // We remove SAIK's signatures and MACs
    σ ← *authenticate(γ, U')
    return (U', (U, U', C, σ, id, γ'.comSecConf))

Input (DeleteMovePebble, U) from id
    St[U] ← ⊥

Input (Receive, (U, U', c, σ, id_s, comSecConf) from id
    γ ← St[U]
    if St[U'] ≠ ⊥ then return Semantics[U']
    (St[U'], x) ← *process(γ, U, U', c, σ, id_s, comSecConf)
    Semantics[U'] ← (U, U', x)
    return (U, U', x)
```

```
Input (Join, (U, U', c, σ, id_s, comSecConf) from id
    if St = ⊥ then St[*], Semantics[*] ← ⊥
    if St[U'] ≠ ⊥ then return Semantics[U']
    (γ', x) ← *process(⊥, U, U', c, σ, id_s, comSecConf)
    St[U'] ← γ'; Semantics[U'] +← (U', x)
    return (U', x)

Input (GetKey, U) from id
    return SAIK.GetKey(St[U])

helper *process(γ, U, U', c, σ, id_s, comSecConf)
    if γ ≠ ⊥ then try (γ', x) ← SAIK.Receive(γ, c)
    else // SAIK only uses c; U is passed to *derive-epoch-keys
        try (γ', x) ← SAIK.Join(c, U)
        // SAIK didn't return (γ', x) ≠ ⊥ so it succeeded
    req *verify(γ, id_s, U', σ)
    if γ' ≠ ⊥ then
        req U' = γ'.eid ∧ comSecConf = γ'.comSecConf
    else // id is removed
        // treeHash' is derived using TreeKEM, γ and c
        ctx ← (treeHash', id_s-'rm'-id, U)
        req U' = HKDF.Exp(ctx, comSecConf)
        γ.initSec ← PPRF.puncture(γ.initSec, U')
    return (γ', x)
```

FREEK: Key schedule

```
helper *derive-keys(γ, γ', pathSec) // SAIK calls this during Join and
    // Receive. The input is the old state γ, the partially initialized new state γ'
    // and pathSec generated by TreeKEM
    γ'.comSecConf ← HKDF.Exp(pathSec, 'conf')
    γ'.eid ← HKDF.Exp(grpCtxt(γ'), γ'.comSecConf)
    initChildSec ← PPRF.eval(γ.initSec, γ'.eid)
    γ'.parEid ← γ.eid
    joinerSec ← *derive-joiner(γ, γ')
    γ' ← *derive-epoch-keys(γ', joinerSec, γ.parEid)
    return (γ', joinerSec)

helper grpCtxt(γ) // treeHash (generated by TreeKEM) binds member set
    return (γ.treeHash, γ.lastAct, γ.parEid)
```

```
helper *derive-epoch-keys(γ', joinerSec, U) //
    // Called by *derive-keys and by SAIK.Join with
    // joinerSec received directly from invitor and U passed
    // from FREEK.*process
    γ'.parEid ← U
    epSec ← HKDF.Ext(joinerSec, grpCtxt(γ'))
    γ'.appSec ← HKDF.Exp(epSec, 'app')
    γ'.membKey ← HKDF.Exp(epSec, 'memb')
    γ'.initSec ← HKDF.Exp(epSec, 'init')
    return γ'

helper *derive-joiner(γ, γ')
    γ.initSec ← PPRF.puncture(γ.initSec, γ'.eid)
    commitSec ← HKDF.Exp(pathSec, 'com')
    return HKDF.Ext(γ'.grpCtxt(), initChildSec, commitSec)
```

FREEK: Message framing

```
helper *authenticate(γ, x)
    return (MAC.tag(γ.membKey, x), Sig.sign(γ.ssk, x))
```

```
helper *verify(γ, id_s, x, (σ, t))
    // In SAIK leafof(id_s).spk is id_s's personal public key
    return ← MAC.vrf(γ.membKey, x, t) ∧ Sig.vrf(γ.leafof(id_s).spk, x, σ)
```

Fig. 7. FREEK algorithms.

Receive and Join. Receive, on input $(U, U', c, σ, id_s, comSecConf)$, first recovers the SAIK's state that will be used to process the incoming message for epoch U $(γ ← St[U])$ and if id has already processed a message that leads to the target epoch, U', the operation returns the values stored in Semantics[U'] (computed the first time id processed a message that led to U'). If not, it processes the message by executing SAIK's Receive or Join operation with c. Internally, (not in Fig. 7) SAIK's Receive algorithm runs TreeKEM to decrypt pathSec which it inputs to our modified *derive-keys function to get the key schedule for $γ'$. Similarly, SAIK's Join operation decrypts joinerSec and runs *derive-epoch-keys.

Predicate P for FREEK

//

P is true if the adversary leaked the (unpunctured) init secret from *any* id′ and exposed id's individual secrets

$P(\mathsf{Eps}, \mathsf{id}, V, \mathsf{Move}^{\mathcal{A}}, *, \mathsf{Visited}^{\mathcal{A}}) \leftrightarrow \exists \mathsf{id}' \big((\mathsf{id}', \mathsf{Eps}[V].\mathsf{par}) \in \mathsf{Move}_i^{\mathcal{A}} \wedge (\mathsf{id}', V) \notin \mathsf{Visited}_i^{\mathcal{A}} \big) \wedge *\texttt{leaked-ind-secs}(\mathsf{id}, V)$

$*\texttt{leaked-ind-secs}(U, \mathsf{id}) \leftrightarrow \big(\exists U' : *\texttt{share-ind-secs}(U, U', \mathsf{id}) \wedge *\texttt{ind-secs-bad}(U', \mathsf{id}) \big) *\texttt{exposed-ind-secs-weak}(U, \mathsf{id})$

$*\texttt{share-ind-secs}(U, U', \mathsf{id}) \leftrightarrow U$ and U' are the same or connected via undirected path of
$\qquad\qquad\qquad\qquad\qquad\qquad$ epochs U'' such that $\mathsf{Eps}[U''].\mathsf{sndr} \neq \mathsf{id} \wedge \mathsf{Eps}[U].\mathsf{act} \notin \{ \textit{'rem'-}\mathsf{id}, \textit{'add'-}\mathsf{id}\}$

$*\texttt{ind-secs-bad}(U, \mathsf{id}) \leftrightarrow \boxed{(\mathsf{id}, U) \in \mathsf{Move}^{\mathcal{A}}} \vee (\mathsf{Eps}[U].\mathsf{packet} = \textit{'inj'} \wedge (\mathsf{Eps}[U].\mathsf{sndr} = \mathsf{id} \vee \mathsf{Eps}[U].\mathsf{act} = \textit{'add'-}\mathsf{id}))$

$*\texttt{exposed-ind-secs-weak}(U, \mathsf{id}) \leftrightarrow \exists U_1, U_2, U_3 :$ all of the following conditions are satisfied:
$\quad$ (1) $U_1 \neq U_2 \wedge *\texttt{ancestor}(U_1, U) \wedge *\texttt{ancestor}(U_2, U_3)$ $\qquad$ (3) $*\texttt{share-ind-secs}(U_1, U, \mathsf{id}) \wedge *\texttt{share-ind-secs}(U_2, U_3, \mathsf{id})$
$\quad$ (2) $\mathsf{Eps}[U_1].\mathsf{act} = \mathsf{Eps}[U_2].\mathsf{act} = \textit{'add'-}\mathsf{id}$ $\qquad\qquad\qquad$ (4) $\mathsf{Eps}[U_2].\mathsf{inj} \wedge \mathsf{id} \in \mathsf{Eps}[U_3].\mathsf{exp}$

Fig. 8. The predicate P instantiating the generic security predicates for FREEK.

Observe that the protocol checks if the sender knows the right epoch id, U', and if the user is removed it directly uses comSecConf to do that check. Removed users also puncture the init secret on the epoch from which they are removed, U'. This prevents the adversary from injecting a message that removes id from U', so that later id cannot transition to an honestly generated epoch U'.

3.2   Security of FREEK

Security Predicate. FREEK's security predicates **conf** and **auth** instantiate the generic security predicates from Fig. 6 with the predicate P defined in Fig. 8.

Recall that according to the optimal predicates ($P(\cdot) = \texttt{false}$), the adversary can put a move pebble for id on V only if it has a move pebble *for* id on V's parent U and there is no visited pebble *for* id on V. At a high level, the reason why FREEK achieves a weaker guarantee is that some secrets used by id (the init secret and the MAC key) are shared among all group members. Therefore, it is enough to have a move pebble on U without a visited pebble on V for *any* id′ to get these secrets. Getting these secrets may break the last line of defense and enable putting a move pebble for id on V.

A bit more precisely, we can distinguish two types of FREEK secrets for each epoch: *group secrets* known to all group members and *individual secrets* known only to some members (e.g., the signing key of id or PKE secret keys generated for it by TreeKEM). FREEK guarantees that the adversary can put a move pebble for id on V only if A) it has the group secrets of its parent U and B) id's individual secrets in V. For A), it is enough for the adversary to have a move pebble on U for any id′ (c.f. the first two literals of P). To decide if B) is satisfied, we use the predicate $*\texttt{leaked} - \texttt{ind} - \texttt{secs}$ which is the same as in SAIK.

It remains to explain $*\texttt{leaked} - \texttt{ind} - \texttt{secs}$. It consists of two clauses, where the latter one considers an edge-case attack on SAIK; we refer to [8] for an explanation and focus here on the former, more interesting case. Roughly, id's secrets are replaced by FREEK whenever it sends a message by (possibly) secure ones. Its secrets are also not present in epochs where it is not a member. We define *share − ind − secs(U, U', id) to capture when id's secrets are the same in U and U'. Now *leaked − ind − secs is true in U if they are the same as in some U' where they are corrupted, as per *ind − secs − bad. The latter is true if id's state is exposed in U', which is marked by $\mathcal{F}_{\text{FR-CGKA}}$ by adding a move pebble, or id's state is created via an injection on its behalf, or an injection that adds it.

FREEK *vs* SAIK. Since FR-CGKA implies CGKA, it makes sense to ask how security of SAIK compares with the security of FREEK when used in the CGKA mode, i.e., when every party has only one move pebble on the "current" epoch (when transitioning, the old move pebble is immediately deleted). It turns out that FREEK in the CGKA mode achieves the same CGKA security as SAIK. In fact, the protocols are almost equivalent, since puncturing becomes void—any keys punctured by FREEK when creating new epochs are immediately deleted.

We note that SAIK uses simplified predicates that do not enforce deleting group keys after outputting them. In our case, this means that key and move pebbles become the same thing and the former are not needed—an epoch is secure if the adversary does not have a move pebble on it. Now, equivalence of SAIK's predicate and our predicate without key pebbles follows by inspection.

Security of FREEK. Informally, the result is stated as follows. For the PPRF, we require one-wayness security (with adaptive corruptions), defined. The TreeKEM component of FREEK, which is the same as in FREEK, also requires a multi-message multi-recipient PKE scheme, mmPKE. At a high level, mmPKE has the functionality (and security) of a parallel composition of standard PKEs. Its goal is to improve efficiency. For mmPKE, we require one-wayness (the adversary's goal is to compute a random encrypted message) RCCA (a relaxation of CCA) security. Due to space limitations, we defer the *exact* security bounds, the proof and security notions for primitives we use to the full version of this paper [11].

Theorem 1 (Informal). *Let $\mathcal{F}_{\text{FR-CGKA}}$ be the functionality from Fig. 5 with predicates conf, auth, defined in Figs. 6 and 8, and assume that FREEK (cf. Fig. 7) is instantiated witch schemes such that mmPKE is mmOW-RCCA secure, PPRF is OW-PPRF secure, Sig and MAC are EUF-CMA secure, and HKDF functions are modeled as a random oracle. Then, for any $\mathcal{A}$, there exists $\mathcal{S}$, such that $\text{IDEAL}_{\mathcal{F}_{\text{FR-CGKA}}, \mathcal{S}}(\mathcal{A})$ is indistinguishable from $\text{REAL}_{\text{FREEK}, \mathcal{F}_{\text{AKS}}}(\mathcal{A})$.*

4   FR-CGKA with Optimal Security

In this section we give an overview of the protocol OSAIK, that achieves *optimal security* predicates, i.e., the predicates from Fig. 6 with P set to false. Due to space limitations, discussion about authenticity, formal description of the protocol and the security proof are deferred to the full version [11]. Roughly, we start with a simplified version of SAIK called PAIK-S which is less efficient but just as secure. We then identify and fix two problems with it: cross-fork and collusion attacks. The first fix uses a known technique from [7], using HIBE. The second fix needs modifying the HIBE fix to *also* deal with new attacks specific to FR-CGKA.

In PAIK-S, each member has a PKE key pair. When an epoch is created, the committer encrypts a random path secret to all members and the new epoch's secrets are derived by mixing it with the (child) init secret. It also generates a new PKE (and signature) key pair for itself.

Weak PCFS and Cross-Fork Attacks. Cross-fork attacks are relevant for CGKA in general (not only FR-CGKA). Roughly, the problem is that parts of the private state of parties in different epochs may be the same. In that case, the same secret may be relevant to two (or more) distinct epochs, and it is impossible to meaningfully delete a move pebble on one epoch but not another.

For concreteness, assume that a protocol execution creates an epoch 1 on which parties A, B and C all have a move pebble. Then a fork is created as follows: A creates (and transitions to) epoch 2 and at the same time B creates epoch 3. Notice that C's PKE key is the same in epochs 1, 2 and 3. Now assume that C transitions to epoch 2, *deletes the move pebble on 1* and then gets corrupted. The adversary can use C's PKE secret key to decrypt the commit secret in epoch 3.

Intuitively, to defend against cross-fork attacks, a protocol needs to ratchet *all key material (of all group members), with each epoch change.* This has to be done in a way such that, secrets in any epoch V do not reveal information about its *ancestors or epochs in other arms of a fork.* Following [7], we achieve this using HIBE. Roughly, the public key of each party in an epoch U is a pair of a HIBE (master) public key and a vector of HIBE identities. The latter contains the identifiers of all epochs since the key was inserted into the state, ordered from the oldest to U. When a party A creates a child epoch of U, it encrypts the fresh commit secret to the HIBE public key and identity vector of each (non-removed) member B in U. Then A computes the public group state in V as follows: the identifier V is the same as in PAIK-S; the public key of each other group member B is the HIBE public key from U and the identity vector from U with V appended; the public key of A is a fresh HIBE master key she chooses and the empty identity vector. When B transitions to V, it updates the HIBE secret key of U with V and stores the resulting secret key that will be used to process incoming messages for V; it also keeps the HIBE key before the update. When later B removes the move pebble on U it simply erases that key (i.e., the key before the update). At a high level, the HIBE secret key of an epoch U enables key generation only for the descendants of U. This prevents the attack described above since all secrets in an epoch V are (computationally) unrelated to the secrets in any epochs other than the descendants of V.

Collusion Attacks. This type of attacks is specific to the way PAIK-S punctures the init secrets to get forward-secure FR-CGKA. In particular, observe that in PAIK-S, if a party A has a move pebble on an epoch U, then it can decrypt the commit secrets of all children of U, even those on which it has visited pebbles. The only thing that protects the children in case A is corrupted is the fact that A punctured the init secret on their identifiers. However, the unpunctured init can be leaked when other members are corrupted, which enables *collusion attacks.* For concreteness, assume that in a protocol execution, A, B and C, are in epoch

1. Then, A creates (and transitions to) epoch 2 by removing C; B transitions to 2, creates epoch 3 as its child, and deletes the group key in epoch 2. He now has move pebbles on epochs 1, 2 and 3, and visited pebbles on 2 and 3. C never sees epoch 2. Now assume B and C get corrupted. The expectation is that epoch 2 is secure since C cannot move there because A removed him, and B has a visited pebble on it and deleted the group key. Unexpectedly, epoch 2 is insecure for the following reason: the adversary can compute the group key in 2 by combining the unpunctured init secret from C and the commit secret decrypted using B's secret key from epoch 1.

Intuitively, puncturing the init secret is insufficient, since it is known to other group members, and the adversary can leak the (unpunctured) key via corruptions of removed users, or group members that lie in other epochs. Therefore, in order for security to be preserved in the presence of collusion attacks we require the following: when B puts a visited pebble on V with parent U, he has to puncture *his own* secret key in U, so that it can no longer decrypt the ciphertext that carries the commit secret of V. To achieve this, we modify the HIBE-version of PAIK-S as follows. The main observation is that HIBE with a binary identity space, called binary-tree encryption, BtPke, (a special case of HIBE [27]) can be used to construct puncturable public key encryption [30], whose goal is exactly to allow A to puncture her secret key. So, we first switch from HIBE to BtPke. Second, we switch the order of encryption and updating the identity vector: when A creates a new epoch V, then for each other member B, she first appends all bits of V to B's identity vector $\vec{U}$ in U and then encrypts the commit secret to B's public key and the identity $\vec{V} = \vec{U} \parallel V$. So, the commit is encrypted to its unique identity vector $\vec{V}$. When later B puts a visited pebble on V, he punctures his secret key in U on the unique $\vec{V}$, as we describe below.

Puncturing in our setting is essentially a public-key version of puncturing a GGM tree. That is, B's secret key in U is a binary tree $\mathsf{eskTree}_U$ of height $|V|$, where each node is labeled by a binary identity vector $\vec{A}$. The root's label is $\vec{U}$ and if a node has label $\vec{A}$, then its left and right children have labels $\vec{A} \parallel 0$ and $\vec{A} \parallel 1$, respectively. In addition, some nodes store the HIBE secret keys corresponding to their labels. We denote the HIBE secret key of a node $\vec{U} \parallel \vec{A}$ by $\mathsf{eskTree}_U[\vec{A}]$. Initially, when U is created, only the root stores a key in $\mathsf{eskTree}_U[\epsilon]$. Notice that $\vec{V} = \vec{U} \parallel V$, is a label on a leaf in $\mathsf{eskTree}_U$. To puncture the tree on $\vec{V}$, B derives and stores HIBE secret keys for all nodes on the copath of that leaf to the root and then deletes all nodes in the path to the root.

5   Natural Fork-Resolution Protocols

In this section, we discuss how any FR-CGKA can be used together with *a natural fork-resolution protocol* to get a complete solution to group management. At a high level, the goal of a natural fork-resolution protocol is to allow group members whose views of the group have diverged to reconcile these views and define the *current* group state. A bit more precisely, a group member can use the fork-resolution protocol to collect information about the group's history graph

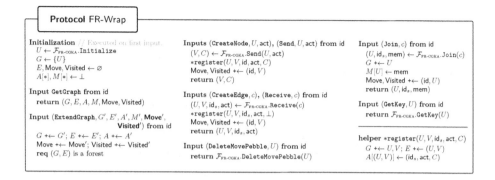

Fig. 9. The protocol FR-Wrap supporting fork-resolution protocols.

from other members (assuming point-to-point channels) and identify (or create) an epoch representing the current state consistent with the collected view.

To support fork-resolution protocols, we construct a simple protocol called FR-Wrap, defined in Fig. 9. The protocol works in the $\mathcal{F}_{\text{FR-CGKA}}$-hybrid model. That is, it makes black-box calls to $\mathcal{F}_{\text{FR-CGKA}}$ and so can be instantiated with any FR-CGKA protocol realizing $\mathcal{F}_{\text{FR-CGKA}}$. FR-Wrap extends the interface of $\mathcal{F}_{\text{FR-CGKA}}$ with methods useful for fork-resolution. Specifically, it curates a representation of a clients local cryptographic state in the form of a DAG G and accompanying node (sub)sets Move and Visited. The idea is to abstract away everything about the client's state leaving only exactly what is relevant for fork-resolution. Nodes in G represent CGKA epochs and edges the CGKA operations that produce one epoch from another.[6] Nodes are included in the set Move to indicate the client can still process new operations leaving that epoch. Nodes are included in Visited set to indicate that the operation leading to them have already been processed.

Now, by comparing the DAGs produced by their respective FR-Wrap protocols a pair of clients A and B can quickly determine which CGKA operations (and resulting epochs), one client has seen that the other has not. Using Move and Visited they can further determine which missing operations they can each still process. Finally, by simply replaying corresponding protocol packets each client can catch up (as far as permitted given their local state).

Once A and B have identified, exchanged and processed missing CGKA operations to synchronize their DAGs it remains to agree on a single *current* epoch to be presented to any higher-level applications using the FR-CGKA as the current group state. Agreeing on this epoch (either by selecting an existing one or creating a new one) is the goal of a type of higher-level (non-cryptographic) scheme called a *state-resolution* algorithm. One example is the State Resolution v2 algorithm of [25]. We refer to the full version of this paper for further discussion.

---

[6] So e.g., all nodes have indegree 1 except the initial epoch's node has indegree 0.

6   Benchmarks

We report on benchmarks and statistics exploring the storage, communication and computational costs of FREEK (in particular, relative to MLS). Concretely, we use Curve25519, SHA2-256 and AES128-GCM (i.e. MLS ciphersuite 1).

Storage. We call a past epoch for which a client stores enough state to process further outgoing CGKA operations a *trailing* epoch (i.e., trailing epochs are those on which the client has a move pebble). Recall that FREEK lets applications decide, at runtime, which epochs to keep as trailing and when to remove them.

In this paragraph, we elucidate how storage grows in the number (and type) of trailing epochs. An interesting special case occurs when the application stores no trailing epochs at all, as then FREEK's storage effectively collapses to that of MLS (in an analogous execution).

Our storage benchmarks are based on the following quite pessimistic assumptions which, if anything, results in overestimating the additional relative cost of keeping trailing epochs introduced by FREEK. To store the ratchet trees of t epochs, the client only stores 1 complete ratchet tree and $t - 1$ delta's each of which is a single new path from a leaf to root. For each node in a ratchet tree (or delta) we only count the cost of storing the PKE public key and a tree hash value at the node. We omit any further data (e.g."parent hash") present in MLS but omitted in this work for simplicity. We also assume that for each group member a credential consisting of a single 1KB big X.509 certificate is stored.[7] The results are highly execution-dependent so we explored a variety of cases which differ along 3 orthogonal axis. First, our executions vary in the number of trailing epochs. For each trailing epoch a ratchet tree delta and a PPRF instance is stored. Second, we considered groups of size $n = 2$ and $n = 128$. Note that $n = 2$ results in the greatest relative overhead of a trailing epoch, as the PPRF state size is independent of n and the ratchet tree delta's only grow logarithmically in n. Meanwhile, other storage which is needed even without any trailing epochs (like the credentials and a full ratchet tree) grow linearly in n.

The third axis varies how many child epochs each trailing epoch has. Each child epoch requires a puncturing of the trailing epoch's PPRF. Note that the more the network delivers packets in a global order the fewer children per trailing epoch we can expect. (MLS requires a perfectly globally ordered network in order to guarantee liveness of the execution.) The results are in Fig. 10.

For instance, for $n = 128$, four trailing epochs with three children, the storage required for the ratchet trees corresponds to the storage of one full ratchet tree plus the cost of the remaining three trailing epochs, which optimistically only requires three paths of logarithmic (in n) number of public keys. The former is approximately $2n|\mathsf{pk}|$ (we consider $|\mathsf{pk}| = 64$ bytes), while the

---

[7] We chose X.509 as a credential type as it's one of two non-trivial credential types mentioned in MLS's RFC and Cisco's WebEx—the only currently deployed instance of MLS we know of—uses X.509 certificates as credentials. As for the size we took 1 KB as just one X.509 SSL cert in the certificate chain of github.com is 4KB large.

Storage					
n	# of Trailing Epochs	Child Epochs per Trailing Epoch	Ratchet Trees (bytes)	PPRF States (bytes)	PPRF Relative Overhead
2	0	0	256	32	0.02%
	1	1	256	1024	31.22%
		2		2048	47.58%
		3		3072	57.66%
		4		4096	64.48%
	2	1	320	2048	46.89%
		2		4096	63.84%
		3		6144	72.59%
		4		8192	77.93%
	4	1	448	4096	62.59%
		2		8192	76.99%
		3		12288	83.39%
		4		16384	87.00%
	8	1	704	8192	75.18%
		2		16384	85.83%
		3		24576	90.09%
		4		32768	92.38%
128	0	0	16384	32	0.02%
	1	1	16384	1024	0.70%
		2		2048	1.40%
		3		3072	2.08%
		4		4096	2.76%
	2	1	16832	2048	1.39%
		2		4096	2.75%
		3		6144	4.07%
		4		8192	5.35%
	4	1	17728	4096	2.73%
		2		8192	5.32%
		3		12288	7.78%
		4		16384	10.11%
	8	1	19520	8192	5.26%
		2		16384	10.00%
		3		24576	14.28%
		4		32768	18.18%

Communication Complexity							
n	2	4	8	16	32	64	128
No Blanks in Ratchet Trees	$469B$ 16.99%	$586B$ 14.0%	$703B$ 12.01%	$820B$ 10.48%	$937B$ 9.29%	$1054B$ 8.34%	$1171B$ 7.57%
Fully Blank Ratchet Trees	$469B$ 16.99%	$668B$ 12.56%	$1031B$ 8.51%	$1722B$ 5.28%	$3069B$ 3.03%	$5728B$ 1.64%	$11011B$ 0.86%

Computation						
n	Send (time)	Send (cycles)	Receive (time)	Receive (cycles)	PPRF (time)	PPRF (cycles)
2	$328.904\mu s$	823912	$557.164\mu s$	1374924		
4	$426.953\mu s$	1101432	$565.914\mu s$	1432578		
8	$526.707\mu s$	1411876	$648.008\mu s$	1633113		
16	$737.515\mu s$	1802282	$761.699\mu s$	1862619	$690.4\mu s$	1579919
32	1.023832ms	2514600	$999.035\mu s$	2410291		
64	1.510185ms	3925638	1.38023ms	3799105		
128	2.302629ms	5911521	2.126117ms	5480508		

Fig. 10. Overhead of FREEK compared to MLS.

latter is $3\log(128)|\mathsf{pk}|$, summing up to 17728 bytes. The size of PPRF states is equal to the number of trailing epochs, times the number of children per epoch, times the size a single PPRF state which is $4\kappa^2$ (where κ is the security parameter, i.e., $16B$), summing up to $4 \cdot 3 \cdot (4 \cdot 16^2) = 12288$ bytes. Finally, the overhead is computed as the PPRF state size divided by the sum of the PPRF state plus the ratchet trees size and the credentials size (which is n times the X.509 certificate size, i.e., 128000 bytes), thus we compute the overhead as $12288/(12288 + 17728 + 128000) \approx 7.78\%$.

Communication. Next, we provide some benchmarks elucidating the communication complexity (i.e. protocol packet size) overhead when switching from MLS to FREEK. Recall that, in an analogous execution, a FREEK packet is identical to an MLS packet except that it has in addition two epoch IDs and the comSecConf value which amounts to $96B$ (regardless of group size n). While this overhead has a fixed size, the rest of the packet grows at least logarithmically in n (if not linearly). So, to establish an upper bound (over all possible executions and CGKA packets) on the relative overhead of FREEK, we considered a group of the smallest reasonable size $n = 2$. To understand how the relative overhead scales, we also looked at sizes $n = 4, 8, \ldots, 128$. All executions use the pessimistic (for FREEK) assumptions that the ratchet tree contains no blanks and so packet sizes scale only logarithmically in n (instead of linearly).

We used OpenMLS [43] to produce MLS packets for both types of execution and measured their size in bytes. To ensure we have an upperbound on FREEK's relative overhead we pessimistically assumed that the smallest type of credential (aka. "basic credential") is used and that no extensions nor capabilities are included. Changing any of these assumptions can only increase parts of the packet shared by MLS and FREEK so decreasing the relative overhead. The results are in Fig. 10;

Computation. Finally, we provide some benchmarks measuring the computational overhead of FREEK relative to MLS. For MLS we used the OpenMLS [43] implementation of MLS written in Rust. Separately, we also implemented (in Rust) the PPRF as used by FREEK and estimated the runtime of FREEK as the sum of the MLS and PPRF runtimes. (Indeed, apart from the PPRF, the two protocols share all other "heavy", e.g. public key, operations both for sending and receiving commit packets.)

As with communication costs, FREEK's absolute overhead is constant in the group size n, while MLS's runtime (e.g. number of public key operations) scales at least logarithmically, if not linearly, in n. So, to understand how the relative overhead decreases in n, we considered groups of sizes $n = 2, 4, 8, \ldots, 128$. To obtain an upper bound on the relative overhead, we made two pessimistic assumptions. First, the ratchet tree contains no blanks. Second, the receiver is in the opposite half of the ratchet tree from the sender, meaning the receiver need only do a small constant number of public key operations independent of n.

The experiments where run on 2.6 GHz 6-Core Intel Core i7 and results are given both in wall clock time and in CPU cycles (measured with Intel's `rdtsc` command). The results are in Fig. 10.

References

1. Albrecht, M.R., Celi, S., Dowling, B., Jones, D.: Practically-exploitable cryptographic vulnerabilities in matrix. In: 2023 2023 IEEE Symposium on Security and Privacy (SP) (SP), pp. 1419–1436, Los Alamitos, CA, USA, May 2023. IEEE Computer Society (2023)

2. Alwen, J., et al.: Grafting key trees: efficient key management for overlapping groups. In: Nissim, K., Waters, B. (eds.) TCC 2021, Part III. LNCS, vol. 13044, pp. 222–253. Springer, Cham (2021). https://doi.org/10.1007/978-3-030-90456-2_8

3. Alwen, J., Auerbach, B., Noval, M.C., Klein, K., Pascual-Perez, G., Pietrzak, K.: DeCAF: decentralizable continuous group key agreement with fast healing. Cryptology ePrint Archive, Report 2022/559 (2022). https://eprint.iacr.org/2022/559

4. Alwen, J., et al.: CoCoA: concurrent continuous group key agreement. In: Dunkelman, O., Dziembowski, S. (eds.) EUROCRYPT 2022, Part II. LNCS, vol. 13276, pp. 815–844. Springer, Heidelberg (2022). https://doi.org/10.1007/978-3-031-07085-3_28

5. Alwen, J., Coretti, S., Dodis, Y., Tselekounis, Y.: Security analysis and improvements for the IETF MLS standard for group messaging. In: Micciancio, D., Ristenpart, T. (eds.) CRYPTO 2020, Part I. LNCS, vol. 12170, pp. 248–277. Springer, Cham (2020). https://doi.org/10.1007/978-3-030-56784-2_9

6. Alwen, J., Coretti, S., Dodis, Y., Tselekounis, Y.: Modular design of secure group messaging protocols and the security of MLS. In: Vigna, G., Shi, E. (eds.) ACM CCS 2021, pp. 1463–1483. ACM Press, November 2021

7. Alwen, J., Coretti, S., Jost, D., Mularczyk, M.: Continuous group key agreement with active security. In: Pass, R., Pietrzak, K. (eds.) TCC 2020, Part II. LNCS, vol. 12551, pp. 261–290. Springer, Cham (2020). https://doi.org/10.1007/978-3-030-64378-2_10

8. Alwen, J., Hartmann, D., Kiltz, E., Mularczyk, M.: Server-aided continuous group key agreement. In: Yin, H., Stavrou, A., Cremers, C., Shi, E. (eds.) ACM CCS 2022, pp. 69–82. ACM Press, November 2022

9. Alwen, J., Jost, D., Mularczyk, M.: On the insider security of MLS. In: Dodis, Y., Shrimpton, T. (eds.) CRYPTO 2022, Part II. LNCS, vol. 13508, pp. 34–68. Springer, Heidelberg (2022). https://doi.org/10.1007/978-3-031-15979-4_2

10. Alwen, J., et al.: Keep the dirt: tainted treekem, an efficient and provably secure continuous group key agreement protocol. In: 42nd IEEE Symposium on Security and Privacy (2021). Full Version: https://ia.cr/2019/1489

11. Alwen, J., Mularczyk, M., Tselekounis, Y.: Fork-resilient continuous group key agreement. Cryptology ePrint Archive, Paper 2023/394 (2023). https://eprint.iacr.org/2023/394

12. Automerge.org. Automerge (2023). https://automerge.org/

13. Balbás, D., Collins, D., Vaudenay, S.: Cryptographic administration for secure group messaging. Cryptology ePrint Archive, Report 2022/1411 (2022). https://eprint.iacr.org/2022/1411

14. Barnes, R., Beurdouche, B., Robert, R., Millican, J., Omara, E., Cohn-Gordon, K.: The messaging layer security (MLS) protocol. Internet-Draft draft-ietf-mls-protocol-17, Internet Engineering Task Force, December 2022. Work in Progress

15. Barnes, R., Millican, J., Omara, E., Cohn-Gordon, K., Robert, R.: Message layer security (mls) wg (2018). https://datatracker.ietf.org/wg/mls/about/

16. Bienstock, A., Dodis, Y., Garg, S., Grogan, G., Hajiabadi, M., Rösler, P.: On the worst-case inefficiency of CGKA. In: Kiltz, E., Vaikuntanathan, V. (eds.) TCC 2022, Part II. LNCS, vol. 13748, pp. 213–243. Springer, Heidelberg (2022). https://doi.org/10.1007/978-3-031-22365-5_8

17. Bienstock, A., Dodis, Y., Tang, Y.: Multicast key agreement, revisited. In: Galbraith, S.D. (ed.) CT-RSA 2022. LNCS, vol. 13161, pp. 1–25. Springer, Cham (2022). https://doi.org/10.1007/978-3-030-95312-6_1

18. Brzuska, C., Cornelissen, E., Kohbrok, K.: Cryptographic security of the MLS RFC, draft 11. Cryptology ePrint Archive, Report 2021/137 (2021). https://eprint.iacr.org/2021/137

19. Brzuska, C., Cornelissen, E., Kohbrok, K.: Security analysis of the MLS key derivation. In: 2022 IEEE Symposium on Security and Privacy, pp. 2535–2553. IEEE Computer Society Press, May 2022

20. Buterin, V.: Ethereum: a next-generation smart contract and decentralized application platform (2014)

21. Chase, M., Perrin, T., Zaverucha, G.: The signal private group system and anonymous credentials supporting efficient verifiable encryption. In: Ligatti, J., Ou, X., Katz, J., Vigna, G. (eds.) ACM CCS 2020, pp. 1445–1459. ACM Press, November 2020

22. Cohn-Gordon, K., Cremers, C.J.F., Garratt, L.: On post-compromise security. In: IEEE 29th Computer Security Foundations Symposium, CSF 2016, Lisbon, Portugal, 27 June–1 July 2016, pp. 164–178. IEEE Computer Society (2016)

23. Cong, K., Eldefrawy, K., Smart, N.P., Terner, B.: The key lattice framework for concurrent group messaging. Cryptology ePrint Archive, Report 2022/1531 (2022). https://eprint.iacr.org/2022/1531

24. Devigne, J., Duguey, C., Fouque, P.-A.: MLS group messaging: how zero-knowledge can secure updates. In: Bertino, E., Shulman, H., Waidner, M. (eds.) ESORICS 2021. LNCS, vol. 12973, pp. 587–607. Springer, Cham (2021). https://doi.org/10.1007/978-3-030-88428-4_29

25. The Matrix.org Foundation: Matrix specification (2023). https://spec.Matrix.org/v1.6

26. The Matrix.org Foundation: Matrix state resolution (2023). https://spec.Matrix.org/v1.6/rooms/v10

27. Gentry, C., Silverberg, A.: Hierarchical ID-based cryptography. In: Zheng, Y. (ed.) ASIACRYPT 2002. LNCS, vol. 2501, pp. 548–566. Springer, Heidelberg (2002). https://doi.org/10.1007/3-540-36178-2_34

28. Wire Swiss GmbH. Wire security whitepaper (2021). https://wire-docs.wire.com/download/Wire+Security+Whitepaper.pdf

29. Google: Google docs (2023). https://docs.google.com/

30. Green, M.D., Miers, I.: Forward secure asynchronous messaging from puncturable encryption. In: 2015 IEEE Symposium on Security and Privacy, pp. 305–320. IEEE Computer Society Press, May 2015

31. Hashimoto, K., Katsumata, S., Postlethwaite, E., Prest, T., Westerbaan, B.: A concrete treatment of efficient continuous group key agreement via multi-recipient PKEs. In: Vigna, G., Shi, E. (eds.) ACM CCS 2021, pp. 1441–1462. ACM Press, November 2021

32. Hashimoto, K., Katsumata, S., Prest, T.: How to hide MetaData in MLS-like secure group messaging: simple, modular, and post-quantum. In: Yin, H., Stavrou, A., Cremers, C., Shi, E. (eds.) ACM CCS 2022, pp. 1399–1412. ACM Press, November 2022

33. Howell, C., Leavy, T., Alwen, J.: Wickr messaging protocol: technical paper (2019). https://wickr.com/wp-content/uploads/2019/12/WhitePaper_WickrMessagingProtocol.pdf
34. Jabber. Jabber (2023). https://www.jabber.org/
35. Kajita, K., Emura, K., Ogawa, K., Nojima, R., Ohtake, G.: Continuous group key agreement with flexible authorization and its applications. Cryptology ePrint Archive, Report 2022/1768 (2022). https://eprint.iacr.org/2022/1768
36. Katsumata, S., Kwiatkowski, K., Pintore, F., Prest, T.: Scalable ciphertext compression techniques for post-quantum KEMs and their applications. In: Moriai, S., Wang, H. (eds.) ASIACRYPT 2020. LNCS, vol. 12491, pp. 289–320. Springer, Cham (2020). https://doi.org/10.1007/978-3-030-64837-4_10
37. Marlinspike, M., Perrin, T.: The double ratchet algorithm, November 2016. https://whispersystems.org/docs/specifications/doubleratchet/doubleratchet.pdf
38. Marlinspike, M., Perrin, T.: Signal - technical information (2022). https://signal.org/docs/
39. Matrix.org. are we MLS yet? (2023). http://arewemlsyet.com/
40. Matrix.org. Decentralised MLS (2023). https://gitlab.matrix.org/matrix-org/mls-ts/-/blob/decentralised2/decentralised.org
41. Nakamoto, S.: Bitcoin: a peer-to-peer electronic cash system, December 2008
42. Oikarinen, J., Reed, D.: Internet relay chat protocol. RFC 1459, RFC Editor (1993)
43. Phoenix R&D and Cryspen. OpenMLS (2023). https://github.com/openmls/openmls
44. Microsoft Teams: Group chat software (2023). https://www.microsoft.com/en-us/microsoft-teams/group-chat-software
45. Wallez, T., Protzenko, J., Beurdouche, B., Bhargavan, K.: TreeSync: authenticated group management for messaging layer security. Cryptology ePrint Archive, Report 2022/1732 (2022). https://eprint.iacr.org/2022/1732
46. Weidner, M.: Group messaging for secure asynchronous collaboration. MPhil dissertation (2019). Advisors: A. Beresford and M. Kleppmann (2019). https://mattweidner.com/acs-dissertation.pdf
47. Weidner, M., Kleppmann, M., Hugenroth, D., Beresford, A.R.: Key agreement for decentralized secure group messaging with strong security guarantees. In: Vigna, G., Shi, E. (eds.) ACM CCS 2021, pp. 2024–2045. ACM Press, November 2021
48. WhatsApp: Whatsapp encryption overview (2023). https://www.whatsapp.com/security/WhatsApp-Security-Whitepaper.pdf

Functional Encryption

Streaming Functional Encryption

Jiaxin Guan[1]($\boxtimes$) (ID), Alexis Korb[2]($\boxtimes$) (ID), and Amit Sahai[2]

[1] Princeton University, Princeton, USA
`jiaxin@guan.io`
[2] UCLA, Los Angeles, USA
`alexiskorb@cs.ucla.edu`

Abstract. We initiate the study of *streaming functional encryption* (sFE) which is designed for scenarios in which data arrives in a streaming manner and is computed on in an iterative manner as the stream arrives. Unlike in a standard functional encryption (FE) scheme, in an sFE scheme, we (1) do not require the entire data set to be known at encryption time and (2) allow for partial decryption given only a prefix of the input. More specifically, in an sFE scheme, we can sequentially encrypt each data point x_i in a stream of data $x = x_1 \ldots x_n$ as it arrives, without needing to wait for all n values. We can then generate function keys for streaming functions which are stateful functions that take as input a message x_i and a state st_i and output a value y_i and the next state st_{i+1}. For any $k \leq n$, a user with a function key for a streaming function f can learn the first k output values $y_1 \ldots y_k$ where $(y_i, \mathsf{st}_{i+1}) = f(x_i, \mathsf{st}_i)$ and $\mathsf{st}_1 = \bot$ given only ciphertexts for the first k elements $x_1 \ldots x_k$.

In this work, we introduce the notion of sFE and show how to construct it from FE. In particular, we show how to achieve a secure sFE scheme for P/Poly from a compact, secure FE scheme for P/Poly, where our security notion for sFE is similar to standard FE security except that we require all function queries to be made before the challenge ciphertext query. Furthermore, by combining our result with the FE construction of Jain, Lin, and Sahai (STOC, 2022), we show how to achieve a secure sFE scheme for P/Poly from the polynomial hardness of well-studied assumptions.

1 Introduction

Functional encryption (FE) [16,40,42] is a powerful extension of public key encryption that restricts users with secret keys to only learning functions of the encrypted data. In an FE scheme, an authority can generate function keys for functions of their choice using a master secret key. Given a function key for f and an encryption of x, one should be able to learn $f(x)$ and nothing else. Functional encryption has been studied extensively (e.g. [4,7,15,18,19,26,28,41,42] [2,5,6,9,14,20,21,32,36–39].) In addition to its many direct applications, FE has also been used to build other cryptographic applications such as reusable garbled circuits [26], adaptive garbling [31], multi-party non-interactive key exchange [21], universal samplers [21], and verifiable random functions [11,13,29]. Importantly, FE can be used to construct $i\mathcal{O}$ [7,14], a powerful tool which can be used to build many cryptographic primitives [41].

H. Handschuh and A. Lysyanskaya (Eds.): CRYPTO 2023, LNCS 14084, pp. 433–463, 2023.
https://doi.org/10.1007/978-3-031-38551-3_14

Now is an exciting time for functional encryption. While early constructions of FE were restricted – for example, some required a bound on the number of function keys [27], or only allowed functions keys for simple functions like inner product [1,3] or quadratic functions [12] – we've recently been able to achieve FE for P/Poly from well-studied assumptions [33,34]. This has also opened the door to extensions such as FE for Turing machines [10] and multi-input FE [25]. In light of these advances, it is natural to consider the feasibility of even stronger notions of functional encryption.

The Streaming Scenario. In many modern applications, the data sets being used might not be available all at once or might be in some ongoing process of being generated. Additionally, data sets are often large, and it can be difficult to store or compute on the entire data set all at once. Using functional encryption in these scenarios can incur a large expense or may not even be possible.

For example, consider a privacy-preserving machine learning algorithm that is being trained on a massive data set provided by a third party. The third party might hope to use FE to protect the training data by encrypting it and providing it to the training algorithm user along with a function key for the algorithm. However, using FE in this manner requires the training set to be fixed at encryption time. If new training data later becomes available, the user cannot continue training the algorithm on this data without re-encrypting the entire data set. Furthermore, the user cannot generate any partial results while training the algorithm but must instead wait until the full decryption finishes, which takes time and space proportional to the size of the data set.

Using FE in these scenarios is additionally infeasible when the data arrives in a streaming fashion either due to the nature of the data or because the data is too large to be stored on the user's computer all at once. As an example, consider a video-processing algorithm. For privacy, the video broadcaster might consider using FE to send an encryption of the video and a function key for the video-processing algorithm to the user. However, if the video is being recorded live or is large in size, then we would ideally like the broadcaster to be able to stream an encryption of the video to the user who could then begin processing the video as the stream arrives. However, this is not possible with regular FE. The broadcaster would have to wait until the video is finished (if it ever is!) to encrypt the video, and then send the entire encryption to the user, who could only then begin processing the video. Furthermore, the user would have to compute on an encryption of the entire video stream, which may be large.

As another example, consider a business that receives data from many internet users. Suppose that an outside company wishes to run an algorithm on this data. To protect the data of the internet users, the business could use FE to send a function key of the algorithm to the other company along with an encryption of the internet users' data. As the internet users are not likely to be concurrently online, the data is unlikely to be available all at once. Ideally, the business could collect, encrypt, and send the data as it becomes available to them, without needing to store it long term. However, if we are using regular FE, then the business would have to store all of the received data until a time when it has received sufficient data from a sufficient number of internet users. Only then could the business encrypt the data and send it to the outside company. At this point, the data set provided to the outside company is fixed, and adding new data to the set is difficult and may require re-encrypting all of the data. As this data set may be very large, it may also be difficult for the business or the outside company to store the data in its entirety or compute FE functionalities on it.

The reason that FE is so expensive in these scenarios is that when using FE, the entire data set must be known at encryption time, and decryption can only be run on a ciphertext for the entire data set. To counter these issues, we put forward a new type of FE which is better suited for these scenarios.

1.1 Our Results

In this work, we introduce the notion of streaming functional encryption (sFE) and show how to construct it from FE. Streaming FE is designed for scenarios where data arrives in a streaming manner and is computed on in an iterative manner as the stream arrives.

First, we define a streaming function to be a stateful function that takes as input a state st_i and a value x_i and outputs the next state st_{i+1} and a value y_i. A streaming FE scheme will compute function keys for streaming functions.

Definition 1.1 (Streaming Function). *A streaming function with state space $\mathcal{S}$, input space $\mathcal{X}$, and output space $\mathcal{Y}$ is a function $f : \mathcal{X} \times \mathcal{S} \to \mathcal{Y} \times \mathcal{S}$.*

- *We define the **output** of f on $x = x_1 \ldots x_n \in \mathcal{X}^n$ (denoted $f(x)$) to be $y = y_1 \ldots y_n \in \mathcal{Y}^n$ where[1] we have $\mathsf{st}_1 = \bot$ and*

$$(y_i, \mathsf{st}_{i+1}) = f(x_i, \mathsf{st}_i)$$

Definition 1.2 (Streaming Function Class). *The streaming function class $\mathcal{F}[\ell_{\mathcal{F}}, \ell_{\mathcal{S}}, \ell_{\mathcal{X}}, \ell_{\mathcal{Y}}]$ is the set of all streaming functions f that have a description $\widehat{f} \in \{0,1\}^{\ell_{\mathcal{F}}}$, state space $\mathcal{S} = \{0,1\}^{\ell_{\mathcal{S}}}$, input space $\mathcal{X} = \{0,1\}^{\ell_{\mathcal{X}}}$, and output space $\mathcal{Y} = \{0,1\}^{\ell_{\mathcal{Y}}}$.*

Now, as we receive the input data $x = x_1 \ldots x_n$ in a streaming manner, we would like to be able to encrypt the input and decrypt the streaming function of the encrypted input as it arrives. For encryption, we require the ability to individually generate ciphertexts ct_i for the ith input x_i given only the master public key, x_i, the index i, and an encryption state (which is generated once for x using only the master public key). The decryption algorithm will itself be a streaming function that takes as input the ith ciphertext ct_i, the index i, the function key sk_f, and the current decryption state $\mathsf{Dec.st}_i$ (which roughly speaking encrypts st_i), and outputs the next output value y_i where $(y_i, \mathsf{st}_{i+1}) = f(x_i, \mathsf{st}_i)$ and the next decryption state $\mathsf{Dec.st}_{i+1}$. We now define streaming FE.

---

[1] We assume that unless specified otherwise, all streaming functions have the same starting state $\bot$ (or the all zero string) which is included in their state space.

Definition 1.3 (Public-Key Streaming FE). *A public-key streaming functional encryption scheme for* P/Poly *is a tuple of PPT algorithms*
sFE = (Setup, EncSetup, Enc, KeyGen, Dec) *defined as follows:*

- Setup($1^\lambda, 1^{\ell_\mathcal{F}}, 1^{\ell_\mathcal{S}}, 1^{\ell_\mathcal{X}}, 1^{\ell_\mathcal{Y}}$): *takes as input the security parameter* λ, *a function size* $\ell_\mathcal{F}$, *a state size* $\ell_\mathcal{S}$, *an input size* $\ell_\mathcal{X}$, *and an output size* $\ell_\mathcal{Y}$, *and outputs the master public key* mpk *and the master secret key* msk.
- EncSetup(mpk): *takes as input the master public key* mpk *and outputs an encryption state* Enc.st[2].
- Enc(mpk, Enc.st, i, x_i): *takes as input the master public key* mpk, *a state* Enc.st, *an index* i, *and a message* $x_i \in \{0,1\}^{\ell_\mathcal{X}}$ *and outputs an encryption* ct_i *of* x_i.
- KeyGen(msk, f): *takes as input the master secret key* msk *and a function* $f \in \mathcal{F}[\ell_\mathcal{F}, \ell_\mathcal{S}, \ell_\mathcal{X}, \ell_\mathcal{Y}]$ *and outputs a function key* sk_f.
- Dec(sk_f, Dec.st$_i$, i, ct_i): *where for each function key* sk_f, Dec($\mathsf{sk}_f, \cdot, \cdot, \cdot$) *is a streaming function that takes as input a state* Dec.st$_i$, *an index* i, *and an encryption* ct_i *and outputs a new state* Dec.st$_{i+1}$ *and an output* $y_i \in \{0,1\}^{\ell_\mathcal{Y}}$.

sFE *satisfies* **correctness** *if for all polynomials* p, *there exists a negligible function* μ *such that for all* $\lambda \in \mathbb{N}$, *all* $\ell_\mathcal{F}, \ell_\mathcal{S}, \ell_\mathcal{X}, \ell_\mathcal{Y} \leq p(\lambda)$, *all* $n \in [2^\lambda]$, *all* $x = x_1 \ldots x_n$ *where each* $x_i \in \{0,1\}^{\ell_\mathcal{X}}$, *and all* $f \in \mathcal{F}[\ell_\mathcal{F}, \ell_\mathcal{S}, \ell_\mathcal{X}, \ell_\mathcal{Y}]$,

$$\Pr\left[\overline{\mathsf{Dec}}(\mathsf{sk}_f, \mathsf{ct}_x) = f(x) : \begin{array}{c} (\mathsf{mpk}, \mathsf{msk}) \leftarrow \mathsf{Setup}(1^\lambda, 1^{\ell_\mathcal{F}}, 1^{\ell_\mathcal{S}}, 1^{\ell_\mathcal{X}}, 1^{\ell_\mathcal{Y}}), \\ \mathsf{ct}_x \leftarrow \overline{\mathsf{Enc}}(\mathsf{mpk}, x) \\ \mathsf{sk}_f \leftarrow \mathsf{KeyGen}(\mathsf{msk}, f) \end{array}\right] \geq 1 - \mu(\lambda)$$

where we define[3]

- *the output of* $\overline{\mathsf{Enc}}(\mathsf{mpk}, x)$ *to be* $\mathsf{ct}_x = (\mathsf{ct}_i)_{i \in [n]}$ *produced by sampling* Enc.st $\leftarrow$ EncSetup(mpk) *and then computing* $\mathsf{ct}_i \leftarrow \mathsf{Enc}(\mathsf{mpk}, \mathsf{Enc.st}, i, x_i)$ *for* $i \in [n]$.
- *the output of* $\overline{\mathsf{Dec}}(\mathsf{sk}_f, \mathsf{ct}_x)$ *to be* $y = (y_i)_{i \in [n]}$ *where* $(y_i, \mathsf{Dec.st}_{i+1}) = \mathsf{Dec}(\mathsf{sk}_f, \mathsf{Dec.st}_i, i, \mathsf{ct}_i)$

For non-triviality, we require that our streaming FE scheme is *streaming efficient*, meaning that the runtime of our algorithms should not depend on the

---

[2] The purpose of the encryption state is to tie elements of the stream together and must be kept secret in order to prevent mix and match attacks. Suppose that the encryption state either did not exist or was made public. Then an adversary given a function key for some streaming function f and ciphertexts $\mathsf{ct}_1, \ldots, \mathsf{ct}_n$ for some stream $x = x_1 \ldots x_n$ could learn the value of f on any extension of the stream. That is, the adversary could encrypt any values $z = z_1 \ldots z_k$ to get ciphertexts $\mathsf{ct}'_1, \ldots, \mathsf{ct}'_k$, and then learn the value of f on any interpolation of x and z (e.g. $x_1 z_2 z_3 x_4 z_k$) by simply decrypting using the corresponding interpolation of $\mathsf{ct}_1 \ldots \mathsf{ct}_n$ and $\mathsf{ct}'_1 \ldots \mathsf{ct}'_k$ (e.g. $\mathsf{ct}_1 \mathsf{ct}'_2 \mathsf{ct}'_3 \mathsf{ct}_4 \mathsf{ct}'_5$). This is much more power than we want the adversary to have. Note that when the encryption state is secret, then this bad behavior is not allowed as decryption will fail on any ciphertexts ct'_i not generated using the secret encryption state.

[3] As with all streaming functions, we assume that Dec.st$_1 = \perp$ by default.

total length n of the message $x = x_1 \ldots x_n$ that we wish to encrypt. More formally, we require that the size and runtime of all algorithms of sFE on security parameter λ, function size $\ell_{\mathcal{F}}$, state size $\ell_{\mathcal{S}}$, input size $\ell_{\mathcal{X}}$, and output size ℓ_y are $\mathsf{poly}(\lambda, \ell_{\mathcal{F}}, \ell_{\mathcal{S}}, \ell_{\mathcal{X}}, \ell_y)$.

Our security notions are the same as in regular FE except that we allow inputs $x = x_1 \ldots x_n$ of arbitrary length n, allow function keys for streaming functions, and replace $\mathsf{Enc}(\mathsf{mpk}, x)$ with $\overline{\mathsf{Enc}}(\mathsf{mpk}, x)$ as defined in the above definition of streaming FE. In particular, our sFE scheme achieves security similar to standard indistinguishability (IND) security, except that we require all function queries to be made before the challenge message query. This makes our security *function-selective*. However, our definition of security is more liberal than the usual definition of function-selective security in that we allow the choice of each function query to depend on the master public key and all previous function queries. For this reason, we say that our scheme achieves *semi-adaptive-function-selective-IND-security* (see Definition 4.6).[4]

We then show how to build sFE from compact FE. Here, compactness means that the runtime of both the setup and encryption algorithms are independent of the function size.[5] This gives us our main theorem.

Theorem 1.4 (Main Theorem). *Assuming a compact, selective-IND-secure, public-key FE scheme for* P/Poly*, there exists a semi-adaptive-function-selective-IND-secure, public-key sFE scheme for* P/Poly*.*

It turns out that the main technical challenge is to build a secret key streaming FE scheme that works even for just one key and one challenge stream to be encrypted. (Please see the Technical Overview for more details.) Our main theorem then follows from this scheme using a bootstrapping approach similar to [10].

Additionally, we can build our sFE scheme from well-studied assumptions, and in fact only require polynomial security of these assumptions (unlike the subexponential security needed for $i\mathcal{O}$). Recently, [33] construct sublinear, single-key FE for P/Poly from well-studied assumptions. We formally define these assumptions in the full version of the paper [30].

Theorem 1.5 ([33]). *If there exists constants* $\delta, \tau > 0$ *such that:*

- δ-*LPN assumption holds*
- *There exists a PRG in* NC_0 *with a stretch of* $n^{1+\tau}$ *where* n *is the length of the input*
- *The DLIN assumption over prime order symmetric bilinear groups holds*

---

[4] We can actually achieve security even when the challenge stream messages depend on the ciphertexts given for the previous stream values. See Remark 4.7.

[5] In other sections of this paper, we refer to this notion as *strong-compactness* since the usual notion of compactness found in the literature only requires the encryption algorithm to be independent of the function size. However, all existing transformations achieving compactness also yield strong compactness.

Then, there exists a sublinear, single-key, selective-IND-secure, public-key FE scheme for P/Poly.

[8,14,22,35] show how to bootstrap this to a compact scheme in an unbounded collusion setting with only a polynomial loss in security.

Theorem 1.6 ([8,14,22,35]). *If there exists a sublinear, single-key, selective-IND-secure, public-key FE scheme for* P/Poly, *then there exists a compact, selective-IND-secure, public-key FE scheme for* P/Poly.

By combining these results, we get the following corollary.

Corollary 1.7. *If there exists constants* $\delta, \tau > 0$ *such that:*

- δ-*LPN assumption holds*
- *There exists a PRG in* NC_0 *with a stretch of* $n^{1+\tau}$ *where* n *is the length of the input*
- *The DLIN assumption over prime order symmetric bilinear groups holds*

Then, there exists a semi-adaptive-function-selective-IND-secure, public-key sFE scheme for P/Poly.

1.2   Related Work

[10] show how to construct FE for Turing machines. While Turing machines internally involve an iterative operation, similar to a streaming function, in contrast to our setting, their final FE scheme still requires the entire input to be known at encryption time and does not produce output until the entire Turing machine computation terminates.

2   Technical Overview

Our goal is to build a public-key sFE scheme for P/Poly. It turns out that it will suffice for us to build a a seemingly weaker primitive: namely a secret-key sFE scheme for P/Poly that works for just one key and one challenge stream to be encrypted. Our main theorem then follows from this scheme using a bootstrapping approach similar to [10]. Thus, we build our scheme in two steps:

1. First, we construct a single-key, single-ciphertext, secret-key sFE scheme One-sFE. We prove the following:

Theorem 2.1. *Assuming a strongly-compact, selective-IND-secure, secret-key FE scheme for* P/Poly, *there exists a single-key, single-ciphertext, function-selective-SIM-secure, secret-key sFE scheme for* P/Poly.

2. Second, we show how to adapt the technique from [10] to bootstrap One-sFE into a public-key, sFE scheme sFE. We prove the following:

Theorem 2.2. *Assuming (1) a selective-IND-secure, public-key FE scheme for* P/Poly, *and (2) a single-key, single-ciphertext, function-selective-IND-secure, secret-key sFE scheme for* P/Poly, *there exists a semi-adaptive-function-selective-IND-secure, public-key sFE scheme for* P/Poly.

Together, these two theorems imply our main theorem.

Our main technical contributions is constructing the first single-key, single-ciphertext, secret-key sFE scheme. We then overcome two major obstacles that arise from our construction paradigm.

- Our first approach requires a recursive definition that breaks streaming efficiency by requiring keys of length proportional to the length of the stream.
- A second more subtle issue is that we end up with circular parameter dependencies.

We eliminate both these issues through careful changes to the construction as shown below.

Notation. For notational convenience, in this section, we may omit the security, input size, output size, message size, function size, or state size parameters from our algorithms. Additionally, we will often refer to schemes as being SIM-secure or IND-secure, without specifying whether they are selectively, function-selectively, semi-adaptive-function-selectively, or adaptively secure. We leave these details to the formal proofs.

2.1 Single-Key, Single-Ciphertext, SIM-Secure, Secret-Key Streaming FE

For our first step, we wish to build a secret-key sFE scheme One-sFE, which is only required to be secure against an adversary who is allowed to make a single function query, followed by a single message query. We will achieve simulation security, meaning that there exists a PPT simulator which can simulate the real function key for f and the real ciphertext for x given only the streaming function f and the output value $y = f(x)$

A Mild Form of SIM-Security for FE. As a warm-up, we first show how to build an *ordinary non-streaming* FE scheme OneSimFE which achieves a mild form of SIM-security from an IND-secure FE scheme FE and a symmetric key encryption scheme Sym. In particular, our simulation security will only hold against an adversary who is allowed to make a single function query and a single message query. This mild form of simulation security will be useful in building streaming FE, and we will use this technique throughout this section.

- OneSimFE.Setup(1^λ):
  1. msk ← FE.Setup(1^λ)
  2. k ← Sym.Setup(1^λ)
  3. Output (mpk$'$ = mpk, msk$'$ = (msk, k))

- OneSimFE.Enc(mpk, x) = FE.Enc(mpk, $(x, 0, \perp, \perp)$)
- OneSimFE.KeyGen((msk, k), f):
  (a) $c \leftarrow$ Sym.Enc($k, 0$)
  (b) Output FE.KeyGen(msk, $g_{f,c}$) where we define

$g_{f,c}(x, \alpha, k, v)$:
- If $\alpha = 0$, output $f(x)$.   //$\alpha = 0$ is the "normal" case.
- Else, output $v \oplus$ Sym.Dec(k, c).
  // This branch is for simulation.

- OneSimFE.Dec(sk_f, ct) = FE.Dec(sk_f, ct)

In our simulation security game, there are two cases:

- **Case 1: The message query x is asked before the function query f.**
  On receiving a message query length n, the simulator Sim outputs a simulated ciphertext ct $\leftarrow$ FE.Enc(mpk, $(0^n, 1, k, 0)$). On receiving a function query f along with $f(x)$, Sim outputs a simulated function key $\mathsf{sk}_f \leftarrow$ FE.KeyGen(msk, $g_{f,c'}$) where $c' \leftarrow$ Sym.Enc($k, f(x)$).
- **Case 2: The function query f is asked before the message query x.**
  On receiving a function query f, the simulator Sim outputs a simulated function key $\mathsf{sk}_f \leftarrow$ FE.KeyGen(msk, $g_{f,c}$) where $c \leftarrow$ Sym.Enc($k, 0$). On receiving a message query length n and $f(x)$, Sim outputs a simulated ciphertext ct $\leftarrow$ FE.Enc(mpk, $(0^n, 1, k, f(x))$.

Simulation security then follows by the IND-security of FE since $g_{f,c}(x, 0, \perp, \perp) = g_{f,c}(0^n, 1, k, f(x)) = g_{f,c'}(x, 0, \perp, \perp) = g_{f,c'}(0^n, 1, k, 0) = f(x)$ and $c \approx c'$ by the security of Sym.

With this simple initial tool in our belt, we now proceed to tackle the main problem – building streaming FE.

First Attempt at Building One-sFE. Each iteration of our streaming FE scheme needs to combine two values: the current input x_i and the current state st_i. Our first observation is that regular FE allows us to securely combine two values: a function and an input. Thus, if we were to place x_i in a FE ciphertext and place st_i (and f) in a corresponding FE function key, then we could hope to use FE to securely combine the two values and compute $f(x_i, \mathsf{st}_i)$. Now, $\mathsf{st}_1 = \perp$ is fixed and known at key generation time. Thus, we can generate the first function key containing f and st_1. But how do we generate keys containing future states? Our main intuition here is to have the function key containing st_i and f not only compute $f(x_i, \mathsf{st}_i)$ and output y_i, but also create the next function key for the next state st_{i+1}. This gives us the following initial construction: The ciphertext for x is $\mathsf{ct}_x = \{\mathsf{ct}_i\}_{i \in [n]}$ where each $\mathsf{ct}_i \leftarrow$ OneSimFE.Enc(msk$_i$, $(x_i, \mathsf{msk}_{i+1})$). The function key for f is $\mathsf{sk}_f = \mathsf{sk}_{g_{f,\mathsf{st}_1}} \leftarrow$ OneSimFE.KeyGen(msk$_1$, g_{f,st_1}) for g_{f,st_1} as defined below. Here, we use a different master secret key msk$_i$ for each iteration i as our simulation security technique only allows us to program a single value into each ciphertext or key. We can generate all of the One-sFE master secret keys $\{\mathsf{msk}_i\}$ from a short PRF key, which will be the master secret key of our streaming FE scheme. Figure 1 below depicts how we can combine ct_x and sk_f to learn $f(x)$.

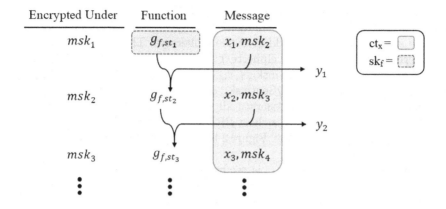

$g_{f,\mathsf{st}_i}(x_i, \mathsf{msk}_{i+1})$:

1. $(y_i, \mathsf{st}_{i+1}) = f(x_i, \mathsf{st}_i)$
2. Output $(y_i, \mathsf{OneSimFE.KeyGen}(\mathsf{msk}_{i+1}, g_{f,\mathsf{st}_{i+1}}))$

Fig. 1. First attempt at building One-sFE.

The idea behind this attempt is that we want to prove security by one by one replacing each $(\mathsf{sk}_{g_{f,\mathsf{st}_i}}, \mathsf{ct}_i)$ with simulated values using the security of OneSimFE. Observe, that simulating $(\mathsf{sk}_{g_{f,\mathsf{st}_i}}, \mathsf{ct}_i)$ removes msk_{i+1} from ct_i, hopefully allowing us to then simulate the next $(\mathsf{sk}_{g_{f,\mathsf{st}_{i+1}}}, \mathsf{ct}_{i+1})$ (as msk_{i+1} is hidden). Unfortunately, this initial scheme does not work and has three main issues:

1. OneSimFE only creates function keys for deterministic functions, but OneSimFE.KeyGen (and thus each g_{f,st_i}) is a randomized function.
2. As OneSimFE is not function-hiding, the value of each intermediate st_i is made public, thus compromising security. (In particular, simulating $(\mathsf{sk}_{g_{f,\mathsf{st}_i}}, \mathsf{ct}_i)$ requires us to know the output value $(y_i, \mathsf{sk}_{g_{f,\mathsf{st}_{i+1}}})$.)
3. The definition of g_{f,st_i} is recursive, and thus the size of our initial function key g_{f,st_1} will depend on the total number n of recursive steps we wish to take. Therefore, our scheme is not streaming efficient as it depends on the length of x.

Solving the Randomization and State Privacy Issues. We can easily fix the first two issues. We can make g_{f,st_i} deterministic by simply giving the randomness r_i needed to compute OneSimFE.KeyGen as input to g_{f,st_i} by placing this randomness in the ith ciphertext. To fix the second issue, instead of giving out function keys with st_i hardcoded into them, we give out function keys with $\widetilde{\mathsf{st}}_i$ hardcoded into them where $\widetilde{\mathsf{st}}_i = \mathsf{st}_i \oplus p_i$ for a random pad p_i. We then simply add p_i and p_{i+1} into the ciphertext for x_i so that we can pad and un-pad states st_i and st_{i+1} in the ith iteration. As each $\widetilde{\mathsf{st}}_i$ is uniformly random when pad p_i is hidden, then giving out $\widetilde{\mathsf{st}}_i$ should not compromise security since p_i is hidden in the ciphertext. This gives us the following intermediate scheme. The ciphertext for x is $\mathsf{ct}_x = \{\mathsf{ct}_i\}_{i\in[n]}$ where each $\mathsf{ct}_i \leftarrow \mathsf{OneSimFE.Enc}(\mathsf{msk}_i, (x_i, \mathsf{msk}_{i+1}, r_{i+1}, p_i, p_{i+1}))$. The function key for f is $\mathsf{sk}_f = \mathsf{sk}_{g_{f,\widetilde{\mathsf{st}}_1}} \leftarrow \mathsf{OneSimFE.KeyGen}(\mathsf{msk}_1, g_{f,\widetilde{\mathsf{st}}_1})$ where $\widetilde{\mathsf{st}}_1 = \mathsf{st}_1 \oplus p_1$ and $g_{f,\widetilde{\mathsf{st}}_1}$ is defined as below. We can generate all of the OneSimFE master secret keys $\{\mathsf{msk}_i\}$ and the pads $\{p_i\}$ from a short PRF key, which will be the master secret key of our streaming FE scheme. Figure 2 below depicts how we can combine ct_x and sk_f to learn $f(x)$.

Again, the definition of g_{f,st_i} is recursive, so this scheme is not streaming efficient. Indeed, achieving streaming efficiency, where the complexity of each encryption and decryption do not grow with n, is the main technical barrier we need to overcome.

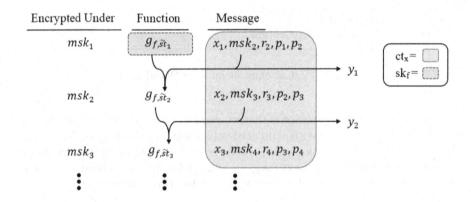

$g_{f,\widetilde{\mathsf{st}}_i}(x_i, \mathsf{msk}_{i+1}, r_{i+1}, p_i, p_{i+1})$:

1. $\mathsf{st}_i = \widetilde{\mathsf{st}}_i \oplus p_i$
2. $(y_i, \mathsf{st}_{i+1}) = f(x_i, \mathsf{st}_i)$
3. $\widetilde{\mathsf{st}}_{i+1} = \mathsf{st}_{i+1} \oplus p_{i+1}$
4. Output $(y_i, \mathsf{OneSimFE.KeyGen}(\mathsf{msk}_{i+1}, g_{f,\widetilde{\mathsf{st}}_{i+1}}; r_{i+1}))$

Fig. 2. Solving the randomization and state privacy issues.

Achieving Streaming Efficiency, Part 1: Removing the Recursive Definition. To fix the issue of the recursive definition, we split each $g_{f,\widetilde{\mathsf{st}}_i}$ into two functions. Rather than having $g_{f,\widetilde{\mathsf{st}}_i}$ generate the function key for $g_{f,\widetilde{\mathsf{st}}_{i+1}}$, we have $g_{f,\widetilde{\mathsf{st}}_i}$ simply generate an encryption of f and $\widetilde{\mathsf{st}}_i$, and have a different function h generate $g_{f,\widetilde{\mathsf{st}}_{i+1}}$ from f and $\widetilde{\mathsf{st}}_i$. This gives us the following scheme. The ciphertext for x is $\mathsf{ct}_x = \{\mathsf{ct}_i, \mathsf{sk}_{h_i}\}_{i \in [n]}$ where each $\mathsf{ct}_i \leftarrow \mathsf{OneSimFE.Enc}(\mathsf{msk}_i, (x_i, \mathsf{msk}'_{i+1}, r'_{i+1}, p_i, p_{i+1}, \mathsf{msk}_{i+1}, r_{i+1}))$ and $\mathsf{sk}_{h_i} \leftarrow \mathsf{OneSimFE.KeyGen}(\mathsf{msk}'_i, h)$ for h defined below. The function key for f is $\mathsf{sk}_f = \mathsf{sk}_{g_{f,\widetilde{\mathsf{st}}_1}} \leftarrow \mathsf{OneSimFE.KeyGen}(\mathsf{msk}_1, g_{f,\widetilde{\mathsf{st}}_1})$ where $\widetilde{\mathsf{st}}_1 = \mathsf{st}_1 \oplus p_1$ and $g_{f,\widetilde{\mathsf{st}}_1}$ is defined below. We can generate all of the One-sFE master secret keys $\{\mathsf{msk}_i, \mathsf{msk}'_i\}$ and the pads $\{p_i\}$ from a short PRF key, which will be the master secret key of our streaming FE scheme. Figure 3 below depicts how we can combine ct_x and sk_f to learn $f(x)$.

Unfortunately, although the definitions of $g_{f,\widetilde{\mathsf{st}}_i}$ (and h) are no longer recursive, the scheme written here has circularly-dependent parameters. In particular, OneSimFE must generate function keys for its own key generation and encryption algorithms as it must generate function keys for h (which contains OneSimFE.KeyGen) and function keys for $g_{f,\widetilde{\mathsf{st}}_i}$, (which contains OneSimFE.Enc).

Achieving Streaming Efficiency, Part 2: Fixing the Circular Dependencies. To remove the circular dependencies among the parameters, we will make two changes:

- Rather than encrypting msk'_i and msk_i in our ciphertexts, we will instead encrypt the randomness r'_{msk_i} and r_{msk_i} used to generate these values. We can then generate $\mathsf{msk}'_i, \mathsf{msk}_i$ from this randomness within $g_{f,\widetilde{\mathsf{st}}_i}$ and h by using the setup algorithm. This will allow us to bound the size of our FE messages as we can assume without loss of generality that the size of all randomness used is λ (if we need additional randomness, our algorithms can simply expand this randomness using a PRG).
- We will use two different FE schemes: one scheme OneSimFE for $g_{f,\widetilde{\mathsf{st}}_i}$, and the other scheme OneSimFE′ for h. Additionally, we will require that OneSimFE′ is strongly-compact, meaning that the setup and encryption algorithms do not depend on the function size and output size.

Now we can instantiate our parameters.

1. Since we are encrypting $r_{\mathsf{msk}_i}, r'_{\mathsf{msk}_i}$ instead of $\mathsf{msk}_i, \mathsf{msk}'_i$, we can bound the size of the inputs to both OneSimFE and OneSimFE′.
2. Since we know the input size of OneSimFE′, by the strong-compactness of OneSimFE′, we can determine the sizes of OneSimFE′.Setup and OneSimFE′.Enc and thus of $g_{f,\widetilde{\mathsf{st}}_i}$.
3. Since we know the function size (i.e. the size of $g_{f,\widetilde{\mathsf{st}}_i}$), input size, and output size of functions of OneSimFE, this allows us to determine the parameters of OneSimFE. Thus, we can determine the sizes of OneSimFE.Setup and OneSimFE.KeyGen and therefore of h.
4. Finally, this allows us to determine the parameters of OneSimFE′ which generates keys for h.

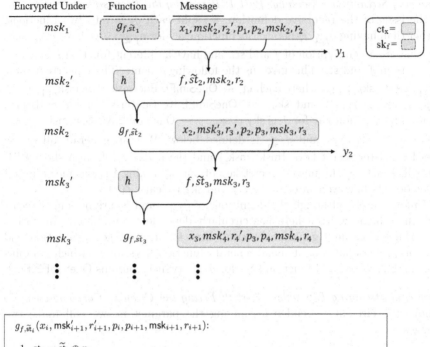

$g_{f,\widetilde{st}_i}(x_i, \mathsf{msk}'_{i+1}, r'_{i+1}, p_i, p_{i+1}, \mathsf{msk}_{i+1}, r_{i+1})$:

1. $\mathsf{st}_i = \widetilde{\mathsf{st}}_i \oplus p_i$
2. $(y_i, \mathsf{st}_{i+1}) = f(x_i, \mathsf{st}_i)$
3. $\widetilde{\mathsf{st}}_{i+1} = \mathsf{st}_{i+1} \oplus p_{i+1}$
4. Output $(y_i, \mathsf{OneSimFE.Enc}(\mathsf{msk}'_{i+1}, (f, \widetilde{\mathsf{st}}_{i+1}, \mathsf{msk}_{i+1}, r_{i+1}); r'_{i+1}))$

$h(f, \widetilde{\mathsf{st}}_{i+1}, \mathsf{msk}_{i+1}, r_{i+1})$:

1. Output $\mathsf{OneSimFE.KeyGen}(\mathsf{msk}_{i+1}, g_{f,\widetilde{\mathsf{st}}_{i+1}}; r_{i+1})$

Fig. 3. Removing the recursive definition.

Now,
we have the following scheme. The ciphertext for x is $\mathsf{ct}_x = \{\mathsf{ct}_i, \mathsf{sk}_{h_i}\}_{i \in [n]}$
where each $\mathsf{ct}_i \leftarrow \mathsf{OneSimFE.Enc}(\mathsf{msk}_i, (x_i, r'_{\mathsf{msk}_{i+1}}, r'_{i+1}, p_i, p_{i+1}, r_{\mathsf{msk}_{i+1}}, r_{i+1}))$
and $\mathsf{sk}_{h_i} \leftarrow \mathsf{OneSimFE'.KeyGen}(\mathsf{msk}'_i, h)$ for h defined below. The function key
for f is $\mathsf{sk}_f = \mathsf{sk}_{g_{f,\widetilde{st}_1}} \leftarrow \mathsf{OneSimFE.KeyGen}(\mathsf{msk}_1, g_{f,\widetilde{st}_1})$ where $\widetilde{\mathsf{st}}_1 = \mathsf{st}_1 \oplus p_1$
and $g_{f,\widetilde{st}_1}$ is defined below. We can generate all of the One-sFE master secret
keys $\{\mathsf{msk}_i, \mathsf{msk}'_i\}$, the randomness $\{r_{\mathsf{msk}_i}, r_{\mathsf{msk}'_i}\}$ needed to compute them, and
the pads $\{p_i\}$ from a short PRF key, which will be the master secret key of our
streaming FE scheme. Figure 4 below depicts how we can combine ct_x and sk_f
to learn $f(x)$.

To prove security, we will iteratively replace each ciphertext and function key with simulated values.

1. First, we use the SIM-security of OneSimFE to replace ct_1 and $\mathsf{sk}_{g_{f,\widetilde{\mathsf{st}}_1}}$ with simulated values. The simulation only requires knowledge of the function $g_{f,\widetilde{\mathsf{st}}_1}$ and the output values y_1 and $\mathsf{ct}_2' = $ OneSimFE$'$.Enc$(\mathsf{msk}_2', (f, \widetilde{\mathsf{st}}_2, r_{\mathsf{msk}_2}, r_2); r_2')$. This change removes the values of x_1 and p_1 from the experiment, which ensures that $\widetilde{\mathsf{st}}_1$ can be made uniformly random and does not leak any information. Additionally, msk_2' (and r_{msk_2}') are now only used to generate ct_2' and sk_{h_2}.
2. Next, we use the SIM-security of OneSimFE$'$ to replace ct_2' and sk_{h_2} with simulated values. The simulation only requires knowledge of the function h and the output value $\mathsf{sk}_{g_{f,\widetilde{\mathsf{st}}_2}} \leftarrow$ OneSimFE.KeyGen$(\mathsf{msk}_2, g_{f,\widetilde{\mathsf{st}}_2}; r_2)$. Now, msk_2 (and r_{msk_2}) are only used to generate ct_2 and $\mathsf{sk}_{g_{f,\widetilde{\mathsf{st}}_2}}$.
3. As in step 1, we replace ct_2 and $\mathsf{sk}_{g_{f,\widetilde{\mathsf{st}}_2}}$ with simulated values. This hides x_2, msk_3', and r_{msk_3}'.
4. As in step 2, we replace ct_2' and sk_{h_2} with simulated values. This hides msk_3 and r_{msk_3}.
5. We then repeat steps 3 and 4 in order for every $(\mathsf{ct}_i, \mathsf{sk}_{g_{f,\widetilde{\mathsf{st}}_i}})$ and $(\mathsf{ct}_i', \mathsf{sk}_{h_i})$.

Once all ciphertexts and function keys have been simulated, then we are in an ideal world, simulator experiment. Thus, we achieve single-key, single-ciphertext, SIM-security, as long as the challenge function f is given before the challenge message x. This is because in order to simulate each sk_{h_i} in the ith ciphertext for x, we must know the output value $\mathsf{sk}_{g_{f,\widetilde{\mathsf{st}}_i}}$ and thus must know f.

Final Scheme. Our final scheme is the same as the previous construction except that we instantiate OneSimFE and OneSimFE$'$ from standard FE, using techniques similar to the one described at the beginning of this technical overview. This requires a little care to ensure that we do not introduce new circular dependencies.

2.2 Bootstrapping to an IND-Secure, Public-Key Streaming FE

Here, we use the same technique that was used in [10] to bootstrap a single-key, single-ciphertext FE scheme for Turing machines into a public-key FE scheme for Turing machine. Our construction is nearly the same as in [10], with only a few minor modifications. Thus, we will only provide an abbreviated overview of this technique.

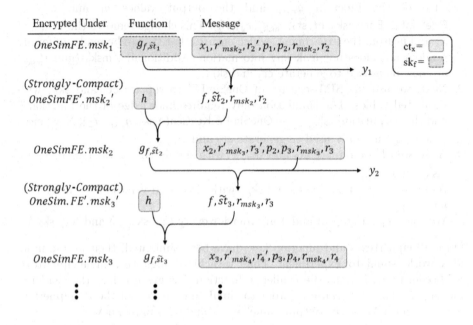

$g_{f,\widetilde{st}_i}(x_i, r'_{\mathsf{msk}_{i+1}}, r'_{i+1}, p_i, p_{i+1}, r_{\mathsf{msk}_{i+1}}, r_{i+1})$:

1. $\mathsf{st}_i = \widetilde{\mathsf{st}}_i \oplus p_i$
2. $(y_i, \mathsf{st}_{i+1}) = f(x_i, \mathsf{st}_i)$
3. $\widetilde{\mathsf{st}}_{i+1} = \mathsf{st}_{i+1} \oplus p_{i+1}$
4. $\mathsf{msk}'_{i+1} \leftarrow \mathsf{OneSimFE'}.\mathsf{Setup}(1^\lambda; r'_{\mathsf{msk}_{i+1}})$
5. Output $(y_i, \mathsf{OneSimFE'}.\mathsf{Enc}(\mathsf{msk}'_{i+1}, (f, \widetilde{\mathsf{st}}_{i+1}, r_{\mathsf{msk}_{i+1}}, r_{i+1}); r'_{i+1}))$

$h(f, \widetilde{\mathsf{st}}_{i+1}, r_{\mathsf{msk}_{i+1}}, r_{i+1})$:

1. $\mathsf{msk}_{i+1} \leftarrow \mathsf{OneSimFE}.\mathsf{Setup}(1^\lambda; r_{\mathsf{msk}_{i+1}})$
2. Output $\mathsf{OneSimFE}.\mathsf{KeyGen}(\mathsf{msk}_{i+1}, g_{f,\widetilde{\mathsf{st}}_{i+1}}; r_{i+1})$

Fig. 4. Fixing the circular dependencies.

Let FE be a selective-IND-secure, public-key FE scheme. Let FPFE be a function-private-selective-IND-secure, secret-key FE scheme. (This can be built from FE using techniques from [17].) Let One-sFE be our single-key, single-ciphertext, function-selective-SIM-secure, secret-key streaming FE scheme. Let PRF and PRF2 be secure PRFs.

At a high level, the idea is to generate a new One-sFE master secret key One-sFE.msk for each message x and function f. This ensures that each One-sFE.msk is only used for one key and one ciphertext, allowing us to then rely on the security of One-sFE. This is implemented in two steps:

1. First, we use FE to combine a PRF key PRF.k from the ciphertext for x with randomness s from the function key for f to securely generate a fresh One-sFE.msk for (x, f). We then use One-sFE.msk to generate a function key One-sFE.sk$_f$ for f and a ciphertext FPFE.ct encrypting One-sFE.msk.

2. Second, our ciphertext for x creates FPFE function keys with values from x hardcoded into them. The function privacy of FPFE will ensure that this does not leak information about x. These function keys can then be combined with FPFE.ct to get an encryption One-sFE.ct$_x$ of x.

This gives us the following scheme, which is close to our actual construction.[6] The ciphertext for $x = x_1 \ldots x_n$ is ct$_x$ = (FE.ct, {FPFE.sk$_{H_{i,x_i,t_i}}\}_{i \in [n]}$) where FE.ct $\leftarrow$ FE.Enc(FE.mpk, (FPFE.msk, PRF.K)) and FPFE.sk$_{H_{i,x_i,t_i}}$ $\leftarrow$ FPFE.KeyGen(FPFE.msk, H_{i,x_i,t_i}) for H_{i,x_i,t_i} defined below and a random t_i. The function key for f is sk$_f$ = FE.sk$_{G_{f,s}}$ $\leftarrow$ FE.KeyGen(FE.msk, $G_{f,s}$) for $G_{f,s}$ defined below. Figure 5 below depicts how we can combine ct$_x$ and sk$_f$ to learn $f(x)$.

To prove security, we will first use a similar simulation technique as in our One-sFE construction to ensure that each One-sFE.msk is securely generated. This is done by programming into each $G_{f,s}$ the output value (One-sFE.msk, One-sFE.Enc.st, PRF2.k) generated by $G_{f,s}$(FPFE.msk, PRF.K). Next, we will move from encrypting $x^{(b)}$ for a random $b \leftarrow \{0,1\}$ to always encrypting $x^{(0)}$. This will prove security as our final hybrid will be independent of b. We will perform this change from $x^{(b)}$ to $x^{(0)}$ one function at a time by utilizing the security of One-sFE and FPFE to switch between different branches of computation within H_{i,x_i,t_i} (which we add into H_{i,x_i,t_i} using the function privacy of FPFE). We leave further details to the formal proof.

---

[6] Our actual scheme adds additional branches of computation to $G_{f,s}$ and H_{i,x_i,t_i} which are only used in the security proof.

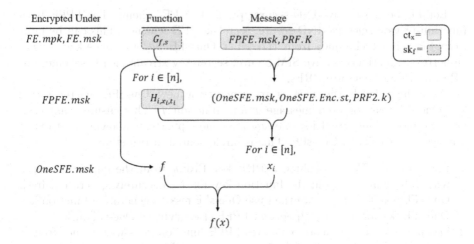

$G_{f,s}(\mathsf{FPFE.msk}, \mathsf{PRF}.K):$

1. $(r_{\mathsf{Setup}}, r_{\mathsf{KeyGen}}, r_{\mathsf{EncSetup}}, r_{\mathsf{PRF2}}, r_{\mathsf{Enc}}) \leftarrow \mathsf{PRF.Eval}(\mathsf{PRF}.K, s)$
2. $\mathsf{One\text{-}sFE.msk} \leftarrow \mathsf{One\text{-}sFE.Setup}(1^\lambda; r_{\mathsf{Setup}})$
3. $\mathsf{One\text{-}sFE.Enc.st} \leftarrow \mathsf{One\text{-}sFE.EncSetup}(\mathsf{One\text{-}sFE.msk}; r_{\mathsf{EncSetup}})$
4. $\mathsf{One\text{-}sFE.sk}_f \leftarrow \mathsf{One\text{-}sFE.KeyGen}(\mathsf{One\text{-}sFE.msk}, f; r_{\mathsf{KeyGen}})$
5. $\mathsf{PRF2}.k \leftarrow \mathsf{PRF2.Setup}(1^\lambda; r_{\mathsf{PRF2}})$
6. $\mathsf{FPFE.ct} \leftarrow \mathsf{FPFE.Enc}(\mathsf{FPFE.msk}, (\mathsf{One\text{-}sFE.msk}, \mathsf{One\text{-}sFE.Enc.st}, \mathsf{PRF2}.k); r_{\mathsf{Enc}})$
7. Output $(\mathsf{One\text{-}sFE.sk}_f, \mathsf{FPFE.ct})$

$H_{i,x_i,t_i}(\mathsf{One\text{-}sFE.msk}, \mathsf{One\text{-}sFE.Enc.st}, \mathsf{PRF2}.k):$

1. $r_i \leftarrow \mathsf{PRF2.Eval}(\mathsf{PRF2}.k, t_i)$
2. Output $\mathsf{One\text{-}sFE.Enc}(\mathsf{One\text{-}sFE.msk}, \mathsf{One\text{-}sFE.Enc.st}, i, x_i; r_i)$

Fig. 5. Bootstrapping to an IND-secure, public-key streaming FE. This is similar, but not identical to our final construction.

3 Preliminaries

Throughout, we will use λ to denote a security parameter.

Notation. – We say that a function $f(\lambda)$ is negligible in λ if $f(\lambda) = \lambda^{-\omega(1)}$, and we denote it by $f(\lambda) = \mathsf{negl}(\lambda)$.
– We say that a function $g(\lambda)$ is polynomial in λ if $g(\lambda) = p(\lambda)$ for some fixed polynomial p, and we denote it by $g(\lambda) = \mathsf{poly}(\lambda)$.
– For $n \in \mathbb{N}$, we use $[n]$ to denote $\{1, \ldots, n\}$.
– If R is a random variable, then $r \leftarrow R$ denotes sampling r from R. If T is a set, then $i \leftarrow T$ denotes sampling i uniformly at random from T.

We will use PRFs and symmetric key encryption schemes with pseudorandom ciphertexts. We defer this definition to the full version [30].

3.1 Functional Encryption

Here we give some fundamental definitions for functional encryption (FE) schemes. We defer this section to the full version [30].

4 Streaming Functional Encryption

We now define our notion of streaming functional encryption which is an FE scheme for streaming functions. First, we define a streaming function.

Definition 4.1 (Streaming Function). *A streaming function with state space $\mathcal{S}$, input space $\mathcal{X}$, and output space $\mathcal{Y}$ is a function $f : \mathcal{X} \times \mathcal{S} \to \mathcal{Y} \times \mathcal{S}$.*

- *We define the **output** of f on $x = x_1 \ldots x_n \in \mathcal{X}^n$ (denoted $f(x)$) to be $y = y_1 \ldots y_n \in \mathcal{Y}^n$ where[7] we have $\mathsf{st}_1 = \bot$ and*

$$(y_i, \mathsf{st}_{i+1}) = f(x_i, \mathsf{st}_i)$$

Definition 4.2 (Streaming Function Class). *The streaming function class $\mathcal{F}[\ell_{\mathcal{F}}, \ell_{\mathcal{S}}, \ell_{\mathcal{X}}, \ell_{\mathcal{Y}}]$ is the set of all streaming functions f that have a description $\widehat{f} \in \{0,1\}^{\ell_{\mathcal{F}}}$, state space $\mathcal{S} = \{0,1\}^{\ell_{\mathcal{S}}}$, input space $\mathcal{X} = \{0,1\}^{\ell_{\mathcal{X}}}$, and output space $\mathcal{Y} = \{0,1\}^{\ell_{\mathcal{Y}}}$.*

Definition 4.3 (Public-Key Streaming FE). *A public-key streaming functional encryption scheme for P/Poly is a tuple of PPT algorithms* $\mathsf{sFE} = (\mathsf{Setup}, \mathsf{EncSetup}, \mathsf{Enc}, \mathsf{KeyGen}, \mathsf{Dec})$ *defined as follows:*[8]

- $\mathsf{Setup}(1^\lambda, 1^{\ell_{\mathcal{F}}}, 1^{\ell_{\mathcal{S}}}, 1^{\ell_{\mathcal{X}}}, 1^{\ell_{\mathcal{Y}}})$: *takes as input the security parameter λ, a function size $\ell_{\mathcal{F}}$, a state size $\ell_{\mathcal{S}}$, an input size $\ell_{\mathcal{X}}$, and an output size $\ell_{\mathcal{Y}}$, and outputs the master public key* mpk *and the master secret key* msk.
- $\mathsf{EncSetup}(\mathsf{mpk})$: *takes as input the master public key* mpk *and outputs an encryption state* $\mathsf{Enc.st}$.
- $\mathsf{Enc}(\mathsf{mpk}, \mathsf{Enc.st}, i, x_i)$: *takes as input the master public key* mpk, *an encryption state* $\mathsf{Enc.st}$, *an index i, and a message $x_i \in \{0,1\}^{\ell_{\mathcal{X}}}$ and outputs an encryption ct_i of x_i.*
- $\mathsf{KeyGen}(\mathsf{msk}, f)$: *takes as input the master secret key* msk *and a function $f \in \mathcal{F}[\ell_{\mathcal{F}}, \ell_{\mathcal{S}}, \ell_{\mathcal{X}}, \ell_{\mathcal{Y}}]$ and outputs a function key sk_f.*
- $\mathsf{Dec}(\mathsf{sk}_f, \mathsf{Dec.st}_i, i, \mathsf{ct}_i)$: *where for each function key sk_f, $\mathsf{Dec}(\mathsf{sk}_f, \cdot, \cdot, \cdot)$ is a streaming function that takes as input a state $\mathsf{Dec.st}_i$, an index i, and an encryption ct_i and outputs a new state $\mathsf{Dec.st}_{i+1}$ and an output $y_i \in \{0,1\}^{\ell_{\mathcal{Y}}}$.*

---

[7] We assume that unless specified otherwise, all streaming functions have the same starting state $\bot$ (or the all zero string) which is included in their state space.

[8] We also allow $\mathsf{Enc}, \mathsf{EncSetup}, \mathsf{KeyGen}$, and Dec to additionally receive parameters $1^\lambda, 1^{\ell_{\mathcal{F}}}, 1^{\ell_{\mathcal{S}}}, 1^{\ell_{\mathcal{X}}}, 1^{\ell_{\mathcal{Y}}}$ as input, but omit them from our notation for convenience.

sFE *satisfies* **correctness** *if for all polynomials* p, *there exists a negligible function* μ *such that for all* $\lambda \in \mathbb{N}$, *all* $\ell_{\mathcal{F}}, \ell_{\mathcal{S}}, \ell_{\mathcal{X}}, \ell_{\mathcal{Y}} \leq p(\lambda)$, *all* $n \in [2^\lambda]$, *all* $x = x_1 \ldots x_n$ *where each* $x_i \in \{0,1\}^{\ell_{\mathcal{X}}}$, *and all* $f \in \mathcal{F}[\ell_{\mathcal{F}}, \ell_{\mathcal{S}}, \ell_{\mathcal{X}}, \ell_{\mathcal{Y}}]$,

$$\Pr\left[\overline{\mathsf{Dec}}(\mathsf{sk}_f, \mathsf{ct}_x) = f(x) : \begin{array}{c} (\mathsf{mpk}, \mathsf{msk}) \leftarrow \mathsf{Setup}(1^\lambda, 1^{\ell_{\mathcal{F}}}, 1^{\ell_{\mathcal{S}}}, 1^{\ell_{\mathcal{X}}}, 1^{\ell_{\mathcal{Y}}}), \\ \mathsf{ct}_x \leftarrow \overline{\mathsf{Enc}}(\mathsf{mpk}, x) \\ \mathsf{sk}_f \leftarrow \mathsf{KeyGen}(\mathsf{msk}, f) \end{array}\right] \geq 1 - \mu(\lambda)$$

where we define[9]

- *the output of* $\overline{\mathsf{Enc}}(\mathsf{mpk}, x)$ *to be* $\mathsf{ct}_x = (\mathsf{ct}_i)_{i \in [n]}$ *produced by sampling* $\mathsf{Enc.st} \leftarrow \mathsf{EncSetup}(\mathsf{mpk})$ *and then computing* $\mathsf{ct}_i \leftarrow \mathsf{Enc}(\mathsf{mpk}, \mathsf{Enc.st}, i, x_i)$ *for* $i \in [n]$.
- *the output of* $\overline{\mathsf{Dec}}(\mathsf{sk}_f, \mathsf{ct}_x)$ *to be* $y = (y_i)_{i \in [n]}$ *where* $(y_i, \mathsf{Dec.st}_{i+1}) = \mathsf{Dec}(\mathsf{sk}_f, \mathsf{Dec.st}_i, i, \mathsf{ct}_i)$

Efficiency. We require our streaming FE schemes to be *streaming efficient*, meaning that the runtime of our algorithms should not depend on the total length n of the message $x = x_1 \ldots x_n$ that we wish to encrypt. More formally, we require that the size and runtime of all algorithms of sFE on security parameter λ, function size $\ell_{\mathcal{F}}$, state size $\ell_{\mathcal{S}}$, input size $\ell_{\mathcal{X}}$, and output size $\ell_{\mathcal{Y}}$ are $\mathsf{poly}(\lambda, \ell_{\mathcal{F}}, \ell_{\mathcal{S}}, \ell_{\mathcal{X}}, \ell_{\mathcal{Y}})$.

Definition 4.4 (Secret-Key Streaming FE). *Secret-key streaming FE is the same as public-key streaming FE except that* Setup *only outputs a master secret key and* EncSetup *and* Enc *require the master secret key instead of the (non-existent) master public key. We defer this definition to the full version [30].*

Remark 4.5. We can also define a relaxed variant of streaming FE in which the encryption function is also a streaming function that takes as input the master public key, a state $\mathsf{Enc.st}_i$, an index i, and an input x_i, and outputs a new state $\mathsf{Enc.st}_{i+1}$, and an encryption ct_i of x_i. We defer this definition to the full version [30].

4.1 Security

All of our definitions of security for streaming FE are exactly the same as the definitions of security for regular FE except that in the security games,

1. The adversary additionally outputs a state size parameter $1^{\ell_{\mathcal{S}}}$.
2. We allow function queries for streaming functions in $\mathcal{F}[\lambda, \ell_{\mathcal{F}}, \ell_{\mathcal{S}}, \ell_{\mathcal{X}}, \ell_{\mathcal{Y}}]$.
3. We allow the challenge message query pairs to be $(x^{(0)}, x^{(1)})$ where $x^{(0)} = x_1^{(0)} \ldots x_n^{(0)}$ and $x^{(1)} = x_1^{(1)} \ldots x_n^{(1)}$ for some length $n \in \mathbb{N}$ chosen by the adversary and where each $x_i^0, x_i^1 \in \{0,1\}^{\ell_{\mathcal{X}}}$.
4. We replace $\mathsf{Enc}(\mathsf{mpk}, x)$ with $\overline{\mathsf{Enc}}(\mathsf{mpk}, x)$ as defined in Definition 4.3.

As an example, we define the following:

---

[9] As with all streaming functions, we assume that $\mathsf{Dec.st}_1 = \bot$ by default.

Definition 4.6 (Semi-Adaptive-Function-Selective-IND-Security). *A public-key streaming FE scheme* sFE *for* P/Poly *is semi-adaptive-function-selective-IND-secure if there exists a negligible function μ such that for all $\lambda \in \mathbb{N}$ and all PPT adversaries $\mathcal{A}$,*

$$\left| \Pr[\text{sFE-Expt}_{\mathcal{A}}^{\text{Semi-Ad-Func-Sel-IND}}(1^\lambda, 0) = 1] \right.$$
$$\left. - \Pr[\text{sFE-Expt}_{\mathcal{A}}^{\text{Semi-Ad-Func-Sel-IND}}(1^\lambda, 1) = 1] \right| \leq \mu(\lambda)$$

where for each $b \in \{0, 1\}$ and $\lambda \in \mathbb{N}$, we define

---

$\text{sFE-Expt}_{\mathcal{A}}^{\text{Semi-Ad-Func-Sel-IND}}(1^\lambda, b)$

1. **Parameters:** $\mathcal{A}$ *takes as input 1^λ, and outputs a function size $1^{\ell_{\mathcal{F}}}$, a state size $1^{\ell_{\mathcal{S}}}$, an input size $1^{\ell_{\mathcal{X}}}$, and an output size $1^{\ell_{\mathcal{Y}}}$.*
2. **Public Key:** *Compute* $(\text{mpk}, \text{msk}) \leftarrow \text{sFE.Setup}(1^\lambda, 1^{\ell_{\mathcal{F}}}, 1^{\ell_{\mathcal{S}}}, 1^{\ell_{\mathcal{X}}}, 1^{\ell_{\mathcal{Y}}})$ *and send* mpk *to $\mathcal{A}$.*
3. **Function Queries:** *The following can be repeated any polynomial number of times:*
   (a) $\mathcal{A}$ *outputs a streaming function query $f \in \mathcal{F}[\ell_{\mathcal{F}}, \ell_{\mathcal{S}}, \ell_{\mathcal{X}}, \ell_{\mathcal{Y}}]$*
   (b) $\text{sk}_f \leftarrow \text{sFE.KeyGen}(\text{msk}, f)$
   (c) *Send* sk_f *to $\mathcal{A}$*
4. **Challenge Message:** *$\mathcal{A}$ outputs a challenge message pair $(x^{(0)}, x^{(1)})$ where $x^{(0)} = x_1^{(0)} \dots x_n^{(0)}$ and $x^{(1)} = x_1^{(1)} \dots x_n^{(1)}$ for some length $n \in \mathbb{N}$ chosen by the adversary and where each $x_i^{(0)}, x_i^{(1)} \in \{0, 1\}^{\ell_{\mathcal{X}}}$.*
5. **Challenge Ciphertext:** *Compute* $\text{ct} \leftarrow \text{sFE.\overline{Enc}}(\text{mpk}, x^{(b)})$ *and send* ct *to $\mathcal{A}$.*
6. **Experiment Outcome:** *$\mathcal{A}$ outputs a bit b'. The output of the experiment is set to 1 if $b = b'$ and $f(x^{(0)}) = f(x^{(1)})$ for all functions f queried by the adversary.*

Remark 4.7. Our definition of security above requires all elements of the challenge streams to be given before the adversary receives any ciphertexts. However, we can actually achieve a slightly more adaptive notion of security where the challenge stream messages can depend on the ciphertexts given for the previous stream values. In particular, in the security game above, the **Challenge Message** and **Challenge Ciphertext** phases can be replaced with one where the adversary iteratively outputs the next challenge message pair $(x_i^{(0)}, x_i^{(1)})$ and receives the next challenge ciphertext: an encryption of $x_i^{(b)}$. We can prove this stronger notion of security using the same proof already in the paper, with only minor modifications. In particular, we modify any intermediate definitions of security to also have this property and reformat the hybrids accordingly.

The rest of the security definitions in both the secret-key and public-key settings follow analogously.

We also define a weak notion of simulation security in the secret-key setting.

Definition 4.8 (Single-Key, Single-Ciphertext, Function-Selective-SIM-Security). *A secret-key streaming FE scheme* sFE *for* P/Poly *is single-key, single-ciphertext, function-selective-SIM-secure if there exists a PPT simulator* Sim *and a negligible function* μ *such that for all* $\lambda \in \mathbb{N}$ *and all PPT adversaries* $\mathcal{A}$,

$$\left| \Pr[\mathsf{RealExpt}_{\mathcal{A}}^{\mathsf{One\text{-}Func\text{-}Sel\text{-}SIM}}(1^\lambda) = 1] - \Pr[\mathsf{IdealExpt}_{\mathcal{A},\mathsf{Sim}}^{\mathsf{One\text{-}Func\text{-}Sel\text{-}SIM}}(1^\lambda) = 1] \right| \leq \mu(\lambda)$$

where for $\lambda \in \mathbb{N}$, *we define*

$\mathsf{RealExpt}_{\mathcal{A}}^{\mathsf{One\text{-}Func\text{-}Sel\text{-}SIM}}(1^\lambda)$

1. **Parameters:** $\mathcal{A}$ *takes as input* 1^λ, *and outputs a function size* $1^{\ell_{\mathcal{F}}}$, *a state size* 1^{ℓ_S}, *an input size* 1^{ℓ_X}, *and an output size* 1^{ℓ_Y}.
2. **Setup:** $\mathsf{msk} \leftarrow \mathsf{sFE.Setup}(1^\lambda, 1^{\ell_{\mathcal{F}}}, 1^{\ell_S}, 1^{\ell_X}, 1^{\ell_Y})$
3. **Function Query:**
   (a) $\mathcal{A}$ *outputs a streaming function query* $f \in \mathcal{F}[\ell_{\mathcal{F}}, \ell_S, \ell_X, \ell_Y]$.
   (b) $\mathsf{sk}_f \leftarrow \mathsf{sFE.KeyGen}(\mathsf{msk}, f)$
   (c) *Send* sk_f *to* $\mathcal{A}$.
4. **Message Query:**
   (a) $\mathcal{A}$ *outputs a message* x *where* $x = x_1 \ldots x_n$ *for some* $n \in \mathbb{N}$ *chosen by the adversary and where each* $x_i \in \{0,1\}^{\ell_X}$.
   (b) $\mathsf{ct} \leftarrow \mathsf{sFE.}\overline{\mathsf{Enc}}(\mathsf{msk}, x)$
   (c) *Send* ct *to* $\mathcal{A}$.
5. **Experiment Outcome:** $\mathcal{A}$ *outputs a bit* b *which is the output of the experiment.*

$\mathsf{IdealExpt}_{\mathcal{A},\mathsf{Sim}}^{\mathsf{One\text{-}Func\text{-}Sel\text{-}SIM}}(1^\lambda)$

1. **Parameters:** $\mathcal{A}$ *takes as input* 1^λ, *and outputs a function size* $1^{\ell_{\mathcal{F}}}$, *a state size* 1^{ℓ_S}, *an input size* 1^{ℓ_X}, *and an output size* 1^{ℓ_Y}. Sim *receives* $(1^\lambda, 1^{\ell_{\mathcal{F}}}, 1^{\ell_S}, 1^{\ell_X}, 1^{\ell_Y})$.
2. **Function Query:**
   (a) $\mathcal{A}$ *outputs a streaming function query* $f \in \mathcal{F}[\ell_{\mathcal{F}}, \ell_S, \ell_X, \ell_Y]$.
   (b) Sim *receives* f *and outputs a function key* sk_f.
   (c) *Send* sk_f *to* $\mathcal{A}$.
3. **Message Query:**
   (a) $\mathcal{A}$ *outputs a message* x *where* $x = x_1 \ldots x_n$ *for some* $n \in \mathbb{N}$ *chosen by the adversary and where each* $x_i \in \{0,1\}^{\ell_X}$.
   (b) Sim *receives* $(1^n, f(x))$ *and outputs a ciphertext* ct.
   (c) *Send* ct *to* $\mathcal{A}$.
4. **Experiment Outcome:** $\mathcal{A}$ *outputs a bit* b *which is the output of the experiment.*

Remark 4.9. In the secret-key setting, single-key, single-ciphertext, function-selective-SIM security implies single-key, single-ciphertext, function-selective-IND security.

5 Single-Key, Single-Ciphertext, SIM-Secure, Secret-Key Streaming FE

In this section, we construct our main building block: a single-key, single-ciphertext, function-selective-SIM-secure, secret-key sFE scheme. We prove the following:

Theorem 5.1. *Assuming a strongly-compact, selective-IND-secure, secret-key FE scheme for* P/Poly, *there exists a single-key, single-ciphertext, function-selective-SIM-secure, secret-key sFE scheme for* P/Poly.

Please refer to the technical overview (Sect. 2) for a high level overview of our construction. To prove Theorem 5.1, we build an sFE scheme from the following tools:

Tools.

- PRF = (PRF.Setup, PRF.Eval): A secure pseudorandom function family.
- PRF2 = (PRF2.Setup, PRF2.Eval): A secure pseudorandom function family.
- Sym = (Sym.Setup, Sym.Enc, Sym.Dec): A secure symmetric key encryption scheme.
- Sym' = (Sym'.Setup, Sym'.Enc, Sym'.Dec): A secure symmetric key encryption scheme.
- OneCompFE = (OneCompFE.Setup, OneCompFE.Enc, OneCompFE.KeyGen, OneCompFE.Dec): A *strongly-compact*, single-key, single-ciphertext, *selective*-IND-secure, secret-key FE scheme for P/Poly.
- OneFSFE   = (OneFSFE.Setup, OneFSFE.Enc, OneFSFE.KeyGen, OneFSFE.Dec): A single-key, single-ciphertext, *function-selective*-IND-secure, secret-key FE scheme for P/Poly.

Instantiation of the Tools. Let SKFE be a strongly-compact, selective-IND-secure, secret-key FE scheme for P/Poly.

- We can build PRF, PRF2, Sym, Sym' from any one-way-function using standard cryptographic techniques (e.g. [23,24]). As FE implies one-way-functions, then we can build these from SKFE.
- SKFE already satisfies the compactness and security requirements needed for OneCompFE.
- We can first build a function-private-selective-IND-secure, secret-key FE scheme FPFE for P/Poly by using the function-privacy transformation of [17] on SKFE. As observed in [17], a single-key, single-ciphertext, function-private-selective-IND-secure, secret-key FE scheme for P/Poly is also a (non-compact) single-key, single-ciphertext, function-selective-IND-secure, secret-key FE scheme for P/Poly as we can simply exchange the roles of the functions and messages using universal circuits. Thus, FPFE can be used to build OneFSFE.

5.1   Parameters

We defer this section to the full version [30].

5.2   Construction

We now construct our streaming FE scheme One-sFE. Recall that for notational convenience, we may omit the security, input size, output size, message size, function size, or state size parameters from our setup and FE algorithms. For information on our parameters, please see the parameter section (Sect. 5.1) in the full version of the paper [30].

- One-sFE.Setup($1^\lambda, 1^{\ell_\mathcal{F}}, 1^{\ell_s}, 1^{\ell_x}, 1^{\ell_y}$):
   1. PRF.$K \leftarrow$ PRF.Setup(1^λ), PRF2.$K \leftarrow$ PRF2.Setup(1^λ)
      * Throughout, for $i \in [2^\lambda]$, we will define

$$r_{\mathsf{msk}_i} = \mathsf{PRF.Eval}(\mathsf{PRF}.K, (i, 0))$$
$$\mathsf{msk}_i = \mathsf{OneFSFE.Setup}(1^\lambda; r_{\mathsf{msk}_i})$$
$$r'_{\mathsf{msk}_i} = \mathsf{PRF.Eval}(\mathsf{PRF}.K, (i, 1))$$
$$\mathsf{msk}'_i = \mathsf{OneCompFE.Setup}(1^\lambda; r'_{\mathsf{msk}_i})$$
$$r_{k_i} = \mathsf{PRF.Eval}(\mathsf{PRF}.K, (i, 2))$$
$$k_i = \mathsf{Sym.Setup}(1^\lambda; r_{k_i})$$
$$r'_{k_i} = \mathsf{PRF.Eval}(\mathsf{PRF}.K, (i, 3))$$
$$k'_i = \mathsf{Sym'.Setup}(1^\lambda; r'_{k_i})$$

Observe that these can all be computed from PRF.K and i. We will also define

$$p_i = \mathsf{PRF2.Eval}(\mathsf{PRF2}.K, i)$$

which can be computed from PRF2.K and i.
   2. Output MSK = (PRF.K, PRF2.K)
- One-sFE.EncSetup(MSK): Output Enc.st = $\perp$.
- One-sFE.Enc(MSK, Enc.st, i, x_i)
   1. Parse MSK = (PRF.K, PRF2.K).
   2. Compute $\mathsf{msk}_i, p_i, p_{i+1}, r'_{\mathsf{msk}_{i+1}}, r_{\mathsf{msk}_{i+1}}, k_i, k'_i, \mathsf{msk}'_i$ from PRF.K, PRF2.K.
   3. $r'_{\mathsf{Enc}_{i+1}}, r_{\mathsf{KeyGen}_{i+1}} \leftarrow \{0, 1\}^\lambda$
   4. $\mathsf{ct}_i \leftarrow \mathsf{OneFSFE.Enc}(\mathsf{msk}_i, (x_i, p_i, p_{i+1}, r'_{\mathsf{msk}_{i+1}}, r'_{\mathsf{Enc}_{i+1}}, r_{\mathsf{msk}_{i+1}}, r_{\mathsf{KeyGen}_{i+1}}, 0, 0^\lambda, 0^{\ell_y}))$
   5. If $i = 1$, output $CT_1 = \mathsf{ct}_1$.
   6. If $i > 1$
      (a) $c_i \leftarrow \mathsf{Sym.Enc}(k_i, 0^{\ell_{\mathsf{Sym}}.m_\lambda})$
      (b) $c'_i \leftarrow \mathsf{Sym'.Enc}(k'_i, 0^{\ell_{\mathsf{Sym'}}.m_\lambda})$
      (c) Let $h_i = h_{c_i, c'_i}$ as defined in Fig. 7.
      (d) $\mathsf{sk}'_{h_i} \leftarrow \mathsf{OneCompFE.KeyGen}(\mathsf{msk}'_i, h_i)$
      (e) Output $CT_i = (\mathsf{ct}_i, \mathsf{sk}'_{h_i})$

- One-sFE.KeyGen(MSK, f)
    1. Parse MSK = (PRF.K, PRF2.K).
    2. Compute msk_1, k_1, p_1 from PRF.K, PRF2.K.
    3. $c_1 \leftarrow \mathsf{Sym.Enc}(k_1, 0^{\ell_{\mathsf{Sym}} \cdot m_\lambda})$
    4. $\widetilde{\mathsf{st}}_1 = p_1$ (Here, we assume $\mathsf{st}_1 = 0^{\ell_s}$ for all streaming functions so that $\mathsf{st}_1 = \widetilde{\mathsf{st}}_1 \oplus p_1$.)
    5. Let $g_1 = g_{f, \widetilde{\mathsf{st}}_1, c_1}$ as defined in Fig. 6.
    6. $\mathsf{sk}_{g_1} \leftarrow \mathsf{OneFSFE.KeyGen}(\mathsf{msk}_1, g_1)$
    7. Output $\mathsf{SK}_f = \mathsf{sk}_{g_1}$.

$g_{f, \widetilde{\mathsf{st}}_i, c_i}(x_i, p_i, p_{i+1}, r'_{\mathsf{msk}_{i+1}}, r'_{\mathsf{Enc}_{i+1}}, r_{\mathsf{msk}_{i+1}}, r_{\mathsf{KeyGen}_{i+1}}, \alpha_i, r_{k_i}, \psi_i)$:
- If $\alpha_i = 0$,
    1. $\mathsf{st}_i = \widetilde{\mathsf{st}}_i \oplus p_i$
    2. $(y_i, \mathsf{st}_{i+1}) = f(x_i, \mathsf{st}_i)$
    3. $\widetilde{\mathsf{st}}_{i+1} = \mathsf{st}_{i+1} \oplus p_{i+1}$
    4. $\mathsf{msk}'_{i+1} = \mathsf{OneCompFE.Setup}(1^\lambda; r'_{\mathsf{msk}_{i+1}})$
    5. $\mathsf{ct}'_{i+1} = \mathsf{OneCompFE.Enc}(\mathsf{msk}'_{i+1}, (f, \widetilde{\mathsf{st}}_{i+1}, r_{\mathsf{msk}_{i+1}}, r_{\mathsf{KeyGen}_{i+1}}, 0, 0^\lambda); r'_{\mathsf{Enc}_{i+1}})$
    6. Output $(y_i, \mathsf{ct}'_{i+1})$.
- Else
    1. $k_i = \mathsf{Sym.Setup}(1^\lambda; r_{k_i})$
    2. $(\theta_i, \mathsf{ct}'_{i+1}) = \mathsf{Sym.Dec}(k_i, c_i)$.
    3. Output $(\theta_i \oplus \psi_i, \mathsf{ct}'_{i+1})$.

Fig. 6. Def of $g_{f, \widetilde{\mathsf{st}}_i, c_i}$.

$h_{c_i, c'_i}(f, \widetilde{\mathsf{st}}_i, r_{\mathsf{msk}_i}, r_{\mathsf{KeyGen}_i}, \alpha'_i, r'_{k_i})$
- If $\alpha'_i = 0$,
    1. $\mathsf{msk}_i = \mathsf{OneFSFE.Setup}(1^\lambda; r_{\mathsf{msk}_i})$
    2. Let $g_i = g_{f, \widetilde{\mathsf{st}}_i, c_i}$ as defined in Fig. 6.
    3. $\mathsf{sk}_{g_i} = \mathsf{OneFSFE.KeyGen}(\mathsf{msk}_i, g_i; r_{\mathsf{KeyGen}_i})$
    4. Output sk_{g_i}.
- Else
    1. $k'_i = \mathsf{Sym'.Setup}(1^\lambda; r'_{k_i})$
    2. Output $\mathsf{sk}_{g_i} = \mathsf{Sym'.Dec}(k'_i, c'_i)$.

Fig. 7. Def of h_{c_i, c'_i}.

- One-sFE.Dec(SK_f, Dec.$\mathsf{ST}_i, i, \mathsf{CT}_i$):
    1. If $i = 1$
        (a) Parse $\mathsf{SK}_1 = \mathsf{sk}_{g_1}$ and $\mathsf{CT}_1 = \mathsf{ct}_1$
        (b) $(y_1, \mathsf{ct}'_2) = \mathsf{OneFSFE.Dec}(\mathsf{sk}_{g_1}, \mathsf{ct}_1)$

(c) Output $(y_1, \mathsf{Dec.ST}_2 = \mathsf{ct}'_2)$

2. If $i > 1$

   (a) Parse $\mathsf{Dec.ST}_i = \mathsf{ct}'_i$ and $\mathsf{CT}_i = (\mathsf{ct}_i, \mathsf{sk}'_{h_i})$.
   (b) $\mathsf{sk}_{g_i} = \mathsf{OneCompFE.Dec}(\mathsf{sk}'_{h_i}, \mathsf{ct}'_i)$.
   (c) $(y_i, \mathsf{ct}'_{i+1}) = \mathsf{OneFSFE.Dec}(\mathsf{sk}_{g_i}, \mathsf{ct}_i)$
   (d) Output $(y_i, \mathsf{Dec.ST}_{i+1} = \mathsf{ct}'_{i+1})$

5.3 Correctness and Efficiency

Efficiency. Using our discussion above on parameters, it is easy to see that the size and runtime of all algorithms of One-sFE on security parameter λ, function size $\ell_{\mathcal{F}}$, state size $\ell_{\mathcal{S}}$, input size $\ell_{\mathcal{X}}$, and output size $\ell_{\mathcal{Y}}$ are $\mathsf{poly}(\lambda, \ell_{\mathcal{F}}, \ell_{\mathcal{S}}, \ell_{\mathcal{X}}, \ell_{\mathcal{Y}})$.

Correctness Intuition. Each sk_{g_i} and ct_i can be combined via OneFSFE decryption to obtain y_i and ct'_{i+1}. We obtain $\{\mathsf{ct}_i\}_{i \in [n]}$ from the ciphertext for x, and get the first function key sk_{g_1} as the function key for f. For $i > 1$, we can use OneCompFE decryption to iteratively combine the ct'_i generated by the previous step with the sk'_{h_i} given in the ciphertext to get the next sk_{g_i}. This lets us continue the process for all $i \in [n]$ and recover $y = y_1 \ldots y_n$.

Correctness. More formally, let p be any polynomial and consider any λ and any $\ell_{\mathcal{F}}, \ell_{\mathcal{S}}, \ell_{\mathcal{X}}, \ell_{\mathcal{Y}} \leq p(\lambda)$. Let SK_f be a function key for function $f \in \mathcal{F}[\ell_{\mathcal{F}}, \ell_{\mathcal{S}}, \ell_{\mathcal{X}}, \ell_{\mathcal{Y}}]$, and let $\{\mathsf{CT}_i\}_{i \in [n]}$ be a ciphertext for x where $x = x_1 \ldots x_n$ for some $n \in [2^\lambda]$ and where each $x_i \in \{0,1\}^{\ell_{\mathcal{X}}}$. When $i = 1$, by correctness of OneFSFE, except with negligible probability,

$$\mathsf{One\text{-}sFE.Dec}(\mathsf{SK}_f, \mathsf{Enc.ST}_1, \mathsf{CT}_1) = \mathsf{One\text{-}sFE.Dec}(\mathsf{sk}_{g_1}, \bot, \mathsf{ct}_1)$$
$$= \mathsf{OneFSFE.Dec}(\mathsf{sk}_{g_1}, \mathsf{ct}_1)$$
$$= g_{f, \mathsf{st}_1 \oplus p_1, c_1}(x_1, p_1, p_2, r'_{\mathsf{msk}_2}, r'_{\mathsf{Enc}_2}, r_{\mathsf{msk}_2}, r_{\mathsf{KeyGen}_2}, 0, 0^\lambda, 0^{\ell_{\mathcal{Y}}})$$
$$= (y_1, \mathsf{Dec.ST}_2 = \mathsf{ct}'_2)$$

where $(y_1, \mathsf{st}_2) = f(x_1, \mathsf{st}_1)$ and $\mathsf{ct}'_2 = \mathsf{OneCompFE.Enc}(\mathsf{msk}'_2, (f, \mathsf{st}_2 \oplus p_2, r_{\mathsf{msk}_2}, r_{\mathsf{KeyGen}_2}, 0, 0^\lambda); r'_{\mathsf{Enc}_2})$ When $i = 2$, by correctness of OneCompFE and OneFSFE, except with negligible probability,

$$\mathsf{One\text{-}sFE.Dec}(\mathsf{SK}_f, \mathsf{Dec.ST}_2, \mathsf{CT}_2) = \mathsf{One\text{-}sFE.Dec}(\mathsf{sk}_{g_1}, \mathsf{ct}'_2, (\mathsf{ct}_2, \mathsf{sk}'_{h_2}))$$
$$= \mathsf{OneFSFE.Dec}(\mathsf{OneCompFE.Dec}(\mathsf{sk}'_{h_2}, \mathsf{ct}'_2), \mathsf{ct}_2)$$
$$= \mathsf{OneFSFE.Dec}(h_{c_2, c'_2}(f, \mathsf{st}_2 \oplus p_2, r_{\mathsf{msk}_2}, r_{\mathsf{KeyGen}_2}, 0, 0^\lambda), \mathsf{ct}_2)$$
$$= \mathsf{OneFSFE.Dec}(\mathsf{OneFSFE.KeyGen}(\mathsf{msk}_2, g_{f, \mathsf{st}_2 \oplus p_2, c_2}; r_{\mathsf{KeyGen}_2}), \mathsf{ct}_2)$$
$$= \mathsf{OneFSFE.Dec}(\mathsf{sk}_{g_2}, \mathsf{ct}_2)$$
$$= g_{f, \mathsf{st}_2 \oplus p_2, c_2}(x_2, p_2, p_3, r'_{\mathsf{msk}_3}, r'_{\mathsf{Enc}_3}, r_{\mathsf{msk}_3}, r_{\mathsf{KeyGen}_3}, 0, 0^\lambda, 0^{\ell_{\mathcal{Y}}})$$
$$= (y_2, \mathsf{Dec.ST}_3 = \mathsf{ct}'_3)$$

where $(y_2, \mathsf{st}_3) = f(x_2, \mathsf{st}_2)$ and $\mathsf{ct}'_3 = \mathsf{OneCompFE.Enc}(\mathsf{msk}'_3, (f, \mathsf{st}_3 \oplus p_3, r_{\mathsf{msk}_3}, r_{\mathsf{KeyGen}_3}, 0, 0^\lambda); r'_{\mathsf{Enc}_3})$. Similarly, by induction, for $i > 2$, except with negligible probability,

$$\mathsf{One\text{-}sFE.Dec}(\mathsf{SK}_f, \mathsf{Dec.ST}_i, \mathsf{CT}_i) = (y_i, \mathsf{Dec.ST}_{i+1} = \mathsf{ct}'_{i+1})$$

where $(y_i, \mathsf{st}_{i+1}) = f(x_i, \mathsf{st}_i)$ and $\mathsf{ct}'_{i+1} = \mathsf{OneCompFE.Enc}(\mathsf{msk}'_{i+1}, (f, \mathsf{st}_{i+1} \oplus p_{i+1}, r_{\mathsf{msk}_{i+1}}, r_{\mathsf{KeyGen}_{i+1}}, 0, 0^\lambda); r'_{\mathsf{Enc}_{i+1}})$. Thus, we correctly output $y = y_1 \ldots y_n$ where $(y_i, \mathsf{st}_{i+1}) = f(x_i, \mathsf{st}_i)$ and $\mathsf{st}_1 = 0^{\ell_S}$.

5.4   Security

We use a hybrid argument to prove that our scheme is single-key, single-ciphertext, function-selective-SIM-secure (see Definition 4.8). Our PPT simulator is defined in the final hybrid ($\mathbf{Hybrid}_8^{\mathcal{A}}$) of the formal security proof. We need to prove that the real world security game $\mathbf{Hybrid}_1^{\mathcal{A}}$ is indistinguishable from the ideal world security game $\mathbf{Hybrid}_8^{\mathcal{A}}$.

Proof Overview. To build intuition, we provide a brief overview of each hybrid below.

- $\mathbf{Hybrid}_1^{\mathcal{A}}$: This is the real world experiment. The adversary first receives the security parameter and chooses the function size, state size, input size, and output size. Then, the adversary submits a function query and receives a function key. Next, the adversary submits a message query and receives the corresponding ciphertext. Finally, the adversary outputs a single bit which is the outcome of this experiment.
- $\mathbf{Hybrid}_2^{\mathcal{A}}$: We exchange the PRF randomness for true randomness. Instead of generating the randomness for $\mathsf{msk}_i, \mathsf{msk}'_i, k_i, k'_i, p_i$ using the master secret key, which consists of PRF keys $\mathsf{PRF}.K$ and $\mathsf{PRF2}.K$, we generate these values using true randomness. The indistinguishability of $\mathbf{Hybrid}_1^{\mathcal{A}}$ and $\mathbf{Hybrid}_2^{\mathcal{A}}$ holds by the security of PRF and PRF2.
- $\mathbf{Hybrid}_3^{\mathcal{A}}$: We adjust the way we sample p_i and $\widetilde{\mathsf{st}}_i$ so that each $\widetilde{\mathsf{st}}_i$ is now sampled uniformly at random. For each i, to hide the intermediate state st_i, our previous hybrid padded st_i with a one time pad p_i to get $\widetilde{\mathsf{st}}_i = \mathsf{st}_i \oplus p_i$. The value $\widetilde{\mathsf{st}}_i$ can then be leaked (and is in fact leaked) as long as p_i remains hidden. In this hybrid, rather than computing $\widetilde{\mathsf{st}}_i = \mathsf{st}_i \oplus p_i$ for a random pad p_i, we compute $p_i = \mathsf{st}_i \oplus \widetilde{\mathsf{st}}_i$ for a random value $\widetilde{\mathsf{st}}_i$. This lets us use $\widetilde{\mathsf{st}}_i$ before knowing the value of the true state st_i. It is easy to see that $\mathbf{Hybrid}_2^{\mathcal{A}}$ and $\mathbf{Hybrid}_3^{\mathcal{A}}$ are identically distributed.
- $\mathbf{Hybrid}_4^{\mathcal{A}}$: We hardcode in values for the $\alpha_i = 1$ branch of g_i. For each i, we hardcode into c_i the values $(y_i, \mathsf{ct}'_{i+1})$ that are output by $g_i = g_{f, \widetilde{\mathsf{st}}, c_i}$ on the $\alpha_i = 0$ branch if we run it on the input generated by the challenge message x. (i.e. $c_i \leftarrow \mathsf{Sym.Enc}(\mathsf{Sym}.k_i, (y_i, \mathsf{ct}'_{i+1})))$. The objective is to later use the security of OneFSFE to switch to the $\alpha_i = 1$ branch of g_i, which does not require knowledge of x in the input. We also need to ensure that this

hardcoding can be done before knowing the value of x (or $y = f(x)$) as we must output $\mathsf{SK}_f = \mathsf{sk}_{g_1}$ before learning x. Observe that the output value of g_i in the $\alpha_i = 0$ branch depends only on y_i, f, $\widetilde{\mathsf{st}}_{i+1}$, and randomness. f is known at this stage and the randomness can be pre-computed. Additionally, because of our previous hybrid, we can compute $\widetilde{\mathsf{st}}_{i+1}$ before knowing x. To deal with y_i, instead of encrypting y_i directly, we encrypt a random value θ_i. We can then correct this value later by substituting in an appropriate $\psi_i = \theta_i \oplus y_i$ into the ciphertext when we switch to the $\alpha_i = 1$ branch. The indistinguishability of $\mathbf{Hybrid}_3^{\mathcal{A}}$ and $\mathbf{Hybrid}_4^{\mathcal{A}}$ holds by the security of Sym.

– $\mathbf{Hybrid}_5^{\mathcal{A}}$: We hardcode in values for the $\alpha_i' = 1$ branch of h_i. For each i, we hardcode into c_i' the value sk_{g_i} that would be output by $h_i = h_{c_i,c_i'}$ in the $\alpha_i' = 0$ branch if we were to run it on the input generated by the challenge message x. (i.e. $c_i' \leftarrow \mathsf{Sym'}.\mathsf{Enc}(\mathsf{Sym'}.k_i, \mathsf{sk}_{g_i})$). The objective is to later use the security of OneCompFE to switch to the $\alpha_i' = 1$ branch of h_i, which does not require knowledge of x in the input. We also need to ensure that this hardcoding can be done without knowing the value of x so that we can later achieve simulation security. Observe that the output value of h_i in the $\alpha_i' = 0$ branch depends only on $g_i = g_{f,\widetilde{\mathsf{st}}_i,c_i}$ and randomness. As we showed in our previous hybrid, we can compute each g_i without knowing x and can precompute the randomness, so there is no dependence on x in this hardcoding of c_i'. The indistinguishability of $\mathbf{Hybrid}_4^{\mathcal{A}}$ and $\mathbf{Hybrid}_5^{\mathcal{A}}$ holds by the security of Sym'.

– We will now go through the following hybrids for $k = 1$ to q where $q = q(\lambda)$ is the runtime of $\mathcal{A}$ so that $q(\lambda) \geq n$ for any challenge message $x = x_1 \ldots x_n$ output by $\mathcal{A}$ on security parameter λ.

  • $\mathbf{Hybrid}_{6,k,1}^{\mathcal{A}}(1^\lambda)$: For the kth ciphertext ct_k, instead of generating

$$\mathsf{ct}_k \leftarrow \mathsf{OneFSFE}.\mathsf{Enc}(\mathsf{msk}_k, (x_k, p_k, p_{k+1}, r'_{\mathsf{msk}_{k+1}},$$
$$r'_{\mathsf{Enc}_{k+1}}, r_{\mathsf{msk}_{k+1}}, r_{\mathsf{KeyGen}_{k+1}}, 0, 0^\lambda, 0^{\ell_y})),$$

we generate

$$\mathsf{ct}_k \leftarrow \mathsf{OneFSFE}.\mathsf{Enc}(\mathsf{msk}_k, (0^{\ell_x}, 0^{\ell_s}, 0^{\ell_s}, 0^\lambda, 0^\lambda, 0^\lambda, 0^\lambda, 1, r_{k_k}, \psi_k))$$

where $\psi_k = \theta_k \oplus y_k$. Observe that the only function key generated under msk_k is

$$\mathsf{sk}_{g_k} \leftarrow \mathsf{OneFSFE}.\mathsf{KeyGen}(\mathsf{msk}_k, g_{f,\widetilde{\mathsf{st}}_k,c_k}; r_{\mathsf{KeyGen}_k})$$

Additionally, because we have hardcoded the correct output value into c_k in a previous hybrid,

$$g_{f,\widetilde{\mathsf{st}}_k,c_k}(x_k, p_k, p_{i+1}, r'_{\mathsf{msk}_{k+1}}, r'_{\mathsf{Enc}_{k+1}}, r_{\mathsf{msk}_{k+1}}, r_{\mathsf{KeyGen}_{k+1}}, 0, 0^\lambda, 0^{\ell_y})$$
$$= g_{f,\widetilde{\mathsf{st}}_k,c_k}(0^{\ell_x}, 0^{\ell_s}, 0^{\ell_s}, 0^\lambda, 0^\lambda, 0^\lambda, 0^\lambda, 1, r_{k_k}, \psi_k)$$

Thus we should be able to swap these ciphertexts by the security of OneFSFE as long as msk_k, r_{msk_k}, and r_{KeyGen_k} remain hidden. Now, except for their appearances in ct_k and sk_{g_k}, msk_k appears nowhere else in the hybrid and r_{msk_k} and r_{KeyGen_k} only appear in ct_{k-1} and in ct'_k (which is used to hardcode c'_{k-1}). (For $k = 1$, r_{msk_1} and r_{KeyGen_1} appear nowhere else as there is no ct_0, and ct'_1 is not used.) However, since we are going through these hybrids iteratively from $k = 1$ to q, then we will do $\mathbf{Hybrid}^{\mathcal{A}}_{6,k-1,1}$ before this hybrid which means that ct_{k-1} will no longer contain r_{msk_k} and r_{KeyGen_k}. Additionally, we will also do $\mathbf{Hybrid}^{\mathcal{A}}_{6,k-1,2}$ before this hybrid which will remove r_{msk_k} and r_{KeyGen_k} from ct'_k (as will be seen shortly). Thus, we have removed all other occurrences of msk_k, r_{msk_k}, r_{KeyGen_k} except for ct_k and sk_{g_k}, so we can argue indistinguishability by the security of OneFSFE.

- $\mathbf{Hybrid}^{\mathcal{A}}_{6,k,2}(1^{\lambda})$: For the $(k+1)^{th}$ ciphertext ct'_{k+1} (which is used to hardcode c'_k), instead of generating

$$\mathsf{ct}'_{k+1} \leftarrow \mathsf{OneCompFE.Enc}(\mathsf{msk}'_{k+1}, (f, \widetilde{\mathsf{st}}_{k+1}, r_{\mathsf{msk}_{k+1}}, r_{\mathsf{KeyGen}_{k+1}}, 0, 0^{\lambda}); r'_{\mathsf{Enc}_{k+1}}),$$

we will generate

$$\mathsf{ct}'_{k+1} \leftarrow \mathsf{OneCompFE.Enc}(\mathsf{msk}'_{k+1}, (0^{\ell_{\mathcal{F}}}, 0^{\ell_{\mathcal{S}}}, 0^{\lambda}, 0^{\lambda}, 1, r'_{k_k}); r'_{\mathsf{Enc}_{k+1}})$$

Observe that the only function key generated under msk'_{k+1} is

$$\mathsf{sk}'_{h_{k+1}} \leftarrow \mathsf{OneCompFE.KeyGen}(\mathsf{msk}'_{k+1}, h_{c_{k+1},c'_{k+1}})$$

Additionally, because we have hardcoded the correct output value into c'_{k+1} in a previous hybrid

$$h_{c_{k+1},c'_{k+1}}(f, \widetilde{\mathsf{st}}_{k+1}, r_{\mathsf{msk}_{k+1}}, r_{\mathsf{KeyGen}_{k+1}}, 0, 0^{\lambda})$$
$$= h_{c_{k+1},c'_{k+1}}(0^{\ell_{\mathcal{F}}}, 0^{\ell_{\mathcal{S}}}, 0^{\lambda}, 0^{\lambda}, 1, r'_{k_k})$$

Thus we should be able to swap these ciphertexts by the security of OneCompFE as long as msk'_{k+1}, $r'_{\mathsf{msk}_{k+1}}$, and $r'_{\mathsf{Enc}_{k+1}}$ remain hidden. Now, except for their appearances in ct'_{k+1} and $\mathsf{sk}'_{h_{k+1}}$, msk'_{k+1} appears nowhere else in the hybrid and $r'_{\mathsf{msk}_{k+1}}$ and $r'_{\mathsf{Enc}_{k+1}}$ only appear in ct_k. However, since we are going through these hybrids iteratively from $k = 1$ to q, then we will do $\mathbf{Hybrid}^{\mathcal{A}}_{6,k,1}$ before this hybrid which means that ct_k will no longer contain $r'_{\mathsf{msk}_{k+1}}$ and $r'_{\mathsf{Enc}_{k+1}}$. Thus, we have removed all other occurrences of msk'_{k+1}, $r'_{\mathsf{msk}_{k+1}}$, $r_{\mathsf{Enc}'_{k+1}}$ except for ct'_{k+1} and $\mathsf{sk}'_{h_{k+1}}$, so we can argue indistinguishability using the security of OneFSFE.

- $\mathbf{Hybrid}^{\mathcal{A}}_7$: This is the same as $\mathbf{Hybrid}^{\mathcal{A}}_{6,q,2}$ where $q = q(\lambda)$ is the runtime of $\mathcal{A}$. We write it explicitly to make the simulator in the next hybrid easier to understand.

- $\mathbf{Hybrid}^{\mathcal{A}}_8$: We formally write the previous hybrid as a simulator. This hybrid acts identically to the previous one. Observe that as $q(\lambda) \geq n$ for all $x = x_1 \ldots x_n$ output by $\mathcal{A}$ on security parameter λ, then we will use the $\alpha_i = \alpha'_i = 1$ branches of all g_i and h_i. Thus, to generate our ciphertexts ct_i and ct'_i, we only need to know $y = f(x)$ (as ψ_i depends on y_i) and don't need to know x. Furthermore to generate our function keys sk_{g_i} and sk_{h_i}, we only need the programmed values of c_i and c'_i, which also do not depend on x. Thus we can simulate this hybrid with y instead of x.

Formal Proof. We defer the full hybrid proof to the full version of the paper [30].

6   Bootstrapping to an IND-Secure, Public-Key Streaming FE Scheme

We defer this section to the full version [30].

Acknowledgments. This research was supported in part from a Simons Investigator Award, DARPA SIEVE award, NTT Research, NSF Frontier Award 1413955, BSF grant 2012378, a Xerox Faculty Research Award, a Google Faculty Research Award, and an Okawa Foundation Research Grant. This material is based upon work supported by the Defense Advanced Research Projects Agency through Award HR00112020024. The views expressed are those of the authors and do not reflect the official policy or position of any funding source or the U.S. Government.

References

1. Abdalla, M., Bourse, F., De Caro, A., Pointcheval, D.: Simple functional encryption schemes for inner products. In: Katz, J. (ed.) PKC 2015. LNCS, vol. 9020, pp. 733–751. Springer, Heidelberg (2015). https://doi.org/10.1007/978-3-662-46447-2_33

2. Agrawal, S.: Indistinguishability obfuscation without multilinear maps: new methods for bootstrapping and instantiation. In: Ishai, Y., Rijmen, V. (eds.) EUROCRYPT 2019. LNCS, vol. 11476, pp. 191–225. Springer, Cham (2019). https://doi.org/10.1007/978-3-030-17653-2_7

3. Agrawal, S., Libert, B., Stehlé, D.: Fully secure functional encryption for inner products, from standard assumptions. In: Robshaw, M., Katz, J. (eds.) CRYPTO 2016. LNCS, vol. 9816, pp. 333–362. Springer, Heidelberg (2016). https://doi.org/10.1007/978-3-662-53015-3_12

4. Ananth, P., Brakerski, Z., Segev, G., Vaikuntanathan, V.: From selective to adaptive security in functional encryption. In: Gennaro, R., Robshaw, M. (eds.) CRYPTO 2015. LNCS, vol. 9216, pp. 657–677. Springer, Heidelberg (2015). https://doi.org/10.1007/978-3-662-48000-7_32

5. Ananth, P., Jain, A., Lin, H., Matt, C., Sahai, A.: Indistinguishability obfuscation without multilinear maps: new paradigms via low degree weak pseudorandomness and security amplification. In: Boldyreva, A., Micciancio, D. (eds.) CRYPTO 2019. LNCS, vol. 11694, pp. 284–332. Springer, Cham (2019). https://doi.org/10.1007/978-3-030-26954-8_10

6. Ananth, P., Jain, A., Sahai, A.: Indistinguishability obfuscation without multilinear maps: IO from LWE, bilinear maps, and weak pseudorandomness. Cryptology ePrint Archive, Paper 2018/615 (2018). https://eprint.iacr.org/2018/615

7. Ananth, P., Jain, A.: Indistinguishability obfuscation from compact functional encryption. In: Gennaro, R., Robshaw, M. (eds.) CRYPTO 2015. LNCS, vol. 9215, pp. 308–326. Springer, Heidelberg (2015). https://doi.org/10.1007/978-3-662-47989-6_15

8. Ananth, P., Jain, A., Sahai, A.: Indistinguishability obfuscation from functional encryption for simple functions. Cryptology ePrint Archive, Paper 2015/730 (2015). https://eprint.iacr.org/2015/730

9. Ananth, P., Sahai, A.: Projective arithmetic functional encryption and indistinguishability obfuscation from degree-5 multilinear maps. In: Coron, J.-S., Nielsen, J.B. (eds.) EUROCRYPT 2017. LNCS, vol. 10210, pp. 152–181. Springer, Cham (2017). https://doi.org/10.1007/978-3-319-56620-7_6

10. Ananth, P., Sahai, A.: Functional encryption for turing machines. In: Kushilevitz, E., Malkin, T. (eds.) TCC 2016. LNCS, vol. 9562, pp. 125–153. Springer, Heidelberg (2016). https://doi.org/10.1007/978-3-662-49096-9_6

11. Badrinarayanan, S., Goyal, V., Jain, A., Sahai, A.: A note on VRFsfrom verifiable functional encryption. IACR Crypt. ePrint Arch. **2017**, 51 (2017)

12. Baltico, C.E.Z., Catalano, D., Fiore, D., Gay, R.: Practical functional encryption for quadratic functions with applications to predicate encryption. In: Katz, J., Shacham, H. (eds.) CRYPTO 2017. LNCS, vol. 10401, pp. 67–98. Springer, Cham (2017). https://doi.org/10.1007/978-3-319-63688-7_3

13. Bitansky, N.: Verifiable random functions from non-interactive witness-indistinguishable proofs. In: Kalai, Y., Reyzin, L. (eds.) TCC 2017. LNCS, vol. 10678, pp. 567–594. Springer, Cham (2017). https://doi.org/10.1007/978-3-319-70503-3_19

14. Bitansky, N., Vaikuntanathan, V.: Indistinguishability obfuscation from functional encryption. In: Guruswami, V. (ed.) 56th FOCS, pp. 171–190. IEEE Computer Society Press (2015). https://doi.org/10.1109/FOCS.2015.20

15. Boneh, D., et al.: Fully key-homomorphic encryption, arithmetic circuit ABE and compact garbled circuits. In: Nguyen, P.Q., Oswald, E. (eds.) EUROCRYPT 2014. LNCS, vol. 8441, pp. 533–556. Springer, Heidelberg (2014). https://doi.org/10.1007/978-3-642-55220-5_30

16. Boneh, D., Sahai, A., Waters, B.: Functional encryption: definitions and challenges. In: Ishai, Y. (ed.) TCC 2011. LNCS, vol. 6597, pp. 253–273. Springer, Heidelberg (2011). https://doi.org/10.1007/978-3-642-19571-6_16

17. Brakerski, Z., Segev, G.: Function-private functional encryption in the private-key setting. J. Cryptol. **31**(1), 202–225 (2017). https://doi.org/10.1007/s00145-017-9255-y

18. Garg, S., Gentry, C., Halevi, S., Raykova, M., Sahai, A., Waters, B.: Candidate indistinguishability obfuscation and functional encryption for all circuits. In: 54th FOCS, pp. 40–49. IEEE Computer Society Press (2013). https://doi.org/10.1109/FOCS.2013.13

19. Garg, S., Gentry, C., Halevi, S., Zhandry, M.: Functional encryption without obfuscation. In: Kushilevitz, E., Malkin, T. (eds.) TCC 2016. LNCS, vol. 9563, pp. 480–511. Springer, Heidelberg (2016). https://doi.org/10.1007/978-3-662-49099-0_18

20. Garg, S., Pandey, O., Srinivasan, A.: Revisiting the cryptographic hardness of finding a nash equilibrium. In: Robshaw, M., Katz, J. (eds.) CRYPTO 2016. LNCS, vol. 9815, pp. 579–604. Springer, Heidelberg (2016). https://doi.org/10.1007/978-3-662-53008-5_20

21. Garg, S., Pandey, O., Srinivasan, A., Zhandry, M.: Breaking the sub-exponential barrier in Obfustopia. In: Coron, J.-S., Nielsen, J.B. (eds.) EUROCRYPT 2017. LNCS, vol. 10212, pp. 156–181. Springer, Cham (2017). https://doi.org/10.1007/978-3-319-56617-7_6

22. Garg, S., Srinivasan, A.: Single-key to multi-key functional encryption with polynomial loss. In: Hirt, M., Smith, A. (eds.) TCC 2016. LNCS, vol. 9986, pp. 419–442. Springer, Heidelberg (2016). https://doi.org/10.1007/978-3-662-53644-5_16

23. Goldreich, O.: Foundations of Cryptography, Volume 1, Basic Tools, vol. 1. Cambridge University Press (2001)

24. Goldreich, O.: Foundations of Cryptography, Volume 2, Basic Applications, vol. 2. Cambridge University Press (2009)

25. Goldwasser, S., et al.: Multi-input functional encryption. In: Nguyen, P.Q., Oswald, E. (eds.) EUROCRYPT 2014. LNCS, vol. 8441, pp. 578–602. Springer, Heidelberg (2014). https://doi.org/10.1007/978-3-642-55220-5_32

26. Goldwasser, S., Kalai, Y.T., Popa, R.A., Vaikuntanathan, V., Zeldovich, N.: Reusable garbled circuits and succinct functional encryption. In: Boneh, D., Roughgarden, T., Feigenbaum, J. (eds.) 45th ACM STOC, pp. 555–564. ACM Press (2013). https://doi.org/10.1145/2488608.2488678

27. Gorbunov, S., Vaikuntanathan, V., Wee, H.: Functional encryption with bounded collusions via multi-party computation. In: Safavi-Naini, R., Canetti, R. (eds.) CRYPTO 2012. LNCS, vol. 7417, pp. 162–179. Springer, Heidelberg (2012). https://doi.org/10.1007/978-3-642-32009-5_11

28. Gorbunov, S., Vaikuntanathan, V., Wee, H.: Predicate encryption for circuits from LWE. In: Gennaro, R., Robshaw, M. (eds.) CRYPTO 2015. LNCS, vol. 9216, pp. 503–523. Springer, Heidelberg (2015). https://doi.org/10.1007/978-3-662-48000-7_25

29. Goyal, R., Hohenberger, S., Koppula, V., Waters, B.: A generic approach to constructing and proving verifiable random functions. In: Kalai, Y., Reyzin, L. (eds.) TCC 2017. LNCS, vol. 10678, pp. 537–566. Springer, Cham (2017). https://doi.org/10.1007/978-3-319-70503-3_18

30. Guan, J., Korb, A., Sahai, A.: Streaming functional encryption. Cryptology ePrint Archive, Report 2022/1599 (2022). https://eprint.iacr.org/2022/1599

31. Hemenway, B., Jafargholi, Z., Ostrovsky, R., Scafuro, A., Wichs, D.: Adaptively secure garbled circuits from one-way functions. In: Robshaw, M., Katz, J. (eds.) CRYPTO 2016. LNCS, vol. 9816, pp. 149–178. Springer, Heidelberg (2016). https://doi.org/10.1007/978-3-662-53015-3_6

32. Jain, A., Lin, H., Matt, C., Sahai, A.: How to leverage hardness of constant-degree expanding polynomials over $\mathbb{R}$ to build $i\mathcal{O}$. In: Ishai, Y., Rijmen, V. (eds.) EUROCRYPT 2019. LNCS, vol. 11476, pp. 251–281. Springer, Cham (2019). https://doi.org/10.1007/978-3-030-17653-2_9

33. Jain, A., Lin, H., Sahai, A.: Indistinguishability obfuscation from LPN over $\mathbb{F}_p$, DLIN, and PRGs in NC^0. In: Dunkelman, O., Dziembowski, S. (eds.) Advances in Cryptology–EUROCRYPT 2022. EUROCRYPT 2022. Lecture Notes in Computer Science, vol. 13275, pp. 670–699. Springer, Cham (2022). https://doi.org/10.1007/978-3-031-06944-4_23

34. Jain, A., Lin, H., Sahai, A.: Indistinguishability obfuscation from well-founded assumptions. In: Khuller, S., Williams, V.V. (eds.) STOC 2021: 53rd Annual ACM SIGACT Symposium on Theory of Computing, Virtual Event, Italy, 21–25 June 2021, pp. 60–73. ACM (2021)

35. Li, B., Micciancio, D.: Compactness vs collusion resistance in functional encryption. In: Hirt, M., Smith, A. (eds.) TCC 2016. LNCS, vol. 9986, pp. 443–468. Springer, Heidelberg (2016). https://doi.org/10.1007/978-3-662-53644-5_17

36. Lin, H.: Indistinguishability obfuscation from constant-degree graded encoding schemes. In: Fischlin, M., Coron, J.-S. (eds.) EUROCRYPT 2016. LNCS, vol. 9665, pp. 28–57. Springer, Heidelberg (2016). https://doi.org/10.1007/978-3-662-49890-3_2

37. Lin, H.: Indistinguishability obfuscation from SXDH on 5-linear maps and locality-5 PRGs. In: Katz, J., Shacham, H. (eds.) CRYPTO 2017. LNCS, vol. 10401, pp. 599–629. Springer, Cham (2017). https://doi.org/10.1007/978-3-319-63688-7_20

38. Lin, H., Tessaro, S.: Indistinguishability obfuscation from trilinear maps and block-wise local PRGs. In: Katz, J., Shacham, H. (eds.) CRYPTO 2017. LNCS, vol. 10401, pp. 630–660. Springer, Cham (2017). https://doi.org/10.1007/978-3-319-63688-7_21

39. Lin, H., Vaikuntanathan, V.: Indistinguishability obfuscation from DDH-like assumptions on constant-degree graded encodings. In: Dinur, I. (ed.) 57th FOCS, pp. 11–20. IEEE Computer Society Press (2016). https://doi.org/10.1109/FOCS.2016.11

40. O'Neill, A.: Definitional issues in functional encryption. IACR Cryptol. ePrint Arch. **2010**, 556 (2010). http://eprint.iacr.org/2010/556

41. Sahai, A., Waters, B.: How to use indistinguishability obfuscation: deniable encryption, and more. In: Shmoys, D.B. (ed.) 46th ACM STOC, pp. 475–484. ACM Press (2014). https://doi.org/10.1145/2591796.2591825

42. Sahai, A., Waters, B.: Fuzzy identity-based encryption. In: Cramer, R. (ed.) EURO-CRYPT 2005. LNCS, vol. 3494, pp. 457–473. Springer, Heidelberg (2005). https://doi.org/10.1007/11426639_27

Attribute-Based Multi-input FE (and More) for Attribute-Weighted Sums

Shweta Agrawal[1]($\boxtimes$), Junichi Tomida[2], and Anshu Yadav[1]

[1] IIT Madras, Chennai, India
shweta@cse.iitm.ac.in
[2] NTT Social Informatics Laboratories, Tokyo, Japan

Abstract. Recently, Abdalla, Gong and Wee (Crypto 2020) provided the first functional encryption scheme for attribute-weighted sums (AWS), where encryption takes as input N (unbounded) attribute-value pairs $\{\mathbf{x}_i, \mathbf{z}_i\}_{i \in [N]}$ where $\mathbf{x}_i$ is public and $\mathbf{z}_i$ is private, the secret key is associated with an arithmetic branching programs f, and decryption returns the weighted sum $\sum_{i \in [N]} f(\mathbf{x}_i)^\top \mathbf{z}_i$, leaking no additional information about the $\mathbf{z}_i$'s.

We extend FE for AWS to the significantly more challenging multi-party setting and provide the first construction for *attribute-based* multi-input FE (MIFE) supporting AWS. For $i \in [n]$, encryptor i can choose an attribute $\mathbf{y}_i$ together with AWS input $\{\mathbf{x}_{i,j}, \mathbf{z}_{i,j}\}$ where $j \in [N_i]$ and N_i is unbounded, the key generator can choose an access control policy g_i along with its AWS function h_i for each $i \in [n]$, and the decryptor can compute

$$\sum_{i \in [n]} \sum_{j \in [N_i]} h_i(\mathbf{x}_{i,j})^\top \mathbf{z}_{i,j} \text{ iff } g_i(\mathbf{y}_i) = 0 \text{ for all } i \in [n]$$

Previously, the only known attribute based MIFE was for the inner product functionality (Abdalla *et al.* Asiacrypt 2020), where additionally, $\mathbf{y}_i$ had to be fixed during setup and must remain the same for all ciphertexts in a given slot.

Our attribute based MIFE implies the notion of multi-input *attribute based encryption* (MIABE) recently studied by Agrawal, Yadav and Yamada (Crypto 2022) and Francati, Friolo, Malavolta and Venturi (Eurocrypt 2023), for a conjunction of predicates represented as arithmetic branching programs (ABP).

Along the way, we also provide the first constructions of multi-client FE (MCFE)[3] and dynamic decentralized FE (DDFE) for the AWS functionality. Previously, the best known MCFE and DDFE schemes were for inner products (Chotard *et al.* ePrint 2018, Abdalla, Benhamouda and Gay, Asiacrypt 2019, and Chotard *et al.* Crypto 2020).

Our constructions are based on pairings and proven selectively secure under the matrix DDH assumption.([3] The literature considers two notions termed as MCFE, one strictly stronger than the other. The stronger notion implies MIFE while the weaker does not. Here, we refer to the stronger notion, making MCFE a strict generalization of MIFE.)

© International Association for Cryptologic Research 2023
H. Handschuh and A. Lysyanskaya (Eds.): CRYPTO 2023, LNCS 14084, pp. 464–497, 2023.
https://doi.org/10.1007/978-3-031-38551-3_15

1   Introduction

Multi-Party Functional Encryption. Functional encryption (FE) [15,35] is a generalization of public key encryption which enables learning specific useful functions of encrypted data via "functional" keys. In FE, a secret key SK_f is associated with a function f, a ciphertext $\mathsf{CT}_\mathbf{x}$ is associated with a message $\mathbf{x}$ and decryption allows to compute $f(\mathbf{x})$ and nothing else. FE has been researched intensely in the community, with a long sequence of works that achieve increasingly powerful functionalities from diverse assumptions – please see [2,4,6,7,9,13,14,25–28,30,32,35,37,38] and references therein.

While initially defined and constructed in the single input setting, i.e. with only one encryptor and one key generator, FE soon began to be generalized to distributed settings to capture the decentralized nature of both data and authority in the modern world. Computation on encrypted data generated independently at multiple sources, with fine-grained control on which data may be combined and with secret keys supporting decryption of meaningful aggregate functionalities, holds the promise of making FE much more relevant for real-world applications. These generalizations took different forms, from multi-input FE [24] to multi-authority FE [16] to multi-client FE [17] to dynamic decentralized FE [19] and such others [8]. These generalizations were captured via the abstraction of multi-party FE [10], which sought to unify these different notions in a single framework.

The Attribute-Weighted Sums Functionality. Recently, Abdalla, Gong, and Wee [6] introduced the functionality of *Attribute-Weighted Sums* (AWS) which supports computation of aggregate statistics on encrypted databases. Concretely, consider a database with N attribute-value pairs $(\mathbf{x}_i, \mathbf{z}_i)_{i \in [N]}$ where $\mathbf{x}_i$ is a public attribute associated with user i, and $\mathbf{z}_i$ is private. Given a function f, the AWS functionality on input $(\mathbf{x}_i, \mathbf{z}_i)_{i \in [N]}$ is defined as

$$\sum_{i \in [N]} f(\mathbf{x}_i)^\top \mathbf{z}_i.$$

The AWS functionality is very natural, and Abdalla, Gong, and Wee suggested several compelling applications for it – for example, when f is a Boolean predicate then AWS can capture (i) the average salaries of minority groups holding a particular job title – here, $\mathbf{z}_i$ represents salary, while $f(\mathbf{x}_i)$ tests for membership in the minority group, (ii) approval ratings of an election candidate amongst specific demographic groups in a particular state – here, $\mathbf{z}_i$ is the rating, while $f(\mathbf{x}_i)$ computes membership in said group. Similarly, when $\mathbf{z}_i$ is Boolean, AWS can capture average age of smokers with lung cancer, where $\mathbf{z}_i$ is lung cancer and f computes average age.

Distributing the Data. In this work, we argue that for several applications of AWS, including the motivating examples provided by [6], the data $(\mathbf{x}_i, \mathbf{z}_i)_{i \in [N]}$ is likely to be distributed across multiple sources which must compute ciphertexts independently. Concretely, in the example of computing average salaries of minority groups holding a particular job title, the data about the individuals would be generated across organizations, which are unlikely to even be in the same location. Similarly, when we compute whether a user is in a specific demographic group in a particular state, it is natural that user data would be distributed across different states, indeed even across different cities in a given state. In the third example, data about patients with lung cancer will naturally be generated and maintained at different hospitals that offer treatment for lung cancer, which would again be distributed geographically.

Thus, to capture data generation by independent sources, we extend FE for AWS to the multi-party setting. Concretely, we focus on the following primitives:

1. *Multi-Input FE (MIFE):* The primitive of multi-input FE (MIFE) [24] allows the input to a function to be distributed among multiple (say n) parties. In more detail, the ith party encrypts its input $\mathbf{z}_i$ to obtain CT_i, a key authority holding a master secret generates a functional key SK_f and these enable the decryptor to compute $f(\mathbf{z}_1, \ldots, \mathbf{z}_n)$ and nothing else.

   We consider a further generalization of MIFE, namely *attribute-based* MIFE introduced by Abdalla *et al.*[4], which enables greater control on the leakage inherent by the functionality of MIFE, making it more suitable for practical applications. In an AB-MIFE for some functionality f, an attribute $\mathbf{y}_i$ is associated with a ciphertext for slot i, in addition to an input $\mathbf{z}_i$. The secret key is associated with an access control policy g in addition to the function input $\mathbf{c}$. Decryption first checks if $g(\mathbf{y}_1, \ldots, \mathbf{y}_n) = 1$, and if so, it computes the MIFE functionality $f(\{\mathbf{z}_i\}, \mathbf{c})$.

2. *Multi-Client FE (MCFE):* MCFE [17,18,24] is a generalization of MIFE. In MCFE, the inputs $\mathbf{z}_i$ are additionally associated with public "labels" L_i and inputs can only be combined with other inputs that share the same label. As in MIFE, a functional key SK_f is provided which allows the decryptor to compute $f(\mathbf{z}_1, \ldots, \mathbf{z}_n)$ as long as the corresponding labels match, i.e. $L_1 = \ldots = L_n$.

3. *Dynamic Decentralized FE (DDFE):* DDFE [19], as the name suggests, is a decentralized variant of FE, where not only can ciphertexts be generated locally and independently but so can the keys. In DDFE for some functionality f, the setup step is localized and run independently by users, letting them generate their private and public keys individually. During encryption, the set of users with whom a given input or key object should be combined can be chosen dynamically. In more detail, each party can specify the set of parties with which its input may be combined, a label that controls which values should be considered together and the input $\mathbf{z}_i$ itself. Similarly, every user can also generate a key object which specifies the set of parties with which the key may be combined, and a key vector $\mathbf{c}_i$. For decryption, the ciphertexts and keys from the parties who mutually agree to combine their inputs and keys are put together to compute $f(\{\mathbf{z}_i\}_i, \{\mathbf{c}_j\}_j)$.

Note that DDFE implies MCFE which implies MIFE[1].

Prior Work. We summarize the state of the art below.

The AWS Functionality. For the AWS functionality, even the weakest multi-input notion, namely MIFE is not known to the best of our knowledge. We note Abdalla et al.[6] did propose a multi-party extension to their FE for AWS. However, this scheme is a much weaker primitive than the standard notion of MCFE (or even MIFE), since this scheme natively only supports a single ciphertext query per slot. To extend it the setting of multiple queries, the authors make use of non-interactive MPC to enable the parties to obtain a random secret sharing of 0.

In more detail, while their scheme supports labels, the difference from standard MCFE schemes is that in their scheme each party uses a one-time secret key for each encryption instead of long-term encryption key, and the one-time keys are generated via non-interactive MPC run between the parties. Specifically, their scheme consists of five algorithms (Setup, OTSKGen, Enc, KeyGen, Dec), and Setup, KeyGen, Dec are the same as those in standard MCFE. $\mathsf{OTSKGen}(1^\lambda)$ is a non-interactive protocol where party i obtains one-time secret key otsk_i as the output of the protocol. $\mathsf{Enc}(\mathsf{otsk}_i, \mathbf{x}_i)$ takes otsk_i and a message $\mathbf{x}_i$ and outputs a ciphertext CT_i for party i. Correctness holds, i.e., decrypting a set $\{\mathsf{CT}_i\}_{i \in [n]}$ of ciphertexts with a secret key for f reveals $f(\mathbf{x}_1, \ldots, \mathbf{x}_n)$, only when the set of ciphertexts are generated under the one-time secret keys $\{\mathsf{otsk}_i\}_{i \in [n]}$ derived from a single running of $\mathsf{OTSKGen}(1^\lambda)$. The one-time secret-key can be used only once for encryption, otherwise security does not hold any more. Thus, this notion is even weaker than the variant of MCFE with one-time labeling restriction [17] and in particular, does not imply MIFE.

Multi-Input Attribute Based Encryption. An attribute based MIFE scheme implies a multi-input attribute based encryption scheme as a special case. In an MIABE scheme, encryptor i encodes a secret message m_i together with an attribute $\mathbf{y}_i$. The function key encodes a circuit g so that decryption outputs $(m_1, \ldots, m_n)$ if $g(\mathbf{y}_1, \ldots, \mathbf{y}_n) = 1$. The generalization to multi-input predicate encryption additionally allows to hide the attributes $\mathbf{y}_i$.

In this setting, Agrawal, Yadav and Yamada [12] recently provided a construction for arbitrary predicates in NC_1 from pairings and Learning With Errors. Additionally, Francati et al.[23] also provided a multi-input predicate encryption scheme for a conjunction of predicates. Their construction supports the class P and is based on the Learning With Errors problem. Moreover, if the arity of the function is restricted to a constant, their security game also supports user corruptions. However, their construction does not support collusions, which is one of the most important and technically challenging aspects of designing attribute based encryption schemes.

---

[1] In this paper, we use the term MCFE as a generalization of MIFE, so that it allows multiple use of labels [18]. In contrast, a weaker notion of MCFE where each label can be used only once does not imply MIFE [17,24].

AB-MIFE, MCFE and DDFE. For AB-MIFE, the best known attribute-based MIFE scheme is for the inner product functionality [4]. Moreover, in the AB-MIFE construction by Abdalla *et al.*[4], the ABE attribute $\mathbf{y}_i{}^2$ associated with the ith slot is fixed in the setup phase and must remain the same for all ciphertexts, instead of being chosen dynamically by the encryptor for each encryption. For MCFE [1] as well as DDFE [19], the largest achievable function class is linear functions (or inner products), albeit with function hiding [10].

1.1 Our Results

In this work, we significantly extend the reach of multi-input functional encryption schemes by providing the first AB-MIFE, MCFE and DDFE schemes that support the AWS functionality. Our constructions satisfy the standard (selective) indistinguishability based security and rely on the matrix DDH assumption on bilinear groups. We discuss each of these contributions below.

AB-MIFE for AWS: We provide the first attribute-based MIFE for the AWS functionality. In our AB-MIFE, each encryptor can choose an attribute $\mathbf{y}_i$ specific to its AWS input $\{\mathbf{x}_{i,j}, \mathbf{z}_{i,j}\}_{j\in[N_i]}$, the key generator can choose an access control policy g_i along with its AWS function h_i for $i \in [n]$ and decryption computes:

$$f((\mathbf{y}_1, \{\mathbf{x}_{1,j}, \mathbf{z}_{1,j}\}_{j\in[N_1]}), \ldots, (\mathbf{y}_n, \{\mathbf{x}_{n,j}, \mathbf{z}_{n,j}\}_{j\in[N_n]}))$$

$$= \begin{cases} \sum_{i\in[n]} \sum_{j\in[N_i]} \langle h_i(\mathbf{x}_{i,j}), \mathbf{z}_{i,j} \rangle & (g_1(\mathbf{y}_1) = \cdots = g_n(\mathbf{y}_n) = 0) \\ \bot & (\text{otherwise}) \end{cases}$$

Here, $\mathbf{y}_i, \mathbf{x}_{i,j}$ are public while $\mathbf{z}_{i,j}$ is private, and g_i, h_i belong to arithmetic branching programs (ABP). We note that the number of slots N_i for $i \in [n]$ can be unbounded, and chosen by the encryptor dynamically.

Connection with Multi-input Attribute-Based Encryption. We observe that this functionality also implies the notion of multi-input attribute-based encryption (MIABE) [12] for a conjunction of predicates represented as ABP. Thus, our construction supports the functionality $g(\mathbf{y}_1, \ldots, \mathbf{y}_n) = \bigwedge(g_i(\mathbf{y}_i) = 0)$, where each g_i is an ABP.

In contrast, the MIABE construction of [12] supports an arbitrary $g \in \mathsf{NC}_1$ but only outputs a fixed message whereas our construction supports the AWS functionality. Additionally, our construction also supports a stronger security model which allows user corruption. In more detail, the MIABE construction of [12] requires all encryptors to share the same master secret key, which obviously cannot be provided to the adversary. In contrast, different encryptors in our construction have different encryption keys, and we allow the adversary to obtain some of these in the security game. By applying the MIABE to MIPE compiler of [12], we obtain a multi-input predicate encryption scheme for constant arity, albeit *without* support for user corruptions, due to the design of the compiler.

---

[2] In their notation, the embedding of access control policy and attribute are swapped to the ciphertext-policy setting – thus, for them $\mathbf{y}_i$ is an access control policy.

Table 1. Comparison with Prior Work in MIABE and MIPE. Note that Koala is a non-standard knowledge type assumption on pairings. For [12,23], the results for MIABE and MIPE are identical, but we achieve different results for the two. We consider CPA-1 sided security for the comparison with [23].

Work	Arity	Corruption	Collusion	Function Class	Assumption
[23]	Poly	No	No	Conjunctions in P	LWE
[23]	Constant	Yes	No	Conjunctions in P	LWE
[12]	2	No	Yes	NC_1	Koala and LWE
This (MIABE)	Poly	Yes	Yes	Conjunctions in NC_1	Matrix DDH
This (MIPE)	Constant	No	Yes	Conjunctions in NC_1	Matrix DDH and LWE

We also compare with the recent work of Francati et al.[23]. As discussed above, their MIABE construction supports no collusions and user corruptions only for constant (not polynomial) arity. In contrast, our construction of AB-MIFE supports unbounded collusions, as well as user corruptions for *polynomial* arity. However, our construction, being based on pairings, only supports the function class NC_1 while they support P. Additionally our construction supports computation of the expressive AWS functionality while theirs just recovers a fixed message (i.e. our scheme is an FE not an ABE). In the setting of MIPE, our construction does not support corruption but does support collusions, while theirs achieves the opposite. Please see Table 1 for a detailed comparison.

Multi-client FE for AWS. We construct the first MCFE for Attribute-Weighted Sums, which generalizes MIFE described above. In more detail, each encryptor can choose input $\{\mathbf{x}_{i,j}, \mathbf{z}_{i,j}\}_{j \in [N_i]}$ together with a label L_i, the key generator can choose ABPs $\{f_i\}_{i \in [n]}$ and decryption computes:

$$f(\{\mathbf{x}_{1,j}, \mathbf{z}_{1,j}\}_{j \in [N_1]}, \ldots, \{\mathbf{x}_{n,j}, \mathbf{z}_{n,j}\}_{j \in [N_n]}) = \sum_{i \in [n]} \sum_{j \in [N_i]} \langle f_i(\mathbf{x}_{i,j}), \mathbf{z}_{i,j} \rangle$$

as long as all the L_i are equal. This is the first MCFE that supports a functionality beyond inner products to the best of our knowledge. Moreover, the number of slots N_i allowed to each party i are unbounded, though the number of parties n is bounded – this feature was not achieved by prior MCFE schemes for inner products as far as we are aware.

This functionality is captured by separable functions defined by Ciampi et al. [20]. A multi-input function f is separable if it can be described as $f(x_1, \ldots, x_n) = f_1(x_1) + \cdots + f_n(x_n)$ for some functions $f_1, \ldots, f_n$. They constructed MCFE for separable functions where $f_1, \ldots, f_n$ belong to poly-size circuits from function-hiding FE for *general circuits*. Their scheme is secure against a priori bounded number of ciphertext queries. Our results differ significantly from theirs because our schemes are secure against unbounded number of ciphertext queries and use only the much weaker MDDH assumption.

Table 2. Prior state of the art and our results. We do not consider function hiding or MCFE schemes with only one time labels. Above, we denote $\mathbf{y} = (\mathbf{y}_1, \ldots, \mathbf{y}_n)$, $\mathbf{z} = (\mathbf{z}_1, \ldots, \mathbf{z}_n)$ or $\mathbf{z} = (\mathbf{z}_i)_{i \in S}$. S is some subset of authorized users for a given key. A function f_i is a monotone span programs fixed in setup. Functions f_i, g_i, h_i are arithmetic branching programs chosen in key generation.

Work	(Pub, Pri) CT	Key	Functionality
MIFE [11]	$(\perp, \mathbf{z}_i)$	$\mathbf{c}$	$\langle \mathbf{c}, \mathbf{z} \otimes \mathbf{z} \rangle$
AB-MIFE [4]	$(\perp, \mathbf{z}_i)$	$\{y_i, \mathbf{c}_i\}_{i \in S}$	$\bigwedge_{i \in S} f_i(y_i) \cdot \sum_{i \in S} \langle \mathbf{z}_i, \mathbf{c}_i \rangle$
AB-MIFE, §4	$((\mathbf{y}_i, \{\mathbf{x}_{i,j}\}_j), \{\mathbf{z}_{i,j}\}_j)$	$\{g_i, h_i\}_{i \in [n]}$	$\bigwedge_i (g_i(\mathbf{y}_i) = 0) \cdot \sum_{i \in [n]} \sum_{j \in [N_i]} h_i(\mathbf{x}_{i,j})^\top \mathbf{z}_{i,j}$
MCFE [1,18]	$(\perp, \mathbf{z}_i)$	$\mathbf{c}$	$\langle \mathbf{c}, \mathbf{z} \rangle$
MCFE, §5	$(\{\mathbf{x}_{i,j}\}_j, \{\mathbf{z}_{i,j}\}_j)$	$\{f_i\}_{i \in [n]}$	$\sum_{i \in [n]} \sum_{j \in [N_i]} f_i(\mathbf{x}_{i,j})^\top \mathbf{z}_{i,j}$
DDFE, [10,19]	$(\perp, \mathbf{z}_i)$	$\mathbf{c}$	$\langle \mathbf{c}, \mathbf{z} \rangle$
DDFE, in full ver	$(\{\mathbf{x}_{i,j}\}_j, \{\mathbf{z}_{i,j}\}_j)$	$\{f_i\}_{i \in S}$	$\sum_{i \in S} \sum_{j \in [N_i]} f_i(\mathbf{x}_{i,j})^\top \mathbf{z}_{i,j}$

Dynamic Decentralized FE for AWS. Next, we extend our MCFE to the much more challenging setting of DDFE. For the setting of AWS, the ith encryptor chooses a set of users $\mathcal{U}_{M,i}$ with whom its input may be combined, some label L_i to constrain which values should be considered together, aside from its AWS inputs $\{\mathbf{z}_{i,j}\}_{j \in [N_i]}$ which are private and $\{\mathbf{x}_{i,j}\}_{j \in [N_i]}$ which are public. For key generation, the ith user also chooses a set of users $\mathcal{U}_{K,i}$ and a set of ABPs $\bar{f}_i = \{f_j\}_{j \in \mathcal{U}_{K,i}}$. If all the sets $\mathcal{U}_{M,i}$ and $\mathcal{U}_{K,i}$ match up (to some $\mathcal{U}'_K$) and if the labels in all n ciphertext slots are equal, then decryption computes the AWS functionality. Formally, for $k_i = (\bar{f}_i, \mathcal{U}_{K,i})$ and $m_i = (\{\mathbf{x}_{i,j}, \mathbf{z}_{i,j}\}_{j \in [N_i]}, \mathcal{U}_{M,i}, L_i)$, the functionality computes:

$$f'(\{i, k_i\}_{i \in \mathcal{U}'_K}, \{i, m_i\}_{i \in \mathcal{U}'_M}) =$$
$$\begin{cases} \sum_{i \in \mathcal{U}'_K} \sum_{j \in [N_i]} \langle f_i(\mathbf{x}_{i,j}), \mathbf{z}_{i,j} \rangle & \text{if the conditions below are satisfied} \\ \perp & \text{otherwise} \end{cases}$$

The conditions are:

1. $\mathcal{U}'_K = \mathcal{U}'_M$ and $\forall\, i \in \mathcal{U}'_K,\ \mathcal{U}_{K,i} = \mathcal{U}_{M,i} = \mathcal{U}'_K$.
2. $\forall_{i,i' \in \mathcal{U}'_K},\ \bar{f}_i = \bar{f}_{i'}$ and $L_i = L_{i'}$.

We summarize prior work in Table 2.

1.2 New Applications

Our attribute-based MIFE enables several new and exciting applications that were not possible before. Let us begin with the example for AWS suggested by [6], of computing average age of smokers who have lung cancer. In this case, the access control layer on top of the MIFE can capture the willingness of a user to even participate in such a study involving their medical data. For example, perhaps a user is willing to participate in this computation if certain criteria are satisfied, for instance if the study is being performed by doctors with certain specializations. Moreover, these criteria can be different for different users. This is exactly the kind of access control that an ABE system is designed to enforce. The required criteria can be specified by each user using its attribute $\mathbf{y}_i$ while the key holder's input g_i must encode her privileges so that she learns the AWS output only if $g_i(\mathbf{y}_i)$ is satisfied for all $i \in [n]$.

In the context of MIABE, Agrawal, Yadav and Yamada [12] provided the following motivating example: a doctor is treating Covid patients and desires to understand the relation between Covid and other medical conditions such as asthma or cancer, each of which are treated at different locations. The records of a given patient are encrypted independently and stored in a central repository, and the doctor can be given a key that filters stored (encrypted) records according to criteria such as condition = 'Covid' and condition = 'asthma' and age group = '60–80' and enables decryption of these. Note that our AB-MIFE can already support a conjunction of predicates and suffices to enable the functionality of the above example. Moreover, in addition to supporting decryption of messages as in MIABE, our AB-MIFE will even allow computing some aggregates on the private data, something beyond the capability of MIABE.

For MCFE and DDFE, generalizing inner products to AWS is clearly meaningful – all applications of AWS in the single input setting are meaningful in the setting with multiple users, with the additional expressiveness offered by MCFE and DDFE. For instance in DDFE, the number of users who can participate in a computation are unbounded and moreover, users can join dynamically – this is useful in real world applications such as the examples involving patients in the lung cancer study or users in the minority group discussed earlier.

1.3 Technical Overview

Recap of AGW. Our starting point is the functional encryption scheme by Abdalla, Gong, and Wee [6], henceforth AGW, which provides the first construction supporting the AWS functionality for ABP from standard assumptions on bilinear maps. In more detail, the encryptor[3] computes a ciphertext encoding $\{\mathbf{x}_j, \mathbf{z}_j\}_{j \in [N]}$ where N is unbounded, $\mathbf{x}_j$ are public and $\mathbf{z}_j$ are private, the key generator computes a secret key encoding an ABP f and decryption recovers $\sum_{j \in [N]} \langle f(\mathbf{x}_j), \mathbf{z}_j \rangle$. At a high level, their construction proceeds in two steps: (i) construct a single slot scheme, i.e. $N = 1$, which supports computation of $\langle f(\mathbf{x}), \mathbf{z} \rangle$, (ii) extend this to support unbounded N by running N instances of the single slot scheme, and cleverly handling leakage and size blowup that occurs along the way. As discussed by AGW, step (i) can be achieved by adapting a framework by Wee [39], and the main conceptual and technical novelty lies in achieving step (ii), especially in supporting unbounded N.

---

[3] Here we discuss the single input construction of AGW, the multi-input construction is discussed later.

We review step (ii) next, as the ideas herein form the basis of our multi-input constructions. As discussed above, the first idea to handle $N > 1$ is to simply run N instances of the single slot scheme but this evidently does not work, since it would allow the decryptor to learn partial sums $\langle f(\mathbf{x}_j), \mathbf{z}_j \rangle$ which are not revealed by the ideal functionality. To address this leakage, the single slot scheme is extended to handle "randomization offsets", namely to add masking values $w_j r$ to the partial sums, where w_j are sampled randomly by the encryptor such that $\sum w_j = 0$, and r is sampled randomly by the key generator. These masking values hide intermediate partial sums $\langle f(\mathbf{x}_j), \mathbf{z}_j \rangle$, but when the partial sums are added, we recover $\sum_{j \in [N]} \langle f(\mathbf{x}_j), \mathbf{z}_j \rangle$ as desired.

To make the secret key size independent of N, AGW construct a hybrid argument over the N slots, collecting "partial sums" along the way – the details of this technique are not relevant for our purposes. They achieve selective simulation based security from the standard k-linear assumption over bilinear groups.

They then extend this construction to a setting where the N slots can be owned by N independent parties – to enforce the constraint that $\sum_{j \in [N]} w_j = 0$, they make use of a non-interactive MPC protocol where the parties communicate to generate these shares prior to each encryption. While this construction provides a first feasibility result for FE supporting the AWS functionality in the multi-party setting, it falls short of achieving the standard notion of MCFE in many important ways:

1. The MPC step introduces an additional round of interaction prior to each encryption[4] – this violates the primary demand of non-interaction that is placed on FE.

2. The ciphertexts constructed in different "iterations", i.e. generated via different runs of the MPC cannot talk to each other, thus failing to satisfy the main functionality requirement of even an MIFE scheme, which explicitly requires supporting such combinations. In more detail, consider a two slot MIFE scheme, where the first slot ciphertexts encode $\mathbf{x}^j$ for $j \in [Q_1]$, the second slot ciphertexts encode $\mathbf{y}^i$ for $i \in [Q_2]$ and the secret key encodes some function f. Then MIFE explicitly requires that $f(\mathbf{x}^j, \mathbf{y}^i)$ should be computable for any pair j, i. Indeed, the standard notion of MCFE *generalizes* MIFE by additionally supporting labels in each ciphertext that dictate how ciphertexts may be combined. The multi-party scheme of AGW does not imply an MIFE.

3. The security game of the multi-client AGW construction does *not* handle the multi-challenge setting, which is the main technical challenge in any MIFE or MCFE construction. Indeed, handling the multi-challenge setting would *disallow* the usage of simulation security due to an impossibility result by Boneh, Sahai and Waters [15] – since the AGW constructions satisfy simulation security, any generalization to the multi-input setting must necessarily take a different route.

---

[4] This can done in a offline phase, but then places a bound on the number of ciphertexts which can be computed.

Thus, the question of even constructing an MIFE for AWS, let alone generalizations to AB-MIFE, MCFE and DDFE, is completely open.

Building MIFE for AWS. In an MIFE for AWS, we have n parties, where the ciphertext computed by the ith party embeds inputs $\{\mathbf{x}_{i,j}, \mathbf{z}_{i,j}\}_{j \in [N_i]}$ where N_i is unbounded, the secret key embeds a set of ABPs $\{f_i\}_{i \in [n]}$, and decryption computes

$$f(\{\mathbf{x}_{1,j}, \mathbf{z}_{1,j}\}_{j \in [N_1]}, \ldots, \{\mathbf{x}_{n,j}, \mathbf{z}_{n,j}\}_{j \in [N_n]}) = \sum_{i \in [n]} \sum_{j \in [N_i]} \langle f_i(\mathbf{x}_{i,j}), \mathbf{z}_{i,j} \rangle$$

Recall that $\mathbf{x}_i$ is public while $\mathbf{z}_i$ is private, i.e., a ciphertext only hides $\mathbf{z}_i$.

A natural idea would be to begin with the multi-party[5] construction of AGW and try to get rid of the MPC. In fact, removing the usage of MPC is not very difficult by using PRFs to compute a secret sharing of 0 for any given label[6], but this would still only lead to a weak variant of MCFE which has the so called "one time label" restriction. Intuitively, an MCFE with a one time label restriction, as the name suggests, allows each label to be used only one time for each input; this primitive therefore no longer implies MIFE. Handling combinations of multiple ciphertexts is the core functionality of MIFE and forms the basis for most applications, so the one time label restriction is quite a significant limitation. Indeed, in the inner product setting, early constructions of MCFE suffered from the one time label restriction [17] and were upgraded to full-fledged MCFE by follow-up work using nontrivial ideas [1,18].

Another point to note is the handling of unbounded slots for each client. Concretely, let us say there are n clients, and the ith one chooses N_i (unbounded) internal slots for their data. Now, the AGW multi-party construction can easily handle unbounded N by instantiating $\sum_{i \in [n]} N_i$ nominal clients and having each client internally handle N_i of these. This trick does not work out of the box anymore in the MIFE setting due to the requirement of supporting combinations of all ciphertexts across slots.

Our Approach. Taking a step back, a natural approach is to ask whether existing transformations of FE from the single to multi-input setting for the inner product functionality can help us overcome the challenges faced in designing this generalization for AWS. Towards this approach, we observe that all IP-MIFE (or IP-MCFE) schemes in the literature are constructed by (explicitly or implicitly) running an IPFE scheme in parallel for each input and handling leakage issues along the way. At a high level, these works can be classified into two categories

---

[5] Since the AGW construction does not satisfy the standard definition of MCFE in several important ways as discussed above, we refer to their construction as a multi-party construction, in the sense of [10].

[6] Consider the 3 party case. Let us say that parties have PRF keys (k_1, k_2), (k_2, k_3), and (k_3, k_1) respectively. Then we can use the fact for every label L, $F(k_1, L) + F(k_2, L), -F(k_2, L) + F(k_3, L), -F(k_3, L) - F(k_1, L)$ are pseudorandom shares of 0 [1,31].

based on which property of the underlying IPFE is required in the security proof: 1) ciphertext homomorphism, e.g., [1,3,5,18] or 2) function-hiding security, e.g., [10,21,36].

While IPFE schemes have ciphertext homomorphism (a ciphertext is a group element, and adding ciphertexts of $\mathbf{x}_1$ and $\mathbf{x}_2$ results in a ciphertext of $\mathbf{x}_1 + \mathbf{x}_2$), this is not the case in FE for AWS due to public inputs for ABPs. Since ABPs are not linear functions, it is hopeless to equip an FE scheme for AWS with ciphertext homomorphism. It is worth noting that the reason that the AB-MIFE scheme in [4] can handle only a limited form of access control, i.e., only secret keys are associated with attributes, and access control is done between the attributes and the public fixed policy, comes from the fact that their scheme relies on the former approach and cannot associate ciphertexts with attributes or a policy as the case of the single input AB-FE schemes.

Fortunately, the latter approach is not ruled out, and indeed, we show that it can be made to work even for the AWS functionality. We observe that works in the latter category use function-hiding security of the underlying scheme to obtain function-hiding in the resultant IP-MIFE scheme. In this work, however, we will use function-hiding for a completely different purpose – to transform a singe-input scheme into a multi-input scheme *without* relying on ciphertext homomorphism of the underlying scheme. In particular, we will not achieve function-hiding security in our final MIFE for AWS scheme.

Recap: Construction of IP-MIFE from IPFE. Our starting point is therefore the FE to MIFE transformation for inner products by Datta, Okamoto and Tomida [21] (henceforth DOT), which we describe next. Recall that IP-MIFE supports functions $f : (\mathbb{Z}_p^d)^n \rightarrow G_T$ specified by $(\mathbf{c}_1, \ldots, \mathbf{c}_n) \in (\mathbb{Z}_p^d)^n$ and defined as $f(\mathbf{x}_1, \ldots, \mathbf{x}_n) = [\sum_{i \in [n]} \langle \mathbf{x}_i, \mathbf{c}_i \rangle]_T$. While the DOT IP-MIFE scheme is a direct construction based on pairings, it can be viewed as a generic construction from a function-hiding FE scheme for inner product (IPFE) as described in the next paragraph. Recall that in an IPFE scheme, the ciphertext and secret key are associated with $\mathbf{x} \in \mathbb{Z}_p^d$ and $\mathbf{c} \in \mathbb{Z}_p^d$ respectively, and decryption reveals $[\langle \mathbf{x}, \mathbf{c} \rangle]_T$. The function-hiding property guarantees that the secret key hides $\mathbf{c}$ along with hiding $\mathbf{x}$ in the ciphertext.

Let iFE = (iSetup, iEnc, iKeyGen, iDec) be a function-hiding IPFE scheme with the vector being $d + 1$. Then the IP-MIFE scheme is constructed as follows. Setup generates master secret keys $\mathsf{iMSK}_1, \ldots, \mathsf{iMSK}_n \leftarrow \mathsf{iSetup}(1^\lambda)$ and sets $\mathsf{EK}_i = \mathsf{iMSK}_i, \mathsf{MSK} = \{\mathsf{iMSK}_i\}_{i \in [n]}$. Encryption of $\mathbf{x}_i$ for slot i computes $\mathsf{iCT}_i \leftarrow \mathsf{iEnc}(\mathsf{iMSK}_i, (\mathbf{x}_i, 1))$ and outputs $\mathsf{CT}_i = \mathsf{iCT}_i$. Key generation, given input $(\mathbf{c}_1, \ldots, \mathbf{c}_n)$, randomly chooses $r_1, \ldots, r_n \leftarrow \mathbb{Z}_p$ such that $\sum_{i \in [n]} r_i = 0$, computes $\mathsf{iSK}_i \leftarrow \mathsf{iKeyGen}(\mathsf{iMSK}_i, (\mathbf{c}_i, r_i))$ for $i \in [n]$, and outputs $\mathsf{SK} = \{\mathsf{iSK}_i\}_{i \in [n]}$. Decryption outputs $\sum_{i \in [n]} \mathsf{iDec}(\mathsf{iCT}_i, \mathsf{iSK}_i) = [\sum \langle \mathbf{x}_i, \mathbf{c}_i \rangle]_T$, since $\sum r_i = 0$. Here, the random element r_i is used to hide partial decryption values $\langle \mathbf{x}_i, \mathbf{c}_i \rangle$.

Let us now turn our attention to the security proof. Since we need neither function hiding nor adaptive security for the multi-input scheme in our purpose, we can make the proof much simpler than that by DOT as follows. We will denote $\mathsf{iEnc}(\mathsf{iMSK}_i, \mathbf{v})$ and $\mathsf{iKeyGen}(\mathsf{iMSK}_i, \mathbf{v})$ by $\mathsf{iCT}_i[\mathbf{v}]$ and $\mathsf{iSK}_i[\mathbf{v}]$, respectively. Now, in the original game, the adversary is given $\mathsf{iCT}_i[(\mathbf{x}_i^{j,\beta}, 1)]$ for the j-th challenge message $(\mathbf{x}_i^{j,0}, \mathbf{x}_i^{j,1})$ and $\{\mathsf{iSK}_i[(\mathbf{c}_i^\ell, r_i^\ell)]\}_{i\in[n]}$ for the ℓ-th secret key of $(\mathbf{c}_1^\ell, \ldots, \mathbf{c}_n^\ell)$, where β is the challenge bit. Thus, the goal of the proof is to delete the information of β from the ciphertexts in an indistinguishable manner. In what follows, we omit index ℓ for conciseness since all secret keys can be handled in the same manner.

The security proof uses two hybrids. In the first hybrid, the j-th ciphertext for slot i is changed to $\mathsf{iCT}_i[(\mathbf{x}_i^{j,0}, 1)]$ while all secret keys are changed to $\{\mathsf{iSK}_i[(\mathbf{c}_i, r_i + \langle \mathbf{x}_i^{1,\beta}, \mathbf{c}_i\rangle - \langle \mathbf{x}_i^{1,0}, \mathbf{c}_i\rangle)]\}_{i\in[n]}$ for *all* i, j. The indistinguishability of the original game and the first hybrid follows from the security of the function-hiding IPFE scheme and the following constraint:

$$\langle \mathbf{x}_i^{j,\beta}, \mathbf{c}_i\rangle - \langle \mathbf{x}_i^{j,0}, \mathbf{c}_i\rangle = \langle \mathbf{x}_i^{1,\beta}, \mathbf{c}_i\rangle - \langle \mathbf{x}_i^{1,0}, \mathbf{c}_i\rangle \quad \text{for all } i, j \qquad (1.1)$$

which follows from the fact that the adversary can inherently learn $\langle \mathbf{x}_i^{j,\beta}, \mathbf{c}_i\rangle - \langle \mathbf{x}_i^{1,\beta}, \mathbf{c}_i\rangle$ from challenge queries (originally observed in [5, page 4]). In the second hybrid, all secret keys are changed to $\{\mathsf{iSK}_i[(\mathbf{c}_i, r_i)]\}_{i\in[n]}$ for all i, which readily follows from the fact that the two distributions are equivalent:

$$\{(r_1, \ldots, r_n) : r_1', \ldots, r_n' \leftarrow \mathbb{Z}_p \text{ s.t. } \sum r_i' = 0, \ r_i = r_i' + \langle \mathbf{x}_i^{1,\beta}, \mathbf{c}_i\rangle - \langle \mathbf{x}_i^{1,0}, \mathbf{c}_i\rangle\}$$

$$\{(r_1, \ldots, r_n) : r_1, \ldots, r_n \leftarrow \mathbb{Z}_p \text{ s.t. } \sum r_i = 0\}$$

This is because we have that $\sum_{i\in[n]}(\langle \mathbf{x}_i^{1,\beta}, \mathbf{c}_i\rangle - \langle \mathbf{x}_i^{1,0}, \mathbf{c}_i\rangle) = 0$ due to the admissibility condition on the queries. At this point, the advantage of the adversary is 0 since its view contains no information about β.

Generalizing the FE to MIFE to support AWS. Next, we show how to generalize the FE to MIFE compiler of DOT to handle the AWS functionality. In this step, we make use of an insight developed by AGW to handle unbounded slots, namely, to leverage a (single input) FE scheme that supports *unbounded-slot* AWS together with randomization offsets. In more detail, a ciphertext is associated with $(\mathbf{v}, \mathbf{p}) \in \mathcal{X} \times \mathbb{Z}_p^m$, a secret key is associated with $(F, \mathbf{q}) \in \mathcal{F} \times \mathbb{Z}_p^m$, and decryption reveals $[F(\mathbf{v}) + \langle \mathbf{p}, \mathbf{q}\rangle]_T$. Here, we assume that $\mathcal{F}$ is a set of functions belong to unbounded-slot AWS and $\mathcal{X}$ is its input space, but observe that the argument below can be applied to any function classes. For security, we require that both $\mathbf{p}, \mathbf{q}$ are hidden. In what follows, we call this functionality AWS with inner product (AWSw/IP).

We emphasize that while this is also the functionality achieved by AGW [6][Sec 6], the security achieved by these is quite different: our construction must satisfy partially function hiding *indistinguishability based* security, while theirs satisfies simulation based security without function hiding. Additionally, our construction will support the additional inner product functionality with respect to unbounded-slot AWS, while AGW support it for only single-slot AWS.

Suppose we have a partially function-hiding FE scheme for the AWSw/IP functionality, denoted as $\mathsf{aFE} = (\mathsf{aSetup}, \mathsf{aEnc}, \mathsf{aKeyGen}, \mathsf{aDec})$. Then, we can construct MIFE that supports functions $F : (\mathcal{X})^n \to G_T$ specified by

$(F_1, \ldots, F_n) \in \mathcal{F}^n$ and defined as $F(\mathbf{v}_1, \ldots, \mathbf{v}_n) = [\sum_{i \in [n]} F_i(\mathbf{v}_i)]_T$ from aFE by following the template of DOT, as described next. Looking ahead, F can be instantiated to capture either AWS or attribute based AWS to obtain MIFE for AWS or AB-MIFE for AWS respectively. For instance, for MIFE, we set $\mathbf{v}_i = \{\mathbf{x}_{i,j}, \mathbf{z}_{i,j}\}_{j \in [N_i]}$, $F = (f_1, \ldots, f_n)$ where f_i are ABPs, and $F(\mathbf{v}_1, \ldots, \mathbf{v}_n) = \sum_{i \in [n]} \sum_{j \in [N_i]} \langle f_i(\mathbf{x}_{i,j}), \mathbf{z}_{i,j} \rangle$.

Construction 1 (MIFE for AWS).

Setup(1^λ): It outputs $\mathsf{EK}_i = \mathsf{aMSK}_i \leftarrow \mathsf{aSetup}(1^\lambda)$ for $i \in [n]$ and $\mathsf{MSK} = \{\mathsf{aMSK}_i\}_i$.

Enc($\mathsf{EK}_i, \mathbf{v}_i$): It outputs $\mathsf{CT}_i = \mathsf{aCT}_i \leftarrow \mathsf{aEnc}(\mathsf{aMSK}_i, (\mathbf{v}_i, 1))$.

KeyGen($\mathsf{MSK}, (F_1, \ldots, F_n)$): It outputs $\mathsf{SK} = \{\mathsf{aSK}_i\}_{i \in [n]}$ where $r_1, \ldots, r_n \leftarrow \mathbb{Z}_p$ s.t. $\sum r_i = 0$ and $\mathsf{aSK}_i \leftarrow \mathsf{aKeyGen}(\mathsf{aMSK}_i, (F_i, r_i))$.

Dec($\mathsf{CT}_1, \ldots, \mathsf{CT}_n, \mathsf{SK}$): It outputs $\sum_{i \in [n]} \mathsf{aDec}(\mathsf{aCT}_i, \mathsf{aSK}_i) = [\sum F_i(\mathbf{v}_i)]_T$.

The security proof is essentially the same as in the case of IP-MIFE, discussed above. We use the following two hybrids: in the first hybrid, the j-th ciphertext for slot i is changed from $\mathsf{aCT}_i[(\mathbf{v}^{j,\beta}, 1)]$ to $\mathsf{aCT}_i[(\mathbf{v}^{j,0}, 1)]$ while all secret keys are changed from $\{\mathsf{aSK}_i[(F_i, r_i)]\}_{i \in [n]}$ to $\{\mathsf{aSK}_i[(F_i, r_i + F_i(\mathbf{v}_i^{1,\beta}) - F_i(\mathbf{v}_i^{1,0}))]\}_{i \in [n]}$. In this step, we leverage the important observation that a constraint similar to Eq. (1.1) holds in MIFE for the function class we consider, where the final output is the summation of the output of each slot. Specifically, we have $F_i(\mathbf{v}_i^{j,\beta}) - F_i(\mathbf{v}_i^{j,0}) = F_i(\mathbf{v}_i^{1,\beta}) - F_i(\mathbf{v}_i^{1,0})$ for all i, j. Hence we can use the function-hiding security of aFE to change the second element of the function in secret keys from r_i to $r_i + F_i(\mathbf{v}_i^{1,\beta}) - F_i(\mathbf{v}_i^{1,0})$ in a indistinguishable manner. In the second hybrid, we bring back all secret keys to the form $\{\mathsf{aSK}_i[(F_i, r_i)]\}_{i \in [n]}$. This transition is possible as the case of IP-MIFE, that is, we use the fact that the following distributions are equivalent:

$$\{(r_1, \ldots, r_n) : r_1', \ldots, r_n' \leftarrow \mathbb{Z}_p \text{ s.t. } \sum r_i' = 0, \ r_i = r_i' + F_i(\mathbf{v}_i^{1,\beta}) - F_i(\mathbf{v}_i^{1,0})\}$$

$$\{(r_1, \ldots, r_n) : r_1, \ldots, r_n \leftarrow \mathbb{Z}_p \text{ s.t. } \sum r_i = 0\}$$

which follows from the query condition $\sum_{i \in [n]} (F_i(\mathbf{v}_i^{1,\beta}) - F_i(\mathbf{v}_i^{1,0})) = 0$. At this point, the advantage of the adversary is 0.

Partial Function Hiding FE for AWS with Inner Product. It remains to construct the single input, unbounded slot FE scheme for the AWSw/IP functionality which satisfies partial function hiding. As discussed, the AGW scheme achieves simulation-based security but not function hiding. Our idea of extending AGW to function-hiding to the multi-challenge setting is to design AGW using a function-hiding IPFE scheme, which is inspired by the constructions of ABE for ABP and FE for AWS from (slotted) function-hiding IPFE in [22, 32].

Recall that AGW first constructs a one-slot scheme that can handle randomization offsets, the construction of which basically follows the ABE scheme by [39], and then converts it to an unbounded-slot scheme in a modular manner.

The spirit of our construction follows their blueprint, that is, we first construct a function-hiding one-slot scheme that can handle randomization offsets using a function-hiding IPFE scheme, and then convert it to a unbounded-slot scheme. However, we present the unbounded construction directly since later we will need to extend this to attribute based FE for AWSw/IP, and the modular construction does not apply to that setting. To see this, note that in an attribute-based FE for AWSw/IP, an attribute is associated with an unbounded-slot message and how to deconstruct the attribute for a one-slot message is unclear.

The key building block of [22,32] is the arithmetic key garbling scheme (AKGS), which is specialized for constructing attribute-based encryption schemes. In our work, however, we use the (extended) partially-garbling scheme (PGS) for ABP [6,29] together with function-hiding IPFE since PGS is more suitable for FE that computes ABPs and AWSs directly. Informally, it uses an algorithm $\mathsf{pgb}(f, \mathbf{x}, \mathbf{z}, \delta; \mathbf{t})$ that takes an ABP $f : \mathbb{Z}_p^{n_0} \to \mathbb{Z}_p^{n_1}$, a public string $\mathbf{x} \in \mathbb{Z}_p^{n_0}$, private strings $\mathbf{z} \in \mathbb{Z}_p^{n_1}$ and $\delta \in \mathbb{Z}_p$, and a random tape $\mathbf{t} \in \mathbb{Z}_p^{t-1}$, and outputs

$$\mathbf{L} = (\langle \mathbf{L}_1 \mathbf{t}, \mathbf{x}' \rangle + \delta, \langle \mathbf{L}_2 \mathbf{t}, \mathbf{x}' \rangle, \dots,, \langle \mathbf{L}_s \mathbf{t}, \mathbf{x}' \rangle, \mathbf{z}[1] + \langle \mathbf{L}_{s+1} \mathbf{t}, \mathbf{x}' \rangle, \dots, \mathbf{z}[n_1] + \langle \mathbf{L}_t \mathbf{t}, \mathbf{x}' \rangle)$$

where $\mathbf{x}' = (\mathbf{x}, 1)$, and $s, t \in \mathbb{N}, \mathbf{L}_i \in \mathbb{Z}_p^{(n_0+1) \times (t-1)}$ are deterministically computed from f. The algorithm pgb satisfies:

Corrrectness: we can efficiently compute a vector $\mathbf{b}_{f,\mathbf{x}} \in \mathbb{Z}_p^t$ from $f, \mathbf{x}$ such that $\langle \mathbf{L}, \mathbf{b}_{f,\mathbf{x}} \rangle = \langle f(\mathbf{x}), \mathbf{z} \rangle + \delta$;
Security: we can efficiently simulate the distribution of $\mathbf{L}$ over $\mathbf{t} \leftarrow \mathbb{Z}_p^{t-1}$ from $(f, \mathbf{x}, \langle f(\mathbf{x}), \mathbf{z} \rangle + \delta)$.

Then, we can construct FE for AWSw/IP as follows. Let iFE be a function-hiding IPFE scheme as above.

Construction 2 (FE for AWSw/IP).

$\mathsf{Setup}(1^\lambda)$: It outputs $(\mathsf{PP}, \mathsf{MSK}) = (\mathsf{iPP}, \mathsf{iMSK}) \leftarrow \mathsf{iSetup}(1^\lambda)$.
$\mathsf{Enc}(\mathsf{MSK}, (\{\mathbf{x}_j, \mathbf{z}_j\}_{j \in [N]}, \mathbf{p}))$: It chooses $u_1, \dots, u_N, w_1, \dots, w_N \leftarrow \mathbb{Z}_p$ s.t. $\sum_{j \in [N]} w_j = 0$. It defines

$$\mathbf{X}_j = \begin{cases} (u_j \mathbf{x}'_j, \mathbf{z}_j, w_j, \mathbf{p}, \ 0^\rho) & (j = 1) \\ (u_j \mathbf{x}'_j, \mathbf{z}_j, w_j, 0^m, 0^\rho) & (j > 1) \end{cases}$$

and computes $\mathsf{iCT}_j \leftarrow \mathsf{iEnc}(\mathsf{iMSK}, \mathbf{X}_j)$ for $j \in [N]$. It outputs $\mathsf{CT} = (\{\mathbf{x}_j, \mathsf{iCT}_j\}_j)$. Note that the last ρ entries are used only for the security proof.
$\mathsf{KeyGen}(\mathsf{MSK}, (f, \mathbf{q}))$: It chooses $r \leftarrow \mathbb{Z}_p, \mathbf{t} \leftarrow \mathbb{Z}_p^{t-1}$ and computes $\mathbf{L}_1, \dots, \mathbf{L}_t$ from f. It defines

$$\mathbf{Y}_j = \begin{cases} (\mathbf{L}_j \mathbf{t}, 0^{n_1}, \ r, \ \mathbf{q}, \ 0^\rho) & (j = 1) \\ (\mathbf{L}_j \mathbf{t}, 0^{n_1}, \ 0, 0^m, 0^\rho) & (1 < j \le s) \\ (\mathbf{L}_j \mathbf{t}, \mathbf{e}_{j-s}, 0, 0^m, 0^\rho) & (s < j \le t) \end{cases} \qquad (1.2)$$

where $\mathbf{e}_i$ is one-hot vector with the i-th element being 1. Finally it computes $\mathsf{iSK}_j \leftarrow \mathsf{iKeyGen}(\mathsf{iMSK}, \mathbf{Y}_j)$ for $j \in [t]$ and outputs $\mathsf{SK} = (f, \{\mathsf{iSK}_j\}_j)$.

Dec(CT, SK): It computes $[d_{j,\ell}]_T = \mathsf{iDec}(\mathsf{iCT}_j, \mathsf{iSK}_\ell)$ for all $j \in [N], \ell \in [t]$ and $\mathbf{b}_{f,\mathbf{x}}$ describe above. It outputs $\sum_{j \in [N]} \sum_{\ell \in [t]} [\mathbf{b}_{f,\mathbf{x}}[\ell] \cdot d_{j,\ell}]_T$.

In decryption, it follows that

$$(d_{j,1}, \ldots, d_{j,t}) = \begin{cases} \mathsf{pgb}(f, \mathbf{x}_j, \mathbf{z}_j, rw_j + \langle \mathbf{p}, \mathbf{q} \rangle; u_j \mathbf{t}) & (j = 1) \\ \mathsf{pgb}(f, \mathbf{x}_j, \mathbf{z}_j, rw_j; u_j \mathbf{t}) & (j > 1) \end{cases}$$

and thus $\sum_{j \in [N]} \sum_{\ell \in [t]} \mathbf{b}_{f,\mathbf{x}}[\ell] \cdot d_{j,\ell} = \sum_{j \in [N]} (\langle f(\mathbf{x}_j), \mathbf{z}_j \rangle + rw_j + (j = 1)\langle \mathbf{p}, \mathbf{q} \rangle) = \sum_{j \in [N]} \langle f(\mathbf{x}_j), \mathbf{z}_j \rangle + \langle \mathbf{p}, \mathbf{q} \rangle$. Roughly speaking, the partially function-hiding security of this scheme follows from the following observations:

- Thanks to the function-hiding property of iFE, what the adversary can learn from CT and SK is $\{[(d_{j,1}, \ldots, d_{j,t})]_T\}_{j \in [N]}$.
- The random tape $\{[u_j \mathbf{t}]_T\}_{j \in [N]}$ used to compute $\{d_{j,\ell}\}$ looks random under the SXDH assumption, and $(d_{j,1}, \ldots, d_{j,t})$ for each j appear to be generated by a fresh random tape.
- Thanks to the security of the PGS, the only information about $(\{\mathbf{z}_j\}, \mathbf{p}, \mathbf{q})$ contained in $(d_{j,1}, \ldots, d_{j,t})$ is $\langle f(\mathbf{x}_j), \mathbf{z}_j \rangle + rw_j + (j = 1)\langle \mathbf{p}, \mathbf{q} \rangle$.
- Under the SXDH assumption, $\{[rw_j]_T\}_{j \in [N]}$ looks random with the constraint that the summation of these is $[0]_T$. Thus, the only information about $(\{\mathbf{z}_j\}, \mathbf{p}, \mathbf{q})$ in $\{[(d_{j,1}, \ldots, d_{j,t})]_T\}_{j \in [N]}$ is $\sum \langle f(\mathbf{x}_j), \mathbf{z}_j \rangle + \langle \mathbf{p}, \mathbf{q} \rangle$.

We remark that we can easily modify the scheme such that Enc and KeyGen take vectors $\mathbf{p}$ and $\mathbf{q}$ as a vector of group elements. We will use this property later in the overview for DDFE for AWS.

Attribute-Based MIFE for AWS. Next, we explain how to make the above MIFE for AWS construction attribute-based. At a high level, we do the following: (i) Make FE for AWSw/IP Attribute-Based, (ii) Use the FE to MIFE compiler discussed above to "lift" this to AB-MIFE for AWS. We expand on these below.

Step 1: Make FE for AWSw/IP Attribute-Based. We extend FE for AWSw/IP such that it incorporates an ABP predicate which controls decryption, similarly to attribute-based encryption. Specifically, we add a public vector $\mathbf{y}$ to the message in the ciphertext and a public ABP g to the function in the secret key, and allow decryption only when $g(\mathbf{y}) = 0$.

A naive idea is to define $\mathbf{x}'_j = (\mathbf{y}, \mathbf{x}_j), \mathbf{z}'_j = (v, \mathbf{z}_j)$ and $f'(\mathbf{x}') = (a \cdot g(\mathbf{y}), f(\mathbf{x}))$ where $a, v \leftarrow \mathbb{Z}_p$ and use $\{\mathbf{x}'_j, \mathbf{z}'_j\}$ and f' as inputs for encryption and key generation of FE for AWSw/IP, respectively. Note that f' is an ABP if f, g in turn are ABPs. Then, decryption outputs $[\sum_{j \in [N]} (av \cdot g(\mathbf{y}) + \langle f(\mathbf{x}_j), \mathbf{z}_j \rangle) + \langle \mathbf{p}, \mathbf{q} \rangle]_T$. Since $[av \cdot g(\mathbf{y})]_T$ looks random if $g(\mathbf{y}) \neq 0$ under the SXDH assumption, the decryptor can learn $[\sum_{j \in [N]} \langle f(\mathbf{x}_j), \mathbf{z}_j \rangle + \langle \mathbf{p}, \mathbf{q} \rangle]_T$ only when $g(\mathbf{y}) = 0$.

However, this idea does not work since a needs to be provided in the clear in the secret key for decryption, and this disallows the reliance on the SXDH assumption (recall that we need f and $\mathbf{x}$ to compute $\mathbf{b}_{f,\mathbf{x}}$ in the decryption of the FE for AWSw/IP). To avoid this, we directly embed a in $\mathbf{Y}_{s+1}$ so that we can perform decryption without the knowledge of a. Concretely, we define f'

as $f'(\mathbf{x}') = (g(\mathbf{y}), f(\mathbf{x}))$ instead of $f'(\mathbf{x}') = (a \cdot g(\mathbf{y}), f(\mathbf{x}))$ and define $\mathbf{Y}_{s+1} = (\mathbf{L}_{s+1}, \underline{a}\mathbf{e}_1, 0, 0^m, 0^\rho)$ in Eq. (1.2). Then, the decryption result is the same as the naive construction, which follows from the correctness of the PGS, but f' does not contain information about a in this construction.

The proof of function-hiding security of this scheme is inspired from the proof in AGW [6, Section 7], but with the following key differences: 1) we need to prove IND-based function-hiding security in the secret-key multi-challenge setting while AGW proves SIM-based security in the public-key setting (thus not function-hiding); 2) Our scheme is attribute-based while AGW is not. Hence we need to handle secret key queries that cannot decrypt some challenge ciphertexts, and for such ciphertexts the function values in $\beta = 0$ and $\beta = 1$ can be different (β is the challenge bit).

Step 2: AB-MIFE for AWS. Suppose we have an FE scheme aFE where a ciphertext is associated with $(c, \mathbf{v}, \mathbf{p})$ while a secret key is associated with $(k, F, \mathbf{q})$, and decryption reveals $[F(\mathbf{v}) + \langle \mathbf{p}, \mathbf{q} \rangle]_T$ if $\mathsf{P}(c, k) = 1$ for some predicate P and $\perp$ otherwise. We also assume that aFE is partially function-hiding, so that the ciphertext hides (a part of) $\mathbf{v}$ and $\mathbf{p}$, and the secret key hides $\mathbf{q}$.

At first glance, it seems that we can construct AB-MIFE for $\mathcal{F}'$ from aFE by using Construction 1, where $\mathcal{F}'$ consists of functions $F' : (\mathcal{C} \times \mathcal{X})^n \to G_T$ specified by $((k_1, F_1), \ldots, (k_n, F_n)) \in (\mathcal{K} \times \mathcal{F})^n$ and defined as

$$F'((c_1, \mathbf{v}_1), \ldots, (c_n, \mathbf{v}_n)) = \begin{cases} [\sum_{i \in [n]} F_i(\mathbf{v}_i)]_T & \mathsf{P}(c_i, k_i) = 1 \text{ for all } i \\ \perp & \text{otherwise} \end{cases}$$

Note that AB-MIFE for AWS corresponds to the case where $c = \mathbf{y}, \mathbf{v} = \{\mathbf{x}_j, \mathbf{z}_j\}_{j \in [N]}$, $k = g$ where g is an ABP, $\mathsf{P}(c, k) = 1$ iff $g(\mathbf{y}) = 0$, and F is specified by an ABP f and defined as $F(\mathbf{v}) = \sum \langle f(\mathbf{x}_j), \mathbf{z}_j \rangle$. We can also observe that aFE for the above setting corresponds to attribute-based FE for AWSw/IP.

However the above construction is insufficient due to the following reason. Let us consider a two-input scheme where an adversary obtains ciphertexts of $(c_1^1, \mathbf{v}_1^1)$ and $(c_1^2, \mathbf{v}_1^2)$ for slot 1 (denoted by $\mathsf{CT}_1^1, \mathsf{CT}_1^2$), a ciphertext of $(c_2^1, \mathbf{v}_2^1)$ for slot 2 (denoted by CT_2^1), and a secret key for $((k_1, F_1), (k_2, F_2))$ (denoted by SK) such that $\mathsf{P}(c_1^j, k_1) = 1$ for both $j \in \{1, 2\}$ while $\mathsf{P}(c_2^1, k_2) = 0$. Note that CT_i^j denotes the j-th ciphertext for slot i. In this case, the adversary should not obtain any information about private inputs, since the predicate of slot 2 is never satisfied. However, the adversary can learn $[F_1(\mathbf{v}_1^2) - F_1(\mathbf{v}_1^1)]_T$ in this construction (recall that it can learn $[F_1(\mathbf{v}_1^1) + r_1]_T$ and $[F_1(\mathbf{v}_1^2) + r_1]_T$ by decryption of aFE in slot 1). This is leakage which we need to avoid.

An important fact is that this leakage is inherent if the adversary additionally obtains a ciphertext of $(c_2^2, \mathbf{v}_2^2)$ for slot 2 (denoted by CT_2^2) such that $\mathsf{P}(c_2^2, k_2) = 1$. This is because it can learn $[F_1(\mathbf{v}_1^2) - F_1(\mathbf{v}_1^1)]_T$ by $\mathsf{Dec}(\mathsf{CT}_1^2, \mathsf{CT}_2^2, \mathsf{SK}) - \mathsf{Dec}(\mathsf{CT}_1^1, \mathsf{CT}_2^2, \mathsf{SK})$. By generalizing this observation, it turns out that such leakage appears only when the adversary obtains an illegitimate secret key, which cannot decrypt any combinations of ciphertexts that the adversary has. More formally, we say a secret key for $((k_1, F_1), \ldots, (k_n, F_n))$

is illegitimate if there exists slot i and the adversary does not have a ciphertext of $(c_i, *)$ for slot i such that $\mathsf{P}(c_i, k_i) = 1$. In other words, the above construction is secure in the model where the adversary never asks for illegitimate secret keys – we refer to this notion as security against legitimate keys.

Achieving Security Against Any Keys. We next show how to remove this restriction and achieve security against any keys starting with a scheme secure against legitimate keys. Our idea is to encrypt all secret keys and allow the adversary to decrypt only legitimate secret keys. We achieve such a construction by leveraging an n-out-of-n secret sharing scheme and an attribute-based encryption scheme ABE for the *dual predicate* of P, denoted by $\overline{\mathsf{P}}$. Note that $\overline{\mathsf{P}} : \mathcal{K} \times \mathcal{C} \to \{0, 1\}$ is defined as $\overline{\mathsf{P}}(k, c) = 1 \Leftrightarrow \mathsf{P}(c, k) = 1$. We describe this conversion next.

Let $\mathsf{wmFE} = (\mathsf{wmSetup}, \mathsf{wmEnc}, \mathsf{wmKeyGen}, \mathsf{wmDec})$ be an AB-MIFE scheme for $\mathcal{F}'$ secure against legitimate keys. The setup algorithm generates n master secret keys $\mathsf{abMSK}_1, \ldots, \mathsf{abMSK}_n$ of ABE and sets $(\mathsf{abMSK}_i, \mathsf{wmEK}_i)$ as an encryption key for slot i. Encryption of $(c_i, \mathbf{v}_i)$ for slot i is the same as wmEnc except that it appends a secret key of ABE for c_i to wmCT_i. Key generation of $\{k_i, F_i\}$ runs $\mathsf{wmSK} \leftarrow \mathsf{wmKeyGen}(\mathsf{wmMSK}, \{k_i, F_i\})$, secret shares wmSK to $\sigma_1, \ldots, \sigma_n$, encrypts σ_i with attribute k_i to abCT_i by ABE, and outputs $\{\mathsf{abCT}_i\}$. In this construction, observe that the adversary cannot obtain illegitimate secret keys. Recall that in AB-MIFE for AWS, an ABE scheme for $\overline{\mathsf{P}}$ corresponds to ciphertext-policy ABE (CP-ABE) for ABPs, which was recently proposed by Lin and Luo [33].

We observe that this security against legitimate vs. any keys in the context of AB-MIFE can be seen as generalization of security against complete vs. incomplete (or zero vs. multiple) queries in the context of MIFE [5]. Recall that incomplete queries refers to the case where an adversary does not make a ciphertext query for some inputs. Therefore, in the context of plain MIFE, all secret keys become illegitimate if the adversary makes incomplete queries and legitimate otherwise. On the other hand, in the context of AB-MIFE, whether each secret key become legitimate or illegitimate crucially depends on which attributes are queried in both ciphertext and secret-key queries, and thus the situation is much more complex. This is why we need an advanced primitive, namely, ABE to upgrade the security of AB-MIFE while MIFE secure against complete queries can be upgraded to that secure against incomplete queries using only symmetric key encryption.

Security Under Corruptions. The above transformation works only in the secret-key setting where the adversary cannot corrupt encryption keys. Intuitively, this limitation arises from the fact that there exist ABPs that never evaluate to 0 (we call such ABPs null ABPs). For the transformation to work in the corruption model, we require the underlying CP-ABE scheme to have the property that the adversary cannot decrypt ciphertexts for null ABPs even if it obtains the master secret key. However, in the only known CP-ABE scheme for ABPs by [33], the master secret key has the ability to decrypt ciphertexts for null ABPs. Indeed, such a CP-ABE scheme implies witness encryption for NP relations verifiable in NC_1, and seems quite challenging to obtain from standard assumptions.

To circumvent this problem, we introduce wildcards for the access-controlling functionality similarly to [23]. In more detail, for the wildcard input $\star$ and all ABPs (including null ABPs) g, we always have $g(\star) = 0$. In this functionality, the adversary that corrupts i-th input can admissibly generate a ciphertext for slot i that satisfies any i-th predicate of secret keys, and the leakage of the master secret key of the CP-ABE scheme does not give any additional information to the adversary. As observed in [23], although multi-input ABE with corruptions in general implies witness encryption, their constructions do not yield witness encryption because of the use of wildcards. The same applies to our work as well.

To allow our AB-MIFE scheme to support wildcards, the underlying AB-FE scheme for AWSw/IP also needs to have the wildcard functionality. This modification is quite simple: just setting $v = 0$ (see step 1 above) in encryption with the wildcard attribute suffices.

Comparison with [34]. Very recently, Nguyen, Phan and Pointcheval proposed an attribute-based MCFE scheme for inner product. Their scheme is in the weaker MCFE model where each label can be used only once per input, and does not imply standard MIFE for the same function class. In [34, Remark 16], they informally state that we can apply 1) the technique in [18] to convert their scheme into the MCFE in the stronger notion and 2) All-or-Nothing Encapsulation [19] to achieve security against incomplete queries. We believe that both claims are false.

Regarding item 1, as we discussed previously, the technique in [18] to remove the one-time restriction requires ciphertext homomorphism of the underlying scheme. However, their underlying single client scheme is not ciphertext homomorphic, and thus how to use the technique in [18] is unclear. Regarding item 2, as discussed above, in the context of the *attribute-based* setting, All-or-Nothing Encapsulation would be insufficient to achieve full-fledged security in the AB-MIFE setting, which can handle only the issue of complete vs. incomplete queries in the non-attribute-based setting. Hence, their result does not appear to imply AB-MIFE scheme as claimed.

Multi-Client FE for AWS. To construct MCFE for AWS, we follow the blueprint by [10] where they construct an MCFE scheme for inner products from a function-hiding IPFE scheme. Roughly speaking, we replace the function-hiding IPFE scheme in their scheme with our FE scheme for AWSw/IP. However, following this approach leads to obstacles in the security proof, to handle which, we need to modify their blueprint. To see this, first consider the MCFE construction for AWS that is obtained by applying their blueprint straightforwardly to our setting. Let $H : \{0,1\}^* \to G_1$ be a hash function and aFE be a FE scheme for AWSw/IP. The scheme is given as follows:

Construction 3 (Candidate MCFE for AWS).

$\mathsf{Setup}(1^\lambda)$: It outputs $\mathsf{EK}_i = \mathsf{aMSK}_i \leftarrow \mathsf{aSetup}(1^\lambda)$ for $i \in [n]$ and $\mathsf{MSK} = \{\mathsf{aMSK}_i\}_i$.

$\mathsf{Enc}(\mathsf{EK}_i, \mathbf{v}_i, L)$: It outputs $\mathsf{CT}_i = \mathsf{aCT}_i \leftarrow \mathsf{aEnc}(\mathsf{aMSK}_i, (\mathbf{v}_i, [(v_L, 0)]_1))$ where $[v_L]_1 = H(L)$.

$\mathsf{KeyGen}(\mathsf{MSK}, (F_1, \ldots, F_n))$: It outputs $\mathsf{SK} = \{\mathsf{aSK}_i\}_{i\in[n]}$ where $r_1, \ldots, r_n \leftarrow \mathbb{Z}_p$
   s.t. $\sum r_i = 0$ and $\mathsf{aSK}_i \leftarrow \mathsf{aKeyGen}(\mathsf{aMSK}_i, (F_i, [(r_i, 0)]_2))$.

$\mathsf{Dec}(\mathsf{CT}_1, \ldots, \mathsf{CT}_n, \mathsf{SK})$: It outputs $\sum_{i\in[n]} \mathsf{aDec}(\mathsf{aCT}_i, \mathsf{aSK}_i) = [\sum F_i(\mathbf{v}_i)]_T$.

Let us try to prove the security of this MCFE candidate similarly to Construction 1. In what follows, we denote $\mathsf{aEnc}(\mathsf{aMSK}_i, (\mathbf{v}, [\mathbf{p}]_1))$ and $\mathsf{aKeyGen}(\mathsf{aMSK}_i, (F, [\mathbf{q}]_2))$ by $\mathsf{aCT}_i[\mathbf{v}, \mathbf{p}]$ and $\mathsf{aSK}_i[F, \mathbf{q}]$, respectively. To see why the security proof does not work in this construction, considering the simple case suffices where an adversary queries only one challenge ciphertext for each slot after which it makes secret-key queries adaptively. In the original game, the adversary is given $\mathsf{aCT}_i[\mathbf{v}_i^\beta, (v_L, 0)]$ for a challenge message $(\mathbf{v}_i^0, \mathbf{v}_i^1, L)$ and $\{\mathsf{aSK}_i[F_i, (r_i, 0)]\}_{i\in[n]}$ for a secret key of $(F_1, \ldots, F_n)$. In the first hybrid, the ciphertext for slot i is changed to $\mathsf{aCT}_i[\mathbf{v}^0, (0, 1)]$ while all secret keys are changed to $\{\mathsf{aSK}_i[F_i, (r_i, v_L r_i + F_i(\mathbf{v}_i^\beta) - F_i(\mathbf{v}_i^0))]\}_{i\in[n]}$. The indistinguishability of the original game and the hybrid follows from the partially function-hiding security of aFE. The next step will be to change $[v_L r_i]_2$ to $[\tilde{r}_i]_2$ where $\tilde{r}_i$ is a random element in $\mathbb{Z}_p$ such that $\sum \tilde{r}_i = 0$. If we can show this indistinguishability, $\tilde{r}_i$ absorbs the term $F_i(\mathbf{v}_i^\beta) - F_i(\mathbf{v}_i^0)$ and we can conclude the proof, but this is not the case. This is because the adversary can compute $[v_L]_1$ by the hash function, and thus we cannot use the SXDH assumption in G_2.

We solve this by modifying Construction 3 as follows: Let $\mathsf{PRF} : \{0,1\}^* \to \mathbb{Z}_p$ be a pseudorandom function with a key space $\mathcal{K}$.

Construction 4 (MCFE for AWS).

$\mathsf{Setup}(1^\lambda)$: It chooses $\mathsf{K}_{i,j} \leftarrow \mathcal{K}$ for $i, j \in [n], i < j$, and sets $\mathsf{K}_{i,j} = \mathsf{K}_{j,i}$ for $j < i$. It outputs $\mathsf{EK}_i = (\mathsf{aMSK}_i \leftarrow \mathsf{aSetup}(1^\lambda), \{\mathsf{K}_{i,j}\}_{i\neq j})$ for $i \in [n]$ and $\mathsf{MSK} = \{\mathsf{aMSK}_i\}_i$.

$\mathsf{Enc}(\mathsf{EK}_i, x_i, L)$: It outputs $\mathsf{CT}_i = \mathsf{aCT}_i \leftarrow \mathsf{aEnc}(\mathsf{aMSK}_i, (x, [(v_{L,i}, 0)]_1))$ where $v_{L,i} = \sum_{j\in[n]\setminus\{i\}} (-1)^{j<i} \mathsf{PRF}^{\mathsf{K}_{i,j}}(L)$.

$\mathsf{KeyGen}(\mathsf{MSK}, (f_1, \ldots, f_n))$: It outputs $\mathsf{SK} = \{\mathsf{aSK}_i\}_{i\in[n]}$ where $r \leftarrow \mathbb{Z}_p$ and $\mathsf{aSK}_i \leftarrow \mathsf{aKeyGen}(\mathsf{aMSK}_i, (f_i, [(r, 0)]_2))$.

$\mathsf{Dec}(\mathsf{CT}_1, \ldots, \mathsf{CT}_n, \mathsf{SK})$: It outputs $\sum_{i\in[n]} \mathsf{aDec}(\mathsf{aCT}_i, \mathsf{aSK}_i) = [\sum f_i(x_i)]_T$.

This construction is inspired by the MIFE scheme in [5], in which the randomizing term v_i in ciphertexts are generated in the setup phase (not by a PRF). Note that this is enough for MIFE, but in our case we extend the technique to generate the term $v_{L,i}$ for each label on the fly via PRF to handle an exponentially large number of labels. Observe that $\sum_{i\in[n]} v_{L,i} = 0$ for all L and correctness holds. Such a usage of PRF in MCFE was first introduced by [1], but again their MCFE construction requires ciphertext homomorphism and is not applicable to AWS functionality. This is why we devise a new construction based on DOT combining ideas from [1,5].

In this construction, the above proof strategy works. At a high level, this is due to the following reasons:

- $\{v_{L,i}\}$ looks random with the constraint $\sum v_{L,i} = 0$ for each label if the PRF is secure.

– In contrast to Construction 3, the adversary cannot compute $v_{L,i}$ publicly.

In fact, Construction 4 is a secure MCFE scheme for AWS. For a detailed description, we refer the reader to Sect. 5.

Dynamic Decentralized FE for AWS. Given an MCFE scheme for AWS, we now convert it to DDFE using the template provided by [10]. The high-level idea of the blueprint is to allow parties in the system to generate an independent MCFE instance in Construction 4 for each user set $\mathcal{U}$ by using a PRF on the fly. First, each party joins the system dynamically by generating a key K_i of a pseudorandom function (PRF) as a master secret key. In encryption and key generation for party set $\mathcal{U}$, party $i \in \mathcal{U}$ generates $\mathsf{aMSK}_{i,\mathcal{U}} = \mathsf{aSetup}(1^\lambda; \mathsf{PRF}^{\mathsf{K}_i}(\mathcal{U}))$, which is unique to $(i, \mathcal{U})$. For key generation of $(\{f_i\}, \mathcal{U})$, party i computes a common random element $r_{i,\mathcal{U}} = H(\{f_i\}, \mathcal{U})$ by a hash function and outputs $\mathsf{aSK}_{i,\mathcal{U}}$ as KeyGen in Construction 4. In encryption of $(x_i, \mathcal{U}, L)$, party i generates $\mathsf{K}_{i,j}$ via non-interactive key exchange, and outputs $\mathsf{aCT}_{i,\mathcal{U}}$ in the same manner as Enc in Construction 4. Observe that $\mathsf{aCT}_{i,\mathcal{U}}/\{\mathsf{aSK}_{i,\mathcal{U}}\}_{i \in \mathcal{U}}$ is a valid ciphertext/secret key of the MCFE scheme in Construction 4 with respect to $\mathcal{U}$.

2 Preliminaries

Notations. We use $[n]$ to denote the set $\{1, \ldots, n\}$. For vector $\mathbf{v}$, $\mathbf{v}[i]$ denotes the i-th element of $\mathbf{v}$. For vectors $\mathbf{v}_1, \ldots, \mathbf{v}_n$, $(\mathbf{v}_1, \ldots, \mathbf{v}_n)$ denotes the vector concatenation as row vectors *regardless of* whether each $\mathbf{v}_i$ is a row or column vector. For a matrix $\mathbf{A} = (a_{j,\ell})_{j,\ell}$ over $\mathbb{Z}_p$, $[\mathbf{A}]_i$ denotes a matrix over G_i whose (j, ℓ)-th entry is $g_i^{a_{j,\ell}}$, and we use this notation for vectors and scalars similarly. We use addition for the group operation in every group in bilinear groups. For vectors $\mathbf{a} \in \mathbb{Z}_p^n$ and $\mathbf{b} \in G^n$ where G is a cyclic group of order p, we abuse the notation of inner product and denote $\sum_{i \in [n]} \mathbf{a}[i][\mathbf{b}[i]]$ by $\langle \mathbf{a}, [\mathbf{b}] \rangle$. For a matrix $\mathbf{M} \in \mathbb{Z}_p^{a \times b}$ and vectors $\mathbf{a} \in \mathbb{Z}_p^a, \mathbf{b} \in \mathbb{Z}_p^b$, we denote a vector $\mathbf{m}$ such that $\langle \mathbf{a} \otimes \mathbf{b}, \mathbf{m} \rangle = \mathbf{a}^\top \mathbf{M} \mathbf{b}$ by $\mathsf{vec}(\mathbf{M})$.

Definition 2.1 (Arithmetic Branching Programs (ABPs)). An arithmetic branching program $f : \mathbb{Z}_p^{n_0} \to \mathbb{Z}_p$ is defined by a prime p, a directed acyclic graph (V, E), two special vertices $v_0, v_1 \in V$, and a labeling function $\sigma : E \to \mathcal{F}^{\mathsf{Affine}}$, where $\mathcal{F}^{\mathsf{Affine}}$ consists of all affine functions $g : \mathbb{Z}_p^{n_0} \to \mathbb{Z}_p$. The size of f is the number of vertices $|V|$. Given an input $\mathbf{x} \in \mathbb{Z}_p^{n_0}$ to the ABP, we can assign a $\mathbb{Z}_p$ element to edge $e \in E$ by $\sigma(e)(\mathbf{x})$. Let P be the set of all paths from v_0 to v_1. Each element in P can be represented by a subset of E. The output of the ABP on input $\mathbf{x}$ is defined as $\sum_{E' \in P} \prod_{e \in E'} \sigma(e)(\mathbf{x})$. We can extend the definition of ABPs for functions $f : \mathbb{Z}_p^{n_0} \to \mathbb{Z}_p^{n_1}$ by evaluating each output in a coordinate-wise manner and denote such a function class by $\mathcal{F}_{n_0,n_1}^{\mathsf{ABP}}$.

Note that we can convert any boolean formula, boolean branching program or arithmetic formula to an arithmetic branching program with a constant blow-up in the representation size. Thus, ABPs are a stronger computational model than all of the above.

Definition 2.2 (Partial Garbling Scheme for $\mathcal{F}_{n_0,n_1}^{\mathsf{ABP}}$). We use the following partial garbling scheme for $\mathcal{F}_{n_0,n_1}^{\mathsf{ABP}}$ [29] (please see Definition 2.1) for the construction of our FE schemes. A partial garbling scheme for $\mathcal{F}_{n_0,n_1}^{\mathsf{ABP}}$ consists of the four algorithms. Note that lgen and rec are deterministic algorithms while pgb and pgb* are probabilistic algorithms.

lgen(f): It takes $f \in \mathcal{F}_{n_0,n_1}^{\mathsf{ABP}}$ and outputs $\mathbf{L}_1, \dots, \mathbf{L}_t \in \mathbb{Z}_p^{(n_0+1) \times (t-1)}$ where t depends on f.

pgb($f, \mathbf{x}, \mathbf{z}; \mathbf{t}$): Let $\mathbf{x'}^\top = (\mathbf{x}, 1)$. It takes $f \in \mathcal{F}_{n_0,n_1}^{\mathsf{ABP}}, \mathbf{x} \in \mathbb{Z}_p^{n_0}, \mathbf{z} \in \mathbb{Z}_p^{n_1}$, and a random tape $\mathbf{t} \in \mathbb{Z}_p^{t-1}$. It then outputs

$$(\mathbf{x'}^\top \mathbf{L}_1 \mathbf{t}, \dots, \mathbf{x'}^\top \mathbf{L}_s \mathbf{t}, \mathbf{z}[1] + \mathbf{x'}^\top \mathbf{L}_{s+1} \mathbf{t}, \dots, \mathbf{z}[n_1] + \mathbf{x'}^\top \mathbf{L}_t \mathbf{t}) \in \mathbb{Z}_p^t$$

where $s = t - n_1$ and $(\mathbf{L}_1, \dots, \mathbf{L}_t) = \mathsf{lgen}(f)$.

pgb*($f, \mathbf{x}, \mu; \mathbf{t}$): It takes $\mu \in \mathbb{Z}_p$ and $f, \mathbf{x}, \mathbf{t}$ as above and outputs

$$(\mathbf{x'}^\top \mathbf{L}_1 \mathbf{t} + \mu, \mathbf{x'}^\top \mathbf{L}_2 \mathbf{t}, \dots, \mathbf{x'}^\top \mathbf{L}_t \mathbf{t}) \in \mathbb{Z}_p^t$$

where $(\mathbf{L}_1, \dots, \mathbf{L}_t) = \mathsf{lgen}(f)$.

rec($f, \mathbf{x}$): It takes $f, \mathbf{x} \in \mathbb{Z}_p^{n_0}$ and outputs $\mathbf{d}_{f,\mathbf{x}} \in \mathbb{Z}_p^t$.

The concrete description of lgen, rec that satisfy the following properties is found in [6, Appendix A]. We slightly modify the format of the output of lgen from [6] for convenience in our construction, but note that they are essentially the same.

Correctness. The garbling scheme is correct if for all $f \in \mathcal{F}_{n_0,n_1}^{\mathsf{ABP}}, \mathbf{x} \in \mathbb{Z}_p^{n_0}, \mathbf{z} \in \mathbb{Z}_p^{n_1}, \mathbf{t} \in \mathbb{Z}_p^{t-1}$, we have

$$\langle \mathsf{pgb}(f, \mathbf{x}, \mathbf{z}; \mathbf{t}), \mathsf{rec}(f, \mathbf{x}) \rangle = \langle f(\mathbf{x}), \mathbf{z} \rangle.$$

Security. The garbling scheme is secure if for all $f \in \mathcal{F}_{n_0,n_1}^{\mathsf{ABP}}, \mathbf{x} \in \mathbb{Z}_p^{n_0}, \mathbf{z} \in \mathbb{Z}_p^{n_1}$, the following distributions are statistically close:

$$\mathsf{pgb}(f, \mathbf{x}, \mathbf{z}; \mathbf{t}) \quad \text{and} \quad \mathsf{pgb}^*(f, \mathbf{x}, \langle f(\mathbf{x}), \mathbf{z} \rangle; \mathbf{t})$$

where the random tape is chosen over $\mathbf{t} \leftarrow \mathbb{Z}_p^{t-1}$.

Extension of Partial Garbling Scheme. We can construct an additional partial garbling algorithm pgb+ with the following properties [6, Appendix A].

pgb+($f, \mathbf{x}, \mathbf{z}, \delta; \mathbf{t}$): Let $\mathbf{x'}^\top = (\mathbf{x}, 1)$. It takes $f \in \mathcal{F}_{n_0,n_1}^{\mathsf{ABP}}, \mathbf{x} \in \mathbb{Z}_p^{n_0}, \mathbf{z} \in \mathbb{Z}_p^{n_1}, \delta \in \mathbb{Z}_p$, and a random tape $\mathbf{t} \in \mathbb{Z}_p^{t-1}$. It then outputs

$$(\mathbf{x'}^\top \mathbf{L}_1 \mathbf{t} + \boxed{\delta}, \mathbf{x'}^\top \mathbf{L}_2 \mathbf{t}, \dots, \mathbf{x'}^\top \mathbf{L}_s \mathbf{t}, \mathbf{z}[1] + \mathbf{x'}^\top \mathbf{L}_{s+1} \mathbf{t}, \dots, \mathbf{z}[n_1] + \mathbf{x'}^\top \mathbf{L}_t \mathbf{t}) \in \mathbb{Z}_p^t$$

where $s = t - n_1$ and $(\mathbf{L}_1, \dots, \mathbf{L}_t) = \mathsf{lgen}(f)$.

Correctness. For all $f \in \mathcal{F}_{n_0, n_1}^{\mathsf{ABP}}, \mathbf{x} \in \mathbb{Z}_p^{n_0}, \mathbf{z} \in \mathbb{Z}_p^{n_1}, \mathbf{t} \in \mathbb{Z}_p^{t-1}$, we have

$$\langle \mathsf{pgb}^+(f, \mathbf{x}, \mathbf{z}, \delta; \mathbf{t}), \mathsf{rec}(f, \mathbf{x}) \rangle = \langle f(\mathbf{x}), \mathbf{z} \rangle + \delta.$$

Security. For all $f \in \mathcal{F}_{n_0, n_1}^{\mathsf{ABP}}, \mathbf{x} \in \mathbb{Z}_p^{n_0}, \mathbf{z} \in \mathbb{Z}_p^{n_1}$, the following distributions are statistically close:

$$\mathsf{pgb}^+(f, \mathbf{x}, \mathbf{z}, \delta; \mathbf{t}) \quad \text{and} \quad \mathsf{pgb}^*(f, \mathbf{x}, \langle f(\mathbf{x}), \mathbf{z} \rangle + \delta; \mathbf{t})$$

where the random tape is chosen over $\mathbf{t} \leftarrow \mathbb{Z}_p^{t-1}$.

Linearlity. Observe that pgb^+ is affine in $\mathbf{z}[1]$, $\mathbf{t}$, δ, and pgb^* is affine in μ.

3   Attribute-Based FE for Attribute-Weighted Sums with Inner Product

In this section, we present an attribute-based FE for attribute-weighted sums with inner product (AB-FE for AWSw/IP).

Definition 3.1 (Inner Product Functional Encryption). Inner product functional encryption (IPFE) is a class of secret-key functional encryption (SK-FE) that supports the following functionality. Let $\mathbb{G}$ be bilinear groups. Let $\mathcal{X} = G_1^m$ be a message space. Let $\mathcal{F} = G_2^m$ be a family of functions, where $f = [\mathbf{c}]_2 \in \mathcal{F}$ represents the function $f : \mathcal{X} \to G_T$ defined as $f([\mathbf{x}]_1) = [\langle \mathbf{x}, \mathbf{c} \rangle]_T$ where $\mathbf{x}, \mathbf{c} \in \mathbb{Z}_p^m$ are both private inputs.

A function-hiding IPFE scheme can be constructed from the MDDH assumption [36, Appendix A].

Definition 3.2 (FE for AWSw/IP). An FE scheme for attribute-weighted sums with inner product (AWSw/IP) is a class of SK-FE that supports the following functionality. Let $\mathbb{G}$ be bilinear groups of order p. Let $\mathcal{X} = \bigcup_{i \in \mathbb{N}} (\mathbb{Z}_p^{n_0} \times \mathbb{Z}_p^{n_1})^i \times G_1^m$ be a message space. Let $\mathcal{F} = \mathcal{F}_{n_0, n_1}^{\mathsf{ABP}} \times G_2^m$ (see Definition 2.1 for $\mathcal{F}_{n_0, n_1}^{\mathsf{ABP}}$) be a family of functions, where $f' = (f, [\mathbf{q}]_2) \in \mathcal{F}$ represents the function $f' : \mathcal{X} \to G_T$ defined as

$$f'((\{\mathbf{x}_i, \mathbf{z}_i\}_{i \in [N]}, [\mathbf{p}]_1)) = [\sum_{i \in [N]} \langle f(\mathbf{x}_i), \mathbf{z}_i \rangle + \langle \mathbf{p}, \mathbf{q} \rangle]_T$$

where $\{\mathbf{x}_i\}, f$ are public elements while $\{\mathbf{z}_i\}, [\mathbf{p}]_1, [\mathbf{q}]_2$ are private elements.

Definition 3.3 (AB-FE for AWSw/IP). An attribute-based FE scheme for attribute-weighted sums with inner product (AB-FE for AWSw/IP) is a class of SK-FE that supports the following functionality. Let $\mathbb{G}$ be bilinear groups. Let $\mathcal{X} = (\mathbb{Z}_p^{n_0'} \cup \{\star\}) \times \bigcup_{i \in \mathbb{N}} (\mathbb{Z}_p^{n_0} \times \mathbb{Z}_p^{n_1})^i \times G_T^m$ be a message space. Let $\mathcal{F} = \mathcal{F}_{n_0',1}^{\mathsf{ABP}} \times \mathcal{F}_{n_0,n_1}^{\mathsf{ABP}} \times G_2^m$ be a family of functions, where $f = (g, h, [\mathbf{q}]_2) \in \mathcal{F}$ represents the function $f : \mathcal{X} \to G_T$ defined as

$$f((\mathbf{y}, \{\mathbf{x}_j, \mathbf{z}_j\}_{j \in [N]}, [\mathbf{p}]_1)) = \begin{cases} [\sum_{j \in [N]} \langle h(\mathbf{x}_j), \mathbf{z}_j \rangle + \langle \mathbf{p}, \mathbf{q} \rangle]_T & g(\mathbf{y}) = 0 \vee \mathbf{y} = \star \\ \bot & g(\mathbf{y}) \neq 0 \end{cases}$$

where $\mathbf{y}, \{\mathbf{x}_i\}, g, h$ are public elements while $\{\mathbf{z}_i\}, [\mathbf{p}]_1, [\mathbf{q}]_2$ are private elements. For notational convenience, we define $g(\star) = 0$ for all ABPs g (even for ABPs g such that $g(\mathbf{y}) \neq 0$ for all $\mathbf{y} \in \mathbb{Z}_p^{n_0'}$).

Remark 3.1. As explained in the introduction, we need the wildcard functionality to make our AB-MIFE scheme secure in the corruption model. This is why we define the functionality of AB-FE for AWSw/IP such that it also supports wildcards, which we will use to construct our AB-MIFE scheme as a building block.

3.1 Construction

Let k be the parameter for the MDDH$_k$ assumption. Let $\mathsf{iFE} = (\mathsf{iSetup}, \mathsf{iEnc}, \mathsf{iKeyGen}, \mathsf{iDec})$ be a function-hiding IPFE scheme with the vector length being $k(n_0' + n_0 + 3) + n_1 + 2m + 2$. The last $m + 2$ elements are used for only the security proof. Let $(\mathsf{lgen}, \mathsf{pgb}, \mathsf{pgb}^+, \mathsf{pgb}^*, \mathsf{rec})$ be a partially garbling scheme for ABPs (Definition 2.2). Our AB-FE scheme for AWSw/IP is given in Fig. 1.

Correctness and Security. In decryption, due to the correctness of iFE, we have

$$\mathbf{d}_j = \begin{cases} \mathsf{pgb}^+(\phi, (\mathbf{y}, \mathbf{x}_j), (\langle \mathbf{s}, \mathbf{v} \rangle, \mathbf{z}_j), \langle \mathbf{r}, \mathbf{w}_j \rangle + \langle \mathbf{p}, \mathbf{q} \rangle; \mathbf{T}u_j) & (j = 1) \\ \mathsf{pgb}^+(\phi, (\mathbf{y}, \mathbf{x}_j), (\quad 0, \quad \mathbf{z}_j), \langle \mathbf{r}, \mathbf{w}_j \rangle \qquad\quad; \mathbf{T}u_j) & (j > 1) \end{cases}$$

where $\mathbf{v} = \mathbf{0}$ if $\mathbf{y}' = \star$. Thanks to the correctness of the partial garbling scheme, we have

$$\langle \mathbf{d}_j, \mathsf{rec}(\phi, (\mathbf{y}, \mathbf{x}_j)) \rangle = \begin{cases} \langle \mathbf{s}, \mathbf{v} \rangle g(\mathbf{y}) + \langle h(\mathbf{x}_j), \mathbf{z}_j \rangle + \langle \mathbf{r}, \mathbf{w}_j \rangle + \langle \mathbf{p}, \mathbf{q} \rangle & (j = 1) \\ \langle h(\mathbf{x}_j), \mathbf{z}_j \rangle + \langle \mathbf{r}, \mathbf{w}_j \rangle & (j > 1) \end{cases}$$

In the above, we use the fact that $\phi((\mathbf{y}, \mathbf{x}_j)) = (g(\mathbf{y}), h(\mathbf{x}_j)) \in \mathbb{Z}_p^{1+n_1}$. Hence $d = \sum_{j \in [N]} \langle h(\mathbf{x}_j), \mathbf{z}_j \rangle + \langle \mathbf{p}, \mathbf{q} \rangle$ if $g(\mathbf{y}') = 0$, since $\sum_{j \in [N]} \langle \mathbf{r}, \mathbf{w}_j \rangle = 0$.

Remark 3.2. A partially-hiding FE scheme for AWSw/IP can be obtained from a partially-hiding AB-FE scheme for AWSw/IP by setting $n_0' = 0$ and g as the constant function that outputs 0.

Setup(1^λ): It runs iPP, iMSK $\leftarrow$ iSetup(1^λ) and outputs (PP, MSK) = (iPP, iMSK).

Enc(MSK, $(\mathbf{y}', \{\mathbf{x}_j, \mathbf{z}_j\}_{j \in [N]}, [\mathbf{p}]_1)$): It samples $\mathbf{u}_1, \ldots, \mathbf{u}_N, \mathbf{w}_1, \ldots, \mathbf{w}_{N-1} \leftarrow \mathbb{Z}_p^k$ and sets $\mathbf{w}_N = -\sum_{j \in [N-1]} \mathbf{w}_j$. If $\mathbf{y}' = \star$, it sets $\mathbf{y} = 0^{n_0'}$ and $\mathbf{v} = 0^k$, otherwise it sets $\mathbf{y} = \mathbf{y}'$ and $\mathbf{v} \leftarrow \mathbb{Z}_p^k$. Then, it defines

$$\boldsymbol{\chi}_j^\top = (\mathbf{y}, \mathbf{x}_j, 1), \quad \mathbf{X}_j = \begin{cases} (\boldsymbol{\chi}_j \otimes \mathbf{u}_j, \mathbf{z}_j, \mathbf{w}_j, \mathbf{v}, \ \mathbf{p}, \ 0^{m+2}) & (j = 1) \\ (\boldsymbol{\chi}_j \otimes \mathbf{u}_j, \mathbf{z}_j, \mathbf{w}_j, 0^k, 0^m, 0^{m+2}) & (j > 1) \end{cases}$$

and computes $\mathsf{iCT}_j \leftarrow \mathsf{iEnc}(\mathsf{iMSK}, [\mathbf{X}_j]_1)$ for all $j \in [N]$. It outputs CT = $(\mathbf{y}, \{\mathbf{x}_j, \mathsf{iCT}_j\}_{j \in [N]})$.

KeyGen(MSK, $(g, h, [\mathbf{q}]_2)$): It samples $\mathbf{r}, \mathbf{s} \leftarrow \mathbb{Z}_p^k$ and defines an ABP $\phi : \mathbb{Z}_p^{n_0' + n_0} \rightarrow \mathbb{Z}_p^{1+n_1}$ as $\phi((\mathbf{y}, \mathbf{x})) = (g(\mathbf{y}), h(\mathbf{x}))$ for $\mathbf{y} \in \mathbb{Z}_p^{n_0'}, \mathbf{x} \in \mathbb{Z}_p^{n_0}$. It computes $\mathbf{L}_1, \ldots, \mathbf{L}_t \leftarrow \mathsf{lgen}(\phi)$ and $\mathbf{T} \leftarrow \mathbb{Z}_p^{(t-1) \times k}$ and defines

$$\mathbf{Y}_j = \begin{cases} (\mathrm{vec}(\mathbf{L}_j \mathbf{T}), 0^{n_1}, & \mathbf{r}, \ 0^k, \mathbf{q}, \ 0^{m+2}) & (j = 1) \\ (\mathrm{vec}(\mathbf{L}_j \mathbf{T}), 0^{n_1}, & 0^k, 0^k, 0^m, 0^{m+2}) & (1 < j \leq s) \\ (\mathrm{vec}(\mathbf{L}_j \mathbf{T}), 0^{n_1}, & 0^k, \mathbf{s}, \ 0^m, 0^{m+2}) & (j = s+1) \\ (\mathrm{vec}(\mathbf{L}_j \mathbf{T}), \mathbf{e}_{j-s-1}, 0^k, 0^k, 0^m, 0^{m+2}) & (s+1 < j) \end{cases}$$

where s is the parameter of the partial garbling scheme defined in Definition 2.2. It computes $\mathsf{iSK}_j \leftarrow \mathsf{iKeyGen}(\mathsf{iMSK}, [\mathbf{Y}_j]_2)$ for all $j \in [t]$ and outputs SK = $(\phi, \{\mathsf{iSK}_j\}_{j \in [t]})$.

Dec(CT, SK): It parse CT, SK as $(\mathbf{y}, \{\mathbf{x}_j, \mathsf{iCT}_j\}_{j \in [N]})$ and $(\phi, \{\mathsf{iSK}_j\}_{j \in [t]})$, respectively. It outputs $\bot$ if $g(\mathbf{y}') \neq 0$. Otherwise, it computes $[d_{j,\ell}]_T = \mathsf{iDec}(\mathsf{iCT}_j, \mathsf{iSK}_\ell)$ for $j \in [N], \ell \in [t]$ and outputs

$$[d]_T = \sum_{j \in [N]} \langle [\mathbf{d}_j]_T, \mathsf{rec}(\phi, (\mathbf{y}, \mathbf{x}_j)) \rangle.$$

where $\mathbf{d}_j = (d_{j,1}, \ldots, d_{j,t})$.

Fig. 1. Attribute-Based FE for AWSw/IP

We argue security via the following theorem.

Theorem 3.1. *If* iFE *is function-hiding, the partial garbling scheme is secure, and the* $MDDH_k$ *assumption holds in* $\mathbb{G}$, *then the proposed AB-FE scheme for AWSw/IP is partially function-hiding.*

Due to space constraints, we present the proof in the full version.

4   Attribute-Based MIFE for Attribute-Weighted Sums

In this section, we present our AB-MIFE for AWS in two steps as discussed in Sect. 1.

Definition 4.1 (Multi-Input Functional Encryption). Let $\mathcal{F}$ be a function family such that, for all $f \in \mathcal{F}$, $f : \mathcal{X}^n \to \mathcal{Z}$.[7] An MIFE scheme for $\mathcal{F}$ consists of four algorithms.

Setup($1^\lambda, 1^n$): It takes a security parameter 1^λ and a number 1^n of slots, and outputs a public parameter PP, encryption keys $\{\mathsf{EK}_i\}_{i \in [n]}$, a master secret key MSK. The other algorithms implicitly take PP.

Enc(EK_i, x_i): It takes EK_i and $x_i \in \mathcal{X}$ and outputs a ciphertext CT_i.

KeyGen(MSK, f): It takes MSK and $f \in \mathcal{F}$, and outputs a secret key SK.

Dec($\mathsf{CT}_1, \ldots, \mathsf{CT}_n, \mathsf{SK}$): It takes $\mathsf{CT}_1, \ldots, \mathsf{CT}_n$ and SK, and outputs a decryption value $d \in \mathcal{Z}$ or a symbol $\bot$.

Correctness. An MIFE scheme is correct if it satisfies the following condition. For all $\lambda, n \in \mathbb{N}$, $(x_1, \ldots, x_n) \in \mathcal{X}^n$, $f \in \mathcal{F}$, we have

$$
\Pr\left[d = f(x_1, \ldots, x_n) : \begin{array}{l} (\mathsf{PP}, \{\mathsf{EK}_i\}, \mathsf{MSK}) \leftarrow \mathsf{Setup}(1^\lambda, 1^n) \\ \mathsf{CT}_i \leftarrow \mathsf{Enc}(\mathsf{EK}_i, x_i) \text{ for } i \in [n] \\ \mathsf{SK} \leftarrow \mathsf{KeyGen}(\mathsf{MSK}, f) \\ d = \mathsf{Dec}(\mathsf{CT}_1, \ldots, \mathsf{CT}_n, \mathsf{SK}) \end{array} \right] = 1.
$$

Security. We consider the case where each $x_i \in \mathcal{X}$ consists of a public part $x_{i,\mathsf{pub}}$ and a private part $x_{i,\mathsf{priv}}$, i.e., $x_i = (x_{i,\mathsf{pub}}, x_{i,\mathsf{priv}})$. An MIFE scheme is selectively partially-hiding if for every stateful PPT adversary $\mathcal{A}$, there exists a negligible function negl such that for all $\lambda, n \in \mathbb{N}$, the following holds

$$
\Pr\left[\beta = \beta' : \begin{array}{l} \beta \leftarrow \{0, 1\} \\ (\mathsf{PP}, \{\mathsf{EK}_i\}, \mathsf{MSK}) \leftarrow \mathsf{Setup}(1^\lambda, 1^n) \\ \beta' \leftarrow \mathcal{A}^{\mathsf{QCor}(), \mathsf{QEnc}^\beta(), \mathsf{KeyGen}(\mathsf{MSK}, \cdot)}(\mathsf{PP}) \end{array} \right] \leq \frac{1}{2} + \mathsf{negl}(\lambda)
$$

where $\mathsf{QCor}(i)$ outputs EK_i, and $\mathsf{QEnc}^\beta(i, x_i^0, x_i^1)$ outputs $\mathsf{Enc}(\mathsf{EK}_i, x_i^\beta)$. Let $q_{c,i}$ be the numbers of queries of the forms of $\mathsf{QEnc}^\beta(i, *, *)$. Let $\mathcal{HS}$ be the set of parties on which the adversary has not queried QCor at the end of the game, and $\mathcal{CS} = [n] \backslash \mathcal{HS}$. Then, the admissible adversary's queries must satisfy the following conditions.

- For $i \in \mathcal{CS}$, the queries $\mathsf{QEnc}^\beta(i, x_i^0, x_i^1)$ must satisfy $x_i^0 = x_i^1$.
- For $i \in \mathcal{HS}$, the queries $\mathsf{QEnc}^\beta(i, x_i^0, x_i^1)$ must satisfy $x_{i,\mathsf{pub}}^0 = x_{i,\mathsf{pub}}^1$.
- $f(x_1^0, \ldots, x_n^0) = f(x_1^1, \ldots, x_n^1)$ for all sequences $(x_1^0, \ldots, x_n^0, x_1^1, \ldots, x_n^1, f)$ that satisfy the two conditions:
  - For all $i \in [n]$, [$\mathsf{QEnc}^\beta(i, x_i^0, x_i^1)$ is queried and $i \in \mathcal{HS}$] or [$x_i^0 = x_i^1 \in \mathcal{X}_i$ and $i \in \mathcal{CS}$].
  - KeyGen(MSK, f) is queried.

---

[7] In general, the domain of each slot can be different, i.e., f can be defined as $f : \mathcal{X}_1 \cdots \times \mathcal{X}_n \to \mathcal{Z}$. In this paper, however, we only handle the case where $\mathcal{X}_i = \mathcal{X}$ for all $i \in [n]$.

- The adversary must make all queries to QCor and QEnc in one shot. That is, first it outputs $(\mathcal{CS}, \{i, x_i^0, x_i^1\})$ and obtains the response: $(\{EK_i\}_{i \in \mathcal{CS}}, \{Enc(EK_i, x_i^\beta)\})$. Only after the one-shot query, the adversary can query KeyGen adaptively.

We formally define attribute-based MIFE scheme for attribute-weighted sums and its security.

Definition 4.2 (AB-MIFE for AWS). Attribute-based MIFE for Attribute-Weighted Sums (AB-MIFE for AWS) is a class of MIFE (Definition 4.1) that supports the following functionality. Let $\mathbb{G}$ be bilinear groups. Let $\mathcal{X} = (\mathbb{Z}_p^{n_0'} \cup \{\star\}) \times \bigcup_{i \in \mathbb{N}} (\mathbb{Z}_p^{n_0} \times \mathbb{Z}_p^{n_1})^i$ be a message space. Let $\mathcal{F} = (\mathcal{F}_{n_0',1}^{\mathsf{ABP}} \times \mathcal{F}_{n_0,n_1}^{\mathsf{ABP}})^n$ be a family of functions, where $((g_1, h_1), \ldots, (g_n, h_n)) \in \mathcal{F}$ represents the function $f : \mathcal{X}^n \to G_T$ defined as

$$f((\mathbf{y}_1, \{\mathbf{x}_{1,j}, \mathbf{z}_{1,j}\}_{j \in [N_1]}), \ldots, (\mathbf{y}_n, \{\mathbf{x}_{n,j}, \mathbf{z}_{n,j}\}_{j \in [N_n]}))$$
$$= \begin{cases} [\sum_{i \in [n]} \sum_{j \in [N_i]} \langle h_i(\mathbf{x}_{i,j}), \mathbf{z}_{i,j} \rangle]_T & (g_i(\mathbf{y}_i) = 0 \text{ for all } i \in [n]) \\ \bot & (\text{otherwise}) \end{cases}$$

where $\mathbf{y}_i, \mathbf{x}_{i,j}$ are public inputs while $\mathbf{z}_{i,j}$ is a private input, and we always have $g_i(\star) = 0$.

Definition 4.3 (Security of AB-MIFE for AWS). We say that an AB-FE scheme for AWS satisfies security against *legitimate* keys if the scheme is secure against adversaries that follows the condition defined below in addition to the conditions defined in Definition 4.1. Let $(\mathcal{CS}, \{i, x_i^{\ell,0}, x_i^{\ell,1}\}_{i \in [n], \ell \in [q_{c,i}]}, \{f^\eta\}_{\eta \in [q_k]})$ be the query of the adversary, where q_k is the number of queries to KeyGen, $x_i^{\ell,\beta} = (\mathbf{y}_i^\ell, \{\mathbf{x}_{i,j}^\ell, \mathbf{z}_{i,j}^\ell\}_{j \in [N_i^\ell]})$ and $f^\eta = \{g_i^\eta, h_i^\eta\}_{i \in [n]}$. We say that f^η is legitimate if for all $i \in \mathcal{HS}$, there exists $\ell_i' \in [q_{c,i}]$ such that $g_i^\eta(\mathbf{y}_i^{\ell_i'}) = 0$. In security against legitimate keys, f^η must be legitimate for all $\eta \in [q_k]$. In contrast, we say that an AB-FE scheme for AWS satisfies security against *any* keys if the scheme is secure against adversaries that follows just the condition defined in Definition 4.1.

4.1 Construction

Let aFE $=$ (aSetup, aEnc, aKeyGen, aDec) be an FE scheme for AB-FE for AWSw/IP. Then our AB-MIFE scheme for AWS is given in Fig. 2.

Correctness and Security. Due to the correctness of aFE, we have

$$d_i = \sum_{j \in [N_i]} \langle f(\mathbf{x}_{i,j}), \mathbf{z}_{i,j} \rangle + r_i$$

Hence $d = \sum_{i \in [n]} \sum_{j \in [N_i]} \langle f(\mathbf{x}_{i,j}), \mathbf{z}_{i,j} \rangle$ since $\sum_{i \in [n]} r_i = 0$.

The proposed scheme is secure against legitimate keys as stated by the following theorem.

Theorem 4.1. *If* aFE *is partially function-hiding, then the proposed AB-MIFE scheme for AWS satisfies security against legitimate keys as per Definition 4.3.*

Due to space limitations, the proof is presented in the full version.

Setup($1^\lambda, 1^n$): It runs $\text{aPP}_i, \text{aMSK}_i \leftarrow \text{aSetup}(1^\lambda)$ for $i \in [n]$ and outputs

$$\text{PP} = \{\text{aPP}_i\}_{i\in[n]}, \quad \text{EK}_i = \text{aMSK}_i \text{ for } i \in [n], \quad \text{MSK} = \{\text{EK}_i\}_{i\in[n]}.$$

Enc($\text{EK}_i, (\mathbf{y}_i, \{\mathbf{x}_{i,j}, \mathbf{z}_{i,j}\}_{j\in[N_i]})$): It outputs

$$\text{CT}_i = \text{aCT}_i \leftarrow \text{aEnc}(\text{aMSK}_i, (\mathbf{y}_i, \{\mathbf{x}_{i,j}, \mathbf{z}_{i,j}\}_{j\in[N_i]}, [1]_1)).$$

KeyGen($\text{MSK}, \{g_i, h_i\}_{i\in[n]}$): It samples $r_1, \ldots, r_{n-1} \leftarrow \mathbb{Z}_p$, sets $r_n = -\sum_{i\in[n-1]} r_i$, and outputs $\text{SK} = \{\text{aSK}_i\}_{i\in[n]}$ where

$$\text{aSK}_i \leftarrow \text{aKeyGen}(\text{aMSK}_i, (g_i, h_i, [r_i]_2)).$$

Dec($\text{CT}_1, \ldots, \text{CT}_n, \text{SK}$): It parse CT_i, SK as $\text{aCT}_i, \{\text{aSK}_i\}_{i\in[n]}$, respectively. If there exists i such that $g_i(\mathbf{y}_i) \neq 0$, it outputs $\perp$. Otherwise, it computes $[d_i]_T = \text{aDec}(\text{aCT}_i, \text{aSK}_i)$ for $i \in [n]$, and outputs $[d]_T = \sum_{i\in[n]} [d_i]_T$.

Fig. 2. Attribute-Based MIFE for AWS

4.2   Security Against Any Keys in AB-MIFE for AWS

In this section, we present how to convert an AB-MIFE scheme for AWS with security against legitimate keys to one with security against any keys. In the conversion, we use a ciphertext-policy ABE (CP-ABE) scheme for ABP and a (n-out-of-n) secret sharing scheme. A CP-ABE scheme for ABP with wildcards is an ABE scheme that supports predicate $\mathsf{P} : \mathcal{X} \times \mathcal{Y} \to \{0,1\}$ where $\mathcal{X} = \mathcal{F}_{n_0,1}^{\text{ABP}}$, $\mathcal{Y} = \mathbb{Z}_p^{n_0} \cup \{\star\}$, and for $g \in \mathcal{X}, \mathbf{y} \in \mathcal{Y}$, P is defined as

$$\mathsf{P}(g, \mathbf{y}) = \begin{cases} 1 & g(\mathbf{y}) = 0 \\ 0 & g(\mathbf{y}) \neq 0 \end{cases}$$

A CP-ABE scheme for ABP with wildcards is easily obtained from the CP-ABE scheme for ABP in [33] just by setting the master secret key as the secret key for the wildcard.

Construction. Let wmFE = (wmSetup, wmEnc, wmKeyGen, wmDec) be an AB-MIFE scheme for AWS with security against legitimate keys, ABE = (abSetup, abEnc, abKeyGen, abDec) be an CP-ABE scheme for ABP, and (Share, Rec) be a secret sharing scheme. Then, an AB-MIFE scheme for AWS can be constructed as in Fig. 3.

Correctness and Security. Due to the correctness of ABE, $\sigma'_1, \ldots, \sigma'_n$ are valid shares of wmSK for $\{g_i, h_i\}_{i \in [n]}$. Thus, thanks to the correctness of wmFE, we have $d = \sum_{i \in [n]} \sum_{j \in [N_i]} \langle f_i(\mathbf{x}_{i,j}), \mathbf{z}_{i,j} \rangle$.

We argue security via the following theorem.

Theorem 4.2. *If* wmFE *has security against legitimate keys,* ABE *is selectively secure, and the secret sharing scheme is secure, then the proposed scheme satisfies security against any keys, i.e., selectively partially-hiding security in Definition 4.1.*

Setup($1^\lambda, 1^n$): It runs wmPP, $\{\text{wmEK}_i\}_{i \in [n}, \text{wmMSK} \leftarrow \text{wmSetup}(1^\lambda)$ and abPK_i, $\text{abMSK}_i \leftarrow \text{abSetup}(1^\lambda)$ for $i \in [n]$. It outputs PP, $\{\text{EK}_i\}_{i \in [n]}$, MSK as follows:

$$\text{PP} = (\text{wmPP}, \{\text{abPK}_i\}_{i \in [n]}), \quad \text{EK}_i = (\text{wmEK}_i, \text{abMSK}_i), \quad \text{MSK} = \text{wmMSK}$$

Enc($\text{EK}_i, (\mathbf{y}_i, \{\mathbf{x}_{i,j}, \mathbf{z}_{i,j}\}_{j \in [N_i]})$): It outputs $\text{CT}_i = (\text{wmCT}_i, \text{abSK}_i)$ where

$$\text{wmCT}_i \leftarrow \text{wmEnc}(\text{wmEK}_i, (\mathbf{y}_i, \{\mathbf{x}_{i,j}, \mathbf{z}_{i,j}\}_{j \in [N_i]})), \quad \text{abSK}_i \leftarrow \text{abKeyGen}(\text{abMSK}_i, \mathbf{y}_i)$$

KeyGen(MSK, $\{g_i, h_i\}_{i \in [n]}$): It outputs SK as follows:

$$\text{wmSK} \leftarrow \text{wmKeyGen}(\text{wmMSK}_i, \{g_i, h_i\}_{i \in [n]}), \quad (\sigma_1, \ldots, \sigma_n) \leftarrow \text{Share}(\text{wmSK}, n)$$
$$\text{abCT}_i \leftarrow \text{abEnc}(g_i, \sigma_i) \text{ for } i \in [n], \quad \text{SK} = \{\text{abCT}_i\}_{i \in [n]}$$

Dec($\text{CT}_1, \ldots, \text{CT}_n, \text{SK}$): It parse CT_i, SK as $(\text{wmCT}_i, \text{abSK}_i), \{\text{abCT}_i\}_{i \in [n]}$, respectively. If there exists i such that $g_i(\mathbf{y}_i) \neq 0$, it outputs $\perp$. Otherwise, it outputs $[d]_T$ as follows:

$$\sigma'_i = \text{abDec}(\text{abCT}_i, \text{abSK}_i) \text{ for } i \in [n], \quad \text{wmSK}' = \text{Rec}(\sigma'_1, \ldots, \sigma'_n)$$
$$[d]_T = \text{wmDec}(\text{wmCT}_1, \ldots, \text{wmCT}_n, \text{wmSK}')$$

Fig. 3. Attribute-Based MIFE for AWS with Standard Security

Due to the space limitations, we present the proof in the full version.

5 Multi-client FE for Attribute-Weighted Sums

We define multi-client functional encryption, which basically follows the definition in [1]. The essential difference from the definition in [1] is that we add the definition of selective security.

Definition 5.1 (Multi-client Functional Encryption). Let $\mathcal{F}$ be a function family such that, for all $f \in \mathcal{F}$, $f : \mathcal{X}^n \rightarrow \mathcal{Z}$. Let $\mathcal{L}$ be a label space. An MCFE scheme for $\mathcal{F}$ and $\mathcal{L}$ consists of four algorithms.

Setup($1^\lambda, 1^n$) : It takes a security parameter 1^λ and a number 1^n of slots, and outputs a public parameter PP, encryption keys $\{EK_i\}_{i \in [n]}$, a master secret key MSK. The other algorithms implicitly take PP.

Enc(EK_i, x_i, L): It takes EK_i, an index $i \in [n]$, $x_i \in \mathcal{X}$, and a label L and outputs a ciphertext CT_i.

KeyGen(MSK, f): It takes MSK and $f \in \mathcal{F}$, and outputs a secret key SK.

Dec($CT_1, \ldots, CT_n, SK$): It takes $CT_1, \ldots, CT_n$ and SK, and outputs a decryption value $d \in \mathcal{Z}$ or a symbol $\perp$.

Correctness. An MCFE scheme is correct if it satisfies the following condition. For all $\lambda, n \in \mathbb{N}$, $(x_1, \ldots, x_n) \in \mathcal{X}^n$, $f \in \mathcal{F}$, $L \in \mathcal{L}$, we have

$$
\Pr \left[d = f(x_1, \ldots, x_n) : \begin{array}{l} (PP, \{EK_i\}, MSK) \leftarrow Setup(1^\lambda, 1^n) \\ CT_i \leftarrow Enc(EK_i, x_i, L) \text{ for } i \in [n] \\ SK \leftarrow KeyGen(MSK, f) \\ d = Dec(CT_1, \ldots, , CT_n, SK) \end{array} \right] = 1.
$$

Security. We consider the case where each $x_i \in \mathcal{X}$ consists of a public part $x_{i,\text{pub}}$ and a private part $x_{i,\text{priv}}$, i.e., $x_i = (x_{i,\text{pub}}, x_{i,\text{priv}})$. An MCFE scheme is xx-yy-partially-hiding (xx $\in \{\text{sel, sta, adt}\}$, yy $\in \{\text{any, pos}\}$) if for every stateful PPT adversary $\mathcal{A}$, there exists a negligible function negl such that for all $\lambda, n \in \mathbb{N}$, the following holds

$$
\Pr \left[\beta = \beta' : \begin{array}{l} \beta \leftarrow \{0,1\} \\ (PP, \{EK_i\}, MSK) \leftarrow Setup(1^\lambda, 1^n) \\ \beta' \leftarrow \mathcal{A}^{QCor(), QEnc^\beta(), KeyGen(MSK, \cdot)}(PP) \end{array} \right] \leq \frac{1}{2} + negl(\lambda)
$$

where QCor(i) outputs EK_i, and $QEnc^\beta(i, x_i^0, x_i^1, L)$ outputs Enc(EK_i, x_i^β, L). Let $q_{c,i,L}$ be the numbers of queries of the forms of $QEnc^\beta(i, *, *, L)$. Let $\mathcal{HS}$ be the set of parties on which the adversary has not queried QCor at the end of the game, and $\mathcal{CS} = [n] \backslash \mathcal{HS}$. Then, the admissible adversary's queries must satisfy the following conditions.

- For $i \in \mathcal{CS}$, the queries $QEnc^\beta(i, x_i^0, x_i^1, L)$ must satisfy $x_i^0 = x_i^1$.
- For $i \in \mathcal{HS}$, the queries $QEnc^\beta(i, x_i^0, x_i^1, L)$ must satisfy $x_{i,\text{pub}}^0 = x_{i,\text{pub}}^1$.
- $f(x_1^0, \ldots, x_n^0) = f(x_1^1, \ldots, x_n^1)$ for all sequences $(x_1^0, \ldots, x_n^0, x_1^1, \ldots, x_n^1, f, L)$ that satisfy the two conditions:
  - For all $i \in [n]$, $[QEnc^\beta(i, x_i^0, x_i^1, L)$ is queried and $i \in \mathcal{HS}]$ or $[x_i^0 = x_i^1 \in \mathcal{X}_i$ and $i \in \mathcal{CS}]$.
  - KeyGen(MSK, f) is queried.
- When xx = sta: the adversary cannot query QCor after querying QEnc or KeyGen even once.
- When xx = sel: the adversary must make all queries to QCor and QEnc in one shot. That is, first it outputs $(\mathcal{CS}, \{i, x_i^0, x_i^1, L\})$ and obtains the response: $(\{EK_i\}_{i \in \mathcal{CS}}, \{Enc(EK_i, x_i^\beta, L)\})$. Only after the one-shot query, the adversary can query KeyGen adaptively.

– When yy = pos: for each $L \in \mathcal{L}$, either $q_{c,i,L} > 0$ for all $i \in \mathcal{HS}$ or $q_{c,i,L} = 0$ for all $i \in \mathcal{HS}$[8].

First, we formally define MCFE for AWS.

Definition 5.2 (MCFE for Attribute-Weighted Sums). MCFE for Attribute-Weighted Sums (AWS) is a class of MCFE (Definition 5.1) that supports the following functionality. Let $\mathbb{G} = (p, G_1, G_2, G_T, g_1, g_2, e)$ be bilinear groups. Let $\mathcal{X} = \bigcup_{i \in \mathbb{N}} (\mathbb{Z}_p^{n_0} \times \mathbb{Z}_p^{n_1})^i$ be a message space. Let $\mathcal{F} = (\mathcal{F}_{n_0,n_1}^{ABP})^n$ be a family of functions, where $(f_1, \ldots, f_n) \in \mathcal{F}$ represents the function $f' : \mathcal{X}^n \to G_T$ defined as

$$f'(\{\mathbf{x}_{1,j}, \mathbf{z}_{1,j}\}_{j \in [N_1]}, \ldots, \{\mathbf{x}_{n,j}, \mathbf{z}_{n,j}\}_{j \in [N_n]}) = [\sum_{i \in [n]} \sum_{j \in [N_i]} \langle f_i(\mathbf{x}_{i,j}), \mathbf{z}_{i,j} \rangle]_T.$$

5.1 Construction

Let aFE = (aSetup, aEnc, aKeyGen, aDec) be an FE scheme for AWSw/IP. Let $\mathsf{PRF}^\mathsf{K} : \mathcal{L} \to \mathbb{Z}_p^k$ be a PRF with key space $\mathcal{K}$. Let k be the parameter for the MDDH_k assumption. Construction of our MCFE scheme for AWS is given in Fig. 4.

$\mathsf{Setup}(1^\lambda, 1^n)$: It runs $\mathsf{aPP}_i, \mathsf{aMSK}_i \leftarrow \mathsf{aSetup}(1^\lambda)$ for $i \in [n]$, chooses $\mathsf{K}_{i,j} \leftarrow \mathcal{K}$ for $i,j \in [n], i < j$, and sets $\mathsf{K}_{i,j} = \mathsf{K}_{j,i}$ for $j < i$. It outputs

$$PP = \{\mathsf{aPP}_i\}_{i \in [n]}, \ \mathsf{EK}_i = (\mathsf{aMSK}_i, \{\mathsf{K}_{i,j}\}_{j \in [n] \setminus \{i\}}) \text{ for } i \in [n], \ \mathsf{MSK} = \{\mathsf{EK}_i\}_{i \in [n]}$$

$\mathsf{Enc}(\mathsf{EK}_i, L, x_i = \{\mathbf{x}_{i,j}, \mathbf{z}_{i,j}\}_{j \in [N_i]})$: It computes $\mathbf{v}_{L,i} = \sum_{j \in [n] \setminus \{i\}} (-1)^{j < i} \mathsf{PRF}^{\mathsf{K}_{i,j}}(L)$ and outputs

$$\mathsf{CT}_i = \mathsf{aCT}_i \leftarrow \mathsf{aEnc}(\mathsf{aMSK}_i, x_i, [(\mathbf{v}_{L,i}, 0)]_1).$$

$\mathsf{KeyGen}(\mathsf{MSK}, \{f_i\}_{i \in [n]})$: It samples $\mathbf{s} \leftarrow \mathbb{Z}_p^k$ and outputs $\mathsf{SK} = \{\mathsf{aSK}_i\}_{i \in [n]}$ where

$$\mathsf{aSK}_i \leftarrow \mathsf{aKeyGen}(\mathsf{aMSK}_i, f_i, [(\mathbf{s}, 0)]_2).$$

$\mathsf{Dec}(\mathsf{CT}_1, \ldots, \mathsf{CT}_n, \mathsf{SK})$: It parse $\mathsf{CT}_i, \mathsf{SK}$ as $\mathsf{aCT}_i, \{\mathsf{aSK}_i\}_{i \in [n]}$, respectively. It computes $[d_i]_T = \mathsf{aDec}(\mathsf{aCT}_i, \mathsf{aSK}_i)$ for $i \in [n]$, and outputs $[d]_T = \sum_{i \in [n]} [d_i]_T$.

Fig. 4. Multi-Client FE for AWS

Correctness and Security. Due to the correctness of aFE, we have

$$d_i = \sum_{j \in [N_i]} \langle f(\mathbf{x}_{i,j}), \mathbf{z}_{i,j} \rangle + \langle \mathbf{v}_{L,i}, \mathbf{s} \rangle$$

---

[8] We can covert a xx-pos-partially-hiding scheme to xx-any-partially-hiding scheme generically [1].

Hence $d = \sum_{i \in [n]} \sum_{j \in [N_i]} \langle f(\mathbf{x}_{i,j}), \mathbf{z}_{i,j} \rangle$ since $\sum_{i \in [n]} \langle \mathbf{v}_{L,i}, \mathbf{s} \rangle = 0$.
We argue security via the following theorem.

Theorem 5.1. *If* aFE *is partially function-hiding, and the MDDH$_k$ assumption holds in* $\mathbb{G}$, *then the proposed MCFE scheme for AWS is sel-pos-partially-hiding as per Definition 5.1.*

Due to space constraints, we present the proof in the full version.

References

1. Abdalla, M., Benhamouda, F., Gay, R.: From single-input to multi-client inner-product functional encryption. In: Galbraith, S.D., Moriai, S. (eds.) ASIACRYPT 2019. LNCS, vol. 11923, pp. 552–582. Springer, Cham (2019). https://doi.org/10.1007/978-3-030-34618-8_19

2. Abdalla, M., Bourse, F., De Caro, A., Pointcheval, D.: Simple functional encryption schemes for inner products. In: Katz, J. (ed.) PKC 2015. LNCS, vol. 9020, pp. 733–751. Springer, Heidelberg (2015). https://doi.org/10.1007/978-3-662-46447-2_33

3. Abdalla, M., Catalano, D., Fiore, D., Gay, R., Ursu, B.: Multi-input functional encryption for inner products: function-hiding realizations and constructions without pairings. In: Shacham, H., Boldyreva, A. (eds.) CRYPTO 2018, Part I. LNCS, vol. 10991, pp. 597–627. Springer, Cham (2018). https://doi.org/10.1007/978-3-319-96884-1_20

4. Abdalla, M., Catalano, D., Gay, R., Ursu, B.: Inner-product functional encryption with fine-grained access control. In: Moriai, S., Wang, H. (eds.) ASIACRYPT 2020, Part III. LNCS, vol. 12493, pp. 467–497. Springer, Cham (2020). https://doi.org/10.1007/978-3-030-64840-4_16

5. Abdalla, M., Gay, R., Raykova, M., Wee, H.: Multi-input inner-product functional encryption from pairings. In: Coron, J.-S., Nielsen, J.B. (eds.) EUROCRYPT 2017, Part I. LNCS, vol. 10210, pp. 601–626. Springer, Cham (2017). https://doi.org/10.1007/978-3-319-56620-7_21

6. Abdalla, M., Gong, J., Wee, H.: Functional encryption for attribute-weighted sums from k-lin. In: Micciancio, D., Ristenpart, T. (eds.) CRYPTO 2020. LNCS, vol. 12170, pp. 685–716. Springer, Cham (2020). https://doi.org/10.1007/978-3-030-56784-2_23

7. Agrawal, S., Boyen, X., Vaikuntanathan, V., Voulgaris, P., Wee, H.: Functional encryption for threshold functions (or fuzzy IBE) from lattices. In: Fischlin, M., Buchmann, J., Manulis, M. (eds.) PKC 2012. LNCS, vol. 7293, pp. 280–297. Springer, Heidelberg (2012). https://doi.org/10.1007/978-3-642-30057-8_17

8. Agrawal, S., Clear, M., Frieder, O., Garg, S., O'Neill, A., Thaler, J.: Ad hoc multi-input functional encryption. In: Vidick, T. (ed.) ITCS 2020, vol. 151, pp. 40:1–40:41. LIPIcs (2020). https://doi.org/10.4230/LIPIcs.ITCS.2020.40

9. Agrawal, S., Freeman, D.M., Vaikuntanathan, V.: Functional encryption for inner product predicates from learning with errors. In: Lee, D.H., Wang, X. (eds.) ASIACRYPT 2011. LNCS, vol. 7073, pp. 21–40. Springer, Heidelberg (2011). https://doi.org/10.1007/978-3-642-25385-0_2

10. Agrawal, S., Goyal, R., Tomida, J.: Multi-party functional encryption. In: Nissim, K., Waters, B. (eds.) TCC 2021, Part II. LNCS, vol. 13043, pp. 224–255. Springer, Cham (2021). https://doi.org/10.1007/978-3-030-90453-1_8

11. Agrawal, S., Goyal, R., Tomida, J.: Multi-input quadratic functional encryption: Stronger security, broader functionality. In: Kiltz, E., Vaikuntanathan, V. (eds.) TCC 2022. LNCS, vol. 13747, pp. 711–740. Springer, Cham (2022). https://doi.org/10.1007/978-3-031-22318-1_25

12. Agrawal, S., Yadav, A., Yamada, S.: Multi-input attribute based encryption and predicate encryption. In: Dodis, Y., Shrimpton, T. (eds.) CRYPTO 2022. LNCS, vol. 13507, pp. 590–621. Springer, Cham (2022). https://doi.org/10.1007/978-3-031-15802-5_21

13. Bethencourt, J., Sahai, A., Waters, B.: Ciphertext-policy attribute-based encryption. In: 2007 IEEE Symposium on Security and Privacy, pp. 321–334. IEEE Computer Society Press (2007). https://doi.org/10.1109/SP.2007.11

14. Boneh, D., et al.: Fully key-homomorphic encryption, arithmetic circuit ABE and compact garbled circuits. In: Nguyen, P.Q., Oswald, E. (eds.) EUROCRYPT 2014. LNCS, vol. 8441, pp. 533–556. Springer, Heidelberg (2014). https://doi.org/10.1007/978-3-642-55220-5_30

15. Boneh, D., Sahai, A., Waters, B.: Functional encryption: definitions and challenges. In: Ishai, Y. (ed.) TCC 2011. LNCS, vol. 6597, pp. 253–273. Springer, Heidelberg (2011). https://doi.org/10.1007/978-3-642-19571-6_16

16. Chase, M.: Multi-authority attribute based encryption. In: Vadhan, S.P. (ed.) TCC 2007. LNCS, vol. 4392, pp. 515–534. Springer, Heidelberg (2007). https://doi.org/10.1007/978-3-540-70936-7_28

17. Chotard, J., Dufour Sans, E., Gay, R., Phan, D.H., Pointcheval, D.: Decentralized multi-client functional encryption for inner product. In: Peyrin, T., Galbraith, S. (eds.) ASIACRYPT 2018, Part II. LNCS, vol. 11273, pp. 703–732. Springer, Cham (2018). https://doi.org/10.1007/978-3-030-03329-3_24

18. Chotard, J., Dufour Sans, E., Gay, R., Phan, D.H., Pointcheval, D.: Multi-client functional encryption with repetition for inner product. Cryptology ePrint Archive, Report 2018/1021 (2018). https://eprint.iacr.org/2018/1021

19. Chotard, J., Dufour-Sans, E., Gay, R., Phan, D.H., Pointcheval, D.: Dynamic decentralized functional encryption. In: Micciancio, D., Ristenpart, T. (eds.) CRYPTO 2020, Part I. LNCS, vol. 12170, pp. 747–775. Springer, Cham (2020). https://doi.org/10.1007/978-3-030-56784-2_25

20. Ciampi, M., Siniscalchi, L., Waldner, H.: Multi-client functional encryption for separable functions. In: Garay, J.A. (ed.) PKC 2021, Part I. LNCS, vol. 12710, pp. 724–753. Springer, Cham (2021). https://doi.org/10.1007/978-3-030-75245-3_26

21. Datta, P., Okamoto, T., Tomida, J.: Full-hiding (unbounded) multi-input inner product functional encryption from the k-linear assumption. In: Abdalla, M., Dahab, R. (eds.) PKC 2018, Part II. LNCS, vol. 10770, pp. 245–277. Springer, Cham (2018). https://doi.org/10.1007/978-3-319-76581-5_9

22. Datta, P., Pal, T.: (Compact) adaptively secure FE for attribute-weighted sums from k-Lin. In: Tibouchi, M., Wang, H. (eds.) ASIACRYPT 2021, Part IV. LNCS, vol. 13093, pp. 434–467. Springer, Cham (2021). https://doi.org/10.1007/978-3-030-92068-5_15

23. Francati, D., Friolo, D., Malavolta, G., Venturi, D.: Multi-key and multi-input predicate encryption from learning with errors. In: Hazay, C., Stam, M. (eds.) EUROCRYPT 2023. LNCS, vol. 14006, pp. 573–604. Springer, Cham (2023). https://doi.org/10.1007/978-3-031-30620-4_19

24. Goldwasser, S., et al.: Multi-input functional encryption. In: Nguyen, P.Q., Oswald, E. (eds.) EUROCRYPT 2014. LNCS, vol. 8441, pp. 578–602. Springer, Heidelberg (2014). https://doi.org/10.1007/978-3-642-55220-5_32

25. Gorbunov, S., Vaikuntanathan, V., Wee, H.: Functional encryption with bounded collusions via multi-party computation. In: Safavi-Naini, R., Canetti, R. (eds.) CRYPTO 2012. LNCS, vol. 7417, pp. 162–179. Springer, Heidelberg (2012). https://doi.org/10.1007/978-3-642-32009-5_11

26. Gorbunov, S., Vaikuntanathan, V., Wee, H.: Attribute-based encryption for circuits. In: Boneh, D., Roughgarden, T., Feigenbaum, J. (eds.) 45th ACM STOC, pp. 545–554. ACM Press (2013). https://doi.org/10.1145/2488608.2488677

27. Gorbunov, S., Vaikuntanathan, V., Wee, H.: Predicate encryption for circuits from LWE. In: Gennaro, R., Robshaw, M. (eds.) CRYPTO 2015. LNCS, vol. 9216, pp. 503–523. Springer, Heidelberg (2015). https://doi.org/10.1007/978-3-662-48000-7_25

28. Goyal, V., Pandey, O., Sahai, A., Waters, B.: Attribute-based encryption for fine-grained access control of encrypted data. In: Juels, A., Wright, R.N., De Capitani di Vimercati, S. (eds.) ACM CCS 2006, pp. 89–98. ACM Press (2006). https://doi.org/10.1145/1180405.1180418, available as Cryptology ePrint Archive Report 2006/309

29. Ishai, Y., Wee, H.: Partial garbling schemes and their applications. In: Esparza, J., Fraigniaud, P., Husfeldt, T., Koutsoupias, E. (eds.) ICALP 2014, Part I. LNCS, vol. 8572, pp. 650–662. Springer, Heidelberg (2014). https://doi.org/10.1007/978-3-662-43948-7_54

30. Katz, J., Sahai, A., Waters, B.: Predicate encryption supporting disjunctions, polynomial equations, and inner products. In: Smart, N. (ed.) EUROCRYPT 2008. LNCS, vol. 4965, pp. 146–162. Springer, Heidelberg (2008). https://doi.org/10.1007/978-3-540-78967-3_9

31. Kursawe, K., Danezis, G., Kohlweiss, M.: Privacy-friendly aggregation for the smart-grid. In: Fischer-Hübner, S., Hopper, N. (eds.) PETS 2011. LNCS, vol. 6794, pp. 175–191. Springer, Heidelberg (2011). https://doi.org/10.1007/978-3-642-22263-4_10

32. Lin, H., Luo, J.: Compact adaptively secure ABE from k-Lin: beyond NC^1 and towards NL. In: Canteaut, A., Ishai, Y. (eds.) EUROCRYPT 2020, Part III. LNCS, vol. 12107, pp. 247–277. Springer, Cham (2020). https://doi.org/10.1007/978-3-030-45727-3_9

33. Lin, H., Luo, J.: Succinct and adaptively secure ABE for ABP from k-Lin. In: Moriai, S., Wang, H. (eds.) ASIACRYPT 2020, Part III. LNCS, vol. 12493, pp. 437–466. Springer, Cham (2020). https://doi.org/10.1007/978-3-030-64840-4_15

34. Nguyen, K., Phan, D.H., Pointcheval, D.: Multi-client functional encryption with fine-grained access control. In: Agrawal, S., Lin, D. (eds.) ASIACRYPT 2022. vol. 13791, pp. 95–125. Springer, Cham (2022). https://doi.org/10.1007/978-3-031-22963-3_4

35. Sahai, A., Waters, B.: Fuzzy identity-based encryption. In: Cramer, R. (ed.) EUROCRYPT 2005. LNCS, vol. 3494, pp. 457–473. Springer, Heidelberg (2005). https://doi.org/10.1007/11426639_27

36. Tomida, J.: Tightly secure inner product functional encryption: multi-input and function-hiding constructions. In: Galbraith, S.D., Moriai, S. (eds.) ASIACRYPT 2019, Part III. LNCS, vol. 11923, pp. 459–488. Springer, Cham (2019). https://doi.org/10.1007/978-3-030-34618-8_16

37. Waters, B.: Functional encryption for regular languages. In: Safavi-Naini, R., Canetti, R. (eds.) CRYPTO 2012. LNCS, vol. 7417, pp. 218–235. Springer, Heidelberg (2012). https://doi.org/10.1007/978-3-642-32009-5_14

38. Wee, H.: Attribute-hiding predicate encryption in bilinear groups, revisited. In: Kalai, Y., Reyzin, L. (eds.) TCC 2017, Part I. LNCS, vol. 10677, pp. 206–233. Springer, Cham (2017). https://doi.org/10.1007/978-3-319-70500-2_8
39. Wee, H.: Attribute-hiding predicate encryption in bilinear groups, revisited. In: Kalai, Y., Reyzin, L. (eds.) TCC 2017. LNCS, vol. 10677, pp. 206–233. Springer, Cham (2017). https://doi.org/10.1007/978-3-319-70500-2_8

How to Use (Plain) Witness Encryption: Registered ABE, Flexible Broadcast, and More

Cody Freitag[1]($\boxtimes$), Brent Waters[2,3], and David J. Wu[2]

[1] Boston University, Boston, USA
freitag@bu.edu
[2] UT Austin, Austin, USA
{bwaters,dwu4}@cs.utexas.edu
[3] NTT Research, Sunnyvale, USA

Abstract. Witness encryption is a generalization of public-key encryption where the public key can be any NP statement x and the associated decryption key is any witness w for x. While early constructions of witness encryption relied on multilinear maps and indistinguishability obfuscation ($i\mathcal{O}$), recent works have provided direct constructions of witness encryption that are more efficient than $i\mathcal{O}$ (and also seem unlikely to yield $i\mathcal{O}$). Motivated by this progress, we revisit the possibility of using witness encryption to realize advanced cryptographic primitives previously known only in "obfustopia."

In this work, we give new constructions of *trustless* encryption systems from *plain* witness encryption (in conjunction with the learning-with-errors assumption): (1) flexible broadcast encryption (a broadcast encryption scheme where users choose their *own* secret keys and users can encrypt to an *arbitrary* set of public keys); and (2) registered attribute-based encryption (a system where users choose their own keys and then register their public key together with a set of attributes with a deterministic and transparent key curator). Both primitives were previously only known from $i\mathcal{O}$. We also show how to use our techniques to obtain an *optimal* broadcast encryption scheme in the random oracle model.

Underlying our constructions is a novel technique for using witness encryption based on a new primitive which we call *function-binding hash functions*. Whereas a somewhat statistically binding hash function statistically binds a digest to a few bits of the input, a function-binding hash function statistically binds a digest to the *output* of a function of the inputs. As we demonstrate in this work, function-binding hash functions provide us new ways to leverage the power of plain witness encryption and use it as the foundation of advanced cryptographic primitives. Finally, we show how to build function-binding hash functions for the class of disjunctions of block functions from leveled homomorphic encryption; this in combination with witness encryption yields our main results.

1 Introduction

In the last decade, indistinguishability obfuscation ($i\mathcal{O}$) [5,31] has emerged as a central hub for cryptography, and in combination with one-way functions or

© International Association for Cryptologic Research 2023
H. Handschuh and A. Lysyanskaya (Eds.): CRYPTO 2023, LNCS 14084, pp. 498–531, 2023.
https://doi.org/10.1007/978-3-031-38551-3_16

somewhere statistically binding hash functions [47], have yielded solutions to a broad range of cryptographic problems [3,7,13,19,22,30,49,53]; we refer to [48, Corollary 1.1] for a more comprehensive list. Witness encryption [32] is another cryptographic notion that is often considered alongside indistinguishability obfuscation, and has been used successfully to construct a number of cryptographic primitives such as public-key encryption, identity-based encryption, attribute-based encryption [32], oblivious transfer [4], laconic arguments [9,27], and null-$i\mathcal{O}$ [41,58]. However, compared to indistinguishability obfuscation, there has been significantly less success in leveraging witness encryption to realize other cryptographic notions, and indeed, many of the notions implied by witness encryption can be achieved directly from standard number-theoretic or lattice-based assumptions.

Witness Encryption. Intuitively, witness encryption [32] is a generalization of public-key encryption where the public key can be any NP statement x and the associated decryption key is any witness w for x. Here, a user can encrypt a message m with respect to the statement x and anyone who knows a witness w for x can decrypt. The security requirement is that if the statement x is false, then the message is computationally hidden.

Although witness encryption appears to be a substantially weaker primitive than $i\mathcal{O}$ (both in terms of its applications and with respect to black-box separations [35]), early constructions nonetheless either relied on $i\mathcal{O}$ [31] or techniques that sufficed for $i\mathcal{O}$ (e.g., assumptions over multilinear maps [32,36]). This state of affairs changed recently with several works providing constructions from lattice-based assumptions [21,54,55] or suggesting new routes from group-based approaches [6]. Of particular note, the recent results [54,55] construct witness encryption from the "evasive LWE" assumption, a new knowledge assumption on lattices [54,57]. These works give a direct construction of witness encryption that is significantly more efficient than existing $i\mathcal{O}$ approaches. Moreover, the current techniques do not seem to extend to give $i\mathcal{O}$.

This Work: Cryptography from *Plain* Witness Encryption. Motivated by the recent progress in constructing witness encryption, our goal in this work is to revisit the possibility of using witness encryption to realize advanced cryptographic primitives. Much like how the punctured programming framework [53] and notions like somewhere statistically binding hash functions [47] allowed us to leverage the power of $i\mathcal{O}$, our goal is to develop analogous techniques in the setting of (plain) witness encryption. Previous approaches to use witness encryption for realizing new cryptographic primitives have focused on augmenting witness encryption with additional properties such as "position-hiding" [36,43] or "extractability" [27,40]. However, positional witness encryption is only known from $i\mathcal{O}$ [36,43] while extractable witness encryption currently relies on a knowledge assumption over multilinear maps or the stronger notion of differing-inputs obfuscation [40]. Moreover, the recent advancements in construction witness encryption seem insufficient for realizing these stronger notions. As such, we focus on techniques that use *plain* witness encryption.

Function-Binding Hash Functions. In this work, we introduce a new cryptographic primitive called a *function-binding hash function*. Similar to how somewhere statistically binding (SSB) hash functions [47] statistically bind to a few bits of an *input* to the hash function, our function-binding hash function statistically binds to the *output* of a *function* of the inputs. In fact, we can view SSB hash functions as a special case of function-binding hash functions for the class of index functions (see Remark 3.2). Similar to the setting of SSB hash function, a function-binding hash function should allow a user to *locally* open one or more bits of the input. The size of the opening should be small compared to the size of the input.

To illustrate the function-binding property, consider a (keyed) hash function H that is statistically binding for the OR function. Suppose that $\mathsf{dig} \leftarrow H(\mathsf{hk}, b_1, \ldots, b_n)$ where hk is the hash key and $b_1 = \cdots = b_n = 0$. If H is (statistically) function-binding for the OR function, then it should not be possible to locally open *any* index i to a value $b_i' = 1$. This is because the output of the OR function on all inputs $(b_1', \ldots, b_n')$ is $1 \neq 0$, irrespective of the values of b_j' for $j \neq i$. More generally, a function-binding hash function only supports local openings to values that are consistent with the output of the associated function (i.e., the locally-opened value(s) can be extended into an input to the function that maps to the value associated with the digest).

We provide a formal definition of this notion in Sect. 3 and a high-level overview in Sect. 1.1. We then show how to construct a function-binding hash function using leveled homomorphic encryption, which can in turn be based on standard lattice assumptions [14,15,17,37]. Our construction here follows a similar structure as the construction of somewhere statistically binding hash functions [47] from leveled homomorphic encryption.

Our Results. Using function-binding hash functions together with plain witness encryption, we are able to realize new *trustless* encryption notions like flexible broadcast encryption and registered attribute-based encryption (for general policies) [46] without indistinguishability obfuscation. These examples are intended to illustrate the usefulness of function-binding hash functions in conjunction with witness encryption, and we expect to see further applications in the future. We summarize our main results below:

- **Flexible broadcast encryption.** In a flexible broadcast encryption scheme, users generate their own public/private key-pair $(\mathsf{pk}, \mathsf{sk})$ (much like in vanilla public-key encryption) and then post their public key pk to a public bulletin board. The encryption algorithm takes a collection of user public keys $S = (\mathsf{pk}_1, \ldots, \mathsf{pk}_n)$ along with a message m and outputs a single ciphertext ct that can be decrypted by any user who possesses a secret key corresponding to a public key in the broadcast set S. The size of the ciphertext ct scales *polylogarithmically* with the size of the broadcast set S. Flexible broadcast encryption generalizes both the traditional notion of broadcast encryption [28] which assumes a central *trusted* authority issues keys to users as well as the notion of distributed broadcast encryption [13]. In distributed broadcast encryption, users generate their own public and private keys, but the syntax stipulates that each user is associated with a particular "index" (like in standard broadcast encryption); in turn, one can only encrypt to users associated with different indices. Flexible broadcast encryption eliminates all user coordination and supports encryption to an arbitrary set of user public keys. Previously, distributed broadcast encryption was only known from $i\mathcal{O}$ [13]. In this work, we show how to construct flexible broadcast encryption from plain witness encryption and function-binding hash functions (which implies a distributed broadcast encryption scheme). Previously, it was not even known how to obtain *vanilla* broadcast encryption from witness encryption; instead, previous approaches relied on the stronger notion of positional witness encryption [36,43].

– **Registered attribute-based encryption.** A second application we show is to registered attribute-based encryption [46]. Much like how flexible broadcast encryption removes the trusted key issuer from broadcast encryption, registered ABE removes the trusted key issuer from traditional ABE [44,52]. In the registered ABE model, instead of a key issuer generating decryption keys for user attributes, users instead generate their own public/secret keys and then *register* their public key along with their attributes with a key curator. The key curator in this case is a deterministic and transparent algorithm that is responsible for aggregating the keys and attributes for the different users into a short master public key (whose size is polylogarithmic in the number of registered users). The aggregated public key functions as a public key for a standard ABE scheme. Since the key curator maintains no long-term secrets and can be publicly audited, registered ABE serves as a new paradigm for enabling the access-control capabilities of ABE without introducing a trusted key-issuing authority into the picture. Previously, the work of [46] showed how to construct registered ABE for an a priori bounded number of users using pairing-based assumptions in a model with a structured common reference string, as well as a scheme for an unbounded number of users in the common *random* string model from $i\mathcal{O}$. In this work, we show how to obtain a registered ABE scheme with the same properties as the previous construction from $i\mathcal{O}$ using plain witness encryption and function-binding hash functions.

– **Optimal broadcast encryption.** As an additional application, we show how to adapt our flexible broadcast encryption scheme to obtain an *optimal* broadcast encryption scheme (in the traditional centralized model with a trusted key issuer) in the random oracle model from plain witness encryption and function-binding hash functions. An optimal broadcast encryption scheme is one where all of the scheme parameters (public key size, secret key size, and ciphertext size) all scale polylogarithmically with the number of users n, and was previously known from multilinear maps [12], *positional* witness encryption [43], on combinations of (non-falsifiable or idealized) pairing-based and lattice-based assumptions [1,2], or from new (non-falsifiable) lattice assumptions [18,57].

By instantiating the underlying witness encryption scheme with the recent constructions [54,55] based on evasive LWE, we realize for the first time flexible (and distributed) broadcast encryption and registered ABE for general policies from lattice assumptions. Previously, these were only known from $i\mathcal{O}$. As we elaborate in Sect. 1.1, our approach to the above problem is to start from an approach that relies on obfuscation and SSB hash functions, and then roughly speaking, replace $i\mathcal{O}$ with plain witness encryption and the SSB hash function with a function-binding hash function. In some sense, we are able to substitute the strong notion of $i\mathcal{O}$ with the comparatively weaker notion of witness encryption by using the more expressive notion of function-binding hash functions in place of an SSB hash function. Broadly speaking, we are optimistic that the techniques we develop will allow us to use witness encryption in place of $i\mathcal{O}$ in other settings, and thus, bring us closer to simpler and more practical realizations of many advanced cryptographic primitives.

Why Witness Encryption? Since witness encryption is often regarded as an "obfustopia" primitive, a natural question one might ask is whether it is interesting to study cryptographic constructions from plain witness encryption. We believe the answer is yes. As noted previously, recent advances have introduced new routes [6,16] and constructions [21,54,55] for building (plain) witness encryption in ways that do not seem sufficient for indistinguishability obfuscation (nor stronger forms of witness encryption). Moreover, these constructions are simpler and far more efficient than all existing constructions of indistinguishability obfuscation. Thus, witness encryption can be an easier primitive to build, and provide a more efficient path towards realizing advanced cryptographic notions that are currently only known from obfuscation. In more detail, [16] show how to construct a non-trivial exponentially-efficient witness encryption assuming sub-exponential hardness of the standard learning with errors (LWE) assumption, and [6] show how to construct witness encryption in the generic (pairing-free) group model under the hypothesis that approximating the minimal distance in linear codes is NP-hard (for super-logarithmic approximation factors). Recent works [54,55] construct witness encryption under a new "evasive LWE" assumption, a new knowledge assumption that conjectures hardness of LWE even given some trapdoor information. Moreover, at least with respect to black-box separations [35], witness encryption is a demonstrably weaker notion than indistinguishability obfuscation.

Paper Organization

In Sect. 1.1, we give a technical overview for our main results and contributions. We overview some preliminary notation and define witness encryption in Sect. 2. Due to space limitations, we use the main body of the paper to focus on our definition and construction of function binding hash functions (Sect. 3, with associated proofs deferred to the full version of this paper [29]) and how it is used with witness encryption to construct distributed broadcast encryption (Sect. 4). We define and construct (slotted) registered ABE from witness encryption and function binding hash in Sect. 6, with the definitions of selective security and proofs of correctness and security of our construction provided in the full version.

The full details for the rest of our results and contributions are provided in the full version of this paper [29], along with additional preliminaries and definitions.

1.1 Technical Overview

In this section, we provide a general overview of our notion of function-binding hash functions and how to combine it with witness encryption to realize new cryptographic applications. To demonstrate our approach, we first introduce our notion of flexible broadcast encryption (which generalizes the notion of distributed broadcast encryption from [13]) and describe a simple construction of flexible broadcast encryption from indistinguishability obfuscation and somewhere statistically binding hash functions. We then show how we instantiate an analogous template using witness encryption and function-binding hash functions.

Flexible Broadcast Encryption. In a traditional broadcast encryption scheme [28], each user is associated with an index $i \in [n]$ and a broadcaster can encrypt a message to a set of recipients $S \subseteq [n]$. Any user in the set S can use their private key to decrypt the encrypted broadcast, while users outside the set S should learn no information about the message (even if they combine their keys together). The efficiency requirement is that the size of the ciphertext should be sublinear in the size of S (ideally, polylogarithmic in $|S|$). Note that we assume that the decrypter knows the set S. In traditional broadcast encryption, a central authority is needed to issue the decryption keys to users. The central authority is fully trusted, and if compromised, their long-term secret key can be used to decrypt all ciphertexts. Broadcast encryption is a well-studied primitive and construction are known from a broad range of cryptographic assumptions [1,2,8,10–13,18,20,25,28,38,43,45, 51,56,57].

Distributed broadcast encryption [13] provides an elegant approach to remove the trusted key issuer in the setting of broadcast encryption. Here, instead of a central authority issuing keys, users generate their own key. Like broadcast encryption, each user in a distributed broadcast encryption is still associated with an index $i \in [n]$, and the implicit assumption is that indices for different users are unique. The encrypter in this case can encrypt a message by specifying a set $S \subseteq [n]$ of user indices. As before, the size of the broadcast ciphertext should be sublinear, or preferably, polylogarithmic, in the number of users in the broadcast set. Anyone in the broadcast set can decrypt using their own secret key. Analogous to broadcast encryption where we assume the decrypter knows the set of users associated with an encrypted broadcast, we assume the decrypter in the distributed broadcast scheme knows the set of public keys associated with the broadcast ciphertext. Unlike the case with traditional broadcast encryption, distributed broadcast is currently only known from $i\mathcal{O}$ [13].

Flexible broadcast encryption is a further generalization of distributed broadcast encryption where we remove the index-dependence for users. Here, users simply generate their public key and post it to the public bulletin board (e.g., a public-key directory). There is no notion of a user "index" and indeed users can generate their keys independently and without any coordination.[1] We do assume that there is a global set of public parameters for the scheme (that users use when generating keys).

An Obfuscation-Based Approach for Flexible Broadcast Encryption. We start by describing a simple approach to construct a flexible broadcast encryption from indistinguishability obfuscation and somewhere statistically binding (SSB) hash functions [47]. The approach we take here is an adaptation of the registered ABE scheme from [46] (rather than the Boneh-Zhandry approach [13] based on a reduction to key-agreement).

- The public parameters $pp = (pk, hk)$ for the scheme contains a public key pk for a standard public-key encryption scheme and a hash key hk for an SSB hash function.
- To join the system, a user samples randomness r and computes an encryption of 1 under pk with randomness r: $c = \mathsf{PKE.Enc}(pk, 1; r)$. The user's public key is the ciphertext c and the decryption key is the randomness r.
- To encrypt a message m to an (ordered) set of public keys $(c_1, \ldots, c_n)$, the encrypter now proceeds as follows:
  - The encrypter starts by hashing the public keys using the SSB hash function to obtain a digest $dig = H(hk, (c_1, \ldots, c_n))$. Recall that in an SSB hash function, one can give a succinct proof (of size $\mathsf{poly}(\lambda, \log n)$ where λ is a security parameter) that the value at index i is c_i (with respect to (hk, dig)).
  - The encrypter now prepares a program $\mathcal{P}$ that has message m, the public parameters $pp = (hk, pk)$, and the digest dig hard-wired inside. The program takes as input an index $i \in [n]$, a public key c, an opening π, and a secret key r and checks the following:
    * **Inclusion in broadcast set:** The opening π is a valid opening for c at index i with respect to (hk, dig).
    * **Knowledge of secret key:** The pair (c, r) is a valid public/secret key-pair: $c = \mathsf{PKE.Enc}(pk, 1; r)$.
    If all of these properties are satisfied, then the program outputs the message m. Otherwise, it outputs $\perp$.
  - The broadcast ciphertext is an obfuscation of program $\mathcal{P}$: $ct \leftarrow i\mathcal{O}(\mathcal{P})$.

---

[1] Note that we can generically obtain a flexible broadcast encryption scheme from a distributed broadcast encryption scheme by having users sample their index randomly. To support a maximum of ℓ users, we would instantiate the scheme with $n = \Omega(\ell^2)$ indices. This is sufficient if the number of users is *a priori* bounded, though it may incur a *quadratic* blowup in the size of some scheme parameters. If the underlying distributed broadcast encryption scheme supports a super-polynomial number of users (i.e., $n = \lambda^{\omega(1)}$), then it directly implies a flexible broadcast encryption for an arbitrary polynomial number of users.

- During decryption, the user know both the ciphertext $\mathsf{ct} = i\mathcal{O}(\mathcal{P})$ and the set of public keys $(c_1, \ldots, c_n)$ associated with ct.[2] Suppose the user's public key is $c_i \in (c_1, \ldots, c_n)$ and let r_i be their secret key. The user starts by computing $\mathsf{dig} = H(\mathsf{hk}, (c_1, \ldots, c_n))$ together with an opening π for (i, c_i) with respect to $(\mathsf{hk}, \mathsf{dig})$. It runs the obfuscated program ct on input (i, c_i, π, r_i).

Correctness of the scheme follows as long as the obfuscation scheme is functionality-preserving. Security follows via a simple hybrid argument:

- In the normal flexible broadcast encryption security game, the challenge ciphertext is an encryption of m to a set $S = (c_1, \ldots, c_n)$, where $c_i = \mathsf{PKE.Enc}(\mathsf{pk}, 1; r)$. Since the adversary cannot be in the broadcast set in the security game, each public key c_i is an *honestly-generated* encryption of 1: $c_i = \mathsf{PKE.Enc}(\mathsf{pk}, 1; r_i)$. We appeal to semantic security of the public-key encryption scheme to replace each c_i with an encryption of 0 (i.e., $c_i = \mathsf{PKE.Enc}(\mathsf{pk}, 0; r_i)$).
- Next, we replace the hash key hk with one that is statistically binding at position 1. This is computationally indistinguishable from the normal hash key if the SSB scheme satisfies index hiding. Now $\mathsf{dig} = H(\mathsf{hk}, (c_1, \ldots, c_n))$ and c_1 is now an encryption of 0. We conclude that every input (i, c, π, r) where $i = 1$ causes the program $\mathcal{P}$ to output $\bot$. This is because the only valid opening for index $i = 1$ is $c = c_1$ (since the hash function is *statistically* binding at index 1). However, c_1 is an encryption of 0, so it cannot be the case that $c_1 = \mathsf{PKE.Enc}(\mathsf{pk}, 1; r)$ by (perfect) correctness of PKE. Then, by $i\mathcal{O}$ security, we can replace $\mathcal{P}$ with an obfuscation of the program $\mathcal{P}_1$ that outputs $\bot$ whenever $i = 1$.
- More generally, we can let $\mathcal{P}_t$ be the program $\mathcal{P}$ that always outputs $\bot$ whenever the input index satisfies $i \leq t$. By the above argument, if we sample hk to be statistically binding at index t, then the obfuscations of programs $\mathcal{P}_{t-1}$ and $\mathcal{P}_t$ are computationally indistinguishable.
- Finally, the program $\mathcal{P}_n$ outputs $\bot$ on all indices $i \leq n$. This program outputs $\bot$ on *all* inputs, so an obfuscation of $\mathcal{P}_n$ is computationally indistinguishable from an obfuscation of the program that outputs $\bot$ on *all* inputs.

In the final hybrid where the ciphertext is an obfuscated program that always outputs $\bot$, the adversary's view is *independent* of the message m, and semantic security holds.

Using Witness Encryption instead of $i\mathcal{O}$**.** Suppose we try to implement the above strategy using witness encryption in place of indistinguishability obfuscation. Observe that the program $\mathcal{P}$ defined above is a program that is checking

---

[2] Note that set of public keys could just be a set of indices if we include a mapping between indices and user public keys (i.e., a public-key directory) as part of the public parameters of the flexible broadcast encryption scheme. This is the setting considered in [13]. More generally, the set of users could admit a succinct description (e.g., "all computer science students") and the decrypter would look up the public keys associated with the members of the set.

membership in an NP language and outputting m if the input is a valid witness. Specifically, we can view the hard-wired components $(\mathsf{hk}, \mathsf{pk}, \mathsf{dig})$ as the statement and the input (i, c, π, r) as the witness. The associated NP relation then checks the inclusion-in-broadcast-set and knowledge-of-secret-key properties defined above. Thus, we can derive the same functionality as above by replacing the obfuscation of $\mathcal{P}$ with a witness encryption of m with respect to the statement $(\mathsf{hk}, \mathsf{pk}, \mathsf{dig})$. Correctness now follows exactly as before.

The challenge is in the security proof. Suppose we try a similar strategy as above where we first replace the public keys $(c_1, \ldots, c_n)$ with encryptions of 0. Let $\mathsf{dig} = H(\mathsf{hk}, (c_1, \ldots, c_n))$ as before. To leverage security of the witness encryption scheme and argue that the message is computationally hidden, we need to show that there does not exist a witness (i, c, π, r) for the statement $(\mathsf{hk}, \mathsf{pk}, \mathsf{dig})$. Certainly, any c where $c \in (c_1, \ldots, c_n)$ cannot be part of a valid witness. However, we cannot rule out inputs where $c \notin (c_1, \ldots, c_n)$ because it is possible for there to *exist* some $c = \mathsf{PKE.Enc}(\mathsf{pk}, 1; r)$ and opening π such that π is a valid opening for (i, c) with respect to $(\mathsf{hk}, \mathsf{dig})$. While finding such an opening is computationally hard (by SSB security), such openings can certainly exist for some *index* $i \in [n]$. The crux of the issue is that SSB hash functions can only bind to a *single* component of the input, whereas to appeal to security of witness encryption, we need to argue that the digest dig rules out invalid openings to *all* indices.

Using $i\mathcal{O}$, the ability to statistically bind to a single index was sufficient to argue security because we are able to "save our progress" within the obfuscated program. Namely, we can iteratively rule out inputs (i, c, π, r) where $i \leq t$, and then just focus on ruling out inputs where $i \leq t+1$. In this step, we only have to consider inputs of the form $(t+1, c, \pi, r)$ which we can handle by programming the SSB hash function to statistically bind on index $t+1$. A similar step-by-step approach does not work if we use witness encryption. While we can certainly embed the threshold t into the NP relation (i.e., only accept witnesses (i, c, π, r) where $i > t$), witness encryption does not provide any hiding property for t in this case. Indeed, the adversary can distinguish between a witness encryption ciphertext encrypted with respect to threshold t and one encrypted with respect to threshold $t+1$. In the case of $i\mathcal{O}$, the thresholds themselves are hidden. In fact, this limitation motivated the formulation of a stronger version of "positional witness encryption" [36,43] which augments witness encryption with an additional "index hiding" property that allows one to secretly embed a threshold within a witness encryption ciphertext. Using positional witness encryption, it is possible to carry out the proof strategy defined above. Unfortunately, positional witness encryption appears to be a much stronger notion than plain witness encryption and the only known instantiations are from $i\mathcal{O}$.

Function-Binding Hash Functions. The key barrier to instantiating the above framework is that SSB hash functions only bind statistically to a *single* input, but to rule out the *existence* of *any* valid tuple (i, c, π, r), we would seemingly need to statistically bind on all inputs simultaneously. The latter is clearly impossible if we require that the digest be compressing. We take a different approach. Instead of statistically binding to part of the *input* to the hash function, we instead statistically bind to the *output* of a function of the inputs. Namely, let $f\colon (\{0,1\}^\ell)^n \to \{0,1\}^t$ be a function. We say that a keyed function H with hash key hk is statistically function-binding for f if for all inputs $x_1, \ldots, x_n \in \{0,1\}^\ell$ and computing $\mathsf{dig} = H(\mathsf{hk}, (x_1, \ldots, x_n))$, there does not exist an opening π for $(j, \hat{x}_j)$ with respect to $(\mathsf{hk}, \mathsf{dig})$ whenever

$$\forall (x_1', \ldots x_{j-1}', x_{j+1}', \ldots, x_n') : f(x_1', \ldots, x_{j-1}', \hat{x}_j, x_{j+1}', \ldots, x_n') \neq f(x_1, \ldots, x_n).$$

In other words, the only possible openings at *any* index j are to values $\hat{x}_j$ where there exists an assignment to the remaining variables that are consistent with an evaluation of $f(x_1, \ldots, x_n)$. As in the case of SSB hash functions, we require succinct local openings to any index. We describe two cases of interest:

- **Index functions:** As a special case, an SSB hash function is a function-binding hash function for the index function $\mathsf{ind}_i\colon (\{0,1\}^\ell)^n \to \{0,1\}^\ell$ where $\mathsf{ind}_i(x_1, \ldots, x_n) := x_i$.
- **Disjunction of predicates:** Let $g\colon \{0,1\}^\ell \to \{0,1\}$ be a binary-valued predicate and let $f_g\colon (\{0,1\}^\ell)^n \to \{0,1\}$ be the block-wise disjunction function

$$f_g(x_1, \ldots, x_n) := \bigvee_{i \in [n]} g(x_i). \tag{1.1}$$

Suppose a hash key hk is statistically binding for the function f_g, and suppose $\mathsf{dig} = H(\mathsf{hk}, (x_1, \ldots, x_n))$ for an input $(x_1, \ldots, x_n)$ where $g(x_i) = 0$ for all $i \in [n]$. Function-binding security now says that there does *not* exist any opening $(j, \hat{x}_j)$ for any $j \in [n]$ and $\hat{x}_j \in \{0,1\}^\ell$ where $g(\hat{x}_j) = 1$.

Like index hiding in the context of SSB hash functions, we additionally require that the hash key hk associated with a predicate f computationally hides the function f. Similarly, we require that given a digest $\mathsf{dig} = H(\mathsf{hk}, (x_1, \ldots, x_n))$, one can efficiently compute a succinct local opening π to any index (j, x_j), where $|\pi| = \mathsf{poly}(\lambda, \ell, \log n)$, where ℓ is the output length of f. We provide the formal definition in Sect. 3.

Using Function-Binding Hash Functions. Consider again our template for constructing flexible broadcast encryption, except we replace the SSB hash function in the construction with a function-binding hash function. Our security reduction now proceeds as follows:

- As before, we start by switching the honest users' public keys $c_1, \ldots, c_n \leftarrow \mathsf{PKE.Enc}(\mathsf{pk}, 0)$ to encryptions of 0.
- Next, we sample the hash key hk to be statistically function-binding for the function $f_g(c_1, \ldots, c_n)$ where f_g is the disjunction-of-predicates function from Eq. (1.1) and $g(c) = \mathsf{PKE.Dec}(\mathsf{sk}, c)$, and sk is the decryption key associated with pk in the public-key encryption scheme. Observe now that in the challenge ciphertext, $f_g(c_1, \ldots, c_n) = 0$ since each c_i is an encryption of 0.

- Security now follows by security of the witness encryption scheme. We claim that with overwhelming probability over the choice of the hash key hk, the statement $(\mathsf{hk}, \mathsf{pk}, \mathsf{dig})$ is false. Take any candidate witness (i, c, π, r). For this to be a valid witness, it must be the case that $c = \mathsf{PKE.Enc}(\mathsf{pk}, 1; r)$ and π is a valid opening for (i, c) with respect to $(\mathsf{hk}, \mathsf{dig})$ where $\mathsf{dig} = H(\mathsf{hk}, (c_1, \ldots, c_n))$. Since c is an encryption of 1, $g(c) = 1$. Since f_g is a disjunction, the output of f_g on any tuple of inputs that includes c is necessarily $1 \neq 0 = f_g(c_1, \ldots, c_n)$. Function-binding security now says that there does not exist any valid π for (i, c) with respect to $(\mathsf{hk}, \mathsf{dig})$.

The use of the function-binding hash function eliminates the need for a step-by-step hybrid strategy. As such, we can rely directly on *plain* witness encryption to complete the analysis. This yields the first flexible (and correspondingly, distributed) broadcast encryption scheme that does not rely on $i\mathcal{O}$. Like the Boneh-Zhandry distributed broadcast encryption scheme from $i\mathcal{O}$, the size of the ciphertexts in our scheme scale with $\mathsf{poly}(\lambda, \log n)$, where n is the number of users in the broadcast set. We provide the full construction and analysis in Sect. 4.

Optimal Broadcast Encryption. A flexible broadcast encryption scheme immediately implies a traditional broadcast encryption scheme with a central key issuer. Here, the central key issuer would generate the public/private keys for all of the users and publish the public keys for each user as the master public key for the broadcast encryption system. Instantiated with our flexible broadcast encryption scheme, this yields a construction with a linear-size public key, but short ciphertexts and secret keys (scaling polylogarithmically with the number of users). It is straightforward to extend our scheme to an *optimal* broadcast encryption where the size of the public key also scales polylogarithmically with the number of users by working in the random oracle model.

The reason our basic approach has a linear-size public key is because we concatenate n user keys $c_1, \ldots, c_n$ to form the master public key for the broadcast encryption scheme. The key idea behind our optimal broadcast encryption scheme is to instead derive each user's public key from a hash of the user index i: that is, we compute $c_i \leftarrow h(i)$, where h is modeled as a random oracle. On the one hand, the master public key only needs to contain the public parameters for our flexible broadcast encryption system, which is now independent of the number of users in the scheme. On the flip side, we need a way to generate decryption keys for the users.

To recover functionality, we start with a more general view of our scheme. Recall that in our scheme, an honestly-generated public key c_i is an encryption of 1 and the associated secret key is a proof that c_i is an encryption of 1. In this case, the proof is the encryption randomness. In the security analysis, each c_i is replaced with an encryption of 0. In this case, there no longer exists a proof (i.e., encryption randomness) that asserts c_i to be an encryption of 1. We can more abstractly view this as implementing a set system where the honestly-generated public keys c_i are elements of some set S (i.e., encryptions of 1 in our case), and the associated secret key is a (statistically sound) proof of membership that

$c_i \in S$. In the security proof, the public keys are sampled from some set T that is disjoint from S (i.e., encryptions of 0 in our case). Finally, we also require that a random element in S should be computationally indistinguishable from a random element in T so we can change the distribution of the honest users' keys in the security proof. Now, suppose we can construct sets $S, T \subseteq \{0,1\}^k$ where S is dense (i.e., a random element in $\{0,1\}^k$ is contained in S with all but negligible probability), and moreover, given a trapdoor, it is possible to construct a proof of membership for any element $c \in S$. We refer to this notion as a "trapdoor proof system." Trapdoor proof systems can be constructed in a straightforward manner from a non-interactive zero-knowledge proof in conjunction with a public-key encryption scheme with pseudorandom ciphertexts (see the full version of this paper [29] for details). Using a trapdoor proof system, we can now adapt our flexible broadcast encryption scheme to obtain an optimal broadcast encryption scheme in the random oracle model:

- The setup algorithm for the broadcast encryption scheme samples a trapdoor td for our trapdoor proof system. Let $S, T \subseteq \{0,1\}^k$ be the sets associated with the trapdoor proof system. Let $h \colon [n] \to \{0,1\}^k$ be a hash function that is modeled as a random oracle.
- The public key for user i is $c_i \leftarrow h(i)$. With overwhelming probability, $c_i \in S$. The secret key r_i is a proof of membership that $c_i \in S$, which can be sampled using the trapdoor td for the trapdoor proof system.
- Encryption and decryption proceed exactly as in the flexible broadcast encryption scheme.

The security analysis also proceeds analogously to that for our flexible broadcast encryption scheme. Namely, we first move the honest users' public keys from S to T (so no proofs of membership exist), and then appeal to statistical function-binding and security of witness encryption. We refer to the full version of this paper [29] for the full details.

Registered Attribute-Based Encryption. In Sect. 6, we show that function-binding hash functions and plain witness encryption can also be used to obtain a registered ABE scheme that supports an arbitrary number of users and supporting general policies. Previously, this was also only known from indistinguishability obfuscation [46]. Non-obfuscation-based constructions of registered ABE could only support a bounded number of users [46] or support less-expressive policies such as Boolean formulas [46] or equality predicates [23,33,34,39,42]. We sketch the basic idea here (which closely parallels the $i\mathcal{O}$-based approach from [46]):

- The common reference string for the registered ABE scheme consists of a public key pk for a public-key encryption scheme and the hash key for a function-binding hash function.
- As in our flexible broadcast encryption scheme, to generate a public key, a user samples randomness r and computes their public key as $c = \mathsf{PKE.Enc}(\mathsf{pk}, 1; r)$. Their secret key is the encryption randomness r.

- Suppose n users register with public keys $(c_1, \ldots, c_n)$ and attributes $(x_1, \ldots, x_n)$. The aggregated public key is a hash of the public keys and associated attributes: $\mathsf{mpk} = \mathsf{dig} = H(\mathsf{hk}, ((c_1, x_1), \ldots, (c_n, x_n)))$. The helper decryption key for user i is an opening π_i for (c_i, x_i) with respect to $(\mathsf{hk}, \mathsf{dig})$.
- An encryption of message m under a policy $\mathcal{P}$ consists of a witness encryption ciphertext for m with respect to the statement $(\mathsf{pk}, \mathsf{hk}, \mathsf{dig}, \mathcal{P})$. A witness (i, c, x, π, r) is valid if the following holds:
  - **Valid opening:** The opening π is a valid opening for (c, x) at index i with respect to $(\mathsf{hk}, \mathsf{dig})$.
  - **Policy satisfiability:** The associated attribute satisfies the policy: $\mathcal{P}(x) = 1$.
  - **Knowledge of secret key:** The pair (c, r) is a valid public/secret key-pair: $c = \mathsf{PKE.Enc}(\mathsf{pk}, 1; r)$.

We show that this scheme is secure in a *selective* model where the adversary commits to its challenge policy $\mathcal{P}$ at the beginning of the security game. The security proof follows a similar hybrid structure as the security proof for our flexible broadcast encryption scheme:

- We first replace the honest users' public keys with encryptions of 0.
- Next, we sample the hash key to be statistically function-binding for the function $f_g((c_1, x_1), \ldots, (c_n, x_n))$ where f_g is the disjunction-of-predicates function from Eq. (1.1) and $g(c, x) \coloneqq \mathsf{PKE.Dec}(\mathsf{sk}, c) \wedge \mathcal{P}(x)$. Since we need to program the challenge policy $\mathcal{P}$ into the hash key, we are only able to argue selective security.
- Security now follows by security of the witness encryption scheme. Specifically, with overwhelming probability over the choice of the hash key, the statement $(\mathsf{hk}, \mathsf{pk}, \mathsf{dig})$ is false. This is because $f_g((c_1, x_1), \ldots, (c_n, x_n)) = 0$ by construction[3] whereas a valid witness (i, c, x, π, r) must satisfy $g(c, x) = 1$.

Constructing Function-Binding Hash Functions. To complete the loop, we finally show how to construct function-binding hash functions. In this work, we describe a construction that supports the disjunction-of-blocks family of functions f_g (for arbitrary g) from Eq. (1.1). This is the function family used in our applications to flexible broadcast encryption and registered ABE. Our construction proceeds very similarly to the construction of SSB hash functions from fully homomorphic encryption [47].

Specifically, let $(x_1, \ldots, x_n)$ be the input to our function-binding hash function; for ease of exposition, suppose that $n = 2^d$ is a power of two. We combine a Merkle tree [50] with a (leveled) homomorphic encryption scheme. We construct a complete binary tree of depth d, where the leaves of the binary tree are associated with the labels $x_1, \ldots, x_n$. At the base level (the leaves), we homomorphically evaluate the function g on the input. Note that the description of g

---

[3] Specifically, if c_i is the public key of an honest user, then $\mathsf{PKE.Dec}(\mathsf{sk}, c_i) = 0$ whereas if x_i belongs to a corrupted user, then $\mathcal{P}(x_i) = 0$ by the admissibility restriction on the registered ABE adversary. In either case, $g(c_i, x_i) = 0$ for all $i \in [n]$.

itself is encrypted as part of the hash key, since we require the hash key to hide the function. The value of each internal node is then obtained by homomorphically evaluated the OR function on its child ciphertexts. Observe that at the end of this process, the root of the tree will be an encryption of $f_g(x_1, \ldots, x_n)$. The function-binding property now follows from (perfect) correctness of the encryption scheme. We provide the full details and proof in Sect. 3.1.

From Selective to Adaptive Security in the Random Oracle Model. The aforementioned constructions of flexible/optimal broadcast encryption and registered ABE all satisfy a selective notion of security where the adversary has to pre-commit to the set of corrupted users in the security game. We do note that our flexible/optimal broadcast encryption schemes, however, satisfy a stronger notion of "semi-static security" [38] where the adversary only needs to commit to a *super-set* of its challenge set (but is not allowed to corrupt any users in its committed set). Previously, Gentry and Waters [38] showed that a broadcast encryption scheme with semi-static security implies an adaptively-secure scheme in the random oracle model. Using the techniques of [38], we show in the full version of this paper [29] how to transform the flexible broadcast encryption scheme above into one that satisfies adaptive security in the random oracle model. Similarly, our registered ABE construction described above satisfies a weaker policy-selective security without corruption queries. Namely, in the security game, the adversary has to declare its challenge policy upfront and it is not allowed to corrupt honestly-generated keys (but it can still generate its own keys and register those). We show in the full version of this paper [29] that in the random oracle model, we can apply a similar approach based on [38] to support corruption queries in our registered ABE scheme.[4] We note that the $i\mathcal{O}$-based construction of registered ABE of [46] achieves full adaptive security. We leave it as an open question to satisfy this stronger notion from plain witness encryption.

Flexible Broadcast Encryption from Registered ABE. As a final contribution, we also show that a registered ABE scheme *generically* implies a flexible broadcast encryption scheme.[5] The idea is simple: the public parameters for the flexible broadcast encryption scheme is the CRS for the registered ABE scheme. Now, to broadcast to a set of public keys $(\mathsf{pk}_1, \ldots, \mathsf{pk}_n)$, the encrypter initializes a registered ABE scheme and registers $\mathsf{pk}_1, \ldots, \mathsf{pk}_n$ to a dummy attribute x to obtain a master public key mpk. It then encrypts the message m with respect to the master public key and a dummy policy P where $P(x) = 1$. To decrypt,

---

[4] The transformed scheme is still policy-selective; however, this can be removed generically via complexity leveraging and assuming subexponential hardness. Note that one cannot use complexity leveraging to handle corruption queries without having the ciphertext size grow with the number of registered users.

[5] Note that the direct approach of encoding the broadcast set as part of the policy in the ABE scheme does *not* yield a flexible broadcast encryption scheme with the required efficiency. Namely, in existing registered ABE schemes (including the one in this work), the size of the ciphertext scales with the size of the policy. Using this to implement broadcast encryption yields a flexible broadcast encryption scheme where the size of the ciphertext scales *linearly* with the number of users.

a user would run the registration algorithm itself, derive the associated helper decryption key, and combine with their own secret key to recover the message m. We describe this transformation in the full version of this paper [29].

By applying the generic transformation to our registered ABE scheme, we obtain another approach for constructing flexible broadcast encryption from witness encryption and function-binding hash functions. We do note though that the flexible broadcast encryption scheme obtained via this generic approach satisfies a *weaker* notion of static security (as opposed to semi-static security). Thus, the generic transformation does not subsume our direct construction of flexible broadcast encryption which satisfies semi-static security. As noted above, a semi-statically secure scheme can be bootstrapped to an adaptively-secure one in the random oracle model, but a similar transformation is not known if we start from a statically-secure scheme.

The transformation described here critically assumes that the key-generation process is "stateless:" namely, users can independently generate their keys without knowledge of the current state of the key curator. In schemes like the pairing-based construction of [46], the registration process is not stateless and users need to know the current number of registered users when registering. In this setting, our transformation can still be applied to obtain a *distributed* broadcast encryption scheme from assumptions over pairing groups. We provide additional details in the full version of this paper [29]. Ultimately, in conjunction with [46], we also obtain the first distributed broadcast encryption scheme from pairing-based assumptions (over a composite-order group). The resulting scheme supports an *a priori bounded* number of users, requires a quadratic-size CRS (inherited from [46]), and satisfies static security.

2   Preliminaries

In this section, we introduce the notation and definitions of standard cryptographic primitives that we use in this paper. We let $\mathbb{N} = \{1, 2, 3, \ldots\}$ denote the set of natural numbers, and for any $n \in \mathbb{N}$, we write $[n]$ to denote the set $[n] = \{1, \ldots, n\}$. For integers $a, b \in \mathbb{Z}$ with $a \leq b$, we write $[a, b]$ to denote the set $\{a, a+1, \ldots, b\}$. For a set Σ, referred to as the *alphabet*, we denote Σ^* the set of strings consisting of 0 or more elements from Σ. We let Σ^n denote the set of n-character strings from Σ and $\Sigma^{\leq n}$ the set of string of length at most n. For a string $s \in \Sigma^*$, we let $|s|$ denote the length of s. Unless specified otherwise, we assume that a string s is defined over the binary alphabet $\{0, 1\}$.

We write $\lambda \in \mathbb{N}$ to denote the security parameter. We say that a function $p \colon \mathbb{N} \to \mathbb{N}$ is in the set $\mathsf{poly}(\lambda)$ and is *polynomially-bounded* if there exists a constant c and an index $i \in \mathbb{N}$ such that $p(\lambda) \leq \lambda^c$ for all $\lambda \geq i$. We say that a function $\mathsf{negl} \colon \mathbb{N} \to \mathbb{R}$ is negligible if for every constant $c > 0$ there exists $i \in \mathbb{N}$ such that $\mathsf{negl}(\lambda) \leq \lambda^{-c}$ for all $\lambda \geq i$.

We use PPT to denote the acronym *probabilistic polynomial time*. We say that an algorithm is *stateful* if when invoked multiple times in succession, it implicitly takes its entire view so far, including previous inputs and random coins used, as input. We say that a function $f \colon \mathbb{N} \to \mathbb{N}$ is efficiently computable if there exists a PPT algorithm that computes f on all inputs.

For a distribution X, we write $x \leftarrow X$ to denote the process of sampling a value x from the distribution X. For a set $\mathcal{X}$, we use $x \xleftarrow{\text{R}} \mathcal{X}$ to denote the process of sampling a value x from the uniform distribution over $\mathcal{X}$. We use $x = A(\cdot)$ to denote the output of a deterministic algorithm and $x \leftarrow A(\cdot)$ to denote the output of a randomized algorithm. We write $x \leftarrow A(y; r)$ to denote the output of running the randomized algorithm A on input y with *explicit* randomness r. We write $x := y$ to denote the assignment of value y to x. For a distribution D, we define $\mathrm{Supp}(D)$ to denote the support of the distribution D.

Boolean Circuits. A Boolean circuit consist of input and output wires (each labeled with a bit) and gates (either AND, OR, or NOT gates unless specified otherwise) that are arranged according to a directed acyclic graph. We define the size of a circuit to be the number of input/output wires and gates in the circuit. We assume a canonical description for all Boolean circuits of a given size. We define the circuit depth to be the depth of the graph representing the circuit.

Message Spaces. For a function $m \colon \mathbb{N} \to \mathbb{N}$, we say that a sequence $\mathcal{M} = \{\mathcal{M}_\lambda\}_{\lambda \in \mathbb{N}}$ is a *message space with message-length* m if for every $\mathsf{msg} \in \mathcal{M}_\lambda$, $|\mathsf{msg}| = m(\lambda)$. We reserve the special character $\bot$ to denote an invalid message.

Languages and Witness Relations. We consider sequences of languages $\mathcal{L} = \{\mathcal{L}_\lambda\}_{\lambda \in \mathbb{N}}$ that are parameterized by a security parameter λ. We say that a language has instance length $m = m(\lambda)$ if for all security parameters $\lambda \in \mathbb{N}$ and statements $x \in \mathcal{L}_\lambda$, we have that $|x| = m(\lambda)$. We say a language $\mathcal{L} = \{\mathcal{L}_\lambda\}_{\lambda \in \mathbb{N}}$ is polynomially-bounded if there exists a polynomial p such that for all $\lambda \in \mathbb{N}$, $\max\{|x| : x \in \mathcal{L}_\lambda\} \leq p(\lambda)$. A witness relation for an NP language $\mathcal{L} = \{\mathcal{L}_\lambda\}_{\lambda \in \mathbb{N}}$ with instances of length m is a deterministic, binary relation $\mathbf{R}_\mathcal{L}$ that can be computed in time $\mathsf{poly}(\lambda, m(\lambda))$ and characterizes $\mathcal{L}$ by $\mathcal{L}_\lambda = \{x : \exists w, (1^\lambda, x, w) \in \mathbf{R}_\mathcal{L}\}$. We say that a string $w \in \{0, 1\}^*$ is a *witness* for an instance $x \in \mathcal{L}_\lambda$ if $(1^\lambda, x, w) \in \mathbf{R}_\mathcal{L}$. We let $\mathbf{R}_\mathcal{L}(1^\lambda, x)$ denote the set of all witnesses for x: namely, $\mathbf{R}_\mathcal{L}(1^\lambda, x) = \{w : \mathbf{R}_\mathcal{L}(1^\lambda, x, w) = 1\}$. We say that $\mathcal{L}$ is efficiently samplable with ℓ uniform bits if there exists an efficient algorithm Sample such that

$$\{x \leftarrow \mathsf{Sample}(1^\lambda; r) : r \xleftarrow{\text{R}} \{0, 1\}^\ell\} \equiv \{x \xleftarrow{\text{R}} \mathcal{L}_\lambda\}.$$

We say that $\mathcal{L}$ is efficiently-recognizable if there exists an efficient algorithm Decide that takes as input the security parameter λ and an instance $x \in \{0, 1\}^m$ and outputs whether $x \in \mathcal{L}_\lambda$.

2.1 Witness Encryption

Witness encryption [32] allows users to encrypt a message with respect to an instance x of an NP language $\mathcal{L}$. Anyone who has a corresponding witness w for x should be able to decrypt, whereas if x is false, the ciphertext should computationally hide the underlying message. We formalize this as follows.

Definition 2.1 (Witness Encryption). *Let* $m \in \text{poly}(\lambda)$ *and* $\mathcal{M} = \{\mathcal{M}_\lambda\}_{\lambda \in \mathbb{N}}$ *be a message space of length* m. *A witness encryption scheme* WE *for an* NP *language* $\mathcal{L} = \{\mathcal{L}_\lambda\}_{\lambda \in \mathbb{N}}$ *with instance length* $n = n(\lambda)$ *and witness relation* $\mathbf{R}_\mathcal{L}$ *consists of polynomial-time algorithms* (Enc, Dec) *with the following syntax:*

- Enc$(1^\lambda, \text{msg}, x) \to \text{ct}$: *A probabilistic algorithm that on input a security param-eter* λ, *a message* $\text{msg} \in \mathcal{M}_\lambda$, *and an instance* x *for the language* $\mathcal{L}$, *outputs a ciphertext* ct. *We implicitly assume that* ct *includes* 1^λ *and* x.
- Dec$(\text{ct}, w) \to \text{msg}$: *A deterministic algorithm that on input a ciphertext* ct *and a witness* w, *outputs a message* $\text{msg} \in \mathcal{M}_\lambda \cup \{\bot\}$.

We require that (Enc, Dec) *satisfy the following properties:*

- *(Perfect) correctness: For all* $\lambda \in \mathbb{N}$, *messages* $\text{msg} \in \mathcal{M}_\lambda$, *and tuples* $(1^\lambda, x, w) \in \mathbf{R}_\mathcal{L}$, *it holds that*

$$\Pr\left[\text{ct} \leftarrow \text{Enc}(1^\lambda, \text{msg}, x) : \text{Dec}(\text{ct}, w) = \text{msg}\right] = 1.$$

- *Message indistinguishability: For all stateful PPT algorithms* A, *there exists a negligible function* negl *such that for all* $\lambda \in \mathbb{N}$, *it holds that*

$$\Pr\left[\begin{array}{l}(x, \text{msg}_0, \text{msg}_1) \leftarrow A(1^\lambda) \\ b \xleftarrow{\text{R}} \{0,1\} \\ \text{ct}^\star \leftarrow \text{Enc}(1^\lambda, \text{msg}_b, x) \\ b' \leftarrow A(\text{ct}^\star)\end{array} : x \notin \mathcal{L}_\lambda \wedge b' = b\right] \leq 1/2 + \text{negl}(\lambda).$$

3   Function-Binding Hash Functions

In this section, we introduce the notion of a *function-binding* hash function. In the following, we consider the setting where the hash function satisfies *statistical function binding* and *computational function hiding*. This is the notion we rely on for our applications. However, we note that we can easily consider alternative notions where function binding is computational or function hiding is statistical.

Definition 3.1 (Function-Binding Hash Function). *Let* $\ell_{\text{blk}} = \ell_{\text{blk}}(\lambda)$ *be the block size,* $\ell_{\text{out}} = \ell_{\text{out}}(\lambda)$ *be the output size. Let* $\mathcal{F} = \{\mathcal{F}_\lambda\}_{\lambda \in \mathbb{N}}$ *be a class of functions where each* $\mathcal{F}_\lambda$ *is a collection of functions* $f \colon (\{0,1\}^{\ell_{\text{blk}}(\lambda)})^* \to \{0,1\}^{\ell_{\text{out}}(\lambda)}$ *implementable by a circuit of size at most* $s(\lambda) \cdot \text{poly}(k)$, *where* k *is the number of input blocks to* f. *A function-binding hash function for* $\mathcal{F}$ *is a tuple of polynomial-time algorithms* (Setup, SetupBinding, Hash, ProveOpen, VerOpen) *with the following syntax:*

- Setup$(1^\lambda, n) \to \text{hk}$: *A probabilistic algorithm that on input a security param-eter* λ *and a bound on the number of input blocks* n *(in* binary*), outputs a hash key* hk. *We implicitly assume that* hk *includes* 1^λ *and* n.
- SetupBinding$(1^\lambda, n, f) \to \text{hk}$: *A probabilistic algorithm that on input a security parameter* λ, *a bound on the number of input blocks* n, *and a function* $f \in \mathcal{F}_\lambda$, *outputs a hash key* hk. *We implicitly assume that* hk *includes* 1^λ *and* n.

- Hash(hk, (hinp$_1$, . . . , hinp$_k$)) → dig: *A deterministic algorithm that on input a hash key* hk *and hash inputs* (hinp$_1$, . . . , hinp$_k$) ∈ $(\{0,1\}^{\ell_{blk}(\lambda)})^k$ *for some* $k \le n$, *outputs a digest* dig.
- ProveOpen(hk, (hinp$_1$, . . . , hinp$_k$), S) → π: *A deterministic algorithm that on input a hash key* hk, *a sequence of hash inputs* (hinp$_1$, . . . , hinp$_k$) ∈ $(\{0,1\}^{\ell_{blk}(\lambda)})^k$ *for any* $k \le n$, *and a subset of indices* $S \subseteq [k]$, *outputs a proof* π.
- VerOpen(hk, dig, S, $\{(i, \text{hinp}_i)\}_{i \in S}$, π) → $\{0,1\}$: *A deterministic algorithm that on input a hash key* hk, *a digest* dig, *a subset* $S \subseteq [k]$ *for any* $k \le n$, *a set of hash inputs* $\{(i, \text{hinp}_i)\}_{i \in S}$ *where each* hinp$_i$ ∈ $\{0,1\}^{\ell_{blk}(\lambda)}$, *and a proof* π, *outputs a bit* $b \in \{0,1\}$.

We require that (Setup, SetupBinding, Hash, ProveOpen, VerOpen) *satisfy the following properties:*

- ***Efficiency:*** *There exist polynomials* p_1, p_2, p_3 *such that for all parameters* $\lambda \in \mathbb{N}$, $k \in \mathbb{N}$, $n \in \mathbb{N}$ *with* $k \le n$, *any function* $f \in \mathcal{F}_\lambda$, *any hash key* hk ∈ Supp$\big($Setup$(1^\lambda, n)\big)$, *any tuple of inputs* (hinp$_1$, . . . , hinp$_k$) ∈ $(\{0,1\}^{\ell_{blk}(\lambda)})^k$, *any digest* dig ∈ Supp$\big($Hash(hk, (hinp$_1$, . . . , hinp$_k$))$\big)$, *any subset* $S \subseteq [k]$, *and any proof* $\pi \in$ Supp$\big($ProveOpen(hk, (hinp$_1$, . . . , hinp$_k$), S)$\big)$, *the following hold:*
  - Setup$(1^\lambda, n)$ *and* SetupBinding$(1^\lambda, n, f)$ *run in time* $p_1(\lambda, s(\lambda), \log n)$;
  - $|\text{dig}| \le p_2(\lambda, \ell_{out}(\lambda), \log k)$; *and*
  - $|\pi| \le |S| \cdot p_3(\lambda, \ell_{out}(\lambda), \log k)$.
- ***Perfect completeness:*** *For all parameters* $\lambda \in \mathbb{N}$, $k \in \mathbb{N}$, $n \in \mathbb{N}$ *with* $k \le n$, *inputs* (hinp$_1$, . . . , hinp$_k$) ∈ $(\{0,1\}^{\ell_{blk}(\lambda)})^k$, *and subsets* $S \subseteq [k]$, *it holds that*

$$
\Pr\left[
\begin{array}{l}
\text{hk} \leftarrow \text{Setup}(1^\lambda, n) \\
\text{dig} = \text{Hash}(\text{hk}, (\text{hinp}_1, \ldots, \text{hinp}_k)) \\
\pi = \text{ProveOpen}(\text{hk}, (\text{hinp}_1, \ldots, \text{hinp}_k), S) \\
b = \text{VerOpen}(\text{hk}, \text{dig}, S, \{(i, \text{hinp}_i)\}_{i \in S}, \pi)
\end{array}
: b = 1 \right] = 1.
$$

- ***Statistical function binding:*** *For all stateful unbounded adversaries A and efficiently-computable functions* $n \in \text{poly}(\lambda)$, *there exists a negligible function* negl *such that for all* $\lambda \in \mathbb{N}$,

$$
\Pr\left[\text{Expt}^{\text{FB}}_{A, n(\lambda)}(\lambda) = 1\right] \le \text{negl}(\lambda),
$$

where $\text{Expt}^{\text{FB}}_{A, n}(\lambda)$ *is defined via the following security game between the adversary A and a challenger on common input* 1^λ:
1. *On input the security parameter* λ, *A outputs a function* $f \in \mathcal{F}_\lambda$.
2. *The challenger samples a hash key* hk ← SetupBinding$(1^\lambda, n, f)$ *for the function* f *and gives* hk *to A.*
3. *Algorithm A outputs a sequences of hash inputs* (hinp$_1$, . . . , hinp$_k$) *where each* hinp$_i$ ∈ $\{0,1\}^{\ell_{blk}(\lambda)}$ *and* $k \le n$. *Additionally, A outputs a set* $S \subseteq [k]$ *with associated values* $\{(i, \text{hinp}_i^\star)\}_{i \in S}$ *and a proof* π.

4. The experiment outputs 0 if there exists an extension of remaining inputs $\{(j, \mathsf{hinp}_j^\star)\}_{j \in [k] \setminus S}$ such that $f(\mathsf{hinp}_1, \ldots, \mathsf{hinp}_k) = f(\mathsf{hinp}_1^\star, \ldots, \mathsf{hinp}_k^\star)$. Otherwise, let $\mathsf{dig} = \mathsf{Hash}(\mathsf{hk}, (\mathsf{hinp}_1, \ldots, \mathsf{hinp}_k))$. *The output of the experiment is* $\mathsf{VerOpen}(\mathsf{hk}, \mathsf{dig}, S, \{(i, \mathsf{hinp}_i^\star)\}_{i \in S}, \pi)$.

- ***Computational function hiding:*** *For all stateful PPT algorithms A and efficiently-computable functions $n \in \mathsf{poly}(\lambda)$, there exists a negligible function* negl *such that for all $\lambda \in \mathbb{N}$, it holds that*

$$\Pr \left[\begin{array}{l} f \leftarrow A(1^\lambda) \\ \mathsf{hk}_0 \leftarrow \mathsf{Setup}(1^\lambda, n(\lambda)) \\ \mathsf{hk}_1 \leftarrow \mathsf{SetupBinding}(1^\lambda, n(\lambda), f) \\ b \xleftarrow{\mathsf{R}} \{0,1\} \end{array} : f \in \mathcal{F}_\lambda \wedge A(\mathsf{hk}_b) = b \right] \leq 1/2 + \mathsf{negl}(\lambda).$$

Remark 3.2 (Somewhere Statistically Binding Hash Functions). Definition 3.1 captures the notion of a somewhere statistically binding hashing [47] as a special case where the function class $\mathcal{F}$ is the class of index functions *(i.e., functions f_i where $f_i(\mathsf{hinp}_1, \ldots, \mathsf{hinp}_n) = \mathsf{hinp}_i$).*

3.1   Function-Binding Hash Functions for Disjunctions of Block Functions

We construct a function-binding hash for the function class consisting of disjunctions of block functions:

Definition 3.3 (Disjunction of Block Functions). *Let $\ell_{\mathsf{blk}} = \ell_{\mathsf{blk}}(\lambda)$ be an input length parameter. We say a function $f_g : (\{0,1\}^{\ell_{\mathsf{blk}}})^* \to \{0,1\}$ is a* disjunction of block function *if we can express it as*

$$f_g(x_1, \ldots, x_k) = \bigvee_{i \in [k]} g(x_i), \tag{3.1}$$

and where the function $g : \{0,1\}^{\ell_{\mathsf{blk}}} \to \{0,1\}$ is a predicate on ℓ_{blk}-bit inputs. We say that $\mathcal{F} = \{\mathcal{F}_\lambda\}_{\lambda \in \mathbb{N}}$ is the class of disjunctions for block functions *with input length $\ell_{\mathsf{blk}} = \ell_{\mathsf{blk}}(\lambda)$, size $s = s(\lambda)$, and depth $d = d(\lambda)$ if $\mathcal{F}_\lambda$ contains all functions $f_g : (\{0,1\}^{\ell_{\mathsf{blk}}})^* \to \{0,1\}$ where the function g can be computed by a Boolean circuit of size s and depth d.*

Our construction closely follows the construction of somewhere statistically binding hash functions of [47], which uses a Merkle tree [50] where the underlying two-to-one hash function is built from a leveled homomorphic encryption scheme. We first introduce some preliminary notation and background on Merkle trees and then describe our full construction.

Merkle Tree Preliminaries. We recall some preliminary definitions regarding Merkle trees [50] that we will use in our construction. A Merkle tree MT with depth α is a complete binary tree with 2^α leaf nodes at level 0 in the tree. Each leaf node is associated with an arbitrary fixed-length value. The values of the intermediate nodes in level $i \in [0, \alpha - 1]$ is defined by applying a two-to-one hash function to the two values associated with its child nodes. As such, there are $2^{\alpha-j}$ nodes at level j in the tree MT, and a single node at level α, which we refer to as the *root* node. We view the Merkle tree MT as a directed acyclic graph with edges running from each node to its parent. We index each node in the tree by a pair $(j,i) \in [0,\alpha] \times [1, 2^{\alpha-j}]$ corresponding to its level j and its index i at level j, ordered from left to right.

Merkle Tree Notation. We also introduce some helpful notation for referring to different sets of nodes in the tree. Our treatment follows the generalization of authentication paths in Merkle trees used by [26]. Let MT be a depth α Merkle tree. For a leaf at index $i \in [2^\alpha]$, we write $\mathsf{path}(i)$ to denote the set of nodes along the directed path from leaf i to the root. For a set of leaves $S \subseteq [2^\alpha]$, we define the subtree corresponding to S, denoted $\mathsf{ST}(S)$, to be the union of all paths associated with the leaf nodes $i \in S$: $\mathsf{ST}(S) = \bigcup_{i \in S} \mathsf{path}(i)$. This is sometimes referred to as the Steiner tree for S (c.f., [51]). We define the sibling of a node (j,i), denoted $\mathsf{sib}((j,i))$, to be the adjacent node in the tree who shares a parent with the node; this is either node $(j, i-1)$ if i is even or node $(j, i+1)$ is i is odd.

Definition 3.4 (Dangling Nodes). *Let* MT *be a depth α Merkle tree, and let $S \subseteq [2^\alpha]$. We define the set $\mathsf{dangling}(S)$ to be the set of nodes "dangling" off of the subtree $\mathsf{ST}(S)$. These are the siblings of nodes in $\mathsf{ST}(S)$ which are not contained in $\mathsf{ST}(S)$. Formally,*

$$\mathsf{dangling}(S) = \{\mathsf{sib}(\mathsf{node}) : \mathsf{node} \in \mathsf{ST}(S) \wedge \mathsf{sib}(\mathsf{node}) \notin \mathsf{ST}(S)\}.$$

Normally, one can prove membership of a leaf node i in a Merkle tree (with respect to a Merkle root) by providing the values associated with $\mathsf{dangling}(\{i\})$; this is referred to as the authenticating path of i. To check the proof of membership, the verifier uses the value of node i together with the values of the nodes in $\mathsf{dangling}(\{i\})$ to compute the root of the Merkle tree and compare with the given value. More generally, $\mathsf{dangling}(S)$ defines an authentication path for a set of leaves. Namely, given the values of the nodes in S together with those in $\mathsf{dangling}(S)$, one can again compute the value of the root. Assuming the underlying two-to-one hash function is collision-resistant, the value at the root is computationally unique, so the values in $\mathsf{dangling}(S)$ can be used to authenticate the values of S with respect to the root.

Construction 3.5 (Function-Binding Hash for Disjunctions). Let $\ell_{\mathsf{blk}} = \ell_{\mathsf{blk}}(\lambda)$ be an input length parameter. Fix a size parameter $s_g = s_g(\lambda)$ and depth parameter $d_g = d_g(\lambda)$. We define the function class $\mathcal{F} = \{\mathcal{F}_\lambda\}_{\lambda \in \mathbb{N}}$ to consist of all disjunction-of-block-functions $f_g \colon (\{0,1\}^{\ell_{\mathsf{blk}}})^* \to \{0,1\}$ where

$$f_g(\mathsf{hinp}_1, \ldots, \mathsf{hinp}_k) = \bigvee_{i \in [k]} g(\mathsf{hinp}_i), \tag{3.2}$$

and $g \colon \{0,1\}^{\ell_{\mathsf{blk}}} \to \{0,1\}$ is a function that can be computed by a Boolean circuit C_g of size s_g and depth d_g. In particular, the function f_g can be computed by a circuit of size at most $s_g(\lambda) \cdot (2k+1) \in s_g(\lambda) \cdot \mathsf{poly}(k)$. Our construction relies on the following building blocks:

- Let $U(\cdot, \cdot)$ be a universal circuit that takes as input a circuit C_g of size s_g and depth d_g as well as an input $x \in \{0,1\}^{\ell_{\text{blk}}}$ and outputs $C_g(x)$. Such a universal circuit exists with size $s \in \text{poly}(s_g)$ and depth $d_0 \in O(d_g)$ [24].

- Let LHE $=$ (KeyGen, Enc, Dec, Eval) be a leveled homomorphic encryption scheme with polylogarithmic depth decryption (see the full version of this paper [29]). Let $d_0(\lambda) \in O(d_g(\lambda))$ be the depth of the universal circuit U defined above, and for $j = 1, 2, \ldots, \lceil \log_2 n \rceil$, we recursively define $d_j(\lambda)$ to be the depth of the decryption circuit LHE.Dec instantiated with security parameter λ and depth parameter $d_{j-1}(\lambda)$. Note that since LHE supports polylogarithmic depth decryption, there exists a polynomial p such that $d_j(\lambda) \leq p(\lambda, \log j)$ for all $j \in [0, \lceil \log_2 n \rceil]$.

We show how to construct a function-binding hash for the function family $\mathcal{F}$. We construct the function-binding hash function FBH $=$ (Setup, SetupBinding, Hash, ProveOpen, VerOpen) for the class of functions $\mathcal{F}$ as follows:

- Setup($1^\lambda, n$): On input the security parameter λ and a bound on the number of inputs $n \in \mathbb{N}$, let $\alpha = \lceil \log_2 n \rceil$. For $j \in [0, \alpha]$, sample encryption keys $(\text{pk}_j, \text{sk}_j) \leftarrow$ LHE.Setup($1^\lambda, 1^{d_j(\lambda)+1}$), where $d_j(\lambda)$ is defined above. Let $c_j \leftarrow$ LHE.Enc($\text{pk}_j, \text{sk}_{j-1}$) for $j \in [\alpha]$. Let $c_g \leftarrow$ LHE.Enc($\text{pk}_0, g_\perp$) where $g_\perp : \{0,1\}^{\ell_{\text{blk}}(\lambda)} \to \{0,1\}$ is a dummy circuit of size $s(\lambda)$ that outputs 0 on all inputs. Output the hash key $\text{hk} = (\text{pk}_0, \ldots, \text{pk}_\alpha, c_1, \ldots, c_\alpha, c_g)$.

- SetupBinding($1^\lambda, n, f_g$): On input the security parameter λ, a bound on the number of inputs n, and a target function $f_g \in \mathcal{F}$, the binding setup function samples $(\text{pk}_0, \ldots, \text{pk}_\alpha, c_1, \ldots, c_\alpha)$ exactly as in Setup($1^\lambda, n$). It then samples $c_g \leftarrow$ LHE.Enc(pk_0, g) and outputs the hash key $\text{hk} = (\text{pk}_0, \ldots, \text{pk}_\alpha, c_1, \ldots, c_\alpha, c_g)$.

- Hash(hk, ($\text{hinp}_1, \ldots, \text{hinp}_k$)): On input the hash key $\text{hk} = (\text{pk}_0, \ldots, \text{pk}_\alpha, c_1, \ldots, c_\alpha, c_g)$, and a tuple of inputs $(\text{hinp}_1, \ldots, \text{hinp}_k) \in (\{0,1\}^{\ell_{\text{blk}}})^k$, the hash algorithm sets $\alpha' = \lceil \log_2 k \rceil$ and $k' = 2^{\alpha'}$. Then, for each $i \in [k']$, it constructs ciphertexts as follows:
  - If $i \leq k$, it homomorphically computes $\text{ct}_i = $ LHE.Eval($\text{pk}_0, U(\cdot, \text{hinp}_i), c_g$) where $U(\cdot, \text{hinp}_i)$ is the universal circuit defined above.
  - If $i > k$, it deterministically sets $\text{ct}_i \leftarrow$ LHE.Enc($\text{pk}_0, 0; 0^\lambda$) using fixed randomness 0^λ.

The hash algorithm now constructs a Merkle tree MT of depth α':
  - It associates leaf i with the value ct_i.
  - It uses the following two-to-one hash function h_j to compute the values of the nodes at level $j \in [0, \alpha']$ in the tree (recall that level 0 corresponds to the leaves):

$$h_j(\text{node}_1, \text{node}_2) := \text{LHE.Eval}\big(\text{pk}_j, f_{\text{node}_1, \text{node}_2, j}, c_j\big), \qquad (3.3)$$

where

$$f_{\text{node}_1, \text{node}_2, j}(\text{sk}) := \begin{cases} 1 & \text{LHE.Dec}(\text{sk}, \text{node}_1) = 1 \ \vee \ \text{LHE.Dec}(\text{sk}, \text{node}_2) = 1 \\ 0 & \text{otherwise.} \end{cases}$$

By design, $f_{\text{node}_1, \text{node}_2, j}$ can be computed by a circuit of depth $d_j(\lambda) + 1$.

Output $\mathsf{dig} = (\mathsf{root}, k)$ where root is the value associated with the root of the Merkle tree MT.

- $\mathsf{ProveOpen}(\mathsf{hk}, (\mathsf{hinp}_1, \ldots, \mathsf{hinp}_k), S)$: On input the hash key hk and a tuple of inputs $(\mathsf{hinp}_1, \ldots, \mathsf{hinp}_k) \in (\{0,1\}^{\ell_{\mathsf{blk}}})^k$, the prove algorithm starts by computing the Merkle tree MT according to the specification of $\mathsf{Hash}(\mathsf{hk}, (\mathsf{hinp}_1, \ldots, \mathsf{hinp}_k))$. Let dvals to be a map consisting of the values associated with the nodes in $\mathsf{dangling}(S)$ in MT. Output $\pi = \mathsf{dvals}$.

- $\mathsf{VerOpen}(\mathsf{hk}, \mathsf{dig}, S, \{(i, \mathsf{hinp}_i)\}_{i \in S}, \pi)$: On input the hash key $\mathsf{hk} = (\mathsf{pk}_0, \ldots, \mathsf{pk}_\alpha, c_1, \ldots, c_\alpha, c_g)$, a digest $\mathsf{dig} = (\mathsf{root}, k)$, a set S, values $\{(i, \mathsf{hinp}_i)\}_{i \in S}$, and a proof $\pi = \mathsf{dvals}$, the verification algorithm first checks that $S \subseteq [k]$ and moreover that dvals corresponds to $\mathsf{dangling}(S)$ for a Merkle tree with $k' = 2^{\lceil \log_2(k) \rceil}$ leaves. If either check fails, it outputs 0. Otherwise, it computes $\mathsf{ct}_i = \mathsf{LHE}.\mathsf{Eval}(\mathsf{pk}_0, U(\cdot, \mathsf{hinp}_i), c_g)$ for each $i \in S$. Then, using the values of $\{\mathsf{ct}_i\}_{i \in S}$ together with the values in dvals for the set $\mathsf{dangling}(S)$, the verification algorithm computes the root root' of the Merkle tree using the two-to-one hash function from the specification of $\mathsf{Hash}(\mathsf{hk}, \cdot)$ (Eq. (3.3)). If $\mathsf{root} = \mathsf{root}'$, it outputs 1. Otherwise, it outputs 0.

Due to space restrictions, we analyze the correctness and security of this construction in the full version of this paper [29].

4   Flexible Broadcast Encryption

In this section, we introduce the notion of flexible broadcast encryption. As described in Sect. 1.1, a flexible broadcast encryption allows anyone to encrypt a message to an arbitrary set of public keys with a ciphertext whose size scales sublinearly with the size of the broadcast set. Unlike traditional broadcast encryption [28], there is no central authority that is responsible for issuing decryption keys to users. Instead, users generate their own public and secret keys, and the encryption algorithm takes in the list of public keys for the users in a broadcast set and outputs a single *short* ciphertext that can be decrypted by every member in the broadcast set. Note that this notion of broadcast encryption implies standard broadcast encryption with short ciphertexts and a long public key (by having a central broadcast authority generate the keys for each user and publishing all of them as part of the master public key). Flexible broadcast encryption also generalizes the notion of distributed broadcast encryption introduced by Boneh and Zhandry [13]. The main difference is that in distributed broadcast encryption, users generate keys with respect to a specific index and one can broadcast to at most one key for each index. Flexible broadcast encryption imposes no requirement on the public keys to which one may broadcast. We now give the formal definition:

Definition 4.1 (Flexible Broadcast Encryption). *Let* $m \in \mathsf{poly}(\lambda)$ *and* $\mathcal{M} = \{\mathcal{M}_\lambda\}_{\lambda \in \mathbb{N}}$ *be a message space for messages of length* m. *A flexible broadcast encryption scheme* FBE *with message space* $\mathcal{M}$ *consists of polynomial-time algorithms* $(\mathsf{Setup}, \mathsf{KeyGen}, \mathsf{Enc}, \mathsf{Dec})$ *with the following syntax:*

- Setup$(1^\lambda, n) \to$ pp: *A probabilistic algorithm that on input a security parameter λ and a bound on the size of the broadcast set n (in binary), outputs public parameters* pp. *We implicitly assume that* pp *contains 1^λ and n.*
- KeyGen$($pp$) \to ($pk$,$ sk$)$: *A probabilistic algorithm that on input public parameters* pp, *outputs a public key* pk *and a secret key* sk.
- Enc$($pp$,$ msg$, ($pk$_1, \ldots,$ pk$_k)) \to$ ct: *A probabilistic algorithm that on input public parameters* pp, *a message* msg $\in \mathcal{M}_\lambda$, *and an ordered sequence of k public keys $($pk$_1, \ldots,$ pk$_k)$ for some $k \leq n$, outputs a ciphertext* ct.[6]
- Dec$($pp$,$ ct$, (j,$ sk$_j), ($pk$_1, \ldots,$ pk$_k)) \to$ msg: *A deterministic algorithm that on input public parameters* pp, *a ciphertext* ct, *an index and secret key pair $(j,$ sk$_j)$, and public keys $($pk$_1, \ldots,$ pk$_k)$ where $k \leq n$, outputs a message* msg $\in \mathcal{M}_\lambda \cup \{\bot\}$.

We require that (Setup, KeyGen, Enc, Dec) *satisfy the following properties:*

- **Succinct ciphertexts:** *There exists a polynomial p such that for all $\lambda \in \mathbb{N}$, $k \in \mathbb{N}$, $n \in \mathbb{N}$ with $k \leq n$, public parameters* pp $\in$ Supp $($Setup$(1^\lambda, n))$, *public/secret keys $($pk$_i,$ sk$_i) \in$ Supp $($KeyGen$($pp$))$ for $i \in [k]$, messages* msg $\in \mathcal{M}_\lambda$, *and ciphertexts* ct $\in$ Supp $($Enc$($pp$,$ msg$, ($pk$_1, \ldots,$ pk$_k)))$, *it holds that $|$ct$| \leq p(\lambda, m(\lambda), \log n)$.*
- **Correctness:** *There exists a negligible function* negl *such that for all $\lambda \in \mathbb{N}$, $n \in$ poly(λ), $k \leq n(\lambda)$, $j \in [k]$, and* msg $\in \mathcal{M}_\lambda$, *it holds that*

$$\Pr\left[\begin{array}{l} \text{pp} \leftarrow \text{Setup}(1^\lambda, n(\lambda)) \\ \forall i \in [k], (\text{pk}_i, \text{sk}_i) \leftarrow \text{KeyGen}(\text{pp}) \\ \text{ct} \leftarrow \text{Enc}(\text{pp}, \text{msg}, (\text{pk}_1, \ldots, \text{pk}_k)) \\ \text{msg}' = \text{Dec}(\text{pp}, \text{ct}, (j, \text{sk}_j), (\text{pk}_1, \ldots, \text{pk}_k)) \end{array} : \text{msg}' = \text{msg}\right] \geq 1 - \text{negl}(\lambda).$$

We say that the scheme satisfies perfect correctness if the above probability is equal to 1.
- **Adaptive security:** *For all stateful PPT adversaries A and all efficiently-computable functions $n \in$ poly(λ), there exists a negligible function* negl *such that for all $\lambda \in \mathbb{N}$,*

$$\Pr\left[\text{Expt}^{\text{FBE}}_{A,n(\lambda)}(\lambda) = 1\right] \leq 1/2 + \text{negl}(\lambda),$$

where Expt$^{\text{FBE}}_{A,n}(\lambda)$ *is defined via the following security game between the adversary A and a challenger on common input 1^λ:*
  - **Setup phase:** *The challenger samples* pp $\leftarrow$ Setup$(1^\lambda, n)$ *and sends* pp *to A. The challenger also initializes a counter* ctr $:= 0$, *a dictionary* D, *and a set of (corrupted) indices $\mathcal{C} = \varnothing$.*
  - **Pre-challenge query phase:** *The adversary A can now issue the following queries:*

---

[6] Here, we assume an ordered list of public keys for simplicity. However, we could have alternatively encrypted to an (unordered) set of public keys by first ordering the public keys in lexicographic order.

* * **Key-generation query:** *In a key-generation query, the challenger increments* ctr := ctr + 1, *samples a key-pair* (pk, sk) ← KeyGen(pp), *and replies to A with* (ctr, pk). *The challenger adds the mapping* ctr ↦ (pk, sk) *to the dictionary* D.
  * * **Corruption query:** *In a corruption query, the adversary specifies a counter value* $c \in$ [ctr]. *In response, the challenger looks up* (pk, sk) := D[c], *replies to A with* sk, *and adds* ctr *to* C.
* **Challenge phase:** *Algorithm A computes two messages* $\mathsf{msg}_0, \mathsf{msg}_1 \in \mathcal{M}_\lambda$ *and an ordered list* $S^\star = (i_1, \dots, i_{k^\star}) \subseteq$ [ctr] *that it sends to the challenger. If* $S^\star \cap C \neq \varnothing$, *the experiment outputs* 0. *Otherwise, the challenger samples a bit* $b \xleftarrow{R} \{0, 1\}$ *and computes an encryption of* msg_b *under the keys corresponding to* $S^\star$: $\mathsf{ct}^\star \leftarrow \mathsf{Enc}(\mathsf{pp}, \mathsf{msg}_b, (\mathsf{pk}_{i_1}, \dots, \mathsf{pk}_{i_{k^\star}}))$. *The challenger sends* $\mathsf{ct}^\star$ *to A.*
* **Output phase:** *Algorithm A outputs a bit* $b' \in \{0, 1\}$. *The experiment outputs* 1 *if* $b' = b$ *and* 0 *otherwise.*

Semi-Static Security. In this work, we also consider a weaker notion of semi-static security introduced by Gentry and Waters [38] in the context of broadcast encryption. In the setting of flexible broadcast encryption, semi-static security corresponds to the setting where the adversary is allowed to make any number of honest key-generation queries, and then declares its challenge set to be some subset of these keys. The adversary cannot make any corruption queries in this model. In the context of broadcast encryption, Gentry and Waters showed that semi-static security implies adaptive security in the random oracle model. In the full version of this paper [29], we show that the same technique also applies in the case of flexible broadcast encryption.

Definition 4.2 (Semi-Static Security [38, adapted]**).** *We say that a flexible broadcast encryption scheme* (Setup, KeyGen, Enc, Dec) *satisfies semi-static security if instead of adaptive security, it satisfies the following:*

- *   **Semi-static security:** *For all stateful PPT adversaries A and all efficiently-computable functions* $n \in \mathsf{poly}(\lambda)$, *there exists a negligible function* negl *such that for all* $\lambda \in \mathbb{N}$,

$$\Pr\left[\mathsf{Expt}_{A, n(\lambda)}^{\mathsf{FBE, SS}}(\lambda) = 1\right] \leq 1/2 + \mathsf{negl}(\lambda),$$

where $\mathsf{Expt}_{A, n}^{\mathsf{FBE, SS}}(\lambda)$ *is identical to the adaptive security game* $\mathsf{Expt}_{A, n(\lambda)}^{\mathsf{FBE}}(\lambda)$, *except the adversary A is not allowed to make any corruption queries.*

4.1 Constructing Flexible Broadcast Encryption

We now show how to construct a flexible broadcast encryption scheme by combining a witness encryption scheme with a function-binding hash function and a vanilla public-key encryption scheme. Note that public-key encryption is implied by combining witness encryption and one-way functions [32]. Thus, the additional assumption of public-key encryption is technically unnecessary (since function-binding hash functions imply one-way functions). Our construction satisfies semi-static security. However, we show in the full version of this paper [29] how to use this to construct an adaptively secure scheme via a transformation following the approach of [38].

Construction 4.3 (Flexible Broadcast Encryption). Let $s = s(\lambda)$, $\ell_{\mathsf{blk}} = \ell_{\mathsf{blk}}(\lambda)$, and $d = d(\lambda)$ be polynomials, and $m = m(\lambda)$ be any function. Let $\mathcal{M} = \{\mathcal{M}_\lambda\}_{\lambda \in \mathbb{N}}$ be a message space for messages of length m. Our construction of flexible broadcast encryption relies on the following primitives:

- Let $\mathsf{PKE} = (\mathsf{PKE.KeyGen}, \mathsf{PKE.Enc}, \mathsf{PKE.Dec})$ be a semantically-secure public-key bit encryption scheme where for $(\mathsf{pk}, \mathsf{sk}) \in \mathsf{Supp}\left(\mathsf{PKE.KeyGen}(1^\lambda)\right)$, ciphertexts have length at most $\ell_{\mathsf{blk}}(\lambda)$ and decryption can be computed by a circuit of size $s(\lambda)$ and depth $d(\lambda)$.
- Let $\mathsf{FBH} = (\mathsf{FBH.Setup}, \mathsf{FBH.SetupBinding}, \mathsf{FBH.Hash}, \mathsf{FBH.ProveOpen}, \mathsf{FBH.VerOpen})$ be a function-binding hash for the class $\mathcal{F}$ of disjunctions of block functions for input length ℓ_{blk}, size s, and depth d (Definition 3.3).
- Let $\mathsf{WE} = (\mathsf{WE.Enc}, \mathsf{WE.Dec})$ be a witness encryption scheme for the language $\mathcal{L} = \{\mathcal{L}_\lambda\}_{\lambda \in \mathbb{N}}$ defined by the relation $\mathbf{R}_\mathcal{L}$ as follows. Instances of the language $\mathcal{L}_\lambda$ are of the form $(\mathsf{hk}, \mathsf{pk}_{\mathsf{PKE}}, \mathsf{dig})$ and the relation $\mathbf{R}_\mathcal{L}$ is given by

$$\mathbf{R}_\mathcal{L}\left(1^\lambda, (\mathsf{hk}, \mathsf{pk}_{\mathsf{PKE}}, \mathsf{dig}), (i, \mathsf{hinp}_i, r, \pi)\right) = 1$$
$$\Leftrightarrow \mathsf{hinp}_i = \mathsf{PKE.Enc}(\mathsf{pk}_{\mathsf{PKE}}, 1; r) \wedge$$
$$\mathsf{FBH.VerOpen}(\mathsf{hk}, \mathsf{dig}, \{i\}, \{(i, \mathsf{hinp}_i)\}, \pi) = 1.$$

We construct a flexible broadcast encryption scheme $\mathsf{FBE} = (\mathsf{Setup}, \mathsf{KeyGen}, \mathsf{Enc}, \mathsf{Dec})$ with message space $\mathcal{M}$ as follows:

- $\mathsf{Setup}(1^\lambda, n)$: On input the security parameter λ and a bound on the broadcast set size n, the setup algorithm samples $(\mathsf{pk}_{\mathsf{PKE}}, \mathsf{sk}_{\mathsf{PKE}}) \leftarrow \mathsf{PKE.KeyGen}(1^\lambda)$, $\mathsf{hk} \leftarrow \mathsf{FBH.Setup}(1^\lambda, n)$, and outputs the public parameters $\mathsf{pp} = (\mathsf{pk}_{\mathsf{PKE}}, \mathsf{hk})$. Note that we implicitly assume that pp contain 1^λ and n.
- $\mathsf{KeyGen}(\mathsf{pp})$: On input the public parameters $\mathsf{pp} = (\mathsf{pk}_{\mathsf{PKE}}, \mathsf{hk})$, the key-generation algorithm samples $r \xleftarrow{R} \{0,1\}^\lambda$ and computes $\mathsf{ct} = \mathsf{PKE.Enc}(\mathsf{pk}_{\mathsf{PKE}}, 1; r)$. Output the public key $\mathsf{pk} = \mathsf{ct}$ and the secret key $\mathsf{sk} = r$.
- $\mathsf{Enc}(\mathsf{pp}, \mathsf{msg}, (\mathsf{pk}_1, \dots, \mathsf{pk}_k))$: On input the public parameters $\mathsf{pp} = (\mathsf{pk}_{\mathsf{PKE}}, \mathsf{hk})$, the message $\mathsf{msg} \in \mathcal{M}_\lambda$, and public keys $\mathsf{pk}_1, \dots, \mathsf{pk}_k$, the encryption algorithm computes the digest $\mathsf{dig} = \mathsf{FBH.Hash}(\mathsf{hk}, (\mathsf{pk}_1, \dots, \mathsf{pk}_k))$ and outputs the ciphertext $\mathsf{ct} \leftarrow \mathsf{WE.Enc}(1^\lambda, \mathsf{msg}, (\mathsf{hk}, \mathsf{pk}_{\mathsf{PKE}}, \mathsf{dig}))$.
- $\mathsf{Dec}(\mathsf{pp}, \mathsf{ct}, (j, \mathsf{sk}_j), (\mathsf{pk}_1, \dots, \mathsf{pk}_k))$: On input the public parameters $\mathsf{pp} = (\mathsf{pk}_{\mathsf{PKE}}, \mathsf{hk})$, the ciphertext ct, an index $j \in [n]$, the associated secret key sk_j, and the public keys $\mathsf{pk}_1, \dots, \mathsf{pk}_k$, the decryption algorithm computes the digest $\mathsf{dig} = \mathsf{FBH.Hash}(\mathsf{hk}, (\mathsf{pk}_1, \dots, \mathsf{pk}_k))$, the opening $\pi = \mathsf{FBH.ProveOpen}(\mathsf{hk}, (\mathsf{pk}_1, \dots, \mathsf{pk}_k), \{j\})$, and finally, outputs the message $\mathsf{msg} = \mathsf{WE.Dec}(1^\lambda, \mathsf{ct}, (j, \mathsf{pk}_j, \mathsf{sk}_j, \pi))$.

Correctness and Security Analysis. We note that efficiency, succinct ciphertexts, and perfect correctness follow from the correctness and efficiency of PKE and WE, and the efficiency and completeness of FBH. Semi-static security in turn follows from security of the witness encryption scheme along with security of the function-binding hash function. Due to space restrictions, we defer the full analysis to the full version of this paper [29].

Remark 4.4 (Transparent Setup). We note that the public parameters in our construction consist of a hash key for the function-binding hash and a public key for a public-key encryption scheme. If we instantiate the function-binding hash function using Construction 3.5, then the hash key consists of a sequence of public keys and ciphertexts for a leveled homomorphic encryption scheme. Using a suitable encryption scheme (e.g., [37]), these are all pseudorandom. In other words, the public parameters in Construction 4.3 is pseudorandom and can be instantiated with a uniform random string. This yields a flexible broadcast encryption scheme with a *transparent* setup.

5   Optimal Broadcast Encryption

As noted in Sect. 4, a flexible broadcast encryption scheme immediately implies a traditional broadcast encryption scheme with a central trusted authority. Namely, to construct a scheme for n users, the central authority would sample n different public/secret keys $(\mathsf{pk}_1, \mathsf{sk}_1), \ldots, (\mathsf{pk}_n, \mathsf{sk}_n)$. The master public key for the broadcast encryption scheme is the concatenation of all n public keys while the secret key for user i is sk_i. While this yields a scheme with short secret keys and ciphertexts, the master public key is very long (scales linearly with the number of users). In the full version of this paper [29], we show a simple adaptation of our approach yields an *optimal* broadcast encryption scheme in the *random oracle mode*. In an optimal broadcast encryption scheme [12], we require that all of the scheme parameters (i.e., the master public key, the user decryption keys, and the ciphertext) to be short (e.g., polylogarithmic with the number of users). We refer to the full version of this paper [29] for the details.

6   Registered Attribute-Based Encryption

In this section, we define and construct a slotted registered ABE scheme from witness encryption and a function-binding hash for disjunctions of block functions. We note that this implies a full registered ABE scheme by the transformation of [46]. Due to space limitations, we refer to the full version of this paper [29] for the definitions of policy-selective security as well as the proof of correctness and security of our construction.

6.1   Slotted Registered ABE Definition

In this section, we recall the notion of a *slotted* registered ABE scheme from [46]. In our setting, each user is associated with an attribute of length $\ell = \ell(\lambda)$ and each ciphertext is associated with a policy $P\colon \{0,1\}^{\ell(\lambda)} \to \{0,1\}$ taken from some policy space $\mathcal{P} = \{\mathcal{P}_\lambda\}_{\lambda\in\mathbb{N}}$. We say that an attribute x satisfies the policy P if $P(x) = 1$. We now recall the formal definition. We present the definition for the setting with a large (i.e., super-polynomial size) attribute universe and for supporting an arbitrary number of users (c.f., [46, Remark 6.10]):

Definition 6.1 (Slotted Registered ABE [46, adapted]**).** *Let $\ell = \ell(\lambda)$ be an attribute length and $\mathcal{P} = \{\mathcal{P}_\lambda\}_{\lambda\in\mathbb{N}}$ be a policy space on ℓ-bit inputs (i.e., $\mathcal{P}_\lambda$ is a set of functions $P\colon \{0,1\}^{\ell(\lambda)} \to \{0,1\}$). Let $m = m(\lambda)$ and $\mathcal{M} = \{\mathcal{M}_\lambda\}_{\lambda\in\mathbb{N}}$ be a message space with message length m. A* slotted registered attribute-based encryption scheme *for attributes of length ℓ, policy space $\mathcal{P}$, and message space $\mathcal{M}$ consists of polynomial-time algorithms* (Setup, KeyGen, Aggregate, Enc, Dec)[7] *with the following syntax:*

- Setup$(1^\lambda, L) \to$ pp*: A probabilistic algorithm that on input a security parameter λ and a number of slots L, outputs public parameters* pp*. We implicitly assume that* pp *contains 1^λ and L.*
- KeyGen$($pp$, i) \to ($pk, sk$)$*: A probabilistic algorithm that on input the public parameters* pp *and a slot index $i \in [L]$, outputs a public key* pk *and a secret key* sk*.*
- Aggregate$($pp$, ($pk$_1, x_1), \ldots, ($pk$_L, x_L)) \to ($mpk, hsk$_1, \ldots,$ hsk$_L)$*: A deterministic algorithm that on input public parameters* pp *and a list of public keys with associated attributes $($pk$_1, x_1), \ldots, ($pk$_L, x_L)$ outputs a master public key* mpk *and a sequence of helper decryption keys* hsk$_1, \ldots,$ hsk$_L$.
- Enc$($mpk$, P,$ msg$) \to$ ct*: A probabilistic algorithm that on input a master public key* mpk*, an access policy $P \in \mathcal{P}_\lambda$, and a message* msg $\in \mathcal{M}_\lambda$*, outputs a ciphertext* ct*.*
- Dec$($mpk, hsk, sk, ct$) \to$ msg*: A deterministic algorithm that on input a master public key* mpk*, a helper decryption key* hsk*, a secret key* sk*, and a ciphertext* ct*, outputs a message* msg $\in \mathcal{M}_\lambda \cup \{\perp\}$*.*

We require that (Setup, KeyGen, Aggregate, Enc, Dec) *satisfy the following properties:*

- **Compactness:** *There exists a polynomial p such that for any $\lambda \in \mathbb{N}$, $L \in \mathbb{N}$, public parameters* pp $\in$ Supp$\big($Setup$(1^\lambda, L)\big)$*, public/secret key-pairs $($pk$_i,$ sk$_i) \in$ Supp$\big($KeyGen$($pp$, i)\big)$, and attributes $x_i \in \{0,1\}^{\ell(\lambda)}$ for each $i \in [L]$, and setting $($mpk, hsk$_1, \ldots,$ hsk$_L) =$ Aggregate$($pp$, ($pk$_1, x_1), \ldots, ($pk$_L, x_L))$, the following holds:*
  - $|$mpk$| \le p(\lambda, \ell, \log L)$*, and*
  - $|$hsk$_i| \le p(\lambda, \ell, \log L)$ *for each $i \in [L]$.*

---

[7] The definition from [46] also includes an algorithm IsValid$($pp$, i,$ pk$_i) \to \{0,1\}$ that checks if a given public key is valid. Our construction does not require this check. However, to match their syntax, we could define it to simply output 1 on any public key of the correct length with respect to the public parameters pp.

This compactness notion requires that the size of the master public key and the helper decryption keys scale polylogarithmically with the size of the attribute universe ($|\{0,1\}^{\ell}| = 2^{\ell}$). We can define a weaker notion of compactness where the size of the master public key and the helper decryption keys scale polynomially with the size of the attribute universe. This weaker notion is the default in [46], as the parameters of their pairing-based construction scale polynomially with the size of the attribute universe.

– **Correctness:** *For any $\lambda \in \mathbb{N}$, $L \in \mathbb{N}$, $i \in [L]$, message $\mathsf{msg} \in \mathcal{M}_{\lambda}$, attributes $x_1, \ldots, x_L \in \{0,1\}^{\ell(\lambda)}$, policy $P \in \mathcal{P}_{\lambda}$ where $P(x_i) = 1$, $\mathsf{pp} \in \mathsf{Supp}\left(\mathsf{Setup}(1^{\lambda}, L)\right)$, $(\mathsf{pk}_i, \mathsf{sk}_i) \in \mathsf{Supp}\left(\mathsf{KeyGen}(\mathsf{pp}, i)\right)$, and any public keys $\{\mathsf{pk}_j\}_{j \neq i \in [L]}$ (which may be correlated with pk_i), let $(\mathsf{mpk}, \mathsf{hsk}_1, \ldots, \mathsf{hsk}_L) = \mathsf{Aggregate}(\mathsf{pp}, (\mathsf{pk}_1, x_1), \ldots, (\mathsf{pk}_L, x_L))$. Then, it holds that*

$$\Pr\left[\begin{matrix} \mathsf{ct} \leftarrow \mathsf{Enc}(\mathsf{mpk}, P, \mathsf{msg}) \\ \mathsf{msg}' = \mathsf{Dec}(\mathsf{mpk}, \mathsf{hsk}_i, \mathsf{sk}_i, \mathsf{ct}) \end{matrix} : \mathsf{msg}' = \mathsf{msg}\right] = 1.$$

– **Adaptive security:** *For all stateful PPT adversaries A and efficiently-computable function $L \in \mathsf{poly}(\lambda)$, there exists a negligible function negl such that for all $\lambda \in \mathbb{N}$,*

$$\Pr\left[\mathsf{Expt}_{A,L(\lambda)}^{\mathsf{srABE}}(\lambda) = 1\right] \leq 1/2 + \mathsf{negl}(\lambda),$$

where $\mathsf{Expt}_{A,L}^{\mathsf{srABE}}(\lambda)$ is defined via the following security game between the adversary A and a challenger on common input 1^{λ}:

- **Setup phase:** *The challenger samples $\mathsf{pp} \leftarrow \mathsf{Setup}(1^{\lambda}, L)$ and sends pp to A. The challenger initializes a counter $\mathsf{ctr} := 0$, a dictionary D, and a set of (corrupted) slot indices $\mathcal{C} := \varnothing$.*
- **Pre-challenge query phase:** *The adversary A can now issue the following queries:*
  * **Key-generation query:** *In a key-generation query, the adversary specifies a slot index $i \in [L]$. The challenger increments the counter value $\mathsf{ctr} := \mathsf{ctr} + 1$, samples $(\mathsf{pk}, \mathsf{sk}) \leftarrow \mathsf{KeyGen}(\mathsf{pp}, i)$ and replies with $(\mathsf{ctr}, \mathsf{pk})$ to A. The challenger adds the mapping $\mathsf{ctr} \mapsto (i, \mathsf{pk}, \mathsf{sk})$ to the dictionary D.*
  * **Corruption query:** *In a corruption query, the adversary specifies a counter value $c \in [\mathsf{ctr}]$. In response, the challenger looks up the tuple $(i, \mathsf{pk}, \mathsf{sk}) := \mathsf{D}[c]$ and replies to A with sk.*
- **Challenge phase:** *For each slot $i \in [L]$, the adversary A specifies a tuple $(c_i, x_i, \mathsf{pk}_i^{\star})$ where either $c_i \in \{1, \ldots, \mathsf{ctr}\}$ to reference a challenger-generated key or $c_i = \perp$ to reference a key outside this set. The adversary also sends a challenge policy $P^{\star} \in \mathcal{P}_{\lambda}$ and two messages $\mathsf{msg}_0, \mathsf{msg}_1 \in \mathcal{M}_{\lambda}$. The challenger responds by first constructing pk_i as follows for each $i \in [L]$:*
  * *If $c_i \in \{1, \ldots, \mathsf{ctr}\}$, then the challenger sets $(i', \mathsf{pk}, \mathsf{sk}) := \mathsf{D}[c_i]$. If $i = i'$, then the challenger sets $\mathsf{pk}_i := \mathsf{pk}$. Moreover, if the adversary previously issued a corruption query on counter c_i, then the challenger*

> adds the slot index i to $\mathcal{C}$. Otherwise, if $i \neq i'$, then the experiment
> halts and outputs 0.

* If $c_i = \bot$, the challenger sets $\mathsf{pk}_i := \mathsf{pk}_i^\star$ and adds the slot index i to $\mathcal{C}$.
  The challenger computes $(\mathsf{mpk}, \mathsf{hsk}_1, \ldots, \mathsf{hsk}_L) = \mathsf{Aggregate}(\mathsf{pp}, (\mathsf{pk}_1, x_1),$
  $\ldots, (\mathsf{pk}_L, x_L))$, samples a random bit $b \leftarrow \{0, 1\}$, known as the challenge
  bit, and replies with the challenge ciphertext $\mathsf{ct}^\star \leftarrow \mathsf{Enc}(\mathsf{mpk}, P^\star, \mathsf{msg}_b)$.[8]

- **Output phase:** At the end of the experiment, the adversary A outputs
  a bit $b' \in \{0, 1\}$. We say that algorithm A is admissible if $P^\star(x_i) = 0$
  for all $i \in \mathcal{C}$ (i.e., the attributes associated with corrupted slots do not
  satisfy the challenge policy). The experiment outputs 1 if $b' = b$ and A is
  admissible. Otherwise, the experiment outputs 0.

6.2   Slotted Registered ABE Construction

We now show how to construct a slotted registered ABE scheme from witness
encryption, function binding hash functions, and public-key encryption. Our
scheme satisfies policy-selective security without corruptions. We show in the full
version of this paper [29] how to use this to generically transform this scheme
into one that satisfies policy-selective security with corruptions in the random
oracle model. As was the case for our flexible broadcast encryption scheme (Construction 4.3), the public parameters for our registered ABE scheme is a uniform
random string, and thus, our scheme supports a transparent setup.

Construction 6.2 (Slotted Registered ABE). Let $\ell = \ell(\lambda)$ be the attribute
length and $m = m(\lambda)$ be the message length. Let $s = s(\lambda, \ell)$, $\ell_{\mathsf{blk}} = \ell_{\mathsf{blk}}(\lambda)$, and
$d = d(\lambda, \ell)$ be polynomials. Let $\mathcal{M} = \{\mathcal{M}_\lambda\}_{\lambda \in \mathbb{N}}$ be a message space for message
of length m. Let $\mathcal{P} = \{\mathcal{P}_\lambda\}_{\lambda \in \mathbb{N}}$ be a set of policies on ℓ-bit attributes (i.e., $\mathcal{P}_\lambda$
consists of functions $P \colon \{0, 1\}^{\ell(\lambda)} \to \{0, 1\}$) where each policy $P \in \mathcal{P}_\lambda$ can be
implemented by a Boolean circuit of size s and depth d. Our construction of
slotted registered ABE relies on the following primitives:

- Let $\mathsf{PKE} = (\mathsf{PKE.KeyGen}, \mathsf{PKE.Enc}, \mathsf{PKE.Dec})$ be a semantically-secure public-
  key bit encryption scheme where, for $(\mathsf{pk}, \mathsf{sk}) \in \mathsf{Supp}\left(\mathsf{PKE.KeyGen}(1^\lambda)\right)$,
  ciphertexts have length at most $\ell_{\mathsf{blk}}(\lambda)$ and decryption can be computed by a
  circuit of size s and depth d.
- Let $\mathsf{FBH} = (\mathsf{FBH.Setup}, \mathsf{FBH.SetupBinding}, \mathsf{FBH.Hash}, \mathsf{FBH.ProveOpen},$
  $\mathsf{FBH.VerOpen})$ be a function-binding hash for the class $\mathcal{F}$ of disjunctions
  of block functions for input length $\ell_{\mathsf{blk}}(\lambda) + \ell(\lambda)$, size $2s + 1$, and depth d
  (Definition 3.3).
- Let $\mathsf{WE} = (\mathsf{WE.Enc}, \mathsf{WE.Dec})$ be a witness encryption scheme for the language
  $\mathcal{L} = \{\mathcal{L}_\lambda\}_{\lambda \in \mathbb{N}}$ defined by the relation $\mathbf{R}_{\mathcal{L}}$ as follows. Instances of the language

---

[8] Note that because $\mathsf{Aggregate}$ is deterministic and can be run by A itself, there is
no need to additionally provide $(\mathsf{mpk}, \mathsf{hsk}_1, \ldots, \mathsf{hsk}_L)$ to A. Similarly, there is no
advantage to allowing the adversary to select the challenge policy and messages
after seeing the aggregated key.

$\mathcal{L}_\lambda$ are of the form $(\mathsf{hk}, \mathsf{pk}_{\mathsf{PKE}}, \mathsf{dig}, P)$ and the relation $\mathbf{R}_\mathcal{L}$ is given by

$$\mathbf{R}_\mathcal{L}((\mathsf{hk}, \mathsf{pk}_{\mathsf{PKE}}, \mathsf{dig}, P), (i, \mathsf{ct}, x, r, \pi)) = 1$$
$$\Leftrightarrow \mathsf{ct} = \mathsf{PKE.Enc}(\mathsf{pk}_{\mathsf{PKE}}, 1; r) \wedge P(x) = 1 \wedge$$
$$\mathsf{FBH.VerOpen}(\mathsf{hk}, \mathsf{dig}, \{i\}, \{(i, (\mathsf{ct}, x))\}, \pi) = 1.$$

We construct a slotted registered ABE scheme $\mathsf{srABE} = (\mathsf{Setup}, \mathsf{KeyGen},$ $\mathsf{Aggregate}, \mathsf{Enc}, \mathsf{Dec})$ with attribute length ℓ, policy space $\mathcal{P}$, and message space $\mathcal{M}$ as follows:

- $\mathsf{Setup}(1^\lambda, L)$: On input the security parameter λ and the number of slots L, the setup algorithm samples $(\mathsf{pk}_{\mathsf{PKE}}, \mathsf{sk}_{\mathsf{PKE}}) \leftarrow \mathsf{PKE.KeyGen}(1^\lambda)$, $\mathsf{hk} \leftarrow \mathsf{FBH.Setup}(1^\lambda, L)$, and outputs public parameters $\mathsf{pp} = (\mathsf{pk}_{\mathsf{PKE}}, \mathsf{hk})$.
- $\mathsf{KeyGen}(\mathsf{pp}, i)$: On input the public parameters $\mathsf{pp} = (\mathsf{pk}_{\mathsf{PKE}}, \mathsf{hk})$ and an index $i \in [L]$, the key-generation algorithm samples $r \xleftarrow{\mathrm{R}} \{0,1\}^\lambda$ and computes $\mathsf{ct} = \mathsf{PKE.Enc}(\mathsf{pk}_{\mathsf{PKE}}, 1; r)$. It then outputs the public key $\mathsf{pk} = \mathsf{ct}$ and secret key $\mathsf{sk} = r$.
- $\mathsf{Aggregate}(\mathsf{pp}, (\mathsf{pk}_1, x_1), \ldots, (\mathsf{pk}_L, x_L))$: On input the public parameters $\mathsf{pp} = (\mathsf{pk}_{\mathsf{PKE}}, \mathsf{hk})$ and a ordered list of public keys pk_i with associated attributes $x_i \in \{0,1\}^\ell$, the aggregation algorithm first computes the digest $\mathsf{dig} = \mathsf{FBH.Hash}(\mathsf{hk}, ((\mathsf{pk}_1, x_1), \ldots, (\mathsf{pk}_L, x_L)))$. Then, for each $i \in [L]$, it computes the proof $\pi_i = \mathsf{FBH.ProveOpen}(\mathsf{hk}, ((\mathsf{pk}_1, x_1), \ldots, (\mathsf{pk}_L, x_L)), \{i\})$. Finally, it outputs the master public key $\mathsf{mpk} = (\mathsf{pp}, \mathsf{dig})$ and the helper decryption key $\mathsf{hsk}_i = (i, \pi_i, \mathsf{pk}_i, x_i)$ for each $i \in [L]$.
- $\mathsf{Enc}(\mathsf{mpk}, P, \mathsf{msg})$: On input the master public key $\mathsf{mpk} = ((\mathsf{pk}_{\mathsf{PKE}}, \mathsf{hk}), \mathsf{dig})$, a policy $P \in \mathcal{P}_\lambda$, and a message $\mathsf{msg} \in \mathcal{M}_\lambda$, the encryption algorithm outputs $\mathsf{ct} \leftarrow \mathsf{WE.Enc}(1^\lambda, \mathsf{msg}, (\mathsf{hk}, \mathsf{pk}_{\mathsf{PKE}}, \mathsf{dig}, P))$.
- $\mathsf{Dec}(\mathsf{mpk}, \mathsf{hsk}, \mathsf{sk}, \mathsf{ct})$: On input the master public key mpk, the helper decryption key $\mathsf{hsk} = (i, \pi, \mathsf{pk}, S)$, a secret key sk, and a ciphertext ct, the decryption algorithm outputs $\mathsf{msg} = \mathsf{WE.Dec}(1^\lambda, \mathsf{ct}, (i, \mathsf{pk}, S, \mathsf{sk}, \pi))$.

Correctness and security analysis. Due to space restrictions, we defer the correctness and security analysis of Construction 6.2 to the full version of this paper [29].

Acknowledgments. We thank Dan Boneh and Hoeteck Wee for helpful pointers on broadcast encryption. Cody Freitag's work was done while at Cornell Tech, and he is supported by the National Science Foundation Graduate Research Fellowship under Grant No. DGE-2139899, DARPA Award HR00110C0086, AFOSR Award FA9550-18-1-0267, NSF CNS-2128519, and DARPA under Agreement No. HR00112020023. Brent Waters is supported by NSF CNS-1908611, a Simons Investigator award, and the Packard Foundation Fellowship. David J. Wu is supported by NSF CNS-2151131, CNS-2140975, a Microsoft Research Faculty Fellowship, and a Google Research Scholar award.

References

1. Agrawal, S., Wichs, D., Yamada, S.: Optimal broadcast encryption from LWE and pairings in the standard model. In: Pass, R., Pietrzak, K. (eds.) TCC 2020. LNCS, vol. 12550, pp. 149–178. Springer, Cham (2020). https://doi.org/10.1007/978-3-030-64375-1_6
2. Agrawal, S., Yamada, S.: Optimal broadcast encryption from pairings and LWE. In: Canteaut, A., Ishai, Y. (eds.) EUROCRYPT 2020. LNCS, vol. 12105, pp. 13–43. Springer, Cham (2020). https://doi.org/10.1007/978-3-030-45721-1_2
3. Ananth, P., Lombardi, A.: Succinct garbling schemes from functional encryption through a local simulation paradigm. In: Beimel, A., Dziembowski, S. (eds.) TCC 2018. LNCS, vol. 11240, pp. 455–472. Springer, Cham (2018). https://doi.org/10.1007/978-3-030-03810-6_17
4. Badrinarayanan, S., Garg, S., Ishai, Y., Sahai, A., Wadia, A.: Two-message witness indistinguishability and secure computation in the plain model from new assumptions. In: Takagi, T., Peyrin, T. (eds.) ASIACRYPT 2017. LNCS, vol. 10626, pp. 275–303. Springer, Cham (2017). https://doi.org/10.1007/978-3-319-70700-6_10
5. Barak, B., et al.: On the (im)possibility of obfuscating programs. In: Kilian, J. (ed.) CRYPTO 2001. LNCS, vol. 2139, pp. 1–18. Springer, Heidelberg (2001). https://doi.org/10.1007/3-540-44647-8_1
6. Barta, O., Ishai, Y., Ostrovsky, R., Wu, D.J.: On succinct arguments and witness encryption from groups. In: Micciancio, D., Ristenpart, T. (eds.) CRYPTO 2020. LNCS, vol. 12170, pp. 776–806. Springer, Cham (2020). https://doi.org/10.1007/978-3-030-56784-2_26
7. Bitansky, N., Paneth, O., Rosen, A.: On the cryptographic hardness of finding a Nash equilibrium. In: FOCS (2015)
8. Boneh, D., Gentry, C., Waters, B.: Collusion resistant broadcast encryption with short ciphertexts and private keys. In: Shoup, V. (ed.) CRYPTO 2005. LNCS, vol. 3621, pp. 258–275. Springer, Heidelberg (2005). https://doi.org/10.1007/11535218_16
9. Boneh, D., Ishai, Y., Sahai, A., Wu, D.J.: Quasi-optimal SNARGs via linear multi-prover interactive proofs. In: Nielsen, J.B., Rijmen, V. (eds.) EUROCRYPT 2018. LNCS, vol. 10822, pp. 222–255. Springer, Cham (2018). https://doi.org/10.1007/978-3-319-78372-7_8
10. Boneh, D., Waters, B.: A fully collusion resistant broadcast, trace, and revoke system. In: ACM CCS (2006)
11. Boneh, D., Waters, B.: Constrained pseudorandom functions and their applications. In: Sako, K., Sarkar, P. (eds.) ASIACRYPT 2013. LNCS, vol. 8270, pp. 280–300. Springer, Heidelberg (2013). https://doi.org/10.1007/978-3-642-42045-0_15
12. Boneh, D., Waters, B., Zhandry, M.: Low overhead broadcast encryption from multilinear maps. In: Garay, J.A., Gennaro, R. (eds.) CRYPTO 2014. LNCS, vol. 8616, pp. 206–223. Springer, Heidelberg (2014). https://doi.org/10.1007/978-3-662-44371-2_12
13. Boneh, D., Zhandry, M.: multiparty key exchange, efficient traitor tracing, and more from indistinguishability obfuscation. In: Garay, J.A., Gennaro, R. (eds.) CRYPTO 2014. LNCS, vol. 8616, pp. 480–499. Springer, Heidelberg (2014). https://doi.org/10.1007/978-3-662-44371-2_27
14. Brakerski, Z.: Fully homomorphic encryption without modulus switching from classical GapSVP. In: Safavi-Naini, R., Canetti, R. (eds.) CRYPTO 2012. LNCS, vol. 7417, pp. 868–886. Springer, Heidelberg (2012). https://doi.org/10.1007/978-3-642-32009-5_50

15. Brakerski, Z., Gentry, C., Vaikuntanathan, V.: (Leveled) fully homomorphic encryption without bootstrapping. In: ITCS (2012)
16. Brakerski, Z., Jain, A., Komargodski, I., Passelègue, A., Wichs, D.: Non-trivial witness encryption and null-iO from standard assumptions. In: Catalano, D., De Prisco, R. (eds.) SCN 2018. LNCS, vol. 11035, pp. 425–441. Springer, Cham (2018). https://doi.org/10.1007/978-3-319-98113-0_23
17. Brakerski, Z., Vaikuntanathan, V.: Efficient fully homomorphic encryption from (standard) LWE. In: FOCS (2011)
18. Brakerski, Z., Vaikuntanathan, V.: Lattice-inspired broadcast encryption and succinct ciphertext-policy ABE. In: ITCS (2022)
19. Canetti, R., Park, S., Poburinnaya, O.: Fully deniable interactive encryption. In: Micciancio, D., Ristenpart, T. (eds.) CRYPTO 2020. LNCS, vol. 12170, pp. 807–835. Springer, Cham (2020). https://doi.org/10.1007/978-3-030-56784-2_27
20. Chen, J., Gay, R., Wee, H.: Improved dual system ABE in prime-order groups via predicate encodings. In: Oswald, E., Fischlin, M. (eds.) EUROCRYPT 2015. LNCS, vol. 9057, pp. 595–624. Springer, Heidelberg (2015). https://doi.org/10.1007/978-3-662-46803-6_20
21. Chen, Y., Vaikuntanathan, V., Wee, H.: GGH15 beyond permutation branching programs: proofs, attacks, and candidates. In: Shacham, H., Boldyreva, A. (eds.) CRYPTO 2018. LNCS, vol. 10992, pp. 577–607. Springer, Cham (2018). https://doi.org/10.1007/978-3-319-96881-0_20
22. Chung, K.-M., Lin, H., Pass, R.: Constant-round concurrent zero-knowledge from indistinguishability obfuscation. In: Gennaro, R., Robshaw, M. (eds.) CRYPTO 2015. LNCS, vol. 9215, pp. 287–307. Springer, Heidelberg (2015). https://doi.org/10.1007/978-3-662-47989-6_14
23. Cong, K., Eldefrawy, K., Smart, N.P.: Optimizing registration based encryption. In: Paterson, M.B. (ed.) IMACC 2021. LNCS, vol. 13129, pp. 129–157. Springer, Cham (2021). https://doi.org/10.1007/978-3-030-92641-0_7
24. Cook, S.A., Hoover, H.J.: A depth-universal circuit. SIAM J. Comput. **14**(4) (1985)
25. Dodis, Y., Fazio, N.: Public key broadcast encryption for stateless receivers. In: ACM CCS (2002)
26. Ephraim, N., Freitag, C., Komargodski, I., Pass, R.: SPARKs: succinct parallelizable arguments of knowledge. In: Canteaut, A., Ishai, Y. (eds.) EUROCRYPT 2020. LNCS, vol. 12105, pp. 707–737. Springer, Cham (2020). https://doi.org/10.1007/978-3-030-45721-1_25
27. Faonio, A., Nielsen, J.B., Venturi, D.: Predictable arguments of knowledge. In: Fehr, S. (ed.) PKC 2017. LNCS, vol. 10174, pp. 121–150. Springer, Heidelberg (2017). https://doi.org/10.1007/978-3-662-54365-8_6
28. Fiat, A., Naor, M.: Broadcast encryption. In: Stinson, D.R. (ed.) CRYPTO 1993. LNCS, vol. 773, pp. 480–491. Springer, Heidelberg (1994). https://doi.org/10.1007/3-540-48329-2_40
29. Freitag, C., Waters, B., Wu, D.J.: How to use (plain) witness encryption: registered ABE, flexible broadcast, and more (2023). https://eprint.iacr.org/2023/812
30. Garg, S., Gentry, C., Halevi, S., Raykova, M.: Two-round secure MPC from indistinguishability obfuscation. In: Lindell, Y. (ed.) TCC 2014. LNCS, vol. 8349, pp. 74–94. Springer, Heidelberg (2014). https://doi.org/10.1007/978-3-642-54242-8_4
31. Garg, S., Gentry, C., Halevi, S., Raykova, M., Sahai, A., Waters, B.: Candidate indistinguishability obfuscation and functional encryption for all circuits. In: FOCS (2013)
32. Garg, S., Gentry, C., Sahai, A., Waters, B.: Witness encryption and its applications. In: STOC (2013)

33. Garg, S., Hajiabadi, M., Mahmoody, M., Rahimi, A.: Registration-based encryption: removing private-key generator from IBE. In: Beimel, A., Dziembowski, S. (eds.) TCC 2018. LNCS, vol. 11239, pp. 689–718. Springer, Cham (2018). https://doi.org/10.1007/978-3-030-03807-6_25

34. Garg, S., Hajiabadi, M., Mahmoody, M., Rahimi, A., Sekar, S.: Registration-based encryption from standard assumptions. In: Lin, D., Sako, K. (eds.) PKC 2019. LNCS, vol. 11443, pp. 63–93. Springer, Cham (2019). https://doi.org/10.1007/978-3-030-17259-6_3

35. Garg, S., Mahmoody, M., Mohammed, A.: Lower bounds on obfuscation from all-or-nothing encryption primitives. In: Katz, J., Shacham, H. (eds.) CRYPTO 2017. LNCS, vol. 10401, pp. 661–695. Springer, Cham (2017). https://doi.org/10.1007/978-3-319-63688-7_22

36. Gentry, C., Lewko, A., Waters, B.: Witness encryption from instance independent assumptions. In: Garay, J.A., Gennaro, R. (eds.) CRYPTO 2014. LNCS, vol. 8616, pp. 426–443. Springer, Heidelberg (2014). https://doi.org/10.1007/978-3-662-44371-2_24

37. Gentry, C., Sahai, A., Waters, B.: Homomorphic encryption from learning with errors: conceptually-simpler, asymptotically-faster, attribute-based. In: Canetti, R., Garay, J.A. (eds.) CRYPTO 2013. LNCS, vol. 8042, pp. 75–92. Springer, Heidelberg (2013). https://doi.org/10.1007/978-3-642-40041-4_5

38. Gentry, C., Waters, B.: Adaptive security in broadcast encryption systems (with short ciphertexts). In: Joux, A. (ed.) EUROCRYPT 2009. LNCS, vol. 5479, pp. 171–188. Springer, Heidelberg (2009). https://doi.org/10.1007/978-3-642-01001-9_10

39. Glaeser, N., Kolonelos, D., Malavolta, G., Rahimi, A.: Efficient registration-based encryption. In: ACM CCS (2023)

40. Goldwasser, S., Kalai, Y.T., Popa, R.A., Vaikuntanathan, V., Zeldovich, N.: How to run Turing machines on encrypted data. In: Canetti, R., Garay, J.A. (eds.) CRYPTO 2013. LNCS, vol. 8043, pp. 536–553. Springer, Heidelberg (2013). https://doi.org/10.1007/978-3-642-40084-1_30

41. Goyal, R., Koppula, V., Waters, B.: Lockable obfuscation. In: FOCS (2017)

42. Goyal, R., Vusirikala, S.: Verifiable registration-based encryption. In: Micciancio, D., Ristenpart, T. (eds.) CRYPTO 2020. LNCS, vol. 12170, pp. 621–651. Springer, Cham (2020). https://doi.org/10.1007/978-3-030-56784-2_21

43. Goyal, R., Vusirikala, S., Waters, B.: Collusion resistant broadcast and trace from positional witness encryption. In: Lin, D., Sako, K. (eds.) PKC 2019. LNCS, vol. 11443, pp. 3–33. Springer, Cham (2019). https://doi.org/10.1007/978-3-030-17259-6_1

44. Goyal, V., Pandey, O., Sahai, A., Waters, B.: Attribute-based encryption for fine-grained access control of encrypted data. In: ACM CCS (2006)

45. Halevy, D., Shamir, A.: The LSD broadcast encryption scheme. In: Yung, M. (ed.) CRYPTO 2002. LNCS, vol. 2442, pp. 47–60. Springer, Heidelberg (2002). https://doi.org/10.1007/3-540-45708-9_4

46. Hohenberger, S., Lu, G., Waters, B., Wu, D.J.: Registered attribute-based encryption. In: Hazay, C., Stam, M. (eds.) EUROCRYPT 2023. LNCS, vol. 14006, pp. 511–542. Springer, Cham (2023). https://doi.org/10.1007/978-3-031-30620-4_17

47. Hubácek, P., Wichs, D.: On the communication complexity of secure function evaluation with long output. In: ITCS (2015)

48. Jain, A., Lin, H., Sahai, A.: Indistinguishability obfuscation from well-founded assumptions. In: STOC (2021)

49. Kalai, Y.T., Rothblum, G.N., Rothblum, R.D.: From obfuscation to the security of Fiat-Shamir for proofs. In: Katz, J., Shacham, H. (eds.) CRYPTO 2017. LNCS, vol. 10402, pp. 224–251. Springer, Cham (2017). https://doi.org/10.1007/978-3-319-63715-0_8

50. Merkle, R.C.: A certified digital signature. In: Brassard, G. (ed.) CRYPTO 1989. LNCS, vol. 435, pp. 218–238. Springer, New York (1990). https://doi.org/10.1007/0-387-34805-0_21

51. Naor, D., Naor, M., Lotspiech, J.: Revocation and tracing schemes for stateless receivers. In: Kilian, J. (ed.) CRYPTO 2001. LNCS, vol. 2139, pp. 41–62. Springer, Heidelberg (2001). https://doi.org/10.1007/3-540-44647-8_3

52. Sahai, A., Waters, B.: Fuzzy identity-based encryption. In: Cramer, R. (ed.) EURO-CRYPT 2005. LNCS, vol. 3494, pp. 457–473. Springer, Heidelberg (2005). https://doi.org/10.1007/11426639_27

53. Sahai, A., Waters, B.: How to use indistinguishability obfuscation: deniable encryption, and more. In: STOC (2014)

54. Tsabary, R.: Candidate witness encryption from lattice techniques. In: Dodis, Y., Shrimpton, T. (eds.) CRYPTO 2022. LNCS, vol. 13507, pp. 535–559. Springer, Cham (2022). https://doi.org/10.1007/978-3-031-15802-5_19

55. Vaikuntanathan, V., Wee, H., Wichs, D.: Witness encryption and null-IO from evasive LWE. In: Agrawal, S., Lin, D. (eds.) ASIACRYPT 2022. LNCS, vol. 13791, pp. 195–221. Springer, Cham (2022). https://doi.org/10.1007/978-3-031-22963-3_7

56. Wee, H.: Broadcast encryption with size $N^{1/3}$ and more from k-Lin. In: Malkin, T., Peikert, C. (eds.) CRYPTO 2021. LNCS, vol. 12828, pp. 155–178. Springer, Cham (2021). https://doi.org/10.1007/978-3-030-84259-8_6

57. Wee, H.: Optimal broadcast encryption and CP-ABE from evasive lattice assumptions. In: Dunkelman, O., Dziembowski, S. (eds.) EUROCRYPT 2022. LNCS, vol. 13276, pp. 217–241. Springer, Cham (2022). https://doi.org/10.1007/978-3-031-07085-3_8

58. Wichs, D., Zirdelis, G.: Obfuscating compute-and-compare programs under LWE. In: FOCS (2017)

Constant Input Attribute Based (and Predicate) Encryption from Evasive and Tensor LWE

Shweta Agrawal[1]($\boxtimes$), Mélissa Rossi[2], Anshu Yadav[3], and Shota Yamada[4]

[1] IIT Madras, Chennai, India
shweta@cse.iitm.ac.in
[2] ANSSI, Paris, France
melissa.rossi@ssi.gouv.fr
[3] IIT Madras, Chennai, India
[4] AIST, Tokyo, Japan
yamada-shota@aist.go.jp

Abstract. Constructing advanced cryptographic primitives such as obfuscation or broadcast encryption from standard hardness assumptions in the post quantum regime is an important area of research, which has met with limited success despite significant effort. It is therefore extremely important to find new, simple to state assumptions in this regime which can be used to fill this gap. An important step was taken recently by Wee (Eurocrypt '22) who identified two new assumptions from lattices, namely evasive LWE and tensor LWE, and used these to construct broadcast encryption and ciphertext policy attribute based encryption for P with optimal parameters. Independently, Tsabary formulated a similar assumption and used it to construct witness encryption (Crypto '22). Following Wee's work, Vaikuntanathan, Wee and Wichs independently provided a construction of witness encryption (Asiacrypt '22).

In this work, we advance this line of research by providing the first construction of multi-input attribute based encryption (miABE) for the function class NC_1 for *any* constant arity from evasive LWE. Our construction can be extended to support the function class P by using evasive and a suitable strengthening of tensor LWE. In more detail, our construction supports k encryptors, for any constant k, where each encryptor uses the master secret key msk to encode its input $(\mathbf{x}_i, m_i)$, the key generator computes a key sk_f for a function $f \in NC_1$ and the decryptor can recover $(m_1, \ldots, m_k)$ if and only if $f(\mathbf{x}_1, \ldots, \mathbf{x}_k) = 1$. The only known construction for miABE for NC_1 by Agrawal, Yadav and Yamada (Crypto '22) supports arity 2 and relies on pairings in the generic group model (or with a non-standard knowledge assumption) in addition to LWE. Furthermore, it is completely unclear how to go beyond arity 2 using this approach due to the reliance on pairings.

Using a compiler from Agrawal, Yadav and Yamada (Crypto '22), our miABE can be upgraded to multi-input *predicate* encryption for the same arity and function class. Thus, we obtain the first constructions for constant-arity predicate and attribute based encryption for a generalized class such as NC_1 or P from simple assumptions that may be conjectured post-quantum secure. Along the way, we show that the tensor LWE

© International Association for Cryptologic Research 2023
H. Handschuh and A. Lysyanskaya (Eds.): CRYPTO 2023, LNCS 14084, pp. 532–564, 2023.
https://doi.org/10.1007/978-3-031-38551-3_17

assumption can be reduced to standard LWE in an important special case which was not known before. This adds confidence to the plausibility of the assumption and may be of wider interest.

Keywords: multi-input attribute based encryption · multi-input predicate encryption · evasive LWE · tensor LWE

1   Introduction

Attribute Based Encryption. Attribute based encryption (ABE) [31,34] enables fine grained access control on encrypted data. In this notion, an encryptor computes a ciphertext encoding a secret message m and a public *attribute* vector $\mathbf{x}$, a key generator computes a secret key associated with a function f, and decryption outputs m if and only if $f(\mathbf{x}) = 1$. Security is formalized using an *indistinguishability* style game, where an adversary is asked to distinguish between an encryption of $(m_0, \mathbf{x}_0)$ and $(m_1, \mathbf{x}_1)$ given secret keys that do not decrypt the challenge. A further strengthening of this notion, traditionally referred to as *predicate* encryption (PE), additionally enables hiding of the attributes $\mathbf{x}$ which are public in ABE.

The Multi-Input Setting. The recent work of Agrawal, Yadav and Yamada [14] (henceforth by AYY) proposed decentralizing these notions to the multi-input setting, where the attribute $\mathbf{x}$ and the message m may be distributed among multiple parties, who must encrypt their inputs independently using uncorrelated random coins. In more detail, we now have k encryptors, who each encrypt their input $\{\mathbf{x}_i, m_i\}_{i \in [k]}$ using a master secret key msk^1, the key generator provides a key sk_f for an arity k function f, and decryption recovers $(m_1, \ldots, m_k)$ if and only if $f(\mathbf{x}_1, \ldots, \mathbf{x}_k) = 1$.

While the notion of multi-input ABE, denoted by miABE, had been studied before [22], this was as a stepping stone to constructing *Witness Encryption*. AYY argue that miABE is an important primitive in its own right and not just as a stepping stone to witness encryption, since it captures the demands of real world data more realistically than single input ABE. At the heart of miABE is the idea that though data may be generated in different places, it may be correlated in meaningful ways and natural access control policies are likely to embed constraints that pertain to the entire data. Hence, all information related to any self-contained unit, such as an individual or organization, should be considered together for the purpose of access control.

As a simple example, consider a dental care facility that has multiple branches in different geographical locations. A patient Alice (say) may visit the branch near her home if she needs a consultation on a Saturday but the branch near her work place if the appointment is on a weekday. Indeed, she may visit a branch in another city if she is travelling and needs dental assistance. In this scenario, each

---

[1] As in multi-input functional encryption, the notion of miABE is primarily meaningful in the secret key setting, due to excessive leakage that occurs in the public key setting.

branch will contain some subset of the data pertaining to Alice's dental history. Yet, all this data must be considered together in order to make decisions about future treatments. To enable this, each branch might encrypt their patient data everyday and upload it to a central repository. Ideally, a doctor should be able access all the information related to Alice's dental history if the doctor's key satisfies the relevant access control policy (for instance if she is one of Alice's designated doctors and all the records correspond to the Alice).

As another example, consider a businessman Bob (say) whose job involves frequent travelling. To stay healthy, he may become a member of a fitness center which has branches in several cities and visit the nearest one in his current location. The fitness center could have reduced rates or other promotional offers for clients depending on their usage, and Bob would wish to benefit from these though his usage is split across locations. As in the example above, each branch can encrypt their local data and upload it to a central location and secret keys could be provided to compute eligibility for the offer by collating this data. If eligible, the personal information can be decrypted and the offer can be extended. Finally, consider a research project which spans multiple universities. Each university could encrypt their findings and upload it to a central server, and keys could be provided for accessing the joint data based on some policy that spans the entire dataset. Please see [14] for several other examples.

1.1 Prior Work

AYY provided the first constructions for multi-input attribute based (and predicate) encryption. Specifically, they provided the first construction for two-input *key-policy* ABE for NC_1 from LWE and pairings by leveraging a surprising connection between the algebraic properties required to build two input ABE and the techniques developed in the context of broadcast encryption [13,15]. They also provided heuristic constructions for 2 input ABE for P and 3 input ABE for NC_1 – we will not discuss these here since our focus will be on constructions that admit a proof. Additionally, they gave a compiler that "lifts" any constant arity ABE scheme to a PE scheme of the same arity using the power of lockable obfuscation, which can be constructed from the Learning With Errors (LWE) assumption. Independently, Francati et al. [27] provided multi-input PE (hence also ABE) schemes for the restricted functionality of conjunctions of (bounded) polynomial depth from LWE. Notably, one of their constructions can support polynomial arity unlike AYY, which is a plus. On the other hand, their security model does not support collusions, which is typically the main technical challenge in constructing ABE and PE even in the single input setting. As another plus, when restricted to constant (though not polynomial) arity, their constructions can support user corruption, which AYY cannot – indeed AYY cannot even support arity for any constant though they support a much more expressive function class which is not restricted to conjunctions.

We briefly mention the stronger notion of multi-input *functional encryption* (miFE) [30], which generalizes multi-input ABE and PE. In contrast to miABE and miPE, miFE has been studied extensively, and admits constructions for various functionalities from a variety of assumptions [2–5,7–9,16,24,25,30,32,35]. However, since multi-input FE for NC_1 implies indistinguishability obfuscation (iO) [20,28], it remains an important area of study to instantiate weaker notions such as miABE and miPE from assumptions not known to imply iO. This is particularly important in the post quantum regime, where constructions of iO are still based on strong, ill-understood assumptions which are often broken [1,6,11,26,29,40]. Several prior works therefore focus on instantiating iO based constructions from weaker assumptions [10,13,15,36,37,39], a direction also followed by the present work.

Table 1. Comparison with Prior Work in miPE. Note that KOALA is a non-standard knowledge type assumption and "heuristic" means that there is no proof of security.

Paper	Arity	Functionality	Corruption	Collusion	Assumption
[27]	Poly	Conjunctions in P	No	No	LWE
[27]	Constant	Conjunctions in P	Yes	No	LWE
[14]	2	NC_1	No	Yes	Koala and LWE
[14]	2	P	No	Yes	Heuristic
This	2	P	No	Yes	Evasive and Tensor LWE
This	Constant	NC_1	No	Yes	Evasive LWE
This	Constant	P	No	Yes	Evasive and strong Tensor LWE

1.2   Our Results

As seen above, current known results for miABE schemes are quite restricted – the result of AYY appears to be fundamentally stuck at arity 2, while the result of Francati et al. [27] is tailored to the restricted functionality of conjunctions, offering no avenue for generalization to arbitrary NC_1 circuits.

In this work, we significantly extend the reach of multi-input ABE schemes by providing the first construction of miABE for the function class NC_1 for *any* constant arity from the recently introduced evasive LWE assumption [36,39]. Our construction can be extended to support the function class P by using evasive and a suitable strengthening of tensor LWE. For the special case of arity 2, we need only the assumptions introduced by Wee, i.e. evasive LWE for NC_1 and evasive plus tensor LWE for P (i.e. we do not need to strengthen tensor LWE).[2]

In more detail, our construction supports k encryptors, for any constant k, where each encryptor uses the master secret key msk to encode its input $(\mathbf{x}_i, m_i)$, the key generator computes a key sk_f for a function $f \in NC_1$ (or P at the cost of a stronger assumption) and the decryptor can recover $(m_1, \ldots, m_k)$ if and only

---

[2]   Actually, our definition of evasive LWE is slightly different from that defined in [39]. Please refer to Assumption 1 and the related discussion.

if $f(\mathbf{x}_1, \ldots, \mathbf{x}_k) = 1$. We prove security in the standard indistinguishability game defined by AYY from the aforementioned assumptions. Using the compiler from AYY, our miABE schemes can be upgraded to multi-input predicate encryption schemes for the same arity and function class. Along the way, we show that the tensor LWE assumption can be reduced to standard LWE in a special case which was not known before. This adds confidence to the plausibility of the assumption and may be of wider interest.

We defer details about our strengthening of tensor LWE for P as well as the new implication discussed above to the technical overview (Sect. 1.3) since stating them formally will require heavy notation which we do not want to introduce here. We provide a comparison with known results in Table 1.

Perspective: Connection to Witness Encryption. Witness encryption (WE) is defined for some NP language L with a corresponding witness relation R. In WE, an encryptor encrypts a message m to a particular problem instance x. The decryptor can recover m if $x \in L$ and it knows a witness w such that $R(x, w) = 1$. Security posits that a ciphertext hides the message m so long as $x \notin L$. Brakerski et al. [22] showed that miABE for polynomial arity implies witness encryption – this may explain in part why constructions of miABE have been so elusive. Even for smaller arity, there are nontrivial implications – for instance, the arity 2 miABE for NC_1 by AYY implies a compression factor of $1/3$ for witness encryption, which may be considered surprising. In the other direction, it is well known that in the single input setting, witness encryption implies attribute based encryption [28]. It is completely unclear however, how to generalize this implication to the multi-input setting – in the setting of single input, the ABE ciphertext contains a WE ciphertext for an NP statement that embeds the attribute. If the attributes are distributed amongst multiple parties, the above approach fails and appears challenging to extend. Thus, miABE implies new results in WE but not the other way around – indeed, in miABE, all encryptors must choose their randomness independently to construct a ciphertext for their respective slot, whereas in WE, there is only one encryptor who constructs the ciphertexts for all slots, making it possible to choose correlated randomness across slots. As we will see, this creates a major technical hurdle in designing miABE, which is not present in WE. Also note that miABE can subsequently be strengthened to miPE using lockable obfuscation, as discussed above.

We also note that single input ABE is the strongest application of the stated definition of WE in [28]. Since the definition of WE given in [28] only hides the message in the ciphertext when the statement is not in the language, the notion is insufficient to give any meaningful security guarantee when the statement is actually believed to be true but the witness is not known, such as solutions to some of the Clay Institute Millennium Prize Problems, as discussed in [28]. Hence, we believe that the primitives of miABE and miPE deserve to be studied even from assumptions that are already known to imply WE, such as evasive LWE [36,37].

1.3   Technical Overview

Recap of AYY. As observed by AYY, the main difficulty in building an miABE scheme is simultaneously fulfilling two opposing requirements: (1) each encryptor should be able to generate its own ciphertexts independently, (2) these independently generated ciphertexts should permit some kind of "joining" that lets them be viewed as multiple components of a single ABE ciphertext, such that decryption can proceed as in the single input setting. To achieve joining of ciphertext components, existing single input schemes generate multiple ciphertext components using common randomness. However, evidently, two independent sources, each generating an unbounded number of ciphertexts (say Q_1 and Q_2 respectively) cannot even store, much less embed, $Q_1 \cdot Q_2$ random strings in the ciphertexts they compute (even if they share a common PRF key).

In the two-input setting, AYY solve this conundrum by using the beautiful synergy between the algebraic structure offered by lattice based single input ABE schemes and pairing based constructions. This synergy was first discovered and harnessed by Agrawal and Yamada [15] in the context of broadcast encryption (a.k.a succinct single input ciphertext policy ABE for NC_1). The work of AYY noticed that the same synergy can be beneficial for the two-input *key* policy ABE setting, albeit for different reasons.

In more detail, AYY achieve the joining of ciphertexts via common randomness by letting each party embed fresh randomness in the exponent of a pairing based group for each ciphertext it computes. Now, party 1 (respectively 2) has Q_1 (respectively Q_2) random elements embedded in its Q_1 (respectively Q_2) ciphertexts. Using the pairing operation, the dercryptor can compute $Q_1 \cdot Q_2$ elements by pairwise multiplication in the exponent. In more detail, for each input, party 1 samples randomness t_1 and encodes it in $\mathbb{G}_1$, party 2 samples randomness t_2 and encodes it in $\mathbb{G}_2$, where $\mathbb{G} : \mathbb{G}_1 \times \mathbb{G}_2 \to \mathbb{G}_T$ is a pairing group with prime order q. Now these ciphertexts may be combined to form a new ciphertext with respect to the randomness $t_1 t_2$ on $\mathbb{G}_T$. This allows to uniquely separate every pair of ciphertexts, since each pair (i, j) where $i \in [Q_1]$ and $j \in [Q_2]$, will have unique randomness $t_1^i t_2^j$. We have by security of pairings that these $Q_1 \cdot Q_2$ correlated terms are indistinguishable from random in the exponent. This allows for generating the requisite randomness and solving the difficulty described above.

Fruitful interplay of pairings and lattices. However, generating joint randomness was not the final goal – the ciphertexts generated using the above joining procedure must behave like an ABE! Note that, having relied on a pairing, whatever we have obtained must live in the exponent of a group. Also note that, pairing based ABE schemes have been rendered unhelpful by this point, since the single multiplication afforded by the pairing has been used up and can no longer participate in the design of the ABE. Here, AYY, similarly to [13,15] are rescued by the serendipitously well-fitting structure of a lattice based ABE scheme constructed by Boneh et al. [21]. In [21] (henceforth BGG$^+$), decryption works as follows: (i) homomorphically compute the circuit f on ciphertext encodings – this step is *linear* even for $f \in P$, (ii) perform a product of the ciphertext matrix and secret key vector, (iii) round the recovered value to recover the message. Hence, the first two steps can be performed "upstairs" in the exponent and the last step may be performed "downstairs" by recovering the exponent brute force.

Structure of BGG^+. Let us recall the structure of the BGG^+ scheme, since this forms the starting point of our construction. As observed in multiple works, in BGG^+, the ciphertext for an attribute $\mathbf{x} \in [\ell]$ in BGG^+ is computed by first generating LWE encodings for all possible values of the attribute $\mathbf{x}$, namely, $\{\psi_{i,b}\}_{i \in [\ell], b \in \{0,1\}}$ and then choosing $\{\psi_{i,x_i}\}_{i \in [\ell]}$ where x_i is the i-th bit of attribute $\mathbf{x}$. Here, $\psi_{i,b} = \mathbf{s}(\mathbf{A}_i - x_{i,b} \cdot \mathbf{G}) + \mathsf{noise}$ where $\mathbf{A}_i \in \mathbb{Z}_q^{n \times m}$ are public matrices, $\mathbf{s} \in \mathbb{Z}_q^n$ is freshly chosen randomness, and $\mathbf{G} \in \mathbb{Z}_q^{n \times m}$ is the special "gadget" matrix which admits a public trapdoor (details not important here). Here, and in the remainder of this overview, we use noise to denote freshly and independently sampled noise terms of appropriate dimension, for each sample. Choosing components based on $\mathbf{x}$ and concatenating the samples yields $\mathbf{s}(\mathbf{A} - \mathbf{x} \otimes \mathbf{G}) + \mathsf{noise}$, where $\mathbf{A} \in \mathbb{Z}_q^{n \times \ell m}$ denotes the concatenation of $\{\mathbf{A}_i\}_{i \in [\ell]}$.

To evaluate a circuit $f \in \mathsf{P}$, BGG^+ observe that there exists an efficiently computable low norm matrix, denoted by $\widehat{\mathbf{H}}_{\mathbf{A},f,\mathbf{x}}$, so that the right multiplication of $(\mathbf{A} - \mathbf{x} \otimes \mathbf{G})$ by $\widehat{\mathbf{H}}_{\mathbf{A},f,\mathbf{x}}$ yields a quantity of the form $\mathbf{A}_f - f(\mathbf{x})\mathbf{G}$ – since the matrix is low norm, this can be right multiplied to $\mathbf{s}(\mathbf{A} - \mathbf{x} \otimes \mathbf{G}) + \mathsf{noise}$ to obtain approximately $\mathbf{s}(\mathbf{A}_f - f(\mathbf{x})\mathbf{G})$ without blowing up the noise. The decryption key for a function f is a low norm vector which, loosely speaking, is used in a matrix vector product that allows to cancel the masking term $\mathbf{s}\mathbf{A}_f$ when $f(\mathbf{x}) = 0$, and this in turn allows to recover the message.

Circling back to AYY, the first encryptor can (roughly speaking) compute $[t_1 \cdot \psi_{\mathbf{x}}]_1$, $[t_1]_1$, the second encryptor can compute $[t_2 \cdot \psi_{\mathbf{y}}]_2$, $[t_2]_2$ and the decryptor can compute $[t_1 t_2 \psi_{\mathbf{x}\|\mathbf{y}}]_T$, $[t_1 t_2]_T$. Note that randomization by $t_1 t_2$ is absolutely essential for security, else the adversary can potentially recover terms like $\mathbf{s}(\mathbf{A} - \mathbf{x} \otimes \mathbf{G}) + \mathsf{noise}$ and $\mathbf{s}(\mathbf{A} - \overline{\mathbf{x}} \otimes \mathbf{G}) + \mathsf{noise}$ in the exponent, which allows to cancel $\mathbf{s}\mathbf{A}$ by subtraction, and leads to a complete break of security. Next, the circuit f can be evaluated in the exponent as described above by right multiplication with a low norm matrix and the secret key can be applied by the matrix vector product to obtain the (scaled) message plus some noise in the exponent. The noise growth can be suitably bounded for the circuit class NC_1, and given $[t_1 t_2]_T$, one can recover the message using brute force discrete log computation.

While AYY takes an important first step towards constructing miABE schemes, it is evident that going beyond degree two is difficult while relying on pairings. Indeed, they do consider arity 3 by additionally relying on ideas from a clever lattice based scheme by Brakerski and Vaikuntanathan [23] but this scheme is heuristic, i.e. does not have a proof based on any clean assumption. Thus, it is completely unclear how to go beyond arity 2 using the techniques of AYY, even for NC_1. A natural idea to overcome the barrier of 2 is to rely on lattices in lieu of pairings.

Towards Lattice Based Constructions. Taking a step back, a promising direction would be to consider the lattice adaptation of the Agrawal-Yamada broadcast encryption scheme [15] recently proposed by Wee [39]. This construction makes important progress in identifying a clean assumption in the lattice regime that captures the functionality provided by the pairing without relying on bilinear groups, and can be used to construct advanced primitives like broadcast encryption and witness encryption without relying on iO (or the messy assumptions needed to build iO in the post quantum regime). In more detail, Wee [39] suggested two new assumptions – the evasive LWE and tensor LWE and used these to construct ciphertext polict ABE schemes with optimal parameters. We describe his approach next.

Overview of Wee's approach. The main idea of Wee is to cleverly replace the randomization in the exponent by tensoring on the ground. In more detail, Wee observes that the transformation of $(\mathbf{A} - \mathbf{x} \otimes \mathbf{G})$ to $(\mathbf{A}_f - f(\mathbf{x})\mathbf{G})$ via right multiplication by $\widehat{\mathbf{H}}_{\mathbf{A},f,\mathbf{x}}$ is preserved under tensoring with random low norm vectors $\mathbf{r}$. To see this, note that

$$\mathbf{s}(\mathbf{A} \otimes \mathbf{r}^\top) + \text{noise} = \underbrace{\mathbf{s}(\mathbf{I} \otimes \mathbf{r}^\top)}_{\text{Randomized secret}} \mathbf{A} + \text{noise}$$

where the latter quantity can be seen as BGG^+ ciphertext with a tensored LWE secret. This easily implies that homomorphism is preserved even with tensoring as desired. Hence, one can homomorphically evaluate f on $(\mathbf{A} - \mathbf{x} \otimes \mathbf{G}) \otimes \mathbf{r}^\top$ to obtain $(\mathbf{A}_f - f(\mathbf{x})\mathbf{G}) \otimes \mathbf{r}^\top$ via right multiplication by $\widehat{\mathbf{H}}_{\mathbf{A},f,\mathbf{x}}$.

Importantly, Wee shows that a very natural adaptation of [15], obtained by replacing randomization in the exponent by tensoring can be shown secure under a new and elegant assumption, which he calls *evasive* LWE. To support NC_1, he shows that evasive LWE suffices, while to support P, one additionally needs another new assumption, which he calls *tensor* LWE. The formulation of a relatively simple and general assumption in the lattice regime that allows to give a proof for a very natural construction of succint ciphertext policy ABE is a very important contribution which is likely to influence many future lattice constructions, including ours. We describe these assumptions next.

Evasive LWE. The evasive LWE assumption, introduced by Wee [39] (and independently Tsabary [36]), is a strengthening of the LWE assumption which says that certain extra information, namely Gaussian preimages to LWE public matrices, can only be used in a "semi-honest" way. Recall that the LWE assumption says that

$$(\mathbf{B}, \mathbf{sB} + \mathbf{e}) \approx_c (\mathbf{B}, \mathbf{c})$$

where $\mathbf{B} \leftarrow \mathbb{Z}_q^{n \times m}$, $\mathbf{s} \leftarrow \mathbb{Z}_q^n$, $\mathbf{e} \leftarrow \chi^m$ for some low norm "noise" distribution χ and $\mathbf{c} \leftarrow \mathbb{Z}_q^m$. Intuitively, the evasive LWE assumption says that if the adversary is additionally given some low norm matrix $\mathbf{K}$ such that $\mathbf{BK} = \mathbf{P}$, which we denote as $\mathbf{B}^{-1}(\mathbf{P})$ (as in the literature, see for instance [39]), for some efficiently sampleable matrix $\mathbf{P}$, then the adversary can exploit this extra information only via the limited means of computing the product $(\mathbf{sB} + \mathbf{e}) \cdot \mathbf{B}^{-1}(\mathbf{P}) \approx \mathbf{sP}$ and trying to distinguish this from uniform. The assumption says that this is the only additional capability that the adversary obtains, besides its existing strategies for breaking LWE.

Evidently, the distribution of $\mathbf{P}$ here is of crucial importance – for instance, if $\mathbf{P} = \mathbf{0}$, then $\mathbf{B}^{-1}(\mathbf{P})$ is a trapdoor for $\mathbf{B}$ and can be used to easily break LWE. On the other extreme, if $\mathbf{P}$ is chosen uniformly, then this assumption reduces to standard LWE. The "playing ground" of evasive LWE is in the middle – namely, when it holds that

$$(\mathbf{B}, \mathbf{P}, \mathbf{s}\mathbf{B} + \mathbf{e}, \mathbf{s}\mathbf{P} + \mathbf{e}') \approx_c (\mathbf{B}, \mathbf{P}, \mathbf{c}, \mathbf{c}')$$

then

$$(\mathbf{B}, \mathbf{s}\mathbf{B} + \mathbf{e}, \mathbf{B}^{-1}(\mathbf{P})) \approx_c (\mathbf{B}, \mathbf{c}, \mathbf{B}^{-1}(\mathbf{P})).$$

Here, the former condition is referred to as the PRE condition and the latter as POST. The actual assumption used by the scheme is more complex and includes more LWE samples that use the same secret $\mathbf{s}$ as well as some (carefully chosen) auxiliary information aux. To formalize the PRE condition, the assumption must specify an efficient sampler Samp which outputs the correlated LWE matrices. We defer the formalization to Sect. 3; here we only remark that the assumption captures in the lattice setting, the guarantees provided by the generic group model for pairings, namely the intuition that an adversary can only use legitimate operations to learn anything. It is therefore very natural (in hidsight) that this assumption should be able to replace the reliance on the generic group model in the constructions of [13, 15].

Tensor LWE. The tensor LWE assumption states that correlated BGG$^+$ samples tensored with different random vectors remain pseudorandom. In more detail, for all $\mathbf{x}_1, \cdots, \mathbf{x}_Q \in \{0,1\}^\ell$, it posits that

$$\mathbf{A}, \left\{ \mathbf{s}(\mathbf{I}_n \otimes \mathbf{r}_i^\top)(\mathbf{A} - \mathbf{x}_i \otimes \mathbf{G}) + \mathbf{e}_i, \ \mathbf{r}_i^\top \right\}_{i \in [Q]} \approx_c \mathbf{A}, \left\{ \mathbf{c}_i, \mathbf{r}_i^\top \right\}_{i \in [Q]}$$

where $\mathbf{A} \leftarrow \mathbb{Z}_q^{n \times \ell m}, \mathbf{s} \leftarrow \mathbb{Z}_q^{mn}, \mathbf{e}_i \leftarrow \mathcal{D}_{\mathbb{Z},\chi}^{\ell m}, \mathbf{r}_i \leftarrow \mathcal{D}_{\mathbb{Z},\gamma}^m, \mathbf{c}_i \leftarrow \mathbb{Z}_q^{\ell m}$.

Note that there are no Gaussian preimages in the above assumption. In our work, we show that for the special case where $\mathbf{x}_i = 0 \ \forall i \in [Q]$, tensor LWE reduces to standard LWE (Lemma 3). In more detail, let $\mathcal{A}$ be an attacker for Tensor LWE with $\mathbf{x}_i = \mathbf{0}$ for all $i \in [Q]$. $\mathcal{A}$ is given either $\mathbf{A}, \left\{ \mathbf{s}(\mathbf{I}_n \otimes \mathbf{r}_i^\top)\mathbf{A} + \mathbf{e}_i, \mathbf{r}_i^\top \right\}_{i \in [Q]}$ or $\mathbf{A}, \left\{ \mathbf{c}_i, \mathbf{r}_i^\top \right\}_{i \in [Q]}$. We prove that under the LWE assumption, $\mathcal{A}$ has a negligible probability of distinguishing the left hand side from the right hand side. This implication was not known before, and increases our confidence in the assumption, which is new and not so well studied. Please see Lemma 3 for details.

Generalizing Tensor LWE. While tensor LWE as stated by Wee suffices for our construction of 2-ABE for P, for extending the arity to any constant k, we require a strengthening of this assumption. In more detail, we require that for all $\mathbf{x}_{j_1,\dots,j_k} \in \{0,1\}^\ell$ indexed by $j_1, \dots, j_k \in [Q]$, it holds that:

$$\mathbf{A}, \left\{ \mathbf{s}(\mathbf{I}_n \otimes \mathbf{r}_{1,j_1}^\top \otimes \cdots \otimes \mathbf{r}_{k,j_k}^\top)(\mathbf{A} - \mathbf{x}_{j_1,\dots,j_k} \otimes \mathbf{G}) + \mathbf{e}_{j_1,\dots,j_k}, \mathbf{r}_{i,j_i} \right\}_{i \in [k], j_1,\dots,j_k \in [Q]}$$

$$\approx_c \mathbf{A}, \left\{ \mathbf{c}_{i,j_i}, \mathbf{r}_{i,j_i} \right\}_{i \in [k], j_1,\dots,j_k \in [Q]}$$

where $\mathbf{A} \leftarrow \mathbb{Z}_q^{n \times \ell m}, \mathbf{s} \leftarrow \mathbb{Z}_q^{nm^k}, \mathbf{e}_{j_1, \dots, j_k} \leftarrow \mathcal{D}_{\mathbb{Z}, \chi}^{\ell m}, \mathbf{r}_{i, j_i} \leftarrow \mathcal{D}_{\mathbb{Z}, \gamma}^m, \mathbf{c}_{i, j_i} \leftarrow \mathbb{Z}_q^{\ell m}.$

It is easy to see that the generalized tensor LWE yields Wee's version of tensor LWE for $k = 1$.

Two Input ABE from evasive and tensor LWE. As a warmup, we first describe our construction of miABE for arity 2. For NC_1, our construction can be proven secure by relying solely on evasive LWE while for P, we additionally need tensor LWE. We will show subsequently how to generalize this to any constant arity. In this work, we consider a modified syntax of miABE where there is only a single encryption slot which is public key, and multiple key generation slots, which require the master secret key. This syntax better fits our construction and easily implies the standard definition of miABE which has multiple encryptors that have as input the master secret key, and a single key generator who also requires the master secret key – please see Sect. 2.1 for details.

Given the above discussion, a natural approach to construct miABE schemes from lattices is to try adapting the ideas in AYY by replacing the use of pairings with tensoring, analogously to Wee's approach of adapting the Agrawal-Yamada broadcast encryption scheme to lattices in Wee. We show that in the end, this approach indeed can be made to work, but via several failed attempts which require new techniques to overcome, and a complex security proof, which requires proving several new lemmas. Below, we outline the pathway to our final construction, detailing the hurdles we encounter and the ideas towards their resolution.

Attempt 1. We attempt to design a scheme using tensor based randomization from Wee to instantiate the template of AYY. We sketch the construction at a high level below. We suppress dimensions for ease of readability in this overview.

1. The master public key is $(\mathbf{A}_0, \mathbf{A}_1, \mathbf{A}_2, \mathbf{B}, \mathbf{u})$ where $\mathbf{A}_1, \mathbf{A}_2, \mathbf{B}$ are sampled uniformly and $\mathbf{u}$ is sampled from the discrete Gaussian distribution. The master key is a trapdoor for $\mathbf{A}_0$ and a trapdoor for $\mathbf{B}$.
2. The encryptor, given input $(\mathbf{x}, \mu)$ where $\mathbf{x}$ is the attribute and μ is the message, samples randomness $\mathbf{s}$ along with requisite noise terms and computes

$$\underbrace{\mathbf{s}\mathbf{A}_0 + \text{noise}}_{\mathbf{c}_0}, \quad \underbrace{\mathbf{s}\big((\mathbf{A}_1 - \mathbf{x} \otimes \mathbf{G}) \otimes \mathbf{I}\big) + \text{noise}}_{\mathbf{c}_1}, \quad \underbrace{\mathbf{s}(\mathbf{G}\mathbf{u}^\top \otimes \mathbf{I}) + \text{noise}}_{\mathbf{c}_2}, \quad \underbrace{\mathbf{s}\mathbf{B} + \text{noise}}_{\mathbf{c}_3}$$

if $\mu = 0$ and else samples random elements of appropriate dimensions if $\mu = 1$. Note that the encryption procedure is public key.
3. The first key generator (to be interpreted as the second encryptor), given input msk and attribute $\mathbf{y}$ samples Gaussian random vector $\mathbf{r}$ and computes

$$\mathsf{sk}_{\mathbf{y}} = \mathbf{B}^{-1}\big((\mathbf{A}_2 - \mathbf{y} \otimes \mathbf{G}) \otimes \mathbf{r}^\top\big), \mathbf{r}^\top$$

It outputs this as the secret key for $\mathbf{y}$. Note that the randomizer $\mathbf{r}$ is used to prevent collusion attacks – in its absence, an attacker can obtain samples corresponding to $\mathbf{y}$ and $\overline{\mathbf{y}}$ (i.e. complement of $\mathbf{y}$) and launch attack as discussed earlier.

4. The second key generator, given msk and function f as input computes $\mathsf{sk}_f = (\mathbf{A}_0\|\mathbf{A}_f)^{-1}(\mathbf{Gu}^\top)$ and outputs this as the secret key for f.
5. The decryptor does the following:
   (a) *Computing ciphertext component for second attribute:* It combines the ciphertext $\mathbf{c}_3$ with the first secret key $\mathsf{sk}_\mathbf{y}$ to obtain $\mathbf{s}((\mathbf{A}_2 - \mathbf{y} \otimes \mathbf{G}) \otimes \mathbf{r}^\top) + \mathsf{noise}$.
   (b) *Randomizing ciphertext component for first attribute:* From $\mathbf{c}_1$ and $\mathsf{sk}_\mathbf{y}$, it computes $(\mathbf{s}((\mathbf{A}_1-\mathbf{x}\otimes\mathbf{G})\otimes\mathbf{I})+\mathsf{noise})(\mathbf{I}\otimes\mathbf{r}^\top) = \mathbf{s}((\mathbf{A}_1-\mathbf{x}\otimes\mathbf{G})\otimes\mathbf{r}^\top)+\mathsf{noise}$
   (c) *Producing a complete* BGG^+ *ciphertext:* Concatenating the results of the previous two steps, we get

$$\mathbf{s}((\mathbf{A}_1\|\mathbf{A}_2) - (\mathbf{x}\|\mathbf{y}) \otimes \mathbf{G}) \otimes \mathbf{r}^\top) + \mathsf{noise}$$

   Note that this looks exactly like a BGG^+ sample except for the tensoring with $\mathbf{r}^\top$. As discussed above, Wee shows that homomorphic computation is preserved under right tensoring with $\mathbf{r}^\top$.
   (d) BGG^+ *Homomorphic evaluation:* Computing the circuit f homomorphically on this BGG^+ sample, we obtain

$$\mathbf{s}((\mathbf{A}_f - f(\mathbf{x},\mathbf{y})\mathbf{G}) \otimes \mathbf{r}^\top) + \mathsf{noise}$$

   If $f(\mathbf{x},\mathbf{y}) = 0$, then we get $\mathbf{s}(\mathbf{A}_f \otimes \mathbf{r}^\top) + \mathsf{noise}$. Concatenating with the ciphertext component $\mathbf{c}_0$, we get

$$\mathbf{s}(\mathbf{A}_0\|\mathbf{A}_f) \otimes \mathbf{r}^\top) + \mathsf{noise}$$

   (e) *Applying* BGG^+ *secret key.* By right multiplying the second slot secret key $(\mathbf{A}_0\|\mathbf{A}_f)^{-1}(\mathbf{Gu}^\top) \otimes \mathbf{I}$ to this, we get

$$\mathbf{s}(\mathbf{Gu}^\top \otimes \mathbf{r}^\top) + \mathsf{noise}$$

   (f) BGG^+ *decryption with tensoring.* Multiplying $\mathbf{c}_2$ with $\mathbf{I} \otimes \mathbf{r}^\top$, we get $\mathbf{s}(\mathbf{Gu}^\top \otimes \mathbf{r}^\top) + \mathsf{noise}$. Subtracting from the output of the previous step, we get a small value when $\mu = 0$. Thus, we recover μ when $f(\mathbf{x},\mathbf{y}) = 0$.

The above scheme provides functionality and does not appear to have any immediate attacks. However, we are unable to prove security of this scheme based on the evasive/tensor LWE assumption. This is because the evasive LWE assumption accommodates Gaussian preimages for fixed matrices, namely terms of the form $\mathbf{B}^{-1}(\mathbf{P})$, where $\mathbf{B}$ is a random matrix and $\mathbf{P}$ is structured, but does not know how to handle terms such as $(\mathbf{A}_0\|\mathbf{A}_f)^{-1}(\mathbf{Gu}^\top)$. Since $\mathbf{A}_f$ is highly structured, this is incompatible with the assumption.

Attempt 2. To handle this barrier, in our next attempt, we use an idea by Wee to remove the problematic term $(\mathbf{A}_0\|\mathbf{A}_f)^{-1}(\mathbf{Gu}^\top)$. Note that the purpose of this term is to create an LWE sample with secret $\mathbf{s}$ and matrix $\mathbf{A}_f$. In more detail, as shown in step 5e, the term $\mathbf{s}(\mathbf{A}_0\|\mathbf{A}_f) \otimes \mathbf{r}^\top) + \mathsf{noise}$ obtained by homomorphic evaluation is combined together with the secret key in the second slot

$(\mathbf{A}_0\|\mathbf{A}_f)^{-1}(\mathbf{Gu}^\top)$ to obtain $\mathbf{s}(\mathbf{Gu}^\top \otimes \mathbf{r}^\top) + $ noise. As shown in step 5f, this term is then used to unmask the ramdomized $\mathbf{c}_2$, i.e. $\mathbf{s}(\mathbf{Gu}^\top \otimes \mathbf{r}^\top) + $ noise by subtraction to recover μ.

So as to do away with the requirement of revealing $(\mathbf{A}_0\|\mathbf{A}_f)^{-1}(\mathbf{Gu}^\top)$, we provide an alternate route to recover μ. We change the second slot secret key sk_f to $\mathbf{B}^{-1}(\mathbf{A}_f\mathbf{u} \otimes \mathbf{I})$, and use this together with the term $\mathbf{sB} + $ noise provided in the ciphertext to obtain $\mathbf{s}(\mathbf{A}_f\mathbf{u} \otimes \mathbf{I}) + $ noise. This allows us to cancel the mask $\mathbf{sA}_f$ obtained via homomorphic evaluation and brings us closer to relying only on evasive and tensor LWE.

Below, we detail only the modifications we make to our previous attempt:

1. The encryptor, given input $(\mathbf{x}, \mu)$ where $\mathbf{x}$ is the attribute and μ is the message, samples randomness $\mathbf{s}$ along with requisite noise terms and computes

$$\underbrace{\cancel{\mathbf{sA}_0 + \text{noise}}}_{c_0}, \quad \underbrace{\mathbf{s}((\mathbf{A}_1 - \mathbf{x} \otimes \mathbf{G}) \otimes \mathbf{I}) + \text{noise}}_{c_1}, \quad \underbrace{\cancel{\mathbf{s}(\mathbf{Gu}^\top \otimes \mathbf{I}) + \text{noise}}}_{c_2}, \quad \underbrace{\mathbf{sB} + \text{noise}}_{c_3}$$

if $\mu = 0$ else samples random elements of appropriate dimensions if $\mu = 1$.
2. The second key generator, given msk and function f computes $\mathsf{sk}_f = \mathbf{B}^{-1}(\mathbf{A}_f\mathbf{u}^\top \otimes \mathbf{I})$. At this junction, we let $\mathbf{u}$ be chosen independently by each user instead of fixing it in the public parameters to prevent the adversary from requesting keys for correlated functions and obtaining correlated LWE samples of the form $\mathbf{sA}_f\mathbf{u}^\top + $ noise with the same $\mathbf{u}$ and same $\mathbf{s}$.
3. During decryption,
   (a) BGG^+ homomorphic evaluation is simplified. We only compute the circuit f homomorphically on this BGG^+ sample, to obtain

$$\mathbf{s}((\mathbf{A}_f - f(\mathbf{x}, \mathbf{y})\mathbf{G}) \otimes \mathbf{r}^\top) + \text{noise}$$

   If $f(\mathbf{x}, \mathbf{y}) = 0$, then we get $\mathbf{s}(\mathbf{A}_f \otimes \mathbf{r}^\top) + $ noise. There is no need to concatenate with $\mathbf{c}_0$ (this is no longer even provided) but we must right multiply by $(\mathbf{u}^\top \otimes \mathbf{I})$ to obtain $\mathbf{s}(\mathbf{A}_f\mathbf{u}^\top \otimes \mathbf{r}^\top) + $ noise. Recall that $\mathbf{u}$ is low norm, hence does not blow up the noise.
   (b) The second slot key $\mathbf{B}^{-1}(\mathbf{A}_f\mathbf{u}^\top \otimes \mathbf{I})$ is right multiplied to $\mathbf{c}_3$ to get $\mathbf{s}(\mathbf{A}_f\mathbf{u}^\top \otimes \mathbf{I}) + $ noise. By right multiplying with $(\mathbf{I} \otimes \mathbf{r}^\top)$, we now recover the masking term $\mathbf{s}(\mathbf{A}_f\mathbf{u} \otimes \mathbf{r}^\top) + $ noise which can be subtracted from the output of the previous step. If this is small, learn that $\mu = 0$.

Importantly, at this point, we can hope to use evasive LWE to "get rid" of the preimages $\mathbf{B}^{-1}((\mathbf{A}_2 - \mathbf{y} \otimes \mathbf{G}) \otimes \mathbf{r}^\top)$ and $\mathbf{B}^{-1}(\mathbf{A}_f\mathbf{u}^\top \otimes \mathbf{I})$ from the distribution seen by the adversary. This essentially reduces the task of proving the security of the scheme to that of proving the pseudorandomness of the terms

$$\mathbf{s}((\mathbf{A}_1 - \mathbf{x} \otimes \mathbf{G}) \otimes \mathbf{I}) + \text{noise}, \quad \mathbf{s}((\mathbf{A}_2 - \mathbf{y} \otimes \mathbf{G}) \otimes \mathbf{r}^\top) + \text{noise}, \quad \mathbf{s}(\mathbf{A}_f\mathbf{u}^\top \otimes \mathbf{I}) + \text{noise}$$

Unfortunately, we are still not done, even by relying additionally on tensor LWE. This is because tensor LWE only posits pseudorandomness of LWE samples with respect to secret $\mathbf{s}(\mathbf{I} \otimes \mathbf{r})$. In particular, the presence of the terms $\mathbf{s}((\mathbf{A}_1 - \mathbf{x} \otimes$

$\mathbf{G}) \otimes \mathbf{I}) +$ noise and $\mathbf{s}(\mathbf{A}_f \mathbf{u}^\top \otimes \mathbf{I}) +$ noise cannot be handled by invoking tensor LWE since they do not have the right form (in particular no $\mathbf{r}$ term appears in these). Therefore, we must handle these next.

Attempt 3. Let us first explain how to deal with the first term $\mathbf{s}((\mathbf{A}_1 - \mathbf{x} \otimes \mathbf{G}) \otimes \mathbf{I}) +$ noise. As in Wee, the idea is to "mask" the problematic term, in this case, $\mathbf{s}((\mathbf{A}_1 - \mathbf{x} \otimes \mathbf{G}) \otimes \mathbf{I}) +$ noise, with a pseudorandom term $\mathbf{s}_0(\mathbf{A}_0 \otimes \mathbf{I}) +$ noise such that there is a way to provide an "unmasking" term using which, we can recover a simulatable term $\mathbf{s}((\mathbf{A}_1 - \mathbf{x} \otimes \mathbf{G}) \otimes \mathbf{r}^\top) +$ noise but nothing else is revealed[3].

In more detail, we make the following changes:

1. We replace $\mathbf{s}((\mathbf{A}_1 - \mathbf{x} \otimes \mathbf{G}) \otimes \mathbf{I}) +$ noise by $\mathbf{c} = \mathbf{s}((\mathbf{A}_1 - \mathbf{x} \otimes \mathbf{G}) \otimes \mathbf{I}) + \mathbf{s}_0(\mathbf{A}_0 \otimes \mathbf{I}) +$ noise.
2. Next, we put some terms so that the ciphertext along with the first slot of the secret key jointly generates $\mathbf{d} := \mathbf{s}_0(\mathbf{A}_0 \otimes \mathbf{r}^\top) +$ noise, which is an "unmasking" term.
3. To obtain the desired term, we compute $\mathbf{c}(\mathbf{I} \otimes \mathbf{r}^\top) - \mathbf{d} = \mathbf{s}((\mathbf{A}_1 - \mathbf{x} \otimes \mathbf{G}) \otimes \mathbf{r}) +$ noise.

Furthermore, it is easy to show that $\mathbf{s}_0(\mathbf{A}_0 \otimes \mathbf{I}) +$ noise is pseudorandom by LWE (since $\mathbf{s}_0$ is a fresh randomness introduced only for this specific purpose), which implies that $\mathbf{c}$ is also pseudorandom. This allows us to conclude that $\mathbf{d}$ does not reveal anything more than the desired term, since $\mathbf{c}$ and the desired term determine $\mathbf{d}$.

At this stage, the scheme looks like the following, where for brevity we again omit to mention components that are unchanged.

1. The encryptor computes $\mathbf{c}_1 = (\mathbf{s}, \mathbf{s}_0) \begin{pmatrix} (\mathbf{A}_1 - \mathbf{x} \otimes \mathbf{G}) \otimes \mathbf{I} \\ \mathbf{A}_0 \otimes \mathbf{I} \end{pmatrix} +$ noise and $\mathbf{c}_2 = (\mathbf{s}, \mathbf{s}_0)\mathbf{B} +$ noise for $\mu = 0$ (and random elements for $\mu = 1$).
2. The first slot key is $\mathsf{sk}_\mathbf{y} \leftarrow \mathbf{B}^{-1} \begin{pmatrix} (\mathbf{A}_2 - \mathbf{y} \otimes \mathbf{G}) \otimes \mathbf{r}^\top \\ \mathbf{A}_0 \otimes \mathbf{r}^\top \end{pmatrix}$
3. The second slot key is $\mathsf{sk}_f \leftarrow \mathbf{B}^{-1} \begin{pmatrix} \mathbf{A}_f \mathbf{u}^\top \otimes \mathbf{I} \\ \mathbf{0} \end{pmatrix}$ and $\mathbf{u}$. This key is essentially unchanged except padding the inner matrix with zeroes to account for the longer secret.
4. Now, from the ciphertext component $\mathbf{c}_2$ and the first slot key, we get terms $\mathbf{s}(\mathbf{A}_2 - \mathbf{y} \otimes \mathbf{G}) \otimes \mathbf{r}^\top) +$ noise and $\mathbf{d} = \mathbf{s}_0(\mathbf{A}_0 \otimes \mathbf{r}^\top) +$ noise. The second term $\mathbf{d}$ is the new term that we will make use of as described above.
5. Now, we compute $\mathbf{c}(\mathbf{I} \otimes \mathbf{r}^\top) - \mathbf{d} = \mathbf{s}((\mathbf{A}_1 - \mathbf{x} \otimes \mathbf{G}) \otimes \mathbf{r}) +$ noise. Using pseudorandomness of $\mathbf{c}$, we can argue that $\mathbf{d}$ did not reveal anything except $\mathbf{s}((\mathbf{A}_1 - \mathbf{x} \otimes \mathbf{G}) \otimes \mathbf{r}) +$ noise.

At this stage, we obtained a term that tensor LWE can handle, namely $\mathbf{s}((\mathbf{A}_1 - \mathbf{x} \otimes \mathbf{G}) \otimes \mathbf{r}) +$ noise.

---

[3] The informed reader may notice the similarity with randomized encodings [17] and pair/predicate encodings [18,38].

Attempt 4. Next, we must deal with the second problematic term $s(\mathbf{A}_f \mathbf{u}^\top \otimes \mathbf{I})$ + noise. It is tempting to try the same strategy as above but unfortunately, this does not work. To see why, let us try to replace $s(\mathbf{A}_f \mathbf{u}^\top \otimes \mathbf{I})$ + noise with $s(\mathbf{A}_f \mathbf{u}^\top \otimes \mathbf{I}) + s_1(\mathbf{D} \otimes \mathbf{I})$ + noise, where $\mathbf{D}$ is some fixed matrix. We can then modify the scheme so that the ciphertext along with the first slot secret key generate the unmasking term $s_1(\mathbf{D} \otimes \mathbf{r}^\top)$ + noise. Similarly to the above, this allows us to derive the desired term $s(\mathbf{A}_f \mathbf{u}^\top \otimes \mathbf{r}^\top)$ + noise which can be handled by tensor LWE. One may hope that this suffices to prove security.

However, we run into another problem, namely, that of collusion resistance. In particular, an adversary may make multiple key queries for the second slot and use the same ciphertext and first slot key for decryption. These allow her to recover $s(\mathbf{A}_f \mathbf{u}^\top \otimes \mathbf{I}) + s_1(\mathbf{D} \otimes \mathbf{r}^\top)$ + noise and $s(\mathbf{A}_{f'} \mathbf{u'}^\top \otimes \mathbf{I}) + s_1(\mathbf{D} \otimes \mathbf{r}^\top)$ + noise for different f and f'. Even though we want to hide two terms $s(\mathbf{A}_f \mathbf{u}^\top \otimes \mathbf{I})$ and $s(\mathbf{A}_{f'} \mathbf{u'}^\top \otimes \mathbf{I})$, there is only a single masking term $s_1(\mathbf{D} \otimes \mathbf{r}^\top)$ + noise, since s_1 would be chosen by the encryptor and $\mathbf{r}$ by the first slot key – this is clearly problematic.

To fix this, we ensure that the masking term is randomized by a user specific randomness corresponding to the second slot key. Namely, we replace $s(\mathbf{A}_f \mathbf{u}^\top \otimes \mathbf{I}) + s_1(\mathbf{D} \otimes \mathbf{I})$ + noise with $s(\mathbf{A}_f \mathbf{u}^\top \otimes \mathbf{I}) + s_1(\mathbf{D} \otimes \mathbf{t}^\top)$ + noise, where $\mathbf{t}$ is user specific randomness. We then use the ideas discussed previously to ensure that the ciphertext and second slot key generate $s_1(\mathbf{D} \otimes \mathbf{t}^\top)$ + noise. This mask is removed similarly to the previous case and we may obtain $s(\mathbf{A}_f \mathbf{u}^\top \otimes \mathbf{I})$ + noise.

Attempt 5. Unfortunately, this still does not suffice. Recall that we wanted to generate the term $s(\mathbf{A}_f \mathbf{u}^\top \otimes \mathbf{r}^\top)$ + noise in order to invoke tensor LWE, which the above term does not let us do. To achieve this, we replace $s(\mathbf{A}_f \mathbf{u}^\top \otimes \mathbf{I}) + s_1(\mathbf{D} \otimes \mathbf{t})$ + noise with $s(\mathbf{A}_f \mathbf{u}^\top \otimes \mathbf{I}) + s_1(\mathbf{D} \otimes \mathbf{t} \otimes \mathbf{I})$ + noise, i.e., we added some space to further randomize the masking term with $\mathbf{r}^\top$. We then let the ciphertext and secret keys for both slots jointly generate $s_1(\mathbf{D} \otimes \mathbf{t}^\top \otimes \mathbf{r}^\top)$ + noise.

To do so, we do the following:

1. Include $s_1 \mathbf{B}$ + noise in the ciphertext and $\mathbf{B}^{-1}(\mathbf{C} \otimes \mathbf{r}^\top)$ in the first slot key. Multiplying them yields $s_1(\mathbf{C} \otimes \mathbf{r}^\top)$ + noise.
2. Include $\mathbf{C}^{-1}(\mathbf{D} \otimes \mathbf{t}^\top)$ in the second slot key.

Putting these together enables us to recover the masking term as:

$$
\begin{aligned}
(s_1(\mathbf{C} \otimes \mathbf{r}^\top) + \text{noise}) \cdot \mathbf{C}^{-1}(\mathbf{D} \otimes \mathbf{t}^\top) &= s_1(\mathbf{I} \otimes \mathbf{r}^\top)\mathbf{C} \cdot \mathbf{C}^{-1}(\mathbf{D} \otimes \mathbf{t}^\top) + \text{noise} \\
&= s_1(\mathbf{I} \otimes \mathbf{r}^\top)(\mathbf{D} \otimes \mathbf{t}^\top) + \text{noise} \\
&= s_1(\mathbf{D} \otimes \mathbf{t}^\top \otimes \mathbf{r}^\top) + \text{noise}
\end{aligned}
$$

The above term contains randomness s_1 chosen by the encryptor, $\mathbf{r}$ chosen by the first slot key and $\mathbf{t}$ chosen by the second slot key. Intuitively, this randomness triple separates the triple of ciphertext, first key and second key, from any other triple even if some components of the triple are reused. This allows to separate the "thread" of computation corresponding to a given triple, from all other threads, and hopefully allows us to prove security. This brings us to our final scheme.

We provide the complete construction below. The vector $\mathbf{u}$ above is now changed to a matrix $\mathbf{U}$ for syntactic reasons.

1. Set $\mathsf{mpk} = (\mathbf{A}_0, \mathbf{A}_1, \mathbf{A}_2, \mathbf{B}, \mathbf{C}, \mathbf{D})$, and msk as trapdoors for $\mathbf{B}$ and $\mathbf{C}$.
2. To encrypt a message μ against attribute $\mathbf{x}$, do the following. If $\mu = 0$, do:
   (a) Compute $\mathbf{c}_1 = (\mathbf{s}, \mathbf{s}_0) \begin{pmatrix} (\mathbf{A}_1 - \mathbf{x} \otimes \mathbf{G}) \otimes \mathbf{I} \\ \mathbf{A}_0 \otimes \mathbf{I} \end{pmatrix} + \text{noise}$
   (b) Compute $\mathbf{c}_2 = (\mathbf{s}, \mathbf{s}_0, \mathbf{s}_1)\mathbf{B} + \text{noise}$
   (c) Output $\mathsf{ct}_{\mathbf{x}} = (\mathbf{c}_1, \mathbf{c}_2)$
   If $\mu = 1$, output random elements in the appropriate space.
3. To compute the first slot key for attribute $\mathbf{y}$, sample

$$\mathsf{sk}_{\mathbf{y}} \leftarrow \mathbf{B}^{-1} \begin{pmatrix} (\mathbf{A}_2 - \mathbf{y} \otimes \mathbf{G}) \otimes \mathbf{r}^{\top} \\ \mathbf{A}_0 \otimes \mathbf{r}^{\top} \\ \mathbf{C} \otimes \mathbf{r}^{\top} \end{pmatrix}$$

4. To compute the second slot key for function f, sample $\mathbf{U}, \mathbf{t}$ and compute

$$\mathsf{sk}_f \leftarrow \mathbf{B}^{-1} \begin{pmatrix} \mathbf{A}_f \mathbf{U} \otimes \mathbf{I} \\ 0 \\ \mathbf{D} \otimes \mathbf{t}^{\top} \otimes \mathbf{I} \end{pmatrix}, \quad \mathbf{C}^{-1}\left(\mathbf{D} \otimes \mathbf{t}^{\top}\right), \quad \mathbf{U}, \quad \mathbf{t}$$

To decrypt, first compute $\mathbf{d}_1 = \mathbf{c}_1(\mathbf{I} \otimes \mathbf{r}^{\top})$, $(\mathbf{d}_2, \mathbf{d}_3, \mathbf{d}_4) = \mathbf{c}_2 \cdot \mathsf{sk}_{\mathbf{y}}$, $\mathbf{d}_5 = \mathbf{c}_2 \cdot \mathsf{sk}_{f,1}$, $\mathbf{d}_6 = \mathbf{d}_5(\mathbf{I} \otimes \mathbf{r}^{\top})$ and $\mathbf{d}_7 = \mathbf{d}_4 \cdot \mathsf{sk}_{f,2}$. Then compute $\mathbf{d}_8 = \mathbf{d}_1 - \mathbf{d}_3$, $\mathbf{d}_9 = (\mathbf{d}_8 \| \mathbf{d}_2)\widehat{\mathbf{H}}_{(\mathbf{A}_1 \| \mathbf{A}_2), f, (\mathbf{x} \| \mathbf{y})} \mathbf{U}$, $\mathbf{d}_{10} = \mathbf{d}_6 - \mathbf{d}_7$. Finally, if $\mathbf{d}_{10} - \mathbf{d}_9 \approx 0$, then output 0, else 1. To see the correctness, observe:

$$\mathbf{d}_1 = \mathbf{s}((\mathbf{A}_1 - \mathbf{x} \otimes \mathbf{G}) \otimes \mathbf{r}^{\top}) + \mathbf{s}_0(\mathbf{A}_0 \otimes \mathbf{r}^{\top}) + \text{noise},$$

$$\mathbf{d}_2 = \mathbf{s}((\mathbf{A}_2 - \mathbf{y} \otimes \mathbf{G}) \otimes \mathbf{r}^{\top}) + \text{noise}, \quad \mathbf{d}_3 = \mathbf{s}_0(\mathbf{A}_0 \otimes \mathbf{r}^{\top}) + \text{noise},$$

$$\mathbf{d}_4 = \mathbf{s}_1(\mathbf{C} \otimes \mathbf{r}^{\top}) + \text{noise}, \quad \mathbf{d}_5 = \mathbf{s}(\mathbf{A}_f \mathbf{U} \otimes \mathbf{I}) + \mathbf{s}_1(\mathbf{D} \otimes \mathbf{t}^{\top} \otimes \mathbf{I}) + \text{noise},$$

$$\mathbf{d}_6 = \mathbf{s}(\mathbf{A}_f \mathbf{U} \otimes \mathbf{r}^{\top}) + \mathbf{s}_1(\mathbf{D} \otimes \mathbf{t}^{\top} \otimes \mathbf{r}^{\top}) + \text{noise},$$

$$\mathbf{d}_7 = \mathbf{d}_4 \cdot \mathbf{C}^{-1}(\mathbf{D} \otimes \mathbf{t}^{\top}) = \mathbf{s}_1(\mathbf{D} \otimes \mathbf{t}^{\top} \otimes \mathbf{r}^{\top}) + \text{noise},$$

$$\mathbf{d}_8 = \mathbf{s}((\mathbf{A}_1 - \mathbf{x} \otimes \mathbf{G}) \otimes \mathbf{r}^{\top}) + \text{noise}$$

$$\mathbf{d}_9 = \mathbf{s}((\mathbf{A}_f - f(\mathbf{x}, \mathbf{y})\mathbf{G}) \otimes \mathbf{r}^{\top})\mathbf{U} + \text{noise}, \quad \mathbf{d}_{10} = \mathbf{s}(\mathbf{A}_f \mathbf{U} \otimes \mathbf{r}^{\top}) + \text{noise}$$

If $f(\mathbf{x}, \mathbf{y}) = 0$, then $\mathbf{d}_{10} - \mathbf{d}_9 = \text{noise}$ when $\mu = 0$, else it is large. Above, the terms $\mathbf{d}_2, \mathbf{d}_8$ in blue mimic the ciphertext components of single input BGG$^+$, computed as if with shared randomness by a single party holding both $\mathbf{x}$ and $\mathbf{y}$. Note that all the machinery developed above was to be able to simulate the single party setting in the two party setting, where the ciphertexts are produced using independent randomness.

Proof Sketch. For ease of exposition, we sketch the proof for the case where only a single key is generated for both the slots. First, we observe that we need to invoke evasive LWE twice, once to handle terms $\mathbf{B}^{-1}(\cdot)$ and once for $\mathbf{C}^{-1}(\cdot)$. Of these, the first application is standard, following Wee while the second one requires more care as it uses a structured LWE, as in [37].

Having removed Gaussian preimages with respect to $\mathbf{B}$ and $\mathbf{C}$, we are required to show pseudorandomness of the following terms:

$$\mathbf{c}_1 = \mathbf{s}((\mathbf{A}_1 - \mathbf{x} \otimes \mathbf{G}) \otimes \mathbf{I}) + \mathbf{s}_0(\mathbf{A}_0 \otimes \mathbf{I}) + \text{noise}, \quad \mathbf{c}_2 = (\mathbf{s}, \mathbf{s}_0, \mathbf{s}_1)\mathbf{B} + \text{noise},$$

$$\mathbf{c}_3 = \mathbf{s}((\mathbf{A}_2 - \mathbf{y} \otimes \mathbf{G}) \otimes \mathbf{r}^\top) + \text{noise} \quad \mathbf{c}_4 = \mathbf{s}_0(\mathbf{A}_0 \otimes \mathbf{r}^\top) + \text{noise},$$

$$\mathbf{c}_5 = \mathbf{s}_1(\mathbf{C} \otimes \mathbf{r}^\top) + \text{noise}, \quad \mathbf{c}_6 = \mathbf{s}(\mathbf{A}_f \mathbf{U} \otimes \mathbf{I}) + \mathbf{s}_1(\mathbf{D} \otimes \mathbf{t}^\top \otimes \mathbf{I}) + \text{noise}$$

$$\mathbf{c}_7 = \mathbf{s}_1(\mathbf{D} \otimes \mathbf{t}^\top \otimes \mathbf{r}^\top) + \text{noise}$$

Above, note that $\mathbf{c}_3, \mathbf{c}_4, \mathbf{c}_5$ are generated using the secret key for the first slot and the ciphertext, $\mathbf{c}_6$ is generated using the ciphertext and secret key of the second slot, and $\mathbf{c}_7$ is generated using evasive LWE with structured secret, namely by combining $\mathbf{C}^{-1}(\mathbf{D} \otimes \mathbf{t}^\top)$ and $\mathbf{c}_5 = \mathbf{s}_1(\mathbf{I} \otimes \mathbf{r}^\top)\mathbf{C} + \text{noise}$. This yields $\mathbf{s}_1(\mathbf{I} \otimes \mathbf{r}^\top)(\mathbf{D} \otimes \mathbf{t}^\top) + \text{noise}$ which is equal to $\mathbf{c}_7$.

We now proceed to sketch the hybrid structure of the proof.

Game 0: This is the real game.

Game 1: Express $\mathbf{c}_4$ in terms of $\mathbf{c}_1$ and a term that tensor LWE can handle:

$$\mathbf{c}_4 = \mathbf{c}_1(\mathbf{I} \otimes \mathbf{r}^\top) - \underbrace{\left(\mathbf{s}((\mathbf{A}_1 - \mathbf{x} \otimes \mathbf{G}) \otimes \mathbf{r}^\top) + \text{noise}\right)}_{\mathbf{c}4'}$$

The only difference between Game 0 and Game 1 is the distribution of the noise term which can be handled by noting that $\mathbf{c}_1(\mathbf{I} \otimes \mathbf{r}^\top) \approx \mathbf{s}((\mathbf{A}_1 - \mathbf{x} \otimes \mathbf{G}) \otimes \mathbf{r}^\top) + \mathbf{s}_0(\mathbf{A}_0 \otimes \mathbf{r}^\top)$ and using the standard smudging lemma.

Game 2: We now change $\mathbf{c}_1$ and $\mathbf{c}_2$ to random by using the power of LWE with secret $\mathbf{s}_0$.

Game 3: Now, we express $\mathbf{c}_7$ in terms of $\mathbf{c}_6$ and a term which is friendly with tensor LWE:

$$\mathbf{c}_7 = \mathbf{c}_6(\mathbf{I} \otimes \mathbf{r}^\top) - \underbrace{\mathbf{s}(\mathbf{A}_f \mathbf{U} \otimes \mathbf{r}^\top) + \text{noise}}_{\mathbf{c}_7'}$$

Again, the change follows using the smudging lemma.

Game 4: Change $\mathbf{c}_5$ and $\mathbf{c}_6$ to random. Note that $\mathbf{c}_6(\mathbf{I} \otimes \mathbf{r}^\top) \approx \mathbf{s}(\mathbf{A}_f \mathbf{U} \otimes \mathbf{r}^\top) + \mathbf{s}_1(\mathbf{D} \otimes \mathbf{t}^\top \otimes \mathbf{r}^\top) + \text{noise}$ and $\mathbf{c}_5 = \mathbf{s}_1(\mathbf{C} \otimes \mathbf{r}^\top) + \text{noise}$. Hence, it suffices to show pseudorandomness of

$$\mathbf{s}_1(\mathbf{C} \otimes \mathbf{r}^\top) + \text{noise}, \quad \mathbf{s}_1(\mathbf{D} \otimes \mathbf{t}^\top \otimes \mathbf{I}) + \text{noise})$$

We argue this via a new lemma by using only (standard) LWE.

Game 5: At this point it remains to argue that $\mathbf{c}_3, \mathbf{c}_4'$ and $\mathbf{c}_7'$ are pseudorandom. These constitute:

$$\mathbf{s}(\mathbf{I} \otimes \mathbf{r}^\top)\left((\mathbf{A}_1 \| \mathbf{A}_2) - (\mathbf{x} \| \mathbf{y}) \otimes \mathbf{G}\right) + \text{noise}, \quad \mathbf{s}(\mathbf{I} \otimes \mathbf{r}^\top)(\mathbf{A}_f \mathbf{U}) + \text{noise}$$

and we can directly plug in the tensor LWE assumption to argue this.

Please see Sect. 4 for the detailed proof.

Extension to Constant Arity. Next, we outline how to extend the above idea to the setting of constant arity. The basic idea is to let the secret key for slot $i \in [k]$ generate

$$\mathbf{s}((\mathbf{A} - \mathbf{x}_i \otimes \mathbf{G}) \otimes \mathbf{I} \otimes \mathbf{r}_i^\top \otimes \mathbf{I}) + \underbrace{\mathbf{s}_i(\mathbf{D} \otimes \mathbf{I} \otimes \mathbf{r}_i^\top \otimes \mathbf{I}) + \mathsf{noise}}_{\text{masking term}}$$

where $\mathbf{r}_i$ is the user specific randomness associated with the secret key for the i-th slot.

In addition, we also prepare other terms so that the ciphertext and secret keys can collaboratively generate the unmasking terms as:

$$\mathbf{s}_i(\mathbf{D} \otimes \mathbf{r}_1^\top \otimes \cdots \otimes \mathbf{r}_k^\top) + \mathsf{noise} \ \forall i \in [k]$$

Given the unmasking term, the decryptor can obtain

$$\mathbf{s}((\mathbf{A}_i - \mathbf{x}_i \otimes \mathbf{G}) \otimes \mathbf{r}_1^\top \otimes \cdots \otimes \mathbf{r}_k^\top) + \mathsf{noise}$$

A similar strategy also works for masking $\mathbf{s}(\mathbf{A}_f \mathbf{U} \otimes \mathbf{I})$ and we can show that the adversary can only obtain

$$\mathbf{s}((\mathbf{A} - \mathbf{x} \otimes \mathbf{G}) \otimes \mathbf{r}_1^\top \otimes \cdots \otimes \mathbf{r}_k^\top) + \mathsf{noise}, \quad \mathbf{s}(\mathbf{A}_f \mathbf{U} \otimes \mathbf{r}_1^\top \otimes \cdots \otimes \mathbf{r}_k^\top) + \mathsf{noise}$$

which are LWE samples w.r.t randomness $\mathbf{s}(\mathbf{I} \otimes \mathbf{r}_1^\top \otimes \cdots \otimes \mathbf{r}_k^\top)$. We refer the reader to Sect. 5 for the complete construction.

On Circuit Depth. As discussed above, for our miABE for NC_1, we rely only on evasive LWE, even for constant arity. For our miABE for P, we require evasive and tensor LWE for arity 2, but for general k, we need to generalize tensor LWE as discussed above.

To remove the need for (any) tensor LWE in the restricted case of NC_1 circuits, we use low norm $\mathbf{A}_i$ and switch out $\mathbf{G}$ for $\mathbf{I}$, as suggested by Wee. We also leverage the observation by Wee, that a weaker version of homomorphic computation is still possible in this setting. In addition, we show that when $\mathbf{A}_i$ and $\mathbf{G}$ are changed as above, LWE samples w.r.t $\mathbf{x}$ obtained by combining ciphertexts and secret keys are indistinguishable from those that are computed using fresh randomness for all combinations of ciphertexts and secret keys.

In more detail, let $\mathbf{i} = (i_1, \ldots, i_k)$ denote the ciphertext queries in the k slots which are being combined for decryption. Then, we show that

$$\left\{ \mathbf{s}((\mathbf{A} - \mathbf{x}^{\mathbf{i}} \otimes \mathbf{I}) \otimes \mathbf{r}_1^{i_1 \top} \otimes \ldots \otimes \mathbf{r}_1^{i_k \top}) + \mathsf{noise} \right\}_{i_1,\ldots,i_k \in [Q]}$$

$$\approx_c \left\{ \mathbf{s}_{i_1,\ldots,i_k}(\mathbf{A} - \mathbf{x}^{\mathbf{i}} \otimes \mathbf{I}) + \mathsf{noise} \right\}_{i_1,\ldots,i_k \in [Q]}$$

where $\mathbf{s}_{i_1,\ldots,i_k}$ is a unique, freshly sampled secret for the combination $\mathbf{i} = (i_1,\ldots,i_k)$. Intuitively, the shortness of $\mathbf{A}$ and $\mathbf{I}$ is used to argue that:

$$\mathbf{s}\left((\mathbf{A}-\mathbf{x}^{\mathbf{i}}\otimes\mathbf{I})\otimes\mathbf{r}_1^{i_1\top}\otimes\ldots\otimes\mathbf{r}_k^{i_k\top}\right)+\text{noise} \approx_c \left(\mathbf{s}(\mathbf{I}\otimes\mathbf{r}_1^{i_1\top}\otimes\ldots\otimes\mathbf{r}_k^{i_k\top})+\text{noise}\right)(\mathbf{A}-\mathbf{x}^{\mathbf{i}}\otimes\mathbf{I})+\text{noise}$$

which in turn allows to express $\mathbf{s}(\mathbf{I}\otimes\mathbf{r}_1^{i_1\top}\otimes\ldots\otimes\mathbf{r}_k^{i_k\top})+\text{noise}$ as $\mathbf{s}_{i_1,\ldots,i_k}$ by iteratively separating out $\mathbf{r}_j^{i_j\top}$, and adding noise to obtain a fresh secret[4]. Please see Sect. 5 for details.

2 Preliminaries

2.1 Multi-Input Attribute Based Encryption

Following [14], we define multi-input Attribute Based Encryption (ABE) below. A k-input ABE scheme is parametrized over an attribute space $\{(A_\lambda)^k\}_{\lambda\in\mathbb{N}}$ and function space $\{\mathcal{F}_\lambda\}_{\lambda\in\mathbb{N}}$, where each function maps $\{(A_\lambda)^k\}_{\lambda\in\mathbb{N}}$ to $\{0,1\}$. Such a scheme is described by procedures (Setup, Enc, $\mathsf{KeyGen}_1,\ldots,\mathsf{KeyGen}_{k-1}$, KeyGen_k, Dec) with the following syntax:

$\mathsf{Setup}(1^\lambda) \to (\mathsf{mpk}, \mathsf{msk})$: The Setup algorithm takes as input a security parameter and outputs a master public key mpk and a master secret key msk.

$\mathsf{Enc}(\mathsf{mpk}, \mathbf{x}_0, \mu) \to \mathsf{ct}_{\mathbf{x}_0,\mu}$: The encryption algorithm takes as input the master public key mpk, an attribute $\mathbf{x}_0 \in A_\lambda$, and message $\mu \in \{0,1\}$, and outputs a ciphertext $\mathsf{ct}_{\mathbf{x}_0,\mu}$. The attribute string $\mathbf{x}_0$ is also included as part of the ciphertext.

$\mathsf{KeyGen}_i(\mathsf{msk}, \mathbf{x}_i) \to \mathsf{sk}_{i,\mathbf{x}_i}$ for $1 \le i \le k - 1$: The KeyGen algorithm for the ith slot where $i \in [k-1]$, takes as input the master secret key msk, and an attribute $\mathbf{x}_i \in A_\lambda$ and outputs a key for slot i, $\mathsf{sk}_{i,\mathbf{x}_i}$. Again, we assume that the attribute string $\mathbf{x}_i$ is included as part of the secret key.

$\mathsf{KeyGen}_k(\mathsf{msk}, f) \to \mathsf{sk}_{k,f}$: The KeyGen algorithm for slot k takes as input the master secret key msk and a function $f \in \mathcal{F}_\lambda$ and outputs a key $\mathsf{sk}_{k,f}$.

$\mathsf{Dec}(\mathsf{mpk}, \mathsf{ct}_{\mathbf{x}_0,\mu}, \mathsf{sk}_{1,\mathbf{x}_1},\ldots,\mathsf{sk}_{k-1,\mathbf{x}_{k-1}},\mathsf{sk}_{k,f}) \to \mu'$: The decryption algorithm takes as input a ciphertext $\mathsf{ct}_{\mathbf{x}_0,\mu}$, k keys $\mathsf{sk}_{1,\mathbf{x}_1},\ldots,\mathsf{sk}_{k-1,\mathbf{x}_{k-1}}$, and $\mathsf{sk}_{k,f}$ and outputs a string μ'.

Next, we define correctness and security. For ease of notation, we drop the subscript λ in what follows.

Correctness: For every $\lambda \in \mathbb{N}, \mu \in \{0,1\}$, $\mathbf{x}_0,\ldots,\mathbf{x}_{k-1} \in A$, $f \in \mathcal{F}$, it holds that if $f(\mathbf{x}_0,\ldots,\mathbf{x}_{k-1}) = 0$,[5] then

$$\Pr\left[\mathsf{Dec}\left(\begin{matrix}\mathsf{mpk},\ \mathsf{Enc}(\mathsf{mpk},\mathbf{x}_0,\mu),\\\mathsf{KeyGen}(\mathsf{msk},\mathbf{x}_1),\ldots,\mathsf{KeyGen}_{k-1}(\mathsf{msk},\mathbf{x}_{k-1}),\mathsf{KeyGen}_k(\mathsf{msk},f)\end{matrix}\right) = \mu\right]$$
$$= 1 - \mathsf{negl}(\lambda)$$

---

[4] The informed reader may be reminded of the Naor-Reingold argument [33] used to construct a PRF from DDH or its lattice analogue [19].

[5] We follow the convention in lattice based cryptography where the decryption condition is reversed with respect to the output of the function.

where the probability is over the choice of $(\mathsf{mpk}, \mathsf{msk}) \leftarrow \mathsf{Setup}(1^\lambda)$ and over the internal randomness of Enc and $\mathsf{KeyGen}_1, \ldots, \mathsf{KeyGen}_k$.

Definition 1 (Ada-IND security for k-ABE). *For a k-ABE scheme* k-ABE = {Setup, Enc, KeyGen_1, ..., KeyGen_{k-1}, KeyGen_k, Dec}, *for an attribute space* $\{(A_\lambda)^k\}_{\lambda \in \mathbb{N}}$, *function space* $\{\mathcal{F}_\lambda\}_{\lambda \in \mathbb{N}}$ *and an adversary* $\mathcal{A}$, *we define the* Ada-IND *security game as follows.*

1. **Setup phase:** *On input* 1^λ, *the challenger samples* $(\mathsf{mpk}, \mathsf{msk}) \leftarrow \mathsf{Setup}(1^\lambda)$ *and gives* mpk *to* $\mathcal{A}$.
2. **Query phase:** *During the game,* $\mathcal{A}$ *adaptively makes the following queries, in an arbitrary order.*
   (a) **Key Queries:** $\mathcal{A}$ *makes polynomial number of key queries for each slot, say* $p = p(\lambda)$. *As a j-th query for slot i,* $\mathcal{A}$ *chooses*

$$\begin{cases} \mathbf{x}_{i,j} & \text{if } i \in [k-1] \\ f_j & \text{if } i = k, \end{cases}$$

   where $\mathbf{x}_{i,j} \in A_\lambda$ *and* $f_j \in \mathcal{F}_\lambda$. *The challenger computes*

$$\begin{cases} \mathsf{sk}_{i,\mathbf{x}_{i,j}} = \mathsf{KeyGen}_i(\mathsf{msk}, \mathbf{x}_{i,j}) & \text{if } i \in [k-1] \\ \mathsf{sk}_{f_j} = \mathsf{KeyGen}_k(\mathsf{msk}, f_j) & \text{if } i = k \end{cases}$$

   and returns it to $\mathcal{A}$.
   (b) **Challenge Query:** $\mathcal{A}$ *issues a challenge query for encryption.* $\mathcal{A}$ *declares* $(\mathbf{x}_0, (\mu_0, \mu_1))$ *to the challenger, where* $\mathbf{x}_0 \in A_\lambda$ *is an attribute and* $(\mu_0, \mu_1) \in \{0,1\} \times \{0,1\}$ *is the pair of messages. Then, the challenger samples* $\beta \leftarrow \{0,1\}$, *computes* $\mathsf{ct}_\beta = \mathsf{Enc}(\mathsf{mpk}, \mathbf{x}_0, \mu_\beta)$ *and returns it to* $\mathcal{A}$.
3. **Output phase:** $\mathcal{A}$ *outputs a guess bit* β' *as the output of the experiment.*

For the adversary to be admissible, *we require that for every* $f_1, \ldots, f_p \in \mathcal{F}$, *it holds that* $f_{j_k}(\mathbf{x}_0, \mathbf{x}_{1,j_1}, \ldots, \mathbf{x}_{k-1,j_{k-1}}) = 1$ *for every* $j_1, \ldots, j_k \in [p]$.

We define the advantage $\mathsf{Adv}^{\mathsf{Ada\text{-}IND}}_{\mathsf{k\text{-}ABE}, \mathcal{A}}(1^\lambda)$ *of* $\mathcal{A}$ *in the above game as*

$$\mathsf{Adv}^{\mathsf{Ada\text{-}IND}}_{\mathsf{k\text{-}ABE}, \mathcal{A}}(1^\lambda) := \left| \Pr[\mathsf{Exp}_{\mathsf{k\text{-}ABE}, \mathcal{A}}(1^\lambda) = 1 | \beta = 0] - \Pr[\mathsf{Exp}_{\mathsf{k\text{-}ABE}, \mathcal{A}}(1^\lambda) = 1 | \beta = 1] \right|.$$

The k-ABE *scheme* k-ABE *is said to satisfy* Ada-IND *security (or simply adaptive security) if for any stateful PPT adversary* $\mathcal{A}$, *there exists a negligible function* $\mathrm{negl}(\cdot)$ *such that* $\mathsf{Adv}^{\mathsf{Ada\text{-}IND}}_{\mathsf{k\text{-}ABE}, \mathcal{A}}(1^\lambda) = \mathrm{negl}(\lambda)$.

Definition 2 (VerSel-IND security for k-ABE). *The definitions for* VerSel-IND *security for* k-ABE *is the same as* Ada-IND *security above except that the adversary* $\mathcal{A}$ *is required to submit the challenge query and key queries to the challenger before it samples the public key.*

For notations and more preliminaries please see the full version [12].

3   Assumptions and New Implications

In this section, we discuss the evasive and tensor LWE assumptions. Our variants of these assumptions differ slightly from the original formulation by [39] as discussed below.

3.1   Evasive LWE

Below, we state a variant of the Evasive-LWE assumption which will be useful for our constructions.

Assumption 1 (Evasive LWE). *Let* $n, m, t, m', q \in \mathbb{N}$ *be parameters and* λ *be a security parameter. Let* χ *and* χ' *be parameters for Gaussian distributions. Let* Samp *be a PPT algorithm that outputs*

$$\mathbf{S} \in \mathbb{Z}_q^{m' \times n}, \mathbf{P} \in \mathbb{Z}_q^{n \times t}, \mathsf{aux} \in \{0,1\}^*$$

on input 1^λ. *For a PPT adversary* Adv, *we define the following advantage functions:*

$$\mathcal{A}_{\mathsf{Adv}}^{\mathrm{PRE}}(\lambda) := \Pr[\mathsf{Adv}_0(\mathbf{B}, \mathbf{SB}{+}\mathbf{E}, \mathbf{SP}{+}\mathbf{E}', \mathsf{aux}) = 1] - \Pr[\mathsf{Adv}_0(\mathbf{B}, \mathbf{C}_0, \mathbf{C}', \mathsf{aux}) = 1]$$

$$\mathcal{A}_{\mathsf{Adv}}^{\mathrm{POST}}(\lambda) := \Pr[\mathsf{Adv}_1(\mathbf{B}, \mathbf{SB} + \mathbf{E}, \mathbf{K}, \mathsf{aux}) = 1] - \Pr[\mathsf{Adv}_1(\mathbf{B}, \mathbf{C}_0, \mathbf{K}, \mathsf{aux}) = 1]$$

where

$$(\mathbf{S}, \mathbf{P}, \mathsf{aux}) \leftarrow \mathsf{Samp}(1^\lambda), \quad \mathbf{B} \leftarrow \mathbb{Z}_q^{n \times m},$$

$$\mathbf{C}_0 \leftarrow \mathbb{Z}_q^{m' \times m}, \mathbf{C}' \leftarrow \mathbb{Z}_q^{m' \times t}, \quad \mathbf{E} \leftarrow \mathcal{D}_{\mathbb{Z}, \chi}^{m' \times m}, \mathbf{E}' \leftarrow \mathcal{D}_{\mathbb{Z}, \chi'}^{m' \times t}$$

$$\mathbf{K} \leftarrow \mathbf{B}^{-1}(\mathbf{P}) \text{ with standard deviation } O(\sqrt{m \log(q)}).$$

We say that the evasive LWE *(EvLWE) assumption holds if for every PPT* Samp *and* Adv_1, *there exists another PPT* Adv_0 *and a polynomial* $Q(\cdot)$ *such that*

$$\mathcal{A}_{\mathsf{Adv}_0}^{\mathrm{PRE}}(\lambda) \geq \mathcal{A}_{\mathsf{Adv}_1}^{\mathrm{POST}}(\lambda) / Q(\lambda) - \mathrm{negl}(\lambda).$$

Remark 1. In the above definition, all the entries of $\mathbf{E}'$ are chosen from the same distribution $D_{\mathbb{Z}, \chi'}$. However, in our security proof, we often consider the case where some entries of $\mathbf{E}'$ are chosen from $D_{\mathbb{Z}, \chi'}$ and others from $D_{\mathbb{Z}, \chi''}$ with different $\chi' \gg \chi''$. The evasive LWE assumption with such a mixed noise distribution for $\mathbf{E}'$ is implied by the evasive LWE assumption with all entries in $\mathbf{E}'$ being chosen from $D_{\mathbb{Z}, \chi'}$ as above definition, since if the precondition is satisfied for the latter case, that for the former case is also satisfied. To see this, it suffices to observe that we can convert the distribution from $D_{\mathbb{Z}, \chi''}$ into that from $D_{\mathbb{Z}, \chi'}$ by adding extra Gaussian noise.

Remark 2. In the above, we chose χ' to be smaller than χ following [37]. This makes the precondition stronger, which in turn makes evasive LWE weaker.

Comparison with the original evasive LWE [39]. Our assumption is closely related to the evasive LWE assumption that appeared in Wee [39] with minor differences. In Wee, the secret $\mathbf{S}$ is chosen uniformly whereas in our assumption, the secret can be structured and output by the sampler, subject to the pre-condition being true. On the other hand, in [37], $\mathbf{S}$ is the public matrix and can be structured, while $\mathbf{B}$ is secret and is random. An additional difference is related to the auxiliary input. In Wee, aux contains all the coin tosses used by the sampler – this suffices to rule out obfuscation based counter-examples where aux may contain information of the trapdoor for $\mathbf{P}$ in a hidden way. On the other hand, in [37], the coins of the sampler are private, and aux contains information including certain Gaussian preimages. They argue that their assumption nevertheless avoids the obfuscation based counter-examples, since their auxiliary input does not contain trapdoor for the matrix $\mathbf{P}$. In both their and our cases, aux is derived from the trapdoor for $\mathbf{P}$ or related information that should be kept hidden, but it does not contain the trapdoor itself. We may therefore expect that there is no space for embedding an obfuscation into our auxiliary input, similarly to [37]. We also note that as observed in [37], Tsabary's variant of evasive LWE is less conservative than ours and theirs, since her definition allows aux to depend on $\mathbf{B}$.

In the security proof of our constructions, we sometimes want to include information dependent on $\mathbf{S}$ into the auxiliary information. However, this makes the corresponding evasive LWE assumption stronger and not desirable. The following lemma allows us to do this without strengthening the assumption under certain conditions. In the lemma, we separate the auxiliary information into two parts aux_1 and aux_2, where aux_1 is typically the part dependent on $\mathbf{S}$. The lemma roughly says that if aux_1 is pseudorandom, then we can apply the evasive LWE with respect to a modified sampler whose aux_1 is replaced with a random string to derive the conclusion on postcondition distribution.

Lemma 1. *Let $n, m, t, m', q \in \mathbb{N}$ be parameters and λ be a security parameter. Let χ and χ' be Gaussian parameters. Let* Samp *be a PPT algorithm that outputs*

$$\mathbf{S} \in \mathbb{Z}_q^{m' \times n}, \mathsf{aux} = (\mathsf{aux}_1, \mathsf{aux}_2) \in \mathcal{S} \times \{0,1\}^* \text{ and } \mathbf{P} \in \mathbb{Z}_q^{n \times t}$$

for some set $\mathcal{S}$. Furthermore, we assume that there exists a public deterministic poly-time algorithm Reconstruct *that allows to derive $\mathbf{P}$ from aux_2, i.e. $\mathbf{P} =$* Reconstruct(aux_2). *We introduce the following advantage functions:*

$$\mathcal{A}_{\mathsf{Adv}}^{\mathrm{PRE}'}(\lambda) := \Pr[\mathsf{Adv}(\mathbf{B}, \mathbf{SB} + \mathbf{E}, \mathbf{SP} + \mathbf{E}', \mathsf{aux}_1, \mathsf{aux}_2) = 1] \\ - \Pr[\mathsf{Adv}(\mathbf{B}, \mathbf{C}_0, \mathbf{C}', \mathbf{c}, \mathsf{aux}_2) = 1]$$

$$\mathcal{A}_{\mathsf{Adv}}^{\mathrm{POST}'}(\lambda) := \Pr[\mathsf{Adv}(\mathbf{B}, \mathbf{SB} + \mathbf{E}, \mathbf{K}, \mathsf{aux}_1, \mathsf{aux}_2) = 1] \\ - \Pr[\mathsf{Adv}(\mathbf{B}, \mathbf{C}_0, \mathbf{K}, \mathbf{c}, \mathsf{aux}_2) = 1]$$

where

$$(\mathbf{S}, \mathsf{aux} = (\mathsf{aux}_1, \mathsf{aux}_2), \mathbf{P}) \leftarrow \mathsf{Samp}(1^\lambda), \quad \mathbf{B} \leftarrow \mathbb{Z}_q^{n \times m}$$

$$\mathbf{C}_0 \leftarrow \mathbb{Z}_q^{m' \times m}, \quad \mathbf{C}' \leftarrow \mathbb{Z}_q^{m' \times t}, \mathbf{c} \leftarrow \mathcal{S}$$

$$\mathbf{E} \leftarrow \mathcal{D}_{\mathbb{Z},\chi}^{m' \times m}, \mathbf{E}' \leftarrow \mathcal{D}_{\mathbb{Z},\chi}^{m' \times t} \quad \mathbf{K} \leftarrow \mathbf{B}^{-1}(\mathbf{P}) \text{ with standard deviation } O(\sqrt{m\log(q)}).$$

*Then, under the Evasive-*LWE *(cited above in Assumption 1) with respect to* Samp′ *that outputs* $(\mathbf{S}, (\mathbf{c}, \mathsf{aux}_2), \mathbf{P})$ *for random* $\mathbf{c}$, *if* $\mathcal{A}_{\mathsf{Adv}}^{\mathrm{PRE}'}(\lambda)$ *is negligible for any PPT adversary* Adv, *so is* $\mathcal{A}_{\mathsf{Adv}}^{\mathrm{PRE}'}(\lambda)$ *for any PPT adversary* Adv.

Due to space constraints, we prove the lemma in the full version of the paper [12].

3.2 Tensor LWE

In this section, we define the tensor LWE assumption introduced by Wee [39]. Then, we provide new arguments supporting the assumption.

Assumption 2 (Tensor LWE). *Let* $n, m, q, \ell, Q \in \mathbb{N}$ *be parameters and* $\gamma, \chi > 0$ *be Gaussian parameters. For all* $\mathbf{x}_1, \cdots, \mathbf{x}_Q \in \{0,1\}^\ell$, *we have*

$$\mathbf{A}, \left\{ \mathbf{s}(\mathbf{I}_n \otimes \mathbf{r}_i^\top)(\mathbf{A} - \mathbf{x}_i \otimes \mathbf{G}) + \mathbf{e}_i, \mathbf{r}_i^\top \right\}_{i \in [Q]} \approx_c \mathbf{A}, \left\{ \mathbf{c}_i, \mathbf{r}_i^\top \right\}_{i \in [Q]}$$

where $\mathbf{A} \leftarrow \mathbb{Z}_q^{n \times \ell m}, \mathbf{s} \leftarrow \mathbb{Z}_q^{mn}, \mathbf{e}_i \leftarrow \mathcal{D}_{\mathbb{Z},\chi}^{\ell m}, \mathbf{r}_i^\top \leftarrow \mathcal{D}_{\mathbb{Z},\gamma}^m, \mathbf{c}_i \leftarrow \mathbb{Z}_q^{\ell m}$.

To gain confidence in the tensor LWE assumption, we study conditions under which it can be reduced to standard LWE. To begin, we recall the following lemma which is implicit in [39]. The lemma says that a variant of the tensor LWE assumption holds under the standard LWE assumption if $\mathbf{A}$ matrices are chosen from Gaussian distribution and $\mathbf{G}$ is replaced with $\mathbf{I}$ in certain parameter settings.

Lemma 2 (Implicitly proved in [39]). *Let* $n, m, q, \ell, Q, \beta \in \mathbb{N}$ *be parameters and* χ_0, χ, *and* γ *be a Gaussian parameter satisfying* $m = \Omega(n\log q)$, $\gamma = \lambda^{\omega(1)}$, $\chi = \chi_0 \gamma \lambda^{\omega(1)}$. *For all* $\mathbf{x}_1, \cdots, \mathbf{x}_Q \in \{0,1\}^\ell$, LWE$(n, Q+m, q, \chi_0)$ *hardness assumption implies*

$$\mathbf{A}, \left\{ \mathbf{s}(\mathbf{I}_n \otimes \mathbf{r}_i^\top)(\mathbf{A} - \mathbf{x}_i \otimes \mathbf{I}_m) + \mathbf{e}_i, \mathbf{r}_i^\top \right\}_{i \in [Q]} \approx_c \mathbf{A}, \left\{ \mathbf{c}_i, \mathbf{r}_i^\top \right\}_{i \in [Q]}$$

where $\mathbf{A} \leftarrow \mathcal{D}_{\mathbb{Z},\gamma}^{n \times \ell m}, \mathbf{s} \leftarrow \mathbb{Z}_q^{mn}, \mathbf{e}_i \leftarrow \mathcal{D}_{\mathbb{Z},\chi}^{\ell m}, \mathbf{r}_i^\top \leftarrow \mathcal{D}_{\mathbb{Z},\gamma}^m, \mathbf{c}_i \leftarrow \mathbb{Z}_q^{\ell m}$.

3.3 New Implications for Tensor LWE

We now introduce a new lemma that also proves the same implication between LWE and Tensor LWE in another particular case. Notably, the lemma shows the hardness for the case where $\mathbf{A}$ is chosen uniformly at random rather than from a Gaussian distribution, albeit with the downside of assuming $\mathbf{x}_i = \mathbf{0}$ for all i.

Lemma 3 (Tensor LWE with $\{\mathbf{x}_i = \mathbf{0}\}_i$). *Let $n, m, q, \ell, Q, \beta \in \mathbb{N}$ be parameters and χ_0, χ, and γ be a Gaussian parameter satisfying $m = \Omega(n \log q)$, $\gamma = \Omega(\sqrt{n \log q})$, and $\chi = \gamma \chi_0 \lambda^{\omega(1)}$. Then, $\mathsf{LWE}(n, m, q, \chi_0)$ hardness assumption implies*

$$\mathbf{A}, \left\{ \mathbf{s}(\mathbf{I}_n \otimes \mathbf{r}_i^\top) \mathbf{A} + \mathbf{e}_i, \mathbf{r}_i^\top \right\}_{i \in [Q]} \approx_c \mathbf{A}, \left\{ \mathbf{c}_i, \mathbf{r}_i^\top \right\}_{i \in [Q]}$$

where $\mathbf{A} \leftarrow \mathbb{Z}_q^{n \times \ell m}$, $\mathbf{s} \leftarrow \mathbb{Z}_q^{mn}$, $\mathbf{e}_i \leftarrow \mathcal{D}_{\mathbb{Z}, \chi}^{\ell m}$, $\mathbf{r}_i^\top \leftarrow \mathcal{D}_{\mathbb{Z}, \gamma}^m$, $\mathbf{c}_i \leftarrow \mathbb{Z}_q^{\ell m}$.

Due to space constraints, we prove the lemma in the full version of the paper [12].

3.4   New Implications from LWE

In this section, we provide new lemmata under the LWE assumption which will be useful for our constructions. We believe these may be of broader applicability. Due to space constraints, we prove these lemmata in the full version of the paper [12].

Lemma 4. *Let $n = n(\lambda)$, $m = m(\lambda)$, $N = N(\lambda)$, $q = q(\lambda)$, $\gamma = \gamma(\lambda)$, $\chi_0 = \chi_0(\lambda) \in \lambda^{\omega(1)}$, $\chi = \chi(\lambda)$, and $k = O(1)$ be parameters satisfying $m = \Omega(n \log q)$, $\chi(\lambda) \geq (m \gamma \chi_0)^k$. If $\mathsf{LWE}(n, Q, q, \chi_0)$ holds, then the following distributions are computationally indistinguishable:*

$$\left\{ \mathbf{c}_{j_1, \ldots, j_k} := \mathbf{s}(\mathbf{I}_N \otimes \mathbf{r}_{1, j_1}^\top \otimes \cdots \otimes \mathbf{r}_{k, j_k}^\top) + \mathbf{e}_{j_1, \ldots, j_k} \right\}_{j_1, \ldots, j_k \in [Q]}$$

$$\approx_c \left\{ \mathbf{w}_{j_1, \ldots, j_k} \right\}_{j_1, \ldots, j_k \in [Q]}$$

where $\mathbf{s} \leftarrow \mathbb{Z}_q^{Nm^k}$, $\mathbf{r}_{i, j_i} \leftarrow \mathcal{D}_{\mathbb{Z}, \gamma}^m$, $\mathbf{e}_{j_1, \ldots, j_k} \leftarrow \mathcal{D}_{\mathbb{Z}, \chi}^N$, $\mathbf{w}_{j_1, \ldots, j_k} \leftarrow \mathbb{Z}_q^N$ for $i \in [k]$ and $j_1, \ldots, j_k \in [Q]$.

Lemma 5. *Let $n = n(\lambda)$, $m = m(\lambda)$, $N = N(\lambda)$, $q = q(\lambda)$, $\chi = \chi(\lambda)$, and $k = O(1)$ be parameters. If $\mathsf{LWE}(n, (m+1)^k N, q, \chi)$ holds, then, the following distributions are computationally indistinguishable:*

$$\left(\{\mathbf{B}_i\}_{i \in [0, k]}, \mathbf{s}(\mathbf{B}_0 \otimes \mathbf{I}_m^{\otimes k}) + \mathbf{e}_0, \ldots, \mathbf{s}(\mathbf{B}_i \otimes \mathbf{I}_m^{\otimes (k-i)}) + \mathbf{e}_i, \ldots, \mathbf{s}\mathbf{B}_k + \mathbf{e}_k \right)$$

$$\approx_c \left(\{\mathbf{B}_i\}_{i \in [0, k]}, \mathbf{c}_0, \mathbf{c}_1, \ldots, \mathbf{c}_k \right)$$

where $\mathbf{B}_i \leftarrow \mathbb{Z}_q^{nm^i \times Nm^i}$, $\mathbf{e}_i \leftarrow \mathcal{D}_{\mathbb{Z}, \chi}^{m^k N}$, and $\mathbf{c}_0, \mathbf{c}_1, \ldots, \mathbf{c}_k \leftarrow \mathbb{Z}_q^{m^k N}$ for $i \in [0, k]$, $\mathbf{s} \leftarrow \mathbb{Z}_q^{nm^k}$.

4   Two-input ABE from Evasive and Tensor LWE

4.1   Construction

In this section, we define our construction of 2ABE for P using evasive LWE (Assumption 1) and tensor LWE (Assumption 2). As discussed in Sect. 1, when restricted to NC_1, our construction can be modified to rely only on evasive LWE. We defer the details of this modification to Sect. 5 and focus on circuit class P for this section.

Let ℓ be the length of the attribute in each slot. The construction supports general circuits with bounded depth d and the decryption is possible when $f(\mathbf{x}_0 \| \mathbf{x}_1) = 0$, where $\mathbf{x}_0$ is the attribute associated with a ciphertext, $\mathbf{x}_1$ is the attribute associated with the first slot key, and f is the function associated with the second slot key. Below $\mathbf{I}$ refers to $\mathbf{I}_m$.

$\mathsf{Setup}(1^\lambda)$: The setup algorithm takes as input the security parameter λ and does the following:

- Sample $\mathbf{A}_0, \mathbf{A}_1, \mathbf{A}_2 \leftarrow \mathbb{Z}_q^{n \times m\ell}$; $(\mathbf{B}, \mathbf{B}_{\tau_B}^{-1}) \leftarrow \mathsf{TrapGen}(1^\lambda, 2nm + nm^2, (2nm + nm^2)w)$; $(\mathbf{C}, \mathbf{C}_{\tau_C}^{-1}) \leftarrow \mathsf{TrapGen}(1^\lambda, nm, nmw)$, where $w \in O(\log q)$; $\mathbf{D} \leftarrow \mathbb{Z}_q^{n \times m}$. Let $\mathbf{A} = (\mathbf{A}_1 \| \mathbf{A}_2)$.
- Output $\mathsf{mpk} = (\mathbf{A}_0, \mathbf{A}, \mathbf{B}, \mathbf{C}, \mathbf{D})$, $\mathsf{msk} = (\mathbf{B}_{\tau_B}^{-1}, \mathbf{C}_{\tau_C}^{-1})$.

$\mathsf{Enc}(\mathsf{mpk}, \mathbf{x}_0, \mu)$: The encryption algorithm takes as input the master public key mpk, an attribute $\mathbf{x}_0$ and message bit $\mu \in \{0, 1\}$ and does the following:

- If $\mu = 1$, sample $\mathbf{c}_1 \leftarrow \mathbb{Z}_q^{m^2\ell}$, $\mathbf{c}_2 \leftarrow \mathbb{Z}_q^{(2nm+nm^2)w}$.
- Else,
  - Sample $\mathbf{s}, \mathbf{s}_0 \leftarrow \mathbb{Z}_q^{nm}$ and $\mathbf{s}_1 \leftarrow \mathbb{Z}_q^{nm^2}$.
  - Sample error vectors $\mathbf{e}_1 \leftarrow \mathcal{D}_{\mathbb{Z}, \chi_1}^{m^2\ell}$, $\mathbf{e}_2 \leftarrow \mathcal{D}_{\mathbb{Z}, \chi_2}^{(2nm+nm^2)w}$.
  - Compute $\mathbf{c}_1 = (\mathbf{s}, \mathbf{s}_0) \begin{pmatrix} (\mathbf{A}_1 - \mathbf{x}_0 \otimes \mathbf{G}) \otimes \mathbf{I} \\ \mathbf{A}_0 \otimes \mathbf{I} \end{pmatrix} + \mathbf{e}_1$.
  - Compute $\mathbf{c}_2 = (\mathbf{s}, \mathbf{s}_0, \mathbf{s}_1)\mathbf{B} + \mathbf{e}_2$.
- Output $\mathsf{ct}_{\mathbf{x}_0} = (\mathbf{c}_1, \mathbf{c}_2)$.

$\mathsf{KeyGen}_1(\mathsf{msk}, \mathbf{x}_1)$: The keygen algorithm for slot 1 takes as input the master secret key msk and the slot attribute $\mathbf{x}_1 \in \{0, 1\}^\ell$ and does the following:

- Sample $\mathbf{r} \leftarrow \mathcal{D}_{\mathbb{Z}, \gamma}^m$.
- Sample $\mathbf{L}_{\mathbf{x}_1} \leftarrow \mathbf{B}^{-1} \left(\begin{pmatrix} (\mathbf{A}_2 - \mathbf{x}_1 \otimes \mathbf{G}) \otimes \mathbf{r}^\top \\ \mathbf{A}_0 \otimes \mathbf{r}^\top \\ \mathbf{C} \otimes \mathbf{r}^\top \end{pmatrix}, \tau_B \right)$.
- Output $\mathsf{sk}_{1,\mathbf{x}_1} = (\mathbf{r}, \mathbf{L}_{\mathbf{x}_1})$.

$\mathsf{KeyGen}_2(\mathsf{msk}, f)$ The keygen algorithm for slot 2 takes as input the master secret key msk and slot function f, which is a function represented as a binary circuit $f : \{0, 1\}^{2\ell} \to \{0, 1\}$ and does the following:

- Sample $\mathbf{t} \leftarrow \mathcal{D}_{\mathbb{Z}, \gamma}^m$, $\mathbf{U} \leftarrow \mathcal{D}_{\mathbb{Z}, \gamma}^{m \times m}$.
- Compute $\mathbf{H}_f = \mathsf{EvalF}(\mathbf{A}, f)$ and $\mathbf{A}_f = \mathbf{A}\mathbf{H}_f$.
- Sample $\mathbf{M}_f \leftarrow \mathbf{B}^{-1} \left(\begin{pmatrix} \mathbf{A}_f \mathbf{U} \otimes \mathbf{I} \\ \mathbf{0}_{nm \times m^2} \\ \mathbf{D} \otimes \mathbf{t}^\top \otimes \mathbf{I} \end{pmatrix}, \tau_B \right)$ and $\mathbf{N}_f \leftarrow \mathbf{C}^{-1} \left((\mathbf{D} \otimes \mathbf{t}^\top), \tau_C \right)$.
- Output $\mathsf{sk}_{2,f} = (\mathbf{t}, \mathbf{U}, \mathbf{M}_f, \mathbf{N}_f)$.

$\mathsf{Dec}(\mathsf{mpk}, \mathsf{ct}_{\mathbf{x}_0}, \mathsf{sk}_{1,\mathbf{x}_1}, \mathsf{sk}_{2,f})$ The decryption algorithm takes as input the ciphertext $\mathsf{ct}_{\mathbf{x}_0}$, key $\mathsf{sk}_{1,\mathbf{x}_1}$ for slot 1, and key $\mathsf{sk}_{2,f}$ for slot 2 and does the following:

- Parse $\mathsf{ct}_{\mathbf{x}_0}$ as $(\mathbf{c}_1, \mathbf{c}_2)$, $\mathsf{sk}_{1,\mathbf{x}_1}$ as $(\mathbf{r}, \mathbf{L}_{\mathbf{x}_1})$ and $\mathsf{sk}_{2,f}$ as $(\mathbf{t}, \mathbf{U}, \mathbf{M}_f, \mathbf{N}_f)$.

- Compute $\widehat{\mathbf{H}}_{\mathbf{A},f,(\mathbf{x}_0\|\mathbf{x}_1)} = \mathsf{EvalFX}(\mathbf{A}, f, (\mathbf{x}_0\|\mathbf{x}_1))$.
- Compute the following:

$$\begin{aligned}
\mathbf{d}_1 &= \mathbf{c}_1, & (\mathbf{d}_2,\ \mathbf{d}_3,\ \mathbf{d}_4) &= \mathbf{c}_2\mathbf{L}_{\mathbf{x}_1}, & \mathbf{d}_5 &= \mathbf{c}_2\mathbf{M}_f, \\
\mathbf{d}_6 &= \mathbf{N}_f, & \mathbf{d}'_1 &= \mathbf{d}_1(\mathbf{I}_{m\ell}\otimes\mathbf{r}^\top) - \mathbf{d}_3, & \mathbf{d}'_5 &= \mathbf{d}_5(\mathbf{I}\otimes\mathbf{r}^\top) - \mathbf{d}_4\mathbf{d}_6, \\
\mathbf{d}_7 &= (\mathbf{d}'_1\|\mathbf{d}_2)\widehat{\mathbf{H}}_{\mathbf{A},f,(\mathbf{x}_0\|\mathbf{x}_1)}\mathbf{U}, & & & \mathbf{d}_8 &= \mathbf{d}_7 - \mathbf{d}'_5.
\end{aligned}$$

Note that $\mathbf{d}_6$ is a matrix of size $nmw \times m$ and $\mathbf{d}_i$ for all $i \neq 6$ are vectors.
- If $\|\mathbf{d}_8\|_\infty \leq \beta_0$ (where β_0 is as defined by the parameters setting - provided in the full version [12], due to space constraints) then output $\mu' = 0$, else output 1.

4.2 Correctness, Parameters and Security

Correctness. Here, we show correctness of the scheme.

When $\mu = 1$: We first show the correctness for the case of $\mu = 1$. For an honest run of the protocol, $\mathbf{d}_1$ is distributed uniformly at random over its domain. Then, since $\mathbf{r} \neq \mathbf{0}$ with overwhelming probability and thus $\mathbf{I}_{m\ell}\otimes\mathbf{r}^\top$ is a full-rank matrix, $\mathbf{d}'_1$ is distributed uniformly at random over its domain. Then, since the topmost m rows of $\widehat{\mathbf{H}}_{\mathbf{A},f,(\mathbf{x}_0\|\mathbf{x}_1)}$ constitutes an identity matrix by [12, Lemma 2.6], $(\mathbf{d}'_1\|\mathbf{d}_2)\widehat{\mathbf{H}}_{\mathbf{A},f,(\mathbf{x}_0\|\mathbf{x}_1)}$ is distributed uniformly at random over its domain. Finally, since each column of $\mathbf{U}$ is chosen from $\mathcal{D}^m_{\mathbb{Z},\gamma}$, with overwhelming probability, there exists $i \in [m]$ such that the i-th column of $\mathbf{U}$ is not a zero vector. This in turn implies that that the i-th entry of $\mathbf{d}_7$ is distributed uniformly at random over $\mathbb{Z}_q$. Since we set $\beta_0/q = \lambda^{-\omega(1)}$, the probability that the decryption algorithm falsely outputs 0 is negligible as desired.

When $\mu = 0$: Next, we show the correctness for the case of $\mu = 0$. For an honest run of the protocol, we have

- $\mathbf{d}_1 = \mathbf{c}_1 = \mathbf{s}((\mathbf{A}_1 - \mathbf{x}_0\otimes\mathbf{G})\otimes\mathbf{I}) + \mathbf{s}_0(\mathbf{A}_0\otimes\mathbf{I}) + \mathbf{e}_1$.
  Let $(\mathbf{e}'_2,\ \mathbf{e}'_3,\ \mathbf{e}'_4) = \mathbf{e}_2 \cdot \mathbf{L}_{\mathbf{x}_1}$.
- $\mathbf{d}_2 = \mathbf{s}((\mathbf{A}_2 - \mathbf{x}_1\otimes\mathbf{G})\otimes\mathbf{r}^\top) + \mathbf{e}'_2$,
- $\mathbf{d}_3 = \mathbf{s}_0(\mathbf{A}_0\otimes\mathbf{r}^\top) + \mathbf{e}'_3$,
- $\mathbf{d}_4 = \mathbf{s}_1(\mathbf{C}\otimes\mathbf{r}^\top) + \mathbf{e}'_4$,
- $\mathbf{d}_5 = \mathbf{s}(\mathbf{A}_f\mathbf{U}\otimes\mathbf{I}) + \mathbf{s}_1(\mathbf{D}\otimes\mathbf{t}^\top\otimes\mathbf{I}) + \mathbf{e}'_5$, where $\mathbf{e}'_5 = \mathbf{e}_2 \cdot \mathbf{M}_f$
- $\mathbf{d}'_1$ is computed as

$$\begin{aligned}
\mathbf{d}'_1 &= \mathbf{d}_1(\mathbf{I}_{m\ell}\otimes\mathbf{r}^\top) - \mathbf{d}_3 \\
&= (\mathbf{s}((\mathbf{A}_1 - \mathbf{x}_0\otimes\mathbf{G})\otimes\mathbf{I}) + \mathbf{s}_0(\mathbf{A}_0\otimes\mathbf{I}) + \mathbf{e}_1)(\mathbf{I}_{m\ell}\otimes\mathbf{r}^\top) - \mathbf{s}_0(\mathbf{A}_0\otimes\mathbf{r}^\top) \\
&\quad -\mathbf{e}'_3 \\
&= \mathbf{s}((\mathbf{A}_1 - \mathbf{x}_0\otimes\mathbf{G})\otimes\mathbf{r}^\top) + \mathbf{s}_0(\mathbf{A}_0\otimes\mathbf{r}^\top) - \mathbf{s}_0(\mathbf{A}_0\otimes\mathbf{r}^\top) + \mathbf{e}''_1 \\
&= \mathbf{s}((\mathbf{A}_1 - \mathbf{x}_0\otimes\mathbf{G})\otimes\mathbf{r}^\top) + \mathbf{e}''_1
\end{aligned}$$

Here $\mathbf{e}''_1 = \mathbf{e}_1(\mathbf{I}_{m\ell}\otimes\mathbf{r}^\top) - \mathbf{e}'_3$

- $\mathbf{d}_5'$ is computed as

$$\begin{aligned}
\mathbf{d}_5' &= \mathbf{d}_5(\mathbf{I} \otimes \mathbf{r}^\top) - \mathbf{d}_4\mathbf{d}_6 \\
&= (\mathbf{s}(\mathbf{A}_f\mathbf{U} \otimes \mathbf{I}) + \mathbf{s}_1(\mathbf{D} \otimes \mathbf{t}^\top \otimes \mathbf{I}) + \mathbf{e}_5')(\mathbf{I} \otimes \mathbf{r}^\top) - (\mathbf{s}_1(\mathbf{C} \otimes \mathbf{r}^\top) + \mathbf{e}_4')\mathbf{N}_f \\
&= \mathbf{s}(\mathbf{A}_f\mathbf{U} \otimes \mathbf{r}^\top) + \mathbf{s}_1(\mathbf{D} \otimes \mathbf{t}^\top \otimes \mathbf{r}^\top) - \mathbf{s}_1(\mathbf{D} \otimes \mathbf{t}^\top \otimes \mathbf{r}^\top) + \mathbf{e}_5'', \\
&= \mathbf{s}(\mathbf{A}_f\mathbf{U} \otimes \mathbf{r}^\top) + \mathbf{e}_5''
\end{aligned}$$

where we use $(\mathbf{C} \otimes \mathbf{r}^\top)\mathbf{N}_f = \mathbf{C}\mathbf{N}_f \otimes \mathbf{r}^\top = \mathbf{D} \otimes \mathbf{t}^\top \otimes \mathbf{r}^\top$ and define $\mathbf{e}_5'' := \mathbf{e}_5'(\mathbf{I} \otimes \mathbf{r}^\top) - \mathbf{e}_4'\mathbf{N}_f$ on the third line.

- $\mathbf{d}_7$ is computed as

$$\begin{aligned}
\mathbf{d}_7 &= (\mathbf{d}_1' \| \mathbf{d}_2) \cdot (\widehat{\mathbf{H}}_{\mathbf{A},f,(\mathbf{x}_0\|\mathbf{x}_1)}\mathbf{U}) \\
&= ((\mathbf{s}((\mathbf{A}_1 - \mathbf{x}_0 \otimes \mathbf{G}) \otimes \mathbf{r}^\top) + \mathbf{e}_1'') \| (\mathbf{s}((\mathbf{A}_2 - \mathbf{x}_1 \otimes \mathbf{G}) \otimes \mathbf{r}^\top) + \mathbf{e}_2')) \\
&\quad \cdot (\widehat{\mathbf{H}}_{\mathbf{A},f,(\mathbf{x}_0\|\mathbf{x}_1)}\mathbf{U}) \\
&= (\mathbf{s}((\mathbf{A}_1 \| \mathbf{A}_2 - (\mathbf{x}_0 \| \mathbf{x}_1) \otimes \mathbf{G}) \otimes \mathbf{r}^\top) + (\mathbf{e}_1'' \| \mathbf{e}_2')) \cdot (\widehat{\mathbf{H}}_{\mathbf{A},f,(\mathbf{x}_0\|\mathbf{x}_1)}\mathbf{U}) \\
&= \mathbf{s}((\mathbf{A}_f - f(\mathbf{x}_0\|\mathbf{x}_1)\mathbf{G}) \otimes \mathbf{r}^\top)\mathbf{U} + \mathbf{e}_7' \\
&= \mathbf{s}((\mathbf{A}_f - f(\mathbf{x}_0\|\mathbf{x}_1)\mathbf{G})\mathbf{U} \otimes \mathbf{r}^\top) + \mathbf{e}_7' \\
&= \mathbf{s}(\mathbf{A}_f\mathbf{U} \otimes \mathbf{r}^\top) + \mathbf{e}_7' \quad \text{if } f(\mathbf{x}_0\|\mathbf{x}_1) = 0
\end{aligned}$$

where we define $\mathbf{e}_7' := (\mathbf{e}_1'' \| \mathbf{e}_2')\widehat{\mathbf{H}}_{\mathbf{A},f,(\mathbf{x}_0\|\mathbf{x}_1)}\mathbf{U}$ on the fourth line.

- $\mathbf{d}_8 = \mathbf{d}_7 - \mathbf{d}_5' = \mathbf{s}(\mathbf{A}_f\mathbf{U} \otimes \mathbf{r}^\top) + \mathbf{e}_7' - \mathbf{s}(\mathbf{A}_f\mathbf{U} \otimes \mathbf{r}^\top) - \mathbf{e}_5'' = \mathbf{e}_7' - \mathbf{e}_5''$ which is small ($\leq \beta_0$).

Therefore, the decryption algorithm outputs 0 as desired.

Due to space constraints, we provide the error bound and parameter settings in the full version of the paper [12].

Security: Here, we prove the following theorem, which asserts the security of our scheme.

Theorem 3. *Assuming evasive* LWE *(Assumption 1), tensor* LWE *(Assumption 2), and* LWE, *our construction for 2-input* ABE *for* P *satisfies very selective security (Definition 2). Moreover, for the restricted class* NC_1, *our construction for 2-input* ABE *relies only on evasive* LWE.

Due to space constraints, we provide the proof in the full version of the paper [12].

5 Multi-Input ABE for Any Constant Arity

In this section, we extend the construction in Sec. 4 to construct k-ABE for any constant k using evasive LWE. Our main construction supports functions in NC_1 and proven secure assuming evasive LWE. We also discuss a variant that supports any polynomial size circuit of bounded depth, which can be proven secure assuming a strengthening of tensor LWE in addition.

5.1   Construction for $\mathbf{NC_1}$ Circuits

Here, we show our construction. Let ℓ be the length of each of the k attributes. Decryption is possible when $f(\mathbf{x}_0, \mathbf{x}_1, \ldots, \mathbf{x}_{k-1}) = 0$, where $\mathbf{x}_0 \in \{0,1\}^\ell$ is the attribute associated with the public encryption, $\mathbf{x}_i \in \{0,1\}^\ell$ is the attribute associated with the slot i, and f is a binary circuit associated with the slot k key. Below $\mathbf{I}$ refers to $\mathbf{I}_m$. We require an upper bound on the depth of the circuit and denote it by d. We require $d = O(\log \lambda)$.

In the construction, we will use the low-norm variant of the lattice evaluation algorithms (EvalF, EvalFX) from [12, Lemma 2.8].

Setup(1^λ): The setup algorithm takes as input the security parameter and does the following:

- Sample $\mathbf{A}_0, \ldots, \mathbf{A}_{k-1} \leftarrow \mathcal{D}_{\mathbb{Z},\gamma}^{m \times m\ell}$; $\mathbf{D}_0, \ldots, \mathbf{D}_{k-1} \leftarrow \mathbb{Z}_q^{n \times m\ell}$, $\mathbf{D}_k \leftarrow \mathbb{Z}_q^{n \times m}$, $\mathbf{U} \leftarrow \mathcal{D}_{\mathbb{Z},\gamma}^{m \times m}$. Let $\mathbf{A} = (\mathbf{A}_0, \ldots, \mathbf{A}_{k-1})$.
- Sample $(\mathbf{B}, \mathbf{B}_{\tau_B}^{-1}) \leftarrow \mathsf{TrapGen}(1^\lambda, m^{k+1} + (k+1)nm^k, (m^{k+1} + (k+1)nm^k)w)$, where $w \in O(\log q)$; $\{(\mathbf{C}_i, \mathbf{C}_{i,\tau_C}^{-1}) \leftarrow \mathsf{TrapGen}(1^\lambda, (k+1)nm^{i-1}, (k+1)nm^{i-1}w)\}_{i \in [2,k]}$
- Set $\mathbf{C}_1 = \begin{pmatrix} \mathbf{D}_0 & & & \\ & \mathbf{D}_1 & & \\ & & \ddots & \\ & & & \mathbf{D}_k \end{pmatrix}$
- Output $\mathsf{mpk} = (\mathbf{A}, \mathbf{B}, \mathbf{C}_1, \ldots, \mathbf{C}_k, \mathbf{D}_0, \ldots, \mathbf{D}_k, \mathbf{U})$, $\mathsf{msk} = (\mathbf{B}, \mathbf{B}_{\tau_B}^{-1}, \mathbf{C}_{2,\tau_C}^{-1}, \ldots, \mathbf{C}_{k,\tau_C}^{-1})$.

Enc$(\mathsf{mpk}, \mathbf{x}_0, \mu)$: The Enc algorithm is a public encryption algorithm. It takes as input the master public key mpk, attribute $\mathbf{x}_0$ and message bit $\mu \in \{0,1\}$ and does the following:

- Sample $\mathbf{s} \leftarrow \mathbb{Z}_q^{m^{k+1}}$, $\mathbf{s}_0, \ldots, \mathbf{s}_k \leftarrow \mathbb{Z}_q^{nm^k}$.

- If $\mu = 1$, sample $\mathbf{c}_1 \leftarrow \mathbb{Z}_q^{\ell m^{k+1}}$, $\mathbf{c}_2 \leftarrow \mathbb{Z}_q^{(m^{k+1} + (k+1)nm^k)w}$.
  Else, compute
  - $\mathbf{c}_1 = \mathbf{s}((\mathbf{A}_0 - \mathbf{x}_0 \otimes \mathbf{I}) \otimes \mathbf{I}^{\otimes k}) + \mathbf{s}_0(\mathbf{D}_0 \otimes \mathbf{I}^{\otimes k}) + \mathbf{e}_1$, where $\mathbf{e}_1 \leftarrow \mathcal{D}_{\mathbb{Z},\chi_1}^{\ell m^{k+1}}$.
  - $\mathbf{c}_2 = (\mathbf{s}, \mathbf{s}_0, \cdots, \mathbf{s}_k)\mathbf{B} + \mathbf{e}_2$, where $\mathbf{e}_2 \leftarrow \mathcal{D}_{\mathbb{Z},\chi_2}^{(m^{k+1} + (k+1)nm^k)w}$.
- Output $\mathsf{ct}_{\mathbf{x}_0} = (\mathbf{c}_1, \mathbf{c}_2)$.

KeyGen$_i(\mathsf{msk}, \mathbf{x}_i)$ for $1 \leq i \leq k-1$: The keygen algorithm for slot $1 \leq i \leq k-1$, takes as input the master secret key msk and attribute $\mathbf{x}_i$ and does the following:

- Samples $\mathbf{r}_i \leftarrow \mathcal{D}_{\mathbb{Z},\gamma}^m$
- Samples $\mathbf{X}_i \leftarrow \mathbf{B}^{-1}\left(\begin{pmatrix} (\mathbf{A}_i - \mathbf{x}_i \otimes \mathbf{I}) \otimes \mathbf{I}^{\otimes(i-1)} \otimes \mathbf{r}_i^\top \otimes \mathbf{I}^{\otimes(k-i)} \\ \mathbf{0}_{inm^k \times \ell m^k} \\ \mathbf{D}_i \otimes \mathbf{I}^{\otimes(i-1)} \otimes \mathbf{r}_i^\top \otimes \mathbf{I}^{\otimes(k-i)} \\ \mathbf{0}_{(k-i)nm^k \times \ell m^k} \end{pmatrix}, \tau_B \right)$,
  and $\mathbf{Y}_i \leftarrow \mathbf{C}_{i+1}^{-1}((\mathbf{C}_i \otimes \mathbf{r}_i^\top), \tau_C)$
- Returns $\mathsf{sk}_{i,\mathbf{x}_i} = (\mathbf{r}_i, \mathbf{X}_i, \mathbf{Y}_i)$

$\mathsf{KeyGen}_k(\mathsf{msk}, f)$: The keygen algorithm for slot k takes as input the master secret key, msk, and k-arity function f and does the following:
- Samples $\mathbf{r}_k \leftarrow \mathcal{D}^m_{\mathbb{Z},\gamma}$
- Computes $\mathbf{H}_f = \mathsf{EvalF}(\mathbf{A}, f)$ and $\mathbf{A}_f = \mathbf{A}\mathbf{H}_f$
- Computes $\mathbf{M}_f \leftarrow \mathbf{B}^{-1}\left(\begin{pmatrix} \mathbf{A}_f\mathbf{U}\otimes\mathbf{I}^{\otimes(k-1)}\otimes\mathbf{r}_k^\top \\ \mathbf{0}_{knm^k\times m^k} \\ \mathbf{D}_k\otimes\mathbf{I}^{\otimes(k-1)}\otimes\mathbf{r}_k^\top \end{pmatrix}, \tau_B\right)$ and

$\mathbf{N}_f \leftarrow \mathbf{B}^{-1}\left(\begin{pmatrix} \mathbf{0}_{m^{k+1}\times(k+1)nm^{k-1}w} \\ \mathbf{C}_k\otimes\mathbf{r}_k^\top \end{pmatrix}, \tau_B\right)$
- Returns $\mathsf{sk}_{k,f} = (\mathbf{r}_k, \mathbf{M}_f, \mathbf{N}_f)$

$\mathsf{Dec}(\mathsf{mpk}, \mathsf{ct}_{\mathbf{x}_0}, \mathsf{sk}_{1,\mathbf{x}_1}, \ldots, \mathsf{sk}_{k-1,\mathbf{x}_{k-1}}, \mathsf{sk}_{k,f})$ The decryption algorithm takes a ciphertext $\mathsf{ct}_{\mathbf{x}_0}$, k keys $\mathsf{sk}_{1,\mathbf{x}_1}, \ldots, \mathsf{sk}_{k-1,\mathbf{x}_{k-1}}$ and $\mathsf{sk}_{k,f}$ and does the following:
- Parse $\mathsf{ct}_{\mathbf{x}_0}$ as $(\mathbf{c}_1, \mathbf{c}_2)$, $\mathsf{sk}_{i,\mathbf{x}_i}$ as $(\mathbf{r}_i, \mathbf{X}_i, \mathbf{Y}_i)$ for $1 \leq i \leq k-1$ and $\mathsf{sk}_{k,f}$ as $(\mathbf{r}_k, \mathbf{M}_f, \mathbf{N}_f)$. Let $\mathbf{x} = (\mathbf{x}_0, \ldots, \mathbf{x}_{k-1})$.
- Compute $\widehat{\mathbf{H}}_{\mathbf{A},f,\mathbf{x}} = \mathsf{EvalFX}(\mathbf{A}, f, \mathbf{x})$.
- Compute the following
  * $\mathbf{d}_0' = \mathbf{c}_1(\mathbf{I}_{m\ell}\otimes\mathbf{r}_1^\top\otimes\cdots\otimes\mathbf{r}_k^\top)$
  * $\mathbf{d}_i' = \mathbf{c}_2\mathbf{X}_i(\mathbf{I}_{m\ell}\otimes\mathbf{r}_1^\top\cdots\otimes\mathbf{r}_{i-1}^\top\otimes\mathbf{r}_{i+1}^\top\otimes\cdots\otimes\mathbf{r}_k^\top)$, for $1 \leq i \leq k-1$,
  * $\mathbf{d}_f' = \mathbf{c}_2\mathbf{M}_f(\mathbf{I}_m\otimes\mathbf{r}_1^\top\cdots\otimes\mathbf{r}_{k-1}^\top)$
  * $(\mathbf{d}_0'', \cdots, \mathbf{d}_{k-1}'', \mathbf{d}_f'') = \mathbf{c}_2\mathbf{N}_f\mathbf{Y}_{k-1}\cdots\mathbf{Y}_1$
  * $\mathbf{d}_i = \mathbf{d}_i' - \mathbf{d}_i''$, for $i = 0$ to $k-1$.
  * $\mathbf{d}_f = \mathbf{d}_f' - \mathbf{d}_f''$
  * $\mathbf{d} = (\mathbf{d}_0|\cdots|\mathbf{d}_{k-1})\widehat{\mathbf{H}}_{\mathbf{A},f,\mathbf{x}}\mathbf{U} - \mathbf{d}_f$
- If $\|\mathbf{d}\|_\infty \leq \beta_0$, where β_0 is as defined by the parameters setting, provided in the full version [12], then return $\mu = 0$, else return $\mu = 1$.

ext, we show the correctness for the case o

5.2   Correctness, Parameters and Security

Correctness. Here, we show the correctness of the scheme.

When $\mu = 1$: We first show the correctness for the case of $\mu = 1$. For an honest run of the protocol, $\mathbf{c}_1$ is distributed uniformly at random over its domain. Then, since $\mathbf{r}_i \neq \mathbf{0}$ for all $i \in [k]$ with overwhelming probability and thus $\mathbf{I}_{m\ell}\otimes\mathbf{r}_1^\top\otimes\cdots\otimes\mathbf{r}_k^\top$ is a full-rank matrix, $\mathbf{d}_0'$ and thus $\mathbf{d}_0$ are distributed uniformly at random over their domains. Then, since the topmost m rows of $\widehat{\mathbf{H}}_{\mathbf{A},f,\mathbf{x}}$ constitutes an identity matrix by [12, Lemma 2.8], $(\mathbf{d}_0\|\cdots\|\mathbf{d}_{k-1})\widehat{\mathbf{H}}_{\mathbf{A},f,\mathbf{x}}$ is distributed uniformly at random over its domain. Finally, since each column of $\mathbf{U}$ is chosen from $\mathcal{D}^m_{\mathbb{Z},\gamma}$, with overwhelming probability, there exists $i \in [m]$ such that the i-th column of $\mathbf{U}$ is not a zero vector. This in turn implies that that the i-th entry of $\mathbf{d}$ is distributed uniformly at random over $\mathbb{Z}_q$. Since we set $\beta_0/q = \lambda^{-\omega(1)}$, the probability that the decryption algorithm falsely outputs 0 is negligible as desired.

When $\mu = 0$: We now show the correctness for the case of $\mu = 0$.

∗ Let us first compute $\mathbf{d}_0'$.

$$
\begin{aligned}
\mathbf{d}_0' &= \mathbf{c}_1(\mathbf{I}_{m\ell} \otimes \mathbf{r}_1^\top \otimes \cdots \otimes \mathbf{r}_k^\top) \\
&= \left(\mathbf{s} \cdot \left((\mathbf{A}_0 - \mathbf{x}_0 \otimes \mathbf{I}_m) \otimes \mathbf{I}^{\otimes k}\right) + \mathbf{s}_0 \cdot (\mathbf{D}_0 \otimes \mathbf{I}^{\otimes k})\right) \cdot \left(\mathbf{I}_{m\ell} \otimes \mathbf{r}_1^\top \otimes \cdots \otimes \mathbf{r}_k^\top\right) + \mathbf{e}_{\mathbf{d}_0'} \\
&= \mathbf{s} \cdot \left((\mathbf{A}_0 - \mathbf{x}_0 \otimes \mathbf{I}_m) \otimes \mathbf{r}_1^\top \otimes \cdots \otimes \mathbf{r}_k^\top\right) + \mathbf{s}_0 \cdot \left(\mathbf{D}_0 \otimes \mathbf{r}_1^\top \otimes \cdots \otimes \mathbf{r}_k^\top\right) + \mathbf{e}_{\mathbf{d}_0'} \\
&\text{where } \mathbf{e}_{\mathbf{d}_0'} := \mathbf{e}_1 \cdot (\mathbf{I}_{m\ell} \otimes \mathbf{r}_1^\top \otimes \cdots \otimes \mathbf{r}_k^\top).
\end{aligned}
$$

∗ Let $1 \leq i \leq k-1$,

$$
\begin{aligned}
\mathbf{d}_i' &= \mathbf{c}_2 \cdot \mathbf{X}_i \cdot \left(\mathbf{I}_{m\ell} \otimes \mathbf{r}_1^\top \cdots \otimes \mathbf{r}_{i-1}^\top \otimes \mathbf{r}_{i+1}^\top \otimes \cdots \otimes \mathbf{r}_k^\top\right) \\
&= ((\mathbf{s}, \mathbf{s}_0, \cdots, \mathbf{s}_k)\mathbf{B} + \mathbf{e}_2)\mathbf{B}^{-1}\left(\begin{pmatrix} (\mathbf{A}_i - \mathbf{x}_i \otimes \mathbf{I}_m) \otimes \mathbf{I}^{\otimes(i-1)} \otimes \mathbf{r}_i^\top \otimes \mathbf{I}^{\otimes(k-i)} \\ \mathbf{0}_{inm^k \times \ell m^k} \\ \mathbf{D}_i \otimes \mathbf{I}^{\otimes(i-1)} \otimes \mathbf{r}_i^\top \otimes \mathbf{I}^{\otimes(k-i)} \\ \mathbf{0}_{(k-i)nm^k \times \ell m^k} \end{pmatrix}, \tau_B\right) \\
&\quad \cdot (\mathbf{I}_{m\ell} \otimes \mathbf{r}_1^\top \cdots \otimes \mathbf{r}_{i-1}^\top \otimes 1 \otimes \mathbf{r}_{i+1}^\top \otimes \cdots \otimes \mathbf{r}_k^\top) \\
&= (\mathbf{s}((\mathbf{A}_i - \mathbf{x}_i \otimes \mathbf{I}_m) \otimes \mathbf{I}^{\otimes(i-1)} \otimes \mathbf{r}_i^\top \otimes \mathbf{I}^{\otimes(k-i)}) + \mathbf{s}_i(\mathbf{D}_i \otimes \mathbf{I}^{\otimes(i-1)} \otimes \mathbf{r}_i^\top \\
&\quad \otimes \mathbf{I}^{\otimes(k-i)})) \cdot (\mathbf{I}_{m\ell} \otimes \mathbf{r}_1^\top \cdots \otimes \mathbf{r}_{i-1}^\top \otimes 1 \otimes \mathbf{r}_{i+1}^\top \otimes \cdots \otimes \mathbf{r}_k^\top) + \mathbf{e}_{\mathbf{d}_i'} \\
&= \mathbf{s} \cdot ((\mathbf{A}_i - \mathbf{x}_i \otimes \mathbf{I}_m) \otimes \mathbf{r}_1^\top \otimes \cdots \otimes \mathbf{r}_k^\top) + \mathbf{s}_i \cdot (\mathbf{D}_i \otimes \mathbf{r}_1^\top \otimes \cdots \otimes \mathbf{r}_k^\top) + \mathbf{e}_{\mathbf{d}_i'}
\end{aligned}
$$

where $\mathbf{e}_{\mathbf{d}_i'} := \mathbf{e}_2 \cdot \mathbf{X}_i(\mathbf{I}_{m\ell} \otimes \mathbf{r}_1^\top \cdots \otimes \mathbf{r}_{i-1}^\top \otimes \mathbf{r}_{i+1}^\top \otimes \cdots \otimes \mathbf{r}_k^\top)$.

∗ Now we compute $\mathbf{d}_f'$.

$$
\begin{aligned}
\mathbf{d}_f' &= \mathbf{c}_2 \mathbf{M}_f(\mathbf{I}_m \otimes \mathbf{r}_1^\top \cdots \otimes \mathbf{r}_{k-1}^\top) \\
&= ((\mathbf{s}, \mathbf{s}_0, \cdots, \mathbf{s}_k)\mathbf{B} + \mathbf{e}_2)\mathbf{B}^{-1}\left(\begin{pmatrix} \mathbf{A}_f \mathbf{U} \otimes \mathbf{I}^{\otimes(k-1)} \otimes \mathbf{r}_k^\top \\ \mathbf{0}_{knm^k \times m^k} \\ \mathbf{D}_k \otimes \mathbf{I}^{\otimes(k-1)} \otimes \mathbf{r}_k^\top \end{pmatrix}, \tau_B\right) \\
&\quad \cdot (\mathbf{I}_m \otimes \mathbf{r}_1^\top \cdots \otimes \mathbf{r}_{k-1}^\top \otimes 1) \\
&= (\mathbf{s}(\mathbf{A}_f \mathbf{U} \otimes \mathbf{I}^{\otimes(k-1)} \otimes \mathbf{r}_k^\top) + \mathbf{s}_k(\mathbf{D}_k \otimes \mathbf{I}^{\otimes(k-1)} \otimes \mathbf{r}_k^\top))(\mathbf{I}_m \otimes \mathbf{r}_1^\top \cdots \otimes \mathbf{r}_{k-1}^\top \otimes 1) \\
&\quad + \mathbf{e}_{\mathbf{d}_f'} \\
&= \mathbf{s} \cdot (\mathbf{A}_f \mathbf{U} \otimes \mathbf{r}_1^\top \otimes \cdots \otimes \mathbf{r}_k^\top) + \mathbf{s}_k \cdot (\mathbf{D}_k \otimes \mathbf{r}_1^\top \otimes \cdots \otimes \mathbf{r}_k^\top) + \mathbf{e}_{\mathbf{d}_f'}
\end{aligned}
$$

where $\mathbf{e}_{\mathbf{d}_f'} := \mathbf{e}_2 \mathbf{M}_f(\mathbf{I} \otimes \mathbf{r}_1^\top \cdots \otimes \mathbf{r}_{k-1}^\top)$.

∗ Next, we compute:

$$
\begin{aligned}
&(\mathbf{d}_0'', \cdots, \mathbf{d}_{k-1}'', \mathbf{d}_f'') \\
&= \mathbf{c}_2 \mathbf{N}_f \mathbf{Y}_{k-1} \cdots \mathbf{Y}_1 \\
&= ((\mathbf{s}, \mathbf{s}_0, \cdots, \mathbf{s}_k)\mathbf{B} + \mathbf{e}_2)\mathbf{B}^{-1}\left(\begin{pmatrix} \mathbf{0}_{m^{k+1} \times (k+1)nm^{k-1}w} \\ \mathbf{C}_k \otimes \mathbf{r}_k^\top \end{pmatrix}, \tau_B\right) \cdot \mathbf{Y}_{k-1} \cdots \mathbf{Y}_1 \\
&= (\mathbf{s}_0, \cdots, \mathbf{s}_k) \cdot (\mathbf{C}_k \otimes \mathbf{r}_k^\top) \cdot \mathbf{Y}_{k-1} \cdots \mathbf{Y}_1 + (\mathbf{e}_{\mathbf{d}_0''}, \cdots, \mathbf{e}_{\mathbf{d}_k''}) \\
&= (\mathbf{s}_0, \cdots, \mathbf{s}_k) \cdot (\mathbf{C}_k \otimes \mathbf{r}_k^\top) \cdot (\mathbf{C}_k^{-1}((\mathbf{C}_{k-1} \otimes \mathbf{r}_{k-1}^\top), \tau_C) \otimes 1) \cdot \mathbf{Y}_{k-2} \cdots \mathbf{Y}_1 \\
&\quad + (\mathbf{e}_{\mathbf{d}_0''}, \cdots, \mathbf{e}_{\mathbf{d}_k''}) \\
&= (\mathbf{s}_0, \cdots, \mathbf{s}_k)(\mathbf{C}_k \cdot \mathbf{C}_k^{-1}((\mathbf{C}_{k-1} \otimes \mathbf{r}_{k-1}^\top), \tau_C) \otimes \mathbf{r}_k^\top)\mathbf{Y}_{k-2} \cdots \mathbf{Y}_1 + (\mathbf{e}_{\mathbf{d}_0''}, \cdots, \mathbf{e}_{\mathbf{d}_k''}) \\
&= (\mathbf{s}_0, \cdots, \mathbf{s}_k) \cdot (\mathbf{C}_{k-1} \otimes \mathbf{r}_{k-1}^\top \otimes \mathbf{r}_k^\top) \cdot \mathbf{Y}_{k-2} \cdots \mathbf{Y}_1 + (\mathbf{e}_{\mathbf{d}_0''}, \cdots, \mathbf{e}_{\mathbf{d}_k''}) \\
&= \vdots \\
&= (\mathbf{s}_0, \cdots, \mathbf{s}_k) \cdot (\mathbf{C}_1 \otimes \mathbf{r}_1^\top \otimes \cdots \otimes \mathbf{r}_k^\top) + (\mathbf{e}_{\mathbf{d}_0''}, \cdots, \mathbf{e}_{\mathbf{d}_k''}) \\
&= (\mathbf{s}_0 \cdot (\mathbf{D}_0 \otimes \mathbf{r}_1^\top \otimes \cdots \otimes \mathbf{r}_k^\top) + \mathbf{e}_{\mathbf{d}_0''}, \cdots, \mathbf{s}_k \cdot (\mathbf{D}_k \otimes \mathbf{r}_1^\top \otimes \cdots \otimes \mathbf{r}_k^\top) + \mathbf{e}_{\mathbf{d}_k''})
\end{aligned}
$$

with $(\mathbf{e}_{\mathbf{d}_0''}, \cdots, \mathbf{e}_{\mathbf{d}_k''}) := \mathbf{e}_2 \mathbf{N}_f \mathbf{Y}_{k-1} \cdots \mathbf{Y}_1$.

* Let $0 \leq i \leq k - 1$,

$$
\begin{aligned}
\mathbf{d}_i &= \mathbf{d}_i' - \mathbf{d}_i'' \\
&= \mathbf{s}((\mathbf{A}_i - \mathbf{x}_i \otimes \mathbf{I}_m) \otimes \mathbf{r}_1^\top \otimes \cdots \otimes \mathbf{r}_k^\top) + \mathbf{s}_i(\mathbf{D}_i \otimes \mathbf{r}_1^\top \otimes \cdots \otimes \mathbf{r}_k^\top) + \mathbf{e}_{\mathbf{d}_i'} \\
&\quad - \mathbf{s}_i(\mathbf{D}_i \otimes \mathbf{r}_1^\top \otimes \cdots \otimes \mathbf{r}_k^\top) - \mathbf{e}_{\mathbf{d}_i''} \\
&= \mathbf{s}((\mathbf{A}_i - \mathbf{x}_i \otimes \mathbf{I}_m) \otimes \mathbf{r}_1^\top \otimes \cdots \otimes \mathbf{r}_k^\top) + \mathbf{e}_{\mathbf{d}_i}
\end{aligned}
$$

with $\mathbf{e}_{\mathbf{d}_i} := \mathbf{e}_{\mathbf{d}_i'} - \mathbf{e}_{\mathbf{d}_i''}$.
* Next, $\mathbf{d}_f = \mathbf{d}_f' - \mathbf{d}_f''$. So,

$$
\begin{aligned}
\mathbf{d}_f &= \mathbf{s}(\mathbf{A}_f \mathbf{U} \otimes \mathbf{r}_1^\top \otimes \cdots \otimes \mathbf{r}_k^\top) + \mathbf{s}_k(\mathbf{D}_k \otimes \mathbf{r}_1^\top \otimes \cdots \otimes \mathbf{r}_k^\top) + \mathbf{e}_{\mathbf{d}_f'} \\
&\quad - \mathbf{s}_k(\mathbf{D}_k \otimes \mathbf{r}_1^\top \otimes \cdots \otimes \mathbf{r}_k^\top) - \mathbf{e}_{\mathbf{d}_f''} \\
&= \mathbf{s}(\mathbf{A}_f \mathbf{U} \otimes \mathbf{r}_1^\top \otimes \cdots \otimes \mathbf{r}_k^\top) + \mathbf{e}_{\mathbf{d}_f}
\end{aligned}
$$

with $\mathbf{e}_{\mathbf{d}_f} := \mathbf{e}_{\mathbf{d}_f'} - \mathbf{e}_{\mathbf{d}_f''}$ where $\mathbf{e}_{\mathbf{d}_f''} := \mathbf{e}_{\mathbf{d}_k''}$.

* And finally, $\mathbf{d} = (\mathbf{d}_0 \| \cdots \| \mathbf{d}_{k-1}) \cdot \widehat{\mathbf{H}}_{\mathbf{A}, f, \mathbf{x}} \mathbf{U} - \mathbf{d}_f$. First,

$$
\begin{aligned}
&(\mathbf{d}_0 \| \cdots \| \mathbf{d}_{k-1}) \\
&= (\mathbf{s}((\mathbf{A}_0 - \mathbf{x}_0 \otimes \mathbf{I}) \otimes \mathbf{r}_1^\top \otimes \cdots \otimes \mathbf{r}_k^\top) \| \cdots \| \mathbf{s}((\mathbf{A}_{k-1} - \mathbf{x}_{k-1} \otimes \mathbf{I}) \otimes \mathbf{r}_1^\top \otimes \cdots \otimes \mathbf{r}_k^\top)) \\
&\quad + (\mathbf{e}_{\mathbf{d}_0} \| \cdots \| \mathbf{e}_{\mathbf{d}_{k-1}}) \\
&= (\mathbf{s}(((\mathbf{A}_0 \| \cdots \| \mathbf{A}_{k-1}) - (\mathbf{x}_0 \| \cdots \| \mathbf{x}_{k-1}) \otimes \mathbf{I}) \otimes \mathbf{r}_1^\top \otimes \cdots \otimes \mathbf{r}_k^\top)) + (\mathbf{e}_{\mathbf{d}_0} \| \cdots \| \mathbf{e}_{\mathbf{d}_{k-1}}) \\
&= (\mathbf{s}((\mathbf{A} - \underbrace{(\mathbf{x}_0 \| \mathbf{x}_1 \| \cdots \| \mathbf{x}_{k-1})}_{=\mathbf{x}} \otimes \mathbf{I}) \otimes \mathbf{r}_1^\top \otimes \cdots \otimes \mathbf{r}_k^\top)) + (\mathbf{e}_{\mathbf{d}_0} \| \cdots \| \mathbf{e}_{\mathbf{d}_{k-1}}).
\end{aligned}
$$

From [12, Lemma 2.8], we deduce $(\mathbf{A} - \mathbf{x} \otimes \mathbf{I})\widehat{\mathbf{H}}_{\mathbf{A}, f, \mathbf{x}} = \mathbf{A}_f - f(\mathbf{x})\mathbf{I} \mod q$. Hence,

$$
\begin{aligned}
&(\mathbf{d}_0 \| \cdots \| \mathbf{d}_{k-1})\widehat{\mathbf{H}}_{\mathbf{A}, f, \mathbf{x}} \mathbf{U} - \mathbf{d}_f \\
&= \mathbf{s}((\mathbf{A} - \mathbf{x} \otimes \mathbf{I}) \otimes \mathbf{r}_1^\top \otimes \cdots \otimes \mathbf{r}_k^\top)(\widehat{\mathbf{H}}_{\mathbf{A}, f, \mathbf{x}} \mathbf{U} \otimes 1 \otimes 1 \cdots \otimes 1) + \mathbf{e}_{\mathbf{d}} \\
&\quad - \mathbf{s}(\mathbf{A}_f \mathbf{U} \otimes \mathbf{r}_1^\top \otimes \cdots \otimes \mathbf{r}_k^\top) - \mathbf{e}_{\mathbf{d}_f} \\
&= \mathbf{s}((\mathbf{A} - \mathbf{x} \otimes \mathbf{I})\widehat{\mathbf{H}}_{\mathbf{A}, f, \mathbf{x}} \mathbf{U} \otimes \mathbf{r}_1^\top \otimes \cdots \otimes \mathbf{r}_k^\top) - \mathbf{s}(\mathbf{A}_f \mathbf{U} \otimes \mathbf{r}_1^\top \otimes \cdots \otimes \mathbf{r}_k^\top) + \mathbf{e}_{\mathbf{d}} - \mathbf{e}_{\mathbf{d}_f} \\
&= \mathbf{s}((\mathbf{A}_f \mathbf{U} - f(\mathbf{x})\mathbf{U}) \otimes \mathbf{r}_1^\top \otimes \cdots \otimes \mathbf{r}_k^\top) - \mathbf{s}(\mathbf{A}_f \mathbf{U} \otimes \mathbf{r}_1^\top \otimes \cdots \otimes \mathbf{r}_k^\top) + \mathbf{e}_{\mathbf{d}} - \mathbf{e}_{\mathbf{d}_f} \\
&= -\mathbf{s}(f(\mathbf{x})\mathbf{U} \otimes \mathbf{r}_1^\top \otimes \cdots \otimes \mathbf{r}_k^\top) + \mathbf{e}_{\mathbf{d}} - \mathbf{e}_{\mathbf{d}_f} \\
&= \mathbf{e}_{\mathbf{d}} - \mathbf{e}_{\mathbf{d}_f} \text{ if } f(\mathbf{x}) = 0.
\end{aligned}
$$

where $\mathbf{e}_{\mathbf{d}} := (\mathbf{e}_{\mathbf{d}_0} \| \cdots \| \mathbf{e}_{\mathbf{d}_{k-1}})\widehat{\mathbf{H}}_{\mathbf{A}, f, \mathbf{x}} \mathbf{U}$. Thus, when $\mu = 0$, $\|\mathbf{d}\|_\infty$ is small ($\leq \beta_0$), and hence, the decryption correctly outputs 0.

We provide the error bound and parameter settings in the full version.
Security. We prove the security of our scheme via the following theorem. Due to space constraints, we provide the proof in the full version [12].

Theorem 4. *Assuming evasive* LWE *(Assumption 1) and* LWE, *our construction for k-input* ABE *for* NC$_1$ *satisfies very selective security (Definition 2).*

Acknowledgements. This collaboration was initiated when Mélissa Rossi was visiting IIT Madras. Such a visit has been made possible thanks to the funding of the cybersecurity center of excellence of IIT Madras and of a L'Oreal-UNESCO 2019 Young

Talent Grant. This work was also supported in part by the DST "Swarnajayanti" fellowship, Cybersecurity Center of Excellence, IIT Madras, National Blockchain Project and the Algorand Centres of Excellence programme managed by Algorand Foundation. Shota Yamada was partially supported by JST AIP Acceleration Research JPMJCR22U5, JST CREST Grant Number JPMJCR22M1, and JSPS KAKENHI Grant Number 19H01109.

References

1. Jain, A., Huijia Lin, P.L., Sahai, A.: Polynomial-time cryptanalysis of the subspace flooding assumption for post-quantum IO. In: Eurocrypt (2023)
2. Abdalla, M., Benhamouda, F., Gay, R.: From single-input to multi-client inner-product functional encryption. In: Galbraith, S.D., Moriai, S. (eds.) ASIACRYPT 2019. LNCS, vol. 11923, pp. 552–582. Springer, Cham (2019). https://doi.org/10.1007/978-3-030-34618-8_19
3. Abdalla, M., Benhamouda, F., Kohlweiss, M., Waldner, H.: Decentralizing inner-product functional encryption. In: Lin, D., Sako, K. (eds.) PKC 2019. LNCS, vol. 11443, pp. 128–157. Springer, Cham (2019). https://doi.org/10.1007/978-3-030-17259-6_5
4. Abdalla, M., Catalano, D., Fiore, D., Gay, R., Ursu, B.: Multi-input functional encryption for inner products: function-hiding realizations and constructions without pairings. In: Shacham, H., Boldyreva, A. (eds.) CRYPTO 2018. LNCS, vol. 10991, pp. 597–627. Springer, Cham (2018). https://doi.org/10.1007/978-3-319-96884-1_20
5. Abdalla, M., Gay, R., Raykova, M., Wee, H.: Multi-input inner-product functional encryption from pairings. In: Coron, J.-S., Nielsen, J.B. (eds.) EUROCRYPT 2017. LNCS, vol. 10210, pp. 601–626. Springer, Cham (2017). https://doi.org/10.1007/978-3-319-56620-7_21
6. Agrawal, S.: Indistinguishability obfuscation without multilinear maps: new techniques for bootstrapping and instantiation. In: Eurocrypt (2019)
7. Agrawal, S., Goyal, R., Tomida, J.: Multi-input quadratic functional encryption from pairings. In: CRYPTO (2021)
8. Agrawal, S., Goyal, R., Tomida, J.: Multi-party functional encryption. In: TCC (2021)
9. Agrawal, S., Goyal, R., Tomida, J.: Multi-input quadratic functional encryption: stronger security, broader functionality. In: TCC (2022)
10. Agrawal, S., Kumari, S., Yadav, A., Yamada, S.: Trace and revoke with optimal parameters from polynomial hardness. In: Eurocrypt (2023)
11. Agrawal, S., Pellet-Mary, A.: Indistinguishability obfuscation without maps: attacks and fixes for noisy linear FE. In: Canteaut, A., Ishai, Y. (eds.) EUROCRYPT 2020. LNCS, vol. 12105, pp. 110–140. Springer, Cham (2020). https://doi.org/10.1007/978-3-030-45721-1_5
12. Agrawal, S., Rossi, M., Yadav, A., Yamada, S.: Constant input attribute based (and predicate) encryption from evasive and tensor LWE. In: Cryptology ePrint Archive (2023). https://eprint.iacr.org
13. Agrawal, S., Wichs, D., Yamada, S.: Optimal broadcast encryption from LWE and pairings in the standard model. In: TCC (2020)

14. Agrawal, S., Yadav, A., Yamada, S.: Multi-input attribute based encryption and predicate encryption. In: Dodis, Y., Shrimpton, T. (eds.) CRYPTO 2022, Part I. LNCS, vol. 13507, pp. 590–621. Springer, Heidelberg (Aug 2022). https://doi.org/10.1007/978-3-031-15802-5_21

15. Agrawal, S., Yamada, S.: Optimal broadcast encryption from pairings and LWE. In: EUROCRYPT (2020)

16. Ananth, P., Jain, A.: Indistinguishability obfuscation from compact functional encryption. In: CRYPTO (2015)

17. Applebaum, B., Ishai, Y., Kushilevitz, E.: Cryptography in NC^0. In: 45th FOCS, pp. 166–175. IEEE Computer Society Press (Oct 2004). https://doi.org/10.1109/FOCS.2004.20

18. Attrapadung, N.: Dual system encryption via doubly selective security: framework, fully secure functional encryption for regular languages, and more. In: Nguyen, P.Q., Oswald, E. (eds.) EUROCRYPT 2014. LNCS, vol. 8441, pp. 557–577. Springer, Heidelberg (2014). https://doi.org/10.1007/978-3-642-55220-5_31

19. Banerjee, A., Peikert, C., Rosen, A.: Pseudorandom functions and lattices. In: Pointcheval, D., Johansson, T. (eds.) EUROCRYPT 2012. LNCS, vol. 7237, pp. 719–737. Springer, Heidelberg (2012). https://doi.org/10.1007/978-3-642-29011-4_42

20. Barak, B., et al.: On the (im)possibility of obfuscating programs. In: CRYPTO (2001)

21. Boneh, D., et al.: Fully key-homomorphic encryption, arithmetic circuit ABE and compact garbled circuits. In: EUROCRYPT (2014)

22. Brakerski, Z., Jain, A., Komargodski, I., Passelègue, A., Wichs, D.: Non-trivial witness encryption and null-io from standard assumptions. In: SCN (2018)

23. Brakerski, Z., Vaikuntanathan, V.: Lattice-inspired broadcast encryption and succinct ciphertext policy ABE. In: ITCS (2022)

24. Chotard, J., Dufour Sans, E., Gay, R., Phan, D.H., Pointcheval, D.: Decentralized multi-client functional encryption for inner product. In: Peyrin, T., Galbraith, S. (eds.) ASIACRYPT 2018. LNCS, vol. 11273, pp. 703–732. Springer, Cham (2018). https://doi.org/10.1007/978-3-030-03329-3_24

25. Datta, P., Okamoto, T., Tomida, J.: Full-hiding (unbounded) multi-input inner product functional encryption from the k-linear assumption. In: Abdalla, M., Dahab, R. (eds.) PKC 2018. LNCS, vol. 10770, pp. 245–277. Springer, Cham (2018). https://doi.org/10.1007/978-3-319-76581-5_9

26. Devadas, L., Quach, W., Vaikuntanathan, V., Wee, H., Wichs, D.: Succinct LWE sampling, random polynomials, and obfuscation. In: Nissim, K., Waters, B. (eds.) TCC 2021. LNCS, vol. 13043, pp. 256–287. Springer, Cham (2021). https://doi.org/10.1007/978-3-030-90453-1_9

27. Francati, D., Friolo, D., Malavolta, G., Venturi, D.: Multi-key and multi-input predicate encryption from learning with errors. In: Eurocrypt (2023)

28. Garg, S., Gentry, C., Halevi, S., Raykova, M., Sahai, A., Waters, B.: Candidate indistinguishability obfuscation and functional encryption for all circuits. In: FOCS (2013). http://eprint.iacr.org/

29. Gay, R., Pass, R.: Indistinguishability obfuscation from circular security. In: Proceedings of the 53rd Annual ACM SIGACT Symposium on Theory of Computing, pp. 736–749 (2021)

30. Goldwasser, S., et al.: Multi-input functional encryption. In: EUROCRYPT (2014)

31. Goyal, V., Pandey, O., Sahai, A., Waters, B.: Attribute-based encryption for fine-grained access control of encrypted data. In: ACM CCS (2006)

564   S. Agrawal et al.

32. Libert, B., Ţiţiu, R.: Multi-client functional encryption for linear functions in the standard model from LWE. In: Galbraith, S.D., Moriai, S. (eds.) ASIACRYPT 2019. LNCS, vol. 11923, pp. 520–551. Springer, Cham (2019). https://doi.org/10.1007/978-3-030-34618-8_18

33. Naor, M., Reingold, O.: Number-theoretic constructions of efficient pseudo-random functions. In: 38th FOCS. pp. 458–467. IEEE Computer Society Press (Oct 1997). https://doi.org/10.1109/SFCS.1997.646134

34. Sahai, A., Waters, B.: Fuzzy identity-based encryption. In: EUROCRYPT (2005)

35. Tomida, J.: Tightly secure inner product functional encryption: multi-input and function-hiding constructions. In: Galbraith, S.D., Moriai, S. (eds.) ASIACRYPT 2019. LNCS, vol. 11923, pp. 459–488. Springer, Cham (2019). https://doi.org/10.1007/978-3-030-34618-8_16

36. Tsabary, R.: Candidate witness encryption from lattice techniques. In: Advances in Cryptology-CRYPTO 2022: 42nd Annual International Cryptology Conference, CRYPTO 2022, Santa Barbara, CA, USA, August 15–18, 2022, Proceedings, Part I, pp. 535–559. Springer (2022). https://doi.org/10.1007/978-3-031-15802-5_19

37. Vaikuntanathan, V., Wee, H., Wichs, D.: Witness encryption and null-IO from evasive LWE. In: ASIACRYPT. pp. 195–221. Springer (2022). https://doi.org/10.1007/978-3-031-22963-3_7

38. Wee, H.: Dual system encryption via predicate encodings. In: Lindell, Y. (ed.) TCC 2014. LNCS, vol. 8349, pp. 616–637. Springer, Heidelberg (2014). https://doi.org/10.1007/978-3-642-54242-8_26

39. Wee, H.: Optimal broadcast encryption and CP-ABE from evasive lattice assumptions. In: Dunkelman, O., Dziembowski, S. (eds.) EUROCRYPT 2022, Part II. LNCS, vol. 13276, pp. 217–241. Springer, Heidelberg (May/Jun 2022). https://doi.org/10.1007/978-3-031-07085-3_8

40. Wee, H., Wichs, D.: Candidate obfuscation via oblivious LWE sampling. In: Canteaut, A., Standaert, F.-X. (eds.) EUROCRYPT 2021. LNCS, vol. 12698, pp. 127–156. Springer, Cham (2021). https://doi.org/10.1007/978-3-030-77883-5_5

Correlated Pseudorandomness

Correlated Pseudorandomness
from the Hardness of Quasi-Abelian
Decoding

Maxime Bombar[1,2]([⊠]) [iD], Geoffroy Couteau[3,4] [iD], Alain Couvreur[1,2] [iD],
and Clément Ducros[2,4]

[1] Laboratoire LIX, École Polytechnique, Institut Polytechnique de Paris, 1 rue
Honoré d'Estienne d'Orves, 91120 Palaiseau Cedex, France
[2] Inria, Saclay, France
{maxime.bombar,alain.couvreur}@inria.fr
[3] CNRS, Paris, France
[4] IRIF, Université Paris Cité, Paris, France
{couteau,cducros}@irif.fr

Abstract. A recent paradigm put forth by Boyle *et al.* (CCS 2018,
Crypto 2019) showed how *pseudorandom correlation generators* (PCG)
can be used to generate large amounts of useful forms of correlated
(pseudo)randomness, using minimal interactions followed solely by local
computations, yielding *silent* secure two-party computation protocols.
This can be extended to N-party using *programmable* PCG's. Previous
works constructed very efficient (non-programmable) PCG's for correlations such as random oblivious transfers. However, the situation is less
satisfying for *random oblivious linear evaluations* (OLE's), their generalisation over large fields. The state-of-the-art work of Boyle *et al.* (Crypto
2020) constructed programmable PCG's for OLE, but their work suffers
from two important downsides: (1) it only generates OLE's over *large
fields*, and (2) it relies on a relatively new "splittable" ring-LPN assumption, which lacks strong security foundations.

In this work, we introduce the *quasi-abelian syndrome decoding problem* (QA-SD), a family of assumptions which generalises the well-
established quasi-cyclic syndrome decoding assumption and allows to
construct new programmable PCG's for OLE over any field $\mathbb{F}_q$ with $q > 2$.
Our analysis also sheds light on the security of the ring-LPN assumption
used in Boyle *et al.*, Crypto 2020). Using our new PCG's, we obtain the
first efficient N-party silent secure computation protocols for computing
general arithmetic circuit over $\mathbb{F}_q$ for any $q > 2$.

Keywords: Pseudorandom correlation generators · oblivious linear
evaluation · quasi-abelian codes · silent secure computation

This work was funded by the French Agence Nationale de la Recherche through
the France 2030 ANR Projects ANR-22-PECY-003 SecureCompute and ANR-22-
PETQ-0008 PQ-TLS, the ANR BARRACUDA (ANR-21-CE39-0009-BARRACUDA),
the ANR SCENE (ANR-20-CE39-0001-SCENE), and by the DIM RFSI through the
project LICENCED.

ⓒ International Association for Cryptologic Research 2023
H. Handschuh and A. Lysyanskaya (Eds.): CRYPTO 2023, LNCS 14084, pp. 567–601, 2023.
https://doi.org/10.1007/978-3-031-38551-3_18

1 Introduction

Correlated randomness is a powerful resource in secure computation. Following the seminal work of Beaver [11], many lightweight, concretely efficient secure computation protocols have been designed in a model where the parties have access to long trusted correlated random strings: $\Omega(n)$-length instances of a simple correlation enable securely computing circuits with n gates. Depending on the setting, various correlations are used: for example, oblivious transfer (OT) correlations are used for two-party (semi-honest) secure computation of Boolean circuits, and oblivious linear evaluation (OLE) correlations, which generalize OT over arbitrary fields, enable 2-party semi-honest secure computation of arithmetic circuits. Eventually, n-party Beaver triples enable n-party semi-honest secure computation of arithmetic circuits, and authenticated Beaver triples enable maliciously secure computation of arithmetic circuits.

Since protocols in the correlated randomness paradigm are lightweight and very efficient, they gave rise to a popular, two-stage approach: first, the parties run an input-independent *preprocessing phase*, which securely generates and distributes the correlated strings, and second, these strings are consumed by an *online* protocol. Traditional approaches for implementing the preprocessing phase had $\Omega(n)$ communication [38,52,54] and formed the efficiency bottleneck of the overall protocol. The situation changed recently with a new approach, introduced in [24,27,30] and further refined in many subsequent works [25,26,28,29,36,68,73], with appealing efficiency features such as a one-time, $o(n)$-communication phase followed solely by local computation. At the heart of this approach is the notion of *pseudorandom correlation generators* (PCG's). Informally, a PCG has two algorithms: $\mathsf{Gen}(1^\lambda)$ outputs two *short correlated keys* $(\mathsf{k}_0, \mathsf{k}_1)$, and $R_\sigma \leftarrow \mathsf{Expand}(\mathsf{k}_\sigma)$ stretches k_σ into a long string R_σ, such that (R_0, R_1) is a pseudorandom instance of a target correlation. PCG's enable an efficient, two-stage *silent* preprocessing phase:

1. First, the parties securely distribute the short PCG seeds, using a small amount of work and communication (often independent of the circuit size).
2. Second, the parties locally stretch the PCG's into long correlated pseudorandom strings: this part is the bulk of the computation, but does not require any further communication among the parties.

This is the model of secure computation with *silent preprocessing* (or *silent secure computation* in short), where most of the preprocessing phase is pushed offline. Previous works gave efficient constructions of PCG's for various correlations such as OT's [25,26,36,68], vector-OLE [24], OLE's over large fields [29], authenticated Beaver triples [29] and many more. These PCG's all build upon a common template, which combines function secret sharing (FSS) for simple function classes with suitable variants of the syndrome decoding assumption.

1.1 PCG's: State of the Art and Challenges

Very efficient constructions of PCG's for the OT correlations have been proposed [25,26,36,68]. The most recent constructions (see [25,36]) allow to generate millions of random OT's per second on one core of a standard laptop. Combined with the GMW protocol, they effectively enable extremely efficient two-party secure computation of Boolean circuits in the semi-honest model, with minimal communication in the preprocessing phase (a few dozen of kilobytes, independent of the circuit size), followed by cheap local computation, and a fast online phase (exchanging four bits per AND gate).

The situation, however, is much less satisfactory in essentially all other standard settings of secure computation, where the OT correlation is not the best choice of correlation[1], and one of the major open problems in this line of work is to improve this state of affair. Concretely, when targeting any one of *multiparty* computation (with $N > 2$ parties), *arithmetic* computation (for arithmetic circuits over a field $\mathbb{F}$ of size $|\mathbb{F}| > 2$), or *malicious* security, the best-known PCG-based solutions lag way behind the state of the art for 2-party, semi-honest secure computation of Boolean circuits. At a high level, the problem is twofold:

- Secure computation of arithmetic circuits requires the OLE correlation rather than the OT correlation, and the constructions of [25,26,36,68] are inherently limited to the OT correlation. To handle OLE, a fundamentally different approach is required.
- Additionally, handling $N > 2$ parties or achieving malicious security both require the underlying PCG for OLE (or OT) to satisfy a property known as *programmability* (at a high level, programmability allows both to generate N-party correlations from $O(N^2)$ 2-party correlations, which is required because all known PCG's are inherently restricted to the 2-party setting, and to *authenticate* 2-party correlations with a MAC, which is needed for malicious security). Unfortunately, the constructions of [25,26,36,68] cannot (by design) achieve programmability.

These two limitations were addressed in the recent work of [29], which introduced the first (reasonably efficient) construction of programmable PCG for the OLE correlation. While not as efficient as the best known PCG's for OT, it can produce around 10^5 OLE's per second on a standard laptop. However, the result of [29] suffers from two important downsides:

- it can only produce OLE's over *large enough fields* (concretely, the field size must be larger than the circuit size). This leaves open the question of designing efficient programmable PCG's for OLE over small fields.
- it relies on a relatively new *ring*-LPN *with splittable polynomial* assumption which states, in essence, that $(a, as + e)$ is hard to distinguish from (a, b), where a, b are random polynomials from a ring $\mathcal{R} = \mathbb{F}_p[X]/(P(X))$ where P splits into $\deg(P)$ linear factors, and s, e are random *sparse* polynomials from $\mathcal{R}$. The ring-LPN assumption was introduced a decade ago in [51] to build

---

[1] While the OT correlation is complete even for N-party malicious secure computation of arithmetic circuits, its use induces large overheads in the online phase: an $\Omega(N^2)$ communication overhead for handling N parties, an $\Omega(\log^2 |\mathbb{F}|)$ overhead for handling larger fields $\mathbb{F}$, and an $\Omega(\lambda)$ overhead for handling malicious parties. In contrast, other choices of correlated randomness can avoid each of these overheads.

efficient authentication protocols, and it has received some attention from the cryptography community [14,21,29,37,48,57]. However, so far, we lack both a principled understanding of *which* choice of the underlying polynomial P yield solid instances (beyond the observation that reducible polynomials seem to enable more efficient attacks [29,48]), and a general methodology to argue the security of ring-LPN assumptions.

At a high level, the construction of PCG for OLE from [29] proceeds by generating a single large pseudorandom OLE correlation over a polynomial ring $\mathcal{R} = \mathbb{F}_p[X]/(P(X))$, assuming the hardness of the ring-LPN assumption over $\mathcal{R}$. When P splits into $N = \deg(P)$ linear factors, the Chinese Remainder Theorem permits to convert this large OLE correlation over $\mathcal{R}$ into N OLE correlations over $\mathbb{F}_p$ (by reducing it modulo each of the factors of P). Note that the condition that P splits requires $|\mathbb{F}_p| \geqslant N$, hence the restriction to large fields. Because the ring-LPN assumption with a splittable polynomial is relatively new, the authors also provided a broad overview of its security against standard attacks and provided an ad-hoc analysis of the relation between the choice of the polynomial P and the security strength of this assumption.

1.2 Our Contributions

In this work, we put forth and analyze a new general family of cryptographic assumptions related to the hardness of decoding codes defined over group algebras. A problem called *quasi-abelian syndrome decoding* (QA-SD). Our family of assumptions builds upon quasi-abelian codes, a well-known family of codes in algebraic coding theory. It generalizes both the ring-LPN assumption from [29] under some conditions on the underlying choice of polynomial and the quasi-cyclic syndrome decoding assumption. The latter assumption was in particular used in several recent works [3,7,26,62], including prominent submissions to the NIST post-quantum competition. We show that working over group algebras presents several advantages:

1. a broad family of possible instantiations;
2. a rich structure that allows stronger security foundations;
3. a group algebra contains a canonical basis given by the group itself, providing a canonical notion of sparsity.

Building on our new family of assumptions, we overcome both downsides of the recent work of [29] and obtain PCG's for OLE's over *general fields* with *solid security foundations*. In more details:

A Template for Building New PCG's. We revisit and generalize the approach of [29] for building pseudorandom correlation generators for OLE from ring-LPN. We show that any choice of quasi-abelian code yields a PCG for OLE over a group algebra $\mathcal{R}$ under the corresponding QA-SD assumption. We identify natural instances of our framework such that the group algebra $\mathcal{R}$:

1. supports fast operations via generalizations of the Fast Fourier Transform (which allows to achieve efficiency comparable to that of [29]), and

2. is isomorphic to a product $\mathbb{F}_q \times \cdots \times \mathbb{F}_q$ of N copies of $\mathbb{F}_q$ for arbitrary small $q > 2$ and arbitrary large N and therefore yields an efficient PCG for generating N copies of OLE over $\mathbb{F}_q$ for any $q > 2$.

Therefore, we obtain new constructions of efficient programmable PCG over small fields, circumventing the main limitation of the work of [29]. Our PCG's enable for the first time secure computation of arithmetic circuits over fields $\mathbb{F}$ of any size $|\mathbb{F}| > 2$ in the silent preprocessing model. This holds for two or more parties, in the semi-honest or in the malicious setting. The concrete efficiency of our construction is comparable to that of [29] (we refer the reader to Table 1 for details on the seed size and stretch of our PCG's). Concretely, our costs are essentially identical, up to the fact that [29] uses FFT's over cyclotomic rings, while our generalization to arbitrary field relies on a generic FFT. Because FFT's over cyclotomic rings have been thoroughly optimized in hundreds of papers, we expect that using generic FFT's will be noticeably slower. Still, we identify some concrete FFT-friendly choices of quasi-abelian codes where fast FFT algorithms comparable to cyclotomic FFT's could in principle be designed. We leave the concrete optimization of these FFT algorithms to future work.

Strong Security Foundations. Building upon recent results on the minimum distance of quasi-abelian codes, we give evidence that the assumptions from our family cannot be broken by any attack from the *linear test framework* [28, 36], a broad framework that encompasses essentially all known attacks on LPN and syndrome decoding (including ISD, Gaussian elimination, BKW, and many more). Our approach also sheds light on the security of the ring-LPN assumption. In essence, a conceptual message from our new approach is that some choices of P in the ring $\mathbb{F}_q[X]/(P(X))$ yield an instance of QA-SD, and as such inherit our arguments of resistance against linear attacks. In contrast, other (seemingly very similar) choices of P yield instances that are *completely broken* by linear attacks. This suggests that choosing instantiations of the ring-LPN assumption should be done with care, and our framework yields a way to do it with strong security guarantees.

In a long version of the present article available on eprint [20], we also complement our security analysis by showing, for all concrete instantiations of our framework that we use in our new PCG constructions, a search-to-decision reduction for the underlying assumption. Therefore, we reduce the security of all our new PCG's to (instances of) the *search* QA-SD assumption.

The Case of $\mathbb{F}_2$. Perhaps intriguingly, the most natural way to instantiate our framework goes all the way to $\mathbb{F}_3$, but breaks down over $\mathbb{F}_2$. We prove a theorem that states that this is in fact inherent to the approach. Basically, the reason why the construction is not adaptable to $\mathbb{F}_2$ is due to the fact that the product ring $\mathbb{F}_2^N = \mathbb{F}_2 \times \cdots \times \mathbb{F}_2$ has only one invertible element and hence can never be realised as a group algebra but in the irrelevant case of $N = 1$. In the long version [20], we further discuss a general methodology toward circumventing this limitation over $\mathbb{F}_2$. While our approach falls short of providing a full-fledged solution, it highlights a possible avenue towards the intriguing goal of one day getting an efficient programmable PCG for OLE's over $\mathbb{F}_2$.

Applications. Building upon our new programmable PCG's, we obtain

- (via Beaver triples) secure N-party computation of arithmetic circuits over $\mathbb{F}_q$, for any $q > 2$, with silent preprocessing and communication $N^2 \cdot \mathsf{poly}(\lambda) \cdot \log s$ bits (preprocessing phase) plus $2Ns$ field elements (online phase), where s is the number of multiplication gates. The silent preprocessing phase involves $O(N\mathsf{poly}(\lambda)s \log s)$ work per party. For small numbers of parties, the $N^2 \cdot \mathsf{poly}(\lambda) \cdot \log s$ is dominated by the $2Ns$ field elements for values of s as low as 2^{25}.
- (via circuit-dependent correlated randomness) secure N-party computation of a batch of T arithmetic circuits over $\mathbb{F}_q$, for any $q > 2$, with silent preprocessing and communication $N^2 \cdot \mathsf{poly}(\lambda) \cdot s \log T$ bits (preprocessing phase) plus NTs field elements (online phase), where s is the number of multiplication gates in each circuit. The silent preprocessing phase involves $O(N\mathsf{poly}(\lambda)sT \log T)$ work per party.

As in [29], our protocols extend to the malicious setting by generating *authenticated* correlated randomness instead, which our PCG's allow as well, and using a maliciously secure seed distribution protocol. Since the extension to authenticated correlated randomness and the seed distribution protocols in [29] are oblivious to the concrete choice of underlying ring $\mathcal{R}$, they directly apply to our new PCG's from QA-SD.

1.3   Related Works

Traditional constructions of OLE protocols require communication for each OLE produced. The work of [47] requires $\Omega(\log |\mathbb{F}|)$ string-OT's per OLE[2]. OLE's can also be produced using state-of-the-art protocols based on homomorphic encryption [50,54], *e.g.* producing 64MB worth of OLE's requires about 2GB of communication with Overdrive [54]. A recent direct construction of OLE from Ring-LWE has also been described in [10]. Using their construction, generating a batch of OLE's has an amortized communication of about 8 elements of $\mathbb{F}$ over a large enough field.

PCG's for OLE's allow removing most of the communication overhead, by generating a large number of pseudorandom OLE's using sublinear communication. The work of [29], which is our starting point, has a computational cost comparable to that of recent OLE protocols [54], but a considerably lower communication; however, it only works over large fields. There has been several attempts to build PCG's for OLE's over small fields, but all suffer from severe downsides. The work of [27] describes a PCG construction that combines BGV-based somewhat homomorphic encryption (under ring-LWE) and a new, ad-hoc variant of

---

[2] This approach crucially requires structured OT's, hence we cannot remove the communication by using pseudorandom OT's.

the multivariate quadratic assumption with sparse secrets. Their PCG's require very large seed sizes and are only efficient when generating huge batches ([27] estimates about 7.000 OLE's per second using a 3 GB seed size when producing 17 GB worth of triples).

In an appendix, the work of [29] shows that the standard variant of syndrome decoding with quasi-cyclic code yields a PCG for OLE's over arbitrary fields (including small fields). At a high level, the construction uses the fact that given two pseudorandom vectors $\mathbf{x}^\mathsf{T} = \mathbf{H} \cdot \mathbf{e}_x^\mathsf{T}$ and $\mathbf{y} = \mathbf{H} \cdot \mathbf{e}_y^\mathsf{T}$, generating shares of their pointwise products (*i.e.* a batch of pseudorandom OLE correlations) reduces to generating shares of the diagonal of $\mathbf{x}^\mathsf{T} \cdot \mathbf{y} = \mathbf{H} \cdot (\mathbf{e}_x^\mathsf{T} \cdot \mathbf{e}_y) \cdot \mathbf{H}^\mathsf{T}$, and the term $(\mathbf{e}_x^\mathsf{T} \cdot \mathbf{e}_y)$ can be shared efficiently with FSS for point functions. However, the computational cost of generating n OLE's this way scales as $\Omega(n^2 \log n)$ (ignoring poly(λ) factors), which makes it entirely impractical in practice (the sublinearity in these protocols only "kicks in" for values of n above about 2^{30}).

Eventually, two recent works on PCG's [25,28] have introduced new variants of syndrome decoding called respectively *variable-density* and *expand-accumulate* LPN. Each of these variants can actually be used to construct programmable PCG's for OLE over small fields (though that was not their primary purpose: VDLPN was introduced to construct pseudorandom correlation *functions*, and EALPN to obtain more efficient "online-offline" PCG's for OT). The intuition is that both assumptions can be formulated as the hardness of distinguishing $\mathbf{H} \cdot \mathbf{e}^\mathsf{T}$ from random, where $\mathbf{H}$ is a *sparse* matrix, and the noise distribution is such that the term $(\mathbf{e}_x^\mathsf{T} \cdot \mathbf{e}_y)$ can still be shared efficiently using some appropriate FSS. In this case, extracting the diagonal of $\mathbf{H} \cdot (\mathbf{e}_x^\mathsf{T} \cdot \mathbf{e}_y) \cdot \mathbf{H}^\mathsf{T}$ does not require computing the full square matrix, and scales only as poly(λ) $\cdot \tilde{\Omega}(n)$. However, the hidden costs remain prohibitively large. Concretely, for both the EALPN assumption and the VDLPN assumption, the row-weight of $\mathbf{H}$ must grow as $\lambda \cdot \log n$ [25,28,35] (for some specific security parameter λ), hence the cost of generating n OLE's boils down to $\lambda^2 \cdot \log^2 n$ invocations of an FSS scheme, where the concrete security parameter λ must be quite large: the recent analysis of [35] estimates $\lambda \approx 350$. For $n = 2^{30}$, this translates to around 10^8 invocation of an FSS scheme for *each* OLE produced, which is nowhere near practical.

1.4   Organization

We provide a technical overview of our results in Sect. 2, and preliminaries in Sect. 3. Section 4 is devoted to introducing group algebras, quasi-abelian codes, and our new QA-SD family of assumptions. Section 5 uses our new QA-SD assumption to build programmable PCG's, adapting and generalising the template of [29]. In the longer version available on eprint [20] we complement our study of QA-SD by providing a search-to-decision reduction for the subset of the QA-SD used to construct our PCG's. We also further analyse the concrete security of QA-SD against various known attacks and in particular against *folding attacks* which exploit the structure of the assumption to reduce the dimension of the instances. Finally, in this longer version we also explore a potential way to extend our framework to the case of $\mathbb{F}_2$, using number theory in function fields and the notion of Carlitz modules.

2 Technical Overview

2.1 Generating Pseudorandom Correlations: A Template

A general template to construct PCG's was put forth in [24], and further refined in subsequent works. At a high level, the template combines two ingredients: a method that uses *function secret sharing* to generate a *sparse* version of the target correlation, and a carefully chosen linear code for which the syndrome decoding problem is conjectured to be intractable. To give a concrete example let us consider the task of generating an OLE correlation over a large polynomial ring $\mathcal{R} = \mathbb{F}_p[X]/(P)$, where P is some degree-N split polynomial, and $\mathbb{F}_p$ is a field. In a ring-OLE correlation, each party P_σ receives $(x_\sigma, y_\sigma) \in \mathcal{R}^2$ for $\sigma = 0, 1$, which are random conditioned on $x_0 + x_1 = y_0 \cdot y_1$.

Sparse Correlations from FSS. Informally, FSS for a function class $\mathcal{F}$ allows to share functions $f : \{0,1\}^\ell \mapsto \mathbb{G}$ (where $\mathbb{G}$ is some group) from $\mathcal{F}$ into $(f_0, f_1) \leftarrow$ Share(f) such that

(1) f_σ hides f (computationally), and
(2) for any $x \in \{0,1\}^\ell$, $f_0(x) + f_1(x) = f(x)$.

Since FSS can always be achieved trivially by sharing the truth table of f, one typically wants the shares to be compact (*i.e.* not much larger than the description of f). Efficient constructions of FSS from a length-doubling pseudorandom generator are known for some simple function classes, such as *point functions* (functions $f_{\alpha,\beta}$ that evaluate to β on $x = \alpha$, and to 0 otherwise). FSS for point functions can be seen as a succinct way to privately share a long unit vector. More generally, FSS for t-point functions yield a succinct protocol for privately sharing a long t-sparse vector.

An FSS for multipoint functions immediately gives a strategy to succinctly distribute a *sparse* ring-OLE correlation: sample two random t-sparse polynomials y_0, y_1 (*i.e.* polynomials with t nonzero coefficients in the standard basis), and define f to be the t^2-point function whose truth table are the coefficients of $y_0 \cdot y_1$ (over $\mathbb{F}_p[X]$). Each party P_σ receives $\mathsf{k}_\sigma = (y_\sigma, f_\sigma)$, where $(f_0, f_1) = \mathsf{Share}(f)$. With standard constructions of multipoint FSS, the size of k_σ is $O(t^2 \cdot \log N)$ (ignoring λ and $\log p$ terms): whenever t is small, this is an exponential improvement over directly sharing $y_0 \cdot y_1$ (which would yield keys of length $O(N)$).

From Sparse to Pseudorandom Using Syndrome Decoding. It remains to convert the sparse correlation into a pseudorandom correlation. This step is done non-interactively, by locally *compressing* the sparse correlation using a suitable linear mapping. Viewing the compressed vector as the syndrome of a linear code $\mathcal{C}$ (the compressive linear mapping is the parity-check matrix of $\mathcal{C}$). The mapping must satisfy two constraints: it should be *efficient* (linear or quasi-linear in its input size), and its output on a sparse vector should be *pseudorandom*. Fortunately, decades of research on coding theory have provided us with many linear mappings which are conjectured to satisfy the latter; the corresponding assumptions are usually referred to as (variants of) the *syndrome decoding* (SD) assumption, or as (variants of) the *learning parity with noise* (LPN) assumption[3].

Going back to our example, we will use two instances $(x_\sigma^0, y_\sigma^0)_{\sigma \in \{0,1\}}$ and $(x_\sigma^1, y_\sigma^1)_{\sigma \in \{0,1\}}$ of a sparse ring-OLE correlation. Fix a random element $a \xleftarrow{\$} \mathcal{R}$. Each party P_σ defines $y_\sigma \leftarrow (1, a) \cdot (y_\sigma^0, y_\sigma^1)^\intercal = y_\sigma^0 + a \cdot y_\sigma^1 \bmod P(X)$. The assumption that y_σ is indistinguishable from random is known in the literature as the *ring*-LPN *assumption*, and has been studied in several previous works [29] (for an appropriate choice of P, it is also equivalent to the quasi-cyclic syndrome decoding assumption, used in NIST submissions such as BIKE [7] and HQC [62]). Furthermore, using FFT, the mapping can be computed in time $\tilde{O}(N)$. Then, observe that we have

$$y_0 y_1 = (y_0^0 + a \cdot y_0^1) \cdot (y_1^0 + a \cdot y_1^1) = y_0^0 \cdot y_1^0 + a \cdot (y_1^0 \cdot y_0^1 + y_0^0 \cdot y_1^1) + a^2 \cdot (y_0^1 \cdot y_1^1),$$

where the polynomials $y_0^0 \cdot y_1^0, y_1^0 \cdot y_0^1, y_0^0 \cdot y_1^1$, and $y_0^1 \cdot y_1^1$ are all t^2-sparse. Hence, each of these four polynomials can be succinctly shared using FSS for a t^2-point function. Therefore, shares of $y_0 y_1$ can be reconstructed using a local linear combination of shares of sparse polynomials, which can be distributed succinctly using FSS for multipoint functions.

Wrapping Up. The final PCG looks as follows: each party P_σ gets (y_σ^0, y_σ^1) together with four FSS shares of t^2-point functions whose domain correspond to these four terms. The PCG key size scales as $O(t^2 \log N)$ overall. Expanding the keys amounts to locally computing the shares of the sparse polynomial products (four evaluations of the FSS on their entire domain, in time $O(N)$) and a few $\tilde{O}(N)$-time polynomial multiplications with a and a^2 (which are public parameters). Observe that when P splits into N linear factors over $\mathbb{F}_p[X]$, a single pseudorandom ring-OLE correlation as above can be locally transformed into N instances of pseudorandom OLE's over $\mathbb{F}_p$: this is essentially the construction of PCG for OLE of [29]. However, this requires p to be larger than N, restricting the construction to generating OLE's over large fields. Furthermore, the requirement of a splitting P makes the construction rely on a less-studied variant of ring-LPN.

---

[3] The name LPN historically refers to the hardness of distinguishing oracle access to samples $(\mathbf{a}, \langle \mathbf{a}, \mathbf{s} \rangle + e)$ (for a fixed secret $\mathbf{s}$) from samples $(\mathbf{a}, b)$ where $\mathbf{a}, \mathbf{s}$ are random vectors, e is a biased random bit, and b is a uniform random bit. This becomes equivalent to the syndrome decoding assumption when the number of calls to the oracle is *a priori bounded*, hence the slight abuse of terminology. Since we will mostly use tools and results from coding theory in this work, we will use the standard coding theoretic terminology "syndrome decoding" to refer to the variant with bounded oracle access, which is the one used in all works on PCG's.

2.2   Quasi-Abelian Codes to the Rescue

We start by abstracting out the requirement of the construction of [29]. In coding theoretic terms, the hardness of distinguishing $(a, a \cdot e + f)$ with sparse (e, f) is an instance of the (decisional) *syndrome decoding problem* with respect to a code with parity check matrix $(1, a)$. At a high level, and sticking to the coding-theoretic terminology, we need a ring $\mathcal{R}$ such that

1. the (decisional) syndrome decoding problem with respect to the matrix $(1, a)$ is intractable with high probability over the random choice of $a \xleftarrow{\$} \mathcal{R}$;
2. given *sparse* elements (e, f) of $\mathcal{R}$, it is possible to succinctly share the element $e \cdot f \in \mathcal{R}$;
3. operations on $\mathcal{R}$, such as products, can be computed efficiently (*i.e.* in time quasilinear in the description length of elements of $\mathcal{R}$);
4. eventually, $\mathcal{R}$ is isomorphic to $\mathbb{F} \times \cdots \times \mathbb{F}$ for some target field $\mathbb{F}$ of interest.

We identify *quasi-abelian codes* as a family of codes that simultaneously satisfy all the above criteria. At a high level, a quasi-abelian code of index ℓ has codewords of the form $\{(\mathbf{m}\Gamma_1, \ldots, \mathbf{m}\Gamma_\ell) \mid \mathbf{m} = (m_1, \ldots, m_\ell) \in (\mathbb{F}_q[G])^k\}$, where each Γ_i is an element of $\mathbb{F}_q[G]^k$. Here, $\mathbb{F}_q[G]$ denotes the *group algebra*: $\mathbb{F}_q[G] \stackrel{\text{def}}{=} \left\{\sum_{g \in G} a_g g \mid a_g \in \mathbb{F}_q\right\}$, where G is a finite abelian group. Quasi-abelian codes generalise quasi-cyclic codes in a natural way: a quasi-cyclic code is obtained by instantiating G with $\mathbb{Z}/n\mathbb{Z}$. We define the *quasi-abelian syndrome decoding problem* (QA-SD) as the natural generalisation of the syndrome decoding problem to quasi-abelian codes. This encompasses both quasi-cyclic syndrome decoding and plain syndrome decoding. The properties of quasi-abelian codes have been studied thoroughly in algebraic coding theory. We elaborate below on why quasi-abelian codes turn out to be precisely the right choice given our constraints 1–4 above.

Security Against Linear Tests. The linear test framework from [28, 36] provides a unified way to study the resistance of LPN-style and syndrome decoding-style assumptions against a wide family of *linear* attacks, which includes most known attacks on LPN and syndrome decoding. We refer the reader to Sect. 3.2 for a detailed coverage. At a high level, in our setting, security against linear attacks boils down to proving that $(1, a)$ generates a code with large minimum distance. On one hand, a recent result of Fan and Lin [42] proves that quasi-Abelian codes asymptotically meet the Gilbert-Varshamov bound when the code length goes to infinity and the underlying group is fixed. On the other hand, Gaborit and Zémor [45] prove a similar result when the size of the group goes to infinity but restricted to the case where the group is cyclic. We conjecture an extension of Gaborit and Zémor result to arbitrary abelian groups. The latter conjecture entails that the QA-SD problem cannot be broken by any attack from the linear test framework, for any choice of the underlying group G. This is the key to circumvent the restrictions of [29].

Distribution of Products of Sparse Elements. Using quasi-abelian codes, the ring $\mathcal{R}$ is therefore a group algebra $\mathbb{F}_q[G]$. Now, given $e = \sum_{g \in G} e_g g$ and $f = \sum_{g \in G} f_g g$ any two t-sparse elements of $\mathcal{R}$ (that is, such that $(e_g)_{g \in G}$ and $(f_g)_{g \in G}$ have Hamming weight t), the product $e \cdot f$ can be rewritten as

$$e \cdot f = \sum_{e_g, f_h \neq 0} e_g f_h \cdot gh,$$

which is a t^2-sparse element of the group algebra. In other words, the product of two sparse elements in a group algebra is always a sparse element. In the context of building PCG's, this implies that we can directly distribute elements $ef \in \mathcal{R}$ using Sum of Point Function Secret Sharing (SPFSS) for t^2-point functions. This allows us to generalise the template PCG construction of [29] to the setting of arbitrary quasi-abelian code, with essentially the same efficiency (in a sense, the template is "black-box" in the ring: it only relies on the ability to distribute sparse elements via FSS).

We note that our generalised template differs slightly from the approach of [29]: in this work, the authors work over rings of the form $\mathcal{R} = \mathbb{F}_p[X]/(P(X))$, where P is some polynomial. However, in general, this ring is not a group algebra, and the product of sparse elements of $\mathcal{R}$ might not be sparse. They circumvented this issue by sharing directly the product over $\mathbb{F}_p[X]$ (where the product of sparse polynomials remains sparse) and letting the parties reduce locally modulo P. Doing so, however, introduces a factor 2 overhead in the expansion (and a slight overhead in the seed size). Our approach provides a cleaner solution, using a structure where sparsity is natively preserved through products inside the ring.

Fast Operations on Group Algebras. We observe that, by folklore results, operations over a group algebra $\mathbb{F}_q[G]$ admit an FFT algorithm (using a general form of the FFT which encompasses both the original FFT of Cooley and Tuckey, and the Number Theoretic Transform). When using this general FFT, setting $G = \mathbb{Z}/2^t\mathbb{Z}$ recovers the usual FFT from the literature. In full generality, given any abelian group G of cardinality n with $\gcd(n, q) = 1$ and exponent d, if $\mathbb{F}_q$ contains a primitive d-th root of unity, then the Discrete Fourier Transform and its inverse can be computed in time $O(n \cdot \sum_i p_i)$, where the p_i are the prime factors appearing in the Jordan-Hölder series of G; we refer the reader to Sect. 4.1 for a more detailed coverage. For several groups of interest in our context, this appears to yield very efficient FFT variants. For example, setting $q = 3$ and $G = (\mathbb{Z}/2\mathbb{Z})^d$, the resulting FFT is a d-dimensional FFT over $\mathbb{F}_3$ and it can be computed in time $O(n \cdot \log n)$ (the group algebra $\mathbb{F}_3[(\mathbb{Z}/2\mathbb{Z})^d]$ is the one that yields a PCG for n copies of OLE over $\mathbb{F}_3$).

We note that FFT's over cyclotomic rings, such as those used in [29], have been heavily optimised in hundreds of papers, due to their wide use (among other things) in prominent cryptosystems. As such, it is likely that even over "FFT-friendly" choices of group algebras, such as $\mathbb{F}_3[(\mathbb{Z}/2\mathbb{Z})^d]$, the general FFT construction described above will be in practice significantly less efficient than the best known FFT's implementations over cyclotomic rings. Hence, computationally, we expect that state-of-the-art implementations of the PCG of [29] over large fields $\mathbb{F}$ using a cyclotomic ring $\mathcal{R}$ for the ring-LPN assumption will be noticeably faster than state-of-the-art implementations of our approach to generate OLE's over a small field, such as $\mathbb{F}_3$. There is however nothing inherent to this: the efficiency gap stems solely from the years of effort that have been devoted to optimising FFT's over cyclotomic rings, but we expect that FFT's over other FFT-friendly group algebra such as $\mathbb{F}_3[(\mathbb{Z}/2\mathbb{Z})^d]$ could be significantly optimised in future works. We hope that our applications to silent secure computation over general fields will motivate such studies in the future.

From Quasi-Abelian Codes to OLE's over $\mathbb{F}_q$. Our general PCG template allows to generate a pseudorandom OLE over an arbitrary group algebra $\mathbb{F}_q[G]$. Then, when using $G = (\mathbb{Z}/(q-1)\mathbb{Z})^d$, we have that $\mathbb{F}_q[G] \simeq \mathbb{F}_q^n$ (with $n = (q-1)^d$). Therefore, a single pseudorandom OLE over $\mathbb{F}_q[G]$ can be *locally* converted by the parties into $(q-1)^d$ copies of a pseudorandom OLE over $\mathbb{F}_q$. Furthermore, for these concrete choices of G, we complement our security analysis by proving a search-to-decision reduction, showing that the decision QA-SD problem over $\mathbb{F}_q[G]$ with $G = (\mathbb{Z}/(q-1)\mathbb{Z})^d$ is as hard as the *search* QA-SD problem. This provides further support for the security of our instantiations.

In addition, our framework provides a way to investigate different instantiations of the ring-LPN problem through the lens of quasi-abelian codes. This turns out to play an important role in understanding the basis for the security of ring-LPN: seemingly very similar choices of the underlying polynomial can yield secure instances in one case, and completely broken instances in the other case. While the work of [29] gave a heuristic cryptanalysis of ring-LPN, it fails to identify the influence of the choice of the polynomial.

Concretely, consider the ring $\mathcal{R} = \mathbb{F}_q[X]/(P(X))$ with either $P(X) = X^{q-1} - 1$ or $P(X) = X^q - X$. The latter is a natural choice, as it has the largest possible number of factors over $\mathbb{F}_q$ (which controls the number of OLE's produced over $\mathbb{F}_q$). $\mathcal{R} = \mathbb{F}_q[X]/(P(X))$ with $P(X) = X^{q-1} - 1$ is a group algebra, and the ring-LPN assumption with ring $\mathcal{R}$ reduces to QA-SD($\mathcal{R}$). Hence, it is secure against all attacks from the linear test framework (and admits a search-to-decision reduction) by our analysis. On the other hand, ring-LPN over the ring $\mathcal{R} = \mathbb{F}_q[X]/(P(X))$ with $P(X) = X^q - X$ does not fit in our framework, and turns out to be *completely broken* by a simple linear attack: given (a, b) where b is either random or equal to $a \cdot e + f \bmod X^q - X$, it holds that $e(0) = f(0) = 0 \bmod X^q - X$ with high probability, because $e(0) = f(0) = 0$ over $\mathbb{F}_q[X]$ with high probability (since e, f are sparse, their constant coefficient is likely to be zero), and reduction modulo $X^q - X$ does not change the constant coefficient. Hence, the adversary can distinguish b from random simply by computing $b(0)$ (since $b(0)$ is nonzero with probability $(q-1)/q$ for a random b).

The above suggests that settling for $\mathcal{R} = \mathbb{F}_q[X]/(X^{q-1} - 1)$ is a conservative choice to instantiate the PCG of [29] with strong security guarantees. We note that [29] recommended instead $\mathcal{R} = \mathbb{F}_p[X]/(X^n + 1)$ with n being a power of 2 and p a large prime for efficiency reasons (since it is a cyclotomic ring, it admits fast FFT's). We believe that a natural generalisation of our framework should also encompass this ring, and allow proving that it also yields a flavor of ring-

LPN which is immune to linear attacks. However, this is beyond the scope of our paper, and we leave it to future work.

Considerations on the Case of $\mathbb{F}_2$. Interestingly, the aforementioned instance allows generating many OLE's over $\mathbb{F}_q$ for any $q > 2$; for $q = 2$, however, the term $n = (q-1)^d$ becomes equal to 1; that is, we only get a single OLE over $\mathbb{F}_2$ this way. This is in fact inherent to our approach: the product ring $\mathbb{F}_2^n$ has only one invertible element, and therefore can never be realised as a group algebra unless $n = 1$. Hence, somewhat surprisingly, our general approach circumvents the size limitation of [29] and gets us all the way to $\mathbb{F}_3$ or any larger field, but fails to provide a construction in the (particularly interesting) case $\mathbb{F}_2$.

Motivated by this limitation of our framework, in the long version [20] we devise a strategy to further generalise our approach through the theory of algebraic function fields (in essence, our generalisation is to quasi-abelian codes what quasi-negacyclic codes are to quasi-cyclic codes; we note that this is also close in spirit to the instance chosen in [29]: for their main candidate, they suggest using the ring $\mathcal{R} = \mathbb{F}_p[X]/(X^n + 1)$, which is a module over a group algebra and yields a *quasi-negacyclic code*). Alas, we did not manage to get a fully working candidate. At a (very) high level, our generalised framework produces pseudorandom elements $x = a \odot e_x + 1 \odot f_x$ and $y = a \odot e_y + 1 \odot f_y$ where e_x, e_y, f_x, f_y are sparse. However, the product $\odot$ is now *not* the same product as the group algebra product $x \cdot y$. Concretely, to share $x \cdot y$, we need to share terms of the form $(u \odot e) \cdot (v \odot f)$ (where u, v can be a or 1). However, unlike the case of our previous instantiation, this does not rewrite as a term of the form $uv \cdot ef$ (which we could then share by sharing the sparse term ef, as uv is public). Still, we believe that our approach could serve as a baseline for future works attempting to tackle the intriguing problem of building efficient programmable PCG's for OLE over $\mathbb{F}_2$. In particular, our unsuccessful attempts show that to get such a PCG, it suffices to find a way to succinctly share terms of the form $(u \odot e) \cdot (v \odot f)$ where u, v are public, and e, f are sparse. While FSS do not provide an immediate solution to this problem, this reduces the goal to a "pure MPC problem" which could admit an efficient solution.

Concrete Cryptanalysis. In the long version [20] we complement our study by a concrete analysis of the security of our assumptions. As in previous works, the bounds derived from the resistance to linear attacks are quite loose, because they cover a *worst-case* choice of linear attack. We cover standard attacks, such as information set decoding. A particularity of both ring-LPN with splittable polynomial and our new family of QA-SD assumption is that it grants the adversary some additional freedom: the adversary can, informally, transform a QA-SD instance into an instance with reduced dimension (in the case of ring-LPN, by reducing modulo factors of P; for QA-SD, by quotienting by subgroups of G). This turns out to be equivalent to the concept of *folding attacks*, which have been recently studied both in the context of code-based cryptography [34] and of lattice-based cryptography [22]. We analyse the effect of folding attacks on our instances and discuss the impact on our parameter choices. In particular, the instances of QA-SD used in our PCG construction closely resemble the Multivariate LWE assumption (with sparse noise instead of small-magnitude noise), which was shown in [22] to be broken by folding attacks. We note (but this is well-known [34]) that folding attacks are much less devastating on LPN- and syndrome decoding-style assumptions, essentially because folding yields a very slight increase of the noise magnitude in the LWE setting (the sum of LWE error terms has small magnitude), but increases the noise rate very quickly in the coding setting (the sum of sparse noises very quickly becomes dense).

3 Preliminaries

Function Secret Sharing. Function secret sharing (FSS), introduced in [31, 32], allows to succinctly share functions. An FSS scheme splits a secret function $f : I \to \mathbb{G}$, where $\mathbb{G}$ is some Abelian group, into two functions f_0, f_1, each represented by a key K_0, K_1, such that: (1) $f_0(x) + f_1(x) = f(x)$ for every input $x \in I$, and (2) each of K_0, K_1 individually hides f.

An SPFSS is an FSS scheme for the class of *sums of point functions*: functions of the form $f(x) = \sum_i f_{s_i,y_i}(x)$ where each $f_{s_i,y_i}(\cdot)$ evaluates to y_i on s_i, and to 0 everywhere else. As in previous works, we will use efficient constructions of SPFSS in our constructions of PCGs. Such efficient constructions are known from any length-doubling pseudorandom generator [32].

Pseudorandom Correlation Generators. A pseudorandom correlation generator (PCG) for some target ideal correlation takes as input a pair of short, correlated seeds and outputs long correlated pseudorandom strings, where the expansion procedure is deterministic and can be applied locally. In slightly more details, a PCG is a pair (Gen, Expand) such that $\text{Gen}(1^\lambda)$ produces a pair of short seeds (k_0, k_1) and $\text{Expand}(\sigma, k_\sigma)$ outputs a string R_σ. A PCG is *correct* if the distribution of the pairs (R_0, R_1) output by $\text{Expand}(\sigma, k_\sigma)$ for $\sigma = 0, 1$ is indistinguishable from a random sample of the target correlation. It is *secure* if the distribution of $(k_{1-\sigma}, R_\sigma)$ is indistinguishable from the distribution obtained by first computing $R_{1-\sigma}$ from $k_{1-\sigma}$, and sampling a uniformly random R_σ conditioned on satisfying the target correlation with $R_{1-\sigma}$ (for both $\sigma = 0$ and $\sigma = 1$). In this work, we will mostly consider the OLE correlation, where the parties P_0, P_1 receive random vectors $\mathbf{x}_0, \mathbf{x}_1 \in \mathbb{F}^n$ respectively, together with random shares of $\mathbf{x}_0 * \mathbf{x}_1$, where $*$ denotes the component-wise (*i.e.* Schur) product.

Eventually, *programmable* PCG's allow generating multiple PCG keys such that part of the correlation generated remains the same across different instances. Programmable PCG's are necessary to construct n-party correlated randomness from the 2-party correlated randomness generated via the PCG. Informally, this is because when expanding n-party shares (e.g. of Beaver triples) into a sum of 2-party shares, the sum will involve many "cross terms"; using programmable PCG's allows maintaining consistent pseudorandom values across these cross terms.

3.1   Syndrome Decoding Assumptions

The syndrome decoding assumption over a field $\mathbb{F}$ states, informally, that no adversary can distinguish $(\mathbf{H}, \mathbf{H} \cdot \mathbf{e}^\mathsf{T})$ from $(\mathbf{H}, \mathbf{b}^\mathsf{T})$, where $\mathbf{H}$ is sampled from the set of parity-check matrices of some family of linear codes, and $\mathbf{e}$ is a *noise vector* sampled from some distribution over $\mathbb{F}$-vectors and typically sparse. The vector $\mathbf{b}$ is a uniform vector over $\mathbb{F}^n$. More formally, we define the SD assumption over a ring $\mathcal{R}$ with dimension k, code length n, w.r.t. a family $\mathcal{F}$ of linear codes, and a noise distribution $\mathcal{D}$:

Definition 1 (Syndrome Decoding). *Let $k, n \in \mathbb{N}$, and let $\mathcal{F} = \mathcal{F}_{n,k} \subset \mathcal{R}^{(n-k) \times n}$ be a family of parity-check matrices of codes over some ring $\mathcal{R}$. Let $\mathcal{D}$ be a noise distribution over $\mathcal{R}^n$. The $(\mathcal{D}, \mathcal{F}, \mathcal{R})$-SD$(k, n)$ assumption states that*

$$\{(\mathbf{H}, \mathbf{H} \cdot \mathbf{e}^\mathsf{T}) \mid \mathbf{H} \xleftarrow{\$} \mathcal{F}, \mathbf{e} \xleftarrow{\$} \mathcal{D}\} \overset{c}{\approx} \{(\mathbf{H}, \mathbf{b}^\mathsf{T}) \mid \mathbf{H} \xleftarrow{\$} \mathcal{F}, \mathbf{b} \xleftarrow{\$} \mathcal{R}^n\},$$

where "$\overset{c}{\approx}$" denotes the computational indistiguishability.

Denoting t a parameter which governs the average density of nonzero entries in a random noise vector, common choices of noise distribution are Bernoulli noise (each entry is sampled from a Bernoulli distribution with parameter t/n), exact noise (the noise vector is uniformly random over the set of vectors of Hamming weight t), and regular noise (the noise vector is a concatenation of t random unit vectors). The latter is a very natural choice in the construction of pseudorandom correlation generators as it significantly improves efficiency [24, 26, 27] without harming security (to the best of our knowledge; the recent work [33] being efficient for very low code rates, which is not our setting).

Many codes are widely believed to yield secure instances of the syndrome decoding assumption, such as setting $\mathbf{H}$ to be a uniformly random matrix over $\mathbb{F}_2$ (the standard SD assumption), the parity-check matrix of an LDPC code [6] (the "Alekhnovich assumption"), a quasi-cyclic code (as used in several recent submissions to the NIST post-quantum competition, see e.g. [3,7,62] and in previous works on pseudorandom correlation generators, such as [26]), Toeplitz matrices [46,59] and more. All these variants generalize naturally to larger fields (and are conjectured to remain secure over arbitrary fields).

In the context of PCG's, different codes enable different applications: advanced PCG constructions, such as PCGs for OLE, require codes with structure. When designing new PCGs, it is common to rely on syndrome decoding for codes which have not been previously analyzed in the literature – hence, unlike the ones listed above, they did not withstand years or decades of cryptanalysis. To facilitate the systematic analysis of new proposals, recent works [28,36] have put forth a framework to automatically establish the security of new variants of the syndrome decoding assumption against a large class of standard attacks.

3.2   The Linear Test Framework

The linear test framework provides a unified template to analyze the security of variants of the LPN or syndrome decoding assumption against the most common attacks. It was first put forth explicitly in [28,36] (but similar observations were implicit in many older works). Concretely, an attack against syndrome decoding in the linear test framework proceeds in two stages:

1. First, a matrix $\mathbf{H}$ is sampled from $\mathcal{F}$, and fed to the (unbounded) adversary $\mathcal{A}$. The adversary returns a (nonzero) *test vector* $\mathbf{v} = \mathcal{A}(\mathbf{H})$.
2. Second, a noise vector $\mathbf{e}$ is sampled. The *advantage* of the adversary $\mathcal{A}$ in the linear test game is the bias of the induced distribution $\mathbf{v} \cdot \mathbf{H} \cdot \mathbf{e}^\mathsf{T}$.

To formalize this notion, we recall the definition of the bias of a distribution:

Definition 2 (Bias of a Distribution). *Given a distribution $\mathcal{D}$ over $\mathbb{F}^n$ and a vector $\mathbf{u} \in \mathbb{F}^n$, the bias of $\mathcal{D}$ with respect to $\mathbf{u}$, denoted $\mathsf{bias}_\mathbf{u}(\mathcal{D})$, is equal to*

$$\mathsf{bias}_\mathbf{u}(\mathcal{D}) = |\mathbb{P}_{\mathbf{x} \sim \mathcal{D}}[\mathbf{u} \cdot \mathbf{x}^\mathsf{T} = 0] - \mathbb{P}_{\mathbf{x} \sim \mathcal{U}_n}[\mathbf{u} \cdot \mathbf{x}^\mathsf{T} = 0]| = \left| \mathbb{P}_{\mathbf{x} \sim \mathcal{D}}[\mathbf{u} \cdot \mathbf{x}^\mathsf{T} = 0] - \frac{1}{|\mathbb{F}|} \right|,$$

where $\mathcal{U}_n$ denotes the uniform distribution over $\mathbb{F}^n$. The bias of $\mathcal{D}$, denoted $\mathsf{bias}(\mathcal{D})$, is the maximum bias of $\mathcal{D}$ with respect to any nonzero vector $\mathbf{u}$.

We say that an instance of the syndrome decoding problem is *secure against linear test* if, with very high probability over the sampling of $\mathbf{H}$ in step 1, for any possible adversarial choice of $\mathbf{v} = \mathcal{A}(\mathbf{H})$, the bias of $\mathbf{v} \cdot \mathbf{H} \cdot \mathbf{e}^\mathsf{T}$ induced by the random sampling of $\mathbf{e}$ is negligible. Intuitively, the linear test framework captures any attack where the adversary is restricted to computing a linear function of the syndrome $\mathbf{b}^\mathsf{T} = \mathbf{H} \cdot \mathbf{e}^\mathsf{T}$, but the choice of the linear function itself can depend arbitrarily on the code. Hence, the adversary is restricted in one dimension (it has to be linear in $\mathbf{b}^\mathsf{T}$), but can run in unbounded time given $\mathbf{H}$.

The core observation made in [28,36] (and also implicit in previous works) is that almost all known attacks against syndrome decoding (including, but not limited to, attacks based on Gaussian elimination and the BKW algorithm [16,41,56,58] and variants based on covering codes [18,19,49,74], the ISD family of information set decoding attacks [12,15,23,41,43,60,61,66,69], statistical decoding attacks [5,40,44,64], generalized birthday attacks [55,70], linearization attacks [13,67], attacks based on finding low weight code vectors [75], or on finding correlations with low-degree polynomials [4,17]) fit in the above framework. Therefore, provable resistance against linear test implies security against essentially all standard attacks.

Security Against Linear Tests. Resistance against linear test is a property of both the code distribution (this is the "with high probability over the choice of $\mathbf{H}$" part of the statement) and of the noise distribution (this is the "the bias of the distribution induced by the sampling of $\mathbf{e}$ is low" part of the statement). It turns out to be relatively easy to give sufficient conditions for resistance against linear tests. At a high level, it suffices that

1. the *code generated by* $\mathbf{H}$ has large minimum distance, and

2. for any large enough subset S of coordinates, with high probability over the choice of $\mathbf{e}$, one of the coordinates of $\mathbf{e}$ indexed by S will be nonzero.

The above characterization works for any noise distribution whose nonzero entries are uniformly random over $\mathcal{R} \setminus \{0\}$, which is the case for all standard choices of noise distributions. To see why these conditions are sufficient, recall that the adversarial advantage is the bias of $\mathbf{v} \cdot \mathbf{H} \cdot \mathbf{e}^{\mathsf{T}}$. By condition (2), if the subset S of nonzero entries of $\mathbf{v} \cdot \mathbf{H}$ is sufficiently large, then $\mathbf{e}$ will "hit" one of these entries with large probabilities, and the output will be uniformly random. But the condition that S is sufficiently large translates precisely to the condition that $\mathbf{v} \cdot \mathbf{H}$ has large Hamming weight for any possible (nonzero) vector $\mathbf{v}$, which is equivalent to saying that $\mathbf{H}$ generates a code with large minimum distance. We recall the formalization below:

Definition 3 (Security against Linear Tests). *Let $\mathcal{R}$ be a ring, and let $\mathcal{D}$ denote a noise distribution over $\mathcal{R}^n$. Let $\mathcal{F} \subset \mathcal{R}^{(n-k) \times k}$ be a family of (parity-check matrices of) linear codes. Let $\varepsilon, \eta : \mathbb{N} \mapsto [0, 1]$ be two functions. We say that the $(\mathcal{D}, \mathcal{F}, \mathcal{R})$-SD$(k, n)$ problem is (ε, η)-secure against linear tests if for any (possibly inefficient) adversary $\mathcal{A}$ which, on input $\mathbf{H}$ outputs a nonzero $\mathbf{v} \in \mathcal{R}^n$, it holds that*

$$\Pr[\mathbf{H} \xleftarrow{\$} \mathcal{F}, \mathbf{v} \xleftarrow{\$} \mathcal{A}(\mathbf{H}) \; : \; \mathsf{bias}_{\mathbf{v}}(\mathcal{D}_{\mathbf{H}}) \geqslant \varepsilon(\lambda)] \leqslant \eta(\lambda),$$

where λ denotes the security parameter and $\mathcal{D}_{\mathbf{H}}$ denotes the distribution which samples $\mathbf{e} \leftarrow \mathcal{D}$ and outputs $\mathbf{H} \cdot \mathbf{e}^{\mathsf{T}}$.

The *minimum distance* of a matrix $\mathbf{H}$, denoted $\mathsf{d}(\mathbf{H})$, is the minimum weight of a nonzero vector in its row-span. Then, we have the following straightforward lemma:

Lemma 4. *Let $\mathcal{D}$ denote a noise distribution over $\mathcal{R}^n$. Let $\mathcal{F} \subset \mathcal{R}^{(n-k) \times k}$ be a family of parity-check matrices of linear codes. Then for any integer $d \in \mathbb{N}$, the $(\mathcal{D}, \mathcal{F}, \mathcal{R})$-SD$(k, n)$ problem is (ε_d, η_d)-secure against linear tests, where*

$$\varepsilon_d = \max_{wt(\mathbf{v}) > d} \mathsf{bias}_{\mathbf{v}}(\mathcal{D}), \quad and \quad \eta_d = \Pr_{\mathbf{H} \xleftarrow{\$} \mathcal{F}} [\mathsf{d}(\mathbf{H}) \geqslant d].$$

The proof is folklore, and can be found e.g. in [36]. For example, using either Bernoulli, exact, or regular noise distributions with expected weight t, for any $\mathbf{v}$ of weight at least d, the bias against $\mathbf{v}$ is bounded by $e^{-2td/n}$. Hence, if the code is a good code (*i.e.* $d = \Omega(n)$), the bias is of the form $2^{-\Omega(t)}$.

When security against linear attacks does not suffice. There are two important cases where security against linear test does not yield security against *all* attacks.

1. When the code is strongly algebraic. For example, Reed-Solomon codes, which have a strong algebraic structure, have high dual minimum distance, but can be decoded efficiently with the Welch–Berlekamp algorithm, hence they do not lead to a secure syndrome decoding instance (and indeed, Welch–Berlekamp does not fit in the linear test framework).

2. When the noise is structured (e.g. for regular noise) and the code length is at least quadratic in the dimension. This opens the door to algebraic attacks such as the Arora-Ge attack [8] or the recent attack from Briaud and Øygarden [33]. However, when $n = O(k)$ (which is the case in all our instances), these attacks do not apply.

The above are, as of today, the only known cases where security against linear attacks is known to be insufficient. Algebraic decoding techniques have a long history and are only known for very restricted families of codes, and the aforementioned algebraic attacks typically never applies in the $n = O(k)$ regime which we usually consider for PCG's. Therefore, a reasonable rule of thumb is that a variant of syndrome decoding yields a plausible assumption if (1) it provably resists linear attacks, and (2) finding an algebraic decoding algorithm is a longstanding open problem.

4   Group Algebras and Quasi-Abelian Codes

4.1   Quasi-Abelian Codes

Quasi-abelian codes have been first introduced in [71], and, since then, have been extensively studied in coding theory.

Group Algebras. Let $\mathbb{F}_q$ denote the finite field with q elements, and let G be a finite abelian group of cardinality n. The group algebra of G with coefficients in $\mathbb{F}_q$ is the free algebra with generators G. More precisely, it is the set $\mathbb{F}_q[G]$ of formal linear combinations

$$\mathbb{F}_q[G] \overset{\text{def}}{=} \left\{ \sum_{g \in G} a_g g \ \middle| \ a_g \in \mathbb{F}_q \right\},$$

endowed with an $\mathbb{F}_q$–vector space structure in the natural way, and the multiplication is given by the convolution:

$$\left(\sum_{g \in G} a_g g \right) \left(\sum_{g \in G} b_g g \right) \overset{\text{def}}{=} \sum_{g \in G} \left(\sum_{h \in G} a_h b_{h^{-1}g} \right) g.$$

It is readily seen that $\mathbb{F}_q[G]$ is commutative if and only if the group G is abelian, which will always be the case in this article.

Once an ordering $g_0, \ldots, g_{n-1}$ of the elements of G is chosen, the group algebra $\mathbb{F}_q[G]$ is isomorphic (as an $\mathbb{F}_q$–linear space) to $\mathbb{F}_q^n$ via $\varphi \colon \sum_{i=0}^{n-1} a_i g_i \mapsto (a_0, \ldots, a_{n-1})$. This isomorphism is not canonical since it depends on the ordering, but changing it only leads to a permutation of the coordinates, and many groups (especially *abelian* groups) come with a canonical ordering. This isomorphism allows us to endow $\mathbb{F}_q[G]$ with the Hamming metric, making φ an *isometry*. The weight $\mathrm{wt}(a))$ of $a \in \mathbb{F}_q[G]$ is defined as the Hamming weight of $\varphi(a)$ (Note that changing the ordering of the group does not impact the weight of an element, which is thus well-defined).

Example 5. The simplest example to have in mind is the case of cyclic groups.

- Let $G = \{1\}$ be the trivial group with one element. Then the group algebra $\mathbb{F}_q[G]$ is isomorphic to the finite field $\mathbb{F}_q$.
- Let $G = \mathbb{Z}/n\mathbb{Z}$ be the cyclic group with n elements. Assuming that q is coprime to n, it is easy to see that the group algebra $\mathbb{F}_q[G]$ is nothing else than the usual polynomial ring $\mathbb{F}_q[X]/(X^n - 1)$. The isomorphism is given by $k \mapsto X^k$ extended by linearity.

Remark 6. The above example shows that our framework will only be a generalisation of known constructions. This generality will be crucial though, because all the instances we introduce in the present article and which will be proved to resist to linear attacks will arise from group algebras.

Example 5 shows that the group algebra of a cyclic group can be seen as a (quotient of a) polynomial ring in one variable. For a general finite abelian group, this is not always so simple, however there is also an explicit nice representation. This uses the following standard fact from the theory of group algebras.

Proposition 7. *Let G_1, G_2 be two finite groups. Then*

$$\mathbb{F}_q[G_1 \times G_2] \simeq \mathbb{F}_q[G_1] \otimes_{\mathbb{F}_q} \mathbb{F}_q[G_2].$$

Example 8. Let $G = \mathbb{Z}/n\mathbb{Z} \times \mathbb{Z}/m\mathbb{Z}$. Then, Proposition 7 entails that

$$\mathbb{F}_q[G] = \mathbb{F}_q[\mathbb{Z}/n\mathbb{Z}] \otimes_{\mathbb{F}_q} \mathbb{F}_q[\mathbb{Z}/m\mathbb{Z}] = \mathbb{F}_q[X]/(X^n - 1) \otimes_{\mathbb{F}_q} \mathbb{F}_q[X]/(X^m - 1)$$
$$= \mathbb{F}_q[X, Y]/(X^n - 1, Y^m - 1).$$

This isomorphism can actually be made explicit by $(k, \ell) \mapsto X^k Y^\ell$ extended by linearity.

Remark 9. More generally, since it is well–known that any finite abelian group G is a product of cyclic group $\mathbb{Z}/d_1\mathbb{Z} \times \cdots \times \mathbb{Z}/d_r\mathbb{Z}$, the previous statement asserts that the group algebra $\mathbb{F}_q[G]$ is isomorphic to a quotient of a multivariate polynomial ring, namely:

$$\mathbb{F}_q[G] = \mathbb{F}_q[\mathbb{Z}/d_1\mathbb{Z} \times \cdots \times \mathbb{Z}/d_r\mathbb{Z}] \simeq \mathbb{F}_q[X_1, \ldots, X_r]/(X_1^{d_1} - 1, \ldots, X_r^{d_r} - 1).$$

Quasi-Abelian Codes. Let $\ell > 0$ be any positive integer, and consider the free $\mathbb{F}_q[G]$–module of rank ℓ:

$$(\mathbb{F}_q[G])^\ell \stackrel{\text{def}}{=} \mathbb{F}_q[G] \oplus \cdots \oplus \mathbb{F}_q[G] = \left\{ (a_1, \ldots, a_\ell) \mid a_i \in \mathbb{F}_q[G] \right\}.$$

Any $\mathbb{F}_q[G]$–submodule of $(\mathbb{F}_q[G])^\ell$ is called a *quasi-group* code of index ℓ of G (or quasi-G code). When the group G is abelian, a quasi-G code is called *quasi-abelian*. More precisely, given a matrix

$$\mathbf{\Gamma} = \begin{pmatrix} \gamma_{1,1} & \cdots & \gamma_{1,\ell} \\ \vdots & \ddots & \vdots \\ \gamma_{k,1} & \cdots & \gamma_{k,\ell} \end{pmatrix} \in (\mathbb{F}_q[G])^{k \times \ell},$$

the quasi-G code defined by $\mathbf{\Gamma}$ is

$$\mathcal{C} \stackrel{\text{def}}{=} \{\mathbf{m\Gamma} = (\mathbf{m\Gamma}_1, \ldots, \mathbf{m\Gamma}_\ell) \mid \mathbf{m} = (m_1, \ldots, m_\ell) \in (\mathbb{F}_q[G])^k\},$$

where $\mathbf{\Gamma}_i$ denotes the column $\begin{pmatrix} \gamma_{1,i} \\ \vdots \\ \gamma_{k,i} \end{pmatrix}$ and $\mathbf{m\Gamma}_i = m_1 \gamma_{1,i} + \cdots + m_k \gamma_{k,i} \in \mathbb{F}_q[G]$.

The matrix $\mathbf{\Gamma}$ is said to be *systematic* if it is of the form $\mathbf{\Gamma} = (I_k \mid \mathbf{\Gamma}')$, where $\mathbf{\Gamma}' \in (\mathbb{F}_q[G])^{k \times (\ell-k)}$ and $I_k \in (\mathbb{F}_q[G])^{k \times k}$ is the diagonal matrix with values 1_G.

Let $a \in \mathbb{F}_q[G]$ and choose an ordering $g_0, \ldots, g_{n-1}$ of the elements of G. Through the aforementioned isomorphism φ, the element a can be represented as a vector $(a_0, \ldots, a_{n-1}) \in \mathbb{F}_q^n$. Now, consider the matrix

$$\mathbf{A} = \begin{pmatrix} \varphi(a \cdot g_0) \\ \vdots \\ \varphi(a \cdot g_{n-1}) \end{pmatrix} \in \mathbb{F}_q^{n \times n},$$

where each row is the vector representation of a shift of a by some element $g_i \in G$. In short, the matrix $\mathbf{A}$ is the matrix representing the multiplication–by-a map $m \mapsto am$ in $\mathbb{F}_q[G]$ in the basis $(g_0, \ldots, g_{n-1})$. An easy computation shows that for $m, a \in \mathbb{F}_q[G]$, the vector representation of the product $m \cdot a$ is the vector-matrix product

$$\varphi(m)\mathbf{A} = (m_0, \ldots, m_{n-1}) \begin{pmatrix} \varphi(a \cdot g_0) \\ \vdots \\ \varphi(a \cdot g_{n-1}) \end{pmatrix}.$$

In other words, any quasi-group code $\mathcal{C}$ of index ℓ can be seen as a linear code of length $\ell \times n$ over $\mathbb{F}_q$. The $\mathbb{F}_q[G]$–module structure endows $\mathcal{C}$ with an additional action of the group G on each block of length n; and $\mathcal{C}$ (seen as a linear code over $\mathbb{F}_q$), admits a generator matrix formed out by $k \times \ell$ square blocks of size n.

Example 10. Let us continue with Example 5.

- If $G = \{1\}$, then any linear code is a quasi-G code.
- If $G = \mathbb{Z}/n\mathbb{Z}$ and q is coprime to n. An element of $\mathbb{F}_q[G] \simeq \mathbb{F}_q[X]/(X^n - 1)$ is a polynomial of degree at most n which can be represented by the vector of its coefficients, and any product $m(X) \cdot a(X) \in \mathbb{F}_q[G]$ can be represented by the *circulant* vector-matrix product

$$(m_0 \ m_1 \ldots m_{n-1}) \begin{pmatrix} a_0 & a_1 & \ldots & a_{n-1} \\ a_{n-1} & a_0 & \ldots & a_{n-2} \\ \vdots & & & \vdots \\ a_1 & a_{n-1} & \ldots & a_0 \end{pmatrix} \in \mathbb{F}_q^n.$$

For simplicity, assume that $k = 1$ and $\ell = 2$. Then, a quasi-$\mathbb{Z}/n\mathbb{Z}$ code of index 2 is defined over $\mathbb{F}_q$ by a double-circulant generator matrix

$$\begin{pmatrix} a_0 & a_1 & \dots a_{n-1} & b_0 & b_1 & \dots b_{n-1} \\ a_{n-1} & a_0 & \dots a_{n-2} & b_{n-1} & b_0 & \dots b_{n-2} \\ \vdots & & \vdots & \vdots & & \vdots \\ a_1 & a_{n-1} & \dots & a_0 & b_1 & b_{n-1} \dots & b_0 \end{pmatrix}.$$

In other words, a quasi-$\mathbb{Z}/n\mathbb{Z}$ code is nothing else than a usual *quasi-cyclic* code with block length n.

Duality. In this work, we mainly use the language of parity-check matrices. The key point is that the dual of a quasi-G code is still a quasi-G code, and therefore any quasi-G code will have a parity-check matrix of a similar shape than the generator matrix introduced above. We refer the reader to the long version of this article [20] for an actual proof of this fact.

Fast-Fourier Transform and Encoding. Our construction crucially uses the fact that some quasi-G codes can be encoded very efficiently by means of a generalisation of the Fast-Fourier Transform (FFT) whose complexity only depends on the Jordan-Hölder series of G. We refer the reader to the long version, and to [63] for all the details.

4.2   The Quasi-Abelian Decoding Problem

In this section, we introduce computationally hard problems related to random quasi-abelian codes. They are variants of the Syndrome Decoding Problem, restricted to this class of codes.

Let G be a finite abelian group and $\mathbb{F}_q$ a finite field with q elements. Given an integer $t \in \mathbb{N}$, we denote by $\mathcal{D}_t(\mathbb{F}_q[G])$ a noise distribution over $\mathbb{F}_q[G]$ such that $\mathbb{E}[\mathrm{wt}(x)] = t$ when $x \xleftarrow{\$} \mathcal{D}_t$, and $\mathcal{D}_{t,n}(\mathbb{F}_q[G]) \overset{\mathrm{def}}{=} \mathcal{D}_t(\mathbb{F}_q[G])^{\otimes n}$ will denote its n-fold tensorization, *i.e.* $\mathbf{e} \xleftarrow{\$} \mathcal{D}_{t,n}(\mathbb{F}_q[G])$ is $\mathbf{e} \in \mathbb{F}_q[G]^n$ and its coordinates are drawn independently according to $\mathcal{D}_t(\mathbb{F}_q[G])$. A *random* quasi-$G$ code of index 2, in *systematic form*, will be a quasi-G code whose parity-check matrix $\mathbf{H} \in (\mathbb{F}_q[G])^2$ is of the form $\mathbf{H} = (\mathbf{1} \mid \mathbf{a})$, where a is uniformly distributed over $\mathbb{F}_q[G]$. Equivalently, it is the dual of the code generated by $\mathbf{H}$. The search Quasi-Abelian Syndrome Decoding problem is defined as follows:

Definition 11 ((Search) QA-SD problem). *Given $\mathbf{H} = (\mathbf{1} \mid \mathbf{a})$ a parity-check matrix of a random systematic quasi-abelian code, a target weight $t \in \mathbb{N}$ and a syndrome $\mathbf{s} \in \mathbb{F}_q[G]$, the goal is to recover an error $\mathbf{e} = (\mathbf{e}_1 \mid \mathbf{e}_2)$ with $\mathbf{e}_i \xleftarrow{\$} \mathcal{D}_t(\mathbb{F}_q[G])$ such that $\mathbf{He}^T = \mathbf{s}$, i.e. $\mathbf{e}_1 + \mathbf{a} \cdot \mathbf{e}_2 = \mathbf{s}$.*

The problem also has a decisional version.

Definition 12 ((Decisional) QA-SD problem). *Given a target weight t, the goal of this decisional QA-SD problem is to distinguish, with a non-negligible advantage, between the distributions*

$$\begin{aligned} \mathcal{D}_0 : \quad & (\mathbf{a}, \mathbf{s}) && \text{where } \mathbf{a}, \mathbf{s} \xleftarrow{\$} \mathbb{F}_q[G] \\ \mathcal{D}_1 : \, & (\mathbf{a}, \mathbf{a} \cdot \mathbf{e}_1 + \mathbf{e}_2) && \text{where } \mathbf{a} \xleftarrow{\$} \mathbb{F}_q[G] \text{ and } \mathbf{e}_i \xleftarrow{\$} \mathcal{D}_t(\mathbb{F}_q[G]). \end{aligned}$$

Both assumptions above generalize immediately to the case of parity-check matrices with more columns and/or rows of blocks. When $\mathbf{H} = (\mathbf{1} \mid \mathbf{a_1} \mid \cdots \mid \mathbf{a_{c-1}})$, for some parameter c, this corresponds to what has been called Module-LPN in the literature. This corresponds to the hardness of syndrome decoding for a quasi-abelian code of larger rate $(c-1)/c$. We call (search, decisional) QA-SD$(c, \mathcal{R})$ this natural generalization of QA-SD.

The QA-SD assumption states that the above decisional problem should be hard (for appropriate parameters). When the group G is the trivial group, this is the usual *plain* SD-assumption, while when the group G is cyclic[4], this is the QC-SD assumption at the core of Round 4 NIST submissions BIKE and HQC. Those problems, especially their search version, have been studied for over 50 years by the coding theory community and to this day, no efficient algorithm is known to decode a random quasi-abelian code. This is even listed as an open research problem in the most recent Encyclopedia of Coding Theory (from 2021) [72, Problem 16.10.5].

Remark 13. In Definition 12, we consider quasi-abelian codes with a parity-check matrix in systematic form. Indeed, assume $\mathbf{H} = (\mathbf{a_1} \mid \mathbf{a_2}) \in \mathbb{F}_q[G]^{1 \times 2}$. A syndrome of $\mathbf{H}$ will be of the form $\mathbf{s} = \mathbf{a_1}\mathbf{e_1} + \mathbf{a_2}\mathbf{e_2}$, and therefore is contained in the ideal $\mathcal{I} = (\mathbf{a_1}, \mathbf{a_2})$ of $\mathbb{F}_q[G]$ generated by $\mathbf{a_1}$ and $\mathbf{a_2}$[5]. Therefore, when this ideal is *not* the full ring, there is an obvious bias. When working over a large field $\mathbb{F}_q$, elements of $\mathbb{F}_q[G]$ are invertible with high probability, and therefore $\mathcal{I} = \mathbb{F}_q[G]$ with overwhelming probability. On the other hand, this is not true anymore when working over small fields. Using parity-check matrices in systematic form ensures that $1_G \in \mathcal{I}$, which removes the bias. This is a standard definition (see for instance [1,2]), though not always formulated like that in the literature.

4.3   Security Analysis

In this paragraph, we provide evidence for the QA-SD-assumption. Note first that for $G = \{1\}$ it is nothing but the SD-assumption, which is well established. Moreover, we argue for security of QA-SD against linear tests (Definition 3). With Lemma 4 in hand, it suffices to show that given the parity-check matrix $\mathbf{H}$ of a quasi-G code $\mathcal{C}$, the minimum distance of the code *generated by* $\mathbf{H}$, *i.e.* the *dual* of $\mathcal{C}$, is large with high probability (over the choice of $\mathbf{H}$). Note that when $G = \{1\}$, it is well-known that random codes are good, *i.e.* meet the Gilbert-Varshamov (GV) bound (see for instance [9,39,65]).

Proposition 14 (Gilbert-Varshamov). *Let* $0 < \delta < 1 - \frac{1}{q}$. *Let* $\varepsilon > 0$, *and let* $\mathcal{C}$ *be a random code of rate* $\frac{k}{n} \leqslant (1 - h_q(\delta) - \varepsilon)$. *Then,*

$$\mathbb{P}\left(d_{min}(\mathcal{C}) > \delta n\right) \geqslant 1 - q^{-\varepsilon n},$$

---

[4] and $\gcd(q, |G|) = 1$.
[5] Beware that $\mathbb{F}_q[G]$ is not necessarily principal.

where the probability is taken over the uniform choice of a generator matrix of $\mathcal{C}$*, and* h_q *denotes the q-ary entropy function*

$$h_q(x) \stackrel{def}{=} -x \log_q \left(\frac{x}{q-1} \right) - (1-x) \log_q(1-x).$$

For the past 50 years, it has been a long trend of research in coding theory to extend such a result for more general quasi-abelian codes. For the class of quasi-cyclic codes which are, by far, the most used quasi-abelian codes in cryptography, a GV-like bound was introduced by Kasami in [53]. Gaborit and Zémor even showed in [45] that various families of random double-circulant codes asymptotically satisfied a logarithmic improvement on this bound. More recently, this state of affairs was extended by Fan and Lin in [42] to *any* quasi-abelian code, even in the modular case where $char(\mathbb{F}_q)$ is *not* coprime to $|G|$. The proof of this result makes use of the theory of representations of finite abelian groups in $\mathbb{F}_q$.

Theorem 15 ([42, **Theorem 2.1**]). *Let* G *be a finite abelian group, and let* $(\mathcal{C}_\ell)_\ell$ *be a sequence of random quasi-G codes of length* $\ell \in \mathbb{N}$ *and rate* $r \in (0,1)$. *Let* $\delta \in (0, 1 - \frac{1}{q})$. *Then,*

$$\lim_{\ell \to \infty} \mathbb{P} \left(\frac{d_{min}(\mathcal{C}_\ell)}{|G|} > \delta \ell \right) = \begin{cases} 1 & \text{if } r < 1 - h_q(\delta); \\ 0 & \text{if } r > 1 - h_q(\delta); \end{cases}$$

and both limits converge exponentially fast. The above probability is taken over the uniform choice of a generator matrix $\mathbf{G}_\ell \in \mathbb{F}_q[G]^{k \times \ell}$ *of* $\mathcal{C}_\ell$.

As it is often the case in coding theory, this result is stated asymptotically, but the convergence speed could be made more precise, the exponent depends on $|G|$: the larger the group G, the higher this probability. Actually, to assert the resistance of QA-SD against linear attacks, it would be more relevant to consider the regime where k, ℓ are constant and $|G|$ goes to infinity as it is done in [45] but such a development is out of reach of this article and we leave it as a conjecture. There is a caveat though. Indeed, as it was noticed in Remark 13, in the case of constant k, ℓ and growing $|G|$ there is a bias in the QA-SD distribution when the ideal generated by the blocks in the input parity-check matrix is not the full ring. This corresponds to the parity-check matrix not being *full-rank* when seen as a matrix over $\mathbb{F}_q[G]$. In this case, the minimum distance could drop, but heuristically a random quasi-G code will have a minimum distance linear in its length as long as this bias is removed, which is the case in our setting since we enforce the systematic form.

Example 16. In order to produce OLE's over the field $\mathbb{F}_p$, [29] proposed to use a ring $\mathcal{R}$ of the form $\mathbb{F}_p[X]/(F(X))$ where $F(X)$ is totally split in $\mathbb{F}_p$.

– The choice of polynomial F that maximizes the number of OLE would be the polynomial $F(X) = X^p - X$ which has precisely all its roots in $\mathbb{F}_p$ (This is *not* the choice recommended by the authors, but is still allowed in their framework). However, this ring does not fit in our setting, and in fact the SD-problem in this ring is vulnerable to a very simple linear attack: given (a, b) where b is either random or equal to $a \cdot e + f \mod X^p - X$, it holds that $e(0) = f(0) = 0 \mod X^q - X$ with high probability, because $e(0) = f(0) = 0$ over $\mathbb{F}_p[X]$ with high probability (since e, f are sparse, their constant coefficient is likely to be zero), and reduction modulo $X^p - X$ does not change the constant coefficient. Hence, the adversary can distinguish b from random simply by computing $b(0)$ (since $b(0)$ is nonzero with probability $(p-1)/p$ for a random b).

- However, by simply removing the X factor and setting $F(X) = X^{p-1} - 1$, which would yield $p - 1$ copies of $\mathbb{F}_p$ instead of p, the ring $\mathcal{R} = \mathbb{F}_p[X]/(X^{p-1} - 1)$ is nothing else than the group ring $\mathbb{F}_p[\mathbb{F}_p^\times]$ and totally fits in our framework. In particular, it resists linear attacks. Note that the previous evaluation at 0 does no longer make sense.

5   Pseudorandom Correlation Generators from QA-SD

In the following we always consider $\mathcal{R} = \mathbb{F}_q[G] = \left\{ \sum_{g \in G} a_g g \mid a_g \in \mathbb{F}_q \right\}$, with G an abelian group. We refer to $\mathcal{R}_t$ as the set of ring elements of $\mathcal{R}$ of maximum weight t.

5.1   A Template for Programmable PCG for OLE from QA-SD

Theorem 17. *Let $\mathcal{R} = \mathbb{F}_q[G]$. Assume that SPFSS is a secure FSS scheme for sums of point functions, and that the QA-SD$(c, \mathcal{R})$ assumption holds. Then there exists a generic construction scheme to construct a PCG to produce one OLE correlation (described on Fig. 3). If the SPFSS is based on a PRG : $\{0, 1\}^\lambda \to \{0, 1\}^{2\lambda+2}$ via the PRG-based construction from [32], we obtain:*

- *Each party's seed has maximum size around : $(ct)^2 \cdot ((\log |G| - \log t + 1) \cdot (\lambda + 2) + \lambda + \log q) + ct(\log |G| + \log q)$ bits*
- *The computation of Expand can be done with at most $(2 + \lfloor (\log q)/\lambda \rfloor)|G|c^2 t$ PRG operations, and $O(c^2 |G| \log |G|)$ operations in $\mathbb{F}_q$.*

The protocol, adapted from the work of Boyle et al. [29], is described on Fig. 3. We first present an overview. Remind that an instance of the OLE correlation consists in giving a random value $x_\sigma \in \mathcal{R}$ to party P_σ as well as an additive secret sharing of $x_0 \cdot x_1 \in \mathcal{R}$ to both. Formally:

$$\left\{ ((x_0, z_0), (x_1, z_1)) \mid x_0, x_1, z_0 \xleftarrow{\$} \mathcal{R}, z_1 + z_0 = x_0 \cdot x_1 \right\}.$$

The core idea of the protocol is to give the two parties a random vector $\mathbf{e}_0$ or $\mathbf{e}_1 \in \mathcal{R}_t^c$, where each element of the vector is sparse. In addition, parties have access to a vector $\mathbf{a} = (1, \dot{\mathbf{a}})$, with $\dot{\mathbf{a}} = (a_1, \cdots, a_{c-1})$, a vector of random elements of $\mathcal{R}$. We see the vector $\mathbf{e}_\sigma$ of party P_σ as an error vector. Using the vector $\mathbf{a}$, parties can locally extend their error vector and construct $x_\sigma = \langle \mathbf{a}, \mathbf{e}_\sigma \rangle$, which is pseudorandom under QA-SD.

We want to give the parties shares of $x_0 \cdot x_1$. Note that $x_0 \cdot x_1$ is a degree 2 function in $(\mathbf{e}_0, \mathbf{e}_1)$; therefore, it suffices to share $\mathbf{e}_0 \otimes \mathbf{e}_1$. We underline a property of the sparse elements in $\mathcal{R}_t$. Let e, f be sparse elements. This means that there exist sets $S_e, S_f \subset G$, such that $e = \sum_{g \in S_e} e_g g, f = \sum_{g \in S_f} f_g g$ with $e_g, f_g \in \mathbb{F}_q$ and $|S_e| = |S_f| = t \leqslant |G|$. It follows that the product of $e \cdot f$ can be expressed using only $S_e \cdot S_f \stackrel{\text{def}}{=} \{ gh \mid g \in S_e, h \in S_f \}$ as basis. We conclude with $|S_e \cdot S_f| < |S_e| \cdot |S_f| = t^2$, to deduce that the product of sparse vectors in $\mathcal{R}$ also gives us sparse vectors (with sparsity t^2 instead of t). We note that here, we deviate from the original construction of [29]: over a ring of the form $\mathbb{F}_q[X]/P(X)$ where P is some polynomial, it is not generally true that the product of sparse elements remains sparse. This is circumvented in [29] by sharing the product over $\mathbb{F}_q[X]$ instead, and reducing locally. When using group algebras as we do, the product preserves sparsity and we can share the product directly within $\mathbb{F}_q[G]$, which is slightly more efficient.

This result enables us to express each element of $\mathbf{e}_0 \otimes \mathbf{e}_1$ as a sum of t^2 point functions. Then, we rely on Sum of Point Function Secret Sharing (SPFSS [29, Definition 2.3]). Recall that an SPFSS takes as input a sequence of points as well as a vector of values, and produces two keys that can be use to find shares of the sum of the implicit point functions. When a party evaluates its key at each point in the domain, it obtains a pseudorandom secret sharing of the coefficients of the sparse element in $\mathcal{R}_t$. The protocol uses c^2 elements of $\mathcal{R}_t$ as a result of the tensor product. This means that we need c^2 instances of SPFSS for t^2 point functions. This gives us a seed size of $O(\lambda(ct)^2 \log |G|) = O(\lambda^3 \log |G|)$.

Proof (of Theorem 17). First, we argue the correctness of the protocol. The coefficient vectors $\mathbf{b}_\sigma^i, \mathbf{A}_\sigma^i$ define a random element in $\mathcal{R}_t$. We can rewrite the product of two of these elements as follows:

$$e_0^i \cdot e_1^j = \sum_{k,l \in [0..t)} \mathbf{b}_0^i[k] \cdot \mathbf{b}_1^j[l] \mathbf{A}_0^i[k] \mathbf{A}_1^j[l].$$

This can indeed be described by a sum of point functions. From this point, $\mathbf{u} = \mathbf{u}_0 + \mathbf{u}_1$, then $\mathbf{u} = \mathbf{e}_0 \otimes \mathbf{e}_1$, each entry being equal to one of those $e_0^i \cdot e_1^j$. The party obtains z_σ as an output, and we can verify:

$$z_0 + z_1 = \langle \mathbf{a} \otimes \mathbf{a}, \mathbf{u}_0 + \mathbf{u}_1 \rangle = \langle \mathbf{a} \otimes \mathbf{a}, \mathbf{e}_0 \otimes \mathbf{e}_1 \rangle = \langle \mathbf{a} \otimes \mathbf{e}_0 \rangle \cdot \langle \mathbf{a} \otimes \mathbf{e}_1 \rangle = x_0 \cdot x_1.$$

The next-to-last equality is straightforward to check. Note that here, $\langle \mathbf{a}, \mathbf{e}_\sigma \rangle$ is a QA-SD sample, with fixed random $\mathbf{a}$ and independent secret e_σ. We now briefly show sketch security (the analysis is essentially identical to [29] since the construction is "black-box" in the ring $\mathcal{R}$, we sketch it for completeness). As the two cases are symmetrical, we assume $\sigma = 1$. Let $(k_0, k_1) \stackrel{\$}{\leftarrow}$ PCG.Gen(1^λ) with associated expanded outputs (x_0, z_0) and (x_1, z_1), we need to show that

$$\{(k_1, x_0, z_0)\} \equiv \left\{ (k_1, \tilde{x}_0, \tilde{z}_0) \mid \tilde{x}_0 \stackrel{\$}{\leftarrow} \mathcal{R}, \tilde{z}_0 = \tilde{x}_0 \cdot x_1 - z_1 \right\}.$$

To show this, we use a sequence of hybrid distributions.

- Replace z_0 by $x_0 \cdot x_1 - z_1$.
- Step by step replace each the FSS key $K_1^{i,j}$ in k_1 by a simulated key generated only with the range and the domain of the function. Due of the correctness and the security properties of the FSS scheme, this distribution is indistinguishable from the original distribution.
- Replace x_0 by a fresh $\tilde{x}_0$. It is also impossible to distinguish this distribution from the previous one, since the $K_1^{i,j}$ are now completely independent of x_0, and we can rely on the QA-SD assumption.
- Reverse step 2 by using the FSS security property once again. □

Regarding the size of the different parameters, we use the optimization suggested in [29], such as assuming that the QA-SD assumption holds also for *regular error distributions* (we note that our proof of resistance against linear tests holds for very general noise distributions, and in particular for the regular noise distribution). We can thus reduce the seeds size to $(ct)^2 \cdot ((\log |G| - \log t + 1) \cdot (\lambda + 2) + \lambda + \log q) + ct(\log N + \log q)$ bits ; and the number of PRG calls in Expand down to $(2 + \lfloor (\log q)/\lambda \rfloor)|G|c^2 t$. Note that to achieve security, choosing $ct = O(\lambda)$ is sufficient. The number of PRG calls can be further reduced to $O(|G|c^2)$ using batch codes to implement the SPFSS.

Theorem 18. *The* PCG *construction for* OLE *from Fig. 3 is programmable.*

Proof. In order to show that our PCG is programmable we have to transform it a little, as the Gen functionality takes additional inputs (ρ_0, ρ_1) in the programmability definition. In our case, we can choose $\rho_\sigma = \{\mathbf{A}_\sigma^i, \mathbf{b}_\sigma^i\}$. In this way, as explained in the description of the protocol, the additional input of the players can be seen as a vector of elements in $\mathcal{R}_t$, $\mathbf{e}_\sigma = (\mathbf{e}_\sigma^0, \cdots, \mathbf{e}_\sigma^{c-1})$. Because $x_\sigma = \langle \mathbf{a}, \mathbf{e}_\sigma \rangle$, the players can compute their first input locally, after expanding their ρ_σ into $\mathbf{e}_\sigma$. This defines functions ϕ_σ, and proves the programmability property. The proof of the correctness property is the same as in the proof of the Theorem 17. The programmable security property can be proven with s sequence of hybrid distribution as in the proof of Theorem 17, using the reduction to FSS scheme and the QA-SD assumption. □

Distributed Seed Generation. The protocol described in Fig. 3 assumes that a trusted dealer has given the parties their seed. What we want to do in practice is to achieve the Gen phase via a distributive setup protocol.

Theorem 19 (From [29]). *There exists a protocol securely realizing the functionality* QA-SD$_{\text{OLE-Setup}}$ *of Fig. 1 against malicious adversaries, with complexity:*

- *Communication costs per party dominated by* $(ct)^2 \cdot ((2\lambda + 3) \log 2|G| + (9t + 2) \log(q - 1))$.
- *Computation is dominated by* $2|G|$ *PRG evaluations.*

Functionality QA-SD$_{\text{OLE}-\text{Setup}}$

PARAMETERS: Security parameter 1^λ, PCG$_{\text{OLE}}$ = (PCG$_{\text{OLE}}$.Gen, PCG$_{\text{OLE}}$.Expand) as per Fig. 3
FUNCTIONALITY:

1. Sample $(k_0, k_1) \leftarrow$ PCG$_{\text{OLE}}$.Gen(1^λ).
2. Output k_σ to party P_σ for $\sigma \in \{0, 1\}$

Fig. 1. Generic functionality for the distributed setup of OLE PCG seeds

---

Functionality QA-SD$_{\text{OLE}-\text{All}}$

PARAMETERS: Security parameter, a group G, and a ring $\mathcal{R} = \mathbb{F}_q[G]$.
FUNCTIONALITY:
If both parties are honest:

- Sample $x_0, x_1 \leftarrow \mathcal{R}$
- Sample $z_0 \xleftarrow{\$} \mathcal{R}$ and let $z_1 = x_0 \cdot x_1 - z_0$.
- Output (x_σ, z_σ) to party P_σ for $\sigma \in \{0, 1\}$.

If party P_σ is corrupted:

- Wait for input $(x_\sigma, z_\sigma) \in \mathcal{R}^2$ from the adversary.
- Sample $x_{1-\sigma} \leftarrow \mathcal{R}$ and set $z_{1-\sigma} = x_0 \cdot x_1 - z_\sigma$
- Output $(x_{1-\sigma}, z_{1-\sigma})$ to the honest party.

Fig. 2. OLE Functionality with Corruption

Taking $ct = O(\lambda)$ is enough to achieve exponential security. With this we can conclude a general result:

Theorem 20. *Let G be a group, and $\mathcal{R} = \mathbb{F}_q[G]$. Suppose that SPFSS is a secure FSS scheme for sums of point functions, and the QA-SD$(c, \mathcal{R})$ assumption. Then there exists a protocol securely realizing the QA-SD$_{\text{OLE}-\text{All}}$ functionality over the ring $\mathcal{R}$ with the following parameters*

- *Communication costs and size of the seed : $O(\lambda^3 \log |G|)$.*
- *Computation costs: $O(\lambda|G|)$ PRG evaluations and $O(c^2|G| \log |G|)$ operations in $\mathbb{F}_q$.*

5.2 Instantiating the Group Algebra

In this section we instantiate our general result with a concrete construction of a PCG for OLE correlation over $\mathbb{F}_q$. Remind that $G = \prod_{i=1}^n \mathbb{Z}/q_i\mathbb{Z}$, $q_i \geqslant 2$. Using

---

Construction QA-SD$_{\mathsf{OLE}}$

PARAMETERS: Security parameter λ, noise weight $t = t(\lambda)$, compression factor $c \geqslant 2$, G a finite abelian group, $\mathcal{R} = \mathbb{F}_q[G]$. An FSS scheme (SPFSS.Gen,SPFSS.FullEval) for sums of t^2 point functions, with domain $[0..|G|)$ and range $\mathbb{F}_q$.

PUBLIC INPUT: $c - 1$ random ring elements $a_1, \cdots, a_{c-1} \in \mathcal{R}$.

CORRELATION: After expansion, outputs $(x_0, z_0) \in \mathcal{R}^2$ and $(x_1, z_1) \in \mathcal{R}^2$ where $z_0 + z_1 = x_0 \cdot x_1$

Gen : On input 1^λ :

1. For $\sigma \in \{0,1\}$ and $i \in [0..c)$, sample random vectors $\mathbf{A}_\sigma^i \leftarrow (g_1, \cdots, g_t)_{g_i \in G}$ and $\mathbf{b}_\sigma^i \leftarrow (\mathbb{F}_q^*)^t$.

2. For each $i, j \in [0..c)$, sample FSS keys
$$(K_0^{i,j}, K_1^{i,j}) \xleftarrow{\$} \mathsf{SPFSS.Gen}(1^\lambda, \mathbf{A}_0^i \otimes \mathbf{A}_1^j, \mathbf{b}_0^i \otimes \mathbf{b}_1^j).$$

3. Let $\mathsf{k}_\sigma = ((K_\sigma^{i,j})_{i,j \in [0..c)}, ((\mathbf{A}_\sigma^i, \mathbf{b}_\sigma^i)_{i \in [0..c)})$.

4. Output $(\mathsf{k}_0, \mathsf{k}_1)$.

Expand : On input $(\sigma, \mathsf{k}_\sigma)$:

1. Parse k_σ as $((K_\sigma^{i,j})_{i,j \in [0..c)}, ((\mathbf{A}_\sigma^i, \mathbf{b}_\sigma^i)_{i \in [0..c)})$

2. For $i \in [0..c)$, define the element of $\mathcal{R}_t$
$$e_\sigma^i = \sum_{j \in [0..t)} \mathbf{b}_\sigma^i[j] \cdot \mathbf{A}_\sigma^i[j].$$

3. Compute $x_\sigma = \langle \mathbf{a}, \mathbf{e}_\sigma \rangle$, where $\mathbf{a} = (1, a_1, \cdot, a_{c-1}), \mathbf{e}_\sigma = (e_\sigma^0, \cdots, e_\sigma^{c-1})$.

4. For $i, j \in [0..c)$, compute $u_{\sigma, i+cj} \leftarrow \mathsf{SPFSS.FullEval}(\sigma, K_\sigma^{i,j})$ and view it as a c^2 vector of element in $\mathcal{R}_{t^2}$.

5. Compute $z_\sigma = \langle \mathbf{a} \otimes \mathbf{a}, \mathbf{u}_\sigma \rangle$.

6. Output x_σ, z_σ .

Fig. 3. PCG for OLE over $\mathcal{R}$, based on QA-SD

Proposition 7 from previous section:

$$\mathbb{F}_q[G] = \mathbb{F}_q \left[\prod_{i=1}^n \mathbb{Z}/q_i\mathbb{Z} \right] \simeq \mathbb{F}_q[\mathbb{Z}/q_1\mathbb{Z}] \otimes_{\mathbb{F}_q} \cdots \otimes_{\mathbb{F}_q} \mathbb{F}_q[\mathbb{Z}/q_n\mathbb{Z}]$$

$$\simeq \bigotimes_{i=1}^n \mathbb{F}_q[X_i]/(X_1^{q_i} - 1) \simeq \mathbb{F}_q[X_1, .., X_n]/(X_1^{q_1} - 1, .., X_n^{q_n} - 1).$$

Batch-OLE over $\mathbb{F}_q$. In the following we let all the q_i be all equal to $q - 1$. We therefore use $\mathcal{R} = \mathbb{F}_q[G] \simeq \mathbb{F}_q[X_1, .., X_n]/(X_1^{q-1} - 1, .., X_n^{q-1} - 1)$. Remark that the elements of $\mathbb{F}_q^*$ are the roots of the polynomial $X_i^{q-1} - 1$. Therefore, we can write $X_i^{q-1} - 1 = \prod_{a \in \mathbb{F}_q^*}(X_i - a)$, for all $1 \leqslant i \leqslant n$ and, by the Chinese Remainder Theorem, we get

$$\mathbb{F}_q[X_1, .., X_n]/(X_1^{q-1} - 1, .., X_n^{q-1} - 1) \simeq \prod_{i=1}^{T} \mathbb{F}_q,$$

where $T = (q-1)^n$ is the number of elements in the group. We can apply our protocol to construct a PCG for the OLE correlation in $\mathcal{R}$. This single OLE over $\mathcal{R}$ can be transformed in T different instances of OLE over $\mathbb{F}_q$. We get:

Theorem 21. *Suppose that* SPFSS *is a secure* FSS *scheme for sums of point functions and that the* QA-SD *assumption holds. Let* $\mathcal{R} = \mathbb{F}_q[X_1, .., X_n]/(X_1^{q-1} - 1, .., X_n^{q-1} - 1)$, *and* $T = (q-1)^n$. *We can construct a* PCG *producing* T *instances for* OLE *over* $\mathbb{F}_p$, *using the* QA-SD$_{\mathsf{OLE}}$ *construction. The parameters we obtain are the following.*

- *Each party's seed has size at most:* $(ct)^2 \cdot ((n\log(q-1) - \log t + 1) \cdot (\lambda + 2) + \lambda + \log q) + ct(n\log(q-1) + \log q)$ *bits*
- *The computation of* Expand *can be done with at most* $(2 + \lfloor (\log q)/\lambda \rfloor)n\log(q-1)c^2t$ PRG *operations, and* $O(c^2(q-1)^n n \log(q-1))$ *operations in* $\mathbb{F}_q$.

Concrete Parameters. We report on Table 1 a set of concrete parameters for our new programmable PCGs from QA-SD, when generating T instances of a pseudorandom OLE over $\mathbb{F}_q$, chosen according to the analysis of the long version [20] available on eprint. We note that our concrete security parameters are very close to the parameters of [29]. This stems from two points:

First, [29] conservatively chose security bounds based on existing attacks over $\mathbb{F}_2$, even though their instantiation is over $\mathbb{F}_p$ with $\log p \approx 128$ (and known attacks on syndrome decoding are less efficient over larger fields). One of the reason for this was to get conservative estimates (syndrome decoding over large fields was less investigated, and attacks could improve in the future); another motivation is that over $\mathbb{F}_2$, tools have been implemented to automatically evaluate the resistance against various flavors of ISD (whose exact cost can be quite tedious to analyze). Because our PCGs can handle fields as low as $\mathbb{F}_3$, and to avoid having to pick different parameters for each field size, we also based our analysis on known bounds for $\mathbb{F}_2$.

Second, the main difference between our analysis and that of [29] is that we must consider folding attacks, which are considerably more diverse in our setting (since an attacker can construct a reduced instance by quotienting with *any* subgroup G', of which there are many). Yet, the *effect* of folding on security does not depend on the fine details of the subgroup G', but only on the *size* of G', which allows to compute the new dimension and the reduced noise weight (via a generalized piling-up lemma). This does not differ significantly from the case of ring-LPN over cyclotomic rings considered in [29], since there the adversary could reduce the dimension to any power of two of their choice: our setting allows the adversary to be slightly more fine grained in its dimension reduction (*i.e.* the adversary is not restricted to a power of two), but this does not make a significant difference on the concrete attack cost (essentially because close dimensions yield near-identical noise reduction via the piling-up lemma, and do not have significantly different impact on the concrete attack cost beyond that).

As our table illustrates, our PCG's offer a non-trivial stretch (computed as the ratio between the seed size and the size of storing the output OLE's) from a target number $T = 2^{25}$ of OLE's.

Table 1. Concrete parameters and seed sizes (per party, counted in bits) for our PCG for OLE over $\mathbb{F}_q$ from QA-SD($\mathcal{R}$), using $\mathcal{R} = \mathbb{F}_q[(\mathbb{Z}/(q-1)\mathbb{Z})^n]$, $\lambda = 128$, target number $T = (q-1)^n$ of OLE's, syndrome compression factor $c \in \{2, 4\}$, and number of noisy coordinates t. 'Stretch', computed as $2T/(\text{seed size})$, is the ratio between storing a full random OLE (i.e., $2T$ field elements) and the smaller PCG seed. The parameter k denotes the dimension of the SD instance after folding, and t' the (expected) noise weight of the folded instance (when heuristically choosing the best possible folding for the adversary). #PRG calls is computed as $4 \cdot Tct$. Parameters are chosen to achieve λ-bits of security against known attacks.

T	c	t	(k, t')	Seed size	Stretch	# R-mults	#PRG calls
2^{25}	2	152	$(2^8, 121)$	$2^{26.0}/\log q$	$\log q$	4	$2^{28.2} \cdot \log q$
2^{25}	4	64	$(3 \cdot 2^8, 60)$	$2^{23.6}/\log q$	$5.3 \log q$	16	$2^{28.0} \cdot \log q$
2^{30}	2	152	$(2^8, 121)$	$2^{26.3}/\log q$	$26 \log q$	4	$2^{33.2} \cdot \log q$
2^{30}	4	64	$(3 \cdot 2^8, 60)$	$2^{24.0}/\log q$	$128 \log q$	16	$2^{33.0} \cdot \log q$
2^{35}	2	152	$(2^8, 121)$	$2^{26.6}/\log q$	$676 \log q$	4	$2^{38.2} \cdot \log q$
2^{35}	4	64	$(3 \cdot 2^8, 60)$	$2^{24.3}/\log q$	$3327 \log q$	16	$2^{38.0} \cdot \log q$

Discussions on Efficient FFTs. Operations over the group algebra can be accelerated using the generalized FFT, which we cover in [20]. Here, we briefly remark that some specific values of q yield "FFT-friendly" instances, where the generalized FFT algorithm is extremely efficient (and could even be competitive with the more well-known FFT over cyclotomic rings, with proper optimizations): this is the case whenever $q - 1$ is a power of 2, since it enables a very efficient divide and conquer algorithm. For example, this is the case over $\mathbb{F}_3[(\mathbb{Z}/2\mathbb{Z})^{2^n}]$, where the FFT reduces to a 2^n-dimensional FFT over $\mathbb{F}_3$.

From Decision-QA-SD to Search-QA-SD. In the long version [20] available on eprint, we give a reduction from the search version of QA-SD to the decision version for all instances over $\mathcal{R} = \mathbb{F}_q[G]$ where $G = (\mathbb{Z}/(q-1)\mathbb{Z})^n$, which is the group which we use to obtain PCG's for OLE's over $\mathbb{F}_q^{(q-1)^n}$. This provides further support for the security of our PCG schemes, by showing that their security reduces to the *search* QA-SD assumption. In a nutshell, the reduction follows exactly the same proof as that of [21].

References

1. Aguilar Melchor, C., et al.: BIKE. Round 4 Submission to the NIST Post-Quantum Cryptography Call, v. 5.1, October 2022. https://bikesuite.org
2. Aguilar Melchor, C., et al.: HQC. Round 4 Submission to the NIST Post-Quantum Cryptography Call, October 2022. https://pqc-hqc.org/
3. Aguilar-Melchor, C., Blazy, O., Deneuville, J.C., Gaborit, P., Zémor, G.: Efficient encryption from random quasi-cyclic codes. IEEE Trans. Inf. Theory **64**(5), 3927–3943 (2018)
4. Akavia, A., Bogdanov, A., Guo, S., Kamath, A., Rosen, A.: Candidate weak pseudorandom functions in AC^0 o MOD_2. In: Naor, M. (ed.) ITCS 2014: 5th Conference on Innovations in Theoretical Computer Science, pp. 251–260. Association for Computing Machinery, Princeton, NJ, USA, 12–14 January 2014
5. Jabri, A.A.: A statistical decoding algorithm for general linear block codes. In: Honary, B. (ed.) Cryptography and Coding 2001. LNCS, vol. 2260, pp. 1–8. Springer, Heidelberg (2001). https://doi.org/10.1007/3-540-45325-3_1
6. Alekhnovich, M.: More on average case vs approximation complexity. In: 44th Annual Symposium on Foundations of Computer Science, pp. 298–307. IEEE Computer Society Press, Cambridge, MA, USA, 11–14 October 2003
7. Aragon, N., et al.: Bike: bit flipping key encapsulation (2017)
8. Arora, S., Ge, R.: New algorithms for learning in presence of errors. In: Aceto, L., Henzinger, M., Sgall, J. (eds.) ICALP 2011. LNCS, vol. 6755, pp. 403–415. Springer, Heidelberg (2011). https://doi.org/10.1007/978-3-642-22006-7_34
9. Barg, A., Forney., G.D.: Random codes: minimum distances and error exponents. IEEE Trans. Inf. Theory **48**(9), 2568–2573 (2002). https://doi.org/10.1109/TIT.2002.800480
10. Baum, C., Escudero, D., Pedrouzo-Ulloa, A., Scholl, P., Troncoso-Pastoriza, J.R.: Efficient protocols for oblivious linear function evaluation from ring-LWE. In: Galdi, C., Kolesnikov, V. (eds.) SCN 2020. LNCS, vol. 12238, pp. 130–149. Springer, Cham (2020). https://doi.org/10.1007/978-3-030-57990-6_7
11. Beaver, D.: Efficient multiparty protocols using circuit randomization. In: Feigenbaum, J. (ed.) CRYPTO 1991. LNCS, vol. 576, pp. 420–432. Springer, Heidelberg (1992). https://doi.org/10.1007/3-540-46766-1_34
12. Becker, A., Joux, A., May, A., Meurer, A.: Decoding random binary linear codes in $2^{n/20}$: how $1 + 1 = 0$ improves information set decoding. In: Pointcheval, D., Johansson, T. (eds.) EUROCRYPT 2012. LNCS, vol. 7237, pp. 520–536. Springer, Heidelberg (2012). https://doi.org/10.1007/978-3-642-29011-4_31
13. Bellare, M., Micciancio, D.: A new paradigm for collision-free hashing: incrementality at reduced cost. In: Fumy, W. (ed.) EUROCRYPT 1997. LNCS, vol. 1233, pp. 163–192. Springer, Heidelberg (1997). https://doi.org/10.1007/3-540-69053-0_13
14. Bernstein, D.J., Lange, T.: Never trust a bunny. In: Hoepman, J.-H., Verbauwhede, I. (eds.) RFIDSec 2012. LNCS, vol. 7739, pp. 137–148. Springer, Heidelberg (2013). https://doi.org/10.1007/978-3-642-36140-1_10
15. Bernstein, D.J., Lange, T., Peters, C.: Smaller decoding exponents: ball-collision decoding. In: Rogaway, P. (ed.) CRYPTO 2011. LNCS, vol. 6841, pp. 743–760. Springer, Heidelberg (2011). https://doi.org/10.1007/978-3-642-22792-9_42
16. Blum, A., Kalai, A., Wasserman, H.: Noise-tolerant learning, the parity problem, and the statistical query model. In: 32nd Annual ACM Symposium on Theory of Computing, pp. 435–440. ACM Press, Portland, OR, USA, 21–23 May 2000

17. Bogdanov, A., Rosen, A.: Pseudorandom functions: three decades later. Cryptology ePrint Archive, Report 2017/652 (2017). https://eprint.iacr.org/2017/652
18. Bogos, S., Tramer, F., Vaudenay, S.: On solving LPN using BKW and variants. Cryptography and Communications 8(3), 331–369 (2016)
19. Bogos, S., Vaudenay, S.: Optimization of LPN solving algorithms. In: Cheon, J.H., Takagi, T. (eds.) ASIACRYPT 2016. LNCS, vol. 10031, pp. 703–728. Springer, Heidelberg (2016). https://doi.org/10.1007/978-3-662-53887-6_26
20. Bombar, M., Couteau, G., Couvreur, A., Ducros, C.: Correlated pseudorandomness from the hardness of Quasi-Abelian decoding (2023). Long version, https://eprint.iacr.org/2023/845
21. Bombar, M., Couvreur, A., Debris-Alazard, T.: On codes and learning with errors over function fields. In: Dodis, Y., Shrimpton, T. (eds.) CRYPTO 2022. LNCS, vol. 13508, pp. 513–540. Springer, Cham (2022). https://doi.org/10.1007/978-3-031-15979-4_18, https://arxiv.org/pdf/2202.13990.pdf
22. Bootland, C., Castryck, W., Vercauteren, F.: On the security of the multivariate ring learning with errors problem. In: ANTS-XIV, Fourteenth Algorithmic Number Theory Symposium, Proceedings. Open Book Series, vol. 4, pp. 57–71. Mathematical Sciences Publishers (2020)
23. Both, L., May, A.: Decoding linear codes with high error rate and its impact for LPN security. In: Lange, T., Steinwandt, R. (eds.) PQCrypto 2018. LNCS, vol. 10786, pp. 25–46. Springer, Cham (2018). https://doi.org/10.1007/978-3-319-79063-3_2
24. Boyle, E., Couteau, G., Gilboa, N., Ishai, Y.: Compressing vector OLE. In: Lie, D., Mannan, M., Backes, M., Wang, X. (eds.) ACM CCS 2018: 25th Conference on Computer and Communications Security, pp. 896–912. ACM Press, Toronto, ON, Canada, 15–19 October 2018
25. Boyle, E., Couteau, G., Gilboa, N., Ishai, Y., Kohl, L., Resch, N., Scholl, P.: Correlated pseudorandomness from expand-accumulate codes. In: Dodis, Y., Shrimpton, T. (eds.) CRYPTO 2022, Part II. LNCS, vol. 13508, pp. 603–633. Springer, Heidelberg (2022). https://doi.org/10.1007/978-3-031-15979-4_21
26. Boyle, E., et al.: Efficient two-round OT extension and silent non-interactive secure computation. In: Cavallaro, L., Kinder, J., Wang, X., Katz, J. (eds.) ACM CCS 2019: 26th Conference on Computer and Communications Security, pp. 291–308. ACM Press, London, UK, 11–15 November 2019
27. Boyle, E., Couteau, G., Gilboa, N., Ishai, Y., Kohl, L., Scholl, P.: Efficient pseudorandom correlation generators: silent OT extension and more. In: Boldyreva, A., Micciancio, D. (eds.) CRYPTO 2019. LNCS, vol. 11694, pp. 489–518. Springer, Cham (2019). https://doi.org/10.1007/978-3-030-26954-8_16
28. Boyle, E., Couteau, G., Gilboa, N., Ishai, Y., Kohl, L., Scholl, P.: Correlated pseudorandom functions from variable-density LPN. In: 61st Annual Symposium on Foundations of Computer Science. pp. 1069–1080. IEEE Computer Society Press, Durham, NC, USA, 16–19 November 2020
29. Boyle, E., Couteau, G., Gilboa, N., Ishai, Y., Kohl, L., Scholl, P.: Efficient pseudorandom correlation generators from ring-LPN. In: Micciancio, D., Ristenpart, T. (eds.) CRYPTO 2020. LNCS, vol. 12171, pp. 387–416. Springer, Cham (2020). https://doi.org/10.1007/978-3-030-56880-1_14
30. Boyle, E., Couteau, G., Gilboa, N., Ishai, Y., Orrù, M.: Homomorphic secret sharing: optimizations and applications. In: Thuraisingham, B.M., Evans, D., Malkin, T., Xu, D. (eds.) ACM CCS 2017: 24th Conference on Computer and Communications Security, pp. 2105–2122. ACM Press, Dallas, TX, USA, 31 October–2 November 2017

31. Boyle, E., Gilboa, N., Ishai, Y.: Function secret sharing. In: Oswald, E., Fischlin, M. (eds.) EUROCRYPT 2015. LNCS, vol. 9057, pp. 337–367. Springer, Heidelberg (2015). https://doi.org/10.1007/978-3-662-46803-6_12

32. Boyle, E., Gilboa, N., Ishai, Y.: Function secret sharing: improvements and extensions. In: Weippl, E.R., Katzenbeisser, S., Kruegel, C., Myers, A.C., Halevi, S. (eds.) ACM CCS 2016: 23rd Conference on Computer and Communications Security, pp. 1292–1303. ACM Press, Vienna, Austria, 24–28 October 2016

33. Briaud, P., Øygarden, M.: A new algebraic approach to the regular syndrome decoding problem and implications for PCG constructions. Cryptology ePrint Archive, Paper 2023/176 (2023). https://eprint.iacr.org/2023/176, https://eprint.iacr.org/2023/176

34. Canto-Torres, R., Tillich, J.: Speeding up decoding a code with a non-trivial automorphism group up to an exponential factor. In: Proceedings of IEEE International Symposium Information Theory - ISIT 2019, pp. 1927–1931 (2019)

35. Couteau, G., Ducros, C.: Pseudorandom correlation functions from variable-density LPN, revisited. In: Boldyreva, A., Kolesnikov, V. (eds.) PKC 2023. LNCS, vol. 13941, pp. 221–250. Springer, Cham (2023). https://doi.org/10.1007/978-3-031-31371-4_8

36. Couteau, G., Rindal, P., Raghuraman, S.: Silver: silent VOLE and oblivious transfer from hardness of decoding structured LDPC codes. In: Malkin, T., Peikert, C. (eds.) CRYPTO 2021. LNCS, vol. 12827, pp. 502–534. Springer, Cham (2021). https://doi.org/10.1007/978-3-030-84252-9_17

37. Damgård, I., Park, S.: How practical is public-key encryption based on LPN and ring-LPN? Cryptology ePrint Archive, Report 2012/699 (2012). https://eprint.iacr.org/2012/699

38. Damgård, I., Pastro, V., Smart, N., Zakarias, S.: Multiparty computation from somewhat homomorphic encryption. In: Safavi-Naini, R., Canetti, R. (eds.) CRYPTO 2012. LNCS, vol. 7417, pp. 643–662. Springer, Heidelberg (2012). https://doi.org/10.1007/978-3-642-32009-5_38

39. Debris-Alazard, T.: Code-based cryptography: lecture notes (2023). https://arxiv.org/abs/2304.03541

40. Debris-Alazard, T., Tillich, J.P.: Statistical decoding. In: 2017 IEEE International Symposium on Information Theory (ISIT), pp. 1798–1802. IEEE (2017)

41. Esser, A., Kübler, R., May, A.: LPN decoded. In: Katz, J., Shacham, H. (eds.) CRYPTO 2017. LNCS, vol. 10402, pp. 486–514. Springer, Cham (2017). https://doi.org/10.1007/978-3-319-63715-0_17

42. Fan, Y., Lin, L.: Thresholds of random quasi-abelian codes. IEEE Trans. Inf. Theory **61**(1), 82–90 (2015)

43. Finiasz, M., Sendrier, N.: Security bounds for the design of code-based cryptosystems. In: Matsui, M. (ed.) ASIACRYPT 2009. LNCS, vol. 5912, pp. 88–105. Springer, Heidelberg (2009). https://doi.org/10.1007/978-3-642-10366-7_6

44. Fossorier, M.P., Kobara, K., Imai, H.: Modeling bit flipping decoding based on nonorthogonal check sums with application to iterative decoding attack of McEliece cryptosystem. IEEE Trans. Inf. Theory **53**(1), 402–411 (2006)

45. Gaborit, P., Zémor, G.: Asymptotic improvement of the Gilbert-Varshamov bound for linear codes. In: Proceedings of IEEE International Symposium Information and Theory - ISIT 2006, pp. 287–291. Seattle, USA, June 2006

46. Gilbert, H., Robshaw, M.J.B., Seurin, Y.: Good variants of HB$^+$ are hard to find. In: Tsudik, G. (ed.) FC 2008. LNCS, vol. 5143, pp. 156–170. Springer, Heidelberg (2008). https://doi.org/10.1007/978-3-540-85230-8_12

47. Gilboa, N.: Two party RSA key generation. In: Wiener, M. (ed.) CRYPTO 1999. LNCS, vol. 1666, pp. 116–129. Springer, Heidelberg (1999). https://doi.org/10.1007/3-540-48405-1_8

48. Guo, Q., Johansson, T., Löndahl, C.: A new algorithm for solving ring-LPN with a reducible polynomial. IEEE Trans. Inf. Theory **61**(11), 6204–6212 (2015)

49. Guo, Q., Johansson, T., Löndahl, C.: Solving LPN using covering codes. J. Cryptol. **33**(1), 1–33 (2020)

50. Hazay, C., Ishai, Y., Marcedone, A., Venkitasubramaniam, M.: LevioSA: Lightweight secure arithmetic computation. In: Cavallaro, L., Kinder, J., Wang, X., Katz, J. (eds.) ACM CCS 2019: 26th Conference on Computer and Communications Security, pp. 327–344. ACM Press, London, UK, 11–15 November 2019

51. Heyse, S., Kiltz, E., Lyubashevsky, V., Paar, C., Pietrzak, K.: LaPiN: an efficient authentication protocol based on ring-LPN. In: Canteaut, A. (ed.) FSE 2012. LNCS, vol. 7549, pp. 346–365. Springer, Heidelberg (2012). https://doi.org/10.1007/978-3-642-34047-5_20

52. Ishai, Y., Kilian, J., Nissim, K., Petrank, E.: Extending oblivious transfers efficiently. In: Boneh, D. (ed.) CRYPTO 2003. LNCS, vol. 2729, pp. 145–161. Springer, Heidelberg (2003). https://doi.org/10.1007/978-3-540-45146-4_9

53. Kasami, T.: A Gilbert-Varshamov bound for quasi-cycle codes of rate 1/2 (corresp.). IEEE Trans. Inf. Theory **20**(5), 679–679 (1974)

54. Keller, M., Pastro, V., Rotaru, D.: Overdrive: Making SPDZ great again. In: Nielsen, J.B., Rijmen, V. (eds.) EUROCRYPT 2018. LNCS, vol. 10822, pp. 158–189. Springer, Cham (2018). https://doi.org/10.1007/978-3-319-78372-7_6

55. Kirchner, P.: Improved generalized birthday attack. Cryptology ePrint Archive, Report 2011/377 (2011). https://eprint.iacr.org/2011/377

56. Levieil, É., Fouque, P.-A.: An improved LPN algorithm. In: De Prisco, R., Yung, M. (eds.) SCN 2006. LNCS, vol. 4116, pp. 348–359. Springer, Heidelberg (2006). https://doi.org/10.1007/11832072_24

57. Lipmaa, H., Pavlyk, K.: Analysis and implementation of an efficient ring-LPN based commitment scheme. In: Reiter, M., Naccache, D. (eds.) CANS 2015. LNCS, vol. 9476, pp. 160–175. Springer, Cham (2015). https://doi.org/10.1007/978-3-319-26823-1_12

58. Lyubashevsky, V.: The parity problem in the presence of noise, decoding random linear codes, and the subset sum problem. In: Chekuri, C., Jansen, K., Rolim, J.D.P., Trevisan, L. (eds.) APPROX/RANDOM -2005. LNCS, vol. 3624, pp. 378–389. Springer, Heidelberg (2005). https://doi.org/10.1007/11538462_32

59. Lyubashevsky, V., Masny, D.: Man-in-the-middle secure authentication schemes from LPN and weak PRFs. In: Canetti, R., Garay, J.A. (eds.) CRYPTO 2013. LNCS, vol. 8043, pp. 308–325. Springer, Heidelberg (2013). https://doi.org/10.1007/978-3-642-40084-1_18

60. May, A., Meurer, A., Thomae, E.: Decoding random linear codes in $\tilde{\mathcal{O}}(2^{0.054n})$. In: Lee, D.H., Wang, X. (eds.) ASIACRYPT 2011. LNCS, vol. 7073, pp. 107–124. Springer, Heidelberg (2011). https://doi.org/10.1007/978-3-642-25385-0_6

61. May, A., Ozerov, I.: On computing nearest neighbors with applications to decoding of binary linear codes. In: Oswald, E., Fischlin, M. (eds.) EUROCRYPT 2015. LNCS, vol. 9056, pp. 203–228. Springer, Heidelberg (2015). https://doi.org/10.1007/978-3-662-46800-5_9

62. Melchor, C.A., et al.: Hamming quasi-cyclic (HQC). NIST PQC Round **2**, 4–13 (2018)

63. Oberst, U.: The fast Fourier transform. SIAM J. Control Optim. **46**(2), 496–540 (2007). https://doi.org/10.1137/060658242

64. Overbeck, R.: Statistical decoding revisited. In: Batten, L.M., Safavi-Naini, R. (eds.) ACISP 2006. LNCS, vol. 4058, pp. 283–294. Springer, Heidelberg (2006). https://doi.org/10.1007/11780656_24

65. Pierce, J.N.: Limit distribution of the minimum distance of random linear codes. IEEE Trans. Inform. Theory **13**(1), 595–599 (1967)

66. Prange, E.: The use of information sets in decoding cyclic codes. IRE Trans. Inf. Theory **8**(5), 5–9 (1962). https://doi.org/10.1109/TIT.1962.1057777

67. Saarinen, M.-J.O.: Linearization attacks against syndrome based hashes. In: Srinathan, K., Rangan, C.P., Yung, M. (eds.) INDOCRYPT 2007. LNCS, vol. 4859, pp. 1–9. Springer, Heidelberg (2007). https://doi.org/10.1007/978-3-540-77026-8_1

68. Schoppmann, P., Gascón, A., Reichert, L., Raykova, M.: Distributed vector-OLE: improved constructions and implementation. In: Cavallaro, L., Kinder, J., Wang, X., Katz, J. (eds.) ACM CCS 2019: 26th Conference on Computer and Communications Security, pp. 1055–1072. ACM Press, London, UK, 11–15 November 2019

69. Stern, J.: A method for finding codewords of small weight. In: Cohen, G., Wolfmann, J. (eds.) Coding Theory 1988. LNCS, vol. 388, pp. 106–113. Springer, Heidelberg (1989). https://doi.org/10.1007/BFb0019850

70. Wagner, D.: A generalized birthday problem. In: Yung, M. (ed.) CRYPTO 2002. LNCS, vol. 2442, pp. 288–304. Springer, Heidelberg (2002). https://doi.org/10.1007/3-540-45708-9_19

71. Wasan, S.K.: Quasi-abelian codes (1977). http://elib.mi.sanu.ac.rs/files/journals/publ/41/31.pdf

72. Willems, W.: Codes in Group Algebras, chap. 16. Chapman and Hall/CRC (2021)

73. Yang, K., Weng, C., Lan, X., Zhang, J., Wang, X.: Ferret: Fast extension for correlated OT with small communication. In: Ligatti, J., Ou, X., Katz, J., Vigna, G. (eds.) ACM CCS 2020: 27th Conference on Computer and Communications Security, pp. 1607–1626. ACM Press, Virtual Event, USA, 9–13 November 2020

74. Zhang, B., Jiao, L., Wang, M.: Faster algorithms for solving LPN. In: Fischlin, M., Coron, J.-S. (eds.) EUROCRYPT 2016. LNCS, vol. 9665, pp. 168–195. Springer, Heidelberg (2016). https://doi.org/10.1007/978-3-662-49890-3_7

75. Zichron, L.: Locally computable arithmetic pseudorandom generators. Master's thesis, School of Electrical Engineering, Tel Aviv University (2017). http://www.eng.tau.ac.il/~bennyap/pubs/Zichron.pdf

Expand-Convolute Codes for Pseudorandom Correlation Generators from LPN

Srinivasan Raghuraman[1(✉)], Peter Rindal[2], and Titouan Tanguy[3]

[1] Visa Research and MIT, Cambridge, USA
srraghur@visa.com
[2] Visa Research, Palo Alto, USA
[3] imec-COSIC, KU Leuven, Leuven, Belgium
titouan.tanguy@kuleuven.be

Abstract. The recent development of pseudorandom correlation generators (PCG) holds tremendous promise for highly efficient MPC protocols. Among other correlations, PCGs allow for the efficient generation of oblivious transfer (OT) and vector oblivious linear evaluations (VOLE) with sublinear communication and concretely good computational overhead. This type of PCG makes use of a so-called LPN-friendly error-correcting code. That is, for large dimensions the code should have very efficient encoding and have high minimum distance.

We investigate existing LPN-friendly codes and find that several candidates are less secure than was believed. Beginning with the recent *expand-accumulate* codes, we find that for their *aggressive* parameters, aimed at good concrete efficiency, they achieve a smaller [pseudo] minimum distance than conjectured. This decreases the resulting security parameter of the PCG but it remains unclear by how much. We additionally show that the recently proposed and extremely efficient *silver* codes achieve only very small minimum distance and result in concretely efficient attacks on the resulting PCG protocol. As such, silver codes should not be used.

We introduce a new LPN-friendly code which we call *expand-convolute*. These codes have provably high minimum distance and faster encoding time than suitable alternatives, e.g. expand-accumulate. The main contribution of these codes is the introduction of a convolution step that dramatically increases the minimum distance. This in turn allows for a more efficient parameter selection which results in improved concrete performance. In particular, we observe a 3 times improvement in running time for a comparable security level.

1 Introduction

The use of correlated randomness has emerged as the de facto method for efficient multiparty computation (MPC) and other cryptographic protocols. One of the most fundamental examples is the oblivious transfer correlation which drives a large fraction of efficient MPC protocols. Therefore the efficient generation of such correlated randomness is of paramount importance for realizing

© International Association for Cryptologic Research 2023
H. Handschuh and A. Lysyanskaya (Eds.): CRYPTO 2023, LNCS 14084, pp. 602–632, 2023.
https://doi.org/10.1007/978-3-031-38551-3_19

the real-world potential of these protocols. The recent development of pseudo-random correlation generators (PCG) [12] has been suggested as the preferred way of generating this correlation due to extremely good communication over-head, typically sublinear, and compelling computational overheads. However, more research is needed to realize the true potential of these techniques. This includes an improved understanding of the underlying security assumptions and better computational efficiency.

A PCG Overview. The two party PCG protocols we will focus on have the following structure. During a concretely efficient setup phase, the parties will interactively generate random vectors $\vec{a'}, \vec{b'}, \vec{c'} \in \mathbb{F}^n$ and a scaler $\Delta \in \mathbb{F}$ such that

$$\vec{a'}\Delta + \vec{b'} = \vec{c'}$$

One party will hold $\vec{a'}, \vec{b'}$ while the other holds $\vec{c'}, \Delta$. These values are uniformly distributed with the caveat that $\vec{a'}$ is extremely sparse. The protocol then trans-forms these $\vec{a'}, \vec{b'}, \vec{c'}$ vectors into uniformly random vectors $\vec{a}, \vec{b}, \vec{c} \in \mathbb{F}^k$ that have the same correlation, $\vec{a}\Delta + \vec{b} = \vec{c}$. Typically, k will be large such as 2^{20}. This correlation is known as vector oblivious linear evaluation (VOLE) which is used by several state of art protocols for zero-knowledge and private set intersection. Alternatively, the VOLE correlation can be efficiently converted into k oblivious transfer (OT) correlations which are used by countless protocols.

The core idea of the transformation is to multiply the $\vec{a'}, \vec{b'}, \vec{c'}$ vectors by the transpose of an error correcting generator matrix G. This effectively *compresses* these vectors to obtain $\vec{a} = \vec{a'}G^\mathsf{T}, \vec{b} = \vec{b'}G^\mathsf{T}, \vec{c} = \vec{c'}G^\mathsf{T}$. Given that the error correcting code G has high minimum distance, the sparse vector $\vec{a'}$ will be compressed into a slightly shorter but uniformly random vector $\vec{a}$. Or more formally, $\vec{a}$ is indistinguishable from uniform if the dual LPN assumption holds for G (see Sect. 2.4).

The main overhead in these protocols is the multiplication with the error correcting code G. Various codes have been proposed with the main challenge being that G must have high minimum distance to argue security while also having efficient multiplication.

1.1 Our Contributions

We propose a new class of error-correcting codes with provably high minimum distance which are optimized for use in very large learning parity with noise (LPN) instances for Pseudorandom Correlation Generators (PCG). We name the codes Expand Convolute after the recent Expand Accumulate codes of Boyle et al. [10] and convolutional codes (see Sect. 2.5 and [7]) that we build on. Our new codes offer several compelling features. First is that they achieve linear minimum distance (in the code length) which implies that our codes can provably prevent a very large class of attacks when used for LPN and pseudorandom correlation generators. At the same time our codes are very efficient. The encoding/matrix multiply time requires near-linear time and concretely outperforms the prior art [10]. Our code takes Expand Accumulate codes as a starting point and replaces the accumulation with a convolutional code that we design. Each step of the convolution is mildly less efficient but allows for a drastically bigger rate, e.g. 0.6 as opposed to 0.2. This in turn allows our code to be much more efficient, approaching a $2.8 = 0.6/0.2$ times improvement in the overall running time of the final pseudorandom correlation generator. Alternatively, our construction can decrease the expander parameter by approximately 2 times which similarly improves performance. Finally we introduce a systematic version of our code that achieves a further $1.5\times$ running time improvement at the expense of a small decrease of minimum distance.

When analyzing the concrete parameters of our new code we observe that the aggressive parameters proposed by [10] for their code fall short of their claimed security level. In particular, we are able to empirically find (pseudo) minimum distances of their code that are $30\times$ smaller than conjectured. It does not appear that this results in a practical attack on their construction but certainly decreased their security margin. Due to having a similar structure, one can apply similar techniques to our code. However, as expected we observe that our introduction of a convolution results in a much higher pseudo minimum distance (i.e. the smallest weight codeword that can efficiently be computed).

Our third contribution is demonstrating that the recent Silver codes [14] achieve only sublinear minimum distance and are unsuitable for use in LPN. The compelling feature of Silver was extremely good computational performance. The techniques used to get this efficiency also made proving bounds on the minimum distance of these codes difficult. The authors instead chose to rely on empirical methods for estimating the minimum distance of small codes and extrapolated the distance for the large codes used by PCGs. The authors conjectured their code achieved linear minimum distance with their empirical bounds as supporting evidence. However, we show that the Silver codes only achieve poly log minimum distance which leads to a concretely efficient distinguisher for their PCG construction based on LPN.

Compared to our new codes, the encoding procedure for Silver is several times faster. However, given the sublinear distance of Silver, some added overhead over the silver codes appears necessary. Moreover, our new codes are the fastest known codes that also achieve provable linear minimum distance. In particular, we are twice as fast as [10] for comparable security.

1.2   Technical Overview of Expand Convolute

Both our new expand convolute code and the prior art of expand accumulate [10] describe the generator matrix $G \in \{0,1\}^{k \times n}$ as the multiplication of two other matrices, an expander $B \in \{0,1\}^{k \times n}$ and a convolution $C \in \{0,1\}^{n \times n}$, such that $G = BC$. The expander B is highly sparse with row (and column) hamming weight being $O(\log k)$. Informally, the expander mixes disparate parts of the message together. The convolution C is an upper triangular matrix with a special structure, see Sect. 2.5. In particular, given $\vec{y} = \vec{x}C$, then for all i, we can write y_i as a linear combination of x_i and $y_{i-1}, \ldots, y_{i-m}$ for some small parameter m. Informally, the convolution can be thought of as performing thorough local mixing of the last m outputs and x_i. Together, the expander and convolution perform both global and local mixing which give it strong minimum distance properties.

The structure of B, C gives a natural algorithm for computing $\vec{x}G$. For $i = 1, \ldots, n$, we sum the $O(\log k)$ positions of $\vec{x}$ that are indexed by the ith column of B, i.e. $t_i = \breve{B}_{.,i} \cdot \vec{x}$ and use that to update the convolution as $y_i = t_i + \sum_{j=1,\ldots,m} \alpha_{i,j} y_{i-j}$, where $\alpha_{i,j}$ are the random coefficients that define the convolution. Setting $vSize = 1$ and all of the convolution coefficients $\alpha_{i,1}$ to be 1, we obtain the expand accumulate codes. In contrast, we will define $m \approx 20$ and uniformly sample the convolution coefficients.

The critical security property that we must guarantee is that the code generated by G has high minimum distance. This is equivalent to requiring that low (non-zero) hamming weight codewords $\vec{y} = \vec{x}G$ do not exist. For some iteration i, we refer to the state $\breve{\sigma}_i$ of the convolution as the previous m outputs, i.e., a column vector $\breve{\sigma}_i = (y_{i-1}, \ldots, y_{i-m})^\mathsf{T}$. For the sake of contradiction, let us assume $\vec{x}$ results in a low weight codeword $\vec{y} = \vec{x}BC$, i.e., $\vec{y}$ is mostly zero. Next observe that when the state σ_i is non-zero, the next output $y_i = 1$ with probability $1/2$ over the random choices of $\alpha_{i,j}$, a.k.a C. Therefore, except with negligible probability, for y to be low weight, the state must be zero most of the time.

This brings us to the core idea of our construction. The probability that convolution state can transition to the zero state from non-zero is roughly proportional to 2^{-m}. Observe that while the state is non-zero there is a $1/2$ probability of getting $y_i = 1$ (over the choices of $\alpha_{i,j}$, a.k.a C). Given that $y_i = 1$, at least m more iterations are required before the state can possibly transition to zero. In particular, if $y_i = 1$ then $y_{i+1} = \ldots = y_{i+m} = 0$ must happen to transition to the zero state $\breve{\sigma}_{i+m+1} = (y_{i+1}, \ldots, y_{i+m}) = \vec{0}$. Given that for $j \in [m]$, $\mathrm{Pr}_C[y_{i+j} = 1 \mid y_i = 1] = 1/2$, we have the probability of transiting to state zero at step $i + m$ given $y_i = 1$ is 2^{-m}, i.e. $\mathrm{Pr}_C[\breve{\sigma}_{i+m+1} = 0 \mid y_i = 1] = 2^{-m}$. We note that formalizing this intuition for all i requires significant nuance due to the fact that these events are not all independent, e.g. when $y_i = 0$.

By setting $m = O(\log k)$, in expectation any given message $\vec{x}$ will not transition to the all zero state and is likely to have high weight. In particular, a larger m results in higher minimum distance. In contrast, the expand accumulate code has $m = 1$ and therefore can easily transition back to the zero state.

While the conceptual idea of making the state larger is simple, the main challenge lies in proving exactly how much increasing m helps. To achieve this we model the process of generating $\vec{y}$ as a walk on a Markov chain, where the randomness is over the choice of B, C. Unfortunately, naively modeling this process results in extremely loose bounds and suggests a larger m is bad. We show a series of transformations between related Markov chains such that a final chain can yield tight bounds on the minimum distance of the code.

Organization. We begin in Sect. 2 by reviewing background material and the closely related expand accumulate codes of [10]. We then introduce the Silver codes of [14] in Sect. 3 and discuss why they achieve sublinear minimum distance.

In Sect. 5 we introduce our new codes. We present two different convolutional codes which we call non-wrapping and wrapping, where the latter achieves better practical performance. Building on these convolutional codes we design our final codes in a manner similar to expand accumulate codes, with the main difference being that our codes achieve a much better rate and or a more efficient expander.

2 Preliminaries

2.1 Notation

$[a, b]$ denotes the set $\{a, ..., b\}$ with $[n]$ being shorthand for $[1, n]$. Let $[a, b]_{\mathbb{R}}$ be the interval a to b over the real values. $(a, b]$ and $[a, b)$ denotes the range excluding the first and last element, respectively. Let $\vec{x} \in \mathcal{R}^n$ be a row vector over a domain $\mathcal{R}$ of length n. x_i denotes the ith element. Alternatively, let $\vec{x} \in \mathcal{R}^V$ for a set V denote a vector of length $|V|$ and is index by elements of V. Let $\vec{y}$ be a column vector. Let $(x_1, ..., x_n)$ denote a row vector. For a set S, let $\vec{x}_S$ denote the subvector index by S, i.e. $(x_{S_1}, ..., x_{S_{|S|}})$. We use upper case to denote matrices, e.g. M. M_i denotes the ith row and $M_{.,i}$ denotes the ith column of M. M^{T} and $\vec{x}^{\mathsf{T}}$ are the transpose of a matrix and vector respectively.

2.2 Background on Markov Chains

Markov Chain. A Markov chain is defined by a finite set V of state space and transition matrix $P \in \mathbb{R}^{V \times V}$ s.t. all rows sum to 1 with > 0 entries. For $\vec{u}, \vec{v} \in V$, $P_{u,v}$ is the probability of transitioning from state $\vec{u}$ to $\vec{v}$. P thus naturally describes a random walk:
Let $\vec{v} \in \mathbb{R}^V$ denote a distribution over the state space, so ν_v is the probability of sampling state v. Sample a state $x_0 \leftarrow \vec{v}$. For $i \in [n]$, sample $x_i \leftarrow P_{x_{i-1}}$.

Stationary Distribution. The stationary distribution $\vec{\nu} \in \mathbb{R}^V$ of a Markov chain is a distribution over V such that $\vec{\nu} P = \vec{\nu}$ (e.g. $= \vec{\nu}$ is a left eigenvector for eigenvalue $\lambda_1 = 1$)

Irreducible. A Markov chain is irreducible if any state can be reached from any other state in a finite number of steps. It is well known that if a chain is irreducible, it has a unique stationary distribution.

Reversible. A chain is irreducible reversible if $\forall u, v \in V$, $\nu_u P_{u,v} = \nu_v P_{v,u}$.

Expander Hoeffding Bound. For a function $f : V \rightarrow [0, 1]$, let $\mu = \mathbb{E}_{x \leftarrow \vec{v}}[f(x)]$ be the expected value under distribution $\vec{v}$. Consider the likelihood that the random variable $S_n = \sum_{i \in [n]} f(x_i)$ deviates a lot from $E_{x \leftarrow \vec{v}}[S_n]$, where $(x_1, \ldots, x_n)$ is an n-step random walk on the chain. This distribution is closely related to the second eigenvalue λ_2 of P by the following theorem.

Theorem 1 (Expander Hoeffding Bound). *Let (V, P) denote a finite, irreducible and reversible Markov chain, with stationary distribution $\vec{\pi}$ and second largest eigenvalue λ_2. Let $f : V \rightarrow [0, 1]$ with $\mu = E_{x \leftarrow \vec{\pi}}[f(x)]$, and consider*

$S_n = \sum_{i \in [n]} f(x_i)$ with $x_0 \leftarrow_{\vec{\pi}} V$ and $x_1, \ldots, x_n$ is a random walk which starts from x_0. Then for $\tilde{\lambda}_2 = \max(0, \lambda_2)$, and any $\epsilon > 0$, the following concentration bounds hold:

$$\Pr\left[S_n > n\mu + \epsilon\right] \le \exp\left(-2\frac{\epsilon^2}{n} \cdot \frac{1 - \tilde{\lambda}_2}{1 + \tilde{\lambda}_2}\right)$$

$$\Pr\left[S_n < n\mu - \epsilon\right] \le \exp\left(-2\frac{\epsilon^2}{n} \cdot \frac{1 - \tilde{\lambda}_2}{1 + \tilde{\lambda}_2}\right)$$

Corollary for Other Starting Distributions. We care about the special case where the starting distribution is fixed to be a specific $v \in V$. The bound for this case is (from the *total probability rule*):

$$\Pr\left[S_n > n\mu + \epsilon\right] \le \frac{1}{\pi_v} \exp\left(-2\frac{\epsilon^2}{n} \cdot \frac{1 - \tilde{\lambda}_2}{1 + \tilde{\lambda}_2}\right)$$

$$\Pr\left[S_n < n\mu - \epsilon\right] \le \frac{1}{\pi_v} \exp\left(-2\frac{\epsilon^2}{n} \cdot \frac{1 - \tilde{\lambda}_2}{1 + \tilde{\lambda}_2}\right)$$

2.3 Coding Theory

Generator Matrix. Let $k < n \in \mathbb{N}$. Let $G \in \mathcal{R}^{k \times n}$ be a $k \times n$ matrix over the field $\mathcal{R}$, it generates the set of codewords $\mathcal{C} := \{\vec{c} = \vec{x}G \mid \vec{x} \in \mathcal{R}^k\}$ where $\vec{c}$ is a codeword of the linear code $\mathcal{C}$, and $\vec{x}$ is any input k-length vector. G is the *generator matrix* of $\mathcal{C}$. Often it will be useful to consider a family of error correcting codes that can be sampled from by some randomized procedure C.

Standard Form. The *standard form* for a generator matrix is, $G = [I_k | P]$ where I_k is the $k \times k$ identity matrix and P is a $k \times m'$ matrix, where $m' = n - k$. When the generator matrix is in standard form, the code $\mathcal{C}$ is said to be *systematic* and the message can be read directly from the first k positions codeword, i.e. $c = G\vec{x} = [\vec{x} | \vec{p}]$ for some parity information $\vec{p} \in \mathcal{R}^m$. An arbitrary generator matrix G' can be placed in standard form by performing elementary row operations and possibly column swaps.

Parity Check Matrix. The matrix $H \in \mathcal{R}^{m' \times n}$ representing a linear function $\phi : \mathcal{R}^n \to \mathcal{R}^{n-k}$ whose kernel is $\mathcal{C}$ is called a *parity check matrix* of $\mathcal{C}$. Equivalently, H is a matrix whose kernel, a.k.a. null space, is $\mathcal{C}$, i.e. $\mathcal{C} = \{\vec{c} \mid H\vec{c}^{\mathsf{T}} = 0\}$. It can be verified that H is a $m' \times n$ matrix. The code generated by H is called the *dual code* of $\mathcal{C}$, denoted by $\mathcal{C}^{\perp}$.

Minimum Distance. The distance d of a linear code $\mathcal{C}$ can be defined as the minimum number of positions of a codeword $\vec{c} \in \mathcal{C}$ which must be modified to produce another codeword $\vec{c}'$. Equivalently, it is the minimum number of linearly dependent columns of the parity check matrix H. Due to the linearity of $\mathcal{C}$, it is easy to see that d is equal to the minimum weight non-zero codeword.

Computing the minimum distance for an arbitrary linear code $\mathcal{C}$ is known to be NP-complete [21].

Relating the Generator and Parity Check Matrices. A generator matrix can be used to construct the parity check matrix for a code (and vice versa). If the generator matrix G is in standard form, $G = [I_k|P]$ then the parity check matrix for $\mathcal{C}$ is $H = [-P^\mathsf{T}|I_{n-k}]$ where P^T is the transpose of the matrix P and I_{n-k} is the $m' \times m'$ identity matrix.

2.4 Syndrome Decoding and Learning Parity with Noise

Our constructions follows the recent line of works [10–12,14] to propose a new variant of the learning parity with noise (LPN) assumption (more accurately, a type of syndrome decoding assumption). The learning parity with noise assumption is one of the most fundamental assumptions of cryptography, introduced in the work of [8]; related problems were used even earlier [18]. The LPN assumption over a field $\mathcal{R}$ states, informally, that $(A, A \cdot \vec{s} + \vec{e})$ can not efficiently be distinguished from $(A, \vec{b})$, where A is sampled from some ensemble of matrices, $\vec{s}$ is a uniform secret vector over $\mathcal{R}$, $\vec{e}$ is a *noise vector* sampled from some distribution over sparse $\mathcal{R}$-vectors. $\vec{b}$ is a uniform vector over $\mathcal{R}$. More formally, we define the LPN assumption over $\mathcal{R}$ with dimension m', number of samples n, w.r.t. a code generation algorithm C, and a noise distribution $\mathcal{D}$:

Definition 1 (Primal LPN [14]). *Let $\mathcal{D}(\mathcal{R}) = \{\mathcal{D}_{m',n}(\mathcal{R})\}_{m',n\in\mathbb{N}}$ denote a sequence of efficiently sampleable distributions indexed by a pair of integers (m', n) over a ring $\mathcal{R}$, such that for any $m', n \in \mathbb{N}$, $\mathsf{Im}(\mathcal{D}_{m',n}(\mathcal{R})) \subseteq \mathcal{R}^n$. Let C be a probabilistic code generation algorithm such that $C(m', n, \mathcal{R})$ outputs a matrix $A \in \mathcal{R}^{n \times m'}$. For dimension $m' = m'(\kappa)$, number of samples (or block length) $n = n(\kappa)$, and ring $\mathcal{R} = \mathcal{R}(\kappa)$, the (primal) $(\mathcal{D}, C, \mathcal{R})$-LPN$(m', n)$ assumption states that*

$$\{(A, \vec{b}) \text{ s.t. } A \leftarrow C(m', n, \mathcal{R}), \vec{e} \leftarrow \mathcal{D}_{m',n}(\mathcal{R}), \vec{s} \leftarrow \mathcal{R}^{m'}, \vec{b} \leftarrow A \cdot \vec{s} + \vec{e}\}$$

$$\overset{c}{\approx} \{(A, \vec{b}) \text{ s.t. } A \leftarrow C(m', n, \mathcal{R}), \vec{b} \leftarrow \mathcal{R}^n\}.$$

This definition captures not only LPN type assumptions but also assumptions such as LWE or the multivariate quadratic assumption. For our purposes, we restrict the assumptions such that the noise distribution outputs sparse vectors with high probability. The standard LPN is obtained by sampling A as $A \leftarrow \{0,1\}^{n \times m'}$, i.e. a uniformly random binary matrix, and sampling the noise distribution as $\vec{e} \leftarrow \mathsf{Ber}_r^n(\{0,1\})$, i.e. the binary Bernoulli distribution where for all i, $\Pr[e_i = 1] = r$. Other distributions such as regular noise have been proposed [11], where $\vec{e}$ is the concatenation of t unit vectors of length N/t, to achieve improved running times for target applications.

The assumption comes in two equivalent forms, the "primal" as described above, and the "dual". The latter formulation considers the linear error correcting code $\mathcal{C}$ where A is the transpose of the parity check matrix of the linear code $\mathcal{C}$. Let $H = A^\mathsf{T}$ and G be the parity and generator matrix of $\mathcal{C}$, the hardness of distinguishing $H^\mathsf{T} \cdot \tilde{x} + \tilde{e}$ from random is equivalent to the hardness of distinguishing $G \cdot (H^\mathsf{T} \cdot \tilde{x} + \tilde{e}) = G \cdot \tilde{e} = \vec{e} \cdot G^\mathsf{T}$ from random (since $G^\mathsf{T} \cdot H = 0$).

The Linear Test Framework. Recent works [10–12,14] have built on the observation that, with a few exceptions, essentially applicable attacks fall within the so called *linear test framework*. These attacks have been based on Gaussian elimination and the BKW algorithm [17] and variants based on covering codes, information set decoding attacks [19,20], statistical decoding attacks [3,15,16], generalized birthday attacks, linearization attacks, attacks based on finding low weight code vectors [22], or on finding correlations with low-degree polynomials [2,9]. The linear test framework essentially states that for each of these distinguishers D, there exists a related adversary $\mathcal{A}$ that takes as input A and outputs a *test vector* $\vec{v}$ such that the distinguishing power of $D(A, \tilde{b})$ is no better than $\vec{v} \cdot \tilde{b}$ where $\tilde{b}$ is the LPN sample.

The linear test framework is useful for two primary reasons. First is that it is expressive enough to capture all relevant attacks on LPN. Secondly, when LPN is instantiated with a code with high minimum distance d, one can prove that the advantage of a linear test distinguisher is negligible. If the weight of $\vec{v}$ is at most d, then the rows of A will be d-wise linearly independent and therefore $\vec{v} \cdot (A\tilde{s} + \tilde{e})$ will be uniformly random because $\tilde{s}$ is uniformly random. Therefore, for the distinguisher to succeed, it must output a test vector $\vec{v}$ with weight greater than d. However, in this case, one can parameterize the noise distribution to be sufficiently high that $\vec{v} \cdot \tilde{e}$ is close to uniform.

We note that there are a few notable exceptions to the linear test framework. These exceptions all take advantage of special algebraic structure within the code (e.g. Reed-Solomon) or noise distribution. However, none of these exceptions are directly applicable to our setting [10].

Pseudo Minimum Distance. The original formulation of the linear test framework focuses on the existence of the minimum weight codeword to argue the security of LPN. The recent work [10] made explicit the observation that it is possible for an LPN instance A to be secure per Definition 2 yet have small minimum distance[1]. In particular, the observation is that if codewords with small weight exist but are computationally infeasible to find, then LPN should remain secure. [10] defines *pseudo minimum distance* to be the weight of the smallest weight codeword that can be efficiently computed. Given that computing the minimum weight codeword is known to be NP-Complete, it is very likely that for some codes the difference between pseudo and actual minimum distance could be quite large, possibly even asymptotically different. [10] formalizes this idea ([10], Definition 3.12) and proposes the use of pseudo minimum distance when performing parameter selection.

Minimum Distance vs. Noise Rate. In this discussion, we have focused on the need for high [pseudo] minimum distance. This raises the question of

---

[1] Or more accurately, have a small enough LPN noise rate such that $\tilde{e}$ does not sufficiently intersect a test vector with minimum distance weight with high probability.

exactly how high it needs to be for LPN to be secure. For any given minimum distance d, one needs to set the noise rate of the error vector $\bar{e}$ sufficiently high so that (linear) attacks with weight at least d are sufficiently likely to intersect with it. As such, one can also consider using a code with a smaller distance $d' < d$ and compensate for this by having a higher noise rate, or vice versa. [10] makes extensive use of this tradeoff and considers the use of relatively moderate minimum distance codes with a high noise rate. This has some impact on the communication complexity and running time of the final protocols.

LPN-friendly Codes. Many codes have been conjectured to result in secure LPN instantiations. As mentioned, the original formulation samples A as a uniformly random linear code. Alekhnovich [4] proposed sampling A as a sparse random matrix, i.e. a random LDPC code. Many works have also proposed LPN-friendly codes in the context of the NIST post-quantum completion [1,5,13] which were also used by [11]. It is believed that these codes offer strong security but fall short of the desired running time performance. The recent works of [10,14] have both proposed new classes of codes LDPC/Turbo code which aim for improved running times. With the exception of [14], all of these codes have instantiations which yield proofs of security in the linear test framework. However, we show that [14] is not LPN-friendly due to having small minimum distance.

2.5   Convolutional Codes

An important building block for the error correcting codes considered in this work are convolutional codes. These codes differ from the previously mentioned block codes in that they are capable of encoding an unbounded stream of data. A convolutional code maintains an internal state $\sigma_i \in \{0,1\}^m$ for each time step i. The length m of this state is referred to as the state size or memory size. There exists a state transition function ST that takes in the current time step i, current state σ_i and the next message bit x_i. ST outputs the codeword bit c_i and the new state σ_{i+1}. That is, for $i \in [n]$, $(c_i, \sigma_{i+1}) = \mathsf{ST}(i, x_i, \sigma_i)$ where $\sigma_1 = 0$. More generally, one can consider a state transition function that takes in multiple message bits at a time and output multiple bits. In this way, one is able to achieve a non-rate 1 code. However, for our purposes, this definition will suffice.

All convolutional codes we consider will be linear and as such there exists a matrix $M_i \in \{0,1\}^{(m+1)\times(m+1)}$ such that $\mathsf{ST}(i, x_i, \sigma_{i+1}) = (x_i || \vec{\sigma}_i) \cdot M_i$. The generator matrix for a convolutional code (for a fixed block size n) is then an upper triangular matrix $A \in \{0,1\}^{n \times n}$. Moreover, all of the convolutions we consider are *recursive* where $\sigma_i = c_{i-[m]}$ and therefore the convolution can be computed using an *update column vector* $\bar{\alpha}_i \in \{0,1\}^m$ such that $c_i = x_i + \bar{\alpha}_i \vec{c}_{i-[m]}$. That is, each codeword bit is a linear combination of the previous m codeword bits and the corresponding message bit.

The simplest convolutional code we consider is an accumulator. This code has a state size of $m = 1$ and for all i, $\bar{\alpha}_i = (1)$, each output $c_i = x_i + c_{i-1}$. Looking forward, we will consider more complicated convolutional codes where $m = O(\log n)$ and $\bar{\alpha}_i$ are sampled at random from some distribution.

3   Minimum Distance of Silver Codes

We begin by presenting the negative result that the Silver codes presented in [14] do not achieve linear [pseudo] minimum distance as conjectured. These codes were specifically designed for high efficiency LPN. The core design criteria were high minimum distance and (near) linear time encoding. We demonstrate that the Silver codes have a minimum distance upper bounded by $mw^2 = O(\log^3(n))$, where $m \in \{47, 63\}$ is the memory size of their convolutional code and $w \in \{5, 11\}$ is the number of diagonals in their left matrix. While Silver gives concrete values for m, w, we assume based on their claims that asymptotically they grow logarithmically, which technically means they obtain a $O(n \log n)$ running time. Next, we present the necessary details on the Silver codes which enable our concretely efficient LPN distinguisher along with identifying structural weaknesses of their construction. On the positive side, we identify sever several good design choices in their construction which we will build off of in Sect. 5.

Silver Codes. Arguably, one reason that the sublinear minimum distance of Silver was not previously observed is due to the somewhat complicated presentation of the code itself. Here we will present a simplified version of the code that has several unnecessary details removed[2].

Silver is a linear systematic code in that the codeword $c \in \{0, 1\}^n$ of message $\vec{x} \in \{0, 1\}^k$ is composed of $\vec{c} = (\vec{x} || \vec{c'})$. Their encoder can be broken into two phases, *linear sums* L and a *recursive convolution* A with a state size of $m \in \{47, 63\}$, where $\vec{c'} = \vec{x}LA$. $L \in \{0, 1\}^{k \times k}$ is an extremely sparse and highly structured matrix that is the addition of w rotations of the identity matrix. The convolution A is an upper triangular matrix with state size $m \approx 16$.

A recursive convolution code offers a more efficient encoding algorithm than naively multiplying by A. In particular, the ith bit of $\vec{y} = \vec{x}A$ is a linear combination of the previous m output bits and x_i, i.e. $y_i = x_i + (y_{i-1}, ..., y_{i-m}) \cdot \bar{\alpha}_i$. For our purposes, we can assume $\bar{\alpha}_i$ is uniformly random. An alternative description of A is with its parity check matrix which essentially consists of a width m diagonal band of zeros and ones defined as a function of the $\bar{\alpha}$ coefficients above.

Sublinear Minimum Distance. The state size m of the convolution immediately places an upper bound on the minimum distance of $I || A$, sometimes referred to as the *free distance* of A in the context of convolutional codes. Consider the following, at some index $x_i = 1$ and for $i' \in [i + 1, i + m]$, set $x_{i'} := (x_{i-1}, ..., x_{i-m}) \cdot \bar{\alpha}$. At all other positions let $\vec{x}$ be zero. Such an $\vec{x}$ will result in the state of the convolution return to all zeros after m iterations. Here we refer to the state of the convolution as the last m outputs which in turn define the next output. As such, the minimum distance of $I || A$ is upper bounded by $m + 1$.

For Silver, it is not as simple to get the state of the convolution to return to zeros. Let us first focus on the code formed by the generator matrix $LA \in$

---

[2] These removals will not influence the minimum distance.

$\{0,1\}^{k \times n}$. Let $q_1, ..., q_w \in [k]$ be the rotations of the identity matrix that form:

$$L = \sum_{j \in [w]} \mathsf{shift}(I_k, q_j).$$

As such $\vec{z} = \vec{x}L$ has the structure that $z_i = \sum_{j \in [w]} x_{i+q_j}$. For simplicity let $q_1 = 0$ and assume that the distances between any pair of q_j is greater than mw. Ostensibly, the logic behind Silver is that one is not able to find a value for $\vec{x}$ such that state of the convolution will quickly return to zero whenever it turns on. Of course one could always choose $x_i, ..., x_{i+m}$ such that the state of convolution at iteration i quickly goes to zero but the other $w - 1$ locations that x_i is mapped to will remain at a non-zero state with high probability.

Unfortunately, this need not be the case. Let $x_i = 1$ and consider $x_{i+1}, ... x_{i+mw}$. Let the rest of $\vec{x}$ be zero. Due to the structure of the convolution the state of the convolution at iterations $i + mw + \{q_1, ..., q_w\}$ will be a linear function F of $x_{i+1}, ... x_{i+mw}$. Moreover, the total size of the convolution states at these w iterations will be mw. As such, assuming F is bijective then one can solve for $x_{i+1}, ..., x_{i+mw}$ such that $F(x_{i+1}, ..., x_{i+mw}) = 0^{mw}$.

Therefore, one can choose $\vec{x}$ such that after mw iterations the convolution will return to the zero state at all of the w iterations that x_i was mapped to. This will contribute at most mw^2 ones to the codeword while the rest is all zeros. Since the overall code is of the form $(\vec{x}||\vec{x}LA)$, the minimum distance will be at most $mw + mw^2$ where the first term is due to $\vec{x}$ itself. Therefore one can conclude the [pseudo] minimum distance is $O(\log^3(n))$. See the full paper for additional comments on Silver.

4   Expand Accumulate Codes

Expand-accumulate codes (EA) were recently introduced by Boyle et al. [10]. Among other compelling features, EA offers concretely good encoding time and provable minimum distance under certain instantiations. To achieve better concrete performance [10] suggests the use of "aggressive" parameters which are not compatible with their proof of minimum distance but are plausibly secure. We show that these parameters fall short of their conjectured pseudo minimum distance by as much as $30\times$ for a code of size $k = 2^{20}$. It is unclear to us if this decrease results is a practical LPN distinguisher but, nonetheless, it is of concern and decreases their security margin. More generally, we show that for an EA code to have linear [pseudo] minimum distance, these parameters must grow with k. EA codes can be described using

- A sparse expander $B \in \{0,1\}^{k \times n}$, each row having approximate w weight.
- An accumulator matrix $A \in \{0,1\}^{n \times n}$.

Encoding is performed as $\vec{c} = (\vec{x}B)A$, i.e. $G = BA$. First the message $\vec{x}$ is expanded by B, i.e. $\vec{y} = \vec{x}B$. Concretely, each position y_i will be a sum of approximately $w(k/n) \approx w/2$ entries in $\vec{x}$. Accumulating as $\vec{c} = \vec{y}A$ correspond to taking the prefix sum of each entry, i.e. $c_i = \sum_{j \in [i]} y_j$.

4.1 On the Minimum Distance of EA

[10] proposes several different distributions for B and error vector $\vec{e}$. [10] proved that their code for certain parameter regimes has high minimum distance, where B is sampled using a Bernoulli distribution. In particular, let $\mathsf{EA}(k, n, p_{\mathsf{w}}) = BA$ refer to the process of sampling $B \in \{0, 1\}^{k \times n}$ where $B_{i,j} \leftarrow \mathsf{Ber}_{p_{\mathsf{w}}}$ with $p_{\mathsf{w}} = w/n$ for $w = \Omega(\log n)$. As such, the rows of B have expected weight w with $\Pr[B_{i,j} = 1] = p_{\mathsf{w}}$. Concretely, $w \approx 2.5 \ln n$ was proposed. Below we will review the proof of high minimum distance for this case. [10] also suggests more aggressive parameters with each row of B being randomly sampled with a small fixed hamming weight, e.g. $w = 7$. Focusing on the Bernoulli distribution, the sequence $(y_1, \ldots, y_n) = \vec{x}(BA)$ can be modeled as a n-step random walk (over the randomness of B) on a Markov chain with state space $\{0, 1\}$. That is, at step i of the walk, the current state will be y_i.

In particular, one can visualize this process by focusing on the state of the accumulator. Instead of first computing $\vec{x}B$ and then accumulating the result, consider the scenario where the accumulator state at iteration i is updated with $\vec{x}\vec{B}_{\cdot i}$. Whenever this update is one, the single bit state of the accumulator will flip and equivalently we will have $y_i = y_{i-1} \oplus 1$. This formulation naturally lends itself to being modeled as a Markov chain with the accumulator state being the state space, i.e. $\{0, 1\}$, and transition probability from $0 \rightarrow 1$ or $1 \rightarrow 0$ being $p_r = \Pr[\vec{x}\vec{B}_{\cdot i}]$. Additionally, recall that the column $\vec{B}_{\cdot i}$ is sampled as $\mathsf{Ber}_{p_{\mathsf{w}}}^k$ and therefore p_r is a function of $r = \mathsf{HW}(\vec{x}), p_{\mathsf{w}}$ when $\vec{B}_{\cdot i}$ is viewed as a random variable. Looking forward, we can bound the value of p_r using the Piling-up lemma (2). The proof perform a case analysis of $r = \mathsf{HW}(\vec{x})$ for $r = 1, r < \Omega(\frac{\log n}{n})$ and otherwise. Analyzing the behavior of the chain for each case, via its *spectral gap* (e.g. convergence rate) and then using an *expander Hoeffding bound* (concentration bound for Markov chains), it can be shown that the random walk $(y_1, \ldots, y_N)$ is unlikely to spend too much time on state 0, or equivalently, $\mathsf{HW}(\vec{x}G)$ is unlikely to be too small. In particular, [10] proved the following.

Lemma 1 (Core EA Lemma). *Let $k, n \in \mathbb{N}$, $k \leq n$. Fix $p_{\mathsf{w}} \in (0, \frac{1}{2})$, $\delta > 0$, $\beta = \frac{1}{2} - \delta$. Let $r \in n$, $x \in \{0, 1\}^k$ s.t. $\mathsf{HW}(x) = r$, define $\xi_r = (1 - 2p_{\mathsf{w}})^r$, then:*

$$\Pr\left[\mathsf{HW}(\vec{x}G) < \delta n \,\middle|\, G \leftarrow EA(k, n, p_{\mathsf{w}})\right] \leq 2 \exp\left(-2n\beta^2 \cdot \left(\frac{1 - \xi_r}{1 + \xi_r}\right)\right)$$

The final proof of minimum distance can then be achieved by taking a union bound over all $\vec{x} \in \{0, 1\}^k$. For $w = \Omega(\log(n))$, EA shows that with probability at least $1 - \frac{1}{poly(n)}$ the code has minimum distance $\Omega(n)$, Concretely, EA suggest the use of $w \approx 2.5 \ln n$ which translates to $w = 36$ for $k = 2^{20}$. Alternatively, setting $w = \Omega(\log^2(n))$ results in linear minimum distance except with negligible probability $1 - O(n^{-\log(n)})$.

In further pursuit of better concrete efficiency, [10] proposes a set of aggressive parameters where w is set to be relatively low. In particular, for code sizes $k \in \{2^{20}, 2^{25}, 2^{30}\}$, [10] proposes the use of $w \in \{7, 9, 11\}$. For each of these 9 combinations, [10] conjecture concrete lower bounds on the pseudo minimum distance of the code (see Fig. 9 [10]). The pseudo minimum distances being conjectured are significantly higher than what can be obtained from their proof of minimum distance. EA reconcile this difference by noting that their proof likely has some slack and with the notion of *pseudo minimum distance* of a code, see Sect. 2.4.

Building on the notion of pseudo minimum distance and intuition from their proof, [10] goes on to conjecture that if they have small pseudo minimum distance, then with high probability these will correspond to weight 1 messages, i.e. a row of $G = EA$ will have small weight. They then sample G 100 times and for $n \in \{2^9, 2^{10}, ..., 2^{15}\}$ and record the minimum weight row. From these they extrapolate that the minimum distance goes as δn where $\delta = 0.4633e^{-0.101 \log_2(n)}$ for $w = 7$. Moreover, they give an informal conjecture that finding a lower weight codeword is hard. Next we show that this is false. In particular, we give an improved analysis that shows how to find higher weight messages that result in lower weight codewords. For example, with a similar number of samples of G we were able to find codewords with a δ 30× smaller than conjectured.

4.2 Smaller Weight EA Codewords

We present a more general analysis that will in fact also apply to our construction. This analysis borrows ideas developed for proving that certain Turbocodes have sublinear distance [6]. Let m be the state size of the convolution, e.g. $m = 1$ for EA. The intuition of the analysis is that when w is small, one can find a small number of small regions over $[n]$ such that many rows of B are non-zero exclusively in the regions. The state space of the accumulator at the *end* of these w regions has a combined size of 2^{mw}. Therefore, if one can find mw rows of B that are non-zero exclusively in the regions, then there must exist as assignment to the corresponding message bits such that the state of the accumulator is zero at the end of these regions. Let x be zero outside this assignment and therefore the overall weight of the codeword can at most be the total size of these small regions. For the special case of an accumulator with $m = 1$, it suffices to find two rows of B that map to the same w regions. Next, we describe the process of finding these regions and show that it implies a sublinear minimum distance when w is a constant and m is sublinear. For $i \in [k], j \in [w]$, let $\sigma_j(i) \in [0, n)$ denote the j'th position that x_i was mapped to by B_i when using zero indexing. That is $B_{i,\sigma_j(i)+1} = 1$ and otherwise is zero. For some parameter $\beta \ll n$, divide the range $[n]$ up into β evenly sized regions, where each region has size $\mu = n/\beta$. For each row B_i, let us define its *signature* as $S_i = \{\sigma_1(i)/\mu, ..., \sigma_w(i)/\mu\}$. Let the domain of S_i be $\mathbb{S}$ and note that $|\mathbb{S}| \leq \beta^w$ since $\sigma_j(i) \in [0, \beta - 1]$. By the pigeon hole principle, there must exist a $U \subset [k], T \in \mathbb{S}$ such that $\forall u \in U, S_u = T$ and $|U| \geq k/\beta^w$. Wlog, let us assume $|T| = w$. Let $t_1, ..., t_w \in [n]$ index the end of these w regions in T. The state space of the convolution at these steps has a combined size of 2^{mw}. There are $2^{|U|}$ assignments to the message bits x_u for $u \in U$ and therefore if $|U| > mw$, then there must exist two distinct input strings $x, y \in \{0, 1\}^k$ which are zero outside U such that their states at steps

$t_1, ..., t_w$ are equal. $x + y$ is then encoded into a codeword with weight at most $\mu w = nw/\beta$. Therefore if we set

$$\beta = \left(\frac{k}{wm}\right)^{1/w} \implies |U| \geq \frac{k}{\left(\left(\frac{k}{wm}\right)^{1/w} - 1\right)^w} \geq \frac{k}{\left(\frac{k}{wm}\right)} = wm,$$

$|U|$ will be sufficiently large and therefore x, y must exist s.t. $\mathsf{HW}(x + y)$ is sublinear. Moreover, for EA, A is an accumulator where all transitions are the same and having $m = 1$, the size of U need only be 2. Concretely, for $k = 2^{20}, w = 7$ we can set $\beta = 7.5$ and obtain a minimum distance upper bound of δn where $\delta = 0.93$. Increasing k to 2^{30} and setting $\beta = 18.6$, we obtain $\delta = 0.38$. These upper bounds on δ are significantly larger than those suggested by the EA empirical analysis. However, these bounds hold with probability 1 and therefore are not tight on average.

To get more accurate average case bounds, we implement the analysis and find that δ decreases significantly. We extend the basic analysis above to consider signatures S_u that are almost equal to T. For example, if S_u is equal to T except in one position it is off by 1. By setting $\beta = 10$, we were able to find that most codes with $k = 2^{20}, w = 7$ have minimum distance at most $\delta = 0.01$ and as small as 0.002 over a few hundred trials. That is a reduction in minimum distance of $6\times$ to $30\times$ over what was reported by [10]. We observed similar trends for other parameters.

Looking forward, one should note that the effectiveness of this search falls off dramatically as we increase the state size m. Even for moderate such as $m = 25, w = 7$, the theoretical bound on δ passes 1 and therefore is not meaningful.

5   Expand Convolute Codes

In this section, we introduce expand-convolute codes, which are defined by the product $G = BC$ for a sparse expanding matrix B and a convolution matrix C. We conjecture that the LPN problem is hard to solve for this matrix ensemble and provide theoretical evidence for this conjecture by demonstrating that it resists attacks in the linear test framework.

5.1   Defining Expand Convolute Codes

Expand Matrix. For a ring $\mathcal{R}$ and parameters $w, k, n \in \mathbb{N}$ with $w \ll k \leq n$, an expanding matrix $B \in \mathcal{R}^{k \times n}$ is an $k \times n$ matrix over $\mathcal{R}$ with each row having (approximately) w non-zero entries. In our provable instantiation, every entry of B is sampled as $B_{i,j} \leftarrow \mathsf{Ber}_{p_w}(\mathcal{R})$, where $p_w = \frac{w}{n}$. Fixed row weight w is also conjectured to have similar minimum distance [10].

Convolute Matrix. For a ring $\mathcal{R}$ and parameters $m, n \in \mathbb{N}$ with $m \leq n$, a convolutional code generator matrix $C \in \mathcal{R}^{n \times n}$ is an $n \times n$ upper-triangular matrix over $\mathcal{R}$ with state size m. That is, C has 1's on its diagonal and entries below the diagonal being some linear combination of the following m columns. Concretely, for any $i \in [n]$, there exist $\alpha_{i,1}, \ldots, \alpha_{i,m} \in \mathcal{R}$ such that

$$C_{\cdot,i} = \vec{\mathrm{id}}_{i,n} + \sum_{j \in [m]} \alpha_{i,j} C_{\cdot,i+j}$$

where $\vec{\mathrm{id}}_{i,n}$ is the $n \times 1$ column vector over $\mathcal{R}$ whose i'th entry is 1 and all other entries are 0. In our provable instantiation, C is to sampled such that each $\alpha_{i,j} \leftarrow \mathsf{Ber}_{p_c}(\mathcal{R})$, for $p_c = \frac{1}{2}$. The expand convolute generator matrix is defined as $G = BC$. We denote this sampling procedure by $\mathsf{ECGen}(w, m, k, n, p_c, \mathcal{R})$.

5.2   The EC-LPN Assumption

In this work, we provide a new (dual) LPN-type assumption connected to expand convolute codes which we term EC-LPN. It is obtained by specializing Definition 1 to the case where the code generation algorithm samples $G \leftarrow \mathsf{ECGen}$.

Definition 2 (EC-LPN). *Let* $\mathcal{D}(\mathcal{R}) = \{\mathcal{D}_n(\mathcal{R})\}_{n \in \mathbb{N}}$ *denote a family of efficiently sampleable distributions over a ring* $\mathcal{R}$, *such that for any* $n \in \mathbb{N}$, $\mathsf{Im}(\mathcal{D}_n(\mathcal{R})) \subseteq \mathcal{R}^n$. *For a dimension* $k = k(\kappa)$, *number of samples* $n = n(\kappa)$, *expansion weight* $w = w(\kappa) \in [n]$, *state size* $m = m(\kappa) \in [n]$, *convolving density* $p_c = p_c(\kappa) \in [0,1]$ *and ring* $\mathcal{R} = \mathcal{R}(\kappa)$, *the* $(\mathcal{D}, \mathcal{R})$-*EC-LPN*$(w, m, k, n, p_c)$ *assumption states that*

$$\{(G, \vec{b}) \text{ s.t. } G \leftarrow \mathsf{ECGen}(w, m, k, n, p_c, \mathcal{R}), \vec{e} \leftarrow \mathcal{D}_n(\mathcal{R}), \vec{b} \leftarrow G\vec{e}\}$$
$$\overset{c}{\approx} \{(G, \vec{b}) \text{ s.t. } G \leftarrow \mathsf{ECGen}(w, m, k, n, p_c, \mathcal{R}), \vec{b} \leftarrow \mathcal{R}^k\}.$$

In order to provide evidence for the EC-LPN assumption, we will show that it is secure against linear tests, at least when $\mathcal{R} = \mathbb{F}_2$, $w, m = \Theta(\log n)$ and $p_c = \frac{1}{2}$. To do this, it suffices to show that the minimum distance of the expand convolute code is large (with high probability). To that end, we try to bound the probability that a message vector is mapped to a codeword of low weight using the roadmap below:

1. We consider a fixed message $\vec{x} \in \mathbb{F}_2^k$ and imagine revealing the coordinates of the random vector $\vec{x}G$ one at a time, where $G \leftarrow \mathsf{ECGen}$, and observe that this can be viewed as a random walk on a Markov chain (Sect. 5.2.1).
2. The state space of this Markov chain exactly corresponds to the various possible values of the internal state σ of the code. In general, this would be of size 2^m. However, when $p_c = \frac{1}{2}$, it turns out that the state space shrinks to be of size $m + 1$, which is easier to analyze (Sect. 5.2.2).
3. However, this Markov chain is not reversible and hence we are not in a position to apply the Hoeffding bound to characterize it (Sect. 5.2.3).
4. We instead resort to analyzing a much simpler reversible chain (Sect. 5.2.4 and Sect. 5.2.6), and comparing the behavior of the two chains via a coupling argument (Sect. 5.2.5).

We formalize all these details ahead, the security analysis in Sect. 5.2.7.

5.2.1 Understanding the Markov Chain

For parameters $w, m, k, n \in \mathbb{N}$ with $w, m, k \leq n$ and $0 \leq p_c \leq 1$, let $G = BC$ be $G \leftarrow \mathsf{ECGen}(w, m, k, n, p_c, \mathbb{F}_2)$. Consider a fixed message $\vec{x} \in \mathbb{F}_2^k$. Define $R = \frac{k}{n}$ to be the rate of the code. Consider the codeword $\vec{y} \in \mathbb{F}_2^n$ given by $\vec{y} = \vec{x}G$. We see that the bits of y can be computed iteratively (in reverse) as follows:

$$y_1 = \vec{x}B_{.,1}$$

$$y_i = \vec{x}B_{.,i} + \sum_{j \in [m]} \alpha_{i,j} y_{i+j} \qquad , \forall i \in [2, n]$$

We can view this as a recursive process with an internal state σ_i at step i given by $\vec{\sigma}_i = (y_{i-1}, \ldots, y_{i-m})$. In step 1, let $y_1 = \vec{x}B_{.,1}$ and add y_1 to $\vec{\sigma}_2$ as $\vec{\sigma}_2 = (0, \ldots, 0, y_1)$. In step $i \in [2, n]$, let $y_i = \vec{x}B_{.,i} + \tilde{\alpha}_i \cdot \vec{\sigma}_i$. Now, note that

$$\Pr[y_i = 1 | \vec{\sigma}_i] = \Pr_{B_{.,i}}[\vec{x}B_{.,i} = 0] \cdot \Pr_{\tilde{\alpha}_i}[\tilde{\alpha}_i \vec{\sigma}_i = 1] + \Pr_{B_{.,i}}[\vec{x}B_{.,i} = 1] \cdot \Pr_{\tilde{\alpha}_i}[\tilde{\alpha}_i \sigma_i = 0]$$

The above follows from a few observations. Firstly, B and C are sampled independently in the sampling of G, which means that $B_{.,i}$ and $\tilde{\alpha}_i$ are independent. Secondly, $\vec{\sigma}_i$ is independent of both $B_{.,i}$ and $\tilde{\alpha}_i$. To estimate the probabilities above, we recall the piling-up lemma below.

Lemma 2 (Piling-up Lemma). *For any $0 < q < \frac{1}{2}$ and $t \in \mathbb{N}$, given t random variables $(X_1, \ldots, X_t)$ that are i.i.d. according to Ber_q, it holds that*

$$Pr\left[\bigoplus_{i=1}^{t} X_i = 0\right] = \frac{1}{2} + \frac{(1 - 2q)^t}{2}$$

Let $r = \mathsf{HW}(\vec{x})$. By Lemma 2, $\Pr_{B_{.,i}}[\vec{x}B_{.,i} = 0] = \frac{1}{2} + \frac{(1-2p_w)^r}{2}$ where $p_w = \frac{w}{n}$. By Lemma 2, we also have that $\Pr_{\tilde{\alpha}_i}[\tilde{\alpha}_i \vec{\sigma}_i = 0] = \frac{1}{2}$ as $p_c = \frac{1}{2}$. We note, however, that the last equation above only holds as long as $\vec{\sigma}_i \neq (0, \ldots, 0)$. Indeed, $\Pr_{\tilde{\alpha}_i}[\tilde{\alpha}_i \sigma_i = 0] = 1$ if $\sigma_i = (0, \ldots, 0)$. Thus, $\Pr[y_i = 1 | \vec{\sigma}_i \neq 0] = \frac{1}{2}$ and $\Pr[y_i = 1 | \vec{\sigma}_i = 0] = \frac{1}{2} - \frac{(1-2p_w)^r}{2}$. We define $p_r := \frac{1}{2} - \frac{(1-2p_w)^r}{2}$.

We now begin to view the recursive encoding process described before as a walk on a Markov chain whose state space is the set of all possible values of the internal state σ. We begin at $\vec{\sigma}_1 = (0, \ldots, 0)$. The random walk of n steps then moves as $\vec{\sigma}_2, \ldots, \vec{\sigma}_n$. Since $\vec{\sigma}_i$ are binary vectors of size m, the size of the state space is 2^m. At any step $i \in [n]$, we move from $\vec{\sigma}_{i-1}$ to $\vec{\sigma}_i$. Note that given $\vec{\sigma}_{i-1}$, $\vec{\sigma}_i$ can be only one of two different values, depending on whether y_i is 0 or 1. We denote these two values by $\vec{\sigma}_i^{(0)}$ and $\vec{\sigma}_i^{(1)}$. From our above calculation,

$$\Pr\left[\vec{\sigma}_{i-1} \to \vec{\sigma}_i^{(1)} | \vec{\sigma}_{i-1} \neq 0\right] = \frac{1}{2}$$

$$\Pr\left[\vec{\sigma}_{i-1} \to \vec{\sigma}_i^{(1)} | \vec{\sigma}_{i-1} = 0\right] = p_r$$

5.2.2   Shrinking the Markov Chain

It turns out that the above Markov chain can be shrunk to have only $m+1$ states as opposed to 2^m. This can be done by combining states in the original chain. We note that this possibility arises specifically because we have considered the case of $p_c = \frac{1}{2}$ which induces a lot of symmetry in the transitions.

We can group states based on the suffix of the m bits representing the state. In particular, all states whose last bit is 1 can be combined. All states whose last two bits are 10 can be combined. All states whose last three bits are 100 can be combined. And so on, until the last remaining state is all zeros 0^m state. We will name these states $1, 0_1, 0_2, \ldots, 0_{m-1}, 0_m$. Note that there are $m + 1$ of them. This chain is described in Fig. 1. From our calculations above, we see that we have only three types of transitions:

$$\Pr\left[0_m \to 1\right] = p_r, \qquad \Pr\left[0_m \to 0_m\right] = 1 - p_r$$

and all other transitions are with probability $\frac{1}{2}$.

To see the correctness, consider the following. Suppose that at a certain point in the random walk, we have internal state σ whose last $\ell + 1$ bits are 10^ℓ and hence we are in the shrunk state 0_ℓ. After one more step in the walk, the internal state will be either $10^{\ell+1}$ or $10^\ell 1$. This means that we will either be in the shrunk state $0_{\ell+1}$ or 1. The transition probabilities of both of these are $\frac{1}{2}$, as long as $\ell < m$. If $\ell = m$, after one more step in the walk, the internal state will be either 0^m or $0^{m-1}1$. This means that we will either be in the shrunk state 0_m or 1. The transition probabilities of these are $1 - p_r$ and p_r respectively.

In other words, the Markov chain does not need to keep tract of the actual state of the convolution (with its 2^m possible states) but instead just if there has been a 1 transition in the last m transitions. Looking forward we will effectively shrink the chain to two via a Markov chain coupling.

5.2.3   Random Walks and Minimum Distance

Recall that our overall goal was to show that the minimum distance of G is large (with high probability) and that we are attempting to show this by arguing that for any message $\vec{x}$, the weight of $\vec{y} = \vec{x}G$ is large (with high probability). It is easy to see that the weight of $\vec{y}$ is the number of steps in the n step random walk in the Markov chain we have in Fig. 1 that we are in the state 1 (this is because the last bit of the state corresponds to the codeword bit). One strategy to estimate the amount of time we spend in a state in a random walk on a Markov chain is to estimate the stationary distribution of the chain and then use a concentration bound of some sort, for instance, the expander Hoeffding bound (Theorem 1). The Markov chain we have in Fig. 1 is unfortunately not reversible, and bounds for irreversible Markov chains are unfortunately not tight enough for our purposes. Therefore, we take a different approach.

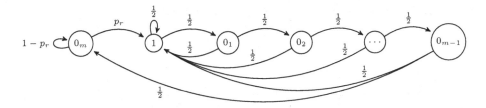

Fig. 1. The $m+1$ state Markov chain representing the encoding process.

5.2.4   A Reversible Markov Chain We will study a different, related, but reversible Markov chain described in Fig. 2. This chain has only two states, namely a 0 state and a ? state, and the following transition probabilities:

$$\Pr[0 \to 0] = 1 - p_r, \qquad \Pr[0 \to ?] = p_r$$

$$\Pr[? \to 0] = 2^{-(m+\theta_m)}, \qquad \Pr[? \to ?] = 1 - 2^{-(m+\theta_m)}$$

At a high level, the 0 state in this reversible chain is meant to capture the 0_m in our previous chain, and the ? state in the reversible chain is meant to *emulate* all the other states of the other chain. Unlike our previous shrinking, this isn't a transformation that preserves functionality. Indeed, the chains in Figs. 1 and 2 are different. However, posit that they are very closed related for the following reason. Firstly note that the states 0_m and 0 in the two chains are identical in a sense. Furthermore, in the chain in Fig. 1, the shortest path that takes you from 1 back to 0_m is a of length m, each transition having a probability of $\frac{1}{2}$, while in the chain in Fig. 2, the transition probability from ? to 0 is $2^{-(m+\theta_m)}$ for some $\theta_m > 0$. Thus, in this reversible Markov chain, leaving the 0 state is about as hard as in our other chain, and hence we hope that we can relate the time spent in states 1 and ? on random walks on the two chains. If we succeed in doing so, then we can use the expander Hoeffding bound to find the time spent in ? in the reversible chain and use that to argue about the time spent in 1 in the other chain, which is what we set out to do.

One final note before we move ahead is regarding the ?. Firstly, the reason for using ? instead of 1 is because the ? emulates states $1, 0_1, \ldots, 0_{m-1}$ in the other chain, and we are actually only interested in the time spent in 1 in the other chain. Looking ahead, we will come up with a way of estimating what fraction of time spent in ? will account for the time spent in 1.

5.2.5   Relating the Two Chains: A Coupling
Recall that our strategy is to relate the behavior of the irreversible chain in Figure 1 with that of the reversible chain in Figure 2, which is much easier to study.

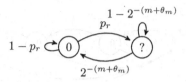

Fig. 2. The 2-state reversible chain which we compare to.

We will consider random walks on both of the Markov chains. In the case of the irreversible chain, we count the number of time steps spent in state 1. In the case of the reversible chain, every time we are in the ? state, we flip a coin and with probability $\frac{1}{2}$, we count it. That is, in expectation, we count approximately half the number of time steps spent in state ?. In this section, we will relate these counts by proving the theorem below.

Theorem 2. *Let n denote the length of the random walks performed on the chains in Figs. 1 and 2, where $m \geq \log n + 2$. Starting from state 0_m of the irreversible chain (Fig. 1), let X_i be the indicator of being in state 1 at step i. Starting from state 0 of the reversible chain (Fig. 2), let Y_i be the indicator of being in state ? at step i and then uniformly mapping ? to $\{0, 1\}$ (with probability $\frac{1}{2}$). Fix $\delta \in [0, 1]$ and $\hat{k} > 0$. Then, there exists $\theta_m \in [0, 1)$ such that*

$$\Pr\left[\sum_{i \in [n]} X_i \leq \delta n - \hat{k}(m-1)\right] \leq \frac{1}{1 - \exp\left(-\frac{\tilde{\delta}_r \hat{k}}{2 + \tilde{\delta}_r}\right)} \Pr\left[\sum_{i \in [n]} Y_i \leq \delta n\right]$$

where $\tilde{\delta}_r = \frac{\hat{k}}{n \cdot 2^{-(m+\theta_m)} \cdot p_r}$.

Conjecture: Theorem 2 holds for all $m \geq 2$.

In order to prove Theorem 2, we will induce a coupling on the random walks on the two Markov chains (Lemma 7). In order to perform the coupling, we walk through a series of lemmas that estimate the required probabilities. We begin with bounding the probability of having a run of length i without returning to the zero state (0 or 0_m)

Lemma 3 (Reversible Run of ?'s). *Starting from state ? in the reversible chain (Fig. 2), let q_i to be the probability of going to state 0 for the first time exactly at step $i + 1$. We have $q_i = \left(1 - 2^{-(m+\theta_m)}\right)^i \cdot 2^{-(m+\theta_m)}$*

Proof. Starting at state ?, the only such possible path stays in the ? for i steps and transitions from state ? to state 0 in the last step.   □

Lemma 4 (Irreversible Run of 1's). *Starting from state 1 in the irreversible chain (Fig. 1), let p_i to be the probability of going to state 0_m for the first time exactly at step $i + m$. Then for $i \in [n]$, $m \geq \log n + 2$ and $\theta_m = 0$,*

$$p_i < q_i$$

Conjecture: For all $m \geq 2$, there exists $\theta_m \in (0,1)$ such that for all $i \geq 1$,

$$\sum_{j \in [i]} p_j < \sum_{j \in [i]} q_j$$

Proof. See the full paper for proof.   □

We are now going to define our coupling. To aid in the description of the coupling, we first describe two processes (Processes 1 and 2) that will faithfully perform random walks on the two chains (Lemmas 5 and 6). In particular, we will first re-characterise the process of performing a random walk to sample the walk as several sub-walks (see full paper). First we will define the function S_0 that will sample the size of the sub-walk with state transitions $0_m \rightarrow \ldots \rightarrow 0_m \rightarrow 1$. Then we will define the function S_1 that will sample the size of the sub-walk with the form $1 \rightarrow \ldots \rightarrow 0_{m-1} \rightarrow 0_m$, that is, start at state 1 and end once state 0_m is reached. Such walks might visit state $1, 0_1, \ldots, 0_{m-1}$ many times but 0_m only once. Constructing the overall walk can then be achieved by alternating calls to S_0 and S_1 (along with sampling a specific sub-walks that is consistent with S_1).

Process 1 (Irreversible Chain). *For each $i \in \mathbb{N}$, let $\tau_i = (1 - p_r)^{i-1} p_r$ and $\eta_i = \sum_{j=1}^{i-1} \tau_j$. So, we have $\eta_1 = 0$, $\eta_2 = \tau_1$, $\eta_3 = \tau_1 + \tau_2$, ...,*

$$\sum_{i=1}^{\infty} \tau_i = p_r \sum_{i=0}^{\infty} (1 - p_r)^i = \frac{p_r}{1 - (1 - p_r)} = 1$$

That is, $\eta_i \rightarrow 1$ as $i \rightarrow \infty$. Also, η_i is trivially monotonically increasing. Define the monotonically increasing step function $S_0 : [0,1]_{\mathbb{R}} \rightarrow \mathbb{N}$ where $S_0(0) = 1$ and for $p \in (0,1]_{\mathbb{R}}$, $S_0(p) = k$ such that $p \in (\eta_k, \eta_{k+1}]$.
   Define $\zeta_1 = 0$ and $\zeta_i = \sum_{j=1}^{i-1} p_j$ for $i \in \mathbb{N}$. We also have

$$\sum_{j=1}^{\infty} p_i = 1$$

That is, $\zeta_i \rightarrow 1$ as $i \rightarrow \infty$. Also, ζ_i is trivially monotonically increasing. Define the monotonically increasing step function $S_1 : [0,1]_{\mathbb{R}} \rightarrow \mathbb{N}$ where $S_1(0) = m$ and $S_1(p) = k + m - 1$ such that $p \in (\zeta_k, \zeta_{k+1}]$.
   Let $\tilde{X}$ be the random variable denoting the output of Algorithm 1 (see full paper) which on input S_0, S_1 samples a walk by alternating calls to S_0, S_1 and constructing sub-walks of that length.

Lemma 5 (Random walk on irreversible Markov chain). *Let $\tilde{X}$ be the random variable described by Process 1. Then $\tilde{X}$ follows the same distribution as a random walk on the irreversible chain (Fig. 1).*

See full paper for a proof of Lemma 5.

Process 2 (Reversible Chain). *Let $S_0' = S_0$. Define $\iota_1 = 0$ and $\iota_i = \sum_{j=0}^{i-1} q_j$ for $i \in \mathbb{N}$. We also have $\sum_{j=1}^{\infty} q_j = 1$ That is, $\iota_i \to 1$ as $i \to \infty$. Also, ι_i is trivially monotonically increasing. Define the monotonically increasing step function $S_1' : [0,1]_{\mathbb{R}} \to \mathbb{N}$ where $S_1'(0) = 1$ and $S_1'(p) = k$ such that $p \in (\iota_k, \iota_{k+1}]$. Let $\tilde{Y}$ be the random variable denoting the output of Algorithm 2 (see full paper) on input S_0', S_1'.*

Lemma 6 (Walk on reversible chain). *Let $\tilde{Y}$ be the random variable described by Process 2. Then $\tilde{Y}$ follows the same distribution as a random walk on the reversible chain (Fig. 2), where the ?'s are set to 1 or 0 with probability $\frac{1}{2}$.*

Proof. Similar to the proof of Lemma 5.   □

We are now ready to define our coupling. We will essentially couple Process 1 and Process 2 that perform random walks on the irreversible and reversible chains, respectively, by having them use the same random coins, which we recall are $(\mathsf{p}_0, \ldots, \mathsf{p}_*), (\mathsf{q}_0, \ldots, \mathsf{q}_*)$. We will use this coupled way of producing random walks on the two chains to compare the hamming weights of the random walks produced by the two processes (Lemma 7). Since $S_0 = S_0'$, most of the work in the proof of Lemma 7 is with regard to relating S_1 and S_1'. In Fig. 3 we give an illustration of how S_1 and S_1' partition the $[0,1]$ interval, annotated with all the possible sub-walks associated with each of the segments. For example, in the segment $p \in (\iota_1, \iota_2]$, $S_1'(p) = 1$, and hence a sub-walk on the reversible chain would correspond to a single ?, while in the segment $p \in (\zeta_1, \zeta_2]$, $S_1(p) = m$, and hence a sub-walk on the irreversible chain would correspond to 10^{m-1}, i.e., the walk $1 \to 0_1 \to \ldots 0_{m-1} \to 0_m$.

Recall that $\iota_i = \sum_{j=1}^{i-1} q_j$ and $\zeta_i = \sum_{j=1}^{i-1} p_j$. From Lemma 4, for all $i \in [n]$, $m \geq \log n + 2$ and $\theta_m = 0$, $p_i < q_i$, and hence $\iota_i < \zeta_i$ for all $2 \leq i \leq n$ (from our conjecture, for all $m \geq 2$, there exists $\theta_m \in (0,1)$ such that for all $i \geq 1$, $\sum_{j \in [i]} p_j < \sum_{j \in [i]} q_j$, i.e., $\iota_i < \zeta_i$ for all $i \geq 2$). The dotted lines materialize the Lemma 4 (and our conjecture). This picture can be used to aid in our conclusion that $\forall p \in [0,1]$, $S_1(p) - (m-1) \geq S_1'(p)$ (where the $m-1$ corresponds to the additional 0^{m-1} that strings annotating the partition of S_1 have), although we will provide a formal proof of this in Lemma 7. This conclusion will allow us to prove that with high probability, the hamming weights of the random walks produced by the two processes cannot be that different, in particular, that the hamming weight of the random walk produced by Process 1, the process of interest, cannot be much smaller than the hamming weight of the random walk produced by Process 2, which we will lower bound in Sect. 5.2.6.

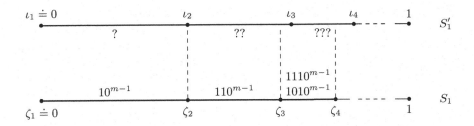

Fig. 3. Example of partitioning $[0, 1]$ by S_1 and S_1' *(not at scale).*

Lemma 7 (Coupling). *Consider the random variable Z which outputs $(Z_{\tilde{X}}, Z_{\tilde{Y}})$ by following Processes 1 and 2 (see full paper) run on the same randomness $p_0, \dots, p_*$ and $q_0, \dots, q_*$. Fix $\hat{k} > 0$. Define $\tilde{\delta}_r = \frac{\hat{k}}{n \cdot 2^{-m} \cdot p_r}$. Then, we have with probability at least $1 - \exp\left(-\frac{\tilde{\delta}_r \hat{k}}{2 + \tilde{\delta}_r}\right)$:*

$$HW(Z_{\tilde{X}}) \geq HW(Z_{\tilde{Y}}) - \hat{k}(m - 1)$$

Proof. The proof of this comes in two parts, first we show that the non-zero sub-walks (of length S_1, S_1') will have the property that the reversible chain (S_1') will be sufficiently shorter. As such, produce fewer ones. Secondly, because the reversible chain's non-zero sub-walks are shorter it will need to perform more sub-walks to reach a walk length of n. We show that this is unlikely to produce more than $k(m - 1)$ additional ones.

Note that the states 0_m and 0 are identical, and S_0 and S_0' are partitioned similarly. Since we use the same randomness for both, the draws on S_0 and S_0' will give the same number of 0s in both $Z_{\tilde{X}}$ and $Z_{\tilde{Y}}$. We also use the same randomness to determine the number of 1s inside the convolution (portion of the walk spent outside the 0_m state) in the irreversible chain and to decide on the real value of ? in the reversible chain. In particular, both processes sample the $\vec{t}$ vectors using randomness $q_1, \dots, q_*$. Therefore, if we concatenate all such $\vec{t}$, they will produce the same string with the exception that the irreversible chain sometimes overwrites the state as a one. However, this only increases the inequality and therefore safe to ignore.

We show that for the same p, we always have $S_1(p) \geq S_1'(p) + (m - 1)$. We have $|S_1(0)| \geq |S_1'(0)| + (m - 1)$ by definition. We have $S_1(p) = k + (m - 1)$ for k such that $p \in (\zeta_k, \zeta_{k+1}]$ and $S_1'(p) = k$ for k such that $p \in (\iota_k, \iota_{k+1}]$. Consider $p \in (\zeta_k, \zeta_{k+1}]$ for some $k \in \mathbb{N}$. The claim is true as long as $p \leq \iota_{k+1}$. We thus show that $\zeta_{k+1} \leq \iota_{k+1}$. We have

$$\zeta_{k+1} = \sum_{j=0}^{k-1} p_j < \sum_{j=0}^{k-1} q_j = \iota_{k+1}$$

as we can bound the sum term by term provably when $m \geq \log n + 2$ from Lemma 4, and bound the sums conjecturally when $m \geq 2$. We thus have that $\forall p, S_1(p) \geq S_1'(p) + (m - 1)$.

However, because a draw on S_1 outputs a sequence with a trailing $m - 1$ 0's, we may have more draws on S_1' than on S_1. Once the $Z_{\bar{X}}$ process has ended, it remains to draw for $Z_{\bar{Y}}$ a number of steps at most equal to the number of times we have reached state 1 for the first time starting from state 1 and going through 0 exactly once. Let us denote by E the Bernoulli random variable for which a success is looping through the simplified chain, we thus have $Pr[E] = \frac{p_r}{2^{m+\theta_m}}$. We now consider $\tilde{E}$ to be the binomial random variable which consists of n independent trials of E. We have $\mathbb{E}[\tilde{E}] = \mu = n2^{-(m+\theta_m)}p_r$. A Chernoff bound gives us that $Pr\left[\tilde{E} \geq (1 + \delta)\mu\right] \leq \exp\left(-\frac{\delta^2\mu}{2+\delta}\right)$. So by setting $\tilde{\delta}_r = \frac{\hat{k}}{\mu}$, we have

$$Pr\left[\tilde{E} \geq \mu + \hat{k}\right] \leq \exp\left(-\frac{\tilde{\delta}_r\hat{k}}{2 + \tilde{\delta}_r}\right)$$

□

We are now ready to prove Theorem 2. Due to lack of space, we defer the proof to the full paper.

5.2.6   Analysis of the Reversible Chain

We now formally analyze the behavior of a random walk on the reversible chain and the conversion of ?'s to 1's in order to bound $Pr\left[\sum_{i\in[n]} Y_i \leq \delta n\right]$. This gives rather tedious expressions that are hard to get a handle on analytically (but they do give significantly better parameters with empirical estimation). And so, we end this section by analyzing another reversible chain which gives bounds that are much more amenable to analytical manipulation.

Bounds for Empirical Estimation. We are trying to bound $Pr\left[\sum_{i\in[n]} Y_i \leq \delta n\right]$ from before, namely, the probability that a random walk on the reversible chain does not produce enough 1's. We bound this by first looking at the number of time steps spent in the ? state and then bounding how many of them get converted to 1's with probability $\frac{1}{2}$. It is easy to check that the 2-state chain is irreducible. One can easily estimate the stationary distribution $\vec{\pi}_r$ and the second largest eigenvalue λ_r as

$$\vec{\pi}_r = \left(\frac{2^{-(m+\theta_m)}}{p_r + 2^{-(m+\theta_m)}}, \frac{p_r}{p_r + 2^{-(m+\theta_m)}}\right)$$

$$\lambda_r = 1 - p_r - 2^{-(m+\theta_m)}$$

We can also then check the detailed balance conditions to ascertain that the chain is also reversible.

Time Spent in the ? State. To bound the time spent in the ? state, we use the corollary of the expander Hoeffding bound for non-uniform starting distributions. Note that the reversible chain is also finite and irreducible. Therefore, the expander Hoeffding bound is applicable. If we consider f such that $f(0) = 0$ and

$f(?) = 1$, $N_?$ counts the number of time steps the random walk spends in the ? state. In this case, $\mu_r = \tilde{\pi}_{r,?}$ and $\tilde{\lambda}_2 = \lambda_r$. We consider a random walk of length n that starts at the $x_0 = 0$ state. From the corollary of the expander Hoeffding bound, we have that for any $\epsilon > 0$,

$$\Pr[N_? < n\mu_r - \epsilon] \leq \left(1 + 2^{m+\theta_m} p_r\right) \exp\left(-2\frac{\epsilon^2}{n} \cdot \frac{1 - \lambda_r}{1 + \lambda_r}\right)$$

Let $\gamma \in [0, \mu_r)_{\mathbb{R}}$ be a parameter. Setting $\epsilon = (\mu_r - \gamma)n$, we have $\Pr[N_? \leq \gamma n] \leq \rho_{\gamma,r}$, where

$$\rho_{\gamma,r} = \left(1 + 2^{m+\theta_m} p_r\right) \exp\left(-2n\left(\frac{p_r}{p_r + 2^{-(m+\theta_m)}} - \gamma\right)^2 \cdot \frac{p_r + 2^{-(m+\theta_m)}}{2 - p_r - 2^{-(m+\theta_m)}}\right)$$

Converting ? 's to 1 's. Now, note that we convert the ?'s to 1's independently with probability $\frac{1}{2}$. Consider the experiment of tossing T independent coins and counting the number of heads ct. This process can be modeled as a Markov chain as described in Fig. 4. It is easy to check that this chain is irreducible. One can easily estimate the stationary distribution $\tilde{\pi}$ and the second largest eigenvalue λ as

$$\tilde{\pi} = \left(\frac{1}{2}, \frac{1}{2}\right), \quad \lambda = 0$$

We can also then check the detailed balance conditions to ascertain that the chain is also reversible. To bound the number of heads ct obtained while tossing T independent coins, we bound the time spent in the 1 state of the chain in Fig. 4 using the expander Hoeffding bound for the uniform starting distribution, which is its stationary distribution. Note that the reversible chain is also finite and irreducible. Therefore, the expander Hoeffding bound is applicable. If we consider f such that $f(0) = 0$ and $f(?) = 1$, S_T counts the number of time steps the random walk spends in the 1 state. In this case, $\mu_r = \tilde{\pi}_{r,?}$ and $\tilde{\lambda}_2 = \lambda_r$. We consider a random walk of length T that starts at a state x_0 sampled according to the uniform distribution, which is the stationary distribution of the chain. From the expander Hoeffding bound, we have that for any $\epsilon > 0$,

$$\Pr\left[S_T < \frac{T}{2} - \epsilon\right] \leq \exp\left(-2\frac{\epsilon^2}{T}\right)$$

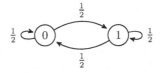

Fig. 4. The 2-state reversible chain that models coin flips.

Let $\beta \in [0, \frac{1}{2})_{\mathbb{R}}$ be a parameter. Let N_1 denote the number of time steps spent in the 1 state. Setting $\epsilon = (\frac{1}{2} - \beta)T$, we have

$$\Pr[N_1 \leq \beta T] \leq \exp\left(-2T\left(\frac{1}{2} - \beta\right)^2\right) = \chi_{\beta,T}$$

Putting It All Together. Thus far, we have estimated separately the probabilities that our random walk on the reversible chain spends too little time in the ? state, and that too few ? are converted into 1's. In theory, we could just add up these failure probabilities and wrap things up. However, this plays against us, particularly for concrete parameters. This is because in order to make the first failure probability, $\rho_{\gamma,r}$ small, we would have to keep γ small. Indeed, the lower γ is, the better our concentration bound works and the lower $\rho_{\gamma,r}$ will be. But, this is antithetical to what we would like in the case of trying to make the second probability, namely, the probability of converting too few ?'s to 1's, small. Indeed, $\Pr[N_1 \leq \beta T]$ will be smaller for larger T. This push and pull in the two failure probabilities makes it difficult to achieve good concrete parameters. To get around this issue, we note that simply adding the probabilities is in a sense performing a worst-case of worst-case analysis. Rather, we must perform a case-by-case analysis. For instance, for large γ, $\rho_{\gamma,r}$ will not be very small, but $\chi_{\beta,\gamma n}$ will be tiny. Similarly, on the other end, if γ is small, $\chi_{\beta,\gamma n}$ will not be very small, but $\rho_{\gamma,r}$ will be tiny. The intuition of the upcoming analysis is that we must leverage this tradeoff in order to estimate $\Pr\left[\sum_{i\in[n]} Y_i \leq \delta n\right]$ tightly.

We divide $[0, 1]$ into K bins of size $\frac{1}{K}$. We then use the law of total probability over the space of the K bins as follows. We have

$$\Pr\left[\sum_{i\in[n]} Y_i \leq \delta n\right] \leq \sum_{i\in[K]} \Pr\left[N_? \in \left[\frac{(i-1)n}{K}, \frac{in}{K}\right]\right] \cdot \Pr\left[N_1 \leq \left(\frac{\delta K}{i-1}\right)\frac{(i-1)n}{K}\right]$$

where $\Pr\left[N_1 \leq \left(\frac{\delta K}{i-1}\right)\frac{(i-1)n}{K}\right] \leq \chi_{\frac{\delta K}{i-1}, \frac{(i-1)n}{K}}$.

Now, we need to estimate $\Pr\left[N_? \in \left[\frac{(i-1)n}{K}, \frac{in}{K}\right]\right]$. A trivial bound would be

$$\Pr\left[N_? \in \left[\frac{(i-1)n}{K}, \frac{in}{K}\right]\right] \leq \Pr\left[N_? \leq \frac{in}{K}\right] = \rho_{\frac{i}{K}, r}$$

This would give us

$$\Pr\left[\sum_{i\in[n]} Y_i \leq \delta n\right] \leq \sum_{i\in[K]} \rho_{\frac{i}{K}, r} \chi_{\frac{\delta K}{i-1}, \frac{(i-1)n}{K}} = \epsilon_{\delta,r}$$

which would work, but we would like to do even better. Due to lack of space, we defer this analysis to the full paper.

Analytical Bounds. In order to estimate $\sum_{i\in[n]} Y_i$ analytically, we consider a different version of the reversible chain, one that implicitly converts ?'s to 0's and 1's independently with probability $\frac{1}{2}$. We present this chain in Fig. 5. It is easy to see that this 3-state chain is identical to the 2-state chain in Fig. 2 where we convert ?'s to 0's and 1's independently with probability $\frac{1}{2}$. Indeed, the 0 states are identical, and we have split up the ? state into two states, namely, $0_?$ and $1_?$ that share the probability masses of the ? state. Indeed, now $\sum_{i\in[n]} Y_i$ is equal to the time spent in the $1_?$ in this new 3-state chain, and we will estimate that using the expander Hoeffding bound.

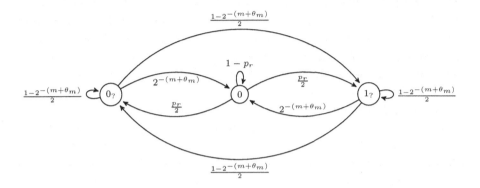

Fig. 5. The 3-state reversible chain which we compare to.

It is easy to check that this 3-state chain is irreducible. One can easily estimate the stationary distribution $\vec{\pi}_r$ and the second largest eigenvalue λ_r as

$$\vec{\pi}_r = \left(\frac{2^{-(m+\theta_m)}}{p_r + 2^{-(m+\theta_m)}}, \frac{1}{2} \cdot \frac{p_r}{p_r + 2^{-(m+\theta_m)}}, \frac{1}{2} \cdot \frac{p_r}{p_r + 2^{-(m+\theta_m)}} \right)$$

$$\lambda_r = 1 - p_r - 2^{-(m+\theta_m)}$$

We can also then check the detailed balance conditions to ascertain that the chain is also reversible. To bound the time spent in the $1_?$ state, we use the corollary of the expander Hoeffding bound for non-uniform starting distributions. Note that the reversible chain is also finite and irreducible. Therefore, the expander Hoeffding bound is applicable. If we consider f such that $f(0) = f(0_?) = 0$ and $f(1_?) = 1$, S_n counts the number of time steps the random walk spends in the $1_?$ state. In this case, $\mu_r = \vec{\pi}_{r,1_?}$ and $\tilde{\lambda}_2 = \lambda_r$. We consider a random walk of length n that starts at the $x_0 = 0$ state. From the corollary of the expander Hoeffding bound, we have that for any $\epsilon > 0$,

$$\Pr[S_n < n\mu_r - \epsilon] \le \left(1 + 2^{m+\theta_m} p_r\right) \exp\left(-2\frac{\epsilon^2}{n} \cdot \frac{1 - \lambda_r}{1 + \lambda_r} \right)$$

Setting $\epsilon = (\mu_r - \delta)n$, we have $\Pr\left[\sum_{i\in[n]} Y_i \le \delta n\right] \le \epsilon_{\delta,r}$, where

$$\epsilon_{\delta,r} = \left(1 + 2^{m+\theta_m} p_r\right) \exp\left(-2n \left(\frac{1}{2} \cdot \frac{p_r}{p_r + 2^{-(m+\theta_m)}} - \delta \right)^2 \cdot \frac{p_r + 2^{-(m+\theta_m)}}{2 - p_r - 2^{-(m+\theta_m)}} \right)$$

5.2.7 Completing the Security Analysis

In the previous section, we determined $\epsilon_{\delta,r}$ such that $\Pr\left[\sum_{i\in[n]} Y_i \leq \delta n\right] \leq \epsilon_{\delta,r}$. Notice that all the analysis up until now has been for a fixed hamming weight $r \in [k]$ (which we occasionally suppress in notion for readability). To complete the analysis, we must perform a union bound over all messages of all possible hamming weights. This way, we bound the probability that any message is mapped to a codeword of low hamming weight. This is because $\sum_{i\in[n]} X_i$ is exactly $\mathsf{HW}(\vec{y}) = \mathsf{HW}(\vec{x}G)$, and through Theorem 2, we have upper bounded $\Pr\left[\sum_{i\in[n]} X_i \leq \delta n - \hat{k}(m-1)\right]$ with $\Pr\left[\sum_{i\in[n]} Y_i \leq \delta n\right]$ (within a multiplicative factor). Since the code is linear, we are effectively bounding the probability that the code has low minimum distance.

Let $\mathsf{d}(G)$ be the minimum distance of $G \leftarrow \mathsf{ECGen}$. By Theorem 2,

$$\Pr[\mathsf{d}(G) < \delta n - \hat{k}(m-1)] \leq \sum_{r\in[k]} \binom{k}{r} \frac{1}{1 - \exp\left(-\frac{\tilde{\delta}_r \hat{k}}{2+\tilde{\delta}_r}\right)} \epsilon_{\delta,r}$$

where $\tilde{\delta}_r = \frac{\hat{k}}{n \cdot 2^{-(m+\theta_m)} \cdot p_r}$. Using our analytically friendly $\epsilon_{\delta,r}$ from before, we prove the following theorem.

Theorem 3. *Let $w, m, k, n \in \mathbb{N}$ with $w, m, k \leq n$. Define $R = \frac{k}{n}$. Fix $\delta \in [0,1]$ and $\hat{k} > 0$. We assume that the following hold: $w = C \ln n$ for some $C > 2$; $m = C_m \log n$ for some $C_m > 1$; $R \leq \frac{2}{e}$, $C\left(\frac{20}{41} - \delta\right)^2 > 2$ and $R < \frac{1}{\ln 2} \cdot \frac{e-1}{e+1}\left(\frac{20}{41} - \delta\right)^2$; $\hat{k} \geq n^{1-C_m}$ and $\hat{k} \geq 2\ln 2$.*
Then, for all sufficiently large n,

$$\Pr\left[\mathsf{d}(G) < \delta n - \hat{k}(m-1) : G \leftarrow \mathsf{ECGen}\left(w, m, k, n, \frac{1}{2}, \mathbb{F}_2\right)\right] \leq 2Rn^{-C\left(\frac{20}{41} - \delta\right)^2 + C_m + 3}$$

Proof. See the full paper for proof.   □

For computing our parameters, we use our tighter analysis from the previous section and empirically estimate the failure probabilities which appear in Table 1. It is evident that we compare rather favorably with [10] boasting much smaller failure probabilities for their choice as parameters, as well as for the enhanced choice of rate $R = \frac{1}{2}$. In the following sections we give additional ways of further improving our results.

Table 1. Comparing failure probabilities for $k = 2^{20}$ between our non-wrapping construction with $m = 25$ and [10]. For both constructions we have expected row weight $w = C \ln n$ and we assume we start at state 0 (see Sect. 5.2.8). For [10] we use δ and for ours $\tilde{\delta}$ such that $\tilde{\delta}n - \hat{k}(m-1) = \delta n$.

	δ	[10] $(R = \frac{1}{5})$	Ours $(R = \frac{1}{5})$	Ours $(R = \frac{1}{2})$
$C = 3$	0.005	$2.77 \cdot 10^{-4}$	$9.39 \cdot 10^{-12}$	$2.56 \cdot 10^{-10}$
	0.02	$1.08 \cdot 10^{-3}$	$3.31 \cdot 10^{-10}$	$7.32 \cdot 10^{-9}$
	0.05	$1.44 \cdot 10^{-2}$	$5.25 \cdot 10^{-8}$	$8.61 \cdot 10^{-7}$
$C = 2.5$	0.005	$1.23 \cdot 10^{-2}$	$1.32 \cdot 10^{-8}$	$2.32 \cdot 10^{-7}$
	0.02	$3.84 \cdot 10^{-2}$	$2.57 \cdot 10^{-7}$	$3.79 \cdot 10^{-6}$
	0.05	$3.58 \cdot 10^{-1}$	$1.75 \cdot 10^{-5}$	$2.01 \cdot 10^{-4}$
$C = 2.3$	0.005	$5.67 \cdot 10^{-2}$	$2.37 \cdot 10^{-7}$	$3.49 \cdot 10^{-6}$
	0.02	$1.65 \cdot 10^{-1}$	$3.65 \cdot 10^{-6}$	$4.57 \cdot 10^{-5}$
	0.05	1	$1.77 \cdot 10^{-4}$	$1.76 \cdot 10^{-3}$
$C = 1.5$	0.005	1	$2.26 \cdot 10^{-2}$	$1.648 \cdot 10^{-1}$
	0.02	1	$1.34 \cdot 10^{-1}$	$8.81 \cdot 10^{-1}$
	0.05	1	1	1

5.2.8 Initializing the Chain with the Stationary Distribution

The corollary of the Hoeffding bound that we apply introduces a noticeable significant multiplicative factor in the failure probability when the starting distribution is not the stationary distribution. When defining $G = BC$ where B is a sparse expander, the initial state of the accumulator is the zero state, which can be far from the stationary distribution due to having small mass on the zero state. One can include this discrepancy in the failure bound (Table 1). Alternatively, one can directly sample the initial state from the stationary distribution to improve the failure bounds (Table 2). Consider the related code $G' = B'C'$ where $B' = R || B$ and $R \in \{0,1\}^{k \times m}$ is the matrix that output the accumulator state after a sufficient number of iterations. In particular, let us assume we have an upper bound q on the number of steps it takes for a random walk on the Markov chain to converge from the zero state to the stationary distribution. We can then sample an expander $\hat{B} \in \{0,1\}^{k \times q}$ and a convolution $\hat{C} \in \{0,1\}^{q \times q}$ and define $R = \hat{B} \cdot \hat{C} \cdot (0^{q-m \times m} || I_m)$ That is, consider the process of performing q iterations of expand accumulate and outputting the state. For the convolution we use, the state is simply the last m outputs which can be obtained by multiplying the whole output by $(0^{q-m \times m} || I_m)$, where I_m is the identity matrix of size m. For irreducible, reversible Markov chains, it is known that the mixing time $\tau(\epsilon) \leq \frac{1}{1-\lambda_2} \ln \left(\frac{1}{\pi_* \epsilon} \right)$ for $\epsilon > 0$, where λ_2 is the second largest eigenvalue of the chain. The mixing time estimates the number of steps needed to get ϵ-close to the stationary distribution. The chains that we have analyzed using the Hoeffding bound are all irreducible, reversible, and have $\lambda_2 = 1 - p_r - 2^{-(m+\theta_m)}$ and $\pi_* = \frac{1}{1+2^m p_r}$. To obtain a failure probability of $2^{-\lambda}$, it suffices to perform

$q = \frac{m+\lambda}{p_r+2^{-(m+\theta m)}}$ additional iterations. Alternatively, we conjecture that sampling R as uniform should produce a similar distribution. These results appear in Table 2[3], where we can now achieve $C = 1.5$ and $R = \frac{4}{7} > \frac{1}{2}$.

Table 2. Comparing failure probabilities for $k = 2^{20}$ between our non-wrapping construction with $m = 25$ and [10]. For both constructions we have expected row weight $w = C \ln n$ and we assume we start in the stationary (see Sect. 5.2.8). For [10] we use δ and for ours $\tilde{\delta}$ such that $\tilde{\delta}n - \hat{k}(m - 1) = \delta n$.

	δ	[10] $(R = \frac{1}{5})$	Ours $(R = \frac{1}{5})$	Ours $(R = \frac{1}{2})$	Ours $(R = \frac{4}{7})$
$C = 3$	0.005	$1.39 \cdot 10^{-4}$	$6.28 \cdot 10^{-14}$	$7.30 \cdot 10^{-13}$	$1.06 \cdot 10^{-12}$
	0.02	$5.39 \cdot 10^{-4}$	$2.22 \cdot 10^{-12}$	$2.09 \cdot 10^{-11}$	$1.29 \cdot 10^{-11}$
	0.05	$7.21 \cdot 10^{-3}$	$3.51 \cdot 10^{-10}$	$2.46 \cdot 10^{-9}$	$1.53 \cdot 10^{-9}$
$C = 2.5$	0.005	$6.16 \cdot 10^{-3}$	$1.06 \cdot 10^{-10}$	$7.93 \cdot 10^{-10}$	$1.08 \cdot 10^{-9}$
	0.02	$1.92 \cdot 10^{-2}$	$2.06 \cdot 10^{-9}$	$1.30 \cdot 10^{-8}$	$8.68 \cdot 10^{-9}$
	0.05	$1.79 \cdot 10^{-1}$	$1.40 \cdot 10^{-7}$	$6.89 \cdot 10^{-7}$	$4.64 \cdot 10^{-7}$
$C = 2.3$	0.005	$2.84 \cdot 10^{-2}$	$2.07 \cdot 10^{-9}$	$1.30 \cdot 10^{-8}$	$1.72 \cdot 10^{-8}$
	0.02	$8.25 \cdot 10^{-2}$	$3.17 \cdot 10^{-8}$	$1.70 \cdot 10^{-7}$	$1.17 \cdot 10^{-7}$
	0.05	$7.81 \cdot 10^{-1}$	$1.54 \cdot 10^{-6}$	$6.56 \cdot 10^{-6}$	$4.56 \cdot 10^{-6}$
$C = 1.5$	0.005	1	$3.00 \cdot 10^{-4}$	$9.35 \cdot 10^{-4}$	$1.11 \cdot 10^{-3}$
	0.02	1	$1.78 \cdot 10^{-3}$	$5.01 \cdot 10^{-3}$	$3.91 \cdot 10^{-3}$
	0.05	1	$2.26 \cdot 10^{-2}$	$5.54 \cdot 10^{-2}$	$4.32 \cdot 10^{-2}$

5.3   Optimizations

We additionally present two optimizations to our code that are proven using natural extensions of our analysis. The first is referred to as wrapping where the last bit of the convolution is always set to one. This makes the convolution less likely to transition to the zero state. Secondly we show that our construction can naturally be made systematic with essentially no loss in minimum distance. This in turn improves our running by 1.5 times. See the full paper for details.

6   Implementation

We implement expand accumulate codes [10] (henceforth EA) and our new expand convolute codes and report on their running time performance. The code can be found in the libOTe repository. Running times were obtained on an Intel $i7$ laptop with 8GB of RAM. It is our intention to open-source the code after publication. Our conclusion is that our code is twice as fast as EA for comparable security. We choose to sample the expander B with fixed row weight w. We

---

[3] The $R = \frac{4}{7}$ case was analyzed with better precision, which explains why the failure probability is sometimes smaller than for smaller rate.

define the rate R of the code as $R = k/n$ and consider R for our code. The unique parameter for our code is the convolution state size m. We only implement the wrapping code where the last convolution state transition bit is always 1. We report our running times of the dual LPN encoding algorithms (i.e. $\bar{y} = G\bar{e}$) in Table 3 for $k = 2^{20}$ outputs. The running time of the associated PCG algorithms for generating OT and VOLE correlations [11,14] scales proportionally to the encoding times due to encoding being the primary overhead. For EA to provably have an acceptable probability of being linear minimum distance (see Table 1) they require an approximate expander weight of $w = 40$. In contrast, our code for the same distance δ, expander weight w, and state size $m = 16$ achieves a 10^{10} times smaller failure probability. Moreover, our code requires 548ms while EA requires 740ms. For a comparable failure probability, we can decrease w to $w = 21$ and obtain a resulting running time of 275ms, a reduction of 2.7×.

EA also proposes aggressive parameters where they set the expander weight w to be in the range of 7 to 11. For these parameters, they empirically estimate the (pseudo) minimums distance and conjecture that it should be hard to find smaller weight codewords. We showed that this is not the case (see 4.2) by finding moderately smaller codewords. However, this appears to only mildly decrease their security guarantees. For example, EA with $w = 7$, we were able to find a minimum distance $n\delta$ for δ as small as $\delta = 0.002$ compared to their conjectured $\delta = 0.06$. When applying the same techniques to our most aggressive parameters of $w = 5, m = 9$, we were able to find a distance as small as $\delta = 0.03$. However, with little runtime overhead, we suggest increasing the state size to $m = 25$ which increases the empirical minimum distance found to $\delta = 0.1$. Moreover, the running time of this code is 74ms compared to the empirically worse minimum distance code of $w = 7$ EA with 143ms. Finally, we also consider the systematic version of our code (see full paper) which gives a further 1.5× speedup with almost no change to minimum distance. In light of these results and Tables 2 and 3 in the full paper, we make the following suggestions for our *wrapping* convolution with $k < 2^{26}$: aggressive parameters $w = 5, m = 25$; moderate parameters $w = 21, m = 21$; conservative parameters $w = 41, m = 25$.

Table 3. The running time of our code in milliseconds compared to related art for $k = 2^{20}$. The codes have rate $R = k/n$, wrapping state size m, and expander weight w (not applicable to [11]). We give the running times for both non-systematic (non-sys) and systematic (sys) version of our codes.

Code	[11]	[10]	Ours non-sys			Ours sys		
m	-	1	9	17	25	9	17	25
w \ R	1/2	1/5		1/2			1/2	
5	2131	–	62	67	74	49	52	54
7		143	82	90	95	62	64	68
11		192	140	145	153	99	101	106
21		357	265	275*	283	175	190	203
41		740*	505	534	548	334	340	346

References

1. Aguilar-Melchor, C., Blazy, O., Deneuville, J.C., Gaborit, P., Zémor, G.: Efficient encryption from random Quasi-cyclic codes. IEEE TIT (2018)
2. Akavia, A., Bogdanov, A., Guo, S., Kamath, A., Rosen, A.: Candidate weak pseudorandom functions in $AC^0 \, o \, MOD_2$, pp. 251–260 (2014). https://doi.org/10.1145/2554797.2554821
3. Al Jabri, A.: A statistical decoding algorithm for general linear block codes (2001)
4. Alekhnovich, M.: More on average case vs approximation complexity, pp. 298–307 (2003). https://doi.org/10.1109/SFCS.2003.1238204
5. Aragon, N., et al.: Bike: bit flipping key encapsulation (2017)
6. Bazzi, L., Mahdian, M., Spielman, D.A.: The minimum distance of turbo-like codes. IEEE Trans. Inf. Theory **55**(1), 6–15 (2009)
7. Berrou, C., Glavieux, A.: Near optimum error correcting coding and decoding: turbo-codes. IEEE Trans. Commun. **44**(10), 1261–1271 (1996)
8. Blum, A., Furst, M.L., Kearns, M.J., Lipton, R.J.: Cryptographic primitives based on hard learning problems, pp. 278–291 (1994). https://doi.org/10.1007/3-540-48329-2_24
9. Bogdanov, A., Rosen, A.: Pseudorandom functions: three decades later. Cryptology ePrint Archive, Report 2017/652 (2017). https://eprint.iacr.org/2017/652
10. Boyle, E., et al.: Correlated pseudorandomness from expand-accumulate codes. In: CRYPTO (2022)
11. Boyle, E., et al.: Efficient two-round OT extension and silent non-interactive secure computation (2019)
12. Boyle, E., Couteau, G., Gilboa, N., Ishai, Y., Kohl, L., Scholl, P.: Efficient pseudorandom correlation generators: silent OT extension and more. Crypto (2019)
13. Carlos, A.M., et al.: Hamming quasi-cyclic (hqc) (2020)
14. Couteau, G., Rindal, P., Raghuraman, S.: Silver: Silent VOLE and oblivious transfer from hardness of decoding structured LDPC codes. In: CRYPTO (2021)
15. Debris-Alazard, T., Tillich, J.P.: Statistical decoding (2017)
16. Fossorier, M.P., Kobara, K., Imai, H.: Modeling bit flipping decoding based on nonorthogonal check sums with application to iterative decoding attack of McEliece cryptosystem (2006)
17. Lyubashevsky, V.: The parity problem in the presence of noise, decoding random linear codes, and the subset sum problem (2005)
18. McEliece, R.J.: A public-key cryptosystem based on algebraic (1978)
19. Prange, E.: The use of information sets in decoding cyclic codes (1962)
20. Stern, J.: A method for finding codewords of small weight (1988)
21. Vardy, A.: The intractability of computing the minimum distance of a code (1997)
22. Zichron, L.: Locally computable arithmetic pseudorandom generators (2017)

Proof Systems in the Discrete-Logarithm Setting

Correlation Intractability and SNARGs from Sub-exponential DDH

Arka Rai Choudhuri[1]([✉]) [iD], Sanjam Garg[1,2], Abhishek Jain[3], Zhengzhong Jin[4], and Jiaheng Zhang[2]

[1] NTT Research, Sunnyvale, USA
arkarai.choudhuri@ntt-research.com
[2] University of California Berkeley, Berkeley, USA
{sanjamg,jiaheng_zhang}@berkeley.edu
[3] Johns Hopkins University, Baltimore, USA
abhishek@cs.jhu.edu
[4] Massachusets Institute of Technology, Cambridge, USA
zzjin@mit.edu

Abstract. We provide the first constructions of SNARGs for Batch-NP and P based solely on the sub-exponential Decisional Diffie Hellman (DDH) assumption. Our schemes achieve poly-logarithmic proof sizes.

We obtain our results by following the correlation-intractability framework for secure instantiation of the Fiat-Shamir paradigm. The centerpiece of our results and of independent interest is a new construction of correlation-intractable hash functions for "small input" product relations verifiable in TC^0, based on sub-exponential DDH.

1 Introduction

Suppose a client wants to learn the outcome of some large computation, but it does not have sufficient resources to perform the computation. Instead, it delegates the computation to an untrusted server. The server returns the output to the client, together with a proof attesting to the correctness of the output. The key requirement is that the client should be able to verify the proof in time that is significantly less than performing the original computation.

Such proofs are referred to as succinct non-interactive arguments (SNARGs). The standard model for SNARGs includes an initial setup, where a common reference string (CRS) is sampled and distributed to the parties. The proof verification procedure is public, and the soundness guarantee is against computationally-bounded provers. Over the years, SNARGs have found numerous applications to the design of advanced cryptographic protocols, and recently seen adoption in the blockchain ecosystem (see, e.g., [1]).

SNARGs from Standard Assumptions. In this work, we focus on the goal of constructing SNARGs from standard cryptographic assumptions. In this direction, [25] demonstrated a barrier to constructing SNARGs for general NP languages based on falsifiable assumptions. To overcome this barrier, a recent line

© International Association for Cryptologic Research 2023
H. Handschuh and A. Lysyanskaya (Eds.): CRYPTO 2023, LNCS 14084, pp. 635–668, 2023.
https://doi.org/10.1007/978-3-031-38551-3_20

of work has focused on the classes P and Batch-NP, where the former refers to deterministic polynomial-time computations, and the latter refers to the setting where a prover wishes to prove multiple (i.e., a batch of) NP statements via a proof of size smaller than the combined witness length.[1] We provide a brief (and incomplete) summary of recent work below; see Sect. 1.2 for details:

- The works of [17,42] demonstrate that SNARGs for Batch–NP imply SNARGs for P.[2]
- SNARGs for Batch-NP (and hence, P) can be obtained from the learning with errors (LWE) assumption [17], decisional linear assumption over bilinear maps [53], and joint assumptions of quadratic residuosity and (sub-exponential) Decisional Diffie-Hellman (DDH) [16,33].

SNARGs based on the *sole* hardness of DDH, however, remain unknown. We ask:

Do there exist SNARGs for P and Batch-NP based on DDH?

Conceptually, this question contributes to a broader goal of understanding the relative power of the discrete-logarithm family of assumptions in cryptography. In recent years, a sequence of results have provided evidence that the gap between this family and the more powerful tools of lattices and bilinear maps is narrower than what was perceived previously. Some examples include succinct secure computation protocols [6], identity based encryption [20], and non-interactive zero-knowledge proofs [34] based on (sub-exponential) DDH. A positive resolution of our question would further consolidate this evidence.

Fiat-Shamir and Correlation Intractability. The aforementioned constructions of SNARGs (with the exception of [53]) rely on the Fiat-Shamir paradigm [22] — a generic method of round-collapsing public-coin interactive protocols. Given a public-coin interactive protocol, the Fiat-Shamir transformation replaces the verifier's messages with the hash of the protocol transcript so far.

The security of Fiat-Shamir was originally proven in the random oracle model. A recent line of work [7,9–11,18,30,31,34,41,52] has demonstrated that the Fiat-Shamir paradigm can be securely instantiated in the standard model using correlation intractable hash functions (CIH) [12]. Intuitively, CIH are hash functions whose input-output pairs behave in a similar way to a random function in that they do not satisfy any "bad" correlations. More specifically, a hash function family $\{\mathcal{H}_k\}_k$ is said to be correlation intractable for a relation class $\mathcal{R}$, if for any relation R in the relation class, given the hash key k to any efficient adversary, it is hard to find an input-output pair of the hash function that satisfies the relation R.

---

[1] SNARGs for Batch-NP are also referred to as non-interactive batch arguments (BARGs).

[2] Their transformations rely on the existence of somewhere extractable hash functions [32], which are known based on many standard assumptions, including the ones considered in this work.

A central goal in this line of research is to expand the class of relations that can be supported by CIH based on standard assumptions. Presently, the best known result is due to [31] who construct CIH for so-called *efficiently verifiable product relations*, based on LWE. This result forms a key ingredient in the work of [17] towards building SNARGs from LWE.

We ask whether such CIH can be constructed from other assumptions, and in particular, DDH:

Do there exist CIH *for efficiently verifiable product relations from* DDH?

While our primary interest is in using CIH for constructing SNARGs, we mention that recent works have explored many other applications of CIH, including counter-examples to zero-knowledge [31,41], non-interactive zero knowledge proofs [7,9,11,18,34,52], establishing hardness of complexity classes such as PPAD [15,35], verifiable delay functions [23,45], error-correcting codes [26], and more. Thus, the above question is of interest beyond our immediate goal.

1.1 Our Results

SNARGs for P & Batch-NP. We construct SNARGs for P and Batch-NP based on the sub-exponential hardness of DDH. Specifically, we assume that there exists a constant $c \in (0,1)$ such that for any non-uniform probabilistic adversary that runs in time $\lambda^{O((\log \log \lambda)^3)}$, its advantage in distinguishing a random tuple and a Diffie-Hellman tuple is at most $2^{-\lambda^c}$.[3]

Theorem 1 (Main Theorem, Informal). *Assuming sub-exponential hardness of* DDH, *there exist:*

- **SNARGs for Batch-NP:** *For every polynomial* $T = T(\lambda)$, *there exists a* SNARG *for proving validity of* T C-SAT *instances* $x_1, \cdots, x_T$ *w.r.t. circuit* C, *where the size of the CRS and proof is* $\mathsf{poly}(\log T, |C|, \lambda)$ *and the verification time is* $\mathsf{poly}(T, |x_i|, \lambda) + \mathsf{poly}(\log T, |C|, \lambda)$.
- **SNARGs for P:** *For every polynomial* $T = T(\lambda)$, *there exists a* SNARG *for* DTIME(T) *where the verifier running time, size of CRS and proof are all* $\mathsf{poly}(\log T, \lambda)$ *and the prover running time is* $\mathsf{poly}(T, \lambda)$.

Both our constructions require a common *random* string (i.e., transparent) setup. The proof-sizes and verifier runtimes match the best-known results (ignoring multiplicative overhead in security parameter).

To prove Theorem 1, we follow the framework of [17] (see Remark 1) that relies on two cryptographic tools: CIH for efficiently verifiable product relations, and somewhere-extractable hash (SEH) functions [32]. Along the way, we obtain new results on CIH and SEH. We discuss them next.

CIH for Efficiently Verifiable Product Relations. We first recall the definition of efficiently verifiable product relations [31]. Let t be an integer, and $\mathcal{X}$

---

[3] Our assumption is slightly stronger than the sub-exponential DDH assumption defined in [34] (and used in [16,33]) that only considers polynomial-time adversaries.

and $\mathcal{Y}$ be two sets of binary strings. We say that a relation $R \subseteq \mathcal{X} \times \mathcal{Y}^t$ is a product relation, if for every $x \in \mathcal{X}$, $R_x = \{\mathbf{y} \mid (x, \mathbf{y}) \in R\}$ can be expressed as the Cartesian product of a series of sets $S_1, S_2, \ldots, S_t$. Further, we say that R is efficiently verifiable, if there exists a circuit C such that for every $i \in [t]$, the set S_i contains exactly all $y_i \in \mathcal{Y}$ such that $C(x, y_i, i) = 1$.

We build CIH for product relations whose verification circuit C is in TC^0 (i.e., constant-depth threshold circuits), based on the sub-exponential DDH assumption. In fact, our construction can support slightly super-constant depth threshold circuits.

Theorem 2 (CIH for Product Relations, Informal). *Assuming the sub-exponential hardness of* DDH, *there exist correlation intractable hash functions for product relations verifiable by threshold circuits of depth $O(\log^* \lambda)$, with running time* $\mathsf{poly}(\lambda, n^{O(\log \log n)}, \log |\mathcal{Y}|)$, *where n is the bit-length of the input to the hash function and $\mathcal{Y}$ is the output space.*

Limitation: Small Inputs. The running time of our CIH is slightly super-polynomial in its input length. Hence, to obtain a polynomial-time hashing algorithm, our construction can only support inputs of size $\lambda^{O(1/\log \log \lambda)}$, which is a sub-polynomial in the security parameter λ. As we discuss later, this poses some additional challenges in adopting the framework of [17] towards proving Theorem 1, and we develop new tools to overcome these challenges.

Our Approach. The recent work of [31] constructed CIH for (all) efficiently verifiable product relations from LWE. At a high-level, their construction involves concatenating list-recoverable codes with CIH for efficiently searchable relations (that are known from LWE [52]). If we restrict ourselves to the sub-exponential DDH assumption, we only know CIH for searchable relations in TC^0 [34]. This means that a direct attempt to port the approach of [31] to the DDH-setting would require list-recoverable codes with *decoding* in TC^0. To the best of our knowledge, it is not known whether such codes exist. We therefore depart from the methodology of [31], and present a new approach to construct CIH for product relations (albeit with the "small input" restriction) without using coding-theory techniques.

Somewhere-Extractable Hash. Another key ingredient in the framework of [17] is the notion of somewhere extractable hash (SEH) with local openings [32]. Roughly speaking, a somewhere extractable hash is a keyed hash function with two indistinguishable modes: a normal mode and an extraction mode. In the extraction mode, the hash key is associated with an index i, and using a trapdoor, it is possible to extract the value committed at index i from the hash value. The local opening property requires that the committer can open to a particular bit in the committed message, with a succinct opening.

The limitations of our CIH for product relations in Theorem 2 dictate additional requirements on SEH for successfully adapting the framework of [17] to the DDH setting:

- TC^0 *extraction*: We require the extraction circuit of SEH to be in TC^0.
- *Large inputs*: We require an SEH that supports input-sizes super-polynomial in the security parameter. Crucially, we still require that the local openings are succinct.

Intuitively, the first property is required since our CIH can only support relations verifiable in TC^0. The second property is dictated by the running time limitation of our CIH; see Sect. 2 for details. We prove the following theorem:

Theorem 3 (Informal). *Assuming sub-exponential hardness of* DDH, *there exists a large-input somewhere extractable hash with local openings and extraction algorithm in* TC^0.

Constructing SEH with the above two properties based on (sub-exponential) DDH turns out to be quite challenging. A natural adaptation of the tree-based approach to construct SEH with local openings used in prior works does not simultaneously achieve both properties. A key technical ingredient in our solution is a new "Bulletproof-style" [5,8] succinct proof in the pre-processing model that can be round-collapsed in the standard model using our CIH.

1.2 Related Work

SNARGs. We start by providing a brief summary of recent work on SNARGs from falsifiable and standard assumptions. [38] gave the first construction of SNARGs for P and Batch-NP from a falsifiable, albeit non-standard assumption over bilinear maps. Independently, [9] constructed SNARGs for bounded-depth deterministic computations assuming the existence of fully homomorphic encryption with optimal circular security. The first construction of SNARGs based on standard assumptions (namely, sub-exponential LWE) was given by [35] for the class of bounded-depth deterministic computations.

Recently, [17] constructed SNARGs for P and Batch-NP with poly-logarithmic proof size from LWE. Their work, as well as [42], also provides a transformation from SNARGs for Batch-NP to SNARGs for P.[4] In a separate work, [16] constructed SNARGs for Batch-NP with proof size $\sqrt{k}$ for batch size k based on quadratic residuosity and sub-exponential DDH (or LWE). Subsequently, [33] improved the proof size to sublinear in k. More recently, [53] constructed SNARGs for Batch-NP with sublinear proof size based on the decisional linear assumption over bilinear maps. Finally, we mention very recent works that devise efficiency boosting compilers for SNARGs for Batch-NP: [19,51] construct rate-1 proofs with applications to incrementally verifiable computation, and [37] show how to achieve strong succinctness (i.e., poly-logarithmic proof size) from weak succinctness (i.e., proof size slightly smaller than the total witness length).

We conclude by mentioning three related lines of research: the first line of work, starting from [47], constructs SNARGs for NP (see, e.g., [2–4,24,27,28,44]) in the Random Oracle model or based on non-falsifiable assumptions [49]. This line of work has led to efficient constructions of SNARGs that are currently used in practice. The second line of work, starting from [39,40], constructs designated-verifier

---

[4] The transformation of [42] also works for NTISP, i.e., bounded-space NP.

SNARGs, where the verifier receives a secret key (sampled together with the common reference string) for verifying proofs. Finally, in the interactive setting (where the prover and the verifier exchange multiple messages), a long sequence of works, starting from [43], have constructed succinct argument and proof systems for various classes. We refer the reader to [17] for a more detailed overview.

CIH. A sequence of works [10,11,18,30,41] constructed CIH for various classes of (not necessarily efficiently searchable) relations from strong assumptions. Recently, [9] constructed CIH for all efficiently searchable relations from circular-secure fully homomorphic encryption, and subsequently, [52] improved the assumption to standard LWE. More recently, [7] constructed CIH for relations that can be approximated by constant-degreee polynomials (over $\mathbb{Z}_2$) based on various standard assumptions, and [34] constructed CIH for TC^0 based on sub-exponential DDH. Finally, [31] constructed CIH for efficiently verifiable product relations from LWE.

While the above works focus on single-input relations, a few works also study multi-input CIH for specific relations [30,46,54]. Finally, we mention [13,48] that investigate the minimal assumptions necessary for CIH.

Concurrent Work. In a concurrent work, Kalai, Lombardi and Vaikuntanathan [36] construct SNARGs for bounded-depth deterministic computations based on sub-exponential DDH (of the flavor considered in [34]). Unlike our work, they also prove the hardness of the complexity class PPAD under the same assumption.

2 Technical Overview

We now provide a technical overview of our results. We organize the discussion in two parts: (i) First, in Sect. 2.1, we describe our construction of CIH for "small input" product relations verifiable in TC^0; (ii) Next, in Sect. 2.2, we describe our constructions of SNARGs for Batch-NP and P. Along the way, we describe our new construction of somewhere extractable hash functions.

2.1 CIH for Product Relations

In this section, we describe the main ideas for the construction of CIH for product relations that are verifiable in TC^0. As noted earlier, our CIH suffers from a limitation that allows us to only support "small input" product relations, and we defer the discussion on how this limitation arises to the end of this section.

Notation. It will be useful to establish some notation for our discussions in this section. Specifically, for any binary relation $R \subseteq \mathcal{X} \times \mathcal{Y}$, we refer to $x \in \mathcal{X}$ as the *input*, and $y \in \mathcal{Y}$ as the *challenge*. We say that a challenge $y \in \mathcal{Y}$ is *bad* with respect to x, if $(x,y) \in R$.[5] We will often refer to such a y as a *witness* for x for the relation R.

---

[5] When x is clear from the context, we simply say that y is bad.

If we consider relations R where every x has a *unique* y such that $(x, y) \in R$, we can define a function f_R that maps x to its corresponding witness. We say that the relation is *searchable* in time T if f_R is computable in time T. In this work, we will require T to be a polynomial in the security parameter λ. Further, we will also consider relations searchable in TC^0, i.e. there exists a polynomial (in λ) size constant-depth threshold circuit C such that f_R is computable by C. A recent work of [34] constructed CIH for relations searchable in TC^0.

For any integer t, we say that a relation $R \subseteq \mathcal{X} \times \mathcal{Y}^t$ is a *product relation*, if for every $x \in \mathcal{X}$, $R_x = \{\mathbf{y} \mid (x, \mathbf{y}) \in R\}$ can be expressed as the Cartesian product of a series of sets $S_1, S_2, \ldots, S_t$. Further, we say that R is verifiable in TC^0, if there exists a constant-depth threshold circuit C such that for every $i \in [t]$, the set S_i contains exactly all $y_i \in \mathcal{Y}$ such that $C(x, y_i, i) = 1$. In this work, $\mathcal{Y}$, and thus each S_i, will be of size that is polynomial in λ.

CIH for Unique-Witness Product Relations. Starting from CIH for relations searchable in TC^0, we construct CIH for a seemingly weak class of product relations $R \subseteq \mathcal{X} \times \mathcal{Y}^t$ where (i) the challenge space $\mathcal{Y}$ has size polynomial in λ; (ii) for each x, there is a *unique* witness $\mathbf{y} \in \mathcal{Y}^t$ such that $R(x, \mathbf{y}) = 1$; and (iii) R is verifiable in TC^0. We start with a simple observation when $t = 1$ (single repetition), namely that the function $f_R : \mathcal{X} \to \mathcal{Y}$ that maps x to its unique witness y can be computed in TC^0. Specifically, to compute f_R, in parallel for every $y \in \mathcal{Y}$ we check if $C(x, y, 1) = 1$, and return the corresponding (unique) y such that the check passes. Since $|\mathcal{Y}|$ is polynomial in λ, the width of the aforementioned circuit remains polynomial, and the depth is (nearly) preserved from the verification circuit C. Given that C can be implemented in TC^0, f_R is searchable in TC^0. In fact this observation generalizes to $t > 1$ due to the existence of a unique witness, since there exists a function $f_R : \mathcal{X} \to \mathcal{Y}$ such that R is searchable by f_R. To see this, for each $i \in [t]$, we repeat in parallel the same process for the single repetition outputting in the i-th repetition y_i such that $C(x, y_i, i) = 1$. Again, if t is polynomial in λ, f_R can be implemented in TC^0.

Thus CIH for relations searchable in TC^0 imply CIH for unique-witness product relations verifiable in TC^0. Combining with the CIH from [34] for relations searchable in TC^0 based on sub-exponential DDH, we have a CIH from the same assumptions for unique-witness product relations verifiable in TC^0.

How to Handle Multiple Witnesses? In general product relations may not have unique witnesses, and it is unclear if the above ideas can be extended to work in this general setting. In fact, the relations of interest in this work fall into this category, and do *not* have unique witnesses. Hence, CIH for unique witness product relations are seemingly of limited interest.

Somewhat surprisingly, we will show that constructing CIH for non-unique-witness product relations can, in fact, be reduced to the task of constructing CIH for a *different but related* unique witness product relations.

For the remainder of this subsection, we first describe the key ideas for the simplified case of a single repetition ($t = 1$), and then show how one handles the more general setting.

Key Idea: Dividing the Challenges. The key idea in the transformation to a unique-witness relation is to treat the challenge string $y \in \mathcal{Y}$ as a binary string, and partition this binary string into d (equal sized) segments. For simplicity, in this overview, we think of the natural partition - if $\rho = \log_2 |\mathcal{Y}|/d$, the i-th segment $y_i := y[(i-1)\rho] \| \cdots \| y[i\rho - 1]$ where $y[j]$ indexes the j-th bit of y (in its binary representation). Given a relation $R \subseteq \mathcal{X} \times \mathcal{Y}$ that is verifiable in TC^0, we shall then define a family of relations $\{\widetilde{R}_i\}_{i \in [d]}$ such that the following two conditions hold: (i) each relation $\widetilde{R}_i$ is unique-witness verifiable in TC^0; and (ii) if $y \in \mathcal{Y}$ is a *bad* challenge for R, then there exists an $i \in [d]$ such that the i-th segment y_i in y is a bad challenge for $\widetilde{R}_i$. This presents a simple method for sampling the challenge - sample each y_i separately and define the challenge string y to be $y_1 \| \cdots \| y_d$. To ensure that the family of $\{\widetilde{R}_i\}_{i \in [d]}$ are indeed unique-witness, we will require that the segments are sampled sequentially, and more importantly, y_i will be defined to be a bad challenge (segment) for the i-th relation $\widetilde{R}_i$ with respect to both the input x *and* the $i - 1$ prefix of segments $y_1 \| \cdots \| y_{i-1}$.

We briefly describe the compilation of the above ideas via CIH hash function Hash. Specifically, let k_i correspond to a key of the hash function that is CIH for the relation $\widetilde{R}_i$ satisfying the aforementioned properties. To compute a challenge $y = y_1 \| \cdots \| y_d$, for each $i \in [d]$, the i-th segment is computed as $y_i := \mathsf{Hash}(\mathsf{k}_i, x, y_1, \cdots, y_{i-1})$. Each application of Hash (with the corresponding key) increases the selected prefix of the final challenge y by ρ bits. To see why this suffices to obtain correlation intractable for R, by property (ii) described above, any bad challenge y for x necessarily implies the existence of an i such that segment y_i is a bad challenge for $\widetilde{R}_i$, which would in turn violate the assumption that k_i was a key that was correlation-intractable for $\widetilde{R}_i$.

We now define the family of relations $\{\widetilde{R}_i\}_{i \in [d]}$, such that they satisfy the aforementioned properties. Given a relation $R \subseteq \mathcal{X} \times \mathcal{Y}$ that is verifiable in TC^0, for any string x we shall keep a count of the number of possible bad challenges y such that $(x, y) \in R$. In constructing the challenge y by incrementally extending the prefix, at the i-th extension of the prefix we can count the number of possible bad challenges y with prefix $y_1 \| \cdots \| y_{i-1}$. Given this prefix, an *i-th segment is bad* if the number of bad challenges with prefix $y_1 \| \cdots \| y_i$ is at least half the number of bad challenges with prefix $y_1 \| \cdots \| y_{i-1}$ (i.e. the i-th segment did not reduce the number of possible bad challenges by at least half). From the pigeonhole principle, it is easy to see that there can only be at most one such bad segment y_i for each i, satisfying the unique witness property as desired. We formalize this description below.

When we partition the challenge string into d segments, for each $i \in [d]$, let $\mathcal{Y}_i \in \{0,1\}^\rho$ where $\rho = \log_2 |\mathcal{Y}|/d$. Thus the challenge space $\mathcal{Y} = \mathcal{Y}_1 \times \cdots \times \mathcal{Y}_d$, and a challenge string y is computed as $y := y_1 \| \cdots \| y_d$ where for each i, $y_i \in \mathcal{Y}_i$. For a relation $R \subseteq \mathcal{X} \times \mathcal{Y}$, define a function BadCnt that counts the number of bad challenges given a prefix, i.e.

$$\mathsf{BadCnt}(x, y_1, y_2, \cdots, y_i) := \left| \{ \hat{y} \mid (x, \hat{y}) \in R \land (\hat{y}_1 = y_1) \land \cdots \land (\hat{y}_i = y_i) \} \right|.$$

This allows us to define for each $i \in [d]$, the relation $\widetilde{R}_i \subseteq (\mathcal{X} \times \mathcal{Y}_1 \times \cdots \times \mathcal{Y}_{i-1}) \times \mathcal{Y}_i$ where statements are of the form $(x, y_1, \cdots, y_{i-1})$ and witnesses of the form y_i. We define $\widetilde{R}_i$ via the set of witnesses for each input, i.e. $\forall x, y_1, \cdots, y_{i-1}$,

$$\widetilde{R}_{i,(x,y_1,\cdots,y_{i-1})} = \left\{ y_i \ \middle| \ \mathsf{BadCnt}(x, y_1, \ldots, y_{i-1}, y_i) > \mathsf{BadCnt}(x, y_1, \ldots, y_{i-1})/2 \right\}.$$

We provide an illustration of the above relation in Fig. 1, and subsequently prove the two properties for the family of relations $\{\widetilde{R}_i\}_{i \in [d]}$.

- We first show that for each $i \in [d]$, $\widetilde{R}_i$ is unique-witness verifiable in TC^0. From our discussion earlier, the uniqueness follows directly from the pigeonhole principle. Verifiability in TC^0 can be shown using ideas previously discussed - in parallel we for all challenges with prefix $y_1 \| \cdots \| y_{i-1}$ we verify using the TC^0 verification in R if they are each bad, and compare the sum with a similarly computed sum for challenges with prefix $y_1 \| \cdots \| y_i$. Since R is verifiable in TC^0, so is the above procedure since the total number of enumerated circuits run in parallel are polynomial in λ (as $|\mathcal{Y}|$ is polynomial in λ).
- Next we show a *cover claim* - for any input x, if y is a bad challenge, then there exists an $i \in [d]$ such that $y_i \in \widetilde{R}_{i,(x,y_1,\cdots,y_{i-1})}$ when y is parsed as $y_1 \| \cdots \| y_d$. We show this for any parameter d such that $2^d > \mathsf{BadCnt}(x)$. The proof proceeds by induction. If the $(d-1)$ parts $y_1, y_2, \ldots, y_{d-1}$ contain a bad challenge, then the claim of the existence of a bad segment is already true. Otherwise, by our definition of $\{\widetilde{R}_i\}_{i \in [d]}$, each selected segment $y_1, \cdots, y_{d-1}$ while extending the prefix (at least) halved the number of possible bad challenges. Thus, the number of possible challenges with prefix $y_1 \| \cdots \| y_{d-1}$ is $\mathsf{BadCnt}(x)/2^{d-1} \leq 1$. Since by assumption, y is bad, it must be the case that $y = y_1 \| \cdots \| y_d$ is indeed the last possible bad challenge identified above. Further given $y_1 \| \cdots \| y_{d-1}$ since y_d is the only choice in $\mathcal{Y}_d$ that leads to a bad challenge in R, it must be the case that y_d is a bad challenge for $\widetilde{R}_d$ (since $1 > (1/2)$).

Generalization to Product Relations. We now want to extend our prior discussion to the setting that $t > 1$, i.e. $R \subseteq \mathcal{X} \times \mathcal{Y}^t$. As with the case of $t = 1$, we partition the challenge into segments by partitioning the challenge for each repetition separately, and then grouping the i-th segment from each repetition to form a larger i-th segment. Specifically, for each $i \in [d]$, $\mathcal{Y}_i \in \{0,1\}^\rho$ where $\rho = \log_2 |\mathcal{Y}|/d$ and a challenge $\mathbf{y} \in \mathcal{Y}^t$ is partitioned into d segments $\mathbf{y} = \mathbf{y}_1 \| \cdots \| \mathbf{y}_d$ where $\mathbf{y}_i \in \mathcal{Y}_i^t$. As before, when compiled via the CIH, to compute a challenge $\mathbf{y} = \mathbf{y}_1 \| \cdots \| \mathbf{y}_d$, for each $i \in [d]$, the i-th segment is computed as $\mathbf{y}_i := \mathsf{Hash}(\mathsf{k}_i, x, \mathbf{y}_1, \cdots, \mathbf{y}_{i-1})$. We shall find it convenient to denote by $y_{i,j} \in \mathcal{Y}_i$ the i-th segment in the j-th repetition.

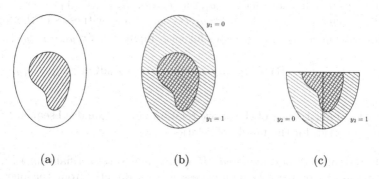

Fig. 1. The challenge space is $\{0,1\}^k$, and the set of bad challenges for a given input x over the entire challenge space is denoted in (a) by ▨ . For this illustration, we set $\rho = 1$ (i.e $d = k$) such that each i-th bit can be *bad* with respect to $\widetilde{R}_i$. In (b), by our new relation $\widetilde{R}_1$, $y_1 = 1$ is bad ▨ , whereas $y_1 = 0$ is not bad ▨ . In (c), conditioned on $y_1 = 1$, $y_2 = 1$ is bad, while $y_2 = 0$ is not bad - this follows from the fact that the there are more bad challenges with prefix 11 than there are with prefix 10.

For each $i \in [d]$, we now define $\widehat{R}_i \subseteq (\mathcal{X} \times \mathcal{Y}_1^t \times \cdots \times \mathcal{Y}_{i-1}^t) \times \mathcal{Y}_i^t$ with similar requirements to the single repetition setting - the relations must be unique witness product relations verifiable in TC^0, and that a bad challenge $\mathbf{y}$ can be mapped to a bad challenge in the family defined. In fact, we shall define $\widehat{R}_i$ to be the product of t relations $\widehat{R}_{i,1} \times \cdots \times \widehat{R}_{i,t}$ where $\forall x, \mathbf{y}_1, \cdots, \mathbf{y}_{i-1}$, $\widehat{R}_{i,j,(x,\mathbf{y}_1,\cdots,\mathbf{y}_{i-1})} := \widetilde{R}_{i,(y_{1,j},y_{2,j},\cdots,y_{i-1,j})}$ for $\widetilde{R}_i$ defined earlier in the $t = 1$ analysis. Since we have already previously argued that $\widetilde{R}_i$ is a unique-witness relation verifiable in TC^0, $\widehat{R}_i$ is thus a unique-witness *product* relation verifiable in TC^0.

All that is left to prove is the following covering claim - for any input x, if $\mathbf{y}$ is a bad challenge $(x, \mathbf{y}) \in R$, then there exists an $i \in [d]$ such that $\mathbf{y}_i \in \widehat{R}_{i,(x,\mathbf{y}_1,\cdots,\mathbf{y}_{i-1})}$ when $\mathbf{y}$ is parsed as $\mathbf{y}_1 \parallel \cdots \parallel \mathbf{y}_d$. For a product relation, $\mathbf{y}$ is *bad* if then every repetition is bad, i.e. for each $j \in [t]$, $\mathbf{y}_j$ is bad. In fact each repetition can be thought to be associated with its own family of relations - the j-th repetition is associated with $\{\widehat{R}_{i,j}\}_{i \in [d]}$. Utilizing our proof from the $t = 1$ setting, we would ideally like to claim is that there must exists an index $i^* \in [d]$ such that for every $j \in [t]$, $y_{i^*,j}$ is a bad challenge for $\widetilde{R}_{i^*,j}$ - this would conclude our proof in a manner similar to $t = 1$. Unfortunately, the only guarantee that our analysis for $t = 1$ provides is that every repetition j has a (possibly different) segment $i_j \in [d]$ such that $y_{i_j,j}$ is a bad challenge for $\widetilde{R}_{i_j,j}$. But from the pigeonhole principle, since there are only d segments but t repetitions, we can still make the claim that there must exists a segment $i^* \in [d]$ such that at least t/d of $(y_{i^*,1}, \cdots, y_{i^*,t})$ are bad (for their corresponding relation). This is illustrated in Fig. 2.

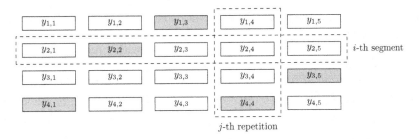

Fig. 2. For illustration, consider the setting where $t = 5$, and $d = 4$. Each column represents a parallel execution, where the concatenation of the values within the same column represents a *single element* of $\mathcal{Y}$. The shaded $y_{i,j}$ elements represent the bad elements, where a bad **y** guarantees the existence of (at least) one bad element per column. By the pigeonhole principle there exists a row (row 4 in the above example) that has at least $\lceil t/d \rceil$ bad elements.

Using the notion of α-approximate product relations introduced in [31], we define for each i, $\widehat{R}_i^\alpha$ to be the super-set of $\widehat{R}_i^\alpha$ containing all vectors all vectors $\mathbf{y}_i \in \mathcal{Y}_i^t$ such that at least $\alpha = (t/d)/t = 1/d$ fraction of repetitions are *bad*. Thus the above performed analysis states that for any input x, if **y** is a bad challenge $(x, \mathbf{y}) \in R$, then there exists an $i \in [d]$ such that $\mathbf{y}_i \in \widehat{R}_{i,(x,\mathbf{y}_1,\cdots,\mathbf{y}_{i-1})}^\alpha$.

The above analysis implies that to handle arbitrary product relations, we require CIH for α-approximate product relations. Fortunately, using small modifications to ideas already discussed, and by observing that the CIH in [34] can be extended to support α-approximate (searchable) relations, we can construct CIH for α-approximate product relations, and the above analysis already suffices. We refer the reader to the full version of the paper for the details.

Running Time of CIH. Let us now compute the running time of our CIH, since this will place some restrictions on the types of relations we can handle. Specifically, we shall show that the size of the challenge $\mathcal{Y}$ is at least d^d, where d is the number of partitions. In our construction, since CIH enumerates over all challenges in $\mathcal{Y}$, this directly translates to the running time of the CIH. Further, since in our earlier analysis we set $2^d > \mathsf{BadCnt}(x)$ for all x, for $\mathcal{Y}$ to be of polynomial size, the above bound on the size of $\mathcal{Y}$ restricts the number (and thus fraction) of bad challenges in a *single repetition* that we can handle. Specifically, for $\mathcal{Y}$ to be polynomial, the number of bad challenges must be bounded above by $\lambda^{O(1/\log\log\lambda)}$ which upper bounds the fraction of bad challenges in the entire challenge space to be $\lambda^{o(1)}/|\mathcal{Y}| = o(1)$. Unfortunately, for our applications we will need to support a larger fraction of bad challenges, and it remains an interesting open question if the above CIH can already be made sufficient for our application. Looking ahead we show that it is possible to support an arbitrary fraction of bad challenges at the cost of restricting the size of the input domain.

First, let us see how we derive this bound on the size of $\mathcal{Y}$. In fact, we prove that $\mathcal{Y}_i$ must of size at least d, which by definition of $\mathcal{Y}_i$ implies that $\mathcal{Y}$ is of size at least d^d. To see this, we make the observation that for a CIH for α-approximate relation $\widehat{R}_i^\alpha$ to exist, α needs to be at least $1/|\mathcal{Y}_i|$. To see why this is true, note that a uniform random challenge $y_i \leftarrow \mathcal{Y}_i$ is bad with probability $1/|\mathcal{Y}_i|$, by linearity of expectation there are on average $1/|\mathcal{Y}_i|$ fraction of bad coordinates in a random $\mathbf{y}_i \leftarrow \mathcal{Y}_i^t$. Thus, for a CIH to exist, the fraction parameter α (at the very least) needs to be non-trivial - i.e. $\alpha > 1/|\mathcal{Y}_i|$. Further, recall that in our covering claim, we set $\alpha = 1/d$. This implies that $|\mathcal{Y}_i|$ needs to be at least d.

Restricting to Small Inputs. To handle relations with an arbitrary fraction of bad challenges, we use ideas of sub-sampling present in [31]. By sub-sampling, we can reduce a relation with an arbitrary fraction of bad challenges to the setting we can handle - relations where the fraction of bad challenges are indeed $o(1)$. As previously alluded to, this comes at a cost, and we need to restrict the size of the input domain for $|\mathcal{Y}|$, and thus our CIH running time, to be polynomial in λ.

The key idea is to divide the t parallel execution into L blocks, where each block consists of $\ell = t/L$ parallel executions. For each of these L blocks, we sample a set of random challenges $\mathbf{q}_1, \mathbf{q}_2, \ldots, \mathbf{q}_N \leftarrow \mathcal{Y}^\ell$. We show that for any arbitrary fraction of bad challenges, we can set the parameter L appropriately (and invoke the union bound over all possible inputs $\mathcal{X}$) to argue that for any input, at most $\approx \log |\mathcal{X}|$ of those N challenges (i.e. $\log |\mathcal{X}|/N$) are bad. Now, one can view $[N]$ as a new challenge space, where each challenge is an index $i \in [N]$ mapping to the set of sampled challenges $\mathbf{q}_i$.

We can then define a new relation $R' \subseteq \mathcal{X} \times [N]^L$ that consists of all of the *bad* tuples of indices. Thus a CIH for R' implies a CIH for R since we simply select the corresponding $\mathbf{q}_i$ based on the output of the CIH for R'. Since we have sub-sampled to ensure that the fraction of bad challenges is small, we can utilize the observations in our earlier discussion. Specifically, if $B \approx \log |\mathcal{X}|$ is the number of bad challenges among the $\mathbf{q}_i$s, we get N to be of the form $(\log B)^{\log B}$. If we restrict the input domain such that $\log |\mathcal{X}| \leq \lambda^{O(1/\log\log\lambda)}$, both N and the running time of our CIH construction becomes polynomial in λ. For more details, see the full version of the paper.

2.2 SNARGs for P and Batch-NP

We now describe applications of our CIH to SNARGs for P and Batch-NP. Recent works of [17,42] demonstrated that SNARGs for Batch-NP are "complete" for constructing SNARGs for P. In fact, [17] reduces the task of constructing SNARGs for DTIME(T) computation to constructing SNARGs for a special Batch-NP language called the *batch-index* language. A batch-index language is associated with a circuit C where the instances are simply indices i that can be represented in $\log k$ bits for a batch of size k. Unlike Batch-NP where the verifier has to read all the instance, one can make a strong verification requirement from SNARGs for batch-index language, namely, that the *total* verification time (including the time to "read" instances) is poly($\lambda, \log k, |C|$).

In the rest of this subsection, we restrict our attention to constructing SNARGs for batch-index.

A Brief Primer on [17]. We start by describing the high level paradigm in [17] for the construction of SNARGs for batch index. Our construction will be identical except for a few key changes that we shall explain later. A reader who is familiar with the prior work can choose to skip this discussion.

PCP Generation: Using witnesses $\omega_1, \cdots, \omega_T$, the prover generates T PCPs $\pi_1, \cdots, \pi_T$.

Succinct Column-wise Hash: The prover arranges $\pi_1, \cdots, \pi_T \in \{0,1\}^\ell$ into rows, and hashes them in a column-wise manner (i.e. ℓ hashes each hashing vectors of length T) using a somewhere extractable hash (to be discussed shortly). Let this hash be denoted by $c = (c_1, \cdots, c_\ell)$.

Challenge Generation via CIH: The prover applies the CIH (different from the hash scheme in the previous step) to (C, c) to generate the PCP queries Q.

Two-to-one Compression: The prover then defines a new circuit C' for the index language that hardcodes the $\{c_j\}_{j \in Q}$ (the hash c restricted only on "columns" specified by Q), and takes as input index i and witness ω_i - where ω_i corresponds to the *local* openings of $\{\pi_{i,j}\}_{j \in Q}$. C' checks (i) that the local openings verify; and (ii) the PCP verifier accepts given the PCP responses $\{\pi_{i,j}\}_{j \in Q}$. The prover further reduces the total number of (index) instances from T to $T/2$ applying a 2-to-1 reduction to C' by defining a circuit $C''(i, (\omega_{2i-1}, \omega_{2i})) := C'(2i-1, \omega_{2i-1}) \wedge C'(2i-1, \omega_{2i-1})$.

Recursion: The prover finally recurses by repeating the above steps, sending witnesses in the clear when the witnesses are small enough.

To ensure that the recursion reduces the size of the circuit and the number of instances, one needs to demonstrate that C'' defined above is "small" with respect to C. The size of C' (and thus of C'') is determined by: (i) size of the hash and local opening; and (ii) size of the PCP verification circuit.

For (1), [17] used a somewhere extractable hash (SEH) [32] with local openings. In such a hashing scheme, a trapdoor td is generated along with the key K on input i^* — td can then be used to extract, from c, the uniquely value at index i^* where the resultant hash is c.[6] The SEH used in the aforementioned work has hash size, local opening size and verification time all to be polylogarithmic in T. For (2), [17] observed that existing PCP schemes can be viewed in an offline/online verification model where the offline verifier pre-processes the circuit C to produce PCP queries and a small state st such that the online verification depends only polylogarithmically on T and $|C|$ given the PCP responses.

It was shown in [17] that CIH for *efficiently verifiable product relations* (as defined in [31]) suffices to prove security of the above described SNARG for batch index. Such a CIH was instantiated from the work of [31] assuming the hardness of LWE.

---

[6] An SEH implies *somewhere binding* at the same index.

Key Challenges. The [17] template uses two cryptographic primitives based on LWE, namely, SEH and CIH. Thus, a natural idea to port the [17] approach to our DDH-setting is as follows: replace the CIH used in [17] with our new CIH from Sect. 2.1, and instantiate the SEH used in their scheme with one based on DDH [21,50].

This simple strategy, however, does not work right out of the box due to the limitations of our new CIH. We describe the key challenges that arise in the process:

Input Size: As described in Sect. 2.1, our new CIH is restricted by its input size being *small*, i.e. for security parameter λ, the input size is bounded by $\mathsf{poly}(\lambda_0)$ where $\lambda_0^{O(\log \log \lambda_0)} = \lambda$. From the above description of the [17] protocol, we have that the input to the CIH consists of the circuit C (for the batch-index language) and the output of SEH. This means that *both the circuit size and the hash size are bounded by* $\mathsf{poly}(\lambda_0)$.

  1. **Bound on size of C:** The restriction on C is pretty significant since for obtaining a general result, we would like to allow for circuits that are of size $\mathsf{poly}(\lambda) = \mathsf{poly}(\lambda_0^{O(\log \log \lambda_0)})$.
     Despite this seemingly strong restriction, we show that: **(i)** It is already sufficient to achieve SNARGs for P — intuitively, this is because the circuit for batch-index language defined in the transformation from SNARGs for batch-index to SNARGs for P [17] are already "small"; **(ii)** With the help of SEH, we can bootstrap SNARGs for *small circuit* batch-index languages to achieve SNARGs for general batch-index languages. At a high level, we split the large circuit C into many smaller components $C_1, \cdots, C_\ell$ such that each such component is of size $\mathsf{poly}(\lambda_0)$, and send ℓ proofs for each corresponding circuit. Care must be taken to ensure that the smaller components are not disparate, but in fact "connect" to verify a batch claim about the original circuit C. We do not discuss the details in this overview and refer the reader to the full version of our paper.
  2. **Bound on hash size:** The bound on the hash size necessitates that we must set the security parameter of SEH to be λ_0. Note, however, that the number of instances T remains polynomial in λ. This means that the SEH must support **large inputs**, i.e. *inputs that are of length super-polynomial in its security parameter*.
     Further, recall that in the [17] template discussed earlier, the size of the circuit C' — that is recursed in the next step — is determined by the size of the local opening of SEH. Putting this together with the bound on the circuit size, we have the restriction that the size of the local opening of SEH can depend on $\mathsf{poly}(\lambda_0)$ and only poly-logarithmically on the large input length.

Verification in TC^0: In addition to the restriction on input size, for a secure application of our new CIH, we require that the bad challenge relation circuit be verifiable in TC^0. The bad challenge relation circuit involves the following key steps:

1. **Extraction of PCP:** The PCP is extracted from the SEH.
2. **PCP Verification:** The online verification of the PCP is executed given its queries.
3. **Checking satisfiability of the circuit:** To ascertain if the i-th instance is true, check circuit satisfiability of C using witness extracted from the PCP.

Thus, we require that each of the above three steps can be performed in TC^0. By choosing an appropriate field, we extend the analysis of [17] to show that both the extraction of the witness from the PCP and online PCP verification can be computed in TC^0. Further, given a witness corresponding to a circuit C, checking if the circuit is satisfiable can be done in TC^0 by checking all the gates in parallel. Thus steps 2 and 3 can be performed in TC^0. This leaves us with step 1, namely, we need SEH that supports **extraction in** TC^0.

In summary, we are left with the task of constructing an SEH with the following key requirements:

– **Large Inputs:** The SEH must support inputs of length super-polynomial in the security parameter, but nevertheless have succinct local openings.
– TC^0 **extraction:** The SEH must support extraction in TC^0.

In the remainder of this overview, we describe the key ideas underlying our construction of such a SEH based on sub-exponential DDH.

Remark 1. Before we proceed, we note that a recent work of Waters and Wu [53] construct SNARGs for P and Batch-NP based on the decisional linear assumption over bilinear maps. Notably, their work avoids the use of correlation intractable hash functions altogether, and thus provides a compelling alternative to [17] for constructing SNARGs. While it is desirable to extend their framework to rely on other assumptions (such as DDH), we believe there are are technical barriers to this approach. The Waters-Wu framework builds upon techniques previously used for constructing NIZKs from bilinear maps [29]. Till date, there is no known analogue of those techniques in other settings without pairings. Indeed, for similar reasons, known constructions of NIZKs from DDH [34] (and LWE [9,52]) rely on the route of CIH.

2.3   Somewhere Extractable Hash from DDH

We start by recalling prior approaches to constructing SEH. We then discuss the main technical challenge towards achieving the two properties we require. Finally, we present our solution.

Background. We follow the standard *tree-based approach* from prior work for constructing SEH with short local openings. To hash a vector of length T, the idea is to build a hash tree (akin to a Merkle tree) with the leaves corresponding to the vector being hashed, and the root corresponding to the resultant hash. We shall refer to the hash used in the construction of the tree to be the *base hash*, and the overall construction simply by SEH. The local opening to a bit (a leaf in the tree) consists of all siblings nodes on the path from the leaf to the root, where verification involves recomputing the hash values along the path from the claimed leaf to the root (using the siblings present in the proof) and comparing against the stored root. Thus the size of the opening is determined by the number of siblings and the depth of the tree, both of which are fixed for a given vector length T by the arity (or degree) of the tree. Thus, if we were to set the arity of the tree to be bounded by $\mathsf{poly}(\lambda_0)$, where λ_0 is the security parameter of SEH, the proof of local opening would be bounded by $\mathsf{poly}(\lambda_0, \log_{\lambda_0} T)$.

Main Challenge. Recall that our requirements from SEH are: (1) extraction in TC^0, (2) support for inputs of length super-polynomial in the security parameter λ_0, while still allowing for short local openings.

Let us consider the first requirement. In the context of tree based construction, extraction from SEH translates to the extraction of a leaf value from the hashed root. The extraction procedure (on input the trapdoor) starts from the root and works down to the (desired) leaf by extracting each hash value along the path, one level at a time. The number of sequential steps in the extraction procedure is proportional to the depth of the tree. Thus for extraction to be computable in TC^0, the depth of the tree must be a *constant*.

Now, let us consider the second requirement on SEH. Note that in order to support large inputs, we can no longer set the arity of the tree to be $\mathsf{poly}(\lambda_0)$. This follows from the fact that for a constant depth tree with arity $\mathsf{poly}(\lambda_0)$, the total number of leaves is limited to be polynomial in λ_0. One way to circumvent this, and support inputs of size $\mathsf{poly}(\lambda)$, would be to set the arity in the tree based construction to be $\mathsf{poly}(\lambda) = \mathsf{poly}(\lambda_0^{O(\log \log \lambda_0)})$. While this does support large inputs in constant depth, a local opening, which constitutes sending all the siblings along the path is now of size $\mathsf{poly}(\lambda_0^{O(\log \log \lambda_0)})$, i.e. we lose succinctness. This constitutes the main challenge that we need to overcome in our construction, namely, devising succinct local openings when the arity of the tree is large.

Sibling Compression. Our key idea is to compress the large number of siblings into a single "effective" sibling. The effective sibling must allow for recomputation of the hash, but it must not be possible to manipulate the effective sibling to produce inconsistent local openings.

To explain the idea, we first describe the *base hash* scheme that we use in our tree based construction. The scheme closely follows the construction of trapdoor hash functions based on DDH [21]. The hash function Hash takes as input $\mathbf{m} \in \{0,1\}^N$, a key $K \in \mathbb{G}^{2 \times N}$ and produces a hash output $c \in \mathbb{G}^2$. To generate a hash key that allows for somewhere extraction of the input bit at index i^{*}[7], the key generation, hashing and extraction algorithms are described below

---

[7] We refer the reader to the technical sections for discussion on the extension of the somewhere extraction property to multiple bits.

Key Generation: On input i^*, the key K is generated as

$$K = \begin{bmatrix} g_1 \ g_2 \ \cdots \ g_N \\ h_1 \ h_2 \ \cdots \ h_N \end{bmatrix} = \begin{bmatrix} g_1 \ \cdots \ g_{i^*-1} & g_{i^*} & g_{i^*+1} \ \cdots \ g_N \\ g_1^s \ \cdots \ g_{i^*-1}^s & \boxed{g_{i^*}^s \cdot g} & g_{i^*+1}^s \ \cdots \ g_N^s \end{bmatrix}$$

where for every $j \in \{1, \cdots, N\}$, g_j is a random group element from $\mathbb{G}$, g is the group generator, and s is randomly sampled. The trapdoor for this generated key is s. At a high level, h_j at every position other than i^* is computed by the exponentiation of g_j to the trapdoor s, whereas h_{i^*} has an additional product term of g. This structure will be exploited for the extraction.

Hashing: On input $\mathbf{m} = (m_1, \cdots, m_N) \in \{0,1\}^N$, and key K, compute the hash $c = (g', h') = \mathsf{Hash}(K, \mathbf{m})$ as $g' := \prod_{j=1}^N g_j^{m_j}$ and $h' := \prod_{j=1}^N h_j^{m_j}$.

Extraction: On input a hash $c = (g', h')$ and trapdoor s, output m_{i^*} to be 0 if $g'^s = h'$, and 1 otherwise. Intuitively, the correctness of extraction follows from the fact that if m_{i^*} is 0, the additional g term in h_{i^*} will disappear.

Assuming DDH, one can argue (as in [21]) that the index i^* is hidden in the generated hash key K. Before we discuss the local opening properties of the base scheme, note that the extraction involves computing a group exponentiation g'^s. With an appropriate pre-processing of g', the exponentiation, and thus the extraction can be computed in TC^0, and we refer the reader to the technical section for details.

Now, given a hash value c, instead of computing the naive local opening to x_{i^*} for some index i^* (of size proportional to the arity of the tree), we compute an "effective" sibling $(g'', h'') = (\prod_{j \neq i^*} g_j^{\tilde{x}_j}, \prod_{j \neq i^*} h_j^{\tilde{x}_j})$, and use this as the proof of local opening to x_{i^*}. Given this effective sibling, the verification of local opening now reduces to checking if $c = (g', h')$ is the same as $(g_{i^*}^{x_{i^*}} \cdot g'', h_{i^*}^{x_{i^*}} \cdot h'')$.

While the above effective sibling idea does indeed satisfy correctness and reduce the cost of local opening to be of size $O(1)$, the security of local opening breaks down. Let us elaborate. An adversary trying to cheat by sending inconsistent local opening can efficiently compute two distinct (pairs of) effective siblings (g'', h'') and $(\tilde{g}'', \tilde{h}'')$. Specifically, given a hash value (g', h'), if an adversary wants to open index i^* of the input to two *distinct* values, x_{i^*} and $\tilde{x}_{i^*}$, then it can compute the effective siblings as

$$(g'' = g'/g_{i^*}^{x_{i^*}}, h'' = h'/h_{i^*}^{x_{i^*}}) \text{ and } (\tilde{g}'' = g'/g_{i^*}^{\tilde{x}_{i^*}}, \tilde{h}'' = h'/h_{i^*}^{\tilde{x}_{i^*}}).$$

The computation of these inconsistent openings are efficient, and it is easy to see from construction that both proofs verify, allowing for openings to different values. Thus the effective sibling, as defined, cannot function as a proof of local opening since there is no guarantee that the extracted value corresponds to the value that an adversary provides a local opening for.

Proofs of Well-Formedness. To address this problem, we modify the above construction such that a local opening now includes a succinct proof (of size $\mathrm{poly}(\log N)$) that the "effective" sibling was computed correctly, i.e. a proof of well-formedness of the effective sibling. At a high level, the security of the proof system would allow us to reduce the security of the local opening to the *uncompressed* case.

Note that the statement of correct computation includes the key $((g_1, \cdots, g_N), (h_1, \cdots, h_N))$. Then, any proof system we construct will need the local opening verifier to read the statement, which would incur a $O(N)$ cost and thus verification would no longer be succinct. To circumvent this issue, we construct an SEH where the verification of the local opening is in the offline/online model - the offline phase is run *once* by the verifier given the SEH key to produce a short state of size $\mathsf{poly}(\lambda_0)$, and the online verification of the local opening can be done in size (and time) *independent* of the arity of the tree. Further, the offline phase runs in time N^k for some fixed constant k.

Putting it all together, when we set $N = \lambda^d$, we have that the verifier computes the pre-processed state in time λ^{kd}, which is independent of the exact value of T since d is a fixed constant. Since the pre-processing is done once (per level) and depends solely on the keys present in the CRS, it is sufficient to consider the efficiency restriction only on the *online* verification of the local opening. Thus, as required, (i) the proof of local opening and its online verification can be done in time $\mathsf{poly}(\lambda_0)$; and (ii) since the depth of the tree remains constant, we can achieve extraction in TC^0. We next discuss the construction of our proof of well-formedness based on the (sub-exponential) hardness of DDH.

2.4   Construction of Proofs of Well-Formedness

We now describe our construction for the proof of well-formedness of effective siblings. For the sake of brevity, we only describe some of the steps in our construction below, and refer the reader to the relevant technical sections for complete details.

Before we proceed, we make the observation that the computation of the effective sibling corresponds to computing the *base hash* using a different key K', derived from the *base key* K. Specifically, to compute the effective sibling for the i-th index, we first exclude the i-th column of K to define K' (i.e. K' has $N - 1$ columns). Next, the effective sibling (g'', h'') can be computed as $\mathsf{Hash}(K', \mathbf{m}')$ where $\mathbf{m}'$ excludes m_i from $\mathbf{m}$. We shall use this observation to define the language for proofs of well formedness.

Reduction to a Promise Language $\mathcal{L}$. From the observation above, we want to define the 'yes' instances of $\mathcal{L}$ to correspond to the correct computation of the base hash using the derived key. We shall shortly see that for the 'no' instances, we only care about arguing security when there is a claim about the effective siblings of index i^* that was used to derive the *base hash* key K. Specifically, in this case, from the definition of K, the derived key K' is such that for each $j \in [N]$, $h_j = g_j^s$. Thus, the effective sibling hash for such a key K' will satisfy the relation $(g')^s = h'$. We define the violation of this relation to be the 'no' instance. Formally, we define $\mathcal{L} = (\mathcal{L}_{\mathsf{YES}}, \mathcal{L}_{\mathsf{NO}})$ below,

$$\mathcal{L}_{\mathsf{YES}} := \left\{ (K, v = (g', h')) \mid \exists \mathbf{m} \in \{0,1\}^n \text{ s.t. } \mathsf{Hash}(K, \mathbf{m}) = v \right\}$$

$$\mathcal{L}_{\mathsf{NO}} := \left\{ (K, v = (g', h')) \mid \exists s \text{ s.t. } \forall j \in [n], \ h_j = g_j^s \wedge (h' \neq (g')^s) \right\}.$$

From our description above, it should be clear that the languages are indeed disjoint, as required.

Before we discuss the construction of the proof system for $\mathcal{L}$, we shall see how one utilizes such a proof to argue well-formedness of the effective sibling. If the effective sibling was computed correctly, (i.e. $v = \mathsf{Hash}(K', \mathbf{m}')$) then it is a 'yes' instance, and the prover can utilize the proof system for $\mathcal{L}$ to prove well-formedness. For security, we will argue "extraction correction" - if the prover provides an opening m_{i^*} with effective sibling $v = (g'', h'')$ such that the extracted value at i^* from the hash c does not match m_{i^*} (i.e. $\mathsf{Ext}(c, i^*, \mathsf{td}) \neq m_{i^*}$), then it must be the case that $(K', v) \in \mathcal{L}_{\mathsf{NO}}$. If the above holds, then we can rely on the soundness of the proof system for $\mathcal{L}$ to show that the prover will not be able to produce an accepting proof of well-formedness for $v = (g'', h'')$. We argue extraction correctness in two cases (i) If the extracted value $\widetilde{m}_{i^*} = 0$, then from the description of the extraction algorithm, $g'^s = h'$. An opening to $m_{i^*} = 1$ implies $(g'' \cdot g_{i^*}^{m_{i^*}})^s = h_1'' \cdot h_{i^*}^{m_{i^*}}$ (from the check that $(g', h') = (g_{i^*}^{x_{i^*}} \cdot g'', h_{i^*}^{x_{i^*}} \cdot h'')$), where cancelling terms yields i.e. $(g'')^s \neq h''$; (ii) if the extracted value $\widetilde{m}_{i^*} = 1$, then $g'^{s_1} \neq h_1'$. Thus opening $m_{i^*} = 1$ implies $(g'' \cdot g_{i^*}^{m_{i^*}})^s \neq h_1'' \cdot h_{i^*}^{m_{i^*}}$, yielding $(g'')^s \neq h''$. In both cases, we have $(g'')^s \neq h''$, thus if the adversary attempts to break extraction correctness, $(K', v) \in \mathcal{L}_{\mathsf{NO}}$.

Proof System for $\mathcal{L}$. To complete the proof of well-formedness it suffices to construct a non-interactive argument in the CRS model for $\mathcal{L}$. We shall do this in a three step process: (i) first, we shall construct an efficient interactive proof where the verifier has oracle access to a large string $\mathcal{O}$ - this string will correspond to some pre-computed information about the hash key K, that the verifier will query *once* at the end of the interactive proof; (ii) second, we will apply the Fiat-Shamir transform to round collapse the interactive protocol and make it non-interactive - we will use our constructed CIH by demonstrating that the interactive protocol satisfies the necessary properties to work; (iii) finally, we will remove the need for the oracle by having the verifier pre-compute on the key K in an offline mode to generate the oracle $\mathcal{O}$, and then produce a small digest to this oracle (think Merkle tree root) - at the end of the protocol, when the verifier needs to query $\mathcal{O}$, it delegates the opening at the queried location to the prover.

We leave the details of steps (ii) and (iii) to the technical sections (Section 5.2.3), and discuss below the construction of our interactive proof $(\mathsf{P}, \mathsf{V}^{\mathcal{O}})$ for $\mathcal{L}$, where V has oracle access to a large string $\mathcal{O}$. Our protocol design is inspired by 'Bulletproof-style' protocols [5,8].

Interactive Proof $(\mathsf{P}, \mathsf{V}^{\mathcal{O}})$ for $\mathcal{L}$. Instead of defining the oracle $\mathcal{O}$ upfront, we shall describe the protocol first, which will specify $\mathcal{O}$. As stated, the protocol follows the 'folding' paradigm. Specifically, we describe a recursive protocol, where we fold a statement of length n (i.e. size of the key K is $O(n)$) to a statement of size n/D. In this high level overview, we shall describe a single step of the folding procedure for $n = 2$ and $D = 2$. The more general setting, along with the full description of the protocol is presented in the technical section.

Let us set some notation. We represent $\mathbf{m}$ as (m_L, m_R), and partition the key as $K = \begin{bmatrix} g_L & g_R \\ h_L & h_R \end{bmatrix}$.

As a part of the folding step, the prover is going to fold K, into a key with half the number of columns, using the random challenge γ sent by the verifier. Let the common input by (K, v), and the prover's auxiliary input be $\mathbf{m}$. One step of the folding is presented below:

1. Prover P computes
   (a) $v_L = (g_L^{m_L}, h_L^{m_L})$ and $v_R = (g_R^{m_R}, h_R^{m_R})$.
   (b) $\tilde{v}_1 = (g_L^{m_R}, h_L^{m_R})$, $\tilde{v}_2 = v$, $\tilde{v}_3 = (g_R^{m_L}, h_R^{m_L})$.
   send (v_L, v_R) and $(\tilde{v}_1, \tilde{v}_2, \tilde{v}_3)$ to verifier $V^{\mathcal{O}}$.
2. Verifier $V^{\mathcal{O}}$
   (a) Checks if $v = v_L \cdot v_R$, and $v = \tilde{v}_2$.
   (b) Sample $\gamma \in \mathscr{C}$ from a challenge space $\mathscr{C}$ to be determined.
   send γ_i to P.
3. P and V set $v = \tilde{v}_1 \cdot \tilde{v}_2^{\gamma}, \tilde{v}_3^{\gamma^2}$.
4. P sets $m' = m_R + \gamma m_L$ and $K = (g_L \cdot g_R^{\gamma}, h_L \cdot h_R^{\gamma})$.

Finally, when $n = 1$ (as is the case above), the prover sends its reduced witness x in the clear, at which point the verifier wants to recompute the hash and check against v. To do so the verifier needs the folded key, which it obtains by querying the oracle $\mathcal{O}$ on the randomness γ to get the corresponding folded key. On receiving key $K = (g, h)$ from the oracle, the verifier simply checks if $v = (g^x, h^x)$ for the reduced statement v. The oracle $\mathcal{O}$ thus pre-processes the n-length key K, and stores a folded key for every possible verifier randomness γ. We describe the parameters to enable the verifier to do compute the pre-computation shortly. We now argue completeness and soundness of the above folding procedure.

Completeness: For completeness, note that $(g')^{m'} = (g')^{m_R + \gamma m_L} = (g_L \cdot g_R^{\gamma})^{m_R + \gamma m_L}$, and similarly for $(h')^{m'}$. Thus, from definition, it follows that $((g')^{m'}, (h')^{m'}) = \tilde{v}_1 \cdot \tilde{v}_2^{\gamma}, \tilde{v}_3^{\gamma^2}$

Soundness: To argue soundness, we will argue that if the (K, v) before the folding is in $\mathcal{L}_{\mathsf{NO}}$, then with high probability over the choice of the verifier randomness γ, the (K, v) at the end of the folding procedure is in $\mathcal{L}_{\mathsf{NO}}$ (also referred to as round-by-round soundness [9]). We denote each $\tilde{v}_i = (g^{\alpha_i}, g^{\beta_i})$ for some α_i, β_i. Since $\tilde{v}_2 = v$, if $(K, v) \in \mathcal{L}_{\mathsf{NO}}$, from the description of the folding procedure it must be the case that $g^{\beta_2} \neq g^{s\alpha_2}$. The newly computed v,

$$\tilde{v}_1 \cdot \tilde{v}_2^{\gamma}, \tilde{v}_3^{\gamma_i^2} = (g'', h'') = (g^{\alpha_1 + \gamma\alpha_2 + \gamma^2\alpha_3}, g^{\beta_1 + \gamma\beta_2 + \gamma_i^2\beta_3}).$$

Then $(g'')^s/h'' = g^{(s\alpha_1-\beta_1)+\gamma(s\alpha_2-\beta_2)+\gamma_i^2(s\alpha_3-\beta_3)} = g^{P(\gamma)}$ where $P(X)$ is a polynomial of degree at most 2. Since $s\alpha_2 \neq \beta_2$, P is not a zero polynomial, and thus $\Pr[P(\gamma) = 0] \leq 2/|\mathscr{C}|$. Therefore overly a randomly sampled γ, $(g'')^s = h''$ only with probability $2/|\mathscr{C}|$.

Lastly, we discuss the parameters that will allow the verifier to compute the oracle $\mathcal{O}$ as a part of its pre-processing in time $\mathsf{poly}(n)$. By our description above, the size of $\mathcal{O}$ is $|\mathscr{C}|^r$, where r is the total number of recursive calls to folding, i.e. for every tuple $\in \mathscr{C}^r$, the verifier needs to store a key. In the above description, $D = 2$, $r = \log(n)$, and thus, to ensure $|\mathscr{C}|^r$ is of size $\mathsf{poly}(n)$, we can set $|\mathscr{C}|$ to be a constant, which results in a high soundness error. Instead, if we pick $D = \log(n)$, and $|\mathscr{C}| = \log^2(n)$, this gives us $|\mathscr{C}|^r = n^2$.

Remark 2. An observant reader may note that since the proof of local opening only satisfies computational soundness, it is possible that the value extracted differs from the local opening sent by a cheating prover. This event happens only with negligible probability, and the extracted value is indeed the unique value (at the specified location) hashed by the cheating prover. Thus in our applications, we condition on the non-occurrence of the event and argue soundness as if it is the extracted value and the opened value always match.

2.5 Roadmap to the Paper

In Sect. 3, we define the necessary preliminaries. We then construct correlation intractable hash functions (CIH) for product relations based on sub-exponential hardness of DDH in Sect. 4. Next in Sect. 5 we construct somewhere extractable hash (SEHash) with succinct local openings based on sub-exponential hardness of DDH. Due to the lack of space, the details are deferred to the full version of the paper [14]. The full version also shows applications of the constructed CIH and SEHash to constructing SNARGs for P and batch NP.

3 Preliminaries

For any positive integer n, denote $[n] = \{1, 2, \ldots, n\}$. For any positive integer n, any vector $x = (x_1, x_2, \ldots, x_n)$, and any subset $S \subseteq [n]$, we denote $x|_S = \{x_i\}_{i \in S}$. We will say that a cryptographic primitive is (T, ρ)-secure if any T time adversary breaks the primitive with probability $\leq \rho$. Thus, for schemes that satisfy "standard" security for a security parameter λ, we say that it is $(\mathsf{poly}(\lambda), \mathsf{negl}(\lambda))$. Additional preliminaries are defined in the full version.

3.1 Decisional Diffie-Hellman Assumption

In the following, we state the decisional Diffie-Hellman (DDH) assumption.

Definition 1 (Decisional Diffie-Hellman). *A prime-order group generator is an algorithm $\mathcal{G}$ that takes the security parameter λ as input, and outputs a tuple $(\mathbb{G}, p, g)$, where $\mathbb{G}$ is a cyclic group of prime order $p(\lambda)$, and g is a generator of $\mathbb{G}$.*

Let $\mathcal{G}$ be a prime-order group generator. We say that $\mathcal{G}$ satisfies the DDH assumption if for any n.u. PPT distinguisher $\mathcal{D}$, there exists a negligible function $\nu(\lambda)$ such that

$$\left| \Pr\left[(\mathbb{G}, p, g) \leftarrow \mathcal{G}(1^\lambda), a, b \leftarrow \mathbb{Z}_p : \mathcal{D}(1^\lambda, \mathbb{G}, p, g, g^a, g^b, g^{ab}) = 1 \right] - \right.$$

$$\left. \Pr\left[(\mathbb{G}, p, g) \leftarrow \mathcal{G}(1^\lambda), a, b, u \leftarrow \mathbb{Z}_p : \mathcal{D}(1^\lambda, \mathbb{G}, p, g, g^a, g^b, g^u) = 1 \right] \right| \le \nu(\lambda)$$

Sub-exponential DDH Assumption. In this work, we use the following version of sub-exponential DDH assumption. Specifically, we say that $\mathcal{G}$ satisfies the sub-exponential DDH assumption, if there exists a constant $0 < c < 1$ such that for any non-uniform distinguisher D that runs in time $\lambda^{O((\log\log\lambda)^3)}$, the advantage $\nu(\lambda)$ is bounded by $2^{-\lambda^c}$ for any sufficiently large λ.

3.2   Correlation Intractable Hash

We start by describing a hash family $\mathcal{H} = \{\mathcal{H}_\lambda\}_{\lambda \in \mathbb{N}}$, which is defined by the two following algorithms:

Gen: a PPT algorithm that on input the security parameter 1^λ, outputs key k.
Hash: a *deterministic* polynomial algorithm than on input a key $k \in \mathsf{Gen}(1^\lambda)$, and an element $x \in \{0,1\}^{n(\lambda)}$ outputs an element $y \in \{0,1\}^\lambda$.

Given a hash family $\mathcal{H}$, we are now ready to define what it means for $\mathcal{H}$ to be correlation intractable.

Definition 2 ([12]). *A hash family $\mathcal{H} = (\mathcal{H}.\mathsf{Gen}, \mathcal{H}.\mathsf{Hash})$ is said to be correlation intractable (CI) for a relation family $\mathcal{R} = \{\mathcal{R}_\lambda\}_{\lambda \in \mathbb{N}}$ if the following property holds: for every PPT adversary $\mathcal{A}$, there exists a negligible function $\mathsf{negl}(\cdot)$ such that for every $R \in \mathcal{R}_\lambda$,*

$$\Pr_{\substack{k \leftarrow \mathcal{H}.\mathsf{Gen}(1^\lambda) \\ x \leftarrow \mathcal{A}(k)}} [(x, \mathcal{H}.\mathsf{Hash}(k, x)) \in R] \le \mathsf{negl}(\lambda).$$

Efficiently Verifiable Product Relations. We take the following definitions of product relations, and efficiently verifiable relations, from [31].

Definition 3 (Product Relation, Definition 3.1 [31]). *A relation $R \subseteq \mathcal{X} \times \mathcal{Y}^t$ is a product relation, if for any x, the set $R_x = \{y \mid (x, y) \in R\}$ is the Cartesian product of several sets $S_{1,x}, S_{2,x}, \ldots, S_{t,x}$, i.e. $R_x = S_{1,x} \times \ldots \times S_{t,x}$.*

Definition 4 (Efficiently Product Verifiability, Definition 3.3 [31]). *A relation R is efficiently product verifiable, if there exists a circuit C such that, for any x, the sets $S_{1,x}, S_{2,x} \ldots S_{t,x}$ (in Definition 3) satisfy that, for any i, $y_i \in S_{i,x}$ if and only if $C(x, y_i, i) = 1$. Furthermore, if C is a threshold circuit of depth d, then we say R is a d-depth verifiable product relation.*

Definition 5 (Product Sparsity, Definition 3.4 [31]). *A relation $R \subseteq \mathcal{X} \times \mathcal{Y}^t$ has sparsity ρ, if for any x, the sets $S_{1,x}, S_{2,x}, \ldots, S_{t,x}$ (in Definition 3) satisfy $|S_{i,x}| \leq \rho|\mathcal{Y}|$.*

Definition 6 (Approximate Product Relation). *We say a relation $R \subseteq \mathcal{X} \times \mathcal{Y}^t$ is an α-approximate product relation, if for any x, there exists subsets $S_{1,x}, S_{2,x} \ldots, S_{t,x} \subseteq \mathcal{Y}^t$ such that $R_x = \{y \mid (x, y) \in R\}$ consists exactly of all of those $y \in \mathcal{Y}^t$ for which $|\{i \in [t] \mid y_i \in S_{i,x}\}| \geq \alpha t$.*

Definition 7 (Searchable Relation). *We say a relation $R \subseteq \mathcal{X} \times \mathcal{Y}$ is searchable, if there exists a function $f : \mathcal{X} \to \mathcal{Y} \cup \{\perp\}$ such that for every $x \in \mathcal{X}$, we have that $(x, y) \in R$ if and only if $y = f(x)$.*

Definition 8 (Approximate Searchable Relation). *Let $\alpha \in (0, 1)$ be a real and $R \subseteq \mathcal{X} \times \mathcal{Y}^t$ be a relation. We say R is α-approximable by threshold circuits $f_1, f_2, \ldots, f_t : \mathcal{X} \to \mathcal{Y} \cup \{\perp\}$, if $R_x = \{y \mid (x, y) \in R\}$ consists exactly of all of those $y \in \mathcal{Y}^t$ for which $|\{i \in [t] \mid y_i = f_i(x)\}| \geq \alpha t$. Furthermore, If the depth of the threshold circuits $f_1, f_2, \ldots, f_t$ is bounded by d, then we say R is an α-approximate searchable relation of depth d.*

4   CIH for Product Relations

We observe that the parameters of the CIH in [34] can be modified to build the following CIH for α-approximate searchable relations in TC^0. We defer discussion of the appropriate theorem, and proof, to the full version of this paper.

4.1   Construction

Lemma 1. *Let $\mathcal{R} = \{\mathcal{R}_\lambda\}_{\lambda \in \mathbb{N}}$ be a family of relations, where each $R \in \mathcal{R}_\lambda$ is $O(\log^* \lambda)$-depth verifiable product relation (Definition 4) of sparsity ρ_λ defined over $\mathcal{X}_\lambda \times \mathcal{Y}_\lambda^t$. Let $n = \log_2 |\mathcal{X}_\lambda|$ be the length of bit strings representing $\mathcal{X}_\lambda$.*

Assuming sub-exponential DDH assumption, if $t_\lambda = \Omega(\lambda^3 / \log(1/\rho_\lambda))$, there exists a CIH for $\mathcal{R}$ with running time $\mathsf{poly}(\lambda, t_\lambda, n^{O(\log\log n)}, \log |\mathcal{Y}|, |C|, \log(1/\rho_\lambda))$, where C is the circuit that verifies the product relation (See Definition 4).

Furthermore, for any adversary that runs in time $\lambda^{O((\log\log \lambda)^2)}$, its advantage for the aforementioned CIH is at most $2^{-\lambda'}$, where $\lambda' = \lambda^{O(1/\log\log \lambda)}$.

Remark 3. If the sparsity $\rho = 1 - \epsilon$ for some $\epsilon = o(1)$, then the above parameters requirement on t becomes $t = \Omega(\lambda^3/\epsilon)$. The running time of CIH is $\mathsf{poly}(\lambda, t_\lambda, n^{O(\log\log n)}, \log |\mathcal{Y}|, |C|, 1/\epsilon)$.

Ingredients. Our construction will use the CIH for α-approximate searchable relations of depth $O(\log^* \lambda)$ CIH = (CIH.Gen, CIH.Hash).

Construction. We describe our construction of CIH for small input product relations in Fig. 3. As we described in Sect. 2.1, we divide $[N]$ into $\mathcal{Y}_1, \mathcal{Y}_2, \ldots, \mathcal{Y}_{\mathsf{depth}}$, where each $|\mathcal{Y}_i| = 2e \log_2(n + \lambda), \mathsf{depth} = \log_2(n + \lambda)$, and we set $N = \prod_{i \in [\mathsf{depth}]} |\mathcal{Y}_i| = n^{O(\log \log n)}$.

The proof of Lemma 1 and extensions to CIH for product relations can be found in the full version of our paper.

5   Somewhere Extractable Hash from **DDH**

In this section, we define and construct a somewhere extractable hash (with additional properties) assuming the sub-exponential hardness of DDH. We first define the standard notion of a somewhere extractable hash, then specify the additional properties required for our applications, and finally describe our construction.

CIH for Small Input Product Relations

Parameters: $[N] = \mathcal{Y}_1 \times \ldots \times \mathcal{Y}_{\mathsf{depth}}, t = \ell \cdot L.$

- Gen(1^λ):
    - Sample N queries from $\mathcal{Y}^\ell$: $\mathbf{q}_1, \mathbf{q}_2, \ldots, \mathbf{q}_N \leftarrow \mathcal{Y}^\ell.$
    - Sample a series of CIH keys for α-approximate searchable relations in $\mathcal{X}_i \times \mathcal{Y}_i^L$, where $\alpha = 1/\mathsf{depth}, L \geq \lambda^2/\alpha$, and $\mathcal{X}_i = \mathcal{X} \times \mathcal{Y}_1^L \times \ldots \times \mathcal{Y}_{i-1}^L.$

$$\forall i \in [\mathsf{depth}], \quad \mathsf{k}_i \leftarrow \mathsf{CIH.Gen}(1^\lambda),$$

    - Output $\mathsf{k} = (\{\mathbf{q}_i\}_{i \in [N]}, \{\mathsf{k}_i\}_{i \in [\mathsf{depth}]}).$
- Hash(k, x):
    - Parse $\mathsf{k} = (\{\mathbf{q}_i\}_{i \in [N]}, \{\mathsf{k}_i\}_{i \in [\mathsf{depth}]}).$
    - For every $i = 1, 2, \ldots, \mathsf{depth}$, we hash the input x and the hash values we obtained so far.

$$\mathbf{y}_i \leftarrow \mathsf{CIH.Hash}(\mathsf{k}_i, (x, \mathbf{y}_1, \mathbf{y}_2 \ldots, \mathbf{y}_{i-1})).$$

    - Then for every $i \in [\mathsf{depth}]$, we first decompose $\mathbf{y}_i$ as a "row" vector $(y_{i,1}, y_{i,2}, \ldots, y_{i,L})$, where each $y_{i,j} \in \mathcal{Y}_i$ for every $j \in [L]$.
    Then we concatenate those rows to obtain a matrix and then take each column of it. Namely, for each $j \in [L]$, we compose the j-th column of the matrix as $i_j = y_{1,j} \| y_{2,j} \| \ldots \| y_{\mathsf{depth},j} \in \mathcal{Y}_1 \times \ldots \times \mathcal{Y}_{\mathsf{depth}}.$
    - We use i_j's as indices to select the queries in $\{\mathbf{q}_i\}_{i \in [N]}$, and output

$$(\mathbf{q}_{i_1}, \mathbf{q}_{i_2}, \ldots, \mathbf{q}_{i_L}).$$

Fig. 3. Description of CIH for small input product relations.

5.1 Definition

In this subsection, we define a somewhere extractable hash [32], along with the required additional. A somewhere extractable hash has a key with two computationally indistinguishable modes: (i) In the *normal mode*, the key is *uniformly random*; and (ii) in the *trapdoor mode*, the key is generated according to a subset S denoting the coordinates of the message to be hashed.

Furthermore, a standard somewhere extractable hash requires the following properties.

Efficiency: The size of the CRS and hash roughly grows with $|S|$.

Extraction: The trapdoor mode hash key is associated with a trapdoor td, such that given the trapdoor, one can extract the message on coordinates in S. Note that the extraction implies the statistical binding property for the coordinates in S.

Local Opening: We allow the prover to generate a *local opening* for any single coordinate of the message. The local opening needs to have a small size, which only grows poly-logarithmically with the total length of the message. Moreover, we require that the value from the local opening should be consistent with the extracted value.

For our application, we require some additional properties specified below.

Low-depth Extraction: We require that the extraction circuit for the hash can be implemented in TC^0. Specifically, we split the extraction into an *preprocessing* and *online* extraction phase, where the trapdoor td is used *only* in the online phase. We require the online phase of the extraction to be implemented in TC^0.

Large inputs: We require that the somewhere extractable hash scheme to support input sizes that are super-polynomial in the security parameter, i.e. $N = \lambda^{\omega(1)}$. Further, we will continue to require that the local opening is small for such inputs. In a manner similar to the extraction, we will split the local opening verification opening into a pre-processing and online phase, and require that the online verification is *small*.

Formally, somewhere extractable hash scheme for large inputs with extraction in TC^0 is a tuple of algorithms $\mathsf{SEHash} = (\mathsf{Gen}, \mathsf{TGen}, \mathsf{Hash}, \mathsf{Open}, \mathsf{PreVer}, \mathsf{OnlineVer}, \mathsf{PreExt}, \mathsf{OnlineExt})$. We defer the description of these algorithms to the full version of the paper.

As described in the technical overview (Sect. 2), it is *both* additional requirements that necessitates a new construction. Even removing one of the requirements would allow us to directly invoke constructions in prior works [21,50] from *polynomial* hardness of DDH.

Remark 4. We note that we do not impose any efficiency requirements on the pre-computation algorithm PreVer. In fact, in our construction it will be the case that PreVer runs in time $\mathsf{p}(m)$ for some fixed polynomial $\mathsf{p}(\cdot)$, where m is fixed independent of N such that $\log_m(N)$ is a constant. This *weak* efficiency guarantee from PreVer will be sufficient for our applications.

We shall prove the following theorem in the subsequent sections.

Theorem 4. *There exists a construction of somewhere extractable hash for large inputs with extraction in* TC^0 *assuming the sub-exponential hardness of* DDH.

5.2   Construction

We construct the somewhere extractable hash in two steps: (i) *base case:* construct a somewhere extractable hash for N bit messages in the *pre-processing model* where the online verification is $\mathsf{poly}(\lambda, \log N)$ while the pre-processing takes time $O(N^z)$ for some fixed constant z; and then (ii) *extend to a tree* bootstrap the construction by constructing an m-ary tree of depth $\log_m(N)$ to get the pre-processing down to $O(m^z)$, and online verification to be $\mathsf{poly}(\lambda, \log_m(N), \log m)$. Looking ahead, both N and m will both be super-polynomial in λ such that $\log_m(N) = O(1)$. This will ensure that the online verification will continue to be $\mathsf{poly}(\lambda, \log N)$ while the other components will be polynomial in m. We will fix m independent of N.

5.2.1   Construction: Base Hash

We construct below a somewhere extractable hash scheme in the pre-processing model for the base construction. Recall, that here for hashing strings of length N, we allow the pre-processing to depend on N^z for some fixed constant z.

Our construction closely follows the construction of the trapdoor hash based on DDH [21], but to achieve the properties discussed above, namely the succinct local opening in the pre-processing model, we augment the construction with a new *proof* of opening. We start with a discussion of all the algorithms except those pertaining to the proving of local opening, which we describe and prove separately. For the subsequent discussion, let $\ell := |S|$. Let the group be generated on λ_0 where $\lambda = \lambda_0^{O(\log \log \lambda_0)}$ is the security parameter for the scheme.

$\mathsf{Gen}(1^\lambda, 1^N, 1^{|S|})$: Sample $(\mathbb{G}, p, g) \leftarrow \mathcal{G}(1^{\lambda_0})$, $s_1, \cdots, s_\ell \leftarrow\!\!\$ \ \mathbb{Z}_p$, and set the hash key $K \in \mathbb{G}^{(\ell+1) \times N}$ to be,

$$K = \begin{bmatrix} g_1 & g_2 & \cdots & g_N \\ h_{1,1} & h_{1,2} & \cdots & h_{1,N} \\ \vdots & \vdots & \ddots & \vdots \\ h_{\ell,1} & h_{\ell,2} & \cdots & h_{\ell,N} \end{bmatrix}$$

where $\forall j \in [N]$, $g_j \leftarrow\!\!\$ \ \mathbb{G}$, and $\forall i \in [\ell], j \in [N]$, $h_{i,j} = g_j^{s_i}$. Output K.

$\mathsf{TGen}(1^\lambda, 1^N, S)$: Sample $(\mathbb{G}, p, g) \leftarrow \mathcal{G}(1^{\lambda_0})$, $s_1, \cdots, s_\ell \leftarrow\!\!\$ \ \mathbb{Z}_p$, where $\ell := |S|$. Let $S = \{j_1^*, \cdots, j_\ell^*\}$. Set the hash key $K \in \mathbb{G}^{(\ell+1) \times N}$ to be,

$$K^* = \begin{bmatrix} g_1 & g_2 & \cdots & g_N \\ h_{1,1} & h_{1,2} & \cdots & h_{1,N} \\ \vdots & \vdots & \ddots & \vdots \\ h_{\ell,1} & h_{\ell,2} & \cdots & h_{\ell,N} \end{bmatrix}$$

where $\forall j \in [N]$, $g_j \leftarrow_\$ \mathbb{G}$, and $\forall i \in [\ell], j \in [N]$, $h_{i,j} = g_j^{s_i} \cdot g$ if $j = j_i^*$, and $g_j^{s_i}$ otherwise. Let $\mathsf{td} := (s_1, \cdots, s_\ell)$. Output (K^*, td).

$\mathsf{Hash}(K, \mathbf{m} = (m_1, \cdots, m_N) \in \{0,1\}^N)$: Compute the hash $c \in \mathbb{G}^{(\ell+1)}$ as $c := (g', h_1', \cdots, h_\ell')$, where $g' := \prod_{j \in [N]} g_j^{m_j}$, and $\forall i \in [\ell]$, $h_i' := \prod_{j \in [N]} h_{1,j}^{m_j}$. Note that since we don't care about our hash being hiding, we ignore the random coins, i.e. Hash is a deterministic algorithm in our construction.

$\mathsf{PreExt}(1^\lambda, c)$: Parse c as $(g', h_1', \cdots, h_\ell')$ and output $c' = (\{g'^{2^k}\}_{k=0}^{[\lambda_0]-1}, h_1', \cdots, h_\ell')$

$\mathsf{OnlineExt}(c', S, \mathsf{td})$: Parse td as $(s_1, \cdots, s_\ell)$ and let $S = \{j_1^*, \cdots, j_\ell^*\}$. We compute m_S as follows: for each $i \in [\ell]$, $m_{j_i^*} = 0$ if $g'^{s_i} = h_i'$, and 1 otherwise. Output m_S.

Efficiency. Note that the size of the keys are $O(\lambda_0 \cdot N \cdot \ell)$, the size of the commitment $O(\lambda_0 \cdot \ell)$ and the size of the pre-processed value c' is $O(\ell \cdot \mathsf{poly}(\lambda_0))$. The time taken to compute the commitment is $\mathsf{poly}(\lambda_0, N, \ell)$ while the extraction can be done $\mathsf{poly}(\lambda_0, \ell)$. Further note that for each i, g'^{s_i} can be computed in TC^0 given s_i and $\{g'^{2^k}\}_{k=0}^{[\lambda_0]-1}$, contained in the *pre-computed* hash c'. This can be done simply by looking at the binary representation of s, and multiplying the relevant g'^{2^k} - which can be done in TC^0, thus ensuring that $\mathsf{OnlineExt}$ can be computed in TC^0.

Lemma 2. *The above scheme satisfies key indistinguishability.*

We defer the proof sketch to the full version of the paper, and note that since the security parameter for the group in λ_0, we require DDH security in the chosen group to be $(\mathsf{poly}(\lambda_0^{\log \log \lambda_0}), \mathsf{negl}(\lambda_0^{\log \log \lambda_0}))$.

5.2.2 Proof of Local Opening

In this section, we shall describe the proof of local opening in the common references string (CRS) model. As described earlier, we require strong efficiency properties from the proof verification algorithm. We will first define below a promise language $\mathcal{L} = (\mathcal{L}_{\mathsf{YES}}, \mathcal{L}_{\mathsf{NO}})$ for which we shall construct a non-interactive argument system in the CRS model. But before we construct this non-interactive argument, we describe how such an argument system, in conjunction with a hash tree scheme, can be used to achieve computational extraction correctness. We then build a non-interactive argument for $\mathcal{L}$.

Our non-interactive argument for $\mathcal{L}$ is going to involve multiple steps that we outline here, and refer the reader to the relevant technical sections for the details. As a first step, we build an interactive *proof*[8] $(\mathsf{P}, \mathsf{V}^L)$ for $\mathcal{L}$ where the verifier V^L will have access to an oracle L, and will otherwise be extremely efficient - the efficiency will in fact be very close to the requirement from $\mathsf{OnlineVer}$. Our interactive protocol is inspired by Bulletproof-style protocols [5,8], but our parameters are such that soundness of the protocol is quite large. We thus parallel repeat and show that it satisfies the necessary requirements to apply the Fiat-Shamir transformation to make it non-interactive. This obtain a non-interactive

---

[8] Statistically sound interactive protocol.

argument system $(\mathsf{P_{FS}}, \mathsf{V_{FS}^L})$ in the CRS (and oracle) model. Finally, we show how to remove the need for an oracle access in the non-interactive argument by the way of verifier pre-processing, and the use of hash trees. The final non-interactive argument we denote by $(\mathsf{P'}, (\mathsf{V_1'}, \mathsf{V_2'}))$ for $\mathcal{L}$ with CRS $\mathsf{crs}_{\mathcal{L}}$. $\mathsf{V_1'}$ will run in time $N^z \mathsf{poly}(\lambda_0, \lambda)$ for a fixed constant z. The output produced is of size $\mathsf{poly}(\lambda)$. The running time of $\mathsf{V_2'}$ is $\mathsf{poly}(\lambda)$. Further, $\mathsf{V_1'}$ is a *deterministic* procedure.

Remark 5. Note that to handle arbitrary polynomial many instances T, we cannot choose a fixed constant depth. Since the number of keys correspond the depth of the hash tree, we set the number of keys to a super-constant depth, $\log^* \lambda$. When running the protocol for any polynomial T, the prover and verifier will select the appropriate constant c such that $T \leq \lambda^c$. But since the CIH needs to be able to handle arbitrary polynomial computation, the CIH is constructed to allow $\mathcal{B}_{C,c}$ that can be verified by threshold circuits of depth $O(\log^* \lambda)$. It is a technicality of our construction, and explains the reasoning behind our CIH theorem allowing for $O(\log^* \lambda)$ verification, but we will not discuss it further in this overview, and assume for further discussion $\mathcal{B}$ verifiable via constant depth threshold circuits, i.e. TC^0.

Promise Language. We start by defining the following promise language $\mathcal{L} = (\mathcal{L}_{\mathsf{YES}}, \mathcal{L}_{\mathsf{NO}})$ where $K = \begin{bmatrix} g_1 \cdots g_n \\ h_1 \cdots h_n \end{bmatrix}$, and $v = (g', h')$

$$\mathcal{L}_{\mathsf{YES}} := \left\{ (K, v) \in \mathbb{G}^{2 \times n} \times \mathbb{G}^2 \mid \exists \mathbf{m} \in \{0,1\}^n \text{ s.t. } \mathsf{Hash}(K, \mathbf{m}) = v \right\}$$

$$\mathcal{L}_{\mathsf{NO}} := \left\{ (K, v) \in \mathbb{G}^{2 \times n} \times \mathbb{G}^2 \mid \exists s \in \mathbb{Z}_p \text{ s.t. } \forall j \in [n], \ h_j = g_j^s \wedge (h' \neq (g')^s) \right\}$$

First note that the above languages are indeed disjoint. This is fairly easy to see - when K is such that $\exists s \in \mathbb{Z}_p$ such that $\forall j \in [n], h_j = g_j^s$, then by construction, for any $\mathbf{m} \in \{0,1\}^n$, $g' = \prod_{j \in [n]} g_j^{m_j}$ and $h' = \prod_{j \in [n]} h_j^{m_j} = \prod_{j \in [n]} (g_j^{m_j})^s$ satisfy $h' = (g')^s$.

We defer discussion to the full version of the paper on how the SNARG in the pre-processing model for the above promise languages is sufficient to provide a proof of local opening, and the *somewhere soundness* property it satisfies.

5.2.3   Non-interactive Argument for $\mathcal{L} = (\mathcal{L}_{\mathsf{YES}}, \mathcal{L}_{\mathsf{NO}})$

In this section, we will construct non-interactive arguments for $\mathcal{L} = (\mathcal{L}_{\mathsf{YES}}, \mathcal{L}_{\mathsf{NO}})$. As described earlier, our construction will proceed in multiple steps. We first define notation that will be instructive for this section.

Notations. In the following discussion, we will require that keys and inputs are partitioned into blocks, with operations performed on the entire block. To improve readability, we will define some shorthand notations below. We will consider the setting where the number of blocks are fixed to be some parameter D.

Further, for simplicity, we assume that the parameter n is some power of D. Consider a vector $\mathbf{x} = (x_1, \cdots, x_n) \in \mathbb{Z}_p^n$, we represent $\mathbf{x}$ by partitioning into D vectors $(\mathbf{x}_1, \cdots, \mathbf{x}_D)$ such that $\mathbf{x}_{j+1} = (x_{1+jn/D}, x_{2+jn/D}, \cdots, x_{(j+1)n/D}) \in \mathbb{Z}_p^{n/D}$.

We extend this analogously to partitioning the key $K \in \mathbb{G}^{2\times n}$ as $\begin{bmatrix} \mathbf{g}_1 \cdots \mathbf{g}_D \\ \mathbf{h}_1 \cdots \mathbf{h}_D \end{bmatrix}$

where each $\mathbf{g}_{j+1} = (g_{1+jn/D}, g_{2+jn/D}, \cdots, g_{(j+1)n/D}) \in \mathbb{G}^{n/D}$ and $\mathbf{h}_{j+1}$ is defined similarly. Further, $\mathbf{g}_{j+1}^{\mathbf{x}_{i+1}} = \prod_{k=1}^{n/D} g_{k+jn/D}^{x_{k+in/D}} \in \mathbb{G}$, and for every scalar $\gamma \in \mathbb{Z}_p$, $\mathbf{g}_{j+1}^{\gamma} = (g_{1+jn/D}^{\gamma}, g_{2+jn/D}^{\gamma}, \cdots, g_{(j+1)n/D}^{\gamma}) \in \mathbb{G}^{n/D}$. Lastly, $\mathbf{g}_{j+1}^{\gamma} \cdot \mathbf{g}_{i+1} = \left(g_{1+jn/D}^{\gamma} \cdot g_{1+in/D}, g_{2+jn/D}^{\gamma} \cdot g_{2+in/D}, \cdots, g_{(j+1)n/D}^{\gamma} \cdot g_{1+(i+1)n/D} \right) \in \mathbb{G}^{n/D}$. Note that we will overload notation and use $\prod$ over both for elements in $\mathbb{G}$ and $\mathbb{G}^{n/D}$, where the resultant element will be in $\mathbb{G}$ and $\mathbb{G}^{n/D}$ respectively. The usage will be clear from context.

Interactive Protocol. We start with the interactive protocol where the prover P and V will start with a key $K \in \mathbb{G}^{2\times n}$, and at each step *fold* it into a new key $K' \in \mathbb{G}^{2\times n/2}$ of half the size based on the verifier challenge γ. After $\log_D(n)$ steps, only the final folded key $K \in \mathbb{G}^{2\times D}$ is used by the verifier to perform checks, and thus V *does not* need access to the intermediate folded keys during the protocol. From the description of our protocol, it will become evident that the folded key depends solely on the starting key K, and the verifier randomness $(\gamma_1, \cdots, \gamma_n)$. To simplify the protocol and analysis, we describe the interactive protocol in the pre-processing model where the verifier V has oracle access to a *pre-processed* string denoted by V^L. The string L depends on K, and our protocol will require the verifier to make a *single query* on the randomness used during the protocol, i.e. $(\gamma_1, \cdots, \gamma_n)$, which returns the appropriate folded key. We will subsequently discuss (i) how to compute the string L; and (ii) how to enable the prover to P to provide read access to the appropriate location of L.

The interactive protocol is presented in Fig. 4. Due to a lack of space, we prover the necessary properties of our protocol in the full version of our paper and additionally discuss the parameters, round-collapse via Fiat-Shamir, pre-processing Phase, and how we get rid of the verifier oracle.

6   SNARGs for P

For completeness, we specify below the main theorem statement in this work. The details for which can be found in the full version of our paper.

Theorem 5. *Assuming the sub-exponential hardness of* DDH, *for every polynomial* $T = T(\lambda)$, *there exists a publicly verifiably non-interactive RAM delegation scheme with CRS size, proof size and verifier time all* $\mathsf{poly}(\lambda, \log T)$ *while the prover running time is* $\mathsf{poly}(\lambda, T)$.

Protocol: Interactive Protocol $(\mathsf{P}, \mathsf{V}^L)$ for $\mathcal{L}_{\mathsf{YES}}$

Common input: input $(K, v) \in \mathbb{G}^{2 \times n} \times \mathbb{G}^2$, security parameter 1^λ.
P's auxiliary input: input $\mathbf{x} = (x_1, \cdots, x_n)$

1. Set $i = 1$.
2. if $n > D$ repeat:
   (a) Prover does the following:
      i. Parse K as $\begin{bmatrix} \mathbf{g}_1 \cdots \mathbf{g}_D \\ \mathbf{h}_1 \cdots \mathbf{h}_D \end{bmatrix}$ and $\mathbf{x}$ as $(\mathbf{x}_1, \cdots, \mathbf{x}_D)$
      ii. For each $j \in [D]$, set $v_j := \begin{bmatrix} \mathbf{g}_j^{\mathbf{x}_j} \\ \mathbf{h}_j^{\mathbf{x}_j} \end{bmatrix}$.
      iii. For each $j \in [D - 1]$, set

$$\widetilde{v}_j = \left[\prod_{i=1}^{j} \begin{matrix} \mathbf{g}_i^{\mathbf{x}_{D-j+i}} \\ \mathbf{h}_i^{\mathbf{x}_{D-j+i}} \end{matrix} \right] \quad \text{and} \quad \widetilde{v}_{D+j} = \left[\prod_{i=1}^{D-j} \begin{matrix} \mathbf{g}_{j+i}^{\mathbf{x}_i} \\ \mathbf{h}_{j+i}^{\mathbf{x}_i} \end{matrix} \right]$$

      iv. Set $\widetilde{v}_D := v$.
      v. Send $(v_1, \cdots, v_D)$ and $((\widetilde{v}_1, \cdots, \widetilde{v}_{2D-1}))$ to V.
   (b) Verifier V^L does the following:
      i. Checks if $v = \prod_{j=1}^{D} v_j$ and $\widetilde{v}_D = v$.
      ii. Sample $\gamma_i \leftarrow_\$ \mathscr{C}$ from the challenge space $(\subset \mathbb{Z}_p)$.
      iii. Send γ_i to P.
   (c) P and V set $\gamma = \gamma_i$ and $v = \prod_{j=1}^{2D-1} \widetilde{v}_j^{\gamma^{j-1}}$.
   (d) P sets $\mathbf{x} = \sum_{j=1}^{D} \mathbf{x}_{D-j+1} \cdot \gamma^{j-1}$, and $K = \left[\prod_{j=1}^{D} \begin{matrix} \mathbf{g}_j^{\gamma^{j-1}} \\ \mathbf{h}_j^{\gamma^{j-1}} \end{matrix} \right]$
   (e) $n := n/D$, $i := i + 1$
3. Let $h := i$
4. Prover sends $\mathbf{x} = (x_1, \cdots, x_D)$ to V^L.
5. Verifier V^L does the following:
   (a) Query L at $(\gamma_1, \cdots, \gamma_h)$ and receive $K = \begin{bmatrix} \mathbf{g} \\ \mathbf{h} \end{bmatrix} \in \mathbb{G}^{2 \times D}$ as response.
   (b) Check $v = \begin{bmatrix} \mathbf{g}^{\mathbf{x}} \\ \mathbf{h}^{\mathbf{x}} \end{bmatrix}$
   Accept if none of the checks have failed.

Fig. 4. Interactive Protocol $(\mathsf{P}, \mathsf{V}^L)$ for $\mathcal{L}_Y$

Acknowledgments. Abhishek Jain and Zhengzhong Jin were supported in part by NSF CNS-1814919, NSF CAREER 1942789 and Johns Hopkins University Catalyst award. Abhishek Jain was also supported in part by AFOSR Award FA9550-19-1-0200 and the Office of Naval Research Grant N00014-19-1-2294. Zhengzhong Jin was additionally supported in part by NSF CAREER 1845349 and by DARPA under Agreement No. HR00112020023 and by an NSF grant CNS-2154149.

The second author is supported in part by DARPA under Agreement No. HR00112020026, AFOSR Award FA9550-19-1-0200, NSF CNS Award 1936826, and research grants by the Sloan Foundation, and Visa Inc.

This research was conducted in part when Arka Rai Choudhuri was at UC Berkeley, and Jiaheng Zhang was an intern at NTT Research.

References

1. Ben-Sasson, E., et al.: Zerocash: decentralized anonymous payments from bitcoin. In: 2014 IEEE Symposium on Security and Privacy, pp. 459–474. IEEE Computer Society Press (May 2014)
2. Bitansky, N., et al.: The hunting of the SNARK. J. Cryptol. **30**(4), 989–1066 (2017)
3. Bitansky, N., Canetti, R., Chiesa, A., Tromer, E.: Recursive composition and bootstrapping for SNARKS and proof-carrying data. In: Boneh, D., Roughgarden, T., Feigenbaum, J. (eds.) 45th ACM STOC, pp. 111–120. ACM Press (Jun 2013)
4. Bitansky, N., Chiesa, A., Ishai, Y., Ostrovsky, R., Paneth, O.: Succinct noninteractive arguments via linear interactive proofs. In: Sahai, A. (ed.) TCC 2013. LNCS, vol. 7785, pp. 315–333. Springer, Heidelberg (2013). https://doi.org/10.1007/978-3-642-36594-2_18
5. Bootle, J., Cerulli, A., Chaidos, P., Groth, J., Petit, C.: Efficient zero-knowledge arguments for arithmetic circuits in the discrete log setting. In: Fischlin, M., Coron, J.S. (eds.) EUROCRYPT 2016, Part II. LNCS, vol. 9666, pp. 327–357. Springer, Heidelberg (2016). https://doi.org/10.1007/978-3-662-49896-5_12
6. Boyle, E., Gilboa, N., Ishai, Y.: Breaking the circuit size barrier for secure computation under DDH. In: Robshaw, M., Katz, J. (eds.) CRYPTO 2016, Part I. LNCS, vol. 9814, pp. 509–539. Springer, Heidelberg (2016). https://doi.org/10.1007/978-3-662-53018-4_19
7. Brakerski, Z., Koppula, V., Mour, T.: NIZK from LPN and trapdoor hash via correlation intractability for approximable relations. In: Micciancio, D., Ristenpart, T. (eds.) CRYPTO 2020, Part III. LNCS, vol. 12172, pp. 738–767. Springer, Heidelberg (2020). https://doi.org/10.1007/978-3-030-56877-1_26
8. Bünz, B., Bootle, J., Boneh, D., Poelstra, A., Wuille, P., Maxwell, G.: Bulletproofs: short proofs for confidential transactions and more. In: 2018 IEEE Symposium on Security and Privacy, pp. 315–334. IEEE Computer Society Press (May 2018)
9. Canetti, R., et al.: Fiat-Shamir: from practice to theory. In: Charikar, M., Cohen, E. (eds.) 51st ACM STOC, pp. 1082–1090. ACM Press (Jun 2019)
10. Canetti, R., Chen, Y., Reyzin, L.: On the correlation intractability of obfuscated pseudorandom functions. In: Kushilevitz, E., Malkin, T. (eds.) TCC 2016-A, Part I. LNCS, vol. 9562, pp. 389–415. Springer, Heidelberg (2016). https://doi.org/10.1007/978-3-662-49096-9_17
11. Canetti, R., Chen, Y., Reyzin, L., Rothblum, R.D.: Fiat-Shamir and correlation intractability from strong KDM-secure encryption. In: Nielsen, J.B., Rijmen, V. (eds.) EUROCRYPT 2018, Part I. LNCS, vol. 10820, pp. 91–122. Springer, Heidelberg (2018). https://doi.org/10.1007/978-3-319-78381-9_4
12. Canetti, R., Goldreich, O., Halevi, S.: The random oracle methodology, revisited. J. ACM **51**(4), 557–594 (Jul 2004). https://doi.org/10.1145/1008731.1008734

13. Chen, Y., Lombardi, A., Ma, F., Quach, W.: Does fiat-shamir require a cryptographic hash function? In: Malkin, T., Peikert, C. (eds.) CRYPTO 2021, Part IV. LNCS, vol. 12828, pp. 334–363. Springer, Heidelberg (2021). https://doi.org/10.1007/978-3-030-84259-8_12

14. Choudhuri, A.R., Garg, S., Jain, A., Jin, Z., Zhang, J.: Correlation intractability and SNARGs from sub-exponential DDH. Cryptology ePrint Archive, Report 2022/1486 (2022). https://eprint.iacr.org/2022/1486

15. Choudhuri, A.R., Hubácek, P., Kamath, C., Pietrzak, K., Rosen, A., Rothblum, G.N.: Finding a nash equilibrium is no easier than breaking Fiat-Shamir. In: Charikar, M., Cohen, E. (eds.) 51st ACM STOC, pp. 1103–1114. ACM Press (Jun 2019)

16. Choudhuri, A.R., Jain, A., Jin, Z.: Non-interactive batch arguments for NP from standard assumptions. In: Malkin, T., Peikert, C. (eds.) CRYPTO 2021, Part IV. LNCS, vol. 12828, pp. 394–423. Springer, Heidelberg (2021). https://doi.org/10.1007/978-3-030-84259-8_14

17. Choudhuri, A.R., Jain, A., Jin, Z.: SNARGs for $\mathcal{P}$ from LWE. In: 62nd FOCS, pp. 68–79. IEEE Computer Society Press (Feb 2022)

18. Couteau, G., Katsumata, S., Ursu, B.: Non-interactive zero-knowledge in pairing-free groups from weaker assumptions. In: Canteaut, A., Ishai, Y. (eds.) EURO-CRYPT 2020, Part III. LNCS, vol. 12107, pp. 442–471. Springer, Heidelberg (2020). https://doi.org/10.1007/978-3-030-45727-3_15

19. Devadas, L., Goyal, R., Kalai, Y., Vaikuntanathan, V.: Rate-1 non-interactive arguments for batch-NP and applications. In: 63rd FOCS, pp. 1057–1068. IEEE Computer Society Press (Oct/Nov 2022)

20. Döttling, N., Garg, S.: Identity-based encryption from the Diffie-Hellman assumption. In: Katz, J., Shacham, H. (eds.) CRYPTO 2017, Part I. LNCS, vol. 10401, pp. 537–569. Springer, Heidelberg (2017). https://doi.org/10.1007/978-3-319-63688-7_18

21. Döttling, N., Garg, S., Ishai, Y., Malavolta, G., Mour, T., Ostrovsky, R.: Trapdoor hash functions and their applications. In: Boldyreva, A., Micciancio, D. (eds.) CRYPTO 2019, Part III. LNCS, vol. 11694, pp. 3–32. Springer, Heidelberg (Aug 2019)

22. Fiat, A., Shamir, A.: How to prove yourself: Practical solutions to identification and signature problems. In: Odlyzko, A.M. (ed.) CRYPTO'86. LNCS, vol. 263, pp. 186–194. Springer, Heidelberg (1987)

23. Freitag, C., Pass, R., Sirkin, N.: Parallelizable delegation from LWE. In: Kiltz, E., Vaikuntanathan, V. (eds.) TCC 2022, Part II. LNCS, vol. 13748, pp. 623–652. Springer, Heidelberg (2022)

24. Gennaro, R., Gentry, C., Parno, B., Raykova, M.: Quadratic span programs and succinct NIZKs without PCPs. In: Johansson, T., Nguyen, P.Q. (eds.) EURO-CRYPT 2013. LNCS, vol. 7881, pp. 626–645. Springer, Heidelberg (2013). https://doi.org/10.1007/978-3-642-38348-9_37

25. Gentry, C., Wichs, D.: Separating succinct non-interactive arguments from all falsifiable assumptions. In: Fortnow, L., Vadhan, S.P. (eds.) 43rd ACM STOC, pp. 99–108. ACM Press (Jun 2011)

26. Grossman, O., Holmgren, J., Yogev, E.: Transparent error correcting in a computationally bounded world. In: Pass, R., Pietrzak, K. (eds.) TCC 2020, Part III. LNCS, vol. 12552, pp. 530–549. Springer, Heidelberg (2020). https://doi.org/10.1007/978-3-030-64381-2_19

27. Groth, J.: Short pairing-based non-interactive zero-knowledge arguments. In: Abe, M. (ed.) ASIACRYPT 2010. LNCS, vol. 6477, pp. 321–340. Springer, Heidelberg (2010). https://doi.org/10.1007/978-3-642-17373-8_19

28. Groth, J.: On the size of pairing-based non-interactive arguments. In: Fischlin, M., Coron, J.S. (eds.) EUROCRYPT 2016, Part II. LNCS, vol. 9666, pp. 305–326. Springer, Heidelberg (2016). https://doi.org/10.1007/978-3-662-49896-5_11

29. Groth, J., Ostrovsky, R., Sahai, A.: Perfect non-interactive zero knowledge for NP. In: Vaudenay, S. (ed.) EUROCRYPT 2006. LNCS, vol. 4004, pp. 339–358. Springer, Heidelberg (2006). https://doi.org/10.1007/11761679_21

30. Holmgren, J., Lombardi, A.: Cryptographic hashing from strong one-way functions (or: One-way product functions and their applications). In: Thorup, M. (ed.) 59th FOCS, pp. 850–858. IEEE Computer Society Press (Oct 2018)

31. Holmgren, J., Lombardi, A., Rothblum, R.D.: Fiat-Shamir via list-recoverable codes (or: parallel repetition of GMW is not zero-knowledge). In: Khuller, S., Williams, V.V. (eds.) 53rd ACM STOC, pp. 750–760. ACM Press (Jun 2021)

32. Hubacek, P., Wichs, D.: On the communication complexity of secure function evaluation with long output. In: Roughgarden, T. (ed.) ITCS 2015, pp. 163–172. ACM (Jan 2015)

33. Hulett, J., Jawale, R., Khurana, D., Srinivasan, A.: SNARGs for P from sub-exponential DDH and QR. In: Dunkelman, O., Dziembowski, S. (eds.) EURO-CRYPT 2022, Part II. LNCS, vol. 13276, pp. 520–549. Springer, Heidelberg (2022). https://doi.org/10.1007/978-3-031-07085-3_18

34. Jain, A., Jin, Z.: Non-interactive zero knowledge from sub-exponential DDH. In: Canteaut, A., Standaert, F.X. (eds.) EUROCRYPT 2021, Part I. LNCS, vol. 12696, pp. 3–32. Springer, Heidelberg (2021). https://doi.org/10.1007/978-3-030-77870-5_1

35. Jawale, R., Kalai, Y.T., Khurana, D., Zhang, R.Y.: SNARGs for bounded depth computations and PPAD hardness from sub-exponential LWE. In: Khuller, S., Williams, V.V. (eds.) 53rd ACM STOC, pp. 708–721. ACM Press (Jun 2021)

36. Kalai, Y.T., Lombardi, A., Vaikuntanathan, V.: SNARGs and PPAD hardness from the decisional diffie-hellman assumption. Cryptology ePrint Archive, Report 2022/1409 (2022). https://eprint.iacr.org/2022/1409

37. Kalai, Y.T., Lombardi, A., Vaikuntanathan, V., Wichs, D.: Boosting batch arguments and RAM delegation. Cryptology ePrint Archive, Report 2022/1320 (2022). https://eprint.iacr.org/2022/1320

38. Kalai, Y.T., Paneth, O., Yang, L.: How to delegate computations publicly. In: Charikar, M., Cohen, E. (eds.) 51st ACM STOC, pp. 1115–1124. ACM Press (Jun 2019)

39. Kalai, Y.T., Raz, R., Rothblum, R.D.: Delegation for bounded space. In: Boneh, D., Roughgarden, T., Feigenbaum, J. (eds.) 45th ACM STOC, pp. 565–574. ACM Press (Jun 2013)

40. Kalai, Y.T., Raz, R., Rothblum, R.D.: How to delegate computations: the power of no-signaling proofs. In: Shmoys, D.B. (ed.) 46th ACM STOC, pp. 485–494. ACM Press (May/Jun 2014)

41. Kalai, Y.T., Rothblum, G.N., Rothblum, R.D.: From obfuscation to the security of Fiat-Shamir for proofs. In: Katz, J., Shacham, H. (eds.) CRYPTO 2017, Part II. LNCS, vol. 10402, pp. 224–251. Springer, Heidelberg (2017). https://doi.org/10.1007/978-3-319-63715-0_8

42. Kalai, Y.T., Vaikuntanathan, V., Zhang, R.Y.: Somewhere statistical soundness, post-quantum security, and SNARGs. In: Nissim, K., Waters, B. (eds.) TCC 2021, Part I. LNCS, vol. 13042, pp. 330–368. Springer, Heidelberg (2021). https://doi.org/10.1007/978-3-030-90459-3_12

43. Kilian, J.: A note on efficient zero-knowledge proofs and arguments (extended abstract). In: 24th ACM STOC, pp. 723–732. ACM Press (May 1992)

44. Lipmaa, H.: Progression-free sets and sublinear pairing-based non-interactive zero-knowledge arguments. In: Cramer, R. (ed.) TCC 2012. LNCS, vol. 7194, pp. 169–189. Springer, Heidelberg (2012). https://doi.org/10.1007/978-3-642-28914-9_10

45. Lombardi, A., Vaikuntanathan, V.: Fiat-shamir for repeated squaring with applications to PPAD-hardness and VDFs. In: Micciancio, D., Ristenpart, T. (eds.) CRYPTO 2020, Part III. LNCS, vol. 12172, pp. 632–651. Springer, Heidelberg (2020). https://doi.org/10.1007/978-3-030-56877-1_22

46. Lombardi, A., Vaikuntanathan, V.: Correlation-intractable hash functions via shift-hiding. In: Braverman, M. (ed.) 13th Innovations in Theoretical Computer Science Conference, ITCS 2022, January 31 - February 3, 2022, Berkeley, CA, USA. LIPIcs, vol. 215, pp. 102:1–102:16. Schloss Dagstuhl - Leibniz-Zentrum für Informatik (2022)

47. Micali, S.: CS proofs (extended abstracts). In: 35th FOCS, pp. 436–453. IEEE Computer Society Press (Nov 1994)

48. Mour, T.: Correlation intractability vs. one-wayness. Cryptology ePrint Archive, Report 2021/057 (2021). https://eprint.iacr.org/2021/057

49. Naor, M.: On cryptographic assumptions and challenges (invited talk). In: Boneh, D. (ed.) CRYPTO 2003. LNCS, vol. 2729, pp. 96–109. Springer, Heidelberg (2003). https://doi.org/10.1007/978-3-540-45146-4_6

50. Okamoto, T., Pietrzak, K., Waters, B., Wichs, D.: New realizations of somewhere statistically binding hashing and positional accumulators. In: Iwata, T., Cheon, J.H. (eds.) ASIACRYPT 2015, Part I. LNCS, vol. 9452, pp. 121–145. Springer, Heidelberg (2015)

51. Paneth, O., Pass, R.: Incrementally verifiable computation via rate-1 batch arguments. In: 63rd FOCS, pp. 1045–1056. IEEE Computer Society Press (Oct/Nov 2022)

52. Peikert, C., Shiehian, S.: Noninteractive zero knowledge for NP from (plain) learning with errors. In: Boldyreva, A., Micciancio, D. (eds.) CRYPTO 2019, Part I. LNCS, vol. 11692, pp. 89–114. Springer, Heidelberg (2019). https://doi.org/10.1007/978-3-030-26948-7_4

53. Waters, B., Wu, D.J.: Batch arguments for sfNP and more from standard bilinear group assumptions. In: Dodis, Y., Shrimpton, T. (eds.) CRYPTO 2022, Part II. LNCS, vol. 13508, pp. 433–463. Springer, Heidelberg (2022)

54. Zhandry, M.: The magic of ELFs. In: Robshaw, M., Katz, J. (eds.) CRYPTO 2016, Part I. LNCS, vol. 9814, pp. 479–508. Springer, Heidelberg (2016)

Algebraic Reductions of Knowledge

Abhiram Kothapalli$^{(\boxtimes)}$ and Bryan Parno

Carnegie Mellon University, Pittsburgh, USA
{akothapalli,parno}@cmu.edu

Abstract. We introduce *reductions of knowledge*, a generalization of arguments of knowledge, which reduce checking knowledge of a witness in one relation to checking knowledge of a witness in another (simpler) relation. Reductions of knowledge unify a growing class of modern techniques as well as provide a compositional framework to modularly reason about individual steps in complex arguments of knowledge. As a demonstration, we simplify and unify recursive arguments over linear algebraic statements by decomposing them as a sequence of reductions of knowledge. To do so, we develop the *tensor reduction of knowledge*, which generalizes the central reductive step common to many recursive arguments. Underlying the tensor reduction of knowledge is a new information-theoretic reduction, which, for any modules U, U_1, and U_2 such that $U \cong U_1 \otimes U_2$, reduces the task of evaluating a homomorphism in U to evaluating a homomorphism in U_1 and evaluating a homomorphism in U_2.

Keywords: Arguments of knowledge · Composition

1 Introduction

Arguments of knowledge [27] are powerful cryptographic primitives that allow a verifier to efficiently check that a prover *knows* a satisfying witness for a claimed statement. Such arguments provide strong integrity and privacy guarantees that enable a large class of cryptographic applications [21, 28, 37, 40, 43].

However, a growing body of work challenges the traditional paradigm by describing interactions in which the verifier does not fully resolve the prover's statement to true or false, but rather reduces it to a simpler statement to be checked:

- The well-studied *inner-product argument* [10] (along with subsequent optimizations [13] and generalizations [11, 16]) relies on recursively applying an interactive reduction from the task of checking knowledge of size n vectors to the task of checking knowledge of size $n/2$ vectors.

Abhiram Kothapalli was supported by a fellowship from Protocol Labs, a gift from Bosch, NSF Grant No. 1801369, and the CONIX Research Center, one of six centers in JUMP, a Semiconductor Research Corporation program sponsored by DARPA. An extended version of this work is available on the Cryptology ePrint Archive [30].

© International Association for Cryptologic Research 2023
H. Handschuh and A. Lysyanskaya (Eds.): CRYPTO 2023, LNCS 14084, pp. 669–701, 2023.
https://doi.org/10.1007/978-3-031-38551-3_21

- *Aggregation schemes* for polynomial commitments [9,12] and *unbounded aggregation schemes* for linear-map vector commitments [18] can both be viewed as interactive reductions from checking proofs of several openings of a commitment to checking a proof of a single opening of a commitment.
- *Split-accumulation schemes* [14] can be viewed as interactive reductions from checking several proofs of knowledge and several accumulators to checking a single accumulator. *Folding schemes* [31] can be viewed as interactive reductions from checking knowledge of two instances in a relation to checking knowledge of a single instance in the relation.
- As observed by Ràfols and Zapico [35], most argument systems with universal and updatable trusted setups [17,19,29,39] construct an interactive reduction from the task of checking knowledge of a preimage of a matrix evaluation to the task of checking knowledge of a preimage of a vector evaluation.

Such interactive reductions, although central to modern arguments, lack a unifying theoretical foundation. As evidenced above, these reductions typically have case-by-case security definitions (if any at all) that are tailored towards the larger systems that rely on them. The lack of a common language makes it difficult to relate comparable techniques hidden under incomparable abstractions. Moreover, stitching together various techniques requires remarkably delicate (and often tedious) reasoning for how the soundness of the larger protocol reduces to the soundness of each subprotocol.

Contributions. Towards a unifying language, we formalize the notion of an interactive reduction over statements of knowledge, in which the verifier reduces the task of checking the original statement to the task of checking a new (simpler) statement. We refer to such a protocol as a *reduction of knowledge*. We prove that reductions of knowledge can be composed sequentially and in parallel. As such, reductions of knowledge serve as both a crisp abstraction and a theory of composition. In particular, they can be stitched together to modularly construct complex arguments of knowledge. Under this treatment, each step of an argument is instilled with a meaningful (and composable) soundness guarantee. This enables significantly simpler soundness proofs and allows each subcomponent to be reused independently in other protocols.

As a technical contribution, we employ reductions of knowledge to unify recursive algebraic arguments and simplify the corresponding analysis. In particular, we develop the *tensor reduction of knowledge* as a generalization of the central recursive step for arguments in this class. By instantiating and recursively composing the tensor reduction of knowledge over appropriate spaces, we derive both new and existing arguments of knowledge for various linear algebraic structures. Most notably, we derive a new argument of knowledge for *bilinear forms* which are expressive enough to encode weighted (and permuted) inner-products and more generally any degree-two gate over vectors of inputs.

Throughout our development, we provide various examples to demonstrate how reductions of knowledge offer a promising route towards taming the complexity of modern arguments. Most notably, we compose our linear algebraic reductions to construct an argument of knowledge for NP with logarithmic communication with minimal additional reasoning.

1.1   Reductions of Knowledge

Recall that arguments of knowledge are defined over a relation $\mathcal{R}$ and allow a prover to show for some statement u that it knows witness w such that $(u, w) \in \mathcal{R}$. In contrast, a reduction of knowledge is defined over a pair of relations $\mathcal{R}_1$ and $\mathcal{R}_2$, and enables a verifier to reduce the task of checking knowledge of a satisfying witness for a statement in $\mathcal{R}_1$ to the task of checking knowledge of a satisfying witness for a new statement in $\mathcal{R}_2$.

Definition 1 (Reduction of Knowledge, Informal). *A reduction of knowledge from $\mathcal{R}_1$ to $\mathcal{R}_2$ is an interactive protocol between a prover and a verifier. Both parties take as input a claimed statement u_1 to be checked, and the prover additionally takes as input a corresponding witness w_1 such that $(u_1, w_1) \in \mathcal{R}_1$. After interaction, the prover and verifier together output a new statement u_2 to be checked in place of the original statement, and the prover additionally outputs a corresponding witness w_2 such that $(u_2, w_2) \in \mathcal{R}_2$. A reduction of knowledge satisfies the following properties.*

(i) Completeness: If the prover is provided a satisfying witness w_1 for the verifier's input statement u_1, then the prover outputs a satisfying witness w_2 for the verifier's output statement u_2.

(ii) Knowledge Soundness: If an arbitrary prover provides a satisfying witness w_2 for the verifier's output statement u_2, then the prover almost certainly knows a satisfying witness w_1 for the verifier's input statement u_1.

We write $\Pi : \mathcal{R}_1 \to \mathcal{R}_2$ to denote that protocol Π is a reduction of knowledge from $\mathcal{R}_1$ to $\mathcal{R}_2$.

There are two ways to conceptually reconcile reductions of knowledge with arguments of knowledge. First, arguments of knowledge can be viewed as a special case of reductions of knowledge where the second relation $\mathcal{R}_2$ is fixed to encode true or false. This interpretation helps naturally translate existing tooling used to study arguments of knowledge to study reductions of knowledge. For instance, we can expect reductions of knowledge to be compatible with idealized soundness models such as the random oracle model [5] and the algebraic group model [23], idealized communication models such as interactive oracle proofs [6] and variants [15,17,19], and heuristic transformations such as Fiat-Shamir [22].

Second, reductions of knowledge can be interpreted as arguments for *conditional* statements in which a prover shows for some u_1 that it knows w_1 such that $(u_1, w_1) \in \mathcal{R}_1$ *contingent* on the fact that for u_2 output by the verifier it knows w_2 such that $(u_2, w_2) \in \mathcal{R}_2$. Put more plainly, reductions of knowledge are arguments for statements of the form "If you believe that I know a witness for statement u_2 in $\mathcal{R}_2$, then you should believe that I know a witness for statement

u_1 in $\mathcal{R}_1$". This interpretation helps characterize statements that reductions of knowledge can handle more naturally than arguments of knowledge.

Reductions of knowledge can also be viewed as a probabilistic variant of Levin reductions [2] (i.e., Karp reductions [2] that map witnesses as well as statements) that verifiably proceed through interaction. Under this interpretation, Levin reductions can be understood as deterministic reductions of knowledge with no interaction. Just as standard reductions are used for principled algorithm design, reductions of knowledge are intended for principled argument design.

Under any interpretation, we are interested in proving that reductions of knowledge can be composed sequentially and in parallel. Such a requirement holds immediately for standard notions of reductions, but requires subtle reasoning when considering knowledge soundness: To ensure that sequential composability holds, we additionally require that reductions of knowledge are *publicly reducible*. That is, given the input statement u_1 and the interaction transcript, any party should be able to reconstruct the output statement u_2. As we detail in Sect. 4, this seemingly innocuous requirement becomes the linchpin in arguing sequential composability. With public reducibility, we have the following.

Theorem 1 (Sequential Composition, Informal). *Consider relations $\mathcal{R}_1$, $\mathcal{R}_2$, and $\mathcal{R}_3$. For reductions of knowledge $\Pi_1 : \mathcal{R}_1 \to \mathcal{R}_2$ and $\Pi_2 : \mathcal{R}_2 \to \mathcal{R}_3$ we have that $\Pi_2 \circ \Pi_1$ is a reduction of knowledge from $\mathcal{R}_1$ to $\mathcal{R}_3$ where $\Pi_2 \circ \Pi_1$ denotes the protocol that first runs Π_1, and then runs Π_2 on the statement and witness output by Π_1.*

By parallel composition, we do not mean running both protocols at the same time, but rather that the composed protocol takes as input instance-witness pairs in parallel and and outputs instance-witness pairs in parallel. For relations $\mathcal{R}_1$ and $\mathcal{R}_2$, let relation $\mathcal{R}_1 \times \mathcal{R}_2$ be such that $((u_1, u_2), (w_1, w_2)) \in \mathcal{R}_1 \times \mathcal{R}_2$ if and only if $(u_1, w_1) \in \mathcal{R}_1$ and $(u_2, w_2) \in \mathcal{R}_2$. Then, we have the following.

Theorem 2 (Parallel Composition, Informal). *Consider relations $\mathcal{R}_1$, $\mathcal{R}_2$, $\mathcal{R}_3$, and $\mathcal{R}_4$. For reductions of knowledge $\Pi_1 : \mathcal{R}_1 \to \mathcal{R}_2$ and $\Pi_2 : \mathcal{R}_3 \to \mathcal{R}_4$ we have that $\Pi_1 \times \Pi_2$ is a reduction of knowledge from $\mathcal{R}_1 \times \mathcal{R}_3$ to $\mathcal{R}_2 \times \mathcal{R}_4$ where $\Pi_1 \times \Pi_2$ denotes the protocol that runs Π_1 on the statement-witness pair in $\mathcal{R}_1$, runs Π_2 on the statement-witness pair in $\mathcal{R}_3$, and outputs the pair of results.*

1.2   A Theory of Composition for Arguments of Knowledge

Reductions of knowledge can be viewed as a minimal compositional framework that can feasibly capture and tame the growing complexity of modern arguments. Regardless of how reductions are stitched together, our composition results abstract out the pedantic reasoning for how exactly to use the soundness of each subcomponent to prove the soundness of the composed reduction. We develop several examples to concretely demonstrate how the reductions of knowledge framework opens up new possibilities.

In more detail, the requirement that the prover *knows* a witness is formally stated as an extractability property: Given an expected polynomial-time prover that can produce a satisfying interaction, there must exist a corresponding expected polynomial-time extractor that can extract the alleged witness (e.g., by running and rewinding the prover internally). This definition, while undoubtedly natural, requires subtle reasoning when constructing large arguments which rely on several sub-arguments: In general, the soundness analysis must meticulously detail how to use the successful prover to construct successful provers for each sub-argument and then use the corresponding extractors to derive an extractor for the overall argument.

In the public-coin setting (where the verifier only sends random challenges), Bootle et al. [10] abstract away some low-level reasoning by proving that *tree special soundness* implies the standard notion of knowledge soundness. Tree special soundness holds when a *tree of accepting transcripts* contains sufficient information to reconstruct the witness, with each path representing a unique transcript and each branch representing diverging verifier randomness. Both Lee [32] and Attema and Cramer [3] show that tree special soundness implies modularity by observing that tree special sound protocols can be sequentially composed to produce a tree special sound protocol.

As demonstrated by these works, tree special soundness is a remarkably useful abstraction for simplifying sequentially composed, uniformly structured arguments (e.g., arguments that recursively invoke themselves). However, when dealing with larger arguments that invoke various *independent* sub-arguments, such as modern arguments for NP, tree special soundness is no longer an appropriate abstraction: having a single transcript that weaves through all such sub-arguments and globally forks with each local challenge undermines the intended semantics and unnecessarily blows up the knowledge error (i.e., the extractor's failure probability).

Reductions of knowledge are designed precisely to reason about such arguments. Unlike prior work, our parallel composition operator enables us to capture arguments with arbitrary dependence topologies. For instance, most argument systems for NP, such as Spartan [39], Poppins [29], and Marlin [19], reduce a statement in an NP-complete relation such as R1CS [25] to several simpler linear algebraic statements (such as inner-product and polynomial evaluation claims), each of which is then checked using a tailored argument [35]. As a concrete example, we show that an argument for NP can be captured modularly in our framework by utilizing both sequential and parallel composition.

Moreover, because we demonstrate that *any* two publicly verifiable reductions can be composed, this opens up the ability to modularly reason about knowledge-assumption-based succinct non-interactive arguments of knowledge (SNARKs [7, 26]) and incrementally verifiable computation [41], which currently fall back on composing extractors in intricate ways [14,29,31]. As a concrete example, we demonstrate how to succinctly express non-interactive ℓ-*folding schemes* [31, 36] (i.e., folding schemes reducing ℓ initial instances) by utilizing a tree-like dependence topology in our reductions of knowledge framework.

In the public-coin setting, we incorporate prior progress into our framework by proving that tree special soundness implies our notion of knowledge soundness. As such, public-coin reductions can be analyzed using standard techniques.

1.3 A Unified Theory for Recursive Algebraic Arguments

Reductions of knowledge provide the necessary abstraction to view various techniques under a unifying lens. As a demonstration, we consolidate recursive arguments over homomorphic structures by recasting their central recursive step as instantiations of the tensor reduction of knowledge.

In more detail, modern arguments are designed around leveraging homomorphic structure to achieve better asymptotics and concrete efficiency. An influential line of work [3,4,10,13,32] studies the consequences of arguments over structurally nested homomorphic objects such as vectors, matrices and hypercubes. A key insight is that such objects contain sufficient algebraic structure for *recursive* arguments in which larger composed statements can be reduced to smaller constituent statements of the same form. For instance, Bootle et al. [10] show that the task of checking an inner-product over committed size n vectors can be split into the task of checking two inner-products over committed size $n/2$ vectors which can then be "folded" into the task of checking a single inner-product over committed size $n/2$ vectors. Homomorphic structures that enable recursive techniques have become a staple in constructing efficient argument systems for NP [13,29,39,42]. However, while arguments over recursive homomorphic structures have become an essential tool in practice, the literature detailing such techniques is becoming increasingly dissonant with sparse progress on unifying the disparate approaches.

Bünz et al. [16] initiate the study of a unified theory by observing that existing inner-product arguments [10,13] only require a commitment scheme that is homomorphic over both the commitment keys and messages. Thus, such inner-product arguments can be viewed as instantiations of a generic inner-product argument that only leverages these properties. Bootle, et al. [11] further relax this requirement by observing that split-and-fold style techniques in general [3,13,15,16] only require a commitment scheme that can be computed by summing over a hypercube. Leveraging this insight, Bootle et al. show that such techniques can be interpreted as instantiations of the familiar sum-check protocol [33].

We considerably sharpen the sufficient conditions with the following observation: Protocols such as the sumcheck protocol and the inner-product argument only require that the underlying linear-algebraic objects (e.g., polynomials, vectors, and matrices) form a module (i.e., have a notion of addition and scalar multiplication). Abstracting away the specific details of the associated modules, all such protocols reduce a claim in a "tensored" module to claims in constituent modules. Leveraging this insight, we design an information-theoretic protocol, the *tensor reduction*, as a sweeping generalization of protocols in this class. Conceptually, the tensor reduction explains why such a broad class of protocols look different but feel the same.

Theorem 3 (Tensor Reduction, Informal). *For modules U, U_1, and U_2 such that $U \cong U_1 \otimes U_2$, there exists an interactive reduction that reduces the task of evaluating a homomorphism in U to the task of evaluating a homomorphism in U_1 and evaluating a homomorphism in U_2.*

We explain in detail how the tensor reduction generalizes familiar patterns in Sect. 5. Essentially, the versatility of the tensor reduction stems from its ability to work over any pair of modules and any valid notion of a tensor product between these modules. In particular, the tensor product can be defined as *any* operator that satisfies the prescribed universality property: the tensor product of any two modules U_1 and U_2 must result in a new module, denoted $U_1 \otimes U_2$, such that any bilinear mapping $\varphi : U_1 \times U_2 \to V$ induces a unique homomorphism $\widetilde{\varphi} : U_1 \otimes U_2 \to V$ such that $\widetilde{\varphi}(u_1 \otimes u_2) = \varphi(u_1, u_2)$.

For instance, for field $\mathbb{F}$, let the tensor product denote the outer product and consider an arbitrary vector in $\mathbb{F}^n$. This vector can be interpreted as a matrix in $\mathbb{F}^{(n/2) \times 2}$ or equivalently as an element of $\mathbb{F}^{n/2} \otimes \mathbb{F}^2$ which consists of sums of outer products of vectors in $\mathbb{F}^{n/2}$ and $\mathbb{F}^2$. Thus, the tensor reduction can reduce a claim over a vector in $\mathbb{F}^n$ to a claim over a vector in $\mathbb{F}^{n/2}$ and a vector in $\mathbb{F}^2$. Similarly, by taking the tensor product to be polynomial multiplication, the tensor reduction can reduce a claim over a degree (m, n) bivariate polynomial in $\mathbb{F}[X, Y] \cong \mathbb{F}[X] \otimes \mathbb{F}[Y]$ to a claim over a degree m univariate polynomial in $\mathbb{F}[X]$ and a degree n univariate polynomial in $\mathbb{F}[Y]$. By taking the tensor product to be the Kronecker product, the tensor reduction can reduce a claim over a matrix in $\mathbb{F}^{mp \times nq}$ to a claim over a matrix in $\mathbb{F}^{m \times n}$ and a matrix in $\mathbb{F}^{p \times q}$. By taking the tensor product to be a pairing operation mapping groups $\mathbb{G}_1$ and $\mathbb{G}_2$ to $\mathbb{G}_T$, the tensor reduction can reduce a claim over $\mathbb{G}_T$ to claims over $\mathbb{G}_1$ and $\mathbb{G}_2$.

Just as the sum-check protocol can be used to design arguments of knowledge, the tensor reduction can be used to design reductions of knowledge. By instantiating the tensor reduction over vector spaces, we derive the *tensor reduction of knowledge*, an unconditionally secure protocol that generalizes the central reductive step common to most recursive algebraic arguments.

Theorem 4 (Tensor Reduction of Knowledge, Informal). *For vector space $\mathrm{hom}(W, V)$, denoting homomorphisms from vector space W to vector space V, and length n, there exists a reduction of knowledge that reduces the task of checking knowledge of $w \in W^n$ such that $u(w) = v$ for $u \in \mathrm{hom}(W^n, V)$ and $v \in V$ to the task of checking knowledge of $w' \in W$ such that $u'(w') = v'$ for $u' \in \mathrm{hom}(W, V)$ and $v' \in V$.*

Leveraging our composition result, we show that tensor reductions of knowledge can be recursively composed to recover various recursive arguments. In particular, we appropriately instantiate the vector spaces to recover a family of reductions of knowledge for vector commitments [9–11], and linear forms [3,4]. Table 1 summarizes the concrete protocols synthesized under the various instantiations of the tensor reduction of knowledge.

We also develop a new family of arguments for bilinear forms which falls out naturally from our prior generalizations. In particular, consider prime order group $\mathbb{G}$ and corresponding scalar field $\mathbb{F}$. For public key $G \in \mathbb{G}^m$, public matrix $M \in \mathbb{F}^{m \times m}$, commitments $\overline{A}, \overline{B} \in \mathbb{G}$, and scalar $\sigma \in \mathbb{F}$, a bilinear forms argument allows a verifier to check that a prover knows $A, B \in \mathbb{F}^m$ such that $A^\top M B = \sigma$, $\langle G, A \rangle = \overline{A}$ (i.e., the inner-product of G and A is $\overline{A}$), and $\langle G, B \rangle = \overline{B}$.

In practice, the matrix M in the bilinear forms relation can encode a variety of constraints. For instance, if M is the identity matrix then the verifier can check the inner-product of A and B (and more generally the inner product of any rearrangement of A and B). If instead M assigns weights to the diagonal, then the verifier can check a weighted inner-product [16,20]. More generally, M can encode any degree-two custom-gate [24], enabling an expressive constraint system for NP as we show in Sect. 7.

Table 1. Protocols synthesized by instantiating the tensor reduction of knowledge. We denote previously unexplored protocols with ✓. PO Group indicates prime order groups and Bil Group indicates symmetric bilinear groups. The parameter k denotes the number of chunks tensors are decomposed into in the tensor reduction of knowledge. For vectors of size n, $k = 2$ results in protocols with $O(\log n)$ rounds of communication and $O(1)$ messages per round. Alternatively, $k = \sqrt[4]{n}$ results in protocols with $O(1)$ rounds of communication and $O(\sqrt{n})$ messages per round.

Structure	Module	Decomposition	
		$k = 2$	$k = \sqrt[4]{n}$
Vector Commitment	PO Groups	[10]	✓
	Bil Groups	[11]	✓
Linear Forms	PO Groups	[3]	[3]
	Bil Groups	[4]	✓
Bilinear Forms	Bil Groups	✓	✓

1.4 Overview of the Upcoming Sections

The remainder of this work formally treats all of the introduced concepts. In Sect. 2, we study two concrete examples, the vector commitment argument [10] and ℓ-folding schemes [31,36], to both preface the tensor reduction of knowledge and demonstrate how our framework simplifies the corresponding analysis. In Sect. 4, we formally treat reductions of knowledge and the corresponding composition results. In Sect. 5, we formally introduce the tensor reduction, followed by the tensor reduction of knowledge as a generalization of the core reductive step common to most recursive algebraic arguments. In Sect. 6, we instantiate the tensor reduction of knowledge to derive arguments for vector commitments, linear forms, and bilinear forms. In Sect. 7, we show that the linear algebraic reductions derived from the tensor reduction of knowledge can be composed to derive an argument of knowledge for NP with minimal effort.

2   Technical Overview

In this section, we demonstrate how reductions of knowledge can be used to modularly reason about the vector commitment argument of Bootle et al. [10] and folding schemes [31] in the non-interactive setting [36]. The former example, being a special case of the tensor reduction of knowledge, provides an introductory overview of its mechanics. The latter example demonstrates how the reductions of knowledge framework can significantly simplify arguments with non-linear dependence topologies. We additionally demonstrate how reductions of knowledge provide a unifying language by formally defining arguments of knowledge and folding schemes as particular types of reductions.

2.1   First Example: A Vector Commitment Argument

The vector commitment argument allows a prover to show that it knows the opening to a Pedersen vector commitment [34]. In particular, consider group $\mathbb{G}$ of prime order p and corresponding scalar field $\mathbb{F} = \mathbb{Z}_p$. Consider some public key $G \in \mathbb{G}^n$ where $n = 2^i$ for some $i \in \mathbb{N}$. Suppose a prover would like to *succinctly* demonstrate to a verifier that it knows $A \in \mathbb{F}^n$ such that $\langle G, A \rangle = \overline{A}$ (i.e., the inner-product of G and A is $\overline{A}$). That is, we would like to design an argument of knowledge for the following relation.

Definition 2 (Vector Commitment Relation). *The vector commitment relation is defined as* $\mathcal{R}_{\mathsf{VC}}(n) = \{((G, \overline{A}), A) \in ((\mathbb{G}^n, \mathbb{G}), \mathbb{F}^n) \mid \langle G, A \rangle = \overline{A}\}$.

Bootle et al. [10] provide an argument system with sublinear communication cost for the above relation. At a high level, the verifier splits the task of checking knowledge of vector A into the task of checking knowledge of the first and second half of A. Instead of checking each separately, the verifier "folds" the two checks into a single check using a random linear combination. The prover computes the corresponding random linear combination of the first and second half of A to produce a folded witness vector that is half the original size. This folding procedure is recursively run until the length of the vector to be checked is 1. At this point the prover directly sends the vector to the verifier.

While the vector commitment argument can be described in a straightforward manner, proving its soundness is considerably more involved. Recursive arguments typically require recursive extractors, and the vector commitment argument is no exception. To prove knowledge soundness, the malicious prover, which produces a length one witness vector as its final message, is used to build an extractor that can produce a length two folded witness vector (which is allegedly the result of folding the original witness vector $\log n - 1$ times). Such an extractor is recursively used to produce an extractor that can produce a length four vector, and so on. Ensuring that the extractor can successively unfold in each recursive step while also ensuring that its runtime remains expected polynomial-time requires tedious low-level reasoning. Bootle et al. [10] and following works [3,13,32] use tree special soundness precisely to avoid such reasoning.

We show that the reductions of knowledge framework is equally as effective in simplifying the analysis for the vector commitment argument. In particular, we start with the simpler goal of designing a reduction of knowledge that reduces the task of checking knowledge of a size n vector to checking knowledge of a size $n/2$ vector. We can recursively compose such a reduction to design an argument of knowledge for the vector commitment relation.

Construction 1 (Vector Commitment Reduction of Knowledge). We construct a reduction of knowledge from $\mathcal{R}_{VC}(n)$ to $\mathcal{R}_{VC}(n/2)$ for $n = 2^i$ where $i \geq 1$. Suppose that the prover $\mathcal{P}$ and verifier $\mathcal{V}$ take as input statement $(G, \overline{A}) \in (\mathbb{G}^n, \mathbb{G})$ and that the prover additionally takes as input alleged witness vector $A \in \mathbb{F}^n$ such that

$$((G, \overline{A}), A) \in \mathcal{R}_{VC}(n).$$

The reduction proceeds as follows.

1. $\mathcal{P}$: Let G_1 and G_2 (respectively A_1 and A_2) denote the first and second half of vector G (respectively A). The prover begins by sending $\overline{A}_{ij} \leftarrow \langle G_i, A_j \rangle$ for $i, j \in \{1, 2\}$. Here, $\overline{A}_{11}$ and $\overline{A}_{22}$ represent the first and second "half" of the original commitment $\overline{A}$, and $\overline{A}_{12}$ and $\overline{A}_{21}$ represent cross terms which will assist the verifier in folding the original statement.
2. $\mathcal{V}$: The verifier first checks the consistency of $\overline{A}_{11}$ and $\overline{A}_{22}$ with $\overline{A}$ by checking that $\overline{A}_{11} + \overline{A}_{22} = \overline{A}$. The verifier must still check that the prover knows A_1 and A_2 such that $\overline{A}_{11} = \langle G_1, A_1 \rangle$ and $\overline{A}_{22} = \langle G_2, A_2 \rangle$. Instead of checking each individually, the verifier folds them into a single check by using a random linear combination. In particular, the verifier sends random $r \in \mathbb{F}$ to $\mathcal{P}$.
3. $\mathcal{P}, \mathcal{V}$: Together, the prover and verifier output the folded key and corresponding commitment $(G', \overline{A}') \in (\mathbb{G}^{n/2}, \mathbb{G})$ where $G' \leftarrow G_1 + r \cdot G_2$ and $\overline{A}' \leftarrow \overline{A}_{11} + r \cdot (\overline{A}_{12} + \overline{A}_{21}) + r^2 \cdot \overline{A}_{22}$.
4. $\mathcal{P}$: The prover outputs the folded witness $A' \in \mathbb{F}^{n/2}$ where $A' \leftarrow A_1 + r \cdot A_2$.

Now, to check the original statement, it is sufficient for the verifier to check that the prover knows A' such that

$$((G', \overline{A}'), A') \in \mathcal{R}_{VC}(n/2).$$

To prove knowledge soundness, we must show that given a prover that produces a witness for the output statement with non-negligible probability, we can derive an extractor that can use this prover to derive a witness for the input statement with nearly the same probability. Because the above reduction is public-coin, it suffices to show that there exists an extractor that can derive a satisfying input witness given a tree of transcripts and corresponding satisfying outputs (Lemma 6). Intuitively, the original extractor can generate such a tree by repeatedly rewinding the prover and collecting transcripts in which the prover outputs a satisfying witness.

Lemma 1 (Vector Commitment Reduction of Knowledge). *For $n = 2^i$ where $i \geq 1$, Construction 1 is a reduction from $\mathcal{R}_{\mathsf{VC}}(n)$ to $\mathcal{R}_{\mathsf{VC}}(n/2)$.*

Proof. We reason via tree extractability (Lemma 6). Suppose an extractor is provided with a tree of transcripts which consists of three transcripts, where the kth transcript has the same initial message $\overline{A}_{ij}$ for $i, j \in \{1, 2\}$, random challenge r_k, and satisfying output instance-witness pairs $((G'_k, \overline{A}'_k), A'_k) \in \mathcal{R}_{\mathsf{VC}}(n/2)$. The extractor first solves for a_k for $k \in \{1, 2, 3\}$ such that

$$\begin{pmatrix} 1 & 1 & 1 \\ r_1 & r_2 & r_3 \\ r_1^2 & r_2^2 & r_3^2 \end{pmatrix} \begin{pmatrix} a_1 \\ a_2 \\ a_3 \end{pmatrix} = \begin{pmatrix} 1 \\ 0 \\ 1 \end{pmatrix}$$

using an inverse Vandermonde matrix. The extractor then computes and outputs the unfolded witness $A = \left(\sum_k a_k \cdot A'_k, \sum_k a_k r_k \cdot A'_k \right)$. Indeed, by textbook algebra, we have that $\langle G, A \rangle = \overline{A}$ (we explicitly demonstrate this in the extended version [30]). Thus, we have that $((G, \overline{A}), A) \in \mathcal{R}_{\mathsf{VC}}(n)$. $\qquad\square$

Later, in Sect. 6, we show that the vector commitment reduction of knowledge is precisely the tensor reduction of knowledge from homomorphisms in $\mathbb{G}^n \cong (\mathbb{G}^{n/2})^2$ to homomorphisms in $\mathbb{G}^{n/2}$.

We are still tasked with isolating the base case of the original vector commitment argument. Below we specify an *argument of knowledge* for $\mathcal{R}_{\mathsf{VC}}(1)$. An argument of knowledge can be succinctly formalized as a reduction of knowledge that reduces to the relation $\mathcal{R}_\top$ encoding true. A verifier reducing to $\mathcal{R}_\top$ can output true if it accepts and any other string (e.g., false) otherwise.

Definition 3 (Argument of Knowledge). *Let $\mathcal{R}_\top = \{(\mathsf{true}, \bot)\}$. An argument of knowledge for relation $\mathcal{R}$ is a reduction of knowledge from $\mathcal{R}$ to $\mathcal{R}_\top$.*

Construction 2 (Base Case). We construct an argument of knowledge for $\mathcal{R}_{\mathsf{VC}}(1)$. Given statement $(G, \overline{A})$ and corresponding witness A, the prover sends A directly to the verifier. The verifier outputs true if $\langle G, A \rangle = \overline{A}$.

We can compose the above reductions to modularly recover the original argument of knowledge for the vector commitment relation. By formalizing each step as a reduction of knowledge, our composition result abstracts away the brunt of the proof effort. In particular, the following corollary holds immediately.

Corollary 1 (Vector Commitment Argument of Knowledge). *Let Π_{VC} denote a reduction of knowledge from $\mathcal{R}_{\mathsf{VC}}(n)$ to $\mathcal{R}_{\mathsf{VC}}(n/2)$ and let Π_{base} denote an argument of knowledge for $\mathcal{R}_{\mathsf{VC}}(1)$. Then*

$$\Pi_{\mathsf{base}} \circ \underbrace{\Pi_{\mathsf{VC}} \circ \ldots \circ \Pi_{\mathsf{VC}}}_{\log n \text{ times}}$$

is an argument of knowledge for $\mathcal{R}_{\mathsf{VC}}(n)$ where $n = 2^i$ for $i \in \mathbb{N}$.

2.2   Second Example: Folding Schemes

The vector commitment reduction of knowledge can be further decomposed into two reductions of knowledge: The first reduction of knowledge splits the original instance into two half-sized instances (i.e., a reduction from $\mathcal{R}_{VC}(n)$ to $\mathcal{R}_{VC}(n/2) \times \mathcal{R}_{VC}(n/2)$). The second folds the two instances into a single instance of the same size (i.e., a reduction from $\mathcal{R}_{VC}(n/2) \times \mathcal{R}_{VC}(n/2)$ to $\mathcal{R}_{VC}(n/2)$).

Kothapalli, Setty, and Tzialla [31] abstract the latter pattern to arbitrary relations and refer to such protocols as *folding schemes*. In particular, a folding scheme is an interactive protocol that reduces the task of checking two instances in a relation to the task of checking a single instance in the relation. Folding schemes provide a minimal abstraction for various protocols in the literature. For instance, Kothapalli et al. show that there exists a folding scheme for NP instances with some fixed size and show that such a construction implies incrementally verifiable computation [41].

More recently, Ràfols and Zacharakis [36] provide non-interactive ℓ-folding schemes (i.e., folding schemes for ℓ initial statements) for the vector commitment relation, inner-product relation, and polynomial commitment relation. Such folding schemes help amortize the verifier's work over multiple instances in larger non-interactive arguments of knowledge which typically involve checking multiple instances of the same form.

As these folding schemes rely on knowledge assumptions rather than interaction, prior techniques cannot help modularize the corresponding soundness analysis. As promised, we can still achieve modularity by decomposing them as a sequence of *non-interactive* reductions of knowledge. Formally, a non-interactive reduction of knowledge is one in which the interaction only consists of messages from the prover. Non-interactive ℓ-folding schemes can be succinctly formalized as a particular class of non-interactive reductions of knowledge. Letting $\mathcal{R}^\ell$ denote $\mathcal{R} \times \ldots \times \mathcal{R}$ for ℓ times, we define the following.

Definition 4 (ℓ-Folding Schemes). *A (non-interactive) ℓ-folding scheme for relation $\mathcal{R}$ is a (non-interactive) reduction of knowledge from $\mathcal{R}^\ell$ to $\mathcal{R}$.*

Ràfols and Zacharakis achieve ℓ-folding schemes for various relations by recursively composing 2-folding schemes in a tree-like fashion. In particular, ℓ instances are treated as leaves in a tree. A 2-folding scheme is then used to fold each pair of adjacent instances to produce a total of $\ell/2$ instances. These $\ell/2$ instances are once more folded in a pairwise fashion to produce $\ell/4$ instances and so on until a single instance remains.

Once again, as demonstrated by Ràfols and Zacharakis, while the tree-folding protocol can be stated in a straightforward manner, the corresponding knowledge soundness analysis requires careful attention to detail. In particular, the corresponding proof involves demonstrating that the malicious prover induces a corresponding expected polynomial-time extractor that unfolds once. Such an extractor is then shown to induce a pair of expected polynomial-time malicious provers for the previous layer of the tree, and so on. Alternatively, by working in the reductions of knowledge framework, nearly all of this reasoning is abstracted away. Indeed, we condense the original three-page proof into several lines.

Lemma 2 (ℓ-Folding Scheme). *Consider a (non-interactive) 2-folding scheme Π_{TF} for relation $\mathcal{R}$ and $\ell = 2^i$ for $i \in \mathbb{N}$ where $i \geq 1$. Then, Π_ℓ, inductively defined as follows, is a (non-interactive) ℓ-folding scheme for $\mathcal{R}$.*

$$\Pi_\ell = \Pi_{\mathsf{TF}} \circ (\Pi_{\ell/2} \times \Pi_{\ell/2})$$
$$\Pi_2 = \Pi_{\mathsf{TF}}$$

Proof. We reason inductively over i. In the base case, suppose $i = 1$. Then, by construction, Π_2 is a 2-folding scheme. Suppose instead $i \geq 2$. Suppose that for $\ell = 2^i$ we have that $\Pi_{\ell/2}$ is a $(\ell/2)$-folding scheme. Then, $\Pi_{\ell/2} \times \Pi_{\ell/2}$ is a reduction of knowledge from $\mathcal{R}^{\ell/2} \times \mathcal{R}^{\ell/2} = \mathcal{R}^\ell$ to $\mathcal{R}^2$. Thus, $\Pi_{\mathsf{TF}} \circ (\Pi_{\ell/2} \times \Pi_{\ell/2})$ is a reduction of knowledge from $\mathcal{R}^\ell$ to $\mathcal{R}$. $\qquad\square$

3   Preliminaries

3.1   Module Theory

In this section, we introduce our notation, intuit the direct sum and tensor product, and recall several useful properties. In the extended version [30], we present formal definitions for rings, modules, direct sums, and tensor products.

Notation (Module Theory). We assume finite, unital, commutative rings and modules with a finite basis throughout. We use $\cong$ to denote that two modules are isomorphic. For ring R and R-modules W and V, let $\hom(W, V)$ denote the R-module of homomorphisms from W to V. For $n \in \mathbb{N}$, we let W^n denote $W \otimes \mathsf{R}^n$ (equivalently $W \oplus \ldots \oplus W$ for n times). We use $\{\delta_i\}$ to denote an orthonormal basis. We refer to elements of modules as tensors. As we use tensors to represent both homomorphisms and objects, for tensors g and a, we use $g(a)$ to denote evaluating the homomorphism tensor g on the object tensor a. For $n \in \mathbb{N}$, let $[n]$ denote $\{1, 2, \ldots, n\}$ and let $[i, n]$ for $i \leq n$ denote $\{i, i+1, \ldots, n\}$. When summing over a variable, we will omit the bounds when clear from context. We write $\langle a, b \rangle$ to denote the inner-product of a and b.

Modules. Intuitively, modules are vector spaces over rings. That is, they support a notion of addition, can be scaled by ring elements, and have an identity element. We say a module is an R-module if it is scaled by ring R. Vectors, polynomials, matrices, tensors and scalars all form modules.

The Direct Sum. Intuitively, a *direct sum* of two R-modules U and V, forms a new R-module denoted $U \oplus V$, which is essentially a Cartesian product of the original modules. Elements of $U \oplus V$ consist of pairs of elements in U and V which are denoted as $u \oplus v$ for $u \in U$ and $v \in V$. For example, for field $\mathbb{F}$, if $U \cong \mathbb{F}^n$ and $V \cong \mathbb{F}^m$ we have that $U \oplus V \cong \mathbb{F}^{n+m}$. We have that $U \oplus V$ forms a module, because we can naturally compute $u_1 \oplus v_1 + u_2 \oplus v_2 = (u_1 + u_2) \oplus (v_1 + v_2)$ and $r \cdot (u \oplus v) = (r \cdot u) \oplus (r \cdot v)$ for $r \in \mathsf{R}$.

The Tensor Product. Intuitively, the tensor product, denoted $\otimes$, can be considered a generalized outer-product that distributes with respect to the direct sum. The tensor product of two modules U and V, forms a new module denoted $U \otimes V$. Elements of $U \otimes V$ include *simple tensors* which are outer products of elements in U and V and are denoted as $u \otimes v$ for $u \in U$ and $v \in V$. The module $U \otimes V$ also contains arbitrary sums of these simple tensors, which are denoted as $\sum_{i \in [\ell]} u_i \otimes v_i$ for $u_1, \dots, u_\ell \in U$ and $v_1, \dots, v_\ell \in V$. If $U \cong \mathbb{F}^n$ and $V \cong \mathbb{F}^m$ we have that $U \otimes V \cong \mathbb{F}^{n \times m}$ (i.e., $n \times m$ matrices over $\mathbb{F}$). Simple tensors in $\mathbb{F}^n \otimes \mathbb{F}^m$ consist of outer products of vectors in $\mathbb{F}^n$ and $\mathbb{F}^m$; however, the entire space is generated by sums over such outer products. We have that $U \otimes V$ forms a module because we can naturally add two sums and compute $r \cdot \sum_i u_i \otimes v_i = \sum_i (r \cdot u_i) \otimes v_i = \sum_i u_i \otimes (r \cdot v_i)$.

Abstracting the Direct Sum and Tensor Product. Formally, the particular definitions of the direct sum and tensor product depend on the particular modules they are working over. For instance, the tensor product could mean the outer product when working over vectors and the Kronecker product when working over matrices. Even for a fixed pair of modules, there could exist multiple valid definitions. For instance, for vectors $v_1, v_2 \in \mathbb{F}^n$, we can define $v_1 \oplus v_2$ to be a vector in $\mathbb{F}^{2n}$ or a matrix in $\mathbb{F}^{2 \times n}$. To account for these considerations, we treat the direct sum and tensor product as *abstract* operations that can be implemented by any concrete operations that satisfy certain axioms (which we detail in the extended version [30]). In practice, much like how abstract groups and rings must be instantiated with concrete objects such as elliptic curves and polynomials, the direct sum and tensor product must be instantiated with concrete operations that respect the prescribed properties.

For the majority of our development, we are interested in taking the direct sum and tensor product of homomorphisms (represented as tensors). In this situation, we do not need to invoke the abstract definitions of these operations, but rather the identities that follow from their axioms.

Lemma 3 (Direct Sum of Homomorphisms). *Consider homomorphisms $r \in \hom(U_1, V)$ and $s \in \hom(U_2, V)$ over R-modules (where R is a commutative ring). Then $r \oplus s \in \hom(U_1 \oplus U_2, V)$ is a homomorphism where $(r \oplus s)(u_1 \oplus u_2) = r(u_1) + s(u_2)$. Symmetrically, homomorphisms $r \in \hom(U, V_1)$ and $s \in \hom(U, V_2)$ over R-modules induce a homomorphism $r \oplus s \in \hom(U, V_1 \oplus V_2)$ where $(r \oplus s)(u) = r(u) \oplus s(u)$.*

Example 1 (Direct Sum of Homomorphisms). Consider group $\mathbb{G}$ of prime order p and corresponding scalar field $\mathbb{F} \cong \mathbb{Z}_p$. We can interpret $\mathbb{G}^n$ as the module of homomorphisms from $\mathbb{F}^n$ to $\mathbb{G}$. In particular, for $g \in \mathbb{G}^n$ we can define $g(a) = \langle g, a \rangle$ for $a \in \mathbb{F}^n$. Then, for $g \in \mathbb{G}^n$ and $h \in \mathbb{G}^m$ we have that $g \oplus h \in \mathbb{G}^n \oplus \mathbb{G}^m \cong \mathbb{G}^{n+m}$ can be interpreted as a map from $\mathbb{F}^{n+m} \cong \mathbb{F}^n \oplus \mathbb{F}^m$ to $\mathbb{G}$. By definition, for $u \in \mathbb{F}^n$ and $v \in \mathbb{F}^m$, we have $(g \oplus h)(u \oplus v) = \langle g \oplus h, u \oplus v \rangle = \langle g, u \rangle + \langle h, v \rangle = g(u) + h(v)$.

Lemma 4 (Tensor Product of Homomorphisms). *Homomorphisms* $r \in$ $\hom(U, X)$ *and* $s \in \hom(V, Y)$ *over* R-*modules (where* R *is a commutative ring) induce a homomorphism* $r \otimes s \in \hom(U \otimes V, X \otimes Y)$, *such that* $(r \otimes s)(u \otimes v) = r(u) \otimes s(v)$. *By linearity, we have that*

$$\left(\sum_{i \in [I]} r_i \otimes s_i \right) \left(\sum_{j \in [J]} u_i \otimes v_i \right) = \sum_{i \in [I], j \in [J]} r_i(u_j) \otimes s_i(v_j).$$

Example 2 (Tensor Product of Homomorphisms). Let $\otimes$ denote the outer product. For prime p and field $\mathbb{F} \cong \mathbb{Z}_p$ we can interpret $\mathbb{F}^n$ as the module of homomorphisms from $\mathbb{F}^n$ to $\mathbb{F}$. In particular, for $f \in \mathbb{F}^n$ we can define $f(a) = \langle f, a \rangle$ for $a \in \mathbb{F}^n$. Then, $f \in \mathbb{F}^n$ and $g \in \mathbb{F}^m$ induce a new map $f \otimes g \in \mathbb{F}^n \otimes \mathbb{F}^m \cong \mathbb{F}^{nm}$ from $\mathbb{F}^{nm}$ to $\mathbb{F} \otimes \mathbb{F} \cong \mathbb{F}$. By definition, for $u \in \mathbb{F}^n$ and $v \in \mathbb{F}^m$, we have $(f \otimes g)(u \otimes v) = (f \cdot g_1 \oplus \ldots \oplus f \cdot g_m)(u \cdot v_1 \oplus \ldots \oplus u \cdot v_m) = \sum_{j \in [m]} f(u) \cdot g_i(v_i) = f(u) \otimes g(v)$.

Lemma 5 (Useful Identities). *For commutative ring* R *and* R-*modules* U, V, *and* W, *we have that* $(U \otimes V) \otimes W \cong U \otimes (V \otimes W)$, $U \otimes V \cong V \otimes U$, $U \otimes (V \oplus W) \cong (U \otimes V) \oplus (U \otimes W)$, *and* $R \otimes U \cong U \otimes R \cong U$.

3.2 Cryptographic Preliminaries

Notation (Cryptography). We use λ globally to denote the security parameter, and negl to denote negligible functions. For events A and B, we let $\Pr[A] \approx \Pr[B]$ denote that $|\Pr[A] - \Pr[B]| = \mathsf{negl}(\lambda)$. We let PPT denote probabilistic polynomial-time. We write _ to denote unused terms.

For soundness to hold when randomly sampling over rings, the set of admissible values must be constrained. We define a valid sampling set over rings.

Definition 5 (Sampling Set [11]). *For ring* R *and* R-*module* M, *subset* $Q \subseteq R$ *is a sampling set for* M *if for every* $q_1, q_2 \in Q$, *the map* $\varphi_{q_1,q_2}(m) = (q_1 - q_2) \cdot m$ *for* $m \in M$ *is injective.*

For certain relations, to be able to prove knowledge soundness, we will need to rely on computational hardness assumptions. We adapt the bilinear relation assumption [11], which can be viewed as a generalization of the discrete logarithm assumption, and the double pairing assumption [1].

Definition 6 (Bilinear Relation Assumption). *For ring* R, *length parameter* n, *and security parameter* λ, *consider* R-*modules* U *and* V *such that* $|U| = O(2^\lambda)$ *and* $|V| = O(2^\lambda)$. *The bilinear relation assumption holds for* (U, V) *(w.r.t. tensor product* $\otimes$*) if given random* $u_1, \ldots, u_n \in U$, *there exists no polynomial-time algorithm to find non-trivial* $v_1, \ldots, v_n \in V$ *such that* $\sum_{i \in [n]} u_i \otimes v_i = 0$.

Symmetrically, we can consider composite spaces such that given elements from both of the constituent spaces, it is *easy* to check that they satisfy the above relation. This ensures that the verifier is able to perform its requisite checks efficiently. Throughout our development, we assume the coset equality assumption holds as necessary.

Definition 7 (Coset Equality Assumption). *For ring* R *and length parameter* n, *consider* R-*modules* U *and* V. *The coset equality assumption holds for* (U, V) *(w.r.t. tensor product* $\otimes$) *if for any* $u_1, \ldots, u_n \in U$ *and* $v_1, \ldots, v_n \in V$, *there exists a polynomial-time algorithm to check* $\sum_{i \in [n]} u_i \otimes v_i = 0$.

Example 3 (Bilinear Relation Assumption). Suppose U is a group of prime order p and V is the corresponding scalar field $\mathbb{Z}_p$. Let the tensor product between these two modules be defined as scalar multiplication. In this setting, the bilinear relation assumption is equivalent to the discrete logarithm assumption. Alternatively, suppose U and V are prime order groups such that there exists a corresponding pairing operation e from $U \times V$ into some target group. Let the tensor product be defined as this pairing operation. In this setting, the bilinear relation assumption is equivalent to the double pairing assumption.

4 Reductions of Knowledge

Recall that in contrast to arguments of knowledge, reductions of knowledge are defined over a pair of relations $\mathcal{R}_1$ and $\mathcal{R}_2$. A prover can use a reduction of knowledge to show for some u_1 that it knows w_1 such that $(u_1, w_1) \in \mathcal{R}_1$ contingent on the fact that it knows w_2 for some statement u_2 (derived from its interaction with the verifier) such that $(u_2, w_2) \in \mathcal{R}_2$. We start by intuiting the desired notion of knowledge soundness needed to capture such an interaction, before presenting a formal definition (Definition 8). We show that any two reductions of knowledge that respect this definition can be composed sequentially and in parallel (Theorems 5 and 6). We then observe that a more restricted — but simpler — notion of soundness, known as tree extractability, implies our definition of knowledge soundness (Lemma 6). In the following sections, we leverage this observation to prove that our reductions of knowledge for linear-algebraic statements are secure.

4.1 Defining Reductions of Knowledge

Intuitively, we would like that if a prover is able to convince a verifier on input u_1 to output some derived statement u_2 such that it knows a corresponding satisfying witness w_2, then it must have known a corresponding satisfying witness w_1 for u_1. We can capture this notion formally by stating that if a malicious prover can output a satisfying witness w_2 for the verifier's output statement u_2, then there must exist a corresponding extractor that can output a satisfying witness w_1 for the verifier's input statement u_1.

While this presents a stand-alone notion of knowledge soundness, we require a more nuanced definition to capture technical difficulties that arise when reasoning about sequential composability. In particular, existing definitions implicitly assume that the environment is provided access to the inputs and outputs of the prover and the verifier, and that some of this material (such as an adversarially chosen statement) is forwarded to the extractor. Unfortunately, when composing such arguments, we end up in situations where intermediate inputs expected by the extractor are never exposed to the environment.

Concretely, consider a reduction of knowledge Π_1 with prover $\mathcal{P}_1$, verifier $\mathcal{V}_1$, and extractor $\mathcal{E}_1$, and a second reduction of knowledge Π_2 with corresponding $\mathcal{P}_2$, $\mathcal{V}_2$, and $\mathcal{E}_2$. Ideally, we would want to use $\mathcal{E}_1$ and $\mathcal{E}_2$ in a black-box manner to construct an extractor $\mathcal{E}$ for $\Pi_2 \circ \Pi_1$. A typical knowledge soundness definition would dictate that the statement provided to the verifier is forwarded to the extractor as well. Unfortunately, in the composed setting, the statement u_2 output by $\mathcal{V}_1$ as input to $\mathcal{V}_2$ is never exposed to the environment, and thus it is unclear how $\mathcal{E}$ can simulate the intermediate statement u_2 expected by $\mathcal{E}_2$.

To alleviate this issue, we stipulate an additional requirement that the verifier's output statement can be deterministically recovered from the mutual view of both the prover and verifier. Specifically, the mutual view consists of the public parameters, initial input statement, and interaction transcript. We refer to this property as *public reducibility*, which can be viewed as analogous to the public verifiability property common to most modern arguments. With public reducibility, we are afforded sequential composability.

We formally define reductions of knowledge as interactive protocols in the global common reference string model.

Definition 8 (Reduction of Knowledge). *Consider ternary relations $\mathcal{R}_1$ and $\mathcal{R}_2$ consisting of public parameters, statement, witness tuples. A reduction of knowledge from $\mathcal{R}_1$ to $\mathcal{R}_2$ is defined by* PPT *algorithms $(\mathcal{G}, \mathcal{P}, \mathcal{V})$ denoting the generator, the prover, and the verifier respectively with the following interface.*

- *$\mathcal{G}(\lambda) \rightarrow$ pp: Takes security parameter λ. Outputs public parameters pp.*
- *$\mathcal{P}(\mathsf{pp}, u_1, w_1) \rightarrow (u_2, w_2)$: Takes as input public parameters pp, and statement-witness pair (u_1, w_1). Interactively reduces the statement $(\mathsf{pp}, u_1, w_1) \in \mathcal{R}_1$ to a new statement $(\mathsf{pp}, u_2, w_2) \in \mathcal{R}_2$.*
- *$\mathcal{V}(\mathsf{pp}, u_1) \rightarrow u_2$: Takes as input public parameters pp, and statement u_1 associated with $\mathcal{R}_1$. Interactively reduces the task of checking u_1 to the task of checking a new statement u_2 associated with $\mathcal{R}_2$.*

Let $\langle \mathcal{P}, \mathcal{V} \rangle$ denote the interaction between $\mathcal{P}$ and $\mathcal{V}$. We treat $\langle \mathcal{P}, \mathcal{V} \rangle$ as a function that takes as input (pp, u_1, w_1) and runs the interaction on prover input (pp, u_1, w_1) and verifier input (pp, u_1). At the end of the interaction, $\langle \mathcal{P}, \mathcal{V} \rangle$ outputs the verifier's statement u_2 and the prover's witness w_2. A reduction of knowledge $(\mathcal{G}, \mathcal{P}, \mathcal{V})$ satisfies the following conditions.

(i) *Completeness: For any* PPT *adversary $\mathcal{A}$, given pp $\leftarrow \mathcal{G}(\lambda)$ and $(u_1, w_1) \leftarrow \mathcal{A}(\mathsf{pp})$ such that $(\mathsf{pp}, u_1, w_1) \in \mathcal{R}_1$, we have that the prover's output statement is equal to the verifier's output statement and that*

$$(\mathsf{pp}, \langle \mathcal{P}, \mathcal{V} \rangle(\mathsf{pp}, u_1, w_1)) \in \mathcal{R}_2.$$

(ii) *Knowledge Soundness: For any expected polynomial-time adversaries $\mathcal{A}$ and $\mathcal{P}^*$, there exists an expected polynomial-time extractor $\mathcal{E}$ such that given pp $\leftarrow \mathcal{G}(\lambda)$ and $(u_1, \mathsf{st}) \leftarrow \mathcal{A}(\mathsf{pp})$, we have that*

$$\Pr[(\mathsf{pp}, u_1, \mathcal{E}(\mathsf{pp}, u_1, \mathsf{st})) \in \mathcal{R}_1] \approx \Pr[(\mathsf{pp}, \langle \mathcal{P}^*, \mathcal{V} \rangle(\mathsf{pp}, u_1, \mathsf{st})) \in \mathcal{R}_2].$$

(iii) Public Reducibility: There exists a deterministic polynomial-time function φ such that for any PPT adversary $\mathcal{A}$ and expected polynomial-time adversary $\mathcal{P}^*$, given $pp \leftarrow \mathcal{G}(\lambda)$, $(u_1, st) \leftarrow \mathcal{A}(pp)$, and $(u_2, w_2) \leftarrow \langle \mathcal{P}^*, \mathcal{V} \rangle(pp, u_1, st)$ with interaction transcript tr, we have that $\varphi(pp, u_1, tr) = u_2$.

We write $\Pi : \mathcal{R}_1 \rightarrow \mathcal{R}_2$ to denote that protocol Π is a reduction of knowledge from relation $\mathcal{R}_1$ to relation $\mathcal{R}_2$.

Definition 9 (Public-Coin). *A reduction of knowledge is public-coin if the verifier only sends uniformly random challenges to the prover.*

4.2   Composing Reductions of Knowledge

We now prove sequential and parallel composition theorems for reductions of knowledge. This allows us to construct complex arguments by stitching together simpler reductions sequentially and in parallel. In the case of sequential composition, much like recursive composition techniques [8,14,31,41], each composition step induces a polynomial blowup in the corresponding extractor. Thus, sequential composition cannot be used more than a constant number of times without additional computational assumptions.[1] Our parallel composition operator is not parallel in the sense that both protocols are being run at the same time, but rather parallel in the sense that the composed protocol takes incoming instance-witness pairs in parallel and produces outgoing instance-witness pairs in parallel.

Theorem 5 (Sequential Composition). *Consider ternary relations $\mathcal{R}_1$, $\mathcal{R}_2$, and $\mathcal{R}_3$. For reductions of knowledge $\Pi_1 = (\mathcal{G}, \mathcal{P}_1, \mathcal{V}_1) : \mathcal{R}_1 \rightarrow \mathcal{R}_2$ and $\Pi_2 = (\mathcal{G}, \mathcal{P}_2, \mathcal{V}_2) : \mathcal{R}_2 \rightarrow \mathcal{R}_3$, we have that $\Pi_2 \circ \Pi_1 = (\mathcal{G}, \mathcal{P}, \mathcal{V})$ is a reduction of knowledge from $\mathcal{R}_1$ to $\mathcal{R}_3$ where*

$$\mathcal{P}(pp, u_1, w_1) = \mathcal{P}_2(pp, \mathcal{P}_1(pp, u_1, w_1))$$
$$\mathcal{V}(pp, u_1) = \mathcal{V}_2(pp, \mathcal{V}_1(pp, u_1, w_1)).$$

Proof Intuition. Completeness and public reducibility follow by observation. As for knowledge soundness, assume there exists an adversarial prover $\mathcal{P}^*$ for Π that succeeds in producing an accepting witness w_3 with non-negligible probability. Using the second half of $\mathcal{P}^*$ (i.e., the part that interacts with $\mathcal{V}_2$), we can construct an adversary $\mathcal{P}_2^{**}$ for Π_2 that succeeds in producing an accepting witness w_3 with the same probability. By the knowledge soundness of Π_2, this implies an extractor $\mathcal{E}_2$ that succeeds in producing an intermediate witness w_2 with nearly the same probability. We can then leverage $\mathcal{E}_2$ to construct an adversary $\mathcal{P}_1^{**}$ for Π_1 that succeeds in producing an accepting witness w_2 with nearly the same probability. In particular, $\mathcal{P}_1^{**}$ first runs the first half of $\mathcal{P}^*$ and then runs extractor $\mathcal{E}_2$ on the intermediate statement u_2 (derived by the public reducibility of Π_1) and the intermediate state of $\mathcal{P}^*$ to produce the output

---

[1] We recommend Bitansky et al. [8, Remark 6.3] for details on such assumptions.

w_2. By the knowledge soundness of Π_1, this implies the desired extractor $\mathcal{E}_1$ that succeeds in producing the witness w_1 with nearly the same probability. We present a formal proof in the extended version [30]. $\qquad\square$

Definition 10 (Relation Pair). *Consider ternary relations $\mathcal{R}_1$ and $\mathcal{R}_2$ over public parameters, statement, witness tuples. We define the relation $\mathcal{R}_1 \times \mathcal{R}_2 = \{(\mathsf{pp}, (u_1, u_2), (w_1, w_2)) \mid (\mathsf{pp}, u_1, w_1) \in \mathcal{R}_1, (\mathsf{pp}, u_2, w_2) \in \mathcal{R}_2\}$. We let $\mathcal{R}^\ell$ denote $\mathcal{R} \times \ldots \times \mathcal{R}$ for ℓ times.*

Theorem 6 (Parallel Composition). *Consider ternary relations $\mathcal{R}_1$, $\mathcal{R}_2$, $\mathcal{R}_3$, and $\mathcal{R}_4$. For reductions of knowledge $\Pi_1 = (\mathcal{G}, \mathcal{P}_1, \mathcal{V}_1) : \mathcal{R}_1 \to \mathcal{R}_2$ and $\Pi_2 = (\mathcal{G}, \mathcal{P}_2, \mathcal{V}_2) : \mathcal{R}_3 \to \mathcal{R}_4$, we have that $\Pi_1 \times \Pi_2 = (\mathcal{G}, \mathcal{P}, \mathcal{V})$ is a reduction of knowledge from $\mathcal{R}_1 \times \mathcal{R}_3$ to $\mathcal{R}_2 \times \mathcal{R}_4$ where*

$$\mathcal{P}(\mathsf{pp}, (u_1, u_3), (w_1, w_3)) = (\mathcal{P}_1(\mathsf{pp}, u_1, w_1), \mathcal{P}_2(\mathsf{pp}, u_3, w_3))$$
$$\mathcal{V}(\mathsf{pp}, (u_1, u_3)) = (\mathcal{V}_1(\mathsf{pp}, u_1), \mathcal{V}_2(\mathsf{pp}, u_3)).$$

Proof Intuition. For $i \in \{1, 2\}$, we leverage a malicious prover $\mathcal{P}^*$ for Π to construct a prover $\mathcal{P}_i^*$ for protocol Π_i that succeeds in producing a satisfying output witness with the same probability. By the knowledge soundness of Π_i, this implies a corresponding extractor $\mathcal{E}_i$ that succeeds in producing a satisfying input witness with nearly the same probability. These extractors imply the desired extractor $\mathcal{E}$. We present a formal proof in the extended version [30]. $\qquad\square$

4.3   Knowledge Soundness from Tree Extraction

When proving constructions secure, reasoning about knowledge soundness directly is typically cumbersome. To alleviate this issue, prior work [10] observes that most protocols are algebraic: The corresponding extractor typically runs the malicious prover multiple times with refreshed verifier randomness to retrieve accepting transcripts, which can be interpolated to retrieve the witness. Leveraging this insight, Bootle et al. [10] provide a general extraction lemma, which states that to prove knowledge soundness for algebraic protocols, it is sufficient to show that there exists an extractor that can produce a satisfying witness when provided a *tree of accepting transcripts* with refreshed verifier randomness at each layer. This proof technique has been adapted to various settings [11,13,14,31], and we similarly provide the corresponding lemma for reductions of knowledge.

Definition 11 (Tree of Transcripts). *Consider an m-round public-coin interactive protocol $(\mathcal{G}, \mathcal{P}, \mathcal{V})$ that satisfies the interface described in Definition 8. A $(n_1, \ldots, n_m)$-tree of accepting transcripts for statement u_1 is a tree of depth m where each vertex at layer i has n_i outgoing edges such that (1) each vertex in layer $i \in [m]$ is labeled with a prover message for round i; (2) each outgoing edge from layer $i \in [m]$ is labeled with a different choice of verifier randomness for round i; (3) each leaf is labeled with an accepting statement-witness pair output by the prover and verifier corresponding to the interaction along the path.*

Lemma 6 (Tree Extraction [11]). *Consider an m-round public-coin interactive protocol $(\mathcal{G}, \mathcal{P}, \mathcal{V})$ that satisfies the interface described in Definition 8 and satisfies completeness. Then $(\mathcal{G}, \mathcal{P}, \mathcal{V})$ is a reduction of knowledge if there exists a PPT extractor χ that, for all instances u_1, outputs a satisfying witness w_1 with probability $1 - \mathsf{negl}(\lambda)$, given an $(n_1, \ldots, n_m)$-tree of accepting transcripts for u_1 where the verifier's randomness is sampled from space Q such that $|Q| = O(2^\lambda)$, and $\prod_i n_i = \mathsf{poly}(\lambda)$.*

Proof Intuition. Our proof closely follows that of Bootle et al. [10]. At a high level, we construct an expected polynomial-time extractor $\mathcal{E}$ that repeatedly runs the malicious prover $\mathcal{P}^*$ and collects corresponding accepting transcripts and associated output statement-witness pairs. The extractor then passes these collected transcripts to χ which retrieves the desired witness by assumption. We present a formal proof in the extended version [30]. □

5   The Tensor Reduction of Knowledge

We start by defining a general tensor-based language to capture a large class of linear algebraic statements. We then design a general reduction, the tensor reduction, for such statements, by extending the sum-check protocol [33]. Next, we leverage the tensor reduction to construct the tensor reduction of knowledge, which, for any length vector space of homomorphisms $\mathrm{hom}(W, V)$ and length n, reduces the task of checking knowledge of a preimage of a vector in $\mathrm{hom}(W^n, V)$ to checking knowledge of a preimage in $\mathrm{hom}(W, V)$.

5.1   Tensor Evaluation Statements

We observe that arguments of knowledge built around statements over linear algebraic objects — such as matrices, vectors, polynomials, and homomorphisms — typically share hints of symmetry. Our goal is to generalize such statements, and more interestingly generalize interactive reductions for such statements.

Regardless of the underlying linear-algebraic objects, arguments over them tend to only rely on the fact they support some notion of addition and that they can be scaled by elements in a field (and more generally rings). This seems to suggest that designing a reduction over the most general objects that support these operations, namely tensors, would give a single universal protocol for such objects. From an algebraic standpoint, tensors unify objects such as scalars, vectors, matrices, and polynomials. More generally, tensors provide a unifying algebraic object for describing both functions (when viewed as homomorphisms) and objects (when viewed as elements of a module).

Take for instance the vector commitment relation: Given a prime order group $\mathbb{G}$ and an underlying scalar field $\mathbb{F}^n$, a prover claims that for public commitment key $G \in \mathbb{G}^n$ and commitment $\overline{A}$, it knows a vector $A \in \mathbb{F}^n$ such that $\langle G, A \rangle = \overline{A}$. As the spaces $\mathbb{G}^n$, $\mathbb{F}^n$ and $\mathbb{G}$ are all modules, we can build a corresponding "tensor evaluation" statement

$$G(A) = \overline{A}$$

where G is a tensor in $\mathbb{G}^n$ that maps tensors in $\mathbb{F}^n$ to tensors in $\mathbb{G}$.

Alternatively, suppose in addition to claiming that it knows a vector A underlying a commitment $\overline{A}$ with respect to commitment key G, the prover additionally claims that taking the inner-product of A against some public vector $B \in \mathbb{F}^n$ results in a scalar $\sigma \in \mathbb{F}$. Following our prior reasoning, this can be represented as two tensor evaluation statements: A claim that $G(A) = \overline{A}$ and a claim that $B(A) = \sigma$. But, under the rules of the direct sum (which can be interpreted as a Cartesian product), this is equivalent to applying the tensor $G \oplus B \in \mathbb{G}^n \oplus \mathbb{F}^n$ to A and checking that this results in $\overline{A} \oplus \sigma \in \mathbb{G} \oplus \mathbb{F}$. Namely, we have that the composite statement can be encoded as the following tensor evaluation statement:

$$(G \oplus B)(A) = \overline{A} \oplus \sigma.$$

The flexibility of tensor evaluation statements becomes more salient with the sum-check protocol [33]. In the sum-check protocol, the prover claims for multivariate polynomial $P : \mathbb{F}^n \to \mathbb{F}$ with degree d in each variable that

$$\sum_{x_1,\ldots,x_n \in \{0,1\}} P(x_1,\ldots,x_n) = \sigma \tag{1}$$

for some claimed sum $\sigma \in \mathbb{F}$. For $i \in [n]$, consider the tensor $\bigoplus_{j \in [0,d]} x_i^j$ which is just shorthand for the vector $(x_i^0, x_i^1, \ldots, x_i^d)$. Now, consider $\bigotimes_{i \in [n]} \bigoplus_{j \in [0,d]} x_i^j$, which is an n-dimensional matrix populated with all possible products of powers of $x_1, \ldots, x_n$. We can now define a tensor $\boldsymbol{X} = \sum_{x_1,\ldots,x_n \in \{0,1\}} \bigotimes_{i \in [n]} \bigoplus_{j \in [0,d]} x_i^j \in (\mathbb{F}^{d+1})^n$ which encodes all desired evaluation points. Additionally, let $\boldsymbol{P} \in (\mathbb{F}^{d+1})^n$ denote an n-dimensional tensor constituting of the coefficients of P. Specifically, let $\boldsymbol{P}$ contain at index $(j_1, \ldots, j_n)$ the coefficient of P associated with term $x_1^{j_1} x_2^{j_2} \ldots x_n^{j_n}$. Now, we have that checking the original sum-check statement is equivalent to checking the tensor evaluation statement

$$\boldsymbol{P}(\boldsymbol{X}) = \sigma.$$

The three examples above suggest that seemingly disparate linear-algebraic claims can be uniformly viewed as tensor evaluation claims. In light of this, we are interested in designing a reduction for statements of the form $u(w) = v$ for tensors u, w, and v.

5.2   The Tensor Reduction

To design a general reduction for tensor statements of the form $u(w) = v$, we start by generalizing the sum-check protocol for tensor evaluation statements. Recall that the sum-check protocol reduces the task of checking the claim in Eq. (1) to the task of checking a sum-check claim over a polynomial with one less variable. In particular, the prover begins by sending

$$p(X) = \sum_{x_1,\ldots,x_{n-1} \in \{0,1\}} P(x_1,\ldots,x_{n-1},X)$$

The verifier then checks that $p(0) + p(1) = \sigma$. The verifier must now check that p is consistent with P. To do so, the verifier samples a random $r \leftarrow \mathbb{F}$, and reduces to checking

$$\sum_{x_1,\ldots,x_{n-1}} P(x_1,\ldots,x_{n-1},r) = p(r).$$

In essence, the sum-check protocol leverages the nested structure of polynomials to reduce the task of checking n-variate polynomials to checking $(n-1)$-variate polynomials. This intuition can be more lucidly expressed with the corresponding tensor evaluation statements: the sum-check protocol reduces the task of checking the evaluation of $\boldsymbol{P} \in (\mathbb{F}^{d+1})^n \cong (\mathbb{F}^{d+1})^{n-1} \otimes \mathbb{F}^{d+1}$ (representing P) to the task of checking the evaluation of $\boldsymbol{P_r} \in (\mathbb{F}^{d+1})^{n-1}$ (representing P evaluated on r) and $\boldsymbol{p} \in \mathbb{F}^{d+1}$ (representing p). That is, the sum-check protocol factors the original statement with respect to the tensor product.

The tensor reduction, which we detail below, follows from generalizing the involved spaces to handle arbitrary tensor evaluation statements: for any modules U, U_1, and U_2 such that $U \cong U_1 \otimes U_2$, we derive a mechanism to reduce an evaluation claim in U to an evaluation claim in U_1 and an evaluation claim in U_2. In the extended version [30], we show that we can recover the sum-check protocol when instantiating the tensor reduction over multivariate polynomials.

Construction 3 (Tensor Reduction). Suppose for tensors $u \in \hom(W_1, V_1) \otimes \hom(W_2, V_2)$ of rank I, $w \in W_1 \otimes W_2$ of rank J, and $v \in V_1 \otimes V_2$ over ring R, a verifier would like to check

$$u(w) = v \tag{2}$$

where $u = \sum_{i \in [I]} u_{1,i} \otimes u_{2,i}$, and $w = \sum_{j \in [J]} w_{1,j} \otimes w_{2,j}$. By definition, the verifier can check (2) by checking $\sum_{i,j} u_{1,i}(w_{1,j}) \otimes u_{2,i}(w_{2,j}) = v$. Therefore, the prover begins by computing and sending $v_{1,ij} \leftarrow u_{1,i}(w_{1,j})$ and $v_{2,ij} \leftarrow u_{2,i}(w_{2,j})$ for all $i \in [I], j \in [J]$. The verifier directly checks

$$\sum_{i \in [I], j \in [J]} v_{1,ij} \otimes v_{2,ij} = v.$$

The verifier must still check that $v_{1,ij} = u_{1,i}(w_{1,j})$ and $v_{2,ij} = u_{2,i}(w_{2,j})$ for all i, j. To do so, the verifier takes a random linear combination of these checks by sending random α, β from a valid sampling set $Q \subseteq \mathsf{R}$, and computing $v_1 = \sum_{i,j} \alpha^i \beta^j v_{1,ij}$ and $v_2 = \sum_{i,j} \alpha^i \beta^j v_{2,ij}$. The verifier then outputs $(\alpha, \beta, v_1, v_2)$, reducing the original check to the task of checking

$$\left(\sum_i \alpha^i u_{1,i}\right)\left(\sum_j \beta^j w_{1,j}\right) = v_1 \quad \text{and} \quad \left(\sum_i \alpha^i u_{2,i}\right)\left(\sum_j \beta^j w_{2,j}\right) = v_2.$$

Theorem 7 (Tensor Reduction). *For tensors* $u = \sum_i u_{1,i} \otimes u_{2,i} \in \hom(W_1, V_1) \otimes \hom(W_2, V_2)$ *of rank* I, $w = \sum_j w_{1,j} \otimes w_{2,j} \in W_1 \otimes W_2$ *of rank* J, *and* $v \in V_1 \otimes V_2$ *over ring* R, *the tensor reduction reduces the task of checking*

$$u(w) = v$$

to the task of checking

$$\left(\sum_i \alpha^i u_{1,i}\right)\left(\sum_j \beta^j w_{1,j}\right) = v_1 \quad and \quad \left(\sum_i \alpha^i u_{2,i}\right)\left(\sum_j \beta^j w_{2,j}\right) = v_2$$

for verifier output $(\alpha, \beta, v_1, v_2)$. Formally, if the former is true, then the latter is true with probability 1, and if the former is false, then the latter is false with probability at least $1 - \frac{IJ}{|Q|}$. The prover complexity, verifier complexity, and communication complexity are all proportional to IJ.

Proof. This follows from the Schwartz-Zippel Lemma [38] extended to modules [11]. □

At first glance, it may seem that the communication cost of the tensor reduction is *greater* than the size of the witness: the witness only consists of J elements in $W_1 \otimes W_2$, but the prover sends IJ elements in V_1 and V_2. This is reconciled by the fact that elements of V_1 and V_2 are intended to be significantly smaller than elements in $W_1 \otimes W_2$. For instance, elements in $W_1 \otimes W_2$ may be long vectors that are mapped to short commitments in V_1 and V_2.

To build intuition for where tensor reductions are useful, we explain how to instantiate the tensor reduction to reconstruct the vector commitment reduction of knowledge presented in Sect. 2.

Example 4 (Vector Commitment Reduction of Knowledge). We construct a reduction of knowledge from $\mathcal{R}_{\mathsf{VC}}(n)$ to $\mathcal{R}_{\mathsf{VC}}(n/2)$ for $n = 2^i$ where $i \geq 1$. Consider group $\mathbb{G}$ of prime order p, and corresponding scalar field $\mathbb{F} \cong \mathbb{Z}_p$. Consider some public key $G \in \mathbb{G}^n$. Suppose a verifier would like to check for some commitment $\overline{A} \in \mathbb{G}$, that the prover knows vector $A \in \mathbb{F}^n$ such that $G(A) = \overline{A}$ where $G(A)$ is defined to be $\langle G, A \rangle$.

We observe that $\mathbb{G}^n \cong \mathbb{G}^{n/2} \otimes \mathbb{F}^2$ and $\mathbb{F}^n \cong \mathbb{F}^{n/2} \otimes \mathbb{F}^2$. Let $\{\delta_1, \delta_2\}$ be an orthonormal basis for $\mathbb{F}^2$ (i.e., we have that $\delta_i(\delta_j) = 1$ when $i = j$ and 0 otherwise). Then, we have that $G = G_1 \otimes \delta_1 + G_2 \otimes \delta_2$ and $A = A_1 \otimes \delta_1 + A_2 \otimes \delta_2$ for some $G_1, G_2 \in \mathbb{G}^{n/2}$ and $A_1, A_2 \in \mathbb{F}^{n/2}$. These terms can be interpreted as the first and second half of vectors G and A. Therefore, the verifier can equivalently check

$$\left(\sum_i G_i \otimes \delta_i\right)\left(\sum_j A_j \otimes \delta_j\right) = \overline{A}.$$

Applying the tensor reduction with respect to this decomposition, we have that the prover sends to the verifier $G_i(A_j), \delta_i(\delta_j)$ for $i, j \in \{1, 2\}$. Explicitly, letting $\overline{A}_{ij} = G_i(A_j)$, the prover sends the terms $(\overline{A}_{11}, 1)$, $(\overline{A}_{12}, 0)$, $(\overline{A}_{21}, 0)$, and $(\overline{A}_{22}, 1)$. We recognize that the first and last terms correspond with the first and second half of commitment $\overline{A}$, and the middle two terms are cross terms.

Upon receiving these terms, the verifier checks that

$$\overline{A}_{11} \otimes 1 + \overline{A}_{12} \otimes 0 + \overline{A}_{21} \otimes 0 + \overline{A}_{22} \otimes 1 = \overline{A}.$$

The verifier then samples and sends random $\alpha, \beta \leftarrow \mathbb{F}$, and sets the new statements to be checked to be $(G_1 + \alpha G_2)(A_1 + \beta A_2) = \sum_{i,j \in \{1,2\}} \overline{A}_{ij} \cdot \alpha^i \beta^j$ and $(\delta_1 + \alpha \delta_2)(\delta_1 + \beta \delta_2) = 1 + (\beta + \alpha) \cdot 0 + \alpha \beta \cdot 1$. The latter check holds immediately. As for the former check, the prover and verifier compute and output the new statement $G' \leftarrow G_1 + \alpha \cdot G_2 \in \mathbb{G}^{n/2}$ and $\overline{A} \leftarrow \sum_{i,j \in \{1,2\}} \overline{A}_{ij} \cdot \alpha^i \beta^j$. The prover privately computes and outputs the new witness vector $A' \leftarrow A_1 + \beta A_2 \in \mathbb{F}^{n/2}$. Now, it is sufficient for the verifier to check that the prover knows $A' \in \mathbb{F}^{n/2}$ such that $G'(A') = \overline{A}'$.

5.3   The Tensor Reduction of Knowledge

By generalizing Example 4 for arbitrary tensor statements, we arrive at the tensor reduction of knowledge, which is unconditionally secure. We start by defining the tensor relation which fixes the homomorphism and image as a statement and the preimage as the witness.[2] We then construct the tensor reduction of knowledge, which for a vector space of homomorphisms U and length n, reduces the task of checking knowledge of a preimage of a homomorphism in U^n to the task of checking knowledge of a preimage of a homomorphism in U. In the upcoming section, we show that the tensor reduction of knowledge can be instantiated to derive reductions of knowledge for various linear algebraic statements.

Definition 12 (Tensor Relation). *For R-modules U, W and V, such that $U \cong \hom(W, V)$ we define the tensor relation for U as follows*

$$\mathcal{R}(U) = \left\{ ((u, v), w) \,\middle|\, \begin{array}{l} u \in U, v \in V, w \in W, \\ u(w) = v \end{array} \right\}$$

Construction 4 (Tensor Reduction of Knowledge). Consider field $\mathbb{F}$, length parameter n, and $\mathbb{F}$-modules W and V. We construct a reduction of knowledge from $\mathcal{R}(\hom(W^n, V))$ to $\mathcal{R}(\hom(W, V))$. Let $\{\delta_i\}$ be an orthonormal basis for $\mathbb{F}^n$. Suppose the prover and verifier are provided statement $u = \sum_i u_i \otimes \delta_i \in \hom(W^n, V)$, and $v \in V$. Additionally, suppose the prover is provided an alleged witness $w = \sum_j w_j \otimes \delta_j \in W^n$ such that

$$((u, v), w) \in \mathcal{R}(\hom(W^n, V)).$$

The prover and verifier run a single tensor reduction on the equivalent statement

$$\left(\sum_{i \in [n]} u_i \otimes \delta_i \right) \left(\sum_{j \in [n]} w_j \otimes \delta_j \right) = v.$$

At the end of tensor reduction, the verifier outputs $(\alpha, \beta, v', \_)$. The prover and verifier compute $u' = \sum_i \alpha^i \cdot u_i$ and set the output statement to be (u', v'). The

---

[2] The tensor relation can be formally understood as a ternary relation where any public parameters are ignored. This makes it compatible with the reductions of knowledge framework which works over ternary relations defined over public parameter, statement, and witness tuples.

prover additionally computes the output witness $w' = \sum_j \beta^j \cdot w_j$ as dictated by the tensor reduction. Now, to check the original statement, it is sufficient for the verifier to check that the prover knows w' such that

$$((u', v'), w') \in \mathcal{R}(\hom(W, V)).$$

Theorem 8 (Tensor Reduction of Knowledge). *For field $\mathbb{F}$, length parameter n, and $\mathbb{F}$-modules W and V, Construction 4 is a reduction of knowledge from $\mathcal{R}(\hom(W^n, V))$ to $\mathcal{R}(\hom(W, V))$.*

We present a formal proof of Theorem 8 in the extended version [30].

6 Instantiating the Tensor Reduction of Knowledge

In this section, we demonstrate a unifying view of existing recursive algebraic arguments by deriving them by instantiating the tensor reduction of knowledge over the appropriate structures. We additionally derive new reductions of knowledge for bilinear forms by extending our techniques. In the extended version [30], we additionally discuss concrete modules each of these reductions can be instantiated over. In Sect. 7, we show how to stitch together these reductions to derive an argument for NP.

6.1 Vector Commitments and Linear Forms

We start by generalizing the vector commitment relation from Sect. 2 and then discuss how succinctly derive the vector commitment reduction of knowledge via the tensor reduction of knowledge. We then adapt the vector commitment reduction for linear forms. The high level approach is to first split all checks over size n vectors into k checks over size n/k vectors. These checks are then folded using a random linear combination. How exactly the vectors are split and folded is abstracted away by the tensor reduction of knowledge.

Consider size parameter $n \in \mathbb{N}$, and consider $\mathbb{F}$-modules $\mathbb{G}$ and $\mathbb{H}$ for field $\mathbb{F}$ such that $\mathbb{G} \cong \hom(\mathbb{H}, \mathbb{G} \otimes \mathbb{H})$. For public key $G \in \mathbb{G}^n$, and commitment $\overline{H} \in \mathbb{G} \otimes \mathbb{H}$, suppose a verifier would like to check that a prover knows $H \in \mathbb{H}^n$ such that $\sum_i G_i \otimes H_i = \overline{H}$. For example, suppose $\mathbb{G}$ is a group of prime order p where the discrete logarithm is hard, $\mathbb{H}$ and $\mathbb{F}$ are $\mathbb{Z}_p$, and $\otimes$ represents scalar multiplication. Then, this amounts to checking knowledge of the opening for a Pedersen commitment. Recall that the prover's claim can be expressed as a tensor statement $G(H) = \overline{H}$. Therefore, because $G \in \mathbb{G}^n$, we define the generalized vector commitment relation as the tensor relation over homomorphisms in $\mathbb{G}^n$.

Definition 13 (Generalized Vector Commitment Relation). *For length $n \in \mathbb{N}$ and group $\mathbb{G}$, the vector commitment relation is defined to be $\mathcal{R}(\mathbb{G}^n)$.*

Construction 5 (Vector Commitment Reduction of Knowledge). Because $\mathbb{G}^n \cong (\mathbb{G}^{n/k})^k$, we can directly apply the tensor reduction of knowledge to get a reduction from $\mathcal{R}(\mathbb{G}^n)$ to $\mathcal{R}(\mathbb{G}^{n/k})$.

Suppose that in addition to checking that the prover knows a vector opening to a commitment, the verifier would like to additionally check some public linear combination of the prover's opening. In particular, for public vector $A \in \mathbb{F}^n$, and $\sigma \in \mathbb{H}$, suppose the verifier would like to additionally check that $A(H) = \sigma$ where $A(H)$ is defined to be $\sum_{i \in [n]} A_i \otimes H_i$. For example, if $\otimes$ represents scalar multiplication, then this amounts to checking an inner-product. Recall, from Sect. 5, that this is equivalent to checking $(G \oplus A)(H) = \overline{H} \oplus \sigma$. Because $G \oplus A \in \mathbb{G}^n \oplus \mathbb{F}^n$, we define the linear forms relation as follows.

Definition 14 (Linear Forms Relation). *For length n and $\mathbb{F}$-module $\mathbb{G}$ for field $\mathbb{F}$, let $\mathsf{LF}_n = \mathbb{G}^n \oplus \mathbb{F}^n$. The linear forms relation is defined to be $\mathcal{R}(\mathsf{LF}_n)$.*

Construction 6 (Linear Forms Reduction of Knowledge). Consider $n, k \in \mathbb{N}$ such that k divides n. We construct a reduction of knowledge from $\mathcal{R}(\mathsf{LF}_n)$ to $\mathcal{R}(\mathsf{LF}_{n/k})$. In particular, we have that $\mathsf{LF}_n = (\mathbb{G} \oplus \mathbb{F})^n \cong (\mathbb{G} \oplus \mathbb{F})^{(n/k) \cdot k} = (\mathsf{LF}_{n/k})^k$. Therefore, the prover and verifier can apply the tensor reduction of knowledge with respect to this decomposition to reduce the task of checking a statement in $\mathcal{R}(\mathsf{LF}_n)$ to the task of checking a statement in $\mathcal{R}(\mathsf{LF}_{n/k})$.

Lemma 7 (Linear Forms Reduction of Knowledge). *Construction 6 is a reduction of knowledge from LF_n to $\mathsf{LF}_{n/k}$ with $O(n)$ prover and verifier time complexity and $O(k^2)$ communication complexity.*

As discussed in Sect. 2, we can construct a base case argument for LF_1 where the prover directly reveals the witness. Thus, we have the following.

Corollary 2 (Linear Forms Argument of Knowledge). *Consider $n, k \in \mathbb{N}$ such that k divides n. Let Π_{LF} be a reduction of knowledge from $\mathcal{R}(\mathsf{LF}_n)$ to $\mathcal{R}(\mathsf{LF}_{n/k})$. Let Π_{base} be an argument of knowledge for $\mathcal{R}(\mathsf{LF}_1)$. Then*

$$\Pi_{\mathsf{base}} \circ \underbrace{\Pi_{\mathsf{LF}} \circ \ldots \circ \Pi_{\mathsf{LF}}}_{\log_k n \text{ times}}$$

is an argument of knowledge for LF_n with $O(n)$ prover and verifier time complexity and $O(k^2 \cdot \log_k n)$ communication complexity.

6.2   Bilinear Forms

We extend the above methodology to develop a new reduction for bilinear forms. Recall that the public parameters consist of public key $G \in \mathbb{G}^m$, and the statement consists of matrix $M \in \mathbb{F}^{m \times m}$, commitments $\overline{A}, \overline{B} \in \mathbb{G}$, and scalar $\sigma \in \mathbb{F}$. A witness $(A, B) \in \mathbb{F}^m$ is satisfying if $A^\top M B = \sigma$, $\langle G, A \rangle = \overline{A}$, and $\langle G, B \rangle = \overline{B}$.

Below, we define a slight generalization where the length n of the vector B is some fraction of the length m. The key G is first (partially) compressed with respect to some public random vector $r \in \mathbb{F}^{m/n}$ to produce a new key $H \in \mathbb{G}^n$. This key is instead used to commit to the vector B. Our bilinear forms reduction will recursively compress G and B until $n = 1$. At this point the bilinear forms statement can be reduced to a linear forms statement.

Definition 15 (Bilinear Forms, Original). *Consider $\mathbb{F}$-module $\mathbb{G}$ for field $\mathbb{F}$. We define the bilinear forms relation, $\mathcal{R}_{\mathsf{Bil}}$, characterized by m rows and n columns as follows. The public parameters consist of key $G \in \mathbb{G}^m$. The statement consists of matrix $M \in \mathbb{F}^{m \times n}$, public randomness $r \in \mathbb{F}^{m/n}$, commitments $(\overline{A}, \overline{B}) \in \mathbb{G}$, and $\sigma \in \mathbb{F}$. A witness (A, B) is satisfying if $A^\top M B = \sigma$, $G(A) = \overline{A}$, and $G(r \otimes B) = \overline{B}$.*

Unlike vector commitments and linear forms, the bilinear forms relation cannot be encoded directly as a tensor evaluation statement. Our approach is to encode the original statement as the *related* statement,

$$(G \otimes H \oplus M)(A \otimes B) = (\overline{A} \otimes \overline{B} \oplus \sigma), \tag{3}$$

where $M \in \mathbb{F}^m \otimes \mathbb{F}^n$ is a tensor such that $M(A \otimes B) = A^\top M B$ and $H = G(r) \in \mathbb{G}^n$. The tensor-based statement implies checking the original statement so long as we additionally stipulate that the bilinear relation assumption holds for $(\mathbb{G}, \mathbb{F})$, and $(\mathbb{G}, \mathbb{G})$. Then, we can utilize the tensor reduction of knowledge to reduce the corresponding tensor relation $\mathcal{R}(\mathbb{G}^m \otimes \mathbb{G}^n \oplus \mathbb{F}^m \otimes \mathbb{F}^n)$.

In practice, $\mathbb{G}$ can be a symmetric bilinear group with the pairing operation acting as the tensor product and $\mathbb{G} \otimes \mathbb{G}$ denoting the target group. In this setting, the bilinear relation assumptions are equivalent to the discrete logarithm assumption over $\mathbb{G}$ and the double pairing assumption [1] over $(\mathbb{G}, \mathbb{G})$.

The computational hardness assumptions are a critical detail for arguing that checking Eq. (3) is sufficient to check the original relation: the unconditional knowledge soundness property of the tensor reduction of knowledge only guarantees that the prover knows *some* satisfying witness in $\mathbb{F}^m \otimes \mathbb{F}^n$ which may be of the form $\sum_i A_i \otimes B_i$ (i.e., not a simple tensor). While this is a valid witness for the corresponding tensor statement, it is *not* a valid witness for the original statement. However, by assuming that the commitment scheme is computationally binding, we can argue that all A_i values must be the same. Leveraging this, we can show that the prover must know a single A and B vector that satisfies the statement. Formally, we define the bilinear forms relation as follows.

Definition 16 (Bilinear Forms, Tensor). *Consider $n, m \in \mathbb{N}$, and consider $\mathbb{F}$-module $\mathbb{G}$ for field $\mathbb{F}$ such that the bilinear relation assumption holds for $(\mathbb{G}, \mathbb{F})$, and $(\mathbb{G}, \mathbb{G})$. Let $\mathsf{BF}_{m,n} = (\mathbb{G}^m \otimes \mathbb{G}^n) \oplus (\mathbb{F}^m \otimes \mathbb{F}^n)$. We define the (tensor-based) bilinear form relation as the corresponding tensor relation $\mathcal{R}(\mathsf{BF}_{m,n})$.*

Next, we show how to recursively reduce $\mathcal{R}_{\mathsf{Bil}(m,n)}$ to $\mathcal{R}(\mathsf{LF}_m)$. To do so, we construct a reduction from $\mathcal{R}_{\mathsf{Bil}(m,n)}$ to $\mathcal{R}_{\mathsf{Bil}(m,n/k)}$, which internally uses the tensor reduction of knowledge from $\mathcal{R}(\mathsf{BF}_{m,n})$ to $\mathcal{R}(\mathsf{BF}_{m,n/k})$. We then construct a base case reduction from $\mathcal{R}_{\mathsf{Bil}(m,1)}$ to $\mathcal{R}(\mathsf{LF}_m)$.

Construction 7 (Bilinear Forms Reduction of Knowledge). Consider $n, k \in \mathbb{N}$ such that k divides n. We reduce from $\mathcal{R}_{\mathsf{Bil}(m,n)}$ to $\mathcal{R}_{\mathsf{Bil}(m,n/k)}$.

The generator samples public key $G \leftarrow \mathbb{G}^m$. Suppose that the prover and verifier take as input statement $(M, r, \overline{A}, \overline{B}, \sigma)$ and the prover additionally takes as input and witness (A, B) such that

$$(G, (M, r, \overline{A}, \overline{B}, \sigma), (A, B)) \in \mathcal{R}_{\mathsf{Bil}(m,n)}$$

The prover and verifier begin by encoding the statement and witness as

$$((G \otimes H \oplus M, \overline{A} \otimes \overline{B} \oplus \sigma), A \otimes B) \in \mathcal{R}(\mathsf{BF}_{m,n})$$

where $M \in \mathbb{F}^m \otimes \mathbb{F}^n$ is such that $M(A \otimes B) = A^\top M B$ and $H = G(r) \in \mathbb{G}^n$.
    We observe that

$$\mathsf{BF}_{m,n} = \mathbb{G}^m \otimes \mathbb{G}^n \oplus \mathbb{F}^m \otimes \mathbb{F}^n \cong (\mathbb{G}^m \otimes \mathbb{G}^{n/k} \oplus \mathbb{F}^m \otimes \mathbb{F}^{n/k})^k = (\mathsf{BF}_{m,n/k})^k.$$

Therefore, the prover and verifier can apply the tensor reduction of knowledge with respect to this decomposition and reduce to the task of checking a statement in $\mathcal{R}(\mathsf{BF}_{m,n/k})$. At a high level, the tensor reduction prover and verifier partition M and H into k sets of columns and the prover partitions B into k corresponding sets of rows. The prover and verifier then take a random linear combination of these sets against weights $(s, s^2, \ldots, s^k)$ for some randomness $s \in \mathbb{F}$. By linearity, we have that the output statement is of the form

$$((G \otimes H' \oplus M', \overline{A} \otimes \overline{B}' \oplus \sigma'), A \otimes B') \in \mathcal{R}(\mathsf{BF}_{m,n/k})$$

for some $H' = H((s, \ldots, s^k)) \in \mathbb{G}^{n/k}$, $M' = M((s, \ldots, s^k)) \in \mathbb{F}^m \otimes \mathbb{F}^{n/k}$, $\overline{B}' \in \mathbb{G}$, $\sigma' \in \mathbb{F}$, and $B' \in \mathbb{F}^{n/k}$. Together, the prover and verifier output the decoded statement $(M', (r \otimes (s, \ldots, s^k)), \overline{A}, \overline{B}', \sigma')$ and witness (A, B'). Now it is sufficient for the verifier to check that the prover knows (A, B') such that.

$$(G, (M', (r \otimes (s, \ldots, s^k)), \overline{A}, \overline{B}', \sigma'), (A, B')) \in \mathcal{R}_{\mathsf{Bil}(m,n/k)}.$$

Lemma 8 (Bilinear Forms Reduction of Knowledge). *Construction 7 is a reduction of knowledge from $\mathcal{R}_{\mathsf{Bil}(m,n)}$ to $\mathcal{R}_{\mathsf{Bil}(m,n/k)}$ with $O(mn)$ prover and verifier time complexity and $O(k^2)$ communication complexity.*

We present a formal proof of Lemma 8 in the extended version [30]. We now present the base case reduction.

Construction 8 (Bilinear Forms Base Case). We construct a reduction of knowledge from $\mathcal{R}_{\mathsf{Bil}(m,1)}$ to $\mathcal{R}(\mathsf{LF}_m)$. Once again the generator samples public key $G \leftarrow \mathbb{G}^m$. Consider statement $(M, r, \overline{A}, \overline{B}, \sigma)$ and alleged witness (A, B). The prover begins the reduction by directly sending B to the verifier. The verifier immediately checks that $H(B) = \overline{B}$ for $H = G(r)$. Additionally, as $M \in \mathbb{F}^m$ and $B \in \mathbb{F}$, the verifier computes the vector $V \leftarrow M \cdot B$. The verifier is left with checking that the prover knows $A \in \mathbb{F}^m$ such that $G(A) = \overline{A}$ and $V(A) = \sigma$. This is equivalent to checking that $((G \oplus V, \overline{A} \oplus \sigma), A) \in \mathcal{R}(\mathsf{LF}_m)$.

Lemma 9 (Bilinear Forms Base Case). *Construction 8 is a reduction of knowledge from $\mathcal{R}_{\mathsf{Bil}(m,1)}$ to $\mathcal{R}(\mathsf{LF}_m)$ with $O(m)$ prover and verifier time complexity and $O(1)$ communication complexity.*

Corollary 3 (Bilinear Forms to Linear Forms). *Consider* $n, k \in \mathbb{N}$ *such that* k *divides* n. *Let* Π_{Bil} *be the reduction of knowledge from* $\mathcal{R}_{\mathsf{Bil}(m,n)}$ *to* $\mathcal{R}_{\mathsf{Bil}(m,n/k)}$. *Let* Π_{base} *be the reduction of knowledge from* $\mathcal{R}(\mathsf{Bil}(m, 1))$ *to* $\mathcal{R}(\mathsf{LF}_m)$. *Then*

$$\Pi_{\mathsf{base}} \circ \underbrace{\Pi_{\mathsf{Bil}} \circ \ldots \circ \Pi_{\mathsf{Bil}}}_{\log_k n \text{ times}}$$

is a reduction of knowledge from $\mathcal{R}_{\mathsf{Bil}(m,n)}$ *to* $\mathcal{R}(\mathsf{LF}_m)$ *with* $O(mn)$ *prover and verifier time complexity and* $O(k^2 \cdot \log_k n)$ *communication complexity.*

7   An Argument of Knowledge for NP

In this section, we develop an argument of knowledge for NP with logarithmic communication by leveraging our reductions of knowledge for linear algebraic statements. In particular, we first show that an NP-complete relation, $\mathcal{R}_{\mathsf{ACS}}$, can be encoded as a sequence of linear and bilinear forms constraints over the same commitment. We then develop helper reductions of knowledge that reduce the task of checking many linear and bilinear forms over the same commitment to a single linear and bilinear form. We then apply our reductions of knowledge for linear forms and bilinear forms.

Definition 17 (Algebraic Constraint System [29]). *Consider group* $\mathbb{G}$ *and corresponding field* $\mathbb{F}$ *such that the bilinear relation assumption holds for* $(\mathbb{G}, \mathbb{F})$ *and* $(\mathbb{G}, \mathbb{G})$. *We define the NP-complete algebraic constraint relation,* $\mathcal{R}_{\mathsf{ACS}}$, *characterized by* n *variables,* $m = O(n)$ *constraints, and* ℓ *inputs as follows. The public parameters consist of* $G \in \mathbb{G}^n$. *The statement consists of* m *sparse constraint matrices* $M_1, \ldots, M_m \in \mathbb{F}^{n \times n}$ *such that the total number of non-zero values in all matrices combined is* $O(n)$, *public inputs and outputs vector* $X \in \mathbb{F}^\ell$, *and witness commitment* $\overline{Z} \in \mathbb{G}$. *A witness vector* $W \in \mathbb{F}^{n-\ell}$ *is satisfying if for* $Z = (X, W)$, $Z^\top M_i Z = 0$ *for all* $i \in [m]$, *and* $G(Z) = \overline{Z}$.

We can encode $\mathcal{R}_{\mathsf{ACS}}$ to tensor relations as follows: First, the verifier can check that $((G \oplus \delta_i, \overline{Z} \oplus X_i), Z) \in \mathcal{R}(\mathsf{LF}_n)$ for all $i \in [\ell]$ to ensure that Z contains public vector X. To check the commitment and constraints, it is sufficient for the verifier to check that the prover knows $Z_1, Z_2 \in \mathbb{F}^n$ such that $(G, (M_i, 1, \overline{Z}, \overline{Z}, 0), (Z_1, Z_2)) \in \mathcal{R}_{\mathsf{Bil}(n,n)}$ for all $i \in [m]$. The bilinear relation assumptions ensure that Z, Z_1 and Z_2 are equal.

Next, we leverage the fact that all linear form checks and all bilinear form checks are over the same commitment to reduce these checks. We formally capture the set of linear and bilinear form checks over the same commitment as the multiple linear and bilinear forms relations.

Definition 18 (Multiple Linear Forms). *We define* $\mathcal{R}_{\mathsf{MLF}(n,\ell)}$ *such that* $((G, (V_1, \ldots, V_\ell), (\sigma_1, \ldots, \sigma_\ell), \overline{Z}), Z) \in \mathcal{R}_{\mathsf{MLF}(n,\ell)}$ *if and only if* $((G \oplus V_i, \overline{Z} \oplus \sigma_i), Z) \in \mathcal{R}(\mathsf{LF}_n)$ *for all* i *in* $[\ell]$.

Definition 19 (Multiple Bilinear Forms). *We define* $\mathcal{R}_{\mathsf{MBil}(m,n,\ell)}$ *such that* $(G, ((M_1, \ldots, M_\ell), r, (\sigma_1, \ldots, \sigma_\ell), \overline{Z}_1, \overline{Z}_2), (Z_1, Z_2)) \in \mathcal{R}_{\mathsf{MBil}(m,n,\ell)}$ *if and only if* $(G, (M_i, r, \overline{Z}_1, \overline{Z}_2, \sigma_i), (Z_1, Z_2)) \in \mathcal{R}_{\mathsf{Bil}(m,n)}$ *for all* i *in* $[\ell]$.

With these relations, the above encoding can be captured as a reduction of knowledge in which the prover and verifier do not interact but rather take as input an $\mathcal{R}_{\mathsf{ACS}}$ statement-witness pair and output the corresponding tensor-based statements and witnesses in the multiple linear forms and bilinear forms relations. This step can be interpreted as a Levin reduction.

Lemma 10 (Encoding NPas Tensor Relations). *There exists a reduction of knowledge from* $\mathcal{R}_{\mathsf{ACS}(m,n,\ell)}$ *to* $\mathcal{R}_{\mathsf{MBil}(n,n,m)} \times \mathcal{R}_{\mathsf{MLF}(n,\ell)}$ *with* $O(n)$ *prover and verifier complexity, and no communication.*

Because all ℓ checks for $\mathcal{R}_{\mathsf{MLF}(n,\ell)}$ concern the same committed value, we observe that they can be batched into a single check for $\mathcal{R}(\mathsf{LF}_n)$ using a random linear combination. In particular, the verifier can send a random challenge $r \in \mathbb{F}$. Together the prover and verifier can compute $V \leftarrow \sum_i V_i \cdot r^i$ and $\sigma \leftarrow \sum_i \sigma_i \cdot r^i$ and reduce to checking that the prover knows Z such that $((G \oplus V, \overline{Z} \oplus \sigma), Z) \in \mathcal{R}(\mathsf{LF}_n)$. Similarly, we can reduce multiple bilinear forms over the same commitment to a single bilinear form. Formally, we have the following reductions.

Lemma 11 (Linear Forms Batch Reduction). *For* $n, m, \ell \in \mathbb{N}$, *there exists a reduction of knowledge from* $\mathcal{R}_{\mathsf{MLF}(n,\ell)}$ *to* $\mathcal{R}_{\mathsf{LF}(n)}$ *with* $O(n\ell)$ *prover and verifier time complexity, and* $O(1)$ *communication complexity.*

Lemma 12 (Bilinear Forms Batch Reduction). *For* $n, m, \ell \in \mathbb{N}$, *there exists a reduction of knowledge from* $\mathcal{R}_{\mathsf{MBil}(m,n,\ell)}$ *to* $\mathcal{R}_{\mathsf{Bil}(m,n)}$ *with* $O(mn\ell)$ *prover and verifier time complexity, and* $O(1)$ *communication complexity.*

Putting everything together, we arrive at an argument of knowledge for NP.

Corollary 4 (An Argument of Knowledge for NP). *Let* Π_{encode} *be the reduction of knowledge from* $\mathcal{R}_{\mathsf{ACS}(n,m,\ell)}$ *to* $\mathcal{R}_{\mathsf{MBil}(n,n,m)} \times \mathcal{R}_{\mathsf{MLF}(n,\ell)}$ *(Lemma 10). Let* Π_{batchLF} *be the batching scheme for linear forms (Lemma 11). Let* Π_{batchBil} *be the batching scheme for bilinear forms (Lemma 12). Let* Π_{LF_n} *be the argument of knowledge for* $\mathcal{R}(\mathsf{LF}_n)$ *with decomposition parameter* k *(Construction 2). Let* $\Pi_{\mathsf{Bil}(n,n)}$ *be the reduction of knowledge from* $\mathcal{R}_{\mathsf{Bil}(n,n)}$ *to* $\mathcal{R}_{\mathsf{LF}(n)}$ *with decomposition parameter* k *(Corollary 3). Let* Π_{id} *be the identity reduction of knowledge (i.e., the prover and verifier output their inputs). Let* Π_{foldBool} *be a 2-folding scheme for* $\mathcal{R}_{\mathsf{T}}$ *(i.e., the verifier outputs* true *if both its inputs are* true*). Then*

$$\Pi_{\mathsf{foldBool}} \circ (\Pi_{\mathsf{id}} \times \Pi_{\mathsf{LF}_m}) \circ (\Pi_{\mathsf{LF}_n} \times \Pi_{\mathsf{Bil}(n,n)}) \circ (\Pi_{\mathsf{batchLF}} \times \Pi_{\mathsf{batchBil}}) \circ \Pi_{\mathsf{encode}}$$

is an argument of knowledge for $\mathcal{R}_{\mathsf{ACS}(n,m,\ell)}$ *with* $O(n)$ *prover and verifier time complexity, and* $O(k^2 \log_k n)$ *communication complexity.*

Acknowledgments. We thank Jonathan Bootle, Quang Dao, Vipul Goyal, Yael Tauman Kalai, Jonathan Lee, Srinath Setty, Elaine Shi, and Zoe Wellner for comments on earlier versions of this work.

References

1. Abe, M., Fuchsbauer, G., Groth, J., Haralambiev, K., Ohkubo, M.: Structure-preserving signatures and commitments to group elements. In: Rabin, T. (ed.) CRYPTO 2010. LNCS, vol. 6223, pp. 209–236. Springer, Heidelberg (2010). https://doi.org/10.1007/978-3-642-14623-7_12
2. Arora, S., Barak, B.: Computational complexity: a modern approach. Cambridge University Press (2009)
3. Attema, T., Cramer, R.: Compressed Σ-protocol theory and practical application to plug & play secure algorithmics. In: Micciancio, D., Ristenpart, T. (eds.) CRYPTO 2020. LNCS, vol. 12172, pp. 513–543. Springer, Cham (2020). https://doi.org/10.1007/978-3-030-56877-1_18
4. Attema, T., Cramer, R., Rambaud, M.: Compressed Σ-protocols for bilinear group arithmetic circuits and application to logarithmic transparent threshold signatures. In: Tibouchi, M., Wang, H. (eds.) ASIACRYPT 2021. LNCS, vol. 13093, pp. 526–556. Springer, Cham (2021). https://doi.org/10.1007/978-3-030-92068-5_18
5. Bellare, M., Rogaway, P.: Random oracles are practical: a paradigm for designing efficient protocols. In: Proceedings of the 1st ACM Conference on Computer and Communications Security, pp. 62–73 (1993)
6. Ben-Sasson, E., Chiesa, A., Spooner, N.: Interactive oracle proofs. In: Hirt, M., Smith, A. (eds.) TCC 2016. LNCS, vol. 9986, pp. 31–60. Springer, Heidelberg (2016). https://doi.org/10.1007/978-3-662-53644-5_2
7. Bitansky, N., Canetti, R., Chiesa, A., Tromer, E.: From extractable collision resistance to succinct non-interactive arguments of knowledge, and back again. In: Proceedings of the 3rd Innovations in Theoretical Computer Science Conference, pp. 326–349 (2012)
8. Bitansky, N., Canetti, R., Chiesa, A., Tromer, E.: Recursive composition and bootstrapping for SNARKs and proof-carrying data. In: Proceedings of the Forty-Fifth Annual ACM Symposium on Theory of Computing, pp. 111–120 (2013)
9. Boneh, D., Drake, J., Fisch, B., Gabizon, A.: Halo Infinite: proof-carrying data from additive polynomial commitments. In: Malkin, T., Peikert, C. (eds.) CRYPTO 2021. LNCS, vol. 12825, pp. 649–680. Springer, Cham (2021). https://doi.org/10.1007/978-3-030-84242-0_23
10. Bootle, J., Cerulli, A., Chaidos, P., Groth, J., Petit, C.: Efficient zero-knowledge arguments for arithmetic circuits in the discrete log setting. In: Fischlin, M., Coron, J.-S. (eds.) EUROCRYPT 2016. LNCS, vol. 9666, pp. 327–357. Springer, Heidelberg (2016). https://doi.org/10.1007/978-3-662-49896-5_12
11. Bootle, J., Chiesa, A., Sotiraki, K.: Sumcheck arguments and their applications. In: Malkin, T., Peikert, C. (eds.) CRYPTO 2021. LNCS, vol. 12825, pp. 742–773. Springer, Cham (2021). https://doi.org/10.1007/978-3-030-84242-0_26
12. Bowe, S., Grigg, J., Hopwood, D.: Recursive proof composition without a trusted setup. Cryptology ePrint Archive, Paper 2019/1021 (2019)
13. Bünz, B., Bootle, J., Boneh, D., Poelstra, A., Wuille, P., Maxwell, G.: Bulletproofs: Short proofs for confidential transactions and more. In: 2018 IEEE Symposium on Security and Privacy (SP), pp. 315–334. IEEE (2018)
14. Bünz, B., Chiesa, A., Lin, W., Mishra, P., Spooner, N.: Proof-carrying data without succinct arguments. In: Malkin, T., Peikert, C. (eds.) CRYPTO 2021. LNCS, vol. 12825, pp. 681–710. Springer, Cham (2021). https://doi.org/10.1007/978-3-030-84242-0_24

15. Bünz, B., Fisch, B., Szepieniec, A.: Transparent SNARKs from DARK compilers. In: Canteaut, A., Ishai, Y. (eds.) EUROCRYPT 2020. LNCS, vol. 12105, pp. 677–706. Springer, Cham (2020). https://doi.org/10.1007/978-3-030-45721-1_24

16. Bünz, B., Maller, M., Mishra, P., Tyagi, N., Vesely, P.: Proofs for inner pairing products and applications. In: Tibouchi, M., Wang, H. (eds.) ASIACRYPT 2021. LNCS, vol. 13092, pp. 65–97. Springer, Cham (2021). https://doi.org/10.1007/978-3-030-92078-4_3

17. Campanelli, M., Faonio, A., Fiore, D., Querol, A., Rodríguez, H.: Lunar: a toolbox for more efficient universal and updatable zkSNARKs and commit-and-prove extensions. In: Tibouchi, M., Wang, H. (eds.) ASIACRYPT 2021. LNCS, vol. 13092, pp. 3–33. Springer, Cham (2021). https://doi.org/10.1007/978-3-030-92078-4_1

18. Campanelli, M., Nitulescu, A., Ràfols, C., Zacharakis, A., Zapico, A.: Linear-map vector commitments and their practical applications. In: Agrawal, S., Lin, D. (eds.) Advances in Cryptology - ASIACRYPT 2022, pp. 189–219. Springer, Cham (2022). https://doi.org/10.1007/978-3-031-22972-5_7

19. Chiesa, A., Hu, Y., Maller, M., Mishra, P., Vesely, N., Ward, N.: Marlin: preprocessing zkSNARKs with universal and updatable SRS. In: Canteaut, A., Ishai, Y. (eds.) EUROCRYPT 2020. LNCS, vol. 12105, pp. 738–768. Springer, Cham (2020). https://doi.org/10.1007/978-3-030-45721-1_26

20. Chung, H., Han, K., Ju, C., Kim, M., Seo, J.H.: Bulletproofs+: shorter proofs for a privacy-enhanced distributed ledger. IEEE Access **10**, 42067–42082 (2022)

21. Delignat-Lavaud, A., Fournet, C., Kohlweiss, M., Parno, B.: Cinderella: turning shabby X. 509 certificates into elegant anonymous credentials with the magic of verifiable computation. In: 2016 IEEE Symposium on Security and Privacy (SP), pp. 235–254. IEEE (2016)

22. Fiat, A., Shamir, A.: How to prove yourself: practical solutions to identification and signature problems. In: Odlyzko, A.M. (ed.) CRYPTO 1986. LNCS, vol. 263, pp. 186–194. Springer, Heidelberg (1987). https://doi.org/10.1007/3-540-47721-7_12

23. Fuchsbauer, G., Kiltz, E., Loss, J.: The algebraic group model and its applications. In: Shacham, H., Boldyreva, A. (eds.) CRYPTO 2018. LNCS, vol. 10992, pp. 33–62. Springer, Cham (2018). https://doi.org/10.1007/978-3-319-96881-0_2

24. Gabizon, A., Williamson, Z.J., Ciobotaru, O.: PLONK: Permutations over lagrange-bases for oecumenical noninteractive arguments of knowledge. Cryptology ePrint Archive, Report 2019/953 (2019)

25. Gennaro, R., Gentry, C., Parno, B., Raykova, M.: Quadratic span programs and succinct NIZKs without PCPs. In: Johansson, T., Nguyen, P.Q. (eds.) EUROCRYPT 2013. LNCS, vol. 7881, pp. 626–645. Springer, Heidelberg (2013). https://doi.org/10.1007/978-3-642-38348-9_37

26. Gentry, C., Wichs, D.: Separating succinct non-interactive arguments from all falsifiable assumptions. In: Proceedings of the forty-third annual ACM symposium on Theory of computing, pp. 99–108 (2011)

27. Goldwasser, S., Micali, S., Rackoff, C.: The knowledge complexity of interactive proof-systems. In: Providing Sound Foundations for Cryptography: On the Work of Shafi Goldwasser and Silvio Micali, pp. 203–225 (2019)

28. Kosba, A., Miller, A., Shi, E., Wen, Z., Papamanthou, C.: Hawk: the blockchain model of cryptography and privacy-preserving smart contracts. In: 2016 IEEE Symposium on Security and Privacy (SP), pp. 839–858. IEEE (2016)

29. Kothapalli, A., Masserova, E., Parno, B.: Poppins: A direct construction for asymptotically optimal zkSNARKs. Cryptology ePrint Archive, Report 2020/1318 (2020)

30. Kothapalli, A., Parno, B.: Algebraic reductions of knowledge. Cryptology ePrint Archive, Paper 2022/009 (2022)

31. Kothapalli, A., Setty, S., Tzialla, I.: Nova: Recursive zero-knowledge arguments from folding schemes. In: Dodis, Y., Shrimpton, T. (eds.) CRYPTO 2022, Part IV, pp. 359–388. Springer, Cham (2022). https://doi.org/10.1007/978-3-031-15985-5_13

32. Lee, J.: Dory: efficient, transparent arguments for generalised inner products and polynomial commitments. In: Nissim, K., Waters, B. (eds.) TCC 2021. LNCS, vol. 13043, pp. 1–34. Springer, Cham (2021). https://doi.org/10.1007/978-3-030-90453-1_1

33. Lund, C., Fortnow, L., Karloff, H., Nisan, N.: Algebraic methods for interactive proof systems. J. ACM (JACM) **39**(4), 859–868 (1992)

34. Pedersen, T.P.: Non-interactive and information-theoretic secure verifiable secret sharing. In: Feigenbaum, J. (ed.) CRYPTO 1991. LNCS, vol. 576, pp. 129–140. Springer, Heidelberg (1992). https://doi.org/10.1007/3-540-46766-1_9

35. Ràfols, C., Zapico, A.: An algebraic framework for universal and updatable SNARKs. In: Malkin, T., Peikert, C. (eds.) CRYPTO 2021. LNCS, vol. 12825, pp. 774–804. Springer, Cham (2021). https://doi.org/10.1007/978-3-030-84242-0_27

36. Ràfols, C., Zacharakis, A.: Folding schemes with selective verification. Cryptology ePrint Archive, Paper 2022/1576 (2022)

37. Sasson, E.B., et al.: Zerocash: decentralized anonymous payments from bitcoin. In: 2014 IEEE Symposium on Security and Privacy, pp. 459–474. IEEE (2014)

38. Schwartz, J.T.: Fast probabilistic algorithms for verification of polynomial identities. J. ACM (JACM) **27**(4), 701–717 (1980)

39. Setty, S.: Spartan: efficient and general-purpose zkSNARKs without trusted setup. In: Micciancio, D., Ristenpart, T. (eds.) CRYPTO 2020. LNCS, vol. 12172, pp. 704–737. Springer, Cham (2020). https://doi.org/10.1007/978-3-030-56877-1_25

40. Tzialla, I., Kothapalli, A., Parno, B., Setty, S.: Transparency dictionaries with succinct proofs of correct operation. In: Network and Distributed System Security (NDSS) 2022, April 2022

41. Valiant, P.: Incrementally verifiable computation or proofs of knowledge imply time/space efficiency. In: Canetti, R. (ed.) TCC 2008. LNCS, vol. 4948, pp. 1–18. Springer, Heidelberg (2008). https://doi.org/10.1007/978-3-540-78524-8_1

42. Wahby, R.S., Tzialla, I., Shelat, A., Thaler, J., Walfish, M.: Doubly-efficient zksnarks without trusted setup. In: 2018 IEEE Symposium on Security and Privacy (SP), pp. 926–943. IEEE (2018)

43. Zhang, Y., Katz, J., Papamanthou, C.: IntegriDB: verifiable SQL for outsourced databases. In: Proceedings of the 22nd ACM SIGSAC Conference on Computer and Communications Security, pp. 1480–1491 (2015)

On the Impossibility of Algebraic NIZK
in Pairing-Free Groups

Emanuele Giunta[1,2]([✉])([iD])

[1] IMDEA Software Institute, Madrid, Spain
emanuele.giunta@imdea.org
[2] Universidad Politecnica de Madrid, Madrid, Spain

Abstract. Non-Interactive Zero-Knowledge proofs (NIZK) allow a prover to convince a verifier that a statement is true by sending only one message and without conveying any other information. In the CRS model, many instantiations have been proposed from group-theoretic assumptions. On the one hand, some of these constructions use the group structure in a black-box way but rely on pairings, an example being the celebrated Groth-Sahai proof system. On the other hand, a recent line of research realized NIZKs from sub-exponential DDH in pairing-free groups using Correlation Intractable Hash functions, but at the price of making non black-box usage of the group.

As of today no construction is known to *simultaneously* reduce its security to pairing-free group problems and to use the underlying group in a black-box way.

This is indeed not a coincidence: in this paper, we prove that for a large class of NIZK either a pairing-free group is used non black-box by relying on element representation, or security reduces to external hardness assumptions. More specifically our impossibility applies to two incomparable cases. The first one covers Arguments of Knowledge (AoK) which proves that a preimage under a given one way function is known. The second one covers NIZK (not necessarily AoK) for hard subset problems, which captures relations such as DDH, Decision-Linear and Matrix-DDH.

1 Introduction

Zero-Knowledge proofs are protocols through which a *prover* can convince a *verifier* that a given statement is true without revealing any other information. *Non-interactive* zero-knowledge proofs (NIZK) [3] are often preferable in concrete applications but it is well known that instantiating them in the standard model is impossible. To overcome this limitations instantiations in the random oracle model (ROM) and the common reference string (CRS) model have been studied.

In the ROM a public hash function is modeled as being truly random, used in the Fiat-Shamir transform [13] to replace interaction with a public coin verifier. In the CRS model a set of public parameters are set up by a trusted party before the protocol starts. In these two settings, a variety of techniques to build NIZK

© International Association for Cryptologic Research 2023
H. Handschuh and A. Lysyanskaya (Eds.): CRYPTO 2023, LNCS 14084, pp. 702–730, 2023.
https://doi.org/10.1007/978-3-031-38551-3_22

for NP-complete relations have been put forward. However, when applying them to languages of interest in cryptographic applications, for instance those based on prime order (pairing) groups, the reduction to a target NP-complete problem introduces overheads which limit applicability. This typically occurs when proving statements related to ElGamal ciphertexts or Pedersen commitments. For this reason NIZK that operate efficiently for group-theoretic statements, and whose hardness only relied on group-theoretic problems have been studied.

In the ROM, positive results came from the Schnorr sigma protocol [40], and its subsequent generalizations [11,35], which eventually led to sub-linear arguments [4,5] for all NP solely based on hard problems over groups. This approach, however, can provide at best *computationally* sound arguments in the ROM and unclear security guarantees when replacing the RO with a hash function.

For these reasons a parallel line of research investigated NIZKs from group assumptions in the CRS model. Early work proved feasibility in the pairing setting [22–24] eventually leading to the celebrated *statistically sound* Groth-Sahai proof system [25]. Still in the pairing setting [10] recently proposed different techniques to compile Schnorr-like sigma-protocols [11,35,40] capturing linear languages. Interestingly, both constructions only make black-box usage of the underlying group, which makes the resulting NIZK simpler, randomizable and able to support aggregation for specific languages.

A more recent approach is to instantiate the Fiat-Shamir transform through correlation-intractable hash (CIH) functions [6]. Recently [27] realized CIH and NIZK only assuming sub-exponential DDH. This sparkled renewed interest and led to new constructions including designated-verifier NIZK from CDH [30], SNARGs for P and batch-NP [9] and for log-space bounded-depth circuits [28]. On the one hand, this proved once again that the gap between pairing-based assumptions and plain prime order group ones is thinner than we expected. On the other hand, as opposed to Groth-Sahai, all CIH-based NIZKs make non black-box usage of the underlying group by relying on element representations, for instance to hash group elements, and thus breaking the algebraic structure. Given the state of the art we therefore ask whether "best of both worlds" constructions are possible, i.e.

Do there exist NIZK based only on pairing-free prime-order group problems and that only use the group in a black-box way?

A positive answer would be interesting in practice since pairing-free groups are generally more efficient than their pairing-friendly counterpart, possibly providing faster NIZKs that Groth-Sahai. Moreover, black-box usage of the group may preserve the algebraic structure yielding NIZK with homomorphic properties, something currently not known to be possible via CIH.

Our Result. We answer the above question in the negative by showing that for a large class of relations defined over a known prime order pairing free group, any NIZK satisfies at least one of the following:

1. Relies on group element representations, thus using the group in a non black-box way.
2. Its security does not *only* depend on hard problems over the group.
3. It assumes additional algebraic structure (such as pairings).

This informally implies that the usage of pairing in black-box constructions such as Groth-Sahai cannot be removed without relying on group elements representation. Analogously, the usage of elements representation in all recent constructions from sub-exponential DDH cannot be removed without introducing more structure (like pairings or unknown order) or assumptions (like LWE).

Following the approach of recent negative results [8,12], we formalize *black-box* access to the group by assuming all procedures to be defined in Maurer's Generic Group Model (GGM) [34], where the group is replaced by addition and equality check oracles, and no representation is ever given (as opposed to Shoup's Group Model [42]). In this model, we isolate hard group-theoretic problems by assuming unbounded adversaries that are constrained to use the group efficiently, as done in [8,12,41]. We will later refer to this class of adversaries as GPPT, standing for *Generic-Group* PPT. More in detail, we prove two independent impossibility results:

Impossibility for Arguments of Knowledge. Our first result shows that, in Maurer's GGM, given a one-way function (family) $f_k : \{0,1\}^n \to \mathbb{G}^m$ whose hardness reduces to hard group problems, there exists no NIZK-Argument of Knowledge (NIZK-AoK) to prove that a preimage x of y for the function f_k is known. In other words there exists no NIZK-AoK for the NP-relation

$$\mathcal{R} = \{((k,y),x) \ : \ f_k(x) = y\}.$$

If f_k is a one-way function family, we need to further assume that the key k only contains uniformly random group elements for the proof to go through. Although this mildly affects generality, we capture virtually all cases of interest. Examples are discrete logarithm and linear maps $f : \mathbb{F}_q^n \to \mathbb{G}^m$, KZG [29] "powers of τ" setup where $f_G : \mathbb{F}_q \to \mathbb{G}^n$ with key the group generator G and $f_G(\tau) = (\tau^i \cdot G)_{i=1}^n$, PST [37] multivariate CRS and range proofs.

Impossibility for Computationally Sound NIZK. Our second negative result addresses a class of relations $\mathcal{R}$ for which it is possible to sample statements inside and outside the associated language[1] so that distinguishing the two distributions is computationally hard. An example is the DDH relation, for which distinguishing DDH tuples[2] from random ones is hard. These relations were called in [17] *hard subset membeship problems* and for them we show that in Maurer's GGM no NIZK (not necessarily AoK) exists. This essentially captures all group-theoretic decisional problems including DDH, DLin, Matrix DDH and others.

---

[1] Or, more generally, so that with overwhelming probability the sampled elements lies inside and outside the language respectively.

[2] i.e. tuples of the form $(G, a \cdot G, b \cdot G, ab \cdot G)$ for random a, b.

Results Comparison. Finally, we remark that these two results are incomparable. The impossibility of NIZK-AoK for the discrete logarithm relation cannot follow from our second result, as the language associated to the discrete logarithm problem is trivial (every group element admits a discrete logarithm), and therefore is not a hard subset membership problem. Conversely, our second result is not implied by the first one because it addresses a weaker class of NIZKs, which only need to satisfy soundness but need not to be extractable.

Our Techniques. We now give an overview of the ideas and challenges involved in our result. Our starting point are two recent papers by Döttling, Hartmann, Hofeinz, Kliz, Schäge, Ursu [12] and Catalano, Fiore, Gennaro, Giunta [8] which respectively proved impossibility of Algebraic Signatures and Vector Commitments (VC) [7,33] in Maurer's GGM.

Techniques for Arguments of Knowledge. Regarding our first result, the main idea is to reduce NIZK-AoK for a one way function f to VC in such a way that the impossibility in [8] carries over to NIZKs. More specifically, in order to contradict [8] one would have to produce a VC for n messages with commitment c and opening Λ of bit length $|c|$ and $|\Lambda|$ respectively such that $|c| \cdot |\Lambda| = o(n)$. Unfortunately, the only compressing commitments known over groups are variations of Pedersen scheme [38], which comply with the lower bound, and NIZKs do not seem to provide an edge for compression as we do not assume succinctness.

We overcome this limitation with the following critical observation. If the VC *hides* unopened entries, the lower bound in [8] can be improved to $\ell_c \geq n$, with ℓ_c being the number of group elements in the commitment and n the length of the committed vector. This clears the path for the following strategy: committing to a vector of field elements via Pedersen, and then relying on a NIZK-AoK to prove knowledge of the openings. Notice that opening proofs in this case may be of linear size, which does not contradict [8]. However, since the commitment would have constant size, we do violate our improved lower bound.

In order to build intuition and illustrate the challenges that arise in this construction let us present a toy instantiation for the simple case in which $f_{G_i}(x_i) = x_i \cdot G_i$ is the group exponentiation with $G_i \in \mathbb{G}$. Applying directly the idea above a commitment C to $(x_1, \ldots, x_n)$ and an opening Λ at position i should be set as

$$C = f_{G_1}(x_1) + \ldots + f_{G_n}(x_n) = x_1 G_1 + \ldots + x_n G_n$$
$$\Lambda_i = (f_{G_j}(x_i), \pi_j)_{j \neq i} = (x_j G_j, \pi_j)_{j \neq i}$$

with π_j being an AoK for x_j. This approach however fails to hide x_j as it leaks $x_j G_j$. To overcome this issue we rely on the Goldreich-Levin hardcore predicate [20]. Their result informally says that for any OWF f, sampling an input x (viewed as a bit-string) and a random string of the same length r, is hard to guess the bit-wise inner product $x^\top r$ modulo 2 given only $f(x)$ and r. With this tool we can turn the above construction into a VC to bits, where each committed bit is a Goldreich-Levin hardcore predicate, which remains hidden even after leaking $f(x)$.

In the toy example with f being the group exponentiation, the resulting commitment for $b_1, \ldots, b_n$ is obtained by sampling x_i, r_i with $x_i^\top r_i = b_i$ and x_i field element and setting

$$C = (x_1 G_1 + \ldots + x_n G_n, \ r_1, \ldots, r_n), \qquad \Lambda_i = (x_j G_j, \pi_j)_{j \neq i}.$$

Another challenge is that we need our OWF f to be collision resistant, which is trivially true for the exponentiation, but false in general. We address this by showing a rather technical way to make any OWF family whose key consist of random group elements collision resistant. Although this transformation renders f computable only in GPPT time, more specifically in exponential space[3] but only polynomially many group operations, this suffices to obtain our result.

Techniques for Computationally Sound NIZK. Regarding our second result, we fail to provide a simple reduction to primitives known to be impossible and instead we directly adapt the approach of [8,12]. Their attack in the setting of digital signatures works as follows: initially the adversary is given a verification key vk. For each message it then attempts to extract a signature by brute-force running the verifier on all possible inputs. Eventually, either a forgery is found or a signature query reveals a linear relation on the group elements of vk. Thus after sufficiently many attempts a forgery will be found.

We begin by sketching an adaptation to the simpler case of *simulation-sound* NIZKs, where the adversary has to prove a false statement given oracle access to the simulator. In this case one may hope that replacing the signature and verification procedures with the NIZK simulator and verifier, the attack would carry over by letting the adversary try to produce a proof for false statements in the same way.

One issue though is that the simulator is not guaranteed to work with *false* statements, and may simply return an error if it recognizes one as such. We therefore restrict our focus on hard subset membership problems, in which false statements can be sampled so that deciding their correctness is hard. In this way the simulator almost always returns an accepting proof, and in particular the attack eventually succeeds.

The final challenge is using this adversary, let us call it $\mathcal{A}$, to break regular soundness where no simulator oracle is provided. Our solution is reminiscent of the strategy to simulate the folklore proof for graph isomorphism against malicious verifiers: Given the crs, we begin by tossing a coin b, that is a guess on the behavior of $\mathcal{A}$: If $b = 1$ we sample a true statement with its witness (x_1, w_1), otherwise we sample a false one x_0. Next we run $\mathcal{A}$ on x_b. If $\mathcal{A}$ returns a proof and we guessed $b = 0$, then this breaks soundness. Conversely if $\mathcal{A}$ asks for a simulated proof and we guessed $b = 1$, the proof can be computed with the NIZK prover using w_1. In this second case $\mathcal{A}$'s output will contain a linear relation among the group elements in the crs. If the guess is not correct we can resample a fresh b and x_b and repeat. Since distinguishing x_0 from x_1 is hard, each guess is correct with probability close to $1/2$ and with sufficiently many guesses the attack succeeds with significant probability.

---

[3] which explains why we do not violate the black-box separation of [43].

Related Work. Since the seminal work by Impagliazzo and Rudich [26], many papers studied the relations among cryptographic primitives through black-box reduction, and, on the negative side, black-box separations [15,16,18,19,31,43].

This includes the study of what primitives can and cannot be built over black-box pairing-free known prime order groups, typically modeled as Maurer's or Shoup's GGM. Papakonstantinou, Rackoff and Vahlis [36] were the first to study the impossibility of Identity-Based Encryption in the Shoup GGM, result later tightened by [41] in Maurer's GGM and fully proved in [44] in Shoup's Model. Recent works showed impossibility in Maurer's GGM for several other primitives, such as verifiable delay functions [39], digital signatures [12] and vector commitments [8], where the last two are known to exist in Shoup's GGM. In this view our work places NIZK as another primitive which separates Maurer's model from Shoup's one.

Regarding general impossibility results for NIZK, Gentry and Wichs's celebrated result [17] shows that succinct arguments cannot be based on falsifiable assumption assuming sub-exponential hardness. We stress that our problem is orthogonal to their result as we don't assume succinctness. However, we ask for black box usage of a group, which is more restrictive than simply assuming a reduction to (falsifiable) group-theoretic problems.

Abe, Camenisch, Dowsley, Dubovitskaya proved in [1] a general impossibility result for deterministic structure-preserving primitives which captures among others PRF, VRF and unique signatures. Their result however does not cover NIZKs as proofs may not be unique.

More recently Ganesh, Khoshakhlagh, Parisella [14] showed that the Couteau-Hartmann framework [10] to instantiate the Fiat-Shamir transform in pairing groups fails to achieve a stronger notion of extraction when no knowledge assumption is used.

We finally remark that Bellare and Goldwasser [2] and later Goldwasser and Ostrovsky [21] proved the equivalence between NIZKs and invariant signatures. This, in combination with the impossibility result for digital signatures in Maurer's GGM [8,12], yields a weaker version of our second result, excluding *simulation sound* NIZKs only for certain expressive relations[4]

2 Preliminaries

2.1 Notation

In the following we denote $[n] = \{1, \ldots, n\}$. $\mathbb{F}_q$ for a prime q is the field of order q, isomorphic to the integers modulo q. $V \leq \mathbb{F}_q^n$ means that V is an affine subspace of $\mathbb{F}_q^n$. Given a group $\mathbb{G}$ of known prime order q, we call G its canonical generator. Although we will use additive notation for groups, given $a \in \mathbb{F}_q$ and $H \in \mathbb{G}$ we will refer to the operation $a \cdot H$ as an *exponentiation*. We also assume operations on vectors and sets are entry-wise, that is given $\mathbf{v} \in \mathbb{F}_q^n$, $V \leq \mathbb{F}_q^n$ and

---

[4] More specifically given a PRF f, a perfectly binding commitment c to a PRF key k, and public inputs x and y the NIZK has to prove that $y = f_k(x)$.

$H \in \mathbb{G}$, $\mathbf{v} \cdot G = (v_1 G, \ldots, v_n G)$ and $V \cdot G = \{\mathbf{v} \cdot G : \mathbf{v} \in V\}$. For a set $\mathcal{X}$, $x \sim \mathcal{X}$ means x is a random variable with support in $\mathcal{X}$ whereas $x \sim U(\mathcal{X})$ means x is uniformly distributed over $\mathcal{X}$. Given $x, y \sim \mathcal{X}$ we denote $\Delta(x, y)$ their statistical distance

$$\Delta(x, y) \;=\; \frac{1}{2} \sum_{t \in \mathcal{X}} \left| \Pr\left[x = t\right] - \Pr\left[y = t\right] \right|.$$

2.2   Maurer's Generic Group Model

Maurer's Generic Model, introduced in [34] and revised in [44], is a framework to describe generic computation. Since we are interested in procedures defined over a group we will refer to this special case as the Generic Group Model (GGM). In this setting, a group $\mathbb{G}$ of known prime order q is modeled by a stateful oracle machine $\mathcal{O}$ along with an internal list of group elements V of length n. The list initially only contains one generator, i.e. $V = (G)$ and $n = 1$. Operations over the group can be performed through oracle queries $\mathcal{O}_{\mathsf{add}}$, $\mathcal{O}_{\mathsf{eq}}$ to $\mathcal{O}$. More specifically

- When $\mathcal{O}_{\mathsf{add}}(i, j)$ is queried with $i, j \leq n$, $\mathcal{O}$ computes $V_{n+1} \leftarrow V_i + V_j$ and appends the result to V.
- When $\mathcal{O}_{\mathsf{eq}}(i, j)$ is queried with $i, j \leq n$, $\mathcal{O}$ computes the bit $b \leftarrow V_i == V_j$ and returns b.

We remark that the above description follows [44] revision, which removes the possibility to specify in $\mathcal{O}_{\mathsf{add}}$ queries in which entry of V the result should be stored, appending it instead at the end of the list by default. Throughout the rest of this paper, to improve readability, we will use $\mathcal{O}_{\mathsf{add}}$ and $\mathcal{O}_{\mathsf{eq}}$ with group elements instead of indices (implicitly associating group elements to indices).

An important class of adversaries in the GGM used to isolate hard problems in the group from other source of hardness is the following.

Definition 1. GPPT *is the class of all (unbounded) probabilistic Turing Machines with access to $\mathcal{O}_{\mathsf{add}}$, $\mathcal{O}_{\mathsf{eq}}$ whose number of oracle queries is polynomially bounded in their input length.*

This class was implicitly introduced when proving lower bound for computational and decisional problems such as discrete logarithm, DDH and CDH, as well as in recent impossibility result [8,12,39].

2.3   NIZK-AoK

A Non-Interactive Zero-Knowledge argument (NIZK) for a relation $\mathcal{R}$ is a tuple of three algorithms $(\mathsf{G}, \mathsf{P}, \mathsf{V})$ that allow a prover to convince a verifier about the validity of a statement without leaking any other information. Given $\mathsf{crs} \leftarrow \mathsf{G}(1^\lambda)$ and $(x, w) \in \mathcal{R}$ a valid statement, the prover can compute a proof running $\pi \leftarrow \mathsf{P}(\mathsf{crs}, x, w)$ which can later be verified by $b \leftarrow \mathsf{V}(\mathsf{crs}, x, \pi)$. The proof is accepted if $b = 1$, or rejected otherwise. Below we revise formally the main properties NIZKs can satisfy.

Completeness: $\forall (x, w) \in \mathcal{R}$

$$\Pr\left[1 \leftarrow \mathsf{V}(\mathsf{crs}, x, \pi) \mid \mathsf{crs} \leftarrow \mathsf{G}(1^\lambda), \pi \leftarrow \mathsf{P}(\mathsf{crs}, x, w)\right] = 1.$$

Soundness: $\exists \varepsilon$ negligible such that $\forall x : \nexists w : (x, w) \in \mathcal{R}$ and $\forall \mathcal{A}$ PPT

$$\Pr\left[1 \leftarrow \mathsf{V}(\mathsf{crs}, x, \pi) \mid \mathsf{crs} \leftarrow \mathsf{G}(1^\lambda), \pi \leftarrow \mathcal{A}(\mathsf{crs}, x)\right] \leq \varepsilon(\lambda).$$

Argument of Knowledge: For any PPT adversary $\mathcal{A}$ there exists a PPT extractor E such that

1. $\exists \varepsilon$ negligible such that $\forall \mathcal{D}$ PPT, given $\mathsf{crs}_0, \mathsf{td} \leftarrow \mathsf{E}(1^\lambda)$, $\mathsf{crs}_1 \leftarrow \mathsf{G}(1^\lambda)$

$$|\Pr\left[1 \leftarrow \mathcal{D}(\mathsf{crs}_0)\right] - \Pr\left[1 \leftarrow \mathcal{D}(\mathsf{crs}_1)\right]| \leq \varepsilon(\lambda).$$

2. There exists a negligible function ε such that

$$\Pr\left[\begin{array}{c} \mathsf{V}(\mathsf{crs}, x, \pi) \to 1 \\ (x, w) \notin \mathcal{R} \end{array} \,\middle|\, \begin{array}{c} \mathsf{crs}, \mathsf{td} \leftarrow \mathsf{E}(1^\lambda), \ (x, \pi) \leftarrow \mathcal{A}(\mathsf{crs}) \\ w \leftarrow \mathsf{E}(\mathsf{td}, x, \pi) \end{array}\right] \leq \varepsilon(\lambda).$$

Zero-Knowledge: There exists a PPT simulator S such that, up to negligible probability ε, for all $(x, w) \in \mathcal{R}$ and PPT adversary $\mathcal{A}$, given

$$\mathsf{crs}_0, \mathsf{td} \leftarrow \mathsf{S}(1^\lambda), \quad \pi_0 \leftarrow \mathsf{S}(\mathsf{td}, x), \quad \mathsf{crs}_1 \leftarrow \mathsf{G}(1^\lambda), \quad \pi_1 \leftarrow \mathsf{P}(\mathsf{crs}_1, x, w)$$

$$\Rightarrow \quad |\Pr\left[1 \leftarrow \mathcal{A}(\mathsf{crs}_0, \pi_0)\right] - \Pr\left[1 \leftarrow \mathcal{A}(\mathsf{crs}_1, \pi_1)\right]| \leq \varepsilon(1^\lambda).$$

In the rest of the paper we will say that in Maurer's Generic Group Model, a NIZK is *algebraic* if soundness and zero-knowledge hold against any GPPT adversary, i.e. with unbounded computational power but limited to perform a polynomially bounded number of queries to the GGM oracles. Analogously an Algebraic NIZK-AoK is an argument of knowledge against GPPT adversaries.

2.4   Digital Signatures

A Digital Signature scheme is a tuple of three algorithms (S.Setup, S.Sign, S.Vfy) along with a set S.M such that

- S.Setup$(1^\lambda) \to \mathsf{vk}, \mathsf{sk}$ generates the verification signature key
- S.Sign$(\mathsf{sk}, m) \to \sigma$ with $m \in \mathsf{S.M}$, signs the message m.
- S.Vfy$(\mathsf{vk}, m, \sigma) \to 0/1$ check the validity of the signature.

A signature scheme is correct if given vk, sk generated by the setup procedure and for all $m \in \mathsf{S.M}$, computing $\sigma \leftarrow \mathsf{S.Sign}(\mathsf{sk}, m)$ yields a valid signature, i.e. such that $\Pr\left[\mathsf{S.Vfy}(\mathsf{vk}, m, \sigma) \to 1\right] = 1$.

A signature scheme is *unforgeable* against a class of adversaries, if no adversary in this class on input vk and oracle access to $\mathsf{S.Sign}(\mathsf{sk}, \cdot)$ can return a signature on a message that was not queried with non negligible probability.

2.5   Vector Commitments

Vector Commitment (VC) [7,33] is a primitive that allows a user to commit to a vector of messages and later on reveal entries of its choice. A VC scheme consists of four algorithms (VC.Setup, VC.Com, VC.Open, VC.Vfy) and a message space VC.M such that

- VC.Setup(1^λ) $\to$ pp generates the public parameters.
- VC.Com(pp, $x_1, \ldots, x_n$) $\to$ (c, aux) with $x_1, \ldots x_n \in$ VC.M.
- VC.Open(pp, i, aux) $\to$ Λ produces an opening proof for position i.
- VC.Vfy(pp, c, x, i, Λ) $\to$ 0/1 check the validity of the opening proof.

A vector commitment is correct if, given pp generated by the setup algorithm, c a commitment to $(x_1, \ldots, x_n)$ with auxiliary information aux and Λ an opening proof for position i, then $\Pr\left[\text{VC.Vfy}(\text{pp}, c, x, i, \Lambda) \to 1\right] = 1$.

The main notion of security for VC is *position binding*. This generalizes the analogous notion for standard commitments as it requires that opening a position to two different messages is computationally hard. More formally, given pp $\leftarrow$ VC.Setup(1^λ), for all adversary $\mathcal{A}$ there exists a negligible ε such that

$$\Pr\left[\begin{array}{l} \mathcal{A}(1^\lambda, \text{pp}) \to (c, i, x_0, \Lambda_0, x_1, \Lambda_1), \\ \forall b \in \{0,1\} \quad \text{VC.Vfy}(\text{pp}, c, x_b, i, \Lambda_b) \to 1 \end{array}\right] \leq \varepsilon(\lambda).$$

Although VC in applications are also required to be *succinct* we will not impose that restriction in this work. The reason behind this choice is that known impossibility results in Maurer's GGM [8] applies also to VC that are not succinct in the traditional sense (i.e. with logarithmic commitment and opening size).

3   One Way Functions in Maurer GGM

3.1   Definition

In this section we provide definitions that allow us to capture one way functions that only uses a black-box group and whose hardness reduces only to hard problems in the group. The first notion is easily captured by assuming f access the group through the oracles $\mathcal{O}_{\text{add}}$ and $\mathcal{O}_{\text{eq}}$. To capture the second one we follow the approach of [8,12] where security is provided against all GPPT adversaries, i.e. unbounded machines restricted to perform a polynomially bounded number of queries to the GGM random oracles.

Definition 2. *We define Algebraic OWF Family a couple* (Gen, f) *of* PPT *algorithms with*

$$k \leftarrow^{\$} \text{Gen}(1^\lambda), \qquad f_k : \{0,1\}^{n_1} \times \mathbb{G}^{n_2} \to \{0,1\}^{m_1} \times \mathbb{G}^{m_2}.$$

such that for all GPPT *adversaries* $\mathcal{A}$ *there exists a negligible* ε *such that*

$$\Pr\left[\mathcal{A}(y) \to z, \ f_k(z) = y \ \middle| \ x \leftarrow^{\$} \{0,1\}^{n_1} \times \mathbb{G}^{n_2}, \ y \leftarrow f(x)\right] \leq \varepsilon(\lambda).$$

The simplest example of algebraic OWF is the group exponentiation $f : \mathbb{F}_q \to \mathbb{G}$ with $f(x) = x \cdot G$, whose hardness in the GGM was proved in [34].

Without loss of generality we can assume that f_k outputs only group elements, as the output bits can be encoded *in the exponent*. More precisely given f as in the definition above we can define for each key k

$$f'_k : \{0,1\}^{n_1} \times \mathbb{G}^{n_2} \to \mathbb{G}^{m_1+m_2} \; : \; f_k(x) = ((b_i)_{i=1}^{m_1}, \mathbf{H}) \;\Rightarrow\; f'_k(x) = ((b_i \cdot G)_{i=1}^{m_1}, \mathbf{H}).$$

In the GGM $f'(x)$ can be computed from $f(x)$ and vice versa.

3.2   Collision Resistance

Our first impossibility result for NIZK-AoK will apply to NP relations defined for a large family of OWF, but we will need the OWF to be collision resistant. This is problematic as not every OWF is collision resistant, effectively restricting the scope of our result.

To address this issue we show that any *algebraic* OWF family with domain $\{0,1\}^n$ and Gen returning only random group elements can be transformed to achieve collision resistance by simply restricting its domain. The idea is that, with unbounded computation, we could find for a given key k a subset $\mathcal{X} \subseteq \{0,1\}^n$ such that $f_k(\mathcal{X}) = \text{Im } f_k$ and f_k is injective over $\mathcal{X}$. However this would be inefficient in terms of group operations[5]. Therefore we show that if the OWF key is a vector of random group elements, it is possible to restrict the function's domain in GPPT time so that finding collisions implies finding linear relations among the group elements in the key.

Concretely in the following lemma we provide two GPPT algorithm, Memb and Samp, respectively testing membership with the restricted domain $x \in \mathcal{X}$ and sampling elements from $\mathcal{X}$. A proofs appears in the full version.

Lemma 1. *Given* (Gen, f) *algebraic OWF family with* $f : \{0,1\}^n \to \mathbb{G}^m$ *and* Gen *returning a uniformly distributed key* $k \sim U(\mathbb{G}^\kappa)$, *there exists a set* $\mathcal{X} \subseteq \{0,1\}^n$ *and two* GPPT *algorithm* Memb *and* Samp *such that*

- **Correctness 1:** Memb$(x) \to 1 \Leftrightarrow x \in \mathcal{X}$.
- **Correctness 2:** $x \leftarrow^\$ $ Samp$(1^\lambda) \Rightarrow x \in \mathcal{X}$.
- **Indistinguishability:** $\exists \varepsilon$ *negligible s.t. for* $k \leftarrow^\$ $ Gen(1^λ), $x_1 \leftarrow^\$ \{0,1\}^n$ *and* $x_2 \leftarrow^\$ $ Samp(1^λ),

$$\Delta((k, f_k(x_1)), (k, f_k(x_2))) \le \varepsilon(\lambda).$$

- **Collision Resistance:** $\exists \varepsilon$ *negligible s.t. for all* GPPT *adversaries* $\mathcal{A}$, *given* $k \leftarrow^\$ $ Gen(1^λ),

$$\Pr[\mathcal{A}(k) \to (x_1, x_2), \; x_1, x_2 \in \mathcal{X}, \; x_1 \neq x_2, \; f_k(x_1) = f_k(x_2)] \le \varepsilon(\lambda).$$

---

[5] Each evaluation of f_k would required access to the GGM, implying exponentially many queries.

We remark that the above Lemma could be extended to $k \sim \mathbb{G}^\kappa$ (not necessarily uniform) such that finding non-trivial linear relations among its group elements is hard for GPPT adversary. This holds as in the GGM such a vector k would be indistinguishable from $k' \sim U(\mathbb{G}^\kappa)$, implying that f can be extended to f' with key space $\mathbb{G}^\kappa$ by running the evaluation algorithm for f also for those keys for which f is not formally defined. Since Memb and Samp exists for f', they satisfy the above properties also for f (or else we could build a distinguisher for k and k').

3.3 Hard-Core Predicates

In [20] Goldreich and Levin proved that in the standard model, any OWF f with domain in $\{0,1\}^n$ can be transformed into another OWF $f'(\mathbf{x}, \mathbf{r}) = (f(\mathbf{x}), \mathbf{r})$ that admits the hard-core predicate $\mathbf{x}^\top \mathbf{r}$.

We observe that, given an algebraic OWF family, that is secure against any GPPT adversary, even when the function's domain is restricted as discussed in the previous section, the same result applies.

Theorem 1. *Let* (Gen, f) *an algebraic OWF familty with* $f : \{0,1\}^n \to \mathbb{G}^m$ *and* Gen *returning* $k \sim U(\mathbb{G}^\kappa)$. *Then there exists* ε *negligible such that for all* GPPT *adversaries* $\mathcal{A}$

$$\Pr\left[\mathcal{A}(k, y, \mathbf{r}) \to b, \quad b = \mathbf{x}^\top \mathbf{r} \;\middle|\; \begin{array}{l} k \xleftarrow{\$} \mathsf{Gen}(1^\lambda), \quad \mathbf{r} \xleftarrow{\$} \{0,1\}^n \\ \mathbf{x} \xleftarrow{\$} \mathsf{Samp}(1^\lambda), \quad y \leftarrow f_k(\mathbf{x}) \end{array}\right] \leq \varepsilon(\lambda)$$

The proof is identical to the original result up to observing that in this case the function's input is sampled with a different distribution than the uniform one and that the reduction only needs black-box access to the group. For completeness a proof is presented in the full version.

4 Impossibility of Algebraic NIZK-AoK

4.1 Hiding Vector Commitments

Our first step toward the impossibility of algebraic NIZK-AoK will be to prove a tighter lower bound than the one presented in [8] for the class of algebraic VC which *hides* unopened entries. In this section we define the *hiding* property in a game-based way. The approach we take is inspired by IND security for functional encryption schemes: for any two vectors $\mathbf{x}^0$, $\mathbf{x}^1$ provided by the adversary, we ask that guessing which one was committed is hard even when those positions in which $\mathbf{x}^0$ and $\mathbf{x}^1$ match are opened.

Definition 3. *Given a Vector Commitment and an adversary* $\mathcal{A}$ *we define its advantage at the hiding game, described in Fig. 1, as*

$$\mathsf{Adv}(\mathcal{A}) = \left| \frac{1}{2} - \Pr\left[\mathsf{ExpHide}^{\mathcal{A}}(1^\lambda) = 1\right] \right|.$$

A VC (resp. Algebraic VC) is hiding if there exists ε *negligible such that for all* PPT *(resp. GPPT) adversaries* $\mathcal{A}$, $\mathsf{Adv}(\mathcal{A}) \leq \varepsilon(\lambda)$.

$\mathsf{ExpHide}^{\mathcal{A}}(1^\lambda)$

---

1 : $\mathsf{pp} \leftarrow \mathsf{VC.Setup}(1^\lambda), \quad \beta \leftarrow^\$ \{0,1\}$

2 : $(\mathbf{x}^0, \mathbf{x}^1) \leftarrow \mathcal{A}(\mathsf{pp})$ such that $\mathbf{x}^0, \mathbf{x}^1 \in (\mathsf{VC.M})^n$

3 : $c, \mathsf{aux} \leftarrow \mathsf{VC.Com}(\mathsf{pp}, \mathbf{x}^\beta), \quad \mathcal{A} \leftarrow c$

4 :   **When** $\mathcal{A}$ queries $i \in \{1, \ldots, n\}$:

5 :   If $x_i^0 = x_i^1$: $\Lambda_i \leftarrow \mathsf{VC.Open}(\mathsf{pp}, i, \mathsf{aux}), \quad \mathcal{A} \leftarrow \Lambda_i$

6 :   **When** $\beta' \leftarrow \mathcal{A}$:

7 :   Return $\beta' == \beta$

Fig. 1. Vector Commitment's hiding game with adversary $\mathcal{A}$

As a sanity check we observe that combining any (non necessarily algebraic) VC with a commitment scheme yields an hiding VC as informally stated in [7]. We further notice that, viewing VCs as a special class of Functional Commitments [32], the game in Fig. 3 could be rephrased for this general primitive by letting $\mathcal{A}$ query functions f and receive an opening for f only if $f(\mathbf{x}^0) = f(\mathbf{x}^1)$.

While the above definition is given in a way that can be easily generalized, when applied to VC it becomes equivalent to a simpler notion, given through the game described in Fig. 2. The two main differences from the previous definition are that $\mathbf{x}^0$ and $\mathbf{x}^1$ are allowed to differ in at most one position, and that opening proofs for all other positions are given directly without oracle queries.

$\mathsf{ExpHideVC}^{\mathcal{A}}(1^\lambda)$

---

1 : $\mathsf{pp} \leftarrow \mathsf{VC.Setup}(1^\lambda), \quad \beta \leftarrow^\$ \{0,1\}$

2 : $(\mathbf{x}^0, \mathbf{x}^1) \leftarrow \mathcal{A}(\mathsf{pp})$ with $\mathbf{x}^0, \mathbf{x}^1$ differing only in position i

3 : $c, \mathsf{aux} \leftarrow \mathsf{VC.Com}(\mathsf{pp}, \mathbf{x}^\beta), \quad \Lambda_j \leftarrow \mathsf{VC.Open}(\mathsf{pp}, j, \mathsf{aux})$ for all $j \neq i$.

4 :   **When** $\beta' \leftarrow \mathcal{A}(c, (\Lambda_j)_{j \neq i})$

5 :   Return $\beta' == \beta$

Fig. 2. Simpler Vector Commitment's hiding game with adversary $\mathcal{A}$

Proposition 1. *A (resp. algebraic) VC is hiding if and only if there exists a negligible ε such that for each* PPT *(resp.* GPPT*) adversary $\mathcal{A}$, its advantage in the game described in Fig. 2 is*

$$\mathsf{Adv}(\mathcal{A}) = \left| \frac{1}{2} - \Pr\left[\mathsf{ExpHideVC}^{\mathcal{A}}(1^\lambda) = 1\right] \right| \leq \varepsilon(\lambda).$$

A proof of this Proposition appears in the full version.

4.2   Reduction to Signatures

Having introduced the notion of hiding VC we now show that the reduction from VC to Signatures provided in [8] transform hiding VCs into unforgeable signature schemes. We recall their construction in Fig. 3. Their idea is to sign the indices from 1 to n by letting the verification key of the scheme be the VC's common reference string and a commitment to n random messages. A signature for message i is then an opening of the i-th position, whose correctness can be verified through VC.Vfy.

$S^*.\mathsf{Setup}(1^\lambda)$:

1 : $\mathsf{VC.Setup}(1^\lambda) \to \mathsf{pp}$
2 : $m_1, \ldots, m_n \leftarrow^\$ \mathsf{VC.M}$
3 : $c, \mathsf{aux} \leftarrow^\$ \mathsf{VC.Com}(\mathsf{pp}, m_1, \ldots, m_n)$
4 : $\mathsf{vk} \leftarrow (\mathsf{pp}, c),\quad \mathsf{sk} \leftarrow \mathsf{aux}$
5 :   Return vk, sk

$S^*.\mathsf{Sign}(\mathsf{sk}, i)$:

1 : $\pi \leftarrow \mathsf{VC.Open}(\mathsf{pp}, i, \mathsf{aux})$
2 :   Return $\sigma \leftarrow (m_i, \pi)$

$S^*.\mathsf{Vfy}(\mathsf{vk}, i, \sigma)$:

1 :   Return $\mathsf{VC.Vfy}(\mathsf{pp}, c, m_i, i, \pi)$

Fig. 3. Generic transformation from VCs to signature schemes

Unforgeability is proven as follows. Assume an adversary forges a signature for message i, that is an opening of c at position i to some message m_i', with c being a commitment to $m_1, \ldots, m_n$. Then $m_i' \neq m_i$ only with negligible probability, or else $\mathcal{A}$ would break position binding. Therefore $\mathcal{A}$ can be used to break the hiding property. This is done by guessing the position i it will forge, querying in the hiding game, Fig. 2, two random vectors differing in that position, answering signature queries with the received opening values and finally returning the bit corresponding to the vector containing m_i' in position i.

A more detailed proof appears in the full version.

Proposition 2. *Given a position-binding and hiding (Algebraic) Vector Commitment, the (Algebraic) Signature scheme in Fig. 3 is unforgeable.*

4.3   Lower Bound

As Proposition 2 implies that Algebraic VC can be transformed into Algebraic Signatures, for which lower bounds on the parameter size are known [8,12], we now derive a lower bound for position-binding and hiding vector commitments.

In [8] it is proven that any algebraic signature satisfying a weaker security notion, which they call ϑ unforgeability, with message space of size n and a verification key with m group elements[6] must satisfy $m \geq n + \vartheta$. As observed in that paper, the standard Unforgeability notion is equivalent to their ϑ-unforgeability

---

[6] Excluding those group elements contained in the CRS for which the signer has no trapdoor information.

when $\vartheta = 0$. Moreover, in the reduction provided in Fig. 3, the verification key only consist of the public parameters (that can be given in the CRS) and one commitment. We thus conclude that

Theorem 2. *Any position-binding and hiding Algebraic Vector Commitment with* GPPT *computable procedures, whose commitment for a vector of length n contains $\ell_c = \ell_c(\lambda, n)$ group elements, satisfies $\ell_c \geq n$.*

Notice that an Algebraic VC that is both position-binding and hiding with linear opening proof size and constant commitment size would violate this Theorem, but not the results presented in [8]. Indeed in the rest of this sections we show that if Algebraic NIZK-AoK exists for certain relations, VC of this form could be built in the GGM.

We finally remark that the above Theorem also captures VC scheme that are efficient only with respect to group operations. This follows as the proof in [8] also captures this corner case and will be extremely useful in the rest of this section in order to apply our Lemma 1.

4.4   Intuition on NIZK-AoK Impossibility

The final step to obtain our claimed result on Algebraic NIZK-AoK is to show that it would allow to construct a vector commitment in GPPT violating the negative result of Theorem 2.

To build up intuition we first provide a toy construction assuming we have a NIZK-AoK $(\mathsf{G}, \mathsf{P}, \mathsf{V})$ for the discrete logarithm relation, i.e. that given $K, H \in \mathbb{G}$ proves knowledge of x such that $H = x \cdot K$. The idea is to tweak a regular Petersen commitment for n field elements until we make it hiding. An initial approach is, given $x_1, \ldots, x_n \in \mathbb{F}_q$, to commit to them by sending $C = x_1 K_1 + \ldots + x_n K_n$ with K_i random group elements in the public parameters. To open position i we can send, together with x_i, the elements $x_j K_j$ along with a proof of knowledge of x_j.

This would be position binding, as from any two opening of the same position a challenger can extract (using the NIZK extractor) two different representations of C in base $K_1, \ldots, K_n$, which would break the security of standard Petersen commitments. However this would not yet be hiding, even if the argument used is zero knowledge. The issue is that $x \cdot K$ does not hide x. More concretely, in the hiding game, an adversary could send $\mathbf{x}^0 = (1, 0, \ldots 0)$ and $\mathbf{x}^1 = (2, 0, \ldots, 0)$. Later, testing if C is equal to K_1 or $2K_1$, it would be able to understand which was the committed vector.

A way to address this issue is resorting to an hard-core predicate $\ell : \mathbb{F}_q \to \{0, 1\}$ for the discrete logarithm OWF, such as the least significant bit. This time, instead of committing to $x_1, \ldots, x_n$, we present a commitment to bits: given $b_1, \ldots, b_n$ the committer samples

$$x_i \xleftarrow{\$} \mathbb{F}_q \ : \ \ell(x_i) = b_i \qquad C = x_1 K_1 + \ldots + x_n K_n.$$

An opening to b_i can again be the message x_i together with $x_j K_j$ and a proof of knowledge for x_j, but now the verifier has to further verify that $\ell(x_i) = b_i$.

This scheme would be binding as before, up to observing that $\ell(x_i^0) \neq \ell(x_i^1)$ implies $x_i^0 \neq x_i^1$. Conversely the scheme is hiding because until position i is opened, nothing about x_i is revealed apart from $x_i K_i$, also because our argument is zero-knowledge. Thus guessing the message at position i reduces to the hardness of predicting the hard-core predicate ℓ.

4.5   Vector Commitments from NIZK-AoK

We now discuss how to generalize the construction in Sect. 4.4 to algebraic OWF families.

The first issue is that not all OWFs admit hard-core predicates. We address this using the Goldreich-Levin transformation, see Sect. 3.3, $f_k'(\mathbf{x}, \mathbf{r}) = (f_k(\mathbf{x}), \mathbf{r})$ which admits the hard-core bit $\mathbf{x}^\top \mathbf{r}$.

The second issue is that OWF may not be collision resistant[7]. An example is $f_K : \{0, \ldots, 2q - 1\} \rightarrow \mathbb{G}$ such that $f_K(x) = x \cdot K$ where $f_K(0) = f_K(q)$. This may allow an adversary to break position-binding by finding two $\mathbf{x}, \mathbf{x}'$ with $f_k(\mathbf{x}) = f_k(\mathbf{x}')$ and different hard-core bits. To address this we introduced in Sect. 3.2 two GPPT procedures Memb and Samp to restrict the domain of a OWF in order to make it collision resistant and to sample from this restricted domain.

Given these observations, in Fig. 4 we provide a complete description of the resulting VC, with (Gen, f) being an algebraic OWF where $f : \{0,1\}^\mu \rightarrow \mathbb{G}^m$ and Gen samples uniformly from $\mathbb{G}^\kappa$, and (G, P, V) is a NIZK-AoK for the relation

$$\mathcal{R} = \{((k, y), x) : f_k(x) = y\}.$$

Theorem 3. *If* (G, P, V) *is a NIZK-AoK, the VC described in Fig. 4 is computable in* GPPT *time, position-binding, hiding and returns commitments with* $O(1)$ *group elements.*

Proof. **Efficiency**: To show that all procedures can be computed in GPPT time it suffices to observe that all steps are efficiently computable, and by Lemma 1 Samp, Memb are computable in GPPT time.

Constant Group-Elements Commitment: Commitments only contains m group elements in $C \in \mathbb{G}^m$ with $\mathbb{G}^m$ being the domain of f. Because m does not depend on n, the commitment only contains a constant number of group elements in n (although it may depends on λ).

Position Binding: Given $\mathcal{A}$ breaking position binding we build $\mathcal{B}$ which, given κn random group elements in $\mathbb{G}$, finds a linear relation among them. Note that this is equivalent to breaking the discrete logarithm problem, which in Maurer's GGM is known to be hard [34].

---

[7] In the previous example $x \mapsto x \cdot K$ is collision resistant because it is a bijection.

VC*.Setup($1^\lambda, n$):	VC*.Com(pp, $b_1, \ldots, b_n$):
1 : $\mathsf{crs}_{i,j} \leftarrow \mathsf{G}(1^\lambda)$	1 : $\mathbf{x}_i \leftarrow^\$ \mathsf{Samp}(1^\lambda)$
2 : $k_i \leftarrow \mathsf{Gen}(1^\lambda)$	2 : $\mathbf{r}_i \leftarrow^\$ \{0,1\}^\mu$ such that $\mathbf{x}_i^\top \mathbf{r}_i = b_i$
3 : $\mathsf{pp} \leftarrow \{\mathsf{crs}_{i,j}, k_i : i,j \in [n]\}$	3 : $C \leftarrow \sum_{i=1}^n f_{k_i}(\mathbf{x}_i)$
	4 : $\mathsf{aux} \leftarrow (\mathbf{x}_i)_{i=1}^n$
	5 : Return $(C, (\mathbf{r}_j)_{j=1}^n), \mathsf{aux}$

VC*.Open(pp, i, aux):	VC*.Vfy(pp, $(C,D), b_i, i, \Lambda_i$)
1 : $\pi_{i,j} \leftarrow \mathsf{P}(\mathsf{crs}_{i,j}, k_j, f_{k_j}(\mathbf{x}_j), \mathbf{x}_j)$	1 : Parse $\Lambda_i = (\mathbf{x}_i, (\mathbf{Y}_j, \pi_{i,j})_{j\neq i})$
2 : $\Lambda_i = (\mathbf{x}_i, (f_{k_j}, \pi_{i,j})_{j\neq i})$	2 : Accept if and only if:
3 : Return Λ_i	3 : $C = f_{k_i}(\mathbf{x}_i) + \sum_{j\neq i} \mathbf{Y}_j$
	4 : $1 = \mathsf{V}(\mathsf{crs}_j, k_j, \mathbf{Y}_j, \pi_j)$
	5 : $1 = \mathsf{Memb}(\mathbf{x}_i), \quad b_i = \mathbf{x}_i^\top \mathbf{r}_i$

Fig. 4. Hiding Vector Commitment from a NIZK-AoK for $\mathcal{R}$.

We preliminary notice that in line 7, A_j^β can be computed efficiently. A way to achieve this is locally storing during the execution of $f_{k_j}(\mathbf{x}_j^\beta)$ a representation for each element queried to the GGM oracle as a linear combination of the group elements in $\mathbf{k}_j$. Doing so, the matrix A_j^β is given by the output elements' representations (Fig. 5).

Next we define the following events:

$\mathcal{B}$ wins	: $\sum_{j=1}^n (A_j^0 - A_j^1)\mathbf{k}_j = \mathbf{0}$ and $(A_j^0 - A_j^1)_{j=1}^n$ is a non-zero matrix
$\mathcal{A}$ wins	: $\mathcal{A}$ breaks position-binding
Ext	: $f_{k_j}(\mathbf{x}_j^\beta) = \mathbf{Y}_j^\beta$ for all $j \neq i$ and $\beta \in \{0,1\}$
Coll	: $\mathbf{x}_i^0 \neq \mathbf{x}_i^1 \wedge f_{k_i}(\mathbf{x}_i^0) = f_{k_i}(\mathbf{x}_i^1) \wedge 1 = \mathsf{Memb}(\mathbf{x}_i^0) = \mathsf{Memb}(\mathbf{x}_i^1)$

Since $\mathcal{A}$ wins only if the openings are correct, $\pi_{i,j}^\beta$ are all accepted. Calling ε_1 the extractor error, see Sect. 2.3, we have that

$$\Pr\left[\mathsf{Ext} \mid \mathcal{A} \text{ wins}\right] = 1 - \Pr\left[\bigvee_{j\neq i} \bigvee_{\beta=0}^1 f_{k_j}(\mathbf{x}_j^\beta) \neq \mathbf{Y}_j^\beta \mid \mathcal{A} \text{ wins}\right]$$
$$\geq 1 - \sum_{j\neq i} \sum_{\beta=0}^1 \Pr\left[f_{k_j}(\mathbf{x}_j) = \mathbf{Y}_j^\beta \mid \mathcal{A} \text{ wins}\right]$$
$$\geq 1 - (2n-2)\varepsilon_1(\lambda) = 1 - \varepsilon_1^*(\lambda).$$

with $\varepsilon_1^* = (2n-2)\varepsilon_1$ being a negligible function. By Lemma 1 we also have that $\Pr\left[\mathsf{Coll}\right] \leq \varepsilon_2(\lambda)$. Next, we notice that $\mathcal{B}$ wins if $\mathcal{A}$ wins, Ext and $\neg$Coll occurs. Indeed in this case

$$C = f_{k_i}(\mathbf{x}_i^\beta) + \sum_{j\neq i} \mathbf{Y}_j^\beta = \sum_{j=1}^n f_{k_j}(\mathbf{x}_j^\beta) = \sum_{j=1}^n A_j^\beta \mathbf{k}_j$$

$\mathcal{B}(\mathbf{V})$:

1 : Parse the input as n OWF keys $\mathbf{V} = (\mathbf{k}_1, \ldots, \mathbf{k}_n) \in (\mathbb{G}^\kappa)^n$

2 : Sample with the NIZK extractor $(\mathsf{crs}_{i,j}, \mathsf{td}_{i,j}) \leftarrow \mathsf{E}(1^\lambda)$

3 : $\mathsf{pp} \leftarrow \{\mathsf{crs}_{i,j}, \mathbf{k}_i \ : \ i, j \in [n]\}$

4 : $\mathcal{A}(\mathsf{pp}) \rightarrow (c, i, b_0, \Lambda_0, b_1, \Lambda_1)$

5 : Parse $c = (C, (\mathbf{r}_j)_{j=1}^n)$ and $\Lambda_\beta = (\mathbf{x}_i^\beta, (\mathbf{Y}_j^\beta, \pi_{i,j}^\beta)_{j \neq i})$ for $\beta \in \{0, 1\}$

6 : Extract $\mathbf{x}_j^\beta \leftarrow \mathsf{E}(\mathsf{td}_{i,j}, \mathbf{k}_j, \mathbf{Y}_j^\beta, \pi_{i,j}^\beta)$ for $j \in [n] \setminus \{i\}$

7 : Compute $A_j^\beta \in \mathbb{F}_q^{m,\kappa}$ such that $f_{\mathbf{k}_j}(\mathbf{x}_j^\beta) = A_j^\beta \cdot \mathbf{k}_j$ for $j \in [n]$

8 : Return $(A_j^0 - A_j^1)_{j=1}^n$

Fig. 5. $\mathcal{B}$ reducing position binding to the discrete logarithm problem.

for both $\beta \in \{0, 1\}$, where the first equality follows by $\mathcal{A}$ wins, the second one from Ext and the third one by construction. This implies $\sum_{j=1}^n (A_j^0 - A_j^1)\mathbf{k}_j = \mathbf{0}$. Moreover this relation is non trivial since, as $\mathcal{A}$ wins, we must have

$$b^0 \neq b^1 \quad \Rightarrow \quad (\mathbf{x}_i^0)^\top \mathbf{r}_i \neq (\mathbf{x}_i^1)^\top \mathbf{r}_i \quad \Rightarrow \quad \mathbf{x}_i^0 \neq \mathbf{x}_i^1 \quad \Rightarrow$$
$$\Rightarrow \quad f_{\mathbf{k}_i}(\mathbf{x}_i^0) \neq f_{\mathbf{k}_i}(\mathbf{x}_i^1) \quad \Rightarrow \quad A_i^0 \mathbf{k}_i \neq A_i^1 \mathbf{k}_i \quad \Rightarrow \quad A_i^0 - A_i^1 \neq \mathbf{0}.$$

Where the fourth implication comes from $\neg\mathsf{Coll}$. To conclude we finally bound the advantage of $\mathcal{A}$ with the probability that $\mathcal{B}$ successfully finds a linear relation.

$$\begin{aligned}
\Pr[\mathcal{B} \text{ wins}] &\geq \Pr[\mathcal{A} \text{ wins}, \mathsf{Ext}, \neg\mathsf{Coll}] \\
&\geq \Pr[\mathcal{A} \text{ wins}, \mathsf{Ext}] - \Pr[\mathsf{Coll}] \\
&\geq \Pr[\mathsf{Ext} \mid \mathcal{A} \text{ wins}] \cdot \Pr[\mathcal{A} \text{ wins}] - \varepsilon_2(\lambda) \\
&\geq (1 - \varepsilon_1^*(\lambda)) \Pr[\mathcal{A} \text{ wins}] - \varepsilon_2(\lambda).
\end{aligned}$$

Since $\mathcal{B}$ succeeds with negligible probability, the advantage of $\mathcal{A}$ must be negligible as well.

Hiding: We show that given any GPPT adversary $\mathcal{A}$ executed in the game described in Fig. 2, we can build an adversary $\mathcal{B}$ guessing the Goldreich-Levin hard-core predicate for f.

The idea is, given $(\mathbf{k}, \mathbf{Y}, \mathbf{r})$, to setup the VC parameters with the simulator, and use $\mathbf{k}$ as the OWF key for a randomly guessed entry i. Next $\mathcal{A}$ proposes its two vectors of bits $\mathbf{b}_0, \mathbf{b}_1$. If they differ on the guessed position i, $\mathcal{B}$ proceeds computing the commitment, where it uses $\mathbf{Y}, \mathbf{r}$ as the OWF image for the i-th entry, and simulating the required openings. Finally, once $\mathcal{A}$ guesses a bit, it returns the same value. A detailed description appears in Fig. 6.

First we observe that due to the Zero-Knowledge property, distinguishing $\mathsf{crs}_{\ell,j}, \pi_{\ell,j}$ generated by $\mathcal{B}$ from the ones returned by real challenger of ExpHideVC

$\mathcal{B}(\mathbf{k}, \mathbf{Y}, \mathbf{r})$:

1 : Sample $i \leftarrow^{\$} \{1, \dots, n\}$ a guess on the position $\mathcal{A}$ will choose
2 : Sample $k_j \leftarrow \mathsf{Gen}(1^{\lambda})$ for $j \neq i$ and set $k_i \leftarrow \mathbf{k}$
3 : Sample with the NIZK simulator $(\mathsf{crs}_{\ell,j}, \mathsf{td}_{\ell,j}) \leftarrow \mathsf{S}(1^{\lambda})$ with $\ell, j \in [n]$
4 : $\mathsf{pp} \leftarrow \{\mathsf{crs}_{\ell,j}, k_j : \ell, j \in [n]\}$
5 : $\mathcal{A}(\mathsf{pp}) \rightarrow \mathbf{b}^0, \mathbf{b}^1$ differing only at position i' (wlog $b_{i'}^0 = 0$ and $b_{i'}^1 = 1$)
6 : **If** $i \neq i'$: Return $\bot$

    // Simulate the commitment

7 : **For** $j \neq i$:
8 :   Sample $\mathbf{x}_j \leftarrow^{\$} \mathsf{Samp}(1^{\lambda})$ and $\mathbf{r}_j \leftarrow^{\$} \{0,1\}^{\mu}$ with $\mathbf{x}_j^{\top} \mathbf{r}_j = b_j^0 = b_j^1$
9 : Set $\mathbf{r}_i \leftarrow \mathbf{r}$
10 : Compute $C \leftarrow \mathbf{Y} + \sum_{j \neq i} f_{k_j}(\mathbf{x}_j)$
11 : Create the commitment $c \leftarrow (C, (\mathbf{r}_j)_{j=1}^n)$

    // Simulate the openings

12 : **For** $\ell \neq i$:
13 : $\pi_{\ell,j} \leftarrow \mathsf{S}(\mathsf{td}_{\ell,j}, k_j, f_{k_j}(\mathbf{x}_j))$ for all $j \neq \ell$
14 : $\Lambda_{\ell} = (\mathbf{x}_{\ell}, (f_{k_j}(\mathbf{x}_j), \pi_{\ell,j})_{j \neq \ell})$

    // Execute $\mathcal{A}$ to guess the hard-core bit

15 : Execute $\mathcal{A}(\mathsf{pp}, C, (\Lambda_{\ell})_{\ell \neq i}) \rightarrow b$ and return b

Fig. 6. Reduction $\mathcal{B}$ guessing the Goldwasser-Levin hardcore predicate of $f_{\mathbf{k}}$.

in Fig. 2 cannot be done with advantage greater than a negligible ε by any GPPT adversary.

Next, assume $i = i'$. Calling β the hard-core predicate $\mathcal{B}$ has to guess, $\mathcal{B}$ correctly commits to $\mathbf{b}_{\beta}$ since its challenger sets $\mathbf{Y} = f_{\mathbf{k}}(\mathbf{x}) = f_{k_i}(\mathbf{x})$ with[8] $b_i^{\beta} = \beta = \mathbf{x}^{\top} \mathbf{r}$, $\mathbf{x} \leftarrow \mathsf{Samp}(1^{\lambda})$ and $\mathbf{r} \leftarrow^{\$} \{0,1\}^{\mu}$. Thus $\mathcal{B}$ wins if $\mathcal{A}$ correctly guesses β, and the initial guess is correct, i.e. $i = i'$. We conclude that

$$\begin{aligned}
\mathsf{Adv}(\mathcal{B}) &= |\Pr[\mathcal{A} \rightarrow 0, \; i = i' | \beta = 0] - \Pr[\mathcal{A} \rightarrow 0, \; i = i' | \beta = 1]| \\
&= \Pr[i = i'] \cdot |\Pr[\mathcal{A} \rightarrow 0 | \beta = 0] - \Pr[\mathcal{A} \rightarrow 0 | \beta = 1]| \\
&\geq \frac{\mathsf{Adv}(\mathcal{A}) - \varepsilon(\lambda)}{n}.
\end{aligned}$$

where the third inequality uses $\Pr[i = i'] = 1/n$, which follows as $\mathcal{A}$ has no information on i when it computes $\mathbf{b}_0, \mathbf{b}_1$ (and in particular i').

4.6 Impossibility of Algebraic NIZK-AoK

Combining Theorem 3 and Theorem 2 we can eventually derive the following

---

[8] note that we assumed without loss of generality $b_i^0 = 0$ and $b_i^1 = 1$.

Theorem 4. *Given* (Gen, f) *a one way function family with* Gen *returning a uniformly sampled vector in* $\mathbb{G}^\kappa$ *and* $f : \{0,1\}^\mu \to \mathbb{G}^m$, *then there exists no Algebraic NIZK-AoK for the relation*

$$\mathcal{R} = \{((k,y),x) \; : \; f_k(x) = y\}.$$

5   Impossibility of Algebraic NIZK

5.1   Hard Subset Membership Problem

In this section we recall the definition of Hard Subset Membership Problem, presented in [17]. Given an NP relation $\mathcal{R}$, its associated language $\mathcal{L}$ is the set of all statements x for which $(x,w) \in \mathcal{R}$ for some witness w. Informally, the relation $\mathcal{R}$ is a hard subset problem if there are two ways to sample from $\mathcal{L}$ and its complement $\{0,1\}^* \setminus \mathcal{L}$ that are computationally hard to distinguish. As mentioned this captures DDH since the distributions (G, aG, bG, abG) and (G, aG, bG, cG) with a,b,c random field elements and $c \neq a \cdot b$ are hard distinguish. More generally this captures decisional assumptions and their related relations such as Decision Linear and Matrix-DDH. More formally:

Definition 4. *A Subset Membership Problem is a tuple* $(\mathcal{R}, \mathsf{SampGood}, \mathsf{SampBad})$ *with* $\mathcal{R}$ *an NP relation, and* $\mathsf{SampGood}, \mathsf{SampBad}$ *such that*

- $\mathsf{SampGood}(1^\lambda) \to (x,w) \quad \Rightarrow \quad (x,w) \in \mathcal{R}.$
- $\mathsf{SampBad}(1^\lambda) \to x \quad\;\; \Rightarrow \quad \nexists w : (x,w) \in \mathcal{R}.$

A subset membership problem is called hard (against GPPT *adversaries) if* $\exists \varepsilon$ *negligible such that for all* $\mathcal{A}$ GPPT

$$x_0 \leftarrow^\$ \mathsf{SampBad}(1^\lambda), \quad (x_1, w_1) \leftarrow^\$ \mathsf{SampGood}(1^\lambda)$$
$$\Rightarrow \quad |\Pr[\mathcal{A}(x_0) \to 0] - \Pr[\mathcal{A}(x_1) \to 0]| \; \leq \; \varepsilon(1^\lambda).$$

In the rest of this section we will also use the following Lemma, saying that the probability of correctly guessing λ independent instances of a subset problem is negligible. A proof appears in the full version.

Lemma 2. *If* $(\mathcal{R}, \mathsf{SampGood}, \mathsf{SampBad})$ *is a Hard Subset Membership Problem, then* $\exists \varepsilon$ *negligible such that for all* GPPT *adversaries* $\mathcal{A}$, *setting for* $i \in [\lambda]$

$$x_i^0 \leftarrow^\$ \mathsf{SampBad}(1^\lambda), \quad (x_i^1, w_i^1) \leftarrow^\$ \mathsf{SampGood}(1^\lambda), \quad b_i \leftarrow^\$ \{0,1\}$$
$$\Rightarrow \Pr\left[\mathcal{A}(x_1^{b_1}, \ldots, x_\lambda^{b_\lambda}) \to (b_1', \ldots, b_\lambda'), \qquad b_i = b_i' \;\; \forall i \in [\lambda]\right] \; \leq \; \varepsilon(\lambda).$$

5.2 Preliminary Adversary

Having defined relations with a hard subset problem against GPPT adversaries, in the rest of this section we show that these relations do not admit a NIZK argument in Maurer's GGM. Toward this goal we first construct an adversary $\mathcal{A}$ that, given a NIZK crs and oracle access to the simulator, either returns a proof of a false statement or it finds a linear relation among the group elements in the CRS. In order to ensure sequential executions of $\mathcal{A}$ we give it an affine space V in input, containing linear relations already found among the crs elements. Finally, we will allow $\mathcal{A}$ to fail with an arbitrary small (but non-negligible) probability $1/p$ with $p = \mathsf{poly}(\lambda)$. More formally

Lemma 3. *Let* $(\mathcal{R}, \mathsf{SampGood}, \mathsf{SampBad})$ *be a hard subset problem and* $(\mathsf{G}, \mathsf{P}, \mathsf{V})$ *a NIZK argument for* $\mathcal{R}$ *with simulator* S*. Then, for any* $p = \mathsf{poly}(\lambda)$*, there exists a* GPPT *adversary* $\mathcal{A}$ *such that: given*

$$(\mathsf{crs}, \mathsf{td}) \leftarrow \mathsf{S}(1^\lambda), \quad x \leftarrow \mathsf{SampBad}(1^\lambda) \quad : \quad \begin{array}{l} \mathsf{crs} = (\mathbf{Y}, c') \in \mathbb{G}^n \times \{0,1\}^* \\ x = (\mathbf{Z}, z') \in \mathbb{G}^m \times \{0,1\}^* \end{array}$$

and $V \leq \mathbb{F}_q^n$ *such that* $\mathbf{Y} \in V \cdot G$*, calling* $\mathbf{Z} = \mathbf{z} \cdot G$ *then either:*

1. $\mathcal{A}(V, \mathsf{crs}, x) \rightarrow (\mathsf{proof}, \pi)$ *such that* $1 \leftarrow \mathsf{V}(\mathsf{crs}, x, \pi)$*.*
2. $\mathcal{A}(V, \mathsf{crs}, x) \rightarrow$ query*. Then setting* $\pi \leftarrow \mathsf{S}(\mathsf{td}, x)$, $\mathcal{A}(V, \mathsf{crs}, x, \pi)$ *either aborts with probability smaller than* $1/p(\lambda)$ *or it returns* L *such that*

$$(\mathbf{Y}, \mathbf{Z}) \in L \cdot G \quad \wedge \quad L \cap \left(\mathbb{F}_q^n \times \{\mathbf{z}\}\right) \lneq (V \times \{\mathbf{z}\})$$

First of all we remark that the second condition simply states that the affine space L contains a new linear relation among the elements $\mathbf{Y}, \mathbf{Z}$ that is non-trivial with respect to $\mathbf{Y}$. Next, we observe that this adversary could be trivially used to break the *simulation soundness* property of the underlying NIZK. This is a stronger version of soundness in which the adversary has oracle access to a simulator and wins if it returns a proof for a false statement that was not queried. The way to use $\mathcal{A}$ is sampling $n + 1$ independent elements with $\mathsf{SampBad}(1^\lambda)$ and sequentially passing them to $\mathcal{A}$, using the simulation oracle to reply query requests. At each step (assuming $\mathcal{A}$ does not abort) either $\mathcal{A}$ finds a new linear relationship on the CRS' group elements, reducing the dimension of V by 1, or it returns a proof for x breaking soundness. Calling n the number of group elements in the CRS, $\mathcal{A}$ can find at most n linear relations, implying by the pigeonhole principle that eventually it has to return a valid proof. However, note that using $\mathcal{A}$ to break the standard notion of soundness is not as trivial since in that case no simulator oracle is provided.

Although the construction of $\mathcal{A}$ is rather technical, we simply adapt the approach of [8]. First, we describe an adversary $\mathcal{B}$ that on input (crs, x) either return a proof or, with one simulation query, finds a linear relation among the group elements in (crs, x). Next, using $\mathcal{B}$ we build $\mathcal{A}$ which ensures that the linear relation found is non-trivial for those elements in the crs with probability $1 - 1/p$. A detailed presentation appears in the full version.

5.3   Attack Description

As mentioned, the main difficulty of using $\mathcal{A}$ to break soundness is the absence of a simulator oracle. In this section we explain how to circumvent this issue, describing an adversary $\mathcal{Z}$ that breaks soundness using $\mathcal{A}$, and eventually derive our second impossibility result for algebraic NIZKs.

The core idea is that NIZKs for hard subset problem allow to produce proofs in two indistinguishable ways, that is either

1. sampling $\mathsf{crs} \leftarrow \mathsf{G}(1^\lambda)$, $(x, w) \leftarrow^{\$} \mathsf{SampGood}(1^\lambda)$ and producing the proof using P and the witness w
2. sampling $(\mathsf{crs}, \mathsf{td}) \leftarrow \mathsf{S}(1^\lambda)$, $x \leftarrow^{\$} \mathsf{SampBad}(1^\lambda)$ and producing the proof using the simulator.

Thus, assuming we were able to predict whether $\mathcal{A}$ is going to return proof or query, our adversary $\mathcal{Z}$ could

1. sample $(x, w) \leftarrow \mathsf{SampGood}(1^\lambda)$ when $\mathcal{A}$ is going to ask a query. In this way it can simulate $\mathsf{S}(x)$ with $\mathsf{P}(x, w)$ and get a linear relation on the CRS' elements.
2. sample $x \leftarrow \mathsf{SampBad}(1^\lambda)$ when $\mathcal{A}$ is going to return a proof π. In this way π proves a false statement and $\mathcal{Z}$ breaks soundness

Unfortunately we don't have a way to predict $\mathcal{A}$'s behavior. However, since the only difference in the two approaches above is how x is sampled, $\mathcal{A}$ cannot distinguish between them. Hence by flipping a random coin $\mathcal{Z}$ can guess $\mathcal{A}$'s reply and act accordingly. Since $\mathcal{A}$ replies almost independently from $\mathcal{Z}$'s choice, its guess is correct with probability close to $1/2$. Amplifying this in a way that makes $\mathcal{Z}$ guess correctly at least $n + 1$ times allows us to conclude that $\mathcal{A}$ proves a false statement at least once, because at most n linear relations can be found on the CRS' elements. A complete description of $\mathcal{Z}$ appears in Fig. 7.

We remark that the computation of $\mathbf{z}$ in line 5 can be done in polynomial time since $\mathsf{SampBad}$ and $\mathsf{SampGood}$ are generic algorithm: Therefore, by reading their queries to the GGM oracles, it is possible to locally store the discrete logarithm in base G of any queried group element during their execution, and in particular of output's group elements.

5.4   Impossibility of Algebraic NIZK

Given a description of the adversary $\mathcal{Z}$ we finally state and prove our second impossibility result for NIZK in Maurer's GGM.

Theorem 5. *Let* $(\mathcal{R}, \mathsf{SampGood}, \mathsf{SampBad})$ *be a subset membership problem hard against* GPPT *adversaries. Then there exists no algebraic NIZK for* $\mathcal{R}$.

Proof. We show that given a complete and zero-knowledge non-interactive argument, $\mathcal{Z}$ breaks soundness. First let us fix some notation. $\mathbf{Y}$ will be the vector of group elements in crs, i.e. $\mathsf{crs} = (\mathbf{Y}, c') \in \mathbb{G}^n \times \{0, 1\}^*$. $\mathcal{A}$ will be the adversary from Lemma 3 chosen with failure probability

$$\frac{1}{p(\lambda)} = \frac{1}{4\lambda(n + 1)}$$

and for the i-th execution of the for-loop in $\mathcal{Z}$ we define the events:

$\mathcal{Z}(\text{crs})$:

---

1 :   Initialize $V \leftarrow \mathbb{F}_q^n$ and $\pi^* \leftarrow \perp$

2 :   **For** $i \in \{1, \ldots, \lambda(n+1)\}$: // $\lambda(n+1)$ iterations to guess correctly $n+1$ times

3 :   Sample $\beta_i \leftarrow^{\$} \{0,1\}$

4 :   **If** $\beta_i = 0$: $x \leftarrow \text{SampBad}(1^\lambda)$; **Else** $(x, w) \leftarrow \text{SampGood}(1^\lambda)$

5 :   Parse $x = (\mathbf{Z}, z') \in \mathbb{G}^m \times \{0,1\}^*$ and get $\mathbf{z}$ such that $\mathbf{Z} = \mathbf{z} \cdot G$

6 :   **If** $\mathcal{A}(V, \text{crs}, x) \rightarrow$ query:

7 :   **If** $\beta_i = 0$: Continue the for loop

8 :   **Else**:

9 :   Create a proof $\pi \leftarrow \text{P}(\text{crs}, x, w)$

10 :   Get $\mathcal{A}(V, \text{crs}, x, \pi) \rightarrow L$ and let V' be s.t. $L \cap (\mathbb{F}_q^n \times \{\mathbf{z}\}) = V' \times \{\mathbf{z}\}$

11 :   Update $V \leftarrow V'$

12 :   **Elif** $\mathcal{A}(V, \text{crs}, x) \rightarrow (\text{proof}, \pi)$:

13 :   **If** $\beta_i = 0$ and $1 \leftarrow \text{V}(\text{crs}, x, \pi)$: store $\pi^* \leftarrow \pi$

14 : Return π^*

Fig. 7. GPPT Adversary $\mathcal{Z}$ breaking soundness using $\mathcal{A}$ from Lemma 3.

$$\begin{aligned}
\text{GoodProof}_i & : \beta_i = 0 \text{ and } \mathcal{A}(V, \text{crs}, x) \rightarrow (\text{proof}, \pi) \\
\text{BadProof}_i & : \beta_i = 1 \text{ and } \mathcal{A}(V, \text{crs}, x) \rightarrow (\text{proof}, \pi) \\
\text{GoodQuery}_i & : \beta_i = 1 \text{ and } \mathcal{A}(V, \text{crs}, x) \rightarrow \text{query} \\
\text{BadQuery}_i & : \beta_i = 0 \text{ and } \mathcal{A}(V, \text{crs}, x) \rightarrow \text{query} \\
\text{Bad}_i & : \text{BadProof}_i \vee \text{BadQuery}_i \\
\text{Fail}_i & : \mathcal{A}(V, \text{crs}, x) \rightarrow \perp \text{ or } \mathbf{Y} \notin V \cdot G
\end{aligned}$$

We further define Fail the event $\exists i : \text{Fail}_i$. Next, we break the proof into the following sequence of claims.

Claim 1. $\Pr[\text{Fail}] \leq 1/2$.

Claim 2. *The probability of happening λ sequential Bad events is negligible, i.e. there exist a negligible ε_0 such that*

$$\forall j_0 \leq n\lambda \qquad \Pr\left[\bigwedge_{i=1}^{\lambda} \text{Bad}_{j_0+i} \mid \neg\text{Fail} \right] \leq \varepsilon_0.$$

Claim 3. *The probability that $\neg\text{Bad}$ occurs less than $n+1$ times is negligible, i.e.*

$$\Pr[\, |\{i : \text{Bad}_i\}| \leq n \mid \neg\text{Fail}] \leq (n+1) \cdot \varepsilon_0.$$

Claim 4. *If GoodQuery_i occurs, then at step 11 of Fig. 7, the dimension of V decreases with overwhelming probability, i.e. there exists a negligible ε_1 such that*

$$\Pr[\text{GoodQuery}_i \wedge \neg(V' \lneq V) \mid \neg\text{Fail}] \leq \varepsilon_1.$$

Claim 5. *If* GoodProof$_i$ *occurs, then at step 13 of Fig. 7, the proof* π *is correct with overwhelming probability, i.e. there exists a negligible* ε_2 *such that*

$$\Pr\left[\text{GoodProof}_i \wedge 0 \leftarrow \mathsf{V}(\mathrm{crs}, x, \pi) \mid \neg\mathsf{Fail}\right] \leq \varepsilon_2.$$

Before proving these claims we show they imply that with significant probability $\mathcal{Z}$ produces a proof for a false statement. From Claim 3, $1 - (n+1)\varepsilon_0 \leq$

$$\leq \Pr\left[\exists i_1, \ldots, i_{n+1} : \neg\mathsf{Bad}_{i_j} \mid \neg\mathsf{Fail}\right]$$

$$\leq \Pr\left[\exists i_1, \ldots, i_{n+1} : \mathsf{GoodQuery}_{i_j} \mid \neg\mathsf{Fail}\right] + \Pr\left[\exists i : \mathsf{GoodProof}_i \mid \neg\mathsf{Fail}\right].$$

Regarding the first term, if GoodQuery occurs $n + 1$ times, in at least one of these events the affine space returned by $\mathcal{A}$ does not yield $V' < V$, because the dimension of V can decrease at most n times. Hence, calling wrong$_i$ the event $\neg(V' < V)$ at iteration i, we have that for some j, wrong$_{i_j}$ occurs. Then

$$\Pr\left[\exists i_1, \ldots, i_{n+1} : \mathsf{GoodQuery}_{i_j} \mid \neg\mathsf{Fail}\right]$$

$$= \Pr\left[\exists i_1, \ldots, i_{n+1} : \mathsf{GoodQuery}_{i_j} \wedge \exists j : \mathsf{wrong}_{i_j} \mid \neg\mathsf{Fail}\right]$$

$$\leq \Pr\left[\exists i : \mathsf{GoodQuery}_i \wedge \mathsf{wrong}_i \mid \neg\mathsf{Fail}\right]$$

$$\leq \sum_{i=1}^{\lambda(n+1)} \Pr\left[\mathsf{GoodQuery}_i \wedge \mathsf{wrong}_i \mid \neg\mathsf{Fail}\right] \leq \lambda(n+1)\varepsilon_1.$$

Regarding the second term, calling valid$_i$ the event that a proof returned at step i is accepted by the verifier.

$$\Pr\left[\exists i : \mathsf{GoodProof}_i \mid \neg\mathsf{Fail}\right]$$
$$\leq \Pr\left[\exists i : \mathsf{GoodProof}_i \wedge \mathsf{valid}_i \mid \neg\mathsf{Fail}\right] + \Pr\left[\exists i : \mathsf{GoodProof}_i \wedge \neg\mathsf{valid}_i \mid \neg\mathsf{Fail}\right]$$
$$\leq \Pr\left[1 \leftarrow \mathsf{V}(\mathrm{crs}, x, \pi^*) \mid \neg\mathsf{Fail}\right] + \lambda(n+1)\varepsilon_2$$

Combining this two upper bounds together we get that $\mathcal{Z}$ returns a correct proof with probability negligibly close to $1/2$.

$$\Pr\left[1 \leftarrow \mathsf{V}(\mathrm{crs}, x, \pi^*)\right] \geq (1 - (n+1)(\varepsilon_0 + \lambda\varepsilon_1 + \lambda\varepsilon_2)) \cdot \Pr\left[\neg\mathsf{Fail}\right]$$
$$\geq \frac{1 - (n+1)(\varepsilon_0 + \lambda\varepsilon_1 + \lambda\varepsilon_2)}{2}.$$

Proof of Claim 1. Calling $\varepsilon_{\mathsf{zk}}$ the advantage of distinguishing a crs generated by G from one produced by S and $\varepsilon_{\mathcal{R}}$ the advantage of guessing an instance of a hard subset membership problem, we will show that

$$\Pr\left[\mathsf{Fail}_i \mid \neg\mathsf{Fail}_1 \wedge \ldots \wedge \neg\mathsf{Fail}_{i-1}\right] \leq \frac{1}{4\lambda(n+1)} + 2(\varepsilon_{\mathsf{zk}} + \varepsilon_{\mathcal{R}}).$$

Summing all this $\lambda(n+1)$ terms will give an upper bound $\Pr\left[\mathsf{Fail}\right] \leq 1/4 + \mathsf{negl}(\lambda)$ that for sufficiently large values of λ is less that $1/2$. To show this we study two cases:

- $\beta_i = 0$. Then $\mathcal{A}$ receives (V, crs, x) with $\mathsf{crs} \leftarrow \mathsf{G}(1^\lambda)$ and $x \leftarrow \mathsf{SampBad}(1^\lambda)$. By Zero-Knowledge, we have that any $\mathcal{D}$ distinguishing (crs_0, π_0) generated with G and P from (crs_1, π_1) generated by S has advantage at most $\varepsilon_{\mathsf{zk}}$. This holds for any statement, and in particular also for (x, w) chosen by $\mathcal{D}$ (not depending on the crs).

  Next we sketch a distinguisher $\mathcal{D}$ using $\mathcal{A}$. Initially $\mathcal{D}$ samples (x_i, w_i) from $\mathsf{SampGood}$, set it as the challenge statement and receives (crs, π_i) either generated correctly using w_i or simulated. For the first $i - 1$ rounds $\mathcal{D}$ behaves as $\mathcal{Z}$. At the i-th round if $\mathcal{A}$ outputs query it replies with π_i. If $\mathcal{A}$ fails $\mathcal{D}$ returns 1, otherwise it returns 0. When the (crs, π_i) is honestly generated, $\mathcal{A}$ fails with probability $1/p(\lambda)$ by Lemma 3. Hence when (crs, π_i) is simulated $\mathcal{A}$ fails with probability smaller than $1/p(\lambda) + \mathsf{Adv}(\mathcal{D}) \le 1/p(\lambda) + \varepsilon_{\mathsf{zk}}$.

  In conclusion $\Pr\left[\mathsf{Fail}_i \mid \neg\mathsf{Fail}_1 \wedge \ldots \wedge \neg\mathsf{Fail}_{i-1}\right] =$

$$\Pr\left[\mathcal{A}(V, \mathsf{crs}, x) \to \perp \;\middle|\; \bigwedge_{j=1}^{i-1} \neg\mathsf{Fail}_j\right] \le \frac{1}{p(\lambda)} + \varepsilon_{\mathsf{zk}} \le \frac{1}{4\lambda(n+1)} + 2(\varepsilon_{\mathsf{zk}} + \varepsilon_{\mathcal{R}}).$$

- $\beta_i = 1$. Then $\mathcal{A}$ receives (V, crs, x) with $\mathsf{crs} \leftarrow \mathsf{G}(1^\lambda)$, $(x, w) \leftarrow \mathsf{SampGood}(1^\lambda)$. By Definition 4 the advantage of distinguishing (crs, x) from (crs, x') with $x' \leftarrow \mathsf{SampBad}(1^\lambda)$ is less than $\varepsilon_{\mathcal{R}}$. The previous argument allow us to conclude

$$\Pr\left[\mathcal{A}(V, \mathsf{crs}, x) \to \perp \mid \neg\mathsf{Fail}_1 \wedge \ldots \wedge \neg\mathsf{Fail}_{i-1}\right] \le \frac{1}{4\lambda(n+1)} + \varepsilon_{\mathsf{zk}} + \varepsilon_{\mathcal{R}}.$$

Analogously, since $(\mathbf{Y}, \mathbf{Z}) \in L \cdot G$ if and only if $\mathbf{Y} \in V' \cdot G$, $\Pr\left[\mathbf{Y} \notin V' \cdot G\right] \le \varepsilon_{\mathsf{zk}} + \varepsilon_{\mathcal{R}}$, or else $\mathcal{A}$ could be used as a distinguisher as shown before. Using a union bound yields again the claimed inequality.

Proof of Claim 2. We describe $\mathcal{M}$ using $\mathcal{A}$ to guess λ instances of a hard subset membership problem.

By inspection $\mathcal{M}$ perfectly emulates the behavior of $\mathcal{Z}$ for the first j_0 executions of the initial For-loop. Regarding the subsequent λ calls to $\mathcal{A}$ we proceed inductively assuming $\mathcal{M}$ correctly guessed all challenges and simulated $\mathcal{Z}$ until the $(i - 1)$-th step. Let b'_i be the challenger's bit, such that if $b'_i = 0$ then x_i is generated with $\mathsf{SampBad}$ or else $\mathsf{SampGood}$ was used. When $b'_i = 0$, $\mathcal{M}$ correctly executes $\mathcal{A}(V, \mathsf{crs}, x_i)$ as $\mathcal{Z}$ would with $\beta_{j_0+i} = 0$. Similarly when b'_0, $\mathcal{M}$ correctly run $\mathcal{A}(V, \mathsf{crs}, x_i)$ as $\mathcal{Z}$ would with $\beta_{j_0+i} = 1$. Thus, assuming $\neg\mathsf{Fail}$

$$b_i = b'_i \quad \Leftrightarrow \quad (b'_i = 0 \to b_i = 0) \wedge (b'_i = 1 \to b_i = 1) \quad \Leftrightarrow$$
$$\Leftrightarrow \quad \mathsf{BadQuery}_{j_0+i} \wedge \mathsf{BadProof}_{j_0+i} \quad \Leftrightarrow \quad \mathsf{Bad}_{j_0+i}.$$

As a consequence, if $\mathcal{M}$ correctly guesses b'_i, not updating V keeps its behavior identical to $\mathcal{Z}$, which only updates V if $\mathsf{GoodQuery}_{j_0+i}$ occurs. Therefore

$$\Pr\left[b_i = b'_i, \ i \in [\lambda]\right] \ge \Pr\left[\neg\mathsf{Fail}\right] \cdot \Pr\left[b_i = b'_i, \ i \in [\lambda] \mid \neg\mathsf{Fail}\right]$$
$$= \Pr\left[\neg\mathsf{Fail}\right] \cdot \Pr\left[\neg\mathsf{Bad}_{j_0+i}, \ i \in [\lambda] \mid \neg\mathsf{Fail}\right]$$

$\mathcal{M}(x_1, \ldots, x_\lambda)$:

---

1 :   Initialize $\mathsf{crs} \leftarrow \mathsf{G}(1^\lambda)$, $V \leftarrow \mathbb{F}_q^n$

2 :   **For** j_0 times: // Behave as $\mathcal{Z}$

3 :   Sample $\beta \xleftarrow{\$} \{0,1\}$

4 :   **If** $\beta = 0$: $x \leftarrow \mathsf{SampBad}(1^\lambda)$; **Else** $(x, w) \leftarrow \mathsf{SampGood}(1^\lambda)$

5 :   **If** $\mathcal{A}(V, \mathsf{crs}, x) \rightarrow$ query:

6 :   **If** $\beta = 1$:

7 :   Create a proof $\pi \leftarrow \mathsf{P}(\mathsf{crs}, x, w)$

8 :   Get $\mathcal{A}(V, \mathsf{crs}, x, \pi) \rightarrow V'$ and update $V \leftarrow V'$

9 :   // After the For-loop, pass for λ times the challenges to $\mathcal{A}$

10 :   **For** $i \in \{1, \ldots, \lambda\}$:

11 :   **If** $\mathcal{A}(V, \mathsf{crs}, x_i) \rightarrow$ proof: Set $b_i \leftarrow 1$

12 :   **Else**: Set $b_i \leftarrow 0$

13 :   Return $(b_1, \ldots, b_\lambda)$

Fig. 8. Reduction $\mathcal{M}$ guessing λ instances of a Hard Subset Membership Problem.

Since by Lemma 2 the probability of $b_i' = b_i$ is negligible, and by Claim 1 $\Pr[\neg\mathsf{Fail}] \geq 1/2$ we conclude that the claim is true (Fig. 8).

Proof of Claim 3. If $\neg\mathsf{Bad}$ occurs less than $n+1$ times, by the pigeonhole principle for at least one of the intervals $I_k = \{\lambda k + 1, \ldots, \lambda(k+1)\}$ Bad_i occurs for all $i \in I_k$. A union bound yields

$$\Pr\left[\left|\{i : \neg\mathsf{Bad}_i\}\right| < n + 1 \mid \neg\mathsf{Fail}\right] \leq \sum_{k=0}^{n} \Pr\left[\forall i \in I_k, \mathsf{Bad}_i \mid \neg\mathsf{Fail}\right]$$
$$\leq (n+1) \cdot \varepsilon(\lambda).$$

Proof of Claim 4. We first observe that if (crs, x) is generated with S and $\mathsf{SampBad}$, if $\mathcal{A}(V, \mathsf{crs}, x) \rightarrow$ query the affine space L it returns satisfies by Lemma 3 $L \cap (\mathbb{F}_q^n \times \{\mathbf{z}\}) \not\leq V \times \{\mathbf{z}\}$. By definition then

$$V' \times \{\mathbf{z}\} = L \cap \left(\mathbb{F}_q^n \times \{\mathbf{z}\}\right) \not\leq V \times \{\mathbf{z}\} \quad \Rightarrow \quad V' \not\leq V.$$

Therefore, borrowing notation from the proof of Claim 1, when $\beta_i = 1$, the probability that $\mathsf{GoodQuery}_i \wedge \neg(V' \leq V)$ is smaller than $\varepsilon_{\mathsf{zk}} + \varepsilon_{\mathcal{R}}$, or else $\mathcal{A}$ could be used to distinguish (crs, x) from (crs', x') respectively generated with $\mathsf{G}, \mathsf{SampGood}$ and $\mathsf{S}, \mathsf{SampBad}$. Finally since $\neg\mathsf{Fail}$ occurs with significant probability,

$$\Pr[\mathsf{GoodQuery}_i \wedge \neg(V' \leq V) \mid \neg\mathsf{Fail}] \leq \frac{\Pr[\mathsf{GoodQuery}_i \wedge \neg(V' \leq V)]}{\Pr[\neg\mathsf{Fail}]}$$
$$\leq \frac{\varepsilon_{\mathsf{zk}} + \varepsilon_{\mathcal{R}}}{\Pr[\neg\mathsf{Fail}]} \leq \frac{\varepsilon_{\mathsf{zk}} + \varepsilon_{\mathcal{R}}}{2}.$$

Proof of Claim 5. Analogous to the proof of Claim 4.

6   Conclusion

In conclusion we proved that in Maurer's GGM the following primitives are impossible:

- NIZK-AoK for the preimage relation of algebraic OWF families whose domain is the set of string $\{0, 1\}^n$ and key consists of random group elements.
- NIZK for any hard subset membership problem.

Although these cover virtually all cases for which NIZKs are currently used in practice, our results leave a small gap open for technical reasons. The mainly theoretical problem of understanding whether NIZK-AoK impossibility extends to all computationally hard relations, for which finding a witness for a given statement x is (worst-case) hard for GPPT adversaries, is thus left for future work. We also leave open the analogous problem of extending our impossibility for NIZK (not necessarily AoK) to all relations $\mathcal{R}$ whose associated language is (worst-case) hard to decide for GPPT adversaries.

Acknowledgments. This work has been partially supported by SECURING Project (PID2019-110873RJ-I00/MCIN/AEI/10.13039/501100011033) and by PRODIGY Project (TED2021-132464B-I00) funded by MCIN/AEI/10.13039/501100011033 and the European Union NextGenerationEU/PRTR. The authors further wish to thank the anonymous reviewers for their comments as well as Dario Fiore, Dario Catalano, David Balbas and Daniele Cozzo for the helpful discussions.

References

1. Abe, M., Camenisch, J., Dowsley, R., Dubovitskaya, M.: On the impossibility of structure-preserving deterministic primitives. J. Cryptology **32**(1), 239–264 (2018). https://doi.org/10.1007/s00145-018-9292-1
2. Bellare, Mihir, Goldwasser, Shafi: New paradigms for digital signatures and message authentication based on non-interactive zero knowledge proofs. In: Brassard, Gilles (ed.) CRYPTO 1989. LNCS, vol. 435, pp. 194–211. Springer, New York (1990). https://doi.org/10.1007/0-387-34805-0_19
3. Blum, M., Feldman, P., Micali, S.: Non-interactive zero-knowledge and its applications (extended abstract). In: 20th ACM STOC, pp. 103–112. ACM Press, May 1988. https://doi.org/10.1145/62212.62222
4. Bootle, Jonathan, Cerulli, Andrea, Chaidos, Pyrros, Groth, Jens, Petit, Christophe: Efficient zero-knowledge arguments for arithmetic circuits in the discrete log setting. In: Fischlin, Marc, Coron, Jean-Sébastien. (eds.) EUROCRYPT 2016. LNCS, vol. 9666, pp. 327–357. Springer, Heidelberg (2016). https://doi.org/10.1007/978-3-662-49896-5_12
5. Bünz, B., Bootle, J., Boneh, D., Poelstra, A., Wuille, P., Maxwell, G.: Bulletproofs: Short proofs for confidential transactions and more. In: 2018 IEEE Symposium on Security and Privacy. pp. 315–334. IEEE Computer Society Press, May 2018. https://doi.org/10.1109/SP.2018.00020
6. Canetti, R., Goldreich, O., Halevi, S.: The random oracle methodology, revisited. J. ACM (JACM) **51**(4), 557–594 (2004)

7. Catalano, Dario, Fiore, Dario: Vector commitments and their applications. In: Kurosawa, Kaoru, Hanaoka, Goichiro (eds.) PKC 2013. LNCS, vol. 7778, pp. 55–72. Springer, Heidelberg (2013). https://doi.org/10.1007/978-3-642-36362-7_5

8. Catalano, D., Fiore, D., Gennaro, R., Giunta, E.: On the impossibility of algebraic vector commitments in pairing-free groups. In: Theory of Cryptography: 20th International Conference, TCC 2022, Chicago, IL, USA, November 7–10, 2022, Proceedings, Part II, pp. 274–299. Springer (2023). https://doi.org/10.1007/978-3-031-22365-5_10

9. Choudhuri, A.R., Garg, S., Jain, A., Jin, Z., Zhang, J.: Correlation intractability and snargs from sub-exponential ddh. Cryptology ePrint Archive (2022)

10. Couteau, G., Hartmann, D.: Shorter non-interactive zero-knowledge arguments and ZAPs for algebraic languages. In: Micciancio, D., Ristenpart, T. (eds.) CRYPTO 2020, Part III. LNCS, vol. 12172, pp. 768–798. Springer, Heidelberg (2020). https://doi.org/10.1007/978-3-030-56877-1_27

11. Cramer, R.: Modular design of secure yet practical cryptographic protocols. Ph. D.-thesis, CWI and Uni. of Amsterdam (1996)

12. Döttling, N., Hartmann, D., Hofheinz, D., Kiltz, E., Schäge, S., Ursu, B.: On the impossibility of purely algebraic signatures. In: Nissim, K., Waters, B. (eds.) TCC 2021, Part III. LNCS, vol. 13044, pp. 317–349. Springer, Heidelberg (2021). https://doi.org/10.1007/978-3-030-90456-2_11

13. Fiat, A., Shamir, A.: How to prove yourself: practical solutions to identification and signature problems. In: Odlyzko, A.M. (ed.) CRYPTO'86. LNCS, vol. 263, pp. 186–194. Springer, Heidelberg (1987). https://doi.org/10.1007/3-540-47721-7_12

14. Ganesh, C., Khoshakhlagh, H., Parisella, R.: Niwi and new notions of extraction for algebraic languages. In: Security and Cryptography for Networks: 13th International Conference, SCN 2022, Amalfi (SA), Italy, September 12–14, 2022, Proceedings, pp. 687–710. Springer (2022). https://doi.org/10.1007/978-3-031-14791-3_30

15. Gennaro, R., Gertner, Y., Katz, J.: Lower bounds on the efficiency of encryption and digital signature schemes. In: 35th ACM STOC, pp. 417–425. ACM Press, June 2003. https://doi.org/10.1145/780542.780604

16. Gennaro, R., Trevisan, L.: Lower bounds on the efficiency of generic cryptographic constructions. In: 41st FOCS, pp. 305–313. IEEE Computer Society Press, November 2000. https://doi.org/10.1109/SFCS.2000.892119

17. Gentry, C., Wichs, D.: Separating succinct non-interactive arguments from all falsifiable assumptions. In: Fortnow, L., Vadhan, S.P. (eds.) 43rd ACM STOC, pp. 99–108. ACM Press, June 2011.https://doi.org/10.1145/1993636.1993651

18. Gertner, Y., Kannan, S., Malkin, T., Reingold, O., Viswanathan, M.: The relationship between public key encryption and oblivious transfer. In: 41st FOCS, pp. 325–335. IEEE Computer Society Press, November 2000. https://doi.org/10.1109/SFCS.2000.892121

19. Gertner, Y., Malkin, T., Reingold, O.: On the impossibility of basing trapdoor functions on trapdoor predicates. In: 42nd FOCS, pp. 126–135. IEEE Computer Society Press, October 2001. https://doi.org/10.1109/SFCS.2001.959887

20. Goldreich, O., Levin, L.A.: A hard-core predicate for all one-way functions. In: 21st ACM STOC, pp. 25–32. ACM Press, May 1989. https://doi.org/10.1145/73007.73010

21. Goldwasser, S., Ostrovsky, R.: Invariant signatures and non-interactive zero-knowledge proofs are equivalent (extended abstract). In: Brickell, E.F. (ed.) CRYPTO'92. LNCS, vol. 740, pp. 228–245. Springer, Heidelberg (1993). https://doi.org/10.1007/3-540-48071-4_16

22. Groth, J.: Simulation-sound NIZK proofs for a practical language and constant size group signatures. In: Lai, X., Chen, K. (eds.) ASIACRYPT 2006. LNCS, vol. 4284, pp. 444–459. Springer, Heidelberg (2006). https://doi.org/10.1007/11935230_29

23. Groth, J., Ostrovsky, R., Sahai, A.: Non-interactive zaps and new techniques for NIZK. In: Dwork, C. (ed.) CRYPTO 2006. LNCS, vol. 4117, pp. 97–111. Springer, Heidelberg (2006). https://doi.org/10.1007/11818175_6

24. Groth, J., Ostrovsky, R., Sahai, A.: Perfect non-interactive zero knowledge for NP. In: Vaudenay, S. (ed.) EUROCRYPT 2006. LNCS, vol. 4004, pp. 339–358. Springer, Heidelberg (2006). https://doi.org/10.1007/11761679_21

25. Groth, J., Sahai, A.: Efficient non-interactive proof systems for bilinear groups. In: Smart, N.P. (ed.) EUROCRYPT 2008. LNCS, vol. 4965, pp. 415–432. Springer, Heidelberg (2008). https://doi.org/10.1007/978-3-540-78967-3_24

26. Impagliazzo, R., Rudich, S.: Limits on the provable consequences of one-way permutations. In: 21st ACM STOC. pp. 44–61. ACM Press, May 1989. https://doi.org/10.1145/73007.73012

27. Jain, A., Jin, Z.: Non-interactive zero knowledge from sub-exponential DDH. In: Canteaut, A., Standaert, F.X. (eds.) EUROCRYPT 2021, Part I. LNCS, vol. 12696, pp. 3–32. Springer, Heidelberg (2021). https://doi.org/10.1007/978-3-030-77870-5_1

28. Kalai, Y.T., Lombardi, A., Vaikuntanathan, V.: Snargs and ppad hardness from the decisional diffie-hellman assumption. Cryptology ePrint Archive (2022)

29. Kate, Aniket, Zaverucha, Gregory M.., Goldberg, Ian: Constant-size commitments to polynomials and their applications. In: Abe, Masayuki (ed.) ASIACRYPT 2010. LNCS, vol. 6477, pp. 177–194. Springer, Heidelberg (2010). https://doi.org/10.1007/978-3-642-17373-8_11

30. Katsumata, S., Nishimaki, R., Yamada, S., Yamakawa, T.: Compact designated verifier NIZKs from the CDH assumption without pairings. J. Cryptology $34(4)$, 1–71 (2021). https://doi.org/10.1007/s00145-021-09408-w

31. Kim, J.H., Simon, D.R., Tetali, P.: Limits on the efficiency of one-way permutation-based hash functions. In: 40th FOCS, pp. 535–542. IEEE Computer Society Press, October 1999. https://doi.org/10.1109/SFFCS.1999.814627

32. Libert, B., Ramanna, S.C., Yung, M.: Functional commitment schemes: From polynomial commitments to pairing-based accumulators from simple assumptions. In: Chatzigiannakis, I., Mitzenmacher, M., Rabani, Y., Sangiorgi, D. (eds.) ICALP 2016. LIPIcs, vol. 55, pp. 30:1–30:14. Schloss Dagstuhl (July 2016). https://doi.org/10.4230/LIPIcs.ICALP.2016.30

33. Libert, B., Yung, M.: Concise mercurial vector commitments and independent zero-knowledge sets with short proofs. In: Micciancio, D. (ed.) TCC 2010. LNCS, vol. 5978, pp. 499–517. Springer, Heidelberg (2010). https://doi.org/10.1007/978-3-642-11799-2_30

34. Maurer, Ueli: Abstract models of computation in cryptography. In: Smart, Nigel P.. (ed.) Cryptography and Coding 2005. LNCS, vol. 3796, pp. 1–12. Springer, Heidelberg (2005). https://doi.org/10.1007/11586821_1

35. Maurer, U.M.: Unifying zero-knowledge proofs of knowledge. In: Preneel, B. (ed.) AFRICACRYPT 09. LNCS, vol. 5580, pp. 272–286. Springer, Heidelberg (Jun 2009)

36. Papakonstantinou, P.A., Rackoff, C., Vahlis, Y.: How powerful are the DDH hard groups? Electron. Colloquium Comput. Complex, p. 167 (2012). https://eccc.weizmann.ac.il/report/2012/167

37. Papamanthou, C., Shi, E., Tamassia, R.: Signatures of correct computation. In: Sahai, A. (ed.) TCC 2013. LNCS, vol. 7785, pp. 222–242. Springer, Heidelberg (2013). https://doi.org/10.1007/978-3-642-36594-2_13

38. Pedersen, T.P.: Non-interactive and information-theoretic secure verifiable secret sharing. In: Feigenbaum, J. (ed.) CRYPTO'91. LNCS, vol. 576, pp. 129–140. Springer, Heidelberg (1992). https://doi.org/10.1007/3-540-46766-1_9

39. Rotem, L., Segev, G., Shahaf, I.: Generic-group delay functions require hidden-order groups. In: Canteaut, A., Ishai, Y. (eds.) EUROCRYPT 2020, Part III. LNCS, vol. 12107, pp. 155–180. Springer, Heidelberg (2020). https://doi.org/10.1007/978-3-030-45727-3_6

40. Schnorr, C.P.: Efficient identification and signatures for smart cards. In: Brassard, G. (ed.) CRYPTO'89. LNCS, vol. 435, pp. 239–252. Springer, Heidelberg (1990). https://doi.org/10.1007/0-387-34805-0_22

41. Schul-Ganz, G., Segev, G.: Generic-Group Identity-Based Encryption: A Tight Impossibility Result. In: Tessaro, S. (ed.) 2nd Conference on Information-Theoretic Cryptography (ITC 2021). Leibniz International Proceedings in Informatics (LIPIcs), vol. 199, pp. 26:1–26:23. Schloss Dagstuhl - Leibniz-Zentrum für Informatik, Dagstuhl, Germany (2021). https://doi.org/10.4230/LIPIcs.ITC.2021.26, https://drops.dagstuhl.de/opus/volltexte/2021/14345

42. Shoup, V.: Lower bounds for discrete logarithms and related problems. In: Fumy, W. (ed.) EUROCRYPT'97. LNCS, vol. 1233, pp. 256–266. Springer, Heidelberg (1997). https://doi.org/10.1007/3-540-69053-0_18

43. Simon, D.R.: Finding collisions on a one-way street: can secure hash functions be based on general assumptions? In: Nyberg, K. (ed.) EUROCRYPT'98. LNCS, vol. 1403, pp. 334–345. Springer, Heidelberg (1998). https://doi.org/10.1007/BFb0054137

44. Zhandry, M.: To label, or not to label (in generic groups). In: Dodis, Y., Shrimpton, T. (eds.) CRYPTO 2022, Part III. LNCS, vol. 13509, pp. 66–96. Springer, Heidelberg (2022). https://doi.org/10.1007/978-3-031-15982-4_3

A Note on Non-interactive
Zero-Knowledge from CDH

Geoffroy Couteau[1]([⊠]), Abhishek Jain[2], Zhengzhong Jin[3], and Willy Quach[4]

[1] Université Paris Cité, CNRS, IRIF, Paris, France
couteau@irif.fr
[2] Johns Hopkins University, Baltimore, MD, USA
abhishek@cs.jhu.edu
[3] MIT, Cambridge, MA, USA
zzjin@mit.edu
[4] Northeastern University, Boston, MA, USA
quach.w@northeastern.edu

Abstract. We build non-interactive zero-knowledge (NIZK) and ZAP arguments for all NP where soundness holds for infinitely-many security parameters, and against uniform adversaries, assuming the subexponential hardness of the Computational Diffie-Hellman (CDH) assumption. We additionally prove the existence of NIZK arguments with these same properties assuming the polynomial hardness of both CDH and the Learning Parity with Noise (LPN) assumption. In both cases, the CDH assumption does not require a group equipped with a pairing.

Infinitely-often uniform security is a standard byproduct of commonly used non-black-box techniques that build on disjunction arguments on the (in)security of some primitive. In the course of proving our results, we develop a new variant of this non-black-box technique that yields improved guarantees: we obtain explicit constructions (previous works generally only obtained existential results) where security holds for a relatively dense set of security parameters (as opposed to an arbitrary infinite set of security parameters). We demonstrate that our technique can have applications beyond our main results.

1 Introduction

Zero-knowledge (ZK) proofs [30] allow a prover to convince a verifier about the validity of a statement without revealing any other information. They are studied in two flavors – interactive proofs, where the prover and the verifier exchange messages in a protocol, and non-interactive proofs, where the prover sends a single message to the verifier. The latter notion, referred to as *non-interactive zero knowledge* (NIZK) [6,19], has been central to the popularity of ZK proofs due to its wide-ranging applications, including advanced encryption schemes [21,42], signature schemes [2,5] and anonymous blockchains [4].

NIZKs are a fascinating object in cryptography. Despite a long line of research starting more than three decades ago [3,6,9–13,17,19,25,29,32,33,35,46,51],

© International Association for Cryptologic Research 2023
H. Handschuh and A. Lysyanskaya (Eds.): CRYPTO 2023, LNCS 14084, pp. 731–764, 2023.
https://doi.org/10.1007/978-3-031-38551-3_23

remarkably, the cryptographic complexity of NIZKs is not well understood. We do not yet know whether NIZKs are in Minicrypt or Cryptomania.[1] In fact, we do not even know how to construct NIZKs from all standard assumptions known to imply public-key encryption. Significant progress, however, has recently been made on this front: we now know NIZKs for NP from learning with errors [10,46] as well as the (sub-exponential) Decisional Diffie Hellman (DDH) assumption [35], which substantially adds to the prior list of assumptions known to imply NIZKs.

DDH is the strongest assumption in the discrete-logarithm family of assumptions. A weaker assumption – known to imply public-key encryption – is the Computational Diffie Hellman (CDH) assumption. With the aim of further enhancing our understanding of the relationship between NIZKs and public-key encryption, we ask the following question:

Do there exist NIZKs for NP based on CDH?

A positive resolution to this question would also help diminish the gap between NIZKs and their designated-verifier[2] counterpart [44]. Indeed, the latter are already known from CDH [15,36,48] as well as all other assumptions known to imply NIZKs (see [38] and references therein).

ZAPs. ZAPs [24] are two-round public-coin proof systems in the plain model that guarantee witness indistinguishability (WI) [26], i.e., a proof for a statement with two or more witnesses does not reveal which of the witnesses was used in the computation of the proof.

Dwork and Naor [24] proved that ZAPs are equivalent to NIZK *proofs* in the common random string model. Thus, ZAPs are known from the same assumptions also known to imply NIZK proofs. Very recently, computationally-sound ZAPs, aka ZAP *arguments* were constructed based on quasi-polynomial LWE [1,31,39], and subexponential DDH (and variants) [16,35]. As in the case of NIZKs, however, constructing ZAP arguments based on CDH remains an open problem.

CDH vs DDH. Our work follows a well-established line of research on building cryptographic primitives from CDH, when feasibility from DDH is already known. The motivation for this line of work stems from the relative gap between CDH and DDH and the difficulty of building cryptography from CDH.

CDH is a weaker assumption than DDH, and believed to be strictly weaker for some choices of groups, e.g. $\mathbb{G} = \mathbb{Z}_q^*$ or the source group $\mathbb{G}$ of a symmetric pairing $e : \mathbb{G} \times \mathbb{G} \to \mathbb{G}_T$ (where, in both cases, DDH is broken). In fact, the hardness of CDH is closely related to that of the discrete logarithm assumption: [41]

---

[1] Throughout this work, we focus on NIZKs in the common reference string (CRS) model. In the Random Oracle model, NIZKs are known to be in Minicrypt.

[2] In a designated-verifier NIZK, the verifier receives a private verification key that is sampled together with the CRS, which can be used to verify many proofs.

proved that the non-uniform hardness of CDH in any group $\mathbb{G}$ of known order q is equivalent to the non-uniform hardness of computing discrete logarithms in $\mathbb{G}$, and [7] proved that the uniform versions are equivalent in the (large) subexponential regime, both results assuming a plausible and widely believed conjecture on the distribution of smooth numbers. In that sense, despite being a public-key assumption, CDH is morally equivalent to the hardness of computing discrete logarithms, while there are no such connections for DDH (unless computing discrete logarithm is easy in all groups where DDH is known not to hold).

Furthermore, CDH seems to be significantly less expressive than DDH in terms of enabling advanced functionalities. While there has been recent progress on building CDH counterparts to fundamental primitives known from DDH, (e.g. trapdoor functions [27], maliciously-secure oblivious transfer [22], or private information retrieval [8]), there are still many fundamental primitives known from DDH that have no CDH counterpart (e.g. lossy trapdoor functions [47], somewhere statistically-binding hash functions [43], or 2-round private information retrieval [23], and more generally, most primitives that are built from the dual mode paradigm).

1.1 Our Main Result

In this work, we make progress towards resolving the above question. We demonstrate that NIZKs and ZAP arguments for NP with infinitely-often security against uniform adversaries do exist based on the subexponential CDH assumption, without requiring the existence of a pairing.

Theorem 1 (Informal). *Under the subexponential CDH assumption, there exist:*

- *a subexponentially-often secure, uniform NIZK argument for all* NP *in the common random string model;*
- *a subexponentially-often secure, uniform ZAP argument for all* NP.

More precisely, our assumption in Theorem 1 states that no subexponential-time adversary can compute random Diffie-Hellman tuples, either over $\mathbb{Z}_q^*$ (or any subgroup, or, even more generally, over any group (family) with exponentiation computable in TC^0) or any (family of) elliptic curves (without requiring a pairing), with better than subexponential probability. Note that similar restrictions on cryptographic groups appear in the construction of NIZKs and ZAP arguments from DDH [35].

Our NIZK satisfies (1) *infinitely-often* adaptive soundness against *uniform* efficient cheating provers, and (2) (standard, computational) adaptive, multi-theorem zero-knowledge. Our ZAP argument satisfies (1) *infinitely-often* non-adaptive soundness against *uniform* efficient cheating provers, and (2) (standard, computational) adaptive witness indistinguishability. Moreover, the set of security parameters where we argue soundness is at least *subexponentially dense*, in a sense we specify below.

1.2   On Infinitely-Often Security

Infinitely-often security refers to a setting where a primitive is secure on infinitely-many security parameters (as opposed to the traditional notion of almost everywhere security, where security holds for all large enough parameters). It shows up naturally as a consequence of a common non-black-box technique where the *insecurity* of a cryptographic primitive is used to argue the *security* of another primitive (where the attacker against the insecure primitive is used either explicitly in the construction, or implicitly in the security analysis), since (the standard notion of) insecurity of a primitive only guarantees the existence of an attacker successful on infinitely-many security parameters. This behavior shows up in many recent works, where it is sometimes explicitly pointed out, and sometimes disregarded as a minor technical subtlety. Early examples include the work of [49] (which shows that if there is a reduction of key-agreement to OWFs, then there exists a mildly-blackbox reduction of infinitely often key-agreement to OWFs) and the work of [40] (infinitely often one-way functions from constant-round weak coin-flipping protocol). There are also many recent examples, such as [34] (infinitely-often key agreement from nontrivially-correlated 2-party protocols), [20] (either the Feige-Shamir protocol is concurrent zero-knowledge, or injective one-way functions imply an infinitely often key agreement), [52] (a post-quantum collision-resistant hash function is either "collapsing", or it implies infinitely often quantum lightning schemes), or the works of [37,50] (which construct (distributional and standard, respectively) collision-resistant hash functions from multi-collision-resistant hash functions). A recent work of [45] shows that hard-on-average NP languages imply infinitely-often hard-on-average *promise-true* NP search problems. Closer in spirit to our work, [17] gives a construction of infinitely-often NIZK from an exponentially-strong KDM-style variant of the discrete logarithm assumption.

In all these works, the existential result is generally non-constructive (whenever the construction itself relies on the *existence* of an adversary against some primitive) and holds only for infinitely many security parameters, with no guarantee on the *density* of these parameters (*i.e.* the secure parameters could be separated by arbitrarily fast-growing gaps).

Our Work. In contrast, a surprising and interesting feature of our work is that we manage to improve significantly on both these caveats: while we employ a non-black-box technique similar in spirit to these works, our constructions

- are fully explicit (*i.e.*, our result is constructive)
- are proven secure on a set E of security parameters which can be shown to be *reasonably dense* in $\mathbb{N}$.

Concretely, in our main construction of NIZKs and ZAP arguments from the subexponential hardness of CDH, the set E of secure security parameters for our NIZKs and ZAPs is at least *subexponentially dense*: there exists a constant $0 < K < 1$ such that, for all $\lambda \in \mathbb{N}$, $\left[\lambda, 2^{\lambda^K}\right] \cap E \neq \emptyset$. In that sense, we say that the constructions of Theorem 1 are *subexponentially-often secure*.

A caveat of our technique is that soundness only holds against *uniform* cheating provers, while usual notions of security allow adversaries to use a non-efficiently computable advice. This seems an unavoidable consequence of aiming for uniform NIZK algorithms (so that honest parties do not require non-uniform advice to run our NIZK). Consequently, our construction can only use the existence of a *uniform* attacker against some primitive, which turns into building soundness on uniform computational assumptions. We refer to the technical overview for more details.

Looking ahead, we prove Theorem 1 by carefully combining two central ingredients. The first is a NIZK (resp. ZAP argument) which is secure assuming the subexponential hardness of DDH [35]. The second is a template to build NIZKs from cryptographic groups, introduced in [15,36,48] (resp. ZAPs, when combined with [24]). Our main technical tool is the construction of a *universal breaker*, which we believe to be of independent interest. In our setting, our universal breaker allows to somewhat efficiently test, given a security parameter λ, whether DDH is "secure" with respect to λ, for a specific definition of security. We refer to the technical overview and Sect. 5.1 for more precise statements.

On the Generality of Our Approach. While we mostly focus on NIZKs and ZAP arguments, our approach is modular, and we believe that a similar technique could be used to refine the results of many of the previous works that achieved infinitely often security, such as those listed above. In general, when our approach can be applied, it should lead to explicit constructions with security on a dense set of security parameters, but with two caveats: it would only prove security against uniform adversaries, and would rely on superpolynomial hardness assumptions (because our techniques inherently require some mild use of complexity leveraging). Though the results stated in Theorem 1 are our main results, we believe that our new techniques are a conceptual contribution of independent interest. Below, we further illustrate the generality of our techniques and obtain some additional results, both within and outside the setting of NIZKs.

1.3 Further Results

NIZKs from CDH+LPN. First, replacing the NIZK of [35] with the one of [9], we directly obtain the following:

Theorem 2 (Informal). *Under both the superpolynomial CDH and polynomial Learning Parity with Noise (LPN) assumptions, there exists a NIZK argument for all NP satisfying (1) superpolynomially-often adaptive soundness against uniform efficient cheating provers, and (2) (standard, computational) adaptive, multi-theorem zero-knowledge.*

We also show, through a different argument, the following existential (non-constructive) result. We refer to Sect. 6 for more details.

Theorem 3 (Informal). *At least one of the following two statements holds:*

- *Under the polynomial LPN assumption, there exists a NIZK argument for all NP satisfying (1) infinitely-often non-adaptive soundness against uniform efficient cheating provers and (2) statistical zero-knowledge;*
- *Under the polynomial CDH assumption, there exists a NIZK proof for all NP satisfying (1) statistical adaptive soundness and (2) (standard, computational) adaptive, multi-theorem zero-knowledge.*

Unlike Theorem 1, neither Theorem 2 nor Theorem 3 suffer from restrictions over cryptographic groups supported.

Promise-true Hard-on-average Search Problems from Hard-on-average Languages. Eventually, we revisit in the full version the recent work of [45], which showed that if there exists a hard-on-average NP language, then there also exists an (infinitely-often) hard-on-average *promise-true* distributional NP search problem – or, using their terminology, proving theorems that are guaranteed to be true is no easier than proving theorems in general. Applying our new technique, we obtain an explicit variant of their main theorem that starts from a (mildly superpolynomially) hard-on-average NP language, and builds a promise-true distributional NP search problem which is sound on a *superpolynomially dense* set of security parameters:

Theorem 4 (Informal). *Given any superpolynomially-secure uniformly hard-on-average NP language, there is an explicit construction of a promise-true distributional NP search problem which is uniformly superpolynomially-often hard-on-average.*

1.4   Roadmap

We present an overview of our techniques in Sect. 2. We introduce notations and recall useful results from prior work in Sect. 3. In Sect. 4, we present generic constructions related to DDH breakers and $\overline{\text{DDH}}$-based NIZKs. In Sect. 5, we present our main construction along with our main technical tools. In Sect. 6, we present a purely existential result corresponding to Theorem 3. We refer to the full version of the paper for a construction of promise-true NP search problem from a hard-on-average NP language, and how to adapt our main theorem to the setting of elliptic curves (without requiring pairings).

2   Technical Overview

Designated-Verifier NIZKs from CDH. Our starting point is the construction of designated-verifier NIZKs for NP from CDH [15,36,48]. In a nutshell, these works, assuming CDH, reduce building a NIZK for all NP to the task of building a NIZK for the DDH language: an instance $(g, g^\alpha, g^\beta, g^\gamma)$ belongs to the language if $\gamma = \alpha \cdot \beta \bmod p$, where p is the order of the group. Unfortunately, we do not know how to build NIZKs for the DDH language assuming only the hardness of CDH. Instead, [15,36,48] observe that *designated-verifier* NIZKs for the DDH language can be constructed [18], which in turn, yields a designated-verifier NIZK for NP from CDH.

In fact, this approach can yield *publicly-verifiable* NIZKs for NP if the verifier can efficiently check whether group elements form DDH tuples. This observation already yields a NIZK for NP when the group is equipped with a (symmetric) bilinear map: the verifier can check whether an input from the source group is a DDH tuple by comparing the appropriate pairings $e(g, g^\gamma)$ and $e(g^\alpha, g^\beta)$ [12,48]. Notably, the bilinear map and the target group are only used in the verification algorithm, and security properties of the NIZK only rely on the hardness of CDH in the source group.

Alternatively, *if DDH were broken over the group* (without pairings), then we could also obtain NIZKs for NP based on CDH via this approach. In this case, the verifier could perform the required checks using the DDH breaker. For convenience, we refer to NIZKs obtained in this manner as $\overline{\text{DDH}}$-based NIZKs.

NIZKs from DDH, and a Disjunction Argument. Recently, [35] provided a construction of NIZK for all NP from (subexponential) DDH.[3],[4] For convenience, we will refer to this NIZK as a DDH-based NIZK.

This brings us to the following attempt for constructing NIZKs for NP from CDH. Fix a single (family of) cryptographic groups for which CDH holds. Then,

– either "DDH is secure", in which case the DDH-based NIZK of [35] is secure,
– or "DDH is broken", which allows to build a $\overline{\text{DDH}}$-based NIZK, assuming CDH!

One could be tempted to conclude that this disjunction approach yields a NIZK for all of NP from CDH. Unfortunately, this conclusion does not directly hold, because the statements "DDH is secure" and "DDH is broken", as (imprecisely) stated above, are not negations of each other. Nevertheless, this dichotomy serves as the key starting point behind our result.

A Closer Look. There are several mismatches in the definitions of "secure" and "broken" above.

1. A first mismatch relates to the *success probabilities* of breakers. An adversary falsifying the security of DDH is only ensured to work with some small,

---

[3] [35] actually provides two NIZKs. The first one provides statistical zero-knowledge, but only non-adaptive soundness. The second is adaptively-sound and computationally zero-knowledge. Because our approach can only yield computational zero-knowledge, we will use the second version.

[4] Technically, [35] imposes mild restrictions on the supported cryptographic groups, that we also inherit. We will ignore this for the sake of this overview, and refer to Sect. 3.1 for more details.

non-negligible (or even subexponentially small) probability. In contrast, the breaker needed to instantiate the $\overline{\text{DDH}}$-based NIZK from CDH needs to work *with very high probability* on *worst-case* inputs (since the breaker is used by the verifier).

2. A second mismatch is that hardness assumptions are usually stated as to handle *non-uniform* adversaries. Consequently, an adversary falsifying the security of DDH would only yield a non-uniform DDH breaker, and thus the resulting verifier for the $\overline{\text{DDH}}$-based NIZK would be non-uniform.

3. A third mismatch is that, in order to falsify DDH being secure in the usual sense, it suffices to exhibit an adversary that breaks DDH with sufficiently good advantage on *infinitely many* security parameters. In fact, it is not even clear, given such an adversary, how to efficiently determine on which security parameters the breaker works, without, say, a bound on its runtime. Such a bound could be provided as non-uniform advice to the verification algorithm, but would again result again in a $\overline{\text{DDH}}$-based NIZK with a non-uniform verifier. Furthermore, such an adversary would only help in constructing a $\overline{\text{DDH}}$-based NIZK on only infinitely many security parameters.

The first mismatch can be taken care of using the random self-reducibility of DDH,[5] which allows us to amplify the success probability of any "weak" breaker to a "strong" one. Given that the DDH-based NIZK of [35] relies on the subexponential hardness of DDH, the resulting amplified breaker runs in subexponential time. Then, after relying on complexity leveraging for the resulting $\overline{\text{DDH}}$-based NIZK in order to make this breaker efficient, soundness follows from the (mildly stronger) subexponential hardness of CDH.

It is unfortunately less clear how to handle the two other issues. Still, the approach above already gives a NIZK with *non-uniform, non-explicit* algorithms, which is *infinitely-often* secure based on the subexponential hardness of CDH — an already interesting result.[6]

A Universal DDH Breaker. Towards tackling the drawbacks of the previous construction, our first step is to characterize more precisely subsets of security parameters such that DDH is secure, and ones such that DDH is broken. Doing so opens the hope of obtaining a new construction which, for every security parameter, uses either the DDH-based NIZK if the security parameter is secure, and the $\overline{\text{DDH}}$-based NIZK otherwise.

Our crucial observation is that, for a suitable notion of security, one can somewhat efficiently test whether a security parameter is secure. We do so through the construction of a *universal breaker* UnivBreak, which (with overwhelming probability) breaks DDH on every security parameter such that *some* good breaker exists, and fails only when no good enough breaker exists. Our construction

---

[5] Assuming the (family of) group is of prime order.

[6] Formalizing such a statement turns out to require quite a bit of care, because of subtleties specific to the precise soundness statement of [35]. We will not develop these difficulties further here, as we will directly prove a stronger statement below.

is inspired by classic constructions of universal cryptographic objects. Namely, it iterates through all small Turing machines of size say $\leq \lfloor \log \lambda \rfloor$, and tests whether they efficiently break DDH. If a good breaker exists, it uses one of them to break DDH, and otherwise states that the security parameter is secure. Standard concentration bounds intuitively ensure that if a good breaker exists, then UnivBreak finds a good breaker (with overwhelming probability), and if no good breakers exist, then UnivBreak is not fooled into using a bad breaker (with overwhelming probability). Still, in order to fully define our universal breaker, we need to define more precisely the set of "small Turing machines" it will consider. Equivalently, we now seek to formally define a set SECURE of security parameters for which DDH is secure.

We observe that if SECURE relates to the *uniform* security of DDH, then breakers on $\overline{\text{SECURE}} := \mathbb{N} \setminus \text{SECURE}$ are also uniform. The intuition is then that, fixing any uniform breaker $\mathcal{A}$ on $\overline{\text{SECURE}}$, UnivBreak will eventually run $\mathcal{A}$ when given as input a large enough security parameter $\lambda \geq 2^{|\mathcal{A}|}$, allowing us to use the $\overline{\text{DDH}}$-based NIZK. Furthermore, we can show that the DDH-based NIZK is sound on SECURE, albeit only against *uniform* cheating provers. Ultimately, this is the reason our constructions are only sound against uniform cheating provers.

This is unfortunately not yet sufficient. The reason is that UnivBreak is called on a fixed security parameter λ, and that security on any *fixed* security parameter is an inherently *non-uniform* notion of security. For instance, there could exist a family of uniform breakers $\mathcal{A}_i$ that respectively break DDH on all *large enough* parameters in $\{\lambda \notin \text{SECURE} \mid \lambda \geq \lambda_i\}$ but such that λ_i grows with their size $|\mathcal{A}_i|$ as Turing machines, e.g. $\lambda_i = |\mathcal{A}_i|$. In particular, we cannot rule out that, for *all* $\lambda \notin \text{SECURE}$, UnivBreak never runs any $\mathcal{A}_i$ on input $\lambda \geq \lambda_i$. This, in turn, could imply that for all security parameters, UnivBreak has low advantage, or even wrongly concludes that some input parameter is secure.

Our solution is to modify the definition of SECURE to bound the "non-uniformity" of breakers. Namely, whether some fixed security parameter λ belongs to SECURE now only depends on whether there exists an adversary with small description $\leq \lfloor \log \lambda \rfloor$ as a Turing machine that breaks DDH on λ.

A separate issue is that iterating over polynomial-time adversaries with non-negligible advantage is not well defined, because the notions of polynomial-time and negligible advantage are *asymptotic*. For instance, for any fixed λ, there will always exist a (uniform) polynomial-time machine breaking DDH on λ with non-negligible advantage. Instead, we define SECURE using $(t(\lambda), \varepsilon(\lambda))$-security (namely, considering adversaries running in time $t(\lambda)$ with advantage $\varepsilon(\lambda)$) with *fixed* functions $t = t(\lambda)$ and $\varepsilon = \varepsilon(\lambda)$, where t is superpolynomial, and ε is inverse superpolynomial, so that (t, ε)-security (asymptotically) implies standard polynomial security. Importantly, we can argue that DDH is uniformly hard on the set SECURE, which will allow us to argue *uniform* soundness of the DDH-based NIZK.

Summing up, our universal breaker UnivBreak, on input a security parameter λ, tests all $t(\lambda)$-time machines of size $\leq \lfloor \log \lambda \rfloor$, and checks whether their advantage in breaking DDH is larger than $\varepsilon(\lambda)$, using $\approx 1/\varepsilon^2(\lambda)$ runs. If some machine has enough advantage, UnivBreak uses this machine to compute its output; and if no such machine exists, UnivBreak indicates that λ is secure. Note that UnivBreak is somewhat efficient in that it runs in superpolynomial time $\approx t(\lambda)/\varepsilon^2(\lambda)$. Intuitively, UnivBreak indicates that λ is secure whenever $\lambda \in$ SECURE, and breaks DDH with advantage $\approx \varepsilon(\lambda)$ whenever $\lambda \notin$ SECURE. It turns out this intuition is slightly inaccurate, but will suffice for the purpose of this overview. We refer to Sect. 5.1 for more details, and a formal treatment.

A Subexponentially-Often NIZK from Subexponential CDH. We now use our universal breaker to build a (weak) NIZK from CDH. A proof in our scheme simply consists of both a DDH-based proof π_{DDH} and a $\overline{\mathsf{DDH}}$-based proof $\pi_{\overline{\mathsf{DDH}}}$. The verifier, given the security parameter λ, tests the universal breaker UnivBreak on λ. If the universal breaker fails to produce an output bit, the verifier verifies π_{DDH}. Otherwise, it amplifies the advantage of UnivBreak in order to verify $\pi_{\overline{\mathsf{DDH}}}$. Note that the construction is *fully explicit*, and features *uniform* algorithms.

Completeness and zero-knowledge follow from correctness of UnivBreak (which is ensured to produce outputs with good advantage whenever it produces an output) and the completeness and zero knowledge properties of the DDH-based NIZK and the $\overline{\mathsf{DDH}}$-based NIZK.

One could hope that the NIZK above satisfies *uniform* soundness on *all* security parameters, Indeed, the *uniform* hardness of DDH holds over the set of parameters SECURE by definition: given any PPT uniform adversary $\mathcal{A}$ of size s, thanks to $t(\lambda)$ (resp. $\varepsilon(\lambda)$) being superpolynomial (resp. inverse superpolynomial), we have that for all large enough $\lambda \geq 2^s$ such that $\lambda \in$ SECURE, the advantage of $\mathcal{A}$ on λ is at most $\varepsilon(\lambda)$. Conversely, if $\lambda \notin$ SECURE, then soundness holds thanks to guarantees on UnivBreak and soundness of the $\overline{\mathsf{DDH}}$-based NIZK.

Unfortunately, the argument above does not hold, because the (amplified) DDH breaker given by UnivBreak runs in super-polynomial time $\approx t(\lambda)/\varepsilon^2(\lambda)$. In fact, the security of the DDH-NIZK of [35] requires assuming the *subexponential security* of DDH, which requires to set ε as inverse subexponential. Thus, the resulting verification algorithm building on UnivBreak actually runs in subexponential time. As a result, we need to rely on complexity leveraging whenever calling the $\overline{\mathsf{DDH}}$-based NIZK to make the verification algorithm efficient. Namely, our NIZK for security parameter λ calls the $\overline{\mathsf{DDH}}$-based NIZK on security parameter $\lambda' := \lfloor \log^{1/c}(\lambda) \rfloor$ for some constant $0 < c < 1$. First, this introduces the need to assume subexponential hardness of CDH (to argue zero-knowledge of the $\overline{\mathsf{DDH}}$-based NIZK). Second, this resulting mismatch of the security parameters used by the DDH-based NIZK and the $\overline{\mathsf{DDH}}$-based NIZK prevents us from arguing soundness on all security parameters: it could be that $\lambda \notin$ SECURE and $\lambda' \in$ SECURE, in which case we do not know how to argue soundness of any of the two NIZKs, whenever running our NIZK on security parameter λ.

Still, we obtain a NIZK which is secure on infinitely-many security parameters. In fact, we can argue that the set of secure parameters for the NIZK is *subexponentially dense* in the following sense. For every security parameter λ, either $\lambda \in$ SECURE or $\lambda \notin$ SECURE. Consequently, either our NIZK is sound on λ (corresponding to $\lambda \in$ SECURE), or it is sound on $\overline{\lambda} := 2^{\lambda^c}$ (corresponding to $\lambda \notin$ SECURE). This is because, in that latter case, on input $\overline{\lambda}$, our NIZK calls the $\overline{\text{DDH}}$-based NIZK and UnivBreak on parameter $\lfloor \log^{1/c}(\overline{\lambda}) \rfloor = \lambda \notin$ SECURE, and therefore soundness of the $\overline{\text{DDH}}$-based NIZK applies.[7] Overall, this ensures that the *relative gap* between two consecutive parameters for which our NIZK is secure is at most subexponential. We refer to Theorem 20 for a formal statement.

Variant: NIZK from CDH and LPN. Our approach is quite modular in the DDH-based NIZK we start from. In particular, starting with the construction of [9] which is secure assuming both the polynomial hardness of DDH and LPN, we obtain a "superpolynomially dense" NIZK where the gap between secure parameters is only superpolynomial, and where security holds assuming both the superpolynomial hardness of CDH and the polynomial hardness of LPN.[8]

Variant: ZAP Arguments from CDH. We observe that, given a DDH breaker, the $\overline{\text{DDH}}$-based NIZKs from [15,36,48] use a uniform common random string, and are statistically sound. Thus, any efficient DDH breaker implies a ZAP for all NP based on CDH via [24]. Moreover, [35] builds ZAP arguments for all NP assuming the subexponential hardness of DDH. Thus, we can apply the same blueprint as for the construction of NIZK. The verifier message consists of verifier messages for both the DDH-based ZAP argument and the (complexity-leveraged) $\overline{\text{DDH}}$-based ZAP, and the prover replies with two proofs. The verifier then runs UnivBreak, and verifies one of the proofs accordingly. A similar analysis gives that the resulting ZAP argument is subexponentially often (non-adaptively) sound against uniform cheating provers,[9] and witness indistinguishable assuming the subexponential hardness of CDH.

3 Preliminaries

Notation. Throughout this paper, λ denotes the security parameter. A probabilistic polynomial time algorithm (PPT, also denoted *efficient* algorithm) runs in time polynomial in the (implicit) security parameter λ. A function f is *negligible* if for any positive polynomial p there exists a bound $B > 0$ such that, for

---

[7] The actual statement we prove is slightly more technical, due to subtleties in the proof of soundness of [35]. We refer to Theorem 20 for more details.

[8] We only know how to instantiate our universal breaker using a superpolynomial (resp. inverse superpolynomial) function t (resp. ε) so that $\lambda \in$ SECURE implies that DDH is polynomially hard on λ against uniform adversaries. We therefore still need to rely on complexity leveraging, resulting in a superpolynomial gap.

[9] This is because the ZAP argument of [35] is only non-adaptively sound.

any integer $k \geq B$, $|f(k)| \leq 1/|p(k)|$. Given a finite set S, the notation $x \xleftarrow{\$} S$ means a uniformly random assignment of an element of S to the variable x. For a positive integer n, m such that $n < m$, we denote by $[n]$ the set $\{1, \cdots, n\}$. We will sometimes explicitly refer to the random coins r used by a probabilistic algorithm M by writing $M(\cdot; r)$.

3.1 Diffie-Hellman Assumptions

Cryptographic Groups. Let DHGen be a deterministic algorithm which on input 1^λ returns a description $\mathcal{G} = (\mathbb{G}, p)$ where $\mathbb{G}$ is a cyclic group of prime order p. Throughout the paper, we will fix DHGen, and therefore a family of groups $\{\mathcal{G}_\lambda\}_{\lambda \in \mathbb{N}}$. Unless specified otherwise, we will assume throughout this work that the prime-order group $\mathbb{G}$ has exponentiation in TC^0. This notably includes (subgroups of) $\mathbb{Z}_q^*$ for $q \in \mathbb{N}$, which includes its subgroup of quadratic residues. We consider in the full version a variant for elliptic curves.

As is usually (implicitly) assumed for cryptographic groups, we will suppose that, for all $\lambda \in \mathbb{N}$, there exists an efficient *oblivious sampling algorithm* $\mathsf{Sample}(1^\lambda; r) \mapsto g$ which we denote $g \xleftarrow{\$} \mathbb{G}_\lambda$. Formally, this requires that there exists an efficient algorithm Equivocate such that the two following distributions are within negligible statistical distance: $(r, \mathsf{Sample}(1^\lambda; r)) \approx_s$ (Equivocate$(g), g \leftarrow \mathbb{G}$), where r is uniformly random. Note that this follows whenever the description of a uniformly random group element is itself a uniformly random string. This allows to securely view uniformly random group elements as uniformly random strings (up to considering the internal random coins used by Sample).

The computational Diffie-Hellman assumption is defined as follows.

Definition 5 (CDH Assumption). *We say that the computational Diffie-Hellman (CDH) assumption holds relative to DHGen if for all PPT adversaries $\mathcal{A}$ and all large enough security parameters λ,*

$$\Pr\left[\mathcal{G} = \mathsf{DHGen}(1^\lambda), g \xleftarrow{\$} \mathbb{G}, \alpha, \beta \xleftarrow{\$} \mathbb{Z}_p : g^{\alpha\beta} \xleftarrow{\$} \mathcal{A}(1^\lambda, \mathcal{G}, g, g^\alpha, g^\beta)\right] \leq \mathsf{negl}(\lambda).$$

We also define similarly the decisional Diffie-Hellman assumption:

Definition 6 (DDH Assumption). *We say that the decisional Diffie-Hellman (DDH) assumption holds relative to DHGen if for all PPT adversaries $\mathcal{A}$ and all large enough security parameters λ,*

$$\Pr\left[\begin{array}{l} \mathcal{G} = \mathsf{DHGen}(1^\lambda), g \xleftarrow{\$} \mathbb{G}, \alpha, \beta, \gamma \xleftarrow{\$} \mathbb{Z}_p, b \xleftarrow{\$} \{0,1\}, \\ \delta \leftarrow b\gamma + (1-b)\alpha\beta, b' \xleftarrow{\$} \mathcal{A}(1^\lambda, \mathcal{G}, g, g^\alpha, g^\beta, g^\delta) \end{array} : b = b'\right] \leq \frac{1}{2} + \mathsf{negl}(\lambda).$$

Throughout the paper, whenever there are no ambiguities about DHGen, we will denote by $\mathsf{Adv}_\mathcal{A}^{\mathsf{DDH}}(1^\lambda)$, for any adversary $\mathcal{A}$ and security parameter λ, the probability

$$\mathsf{Adv}_\mathcal{A}^{\mathsf{DDH}}(1^\lambda) := \Pr\left[\begin{array}{l} \mathcal{G} = \mathsf{DHGen}(1^\lambda), g \xleftarrow{\$} \mathbb{G}, \alpha, \beta, \gamma \xleftarrow{\$} \mathbb{Z}_p, b \xleftarrow{\$} \{0,1\}, \\ \delta \leftarrow b\gamma + (1-b)\alpha\beta, b' \xleftarrow{\$} \mathcal{A}(1^\lambda, \mathcal{G}, g, g^\alpha, g^\beta, g^\delta) \end{array} : b = b'\right] - \frac{1}{2}.$$

Subexponential Security. In the definition of CDH (resp. DDH), if the inequality is strengthened to hold against all probabilistic 2^{λ^c}-time adversaries $\mathcal{A}$ with advantage at most $2^{-\lambda^c}$ for some constant $0 < c < 1$, we refer to the corresponding assumption as the $(2^{\lambda^c}$-)subexponential CDH (resp. DDH) assumption.

Infinitely-often Security. In the definition of CDH (resp. DDH), if the inequality is instead required to hold only for (all large enough elements of) an infinite set of security parameters $E \subseteq \mathbb{N}$, we refer to the corresponding assumption as the infinitely-often CDH (resp. DDH) assumption with respect to E, and denote it io-CDH (resp. io-DDH).

Uniform Security. By default, when we quantify over PPT adversaries $\mathcal{A}$, PPT refers to *non-uniform* adversaries: families $\{\mathcal{A}_\lambda\}_{\lambda \in \mathbb{N}}$ of boolean circuits such that $|\mathcal{A}_\lambda| = \mathsf{poly}(\lambda)$ for every $\lambda \in \mathbb{N}$. In this work, we will in fact mostly consider a weaker, *uniform* notion of security, where the adversaries $\mathcal{A}$ are modelled as probabilistic Turing machines. When the CDH (resp. DDH) assumption is only required to hold against all uniform PPT adversaries, we call *uniform CDH* (resp. *uniform DDH*) the corresponding assumption.

3.2 Non-interactive Zero-Knowledge

A (publicly-verifiable) non-interactive zero-knowledge (NIZK) argument system for an NP relation R, with associated language $\mathscr{L}(R) = \{x \mid \exists w, (x, w) \in R\}$ is a 3-tuple of efficient algorithms $(\mathsf{Setup}, \mathsf{Prove}, \mathsf{Verify})$, where Setup outputs a common reference string, $\mathsf{Prove}(\mathsf{crs}, x, w)$, given the crs, a statement x, and a witness w, outputs a proof π, and $\mathsf{Verify}(\mathsf{crs}, x, \pi)$, on input the crs, a word x, and a proof π, outputs a bit indicating whether the proof is accepted or not. A NIZK argument system satisfies the following: completeness, adaptive soundness, and adaptive multi-theorem zero-knowledge properties:[10]

- A non-interactive argument system $(\mathsf{Setup}, \mathsf{Prove}, \mathsf{Verify})$ for an NP relation R satisfies *completeness* if for every $(x, w) \in R$,

$$\Pr[\mathsf{crs} \xleftarrow{\$} \mathsf{Setup}(1^\lambda, 1^{|x|}), \pi \leftarrow \mathsf{Prove}(\mathsf{crs}, x, w) : \mathsf{Verify}(\mathsf{crs}, x, \pi) = 1] \geq 1 - \mathsf{negl}(\lambda).$$

- A non-interactive argument system $(\mathsf{Setup}, \mathsf{Prove}, \mathsf{Verify})$ for an NP relation R satisfies *adaptive soundness* if for any PPT $\mathcal{A}$ and any large enough security parameter λ,

$$\Pr\left[\begin{array}{l}\mathsf{crs} \xleftarrow{\$} \mathsf{Setup}(1^\lambda, 1^{|x|}), (x, \pi) \xleftarrow{\$} \mathcal{A}(\mathsf{crs}) : \\ \mathsf{Verify}(\mathsf{crs}, x, \pi) = 1 \wedge x \notin \mathscr{L}\end{array}\right] \leq \mathsf{negl}(\lambda).$$

---

[10] Intuitively, multi-theorem zero-knowledge ensures that a simulator can provide *many* simulated proofs under a *common* simulated CRS.

– A non-interactive argument system (Setup, Prove, Verify) for an NP relation R satisfies (computational, statistical) *adaptive multi-theorem zero-knowledge* if for all (computational, statistical) $\mathcal{A}$, there exists a PPT simulator Sim = $(\mathsf{Sim}_1, \mathsf{Sim}_2)$ such that if we run $\mathsf{crs} \xleftarrow{\$} \mathsf{Setup}(1^\lambda, 1^{|x|})$ and $\overline{\mathsf{crs}} \xleftarrow{\$} \mathsf{Sim}_1(1^\lambda, 1^{|x|})$, then we have $|\Pr[\mathcal{A}^{\mathcal{O}_0(\mathsf{crs},\cdot,\cdot)}(\mathsf{crs}) = 1] - \Pr[\mathcal{A}^{\mathcal{O}_1(\overline{\mathsf{crs}},\cdot,\cdot)}(\mathsf{crs}) = 1]| = \mathsf{negl}(\lambda)$, where $\mathcal{O}_0(\mathsf{crs}, x, w)$ outputs $\mathsf{Prove}(\mathsf{crs}, x, w)$ if $(x, w) \in R$ and $\perp$ otherwise, and $\mathcal{O}_1(\overline{\mathsf{crs}}, x, w)$ outputs $\mathsf{Sim}_2(\overline{\mathsf{crs}}, x)$ if $(x, w) \in R$ and $\perp$ otherwise.

Whenever $\mathsf{Setup}(1^\lambda)$ outputs a uniformly random string crs, we say that the NIZK is in the *common random string* model.

Infinitely-Often, Uniform, Subexponential NIZKs. If we relax the definition of correctness (resp. adaptive soundness) to hold only for (all large enough elements of) an infinite set of security parameters $E \subseteq \mathbb{N}$, we say that the NIZK satisfies *infinitely-often correctness* (resp. *infinitely-often adaptive soundness*) *with respect to* E, and refer to the NIZK as an *infinitely-often NIZK*. One could analogously define infinitely-often zero-knowledge, but we will not need it in this work.

If soundness holds only against uniform PPT adversaries, we say that the NIZK is a *uniform NIZK* (similarly, we will not need to consider uniform zero-knowledge in this work).

Finally, if soundness and zero-knowledge hold against subexponential-time adversaries (resp. subexponential-time adversaries with subexponential advantage), we say that the NIZK is subexponentially secure (resp. strongly subexponentially secure).

NIZKs in the Hidden-Bits Model. We use the following result regarding the existence of NIZKs in the hidden-bits model (HBM). Since the full definition of NIZK in the HBM will not be required in our work, we refer the readers to [25] for more details.

Theorem 7 (NIZKs for all of NP in the HBM [25]). *Let λ denote the security parameter and let $k = k(\lambda)$ be any positive integer-valued function. Then, unconditionally, there exists NIZK proof systems for any NP language $\mathscr{L}$ in the HBM that uses $\mathsf{hb} = k \cdot \mathsf{poly}(\lambda, |x|)$ hidden bits with soundness error $\varepsilon \leq 2^{-k \cdot \lambda}$, where λ denotes the security parameter and poly is a function related to the NP language $\mathscr{L}$, and that are perfectly zero-knowledge.*

3.3 Verifiable Pseudorandom Generators

Verifiable pseudorandom generators have been introduced in [24]. Their definition has been refined in [15,36,48], and slightly relaxed in [17]. Below, we recall the definition from [17].

Definition 8 (Verifiable Pseudorandom Generator). *Let $\delta(\lambda)$ and $s(\lambda)$ be positive valued polynomials. A $(\delta(\lambda), s(\lambda))$-verifiable pseudorandom generator (VPRG) is a four-tuple of efficient algorithms (Setup, Stretch, Prove, Verify) such that*

- Setup($1^\lambda, m$), *on input the security parameter (in unary) and a polynomial bound $m(\lambda) \geq s(\lambda)^{1+\delta(\lambda)}$, outputs a set of public parameters* pp *(which contains 1^λ);*
- Stretch(pp), *on input the public parameters* pp, *outputs a triple* (pvk, x, aux), *where* pvk *is a public verification key of length $s(\lambda)$, x is an m-bit pseudorandom string, and* aux *is an auxiliary information;*
- Prove(pp, aux, i), *on input the public parameters* pp, *auxiliary informations* aux, *an index $i \in [m]$, outputs a proof π;*
- Verify(pp, pvk, i, b, π), *on input the public parameters* pp, *a public verification key* pvk, *an index $i \in [m]$, a bit b, and a proof π, outputs a bit β;*

which is in addition complete, hiding, and binding, as defined below.

Definition 9 (Completeness of a VPRG). *For any $i \in [m]$, a complete* VPRG *scheme* (Setup, Stretch, Prove, Verify) *satisfies, for all large enough λ:*

$$
\Pr \left[\begin{array}{l} \text{pp} \xleftarrow{\$} \text{Setup}(1^\lambda, m), \\ (\text{pvk}, x, \text{aux}) \xleftarrow{\$} \text{Stretch}(\text{pp}), : \text{Verify}(\text{pp}, \text{pvk}, i, x_i, \pi) = 1 \\ \pi \xleftarrow{\$} \text{Prove}(\text{pp}, \text{aux}, i), \end{array} \right] \geq 1 - \text{negl}(\lambda).
$$

Definition 10 (Statistical Binding Property of a VPRG). *Let* (Setup, Stretch, Prove, Verify) *be a* VPRG. *A* VPRG *is statistically binding if there exists a (possibly inefficient) extractor* Ext *such that for any (potentially unbounded) $\mathcal{A}$ and for all large enough λ, it holds that*

$$
\Pr \left[\begin{array}{l} \text{pp} \xleftarrow{\$} \text{Setup}(1^\lambda, m), \\ (\text{pvk}, i, \pi) \xleftarrow{\$} \mathcal{A}(\text{pp}), : \text{Verify}(\text{pp}, \text{pvk}, i, 1 - x_i, \pi) = 1 \\ x_i \leftarrow \text{Ext}(\text{pp}, \text{pvk}) \end{array} \right] \leq \text{negl}(\lambda).
$$

Definition 11 (Hiding Property of a VPRG). *A* VPRG *scheme* (Setup, Stretch, Prove, Verify) *is hiding if for any $i \in [m]$ and any PPT adversary $\mathcal{A}$ that outputs bits, and for all large enough λ, it holds that:*

$$
\Pr \left[\begin{array}{l} \text{pp} \xleftarrow{\$} \text{Setup}(1^\lambda, m), \\ (\text{pvk}, x, \text{aux}) \xleftarrow{\$} \text{Stretch}(\text{pp}), : \mathcal{A}(\text{pp}, \text{pvk}, i, (x_j, \pi_j)_{j \neq i}) = x_i \\ (\pi_j \xleftarrow{\$} \text{Prove}(\text{pp}, \text{aux}, j))_j \end{array} \right] \leq 1/2 + \text{negl}(\lambda).
$$

Infinitely-Often, Subexponential VPRGs. If we relax the definition of completeness (resp. binding) to hold only for (all large enough elements of) an infinite set of security parameters $E \subseteq \mathbb{N}$, we say that the VPRG satisfies *infinitely-often completeness* (resp. *infinitely-often binding*) *with respect to E*, and refer to the VPRG as an *infinitely-often VPRG*. We note that one can analogously define infinitely-often hiding, but we will not need it in this work. We furthermore say that a VPRG is a subexponential VPRG, if (1) completeness error (resp. binding error, distinguishing advantage against hiding) are all inverse subexponential, and (2) if hiding holds against subexponential-time adversaries $\mathcal{A}$.

From VPRGs to NIZKs for NP. The following shows that VPRG are sufficient to construct NIZKs for all of NP.

Theorem 12 $((\delta, s)$**-VPRGs $\Rightarrow$ NIZKs for all of NP).** *Fix an NIZK proof system for any* NP *language $\mathscr{L}$ in the HBM that uses* hb $=$ hb$(\lambda, |x|)$ *hidden bits with soundness error $\varepsilon \leq 2^{-\lambda}$ where* hb $\geq \lambda$ *w.l.o.g. Suppose that a $(\delta(\lambda), s(\lambda))$-verifiable pseudorandom generator where $s(\lambda) \geq \max\{\lambda, (\text{hb}^2/\lambda)^{1/\delta(\lambda)}\}$ exists. Then, there exist statistically adaptively sound with soundness error $2^{-\lambda}$ and adaptively multi-theorem zero-knowledge* NIZK *proofs for the* NP *relation $\mathscr{L}$.*

If instead the $(\delta(\lambda), s(\lambda))$-VPRG satisfies infinitely-often completeness and infinitely-often binding with respect to some infinite subset $E \subseteq \mathbb{N}$, then there exists an infinitely-often NIZK which is statistically, adaptively sound with soundness error $2^{-\lambda}$ with respect to E, and adaptively multi-theorem zero-knowledge.

Furthermore, if the public parameters of the verifiable pseudorandom generator are uniformly random, then the resulting NIZK is in the common random string model.

Proof. The proof follows readily from [15,24,25]. It can be checked from Theorem 16 of [15] that we can combine the NIZK in the HBM for the NP relation $\mathscr{L}$ with any VPRG that satisfies $s^{1+\delta} > (1 + s/\lambda)\text{hb} + \text{hb}^2/\lambda$ in order to construct a statistically sound, adaptive single-theorem non-interactive witness indistinguishable (NIWI) proof for the NP relation $\mathscr{L}$. Working out the equation and taking into account that s needs to be at least λ-bits, the condition on s in our statement is sufficient. Then, by using [25], we can convert an adaptive single-theorem NIWI proof into an adaptive multi-theorem NIZK proof assuming the existence of pseudorandom generators (which are by definition implied by VPRGs). To obtain a NIZK with soundness error $2^{-\lambda}$, we use a λ-wise parallel repetition, using that the construction above is statistically sound.

The proof extends directly to VPRGs that are correct and binding on any infinite subset $E \subseteq \mathbb{N}$, giving an infinitely-often NIZK with respect to E.

Since the existence of an NIZK in the HBM for any NP language $\mathscr{L}$ is implied by Theorem 7, the above shows that VPRGs with some mild condition on $\delta(\lambda)$ and $s(\lambda)$ implies existence of NIZKs for any NP language $\mathscr{L}$.

Remark 13 (NIZKs for Large Statements). Theorem 12 can be readily extended to the setting of NIZKs with statements of size *subexponential* in the security parameter, namely $|x| = 2^{\lambda^c}$ for some constant c satisfying $0 < c < 1$, assuming an appropriately strong VPRG. More precisely, assume the existence of a subexponential VPRG with quantitatively stronger completeness, binding, and hiding $2^{-\lambda^{c'}}$, where $c < c' < 1$ is a constant. Then there exists a NIZK with honest algorithms running in time $\text{poly}(\lambda, |x|)$, with completeness error (resp. zero-knowledge distinguishing advantage) $2^{-O(\lambda^{c'})} = \text{negl}(\lambda, |x|)$, and statistical soundness error $2^{-\lambda}$. Moreover, if hiding of the VPRG hiding holds against $2^{-\lambda^{c'}}$-time adversaries, then the resulting NIZK is zero-knowledge against adversaries running in time $2^{O(\lambda^{c'})}$.

The statement above is directly obtained by adapting the proof of Theorem 12, starting instead with a VPRG with subexponential-length output $s^{1+\delta} \geq (1 + s/\lambda)\mathsf{hb}(\lambda, |x|) + \mathsf{hb}^2(\lambda, |x|)/\lambda$, where we recall that hb is a polynomial in $\lambda, |x|$.

3.4 NIZKs and ZAP Arguments from DDH

We recall here the result of [35], which we adapt to our setting. Recall that we assume our cryptographic groups to have exponentiation in TC^0 (Sect. 3.1). We refer to the full version for elliptic curve counterparts (without requiring a pairing).

Theorem 14 (NIZK from DDH [35]). *There exists a constant $L > 0$ such that the following holds. For any constant $0 < c < 1$, and for all $\lambda \in \mathbb{N}$, define the set $\mathsf{TOWER}_\lambda = \mathsf{TOWER}_\lambda(c, L) := \{\lambda\} \cup \{\lambda^{(c/2)^{i/2}}\}_{i \in [L]}$. For any infinite set $E \subseteq \mathbb{N}$, define:*

$$E_{\mathsf{TOWER}} = \bigcup_{\lambda \in E} \mathsf{TOWER}_\lambda.$$

Suppose that, for any (uniform) PPT adversary $\mathcal{A}$, there exists λ^* such that for all $\lambda_{\mathsf{TOWER}} \in E_{\mathsf{TOWER}}$ satisfying $\lambda_{\mathsf{TOWER}} \geq \lambda^*$:

$$\mathsf{Adv}_{\mathcal{A}}^{\mathsf{DDH}}(1^{\lambda_{\mathsf{TOWER}}}) \leq 2^{-(\lambda_{\mathsf{TOWER}})^c}.$$

Then:

- *there exists a NIZK for all NP satisfying perfect completeness, infinitely-often adaptive soundness w.r.t. E (against uniform cheating provers),[11] and computational zero-knowledge against non-uniform verifiers;*
- *there exists a ZAP argument for all NP satisfying perfect completeness, infinitely-often non-adaptive soundness w.r.t. E, and statistical adaptive witness indistinguishability.*

In other words, [35] builds, given a (uniform) cheating prover on security parameter λ, a (uniform) DDH breaker for at least one security parameter in TOWER_λ. Then, the theorem above captures the resulting security statement associated to infinitely-often soundness.

4 DDH Breakers and VPRGs

In this section, we introduce building blocks that we use in our constructions. Throughout this section, we only assume that our cryptographic groups are of prime order, and we do not assume that exponentiation can be computed in TC^0. We mainly prove the following result, which intuitively states that algorithms breaking DDH can be turned into an appropriate NIZK:

---

[11] See the paragraph on infinitely-often security in Sect. 3.2 for a definition of soundness w.r.t. an infinite set E.

Lemma 15. *Let* $t = t(\lambda)$ *be any positive integer-valued function, and* $0 < \varepsilon = \varepsilon(\lambda) < 1/2$ *be any function such that, for all* λ, $t(\lambda)/\varepsilon^2(\lambda) \leq 2^{\lambda^c}$ *for some constant* $0 < c < 1$.

Assume $\mathcal{A}$ *is a Turing machine running in time* $t(\lambda)$, *such that there exists an infinite set* $E \subseteq \mathbb{N}$ *such that for all* $\lambda \in E$:

$$\mathsf{Adv}^{\mathsf{DDH}}_{\mathcal{A}}(1^\lambda) \geq \varepsilon(\lambda).$$

Let $E' = \{2^{\lambda^c}\}_{\lambda \in E}$, *and let* c' *be any constant such that* $c < c' < 1$.

Then, assuming the $2^{\lambda^{c'}}$-*subexponential hardness of CDH (Sect. 3.1), there exists a NIZK in the common random string model, which is infinitely-often correct and statistically adaptively sound with respect to* E', *and satisfying computational, adaptively, multi-theorem zero-knowledge.*

Furthermore, if for all λ, $t(\lambda)/\varepsilon^2(\lambda) = \mathsf{poly}(\lambda)$, *then assuming the polynomial hardness of CDH, there exists a NIZK in the common random string model, which is infinitely-often correct and statistically adaptively sound with respect to* E, *and computationally adaptively, multi-theorem zero-knowledge.*

Remark 16 (Large Statement Sizes). Similar to Remark 13, the resulting NIZK, when ran over input statements of size up to $|x| = 2^{\lambda^c}$, remains correct, statistically sound, and subexponentially zero-knowledge, and where the running time of the honest algorithms is $\mathsf{poly}(\lambda, |x|)$. Looking ahead, this is done by combining the subexponential VPRG of Lemma 18 with the proof of Theorem 12.

In Sect. 4.1, we show how to amplify the success probability of weak DDH breakers. In Sect. 4.2, we show to build a VPRG from strong DDH breakers.

4.1   Amplification of DDH Breakers

First, we prove a generic result on amplifying the success probability of (weak) DDH breakers.

Given a group description $\mathcal{G} = (\mathbb{G}, p) = \mathsf{DHGen}(1^\lambda)$ and a security parameter λ, let $\mathcal{S}_{\mathsf{DH}}(\lambda)$ be the set of DDH four-tuples: $\mathcal{S}_{\mathsf{DH}}(\lambda) = \{(g, g^\alpha, g^\beta, g^\gamma) : \gamma = \alpha\beta\}$. Let $T(\lambda) = \mathsf{poly}(\lambda)$ be such that $|\mathbb{G}| < 2^{T(\lambda)}$.

Lemma 17 (Amplification of DDH Breakers). *Let* $t = t(\lambda)$ *be any positive integer-valued function, and* $\varepsilon = \varepsilon(\lambda)$ *be any function such that* $0 < \varepsilon(\lambda) < 1/2$ *for all* λ.

Assume $\mathcal{A}$ *is a Turing machine running in time* $t(\lambda)$, *such that there exists an infinite set* $E \subseteq \mathbb{N}$ *such that for all* $\lambda \in E$:

$$\mathsf{Adv}^{\mathsf{DDH}}_{\mathcal{A}}(1^\lambda) \geq \varepsilon(\lambda).$$

Then there exists a Turing machine $\overline{\mathcal{A}} = \overline{\mathcal{A}}(t, \varepsilon)$ *running in time* $t(\lambda)/\varepsilon^2(\lambda) \cdot \mathsf{poly}(\lambda)$ *such that, for all large enough security parameters* $\lambda \in E$ *and all DDH tuples* $(g, g^\alpha, g^\beta, g^\gamma) \in \mathcal{S}_{\mathsf{DH}}(\lambda)$:

$$\Pr_r\left[b \xleftarrow{\$} \overline{\mathcal{A}}(1^\lambda, \mathcal{G}, g, g^\alpha, g^\beta, g^\gamma; r) : b = 1\right] \geq 1 - \mathsf{negl}(\lambda) \cdot 2^{-4T(\lambda)}.$$

Furthermore, for all large enough security parameters $\lambda \in E$, and all non-DDH tuples $(g, g^\alpha, g^\beta, g^\gamma) \in \mathbb{G}^4 \setminus \mathcal{S}_{\mathsf{DH}}(\lambda)$,

$$\Pr_r \left[b \xleftarrow{\$} \overline{\mathcal{A}}(1^\lambda, \mathcal{G}, g, g^\alpha, g^\beta, g^\gamma; r) : b = 0 \right] \geq 1 - \mathsf{negl}(\lambda) \cdot 2^{-4T(\lambda)},$$

We call any machine satisfying these properties a strong DDH breaker *with respect to E.*

Brief Overview. The proof is slightly more involved than the standard DDH amplification approach. We start from the default strategy: we run the weak DDH breaker $\mathcal{A}$ on many rerandomized versions of the input to $\overline{\mathcal{A}}$ (using an appropriate rerandomization such that a DDH tuple becomes a fresh DDH tuple, and a non-DDH tuple becomes a fresh random tuple). However, the inputs to $\mathcal{A}$ are now either all random, or all DDH tuples. So we further randomize the inputs, by randomly switching them to a freshly uniform tuple, with probability $1/2$, and check whether $\mathcal{A}$ correctly guesses whether the input was switched. We then check whether these guesses deviate significantly from the distribution of uniform bits using concentration bounds: they should not deviate when starting with a random DDH tuple, as the output to $\mathcal{A}$ is then independent of the switch, and should deviate significantly otherwise by assumption on $\mathcal{A}$. We refer to the full version of the paper for a formal proof.

Next, we make a simple observation:

Claim. For all sufficiently large security parameter λ, denoting $\mathcal{G} = (\mathbb{G}, p) \leftarrow \mathsf{DHGen}(1^\lambda)$, and under the same assumption on $\mathcal{A}$ as in Lemma 17:

$$\Pr_r \left[\exists (g, g^\alpha, g^\beta, g^\gamma) \in \mathcal{S}_{\mathsf{DH}} : \overline{\mathcal{A}}(1^\lambda, \mathcal{G}, g, g^\alpha, g^\beta, g^\gamma; r) \right] = 0] \leq \mathsf{negl}(\lambda), \text{ and}$$

$$\Pr_r \left[\exists (g, g^\alpha, g^\beta, g^\gamma) \in \mathbb{G}^4 \setminus \mathcal{S}_{\mathsf{DH}} : \overline{\mathcal{A}}(1^\lambda, \mathcal{G}, g, g^\alpha, g^\beta, g^\gamma; r) \right] = 1] \leq \mathsf{negl}(\lambda).$$

Proof. This follows immediately from a straightforward union bound over all elements of $\mathcal{S}_{\mathsf{DH}}$ and of $\mathbb{G}^4 \setminus \mathcal{S}_{\mathsf{DH}}$, using the fact that $|\mathcal{S}_{\mathsf{DH}}| < |\mathbb{G}^4 \setminus \mathcal{S}_{\mathsf{DH}}| < 2^{4T(\lambda)}$ since $|G| < 2^{T(\lambda)}$. $\qquad\square$

4.2 VPRGs from Strong DDH Breakers

Next, we show that the existence of the strong DDH breaker $\overline{\mathcal{A}}$, with the specifications of Lemma 17, suffices to construct a verifiable pseudorandom generator under the CDH assumption.

Lemma 18 (a VPRG from subexponential CDH). *Let $0 < c < 1$ be a constant. Assume $\overline{\mathcal{A}}$ is a Turing machine running in time $2^{\lambda^c} \cdot \mathsf{poly}(\lambda)$, and an $E \subseteq \mathbb{N}$ is an infinite set such that $\overline{\mathcal{A}}$ is a strong DDH breaker with respect to E (Lemma 17), and let $E' = \{2^{\lambda^c}\}_{\lambda \in E}$.*

Then, assuming the subexponential 2^{λ^c}-hardness of CDH for any constant $c < c' < 1$, there exists a subexponential, infinitely-often statistically binding VPRG with respect to E'.

Furthermore, if $\overline{\mathcal{A}}$ runs in polynomial time, then assuming the polynomial hardness of CDH, there exists an infinitely-often statistically binding VPRG *with respect to E.*

Let $B : \mathbb{G}^3 \mapsto \{0,1\}$ be a predicate satisfying the following property: given (g^a, g^b, g^c), computing $B(g^a, g^{ab}, g^{ac})$ should be as hard (up to polynomial factors) as computing (g^a, g^{ab}, g^{ac}). Note that this implies that distinguishing $B(g^a, g^{ab}, g^{ac})$ from a random bit given a random triple (g^a, g^b, g^c) is as hard as solving CDH. There are standard method to build this predicate using e.g. the Goldreich-Levin construction [28], see e.g. [14] for an illustration in the specific case of CDH. Our construction proceeds as follows.

Let $\lambda' = \lambda$ if $\overline{\mathcal{A}}$ runs in polynomial time, and $\lambda' = \lfloor \log^{1/c}(\lambda) \rfloor$ if $\overline{\mathcal{A}}$ runs in time 2^{λ^c} for some constant $0 < c < 1$.

- Setup($1^\lambda, m$) : Sample $\mathcal{G} = \mathcal{G}_{\lambda'} = \mathsf{DHGen}(1^{\lambda'})$ and $g \xleftarrow{\$} \mathbb{G}$. For $i = 1$ to m, pick $a_i \xleftarrow{\$} \mathbb{Z}_p$ and set $h_i \leftarrow g^{a_i}$. Pick a random tape R for $\overline{\mathcal{A}}$. Set $\mathsf{pp} = (1^\lambda, \mathcal{G}, g, (h_i)_{i \leq m}, R)$.
- Stretch(pp) : pick $r \xleftarrow{\$} \mathbb{Z}_p$, set $\mathsf{pvk} \leftarrow g^r$, and for $i \leq m$, set $x_i \xleftarrow{\$} B(\mathsf{pvk}, h_i^r)$. Output $(\mathsf{pvk}, x, \mathsf{aux} = r)$.
- Prove($\mathsf{pp}, \mathsf{aux}, i$) : output $\pi \leftarrow h_i^r$.
- Verify($\mathsf{pp}, \mathsf{pvk}, \mathcal{T}, i, \sigma, \pi$) : output 1 iff $(B(\mathsf{pvk}, \pi) = \sigma) = 1$ and $(\overline{\mathcal{A}}(1^\lambda, \mathcal{G}, g, \mathsf{pvk}, h'; R) = 1)$.

Theorem 19. *If the subexponential CDH assumption holds relative to* DHGen, *then the above construction is a computationally, subexponentially hiding and statistically binding* VPRG.

Proof. Observe that $\lambda \in E'$ implies $\lambda' \in E$. Completeness on E' and efficiency $\mathsf{poly}(\lambda, m)$ follows easily by inspection, noting that $\overline{\mathcal{A}}$, on input λ', runs in time $\mathsf{poly}(\lambda)$ by assumption. Furthermore, the VPRG can have arbitrary polynomial stretch $m(\lambda)$, independently of the length of pvk (the latter is a single element of $\mathbb{G}$).

We now show that the construction is infinitely-often statistically binding with respect to E'. Let $\lambda \in E'$. Let $\mathcal{B}$ be an adversary against the binding property: on input pp, $\mathcal{B}$ outputs a triple (pvk, i, π). We must exhibit an extractor Ext that finds bit x_i such that $\mathsf{Verify}(\mathsf{pp}, \mathsf{pvk}, i, 1 - x_i, \pi) = 0$ with overwhelming probability. Ext extracts x_i as follows: it parses pp as $(1^\lambda, \mathcal{G}, g, (h_i)_{i \leq m})$, computes $r \leftarrow \mathsf{dlog}_g(\mathsf{pvk})$ and sets $x_i \leftarrow B(\mathsf{pvk}, \pi)$. To make Verify accept, $\mathcal{B}$ must find a triple (pvk, h_i, π) such that $\overline{\mathcal{A}}(1^\lambda, \mathcal{G}, g, \mathsf{pvk}, h_i, \pi; R) = 1$, yet $B(\mathsf{pvk}, \pi) = 1 - x_i$. The latter implies in particular that $(g, \mathsf{pvk}, h_i, \pi) \notin \mathcal{S}_{\mathsf{DH}}$. But with overwhelming probability over the choice of R, there cannot exist an element of $\mathbb{G}^4 \setminus \mathcal{S}_{\mathsf{DH}}$ where $\overline{\mathcal{A}}$ outputs 1, which concludes the proof.

We now discuss the hiding property. We show that a 2^{λ^c}-time adversary $\mathcal{B}$ against the hiding property with advantage greater than $2^{-\lambda^c}$ of the above scheme contradicts the subexponential CDH assumption. Let $\lambda \in E'$. Given a position i, the reduction receives a CDH challenge on security parameter λ', of the form $(1^{\lambda'}, \mathcal{G}, g, g^\alpha, g^\beta)$ and attempts to guess the predicate $x = B(g^\alpha, g^{\alpha\beta})$.

It defines $h_i \leftarrow g^\beta$ and samples the rest of pp honestly, picking $a_j \xleftarrow{\$} \mathbb{Z}_p$ and setting $h_j \leftarrow g^{a_j}$ for $j \neq i$. Then, it sets pvk $\leftarrow g^\alpha$, and computes π_j as $(g^\alpha)^a_j$ and x_j as $B(\text{pvk}, \pi_j)$ for every $j \neq i$. Observe that the input $(\text{pp}, \text{pvk}, (x_j, \pi_j)_{j \neq i})$ to $\mathcal{B}$ is distributed exactly as in the hiding game. The reduction outputs whatever $\mathcal{B}$ outputs. Observe that $x_i = B(g^\alpha, g^{\alpha\beta})$ by construction, hence the advantage of the reduction in this game is exactly the advantage of $\mathcal{B}$ against the hiding property of the VPRG. Since the reduction runs in time $\text{poly}(\lambda) = \text{poly}(2^{\lambda'^c}) < 2^{\lambda^{c'}}$ for any $c < c' < 1$ for all large enough λ and recovers the hardcore predicate of the CDH challenge with subexponential advantage $2^{-\lambda^c}$, this contradicts the $2^{\lambda^{c'}}$-subexponential CDH assumption. The argument extends directly to the setting where $\lambda' = \lambda$ assuming only the polynomial hardness of CDH. $\square$

Combining Lemma 17 and Lemma 18 with Theorem 12 concludes the proof of Lemma 15, where the resulting CRS is a uniformly random string thanks to the oblivious samplability of the group. We note that the construction above is not new: the works of [12, 48] constructed a NIZK by compiling a NIZK in the HBM under the CDH assumption over pairing-friendly groups. Our construction can be viewed as abstracting out their compiler as a VPRG, and replacing the pairing (which is used solely to check a DDH relation in their construction) by the efficient DDH breaker $\overline{\mathcal{A}}$.

5 A Subexponentially-Often NIZK from Subexponential CDH

In this section we prove our main theorem:

Theorem 20. *Assume the subexponential hardness of CDH. Then for any* NP *language $\mathscr{L}$, there exists a non-interactive zero-knowledge proof for $\mathscr{L}$ which is infinitely-often secure in the following sense:*

- *Subexponentially-often uniform soundness: There exists a constant $0 < K < 1$, and an infinite set $E \subseteq \mathbb{N}$, such that the following properties hold:*
  - *(Relative density of E): For all $\lambda \in \mathbb{N}$, $\left[\lambda, 2^{\lambda^K}\right] \cap E \neq \emptyset$.*
  - *(Infinitely-often uniform soundness w.r.t. E): For all uniform PPT adversary $\mathcal{A}$ and all $\lambda_i \in E$:*

$$\Pr\left[\begin{array}{l} \text{crs} \xleftarrow{\$} \text{Setup}(1^{\lambda_i}), (x, \pi) \xleftarrow{\$} \mathcal{A}(\text{crs}) \ : \\ \text{Verify}(\text{crs}, x, \pi) = 1 \wedge x \notin \mathscr{L} \end{array}\right] \leq \text{negl}(\lambda_i).$$

- *Standard adaptive, multi-theorem zero-knowledge against non-uniform verifiers.*

In particular, defining $E = \{\lambda_i\}_{i \in \mathbb{N}}$ as an increasing sequence (namely $\lambda_i < \lambda_j$ whenever $i < j$), we have that for all $i \in \mathbb{N}$: $\lambda_{i+1} \leq 2^{(\lambda_i+1)^K}$.

Remark 21 (Restriction on cryptographic groups). We recall that we consider here cryptographic groups with exponentiation in TC^0, typically including $\mathbb{Z}_q^*$ or its subgroup of quadratic residues (see also Sect. 3.1). This is a similar restriction to the one made in [35]. We refer to the full version for a sketch of how to extend Theorem 20 to families of elliptic curves (without requiring a pairing).

Remark 22 (Subexponential security). The proof of Theorem 20 can be directly modified to achieve various forms of subexponential soundness and zero-knowledge. Soundness with *subexponential advantage* follows from [35], by relying on an appropriately stronger subexponential hardness of DDH (which in turns requires a stronger CDH assumption). Zero-knowledge against *subexponential time* verifiers follows from relying on an appropriately stronger subexponential hardness of CDH. The constant K will increase with the strength of the subexponential soundness claim, and the exact subexponential hardness of CDH needed will both grow with K and the strength of the subexponential zero-knowledge claim.

In Sect. 5.1, we build a universal DDH breaker. We then present our NIZK construction in Sect. 5.2. We discuss additional results in Sect. 5.3.

5.1 A Universal DDH Breaker

In order to prove Theorem 20, our main building block is a *universal DDH breaker*. Very imprecisely, the universal breaker (1) efficiently breaks DDH on all security parameters such that *some* efficient breaker exists, and such that (2) DDH holds otherwise. For technical reasons (briefly discussed in Remark 26), we split the construction of a universal breaker into two procedures: a *tester* which tests whether some input security parameter is secure or broken (Lemma 24), and a universal DDH breaker which breaks DDH with large probability whenever any weak breaker exists (Lemma 25).

Notation. Throughout the section, $t = t(\lambda)$, $\varepsilon = \varepsilon(\lambda)$ will denote functions such that $t(\lambda)$ is positive-integer-valued, and $0 < \varepsilon(\lambda) < 1/2$. Define the two following machines:

- $M_{(t)}$: on input $(1^\lambda, x)$, run $M(1^\lambda, x)$ for up to $t(\lambda)$ steps. If M terminates and outputs a bit, define that bit as the output of $M_{(t)}(1^\lambda, x)$; otherwise output a random bit $b \leftarrow \{0,1\}$. Note that by definition, $M_{(t)}$ runs in time at most $t(\lambda)$.
- $\overline{M_{(t)}} = \overline{M_{(t)}}(t, \varepsilon/6)$ is the machine defined in Lemma 17 starting with $M_{(t)}$, with functions t and $\varepsilon/6$. In particular, if $\mathsf{Adv}_{M_{(t)}}^{\mathsf{DDH}} \geq \varepsilon/6$, then $\mathsf{Adv}_{\overline{M_{(t)}}}^{\mathsf{DDH}} \geq 1 - \mathsf{negl}(\lambda) \cdot 2^{-4T(\lambda)}$.

Next, we define our sets of secure and broken security parameters.

Definition 23 (Secure and Broken DDH parameters). *Let* $t = t(\lambda)$, $\varepsilon = \varepsilon(\lambda)$ *be functions such that* $t(\lambda)$ *is positive-integer-valued, and* $0 < \varepsilon(\lambda) < 1/2$.

We define SECURE $=$ SECURE$(t, \varepsilon) \subseteq \mathbb{N}$ *as the set of security parameters* λ *such that, for all uniform Turing machines* $\mathcal{A}$ *of size at most* $\lfloor \log \lambda \rfloor$ *running in time at most* $t(\lambda)$:

$$\mathsf{Adv}^{\mathsf{DDH}}_{\mathcal{A}}(1^\lambda) < \varepsilon(\lambda),$$

where $\mathsf{Adv}^{\mathsf{DDH}}_{\mathcal{A}}(1^\lambda)$ *is defined in Definition 6.*

We define BROKEN $=$ BROKEN$(t, \varepsilon) \subseteq \mathbb{N}$ *as the set of security parameters* λ, *such that there exists a uniform machine* $\mathcal{A}^*$ *of size at most* $\lfloor \log \lambda \rfloor$ *such that:*

$$\mathsf{Adv}^{\mathsf{DDH}}_{\mathcal{A}^*_{(t)}}(1^\lambda) \geq \frac{\varepsilon(\lambda)}{2},$$

where $\mathcal{A}^*_{(t)}$ *is defined above.*

Let us make a few comments on this definition. First, SECURE $\cup$ BROKEN $= \mathbb{N}$. This is because if $\lambda \notin$ SECURE, then any machine $\mathcal{A}^*$ contradicting $\lambda \in$ SECURE is a "witness" for $\lambda \in$ BROKEN. However, SECURE and BROKEN are not necessarily complementary sets. This is because (1) the advantage requirements are potentially compatible, and (2) BROKEN quantifies over a slightly larger set of Turing machines, as $\mathcal{A}^*_{(t)}$ can have description size (slightly) larger than $\lfloor \log \lambda \rfloor$.

The following gives an algorithm which, on input a security parameter, efficiently determines whether DDH is secure or not, in the sense of Definition 23.

Lemma 24 (Security Parameter Tester). *Let* $t = t(\lambda)$, $\varepsilon = \varepsilon(\lambda)$ *be functions such that* $t(\lambda)$ *is positive-integer-valued, and* $0 < \varepsilon(\lambda) < 1/2$.

Then there exists an algorithm Test $=$ Test(t, ε) *which takes as input* 1^λ *where* $\lambda \in \mathbb{N}$, *runs in time* $t(\lambda)/\varepsilon^2(\lambda) \cdot \mathsf{poly}(\lambda)$, *and satisfying the following properties:*

– *For any* $\lambda \in \mathbb{N}$:

$$\Pr\left[\lambda \notin \mathsf{SECURE} \wedge \mathsf{Test}(1^\lambda) = 1\right] \leq 2^{-\lambda},$$

over the randomness of Test;
– *For any* $\lambda \in \mathbb{N}$:

$$\Pr\left[\lambda \notin \mathsf{BROKEN} \wedge \mathsf{Test}(1^\lambda) = 0\right] \leq \lambda \cdot 2^{-\lambda},$$

over the randomness of Test.

Intuitively, the algorithm Test can ensure, with overwhelming probability, that some input security parameter is secure (corresponding to output 1) or broken (corresponding to output 0) with respect to Definition 23. Note that Test can potentially produce both outcomes with large probability whenever $\lambda \in$ SECURE $\cap$ BROKEN.

Proof. We define Test as follows. On input (1^λ):

- For $M \in \{0,1\}^{\lfloor \log \lambda \rfloor}$, parse M as the description of a Turing Machine. Let $C(\lambda) = \left\lceil 100 \cdot \frac{\lambda}{\varepsilon^2(\lambda)} \right\rceil$
  - For $i = 1$ to $C(\lambda)$, sample $\alpha_i, \beta_i, \gamma_i \leftarrow \mathbb{Z}_p$, and $b_i \leftarrow \{0,1\}$. Set $\delta_i = b\gamma_i + (1-b)\alpha_i\beta_i$. Compute $b'_i \leftarrow M_{(t)}((1^\lambda, \mathcal{G}, g, g^{\alpha_i}, g^{\beta_i}, g^{\delta_i})$. Let

$$c_M = \sum_{i=1}^{C(\lambda)} 1 \oplus b_i \oplus b'_i$$

  be the number of indices i such that $b_i = b'_i$.
  If $c_M \geq \left(\frac{1}{2} + \frac{3\varepsilon(\lambda)}{4}\right) \cdot C(\lambda)$, then output 0.
  Otherwise continue to the next $M \in \{0,1\}^{\lfloor \log \lambda \rfloor}$.
- If no output has been produced so far, output 1.

Note that Test runs in time $t(\lambda)/\varepsilon^2(\lambda) \cdot \mathsf{poly}(\lambda)$.
We first prove that, for any $\lambda \in \mathbb{N}$:

$$\Pr\left[\lambda \notin \mathsf{SECURE} \wedge \mathsf{Test}(1^\lambda) = 1\right] \leq 2^{-\lambda},$$

over the randomness of Test.

Suppose $\lambda \notin \mathsf{SECURE}$. Then there exists a uniform adversary $\mathcal{A}^*$ with size at most $\lfloor \log \lambda \rfloor$ running in time $t(\lambda)$ such that:

$$\mathsf{Adv}_{\mathcal{A}}^{\mathsf{DDH}}(1^\lambda) \geq \varepsilon(\lambda).$$

Because $\mathcal{A}^*$ runs in time $t(\lambda)$, note that $\mathcal{A}^*_{(t)} \equiv \mathcal{A}^*$. In order to output $\perp$, Test has to loop through $M = \mathcal{A}^*$. When $M = \mathcal{A}^*$, all the b_i and b'_i for all $1 \leq i \leq C(\lambda)$ are independent from each other, and $\Pr[b_i = b'_i] \geq \frac{1}{2} + \varepsilon(\lambda)$ by assumption on $\mathcal{A}^*$, so that $\mathbb{E}[c_M] \geq \left(\frac{1}{2} + \varepsilon(\lambda)\right) \cdot C(\lambda)$. A standard Chernoff bound gives:

$$\Pr\left[c_M \leq \left(\frac{1}{2} + \frac{3\varepsilon(\lambda)}{4}\right) \cdot \left\lceil \frac{\lambda}{\varepsilon^2(\lambda)} \right\rceil\right] \leq \exp\left(-\frac{100\lambda}{64}\right) \leq 2^{-\lambda},$$

so with probability at least $1 - \exp(-\lambda/64)$, Test outputs 0 when looping on $\mathcal{A}^*$ (or some other machine, if it produces an output bit before reaching $\mathcal{A}^*$).

Next, we prove that for all $\lambda \in \mathbb{N}$:

$$\Pr\left[\lambda \notin \mathsf{BROKEN} \wedge \mathsf{Test}(1^\lambda) = 0\right] \leq \lambda \cdot 2^{-\lambda}$$

over the randomness of Test.

Suppose $\lambda \notin \mathsf{BROKEN}$, that is, for all Turing machines M of size at most $\lfloor \log \lambda \rfloor$:

$$\mathsf{Adv}_{M_{(t)}}^{\mathsf{DDH}}(1^\lambda) < \frac{\varepsilon(\lambda)}{2}.$$

Then $\mathbb{E}[c_M] \leq \left(\frac{1}{2} + \frac{\varepsilon(\lambda)}{2}\right) \cdot \left\lceil \frac{\lambda}{\varepsilon^2(\lambda)} \right\rceil$. A standard Chernoff bound gives:

$$\Pr\left[c_M \geq \left(\frac{1}{2} + \frac{3\varepsilon(\lambda)}{4}\right) \cdot \left\lceil \frac{\lambda}{\varepsilon^2(\lambda)} \right\rceil\right] \leq \exp\left(-\frac{100\lambda}{20}\right) \leq 2^{-\lambda}.$$

Using a union bound, the probability that Test outputs 1 on any machine M of size at most $\lfloor \log \lambda \rfloor$ is at most $\lambda \cdot 2^{-\lambda}$. □

Next, we build a universal breaker that breaks DDH on any $\lambda \in$ BROKEN:

Lemma 25 (Universal DDH Breaker). *Let $t = t(\lambda)$ and $\varepsilon = \varepsilon(\lambda)$ be positive functions defined in the beginning of the section.*

Then there exists an algorithm UnivBreak $=$ UnivBreak(t, ε) *which runs in time* $t(\lambda)/\varepsilon^2(\lambda) \cdot \mathsf{poly}(\lambda)$, *such that for all* $\lambda \in$ BROKEN:

$$\Pr \left[\begin{array}{l} \mathcal{G} = \mathsf{DHGen}(1^\lambda), g \xleftarrow{\$} \mathbb{G}, \alpha, \beta, \gamma \xleftarrow{\$} \mathbb{Z}_p, \\ b \xleftarrow{\$} \{0,1\}, \delta \leftarrow b\gamma + (1-b)\alpha\beta, \quad : b = b' \\ b' \xleftarrow{\$} \mathsf{UnivBreak}(1^\lambda, \mathcal{G}, g, g^\alpha, g^\beta, g^\delta) \end{array} \right] \geq 1 - \mathsf{negl}(\lambda) \cdot 2^{-4T(\lambda)}.$$

Proof. We define UnivBreak as follows. On input $(1^\lambda, \mathcal{G}, g, g^\alpha, g^\beta, g^\delta))$:

- For $M \in \{0,1\}^{\lfloor \log \lambda \rfloor}$, parse M as the description of a Turing Machine. Let $C'(\lambda) = \left\lceil 400 \cdot \frac{T(\lambda)+\lambda}{\varepsilon^2(\lambda)} \right\rceil$
  - For $i = 1$ to $C(\lambda)$, sample $\alpha_i, \beta_i, \gamma_i \leftarrow \mathbb{Z}_p$, and $b_i \leftarrow \{0,1\}$. Set $\delta_i = b\gamma_i + (1-b)\alpha_i\beta_i$. Compute $b'_i \leftarrow M_{(t)}((1^\lambda, \mathcal{G}, g, g^{\alpha_i}, g^{\beta_i}, g^{\delta_i})$. Let

$$c_M = \sum_{i=1}^{C(\lambda)} 1 \oplus b_i \oplus b'_i$$

  be the number of indices i such that $b_i = b'_i$.
  If $c_M \geq \left(\frac{1}{2} + \frac{\varepsilon(\lambda)}{3} \right) \cdot C(\lambda)$, then output $\overline{M_{(t)}}(1^\lambda, \mathcal{G}, g, g^\alpha, g^\beta, g^\delta)$.
  Otherwise continue to the next $M \in \{0,1\}^{\lfloor \log \lambda \rfloor}$.
- If no output has been produced so far, output a random bit $b \leftarrow \{0,1\}$.

Note that UnivBreak runs in time $t(\lambda)/\varepsilon^2(\lambda) \cdot \mathsf{poly}(\lambda)$.

Let $\lambda \in$ BROKEN, and let M^* be a machine of size at most $\lfloor \log \lambda \rfloor$ such that:

$$\mathsf{Adv}_{M_{(t)}}^{\mathsf{DDH}}(1^\lambda) \geq \frac{\varepsilon(\lambda)}{2}.$$

We first argue that the probability that UnivBreak outputs a random bit (because of skipping all Turing machines of size at most $\lfloor \log \lambda \rfloor$) is at most $2^{-\lambda} \cdot 2^{-4T(\lambda)}$. This only occurs whenever UnivBreak ignores M^*, which happens with probability at most $2^{-\lambda} \cdot 2^{-4T(\lambda)}$ by a standard Chernoff bound similar to Lemma 24.

Next, we claim that the probability that UnivBreak produces an output using a machine M such that $\mathsf{Adv}_{M_{(t)}}^{\mathsf{DDH}} < \varepsilon/6$ is at most $\lambda \cdot 2^{-\lambda} \cdot 2^{-4T(\lambda)}$, again using a standard Chernoff bound similar to Lemma 24. Finally, by definition of $\overline{M_{(t)}} = \overline{M_{(t)}}(t, \varepsilon/6)$ (defined at the beginning of Sect. 5.1 and Lemma 17), we obtain:

$$\Pr \left[\begin{array}{l} \mathcal{G} = \mathsf{DHGen}(1^\lambda), g \xleftarrow{\$} \mathbb{G}, \alpha, \beta, \gamma \xleftarrow{\$} \mathbb{Z}_p, \\ b \xleftarrow{\$} \{0,1\}, \delta \leftarrow b\gamma + (1-b)\alpha\beta, \quad : b = b' \\ b' \xleftarrow{\$} \mathsf{UnivBreak}(1^\lambda, \mathcal{G}, g, g^\alpha, g^\beta, g^\delta) \end{array} \right] \geq 1 - (2^{-\lambda} + \lambda \cdot 2^{-\lambda} + \mathsf{negl}(\lambda)) \cdot 2^{-4T(\lambda)}.$$

$$\geq 1 - \mathsf{negl}(\lambda) \cdot 2^{-4T(\lambda)}.$$

$\square$

Remark 26 (Splitting tester and universal breaker). We introduced separate constructions of testers and breakers, even though the algorithms are very similar: this is done so that they can use different thresholds. Then, the behavior of UnivBreak becomes fully characterized by whether its input security parameter belongs to BROKEN. Using the same threshold for the tester and the breaker would instead result in a universal breaker which, on input some security parameters in SECURE ∩ BROKEN, could potentially "fail" with high (say constant) probability and use some good enough breaker with also high constant probability.

5.2   A Subexponentially-Often NIZK

We now prove Theorem 20. We first provide an outline of our construction. We use both a DDH-based NIZK, and a VPRG-based NIZK based on the universal breaker of Sect. 5.1. Given a fixed security parameter λ, a proof consists of both proofs (which does not hurt zero-knowledge, as both constructions are zero-knowledge almost-everywhere), where we use complexity leveraging on the VPRG-based one (namely, we run it on a smaller security parameter λ'). In order to verify a proof, we use our "universal tester" from Sect. 5.1 to check whether (the complexity leveraged version of) DDH is broken; if it is, then the VPRG-based NIZK, using the universal breaker of Sect. 5.1, ensures completeness and (statistical) soundness. Note that the testing step, and the verification algorithm of the VPRG-based NIZK, are made efficient thanks to complexity leveraging. Otherwise, we do not know how to directly argue that the DDH-based NIZK provides soundness; instead, we argue that there exists a "relatively close" security parameter $\overline{\lambda}$ for which the DDH-based NIZK allows to argue soundness. The formal construction and proof follow.

Let $\varepsilon = \varepsilon(\lambda) = 2^{-\lambda^c}$ be an inverse subexponential function, where $0 < c < 1$ is a constant and $t = t(\lambda)$ be any superpolynomial, positive-integer-valued function such that $t(\lambda) \leq 2^{\lambda^c}$.[12]

We use the following building blocks:

- A DDH-based NIZK (DDH.Setup, DDH.Prove, DDH.Verify) given by Theorem 14 using the constant c.
- A VPRG-based NIZK (VPRG.Setup, VPRG.Prove, VPRG.Verify) from Lemma 15, instantiated with the universal breaker UnivBreak from Lemma 25.[13]
- A DDH tester Test given by Lemma 24.

---

[12] Taking any other subexponential upper-bound for t would suffice for us, but would result in additional unnecessary notation.

[13] The universal breaker from Lemma 25 is already a strong breaker, so the proof of Lemma 15 can directly argued combining Lemma 18 with Theorem 12, without explicitly using Lemma 17. This is because we internally amplified the success probability of UnivBreak in Lemma 25 (using Lemma 17).

Construction. Define the following NIZK (Setup, Prove, Verify):

- Setup$(1^\lambda, 1^{|x|})$: Define $\lambda' = \left\lfloor \log^{1/c}(\lambda) \right\rfloor$. Compute $\mathsf{crs}_{\mathsf{DDH}} \leftarrow \mathsf{DDH.Setup}$ $(1^\lambda, 1^{|x|})$, $\mathsf{crs}_{\mathsf{VPRG}} \leftarrow \mathsf{VPRG.Setup}(1^{\lambda'}, 1^{|x|})$,[14] and output $\mathsf{crs} = (\mathsf{crs}_{\mathsf{DDH}}, \mathsf{crs}_{\mathsf{VPRG}})$.
- Prove(crs, x, w) : Compute $\pi_{\mathsf{DDH}} \leftarrow \mathsf{DDH.Prove}(\mathsf{crs}_{\mathsf{DDH}}, x, w)$ and $\pi_{\mathsf{VPRG}} \leftarrow \mathsf{VPRG.Prove}(\mathsf{crs}_{\mathsf{VPRG}}, x, w)$. Output $\pi = (\pi_{DDH}, \pi_{\mathsf{VPRG}})$.
- Verify(crs, x, π): Compute $b \leftarrow \mathsf{Test}(1^{\lambda'})$. If $b = 0$, output $\mathsf{VPRG.Verify}$ $(\mathsf{crs}_{\mathsf{VPRG}}, x, \pi_{\mathsf{VPRG}})$ using UnivBreak. If $b = 1$, output $\mathsf{DDH.Verify}(\mathsf{crs}_{\mathsf{DDH}}, x, \pi_{\mathsf{DDH}})$.

We first tie the definitions of Definition 23 with security properties of the NIZKs above. Recall that for any $\lambda \in \mathbb{N}$, we defined in Theorem 14 the set $\mathsf{TOWER}_\lambda = \mathsf{TOWER}_\lambda(c, L) := \{\lambda\} \cup \{\lambda^{(c/2)^{i/2}}\}_{i \in [L]}$, where $L > 0$ is a constant given by Theorem 14.

Lemma 27 (Security of the DDH-based NIZK). *Define the set*

$$E_{\mathsf{DDH}} := \bigcup_{\lambda \in \mathbb{N}} \{\lambda \mid \mathsf{TOWER}_\lambda \subseteq \mathsf{SECURE}\},$$

where $\mathsf{SECURE} = \mathsf{SECURE}(t, \varepsilon)$ *is defined in Definition 23. Then* $(\mathsf{DDH.Setup}, \mathsf{DDH.Prove}, \mathsf{DDH.Verify})$ *satisfies perfect completeness, infinitely-often soundness w.r.t.* E_{DDH} *(against uniform cheating provers), and statistical zero-knowledge against non-uniform verifiers.*

Proof. First, observe that the construction of E_{DDH} implies:

$$\bigcup_{\lambda \in E_{\mathsf{DDH}}} \mathsf{TOWER}_\lambda \subseteq \mathsf{SECURE}.$$

In particular, for any $\lambda \in E_{\mathsf{DDH}}$ and any $\lambda_i \in \mathsf{TOWER}_\lambda$, $\lambda_i \in \mathsf{SECURE}$.

Therefore, by Theorem 14, it suffices to check that, for any uniform PPT adversary $\mathcal{A}$, there exists λ^* such that for all $\lambda \in \mathsf{SECURE}$ such that $\lambda \geq \lambda^*$:

$$\mathsf{Adv}_{\mathcal{A}}^{\mathsf{DDH}}(1^\lambda) \leq 2^{-\lambda^c}. \tag{1}$$

Let $\mathcal{A}$ be a uniform adversary, and let $q(\lambda) = \mathsf{poly}(\lambda)$ denote its runtime, and s its size as a Turing machine. By construction of SECURE (Definition 23), Equation (1) holds for all $\lambda \in \mathsf{SECURE}$ such that $t(\lambda) \geq q(\lambda)$ and $\lambda \geq 2^s$, which in turn hold for all large enough $\lambda \in \mathsf{SECURE}$ as t is a super-polynomial function. $\square$

Lemma 28 (Security of the VPRG-based NIZK). *Define, for all* $\lambda \in \mathbb{N}$, $\overline{\mathsf{VPRG.Setup}}(1^\lambda) := \mathsf{VPRG.Setup}(1^{\lambda'})$, *where* $\lambda' = \left\lfloor \log^{1/c}(\lambda) \right\rfloor$. *Define the set*

$$E_{\mathsf{VPRG}} = \left\{ \lambda \quad \middle| \quad \left\lfloor \log^{1/c}(\lambda) \right\rfloor \in \mathsf{BROKEN} \right\}.$$

---

[14] We use the VPRG-based NIZK to prove statements of size $|x| = \mathsf{poly}(\lambda)$ which are subexponential in its internal security parameter λ'. The VPRG-based NIZK of Lemma 15 remains subexponentially secure in that setting; see Remarks 13 and 16.

Let c' be any constant such that $c < c' < 1$. Assuming the $2^{\lambda^{c'}}$-subexponential hardness of CDH (Sect. 3.1), (VPRG.$\overline{\text{Setup}}$, VPRG.Prove, VPRG.Verify) is infinitely often correct and statistically adaptively sound with respect to E_{VPRG}[15], and computationally adaptively, multi-theorem zero-knowledge.

Proof. By definition of λ', and by assumption on the functions t, ε, UnivBreak on input $(1^{\lambda'}, x)$ for any x runs in time $t(\lambda')/\varepsilon^2(\lambda') \cdot \text{poly}(\lambda') = \text{poly}(\lambda)$, and therefore the algorithms (VPRG.$\overline{\text{Setup}}$, VPRG.Prove, VPRG.Verify) run in polynomial time.

The rest follows by instantiating Lemma 15 starting with $\mathcal{A} = $ UnivBreak, which runs on security parameter $\lambda' \in$ BROKEN by definition of E_{VPRG}, and using that $\text{Adv}_{\text{UnivBreak}}^{\text{DDH}}(1^{\lambda'}) \geq 1 - \text{negl}(\lambda') \cdot 2^{-4T(\lambda')}$ thanks to Lemma 25.   □

Next, we tie Lemma 27 and Lemma 28 together thanks to the properties of our tester Test. Let $\lambda \in \mathbb{N}$. We distinguish several cases:

Case 1: If $\lambda \notin E_{\text{DDH}}$, there exists some $\lambda_i \in$ TOWER$_\lambda$ such that $\lambda_i \notin$ SECURE, so that $\lambda_i \in$ BROKEN and $\overline{\lambda} := 2^{\lambda_i^c} \in E_{\text{VPRG}}$ by definition. Furthermore, because $\lambda_i \notin$ SECURE, Test(1^{λ_i}) outputs 0 except with probability $2^{-\lambda_i}$ by Lemma 24, and therefore (Setup, Prove, Verify) on security parameter $\overline{\lambda} = 2^{\lambda_i^c}$ will call VPRG.Verify with overwhelming probability. Soundness on $\overline{\lambda}$ then follows by soundness of the VPRG-based NIZK (VPRG.$\overline{\text{Setup}}$, VPRG.Prove, VPRG.Verify) on E_{VPRG} (Lemma 28).

Case 2: If $\lambda \in E_{\text{DDH}}$, namely if TOWER$_\lambda \subseteq$ SECURE, we distinguish two subcases:

    Case 2.1: $\lambda' \notin$ BROKEN then Test($1^{\lambda'}$) outputs 1 except with probability at most $\lambda \cdot 2^{-\lambda}$ by Lemma 24, and therefore (Setup, Prove, Verify) on security parameter λ will call DDH.Verify with overwhelming probability. Soundness on λ then follows by soundness of the DDH-based NIZK (DDH.Setup, DDH.Prove, DDH.Verify) on E_{DDH} (Lemma 27).

    Case 2.2: Last, if $\lambda' \in$ BROKEN, then $\lambda \in E_{\text{DDH}} \cap E_{\text{VPRG}}$, and therefore (Setup, Prove, Verify) is sound regardless of the outcome of Test($1^{\lambda'}$) by soundness of both NIZKs (VPRG.$\overline{\text{Setup}}$, VPRG.Prove, VPRG.Verify) and (DDH.Setup, DDH.Prove, DDH.Verify).

Summing up, define a set $E \subseteq \mathbb{N}$ as follows. For all $\lambda \in \mathbb{N}$, define $\lambda \in E$ if either Case 2.1 or Case 2.2 occurs, and define $\overline{\lambda} = 2^{\lambda_i^c} \in E$ if Case 1 or Case 2.2 occurs, for all $\lambda_i \in$ TOWER$_\lambda$ such that $\lambda_i \in$ BROKEN. We obtain that (Setup, Prove, Verify) is infinitely-often adaptively sound with respect to E, and satisfies adaptive, multi-theorem zero-knowledge against non-uniform verifiers. Finally, by construction of E, for all $\lambda \in \mathbb{N}$, $E \cap (\{\lambda\} \cup 2^{\text{TOWER}_\lambda^c}) \neq \emptyset$, and therefore, by construction of TOWER$_\lambda$, $E \cap [\lambda, 2^{\lambda^c}] \neq \emptyset$. Setting $K = c$, we obtain the relative density of E as stated in Theorem 20. This concludes the proof.   □

---

[15] See the paragraph on infinitely-often security in Sect. 3.2 for a definition of soundness w.r.t. an infinite set E.

5.3 Additional Results

Modifying specific building blocks directly yields the following theorems.

Theorem 29 (NIZKs from CDH and LPN). *Assume the superpolynomial hardness of CDH and the polynomial hardness of LPN. Then for any NP language $\mathscr{L}$, there exists a superpolynomially-often uniform non-interactive zero-knowledge proof for $\mathscr{L}$.*

Note that the construction above can be instantiated in *any* (candidate) prime-order groups (that is, without restrictions similar to [35]).

Proof (Sketch). This follows from the same construction as in Sect. 5.2, but instantiating the DDH-based NIZK with the construction of [9] which is secure under the polynomial hardness of both DDH and LPN. We then set t (resp. ε) as any superpolynomial (resp. inverse superpolynomial) function. The only notable differences in the proof are (1) the complexity leveraging is consequently milder, and we therefore only need to rely on the superpolynomial hardness of CDH, and (2) $E_{\mathsf{DDH}} = \mathsf{SECURE}$.

Theorem 30 (ZAP Arguments from Subexponential CDH). *Assume the subexponential hardness of CDH. Then for any NP language $\mathscr{L}$, there exists a ZAP argument for $\mathscr{L}$ satisfying (1) subexponentially-often, non-adaptive soundness against uniform efficient cheating provers and (2) (standard) adaptive witness indistinguishability.*

Proof (Sketch). We start with the existence of DDH-based ZAPs which is secure assuming DDH (Theorem 14; note that it only satisfies non-adaptive soundness), and VPRG-ZAPs built on any DDH breaker, which are secure assuming CDH (this follows noting that Lemma 15 gives a statistically sound NIZK with a common random string, which yields a ZAP by [24]). The construction simply defines the first (resp. second) message of the ZAP as the concatenation of the first (resp. second) messages two ZAPs. Verification proceeds as in Sect. 5.2. The analysis is identical to the one in Sect. 5.2.

6 An Infinitely-Often NIZK from CDH+LPN

In this section, we prove the following theorem:

Theorem 31 (io-NIZK from CDH+LPN). *Assume that CDH and (uniform) LPN both hold. Then for any NP language $\mathscr{L}$, there exists an infinitely-often uniform non-interactive zero-knowledge proof for $\mathscr{L}$.*

Compared to Theorem 29, Theorem 31 only requires the *polynomial* hardness of CDH and LPN. This is, however, at the cost of having a non-constructive result, and losing superpolynomial-oftenness. In fact, we prove the following statement:

Theorem 32. *At least one of the following statements is necessarily true:*

- *the (uniform) LPN assumption implies the existence of an infinitely-often non-interactive zero-knowledge argument system for* NP *with uniform adaptive soundness and standard zero-knowledge, or*
- *the CDH assumption implies the existence of a non-interactive zero-knowledge proof for* NP *with statistical adaptive soundness, and adaptive multi-theorem zero-knowledge.*

In order to prove Theorems 31 and 32, consider the following hypothesis H:

> For all uniform PPT adversary $\mathcal{A}$, all polynomials q, and for infinitely many security parameters $\lambda \in \mathbb{N}$,
>
> $$\mathsf{Adv}_{\mathcal{A}}^{\mathsf{DDH}}(1^\lambda) \leq 1/q(\lambda).$$

Theorems 31 and 32 follow directly from the combination of Lemma 33 and Lemma 34 below, which show the existence of NIZKs when H holds and when $\neg H$ holds, respectively.

Lemma 33. *If H holds, then assuming the (uniform) hardness of LPN, there exists an infinitely-often non-interactive zero-knowledge argument system with uniform non-adaptive soundness and statistical zero-knowledge.*

Proof. This is directly implied by the NIZK of [9] which is statistically zero-knowledge, and (uniformly, non-adaptively) sound assuming the polynomial (uniform) hardness of LPN and DDH; their claim extends directly to the infinitely-often, uniform setting.

Lemma 34. *If H does not hold, then assuming the hardness of CDH, there exists a non-interactive zero-knowledge proof with statistical adaptive soundness, and adaptive multi-theorem zero-knowledge.*

Proof. Assuming $\neg H$, there exists a uniform PPT $\mathcal{A}$, along with a polynomial q, such that for all $\lambda \in \mathbb{N}$, $\mathsf{Adv}_{\mathcal{A}}^{\mathsf{DDH}}(1^\lambda) > 1/q(\lambda)$. The lemma then follows directly from Lemma 15.

Acknowledgements. G. Couteau is supported by the French Agence Nationale de la Recherche (ANR), under grant ANR-20-CE39-0001 (project SCENE), and the France 2030 ANR Project ANR22-PECY-003 SecureCompute. The second author was supported in part by NSF CNS-1814919, NSF CAREER 1942789, Johns Hopkins University Catalyst award, JP Morgan Faculty Award, and research gifts from Ethereum, Stellar and Cisco. Zhengzhong Jin was supported in part by DARPA under Agreement No. HR00112020023 and by an NSF grant CNS-2154149. Willy Quach was supported by NSF grant CNS-1750795, CNS-2055510

References

1. Badrinarayanan, S., Fernando, R., Jain, A., Khurana, D., Sahai, A.: Statistical ZAP arguments. In: Canteaut, A., Ishai, Y. (eds.) EUROCRYPT 2020. LNCS, vol. 12107, pp. 642–667. Springer, Cham (2020). https://doi.org/10.1007/978-3-030-45727-3_22

2. Bellare, M., Micciancio, D., Warinschi, B.: Foundations of group signatures: formal definitions, simplified requirements, and a construction based on general assumptions. In: Biham, E. (ed.) EUROCRYPT 2003. LNCS, vol. 2656, pp. 614–629. Springer, Heidelberg (2003). https://doi.org/10.1007/3-540-39200-9_38

3. Bellare, M., Yung, M.: Certifying cryptographic tools: the case of trapdoor permutations. In: Brickell, E.F. (ed.) CRYPTO 1992. LNCS, vol. 740, pp. 442–460. Springer, Heidelberg (1993). https://doi.org/10.1007/3-540-48071-4_31

4. Ben-Sasson, E., et al.: Zerocash: decentralized anonymous payments from bitcoin. In: 2014 IEEE Symposium on Security and Privacy, SP 2014, Berkeley, CA, USA, May 18–21, 2014, pp. 459–474. IEEE Computer Society (2014)

5. Bender, A., Katz, J., Morselli, R.: Ring signatures: stronger definitions, and constructions without random Oracles. In: Halevi, S., Rabin, T. (eds.) TCC 2006. LNCS, vol. 3876, pp. 60–79. Springer, Heidelberg (2006). https://doi.org/10.1007/11681878_4

6. Blum, M., Feldman, P., Micali, S.: Non-interactive zero-knowledge and its applications (extended abstract). In: 20th ACM STOC, pp. 103–112. ACM Press, May 1988

7. Boneh, D., Lipton, R.J.: Algorithms for black-box fields and their application to cryptography. In: Koblitz, N. (ed.) CRYPTO 1996. LNCS, vol. 1109, pp. 283–297. Springer, Heidelberg (1996). https://doi.org/10.1007/3-540-68697-5_22

8. Boyle, E., Couteau, G., Meyer, P.: Sublinear secure computation from new assumptions. In: TCC 2022, Part II, pp. 121–150. LNCS, Springer, Heidelberg (2022). https://doi.org/10.1007/978-3-031-22365-5_5

9. Brakerski, Z., Koppula, V., Mour, T.: NIZK from LPN and trapdoor hash via correlation intractability for approximable relations. In: Micciancio, D., Ristenpart, T. (eds.) CRYPTO 2020. LNCS, vol. 12172, pp. 738–767. Springer, Cham (2020). https://doi.org/10.1007/978-3-030-56877-1_26

10. Canetti, R., Chen, Y., Holmgren, J., Lombardi, A., Rothblum, G.N., Rothblum, R.D., Wichs, D.: Fiat-Shamir: from practice to theory. In: Charikar, M., Cohen, E. (eds.) 51st ACM STOC, pp. 1082–1090. ACM Press (June 2019)

11. Canetti, R., Chen, Y., Reyzin, L., Rothblum, R.D.: Fiat-Shamir and correlation intractability from strong KDM-secure encryption. In: Nielsen, J.B., Rijmen, V. (eds.) EUROCRYPT 2018. LNCS, vol. 10820, pp. 91–122. Springer, Cham (2018). https://doi.org/10.1007/978-3-319-78381-9_4

12. Canetti, R., Halevi, S., Katz, J.: A forward-secure public-key encryption scheme. In: Biham, E. (ed.) EUROCRYPT 2003. LNCS, vol. 2656, pp. 255–271. Springer, Heidelberg (2003). https://doi.org/10.1007/3-540-39200-9_16

13. Canetti, R., Lichtenberg, A.: Certifying trapdoor permutations, revisited. In: Beimel, A., Dziembowski, S. (eds.) TCC 2018. LNCS, vol. 11239, pp. 476–506. Springer, Cham (2018). https://doi.org/10.1007/978-3-030-03807-6_18

14. Cash, D., Kiltz, E., Shoup, V.: The Twin Diffie-Hellman problem and applications. In: Smart, N. (ed.) EUROCRYPT 2008. LNCS, vol. 4965, pp. 127–145. Springer, Heidelberg (2008). https://doi.org/10.1007/978-3-540-78967-3_8

15. Couteau, G., Hofheinz, D.: Designated-verifier pseudorandom generators, and their applications. In: Ishai, Y., Rijmen, V. (eds.) EUROCRYPT 2019. LNCS, vol. 11477, pp. 562–592. Springer, Cham (2019). https://doi.org/10.1007/978-3-030-17656-3_20

16. Couteau, G., Katsumata, S., Sadeghi, E., Ursu, B.: Statistical ZAPs from group-based assumptions. In: Nissim, K., Waters, B. (eds.) TCC 2021. LNCS, vol. 13042, pp. 466–498. Springer, Cham (2021). https://doi.org/10.1007/978-3-030-90459-3_16

17. Couteau, G., Katsumata, S., Ursu, B.: Non-interactive zero-knowledge in pairing-free groups from weaker assumptions. In: Canteaut, A., Ishai, Y. (eds.) EURO-CRYPT 2020. LNCS, vol. 12107, pp. 442–471. Springer, Cham (2020). https://doi.org/10.1007/978-3-030-45727-3_15

18. Cramer, R., Shoup, V.: Universal hash proofs and a paradigm for adaptive chosen ciphertext secure public-key encryption. In: Knudsen, L.R. (ed.) EUROCRYPT 2002. LNCS, vol. 2332, pp. 45–64. Springer, Heidelberg (2002). https://doi.org/10.1007/3-540-46035-7_4

19. De Santis, A., Micali, S., Persiano, G.: Non-interactive zero-knowledge proof systems. In: Pomerance, C. (ed.) CRYPTO 1987. LNCS, vol. 293, pp. 52–72. Springer, Heidelberg (1988). https://doi.org/10.1007/3-540-48184-2_5

20. Deng, Y.: Magic adversaries versus individual reduction: science wins either way. In: Coron, J.-S., Nielsen, J.B. (eds.) EUROCRYPT 2017. LNCS, vol. 10211, pp. 351–377. Springer, Cham (2017). https://doi.org/10.1007/978-3-319-56614-6_12

21. Dolev, D., Dwork, C., Naor, M.: Non-malleable cryptography (extended abstract). In: 23rd ACM STOC, pp. 542–552. ACM Press, May 1991

22. Döttling, N., Garg, S., Hajiabadi, M., Masny, D., Wichs, D.: Two-round oblivious transfer from CDH or LPN. In: Canteaut, A., Ishai, Y. (eds.) EUROCRYPT 2020. LNCS, vol. 12106, pp. 768–797. Springer, Cham (2020). https://doi.org/10.1007/978-3-030-45724-2_26

23. Döttling, N., Garg, S., Ishai, Y., Malavolta, G., Mour, T., Ostrovsky, R.: Trapdoor hash functions and their applications. In: Boldyreva, A., Micciancio, D. (eds.) CRYPTO 2019. LNCS, vol. 11694, pp. 3–32. Springer, Cham (2019). https://doi.org/10.1007/978-3-030-26954-8_1

24. Dwork, C., Naor, M.: Zaps and their applications. In: 41st FOCS, pp. 283–293. IEEE Computer Society Press, November 2000

25. Feige, U., Lapidot, D., Shamir, A.: Multiple non-interactive zero knowledge proofs based on a single random string (extended abstract). In: 31st FOCS, pp. 308–317. IEEE Computer Society Press, October 1990

26. Fiat, A., Shamir, A.: How to prove yourself: practical solutions to identification and signature problems. In: Odlyzko, A.M. (ed.) CRYPTO 1986. LNCS, vol. 263, pp. 186–194. Springer, Heidelberg (1987). https://doi.org/10.1007/3-540-47721-7_12

27. Garg, S., Hajiabadi, M.: Trapdoor functions from the computational Diffie-Hellman assumption. In: Shacham, H., Boldyreva, A. (eds.) CRYPTO 2018. LNCS, vol. 10992, pp. 362–391. Springer, Cham (2018). https://doi.org/10.1007/978-3-319-96881-0_13

28. Goldreich, O., Levin, L.A.: A hard-core predicate for all one-way functions. In: 21st ACM STOC, pp. 25–32. ACM Press, May 1989

29. Goldreich, O., Rothblum, R.D.: Enhancements of trapdoor permutations. J. Cryptol. **26**(3), 484–512 (2013)

30. Goldwasser, S., Micali, S., Rackoff, C.: The knowledge complexity of interactive proof-systems (extended abstract). In: 17th ACM STOC, pp. 291–304. ACM Press, May 1985

31. Goyal, V., Jain, A., Jin, Z., Malavolta, G.: Statistical zaps and new oblivious transfer protocols. In: Canteaut, A., Ishai, Y. (eds.) EUROCRYPT 2020. LNCS, vol. 12107, pp. 668–699. Springer, Cham (2020). https://doi.org/10.1007/978-3-030-45727-3_23

32. Groth, J., Ostrovsky, R., Sahai, A.: Non-interactive zaps and new techniques for NIZK. In: Dwork, C. (ed.) CRYPTO 2006. LNCS, vol. 4117, pp. 97–111. Springer, Heidelberg (2006). https://doi.org/10.1007/11818175_6

33. Groth, J., Ostrovsky, R., Sahai, A.: Perfect non-interactive zero knowledge for NP. In: Vaudenay, S. (ed.) EUROCRYPT 2006. LNCS, vol. 4004, pp. 339–358. Springer, Heidelberg (2006). https://doi.org/10.1007/11761679_21

34. Haitner, I., Nissim, K., Omri, E., Shaltiel, R., Silbak, J.: Computational two-party correlation: a dichotomy for key-agreement protocols. In: Thorup, M. (ed.) 59th FOCS, pp. 136–147. IEEE Computer Society Press, October 2018

35. Jain, A., Jin, Z.: Non-interactive Zero Knowledge from Sub-exponential DDH. In: Canteaut, A., Standaert, F.-X. (eds.) EUROCRYPT 2021. LNCS, vol. 12696, pp. 3–32. Springer, Cham (2021). https://doi.org/10.1007/978-3-030-77870-5_1

36. Katsumata, S., Nishimaki, R., Yamada, S., Yamakawa, T.: Designated verifier/prover and preprocessing NIZKs from Diffie-Hellman assumptions. In: Ishai, Y., Rijmen, V. (eds.) EUROCRYPT 2019. LNCS, vol. 11477, pp. 622–651. Springer, Cham (2019). https://doi.org/10.1007/978-3-030-17656-3_22

37. Komargodski, I., Yogev, E.: On distributional collision resistant hashing. In: Shacham, H., Boldyreva, A. (eds.) CRYPTO 2018. LNCS, vol. 10992, pp. 303–327. Springer, Cham (2018). https://doi.org/10.1007/978-3-319-96881-0_11

38. Lombardi, A., Quach, W., Rothblum, R.D., Wichs, D., Wu, D.J.: New constructions of reusable designated-verifier NIZKs. In: Boldyreva, A., Micciancio, D. (eds.) CRYPTO 2019. LNCS, vol. 11694, pp. 670–700. Springer, Cham (2019). https://doi.org/10.1007/978-3-030-26954-8_22

39. Lombardi, A., Vaikuntanathan, V., Wichs, D.: 2-message publicly verifiable WI from (subexponential) LWE. Cryptology ePrint Archive, Report 2019/808 (2019). https://eprint.iacr.org/2019/808

40. Maji, H.K., Prabhakaran, M., Sahai, A.: On the computational complexity of coin flipping. In: 51st FOCS, pp. 613–622. IEEE Computer Society Press, October 2010

41. Maurer, U.M.: Towards the equivalence of breaking the Diffie-Hellman protocol and computing discrete logarithms. In: Desmedt, Y.G. (ed.) CRYPTO 1994. LNCS, vol. 839, pp. 271–281. Springer, Heidelberg (1994). https://doi.org/10.1007/3-540-48658-5_26

42. Naor, M., Yung, M.: Public-key cryptosystems provably secure against chosen ciphertext attacks. In: 22nd ACM STOC, pp. 427–437. ACM Press, May 1990

43. Okamoto, T., Pietrzak, K., Waters, B., Wichs, D.: New realizations of somewhere statistically binding hashing and positional accumulators. In: Iwata, T., Cheon, J.H. (eds.) ASIACRYPT 2015. LNCS, vol. 9452, pp. 121–145. Springer, Heidelberg (2015). https://doi.org/10.1007/978-3-662-48797-6_6

44. Pass, R., shelat, Vaikuntanathan, V.: Construction of a non-malleable encryption scheme from any semantically secure one. In: Dwork, C. (ed.) CRYPTO 2006. LNCS, vol. 4117, pp. 271–289. Springer, Heidelberg (2006). https://doi.org/10.1007/11818175_16

45. Pass, R., Venkitasubramaniam, M.: Is it easier to prove theorems that are guaranteed to be true? In: 61st FOCS, pp. 1255–1267. IEEE Computer Society Press, November 2020

46. Peikert, C., Shiehian, S.: Noninteractive zero knowledge for np from (plain) learning with errors. In: Boldyreva, A., Micciancio, D. (eds.) CRYPTO 2019. LNCS, vol. 11692, pp. 89–114. Springer, Cham (2019). https://doi.org/10.1007/978-3-030-26948-7_4
47. Peikert, C., Waters, B.: Lossy trapdoor functions and their applications. In: Ladner, R.E., Dwork, C. (eds.) 40th ACM STOC, pp. 187–196. ACM Press (May 2008)
48. Quach, W., Rothblum, R.D., Wichs, D.: Reusable designated-verifier NIZKs for all NP from CDH. In: Ishai, Y., Rijmen, V. (eds.) EUROCRYPT 2019. LNCS, vol. 11477, pp. 593–621. Springer, Cham (2019). https://doi.org/10.1007/978-3-030-17656-3_21
49. Reingold, O., Trevisan, L., Vadhan, S.: Notions of reducibility between cryptographic primitives. In: Naor, M. (ed.) TCC 2004. LNCS, vol. 2951, pp. 1–20. Springer, Heidelberg (2004). https://doi.org/10.1007/978-3-540-24638-1_1
50. Rothblum, R.D., Vasudevan, P.N.: Collision-resistance from multi-collision-resistance. In: CRYPTO 2022, Part III, pp. 503–529. LNCS, Springer, Heidelberg (2022). https://doi.org/10.1007/978-3-031-15982-4_17
51. Sahai, A., Waters, B.: How to use indistinguishability obfuscation: deniable encryption, and more. In: Shmoys, D.B. (ed.) 46th ACM STOC, pp. 475–484. ACM Press (May/June 2014)
52. Zhandry, M.: Quantum lightning never strikes the same state twice. In: Ishai, Y., Rijmen, V. (eds.) EUROCRYPT 2019. LNCS, vol. 11478, pp. 408–438. Springer, Cham (2019). https://doi.org/10.1007/978-3-030-17659-4_14

Author Index

A

Agrawal, Shweta 464, 532
Alwen, Joël 396

B

Bae, Youngjin 37
Barooti, Khashayar 362
Bombar, Maxime 567

C

Cheon, Jung Hee 37
Choudhuri, Arka Rai 635
Collins, Daniel 362
Colombo, Simone 362
Couteau, Geoffroy 567, 731
Couvreur, Alain 567

D

Dai, Yiran 3
Davies, Gareth T. 330
Deng, Yi 3
Ducros, Clément 567

F

Faller, Sebastian 330
Feng, Dengguo 3
Freitag, Cody 498

G

Garg, Sanjam 635
Gellert, Kai 297, 330
Giunta, Emanuele 702
Gjøsteen, Kristian 297
Guan, Jiaxin 433

H

Handirk, Tobias 330
Heath, David 128
Hesse, Julia 330
Horváth, Máté 330
Huguenin-Dumittan, Loïs 362

I

Ishai, Yuval 263

J

Jacobsen, Håkon 297
Jager, Tibor 297, 330
Jain, Aayush 233, 263
Jain, Abhishek 635, 731
Jin, Zhengzhong 635, 731

K

Kim, Jaehyung 37
Kim, Miran 70
Kolesnikov, Vladimir 128
Korb, Alexis 433
Kothapalli, Abhiram 669

L

Lee, Dongwon 70
Lin, Huijia 233
Lou, Paul 263
Luo, Ji 233

M

Mathialagan, Surya 95
Mularczyk, Marta 396

O

Ostrovsky, Rafail 128

P

Park, Jai Hyun 37
Parno, Bryan 669
Persiano, Giuseppe 161

Q

Quach, Willy 731

R

Raghuraman, Srinivasan 602
Rindal, Peter 602
Rossi, Mélissa 532

© International Association for Cryptologic Research 2023
H. Handschuh and A. Lysyanskaya (Eds.): CRYPTO 2023, LNCS 14084, pp. 765–766, 2023.
https://doi.org/10.1007/978-3-031-38551-3

S
Sahai, Amit   263, 433
Seo, Jinyeong   70
Song, Yongsoo   70
Stehlé, Damien   37

T
Tanguy, Titouan   602
Tomida, Junichi   464
Tselekounis, Yiannis   396

V
Vafa, Neekon   95
Vaudenay, Serge   362

W
Waters, Brent   498
Wichs, Daniel   233
Wu, David J.   498

X
Xiang, Binwu   3

Y
Yadav, Anshu   464, 532
Yamada, Shota   532
Yeo, Kevin   161, 197

Z
Zhandry, Mark   263
Zhang, Jiaheng   635
Zhang, Jiang   3